IMPERIAL CHINA
900–1800

CAMBRIDGE, MASSACHUSETTS, AND LONDON, ENGLAND

F. W. MOTE

IMPERIAL CHINA
900–1800

HARVARD UNIVERSITY PRESS

Overleaf: *The Kangxi Emperor's Southern Inspection Tour,
Scroll Seven: Wuxi to Suzhou.* Wang Hui (1632–1717)
and assistants. CEMAC Ltd., Alberta, Canada;
used with permission.

First Harvard University Press paperback edition, 2003

Third printing, 2003

Publication of this book has been supported through
the generous provisions of the
Maurice and Lula Bradley Smith Memorial Fund.

Library of Congress Cataloging-in-Publication Data

Mote, Frederick W., 1922–
Imperial China 900–1800 / F. W. Mote.
p. cm.
Includes bibliographical references and index.
ISBN 0-674-44515-5 (cloth)
ISBN 0-674-01212-7 (paper)
1. China—History—960–1644. 2. China—History—1644–1795.
I. Title.
DS750.64.M67 2009
951'.02—dc21   99-31840

CONTENTS

Preface   xv

Acknowledgments   xix

PART ONE

CONQUEST DYNASTIES AND THE NORTHERN SONG
900–1127

1. The Five Dynasties   3
 I. Later Imperial China's Place in History   3
 II. The Course of Five Dynasties History   8
 III. The Eastward Shift of the Political Center   17
 IV. Simultaneous Developments in the Ten States   21
 V. China and Inner Asia in Geographic and Historical
   Perspective   23

2. Abaoji   31
 I. The Khitans and Their Neighbors   32
 II. Ethnic Diversity and Language Community   33
 III. The Lessons of History   36
 IV. The New Leader Emerges   37
 V. The Significance of Khitan Acculturation   42
 VI. Abaoji Receives Yao Kun, Envoy of the Later Tang Dynasty   44

3. Building the Liao Empire   49
 I. Succession Issues after Abaoji   49
 II. The Meaning of the Early Liao Succession Crises   54
 III. The Khitans' Inner Asian Tribal Empire   56
 IV. Liao-Korean Relations   60
 V. Expansion into North China   62
 VI. Liao-Song Relations   68

4. Liao Civilization   72
 I. Multicultural Adaptations   72
 II. Khitan Society   75

III. Patterns of Acculturation   76
IV. Buddhism in Khitan Life   81
V. Interpretations of Liao Success   86

5. Creating the Song Dynasty   92
    I. The Vigor of the Later Zhou and the Founding of the Song   92
    II. On Being the Emperor in Tenth-Century China   98
    III. Governing China   101
    IV. The Military Problem   112

6. The World of Ideas in Northern Song China   119
    I. The Man of the Age: Ouyang Xiu   119
    II. The Course of a Song Dynasty Official Career   122
    III. The Civil Service Examination System   126
    IV. The Social Impact of the Song Examination System   131
    V. Political Reform and Political Thought   135
    VI. Neo-Confucian Philosophical Thought   144

7. Dimensions of Northern Song Life   150
    I. High Culture   150
    II. The Example of Su Shi   153
    III. The New Elite and Song High Culture   156
    IV. Religion in Song Life   157
    V. Song Society   164

8. Origins of the Xi Xia State   168
    I. The Tangut People: Names and Ethnic Identities   168
    II. Early History of the Tangut Tribal People   170
    III. The Tanguts Come into the Song Orbit   171
    IV. Yuanhao Proclaims the Xia Dynasty   179
    V. The Xi Xia as an Imperial Dynasty   182

PART TWO

CONQUEST DYNASTIES AND THE SOUTHERN SONG
1127–1279

9. The "Wild Jurchens" Erupt into History   193
    I. Aguda's Challenge   194
    II. The End of the Liao Dynasty   199
    III. The Northern Song Falls to the Jurchens   206
    IV. Who Were These Jurchens?   211
    V. Explaining the Jurchens' Success   216

10. The Jurchen State and Its Cultural Policy   222
    I. The Conquerors Turn to Governing   222
    II. The Period of Dual Institutions, 1115–1135   225

III. The Era of Centralization, 1135–1161   229
IV. The Period of Nativist Reaction, 1161–1208   236
V. The End of the Jin Dynasty, 1208–1234   243

11. The Later Xi Xia State   249
    I. Xi Xia in the Era of the Jin Dynasty, 1115–1227   249
    II. The Crisis of the "Partition of the State"   252
    III. The Destruction of the Xi Xia State   254
    IV. The Tangut Achievement   257
    V. Xia Buddhism   261

12. Trends of Change under Jin Alien Rule   265
    I. Divisions: North and South, Chinese and Non-Chinese   265
    II. Jurchen Dominance   271
    III. The Impact of the Civil Service Examinations   272
    IV. High Culture during the Jin Dynasty   277
    V. Economic Life under the Jin   283

13. The Southern Song and Chinese Survival   289
    I. A Fleeing Prince—A New Emperor   289
    II. War versus Peace   298
    III. Patterns of High Politics after the Treaty of 1141   307

14. Chinese Civilization and the Song Achievement   323
    I. New Social Factors   323
    II. Elite Lives and Song High Culture   325
    III. Confucian Thinkers   333
    IV. Other Kinds of Elite Lives   346
    V. Some Generalizations about the Song Elite   347

15. Southern Song Life—A Broader View   351
    I. Calculating Song China's Population   351
    II. Governing at the Local Level   354
    III. Paying for Government   359
    IV. Status in the Chinese Population   364
    V. Urban and Rural   367
    VI. Families, Women, and Children   368
    VII. A Poet's Observations   370

16. A Mid-Thirteenth-Century Overview   375
    I. The Heritage of the Liao, Xi Xia, and Jin Periods   375
    II. The System of Ritualized Interstate Relations   378
    III. The Growing Scope of International Trade   389
    IV. Cultural Interaction   394

Contents

PART THREE

CHINA AND THE MONGOL WORLD

17. The Career of the Great Khan Chinggis   403
    I. Backgrounds of Mongol History   403
    II. The Ethnic Geography of Inner Asia in the Late Twelfth
        Century   407
    III. Mongol Nomadic Economy and Social Life   410
    IV. The Mongols Emerge into History   413
    V. The Youth of Temüjin   414
    VI. Chinggis Khan as Nation Builder   419

18. Forging the Mongol World Empire, 1206–1260   425
    I. The Nearer Horizons of Empire, 1206–1217   425
    II. The First Campaign to the West, 1218–1225   428
    III. Chinggis Khan, the Man   433
    IV. The Second Campaign to the West, 1236–1241   434
    V. Mongol Adaptations to China under Chinggis and Ögödei   436
    VI. Möngke Khan and the Third Campaign to the West   439
    VII. Relations among the Four Khanates   442

19. Khubilai Khan Becomes Emperor of China   444
    I. The Early Life of Khubilai   445
    II. Khubilai and His Chinese Advisers before 1260   448
    III. Möngke's Field General in China   452
    IV. Maneuvering to Become the Great Khan   455
    V. The Great Khan Khubilai Becomes Emperor of China   456
    VI. The Conquest of the Southern Song, 1267–1279   460
    VII. The War against Khaidu   465
    VIII. Khubilai's Later Years   466
    IX. Khubilai Khan's Successors, 1294–1370   467

20. China under Mongol Rule   474
    I. Yuan Government   474
    II. Managing Society and Staffing the Government   489
    III. Religions   497
    IV. China's People under Mongol Rule   503
    V. The Yuan Cultural Achievement   507

PART FOUR
THE RESTORATION OF NATIVE RULE UNDER THE MING
1368–1644

21. From Chaos toward a New Chinese Order   517
    I. Disintegration   517
    II. Competitors for Power Emerge   521
    III. Rival Contenders, 1351–1368   533
    IV. Zhu Yuanzhang, Boy to Young Man   541

22. Zhu Yuanzhang Builds His Ming Dynasty   549
    I. Learning to Be an Emperor   549
    II. Setting the Pattern of His Dynasty   563
    III. Constructing a Capital and a Government   566
    IV. The Enigma of Zhu Yuanzhang   575

23. Civil War and Usurpation, 1399–1402   583
    I. The New Era   583
    II. The Thought of Fang Xiaoru: What Might Have Been   591
    III. From Prince to Emperor   594

24. The "Second Founding" of the Ming Dynasty   598
    I. Ming Chengzu's Imprint on Ming Governing   598
    II. The Eunuch Establishment and the Imperial Bodyguard   602
    III. Defending Throne and State   606
    IV. Securing China's Place in the Asian World   612
    V. The New Capital   617

25. Ming China in the Fifteenth Century   622
    I. Successors to the Yongle Emperor   622
    II. The Mechanics of Government   636
    III. The Grand Canal in Ming Times   646

26. The Changing World of the Sixteenth Century   654
    I. Emperor Wuzong, 1505–1521   654
    II. Emperor Shizong's Accession   658
    III. The Rites Controversy   663
    IV. Emperor Shizong and Daoism   668
    V. The Emperor Shizong and His Officials   669
    VI. Wang Yangming and Sixteenth-Century Confucian
    Thought   673

27. Ming China's Borders   685

    I. Border Zones, Zones of Interaction   685
    II. Tension and Peril on the Northern Borders   687
    III. Tibet and the Western Borders   698
    IV. The "Soft Border" of the Chinese South   702
    V. The Maritime Borders of Eastern China   717

28. Late Ming Political Decline, 1567–1627   723

    I. The Brief Reign of Emperor Muzong, 1567–1572   723
    II. Zhang Juzheng's Leadership and the Wanli Reign   727
    III. The Wanli Emperor's Successors   738

29. The Lively Society of the Late Ming   743

    I. The Population of Ming China   743
    II. The Organization of Rural Society   750
    III. Ming Cities, Towns, and Urban People: The Question of
        Capitalism   760
    IV. Late Ming Elite Culture   769

30. The Course of Ming Failure   776

    I. Launching the Chongzhen Reign: Random Inadequacies,
        Persistent Hopes   776
    II. The Manchu Invaders   784
    III. The "Roving Bandits"   795
    IV. Beijing, Spring 1644   801

PART FIVE

CHINA AND THE WORLD IN EARLY QING TIMES

31. Alien Rule Returns   813

    I. Beijing: The City Ravaged   813
    II. The Drama at Shanhai Guan, April–May 1644   815
    III. Beijing Becomes the New Qing Capital   818
    IV. The Shunzhi Emperor, 1644–1662   821
    V. The Southern Ming Challenge to Qing Hegemony,
        1644–1662   824
    VI. The Manchu Offensive   827
    VII. The Longwu Regime: Fuzhou, July 1645–October 1646   833
    VIII. Ming Loyalist Activity after 1646   837

32. The Kangxi Emperor: Coming of Age   841

    I. Difficult Beginnings   841
    II. Rebellion, 1673–1681   844
    III. The Conquest of Taiwan   848
    IV. Ming Loyalism and Intellectual Currents in the Early Qing   850

33. The Kangxi Reign: The Emperor and His Empire 856
    I. Banner Lands and the Manchu Migration into China 857
    II. Recruitment and the Examination System 861
    III. The Mongols on the Northern Borders 868
    IV. Manchu/Qing Power and the Problem of Tibet 876
    V. Court Factions 879
    VI. The Succession Crisis 883

34. The Yongzheng Emperor as Man and Ruler 887
    I. Imperial Style, Political Substance 887
    II. Changing the Machinery of Government 892
    III. Other Governing Measures 897
    IV. Military Campaigns and Border Policies 901
    V. Population Growth and Social Conditions 903
    VI. Taxation and the Yongzheng Reforms 908

35. Splendor and Degeneration, 1736–1799 912
    I. Changing Assessments 912
    II. Hongli 914
    III. Political Measures 918
    IV. Cultural Control Measures 922
    V. A Late Flowering of Thought and Learning 928
    VI. The Qianlong Emperor's Military Campaigns 935
    VII. China in the Eighteenth Century 940

36. China's Legacy in a Changing World 949
    I. The Background of China's International Relations 949
    II. Mutual Recognition 951
    III. Economic Interactions 953
    IV. Broadened Horizons of Religion, Philosophy, and Practical Knowledge 956
    V. Diplomatic and Military Threats 961
    VI. An Old Civilization in a New World 963

Appendix: Conversion Table, Pinyin to Wade-Giles 975
Notes 979
Bibliography 1057
Index 1085

CHARTS AND MAPS

DYNASTIC SUCCESSION CHARTS

1. The Liao imperial succession   53
2. The Northern Song imperial succession   105
3. The Xi Xia succession, 1032–1227   184
4. The Jin imperial succession   215
5. The Southern Song imperial succession   309
6. Chinggis Khan's lineage to 1294   415
7. Mongol emperors of the Yuan dynasty   468
8. The Ming imperial succession   624
9. The Qing imperial succession to 1800   822

MAPS

1. The Five Dynasties   11
2. Canals in North China in Late Tang   18
3. China Proper and Chinese Inner Asia, 1800   24
4. The Khitan Liao and Song, 1100   58
5. Early Liao expansion into North China   108
6. Administrative divisions of Northern Song   111
7. The Xi Xia state's core region, 1100   171
8. The Jin State and Southern Song, 1200   230
9. Aggressive Jin and Evasive Song, 1126–1130   294
10. Administrative divisions of Jin and Southern Song, 1200   356
11. Major ethnic groups in Mongolia, 1160s   406
12. Mongol westward expansion across Eurasia   430
13. Yuan dynasty provinces (Xingsheng)   486
14. The rival contenders' base areas at the end of Yuan   531
15. The provinces of Ming China, 1580   640
16. The Grand Canal in Ming and Qing   648
17. Ming China's northern border zone   694
18. Ming China's western border zone   699

19. Ming China's southern border zone 704
20. Ming China's coastline 718
21. Manchu-Russian rivalry for Inner Asian empire 872
22. The administrative geography of Qing China, 1800 944

PREFACE

The present volume is derived directly from my experience as a teacher of later imperial Chinese history to undergraduate and graduate students at Princeton University since 1956. Long contact with intelligent students who frequently challenged me to clarify and defend both my information and my interpretations of it has created a debt of gratitude that must first of all be acknowledged here.

In addition to my graduate seminars, which usually focused on Yuan and Ming history, I also taught early Chinese intellectual history, and occasionally lectured on twentieth-century China. But the period from 900 to 1799, the latter the year in which the Qianlong emperor died, was my "field" in the vast expanses of Chinese civilization, although I did not attempt to cultivate all of it with equal intensity. The Yuan and Ming dynasties were the core of that field. I am committed to the idea that historians of China must engage the entire scope of pre–nineteenth-century Chinese civilization in order to study any segment of it. The present volume is, among other things, an effort to demonstrate that some measure of knowledge about earlier China is essential even to those who focus on the more recent past.

True, we all need a better understanding of contemporary China, an ever larger factor in the world in which we live, but I believe that we will never adequately gain this understanding unless we engage the study of its history. To state the matter quite directly, I believe that ignorance of China's cultural tradition and historical experience is an absolute barrier to comprehending China today. The "sinological" approach to the study of China, the approach by way of serious language study and humanistic investigation of the cultural tradition in historical depth, does not conflict with but strengthens the modern "disciplines" by which our field organizes research on China today.

To turn to the practical experience that led me to write the present volume, when teaching about the later Chinese empire I found that some large aspects of it lacked readily available reading materials. I began more than fifteen years ago to write essays on the so-called conquest dynasties, the Liao, the Xi Xia, the Jin, and the Yuan, where the need was the greatest, and duplicated them for my students. The predecessors of the present chapters on those dynastic eras all were presented to my students starting in the spring semester of 1983. They proved to be useful enough to me as a teacher that I determined to turn them into a book, and expanded that plan to cover the span of time represented here. For some parts of the period there are indeed usable secondary readings as well as translations, if not always general historical surveys. Many more such specialized publications of great value to the field have since appeared. To cite an example, the entire sub-field of Song dynasty history (960–1279), which was quite recently almost barren, today has become one of the most sophisticated fields in Western studies of China. The work of my late colleague and valued friend James T. C. Liu contributed much to that growth of Song studies.

Despite the growing strength of some sub-fields of Chinese history, I nevertheless have attempted to offer here an integrated treatment, representing one point of view. If nothing else, the present volume redresses in some measure the unfortunate imbalance I have referred to: the relative neglect, in historical writing about China, of those peoples of the "conquest dynasties"—the Khitans, the Tanguts, the Jurchens, and the Mongols. The Manchus have fared better at the hands of historians, so my task has been simpler with respect to Manchu and Qing dynasty history. In all of these cases, to be sure, the separate histories of these important peoples are presented here as a significant dimension of China's history, not as rounded histories in their own right, as they also deserve to be presented. But this is a history of China, and I have tried at least to show how important those peoples have been in Chinese history. I have not been able to do as much with regard to the even more commonly ignored non-Chinese peoples and polities of South and Southwest China, but I am confident that deficiency will soon be addressed by other scholars known to me.

Since I began teaching, the principal task has been to work out ways of making China intelligible to American students. The present volume is an end product of that long effort. I hope also that teachers will find this book useful by freeing them of the need to impart much of the basic information so that they can supplement and correct it with lectures and readings closer to their interests. And this book is intended for general readers who are interested in the great civilizations, who will want to encounter more than simple answers and will bring their own questions and experiences to their reading of this book.

To all such readers I must explain the choices made in preparing this book. It is impossible in one volume to give due attention to all aspects of the history of Chinese civilization through nine hundred years. Here I have concentrated first on the political narrative, believing that I can best make the civilization's development throughout history coherent by informing the reader about that central element. That is an arbitrary decision; other ways of organizing a history are equally valid, but not perhaps equally effective for my purposes. Within that political narrative I have selected those actors and events that appear to me to possess intrinsic interest for a modern reader, and that simultaneously reveal the larger course of history.

Other aspects of the civilization have been introduced: the structure of government, the nature of the social system, economic and military factors, the forms of artistic and literary expression, and major patterns in thought and religion. In all of those fields it is essential that one also read more specialized writings; as one's interests dictate, one should read translations, look at works of art, examine critically other arguments and other interpretations. A great quantity of the literature produced through these nine centuries is available in good translations. The essential writings in the philosophical traditions have been translated and explained in a profusion of publications. There are wonderful books and articles on the art and architecture, as on the crafts and material components of life; the religions and philosophies of the age are receiving increasing attention from scholars. Much of that writing is mentioned in the notes, more fully identified in the bibliography, yet it has not been possible to do full justice to all the supporting scholarship. The scholarship cited in the notes is primarily that published in Chinese and in English. No more than a handful of works in Japanese, in German, in French, and in other languages has been cited, not because there are not quantities of such works that could have been listed (and not a few of which have in fact contributed to the author's knowledge), but because I believe that the already extensive bibliography serves most directly the needs of the intended audience by concentrating on scholarship in the two languages, Chinese and English, which constitute the "first line of reference" in this field for Western students.

Except in two or three instances otherwise noted, the translations from Chinese included in this volume were made by the author especially for inclusion here. Translations from the reconstructed Mongolian of the *Secret History* in Chapter 16 are the principal exception; those are borrowed, with permission, from the admirable poetic rendering made by Paul Kahn. My translations from Chinese originals include, alas, no poems, no masterworks of belles lettres or philosophy, no extensive selections from the great historians or other genres of traditional Chinese writing. All such expressions of China's civilization must be directly encountered elsewhere. The sheer limitations of space would not allow it to be otherwise. The translations included here, moreover, are offered for cursory reading so are not accompanied by detailed explanation and documentation. The methods employed in making these translations, as in writing the text, are not technically "sinological" in the strictest sense. Yet I have attempted not to distort by oversimplifying. Although this volume may help some find their way on to further studies of the subject, this volume is intended for reading, for browsing, for the pleasures of the mind, not to provide professional scholars with a source of footnotes.

A few technical matters require explanation. Chinese names and terms are spelled here in the increasingly standard pinyin system, official in Mainland China. The other choice would have been the Wade-Giles system, familiar as the spelling used in most works on the subject published before 1970 and still widely used. Both are abominable as transcription systems; there is little to choose between them, but publishers now mostly have adopted pinyin. I have tried to help the reader by presenting the corresponding Wade-Giles spellings of all the individual syllables possible in modern standard Chinese (*putong hua*) in a table of correpondences of single syllables as an appendix to this volume, to allow the reader to find the Wade-Giles equivalents. Library catalogs and reference systems still mostly use the Wade-Giles spellings. The necessity of encountering all those unfamiliar names and words in two spellings may only complicate the matter for many readers, but sadly there seems to be no other way. I regret that I have been forced to omit the use of Chinese and other East Asian scripts, but that may incidentally reduce the irritations that are aroused by a plenitude of strange words and names.

Finally, I must say that I offer this volume as a preliminary effort. I am aware that errors must exist and that corrections should be made. I fully welcome corrections, and even more I anticipate more successful efforts of this kind that are sure to come from my fellow historians.

ACKNOWLEDGMENTS

In addition to the general acknowledgments of intellectual debts, I also must make specific acknowledgment of help received in preparing the final text of this work. Special thanks are owed to four scholars whose names are not known to me who read a dozen or more earlier versions of chapters and provided uncommonly intelligent and helpful criticisms and advice to me. Two readers for the Harvard University Press offered detailed and perceptive criticism, in the most constructive spirit; I have benefited greatly from their efforts. Parts of this volume also were read in final draft form by two colleagues of many years' standing, William S. Atwell and James P. Geiss. Their specialized researches in aspects of Ming history in particular have added to my knowledge. In addition, James Geiss expended great effort to work over some chapters, greatly improving clarity and style and offering sound advice on content. Naomi Noble Richard, a remarkable editor, while not responsible for editing this volume, nevertheless succeeded in imparting a general sense of her editing standards; I happily express gratitude for the pleasure of having learned from her. Most particularly, however, the entire manuscript was read while I was putting it into final form by my friend and colleague Michael Gasster of Rutgers University; his often detailed and always insightful written comments and oral communications have been indispensable in helping me focus on problems of analysis and of presentation. I have written the later portions of this volume in particular with the hope that they would be followed, supplemented, and further clarified by his own writings on modern Chinese history. Philip Schwartzberg of Meridian Maps in Minneapolis, Minnesota, has turned my crude sketches into the excellent cartography used throughout this volume. Maxwell Hearn, Curator of Asian Art at the Metropolitan Museum in New York, has given invaluable help in selecting and arranging permissions to use the works of art adopted for illustrations. Members of the staff of the Harvard University Press, and its Editor-in-Chief, Aïda D. Donald, have graciously extended their help and advice throughout the process of preparing the manuscript for publication. To all of these persons I must acknowledge my deepest gratitude. The many shortcomings that remain are of course my own responsibility.

IMPERIAL CHINA
900–1800

PART ONE

CONQUEST DYNASTIES AND THE NORTHERN SONG, 900–1127

Overleaf:

Stag Hunt

Attributed to Huang Zongdao, active ca. 1120. Handscroll, ink and color on paper. Metropolitan Museum of Art, New York. Edward Elliott Family Collection. The Dillon Fund gift, 1982. Used with permission.

"A handsome Khitan youth riding a menacing dark brown horse charges in full gallop after a fleeing stag that has just been pierced by an arrow . . . The injured victim, a stunning animal with melting features and soft fur, drops to the ground in a final, desperate leap. The treadmill effect of the horse's hooves, all four spinning in the air, is not unlike the experiments of the Futurists, with simultaneous images to suggest dynamic speed and motion" (Fong 1992, pp. 32–33). Traditionally this painting was attributed to Prince Bei, son of Abaoji, named Prince of Dongdan in 926, also known by the Chinese name Li Zanhua; see Chapters 2 and 3.

1

THE FIVE DYNASTIES

Later imperial China can be said to begin in the half-century of deep changes that occurred between the fall of the Tang dynasty and the subsequent founding of the Song, two of imperial China's longest and most important dynastic periods. Those changes were hastened by the fragmentation and turbulence that marked this period of political disorder and military conflict. One consequence was that in the age which followed, North China became the object of Inner Asian military expansion. Simultaneously, while resisting that expansion, the Song dynasty gave new shape to the course of Chinese civilization. Despite political disorder and military involvement, the tenth century was an age rich in cultural development. Here the political outlines of the Five Dynasties and the concurrent Ten States are briefly summarized. Finally, as prelude to the profound interaction of China and Inner Asia in the centuries that followed, background information on Inner Asia is introduced.

1. LATER IMPERIAL CHINA'S PLACE IN HISTORY

Imperial China was more than a thousand years old when the great Tang dynasty came to its end in the year 907 of our Common Era (C.E.). Chinese high civilization was much older; its documented history as a literate civilization extends back a thousand years before its "imperial" history began in the third century before our Common Era (B.C.E.). That was when the Qin dynasty's "First Emperor," or Shihuangdi, as he insisted on being called, unified all the Chinese states in 221 B.C.E. and launched the new phase in history that we call imperial China.

Throughout the eleven centuries of early imperial China prior to our beginning point in this volume, the imperial Chinese state acquired its characteristic features. The brief Qin dynasty and its successor, the Han (206 B.C.E.–220 C.E.), accomplished the basic steps. Some of early imperial China's social and political features are rare in the histories of early peoples: all political power was highly centralized; its government was a bureaucracy of highly literate administrators who were men selected in principle for their individual qualifications of learning and ability; and its imperial institution, while linked to no church or organized religion, yet claimed that its right to rule was bestowed by heaven's mandate—however that might be interpreted. At the very least, it was taken to mean that the mandate to rule had to be earned, and would be withdrawn when the legitimate rulers showed that, by the standard of serving the "popular good," they were no longer worthy of it. Dynasties, meaning the succession of rulers directly descended from a founding emperor, rose and fell through military action, but the imperial state was a civil government in which, nominally at least, the civil virtues were held to be superior to the military. There was no hereditary military aristocracy in the strict sense of the word, nor even a civil aristocracy. Inherited titles and privileges were, to be sure, more numerous in those earlier centuries, but at no time did they entail fiefs with hereditary political rights. In practice, imperial China was from the beginning largely governed by men (other than the successor emperors themselves) who gained their positions by their individual qualities, not by inheritance. They were drawn from a society that had no legally established class distinctions. Those principles, and the initial experience in practicing them, were clearly established under the radical Qin dynasty in the late third century B.C.E. China's long subsequent experience in working out ways to maintain and enlarge in practice the basic social conditions which they imply gives its history special interest in the comparative study of human civilizations.

Following the Han dynasty, and after a further century of weak governing, a long period of division into simultaneous Northern and Southern Dynasties (317–589) led at last to a new unification. That verified Chinese expectations that their cultural realm constituted one society that should have one ruler. Again, a brief but powerful dynasty like the third-century B.C.E. Qin, in this case the Sui (581–618), accomplished the military reunification, to be followed by the long and glorious flowering of Chinese civilization under the Tang dynasty (618–907).

The year 900 C.E. makes a meaningful beginning point for this volume devoted to the later centuries of China's imperial rule. True, the idea that there could be a "Common Era" *not* based on the Chinese calendar is completely foreign to traditional Chinese civilization; China adopted that idea only in the twentieth century, when the term *gongyuan*, meaning something essentially like "common era," slowly came into widespread use, and even today has not completely superseded the traditional Chinese dating system. In recent decades many historians have come to use this Western, or "Common Era," dating for events in Chinese history, so we may do the same here, even though at that time, in the minds of the Chinese and their neighbors in East and Inner Asia, the year that closely matches 900, (actually, it began on February 4, 900, and ended on January 22, 901) was thought of as the third year of the Guanghua reign period of the late Tang dynasty emperor Zhaozong; that year did not begin a century or precisely correspond to any recognized turning point in history. Nevertheless, the year 900 loosely corresponds to a genuine turning point, marked by the end of the Tang dynasty (formally dated to the year 907). In the last decades of the ninth century C.E. and the first decades of the tenth, we clearly see the beginnings of far-reaching changes that have great significance for defining the subsequent age in Chinese as well as Inner Asian history. It is for this reason that I have chosen the year 900 as our arbitrary beginning point.

The Sui and Tang dynasties, coming to power in the sixth and seventh centuries, faced the problem of consolidating the Chinese state after almost three centuries of north-south division, caused by the incursions of Inner Asian peoples long in contact with the Chinese culture area. When the Sui and then the Tang established their dynasties, they were able to fend off those invasions, but China's interaction with non-Chinese peoples on all of its land borders continued. Other Inner Asian peoples again came to play crucial roles in the life of China after 900, if in a new way. The interplay of China and Inner Asia is a consistent element in the development of both, extending far back into the prehistoric millennia; that is abundantly and ever more clearly revealed by recent systematic archaeological explorations. The Inner Asian peoples occupied regions lying just north of the Chinese cultural area, defined by an ecological boundary that separated the conditions of sedentary farming life of the Chinese people from the harsher conditions farther north and northwest, under which hunting and herding were basic to people's livelihood. In Tang and later times those northern peoples were predominantly "Turkic," insofar as we can determine from our knowledge of the languages their descendants spoke, but by the same measure, some also were Aryan peoples whose languages were related to Persian, and some spoke languages with affinities for present-day Tibetan; there probably were others of still different linguistic and cultural identities.

The sedentary Chinese also interacted with non-Chinese (in present-day usage, non-Han) peoples on its other land frontiers in the south, southwest, and southeast. Those non-Chinese were mostly sedentary farming peoples who, like the Chinese, practiced intensive village-based agriculture. The long centuries of interaction with them, and Chinese infiltration into their lands, did not involve crossing any ecological barriers, and went on continuously, more or less unnoticed by writers of history.

It was the martial tribal peoples of Inner Asia, who developed military and organizational skills based on their lives as hunters and herders, who alone among all of China's neighbors had the power to threaten the existence of the Chinese state. They were always potential raiders, invaders, conquerors, and rulers. Both the Sui and the Tang ruling houses arose in the northwest border zone, having intermarried with Turkic princely families and used warrior skills developed in that interaction to found their dynasties. Through the more than three centuries of Sui and Tang, China remained strongly oriented toward its northern and northwestern frontier. It extended control and influence deep into Inner Asia, and benefited from the cultural and commerical contacts with more distant Central Asia and regions beyond, to India, Persia, and western Asia. It was the age when the ancient Silk Roads came to their greatest importance, connecting the Tang capital to what the Chinese called the Western Regions, to the homeland of Buddhism (which had been present in China from Han times onward), and to the religious and cultural traditions still farther west—Zoroastrian, Manichaean, Islamic, Jewish, Nestorian Christian, among others that came into Tang China. There they established communities of their co-believers. Those immigrant peoples helped to mediate between eastern and western Asia in this most cosmopolitan period of China's 2,000-year-long imperial era. While Chinese interests in Inner Asia led to an extension of China's military and political control there, Chinese population was not significantly extended into Inner Asia at that time. An ecological boundary separated China Proper and the Inner Asian territories, whose grasslands, deserts, and oases did not attract Chinese farmers. Throughout the Tang period's westward extension of Chinese interest and influence, the Chinese presence in Inner Asia was limited to military garrisons and small merchant communities in the oases along the nearer Silk Road routes.

The Tang was, however, a period during which the Chinese people greatly extended the areas of their demographic dominance by migration to the south, where no such ecological barriers existed. Increased numbers of Chinese filled out the Yangzi River drainage basin of Central China and further south, into the Southeast China coastal regions as far as present-day Guangdong (Canton) and Vietnam. The centuries-long process of Chinese southward migration seldom involved large-scale military confrontation, even though it was not always peaceable.

Armed conflict, in contrast, was a constant feature on the northern borders with Inner Asia, where the non-Chinese peoples possessed the means to sorely test Chinese military capacities. Their striking force enabled the northern peoples to take active parts in Tang China's internal power struggles: they supplied the Tang government, or its domestic opponents, with cavalry forces in return for political rewards. Inner Asian military power became a component of Tang internal politics, of increasing importance from the mid-eighth century onward. When the later Tang emperors chose to strengthen their rule by granting military governorships both in the provinces and along the northern borders, these often went to the non-Chinese tribal leaders. During the rebellion of Huang Chao that grew out of widespread bandit operations in the 870s, the capital was sacked and half the provinces of China, as far south as Guangdong, were ravaged by Huang Chao's roaming armies. That massive rebellion was finally suppressed in 884 with the aid of a chieftain of the Shatuo Turks. The Shatuo were one of several Turkic nations with whom the Tang court had been involved. This man bore the Chinese name Li Keyong. His reward for intervening with the might of Turkic cavalry was the grant of a base in northern Shanxi, which he turned into a bastion of Turkic military power, using it to play a major role in the struggles among regional warlords to impose control over the Tang imperial court. Forced to grant local authority to the regional military leaders, whether Chinese or Turkic, including authority for civil governing and tax collection, in return for unreliable professions of loyalty, the later Tang emperors never regained full control over their country. The character of governing was changed. Among those holders of real power who were Chinese (as most were), they had come from the defeated forces of Huang Chao or from other bandit uprisings. The great families of the Tang civil and bureaucratic elite played almost no part in the final struggles of the Tang to survive. As a sector of elite society, they had been largely nullified if not eliminated.

The later Tang emperors were thus little more than pawns of contesting military leaders. One such leader, a Chinese named Zhu Wen, a former captain in Huang Chao's rebel armies, seized the capital in 901. Then in 905 he killed the emperor and most of the Tang imperial family and placed a teenage imperial prince on the throne as his puppet. Finally, in 907 he abandoned all pretenses and declared himself the founding emperor of a new dynasty. In 908 he killed the deposed last Tang emperor, a boy of sixteen. That cycle of violence began the Liang (Later Liang), the first of the Five Dynasties. The fall of the Tang dynasty is one of the more obvious reasons for taking the year 900, more precisely 907, to mark the beginning of the long period that in this volume is called later imperial China.

The half-century-long Five Dynasties period, from the Later Liang in 907 to the founding of the Song dynasty in 960, appears on the surface to have been an age of utter chaos, violence, and political disorder. None of the Five Dynasties, based in North China, was able to reunify China; all coexisted with province-size Chinese states in Central and South China. Three of the five were established by non-Chinese leaders who had become part of the Chinese military and political scene. Despite that surface appearance of unending disorder, the reality underlying this half-century is one of deep and transforming change. A new structure of state power emerged, and a new relationship of military power to civil administrative authority took shape in reaction against the long-accumulated political weaknesses of the late Tang. In civil society, the centuries-long dominance of the established "great families" within officialdom and in the society of their home localities was utterly broken, to be replaced by a new class of civil bureaucrats who used office to gain social status, not the other way around. In economic spheres, the "commercial revolution" of late Tang times continued to alter patterns of trade and economic behavior throughout society, and to provide the state with the means to a strengthened fiscal base.

Also starting in the late Tang, a new understanding of what should constitute the Confucian ethical basis of governing and of social life was forcefully demanded by a few thinkers and statesmen.[1] That became a full-scale movement in Confucian thought in early Northern Song times, some 200 years later, when it produced the flowering of philosophical debate and speculation that we call Neo-Confucianism. That reorientation of the ancient Confucian thought system dominated Chinese civilization for a millennium. It complemented and reinforced other changes in the social development of post-Tang China. These included a spread of learning aided by the Tang invention of printing from engraved wooden blocks, a technology that reached great

heights from the Five Dynasties period onward, with profound social consequences, and one that invites comparison with the appearance of printing
technology in fifteenth-century Europe. Amidst those profound changes, the
flamboyant, cosmopolitan, outward-looking, and expansive age of Sui and
Tang was succeeded by a markedly different cultural tone and outlook in the
Song dynasty, including both the earlier Northern Song phase (960–1126)
and the Southern Song continuation of that long dynasty (to 1279). The implications of that cultural change, leading to the "new culture of Song" that
followed, will be an important focus of the chapters to come.

There also are strong elements of continuity through the transition from
Tang to Song. I have noted that one important element of continuity from
the late Tang into the next several centuries is China's involvement with Inner
Asia. Just as the Tang was being brutally terminated, a rival dynasty was
being created on China's northern borders, the Liao dynasty, formed by the
Khitan tribal nation,[2] taking Tang China's "universal" imperial system as its
political model. By acquiring the means to play a direct role in the politics
of the Five Dynasties, the Khitan nation's Liao state would acquire control
over a strategic border zone within China Proper; that foothold would gain
for it an integral place in the functioning of the Chinese state. The Liao established the precedent for a succession of what are called the "conquest dynasties," first the Liao, then the Tangut Xi Xia, and then the Jurchen Jin, each of
which extended alien control further into North China. The Mongols' Yuan
dynasty then completed the absorption of the entire Chinese culture realm
into their world empire in the thirteenth century. There was a vigorous resurgence of native rule under the Ming dynasty (1368–1644), to be followed by
the final alien dynasty in Chinese later imperial history, the Manchu Qing
dynasty (1644–1911).

That brief outline shows how deeply the history of this long period from
900 to 1800 is intertwined with the histories of Inner Asian peoples, in a
story that will occupy much of this volume. The era of the Five Dynasties
thus brings our attention to the deep changes brought about by the manner
in which the Tang dynasty declined and lost the capacity to rule. It leads
us to consider the changing character of Chinese civilization that emerged
thereafter, and it introduces the element of a new level of Chinese interaction
with the non-Chinese tribal nations of Inner Asia.

II. THE COURSE OF FIVE DYNASTIES HISTORY

In traditional Chinese historical writing this period is known as the "Five
Dynasties and Ten States," a catchall designation for what has always been
seen as a confused and troubled age. Each of the Five Dynasties, in quick
succession, occupied most of northern China; nine of the Ten States[3] were
located in Central and southern China. The difference between a "dynasty"
(*chao* or *chaodai*) and a "state" (*guo*) in this usage reflects traditional Chinese
views about the status and legitimacy of governments. Dynasties were held
to have possessed the Mandate of Heaven (Tian ming), and from that were

entitled to a place in the succession of legitimate dynasties. The mere states also were recognized as polities, whether acknowledged by contemporary dynasties or not, openly subservient to them or not, but were not retroactively confirmed in their claims of legitimacy by deciding that they indeed had held the Mandate to rule over all of China. By implication, that claim always was denied to all but one of the claimants then on the scene. Those decisions were verified by statesmen and historians working under a later dynasty; both the facts of history and political interests had to be carefully considered and plausible judgment reached. This period in Chinese imperial history provides illustrations of all the possible variants in the categories of dynasties and states.

At the time, however, it was not certain that any of the Five Dynasties would receive that verification either from contemporaries or from the historians. The first official history of the period, the *Five Dynasties History (Wudai shi)* was compiled in the 960s and 970s by a scholar-official who served at the court of the first Song emperor.[4] A participant in the history whose compilation he directed, he had the interests of the new Song dynasty in mind when he determined that the five northern states should be confirmed as "dynasties," thereby reinforcing the Song dynasty's claim to legitimacy through transmission of the Mandate all the way from the Tang. If the dynasty that reunified the Chinese state had appeared among the Ten States in the south, another chain of transmission from the Tang would have been devised, and it would have included a different set of intermediary "dynasties."

Apart from historians' concern for legitimacy through direct transmission of the Mandate, there are other reasons for looking upon the northern sequence of states as the logical bearers of legitimacy. However brief and unstable, one after another the Five Dynasties controlled all or most of the old heartland of Chinese civilization. Their territory was considerably larger than that of any of the Ten States, making it more probable that one of them might go on to conquer or coerce the remainder of the realm, and thereby meet a crucial demand for making a claim to be the new bearer of the Mandate. The ancient idea of a heavenly or cosmic mandate to rule was the only theoretical verification of legitimacy that traditional Chinese political thinkers and dynastic founders ever agreed upon. To claim that validating mandate demanded more than the power to conquer or coerce. A new aspirant to legitimate rule, besides displaying the raw military power sufficient to suppress all opposition, and thereby to unify the realm, also had to make plausible his claim that heaven had transferred the Mandate to himself and his lineage (his dynasty), and that he had met convincingly the ritual requirements of universal rulership. He had to be successful in commanding the force, to whatever degree was necessary to unify the realm; but he also had to show that he was morally upright, hence in harmony with the moral universe. To be accepted as morally upright meant that the dynastic founder was obliged to acknowledge tradition and conform to venerated patterns. In other words, a dynastic founder needed to show that he both was "correct" *(zheng)* and could achieve "control" *(tong)*. Whatever his real character, he had to project an image.

The founders of these Five Dynasties scarcely met the criteria. First, though each possessed enough military power to seize the capital and overawe resistance nearer at hand in North China, none of them was able to "unify the realm"; the general expectation that China would be reunified lent force to their pretensions, yet the coexistence of other states in Central and South China continued to divide the realm, denying them that necessary element of legitimacy. Second, although they all engaged in elaborate ritual performances, the "correctness" of their imperial claims might be less than obvious to observers. In particular, the brutal behavior of Zhu Wen, the first in a rapid succession of founding dynasts, the usurper who killed off the Tang imperial family and stole their throne, made many thoughtful persons of the time wish to exclude his Later Liang dynasty from the successive bearers of the Mandate. His courtesy name Zhu Quanzhong, "Zhu of perfect loyalty," made a mockery of his behavior, and the violence which he inflicted on underlings and on loyal adherents of the Tang dynasty made him a hated figure. The compiler of the official *Five Dynasties History* had to swallow hard to include him among the bearers of the Mandate. The thoughtful historians' dilemma was real. Later historians, seeking some higher reasoning to maintain the ideal of legitimacy, blamed Zhu's behavior on the extraordinary times.

One can, then, readily see why the entire period from 907 to 960 has been something of an embarrassment to traditional historians: many of the principal actors were morally tarnished or otherwise found lacking. The founders of the three middle dynasties among the five were non-Chinese Shatuo Turks, military leaders who had at one time been allies of the Tang in the role of regional military governors on the northern borders. Some Chinese were disquieted by their alien origins, even though those Shatuo leaders were virtually indistinguishable from their Chinese rivals, and were superior to some of them. In a period of ruthlessly self-serving political behavior, a man like Zhu Wen's mortal enemy Li Keyong, the Prince of Jin (a title conferred in 895 by the Tang court as a reward for his military assistance) and regional warlord of the Shanxi region, was politically ambitious and adept at plotting. He nevertheless stands out as an exemplar of consistent loyalty to his overlords, the Tang dynasty emperors, in an age when loyalty was not much in evidence. It is a noteworthy feature of the underlying Chinese political theory that non-Chinese were not excluded from the possibility of receiving the Mandate of Heaven and thereby being recognized as legitimate rulers over China.

Even though traditional historians have found the Five Dynasties an embarrassment, the period is important to our understanding of the Song dynasty which followed, and to the growth of Chinese civilization. The political narrative is not set forth in detail here, but is encapsulated in the remainder of this section. Map 1 shows the boundaries of the constituent dynasties and states at one point within the period.[5] In the text that follows, regrettably, I can do little more than identify the dynasties and states in this half-century of history.

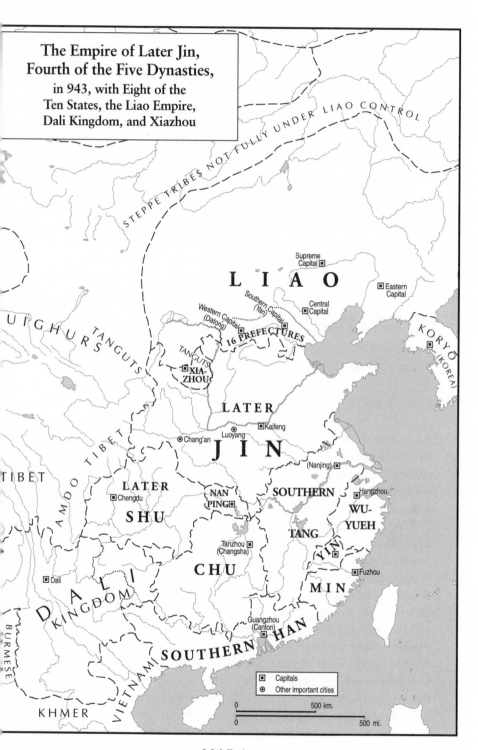

The Empire of Later Jin,
Fourth of the Five Dynasties,
in 943, with Eight of the
Ten States, the Liao Empire,
Dali Kingdom, and Xiazhou

STEPPE TRIBES NOT FULLY UNDER LIAO CONTROL

L I A O

Supreme
Capital ▣

▣ Eastern
Capital

Western Capital
(Datong)

Southern Capital
(Yan)

Central
▣ Capital

16 PREFECTURES

UIGHURS

TANGUTS

TANGUTS
▣ XIA-
ZHOU

KORYO
(KOREA)

LATER

▣ Kaifeng
Luoyang
⊙ Chang'an

J I N

(Nanjing) ▣

TIBET

AMDO TIBET

LATER
▣ Chengdu

SHU

NAN
PING ▣

SOUTHERN

Hangzhou
▣

WU-
YUEH

TANG

Tanzhou ▣
(Changsha)

YIN

D A L I
KINGDOM

▣ Dali

C H U

M I N

▣ Fuzhou

BURMESE

VIETNAM

SOUTHERN HAN

Guangzhou
(Canton) ▣

KHMER

▣ Capitals
⊙ Other important cities

0   500 km.

0   500 mi.

MAP 1

The Five Dynasties (907–959)

Later Liang (16 years, 907–923; 3 rulers). Founder, Zhu Wen (852?–912), also known as Zhu Quanzhong, Zhu Guochang. The Later Liang (the name Liang refers to the Henan region) held much of North China south to the Huai River, and in Hubei south to the Yangzi, but most of Hebei (where Zhu Wen strove unsuccessfully to impose his rule on local warlords), as well as Shanxi and Shaanxi, remained outside his control. Zhu Wen started his career in the 880s as a lieutenant of the rebel Huang Chao; subsequently he took over Huang Chao's best troops and set himself up as warlord of northern Henan, based at Kaifeng, from which he exerted control over the Tang capitals at Luoyang and Chang'an. During twenty years of military and political buildup, he had the Tang emperor Zhaozong murdered in 904 and placed Zhaozong's twelve-year-old son on the throne. In 907 he deposed, and in the following year murdered, that last Tang emperor, known as Ai Di, to proclaim himself emperor of the (Later) Liang. A powerful rivalry existed between the Later Liang on the one hand and, on the other, Li Keyong and his son, leaders of the Shatuo Turks based in Shanxi (see "Later Tang"). That rivalry continued after Zhu Wen was murdered in 912 by his son, who in turn was killed and succeeded by a younger son in 913. The latter reigned until 923 when he was killed by his own soldiers as the attacking Later Tang forces broke into the Liang capital.[6]

Later Tang (13 years, 923–936; 4 rulers). Nominal founder, Li Keyong (856–908), posthumously named "Martial Emperor." Actual founder, his son Li Cunxu (885–926). Capital, Luoyang. The Later Tang held all of North China, its realm considerably expanded to the north and the west beyond the Later Liang territories. Li Keyong was a Shatuo Turk on whom the grateful though always apprehensive Tang court, had bestowed the Tang imperial surname Li, and had further rewarded him with a military governorship in Shanxi, also known by the regional name Jin; in 895 his princely title was elevated to Prince of Jin. Li Keyong controlled the entire region of Shanxi where Shatuo military power was based. From that base he continued loyally (and ambitiously) to support the Tang court, through the once-great Tang dynasty's last decades, against Zhu Wen and other Chinese regional warlord enemies.

In 905, when Zhu Wen's dominant military position at the Tang court threatened Shatuo power, Li Keyong was reinforced by unsolicited aid from Abaoji, the Khitan leader; Abaoji led a vast Khitan cavalry force at full speed from the steppe to Datong in northern Shanxi, where he and Li became "sworn brothers" and military allies. After Li Keyong died in 908, his son Li Cunxu, heir to his regional titles and offices, carried on unremitting and generally successful warfare against the Later Liang, expanding his princely state of Jin. Although he subsequently became a debauched and inattentive governor, he remained militarily strong. In 923 he declared himself emperor of a "restored Tang" dynasty. Shortly thereafter he succeeded in destroying the Liang, whereupon he moved his capital away from Kaifeng west to Luoyang, symbolically important to him because it had been the last Tang capital before 907. At Luoyang he attempted, in form and name at least, to restore the old Tang modes of governing, even its bad features; in relation to the developments of the age, that was an unproductive anachronism.

In 926, after an army officers' rebellion had led to the death of Li Cunxu (he was struck by an unaimed arrow during a riot), an adopted son of Li Keyong, Li Siyuan, succeeded to the throne. By that time the Shatuo leaders were estranged from the Khitans. Nevertheless, in 926 Li Siyuan sent an envoy to Abaoji's court to announce the death of Li Cunxu and his own succession. (See Chapter 2 for a translation of the envoy's report on his meeting with Abaoji.) Li Siyuan died after a reign of eight years, during which the recently conquered region of Shu revolted and declared independence (see "Later Shu" in the next section). His two successors had brief reigns, and the dynasty was terminated in 936 by the rebellion of Shi Jingtang, who, with Khitan aid, made himself the founding emperor of the Later Jin dynasty.

Later Jin (10 years, 936–946; 2 rulers). Founder, Shi Jingtang (892–942), a Shatuo Turk who was the son-in-law of Li Siyuan. Capital, Bian (Kaifeng). The Later Jin controlled the North China territory of the Later Tang dynasty except for the strategic Sixteen Prefectures. The most remarkable event of this founding emperor's reign was his cession to the Khitans of those Sixteen Prefectures which incorporated strategic northeastern border defenses, giving the Liao Empire unimpeded access to North China. The Later Jin was denigrated as a puppet regime. Humiliated by his dynasty's subordination to the Khitans, Shi Jingtang's nephew and successor defied their Khitan patrons, prompting the Khitan invasion of 946–47, which ended the Later Jin dynasty. That conquest was in itself a major turning point in Five Dynasties history. (See Chapter 3.)

Later Han (3 years, 947–950; 2 rulers). Founder, Liu Zhiyuan (895–948). Capital, Bian (Kaifeng). Later Han held the same territories as Later Jin. Liu Zhiyuan was a Shatuo Turk and military governor of Bingzhou, an old name for the area of northern and central Shanxi centered on the city of Taiyuan. This region had long been the stronghold of Turkic military power in North China. Liu Zhiyuan defied the Khitans during their invasion in 946–47. When the Khitan emperor (who had formally adopted the dynastic name Liao at Kaifeng in 947) died suddenly en route back to Liao territory later that year, it left a brief power vacuum in North China. Liu thereupon marched into Kaifeng and proclaimed his new Later Han dynasty. He died a year later, and was succeeded by a teenage son.

Later Zhou (9 years, 951–960; 3 rulers). Founder, Guo Wei (904–954). Capital, Bian (Kaifeng). A well-educated Chinese, the son of a local military leader under the Tang, Guo Wei himself sought a military career, and after 947 became a leading general and Assistant Military Commissioner at the court of the Later Han founder, Liu Zhiyuan. Forced by a military coup to turn against the Later Han, Guo Wei declared himself emperor of the Great Zhou dynasty in Bian, shortly after New Year's Day 951. His rule was from the beginning vigorous and well organized. Early in life he had adopted Chai Rong (921–959), the young son of his wife's elder brother, eventually making the boy his heir. Upon Guo Wei's death from illness in 954 at age fifty, Chai Rong (now known as Guo Rong) ascended the throne as the second emperor. He reigned ably until his early death from an illness at age thirty-eight in 959. His seven-year-old son and heir was placed upon the throne, to reign until the following February, when the second emperor's most trusted senior military commander, Zhao Kuangyin, usurped the throne and declared himself the founder of the Great Song dynasty.

The "Ten States" of the Five Dynasties Period, as Traditionally Counted

Wu (35 years, 902–937; 4 rulers). Founder, Yang Xingmi. Capital, Guangling (Yangzhou), later moved to Jinling (Nanjing). Held major parts of (present-day) Jiangsu and Anhui, as well as adjoining portions of Jiangxi and Hubei. Yang became a military governor in 892 and was named Prince of Wu by the Tang court in 902. His state was taken over from within by the founder of the Southern Tang in 937.

Southern Tang (38 years, 937–975; 3 rulers). Founder, Li Bian (earlier known as Xu Zhigao). Capital, Xidu (Nanjing). Held (present-day) southern Anhui and southern Jiangsu, much of Jiangxi, Hunan, and eastern Hubei, and absorbed the states of Min (Fujian) and Chu (Hunan). Li Bian was reared as Yang Xingmi's stepson, usurped his stepfather's state of Wu, and, claiming to be a descendant of the Tang imperial family, "restored" his surname to Li. At that time he also changed the name of the Wu dynasty to Southern Tang. The second ruler, Li Jing (reigned 943–961), vigorously extended his state at the expense of neighboring Chu and Min, and built a splendid new capital on the site of present-day Nanjing. In 958, coming under pressure, he acknowledged the overlordship of the Later Zhou (of the Five Dynasties) and accepted its calendar. His son Li Yu, the last ruler ("Li Houzhu"), famed as a poet and promoter of the arts, continued to reign as a regional ruler after 961, nominally subordinate to the Song. Song armies invaded his domain in 975 and took him captive; he was poisoned on orders from the second Song emperor in 978.

Former Shu (18 years, 907–925; 2 rulers). Founder, Wang Jian. Capital, Chengdu. Held most of (present-day) Sichuan as well as portions of southern Gansu, Shaanxi, and western Hubei. Wang Jian was named military governor of western Sichuan in 891 by the Tang court; he expanded control to eastern Sichuan and beyond, and took the title of emperor in 907. Wang Jian died in 918, to be succeeded by a profligate and incompetent son. When his state was invaded by the Later Tang in 925, he quickly surrendered.

Later Shu (30 years, 935–965; 2 rulers). Founder, Meng Zhixiang. Capital, Chengdu. Held same area as Former Shu. Meng Zhixiang commanded the invading army of the (Five Dynasties') Later Tang army in 925, and remained there as the military governor while plotting to proclaim himself emperor, which he did in 934. He died six months later and was succeeded by his son, Meng Chang, who ruled very ably for thirty years, until forced to surrender to invading Northern Song armies in 965.

Southern Han (54 years, 917–971; 4 rulers). Capital, Canton. Held (present-day) Guangdong and much of Guangxi. The nominal founder, posthumously so named, was Liu Yin, who had been named Regional Military Governor by the Tang court in 905, and Prince of Nanping in 909. On his death in 917, his brother Liu Yan claimed the more elevated title of emperor, first calling his state Great Yue, then Nan Han, or Southern Han (919).[7] Liu Yan reigned for twenty-five years, until 943, to be followed by his son and two grandsons, until the last was forced to submit to the Song in 971.

Chu (24 years, 927–951; 6 rulers). Founder, Ma Yin, followed by five sons in succession. Capital, Changsha. Held (present-day) Hunan and northeastern Guangxi. Ma Yin was named regional military governor in 896, and Prince of Chu in 907. He was confirmed as Prince of the State of Chu in 927 by the Later Tang of the Five Dynasties. When quarrels among members of the Ma family gave rise to disorder, the ruler sought assistance from the neighboring Southern Tang, whose armies invaded, moved the ruling family to the Southern Tang capital (Nanjing), and absorbed the state.

Wu-Yue (71 years, 907–978; 5 rulers). Founder, Qian Liu. Capital, Xifu (Hangzhou). Held (present-day) Zhejiang and a portion of southern Jiangsu. The Qian family provided regional military leaders from 887 onward. Qian Liu (d. 932) was enfiefed Prince of Yue in 902, to which was added Prince of Wu in 904; he claimed the title King of Wu-Yue in 907 and proclaimed his own reign title; his successors more modestly adhered to the reign titles of the Five Dynasties. The fifth king, Qian Shu, surrendered to the Song in 978.[8] The state of Wu-Yue was noted for high standards of learning, wealth, and cultural development.

Min (36 years, 909–945; 5 rulers). Founder, Wang Shenzhi. Capital, Changle (Fuzhou, in present-day Fujian). Wang Shenzhi's father had held the office of Surveillance Commissioner from 892; Wang Shenzhi became Regional Military Governor and Prince of Min from 909. His son took the title of Emperor of Min in 933; at that time Wang Shenzhi was posthumously named Founding Emperor (Taizu). The state was divided when one of Wang

Shenzhi's fratricidal sons proclaimed himself the independent King of Yin (controlling the northwest portion of the state) in 943. The ruler of Min sought help from the Southern Tang, which first invaded and absorbed the breakaway Yin territory, and ultimately took over most of Min, while local Min leaders in Fuzhou proclaimed allegiance to Wu-Yue. Min was essentially vanquished by 945, although local fighting continued.[9] Its rulers were among the most depraved of the Five Dynasties period.

Nanping (also called Jingnan) (39 years, 924–963; 5 rulers). Founder, Gao Jichang (also known as Gao Jixing). Capital, Jiangling. Held Jiangling and two neighboring districts on the Yangzi southwest of present-day Wuhan in southern Hubei. The founder, Gao Jichang, in service to Zhu Wen, founder of the Later Liang (907–923) of the Five Dynasties, was appointed Regional Military Governor at Jiangling in 907. In 924, shortly after the Later Liang dynasty fell, he and his successors claimed title of King of Nanping. A small and weak state, Nanping tried to remain on proper terms with each of the successive Five Dynasties; it surrendered when Song armies invaded in 963.

Northern Han (28 years, 951–979; 4 rulers). Founder, Liu Min (earlier called Liu Chong). Capital, Taiyuan. Held present-day central Shanxi plus small adjacent portions of Shaanxi and Hebei. The only northern state among the Ten States, the Northern Han was an offshoot of the Later Han, founded in 947 by Liu Min's brother Liu Zhiyuan as the fourth of the Five Dynasties. When the Later Han fell to the Later Zhou at the end of 950, Liu Min formed a small state around the family's military power base in Shanxi and became a client state of the Liao dynasty. Liu Min maintained a fictive nephew-uncle relationship with the Liao emperor, but after 960 he also simultaneously carried on secret communications with the Song founder. When the second Song emperor invaded and captured Taiyuan in 979, Later Han surrendered to the Song.

Other Polities. The term "Ten States" is a loose designation. In addition to those discussed, several other states within the present boundaries of China coexisted for short periods. In the north, two such must be named: Qi, in western Shaanxi, lasted from 907 to 924; and Yan, based at the site of present-day Beijing, existed from 911 to 913. Beyond the regions dominated by Chinese civilization in the southwest, what later became the Ming dynasty province of (also present-day) Yunnan was then an independent kingdom called Nanzhao. It was a federation of six states comprising a number of linguistically distinct non-Chinese peoples, some with histories going back several centuries, who through warfare were amalgamated into the kingdom of Nanzhao in the eighth century.[10] Other portions of southern and southwestern China until very recent times existed under the control of independent polities not recognized by Chinese governments.

III. The Eastward Shift of the Political Center

One trend that is clear-cut by the early tenth century, impelled by reactions to the failures of the Tang and the subsequent disorders of the Five Dynasties, is the shift of China's political power center out of Shaanxi Province in the northwest, eastward to the central Yellow River plain in Henan. The Tang's dual capitals were two hundred miles apart: Chang'an (present-day Xi'an), the "Western Capital," in the Wei River valley of southern Shaanxi, and Luoyang, its "Eastern Capital," in the central Yellow River drainage in Henan. Eighty-five miles still further east in Henan there now emerged a new national administrative center at Bian (present-day Kaifeng). This shift to the east was overdue. The Wei River valley was overpopulated in relation to its economic foundations; it had long been a grain-deficient region, in large part because of Chang'an's immense population and the large garrisons stationed there to protect it. Grain from other regions had to be transported into the capital to sustain its population. The large system of canals linking Luoyang to the lower Yangzi River, and also to points east and northeast, had been constructed in the seventh century by the Sui and the early Tang rulers. To supply the capital at Chang'an, however, there remained the problem of transporting grain overland to the west beyond Luoyang, by overland portage at the San-men Rapids on the Yellow River, and then on through the Tong Pass (Tong Guan) into the Chang'an region. This section of the Yellow River was essentially unnavigable. Land transport was expensive and inefficient. The huge grain supply needed to augment the capital region's production was always subject to interruption: the Tang government had been forced on several occasions to move temporarily to its Eastern Capital at Luoyang, at great expense and disruption, just to avoid starvation.[11] Yet throughout the Tang dynasty (618–907), the force of the capital region's historical identification with the great eras of the past, and the entrenched interests of the elite "eminent clans" based there, prevented a rationalization of the problem.

From the 880s onward, during the massive rebellions of the late Tang, the capital at Chang'an was sacked repeatedly and the region around it thoroughly pillaged. The regional military leaders who came to control the Tang state were not constrained by the previously limiting sentiments; they had to adapt to geopolitical realities. Zhu Wen, who eventually usurped the Tang throne in 907, brought the last Tang emperor east to Luoyang in 904, and soon thereafter moved his own capital still farther east to Kaifeng (Bian). Chang'an would never again be the capital of China. The Chang'an region and all of southern Shaanxi declined in importance thereafter. The administrative center of the Chinese state was fixed in the central Yellow River drainage in Henan through Northern Song times (until 1127).

The old Sui-Tang canal system functioned imperfectly by the tenth century, but it still defined the main routes of domestic trade and linked the economic center of China in the Yangzi River drainage to the North China Plain (Map 2). Water routes connected Hangzhou south of the Yangzi, and other points on the lower Yangzi, to the Huai River a hundred or more miles north of

MAP 2

the Yangzi, and then by canals on to the Yellow River near Kaifeng. Newly important sea routes supplemented the canal system, facilitating both diplomatic travel and economic transport from the Central China coast to Korea, Japan, Liaodong in the Khitan empire, and North China points.[12] By breaking up established patterns of trade and commerce, the political turmoil of the Five Dynasties era hastened the development of sounder economic relationships that came to define an era of prosperous commercial development during the ensuing Song period.

The Impoverishment of the Northwest

Another far-reaching consequence of this period was the desolation which constant civil war brought to the North China region controlled by the Five Dynasties; it stands in contrast to the relative stability and prosperity evident in the nine of the Ten States that lay to the south. None of the Five Dynasties endured for as long as twenty years; some of the Ten States lasted for fifty or sixty years, and some in fact had controlled their territories even longer. The kingdom of Wu-Yue, for example, was created in 907, but its ruling family had controlled the region since the late Tang disorders of the 880s, and they maintained their control until they surrendered to the Song in 978. They provided a century of stability to that economically flourishing region on the Central China coast.[13]

The contrast in economic and social conditions between North China and most of the Ten States in Central and South China is very great. Although at its founding in 960 the Song dynasty placed its capital at Bian (Kaifeng) just south of the Yellow River on the North China Plain, its viability depended on its economic integration with the territories of the former Ten States in Central and South China, not on economic links to the older regions of the north. In this we see a maturation of a pattern that would remain for centuries: considerations of defense were focused on the north, while economic viability depended on relations with Central and South China.

The Five Dynasties period thus hastened the integration of the new and more rationally based political center in the north, the capital at Kaifeng, with economically dominant Central China, especially the lower Yangzi region (China's "historic south"). The newly achieved North China center of power based in Henan not only was necessitated by the economic decline of the old northwest cradle of Chinese civilization centered on Chang'an, but also was relevant to the shift to the east of the steppe powers. China's strategic defense of its northern borders was no longer dominated by threats from the northwest but by new threats coming from the north and northeast, first from the Khitans, thereafter from the Jurchens and Mongols, and, in the seventeenth century, the Manchus. The shift of attention away from the northwest, in fact, helped to create the circumstances that allowed the northwest frontier Tangut state of Xi Xia to fill the vacuum left behind as the Chinese power center moved eastward.

The Political Heritage of Late Tang Decentralization

It is worth repeating here that the political instability reflected in the short-lived Five Dynasties, and in the separate regional power bases that produced the Ten States, was a direct outgrowth of the decentralization of political and military power that marked later Tang history. By the mid-ninth century the centralized Tang state had ceased to exist except in name, the power of emperor and court having been wholly overshadowed by the power of Regional Military Governors (*jiedushi*). At the court, the emperors had become pawns of warring eunuch and civil bureaucrat factions, while the military governors throughout the provinces, independent of Chang'an, developed new and more efficient instruments of regional power in order to enhance their prospects of surviving in the competition among themselves, and in defiance of the center.

Some of the more successful among those regional warlords became emperors during the Five Dynasties; in other cases they became the rulers of the Ten States. Still others remained de facto rulers of smaller units consisting of a prefecture or two, and made no claims to higher political authority. The more important among those who claimed the title of emperor or king on coming to power drew lessons from the political weaknesses of the Tang state. They adopted more effective forms of governing and worked out centralized power structures within their regions in the last decades of the Tang. It is interesting that the object lesson drawn from the example of the weak Tang center, which had made their own usurpation of regional power possible, is what led them to see the need for stronger central authority. A significant shift in the organization of state power on that pragmatic new model was thus accomplished during the half-century of the Five Dynasties era. That paved the way for the succeeding Chinese imperial state under the Song dynasty to attain a centralized power structure that would not be compromised by regional military governors or held hostage to battling court factions. The histories of the Later Zhou (951–960) and its offshoot, the Song dynasty (960–1279), are particularly meaningful in the light of these late Tang and Five Dynasties developments.[14]

Decline of the Old Elite Leadership

Another consequence of the political power realignments of the Five Dynasties era is the disappearance of the old, long-entrenched social elite which had been in existence from well before the Tang dynasty. That stratum had long functioned as a self-perpetuating system of "eminent clans" (or "great lineages"), whose leading members constituted an elite national service corps that could monopolize appointments to the civil bureaucracy so as to dominate the court and overawe their home localities. They directed the disposition of wealth and the retention of privilege; they dominated the access to learning and prestige; and they oversaw the formulation of policy. Their supremacy had begun to erode under the stresses created by late Tang political weaknesses, but it was the prolonged crisis of Tang collapse that permanently displaced those holders of inherited privilege by physically eliminating large numbers of them, and by destroying both their economic base in protected landholding and their ties to political power.[15] This profound social change established the conditions under which a new, more egalitarian elite based on merit was able to emerge under the Song (described in Chapter 6, Section III).

We thus can see that, as was the case in other brief periods of great stress in Chinese history, this half-century of deep social shock resolved many long-standing problems of "institutional lag," by which is meant the typical failure of institutions to adapt rapidly enough to changing conditions. The destabilizing stresses further hastened the pace of change. We should not assume that all the consequences were benign or that the forms they took were somehow inevitable. But that they occurred is undeniable.

IV. SIMULTANEOUS DEVELOPMENTS IN THE TEN STATES

The remnants of Tang dynasty high cultural life declined noticeably in the north under the Five Dynasties. Warfare there was more destructive, and the life of a dynasty was too short to establish the arts of peace under its sponsorship. The greater margin of agricultural productivity in Central and South China produced higher levels of disposable wealth than were possible in the north, supported steady tax revenues, and encouraged the burgeoning trade based on specialized regional crafts and on imported products. That was in sharp contrast to the steady impoverishment of Northwest China. The wealth of the south drew many displaced members of the old Tang elite, as well as migrations of ordinary people, to its more peaceful regions. The courts of the emperors of Former and Later Shu at Chengdu in Sichuan, of the Southern Tang at present-day Nanjing, and of the kings of Wu-Yue at present-day Hangzhou, were particularly important for their large concentrations of poets and scholars, essayists and painters, many drawn from the displaced Tang elite.

The technology of blockprinting used for producing printed books dates back at least to the seventh century and made considerable progress through the Tang, but in many ways it matured into a fully developed art only during the tenth century. The first complete printed edition of the eleven Confucian classics (plus two supplementary works) in 130 volumes was produced at the courts of the Five Dynasties, between 932 and 953, under the uninterrupted sponsorship of a leading minister of state, Feng Dao, who served ten rulers under five successive dynasties. "This was the first time that the Confucian classics were printed, and the beginning of official publications for sale by the National Academy."[16] Despite the disorder of the age, both Luoyang and Kaifeng were major centers of printing in the north. The arts of printing grew even more rapidly in the south. Among the capitals of the Ten States, both Chengdu and Nanjing, and especially Hangzhou under the sponsorship of the kings of Wu-Yue, became centers of fine printing, producing a range of classical, religious, and contemporary secular works for wide distribution throughout the entire country and for export abroad. Printing now extended its range well beyond the numerous printings of Buddhist texts, which had been its principal focus up to this time.

An anthology of lyric poetry *(ci)* compiled and printed during the Five Dynasties is of great importance in literary history. It is the work called *Huajian ji* (Amidst the Flowers Anthology), produced in the state of Later Shu of the Ten States, its preface dated 940. The genre of poetry called *ci* was new in mid-Tang times and flourished greatly during the Five Dynasties and on into the Song. *Huajian ji* is the earliest anthology devoted entirely to this genre, and is important for preserving some of the earliest examples of *ci* songs by the great Tang forerunners, but even more important as evidence of the genre's widespread currency in the early tenth century. This anthology contains some 500 poems by 18 authors, most of whom lived in or had some connection to Sichuan, where the Former and Later Shu states were located.

The name *Huajian* suggests dalliance among the "flowers," here meaning courtesans and prostitutes; the poems are poets' words set to tunes in the new musical forms of mid- and late Tang. The musical patterns of these songs, which entertainers specialized in singing, determined the requirements of *ci* prosody—that is, their distinctive long and short lines of specified syllable length and number—determined where the rhyme words should be placed, and so on. It was an intricate prosody, fixing the poetic form of *ci* that continued to be written even when the form later came to be divorced from the music, the words no longer sung, the poems written as a new standard form of literary expression. In the early phase of this important poetic genre's development, represented in the *Huajian ji*, the poems still reflected their use as entertainers' songs. Not surprisingly, most of them are love poetry—languid, romantic, often erotic. To later Confucian-minded critics the collection was pervaded by the moral degeneracy of the Five Dynasties era, which they saw exemplified not only in the careers of such officials as Feng Dao, who "shamelessly" shifted his loyalty with each change of dynasty,[17] but also in the opulent decadence of elite life at the southern courts.

The Southern Tang court, especially under the second and third of its three emperors, Li Jing and Li Yu (father and son, who together reigned from 943 to 975), was a gathering place for poets and painters. The emperors and some of their literary courtiers are ranked among the most important poets of the entire lyric song *(ci)* tradition, especially Li Yu, the "Last Emperor" (Houzhu) of the Southern Tang. He was captured by the Song armies in 975 and was poisoned in captivity three years later. Unlike his father, who was both a fine poet and an energetic ruler, Li Yu was incompetent as a ruler. Yet he possessed a boundless capacity for aesthetic experience and for literary expression, especially as a lyric poet, and he greatly broadened the scope of the *ci* lyric song genre. He is considered the representative poet of his own age, and one who exerted a powerful influence on the poetry of the succeeding Northern Song period.[18] Even today he ranks among the most widely appreciated poets of all time: his lyrics employ simple and direct language, but in their evocative imagery, sentimentality, and truly profound feelings they are fiendishly difficult to capture in translation.

The unfortunate "Last Emperor" also was a noted calligrapher and prose essayist and, like his father, a patron of painting. Nanjing was at that time the most important center of painting in China. A dozen masters who lived there rank among the best artists of the century. Many of them lived into the early decades of the Song dynasty, and established styles and traditions that profoundly influenced early Song art.[19] Unfortunately, much of their work is known today only through copies made a century or more later. Nevertheless, the distinctive achievement of these artists is well attested.

The court of Wu-Yue, with its capital at the great coastal city of Hangzhou south of modern Shanghai, was rich in economic resources, and used its maritime location to extend its relations with Japan, Korea, North China ports, and the Liao in Manchuria. Its kings, of the Qian family, were great sponsors of Buddhism and of the related arts of architecture, temple decoration, and religious sculpture. Hangzhou began to grow into a great cosmopolitan center, foreshadowing its importance as the national capital in Southern Song times.

Careful study of the Ten States is needed to enlarge our understanding of the transition from the Tang dynasty to the Song; it holds the potential for explaining many things, such as regional distinctiveness, linguistic change, relations of Chinese with non-Chinese populations, developments in material culture, and the like. A brief interlude between two great dynastic eras, and one that has not drawn the sympathies of traditional scholars, it has tended to get lost in the flow of the more momentous events of history. The discussion of the period here can do little more than provide a reference guide to some of the names, dates, and places, but cannot convey the interest and importance that lie there.

v. China and Inner Asia in Geographic and Historical Perspective

Inner Asia assumes so important a place in Chinese later imperial history that it must be defined and explained before we go further into the history of post-Tang China in the tenth and later centuries. The reader will be referred to this section at a number of points. At risk of repeating topics mentioned in Section I of this chapter, some of the geographic and historical contexts of China's relations with Inner Asia will be touched upon again here.

Historians increasingly agree in using "Central Asia" to designate the regions known in the past as Sogdiana, Bactria, Transoxiana, Fergana, and the like. Transoxiana[20] is called that because Alexander the Great crossed the Oxus River in 327 B.C.E. in his eastward campaigns: the area "across the Oxus" was then the ancient kingdom of Sogdiana. Loosely, "Central Asia" means to us today the northern portion of modern Afghanistan and adjoining regions of the former USSR along the Amu Darya (i.e., the ancient Oxus) and the Syr Darya (i.e., the Jaxartes) rivers, lying to the west of the Pamir Mountains and east of the Caspian Sea. The Russians did not establish control there until the nineteenth century, but in modern administrative geography that region now comprises Tajikistan, Turkmenistan, Uzbekistan, Kirghizstan, and southern parts of Kazakhstan of the former USSR, along with northern Afghanistan. During much of China's imperial age that region was the home of flourishing Turkic city-states including Bukhara, Balkh, Merv, Samarkand, and others with similarly evocative historical associations. Many writers, however, continue to use "Central Asia" more loosely to include large parts of what I shall here call Inner Asia.

"Inner Asia," in distinction to "Central Asia," is used here to designate the vast region east of the Pamirs and extending all the way to the Pacific Ocean. It includes Tibet and Xinjiang in the west, north of China Proper from the latitude of China's Great Wall all the way to but not including the Siberian forests and tundra, and east to the Pacific coast. Inner Asia is thus defined as the "interior" of East Asia, whether seen from Russian Siberia or from China.

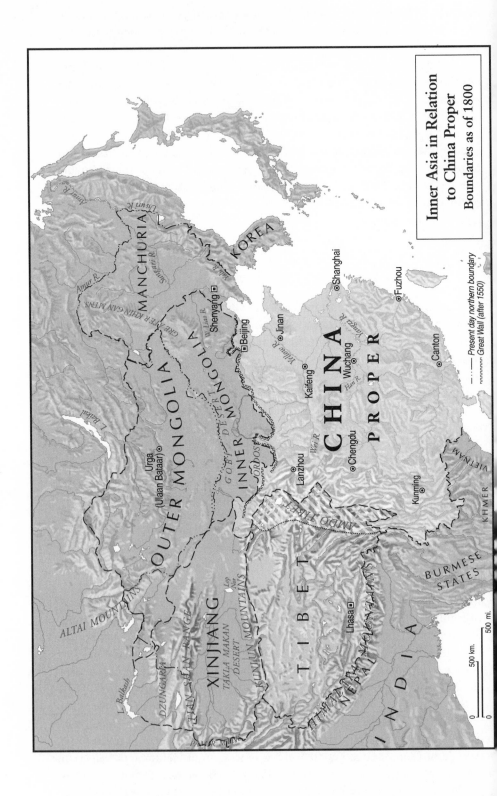

Inner Asia in Relation to China Proper Boundaries as of 1800

From the Pamirs east to Vladivostok is a distance of 3,000 miles; from south to north Inner Asia incorporates a band 1,000 or more miles wide. The core of Inner Asia consists of the regions known, from west to east, as Tibet, Chinese Turkestan or Xinjiang (Sinkiang), Inner and Outer Mongolia, and Manchuria (which the Chinese call "the Northeast," Dongbei). Inner Asia also includes areas of the former USSR east of the Pamirs inhabited today largely by Turkic and Mongolian peoples of the Russian steppe, just to the north of Chinese Turkestan and the Mongolian Republic (formerly Outer Mongolia).[21]

If we include as part of the historical Tibet the Chinese-Tibetan upland comprising the western Chinese border province of Qinghai (or Kokonor) and the former province of Xikang, now largely absorbed into the new boundaries of China's Sichuan Province, that entire area of Inner Asia is well over 4 million square miles in extent (Map 3). About 2 million square miles of that is within the boundaries of China today; by comparison, the area of "China Proper," or "China inside the Wall," is about 1.8 million square miles.[22]

The modern political boundaries in that part of the world have little geographic or cultural relevance for the history of the region; they do not serve any needs of the historian other than to help identify ancient sites on modern maps. Owen Lattimore has used the expressive geographical metaphor of the "Inner Asian Sea" for the steppes and deserts stretching from Manchuria to the Pamirs, seeing its oases as islands and the edges of the sedentary societies encircling it as its shores. This well describes the historical reality of the relationship of the sown (that is, of sedentary agriculture) to the steppe, the sedentary "shore and island dwellers" in relation to the "sea-roaming" nomads.

In Han and Tang times the portions of Inner Asia in which the Chinese were deeply involved lay to their northwest, within the Tibetan borderland and in Chinese Turkestan, the modern province of Xinjiang. From the tenth century on, the areas of China's major involvements in Inner Asia shifted to the east, to the regions known today as Mongolia and Manchuria ("the Northeast"). Simultaneously, but for different reasons, the political and demographic centers of China also shifted eastward, away from the northwest provinces, which had been the locus of China's early capitals and which had been its springboard into Xinjiang.

At its southern and western edges, Inner Asia enfolds Asia's loftiest and most forbidding mountains, the Himalayas and the Pamirs. To the north and east of those great barriers, three mountain chains split off and run to the east, extending into China and Inner Asia for a thousand miles or more: the Kunlun Mountains divide Tibet from Xinjiang; the Tian Shan Range divides Xinjiang into two vast basins, the Tarim Basin on the south and the Dzungaria Basin to the north; and, farther north, the Altai Range divides Xinjiang from Mongolia.

South of the Tian Shan Range, the huge Tarim Basin extends a thousand miles from Kashgar and Yarkand in the west to Hami and Dunhuang in the east, on the edges of China Proper. Most of it is an immense, uninhabited wasteland known as the Takla Makan, a desert of legendary harshness and danger, yet crossed by the fabled Silk Roads connecting China to western Asia. The most important of those routes ran across its northern rim, "island-hopping" from one oasis to the next. Dzungaria, to the north of the Tian Shan, is mostly rolling steppe, and especially at its eastern end it is deep in summer grass on which herds fatten. It is not desert, yet like the Takla Makan to its south, it is subject to extremes of heat and cold and to fierce winter winds. Mongolia, today divided into Inner Mongolia (an administrative region of China) and Outer Mongolia (more correctly, the Republic of Mongolia, recently independent after long being subject to domination by the USSR), lies north and east of the Altai Range. Mongolia is a flatter plateau mostly between 3,000 and 5,000 feet in elevation. That great Mongolian heartland (the Mongol khanate's "hearthland") enfolds vast deserts—the Gobi, the Ordos, and the Alashan—within its southern and western boundaries, but has grassy steppelands farther north and east. The farther east one goes in Mongolia, the more reliable are the rainfall and the grass, but trees are few and forests unknown. Still farther east, beyond the Greater Khingan (Da Xing'an) Mountains in Chahar, just north of Beijing, one crosses into Manchuria, with its rich plains and valleys and, still farther north, its deep forests.

Southern Manchuria was, intermittently, administratively part of China as early as the beginnings of the imperial era, and remained so off and on until the eighth century. Thereafter, its remaining Chinese population was concentrated in the southwestern coastal zone. Except for that narrow zone, Manchuria did not acquire a large Chinese population until nineteenth-century migrations from North China occurred. Not counting that newly populated segment of Inner Asia, the entire core area of Inner Asia, from the Amur River west to the Pamirs, held a population of only about 12 million in the early decades of the twentieth century, when China Proper had a population of around 500 million. In the tenth century China had a population of perhaps 80 million (then a third of the world's population), whereas all of the Inner Asian core area held about 5 million people divided into a very large number of nations and tribal groupings. That is necessarily a rough estimate but it cannot be far wrong. The Khitan population in the tenth century has been carefully estimated to have been less than 1 million. The Mongol population in areas subject to the Yuan dynasty's rule in the late thirteenth century, probably more than half the Mongol population at that time, might be roughly estimated at one-half million.[23] Figures for the Tibetan and Jurchen populations in the twelfth century are not reliable enough to cite even in rough estimate, but could not have been much larger than the estimates for the Mongol and Khitan populations offered here. In short, we cannot know for certain the population of Inner Asia at any point in the span of history covered by this volume, but we can be quite secure in describing the area as one of sparsest habitation, of immense empty distances, with climate often ranging from harsh to worse, conditions testing to the full the toughness and adaptability of its inhabitants, and of all who traveled or campaigned across it.

Yet there were and are rich oases in Xinjiang, favored islands of commerce and agriculture set in the desert sea, often constituting city-states of some importance. The cities and their surrounding oases were links in the chain of supply stations sustaining the caravan routes stretching west from China that crossed the Pamirs, and in a tenuous way linked East Asia to the farther shores of sedentary life in India and Persia and farther west, even to the Black Sea and the Mediterranean. Apart from these important oasis city-states, there were in the tenth century few cities of size and importance in all the rest of Inner Asia. To be sure, three of the five Liao dynasty capitals built early in the tenth century lay north of the Great Wall line (then a line of defended passes, not a continuous wall). Those capital cities, however, were populated by forced migrants, mostly Chinese from the southern coastal rim of Manchuria or North China. Except for the sedentary inhabitants of the oases, the other Inner Asian peoples themselves were not city dwellers.

Agriculture was intensively practiced in the fertile oases of Chinese Turkestan scattered across the Tarim and Dzungaria basins. Some of those were several hundred square miles in extent. They depended on irrigation from short rivers that descended from the mountain ranges; as they flowed farther from their sources in the high mountains, those rivers disappeared in the sands. The agrarian inhabitants were primarily Turkic; some were literate peoples of quite advanced civilizations with strong cultural ties both to China and to places farther west, in Central Asia. Farther east, throughout most of Mongolia agriculture was scarcely possible because the rainfall averages only from three to ten inches a year. Farther on, to the east of the Khingan Mountains in Manchuria, however, the rainfall is a reliable twenty to thirty or more inches a year. The Liao, the Jin, and the Qing dynasties all originated there, among peoples—the Khitans, the Jurchens, and the Manchus—who could easily have practiced agriculture, and sometimes did, but who in their rise from local tribal leadership to military overlordship of enlarged territories, in preparation for conquest, found it advantageous to identify with the potent pattern of militarized steppe nomadism.

Pastoral nomadism appeared in the Inner Asian region perhaps no more than 2,000 years ago. Anthropologists and historians no longer subscribe to theories that saw nomadism as a primitive stage in the development of all mankind, following the stage of hunter-gatherers, and to be followed inevitably by the more advanced stage of sedentary agriculture.[24] Even though Stone Age man everywhere appears to have been nomadic in the sense of wandering about in search of food, pastoral nomadism as it developed in Inner Asia (and some other parts of the world) is quite different. It is an advanced form of social organization, the preference of people whose forebears probably had practiced agriculture, perhaps in regions of quite limited or marginal productivity along the shores of the Inner Asian desert "sea." To those reluctant agriculturalists the alternative of nomadism offered more than did the hard life of growing wheat or millet in arid regions. The Inner Asian core area offered conditions that permitted the highest development of the potential in nomadism, sustained by its wandering herds of cattle and sheep and the use of camels and horses for transport or for war. Only under conditions which to them represented failure would those nomads settle down in one place long enough to scratch out and harvest a summer's crop. They looked with scorn on farmers, and though dependent on neighboring farming peoples for grain, iron, textiles, and other essentials, they much preferred to acquire those by raiding or coercive exploitation. Agriculturalists and nomads thus coexisted in an unbalanced symbiosis, nomads needing items that only stable agricultural communities could provide, while their sedentary neighbors needed nothing from the nomads, yet could not evade their demands. The rich oases were most vulnerable to raids and conquest, and could be forced to provision the first phases of nomadic state development. But beyond that, the scale of their economic support to nomadic power buildups was limited.

Later imperial China is a period of China's and Inner Asia's profound impact on each other. The impact was mutual: it worked in both directions. The historian, however, must write the history of this period primarily from the Chinese record. For these as for most centuries it is the Chinese record that provides the fullest and most factual account of all things affecting China. True, that impressive record distorts events involving non-Chinese peoples by perceiving them as occurring on the periphery of the world's only civilization. For, while not always well informed about other peoples or necessarily unsympathetic to them as fellow human beings, the Chinese nonetheless have disparaged them as people not yet fully within the boundaries of civilized—that is, of Chinese—life. The modern reader may not feel full affinity with that arrogant (even if understandable) prejudice. Yet similar attitudes are familiar in many national histories and are not unknown in our own.

Chinese still have difficulty coming to terms with the long period of invasion and alien domination that began with the Liao dynasty early in the tenth century. Like the ancient Greeks, the Chinese of the past designated peoples who did not use their language and share their cultural values "barbarians." Nevertheless, in recent decades, under ideological imperatives of our time, modern Chinese in China have reversed that narrow view, but only to adopt or retroactively co-opt all the non-Chinese aliens, including those who dominated this period, now classing them as their "non-Han but Chinese" junior partners in the growth of a multiethnic Chinese nation. If this view suits certain modern Chinese political or psychological needs, it is nevertheless strikingly ahistorical, and somewhat disturbing in its patronizing attitude toward peoples who thought of themselves as fiercely independent, and as possessors of cultures having their own integrity despite interactions and influences derived from the Chinese edge of their world. Most modern Chinese historians continue, much like their predecessors throughout several millennia, to accept the preeminence of Chinese cultural values in all periods of East and Inner Asian history. Their arguments can be impressive, if ultimately not convincing to all of their neighboring peoples. "Objectivity" in such matters is difficult to achieve. To repeat, we are perforce almost completely dependent on Chinese sources, and very largely on modern Chinese scholarship, with all the past and present biases and subjective cultural attitudes they embody. Yet there are many Chinese as well as other historians of today who strive to escape the limitations implicit in that circumstance. In this work, difficult though it is given the sources, I shall endeavor to establish a distinct point of view.

When the Inner Asian chieftains scanned their horizons, there were many targets of military expansion to tempt their ambitious warriors. But beyond all the others, China was the great prize, for plunder and for more long-range exploitation. The paramount challenge to Inner Asian tribal peoples in those middle centuries of China's imperial age was to create confederations that could aggregate large enough armies, organized on the supremely efficient steppe nomad model, so that they could prevail over at least a portion of the Chinese nation. During the twelfth and thirteenth centuries the Mongols carried that development to its ultimate heights and conquered not only all of China but all of Central and West Asia and much of Russia as well.

The Mongols' success in conquest is unmatched in history, yet even before them the organization of entire tribal societies for mobility, and the honing of each of their member's skills for warfare, had reached impressive levels of success among their Turkic predecessors. The Kirghiz, the Khazars, and the Oghuz Turks, the Kipchaks and Kumans, and other Turkic-speaking predecessors of the Mongols, all of whom appear to have originated in eastern Inner Asia, began to extend their empires to the west no later than the sixth century C.E. The khanate of the Western Turks controlled most of Central Asia in the sixth century, and at the same time the Khazars, whose language was almost certainly Turkic, and whose rulers converted to Judaism in 740 C.E., had controlled the regions from the northern shores of the Caspian westward into the Ukraine from the sixth century onward. We thus see that the westward spread of Turkic peoples, some reaching as far as Byzantium and eastern Europe, had long preceded the westward expansion of the Mongols in the thirteenth century.[25]

Others moved into the central parts of Inner Asia that we now call Mongolia and created their conquest dynasties in symbiosis with China. The Tangut Xi Xia, whose roots were in the Tibetan uplands of Northwest China, and the Khitan Liao from the Northeast (Manchuria), illustrate the variety of linkages that could be created between advanced nomadism and the Chinese culture area in the tenth century. The Jurchens, the Mongols, and later the Manchus offered further variations on this theme. During the thirteenth century, steppe history fully merged with the mainstream of Chinese history in the Mongol conquest of the entire Chinese culture area and the establishment there of their Yuan dynasty.

That long span of time, roughly half a millennium from the rise of the Khitans to the end of the Mongol Yuan dynasty, was a period of profound changes in Chinese civilization, and of even more remarkable changes in the civilizations and the political organizations of the Inner Asian nations which created the conquest dynasties. Northern tribal states and Chinese dynasties lived in close, continuous interaction. An account of the Inner Asian states is thus properly central to this account of Chinese history. That is not to deny that the Inner Asian civilizations also have their own integral histories—

histories that deserve to be narrated from the point of view of their own states and cultures, and in full consideration of all their other boundaries and their further relations with other nations. They need not be examined *only* from the point of view of their place in Chinese history. But this is a history of China, "China" signifying here, as it has historically, an account of the (Han) Chinese people and of their distinctive civilization. We must start here with the tenth century to trace a coherent story, albeit one that can include only an incomplete and one-sided account of Inner Asian history, distorted by being viewed—for our present purposes—as an extension of Chinese history. That too is a valid point of view, even if it is only one among several that might be adopted.

To begin the story of this phase of Chinese history, I shall then start in the early tenth century, with the brilliant achievements of the Turco-Mongol or Proto-Mongol Khitan nation in creating new forms for exploiting the power of their pastoral nomad state. That extraordinary story follows next.

2

ABAOJI

With the career of Abaoji, a Khitan chieftain who became the founder of the Liao dynasty, a new phase in relations between China and its neighbors to the north began. This remarkable leader set the goal of gaining a foothold within the zone of sedentary life at the edge of China. To incorporate such an addition to his steppe empire, and with the intent to expand it into China, he devised the system of dual administration, the effective tool by which he, his Khitan successors, and subsequent conquerors would govern simultaneously over both nomadic and farming populations, exploiting the wealth of China to build vast empires. Thus began the later millennium of China's imperial era.

"He grew up to be a man nine *chi* tall. The upper part of his face was broad, the lower part sharply chiseled; the flash of his eyes pierced a person. He could draw a bow of three hundred pounds." Those few lines tell us all we know about the physical appearance of Abaoji, the founder of the Liao dynasty. But the Chinese historians recording his life several centuries later also recalled that his birth and early life were marked by portents auguring future greatness: his mother dreamed that the sun fell from the sky into her bosom; she became pregnant thereafter, and when she gave birth to him, the room was filled with mysterious light and extraordinary fragrance. The newborn infant's body was like that of a three-year-old child; at three months he could walk, and at one year could speak. He was able to know things that had not yet come to pass.[1]

Such legends surround the origins of many heroes in East Asian history. Abaoji, the supreme chieftain of the Khitan (Chinese: Qidan) people and founder of the Liao empire, deserves these symbols of greatness. The real achievements of his life were of such magnitude that sober historians were willing to retain legendary corroborations of his exceptional qualities. He was a "man of the steppe" whose heroic qualities in strategy and warfare, whose courage, strength, and cunning, made him an indomitable conqueror. Yet the truly unusual quality of this man lay in his ability to analyze the character of his own and of Chinese civilization and to create instruments for bringing them together into a stable, workable system of empire that his Khitan people could dominate. The Khitan-Liao model of conquest and rule provided a pattern that, if not precisely followed, nonetheless powerfully influenced the successor Jurchen-Jin, the Mongol-Yuan, and, in the seventeenth century, the Manchu-Qing dynasties of conquest.

Did Abaoji possess the "psychic mobility" to imagine a political world that did not yet exist?[2] Perhaps not; it is not necessary to see him as an abstract thinker creating new ideal political forms, for 500 years of Khitan-Chinese interaction lay behind his extraordinary personal achievement. That historical memory provided a base from which to develop new modes and solutions. His achievement resided in drawing on that historical experience as presented to him by his advisers, in making pragmatic decisions to implement new forms, and in his determination to realize a new era through practical institutions for governing. The founders of the subsequent conquest dynasties did not have that depth of experience in their own histories, but Abaoji's achievement became fixed in *their* historical memories as well, and was made credible to them by his untarnished integrity in remaining a true man of the steppe throughout his long involvement with the Chinese. The Liao experience thus possesses great weight in the histories of Inner Asia and of China.

I. THE KHITANS AND THEIR NEIGHBORS

The Khitan people lived on the eastern slopes of the Greater Khingan (Xing-'an) Mountain Range which extends south to north and at the time divided Mongolia from Manchuria.[3] Those well-watered, grassy slopes were ideal for herding cattle and horses, the basic wealth of the Khitans. Their pastoral, nomadic way of life was formed through centuries of conflict and cultural interaction with neighboring steppe and sedentary peoples.

On the western side of the Greater Khingan Mountains lived the more typical nomadic steppe peoples, their economy dependent on sheep and camels and on the necessity to move about to utilize the scantier pastures of the Mongolian plateau. The Khitans were like those peoples to their west in being horse breeders and mounted warriors and were close to them in their way of life. Some of those can be identified by old tribal names such as the Shiwei and the Xi, who had intermarried with the Khitans and provided what we may call the more volatile "Mongol" element in Khitan life. There also were remnants of the Uighurs, Turkic people who in the ninth century had been driven west into Turkestan (Xinjiang) when their great empire occupying what we now call Mongolia was destroyed by another Turkic people, the Kirghiz. The Uighurs had been powerful enemies of the Tang state in the eighth and ninth centuries, yet occasionally had been drawn into military alliances with the Chinese. The Shiwei, the Xi, the Tatars, and other such warlike tribal peoples occupying the endless plains of Mongolia to the west offered the Khitans the challenge of building a great steppe empire by expansion in that direction.

To the east and northeast, all the way to the deep forests of the Amur River basin, dwelt the Jurchens. They lived in small, dispersed tribal groups. Those farther to the north and east still lived by hunting and fishing in the forests; those that had spread south and westward into central Manchuria's open plains combined a woodsman's way of life with simple agriculture and pig rearing. Skilled woodsmen and hunters, when they eventually adapted to the horse and mounted warfare they became dangerous neighbors.

East and southeast from the Khitan homeland, across the Liao River and south to the Yalu River, was the Bohai nation. Some of the Bohai people still lived by hunting and fishing, but in large part they had become a settled agricultural people who also kept in subjugation a farming population made up mainly of conquered Chinese and Koreans. The Koreans pronounced their name Parhae, under which spelling it appears in many histories. The Korean cultural element may have been the dominant one in their civilization. The Bohai had figured importantly in Chinese history in Tang times as a powerful enemy state gradually depriving Tang China of its far northeast territories in what would be modern Liaoning Province of China's Northeast (Manchuria).

On all sides, except to the south, where all these peoples shared a boundary with the stable, sedentary civilization of China, the Khitans were surrounded by a great diversity of tribal nations whose identities and allegiances shifted like the sands of the Gobi. Alignments among tribes could produce federations, rapid buildups of political power capable of assembling mighty military force. The greater their mobility, the greater their striking force; that was their comparative advantage over their more sedentary neighbors. At the acme of their power, the steppe nomads could threaten even China, which, with its massive sedentary population, was the largest, most stable, and wealthiest society in the world. But their threat to China historically had been one of raiding and plundering through incursions at the borders, as yet without well-developed means for occupying and governing. And the Chinese always had the choice of going out into the steppe to fight them on their ground, or devising some sort of compromise to gain a measure of security. The Khitans had observed or had been directly involved in relations of that kind with the Chinese for centuries. They understood the mechanics of relationships between the steppe and the sown.

II. ETHNIC DIVERSITY AND LANGUAGE COMMUNITY

I have referred here to a steppe world inhabited by Turkic, Mongol, and Tungusic peoples. That implies more linguistic confusion than actually existed, for those are the three branches of the Altaic language family. Those languages shared many features. All the Altaic languages appear to have arisen in northwestern Manchuria and northeastern Mongolia, on into the region around Lake Baikal. Speakers of some Turkic branches of Altaic moved westward, into the Mongolian plateau, and eventually on across the

Pamirs into southern Russia and to Anatolia. The modern Turks of Turkey are the westernmost and largest branch of the large Turkic-speaking family. Yet history's earliest known people who called themselves Turks (in Chinese records called Tujue, or Türks, to distinguish them from the modern Turks of Turkey) in the 6th century C.E. had lived on the Orchon River in the central part of today's Mongolia. That is where the Uighur Turks had their capital in the eighth and ninth centuries, before they were driven west into Xinjiang. The Uighurs have remained the largest and historically the most important of Turkic peoples in Chinese Inner Asia. The varieties of the various Turkic languages, from Istanbul all the way to China, have remained linguistically quite similar even where not mutually intelligible.

People clearly identified by the name "Mongol" do not appear in history until the twelfth century. Speakers of the Mongol languages today are divided into three main divisions, found all the way from northern Afghanistan to Manchuria, but mostly concentrated in the central part of Inner Asia, in Inner and Outer Mongolia. The Khitans are sometimes called Turko-Mongols, and their language proto-Mongol, suggesting that those two branches of Altaic had not yet clearly differentiated. Culturally, the Khitans' obvious affinities were with the slightly later Mongols. They were more clearly people of the steppe than were any of the Tungusic peoples to their east. Their ancestral legends link them to the other proto-Mongol peoples, but their language shows a very large number of terms derived from or related to Uighur Turkic. It is quite possible that the population and their ordinary language belonged to the Mongol division of Altaic, but that, as their tribal state interacted with a variety of powerful neighbors, they borrowed much technical language, particularly in government. The Uighurs were the most successful of the Khitans' steppe neighbors in the period of Khitan emergence, from the sixth to the ninth centuries; the pattern of Khitan-Uighur interaction, now friendly, now hostile, could explain a good deal of this language borrowing.

The Tungusic division of the Altaic family of languages includes Jurchen, the later Manchu language, and other remnants of what historically have been large and sometimes powerful tribal confederations originating in the easternmost parts of Inner Asia. The languages of the Bohai, the Koreans, and, according to some scholars, even the Japanese also belong to the Tungusic wing of the Altaic family. Unlike the Khitans and the Mongols to their west, the groups farther east that we can identify as speakers of Tungusic languages, valued the land and did not scorn agriculture, even when they adapted fully to the nomads' methods of mobile warfare. We can include them as "people of the steppe" even though they lived east of the steppe proper, because in their rise to conquest dynasty status they chose to broaden their semi-sedentary way of life by grafting mobile steppe warfare onto it.

But all of the distinctions based on language merely point out the weakness of our ethnic labels. We have no reasonable alternatives to using linguistic identifications for peoples, even though we must recognize that they are tentative labels and that they do not in themselves tell us very much. For most of the Inner Asian peoples, of greater importance than their identification with this or that division of the Altaic language family is the salient fact that all the Altaic languages displayed some degree of homogeneity. Their speakers all recognized one another as users of languages that, to be sure, were in most cases not mutually intelligible, but that they could without too much difficulty learn to understand, and this contributed to a sense of kinship among them. The fellowship shared by all the "people of the steppe" as against the farming Chinese was thus reinforced by their sense of linguistic and cultural community. Those affinities were strongest within the various Turkic languages of the Altaic language family, but were present in some measure throughout all the Altaic languages; extending from one end of Inner Asia to the other, these linguistic affinities underlay the ceaseless process of building confederations of tribes and nations. That, rather than defending and expanding a geographically delimited territorial home, was the characteristic political process of Inner Asian history.

The Khitans and the Uighurs. The Khitan people cherished legends of their past that extended back many centuries into oral tradition. The Khitan language did not have a script until the tenth century; our knowledge of their early history comes from Chinese records, in which we find the name "Khitan" transcribed in Chinese characters that today are pronounced *qidan*. Those references go back as far as the fourth century C.E. They become fuller and more informative two or three centuries later. During the Tang dynasty (618–907), the Khitans became at times subordinate to their powerful neighbor to the west, the Uighurs, in whose formal relations with Tang China they shared. The Uighurs' culture itself underwent rapid changes in the late ninth century, following their evacuation from the Mongolian Plateau after 842. As a nation newly located in Xinjiang, the Uighurs were converted to a new religion—the Manichaean religion founded in third-century Persia. They became literate, adopting from the Indo-European Sogdians a script that had come down via Aramaic from still earlier Semitic scripts. They also at this time gradually abandoned nomadism in favor of living in cities or agricultural city-states based on the oases of Xinjiang. The Khitans' "Uighur connection," heretofore so important to their national development, was not entirely broken off by the geographical movements or the cultural transformations of their Turkic mentors, but they themselves did not take those same paths. Instead, in the tenth century the Khitans moved into the power vacuum in the vast region we now call Mongolia and strove with considerable success to attach that region to their own new empire. Some enclaves of Uighurs who had remained behind when their nation was driven westward in the mid-ninth century came at that time under Khitan rule and continued to be an important source of knowledge to the Khitans as they developed new tools to aid their own national growth. The Uighurs also played important roles in the cultural and political development of other conquest dynasties thereafter.

Khitan leaders in the late ninth century observed how the Uighurs had entered into the Chinese forms of interstate relations with the Tang dynasty court and had successfully coerced the Tang government to pay them subsidies, mainly annual payments of bolts of silk (a bolt of silk was a standard unit of value comparable to standard units of precious metals or to money). For a century or more that gave the Uighurs wealth with which to dominate trade and warfare throughout Inner Asia. The Khitans had also witnessed the intimidating effects of steppe cavalry, whether that of the Shatuo Turks, the Uighurs, the Kirghiz, or their own, in gaining the objectives important to Inner Asian peoples, often at the expense of the less martial Chinese. The Chinese defense usually was to "use the barbarians to control the barbarians." That is, nearer groups among the militarily aggressive peoples at the borders were attached to the Chinese state with subsidies, titles, border zone military offices, and Chinese court honors. Then they were induced to compete with one another and in that process to shield China against enemies farther away.

III. THE LESSONS OF HISTORY

Observing those examples, the Khitans probably saw quite clearly that when a steppe people by degrees gave up its nomadic mobility in exchange for the more comfortable sedentary life, it ran great risks of having to compete with the Chinese on their ground. Losing in that way their comparative advantage inevitably cost the nomads their cultural integrity; they slowly became just "little Chinese." The Koreans, a settled people of high culture, could sinify their social forms and become, as the Korean state of Silla (57 B.C.E.–935 C.E.) was proud to boast, a "little China." Silla could survive that cultural adaptation; its people were too tough, and their land too far away, as early Tang emperors had found out, for them to be annexed to China. But no steppe people on China's borders could become sinified and survive, except by migrating into China and being absorbed—another form of extinction. Under pressure from the conquering Kirghiz, in the mid-ninth century the Uighurs had moved out of the steppe, giving up the comparative advantages of nomadic life; but by going west into Xinjiang and adopting cultural forms drawn from western Asian models, they could remain apart from Chinese civilization. Yet they played an essential part in the Silk Route trade, and were able to serve as cultural intermediaries among peoples on all sides.

Neither the Korean nor the Uighur model was relevant to the Khitan situation. Moreover, the warning to nomadic peoples was clear: they must master the art of drawing resources from China without sacrificing their steppe integrity. Nonetheless, as was true of most Inner Asian peoples, whether they felt drawn to China, or whether they scorned the softer life of the sown, none could ignore China. The wealth that could be wrung from it could give mastery over all of Inner Asia. As the Tang state, fatally weakened following the internal rebellions and subsequent turmoil of the 870s, lost its power to control its neighbors, some of those neighbors were inexorably drawn into China's vortex as aggressors against it, and as rivals against one another in the rush to fatten on the Chinese prize. The stimulus to respond quickly and powerfully to growing opportunities on its southern borders with China forced internal changes on the Khitan nation. The first decades of the tenth century mark the great watershed in Khitan political development.

IV. THE NEW LEADER EMERGES

By the 750s a line of Khitan supreme chieftains, or khans, who used the lineage name or surname Yaolian had risen to dominance. At the triennial councils of all the Khitan chieftains, a leader from their lineage was always "elected," that is, acknowledged as the khan. The Yaolian lineage maintained a monopoly on the supreme chieftainship for a century and a half, during which time they received the full diplomatic treatment from the Tang court. The first Yaolian khan was even awarded the Tang imperial surname, Li, by which he and his descendants are known in Chinese records. But if that counted as high honor at the Tang court, it meant little back in the steppe, where they continued to be known as the Yaolian. The khans appeared at the Chinese court with frequency, carried away honors and titles as well as monetary rewards, and generally served Tang interests quite well—except when they allied themselves with other Inner Asian nomadic peoples to make war on the Chinese.

Chinese sources from that period speak of the "Eight Tribes" of the Khitans, and the "Nine Tents" of the Yaolian lineage. The latter were the descendants of the nine generations of khans who had come from the Yaolian lineage, a spreading clan of royal relatives so numerous that they functioned as a ninth tribe. Among the "Eight Tribes" constituting the bulk of the Khitan nation, the largest and most powerful was the Yila tribe. By the late ninth century its leaders in particular had begun to express dissatisfaction with the Yaolian khans and their management of the China relationship.

Abaoji was born in 872, the son of the elected chieftain of the Yila tribe. In 901 he was himself elected to succeed as the chieftain of the Yila. In this context, "election" means that he presented himself to the triennial council of his tribe's leaders and claimed the right to be acknowledged their chieftain, just as the Yaolian khans were reconfirmed in their khanate every three years, or a successor khan was confirmed by the formality of a tribal chieftains' council. Leaders of a certain status, normally inherited, could expect to be eligible for such formal recognition of their leadership so long as they also displayed the approved personal qualities. This system was not as rigid as a closed aristocracy, and much less so than an inherited kingship, but neither was it as open as a fully democratic process. It well served the leadership needs of nomadic tribal societies, where individual leaders had to merit approval in order to be personally effective in gaining adherents and building intertribal relations. One element of their leadership potential came from inheriting a leading clan's accumulated mystique of power. Yet, of all that clan's potential heirs in any generation, at the triennial assembly, it was the individual who had best displayed the personal qualities of leadership who would be acknowledged the next, or the continuing, chieftain.

Abaoji's clan did not have a surname. Surnames were a feature of Chinese society, not of the steppe. Up to that time, the Yaolian were unique within the Khitan nation in possessing a clan surname. Later, in the 930s, Abaoji's clan began to use the surname Yelü. In keeping with Khitan elite custom, they had long taken their wives exclusively from another clan of their tribe, and at the same time that consort clan began to use the surname Xiao. From the Yelü and Xiao lineages came the royal family and its royal consorts until the end of the Liao dynasty.

The clan that was to adopt the Xiao surname appears to have been of mixed Khitan and Uighur or possibly Xi blood; they had long played a large role as the Tang court's agents in defending Chinese interests north of the border. In addition to managing their China connection, and making use of it in the steppe, they also played a prominent role in tribal affairs to the west, across the crest of the Greater Khingan Mountains. Abaoji's own clan of Yila tribal chieftains also were deeply involved with China, but with an interest in the south. The particular focus of their struggle with the Chinese was the contest to control the defense line that separated the Tang Military Governorships (jiedushi) in northeast China from the steppe powers. The Military Governor in northern Shanxi Province was Li Keyong, a partially sinified Shatuo Turk who also had been granted the title Prince of Jin (Jin meaning the region of Shanxi Province), along with the Tang imperial surname, Li, for military services to the Chinese throne in suppressing the great rebellions of the 870s. As a major player in Tang politics, Li Keyong found it useful to use that surname. He was one of the important warlords in the domestic power struggles that would end the Tang dynasty in 907. Possessing Shanxi, he controlled a bastion within the Tang government's northern defense line of passes and garrisons.[4]

In 905, foreseeing future possibilities, Abaoji led 70,000 of his cavalry in a dash into Datong, Li Keyong's base in northern Shanxi, to swear blood brotherhood in a steppe ritual of exchanging robes and mounts. At a moment when the Tang court threatened the Shatuo base, this act reinforced Li Keyong's hand; it also served as Abaoji's entering wedge into military affairs within China. The Yila tribe was poised to take more aggressive actions on the China front than was the Khitan's Yaolian Great Khan.

In 903 Abaoji had been named the Yüyue, the commander of all the Khitan nation's military forces, second only to the Yaolian Great Khan himself. Early in 907 Abaoji appeared at the triennial council of tribal chieftains to demand that he be acknowledged the new Great Khan (more properly, khaghan, "khan of khans"). To thus displace the Khitan nation's leader was a bold step, but he succeeded in winning the support of the other seven tribal chieftains. Since becoming the Yila chieftain in 901 he had repeatedly raided the China border, capturing cities and taking captives. To the east he had attacked the Jurchens and also taken captives, and through a combination of force and wise diplomacy he had established military superiority over the powerful Xi and Shiwei nomadic confederations in the steppe to the west. Thus, by campaigning and working tirelessly, within a few short years he had established his image as an aggressive new leader on all fronts. With his successes, the Khitans appeared to have a new destiny. The two clans, Abaoji's and his consort's, between them controlled the powerful Yila tribe. Prestige, resources, accomplishment, and force allowed him to prevail in the council of the Eight Tribes' leaders. He challenged the Yaolian, overawed the council, and even obtained the concurrence of the last Yaolian Great Khan himself. Although Abaoji's action had an element of usurpation, it conformed with tribal custom and steppe expectations; it foreshadows the great council or *khuriltai* of 1206, at which Chinggis Khan forced his selection as Supreme Khan of the Mongol nation.

In May of the year 907, down in the North China Plain, the Chinese warlord Zhu Wen, who controlled North China and had murdered the last legitimate Tang ruler in 904 in order to enthrone one of that emperor's young children, now removed his puppet and declared himself the founding emperor of a new Chinese dynasty, called the Later Liang (see Chapter 1, Section II). Zhu's dynasty was short-lived, but it began the succession of short dynasties making up the period of the Five Dynasties that held power in North China for half a century from 907 until 960. Central and South China temporarily went their own way, fragmented into small states. Zhu Wen's usurpation of Tang state power in 907, and Abaoji's takeover of Khitan leadership in 907, each marking significant realignments of power, changed the shape of East Asian history. For one example, China's capital moved eastward from Chang'an to Bian (modern Kaifeng); the Inner Asian pressures on China also shifted from the northwest to the northeast. Moreover, it is of great interest that the middle three of the Five Dynasties were founded in China by remnants of the Shatuo Turks who had been settled inside China's northern boundaries as border zone warlords, and the third of the Five (the Later Jin dynasty created in 936) would be a client state of the Khitans. The reorganized Khitan nation was poised to take a strong hand in Chinese history at a most opportune time.

In light of steppe history, Abaoji's success in becoming the new Great Khan is not difficult to understand. Much more difficult to explain is why, having achieved the position of supreme leader within a strong and warlike nomad nation, he was not content to build an empire of and within the steppe region and thereby also within the expectations of steppe peoples. Instead, he immediately set about transforming the Khitan Grand Khanate, the instrument of rule that he had just gained, into something without precedent in steppe history. He attached a foreign administrative system to the Khitan nomadic state. His was to be a dual empire, part sedentary and part nomad, one part adapting to Chinese modes of governing and the other part remaining true to steppe tradition. The Khitan elite were expected to function in both halves: many became culturally dual in order actually to function and not merely play figurehead roles.

Two pyramids of administrative power were set up side by side, each capped by Abaoji, who served as Khitan Great Khan in the one and as Khitan emperor on the Chinese model in the other. One was a military state composed of the Khitan nation and other directly or indirectly administered tribal groups on the steppe and in Manchuria, presided over by the Northern Chancellery. The other was a civil government administered by sedentary society's (principally Chinese society's) traditional means along the Chinese and Korean borders where conquered farming peoples lived, and was presided over by the Southern Chancellery. The Northern Chancellery managed all military and tribal matters and dealt with tribute from subordinate peoples. The Southern Chancellery engaged in civil governing and focused on collecting agrarian and commercial taxes from non-Khitan subjects. The new government of dual institutions was a brilliant concept. Moreover, in actual practice it functioned with stability for more than two centuries. In 947 the dynastic name Liao, or "The Great Liao," was adopted, in the Chinese manner of naming, and of claiming to be an imperial dynasty; here I shall apply that dynastic name to the entire period starting in 907, as is done in the Chinese records.

However brilliant his achievement might seem in the light of history, Abaoji's new form of the state did not win universal approval from the Khitan tribal nobility of his time. They saw that their interests would be adversely affected. The ordinary tribesmen remained apart from cultural and political affairs of state; we have no way of knowing whether they welcomed, resented, or were indifferent to the new forms of governing. But Abaoji's vision of the stronger and more centralized state that was needed to direct his new system of dual administration required him to transform the Grand Khanate into an institution modeled on the powerful imperial administration of Tang China. That Chinese structure of highly centralized bureaucratic institutions supported by the entire social system with its intellectual and ethical foundations was scarcely within the ken of the Inner Asian observers. To those Khitans close to Abaoji, however, the Chinese emperor's ability to display an unassailable imperial majesty by itself seemed to explain the stability and enduring power of China. Abaoji saw value in that for steppe society, above all for himself as the ruler, and wanted to introduce that kind of strength into his government. Throughout his lifetime much of the tribal nobility opposed his pursuit of emperorship, for that imperial system limited their political roles. In theory, conciliar "election" made all males of the Great Khan's clan eligible for supreme leadership. It also gave leaders in other clans the potential for someday displacing the Great Khan, as Abaoji had done, by proving their individual capacity for leadership. That institutional fluidity was to be superseded by lifelong reigns that would occur in a fixed succession, determined by primogeniture, with a Chinese-style emphasis on family and inheritance. Stability in the ruling institution, they could see, would be gained at the expense of would-be military leaders' ambitions. The underlying ethos of tribal society would be weakened.

Throughout the nine years after 907, Abaoji was beset by serious rebellions, most often led by his own brothers and cousins, who felt that their prerogatives had been preempted and who could easily convince members of other tribes and clans that their opportunities had been diminished. Abaoji sought to convince the Khitan nobility that the new system would bring them different but commensurate rewards. Finally, in 916 he adopted Chinese court ritual formalities that elevated his position even more. He arranged for 200 trusted courtiers to petition him to assume the title of Celestial Emperor and proclaim a Chinese-style reign-period name, thereby imitating the Chinese calendar with its implications of universal sovereignty. He named his eldest son by his principal consort his heir apparent and demanded a display of fealty to him from the entire nobility. And, after 918, his government occupied a newly built walled capital city with broad avenues oriented to the compass points and many large temple compounds. It had a grand park for the imperial tents where the palaces of a Chinese capital would be. Adjoining the city to the south was a second walled "Chinese city" (Han-cheng) with commercial quarters, artisans' shops, and warehouses. The urban population was largely made up of captured people, many of them Chinese, although there was a Uighur quarter and another for residences of diplomats. The imposing new capital was an amenity the Khitans had previously done without, and may not have liked, but its usefulness as a base of wealth and provider of special services was not entirely lost on the Khitan nobility.

Despite Abaoji's new imperial status, he could not behave like a Chinese emperor. In the manner of steppe rulers, he repeatedly forgave the rebels, especially close relatives, and judiciously assigned them posts in the new bureaucracy. It was not an expression of magnanimity; he could be a ruthlessly clear-minded opponent in a struggle. But in matters like this he still had to acknowledge rights of dissenters as defined by tribal custom. His flexibility and skill in enhancing his real bases of power while responding effectively to the many challenges from within gradually allowed his course to prevail.

The new capital, called Shangjing (Supreme Capital) was built at a site hallowed by Khitan legend, near the headwaters of the Shira Muren River, which runs eastward to join the Liao River of central Manchuria. It was one of five capitals eventually established, one for each of the five administrative circuits making up the extended Khitan empire. He also fostered the building of thirty or more small walled cities, or Chinese cities, so called because their inhabitants were largely captured Chinese.[5] They were forced to manufacture salt, smelt and work iron, farm, manufacture many kinds of products, and make the cities into centers of commerce. The Supreme Capital was designed by a Chinese adviser and built with captive Chinese labor. The Eastern Capital was built at the site of modern Liaoyang City in central Manchuria. The Central Capital was built about a hundred miles south of the Supreme Capital, at the site of the newly absorbed Xi tribal people's old ritual center. A century later an imposing new Central Capital city was built there. After 936, as a broad zone 70 to 100 miles wide, lying across the northern boundary of China (the "Sixteen Prefectures" ceded that year), was absorbed into the Liao empire, a Western Capital was created, utilizing the old Chinese fortress city of Datong in northern Shanxi. A new Southern Capital was built at Yan, the site of modern Beijing. Within this populous southern sedentary zone of the Liao state, the preexisting counties and prefectures were taken over and retained in the Chinese pattern of local administration.

The entire administration of the Khitan empire was headed by two prime ministers, one appointed from the Xiao consort clan to head the Northern Chancellery, and one appointed from the Yelü clan to head the Southern Chancellery. The central government had six ministries—for personnel, revenues, rites, war, justice, and works, on the Tang dynasty Chinese model—and many high officials in the Southern Chancellery were appointed from the subject Chinese, Bohai, and Korean populations, all long familiar with the paperwork of Chinese government. Bureaucratic administration on the Chinese model came to be a central component of the Liao state. It even infiltrated the traditional tribal structure of governing among the Khitans and their subject tribal peoples.[6]

V. THE SIGNIFICANCE OF KHITAN ACCULTURATION

Chinese historians always point to these developments as evidence of "sinification," and in a limited and formal sense, they are correct. These were indeed adaptations of Chinese governing techniques, necessitated by the practical requirements of administering sedentary captive populations. But if sinification implies surrender to the superior Chinese culture, one might better use the term "acculturation" to describe this broadening of the cultural models taken over by the Khitans. One should explain Abaoji's measures simply as a realistic, proven means of managing those sources of wealth and power provided by the sedentary sector of his population: they were administrative adaptations to problems of efficient exploitation. We cannot assume that they represented a shift of values, a Khitan acknowledgment of inferiority before China's cultural greatness. No such shift is seen in Abaoji or the nobles of his and the next generation, although there are some individual examples of acculturated Khitan nobles who became devotees of things Chinese. More of those did indeed appear in later Liao history, but even then it did not signify a rejection of "Khitanness," or a significant loss of the solid ground on which adherence to their Khitan cultural heritage rested. The culturally dual Khitan elite, competent in both (and in some cases also in other) cultures, to the end remained Khitan at heart.

Abaoji himself almost certainly spoke Chinese. Yet he kept a certain distance from Chinese cultural influences and stressed Khitan distinctiveness. In 920, wanting for his people the powerful tool of a writing system, he ordered the adoption of a newly devised script. This Khitan "large script," which today's scholars have not yet fully deciphered, looks to an outsider like Chinese, but it was totally unintelligible to the Chinese. It utilizes brush strokes shaped like those that compose Chinese characters, but they form word graphs that arbitrarily add to or reduce or otherwise vary the strokes of the counterpart Chinese characters. The resulting script may have been found clumsy from the beginning. In 925 Abaoji's younger brother Diela appears to have played the essential role in devising a new script. The *Liao History* states: "An Uighur delegation arrived, and there was no one who could understand their language. The Empress said to Emperor Taizu [Abaoji]: 'Diela, who is very intelligent, could be assigned to serve.' He was sent to accompany the delegation. After spending twenty days in their company he had learned their speech and their writing, following which he devised the Khitan small script, which has fewer characters yet is comprehensive."[7] The "small script" for Khitan is assumed to incorporate phonetic writing principles, even though its script still looks like Chinese and not like any of the Semitic scripts from which Uighur phonetic writing was derived.[8] Diela lived up to his reputation for being mentally quick, but it is also evident that while Khitan and Uighur were not mutually intelligible, the distance between them was not great.

The adoption of the second Khitan script was quickly approved. The intention in adopting these scripts, as with the adaptation of the Chinese imperial institution and other elements of Chinese civilization to Khitan needs, was to give the Khitans an advanced social management tool, but without surrendering to sinification by simply taking over the Chinese writing system (along with its classical grammar and literary forms), as the Koreans and the Japanese had done. Khitans would learn to write, but in their own way; Chinese would not be able to read what Khitans wrote without learning their language, and very few Chinese did.

Nonetheless, whatever their intention, Chinese language and writing also were used in administering the Southern Chancellery, and many Khitans of the official elite had to become totally fluent in its use. While the Khitan scripts were prominently used for memorial inscriptions on stone and wood, and for record keeping in the Northern Chancellery, almost no extensive documents written in them have been preserved, and it may well be that few were ever produced.[9] Literate members of the Khitan elite found that they had much to gain by using Chinese; it gave them access to a massive body of writings on all subjects. Inevitably, their elite produced many individuals who became literate, as well as some who were highly learned and who came genuinely to value aspects of Chinese civilization. We need not assume that implied disloyalty to their own Khitan civilization. Rather, through their learning they might experience exhilaration at participating in a broader realm of ideas and values and aesthetic experience.

To cite one particularly important example, many Inner Asian peoples converted to Buddhism, as had the Khitans by the tenth century. For all of them, Chinese translations of the scriptures were the instrument by which they penetrated the teachings of the Lord Buddha. Chinese was not the original language of the Buddha, nor was Buddhism the cultural export of which the Chinese were the most proud. Inner Asians as well as others, being aware of that fact, were if anything the more willing to accept Chinese high culture as a universal vehicle insofar as it was the instrument for gaining access to Buddhism. The Chinese of course thought of Chinese civilization as the world's only high civilization, hence as the universal cultural system. The non-Chinese peoples such as the Khitans who lived within China's orbit also could see Chinese language and learning as in a sense a universal cultural tool without necessarily granting to Chinese values the emotional commitment that Chinese have taken for granted. This subtle difference between acculturation and sinification is one that Chinese today still may not always appreciate. It has parallels in other cases of intercultural relations.

Most important, however, is the simple fact that literacy, whether in Chinese or in the Khitan script, made bureaucratic government possible. It regularized the modes of communication within government and permitted systematic record keeping for administrative purposes. Khitan leaders even before the time of Abaoji had recognized that Silla, the most powerful of the Korean states until its fall in 935, had thoroughly adopted Chinese ways, from its script and its literary traditions to the forms of its government. The kingdom of Bohai was founded about the year 700; thereafter its kings were invested by the Tang court with which it maintained diplomatic relations for more than 200 years. Imitating both Silla and China, Bohai too had created a strongly centralized government on the Chinese model. Although its population was primarily sedentary, it was militarily powerful, at times a threat to Tang China. It was clear to their Khitan counterparts that the Bohai kings and their ruling elite benefited greatly from their cultural borrowing without having surrendered to Chinese domination. Abaoji's sons learned Chinese, at least one of them exceedingly well; their father did not expect them to become less Khitan thereby, although, as we shall see, their mother and others had their doubts about the consequences of deep immersion in Chinese literary culture.

VI. ABAOJI RECEIVES YAO KUN, ENVOY OF THE LATER TANG DYNASTY

Abaoji's own feelings about the Chinese language and about China are revealed in a fascinating conversation he had with a Chinese named Yao Kun who came to him as ambassador from the Later Tang court in 926. The Later Tang, second of the brief Five Dynasties, had been founded in 923 by the son[10] of Li Keyong, the Shatuo Turk warlord of northern Shanxi with whom Abaoji had sworn binding brotherhood in 905. Despite that background, relations between the Shatuo and Khitan states gradually cooled. In 922 and 923 Abaoji had campaigned deep into Hebei, looting cities and taking captives among the Chinese population, and had thus been at war with the Later Tang. Yao, the Chinese ambassador sent by that Turkic Chinese state, carried a diplomatic communication to the Khitan ruler. He went first to the Supreme Capital, where he found the entire court had gone with the armies east into Manchuria. He therefore followed them and late in the summer met Abaoji on campaign, where he had just completed the conquest of the Bohai. The Khitan court was camped at Fuyu, an important Bohai city in what would be present-day Jilin Province in China's Northeast. The ambassador had come to make formal announcement of the Later Tang emperor's death and the accession, by dubious means, of his adopted son. Abaoji, of course, had already heard the news and knew all about the background, for the Shatuo Later Tang dynasty was of the greatest strategic importance to him in his further plans to conquer portions of North China. But the courtesy of a diplomatic announcement was demanded by the elaborate Chinese protocol then observed by all states, even non-Chinese states recently at war with one another. The ambassador's reassembled aide-mémoire preserves the only near–firsthand depiction of Abaoji which offers more than a few scattered phrases.

When Emperor Zhuangzong [of the Later Tang] died [in the spring of 926, his successor] Emperor Mingzong dispatched his Palace Attendant, Yao Kun, to report the late ruler's death to the Khitan state. Yao arrived at Xilou [a fortress adjacent to the Khitan capital] to find that Abaoji was leading a campaign in the east against the Bohai. Yao followed on, meeting up at Shenzhou [near the newly conquered Bohai capital].

[Yao:] After arriving, I was granted an audience. Abaoji invited me into his great tent. Abaoji was nine *chi* tall [very tall!]. He was wearing a long gown of brocade with a wide sash tied at the back. He and his consort sat on facing couches. I was led forth and presented. Before I could deliver my message, Abaoji [mockingly] asked: "I have heard that in your Chinese land you now have one Son of Heaven in Henan and another in Hebei; is that true?" I answered: "The Son of Heaven in Henan died on the first day of the fourth month of this year, in a military uprising at Luoyang. I have come here to bear those woeful tidings. The Regional Commander in Hebei, our Lord General, on command of the late emperor, was just then in the field to suppress a military uprising at Weizhou. By the time he heard of the disaster at court, the loyalties of the armies were wavering, and when he reached the capital it was leaderless. Higher and lower, all insistently petitioned our Lord General to assume charge over the state. Now, in response to the hopes of the people, he has ascended the throne and become the Emperor [Mingzong].

Abaoji uttered a wail of grief, then speaking through his flowing tears he said: "I swore brotherhood with the father of that Lord of Hedong Province; that Son of Heaven in Henan was my son, as the son of my dear friend. Of late I have heard that there were military uprisings in China, and I called up fifty thousand of my armored cavalry intending to go to Luoyang to rescue my son. But at that time I was engaged in Bohai which still had not fallen. That my son should have come to such an end! It is so unjust!" He wept uncontrollably. Then he said to me: "When the present Son of Heaven in China [the new emperor] first heard there were troubles in Luoyang, why did he not rush to the rescue instead of allowing things to come to this pass?"

I replied: "There was no lack of a sense of extreme urgency, but distance and intervening obstructions held him back until it was too late."

Abaoji then spoke again: "When my son died, they should have consulted me. How could the new Son of Heaven just put himself on the throne?" I replied: "My emperor has commanded armies for twenty years and reached the position of Chief Regional Commander. His armies numbered three hundred thousand crack troops. All of them, as with one mind, firmly supported his elevation. If he had removed himself, disaster would have ensued immediately. It is not as if he had not received knowledge of your Majesty's intentions, but what was he to do about the wishes of the people?"

His [Abaoji's] son Tuyu [i.e., Prince Bei], at one side, spoke: "The envoy need not say more. 'He led his ox through another man's field, and the ox was taken from him.' Is that not excessive? [Prince Bei rebukes the envoy by citing an incident from the ancient Chinese *Commentary of Zuo*, where it is told that when a man allowed his ox to damage a neighbor's field, another man who assisted in removing the troublesome ox then seized and kept it, profiting excessively from his good deed. This displays Prince Bei's unexpected command of the Chinese classics. See Legge 1960, 5:310.]

I replied: "'Responding to Heaven and maintaining accord with mankind'—how can that be compared with the petty affairs of some ordinary fellow? For example, when your Majesty gained your rule over your state, and then would not be subject to displacement by some other claimant, could that be called taking the throne by force?" [The Chinese envoy peremptorily rejects the prince's use of an obscure Chinese allusion, and then rather courageously compares his emperor's dubious accession to the new norms Abaoji had imposed on the Khitan rulership.] Abaoji immediately reassured and supported me, saying: "That exactly expresses in a most appropriate fashion the principles involved." Then he went on to say: "That my son in China had come to such troubles, I already knew. But I had heard reports that this son kept two thousand women in his palace, and a thousand musicians, that he spent his days hawking and running his hunting hounds, that he was wallowing in drink and sex; he had no concern for his people, he appointed unworthy men; all this had reached the point where the whole realm was enraged. Since hearing these things, I have been deeply concerned that he might be overthrown. A month ago someone came with news informing me that my son had met calamity. From that time my entire household has given up wines, has turned loose all its hawks and hounds, and has dismissed the court musicians. Throughout all my tribes I too have a thousand households of musicians, but I use them only for banquets of state; I do not dare make inappropriate use of them. If my conduct were to become like that of my son, I too no doubt would be unable to last long. I expect from this time forward to look upon him as a warning to us."

Abaoji again asked: "I have heard that the Chinese ruler has wrested control over Western Sichuan. Is that true?" I answered: "In the ninth month of last year troops were sent forth, and by the eleventh month they had gained control over both Eastern and Western Sichuan, capturing two hundred thousand soldiers and horses, and gold and silk beyond counting. The [new] emperor having just ascended the throne, he has not yet had time to send any of that to you [in tribute], but he will surely dispatch envoys for that purpose." Pleased, Abaoji questioned further: "I have heard that in Western Sichuan there are the perilous precipice roads; how can

troops and horses get through?" I answered: "Although the routes to
Sichuan are indeed perilous, after our late ruler had taken control over
Henan, he possessed four hundred thousand crack troops and one hundred
thousand cavalry. There was no place where he could not advance, and he
looked upon traversing the precipice roads as if crossing flat land!"

Abaoji then went on to say: "I can speak Chinese, but I never speak it
in the presence of my tribal people. I fear that they may emulate the Chinese
and grow soft and timid." And he said further: "My son in China, although
having the son-to-father relationship with me, nonetheless was at times in
a relationship of enmity with me. We even developed an intense mutual
hatred. But I hold no resentment against your present Son of Heaven, so
we may well be able to enjoy friendly relations. You must now report back,
and must say that I intend to continue to lead my generals and tens of
thousands of cavalry to the south, even beyond Youzhou and Zhenzhou
[i.e., beyond present-day Beijing and on into central Hebei]. I shall then
make a face-to-face compact with your sovereign. I demand Hebei and
Youzhou. If my Chinese son will take charge of arranging this, I will have
no cause ever to invade China again."

I replied: "That is a matter beyond my competence to deal with." The
Khitan ruler was enraged. He put me in prison. After something more than
ten days' time, he again summoned me before him and said: "It probably
would be quite difficult to get all of Hebei Province, but if I can have just
Zhenzhou and Youzhou that also would suffice!" He had paper and writing
brushes set before me and ordered me to prepare an account of all this. I
said I could not do that. He wanted to have me killed, but [his trusted
Chinese adviser] Han Yanhui remonstrated against that. Therefore he sent
me back to prison.

Abaoji fell sick with typhoid fever. One evening a large star fell directly
in front of his tent. Abruptly thereafter he died at Fuyu [the former Bohai
capital city] on the twenty-seventh day of the seventh lunar month of the
first year of the Tiancheng reign period [September 6, 926]. His consort,
the Empress of the Shuyu clan, personally led the armies to escort his
funeral cortege back to Xilou. I accompanied them, and after arrival there
was released, and so returned.[11]

Abaoji was fifty-four years old. He had just completed the conquest of the
powerful Bohai state, enfieffing its captured royal family as Khitan nobles
and absorbing its territories and people into the Khitan empire. He had
extended the Khitan boundaries east to the Yalu and Ussuri rivers. He
had also enlarged them westward deep into the Mongolian plateau, and he
had thoroughly studied the problems of extending them southward into
China. Confident in the momentum his armies had achieved, he sought to
exert diplomatic pressure to achieve his next goal. Yao Kun's report on his
embassy, providing firsthand observations of the Khitan ruler's mentality, is
a rare document. We see Abaoji's quick mind comprehending far more than
needs to be spoken. He is capable of anger and of intimidation. But we also

see a breadth of spirit and expressions of emotions ranging from ritual grief to genuine nostalgia, from shrewd badgering to calm reflections on the real state of affairs. And we observe that he could understand the constraints under which others must act, and his willingness to let bygones be bygones. This encounter offers us a fascinating window into his agile mind. No founder of a subsequent conquest dynasty possessed his command of Chinese conditions or his ability to respond so knowingly in a diplomatic encounter.

This strong man stretched the capacities of the Khitan nation even more than he extended its territorial boundaries. He launched his people on a course that forced them to undertake great things. To be sure, it can be argued that his course led two centuries later to their destruction as a dynastic empire. But had his descendants at that later time included another man of his stature, the Liao dynasty might well have taken a different course.

3

BUILDING
THE LIAO EMPIRE

The Khitan state quickly became a vast empire ruling not only over a narrow band of Chinese and other sedentary peoples living along its southern borders but also over dozens of other nomadic and semi-sedentary tribal peoples on its other three borders. Maintaining control required both constant military action and skillful use of diplomacy. Domestically, deeply ingrained Khitan tribal customs repeatedly caused succession crises; they reveal much to us about the processes of social change. Diplomatically, the Liao dynasty's treaty settlements with China opened an unprecedented era in East Asian interstate relations, while its geographic position gave it an important intermediary role in those relations.

1. Succession Issues after Abaoji

Abaoji's death in 926 was sudden and unexpected; he was only fifty-four years old. In 916 he had named his eldest son, Prince Bei, his successor, invoking the principle of primogeniture borrowed from the Chinese social system but alien to the steppe. Was he confident that Prince Bei would succeed him? Bei had accompanied his parents on the campaign against the Bohai nation, and following the victory late in the summer of 926, Abaoji named him Prince of Dongdan, that being the new name given to the conquered Bohai territories; the principality of Dongdan became the eastern circuit of the Khitan realm. Bei was a mature man of twenty-six in a society that considered males to be adults at age fifteen. He was fully capable, we might well think, of carrying on as head of the Khitan state whether that role was defined in Khitan or in Chinese terms. But the hope that an uneventful succession would follow did not take his formidable mother into account. Nor did it estimate correctly the continuing force of traditional Khitan values, which fueled succession crises repeatedly thereafter.

Abaoji's widow is known in the Chinese records as the Empress Yingtian, her posthumous temple name. Few women in history match her independence and determination. We read that she escorted Abaoji's body back to the capital, took over the conduct of both civil and military affairs, and directed the funeral arrangements, assuming full executive powers. A Chinese empress dowager often would assume the role of regent for a young heir because her generational superiority within the imperial clan gave her some authority in clan matters. But no matter how intelligent or well informed, she would "listen from behind a screen" and would defer to ministers of the court or male family members to act for her.

Not so this Khitan empress; we have seen that she accompanied her husband on the campaign against the Bohai and joined him in the audience to receive the ambassador from the Later Tang court. Khitan women, at least those of the elite about whom we know something, were full partners with their menfolk in many things; but even among Khitan women, the Empress Yingtian was exceptional for her strong will, energy, ruthlessness, and martial spirit. Abaoji had been volatile, adaptive, committed to far-reaching cultural change. She, by contrast, was the quintessential Khitan, not only the indomitable virago in her own personality but also the embodiment of conservative tribal values that resisted change. Equally strong-willed and manipulative imperial women were not unknown in Chinese history, but their style had to be quite different. It was inconceivable to the Chinese that a woman could so openly assert herself as the equal of her male relatives; to them such behavior constituted a perverse inversion of the natural order. This strong woman directly took command, whether to lead a campaign at the head of her own units in the armed forces or to impose her will on the councils of state. Many of her own people undoubtedly feared her and sought to limit her powers.

Even so strong a woman as the Empress Yingtian, in many ways the full partner with her husband in ruling, was nonetheless expected to sacrifice herself upon his death. The story is told that when the funeral rites were under way, a Chinese officer at court suggested that she might follow steppe custom and be buried alongside her dead husband. She parried by noting that the officer himself, long in intimate service to the fallen ruler, in all decency might better do that. The ancient Chinese had put aside that custom well over a thousand years earlier, but as the Chinese officer knew, hundreds of Khitan warriors and companions were to be sacrificed and buried with the late emperor. Feeling trapped, he nonetheless bravely replied that in terms of intimacy with the late ruler no one equaled the empress herself, and that if she would go, he would also join those to be entombed. She responded: "I of course do not refuse to join the Emperor underground, but my children are young and the country has no leader, so I am not free to do that."[1] In a gesture to custom, however, she offered her right arm to be cut off and placed in the imperial coffin; when the Khitan nobles protested that such a sacrifice was excessive, she nonetheless had her right hand severed at the wrist to represent her in her husband's mausoleum. By that daunting maneuver she silenced critics and enhanced her powers.

Prince Bei (in his mid-twenties), and his two younger brothers (in their early twenties), were by no means so young that they were still dependent on a mother's guidance. Bei, however, was suspect in her eyes. She was determined to intervene in the succession process and overturn her dead husband's prescript. Her concern was that Prince Bei was culturally dual, addicted to Chinese learning, and therefore in her eyes sadly lacking in Khitan leadership qualities. She ignored the fact that her husband had struggled for two decades to establish stable Chinese principles of rulership and succession. On naming his then seventeen-year-old eldest son his heir in 916, as if anticipating future resistance, Abaoji had demanded that all the Khitan nobles proclaim their loyalty to the prince. That was a radical step. The empress shared the more traditional tribal attitudes. Her second son, called Deguang, and known in history as the Emperor Taizong, was twenty-four in 926, but already had developed all the ideal qualities of the Khitan grand chieftain. Skilled at warfare, he had successfully led a number of campaigns against tribal enemies. Popular with the old nobility, he basked in his mother's favor. The force of circumstances was all too clear; Prince Bei volunteered that his younger brother's qualifications were superior to his own, in effect announcing that he would not contest his mother's decision to elevate him. Perhaps his compliant spirit proved that her judgment was correct. But was he perhaps playing for time? He was by no means a soft stranger to the military life; he too could ride and shoot with his Khitan princely peers, and had performed well at his father's side in distant campaigns, leading forward attack troops in battle. His fatal flaw was that he could function in both cultures. To be the equal of a Chinese courtier at that stage in Khitan history was to raise doubts about his leadership in the steppe. Abaoji had told the ambassador from China that he knew Chinese but would not speak it in the presence of his people lest they "emulate the Chinese and grow soft and timid." Prince Bei, in contrast, had led in persuading his father's government to accept Chinese institutions and rituals, such as the offical veneration of Confucius as patron of the state. He wrote polished essays in both Khitan and Chinese and had even translated a book of ancient Chinese lore.

Forced to abdicate the throne, he nonetheless retained the title of Prince of Dongdan. Could he have been plotting to make that eastern region a base for rebellion? Under suspicion as a potential rival of his younger brother, Deguang, he was kept under surveillance for several years. Eventually, Bei wrote a mournful poem in Chinese accepting the fact that he lived in the shadow of a brother who loomed taller in the eyes of his people. Then in 930 he slipped away and entered China, to live there as a poet and painter. The Later Tang emperor Mingzong (Li Siyuan) received him as an honored guest; the imperial surname Li was bestowed on him together with the Chinese personal name Zanhua, meaning "to exalt China." Yet even in self-imposed exile he remained fiercely loyal to the Khitan cause. In 934 he sent intelligence reports to his brother about conditions in North China urging the Khitans to invade.

Poems and a few of his paintings remain; they display great skill in depicting the mounted hunters and warriors of the steppe and reveal his nostalgia for Khitan life. Prince Bei is an intriguing figure, in some ways one who attracts our sympathies. Yet he was a moody man, on the one hand drawn to books and learning, on the other a man who inflicted violence and petty cruelties on his wives, concubines, and attendants. Unavoidably involved in factional politics at the court in China, he was assassinated there in 936, on orders of the last Later Tang ruler, who felt betrayed by the Khitan invasion that year.[2] Nevertheless, his eldest son, a child of eight when left behind in 926 to be reared by his uncle at the Khitan court, known by his Khitan name Wuyu, had become the model Khitan prince. His uncle Deguang, the Emperor Taizong, is said to have loved him as his own son. He accompanied the emperor on the campaign into China in 947 and was with him when the emperor died in North China on the return from that campaign. The respected position he had achieved in Taizong's entourage made it possible for him to claim the succession, which he did with the support of the army leaders, while escorting the imperial coffin back to the Supreme Capital. He is known in history as the Emperor Shizong.

On the death of her second son during the 947 campaign in China, Empress Dowager Yingtian again wished to name the successor. She denounced his heir, her grandson, this time in favor of her pampered third son, the violent and abhorrent Prince Lihu. She sent an army from the Supreme Capital to intercept the returning forces. In an initial skirmish her army was defeated. Civil war threatened. This time, however, the court failed to support her, though not because her grandson Shizong's claims (as the nephew and favored associate of the dead emperor) to be the legitimate successor were decisive in their minds, for no heir had been formally designated, and Deguang's eligible young sons were not even considered. To the Khitan nobility, Lihu's violent and untrustworthy character had been made all too evident, and thus he lost their support. The new Emperor Shizong, by contrast, was noted for his generosity as well as for being the ideal young martial leader.[3] In this second succession crisis, twenty-one years after Abaoji's death, the principle he had struggled to institute, by which the eldest son should be guaranteed a secure succession, still did not prevail, and again the succession was seriously challenged. Traditional tribal leadership concepts were more meaningful.

After coming to the throne, Shizong quite understandably sent his troublesome grandmother and his uncle Lihu to live far from the capital. Lihu died in prison after several further attempts to rebel. The Empress Yingtian died in 953 at the advanced age of seventy-four.[4] So ended her remarkable career; but the model of the activist (or, as the Chinese would say, the meddlesome) empress remained. One important consequence of her life was that the Khitan custom of sacrificing rulers' wives to be buried with them was thereafter abolished, owing to her repudiation of it in 926.

In the third succession in 951, after Emperor Shizong was killed by a rebellious nephew, the throne passed to Muzong, the son of Prince Bei's younger brother Deguang. The new emperor thus was Shizong's cousin, and so the succession passed to the collateral line in the same generation. Only when Muzong died in 969 did the succession again revert to Prince Bei's line, as Abaoji had intended, to remain there until the end of the dynasty (see Chart 1). It took a

CHART 1. THE LIAO IMPERIAL SUCCESSION

Generations

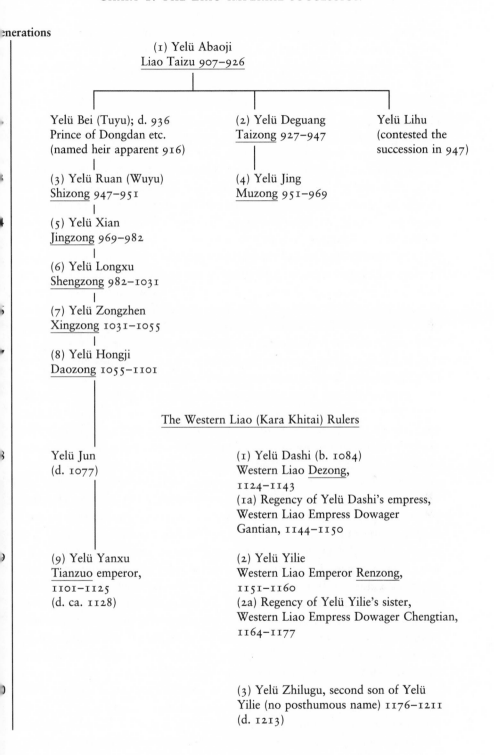

(1) Yelü Abaoji
Liao Taizu 907–926

Yelü Bei (Tuyu); d. 936
Prince of Dongdan etc.
(named heir apparent 916)

(2) Yelü Deguang
Taizong 927–947

Yelü Lihu
(contested the
succession in 947)

(3) Yelü Ruan (Wuyu)
Shizong 947–951

(4) Yelü Jing
Muzong 951–969

(5) Yelü Xian
Jingzong 969–982

(6) Yelü Longxu
Shengzong 982–1031

(7) Yelü Zongzhen
Xingzong 1031–1055

(8) Yelü Hongji
Daozong 1055–1101

The Western Liao (Kara Khitai) Rulers

Yelü Jun
(d. 1077)

(1) Yelü Dashi (b. 1084)
Western Liao Dezong,
1124–1143
(1a) Regency of Yelü Dashi's empress,
Western Liao Empress Dowager
Gantian, 1144–1150

(9) Yelü Yanxu
Tianzuo emperor,
1101–1125
(d. ca. 1128)

(2) Yelü Yilie
Western Liao Emperor Renzong,
1151–1160
(2a) Regency of Yelü Yilie's sister,
Western Liao Empress Dowager Chengtian,
1164–1177

(3) Yelü Zhilugu, second son of Yelü
Yilie (no posthumous name) 1176–1211
(d. 1213)

half-century of conflict and uncertainty to overcome Khitan tribal traditions; the principle of primogeniture that Abaoji had sought to institute as the new pattern of succession slowly began to prevail in the hybrid Liao imperial institution. That it took so long and still remained subject to dispute reveals the tensions underlying the slow process of acculturation that marked early Liao institutional history.

II. THE MEANING OF THE EARLY LIAO SUCCESSION CRISES

As they created large empires needing stable political institutions, all tribal societies in Inner Asian history encountered disruptive succession problems. In the smaller scale of tribal organization, the very instability of leadership could be a source of strength. The individual whose exceptional military skills, clear-mindedness in decisions for short-range action, and charismatic personality won approval of the tribe, in short the "natural leader," would be elevated by acclamation of his peers. That is not quite the same as open "election," even though it is sometimes called that. When the leader lagged in performance, he could be replaced by a more effective successor without creating civil war. That system had great rationality so long as the scope of governing remained small enough for personalities to be the dominant factor.

Abaoji and other steppe leaders who knew China could only envy the profound reverence, loyalty, and obedience that the Chinese displayed toward their imperial throne. Khitan visitors had observed the great court audiences where all the military and civil leaders of the vast Chinese state and the assembled foreign envoys would render servile obeisance, almost without regard for the personal qualities of the ruler. His commands appeared to be unquestioningly obeyed. The observation of that spectacle at the Chinese court always impressed visitors.

At its best, of course, Chinese government embodied many other elements: cultural and institutional limitations on the power of the throne that were not apparent to Inner Asian visitors. A responsible civil bureaucracy, advised by military associates, in possession of systematically assembled information and observing powerful precedents, provided the Chinese throne with judgment and guidance. What appeared to be servile bureaucrats at the Chinese court were in fact self-assured officials carrying out political actions largely of their own making. The Chinese emperor was a despot limited by intricate cultural and bureaucratic restraints; in fact, he shared authority with his scholar-officialdom. It was difficult for the outsider to sense such complex interrelationships behind the pageantry. Yet he would have been correct in perceiving the strength of the Chinese imperial institution, particularly the stability that was provided by normally unchallenged tenure of reign and by predetermined succession. Among all the Inner Asian leaders in history, as they succeeded in building larger states, the only motive in opting for emperorship over the traditional tribal khanate was their desire to enlarge their powers, to increase their authority, and to centralize their governing. In striving for those understandable goals, the Chinese imperial institution and the experience of Inner Asian predecessors in adapting Chinese political forms provided the only alternative model available to the great khans of tribal confederations.

Incongruities lay hidden in the adaptations of Chinese institutions to the structure of nomadic societies. Even the most ambitious and effective leaders such as Abaoji could not abruptly alter the mechanics of their tribal selection procedures or the expectations of their peers in the tribal elite; such change required corresponding adjustments in the structure of the tribal base. As I have argued, to function effectively, tribes needed active chieftains, not symbolic figureheads. The structure of their societies readily accommodated that need. Chinese society also provided outlets by which able individuals could achieve rewards and success, especially in its scholar-officialdom, but that volatile element was balanced against a stable system of imperial authority in which emperors, the supreme leaders once a new dynasty was founded, transcended the pressures of individual competition and selection. Ritually reinforced patterns of reverence for the emperor in the Chinese hierarchy could not just be borrowed and mechanically imposed alongside the personal authority actively commanded by a great chieftain.

The nomad khan's supremacy might be in some measure derived from his clan's status, but essentially it was earned by his individual displays of martial skills, character, and charisma. To Abaoji, who possessed those qualities in abundance, the radical step of borrowing the concept of primogeniture must have seemed the most direct way to strengthen his Khitan state system. But he proposed this solution only *after* he had attained the supreme position; otherwise he himself would not have been able to contest the Yaolian Great Khan in 907. Did tribal resistance to his changes ever arouse doubts in his mind?

Some historians have argued that Abaoji may have come to realize that his second son clearly possessed better qualifications for leadership than did the eldest, whom he had earlier named his successor. The second son had achieved a stronger base of military power, largely because he had so successfully performed the tasks that Abaoji had assigned to him. The tribal leaders liked and wanted him, as the Empress Yingtian clearly saw. However that may be, up to the moment of his untimely death, Abaoji made no move to demote his chosen heir. The empress and the tribal leaders did that after his unexpected death, and old tribal patterns prevailed. The eldest son, too, realized that he could not win. Like an unsuccessful, self-nominated rival in traditional tribal "elections," Prince Bei was not killed or deprived of his dignity and status, even though there may have been suspicions that he might use his princedom in Dongdan as a base from which to contest the throne. Although he left the scene and went to China, where his cultural achievement opened up to him an interesting, perhaps comforting, alternative, he did not flee in fear of his life. His "abdication" under adversity and his continuing demonstration of loyalty to his dynasty demonstrated his "Khitanness," but also made him a model of Confucian virtue to later Chinese historians. Their

comments in the official *Liao History,* written 400 years later, compare him to the upright heir of a debased regime in Chinese antiquity, and they add that Prince Bei's loyalty and virtue were rewarded when his heirs eventually came to the throne. Their rather quaint comments show no understanding of the real circumstances surrounding this succession crisis.[5] When Prince Bei's younger brother, Emperor Taizong, suddenly and unexpectedly died in 947, the succession principles were still being contested. The empress dowager again asserted herself to act as regent. She denounced the new emperor's father, Prince Bei, as a turncoat, and undoubtedly reflected a segment of tribal opinion when she declared that the father's deficiencies made his son unacceptable. She attempted to promote her third son, Lihu, but instead it was Shizong who had gained power and prestige as a military commander and an intimate associate of his uncle, the emperor. That enabled him to be declared the successor.

By this time, conditions had changed somewhat; after coming to the throne, each of the early Liao emperors could see that his security was enhanced by undermining the old system and supporting the new one. As the Emperor Shizong, Bei's son had to banish his grandmother and uncle and purge the elite of potential dissidents. True, rebellions against his rule occurred frequently, and finally he was murdered by a nephew at the head of a faction within the imperial clan that did not accept him or the new pattern. Struggles among dissident factions continued for several years and reappeared during subsequent successions. What had changed was that the cost of contesting the succession had gone up as the rigid Chinese concept gradually displaced the more flexible and accommodating tribal traditions. An ambitious tribal leader who contested the succession now was no longer seen as a legitimate rival: he was a rebel.

The succession issue continued to plague the dynasty to the very end; the basic incongruity between Chinese principles and Khitan social realities remained unresolved. Although primogeniture gave a prospective Liao heir apparent an increasingly strong claim on the succession, it never guaranteed success. The struggles surrounding contested successions became more bloodthirsty because the old process of verifying a new leader by acclamation had been displaced. Instead of being openly accepted as participants in a legitimate selection process, as in the past, rivals were forced into what became, under the new definitions, criminal behavior and desperate acts, often leading to disgrace and death. As we shall see, analogous problems afflicted the imperial successions of later steppe conquerors as well.

III. THE KHITANS' INNER ASIAN TRIBAL EMPIRE

Tribes were the basic building blocks of Inner Asian politics. Amalgamating tribes into confederations of ever larger scope was the typical process of steppe politics. Abaoji inherited the leadership of a Khitan confederation that had existed in relative stability for almost two centuries under the leadership of the Yaolian Great Khans. In the steppe, however, stability was tantamount

to decline; Abaoji was able to wrest leadership from the Yaolian by showing that he could again set the Khitan nation on the road to aggressive expansion. He not only did that with rapid and brilliant success, but also left to his successors the obligation to continue expansion by force, by guile, and by all other means. Throughout the tenth century, most of the Liao rulers exhausted themselves in the restless pursuit of empire.[6] The pace of Khitan aggression slowed somewhat by the mid-eleventh century, but the need to campaign on the frontiers in order to keep neighboring tribes subservient persisted to the end of the dynasty. Liao relations with China, Korea, and the Xi Xia state assumed a more stable pattern during the early eleventh century, but on the boundaries to the north and northwest, when we piece together the Inner Asian history of the Liao from the Chinese records, the fact of incessant campaigning against the empire's tribal components becomes very clear.

The Liao empire forcefully established its presence as a great power in Inner Asia early in the tenth century. Abaoji led campaigns to the west in 916 and again in 924; in the second of those he crossed the "flowing sands" of the Gobi Desert to reach the former capital of the Uighurs on the Orkhon River (far north in present-day Mongolia). The histories say that along the way he subdued the Dangxiang (i.e., the Tanguts), the Tuhun (or Tuyuhun, in modern Gansu Province), and other, mostly Turkic tribes and nations. Vigorous expansion in the north and west continued for a century, as needs and opportunities arose.

The general pattern can be seen in the example offered by Liao relations with the Zubu nation, also called the Dada (Tatars). They had commenced offering tribute to the Khitans after Abaoji displayed the might of his cavalry in his great northern campaign of 924. The Liao emperor Shengzong, who reigned from 982 to 1031, was forced to lead an expeditionary campaign against them in 983. For a decade thereafter they remained turbulent; first they killed their own khan, and then his successors defied the Liao, until the reigning khan surrendered to the Liao in 1003. The Liao decided to impose stricter controls by separating them into several divisions, each under a Liao military governor. They revolted again in 1026 but were again suppressed and forced this time to pay an increased annual tribute of horses, camels, and thousands of sables and other furs. After 1026 they continued to revolt and for a time evaded strict Liao control, growing ever stronger. We know little of them for some decades, but by the 1090s they were invading the Liao empire's northeastern border. In 1100 the Liao forces crushed them in a great battle in which the Zubu khan was taken prisoner; the Khitans took him back to their Supreme Capital and allowed mobs in the market place to hack him to pieces. The battle of 1100 was the only major victory over them in all of later Liao history, and even after it the Zubu remained a potent enemy.

The pattern apparent in this brief sketch of Liao-Zubu relations is typical of Liao relations with a number of the larger and more powerful constituents of their multitribal state. The Liao was an empire constantly being tested by unruly components; its emperors could afford little relaxation. The multitribal structure of the Liao empire was more complex than any other such

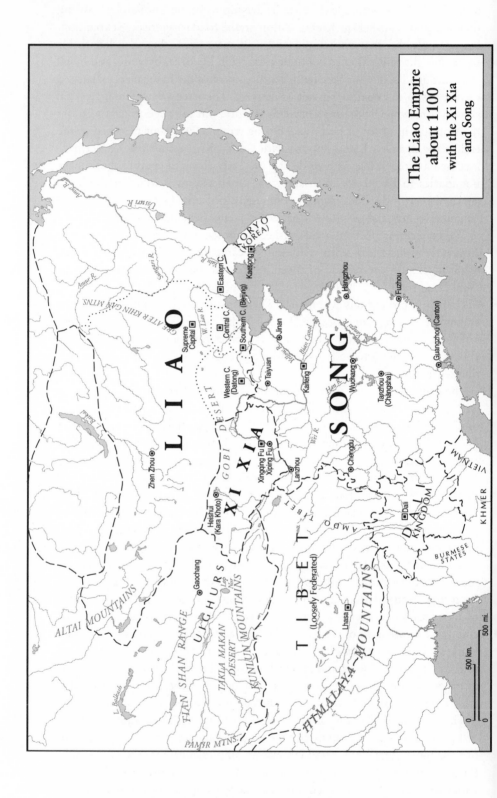

The Liao Empire about 1100 with the Xi Xia and Song

political entity ever developed in East Asian history. The Khitans' ability to formulate a multilayered structure of governing capable of integrating all of its units flexibly and realistically is one of their great achievements, but it required constant military vigilance.

A fact of prime historical importance that emerges from an examination of Liao border affairs is that during the tenth and eleventh centuries there existed a diversity of peoples fragmented into distinct ethnic and political units, mostly small, scattered throughout the length and breadth of Inner Asia. The official *Liao History* reveals scraps of information about many of those units where it lists the offices of Liao government charged with administering their internal affairs or handling their relations with the Liao state.[7] Those relations were directly administered by the military garrison commands to which their tribes were assigned, all under the general supervision of the Northern Chancellery.

The Liao empire in Inner Asia was a military state in which all tribal peoples were organized for total mobilization: each was assigned its place and its duties in an overarching system of military government. The surviving records describing that system therefore afford us a measure of access to the ethnographic complexity of Inner Asia of that age; the record holds many riddles for historians, in the identities, ethnic affinities, and geographic locations of peoples named as nominal or actual subordinates of the Liao Northern Chancellery. The Khitans began a process of amalgamating peoples, absorbing many into their tribal population, in that way probably accounting for the disappearance from history of some ethnic units. A more ruthless simplification of the Inner Asian ethnographic puzzle was accomplished by Chinggis Khan and his successors in the late twelfth and early thirteenth centuries. The Mongols effectively eliminated by absorption half or more of the tribal peoples named in the Liao records. The Khitans employed methods that at times appear to have been ruthless enough, but simply were not as "definitive" as those of their Mongol cousins a century and a half later.

The official *Liao History* (compiled by Chinese historians serving the Mongol Yuan dynasty in the 1340s, utilizing older records) lists fifty-two tribes or tribal divisions that were essentially Khitan by ethnic criteria, and ten "outer tribes" that were ethnically distinct but long considered fully subordinate to the Khitan state. These included some proto-Mongol groups on the northwestern frontiers that had been subordinate to the Khitans even before 907, some Uighur groups remaining on the western slopes of the Greater Khingan Mountains after the collapse of the Uighur state in 840 (before which time the Khitans had been subordinate to them), and some tribes on the eastern borders in Manchuria (see Map 4). This grouping of sixty-two tribal entities and administrative divisions constituted the core of the Khitan state under Abaoji, and remained the center of the empire thereafter.

Beyond those core elements of the Khitan nation and state were clusters of ethnic units possessing more independence, clearly not directly administered by the Liao government but nonetheless subject to administrative restraints and obligations. These numbered six "large tribes" governed by "kings" *(wang)* appointed or approved by the Liao government, and sixty-one "various tribes" for each of which the Northern Chancellery appointed an administrative officer. The "large tribes" included a segment of the Jurchen people living in a Khitan manner, close to the Eastern Capital, as well as some more distant branches of the ten "outer tribes." The category of "various tribes" included, for example, the "wild Jurchen" living farther to the northeast. Others included in this category were remnants of the Bohai nation that had fled beyond direct Liao rule, about twenty-five other units on the eastern and northern boundaries, and about thirty-five tribal units to the west, some as far away as the western borders of Mongolia and the edges of modern Xinjiang. As we examine these long lists of peoples beyond the eastern, northern, and western borders of the Khitan core area, we find names of border tribes whose affairs were nominally supervised by Khitan officials; the same names are duplicated for areas farther out, suggesting that in a number of cases a people was partly within and partly beyond the boundaries of the Liao empire. Those borders appear to have been fluid, changing according to the varying abilities of the Liao armies to control them.

Still farther out beyond the boundaries were seventy-eight "subordinate states," so called in the Chinese-derived usage of the time because at one time or another they had sent envoys to the Liao court offering tribute or requesting diplomatic recognition. In the Chinese view such voluntary requests for recognition and formal relations constituted "subordination." States listed in this category include the states of Korea, Japan, and Xi Xia, the seven more distant divisions of the independent Jurchen peoples (other than those nearer Jurchen units included under direct Liao administration), four divisions of the Zubu or Tatars, five representing the western Uighurs in Xinjiang, and many small units of ethnic or political distinctiveness in western Inner Asia. Diplomatic and commercial relations with many of them were sporadic and marginal, but the fact that the Liao records show contacts with them demonstrates the far-reaching awareness of the Liao empire throughout Inner Asia. The name Khitan, pronounced "Khitai" in western Asia, is the origin of the name Cathay, showing that in western Asia, and eventually in Europe, the Khitan empire was identified with a northern extension of the great civilization of the East, or China. That confusion about Cathay and China was not correctly understood in the West until the sixteenth century.

IV. LIAO-KOREAN RELATIONS

Liao relations with Korea and Xi Xia show how the two great powers in East Asia in the tenth and eleventh centuries, the Chinese Song dynasty and the Khitan Liao dynasty, competed for at least nominal suzerainty over the more important smaller states lying near them. Xi Xia and Korea struggled against both Song China and the Liao to secure their borders and to retain their independence. Liao relations with Xi Xia will be discussed in Chapters 8 and 11, devoted to that state. Here I briefly examine the Korean relationship.

The Liao dynasty and Korea shared a strategic boundary, one that the Liao had pushed south beyond the Yalu River into the Korean peninsula after the conquest of the Bohai state in 926. The Liao aggression as well as cultural interactions had a profound impact on Korean history. Korea was, next to China itself, the oldest of the advanced civilizations in East Asia. It had been both a source from which and the bridge by which Japan derived many cultural elements from the mainland. During the Han dynasty at the beginning of the imperial era, the Chinese had established military outposts on what is today Korean soil. In the Tang period China had tried unsuccessfully to reassert its domination over the Koreans and their Bohai neighbors. Korean belongs to the Tungusic branch of the Altaic languages, but it nonetheless used the Chinese script and employed literary Chinese as its written language of learning and government, in somewhat the same way that medieval northern Europeans used the alien but "classical" Latin. Chinese dynasties were sensitive to that cultural link and placed high importance on their relations with the succession of states created by the Korean people.

Early in the tenth century Korea itself was undergoing great political changes: the rise of the long-lasting kingdom of Koryô (918–1392) culminated in its unification of the Korean peninsula under a single state. The last stage in the unification process was the forced abdication in 935 of the king of the previously powerful Korean state of Silla, founded in 57 B.C.E., which had controlled all of Korea from 668 onward until 935. The Khitans' conquest of the Bohai in 926 intruded into that process of Korean unification; the elimination of the Bohai state gave Liao and Korea a common boundary, but that was on what the Koreans regarded as Korean soil, well south of the Yalu River, which today marks the boundary of China and Korea. The Liao demanded Koryô's submission as a vassal state. In 915, when Abaoji was camped on the Yalu, both the king of Silla and the king of the upstart Koryô state had sent ambassadors to him, offering gifts, as the Koryô king did again in 924.

Despite conflicts of interest, the relations between the new Khitan empire and the new unified kingdom of Koryô seemed to start off well, and the histories say little about their interactions. But late in the tenth century the Liao took up a more aggressive stance, invading Koryô in the 980s and 990s and forcing the Korean king to sue for peace. In 995 the Liao court, following its established pattern, sent a patent of investiture to the new Koryô king, who had just come to the throne. That followed the Chinese protocol in interstate relations as widely observed throughout East Asia.

When a revolt unseated the Korean king in 1010, the Liao therefore intervened to support their "vassal," the legitimate king. The results were disastrous for Korea. The Liao emperor Shengzong, leading the invasion force, entered the Koryô capital at Kaekyong (modern Kaesong, northwest of Seoul) and before leaving it looted and burned the city. Between 1013 and 1019 the Liao sent envoys making territorial demands, which the Koreans resisted. Liao efforts to use force were repeatedly defeated, so the Liao prepared a massive invasion force. Then the Koryô king asked for peaceful negotiations, gaining a settlement generally favorable to Korea.

The two countries exchanged envoys in 1020, and the next year the Liao sent, on request, a Khitan princess to marry into the Koryô royal line. But in 1034 an heir to the displaced Bohai kings revolted against his Liao over-lords and, when defeated, fled to Koryô, where the court granted him sanctuary and bestowed on him the Koryô royal surname, thus pointedly putting him under special protection. The Liao broke off diplomatic relations but did not again threaten to invade. At some point the Koreans resumed tribute submissions to the Liao court, and the two states coexisted more or less amicably to the end of the Liao dynasty.

We see in this relationship a pattern similar to Liao-Song relations: an early phase of aggressive Khitan involvement, followed in the eleventh century by more stable if somewhat passive diplomatic relations. Diplomatic courtesies based on the Chinese model generally defined the relationship, despite the inherent contradictions in that pattern when it was applied simultaneously by more than one state, both or all of which claimed "universal" sovereignty. Cultural contacts throughout the period, however, were by no means passive; they were of great importance to both Korea and Liao.

v. Expansion into North China

After the end of the great Tang dynasty in 907, Chinese political history proceeded through the confusing sequence of the Five Dynasties in North China, discussed in Chapter 1. The disarray in Chinese politics at that time permitted the Liao to expand into North China and create a permanent base there. The interlocking story of the Khitans' Liao dynasty and the ephemeral Chinese dynasties between 907 and 960 must be greatly simplified in the telling here. Reference to Maps 1, 4, and 5, here and in Chapters 1 and 5, will help the reader follow the story.

For the Chinese, defense of the North China Plain, where the capitals of the Five Dynasties were located, depended on control of strategic passes leading through low but often rugged mountains along the line where the Great Wall now stands. Strategic portions of that line had been protected by defended passes and walls since the third century B.C.E., when the first Great Wall of China was built.[8] By this time the Wall itself had crumbled and mostly disappeared, but if not present as a physical monument, the Great Wall line nonetheless was deeply imbedded in people's consciousness; statesmen and historians referred to it in discussing boundaries. Along the eastern end of that line, at the northern edges of the modern provinces of Shanxi and Hebei, there were a dozen or so heavily defended "gates" or barriers *(guan)* at defiles through which traffic had to pass.[9] They supported a defensive line stretching about 400 miles from northern Shanxi eastward to the sea, ending at present-day Shanhai Guan, the great gateway where "the mountains come to the sea." For all of the Five Dynasties (907–960), founded in succession by regional warlords based in North China, the problem was to maintain a northern defense perimeter while maintaining their political base at their capitals, either Luoyang or Kaifeng on the Yellow River in Henan, 400 miles to the south.

For the succeeding Northern Song dynasty (960–1127), the problem was to regain possession of the so-called Sixteen Prefectures on China's side of the Great Wall line, which the Khitans had held since 938. Once the conquest dynasties controlled territory south of the defensible Great Wall line, that line became unimportant. To look ahead, the native Ming dynasty after 1368 again had the problem of holding and defending the line, not only in this eastern extension but all the way across China to its western frontiers. In the late sixteenth century the Ming began building long walls to connect and defend their entire northern boundary; the Great Wall as we know it today is the product of that building project.[10] After 1644 the strategic importance of the Great Wall was again reduced, for the Qing dynasty (1644–1911) created an empire that again controlled both sides of the Wall. In Abaoji's time, while there were at best insignificant remnants of an earlier wall as such, there was a barrier of strong garrisons and fortified passes. Ably defended on the Chinese side, it was enough to deny him easy access to the North China Plain.

Abaoji rose to power just as the unity of China had been temporarily destroyed, offering a possibility that China's northern defense line might be breached. That objective became an obsession with Abaoji; he bequeathed it to his successors, who pursued it with both cunning and force. In 905 Abaoji had rushed off to Datong with an army of seventy thousand cavalry to firm up the resistance of Li Keyong against his rival, the warlord in North China who in 907 would terminate the Tang dynasty and found the first of the Five Dynasties. As we have seen, Li Keyong, a Shatuo Turk, was the warlord of Shanxi, and Abaoji's sworn brother, a relationship conceived by Abaoji with the intention of profiting strategically from it. He hoped it would offer him access into China all the way down to the Yellow River, through Li's military base in the mountains of northern Shanxi.

Far easier than penetrating through mountainous Shanxi would have been to penetrate through the North China Plain in Hebei, lying to the east, directly south of the Khitan core area. Control of Youzhou would allow the Khitan cavalry to sweep south at will across the open plain. But Hebei was defended by a cluster of strong passes controlled from the prefecture of Youzhou, at the site of present-day Beijing, 200 miles east of Datong. The permanently ensconced Chinese military governors based at Youzhou in the early tenth century were among the Khitans' most aggressive and most unrelenting enemies. Another reason for forming the link to Li Keyong was to have an ally just to the west of Hebei in order to isolate and threaten those enemies. The last of those Youzhou warlords fell in battle in 913, not to Abaoji but to Li Keyong's son (who would become the emperor of the Later Tang state),[11] a determined opponent of the Khitans, except when he needed a sudden alliance against some other enemy.

When Abaoji received the ambassador from the Later Tang state in 926, that son of Li Keyong had already been murdered; Li Keyong's stepson Li Siyuan had just succeeded his stepbrother on the Later Tang throne and had sent his ambassador to the Liao court to announce the change of rulers.[12] The stepson's base of power had been precisely in that Hebei region coveted by the Khitans. As the new emperor, known in history as the Later Tang emperor Mingzong, he had departed from that strategic region to take the throne at the capital. In that situation, Abaoji had thought he might intimidate Li Siyuan through his ambassador to relinquish control over Youzhou to the Khitans.

Abaoji died a few days later without having produced the result he desired, but the strategic perceptions underlying his conversation with the ambassador remained fixed in the consciousness of his successors. That is, they would continue the attempt to intimidate the rulers in China to give up their Great Wall line defense bastions; they would intervene politically rather than militarily when they could; and they would use their special but not always untroubled relationship with the assimilated Shatuo Turks in North China, who were the strategically placed regional warlords, to tip the balance when an opportunity presented itself. But if all that failed, they would be prepared to intervene militarily. One way or another the great prize had to be grasped while China was weak and disunited.

Throughout Abaoji's reign he intensified Khitan military action on the North China border, giving that activity an overall direction and an integrated strategic focus previously lacking. He sent embassies with great frequency to the more distant power centers of China, particularly to the Kaifeng court of the first of the Five Dynasties, the Later Liang, until it was overthrown by Li Keyong's son in 923. That he was so unprincipled as to deal with their mutual Chinese enemies had angered Li Keyong and his son. In China, the Khitans were depicted as mercenaries always for hire if properly compensated, ready to intervene on anyone's behalf in the smaller and larger struggles going on throughout China. There seems to have been some truth in that, but it does not mean that Abaoji had no fixed policy; his overall objective was to destabilize all the courts and power centers in China and await opportunities. Even when not ready for a major undertaking he kept up the appearance that he might be about to strike, using annual border raids by small detachments in the time-honored steppe manner. Those raids screened his larger intentions and kept China's defending border zone troops tense and exhausted.

The opportunity to continue those methods and gain a great success came to Abaoji's son Deguang, the Emperor Taizong, in the 930s. After the death of its emperor in 933, the Later Tang dynasty began to disintegrate under pressure of internal revolts. Throughout the realm, disaffected military leaders began to act independently. The most important of those was another Shatuo Turk, the son-in-law of the Later Tang emperor and the military governor of Shanxi. His name was Shi Jingtang. In the disorders of 936–938 in which Prince Bei, the Khitan expatriate resident at the Later Tang court, was assassinated (after having advised his brother Deguang that conditions were ripe for him to invade North China), Shi Jingtang revolted against the Later Tang state and influenced other military leaders to do the same. The Liao emperor, at the head of a large army, entered north Shanxi to aid Shi Jingtang, thereby getting through the passes as an invited guest. In impressive victories over the Later Tang armies he pushed on beyond Datong, reaching Shi's base at Taiyuan, the principal city of Shanxi. Militarily invincible on this occasion, the Liao emperor Taizong now could turn to other goals; he flattered Shi Jingtang into believing that he had the makings of an emperor. Entirely dependent on Khitan military power, Shi was induced to proclaim himself the founder of a new dynasty with its capital at Kaifeng on the Yellow River. He called his dynasty Jin, usually called the Later Jin—Jin being an old name for Shanxi, where Shatuo military power was based. The Liao emperor also arranged for Shi Jingtang to enter into a son-to-father relationship with him. After difficult negotiations, the wily Khitan ruler succeeded in getting his new "son" to grant him the Sixteen Prefectures, including Datong in the west and extending all across the Great Wall line to Youzhou and beyond—in short, the entire North China defense line. In fact, the ceded territory included nineteen, not sixteen, prefectures, but the phrase the "Sixteen Prefectures" became fixed as a symbol and was always used thereafter to designate the ceded territories. With very little cost Taizong thus wrung from his newly adopted relative far more than Abaoji had hoped to get from his Turkic "kinsman" in 926.[13]

The Later Jin dynasty, the third of the Five Dynasties, was seen for what it was: the puppet of the Liao throne. Its ignominious status demoralized its officers and its court. The Later Jin dynasty lasted a mere ten years; but the Liao had gained from it all that they wanted, and their hold on the Sixteen Prefectures was permanent. That proved to be a turning point in Chinese as well as in Khitan history. Datong, at the western end of the ceded zone, was designated the Liao empire's Western Capital, and at Youzhou, approximately on the site of modern Beijing, a new walled city was built to serve as the Liao Southern Capital, thus completing the system of five administrative centers for the five great divisions of the Liao empire. The Khitans now possessed the springboard into North China that they had long sought.

Curiously, however, the Sixteen Prefectures marked the practical limits of the Khitans' southward expansion into China. In 947, after invading and occupying more of North China, they began to experience the complexities of governing an immense area of sedentary population and quickly developed a distaste for that Chinese administrative morass. As we shall see, they used their strategic foothold in North China to intimidate subsequent Chinese regimes and gain many advantages from it. But that pull from the south did not distract the Khitans from their identification with the steppe.

Bizarre events that culminated in 947 were triggered by Shi Jingtang's death in 942 and the succession of his nephew. This new puppet emperor, the adoptive grandson of the Liao ruler, was sensitive to the resentment felt by both his Shatuo and his Chinese subjects against his dynasty's abject submission to the Khitans. Revolt against this puppet Jin ruler seemed imminent; the Liao court had to support him. Taizong, the reigning emperor, again came in at the head of his Khitan cavalry; this time he was forced to engage in inconclusive skirmishes that dragged on for several years. In a rout of his forces in southern Hebei in 945, he barely escaped with his life and had to flee back to his Southern Capital (present-day Beijing) on a camel. He nonetheless kept up pressure on the rebels in the Later Jin state until it collapsed in 946. Finally he forced his way into the Jin capital at Kaifeng. Entering the city in the first month of 947, he took up residence in the imperial palaces.

Then the most curious event in all of Liao history occurred. One day (actually March 25, 947), the Liao emperor Taizong (Deguang) donned the imperial Chinese robes found in the palace apartments, ascended the throne in the great audience hall, and accepted the congratulations of the assembled court, made up of all the officials in his own entourage and all the remaining Jin officials who could be rounded up for this strange display. Early in the following month he issued a proclamation in which he officially adopted the name Liao for his dynasty and announced the beginning of a new reign period, Datong, meaning "great unity." Tantamount to proclaiming himself the emperor of China, this seems nonetheless to have been an ad hoc political decision, not the well-planned objective of his military campaign into China.

Meanwhile, in Shanxi another Shatuo Turk warlord[14] proclaimed himself the founder of the fourth of the Five Dynasties, called the Later Han. In many parts of North China regional leaders announced their loyalty to him as a way of showing their resentment against the Liao presence. Full-scale military suppression of this resistance would have been a larger undertaking than Emperor Taizong was prepared for. He stayed in the Chinese capital for more than three months, until the spring heat became unbearable for northern steppe nomads.

His recently occupied territories in North China, which extended down to the Yellow River, were proving to be ungovernable. In the wake of his conquering progress across the North China Plain, he had failed to put in place local administrators subservient to him who could maintain order and facilitate the extraction of logistical support for his forces. In desperation, he turned his troops loose to pillage and plunder: that is, he adopted the steppe tactics for intimidating a sedentary enemy while drawing needed supplies from the region. His lack of foresight in failing to assign governors to the regions through which his armies had passed left large areas in a state of administrative chaos. All these difficulties quickly escalated, and the China venture, unplanned and ad hoc at best, turned out to be too costly. Unwilling to face all the tasks of ruling in this unfamiliar place, he changed his mind about being emperor of China and in late April left Kaifeng to return to the Khitan homeland. He took along with him vast amounts of material wealth from the Later Jin capital: its astronomical observatory, astronomers, and library; much of the contents of the imperial storehouses and treasuries; hundreds of officials with their families; and thousands of artisan households. With an immense train stretching many miles behind him, he commenced his progress back to the Southern Capital, whence he would push north to the Supreme Capital high on the cool slopes of the Khingan Mountains.

Deep resentments aroused by the rapacious behavior of his troops led to uprisings all along his route across the North China Plain. There were daily attacks on his slowly withdrawing army and its baggage trains. He and his generals did not know how to defend themselves against this kind of guerrilla attack by sedentary populations. According to the *Liao History,* the Emperor Taizong expressed amazement at the ferocity of the "soft and timid" Chinese.

While passing through one of the prefectures east of the Southern Capital, already safely within Khitan-controlled territory, the emperor fell ill and died suddenly on May 18. He was only forty-five years old. His death provoked the succession crisis of 947, discussed in a foregoing section. His nephew Wuyu, the son of Prince Bei, claimed the throne, but the dowager Empress Yingtian resisted his claim. As we have seen, this nephew, known in history as the Emperor Shizong, defied his grandmother and gained the throne. He reigned briefly, spending his energies chiefly on suppressing revolts from within the imperial clan and the Khitan nobility.

The Khitan position in China began to erode, so in 951 Shizong took to the field and successfully repelled Chinese advances. During a second campaign into China in the autumn of that year, the emperor and his mother, another vigorous empress dowager who had accompanied her son into battle, were murdered by a member of the imperial clan who was attempting to usurp the throne. The attempt was unsuccessful. Instead, a son of Taizong, the second emperor, came to the throne to reign as the fourth Liao emperor until he too was murdered in 969. He was given the posthumous title of Muzong. It was at this point that the succession then passed back to a son of Shizong, that is, a grandson of Prince Bei; he is known as Emperor Jingzong (r. 968–982). The succession remained in his line until the end of the dynasty in 1125. Jingzong's son was the Emperor Shengzong, whose forty-nine-year reign, from 982 until 1031, was the longest of the dynasty. It concluded what may be called the century of Liao expansion.

For most of the decade from 951 to 960 the Emperor Muzong was beset by rebellions from within the imperial and consort clans. His ruthless suppression of these clans gradually restored the stability of the throne, giving the Liao state an opportunity to pay more attention to its neighbors.[15] In the meantime the last of the Five Dynasties, called the Later Zhou (951–960), succeeded the very short-lived Later Han and vigorously began to consolidate power in North China. It had little trouble displacing the Later Han, but an offshoot of that Shatuo Turkic dynasty (I shall call it the Northern Han; some accounts call it the Eastern Han) based itself in the mountains of central Shanxi and continued to resist the Zhou. It was situated adjacent to the Liao Western Capital at Datong, and thus was of interest to the Khitans. Because of his addiction to alcohol, Muzong was known to the Chinese as "the dozing emperor." He took no vigorous action to support the Northern Han, but its proximity to Liao territories sufficed to keep it intact.

In China, the Zhou ruler emerged as one of the most able persons to appear on the Chinese political scene in a century. He fully expected that the Khitans would again invade North China on the pretext of sustaining the Eastern Han. Late in the spring of 958 he decided to preempt such a move by striking at Liao positions. He was quite as obsessed with the idea of regaining the Sixteen Prefectures as the Khitans had been with acquiring them. He breached several of the heavily defended passes along the Great Wall line, demonstrating that Chinese armies under able leaders could defeat the Khitans. He succeeded in retaking two of the Sixteen Prefectures in central Hebei; included within these prefectures were three strategic passes that controlled access into Hebei southeast from Shanxi. These two prefectures and their vitally important passes came to be known as the Guannan ("south of the [Waqiao] Pass," the most important of the three passes) area; they remained in Chinese hands and were a major bone of contention with the Liao thereafter. This offensive provoked the "dozing emperor" to prepare for a major military confrontation. He took personally to the field later in the summer of 959 and led a large army to the Southern Capital, but a military confrontation was averted when the Zhou ruler suddenly fell ill and died. Early in 960 the Liao emperor returned to his Supreme Capital. It appeared that nothing had changed.

In China, however, 960 was a momentous year. Zhao Kuangyin, commander in chief of the Zhou ruler's palace guard, usurped the Zhou throne. He had the backing of army leaders who feared that the Zhou state, now headed by an infant heir, would be unable to carry on the promising beginnings of a Chinese resurgence. Zhao Kuangyin immediately began to follow through with the efforts initiated by the unlucky Zhou ruler to reunite North and South China and end a century of dissolution and division. The Khitans had become important players in Chinese domestic affairs by taking advantage of that long period of weakness. Now, a strong Liao empire, firmly entrenched well within the Great Wall defense line on Chinese soil, faced a united and vigorously led Chinese state. Zhao Kuangyin became the founding emperor of the Song dynasty; he was intent on regaining China's territorial integrity.[16] The conditions of the Khitan-Chinese relationship had fundamentally changed.

VI. LIAO-SONG RELATIONS

After the Song dynastic founding in 960, the two large states of East Asia initially entered upon almost two decades of peaceful relations. The Song state was intent on consolidating its control over China and strengthening its forces before trying to deal with its northern enemy. After 974 the two states began to exchange embassies to offer felicitations on New Year's Day, on imperial birthdays, and on other occasions as demanded by Chinese protocol. Profitable trade developed rapidly at crossing points along their shared boundary. Two flaws marred the relationship. One was that the Song rulers and their officials could not accept the Khitans' possession of the Sixteen Prefectures, even though they had held them since 938, long before the Song dynasty came into existence. The other was that the Liao still protected the Turkic Northern Han state, offensive to the Chinese both because it was a holdout against Song reunification of China, and because it had become a place where the displaced Shatuo Turkic military population of North China tended to gather. Like the Later Jin dynasty before it, the Northern Han had become a client state of the Liao and depended on the Khitan military to survive.

When Zhao Kuangyin, the founder of the Song dynasty, seized the throne in 960, there were still half a dozen independent Chinese states scattered across the map, and there were thirty or more military governorships, some dating from the Tang period, that had become hereditary fiefs of petty warlords. Zhao was a cautious man who preferred to win over or coerce those regional leaders without waging war; he was willing to grant generous terms to those who saw the inevitable trend toward unification and surrendered their powers. When he died in 976, the unification of all China under the Song dynasty was on the verge of being completed. The Song court had begun to feel very self-assured in its possession of the Mandate of Heaven. In 976, the last year of his life, the Song founder attacked the last of the holdout states in the north, the despised Northern Han, which, with Khitan assistance, defeated the Song armies. The next year his brother, as the new emperor, again attacked the Northern Han. Negotiations followed, and more than a year passed. Then, early in 979, the Song armies, led by the second emperor, defeated a minor Liao army sent to aid the Northern Han. The latter collapsed, and the Song ruler rejoiced; a contemptible irritation had been removed, and the Liao support had not saved it. Emboldened by this success, the emperor determined to press on against the Liao in the Sixteen Prefectures. Without adequate provisions, and against all his generals' advice, he led the exhausted Chinese troops eastward from Taiyuan and through the Taihang Mountains down onto the North China Plain. They surrounded the Liao Southern Capital (modern Beijing). Alarmed by the defeat of their relief forces and the fall of the Northern Han in July, the Liao court now prepared for battle in earnest. The Liao armies engaged the Song forces on the first of August at the battle of the Gaoliang River in the environs of present-day Beijing. It was a debacle for the Song armies. Completely routed and demoralized despite their exhilarating victory at Taiyuan a month earlier, they straggled back to Kaifeng. The emperor fled the battlefield in a mule cart; military glory had evaded him.[17]

The Khitans then reinforced their positions in the Sixteen Prefectures to prevent another rash effort by the Chinese. In 982 the tyrannical Liao emperor Jingzong died while hunting near the Western Capital. He was succeeded by his eleven-year-old son, the Emperor Shengzong, who reigned until 1031. The youth of the new emperor may have seemed to afford an opportunity to the Song. They failed to reckon with his fiercely aggressive mother; there was no loss of control at the Liao court during that transition. Full of hope, the Song emperor Taizong in 986 tried again to take the offensive; three large armies were sent to attack simultaneously on three different fronts. The Liao forces won decisive victories on all three. The Song offensive was withdrawn and diplomatic relations were resumed.

The Song emperor died in 997 without having ever again attempted military action on the northern borders. He was succeeded by his son, a timid creature known as the Emperor Zhenzong, overall one of the less admirable Song emperors. Relations between the two states worsened through the 990s. Repeatedly the Liao court received information that the Song had attempted to lure the Liao's border zone enemies to join them in coordinated attacks. Border skirmishes in North China increased. Anxious Song envoys sought negotiations but were refused. It seemed clear to all that the young Liao emperor, now approaching thirty, spurred on by his formidably capable mother, was planning to chastise the Song. In 999 he commenced a series of annual campaigns that were largely successful but won him no landmark victories.

In 1004 the Liao emperor Shengzong again launched a major campaign against the Song. Near the end of October, leading a large cavalry force in person, and with his mother following not far behind, he left from the Southern Capital and moved rapidly southward, capturing those cities that surrendered easily but not waiting to bring down those that resisted. Thus the Khitan army bypassed many entrenched Song units, and with lightning speed made the final dash toward Kaifeng, stopping just north of the Yellow River near the small district city of Shanyuan.[18] There they set up camp, waiting, still almost a hundred miles from the Song capital. Emperor Zhenzong, under the influence of a "war party" at his court, had reluctantly marched north at the head of a large army to display resistance to the Khitan invasion; the imperial camp and court were set up within the city walls of Shanyuan. By the end of December the Song court was sending secret messages to Chinese officials serving the Liao, inquiring about terms for peace. As always, the Chinese court was divided between war and peace factions, and their emperor was both fearful and indecisive. The idea of paying the Khitans to go away seems to have originated with the Chinese court; it was not initially a demand of the Khitans.

The Liao emperor's tents and his central command post had been set up a few miles north of Shanyuan. At Shanyuan, as the two emperors at the head of their two armies faced each other, a treaty of peace was worked out between January 13 and 18, 1005, by the modern Western calendar. (History books sometimes date it to the year 1004 because those dates fell within the last lunar month of the year that principally corresponds with 1004 in our calendar.) At first the Liao expected to negotiate a territorial concession— the return of the strategic Guannan area in central Hebei. They abandoned that demand in the face of stubborn Song resistance and the quite unexpected alternative terms offered by the Song court for a negotiated peace settlement. The Chinese agreed to give the Khitans a payment of 200,000 bolts of silk and 100,000 ounces of silver annually. The two rulers would address each other as "emperor," that is, as equals. The two empires would maintain friendly relations, would refrain from building further defenses on their common border, would demarcate their disputed borders and then respect them, would agree to maintain proper relations with regard to certain other issues, and would swear in religious oaths of high solemnity to honor the treaty. The Liao agreed without much hesitation. The Song would call the annual payment a gift while the Liao would label it tribute, an important difference. An additional aspect of the settlement, not specified in the text of the treaty but undoubtedly worked out in detail by the negotiators, was that the two imperial households would establish a fictive kinship relationship by which the two "brother emperors" would address each other as "elder brother" or "younger brother" according to which was actually senior, and would extend the kinship terms to all other members of their immediate clans. Thus the formidable Empress Xiao, the Liao emperor's mother, became the Song emperor's "junior aunt." The kinship relationship was retained to the end of the Liao dynasty.[19]

The timorous Song emperor and some of his courtiers of the "peace party" congratulated themselves on having arranged a clever bargain. By some estimates their self-congratulations were justified. They were not, however, unopposed at the Song court. Chinese military leaders realized that the Liao army was seriously overextended and exposed. They wanted to ignore the treaty settlement and fight. Some high-minded Song scholar-officials of the "war party" agreed with their assessment, and historians have offered a strong case for believing that the Chinese armies could have seriously embarrassed the Khitan invaders. The prevailing sentiment at court was that the settlement would bring them peace in their time: "We shall secure a century of peaceful relations," they boasted confidently. Struggles between war and peace factions were a constant feature of Song dynasty politics thereafter, until the Mongols ended the Song dynasty 270 years later. But for the next century, until the struggle against the Jurchens terminated both the Liao and the Northern Song, the two powers fought no more major wars.

The pattern of indemnified peace established by the Treaty of Shanyuan was thereafter central to Song China's relations with the Liao, the Xi Xia, and the Jin conquest dynasties. The Inner Asian states learned to threaten war, demand territory, or require other concessions, and the Song learned to resist most of those demands by paying ever higher indemnities. In 1042, for example, under pressure from Xi Xia incursions in the northwest and vague threats of impending Liao military action in concert with them, the Song offered to increase the annual payments to 300,000 bolts of silk and 200,000 ounces of silver. The Song court nonetheless adamantly refused to give up the strategic Guannan area in central Hebei, or other territory, or to send a baby daughter of the Song emperor to become the future bride of the Liao emperor's son. The loss of territory and the indignity of sending a princess to marry a foreign ruler were regarded as much less acceptable than the higher annual payments. Throughout all their trials and tribulations with their barbarian foes, the Song court took comfort from the idea that they were exporting civilizing influences to the steppe, and that those influences would eventually work to the advantage of all. The official *Song History* in its "Account of Foreign Countries" (*juan* 485) states: "Could one say that even the kings of antiquity ever exceeded the Song in their policies of extending gentle kindness to faraway peoples in order to win their hearts?" To be sure, the expansive power of the Liao dynasty undoubtedly declined from the mid-eleventh century onward. An answer to whether that was brought about because the subtle infusion of Chinese civilizing influences had "won their hearts" or because of other factors must remain in doubt, though a closer look at the later phases of Liao history may clarify that issue.

4

LIAO
CIVILIZATION

Throughout two centuries of the Khitan Liao dynasty's intimate interaction with the Chinese, the earlier Khitan way of life developed into what we may call "Liao civilization." Throughout that process of change, the Khitan people remained true to their identification with their traditional steppe values. Their invention of dual institutions, realized most notably in their division of government into Northern and Southern Chancelleries, was designed to preserve their distinctiveness; it did much more than that, and was one of the most important breakthroughs in Asian history. The hybrid imperial institution fostered multicultural adaptations in many aspects of life, from laws and regulations governing social practices to the uses of literacy in Khitan and in Chinese among the ruling elite. Above all, the Liao period practice of Buddhism offers us a revealing focus on Liao civilization, in its many-sided interactions among Inner Asian and East Asian peoples. Liao success in creating and managing the empire still defies easy explanation: the concept of "creative misunderstanding" is explored here as a partial explanation of the impressive Khitan historical achievement.

I. MULTICULTURAL ADAPTATIONS

History is a challenge to our imaginations as well as to our skill in assembling and assessing facts. Under the best of circumstances the historian must attempt to reconstruct larger patterns from incomplete information. That is especially true in piecing together the social histories of peoples from records that were not intended to inform us about all the issues we today may consider important. As we might expect, the vast documentation of Chinese history tells us primarily about the things that Chinese of the past considered essential. It tells us much less about the details, for example, of demography, of social practice, of popular custom and belief, about discrepancies between ideal and actual patterns, and many other things that the modern social historian would like to know. Yet carefully imaginative reading of the historical record can provide some important clues even about these matters. A large and important modern work on Liao social history assembles the randomly preserved details of social management as recorded in the Chinese official Liao dynastic history.[1] The following extracts translated from that history invite us to think about the social circumstances to which they refer, and to draw inferences from them:

[921 C.E.:] ". . . all barbarian tribes were now pacified. The high officials were ordered by edict to establish [special] laws for the Khitans and for all barbarians, while the Chinese were sentenced according to [their own] laws and decrees." (Wittfogel 1946, p. 227)

[938–947:] "This was the system of Liao: During the Huitong period [937–945] the emperor's mother and the officials of the Northern Region dressed according to the national [Khitan] style. The emperor and the officials of the Southern Region dressed according to Chinese style." (pp. 227–228)

[941:] "On the day *bingzhen* . . . it was decreed that Khitan individuals who held Chinese offices [i.e., offices in the Southern Chancellery] were to follow Chinese customs and might intermarry with Chinese." (p. 228)

[After 983:] "After [the reign period Qianheng, 978–982], at big ceremonies even officials of the third rank and above in the Northern Region also wore Chinese clothes. After the reign period Chongxi [1032] at big ceremonies all [officials] dressed in the Chinese style." (p. 228)

[989:] "Previously, when a death occurred in a brawl between Khitan and Chinese, justice was not even-handed. Now it was applied impartially." (p. 231)

[994:] "In the twelfth year of Tonghe [994] it was decreed that Khitans who had committed one of the ten grave crimes should also be sentenced according to [Chinese] law." (p. 231)

In the first of these extracts the phrase "for the Khitans and for all barbarians" reflects the Chinese historians' usual way of designating non-Chinese peoples, even though the *Liao History* was officially compiled in the 1340s on command of the Mongol Yuan dynasty, itself a "barbarian" dynasty.[2] The principle that there should be dual systems of law for the two populations was accepted at the beginning, while Abaoji was still alive. The second extract, dated to the first reign after his death, shows that the Northern Chancellery, always directed by appointees from the Xiao clan which provided all imperial consorts, adhered to Khitan tribal ways in important ritual matters such as dress. In contrast, the emperors and their Yelü clan based at the Southern Chancellery accommodated more quickly to Chinese styles.

The last two extracts, concerning law, reveal that Chinese definitions of such matters as "the ten grave crimes" had been extended to all, Chinese and non-Chinese alike, by the end of the tenth century. They appear to indicate that Liao law was moving away from individual-oriented "ethnic law" toward the realization of statewide uniformity in "territorial law," a considerable advance both in terms of legal concepts and as a practical measure for providing uniform conditions throughout the area under the Liao dynasty's administration. The model of codified law was Chinese: it was found in the Tang Code, which continued in force throughout the Five Dynasties, when the Liao first acquired their large Chinese subject population in the Sixteen Prefectures, and was known throughout East Asia where Chinese cultural and political norms had influence. The Liao attempted to supersede its use by compiling their own comprehensive collection of regulations and statutes; their compilation dating from 1036 probably remained in force throughout the remainder of the dynasty.

Despite the promulgation of measures such as those dated 989 and 994, conflicts between Chinese and Khitan law were never fully resolved. The administration of justice remained a haphazard matter, in part because it could not be assumed that all the local administrators would be literate in classical Chinese, the language of the statutes. We find many Chinese complaints about the harshness of Liao legal practice and discrimination against the subject peoples, conditions to be expected wherever conquerors try to maintain their advantages over the conquered. Chinese envoys traveling through Liao territory en route to the capital had opportunities to observe conditions and to talk with the Chinese subjects.[3] They were not unbiased observers, but they reported much dissatisfaction expressed by Chinese over their plight under Khitan rule, complaining both that the laws, when followed, were severe, and that legal protections were not enforced when to do so would not serve Khitan interests.[4] The subject populations were not usually unstable or on the brink of rebellion and disorder, but the Liao government could not fully trust them, for in times of emergency they regularly defied the Khitans' authority over them.[5]

Whether it be in fundamental issues of duality in the country's laws, or seemingly superficial ones of prescribed costume, the multicultural character of the Liao period is apparent. The civilization developed by the Khitan people from the time of their clear emergence into the Chinese historical records during the Tang period, through the rise of Abaoji and the creation of the Liao dynasty in the tenth century, and finally to the collapse of the Liao state in the twelfth century increasingly displays the marks of a hybrid way of life. The Khitans were a nomadic steppe people whose involvement with their sedentary neighbors, as well as with other non-Khitan nomadic peoples, forced them to interact with and accommodate a variety of cultures and institutions. That same challenge faced all the conquest dynasties, but they differed widely in their responses to it. The pattern of Khitan response, in particular the response to Chinese civilization (which the Chinese historical records cover the most fully), reveals the special qualities of the Khitan adaptation. Faced with the need to utilize Chinese means for governing the large sedentary sector of its conquests, whose populations several times outnumbered its own, the Khitans produced what was in many ways a hybrid civilization. Nonetheless, they largely succeeded in that difficult task of governing without giving up the fundamental commitment to their original steppe way of life.

The skill with which the Khitan ruling elite led their people in walking that tightrope for more than two centuries commands our respect. They were the pathbreaking innovators in devising new institutions required for this difficult task. They also were in many ways the most successful of all the steppe practitioners of dual administration. That experience, incidentally, might today be seen as a pertinent historical precedent for current Chinese plans forecasting "one country, two systems" (even though contemporary advocates are ignorant of their history). Be that as it may, the methods worked out by tenth-century Khitans and their advisers for maintaining the integrity of their own civilization, while ruling over and drawing heavily upon the quite different civilizations of sedentary peoples, established the framework within which Khitan civilization developed under the Liao dynasty.

II. KHITAN SOCIETY

We have seen that the official dynastic histories incidentally reveal fascinating bits of information about Khitan society, yet the present state of our knowledge does not permit us to describe it fully or with assurance. We know too little of its kinship terms or other features of base-level social organization. Most of what we know has to do with the larger units of social organization such as the names of tribes and of some clans. Even that information is imprecise because it comes from Chinese historical records, where, of course, Chinese terms for social organization are used. The Chinese term *zu* (lineage, clan) usually means in Chinese society the common descent group from a real ancestor. As the Chinese use the term, it implies that all members of the society possessed surnames, practiced surname exogamy, maintained a ritual focus on ancestors, recognized *zu* leadership based on primogeniture, and observed a hierarchy of authority and deference based on systematically specified degrees of kinship as well as on age and generational place. The term *zu,* when borrowed by Chinese writers as analogue to some form of Khitan tribal or clan organization (probably not well understood by them), becomes quite misleading, for we have no reason to believe that those defining elements of the Chinese *zu* were generally present in Khitan society. In 1074, when a member of the imperial Yelü clan recommended that the practice of using surnames be extended from the Yelü imperial and the Xiao consort clans to include the entire society "so as to make marriages between men and women harmonize with the code of proper behavior," the emperor thought about it and rejected that essentially Chinese idea. He felt that the old Khitan order "should not be suddenly changed." That was a full century and a half after Abaoji's death.[6] We assume that the Khitans reckoned kinship in ways meaningful to them, expressed in religious practices and reflected in authority patterns, but beyond such hypothetical assumptions we can say very little about Khitan social patterns.

It is clear that Khitan women, like women generally in other steppe tribal nations, possessed considerable freedom and authority compared with women in East Asian sedentary societies. Khitan women to be sure lived in a strongly patriarchal society, yet they nonetheless could possess and freely use wealth and property, they could initiate divorce, and divorced women could freely remarry. In the high elite strata of Khitan society, women could hold important civil and even military positions. Empresses were truly co-rulers with their emperor husbands or sons. We can be less sure about the status of women in ordinary households, but it is certain that they shared the heavy work of tending flocks; they rode horseback and drove wagons; and they cared for and defended their settlements when their men were away at war or the hunt. They were not excluded from important positions in the ritual and religious lives of their people. The hard life of the steppe was shared by men and women and children; the women may well have borne more than their share of the heavy work needed to maintain daily life. They had to be competent in many forms of labor, and cope with extremes of hardship and danger that their less free Chinese counterparts were spared. Although the emperor rejected the imposition of Chinese surnames and marriage patterns on Khitan society, we are not told why he hesitated. The old practices must still have had utility in their society.

As early as 940 an imperial decree abolished the traditional practice of requiring a younger sister to take the place in marriage of an older sister who died, but that did not eliminate the sororate[7] as a voluntary pattern in marriage. The levirate[8] too remained a general practice in Khitan as in other steppe tribal societies; it of course encountered strong Chinese ethical objections, yet it never was abolished and was practiced in the imperial family. It kept widowed women and their children within the clan. Polygamy in which multiple wives all were recognized as having equal status probably had been the norm in tribal society. As the imperial clan adopted the idea of primogeniture, however, it became useful to distinguish between principal wives and lesser wives for determining inheritance. That is, in order to lessen disputes about which sons might inherit and in what sequence, it was useful to label wives other than the first wife as lesser wives or "concubines," to place limits on their sons' rights to compete. Thus, although the Chinese institution of concubinage was adopted and became a pattern within the elite, it may not have deeply affected practice among ordinary people in Khitan tribal society. There are other tantalizing but fragmentary bits of information, unfortunately not enough to satisfy our curiosity about many aspects of Khitan society. We have no reason to believe that Khitan social structure changed significantly during the 200 years of the Liao dynasty; it remained a society organized in tribal units, functionally well adapted to the needs of an essentially nomadic, military way of life.

III. PATTERNS OF ACCULTURATION

The advanced pastoral nomadism of tenth-century Inner Asia can in no way be seen as a primitive state of social organization; this point must be repeatedly stressed. Although the nomadic societies were "barbarian" according to Chinese usage, and in our eyes also were significantly "different" as we look at the world from the vantage point of Chinese history, we should take the term "barbarian" merely to mean "different" in specific ways. In examining that difference we should recognize that many sedentary peoples in East Asia at that time possessed skills and capacities which nomadic societies had not needed to develop to high levels. When faced with new needs in governing or in war, nomadic peoples often had to adapt skills and techniques learned from others. New techniques of military organization and warfare tended to be adapted from other steppe peoples, except when specifically non-steppe technical skills were needed. For example, they learned from Chinese associates how to tunnel under fortified city walls, to breach walls with gunpowder, and to construct siege machinery. They had little need for naval skills and made no attempt to adapt them from their seafaring neighbors such as the Koreans; their focus was on the Inner Asian and Chinese frontiers.

In matters of organizing the state, a primary specialization of Chinese civilization, the Khitans, like all Inner Asian nomads, tended to look to China, borrowing either directly or through partially sinified intermediaries such as the Bohai and the Koreans. They learned to borrow concepts and methods they could adapt, and they also learned to co-opt aliens such as surrendered or captured Chinese who could perform specialized services for them. In the succession of conquest dynasties from the Liao to the Mongols' Yuan dynasty (and, looking forward, to the Manchus in the seventeenth century), we see a variety of such adaptations of Chinese patterns to the steppe conquerors' changing needs; we must not overlook influences going from steppe to sedentary China as well.

Relatively few Chinese could shoot a crossbow from the back of a galloping horse, and early in their history very few Khitans could write classical Chinese poetry. Why, indeed, should either try to acquire the other's skills? Eventually, in fact, large numbers of skilled Chinese cavalrymen and Khitan literati appeared. To be more accurate, skilled Chinese cavalry soldiers had appeared throughout Chinese history, since the fourth century B.C.E., when the Chinese first took up cavalry warfare from Inner Asian models. Chinese on the frontier could always adapt in that way, whenever pressed by immediate needs to do so. The Khitan incursions into the northern border zone provided the Chinese there with a new stimulus to borrow steppe fighting skills, but in Chinese society such skills on the whole remained geographically limited to the north and therefore were peripheral to the general populace. It was in the border zones in these centuries that some Chinese became skilled cavalrymen and assimilated fully into steppe society, in some cases even taking steppe surnames and abandoning Chinese beliefs. They were numerous enough to prove the point that Confucius had sadly observed 1,500 years earlier: Chinese could become barbarians.[9] The distinction was cultural, not racial.

As for Khitans learning to write classical Chinese poetry, that too was at first peripheral to the needs of Khitan society; but when that skill came to serve useful functions, Khitan society could produce persons who were accepted as worthy peers by Chinese scholar-officials. Successive conquering steppe peoples varied greatly in their adaptation to the traditional accomplishments of elite Chinese society. For example, by the eleventh century the number of Khitans who could write polished Chinese poetry appears to have been considerably greater than the number of fourteenth-century Mongols who could do the same after ruling in China for a century. Why was that so? We can hypothesize about a number of answers, but none of the possible answers has anything to do with differences in intelligence. The steppe peoples were nothing if not adaptable, educable, and capable of rapid growth in their cultural skills. Their adaptations were not limited to things drawn from China; all the varieties of steppe nomad social experience also contributed in important ways to their brilliant success.

Giving the Khitans and other steppe peoples their due, however, does not demand that we forgo all value judgments. Quite simply, for most of us (though not necessarily for everyone), the norms and the peculiar achievements of Chinese civilization hold more intrinsic value than do those of the nomads. The refinement of their learned, humanistic tradition did not make all Chinese admirable: they neither precluded all heinous acts among Chinese nor prevented such perversions as footbinding, which was imposed on Chinese women for almost a thousand years, starting at about this time in the tenth century. Its faults notwithstanding, most outside observers have always concluded that China's civilization provided better resources for the realization of human potential than did the steppe civilizations. Objectively speaking, the tools that the Chinese had developed for generating, preserving, and transmitting knowledge, and the more stable conditions in which sedentary life developed, gave greater resources to the Chinese people than the Inner Asians enjoyed.

The Khitans themselves, for all their proud self-confidence and attachment to steppe values, nonetheless clearly observed and acknowledged that they could learn from China; they strove to acquire and utilize not only the material goods but also some of the social forms and cultural tools of their sedentary neighbors. A prime example is their creation of their own distinctive writing systems: one, their "large script," adapted elements of Chinese writing; the other, somewhat more phonetic "small script" was based on Uighur writing but still utilized Chinese graphic forms. Yet having accomplished a symbolic independence from Chinese culture while achieving literacy, they at the same time made pragmatic use of Chinese in appropriate contexts, and those occasions probably far outnumbered the situations in which their own writing system was employed. They managed to have it both ways.

All the conquest dynasties were illiterate through their initial rise to power, and all made literacy for their people a priority during the first phases of their conquest regimes. Chinese-style literacy, whether seen as a social tool providing access to and sustenance of the literary tradition that maintained the Chinese ethos, or as an indispensable instrument in managing any large society, or, still more specifically, as the tool for standardizing and regulating procedures, keeping the records of tax levies and disbursements in order to enhance the efficiency and rationality of fiscal systems—all of those, but particularly the more specific applications to state wealth and power—was something the Khitans could admire and envy.

They saw that borrowing literacy and letting it function throughout society would exact a price. That was true where literacy in the Chinese language became necessary for Khitans who worked in their Southern Region; to some extent it was also true where literacy in the Khitan scripts became necessary to the work in the Northern Region, where even the governing of other nomads gradually came to require written records and regularized written procedures. The borrower of cultural tools pays for them in many ways; that is true of all cultural borrowing. If we cannot demonstrate that all the mounted warriors of Inner Asia now became subject to the clerk's and scribe's pens, we know at least that the ways by which nomad governed nomad underwent some changes.

In the case of literacy and the Chinese cultural influences associated with it, the Khitans managed, whether or not by fully conscious design, to prevent the costs to their cultural integrity from becoming too great. Chinese literacy and the service careers dependent on it were restricted within Khitan society to their elite; some members of certain families of nobles and chieftains monopolized the Khitan participation in those functions. Many others of the elite were not so deeply involved, and the common people probably not at all. When the Khitans first adopted the Chinese-style civil service examinations in the 930s and then fully implemented the examination system from 988 onward, participation was limited to non-Khitans, in effect making the examination route to government office the exclusive preserve of Chinese, along with some Bohai, Koreans, and other peripheral subjects of their realm.

The way in which the civil service examination system was made to function informs us about the Khitans' cautious use of borrowed institutions. In Chapter 2 I described their adoption of dual institutions: they used steppe practices for governing themselves and other nomadic tribes and Chinese institutions for governing the sedentary zone of their empire. The resulting system of dual institutions for governing disparate populations making up the two halves of the Khitan empire has been called Abaoji's brilliant achievement, a genuine "breakthrough" conception of how tribal peoples from beyond the Chinese culture sphere could build an integrated empire. Still, they faced the problem of staffing the Chinese side of their empire in as reliable a manner as could be devised.

By Tang times, when the Khitans first became deeply involved with China, the problem of staffing a civil bureaucracy in China had come to be solved by the competitive examinations. The Khitans of course knew all about the Tang dynasty's system of civil service examinations and recruitment, but they could see that it created an official (if "open") elite having its own powerful sense of tradition, and that the proud Chinese holders of the highest civil service degree gained through it a semiautonomous source of authority. The Liao rulers were concerned about problems of control and were hesitant to introduce an institution that might generate its own norms of behavior. They probably were not prepared to state the problem in the terms that we now use, that is, that the Chinese system of civil service examinations and recruitment, with its attendant educational traditions and social prestige (even in Tang times, before the still more open system of Song had come about), was one of the society's principal defining institutions (see Chapter 6). Yet they grasped its implications and were wary of it.

Nevertheless, they had accepted the necessity of governing the sedentary population by Chinese means, and there was a strong desire among their Chinese subjects to implement the examination system as the appropriate way to recruit staff for the Southern Chancellery and local levels of government in Liao-controlled North China. The Khitan rulers waited over sixty years, until 988, before at last implementing an examination system based on the Chinese Tang and Song models: from that date forward they held the highest-level triennial examinations at their Southern Capital fifty-four times until 1123, shortly before the dynasty fell. At first they awarded only three or five degrees at each examination, but from 1014 onward they regularly bestowed from 30 to 130 degrees every three years. The total for the entire period was about 2,000 *jinshi,* or highest-level degrees.[10] That is a much smaller number than in the Jurchen Jin dynasty in the late twelfth and thirteenth centuries, and much smaller than the number of *jinshi* produced in contemporary Northern Song China, or in later Chinese dynasties, as comparisons in later chapters will show.

Not only were the Khitans reluctant to implement the system and allow its full functioning, but also they appear to have appointed to office only a small portion of the *jinshi,* the highest-level degree holders, that it generated. They simultaneously adopted and modified to their social ends Tang systems of "protected" access to office (the *yin* privilege) and methods of sponsorship and recommendation. In Tang, and even more so in Song China, those alternate ways of selecting and appointing carried less prestige than the individually earned degree. But to the Khitans, the direct appointment to persons whose families already had high status seemed to match the norms of their aristocratic society; it seemed proper that persons of high social status should have direct access to government. Persons appointed in that way were rewarded for their families' standing and past service, issues of great import in a tribal aristocracy; their loyalty was more important to the government than other considerations. The numbers of such direct appointees appear to have exceeded the numbers of those who achieved rank and office via the examination route.[11] In short, the Khitans neither ignored the essential instrument of Chinese bureaucratic government nor did they allow it to play a defining role in their dual society.

Khitans were expressly forbidden from taking the examinations, but of course they did not need to do so. All tribesmen who were qualified for official posts, whether those posts would seem to demand knowledge of Chinese or not, could be appointed anywhere in the bureaucracy in accordance with the Khitan-style "inherited privilege," also called *yin,* or "protection," in the Chinese sources. That concept of privilege gave Khitans priority in appointment anywhere within civil or military government; or they might come into inherited offices belonging in their families. In short, Khitans could gain office without the need to display excellence in Chinese learning. Despite that, as time went on the number of them who became the educational peers of the Chinese degree holders steadily increased. To the end of the dynasty such Khitan learned persons were forbidden to take the examinations, so we might ask why they should choose to acquire high educational qualifications. The reasons why men of the Khitan elite chose to acquire deep cultivation in the heritage of Chinese civilization were personal, not to advance political careers. Some developed intellectual interests, others aesthetic pursuits. For many the study of Buddhism also was a powerful motivating factor.

IV. BUDDHISM IN KHITAN LIFE

Prince Bei's biography in the *Liao History* recounts that in 916, when Abaoji first took the title of emperor, he also adopted a calendar and proclaimed a reign title, inserting himself into the Chinese ideal cosmos by assuming these prerogatives of the universal ruler. As emperor of a new dynasty, he also named his eldest son, Prince Bei, his heir. The biography gives the impression that it was during those ceremonies when he turned to his assembled officials and said:

> "The ruler who has received the Mandate of Heaven should be attentive to Heaven and respectful to the great spirits. To those of greatest merit I should offer my veneration. Which among them ranks first?" All present replied that it should be the Buddha. Abaoji responded: "Buddhism is not a Chinese teaching." Then Prince Bei spoke: "Confucius is the great sage, revered for myriad generations. He should rank first." Abaoji was delighted. Thereupon he ordered that a Confucian temple be constructed and decreed that the heir himself should conduct the spring and autumn ritual offerings.[12]

The Chinese historians who compiled the *Liao History* probably thought that the anecdote belonged in Prince Bei's biography instead of in the annals of Abaoji's reign because it contributes to the prince's image as a Confucian paragon, a theme of the biography. It may well be in some measure fanciful, but it is nonetheless interesting for several reasons. We need not doubt that Abaoji thought of the imperial institution which he was at that moment attempting to adapt to Khitan needs as something supported by Chinese teachings, especially by Confucianism. Two years later we read that he ordered the construction of Confucian, Buddhist, and Daoist temples, and later he visited the Confucian temple while ordering the empress and the heir to make offerings at the Buddhist and Daoist temples. Despite the formal continuation of the Confucian cult at the court, after his reign we read, however, almost exclusively about imperial involvement with Buddhism.

We do not know whether Buddhist institutions had been imported into Khitan lands before the time of Abaoji, but the Khitans must have been been familiar with Buddhist practice through their long contact with Tang China before 907. The "great suppression" of Buddhism by the Tang court in 845 may have sharpened their awareness that Buddhism had once been denounced in China as a foreign creed. Abaoji's courtiers clearly expressed their allegiance to it when asked which of the great spirits should be ranked first by the state. That may reflect another point of their resistance to Abaoji's effort to alter the character of Khitan government.

It would be useful to know more about how and when Buddhism became so popular among the Khitan elite. Within a few decades after the dynasty's founding, it clearly had become the most visible of the religions in the records of Liao history. There is a quite noticeable increase of interest during the reign of Emperor Shengzong, which began in 982, and attention to Buddhist activities continued under his successors. Emperors, empresses, and many other members of the imperial clan built Buddhist temples, offered food to immense gatherings of monks, copied sutras in their own Chinese calligraphy, sponsored the study and printing of Buddhist texts, participated in ceremonies, and patronized the Indian religion extravagantly. During one year (1078), for example, local offices of government throughout the realm made offerings of food at Buddhist temples and reported that their offerings had reached a total of 360,000 monks and nuns. It has been estimated that the total population of the Liao empire at that time, including sedentary and tribal populations, was about 3.8 million persons, so if both sets of figures are correct (and they could be), almost one in ten was a monk or nun. The numbers reached by the offerings of food may be exaggerated, but even if they should be discounted by half or more, they still would indicate a very large Buddhist establishment in Liao society.[13]

Throughout the Liao dynasty we can speak of an unending Khitan fascination with Buddhism. It pervaded the Khitan tribal nobility, and it was strong among the almost 3 million Chinese and other sedentary subjects of the Liao state. Support of the Buddhist establishment affected the economy in a number of ways; for example, large numbers of sedentary households were bestowed on temples, where they became indentured laborers who worked the temples' large landholdings and craftsmen for their building projects. There is no evidence that the drain on the economy adversely affected the prosperous Liao state, but the diversion of energies may have affected the society in other ways. We do not know how thoroughly the Khitan tribesmen in the Inner Asian steppe may have become Buddhists; most of the surviving monuments of Liao Buddhism are in the Southern Region, where the population was sedentary and mostly Chinese.

The widespread elite adherence to Buddhism does not mean that the original tribal religion was displaced. The Khitans shared with most of the steppe peoples an animistic religion which we may refer to in general terms as shamanism. In the tribal religion the sun was worshipped, and ritually the emperor sat facing the rising sun in the east (not facing south, in the Chinese manner), thereby giving ritual priority to the north, which was at his left hand, over the south, the direction in which China lay, on his right, for like the Chinese, but unlike the later Mongols, the Khitans gave precedence to the left over the right. The royal tents and most ordinary dwellings faced to the east; Chinese palace layout and ordinary house plans opened to the sun in the south. This ritual priority of the east is reflected throughout the Khitans' arrangements of governing: for example, the Northern Chancellery and the Northern Region (to the left of the seated emperor) took precedence over the Southern Chancellery and the Southern Region; that comfortingly assured them that the tribal homeland was more important to the tribal society than were the throne's Chinese interests.

In addition to the primary focus on the sun, other supreme spirits were those of Heaven and of Earth. The entire natural world was filled with spirits and deities. Spirits of Muye Mountain, the legendary home of the Khitans' ancestors, were most highly honored among terrestrial spirits, but rivers and streams, certain animals, the "Black Mountain" where other guardian spirits of the people dwelled, and other features of the natural world also were venerated.

Shamans, as divinely touched intermediaries, helped man communicate with the powers ruling the natural universe and thus harmonize life. That well-developed system of fundamental religious ideas was proudly retained and probably was of primary importance in the daily life of ordinary people. The elite simply added on the layers of Chinese teachings, those of Confucianism and of Daoism, and especially of Buddhism, known to them in its long-naturalized Chinese forms. Buddhism was not only "non-Chinese" in origin but also was known to the Khitans as the religion of the Uighurs, who had absorbed it via China, and who provided an influential Inner Asian precedent for its adoption. But the situation is made more complex by the fact that just at this time the Uighurs themselves were turning from Buddhism to Manichaeism, a western Asian religion that they had discovered at the Tang capital during the eighth and ninth centuries, and had encountered again after their move to western Inner Asia.

Buddhism and Manichaeism could easily coexist. In fact, neither of these religious and philosophical systems demanded exclusive devotion from its followers. They selectively reinforced each other in the steppe, and parallels for such syncretism were also known in China. The notion of "exclusive truth" was absent from the East Asian mentality; even when the jealous God of monotheism was imported with Judaism, Nestorian Christianity, and Islam during these centuries, it was most difficult to maintain that idea in the prevailing atmosphere of Asian religions' mutual compatibility.

Throughout East Asia, strange though it may seem, the Buddhist religion of compassion that regards the taking of any life as a great evil has often appealed to warrior societies. The Liao emperor, the quintessential exemplar of a tribal warrior for his people, ordered that the Lord Buddha be addressed by the title "The Benevolent King Who Guards the Country." There were well-established Chinese precedents for giving Buddhism the function of guarding the state and thereby gaining imperial patronage. The Khitan rulers appear to have gone well beyond Chinese experience in seeking the religion's protection of the state by associating Buddhism more specifically with the warrior life; they invoked its protection for armies in battle and made massive offerings to celebrate victories while placating the souls of those who had fallen in battle. The state's favor undoubtedly encouraged individuals to make personal commitments to the Buddhist ideal; it came to underlie and sustain the code of the warrior and to leave its mark on all facets of tribal life. For example, during special observances at imperially patronized temples, the hunting and killing of animals might be forbidden for a specified period. A people who lived by hunting were made to acknowledge (although not necessarily to adopt) a higher principle of "taking no life."

When we examine these historical events quite analytically, the incompatibility of Buddhist doctrine with the basic orientations of steppe life would seem to be obvious, but social behavior is seldom governed by detached, rational analysis. The great appeal of Buddhism lay in its accessibility; some measure of its fundamental truth was open to almost any mind, and seeming contradictions between the levels of its truth invited every believer to explore with his own mind the unending vistas of ever-higher truth.

Buddhism enhanced the Liao period's great importance in Inner Asian and East Asian cultural history. The formal study of its scriptures, patronized by the rulers of many states within the orbit of the Liao empire, led to the exchanges of learned monks and of important texts. We read of monks from western Asian regions, from the Xi Xia, from Tibet, from Korea, from Japan, and from China coming to the Liao regions to present sutras for study or to obtain sutras to take back with them. Buddhist monks often served as envoys from one of these countries to others. Buddhism was a world of interstate and intercultural exchange transcending ethnic particularities, using Chinese (at least in its written forms) as its lingua franca, and in that respect paralleling the use of both written and spoken Chinese among the Liao elite. A truly pan-Asian though sinified Buddhism contributed an element of genuine cosmopolitanism to the cultural history of the Liao dynasty.

The principal monuments of Liao Buddhism are religious architecture, sculpture, and painting, tomb art, and the scholarly editing and printing of Buddhist texts. A surprisingly large number of important temple structures dating from Liao times still exist.[14] Their vigorous style represents the late phase of monumental timber frame buildings developed during the Tang dynasty, and they number among the most important examples of historic architecture existing in East Asia today. In addition to these timber halls, twenty or thirty Liao period pagodas (the multistoried towers built of timber or, much more frequently, of masonry, and associated with Buddhist temple complexes) still stand. Many are in a state of near collapse, and many more have collapsed into mounds of rubble, but from them and from the underground treasure rooms over which they were built, scholars have begun to draw large quantities of cultural treasures. In 1970 archaeologists uncovered extensive mural paintings and decorations, a finely sculpted polychromed model of a pagoda, bronze reliquaries, tables and chairs, porcelain objects, items of daily use, mirrors, coins, and carved crystal objects from the rubble mound and the square underground treasury of a pagoda at Nong'an in Jilin Province (in the Northeast), built in the early eleventh century.[15] The large number of recently discovered wall paintings in such pagoda treasuries and in elaborate underground tomb chambers of the period depict all manner of subjects, very directly illustrating many aspects of Liao daily life. The Liao period witnessed an extraordinary burst of elaborate underground tomb construction for Khitans, for Chinese, and for other members of the elite strata. Dozens of such tombs have been excavated, and tomb inscriptions that have been brought to light significantly correct and supplement the data preserved in the *Liao History*.[16] Unfortunately, these discoveries have not been fully published or studied. Yet the study of Liao social history in the broadest sense has a very bright future as these cultural objects receive systematic study.

The commitment to Buddhism is also seen in the large number and high quality of Buddhist sutra printings undertaken during the Liao period. Individual sutras brought from India and written in Pali or Sanskrit had been translated into Chinese since the third century C.E. By Tang times there was a large accumulation of those translated texts, and of new texts written by Chinese. According to their subject matter, the sutras usually were classified into one of three main categories, called the "three baskets," or "tri pitaka" (in Chinese, "San Zang"). Taken together they were known as the *Da-zang,* or *Great Tripitaka,* one vast collection containing the entire corpus of Buddhist canonical writings. Individual sutras had circulated in handwritten copies and as rubbings from texts engraved on stone. From the late sixth or early seventh century those were supplemented with copies made by the newly invented process of woodblock printing. As the printing techniques developed rapidly in late Tang times, it seemed inevitable that the entire *Tripitaka* would be printed in one uniform edition. That was done for the first time under the patronage of the first Song emperor, beginning in 972 and completed in 983. It included 1,076 sutras in 5,048 *juan* (chapters), and required 130,000 individual printing blocks, each engraved on both sides, from each side of which one double page could be printed. Full sets of that vast work soon reached the Liao court, as well as the Korean court and courts of other neighboring countries.

A number of important sutras were engraved and printed at the Liao Southern Capital (modern Beijing) from the 990s onward. Under patronage of the court, the printing of the entire *Tripitaka* in a Liao edition was commenced at the Southern Capital in the mid-eleventh century and was probably completed about 1075. It included 6,000 chapters and may have been printed with Korean ink on high-quality paper also imported from Korea. The quality of the editing surpasses that of the various Song period printings produced in China, a fact long acknowledged by Chinese Buddhist scholars. Buddhist scholarship was taken more seriously in the Liao empire than it was in Song China, where the intellectual repudiation of Buddhism was then under way.

It was long thought that no portions of the Liao *Tripitaka* had survived, but archaeologists are reported to have found some portions of it in a secret hiding place in a pagoda built in 1056 at Yingxian (Ying-hsien) in Shanxi, near the Western Capital.[17] Many other important cultural objects also were found there; it is one of the most important archaeological finds of the late twentieth century. (The building and its statues were undergoing repairs in 1974 after having sustained damage in the widespread destruction caused by the so-called Great Proletarian Cultural Revolution of 1966–1976.) The hidden treasures were concealed inside the great Buddha statue in the pagoda. The statue may have been installed a few years after the pagoda was built, but the 160 important objects concealed within it had safely lain there for nine centuries.

The Koreans also obtained copies of the Liao *Tripitaka*. Using that and the Song printing of 972–983, they undertook their own first printing of the entire *Tripitaka* between 1011 and 1082. It was supplemented in about 1101 by a vast compilation of Korean, Liao, and Song Buddhist writings, further demonstrating the importance of the links among East Asian Buddhist believers and scholars in Liao times, when the Liao empire became the crossroads of Inner Asian cultural exchange.

v. INTERPRETATIONS OF LIAO SUCCESS

An important question arises with regard to the civilization of the Liao period: To what extent are the cultural monuments inspired by Buddhism and the other aspects of Liao period culture, such as the distinctive Liao ceramics, to be credited to the Khitans? They created the state and ordered the society within which those things were produced. They allocated resources for their production, patronized their producers, and developed their own appreciation for them. Most important, perhaps, they created an environment in which exchange and interaction were encouraged. But it is difficult to document any Khitan participation in the tasks of designing and creating the buildings, the sculptures, the tomb art, and other artistic endeavors. The monks and lay scholars working on the Buddhist texts, including the craftsmen engraving the printing blocks and applying the technology of printing and binding the books, all appear to have been Chinese or members of the other sedentary communities incorporated by force into the Liao empire. One can go further and say the same about virtually all the other craftsmen, as well as the farmers and merchants, producers of salt and textiles, processed foods, iron and other metals: the creators of wealth in the society were largely concentrated in the sedentary population.

Although styles and modes distinctive to the period and to the region are evident in some of these arts, and particularly in the ceramics, when we identify them as "Liao" are we simply indicating a time and a place, or are we also crediting the skills and the inspiration behind them to the Khitans? The ceramics, which are in many cases adaptations to Khitan uses and tastes, are clearly different from contemporary Five Dynasties and Song ceramics, although in their techniques they are entirely within the scope of Tang and Song ceramics.[18] It is likely that few if any of the potters who made the representative pieces in the very distinctive "Liao style" were Khitans. We know that the Liao emperors on several occasions specifically ordered that Chinese potters be brought to work in their realm, along with other artisans from China.

Khitan society had developed a limited range of traditional crafts. Khitans were said to be the best saddle makers of the time, and archaeologically recovered examples bear that reputation out. Khitan armorers, cart makers, workers in leather, furriers, and craftsmen producing for other military needs also displayed some specialized skills of a high order. Much Khitan craft production was carried out by women. They sewed skins to make fine boots and clothing, made felt for tents and other uses, and prepared the steppe's distinctive food products. It seems reasonable to assume that a people most famous for its cavalry should have had their own means of supplying and equipping their armed forces. They probably did. Nevertheless, some early documents also suggest that the best of some military items were also made by certain incorporated tribes, especially the closely related Xi tribe. We have no certain answers. Beyond that limited range of traditional tribal craft industries, the civilization's producers and suppliers appear to have been the conquered peoples, not the conquerors.

In general, even by late Liao times the levels of most craft production, including that in the conquered sedentary zone of the Liao state, did not match the levels for the same kinds of activity in Five Dynasties and Song China. Relative to other nomadic societies, the Liao empire was prosperous, in significant part because of the wealth it gained from "tribute" paid to it by China as well as by conquered tribal peoples: its investment in its war machine paid a good rate of return. Measured by the scope and quality of its production activities, however, it was economically backward and remained that way relative to China and to Korea and Japan as well.

Analytically, we can speak of Khitan civilization and Liao civilization. The Khitans created the special conditions that fostered both. Khitan civilization had its special triumphs in building a great empire while preserving the integrity of its own tribal way of life; most of what we mean by "Liao civilization" refers to the period and to the sedentary sector of the Liao empire, not exclusively to the Khitan people themselves.

"Creative Misunderstanding." There are other anomalies in Liao history that are worth exploring. One is the apparent ease with which Liao government was transformed while its traditional tribal structure remained stable throughout the two centuries of the Liao empire. The old Khitan leadership's power, measured by its continuity in decision making and its control over people, was unchanged despite the hybrid government's proliferation of new offices, titles, ranks, and duties. We might think that the Chinese-type institutions superimposed on an at best very slowly changing tribal social base would generate a dysfunctional incongruity between form and reality. Karl A. Wittfogel and Feng Chia-sheng, however, have posed an intriguing explanation: they describe the large-scale borrowing of political forms as "a process of creative misunderstanding."[19] The Khitans, they say, forced the imposition of alien models on an unreconstructed tribal society without fully under-standing the implications inherent in that process. They benefited from the enhanced organizational capacity nonetheless, without knowing that their hybrid forms did not realize the content signified by their foreign names. The resulting forms retained some of the resilience of tribal society while integrat-ing that with the exploitative government imposed over the sedentary popula-tions. They upgraded the continuity and stability of the ruling institution without feeling the need for resolving all the nonrational features of that jux-taposition.

By never stopping to rationalize all these contradictions, they created an imperfect system that nonetheless served Khitan ruling interests very well: it strengthened their tribal empire without undermining their society's struc-tural integrity. The flawed nature of their borrowing does not decrease the importance of the source from which they borrowed; the Chinese component in their civilization was not less important to them because they compre-hended it only imperfectly. The power of the imperial Liao state derived directly from its success in combining the disparate halves of its territories under one integrated government. The imperial clan, strongly identified with the southern interests (the civil governing of sedentary populations), served as the intermediary between those disparate halves of the empire, in the clashes of style and conflicts of interest that were never fully reconciled. By studying the names of those who held the leading northern offices, we can see that the consort clan was identified with northern interests (the adminis-tration of tribal and military affairs). That increased the mother-son (that is, the empress-heir) tensions in the imperial household and led to succession conflicts in some cases. Rebellion against emperors came mostly from within the imperial Yelü clan, some of whose members felt themselves excluded from leadership, while the consort Xiao clan's interests were served only by sup-porting the throne. The integration of those varied interests within one impe-rial institution may have helped keep them in balance and probably served to strengthen the state most of the time.

The division of the state, for administrative purposes, into the Northern and Southern Chancelleries carried to the logical limit the division of Khitan interests, a bifurcation already apparent before the rise of Abaoji. The North-ern Chancellery was given ritual and actual superiority over the Southern. That expressed the reality of Khitan attitudes as well as the preeminence of the military, which drew its manpower from the North. The emperors also recognized that the economic support of war and diplomacy, and the means of intervening in interstate affairs, came from its Southern Region. Moreover, Liao imperial governing became dependent on the services of southerners in all parts of the realm. We can see how "North" and "South" came to have functional as well as regional meanings, and offices for both northern and southern administrators (i.e., for both military and civil governing) came to be established in both the Northern and the Southern Chancelleries. The rele-vance of the southern bureaucracy grew steadily.

Despite that increasing dependence on "southern" resources, tribal interests were never overtaken by the growing role of Chinese-style administration. The tribes were the basic administrative units of Khitan society, and their administration was the principal concern of the Northern Chancellery, where any needed expansion of offices and duties borrowed mostly from Uighur and other steppe society models. The continuing predominance in government of steppe interests can be seen in the conduct of the imperial court. Unlike in the case of imperial China, where the bureaucracy steadily grew at the expense of the cloistered imperial clan's governing powers, the active center of Liao government remained the person of the Khitan emperor and his household, his court with attached officials, his guard, and his entourage. All of those elements remained mobile; the emperors preferred their great felt tents to palaces.

Even after building the Supreme Capital in 916–918, the Khitans continued to observe their annual cycle of nomadic activities. That required them to spend many months each year moving from one camp to another in a fixed sequence of times and places. At those places the ruler and his court engaged in hunting and fishing, in military exercises based on the hunt, and in solidifying personal relationships among tribal leaders. The widely scattered camps and the cycle of attendance at them was called the Nabo. That pattern was maintained, with only slight relaxation, to the end of the dynasty. Twice a year, at the summer and winter Nabo, the emperor summoned all the executive heads of his government into assembly at the Nabo sites, not at the capital cities of the realm. These "great conferences," as they came to be called, decided policy, received nominations for offices, and reviewed all the work of government. Chinese and other non-Khitan officials from the sedentary population were not included in deliberations of military matters, a major focus of the winter Nabo, so most of them did not attend. The summer Nabo, by contrast, concentrated on affairs of the sedentary population.

Parallel but somewhat different administrations for the two parts of the dual empire were required by the different emphases and tasks of governing in the two regions. The throne's announcements stressed this repeatedly: "We, taking into consideration the fact that our country comprises the Khitan and the Chinese, therefore administer them separately through the two Divisions of North and South." So began an edict of 1026. That distinction was established by Abaoji. In the 930s and 940s the Southern Division of the empire expanded greatly with the acquisition of the Sixteen Prefectures, and as we have seen, that required the establishment of a "Southern Chancellery" within the Northern Region, while the Southern Region also acquired a "Northern Chancellery."

The *Liao History* explains these in functional terms. It states that in the Northern Region the Northern Chancellery "administered the affairs of camps, tents, tribes, lineages, and tributary states," and "all the Khitan armies and horses were under its control." At the same time, the Southern Chancellery "was in charge of the Chinese population's prefectures and counties, their taxation, and their local militias and horses," and "the selection of civil officials, and taxation" as it applied to both tribes and lineages, "so that all the

Khitan people [too] were under its control."[20] From this we can see that the terms "Northern" and "Southern" came to have the force of "military" and "civil" aspects of governing. Because the Southern Region became the richest and most populous part of the empire, governing offices proliferated there. Some posts established in the South had no counterpart in the North; for example, the Bureau of Historiography was considered a "southern" kind of activity, so the Liao empire's historical record was kept in the Chinese language by Chinese officials.

The Khitans constructed a well-balanced combination of Chinese and tribal elements. Their example is worth comparing with the experience of other conquerors. Their system absorbed large segments of Chinese culture and acknowledged their usefulness, but they were not overwhelmed by foreign things. In particular, they appear to have fully accepted a division of labor within their tribal society: the court and some of the elite would become culturally dual (perhaps multiple—it is not certain how this worked on frontiers other than the Chinese), and those persons would function in both spheres in the service of the empire. The vast bulk of the Khitan population, including some of the tribal nobility, would stay in "the reservoir" (to use Owen Lattimore's term and the analysis it implies).[21] That is, they would remain in the steppe to retain steppe skills and values undiluted by sedentary influences. In that way the social base of the Khitan nation in the main would not be diverted from tribal military life. That remarkable division of labor gave the Khitan state the flexibility it needed in dealing with its dominant neighbor, China. It also allowed it to incorporate sedentary populations into the Liao empire without threatening the purity of the social base from which its military strength was drawn.

A few historians have tried to show that the Liao government encouraged some Khitan tribesmen to give up full-time nomadism and incorporate agricultural pursuits and craft industry into their steppe way of life. Some of the associated tribes may have developed a measure of what may be called a semi-nomadic, semi-agricultural tribal economy, and in some unusual cases Khitan tribesmen appear to have functioned as managers or supervisors for state-sponsored salt works, iron foundries, and the like. These arguments depend on doubtful readings of the relevant texts and remain unconvincing.

The important fact about the Khitans' exposure to sedentary society is their resistance to its attractions and their unaltered commitment to steppe values. The portion of the elite in which the state's needs demanded cultural duality probably remained a minority, and even among such culturally dual Khitans, few were subverted by their Chinese cultural achievement from their loyalty to Khitanness. If that social management tactic was not fully anticipated in Abaoji's concious planning, it is nonetheless what happened. The early emperors were aware of that development and guided it. Yet such a division of labor could work only if that significant minority portion of the Khitan elite proved capable of developing dual—even multiple—psyches and keeping them in balance. Otherwise they would have been susceptible to a damaging alienation from tribal society and would have lost the acceptance of their own people; then they would have been unable to deliver the political and military leadership expected of them. We do not see evidence of that. In fact, they managed not to be cast aside as useless persons, fatally separated from their social roots; they could still be Khitans to Khitans, people of the steppe to people of the steppe. In that cultural range and flexibility the Khitan elite were truly impressive, virtually unique among all the Inner Asian peoples in these centuries of Chinese and Inner Asian history.

Khitan society's primary orientation to warfare remained fixed. In that sense the selective borrowings and imperfect adaptations from Chinese culture enhanced the rationality of Khitan nomadism, raising its effectiveness to new levels. There were, of course, unforeseen consequences of such borrowing, but those never led to the social crisis that afflicted the Jurchens in similar circumstances, or to the loss of identity that affected a number of other societies in situations of rapid cultural borrowing. Most important, the Khitans' culturally dual elite obviated the necessity for the state to rely too strongly on its Chinese subjects; nor did they become the victims of subordinates in governing imported from elsewhere, as did the Mongols in China, whose solutions of analogous problems were entirely different from the Khitan pattern.

There is in the Khitan cultural accommodation a patience, a calm balance, a sense of being confidently in control, what one is tempted to call an Apollonian tone,[22] a combination of characteristics not seen among other steppe conquerors. Was their cultural policy's one great failure, ironically, not the intended enhancement of the hybrid imperial institution's strength but its political weakness, increasingly evident in the last reigns? And, one may ponder, was it their unintended success in transmitting concepts and tools of enhanced social organization on to others on their periphery that made some of their subject peoples too dangerous for the very survival of the Liao empire? These interpretations of Liao history will be touched upon in Chapter 9, in conjunction with the account of the dynasty's destruction in the early twelfth century. First, however, we must consider other developments in the tenth and eleventh centuries which also contributed centrally to the changing world of China.

CREATING THE
SONG DYNASTY

The circumstances under which Zhao Kuangyin in 960 became the founder of the long-lived and venerated Song dynasty contributed much to the structure and tone which Song rule imparted to China's governance. He was, anomalously, an admired usurper who appeared to embody a widely shared sense of purpose. The story of how he came to power is made more understandable by comparing the event with the founding of the Later Zhou dynasty a mere ten years earlier, in 950. The Song dynasty was the direct offshoot of the Zhou, and continued the latter's efforts to reunify the state and overcome China's fragmentation. Accomplishing that internal military task required the creation of a centrally controlled army system that simultaneously faced external pressures: to defend China against the Khitan Liao dynasty to the north while attempting, albeit without success, to recover the lost Sixteen Prefectures. These challenges—to organize, to govern, and to expand—occupied Zhao Kuangyin and his immediate successors through the first decades of Song rule, during which the new dynasty acquired a form and a political style that made it different from what had been known before.

1. THE VIGOR OF THE LATER ZHOU AND THE FOUNDING OF THE SONG

Important trends of change that are apparent from late Tang times onward into the middle of the tenth century (discussed in Chapter 1) culminated during the brief Later Zhou dynasty (951–960), the last of the Five Dynasties. A strong sense of direction and of forward movement toward the military reunification of China was set in motion by the Zhou founder, Guo Wei. When an illness carried him off in 954, his adopted son Guo Rong (originally called Chai Rong), then in his thirties, continued that incipient dynastic enterprise with great vigor and intelligence. He reorganized the sprawling, undisciplined military machine inherited from the earlier dynasties, and with it won victories on all fronts. His civil governing also gained people's confidence. He convinced the world that great things would inevitably follow. Then, five years later, Guo Rong too died of an illness, leaving an heir of only six. His world could not accept that the longed-for great achievement would be thwarted by the lack of a mature leader. His young heir was placed on the throne late in the summer of 959, and all his father's civil and military officials swore undying allegiance to him and to his mother, who became the regent empress dowager. Yet in February 960 he was deposed, and his father's principal military assistant, Zhao Kuangyin, was proclaimed the founder of the Song dynasty in much the same way that Guo Wei himself had been propelled into the founding of the Later Zhou dynasty a decade earlier.

Clearly, Zhao Kuangyin was a usurper, although that was not an acceptable thing to say during the long Song dynasty. Nor would many serious people of the time have condemned him for that. It is easy for us now to conclude (as some Chinese historians of succeeding times have insisted) that his actions and intentions in that event were "dishonorable," and were predicated on the self-interest typical of Five Dynasties political behavior. Yet there is much more to the story. By comparing Guo Wei's accession as the founding emperor of the Later Zhou in 951 with Zhao Kuangyin's usurpation of Zhou to become the founding emperor of the Song in 960, we can gain some understanding of the military and political conditions that defined political careers at that time.

Guo Wei Becomes Emperor of the Later Zhou: The Traditional Account

Guo Wei (born in 904) was orphaned at the age of three when his father, a military leader, was killed in battle. The young Guo Wei later turned away from education for a civil career to excel in horsemanship, the martial arts, and the study of books on military strategy. He began to achieve prominence as a military captain under the Later Jin dynasty (936–946). There were many predictions that he was destined to achieve great eminence. When the Liao invasion of 947 terminated the Later Jin, Guo Wei was among those officers who urged Liu Zhiyuan, the Shatuo Turk leader, to establish his own Later Han dynasty (947–950), which Guo then served as an outstanding general in the field against the Khitans. When Liu died in 948, he was succeeded by his eighteen-year-old son, known as the Emperor Yin. He appointed Guo Wei to the highest military offices, including commander of his palace guard, the elite core of his army.

The Emperor Yin's courtiers, however, feared Guo because he was popular among the officer corps. They tried to keep him away from the court, at the Khitan front in the North, and even plotted to have him assassinated. In 950 his wife and family, who had remained behind in the capital at Kaifeng, were murdered while Guo was at the head of an army campaigning to the north. On receiving reports that ambitious courtiers surrounding the young emperor were maneuvering to take over the state, Guo Wei heeded an appeal to return to the capital in order to restore proper governance and to free the ruler from those "evil influences." That way of stating the case of course puts Guo in the best possible light, but it may not be too far from the truth. Leaving his adopted son Guo Rong in charge of the northern garrison, he led his army back to the south. Approaching the capital, he encountered the "southern army" of his enemies, the forces arrayed to fend off his return. The young Emperor Yin on occasion visited the camp of the southern army outside the capital gates. Guo Wei sought to confer with the emperor in that setting; it is recorded that, failing to make contact, he admonished his forces: "I have come to punish evildoers; I hold no enmity toward the emperor. You must take pains to initiate no aggressive action against him." Yet many of the soldiers in the emperor's camp deserted to join Guo Wei as suggestions that he would make a better ruler began to circulate.[1]

On the twenty-second day of the eleventh month (January 2, 951) the young emperor, riding outside the city walls, was threatened by hostile troops under unknown command. Blocked from entering the nearby city gate to evade them, he fled to the west with a small guard, apparently seeking to enter by another gate. The hostile troops pursued. The emperor dismounted at a small village to take refuge in a commoner's house, but the pursuing soldiers swarmed in and killed him. Contradictory rumors immediately implicated Guo Wei, as well as some among the emperor's own courtiers, for having arranged the assassination. The facts remain unclear.

Guo Wei, learning the next day of the emperor's death, is reported to have wailed in grief, blaming himself for having failed to protect his ruler. Then he entered the city and went to his residence, where he closed and guarded his gates, as if determined to remain uninvolved. But disorderly soldiers began to pillage and burn the residences of rich people that night, and on the following morning Guo Wei ordered his soldiers to restore order. The courtier responsible for the murder of Guo Wei's wife and family was captured and executed. When asked about how to deal with that man's family, Guo Wei ordered that they were not to be harmed: "True, he killed my family, but if I were to take revenge by killing his, when would the killing ever cease?" On the twenty-fifth day he called on the empress dowager; they discussed the emperor's burial and reached a decision on which of the late emperor's relatives should be called to the capital to take the throne (though, of course, events moved too quickly for that to happen). The empress dowager, who had long-standing family connections with Guo Wei, trusted him and relied on him for support.

On the first day of the twelfth month (January 11) it was reported that the Khitans had invaded; the empress dowager commanded Guo Wei to lead an army northward to repel the enemy. Less than three weeks later, when his army was camped at Shanzhou[2] just north of the Yellow River, Guo Wei's troops rioted and forced their way into his presence, demanding that he assume the throne. They declared that they all hated the Liu imperial family and would not tolerate the accession of the designated Liu heir. Some tore up the army's yellow banners to wrap Guo Wei in the imperial color; others embraced him and shouted, "Ten thousand years to the emperor!" They forced him to lead the army back to the capital.

Five days later (February 3) he was at the outskirts of Kaifeng, the capital. He had previously sent a message to the people of the city saying that order would be maintained and that no one would be harmed; he also had sent a secret message to the empress dowager professing his loyalty to the dynasty and to her personally. The senior civil official of state led the corps of officials out the main gate to welcome Guo and his forces.

Earlier, on the twenty-sixth day of the twelfth month (January 31), the empress dowager had issued a decree naming Guo the regent, but soldiers continued to riot and demand that Guo assume the throne. On the second day of the New Year, the empress dowager issued an edict in which she presented the regalia of imperial office to Guo and asked him to ascend the throne; on the following day (February 11, 951), he proclaimed himself not the new ruler of the Later Han, but the founder of a new dynasty to be called the Great Zhou. The rituals of abdication and of succession by mutual agreement were carried out meticulously. The empress dowager and members of the late emperor's immediate family were guaranteed Guo's protection.

Liu Chong (also called Liu Min), an uncle of the late emperor and a younger brother of Liu Zhiyuan, who commanded the Later Han forces at the base of Shatuo power in northern Shanxi, rejected Guo Wei's usurpation and proclaimed himself the legitimate successor to the Later Han dynasty, calling himself the emperor of the "Northern Han" (in some sources called the "Eastern Han"), and placed himself under the protection of the Khitans.

Zhao Kuangyin Becomes the Founder of the Song Dynasty: The Traditional Account

Zhao Kuangyin was born in 927 in Luoyang, which was then the Later Tang capital. His distinguished family held office for several generations under the Tang, the Later Liang, the Later Tang, and the Later Jin, and his father achieved high military office under the Later Zhou. The surviving record of the young Kuangyin's youth assumes the topos of the emerging hero: he grew up to be a man of imposing bearing and profound judgment; those who knew him recognized that he was no ordinary person. In service under Guo Rong, the second Zhou ruler, he rose to the position of commander of the palace guard, the core of the reorganized Zhou military forces. When Guo Rong's six-year-old son came to the throne in 959, Zhao Kuangyin retained his previous high positions, to which were added new substantial and honorary offices, including Military Governor *(jiedushi)* of Songzhou, in central Henan. He later took the name Song for his dynasty because of its association with this historic Henan locality.[3]

As the court gathered on New Year's Day 960 (January 31) to offer the expected felicitations to the boy emperor, reports came that the Khitans had invaded and the capital was threatened. The ruler's mother, the empress dowager, acting as regent for her son, commanded Zhao Kuangyin, as the highest military officer of the realm, to lead a force north to repel the invasion. A preliminary force left the next day, and Zhao at the head of the main armies left on the third day of the new year (February 2). As the army left the city, it is said that people gathered in the streets and whispered that Zhao should be made emperor. It was noted that he had been the head of the Zhou armies for six years, had distinguished himself in many campaigns, and had won the full trust of soldiers as well as the civilian population. Fortune-tellers noted auspicious omens.

The first day's march brought the main force to Chen's Bridge post-station, across the Yellow River about ten miles north of the capital. The army officers conferred, declaring that the state was leaderless and it was therefore necessary to elevate General Zhao to the throne in order to preserve the gains that had been made. They conveyed these thoughts to Zhao Kuangyin's younger brother, Zhao Guangyi (who later would become the second emperor of the Song dynasty), and to the leading civil official present, Zhao Pu, no kinsman of Zhao Kuangyin but a trusted adviser who had long served as his personal secretary. Zhao Pu advised against any precipitate action that would lose the confidence of the people, and warned that strict military discipline must be observed. The officers concluded that they would have to force Zhao Kuangyin to ascend the throne; they surrounded his residence to wait out the night.

The next morning they pounded on his doors shouting, "We, your generals, are without a ruler; we therefore wish to name you emperor." Zhao Kuangyin, who had drunk too much the night before and was difficult to arouse,[4] now awoke with a start, but made no response. They forced their way in, swords drawn, and threw an imperial yellow robe over his head. They made deep obeisances, shouted "Ten thousand years!" a greeting reserved for an emperor, and led him to the courtyard, where he was assisted onto his mount. Seeing that he had no alternative, Zhao Kuangyin reined in his horse and made the officers swear to obey him, saying: "You all seek riches and noble ranks and hence raise me to the emperorship; when I issue commands, will you then obey?" They all dismounted, again bowed low, and swore to obey him. Then Zhao spoke: "I have devoted myself in service to the empress dowager and the emperor; the high officials of the court are all my colleagues. You must not commit the slightest violence against the palaces and the court, or against the persons or the properties of the officials. If you obey me, you will be well rewarded; if not, you will be executed." They all responded, "We agree." Thereupon he took charge of the forces and led them back to the capital, and no violence or disorder ensued.

The officers led him into Kaifeng, where he dismissed them and went quietly to his offices. He took off the imperial yellow robes, still hesitant and uncertain what to do. When some officers sent as representatives of the army entered, Zhao, choking with emotion and weeping, said: "I have been the recipient of the Emperor Shizong's [i.e., Guo Rong, the second Zhou emperor] most generous favor, but now, forced by the actions of the armies, it has come to this. It shames me to so violate the norms of heaven and earth; what should I do?" They could respond only by silently bowing before him. They led him to the main audience hall of the palace, where before the assembled civil and military officials the stately ritual of abdication and succession was performed. One essential element of the ritual, an edict of abdication from the boy emperor, was lacking; but at the last moment a high Zhou courtier drew such a document from his sleeve so that the ritual could proceed. The Zhou imperial family were given noble titles and granted a palace for their residence. So began the new dynasty of Song.[5]

Analysis of the Two Accounts

We need not assume that these accounts, drawn from traditional historiography, are to be fully believed. Chinese historians in post-Song times have not accepted them uncritically. As for the story of Zhao Kuangyin's having been forced to take the step of usurpation, in fact Bi Yuan, the eighteenth-century writer of the general history heavily drawn upon here, undercuts his own account by noting that the *Liao History* provides no evidence for a Liao invasion early in 960, thus making the campaign led by Zhao Kuangyin look like a device for getting the armed forces out of the capital long enough to bring off the coup at a military camp. Yet he does not go so far as to imply that Zhao himself masterminded the entire plot. We should also not assume that ten years earlier Guo Wei had cynically devised an elaborate charade to conceal his imperial ambitions. In both cases, we might best assume that there are elements both of concealed plot and of genuine force of circumstance at work in the process by which these two ambitious, able leaders betrayed their rulers and seized their thrones. Yet if Guo Rong had not died in 959 but had gone on to complete the work of reunifying the country, we can probably assume that Zhao Kuangyin would have gone down in history as no more than the able military assistant at the founding of a long and glorious Zhou dynasty, and the interim period of the Five Dynasties would have known only four dynasties. History, however, is what really happened, not what might have been.

The histories of these two cases display remarkable similarities, and we may surmise that the former event, which developed more slowly and in a less direct fashion, served as the model for the latter, which was carried out with considerably more dispatch and effectiveness. Several of the participants in the former usurpation in 951 were still on the scene and in important positions in 959–960; it is difficult to imagine that they were not aware that they were reenacting the script of their lifetime's greatest drama. In particular, it appears certain that the new emperor's brother, Zhao Guangyi, and secretary, Zhao Pu, both knew about the plot before it was carried out.

In both of the usurpations, the military emergency of an invasion from the Khitan front provided the setting in which unusual action could be taken. In the second case, the invasion was either a false rumor genuinely believed or a contrived element. In 951 Guo Wei left his adopted son Guo Rong, a very able military commander, with a strong force to guard against any real invasion when he turned back to the capital, while in the 960 case, Zhao Kuangyin and his generals simply abandoned their campaign to the north as if they knew there was no real threat. Both were leaders wholly accepted by the main body of the armed forces; in both cases the rebellious generals' interests lay in enhancing their own careers through their relations with the new emperor of their choice. In both cases the public was prepared: rumors about the need to force a usurpation and about the fitness of the commanding general for that role were spread among the people and noted by astrologers. In both cases the "unsuspecting" protagonist was draped in the imperial yellow and forced into an act of treason. In the first case makeshift yellow robes were utilized, but in the second a complete set of prescribed imperial garments just happened to be in the baggage of some member of the military command, even though under the law their possession in itself constituted prima facie evidence of treason. In both cases the new emperor counted on a good relationship with and the essential instrumental action of the empress dowager in her role as regent, and played to her in ways that induced her assistance.

In a distinct break with then-current patterns, however, in both cases the ritual aspects of a mutually agreed-upon takeover were carried out in a civilized manner, and the displaced imperial family was treated well. Although neither of these usurpers was a paragon of the humane virtues, the refined process of usurpation that they acted out was not typical of the Five Dynasties era. The Zhou and the Song foundings represent a new way of conducting the imperial enterprise. This heralds a new phase in Chinese history, one foretold by the actions and attitudes of these two men throughout the ambiguous events that brought them to power. In the early decades of the Song dynasty, a more reasoned basis for statecraft emerged. This shift away from violent resolutions of political crises contributed directly to the formation of the "new culture of the Song."[6]

II. ON BEING THE EMPEROR IN TENTH-CENTURY CHINA

The Chinese government, in all dynasties from the Qin in the late third century B.C.E. until the end of the Qing in 1911, was headed by a *huangdi*, a supreme ruler whose title we translate as "emperor."[7] His roles were many: he was the state's sole legislator, ultimate executive authority, and highest judge. His pronouncements were, quite literally, the law, and he alone was not bound by his own laws. The emperor was ritual head of the state, analogous to the head of every Chinese clan or lineage, by which every person in society was bound to a surname and to family responsibilities. As the head of the imperial clan, he thus was a model for the maintenance of the atomized, family-based ancestor veneration that held priority among all the forms of religion in the society. And the emperor was held to embody and to have responsibility for upholding all the values of the society. But he was not expected to assume such responsibilities in an open, public manner. He did not interact personally with any sector of society, and did not play a significant political role in public life.

There were two kinds of restraints on the Chinese emperor's seemingly boundless authority: those were ideological and practical. Ideologically, China's rulers, some more effectively than others, were constrained by Confucian norms and the values perpetuated by the scholar-official elite of society. In these respects his authority, while enormous, was not unchallengeable, especially in matters of ethics and of principle that were defined by scholarly interpretations of the past. It might indeed take a brave person to challenge an emperor, who, if he insisted, would prevail. Yet there were many throughout history who had the courage to challenge their rulers on grounds of tradition and classical learning, or in matters of ethics. Song dynasty emperors were unusually broadminded in respecting their scholar-official associates in governing, but they too were despots, whether benign or tyrannical, depending on temper and other contingent circumstances.

The practical restraints on imperial behavior were of still more immediate significance. In all of his imperial roles the ruler was in practice limited by the accumulated precedents established by previous imperial actions, especially within his own dynasty. As the head of a vast governmental apparatus ruling over the world's largest society, he was of course forced to delegate his powers to others who conducted the routine operations of government, and it was the pattern of that delegation that constituted the structure of imperial government. Institutions inherited from previous dynasties were the main vehicles through which he delegated political responsibilities. Strong rulers could create new institutions, modify existing ones, or claim to reinstate antique forms at any time, but seldom did those things. Even new dynasties—including those that announced ambitious "new beginnings"—mostly adopted existing patterns. The pressure to make a new beginning[8] was a useful formula for rejecting the faults of one's immediate predecessors; yet in seeking alternatives to that immediate past, one had no models outside of China to draw upon.

The attractive institutional alternatives were those held to have antique Chinese prototypes. The supreme value of being ancient inhered in them. Nothing could compete in value with or lend more authority to a concept, an institution, or a model of behavior than to claim that it was authentically ancient. The use of names and official titles having evocative associations with ancient models was mostly only a matter of name; borrowing names of offices and titles of office from some revered period in the past could create a validating association with antiquity, but it did not necessarily signify that the substance of historical precedents was being revived.

In reality, Chinese government was continuously evolving, just as Chinese society was continuously changing, though slowly and conservatively. The weight of antiquity notwithstanding, the revered past was something vaguely ideal rather than literally attainable. The best minds in all ages were clearly aware of that.[9] The best statesmen sought the spirit of the past in governing, not its literal re-creation; the same was true in the arts and literature.

Emperors performed their duties within the framework of a slowly changing political system. They were in fact creatures of a venerable tradition that prescribed how they should act. Few emperors took strong issue with that fate. Yet within the vast range of their formal duties, they could make some personal choices that reflected their own personalities and interests. An emperor could choose to be a warrior and could lead his armies in the field, or he could delegate that task to others, whether personally chosen by him or perfunctorily approved by him when his councillors made the choices. An emperor could withdraw from all military involvement to devote himself to civil governing and to overseeing the conduct of his court, its staffing, and its debates on policy. An emperor could even withdraw from involvement in day-to-day political affairs, performing in minimal fashion only his ritually prescribed activities and allowing his seal to be applied to all the documents that kept the paperwork of government flowing, while he devoted his energies to private pursuits within his palace precincts. Those pursuits might range from scholarship or art to mindless frivolity, from sex (bountifully at hand) to the search for immortality via Tantrism, drugs, or arcane practices. While the range of an emperor's choices was broad, he was in most cases bound by precedent, by the influences that his Confucian education and his Confucian advisers exerted on him, by the interests of his consort and her clan, by his religious (as opposed to his ritual) mentors, or even by his close personal relationships with the more important among his eunuch attendants. Most Song dynasty emperors were well-educated men who took their responsibilities seriously, but not all possessed genuine ability and high intelligence; succession was guaranteed to eldest sons born to principal consorts, thereby ensuring that most emperors were predictably dull, reliably conformist. As in all dynasties, after the founding generation of the Song, successors were born and reared within the palace precincts, guaranteeing that they would possess quite limited knowledge of the real world, and were seldom eager to enter into it.

Being the Chinese emperor in China was thus quite different from being a Khitan supreme chieftain who took on the perceived modes of a Chinese-type emperor of the Liao dynasty (as we have seen in Chapters 2 through 4). It also was different from being a highly sinicized Jurchen ruler of the Jin dynasty, or a Mongol Great Khan who doubled as emperor of China (as we shall see in subsequent chapters).

The first two rulers of the Song dynasty came of age in the rough-and-tumble political world of the Five Dynasties, and in some measure they brought to their roles as Chinese emperors the mentality of that milieu, mitigated to be sure by their desire to transcend its limitations. They appear to have very quickly assumed the grandiose posturing of a Son of Heaven, and their close associates from their preimperial younger years just as quickly assumed the servile manner of mere humans in the presence of exalted beings. The first two Song rulers, Taizu and Taizong, in their relations with their court officials and military associates are never presented as having been relaxed and at ease in the company of their highly placed associates; neither behaved as *primus inter pares* among his courtiers, as the early emperors of the Tang dynasty are said to have done. A great gulf separating emperor from servitor became the predominant feature of later imperial history, and it began to take form in the early Song period.

For whatever reasons, a new etiquette of court behavior came into being. A telling example is found in the histories, where it is reported that early in the year 960, Fan Zhi and two other holdover officials of the Later Zhou were appointed to the high position of Chief Councillor at the court of Song Taizu.[10] The following observation is appended:

> The older [pre-Song] system provided that, in considering all major acts of governing with the emperor, the Chief Councillors would always be asked to sit for the discussions, and in an atmosphere of unhurried ease would be offered tea to drink before the meeting concluded. From the Tang through the Five Dynasties this form was always observed. But when Fan Zhi and the others became [Zhao Kuangyin's] Chief Councillors, they were conscious of their all having been courtiers together under the previous Zhou dynasty [when they had been the new emperor's colleagues or superiors]; they felt constrained about how to act and also were overawed by the emperor's overwhelming presence. They therefore requested that they be allowed to prepare brief written summaries of all the matters before them and to submit those in advance as their means of eliciting the emperor's opinions; their request was granted. From this time onward the courtesies of sitting together to discuss matters were abandoned.[11]

In the mind of the recording historian, the collegiality and easy exchange of views between the ruler and his principal advisers was forever lost, and he regretted that.

This very significant change in the way the government operated at the highest level of decision making does not reflect the imperious demand of a new emperor to be more lordly, but reveals the mutual recognition on the part of both ruler and servitors at the beginning of the Song dynasty that this new ruler's position was particularly tenuous. The emperor's own uncertainty about the personal dimensions of his role made these longtime associates uneasy. They all shared an interest in strengthening the new dynasty; a consequence was the adoption of a new etiquette which elevated the ruler to unprecedented heights. Despite that elevation and the elimination of any easy informality in his relations with his chief ministers, in the light of post-Song history, the Song has always been looked back to as an age in which the tone of the court was one of refinement and restraint. High officials surrounding the ruler always were accorded great formal courtesy; it was widely remarked at the time that not even officials guilty of treasonable conduct were executed. For all the evidence of the Song court's refined style, we nonetheless see here, as in other changes in the central government, the institutional steps leading to a considerably enhanced authoritarianism.

III. Governing China

Deeply imbedded in Chinese political thought from Han times onward is the notion that a legitimate new dynasty should be discontinuous with its predecessor even though its Mandate usually was transmitted through that predecessor. It should demonstrate its newness and reinforce its legitimacy by making changes to display a "new beginning" *(gengshi).*[12] Although the justification for proclaiming a thorough break with the immediate past clearly existed in 960, for whatever reasons the early Song emperors did not avail themselves of it. On coming to the throne, Taizu issued no resounding accession proclamation outlining a new era in governing, but he in fact made some significant structural changes. For example, we have seen that Taizu furthered the centralization of military power. The late Tang served as an object lesson in political dissolution; the Song completed the process of subordinating regional military power to central (and hence to civilian) authority which had begun under the Five Dynasties. That major step was taken to correct the most obvious deficiency of Tang government. It was accompanied by many less obvious changes which over time gave Song government its distinctive shape and character. In short, the early Song government was not constructed according to an ideal new plan; it developed gradually in an ad hoc manner that reflects the backgrounds of the first two emperors and the pressures of their times.

The Song dynasty's founder, Zhao Kuangyin, went to great lengths to be "correct" *(zheng),* as the criteria for legitimacy defined correctness, by arranging for the Zhou empress dowager, in the name of her young son, to abdicate in his favor. He accepted the abdication in a court ritual that named him the legitimate successor to the Zhou. He thus could lay claim to be "correct," half of what was required to legitimate the transfer of Heaven's Mandate. He remained under considerable pressure to demonstrate that he also could achieve the other half, the unambiguous "control" *(tong)* over the realm that had eluded all the rulers of the Five Dynasties. Throughout Chinese history, control over the realm had always been won by military force deployed in palace coups, on the field of battle, or by threat of conquest realistic enough to induce capitulation. Although the ancient political theory on which these notions of legitimacy were founded posited that a new ruler should be able to sway all before him with his prepossessing moral force, no ruler ever founded a new dynasty who could not also invoke the sanction behind that sanction: real military power.[13]

Taizu was himself a military leader, albeit one with some pretensions to cultivation; he owed his throne to the generals and colonels who (with or without his connivance) had demanded that he become the emperor. They created the circumstances for his usurpation—circumstances that permitted him to appear nearly blameless yet gave him the leverage to demand absolute obedience from them. In the past these military leaders would have been given full rein to win "control" of the realm for him, while themselves benefiting from the promotions, honors, and rewards coming to them as victors in the field. That is what they now wanted and expected.

Zhao Kuangyin understood all too well the compromises of his authority which would ensue from that course. The lessons of the late Tang, when powerful military governors in the regions tore the state to shreds while pursuing their own interests, were clear in his mind. His mentors, the two Later Zhou emperors whom he had served in high military offices, had begun to purge the military establishment of independent-minded generals and to put the armies under tighter discipline and closer government control. Yet Zhao himself, as the commander of those centralized forces, had still been able to use that disciplined Zhou military establishment to seize power from the Zhou. On the one hand, he needed to reunify the country by extending his control to all the independent regions, especially the states that had been created by autonomous military governors in the late Tang. On the other hand, he could not trust his generals to accomplish that for him in the usual manner.

One of the legendary anecdotes of early Song history recounts that in 961 he commanded all the senior generals to attend a banquet in his palace. During the meal he at first reminisced with them about their shared glories in battle. Then he made a toast to congratulate them on having honorably and safely reached the end of their fighting days: he told them that now they were to be relieved of their commands and allowed to live in luxury at the capital (where he could maintain surveillance over them). This event—"dissolving the militarists' power with a cup of wine," proposing a toast that they could not refuse—may in fact never have taken place; but, in effect, that is what happened.[14] Removing many of the old commanders from power, he determined to accomplish the internal military task, the reunification of the realm, by other means. Where actual fighting was required—and in some cases it was required—he closely supervised it. He selected new, younger generals who were reliably subordinate to him and who were instructed to conduct warfare in a well-publicized "humane" manner: loss of life was to be minimal, and no looting or abuse of the civilian population would be tolerated. Often he campaigned in person, making it clear that the use of force was exclusively an imperial option. Above all, he was patient, giving holdout regional leaders ample opportunity to surrender without coming under attack. On the face of it, the terms that he (and subsequently his younger brother, who succeeded him as the Emperor Taizong) offered to surrendered warlords were as generous as those he gave to the retired generals. (In fact, they sometimes revealed a vindictive spirit, as in the case of the captive last ruler of the Southern Tang dynasty.)[15] It was a well-thought-out strategy; when Taizu died in 976, the reunification of the realm was almost complete, and the element of "control" was not in doubt. The Mandate belonged to his Song dynasty.

He cultivated the image of the magnanimous ruler, one who venerated the humane virtues, and the tone of whose court and government would fully display the supremacy of the civil side of governing over the military. We see in this carefully projected image elements of sincere commitment as well as tactical expediency. The age became one in which civil virtues flourished as never before, in which literary and philosophical achievements were paramount, and in which talent was drawn from a broader social base than had ever been true previously, through the expanded medium of civil service examinations that tested a candidate's command of the classical heritage. All this helped define the "new culture of the Song," something most evident in the morale of the scholar-bureaucrat elite of the age. Benefiting from what probably were neither fully intended nor correctly anticipated consequences of his political choices, the first Song emperor, Zhao Kuangyin, launched an exciting age in the history of China's civilization. The partnership between the holders of power and the possessors of intellect and talent reached new heights during the Song dynasty, especially under the Northern Song (960–1127), the first half of the long Song dynastic era. Chinese have been congratulating themselves ever since on this flowering of the civil virtues.

Yet Chinese also have been troubled by the Song state's failures to defend itself against external threats. Particularly in the present day, newly dominant values of nationalism have altered traditional perceptions and have given rise to doubts about the Song's exalted achievements. In their anachronistic reevaluations of the age, modern Chinese have often regretted that the dynasty never overcame the threat from hostile dynasties on the northern frontier and eventually succumbed to conquest from that quarter; they see weakness where in the past imperishable strengths were seen. Such anomalies in the interpretation of Song history cannot be evaded; but they can be brought into clearer focus by looking into the conduct of government under the Northern Song.

The Reigns of Song Taizu and Taizong, 960–997

The first two Song reigns covered almost forty years; they established the form and the style of Song government. Zhao Kuangyin was posthumously granted the temple name Taizu, "Grand Progenitor," which is the expected designation for a dynastic founder.[16] When Taizu died in 976, two of his four sons survived him (see Chart 2). The elder, twenty-five years old, might have been expected to succeed, but an arrangement had been worked out earlier within the imperial family first to bring the founder's younger brother Guangyi to the throne, after whose reign the succession would then pass to their third brother, Zhao Tingmei, and only then revert to the founder's son or grandson.[17] This most unusual arrangement, supposedly demanded by their mother the empress dowager shortly before her death in 961, acknowledged both the close relationship between the two brothers dating back to the time of the usurpation of the Later Zhou in 960 (in which Zhao Guangyi had played an instrumental role) and the exigencies faced by the Later Han and the Later Zhou dynasties when the succession fell to young and inexperienced heirs. For whatever reasons, it was an irregular succession, one that gave rise to questions of legitimacy and hence one that spawned problems.

Grave doubts about Taizong's character appear to have been circulated widely, and his awareness of these doubts probably influenced at least two aspects of his behavior as emperor: his strenuous efforts to be successful in military leadership, and his personal adherence to popular religious Daoism, through which he sought protection and spiritual support.[18] It undoubtedly also affected his relations with the officials of his court and his susceptibility to advice that would better have been rejected.

CHART 2. THE NORTHERN SONG IMPERIAL SUCCESSION

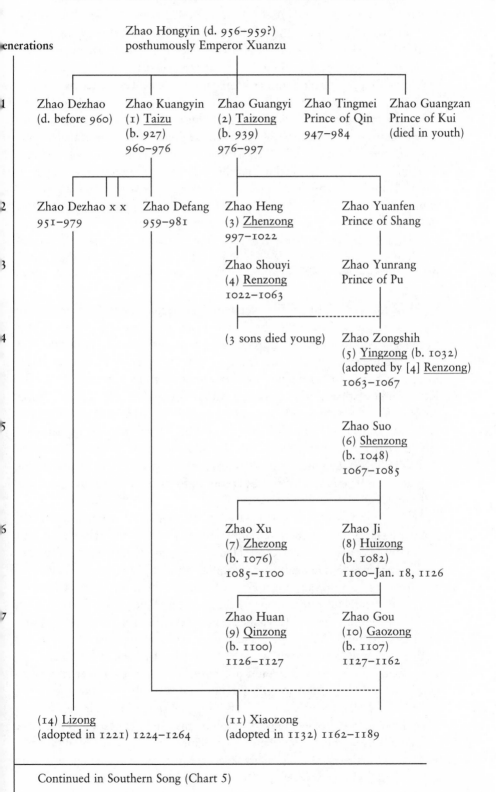

Zhao Hongyin (d. 956–959?)
posthumously Emperor Xuanzu

enerations

1

Zhao Dezhao
(d. before 960)

Zhao Kuangyin
(1) Taizu
(b. 927)
960–976

Zhao Guangyi
(2) Taizong
(b. 939)
976–997

Zhao Tingmei
Prince of Qin
947–984

Zhao Guangzan
Prince of Kui
(died in youth)

2

Zhao Dezhao x x
951–979

Zhao Defang
959–981

Zhao Heng
(3) Zhenzong
997–1022

Zhao Yuanfen
Prince of Shang

3

Zhao Shouyi
(4) Renzong
1022–1063

Zhao Yunrang
Prince of Pu

4

(3 sons died young)

Zhao Zongshih
(5) Yingzong (b. 1032)
(adopted by [4] Renzong)
1063–1067

5

Zhao Suo
(6) Shenzong
(b. 1048)
1067–1085

6

Zhao Xu
(7) Zhezong
(b. 1076)
1085–1100

Zhao Ji
(8) Huizong
(b. 1082)
1100–Jan. 18, 1126

7

Zhao Huan
(9) Qinzong
(b. 1100)
1126–1127

Zhao Gou
(10) Gaozong
(b. 1107)
1127–1162

(14) Lizong
(adopted in 1221) 1224–1264

(11) Xiaozong
(adopted in 1132) 1162–1189

Continued in Southern Song (Chart 5)

Under these first two rulers, the task of reunifying the realm took precedence over other concerns. As we have seen, Taizu accomplished the major
portion of that reunification. Of the surviving Ten States, Nanping on the
central Yangzi surrendered to him in 963, the Later Shu in Sichuan surrendered in 965, the Southern Han in Guangdong surrendered in 971, and the
Southern Tang, the largest and most expansive of the Ten States, which had
previously absorbed Chu (in Hunan) and most of Min (in Fujian), fell before
a Song invasion army in 975. The only holdouts, other than a few independent military governors controlling smaller regions[19] who all eventually came
around, were the state of Wu-Yue, with its capital at Hangzhou (whose kings
had long accepted Song overlordship but who hoped to retain some form of
regional autonomy), and the hated Shatuo state of Northern Han (or "Eastern
Han") in Shanxi, a client state of the Liao. Taizong pressured the king of
Wu-Yue to capitulate in 978, thus virtually completing the reunification of
the entire realm as it was then defined.[20] Only the defiant little state of Northern Han remained to be dealt with, and with it the Liao hold on the Sixteen
Prefectures stretching across the northern frontier from Shanxi eastward to
the sea.[21]

Eager to prove himself the equal of his martial older brother and to
strengthen his legitimacy thereby, Taizong was determined to triumph over
the enemies on the northern borders. He particularly had in mind the Later
Zhou campaign in 959, during which the strategic area in western Hebei
known as the Guannan region had been wrested from Khitan control. The
Later Zhou in that victory had demonstrated that Chinese military power
could defeat the awesome Khitan cavalry. Although the Song emperor Taizong was not a likely candidate for the role of martial hero, he burned with
the desire to prove that he could equal that earlier show of Chinese strength
and in the process complete his "control" over the entire realm of Chinese
civilization. His conduct of this operation informs us about him and about
his governing.

At the beginning of 979 Taizong took to the field. As Taizu frequently had
done, he chose to lead the large imperial army in person.[22] He was at first
successful in penetrating Northern Han territory in modern Shanxi Province
and laying siege to that small state's capital city, Taiyuan. The Liao emperor
was away on a hunt, and his court at first sent only a small relief force to
aid its Shatuo client. The Song army easily defeated that force. Early in June,
after a two-month siege of Taiyuan, the Northern Han ruler surrendered, and
the Liao lost their client state inside China. That finally drew the attention
of the Liao emperor Jingzong, who set a counteroffensive in motion. But Taizong, elated by his success, could not have known that. He determined to
press on to the east, down from the mountains of Shanxi onto the North
China Plain. His troops were severely fatigued after a difficult half-year of
campaigning. Supplies were low. Common sense and the best military advice
argued strongly against the plan, but the emperor would not be dissuaded.
Puffed up by his success and ready to accept the advice of any courtier who
agreed with him, he now decided to strike against the Liao Southern Capital

at present-day Beijing, and then to drive the Khitans north into the steppe beyond the line of the Sixteen Prefectures.

He led his army to the northeast and in mid-July reached the Liao boundary (see Map 5). Pressing on toward the Liao Southern Capital, he encountered only small-scale resistance and took the surrender of several small garrison towns. Once on enemy soil, the emperor donned armor and carried a sword when venturing to the front lines, saying that the soldiers were giving their all so he could not stand back and just look on. The headstrong emperor had transformed himself into the conquering hero, at least in his own eyes. His disgruntled military commanders appear to have been unimpressed. By July 20 the Liao Southern Capital was under attack, the defending Liao soldiers fighting desperately on the walls to prevent the Song forces from scaling or breaching them before the arrival of the main Liao cavalry forces.

When the first contingent of Liao cavalry arrived at dawn on July 30, a pitched battle began on the banks of the Gaoliang River below the western walls of the city. At first the fighting favored the Song forces. Then at dusk the main Khitan cavalry force arrived. The Song troops were exhausted. Their leaders had long been critical of the emperor's poor military judgment, and were further unsettled by soothsayers' inauspicious predictions. The Song forces were disastrously defeated.

In the midst of this engagement, seeing the imminent collapse of his forces, Taizong fled the scene in a mule cart accompanied by a few trusted officers, neither consulting nor informing his generals. He managed to reach safety in Song territory sixty miles to the southwest. The Khitans captured huge amounts of arms and armor and other booty. A subsequent Liao advance into Song territory was stopped by a successful Song stand on the Song-Liao border in October, long after the emperor's return to Kaifeng. Under reasonable conditions the Chinese armies were capable of defeating the Khitans.

Taizong's conduct throughout this campaign reveals unattractive personal qualities. He was overbearing when given unwelcome advice, hot-tempered when he thought he was not being unquestioningly obeyed, full of swagger and bluster when the fighting went well, yet was the irresponsible coward when forced to slink away to safety. Reacting to the crushing defeat, his leading generals, who all along had suppressed their dissatisfaction, now gave vent to their anger. Conferring together, they seriously considered deposing Taizong and replacing him with Zhao Dezhao, Taizu's elder son, who was with the armies in the field.[23] That did not in fact take place, but word of their intent reached the insecure and mean-spirited Taizong. When they later met, the emperor relentlessly harassed and criticized his nephew for his conduct during the campaign, driving him to suicide.[24] Two years later Taizu's other surviving son took ill and died, while Taizu and Taizong's younger brother Zhao Tingmei, also a possible candidate for the succession, was accused of treason in 982 and died in exile in 984. These events removed all possible obstacles and cleared the way for the succession to the Song throne to remain in Taizong's line until 1162, in Southern Song times.[25]

Taizong's unattractive qualities have been stressed here. But it would be

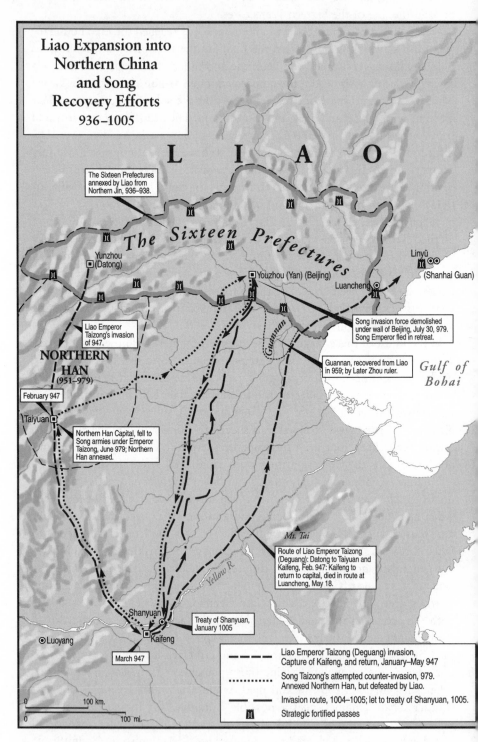

Liao Expansion into Northern China and Song Recovery Efforts 936–1005

L I A O

The Sixteen Prefectures annexed by Liao from Northern Jin, 936–938.

The Sixteen Prefectures

Yunzhou (Datong)

Linyü

(Shanhai Guan)

Youzhou (Yan) (Beijing)

Luancheng

Liao Emperor Taizong's invasion of 947.

Song invasion force demolished under wall of Beijing, July 30, 979. Song Emperor fled in retreat.

NORTHERN HAN (951–979)

February 947

Guannan, recovered from Liao in 959; by Later Zhou ruler.

Gulf of Bohai

Taiyuan

Northern Han Capital, fell to Song armies under Emperor Taizong, June 979; Northern Han annexed.

Mt. Tai

Route of Liao Emperor Taizong (Deguang): Datong to Taiyuan and Kaifeng, Feb. 947; Kaifeng to return to capital, died in route at Luancheng, May 18.

Yellow R.

Shanyuan

Treaty of Shanyuan, January 1005

Luoyang

Kaifeng

March 947

Liao Emperor Taizong (Deguang) invasion, Capture of Kaifeng, and return, January–May 947

Song Taizong's attempted counter-invasion, 979. Annexed Northern Han, but defeated by Liao.

Invasion route, 1004–1005; let to treaty of Shanyuan, 1005.

Strategic fortified passes

0　　100 km.

0　　100 mi.

MAP 5

incorrect to conclude that he was an ineffectual ruler. He was by nature withdrawn and solitary, quite different from his outgoing and popular older brother. He is praised in the official *Song History*[26] for his frugality and personal austerity, for his profound understanding of the obligations of his position, and for his incisive judgment in pursuing his goals. That work also says that later generations would not be without their own judgment about the way he dealt with members of the imperial family, which is about as far as an official history normally would have gone in implying criticism of an emperor. Such traditional moral judgments, however, are not our principal concern here; the first two Song emperors' contributions to civil government were of broad scope and significance. They demand our attention at this point.

Adjusting the Structure of Civil Government, 960–997

The compilers of the official *Song History* find serious fault with the form of the early Song government. The preface to its "Treatise on Offices and Officials" states:

> Song continued the Tang system, while severely curbing its defects. The [high honorary] offices of the Three Preceptors and the Three Dukes were not regularly filled. The Chief Councillors [*zaixiang*] were no longer exclusively appointed from among the heads of the Three Departments [of the imperial secretariat], both the Department of State Affairs and the Chancellery were located on the outside [of the palace precincts], while the Central Secretariat was set up apart from them, inside the palace, where it constituted the Council of State. Together with the Bureau of Military Affairs it shared control over the major acts of governance. Control over the fiscal affairs of the entire realm . . . was wholly subordinate to the State Finance Commission.[27]

This passage succinctly describes the most important structural differences between the early Song and the Tang central government. The very great significance of these changes can be summed up in one word: centralization. In his urgency to achieve that goal, Song Taizu used existing organs of government but bent them to his own purposes. A modern scholar has described early Song government as "overlaid with networks of irregular, sometimes ad hoc agencies and commissions," resulting in "the most complex and confusing pattern of nomenclature of China's whole imperial era."[28] The official *Song History* specifically criticized what it considered chaotic discrepancies between name and reality: leading offices were retained but not properly staffed; high officials bore one title of office but were assigned duties and responsibilities of other offices; some crucial governmental functions implicit in the names of offices that were retained, such as remonstrance and oversight, as well as the keeping of court diaries on which a future official history would be based, simply were not implemented.

Despite the validity of all these criticisms, other scholars have praised the Song founder for the keen administrative ability evident in the way he realized his goal of strengthening his state. Conscious of the weaknesses of the old Tang system, some elements of which had persisted throughout the Five Dynasties, he did not proclaim an elaborate plan to make a "new beginning" but sought instead to overcome these inherited weaknesses *within the existing patterns* by altering the traditional functions of central government institutions. He did that in ways designed to keep what traditional Chinese statecraft calls the "handles of power" *(quan bing)* firmly in his own grasp. His adjustments were to be sure ad hoc; he met his administrative needs without justifying his innovations in any formal sense. He greatly weakened the Chief Councillors' power to initiate and integrate policy by denying them their previous monopoly on the transmission of executive instruments both to and from the emperor, by curtailing their management of both the military and the fiscal arms of the government, and by creating differentiated loci of power in the military, economic, and political appointments and the social management functions of the central government. In this way he eliminated much of the independent discretionary authority of all those components of his central government and simultaneously brought the regional and local offices of government under the center's more direct supervision. The pattern of administrative geography is shown in Map 6.

MAP 6

Circuit name	Administrative seat (city)
1 Jingji, the Metropolitan District	1 Kaifeng
2 Jing Xinan	2 Xiangzhou
3 Jing Xibei	3 Xijing (Luoyang)
4 Jingdong Dong	4 Qingzhou (Yidu)
5 Jingdong Xi	5 Yunzhou (Dongping)
6 Hebei Dong	6 Daming
7 Hebei Xi	7 Zhending
8 Hedong	8 Taiyuan
9 Yongxing Jun	9 Jingzhao (Xi'an)
10 Qinfeng	10 Qinzhou (Tianshui)
11 Huainan Dong	11 Yangzhou
12 Huainan Xi	12 Luzhou
13 Liangzhe	13 Hangzhou
14 Jiangnan Dong	14 Jiangning (Nanjing)
15 Jiangnan Xi	15 Hongzhou (Nanchang)
16 Jinghu Nan	16 Tanzhou (Changsha)
17 Jinghu Bei	17 Jiangling
18 Chengdu Fu	18 Chengdu
19 Zizhou	19 Zizhou (Santai)
20 Lizhou	20 Xingyuan Fu (Hanzhong)
21 Kuizhou	21 Kuizhou
22 Fujian	22 Fuzhou
23 Guangnan Dong	23 Guangzhou (Canton)
24 Guangnan Xi	24 Guiyang

Familiar present-day names are given in parentheses. The 24 Circuits are separately mapped in Tan Xixiang (1991), vol. 6, pp. 12–35.

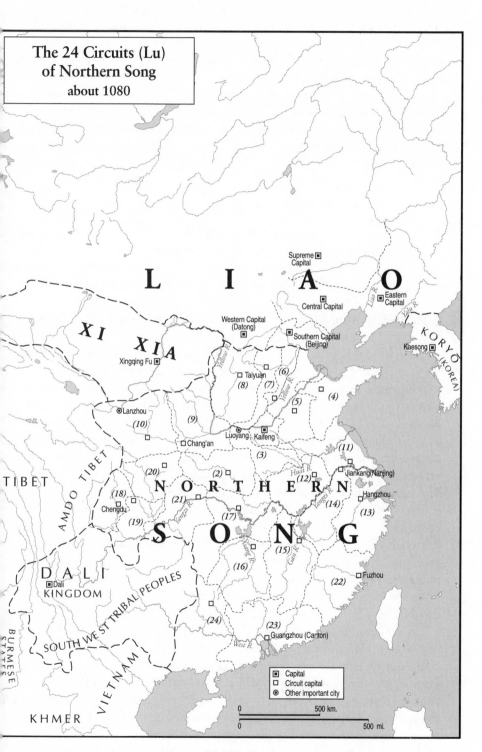

The 24 Circuits (Lu)
of Northern Song
about 1080

LIAO

XI XIA

Xingqing Fu

⊙Lanzhou
(10)

(9)

Supreme ■ Capital

Central Capital ■

Western Capital
(Datong)

□ Southern Capital
(Beijing)

Taiyuan □ *(6)*

(8) *(7)*

(5)

□ *(4)*

Eastern ■ Capital

Kaesong ■

KORYO
(KOREA)

□ Chang'an

Luoyang ⊙ ■ Kaifeng

(3)

TIBET

AMDO TIBET

(20) □

(18) □
Chengdu □

(19)

NORTHERN

(2) □

(21) □

(17) □

(11) □

Hun R.

(12) □

Jiankang (Nanjing) □

Hangzhou □

SONG

(13)

(14)

Yangzi R.

DALI
KINGDOM

■ Dali

SOUTHWEST TRIBAL PEOPLES

(15) □

Gan R.

(16)

(22)

□ Fuzhou

BURMESE STATES

KHMER

VIETNAM

(24)

(23)

□ Guangzhou (Canton)

West R.

■ Capital
□ Circuit capital
⊙ Other important city

0   500 km.

0   500 mi.

MAP 6

Early Song government, notwithstanding its velvet-glove tone and atmosphere, was more and more becoming an instrument capable of iron-fisted despotism; subsequent dynasties would take that development to still further heights while abandoning the restraint and refinement with which the Song state utilized its augmented powers in the day-to-day conduct of government. In the following chapters we shall see the extent to which the structure and tone of early Song government survived the large-scale reorganization implemented by the sixth emperor, Shenzong, in the 1080s, during Wang Anshi's "Major Reform" and subsequent institutional reforms carried out under the Southern Song.

IV. THE MILITARY PROBLEM

Of the five or six major Chinese dynasties,[29] only the Song existed under the ever-present threat of military invasion and conquest. Yet its policy was to curb the role of the military and to coexist with aggressive neighbors. We must go back to the reign of the first Song emperor to trace the factors leading to the dynasty's much-criticized weaknesses in national defense.

The Northern Song's distinctive defense policy was formulated early in the first reign. On coming to the throne, Taizu felt it necessary to maintain peace on the northern borders until he had completed the internal consolidation of the state. That decision implied an eventual second phase of military action to remove the external threat to his realm's security. As early as 974 he sent envoys to the Liao Southern Court to establish peaceful relations and secure his flank. The Liao court responded favorably. The Song set up strong garrisons all along the northern border, but the garrison commanders had no discretionary powers to take any kind of military action on their own, and it was made clear that the Song intended to maintain a passive defense posture. Through its centrally appointed Transport Commissioners (who handled the collection and delivery of tax grains and other revenues to the court), the court also controlled the financial resources of the border regions so that Regional Military Governors could not develop their own resources to support any independent ambitions, as Regional Military Governors had done under the Tang and the Five Dynasties. The Liao court depended on Chinese in its service to keep its policy makers informed about Song intentions and capabilities.

The Emperor Taizu clearly saw the necessity to undertake an eventual second phase, that is, to regain the Sixteen Prefectures, without which the Song could not be militarily secure. He began to build up a secret war chest to draw upon when conditions should become right, but he did not live long enough to attempt an invasion of the Liao. In 979, three years after coming to the throne, Taizong broke the peace established in 974 by leading the disastrous campaign to overthrow the state of Northern Han, and then going on to invade the Liao territory and attack its Southern Capital. In making that decision, Taizong supported a "war faction"[30] at his court initially made up largely of military officers. When he was disgracefully defeated, the "peace faction" at court was strengthened. He continued to nourish the desire to try again. Some officials at his court whose family homes had been in the northern defense zone continued to agitate for an offensive against the Liao. The pro-war group now began to include more civil officials, especially those who espoused the new trends in political thought.[31] They urged joint action with the Bohai and the Koreans, who, they believed, would be eager to throw off their Khitan oppressors. The court sent letters to them suggesting such cooperation. These letters ended up in the hands of the Liao emperors. The Liao court began to be more suspicious of Song intentions.

Seeing that a boy of eleven had come to the Liao throne in 982 and that his mother ruled on his behalf as regent, the Song court mistakenly thought that the Liao would be incapable of mobilizing. It was indeed a tense moment in Liao domestic history, but the Song did not adequately assess the prowess of the formidable empress dowager, a Khitan woman quite prepared to accompany her armies into battle. After watching the situation develop and making secret plans, Taizong launched his second offensive against the Liao Southern Capital in the spring of 986. This time he was dissuaded from leading the armies in person by strong opposition from the peace faction, but he sent three large forces to attack simultaneously three strategic locations in the Sixteen Prefectures. The Song armies had some initial successes, since the Liao southern garrisons normally were not maintained at levels adequate to meet a full-scale offensive. But in June the full force of the Khitan cavalry led by Emperor Shengzong, now fifteen, and his redoubtable mother, rode out of the steppe and descended on the Song armies. The Chinese were roundly defeated with great losses at the battle of Qigou Pass and withdrew in disorder, pursued by the Khitans. For more than a year thereafter the Khitan cavalry continued to raid Song border installations and to inflict further defeats on their Chinese defenders. Some Khitan generals proposed that the time had come to extend their boundary south to the Yellow River, but the empress dowager vetoed that more ambitious plan, probably remembering the unproductive Liao campaign deep into China in 947 (see Chapter 3, Section V).

At the same time, the leader of the Tangut people on China's far northwest border, nominally a vassal of the Song, declared his independence and threatened to attack Chinese border defenses. He also asked the Liao to recognize him as the king of a subordinate state and proposed an alliance with the Khitans to wage war against the Song.[32] That did not happen, but the entire northern border zone, from the Liao in the northeast and north to the Tanguts in the far northwest, was now unsettled and in peril. Fortunately for the Song, the Liao had problems of their own on their other borders and did not want to continue their military involvement deep in China at that time.

At the Song court the emboldened peace faction demanded that those who had advised the court to take up the offensive against the Liao be impeached and the defeated generals be executed for their failure. That, of course, also implied criticism of the emperor. Taizong blamed the generals for their faulty tactics in the field, in that way covering his own culpability for having launched a misguided effort, but he only reluctantly agreed to demote some of them while retaining them in service. The peace party nonetheless was greatly strengthened, its policies vindicated by the emperor's costly defeat. He now seemed resigned to accept the status quo. The terrible defeat suffered at Qigou Pass marked a turning point in Song-Liao relations and in Song foreign policy in general. Taizong died in 997. For more than a century thereafter his successors cautiously avoided aggressive actions against foreign enemies. The "second phase" of Song reunification policy thus took on quite a different character from what the first two rulers had envisioned.

The Emperor Zhenzong (r. 997–1022) succeeded on his father in 997. Internally the realm was united, and its military forces were securely under the central government's control. The conscious policy of favoring the civil side of government over the military had been carried to great lengths. The associated policy of "strengthening the trunk and weakening the branches" was also systematically implemented: appointments to all civil offices including those in county and prefectural government, and to all commands at all levels of the military, as well as regional and local control over fiscal resources, all were brought firmly under central government control. Local officials were allowed little or no discretion even in meeting emergencies. These measures achieved the goal of creating a strongly centralized administrative structure. Yet debate about all of those policies also emerged.

The debates focused with particular intensity on the management of border defense. What I have called the "war faction," which consisted of loose groupings of military and civil officials who favored a more aggressive stance against the Liao and the Xi Xia, became increasingly vocal. There also was a more neutral grouping of middle-of-the-roaders who called for a firm defense of the status quo that would leave the Liao in possession of the Sixteen Prefectures but allow them to go no farther. They argued that Liao demands for the return of the adjacent Guannan region, which were becoming more strident, had to be resisted. Finally, another group of like-minded scholar-officials formed a "peace faction" which represented the interests of those literati, who were prepared to compromise the defense interest further in favor of avoiding warfare.[33] Each faction strove to gain the emperor's ear.

The Song emperor Zhenzong, who came to the throne at the age of thirty, was cautious to the point of pusillanimity. Like his father he put great faith in Daoist miracle workers, but he occasionally also embraced the other extreme in Daoism by citing the philosophical writings of Laozi to justify his passive defense policies. He enjoyed being personally involved in ruling but lacked force of character and the ability to inspire devoted service. His vacillating attitudes encouraged court factions to vie for his favor and prevented the Song state from strongly committing itself, especially on matters of defense. It is therefore surprising that since Taizu's time the size of the armed forces had rapidly increased, from 370,000 late in the founder's reign to 650,000 at the end of Taizong's reign, to almost 1 million (of whom 820,000 belonged to the greatly enlarged imperial guard forces stationed at the capital) by the end of Zhenzong's reign. That steady increase was accompanied by a doubling of civil posts at all levels of governmnent, and the trend continued throughout the dynasty. By Zhenzong's time military expenditures, above all the military establishment's salaries and logistical support, were already crippling the state's budget, consuming three-fourths of the annual tax revenues and thereby limiting the state's ability to implement policy in all areas. That burden continued to grow. We see here a curious contradiction: a state that mistrusted its military leaders and followed pacifist policies was nonetheless severely weakened by the costs of maintaining a swollen military establishment. Because most soldiers were recruited for life from the rural population and served into their sixties, many of them were overaged and militarily useless for at least half their years in service. Soldiers formed a pool of laborers who were used for many of the state's other needs, but they were not kept under military discipline and training, and so did not add to the state's strength.

How best to recruit, train, maintain, and deploy the armed forces is a recurrent theme in Chinese history. An effective solution to those problems never emerged; not even the conquest dynasties, though their people were committed to war as a way of life, found workable solutions to this problem after they came to rule over substantial Chinese populations. How should the Northern Song's military weaknesses by analyzed? The dynasty was from its beginning essentially reactive against the trends toward warlordism in the previous century, and thus committed to inhibiting initiative in its military establishment while grudgingly recognizing an ever-present need for defense. Those conflicting demands led to a compromise: quantity over quality. The Northern Song army degenerated into a system the principal shortcoming of which was waste rather than military inadequacy per se. The Liao possessed what was surely the strongest military force in East Asia through most of the tenth and eleventh centuries, but the Song's overblown, inefficient, often poorly led military establishment still remained second only to the Liao's.

When Emperor Shengzong turned his attention more directly to China in the first years after 1000, the war faction at the Chinese court, led by an able and outspoken Chief Councillor named Kou Zhun (961–1023), faced down the peace faction and its adherents at the court and demanded that the emperor take an unequivocal stand. The Liao emperor was uncertain about the Song court's intentions, so he opted for a first strike. The Liao forces invaded late in 1004 and headed straight toward the Song capital at Kaifeng. By December they had reached the prefecture of Shanyuan north of the Yellow River. At this critical juncture, Kou Zhun demanded that the emperor personally lead the Song armies north to confront the invaders. That action may have prevented further Liao conquest.[34]

The imperial forces set up their base inside the walled prefectural town of Shanyuan. The Khitan army stopped a few miles to the north. The Song emperor was terrified, but acted out the role demanded of him by Kou Zhun: to put up a convincing show of resistance while initiating negotiations that would forestall military action.

Knowing that their fearsome cavalry gave them a negotiating advantage, the Khitans for their part now were willing to talk. They sent Chinese in their service along with high-ranking Khitan nobles to meet the Song negotiators and lay down conditions for peace. Recovery of the Guannan region seemed to be their principal demand. Kou Zhun would not hear of that, or of demands for a Song princess to be married to the Liao heir, or to other demands that seemed to him demeaning to the Chinese.

To break the impasse, the Chinese negotiators offered an alternative: payments of silver, silk, and other valuables in return for the Khitans' withdrawal and their agreement to negotiate a viable peace thereafter. The Khitans adjusted their goals, accepting this offer in principle but haggling over the amounts. The timorous emperor proposed totals that to the Khitans seemed immense, especially when they were offered as *annual* payments. Zhenzong was relieved when his figures were accepted; he had expected to have to go higher. In his own mind he had triumphed; his negotiators had neutralized the Khitans at what he considered a bargain price. Chinese opinion on this issue has been divided ever since. Some Song and later historians have noted that these terms in fact bought a century of peace; others have seen them as a lasting humiliation to be expunged by military successes as soon as possible. Some said that the indemnity impoverished the Chinese state, while others argued that it was trifling in comparison with the costs of war. So the peace versus war policies continued to be debated throughout the remainder of Northern Song, and even to the present day.

The Treaty of Shanyuan, concluded in January 1005, stipulated payments of 200,000 bolts of silk and 100,000 ounces of silver each year (or their monetary equivalent). A bolt of silk was a standard unit of value, by Song times no longer much used as "commodity money" but still employed in levying taxes. Its value was roughly equivalent to one ounce, or tael *(liang)*, of silver, or 1,000 copper cash (one "string" of coins). It is recorded in the histories that the emperor feared he would be overheard by the Khitans' negotiators, who were just beyond a screen partition in an adjoining room. When his representative came to consult on the final settlement, he held up three fingers to signal the maximum beyond which the Chinese side would not go. "Three" was meant to indicate 3 million units of value. When he heard that the Liao had accepted 300,000, he congratulated himself on a great coup.

It is not possible, using the figures that have been preserved, to account precisely for the weight of the indemnity payments in relation to the Northern Song government's revenues and obligatory annual disbursements. Taxes were collected partly in cash—strings nominally of 1,000 copper coins (by convention, actually closer to 800), or in paper currency equivalents of those called *jiaozi*, in several denominations; otherwise taxes were paid in silver bullion, bolts of silk or hempen cloth, and other commodities. During the first century and a half of Northern Song, the percentage of tax revenues collected in money rose from less than 15 to over 50 percent. Both the copper currency (actually an alloy of copper with additions of tin, lead, or zinc) and its paper equivalents were widely counterfeited; in addition, in the mid-eleventh century the costs of wars against the Tanguts caused serious inflation and depreciation of the currency. Given such sources of instability and the scarcity of statistics, it is very difficult to work out details of the fiscal situation. Recent efforts to clarify the basic facts have not produced widely accepted results, but some broad indicators can be cited.

According to the few sets of revenue statistics that have been preserved, it appears that tax revenues calculated in the value of strings of cash were about 16 million strings at the beginning of the dynasty, rose to 26 million in 1121, 36 million in 1056, and 60 million when the inflation was at its worst at some point in the 1070s, then fell to 48 million in 1086. The share of those tax receipts in the same period that came from commercial taxes ranged from 15 to 25 percent.[35] That is, they ranged from the value of 4 million strings to almost 20 million in the extraordinary year 1045 (when the Tangut wars produced a crisis) but usually equaled from 7 to 8 million strings. Because a substantial share of those revenues came from the controlled trade across the Song-Liao borders, it has been said that more than the full amount of the annual indemnity was recovered from that trade alone.

Yet Song sources contain unending complaints, not so much about the burden of paying the indemnity as about the possibly heavier costs of maintaining the diplomatic relationship. That required making lavish annual gifts to the Liao rulers on New Year's Day and on their imperial family birthdays, when no more than token gifts were received in return; there also were substantial expenses of sending and receiving envoys at least twice a year. Was the material burden of maintaining the Khitan relationship, and after 1042 a similar one with the Tangut Xi Xia state, a real cause for concern, or was the psychological component of those humiliating relationships the real cause for the complaints? That interesting problem is worth a closer look at the fiscal realities, insofar as those are discernable.

Using a rather full set of figures reported for 1077, perhaps more or less typical for the later eleventh century, we find that the Song state's total land tax and other tax revenues in that year amounted to 52 million "units of value"—the equivalent of a full string of cash, or one ounce of silver, or one bolt of silk cloth, or one *shi* of grain. That included 60,000 ounces of newly mined silver, almost 3 million bolts of silk cloth, 18 million *shi* (one and one-half bushels) of grain, and other revenues paid in kind. In addition, commercial taxes (including cash collected at the trading barriers between Liao and Song) constituted 8.7 million units of that total. By those figures, the annual outlay to the Liao of 300,000 units of value and associated expenses, and roughly the equivalent of that for the Xi Xia after the 1040s, plus gifts and other associated expenses, may have reached a total of 1 to 2 million units. Yet even calculated generously, those costs could have amounted to no more than 3 or 4 percent of the state's annual revenues.

The cost of the diplomatic relationships is, however, more meaningfully assessed by measuring it against the portion of annual revenues that was not obligated to cover fixed expenditures. As I have mentioned, some historians have stated that the military establishment alone consumed three-fourths of the units of value received in tax revenue each year. Fixed costs for civil officials' salaries and benefits and the costs of procurement and construction for the court and imperial household also were heavy. The remaining funds available for discretionary use could not have amounted to more than a few million. Early in the eleventh century revenues were adequate; thereafter, however, the fixed costs continued to increase, squeezing the narrow margin of unobligated revenues. At less than 10 percent of total revenues in 1077, the costs of the expensive diplomacy would not seem to have constituted a disabling burden on the fiscal system. Much less were such amounts so high as to strain the country's basic economy. One eminent economic historian has summed up a widely held view: the profits on the annual trade with the Liao alone "were more than enough to offset those gift payments."[36]

The problem is that the margin of unobligated revenues was narrowed by the Song's unwise fiscal policies, so that the indemnities and the associated costs may well have come to absorb 30 or 40 percent or even more of the unobligated portion of revenues, and by late in the eleventh century, outgo came to exceed revenues. With that squeeze on discretionary funds, the costs of indemnifying peace did indeed become an intolerable burden. In any event, shrill complaints about them were a constant feature of court discussion. They were, in short, a severe fiscal embarrassment even though not of a size to constitute a strain on the country's economy.

Of greater historical import than the material value of the indemnity payments was the elaborate system of protocol that was established to govern the relations between the two states, which came to define the forms and set the tone of diplomacy among all states within the Chinese orbit. The two principal states at this time, the Song and Liao empires, agreed that their imperial families should regard each other as kin.[37] In this way the complex deference patterns of Chinese society were extended to the Khitan imperial clan. The kinship relationship, fictive though it was, demanded that the two families maintain a busy schedule of ceremonial visits conducted through their diplomatic envoys. The elaborate etiquette of these proceedings was strictly regulated to accord with the conventions of Chinese ritual.

Thus the "second phase" of the relationship between the two states was not one of military recovery of the lost northern border region, as the first two Song emperors had envisaged, but one of diplomacy based on Chinese ritual forms and the establishment of an indemnified peace. The system endured, bringing more than a century of peace in Northern Song times, although revised with an increase of payments in 1042 when the Liao took advantage of a military emergency created by the Tangut Xi Xia state to force a renegotiation of the terms. However distasteful and administratively awkward this system was, it is questionable whether a military solution would have been better than the diplomatic one.

The pattern continued into Southern Song times, when the Jurchen Jin dynasty displaced the Liao and occupied the northern third of China. Until the thirteenth century, when the patterns of buying peace were superseded by the Mongol conquests, Song China continued to participate in this mode of international relations.

6

THE WORLD OF IDEAS IN
NORTHERN SONG CHINA

The Northern Song dynasty, particularly during the eleventh century, witnessed a great flowering of intellectual life, producing not only the intellectual foundations of the "Neo-Confucian" revival that dominated Chinese thought for the remainder of the imperial era, but also a ferment of ideas in all fields, from statecraft to literature. By emphasizing the historical significance of Neo-Confucian ideas rather than any intrinsic philosophical value as such, we see aspects of a self-renewing civilization first in the lives of several leading statesmen, exemplary scholar-bureaucrats who busily engaged the tasks of bringing about a new era in Chinese history. They represented a new kind of elite stratum, both in their social backgrounds and in their intellectual orientations. Yet there are differences of opinion among scholars today on the degree of upward mobility subsequently afforded by the Song examination system. I describe distinct trends in Neo-Confucian thought before concluding with a brief review of the five most important Northern Song cosmologists, the men who worked out the Neo-Confucian system of philosophical ideas that they believed would restore the proper foundations of civilization.

1. THE MAN OF THE AGE: OUYANG XIU

Ouyang Xiu was born in 1007, forty-seven years after the founding of the Northern Song dynasty, and he lived until 1072, forty-five years before its end. His life encompassed much of the eleventh century, during which Song civilization acquired its special character. He led significant developments in every aspect of that transformation—the political, philosophical, literary, and scholarly activities that made the Song dynasty a new age in Chinese history. He was, moreover, a pivotal figure, a man of profound scholarship and profound ideas, who sought out and sponsored talented persons of his own generation and the next, a much-loved yet also deeply resented figure, whose powerful spirit moved the age.

Ouyang Xiu was the "universal man" of his time and one of the small number of such figures in all of Chinese history. No aspect of the great ferment of ideas that marks Northern Song times was foreign to him or untouched by his mind and his personality. He is our most useful and most intriguing key to the spirit of his age. Yet by the end of his life, the forces of change that he had helped set in motion had moved beyond him. In the fractious political life of the Northern Song's last decades, he had become a peripheral figure, remembered more for his achievements in literature and historiography, in thought and learning, than for his lifelong stand as a reforming statesman. We can understand Song China better if we try to recover a sense of his place in history, moving forward with him through the eleventh century, instead of looking back on his life in the light of those subsequent political developments.[1]

The details of his career reflect in significant ways the changes that were occurring in early Northern Song society. He did not stem from one of the great old "eminent lineages" of the previous centuries, nor did he come from the old North China heartland of the Tang and earlier dynasties. He was a southerner as that was then defined: his family was from Luling (modern Ji'an) in Jiangxi, though he was born in Sichuan, where his father was posted as a local official, and never lived in Jiangxi himself. Late in life he chose to make his home north of the Yangzi River at Yingzhou (modern Fuyang) in Anhui, a place where he had served in local office and which appealed to him for its scenery. That rootlessness—his having no binding attachment to an ancestral home and his consequent freedom to decide where "home" should be—was typical of the scholar-officials who were emerging to become the dominant group in Northern Song, but was less common in other times and places. Also typical was his economic status: he received generous salary and supplementary financial rewards for his service as an official, even when he was demoted and sent away from the court in punishment for some political misstep. Yet he never accumulated the great landholdings and wealth that would have made his family independent of the need to render service to the state. Only when the third of his surviving sons received the highest degree by passing the competitive examinations in 1067 was he able to feel assured about his family's status in the succeeding generation.[2] Indeed, a number of his descendants in the following two or three generations achieved rank and office, mostly on their own merit.

"Emergent" describes the social standing of the southern scholar-officialdom in particular, and Ouyang's family was representative of that new social group. His father and three uncles all passed the civil service examinations about the year 1000 and became *jinshi,* or "advanced scholars," bearers of the highest degree in the civil service system, though prior to that no known ancestors had ever held a degree or served in office.[3] His family was of humble origin, yet his mother was literate and is credited with having taught him to write when he was a small boy by using a stick to scratch characters in the dirt (probably an exaggerated reference to their poverty). That anecdote was recounted in a spirit of admiration, for this was a society that honored those who overcame difficult circumstances and got ahead by hard work and native ability.

His father died when Ouyang was only three, after which he and his mother lived with his father's brother, also a *jinshi* who served in a succession of local offices in several of the poorer locales in Central China. The family had few books, so young Ouyang borrowed books from well-off families with whose sons he was friendly and made his own handwritten copies of them. When he was only nine or ten, he found in one of their homes a set of writings by the late Tang literatus Han Yu (768–824), the most important forerunner of the revival movement in Confucianism which Ouyang and his contemporaries carried forward in the eleventh century. "Prose writing must serve as the vehicle for the Dao," that is, it must convey the Great Way of Confucianism; Han Yu was famous for having made that ringing declaration. Han's writings rejected the elaborate stylistic devices of Tang prose in favor of the direct and forceful style of an earlier age. Han Yu thus validated his new stylistic standard by identifying it with a past model (as was typical in Chinese civilization), in this case with what was called "ancient prose," or *gu wen*. Throughout his teens Ouyang immersed himself in studies to prepare for the civil service examinations, which at that time still demanded the use of the elaborate Tang parallel-prose style. He was deeply moved as much by Han Yu's reform ideas as by the force of his clean and powerful literary style; but for the time he had to continue to write in the conventional literary modes if he was to have any chance of passing the examinations.

He sat for the first-level examination when he was sixteen, but was failed for a technical error in his use of rhymes, formal poetry being a major component of the examinations. He sat for the examination again when he was nineteen, and again failed. In 1029, when he was twenty-two, he finally passed the first level; in the following year he gained the *jinshi* degree and was appointed to a minor office at Luoyang, the old Tang dynasty Eastern Capital, which remained a major center of cultural and intellectual life during the Northern Song. There he had time for friends and for literary activity, especially for experimenting, along with like-minded young scholar-officials, in writing the vigorous ancient-style prose advocated by Han Yu—and for developing the philosophical ideas associated with that literary mode. He also began to achieve fame as a poet, along with a degree of notoriety for being somewhat undisciplined in his personal life. He was notorious as a frequenter of the pleasure quarters where young men partied, kept the company of cultivated courtesans, exchanged poems, discussed politics, and encouraged one another's ambitions. Only after the age of thirty did he give up his roistering, saying with regret that he was late in coming to an understanding of the Way.

We see in the young Ouyang a man of irrepressible vitality and generous spirit who was eager to make friends and to know all the talented men of his time. He went out of his way to seek out people who were said to have special literary or intellectual abilities, especially the "new men" who, like himself, had come up through the examination system without relying on the advantages of an eminent family background. At this stage in his young career he simply wanted to interact with interesting people. This habit continued, and when he eventually achieved high office and eminence he continued to seek out the talented, to encourage them and assist them in developing their careers. As a result of this genuinely spontaneous habit of mind (among his other attributes), he became the most influential person of his time. Many young scholars and officials felt gratitude and affection toward him for the help and encouragement he had given them. His help and support were not bestowed in a calculated way, with the intent of building a personal following. He encouraged talent for its own sake and even sponsored people whose philosophical ideas were not congenial to his own. Later, as the burgeoning intellectual life of the age produced philosophical and political factions with which Ouyang became deeply involved, people whom he had sponsored or appointed to office were to be found throughout the full spectrum of factional affiliations. On learning of his death, even some of his political opponents wrote moving tributes to him. The most famous was by Wang Anshi, the leader of the Major Reform of the 1070s. Notwithstanding that Wang's political program had been fiercely opposed by Ouyang, Wang acknowledged him as the greatest literary figure of the age, and though not approving of all of Ouyang's political views, said that he was loved by all who had worked with him at court because he was so fair-minded.[4]

II. THE COURSE OF A SONG DYNASTY OFFICIAL CAREER

The pattern of Ouyang Xiu's public life tells us much about the tone and texture of official life in the eleventh century. Despite their modest circumstances, his father and uncles all received an education that prepared them to sit for and pass the civil service examinations, yet none of them advanced into the higher levels of the imperial bureaucracy. Immediately on passing the *jinshi* examination in 1030, Ouyang Xiu was assigned to a minor secretarial post in the offices of the governor of Luoyang. During his four years in that center of cultivation and wealth, his literary talent attracted so much attention that he soon became famous. He not only found a central place in the widening circle of scholar-officials who made a public cause of promoting the "ancient prose" *(gu wen)* style, with its implications for political and philosophical regeneration, but also gained recognition as a superb poet both in the standard form of "regulated verse" *(lü shi)*, brought to perfection in the preceding Tang dynasty, and in the new lyric mode *(ci)* that had flowered during the Five Dynasties. He first encountered this new genre of lyric poetry in the demimonde of the entertainment quarter, where poets produced lyrics for courtesans to sing. He added much to the development of this lyric song form, moving it away from a narrow focus on romantic passions and broken hearts to encompass the full range of poets' concerns. By the time he reached his late thirties, he was held to be the leading literary figure of the time, a man who in his own lifetime ranked first not only as a prose essayist but also as the reigning master of both the *shi* and *ci* genres of poetry.

Owing to his literary reputation, after having served for four years in the Luoyang post, he was appointed to the Imperial Academy at Kaifeng, the capital. This appointment in 1034 placed his foot on the first rung of the ladder leading to a career in the central government. Literary skill lay at the heart of intellectual life, and at this period of Chinese history, intellectual life came to bear even more directly on political careers and on policy than had previously had been the case. "Scholar" and "official" virtually became terms that, both ideally and practically, defined each other.

Political careers typically were marked by ups and downs. At the capital he began his association with Fan Zhongyan (989–1052),[5] one of the most important of the idealistic "new men" who demanded reforms. Fan was then the Prefect of Kaifeng, the capital city, and thus in a position to express his views on policy. Fan criticized the Chief Councillor for showing favoritism in promotions and submitted a proposal to reform the criteria for advancing and demoting officials. When conservatives denounced Fan, saying that his proposal was intended to sow distrust between the emperor and his court, he was demoted to a post in the regional government. Ouyang then over-stepped his station and submitted a scathing denunciation of Fan's principal critic. For this Ouyang Xiu also was demoted, receiving a very minor post of magistrate in a small county on the upper Yangzi River in western Hubei. Within officialdom, however, this demotion won him approbation as a princi-pled official and made him a central figure in the reform faction.

In 1040 the Liao and the Xi Xia (the Tangut state on the northwest border) threatened to undertake a joint campaign against the Song.[6] Fan Zhongyan and others who had long agitated for a stronger defense policy were now brought back into power to help devise a response to this threat. Ouyang dearly wanted a military post on the frontier so that he might plan strategic defenses, one of his favorite fields of study, but he was denied that. When Fan Zhongyan was sent off to the Xi Xia frontier to take charge of defenses, he offered Ouyang a choice secretarial post on his staff; but Ouyang refused because he did not want to take advantage of his personal connections. Again his principled behavior earned him respect among officials. Brought back to the court, he was assigned to assist in a major scholarly task, the preparation of an annotated catalog of the imperial library, the *Chongwen zongmu* (1041, supplemented 1062). He also delved deeply into archaeological evidence for supplementing the history of antiquity, one of the new fields of learning at the time.

Four decades earlier, during the winter of 1004–5, the Song court had accepted the Treaty of Shanyuan, so called because it was negotiated at the prefectural city of Shanyuan, across the Yellow River north of Kaifeng, where the invading Khitan army had stopped on its way to the Song capital. That landmark treaty established the pattern of indemnified peace between the Song and the Liao. The Song court agreed to make substantial annual pay-ments of silver, silk, and other valuables in return for regularized, peaceful relations between the two states.[7] The Song dynasty's willingness to negotiate such a treaty was looked upon as capitulation. It had been strongly opposed by a war faction in the court, but that activist faction's proponents failed to gain the support of the emperor—whether because he lacked the courage to adopt an aggressive policy or because he was exceptionally farsighted, as the official record claims.

When in the 1040s the Khitan state, this time in conjunction with the Tanguts, once again threatened to invade and demanded an increase in the indemnity, the Xi Xia, who had initially provoked the military crisis, demanded the extension of this policy of payments for peace to themselves. A war faction again opposed the dynasty's "supine" policy of submitting to the "barbarians." This time the faction opposing a treaty settlement linked the military crisis directly to political reform. Fan Zhongyan led what became known as an "idealistic Confucian" reform faction at the court.[8] Ouyang Xiu played an important role in launching this reform movement; his scholarly post at the court allowed him to submit advice to the emperor on political matters. It was on the basis of his counsel that Fan Zhongyan and his principal associates were called to the court in 1043 to offer political advice in the crisis of the alien military threat. Their forceful memorial summarizing their overall plan initiated the "Qingli Reforms," named for the Qingli reign period (1041–1048) during which they were inaugurated. In 1043 Fan and his associates submitted a ten-point proposal covering several aspects of governmental organization. For almost two years they controlled the government and implemented their reform ideas. In 1045, however, the emperor rescinded their reform decrees, and the reformers fell from power. This episode has been called the "Minor Reform" of Northern Song, to contrast it with the much more comprehensive "Major Reform" movement led by Wang Anshi thirty years later.[9] The reform group's fall in 1045 took with it Ouyang, who had made the mistake of defending the group's action as that of a "good political faction," an oxymoron in the context of Chinese political thinking. His role in that reform effort and the concept of "factions" in court politics is discussed later in this chapter.

With the dismissal of Fan Zhongyan and the demise of his reforms, Ouyang was again demoted to a succession of magistracies in the provinces, and for a number of years he remained out of touch with the court.[10] After having served briefly at Yingzhou in Anhui, where he eventually would make his home, in 1049 he was recalled to an advisory post at the court. Shortly thereafter his mother died. That led to his compulsory retirement for the duration of the mourning period, from her death in the third month of 1052 until the fifth month of 1054. That time of enforced idleness was spent at Yingzhou. He had bought property there, and in 1068 he would build on it the residence where his wife and family would have their permanent home.

During the mourning period, late in 1053, he carried out the filial duty of taking his mother's and his father's coffins back to his father's ancestral home in Luling, southern Jiangxi, to bury them amidst the family graves. He wrote a moving tribute to them that became a famous example of the ancient prose style. He never visited his ancestral home again, and this tribute was criticized by some as insincere, for on the one hand he had acknowledged his responsibility to take his parents to their ancestral resting place, while on the other he had abandoned the ancestral tombs and his personal ritual obligations to them by establishing a new home in Anhui. As I have noted, that relative freedom in deciding on the pattern of one's life is evident among the new scholar-official elite in Northern Song times.

Upon completing the obligatory mourning period in 1054, he returned to the court. When the Emperor Renzong (r. 1022–1063) first saw him, he remarked on Ouyang's graying hair and solicitously asked how old he was; by so doing openly he indicated that Ouyang remained in high favor.[11] Shortly thereafter he was appointed Hanlin Academician, a highly ranked, substantive post at court for a person of scholarly eminence; simultaneously he was also chosen to head the commission responsible for compiling a *New Tang History*, a task that was not completed until 1060. Ouyang himself prepared the Basic Annals, the Treatises, and the Tables, which constituted 75 of its 225 chapters *(juan)* but about half of its content. Here he displayed his mastery of the ancient-style prose, seen at its best in the writing of history on the model of the great Han dynasty historian Sima Qian; he also stressed a principle of historical analysis in which ethical considerations were paramount in the consideration of individuals and of events. Later he wrote his own *New History of the Five Dynasties,* in which these literary and historiographical qualities were even more strikingly employed. In 1055 he served as an envoy in the delegation sent to the Liao court to offer the Song emperor's felicitations on the Khitan emperor's birthday, an annual diplomatic requirement under the treaties. He wrote the obligatory report on the journey and some poems complaining about the cold and the discomforts of travel. Thereafter he was regularly appointed to accompany the Liao envoys at the ceremonial dinners offered by the Song emperor when they made their annual visits to the Chinese court. The Liao envoys eagerly sought examples of his calligraphy and copies of his poetry, as did those from Korea. He became internationally famous. His chronological biography for these years is full of references to the many other kinds of ceremonial tasks that fell to him, as they did to all high officials of great prestige, and he himself often mentions that his income rose thanks to the bonuses that the Northern Song court generously bestowed. During these years he also frequently served as examiner for the *jinshi* examinations, and saw these occasions as opportunities to implement his ideas on improving the quality of the examinations (see Section III).

By the early 1060s his concurrent official posts had been raised to the highest levels of actual power and influence at the court; they included Hanlin Academician, Vice Commissioner of Military Affairs, Vice Minister of Revenues, and Assistant Chief Councillor. Along with two or three longtime associates and like-minded statesmen, he had reached the pinnacle of his political power; this group dominated the court and government for six or seven years. But Ouyang was no longer so eager to implement dramatic reforms; a veteran of political struggles, he had become a gradualist. Notwithstanding, he continued to work hard for institutional modifications that would improve the quality of governing, especially by enhancing career opportunities for the "good men" who came up through the substantially reformed examination system.

Great power breeds enmities and jealousies. During these years he frequently came under attack. In 1067, just as Wang Anshi's name came to the attention of the new emperor Shenzong (r. 1067–1085), Ouyang's enemies thought he had become vulnerable. He was charged with several crimes, the most damaging being that of incest with his daughter-in-law. No one—not the new emperor, not even Ouyang's foremost political rivals—deemed the charge credible; but it had to be investigated nonetheless, and thereby it accomplished its purpose. He seemed vulnerable to charges of sexual improprieties because as a young man he had acquired a reputation for being overly fond of keeping company with noted courtesans.

The scurrilous charges now thrown at him hurt him deeply. He repeatedly requested permission to retire, but was always refused. His wish to leave the court did, however, result in his being assigned to various provincial posts, which he received along with concurrent honorary offices and titles and expressions of confidence. He was given posts close enough to Yingzhou that he could reside there while nominally serving in regional offices. In 1071, five years ahead of the then standard retirement age of seventy (by Chinese reckoning, which adds a year to one's life at birth), his formal retirement was granted. He died at home a year later. His third wife, the Lady Xue, the mother of all his children, lived to the age of seventy-three and died there in 1089.[12] His is of course the unique career of an extraordinary man, but it includes many elements that are typical of official careers in his time.

Ouyang Xiu was deeply and consistently committed to ideas about society and government that led him and his contemporaries to demand change. Commitment to renovating changes forms a central thread running through Northern Song intellectual and political history. As he brought his thinking to bear on such issues as the reform of the examination system, he was opposed by men we might label "conservatives," but later on he himself seems to have joined the conservative camp when he strongly opposed the sweeping reforms of Wang Anshi. While those terms are useful, we must define "reformer" and "conservative" in the context of eleventh-century China. By exploring major issues in Northern Song history, we can perhaps come to a more pertinent understanding of the force of ideas in the shaping of Northern Song life. These are the civil service examination system, the impact of that system on society, political reform, and Neo-Confucian political thought.

III. THE CIVIL SERVICE EXAMINATION SYSTEM

In an open society with no elite sector having rights to office by reason of birth or inherited status, the recruitment of men to staff the offices of government is a major problem. By Song times, imperial China had acquired more than a thousand years' experience in solving this problem, but its solutions were still evolving. The long-range trend was away from systems for nominating and appointing the "talented," based on recommendations made at court or throughout the country by individuals possessing some kind of credibility. Such personal nominations, attesting that the nominee possessed both intellectual and moral qualifications for public life, had sometimes produced officials who were ridiculously deficient, thereby arousing opinions critical of the system. More important, through the system of personal recommendations those people in society who possessed wealth and power could attempt to secure the same advantages for other members of their own families, thereby perpetuating a virtual monopoly on officeholding among their own group. For although there was no legally established hereditary aristocracy as such, people who had achieved wealth and power naturally tried to secure those advantages for their descendants.

For these several reasons, there grew throughout Sui and Tang times a widespread sense that this system of subjective judgments had to be supplemented. At first the stress was on forcing the nominators to be legally responsible for the performance of their candidates. But that still allowed the "eminent lineages" to monopolize the appointments and effectively limit them to men of their own social group. Starting in the late sixth century, and continuing through the seventh and the eighth centuries, a number of experiments were made with oral or written examinations to supplement the recommendation system.[13]

Under the Tang, the principal talent pool drawn upon for recommending persons of demonstrated ability was the sub-official corps of staff clerks in administrative offices throughout the country. For that reason, ambitious men with good backgrounds were willing to take clerical posts in government as a way to begin what they hoped would become official careers. The Tang recommendation system at least had the benefit of bringing into officialdom men who had acquired practical office experience. But the idea of using written examinations slowly won out, and they became one major route to officeholding during the later part of the Tang dynasty. Men hoping to start official careers eventually were less willing to apprentice themselves as clerks occupying sub-official positions. They bypassed that accumulation of practical experience as a qualification for the goal of entering into officialdom, turning instead to the new alternative: long years of study undertaken in the hope of qualifying through the written examinations.

The practice of holding oral, and later written, examinations in the palace with the emperor acting as chief examiner also dates from mid-Tang times. This practice was formally institutionalized by the first Song emperor. It was a feature of the emerging civil service examination system that endured until the entire system's final abolition early in the twentieth century. The personal involvement of the ruler emphasized the gravity of the selection process as well as the dignity it bestowed on those who participated. It also made all those examined by the emperor personally loyal to him as their immediate "teacher," thus reinforcing the idea of loyalty to the throne over other loyalties. Many Song emperors took their role as examiner very seriously; in later dynasties it was usually viewed as a mere formality.

By the end of the Tang, regular institutionalized written examinations called *ke ju* had become well established. They were conducted at several levels. The capstone of the system was the palace examinations, which served not to select but to rank those who had been passed and sent on to that highest level of the imperial examination system. As a system it achieved great improvement in rationality and effectiveness, but not without a corresponding price: this system rewarded demonstrated ability in book learning and paid little heed to practical kinds of knowledge that lowly clerks and secretaries learned on the job.[14]

The social impact of the Song examination system, a much-debated topic in current scholarship, will be discussed next. Here I first take note of the mechanics of the system.

Through the first half-century of Song rule the organizational arrangements inherited from Tang continued in place while greater emphasis was given to filling offices through the examinations. Having displaced the recommendation system, the written examinations now became the principal avenue to official status and appointment; in particular, they were the only way to achieve office that carried the full prestige of having individually demonstrated one's merit. While there were some exceptions, in general only the holders of an earned degree could hope for steady advancement into the higher levels or to the more important offices of the imperial bureaucracy. Although in the early Song period a small number of officials were allowed to nominate family members, usually a son, for the direct award of a *jinshi* degree "by grace" (i.e., by the *yin,* or "protection" privilege), without having to sit for the examinations, as was the case with Ouyang Xiu's eldest son, the numbers of such degree holders remained small, and their career opportunities were so limited that this did not become the preferred route into officialdom for men of talent and ambition. Later in the Northern Song, and even more so in the Southern Song, the *yin* privilege was extended to the point that it significantly affected the composition of officialdom, even though it could not compete in prestige with the earned degree.

Examinations were held at three levels. Qualifying examinations were held at the *zhou* or prefectural level and were open to students of almost any background; only the sons of a few "debased" professions, which constituted no more than perhaps 5 percent of the population, were legally excluded, and their exclusion was not rigorously enforced.[15] Examinees in most cases prepared to sit for the examinations by enrolling in local schools and academies. Most of the academies were private establishments, often recognized by the government, and they normally accepted some students too poor to pay more than a token tuition fee. Even so, it was very difficult, hence exceptional, for the poorest families to put a son directly on the educational track that could lead him to officialdom. Practically speaking, a family had to work its way up to a modest level of wealth through several generations before it could begin to plan on educating a son for the examinations, and that son probably would have gained his basic literacy education in a village or temple school, and then would have shared a tutor with sons of other families.

Candidates who passed the qualifying examinations were accepted for enrollment in the county or prefectural Confucian school. More administrative than academic institutions, these schools verified and guaranteed that candidates were fit to advance to the first level of examinations in the prefectures. Their numbers constantly changed as administrative adjustments were made, but for most of the Northern Song period there were about 300 prefectures which had jurisdiction over altogether 1,100 counties. Each prefecture had education officials who loosely oversaw the preparation of students in the counties and who conducted examinations at the seat of the prefectural government. It has been calculated that early in the eleventh century the total number of students sitting for the prefectural examinations was between 20,000 and 30,000; by the end of the century that figure had risen to about 80,000.[16] Success rates were at times as low as 1 percent and were seldom higher than 10 percent; these ratios were fixed by quotas on the number of candidates who could be passed at all levels of the examinations. Just maintaining uniform standards for the prefectural examinations throughout the vast area governed by the Song empire was in itself a very large undertaking.

Those who passed at the prefectural level proceeded to the imperial capital to take the second-level examinations, which were conducted by the Ministry of Rites.[17] Successful candidates remained in the capital to sit for the highest-level examinations, sometimes translated into English as the "doctoral examinations," the analogy being to the doctor of philosophy degree in modern higher education. Most candidates (probably nine out of ten) did not pass at the highest level on their first try, and no shame attended that failure. They could take the examinations again and again, sometimes over a span of many years. By virtue of having been certified as eligible to sit for the Ministry examinations, these candidates were called "elevated men" *(juren),* in Song times an honorific title that did not give them access to official appointments, as that title, earned in a second or provincial-level examination, later did in Ming and Qing times.

Originally, to pass the examinations conducted by the Ministry of Rites marked the final stage in the examination process. In 975, however, the first Song emperor saw the name of someone he felt lacked ability on the list of successful Ministry examination candidates: suspecting some malfeasance, he ordered all the *juren* reexamined in the palace under his direct supervision. This practice became permanently established; only success in the third, or palace examination, conferred on the candidate the degree of "doctor."

Those awarded the highest degree were strictly ranked in order of excellence. The first three names were set apart. To be one of those, especially the man ranked first—the *juangyuan,* sometimes translated *primus* or *optimus*—brought honors of extraordinary significance; the first-ranked name would immediately become known throughout the realm, and that individual could expect to advance into the higher levels of the central government much faster than others. The remaining "doctors" were divided into two categories: an upper group designated as having passed "with distinction," and a lower group designated as "formally qualified." To achieve a place anywhere on the list of the successful was the most important honor that could come to a man. Even the man ranked last was an honored being, suddenly elevated above the common people.

The examination system inherited from the Tang allowed an examinee to select the field of his examinations; the term *jinshi* (advanced scholar) designated only one of those fields, others being classics, history, ritual, law, and mathematics.[18] Instead of being literally translated as "advanced scholar," this term is sometimes translated "doctor of letters" to distinguish it from the degrees earned in the other subject fields. Under the influence of men such as Ouyang Xiu, who wanted to make the content of the examinations bear more practically on real problems in government, the prestige of the doctor of letters examination gradually surpassed that of all the other fields and by the mid-eleventh century had become virtually synonomous with "doctor."

Ouyang Xiu favored this field in the examinations because in all the other fields the candidates were tested only on the ability to memorize classics pertinent to their selected field and compose poetry in several genres. While memorization of classic texts and composing poetry continued to play a significant part in every scholar's preparation, the doctor of letters examinations also contained questions that required the candidate to compose tightly organized essays in which he addressed current social and political issues by discoursing on passages selected from the classics. On several occasions in the 1050s and 1060s when he served as examiner in charge of the Ministry examinations, Ouyang Xiu was able to demand higher quality in those essays, in respect of both their content and the writer's ability to use the forceful "ancient prose" to express forward-looking ideas—albeit entirely through allusions to a remote past. That juxtaposition of "forward-looking" and "remote past" is not as contradictory as it may seem, for Chinese civilization offered no alternative to the understanding gained from knowing the past as a source of rationally derived authority. Intelligent analysis of the past lent conviction to one's views on current and future issues. That was the way renovating change was justified.

By the end of his career in government, these changes in the character and content of the examinations had prevailed, and the doctors of letters *(jinshi)* came to form an elite group that dominated the highest levels of officialdom. In this way the word *jinshi* came thereafter to designate all holders of the highest-level degree. Here the Chinese term usually will be used instead of the translations "doctor," "doctor of letters," and the like.

The examinations at both levels were conducted over a period of days, usually in four (later three) parts, each part requiring one full day of writing, the entire process spread over a span of nine or ten days. Examinations were conducted in large public halls temporarily taken over for this purpose. Only in later dynasties were rows of tiny cells specially built to house the candidates for the duration of their examination ordeal.

There was a very genuine effort to make the process honest. In the early years of the dynasty a number of steps toward that end were rigorously implemented. The candidates' names were removed or pasted over and replaced with numbers to ensure that the examiners could not identify them. By the 1030s this practice had been extended from the palace examinations to the Ministry examinations, and subsequently also to the prefectural examinations. To obviate the possibility of recognizing a candidate by his handwriting, in 1015 a bureau of copyists was established to make uniform copies of the papers for the examiners to read. Each paper had to be read by two examiners; if their opinions were widely disparate, they had to reconcile them before submitting their report to the chief examiner. Elaborate efforts were made to verify the identity of all the candidates sitting for an examination to prevent substitutes from sitting for named candidates, and candidates were searched on entering the hall to prevent memory aids or copies of previously successful answers from being secreted in their clothing. The examinations were too important for the government to tolerate corruption, and when it was discovered, it was punished with severity. Even so, success in the examinations was too crucial in the lives of the candidates and their families for cheating never to be attempted. On balance, however, through the Northern Song as well as during the later Ming and Qing dynasties, the civil service examinations stand out as an institution that operated fairly and with relatively little cheating or corruption.[19]

At the beginning of the Song dynasty, examinations were held irregularly, sometimes every year and sometimes every other year. In 1065 it was decreed that examinations be held every third year, the prefectural examinations in the autumn and the Ministry and palace examinations the following spring. This remained the practice until the examinations were abolished in 1905, although subsequently, under the last two dynasties, the autumn provincial examinations (granting the *juren* degree) were added, with those at the lower prefectural level, making two examination hurdles to qualify candidates for the *jinshi* examinations. Special examination years were sometimes added for ceremonial or other reasons.

The conduct and the content of the civil service examinations underwent constant scrutiny and criticism, and various suggestions for changing and improving them were offered throughout the three centuries of Song rule. The serious concern about them shown by rulers and officials is a measure of their importance to the state and to the entire society.

IV. THE SOCIAL IMPACT OF THE SONG EXAMINATION SYSTEM

How the examination system affected the social order is probably the most contentious issue in historical writing about the Song dynasty today, and its resolution has implications and repercussions for all of subsequent imperial history. Several decades ago, a study measuring upward social mobility concluded that during the first century of Northern Song rule the percentage of "new men" from non-official backgrounds who passed the *jinshi* examinations was very high, reaching over 50 percent of the total number.[20] That appears to be a higher rate of entrance into the official elite than existed in any other premodern society. The study seems to be confirmed by another which measured the mobility from commoner to official status in Ming and Qing times (1368–1911) using the same criteria.[21] Both studies were based on the lists of degree recipients in certain years for which lists are extant; these lists included the information required of each candidate on the status of all his direct forebears in the three generations prior to his own. If any had held civil office, that would be reported, and that information was quantified and analyzed.

Subsequently, objections to this way of measuring upward mobility arose.[22] More recently, several important new studies of the issue during the Song period have been published, all of which further modify the original findings as well as one another's new conclusions.[23] While some of the revised interpretations may have gone too far, they bring us closer to a useful definition of the "openness" of traditional Chinese society.

The recent writers have all attempted to assess the significance of what most of them regard as a methodological fault in earlier studies: defining family as the nuclear family and consequently assuming that if a degree winner's father, grandfather, and great-grandfather all had been "commoners" (that is, men who held no civil service rank or position), then that degree winner represented the entry into official status of a "new man." By that definition Ouyang Xiu's father was a "new man"; and in a sense Ouyang himself came from a background still so humble in his youth that he too could be seen as representing the achievement and the values of the "new men" in officialdom in his time.

These critics have argued that the nuclear family represented by the male line for the three preceding generations is not the relevant social unit to be studied: in their view, "family" should be understood to comprise the lineage, including the extended family with all the uncles, great-uncles, cousins, even relatives by marriage. Any of those more distant relatives who had attained official status could use that status or the family's influence to assist aspiring candidates by financing their preparation over a long period of years, by providing for them a milieu of cultivation and manners, and by influencing the local community to give them preference in admission to the lower-level examinations.

Some of these revisionist studies go so far as to say that when family background is measured more broadly, it can be demonstrated that there was zero social mobility: all recipients of higher degrees benefited from family status and influence and already had taken on the values and attitudes of the elite sector of society. Some even claim that the prefectural examinations at the first rung of the ladder to official status came under the influence of the official families in their locality because these families had the prerogative to certify that candidates were of "good background" and therefore eligible to sit for the examinations in the first place; it is suggested that they used that prerogative to allow only their own kind access to the local examinations. Answers to these claims will require fuller information than is now available. The official examination lists do not provide additional information about a candidate's family background, but that often can be culled from the many types of biographical and informal writing of the period. Careful reconstruction of larger family units to show official connections within a lineage and its marriage affiliations must be based on a painstaking search for data among the vast array of such writings. No study, obviously, can be exhaustive, yet some are careful and broad enough to deserve some credence. We are challenged to rethink the social dynamics of Song dynasty China.

There remain many problems both with the original "high mobility" studies and with the revisionist efforts to lower the figures for mobility. For example, Ouyang Xiu's father's status as a genuine "new man" might be complicated by the fact that some of the posthumous biographical writings on Ouyang Xiu state that his grandfather and great-grandfather held modest civil office and also vaguely link him to a glorious pedigree going back to high antiquity. A more skeptical reading of this information suggests that those statements were fabricated by later writers who, despite proudly acknowledging the poverty of his youth, attempted to make his origins more impressive.[24] If there is significant distortion in the materials, it is of the kind that invents an illustrious background, and not the kind that suppresses it.

Despite the wide range of opinion on the extent to which the examinations facilitated upward mobility from the lower levels of society, scholars all agree that the examination system was the defining institution of the society. Even if the system were manipulated to prevent anyone outside the elite official stratum from entering officialdom by merit (and that view appears to be extreme), in order to attain official status individuals still had to prepare for and succeed in the examinations. There was no way to get around that inescapable requirement, no matter how illustrious a candidate's family might be. Even those who gained *jinshi* status through the privilege of "protection" (a less esteemed method of entry) had to acquire more or less equivalent qualifications. When attempting to account for the vigorous, activist, "Confucian idealist" elite sector of Northern Song society, one might surmise that it was enlivened by the presence of new blood and new attitudes, or one might conclude that their vigorous activism simply resulted from the commitment to learning and to ideas which preparation for the examinations fostered. In either case, the elite constituted through this process dominated Song life—in respect to the operation of government, the formulation of all aspects of policy, the establishment of social standards throughout the realm, the trends in literature and the arts (which became primarily art and literature as practiced and judged by scholar-officials), the definition of ethical standards, and the exploration of new horizons in philosophy. It has been observed that one reason why Western intellectuals have been so enamored of traditional China is that (ideally) it was a society in which power was held by men they can identify with, and was exercised in ways they approve of.[25]

While the debate about the actual incidence of upward mobility from the ranks of the common people to the ranks of officialdom will go on, it can still safely be said that the *jinshi* degree, the highest reward the state could bestow on a subject, was won by individual merit objectively tested, and that therefore the achieving spirit was encouraged at even the highest levels of society. Moreover, the law of the land proclaimed that the recruitment system was open to virtually every male subject in the realm, holding up the ideal of success through individual achievement as an incentive to the entire society. Neither in law nor in popular values was there any basis for discrimination against the newly arrived, so long as their attitudes and behavior, which long years of study for the examinations had imbued in them, accorded with the norms. Finally, there were many ways by which poor but bright men could improve their economic status, if only in slow stages; even though they rarely went in one great leap from poor commoner status to become the Chief Councillor, they might imagine a grandson becoming an official. The examination system as it functioned during the Song dynasty nourished the ideal that success was open to all worthy men. That idea pervaded the society and it contributed in large measure to what is now called the "new culture" of the Song and succeeding ages.

While debate about measuring upward mobility in Song society continues, there is little disagreement about the number of *jinshi* the system produced or about their dominance of officialdom. The total number of civil "official" *(guan)* posts (excluding clerical and sub-official) throughout central and local government initially numbered about 10,000; by the mid-eleventh century the number had reached about 13,000.[26] It has been estimated that on average candidates won their *jinshi* degrees in their early thirties. The life span of these degree holders (who legally could serve until age seventy) allows us to estimate the maximum size of the pool from which officials could be drawn. If the accumulation of those numbers is reckoned by multiplying the average annual addition of 220 by the average service life of thirty-five years, or 7,700, the system produced a pool of 7,000 to 8,000 *jinshi* available for official appointment. Even though not all of them lived that long or were on active service all of the time, those numbers were adequate to fill half the civil offices, and to dominate totally the higher ranks of office where policy was made. The remaining civil offices were filled by men recruited through the other, less prestigious means, the *yin* or "protection" route, or by direct nomination through the schools, or by other means. This dominance of the civil service by examination degree holders was a qualitatively new feature of Song government and of Song society.

More could be said about the social implications of the Song system of "sponsorship" within officialdom. Under the "sponsorship system" established officials identified and sponsored young newcomers, usually degree recipients who had been posted to minor offices, in order to advance their careers more quickly. This system became an important adjunct to the examination system and probably helped maintain the high morale of the civil service.[27] Imperial compassion toward the struggling scholar who sat for the highest-level examination (the Ministry examination) many times without passing also contributed to the vitality of the entire system of elite recruit-ment. Special "facilitated examinations" were given from time to time, usu-ally open to those who had failed five or even more times. The criteria for passing these examinations were relaxed somewhat, and this made the system seem more fair, since the quotas for those allowed to pass in the regular exam-inations were set so low that success involved a large element of luck in addi-tion to ability. It was generally recognized that those who failed might be as competent as those who passed.[28] If the system failed to be fair because at its lowest levels it was not truly open to all, as some recent scholars believe, it nevertheless held up fairness as an ideal, and took into consideration those who had struggled in vain to succeed. There is no reason to believe that cyni-cism about the fairness of the system was widespread in Song society.

V. POLITICAL REFORM AND POLITICAL THOUGHT

The Song, and in particular the Northern Song, was a great age in China's intellectual history. It was the age when "Neo-Confucianism" took form, to remain the dominant philosophical trend throughout late imperial history. "Neo-Confucianism" as a name for the new currents in thought is a recent, and a Western, coinage and usually designates only one aspect of the revived Song Confucianism: a new formulation of Confucian ethics and metaphysics that is called Lixue or Xing li xue, the Learning of Nature and Principle). That major concern of the revived Confucianism produced, to be sure, a brilliant flowering of philosophy. Over several centuries it focused on the nature *(xing)* of humans and of things, and on the mind *(xin)* more than on the more directly practical issues regarding social order and the state which had been central to Confucian thought and practice from its early beginnings. The pro-ponents of Lixue fervently believed, of course, that their new formulation of Confucian principles had significance for the whole life of man in society, and that other things would fall into place when those principles were once again firmly established. The Lixue thinkers in the eleventh century were moved by their urgently perceived need to provide new cosmological founda-tions for Confucian values.

But there also were other powerful spurs to thought in the eleventh century, coming from the new scholarly elite's awareness of political and social issues, and perils to the state arising from the threat of alien invasion from the north. Ouyang Xiu said: "The nature of man and things [*xing*] is *not* the urgent issue for scholars, and is something that the Sage seldom discussed." And "the content of the *Six Classics* is entirely those aspects of human affairs that are relevant to the times, and thus they discuss such issues in great detail. As for the matter of *xing,* it scarcely merits one or two words out of a hundred there."[29] Even as some of Ouyang's contemporaries were delving into the profundities of metaphysics, to give speculative philosophy a Confucian char-acter that would allow it to compete on the ground of debate established by Daoism and Buddhism, others sought what they believed to be a greater Confucian relevance. "The classics talk about real problems," Ouyang was saying, "and so should we." In that attitude he represents men who were just as deeply committed to the regeneration of Confucian thought, but who engaged in the reforms and the political struggles, who focused on institutions and their improvement, and who analyzed the nature of political power and how best to utilize it for the betterment of mankind.

This second trend in Song political thought has been labeled Utilitarian Thought (Gongli sixiang).[30] It will be the subject of this section, leaving the development of Lixue, historically the more significant element in Song dynasty intellectual thought, to be introduced in the next section. Song Utilitarian Thought came to the fore with the Minor Reform of the mid-eleventh century, and reached a high point under the Major Reform of Wang Anshi in his years as Chief Councillor (1069–1076), when he launched his broad-ranging New Policies. After that, it continued as one trend in political thought in later Song times. As a movement in thought, it has scarcely been granted attention in intellectual history, so fully has the Lixue movement dominated philosophical activity in post-Song times. Yet it produced a succession of important thinkers, and it also contributed to practical social thinking that spurred some members of the scholar-bureaucracy to participate in the life of their home communities, without producing philosophical writings as such.

Neo-Confucian Lixue, by contrast, for all its impressive achievements in metaphysics and ethics, made only marginal contributions to political thought and action. Its adherents mostly repeated the old slogans drawn from Confucius and Mencius without developing new social and political ideas. The real ferment of ideas in Song dynasty political thinking belonged to the advocates of Utilitarian Thought, sometimes taken to be the opponents of the Lixue school; Lixue partisans might sometimes go so far as to deride utilitarianism as intrinsically un-Confucian. In the heat of debate, it was at times labeled "deviant," "heterodox," or "Legalist." That animosity obscured the coherence and the importance of this genuinely Confucian trend in thought. A bias against Wang Anshi and against utilitarian or reform thought in general is heavily built into the traditional sources for Song history, and is still reflected in recent scholarship. In what follows, an attempt is made to correct that imbalance.

The Minor Reform of 1043–1045 and the Issue of Factions

We have seen that Ouyang Xiu's early career in the higher levels of the central government led him into association with Fan Zhongyan, leader of the Minor Reform of the 1040s, and that when the conservatives brought Fan down, Ouyang also was demoted to obscure posts in local government. When the conservatives charged that Fan and his associates formed a "faction" and therefore were by definition subversive, Ouyang first replied, a bit off the cuff, that of course they were a faction: good men tend to associate with one another. That got him into real trouble, and forced him to essay a properly Confucian explanation of the true meaning of "faction" (pengdang). He noted that Confucius himself had said that the good persons in society, finding one another congenial, quite naturally will flock together to make the good prevail, just as the bad also band together to realize their unworthy goals. His essay on factions[31] is a brilliant literary exercise, but it did not win the favor of the Song rulers, despots jealous of all independent-minded political forces that might be difficult to control. And, as in many cases, Confucius also could be cited on the emperor's side of the argument as well. The failure of Neo-Confucian thinkers and political activists to break through this formal barrier against concerted political action by groups of like-minded men, by disallowing any distinction between good and bad factions, severely limited Chinese political behavior thereafter, up to the end of the imperial era in the early twentieth century. Most Song political thinkers were like Ouyang in wishing to strengthen the throne, and through it the state, in order to make governing more effective. But they were unable in any practical way to resolve the dilemma created by the juxtaposition of an increasingly powerful imperial institution (largely of their making) and the reinvigorated power of the new Confucian political thinking (which genuinely motivated them). The attempt to redefine "factions" would arise again and again, up to the eighteenth century, but the state's definition always prevailed. Legitimate political parties could not take form, and any who expressed political disagreement were, by definition, morally deficient, hence insidious. "Loyal opposition" could not be acknowledged within a system of politics defined by ethical and personal rather than by operational and institutional norms. China still struggles with the heritage of this eleventh-century political failure.

Fan Zhongyan's reform objectives were set forth in his Ten-Point Memorial that the emperor, at a moment of military crisis, accepted and supported. The ten points can be briefly summarized under three headings: (1) To improve administrative efficiency in the central government by changing personnel management in ways that would reward the able officials and weed out incompetents; to reinforce the laws; and to eliminate favoritism within the bureaucracy. At the same time, the content of the examinations would be shifted away from demonstrating skills in writing correct and ingenious poetry to skills in thinking about practical statecraft issues. (2) To strengthen local government by improving salaries, investing in the infrastructure of agriculture (dykes, canals, land reclamation, and grain transport), and making more equitable the corvée labor requirements imposed on all the rural population. (3) To create militias and improve local defense so as to maintain order in the localities, particularly those on the frontiers that were exposed to the dangers of invasion.

It was the first of these sets of issues that aroused strong opposition at court; groups of bureaucrats felt threatened and fought back. The second set of issues was very farsighted, looking to basic problems in social management and social justice, but they seemed remote from the court and the context of political action there. The third set of issues looked back to the founding of the dynasty and the early Song's overcorrection of military abuses that were held to have destroyed the Tang dynasty. To prevent a repetition, the military's powers were reduced and military forces were placed under secure civil control from the center. Eighty years into the Song dynasty, that reduction seemed to have gone too far in light of the military crisis provoked by Tangut invasion in the northwest and the new Tangut-Khitan alliance. Fan Zhongyan found that there were no adequate regional defense forces posted along the northern and northwestern frontier ready to respond at the discretion of regional commanders. Any decision for a military response had to be made at the center and could only deploy forces based at the center. Both the capacity for quick military response and the basis for maintaining law and order in threatened regions were lacking. Fan's analysis of this danger threatened to open up the most profound challenge to the Song domestic policy. As clearly laid down under the first two emperors, the policy was to weaken the military so as to ensure the stability of the throne, and to be willing to pay the price for inadequate defense against invasion. This would be a recurring and essentially unresolved problem throughout the entire dynasty.

In 1042 an immediate crisis of military invasion was settled by a revision of the treaty arrangements with the Liao, now extended also to the Xi Xia in the northwest. With that pressure removed, even though the humiliation of increased annual indemnity payments for peace frustrated the reform statesmen in particular, there was an anti-reform backlash at court that induced the emperor to abandon the reformers. In 1045 they were sent down from the central government to take postings in the provinces that seemed to them like exile. Yet there remained an acute awareness of the issues and strong support for the reform ideas. Ouyang Xiu and like-minded men, at this later phase of their careers, tended to become evolutionary reformers; they recognized the limits of political action and strove for realistic accommodation to accomplish longer-range goals. In that less confrontational spirit, they continued to press for changes throughout the 1050s and 1060s. They gained some important successes, notably in changing the character of the examinations, hence of the recruitment system. But many real needs in Song society and government remained, and even intensified. In consequence, the far more ambitious Major Reforms designed and led by Wang Anshi in the 1070s addressed basically the same sets of issues.

The Major Reform of Wang Anshi

Wang Anshi (1021–1085) was a man very much like Ouyang Xiu. Although his family, also from Jiangxi, had produced several *jinshi* in the three generations immediately prior to Wang's, he too represented the new elite from the South, and he too first became famous through his remarkable literary and scholarly talent. He gained his *jinshi* degree with high distinction, placing fourth in the palace examinations among 839 degree winners in 1042, the year before Fan Zhongyan submitted his Ten-Point Memorial. Under the influence of reform trends, that examination was one of the first in which prominence was given to questions testing for applied statecraft and knowledge of history over poetry and literary skills, though Wang (like Ouyang when he passed his *jinshi* examination twenty years earlier) excelled in both and would not have been at a disadvantage in either type of examination. For more than twenty years thereafter Wang served in important posts in regional government in the rich lower Yangzi region. His high examination standing ensured that he received substantive posts, even though not at the central government, and he found the practical experience of meeting base-level social and political problems very satisfying.

In 1058 Wang submitted his famous *Wanyan Shu,* or "Ten Thousand Word Memorial," in which he set forth a program of political ideas and called for thorough reforms. While his proposal did not lead to a court appointment, it made him famous for its powerful ideas and gained him a kind of leadership among reformers. With the accession of a new emperor in 1067 (the Emperor Shenzong, who would reign until 1085), advisers to the throne recommended that this ambitious young emperor seek the counsel of Wang Anshi. Wang appeared at court in 1068, where the twenty-year-old ruler found in the forty-seven-year-old Wang precisely the adviser he had been seeking. Early the next year, in 1069, he appointed Wang Vice Chief Councillor in charge of administration, the same post to which Ouyang Xiu had been appointed in 1061 and had held until 1067, when the slanderous attack on him forced his temporary withdrawal from administration. Now the new emperor made a clean break with the politics of his predecessor and appointed a full range of new officials, mostly acting on Wang's advice.

The full trust which Emperor Shenzong gave to Wang Anshi created one of those rare opportunities in all of imperial history: a man of ideas was given virtual free rein to implement them in the name of a ruler who fully respected him.[32]

Wang's analysis of what ailed Song government and society drew on his twenty years of practical experience in regional and local administration. For theoretical justification for his ideas, he drew on his wide-ranging study of classical writings bearing on statecraft and history. In particular, his reform ideas have been associated with the book known as *The Institutes of Zhou,*[33] of which he had made a critical study, finding in it reasons for challenging current modes in governing. But we should not see him as a literal-minded proponent of ancient models. He was glad to use discrepancies between past and present to discredit the present, to make room for sweeping changes. He did not, however, apply ancient models mechanically to Song conditions. In the manner of the best Confucian scholars, he explored all human experience as recorded in history, seeking understanding with which to improve on the past, not to reconstitute it. "Revering the past," to be sure, could produce simpleminded absurdity, or it could inspire subtly nuanced insight into human affairs; Wang Anshi has sometimes been charged with the former, but he is better understood as having a great capacity for the latter.

Although not specifically part of Wang's New Policies, his searching investigation of problems in governing led to a thorough shake-up of the administrative structure, removing most of the anomalous discrepancies between the names of offices and their assigned duties produced by the Song founder's ad hoc approach to administration. The anomalous Finance Commission was demoted and its duties restored to the previously unmanned Ministry of Revenues (Hu Bu). The Department of State Affairs was again fully staffed, as were the combined Central Secretariat and Chancellery; their heads functioned as the Chief Councillors, and in keeping with older precedents, the Central Secretariat was moved out of the palace precincts. The other ministries regained their expected duties and staffing. Any outline of early Song government must be modified to incorporate all the rationalizing changes in structure effected by Wang Anshi.[34]

Wang's principal focus during the first four years he held power, from 1069 to 1073, however, was to formulate and promulgate a dozen or more New Policies *(xinfa)*, setting in motion sweeping changes. These were far more important than the structural rationalization; they constituted his "major reforms." One core group dealt with state finance, money, and trade. These included such fundamental changes as devising new ways to manage the state's procurement system. He proposed paying in cash for labor in place of the traditional levies for labor services to supply the needs of local government. He proposed that landholdings be surveyed to adjust the basic agrarian tax rates on which government revenues principally depended. His proposals also extended to increasing the minting of copper coins, to recognizing the place of the craft and trade guilds, and to improving the management of state trade. He also established a plan to lend farmers cash when they planted, the loans to be repaid at harvest time later the same year; these were called the "green shoots loans." All of those measures were designed to reduce waste, eliminate tax evasion, and improve efficiency. Although he spoke about "enriching the state and strengthening the military," using wording that evokes harsh Legalist practice of earlier times, his fundamental purpose was to focus not on the benefit to the state but on the well-being of the common people. His concern for the state was long-range; he believed it could be rich and strong only when the source of its wealth, the livelihood of the common people, was assured. He was misunderstood in this and condemned for promoting anti-Confucian measures. Such condemnation was either knowingly malicious or ill-informed. His political thought, while incorporating some elements of what we today would call a "managed economy," was entirely Confucian in its conceptual foundations and in its ideals.[35]

A second group of his New Policies had to do with defense and with the means of ensuring social order. Historically the longest lasting of the ideas implemented by Wang Anshi was his plan to institute the so-called *baojia* system, a plan for organizing households into groups of tens *(bao)* and hundreds *(jia)* for collective responsibility to maintain order and report crimes.[36] Later the system also was employed as the basis for organizing militias and strengthening local defense as an adjunct of the regular military. Wang also proposed the creation of systems for increasing the breeding of military horses in the northern frontier zone, for manufacturing weapons more efficiently, and for training the militia. Strengthening the military clearly was more the emperor's priority than it was Wang's, but Wang contributed clear-minded ideas to that cause.

The third group of Wang Anshi's New Policies, those of greatest importance to him, all related to education, and through it to the improvement of governing. One plan was to break down the Song's increasing separation of clerical from official careers to overcome the psychological barrier between the two groups of government servants. He proposed to improve the supervision of the clerks but also to elevate their status. As it was, they could misuse their access to the inner workings of government to carry out corrupt practices, particularly in the county and prefectural governments, where they constituted the enduring element, while the civil service officials came to serve for a few short years before moving on to new posts. Wang proposed ways of rewarding the more able men among the clerical personnel by opening opportunities for the best of them to take examinations and become low-level officials. By such measures he hoped to regain some of the strengths of the Tang system.

Wang's attempts to reform the education and recruitment system were vast and involved every aspect of it. He added tests in the law, military affairs, and medicine; and later, in 1104, during the period when Wang's New Policies were reinstated, tests in mathematics also were added. In establishing some of these minor fields, he hoped to broaden the range of competences among the *jinshi* by recognizing other useful skills. His most important educational New Policies were focused directly on the examinations and the preparation of better-educated men to sit for them. He strongly favored the movement, by his time beginning to succeed, to make practical statecraft questions the core of the examinations; in 1070 he formalized these changes, confirming what Ouyang Xiu and other reformers had striven for a generation to bring about. But Wang went much further. He set in motion a plan to turn the prefectural supervisory offices for Confucian studies into real teaching institutions, to which were allotted buildings for classrooms and dormitories, with teachers and quotas of students who would enroll to undertake formal studies. He also redesigned the National Academy so that it too functioned as a real school, on a higher plane, and not just as a place to hold officials awaiting appointments.

It was his intention then to turn the civil service examinations over to these schools; they would award the degree certification after students had passed the appropriate school examinations, and central government's Ministry of Rites examinations would then serve not to select but only to evaluate and rank the successful candidates for appointment to office. This was the most far-reaching of his ideas about how to build a stronger Confucian government of men by raising the quality of their education. The expansion of the schools, and alteration of the way in which the examinations should function in tandem with them, was strongly pushed throughout Emperor Shenzong's reign (until 1085) but then allowed to lapse.

The education reforms aroused the most deep-seated resistance. They cut directly at the interests of bureaucrats who had arrived under the old system and who had a material stake in continuing it. But other interests of the established elite also were threatened by all the New Policies. The land surveys and taxation reforms threatened their economic hold on their home localities, and their ability to manipulate local conditions to their advantage was undermined by others of the changes. Many groupings, that is, "factions," of conservatives came forth from a spectrum of viewpoints to oppose Wang's New Policies. They denounced his ideas and slandered his character and motives to the emperor; at the center and in the localities they interfered with the implementation of the new measures.

In 1074 a famine in North China drove many poor farmers off their land. Their circumstances seemed to be made worse by their debts under the "green shoots loans," which (probably by malicious design of local officials) were imposed as obligatory on all who planted instead of being a form of assistance for those in need. Farming households were thereby forced to acquire debts which the famine conditions prevented them from paying off. Inept local managers tried to collect the debts even as the suffering people fled their parched lands. A moving description of their suffering, depicted as the result of Wang's inhumane policies, was sent to the emperor; he was a humane man, and his sympathies were deeply stirred. At the same time a cabal composed of the empress dowager and some court eunuchs who disliked Wang and resented his interference in practices from which they benefited also slandered Wang to the emperor.

Wang insisted on resigning. The emperor still supported him, but awarded him high honors and appointed him prefect at Jiangning (Nanjing), where he preferred to live. In 1075, after less than a year, the emperor recalled Wang to court, but now his problems were many. Officials dared to oppose him, seeing that he had been vulnerable. Even close friends and followers began to fall away. Attacks came from various groups of conservatives, some high-minded and some less nobly motivated. These increased in intensity, making life difficult for Wang. He remained in office until late in 1076, then returned to live out the remaining ten years of his life at Nanjing, writing fine poetry and engaging in serious scholarship. He died in 1086, outliving the Emperor Shenzong by a few months.

After the emperor's death an anti-Wang group under the empress dowager (acting as regent for the new nine-year-old emperor Zhezong) vindictively pursued an anti-Wang policy. Wang was defamed, and his New Policies were in large part rescinded during the next eight years, until the empress dowager died and the Emperor Zhezong came into his maturity. As reigning emperor he reversed the anti-Wang policy and reinstated Wang's New Policies, bringing back into power a pro-Wang group. When he was succeeded in 1100 by his younger brother, the pro-Wang forces continued to hold power. The new emperor, Huizong, the artist-emperor, gave at best erratic attention to ruling and allowed strong ministers to run both court and government. Although they continued the so-called later reform or restored reform, Wang's own former associates were gone, and his policies became nothing more than an instrument in bitter political warfare.

The dominant high official at court throughout Huizong's reign was the infamous Cai Jing, a brother of Wang Anshi's son-in-law, thus connected to him in the popular mind. Cai was the very model of the evil "last minister," widely if unfairly held responsible for the fall of the Northern Song to the Jurchen invaders in 1126–27, shortly after he was driven from office.

Cai Jing figures in many works of traditional fiction, and anecdotes about him appear in innumerable informal histories and collections of notes on historical subjects. While the restored reform in fact succeeded in making some of the improvements that Wang Anshi had hoped for, and while much of the evil attributed to Cai is exaggerated, Wang's profound reform ideas no longer mattered. The degenerating political and military circumstances linked Wang's policies to the debased political behavior of Cai Jing's years in power, and thereby to the fall of the dynasty soon thereafter. Thus Wang's New Policies came to a sorry finale forty years after his death.

Wang Anshi's conservative opponents came to regret his fate and their opposition to him after they saw how the anti-reform and the restored reform phases of debased politics were carried out. While his reputation as a scholar and as a literary figure was never challenged, his standing as a political thinker and reform statesman has waited until the present time to be rehabilitated.[37]

Wang Anshi's place in history remains a contentious issue today. His achievements have been evaluated by a scholar who is widely held to be the most important student of Chinese political thought of recent times. Some of his evaluation of Wang Anshi can be cited here, to conclude this brief review of Wang's place in Chinese history:

Wang was superior to the ordinary Confucian scholar-officials in two quite specific ways: the one is his unshakeably positive and constructive attitude; the other is his realistic, fully worked-out planning . . . Wang was fully aware of the Song's accumulated weaknesses and knew that only fundamental reorganization for a new start could bring about any real improvement. In his reform policies, therefore, he started out by making the most thoroughgoing investigations, settling on comprehensive plans; then he followed through by implementing the broadest scale of actions. Seen in this light, he truly merits inclusion in the ranks of the all-time great statesmen . . .

The content of the New Policies, seen from a modern point of view, included some not fully practical features. Yet insofar as he aimed to restrict the actions of the power-holding sector in society, he cannot be faulted. But the reason his policies ultimately were so difficult to implement would seem to be that their spirit ran contrary to the tradition's long-entrenched laissez-faire practices and, further, that they took away advantages that the scholar-officials had by that time secured to themselves. Inevitably, therefore, they bore attack from all sides. In addition, his policies of regulation and control had to be carried out quickly, without adequate human resources or institutional means; those circumstances largely doomed them to failure. The remarkable aspect of it all is that Wang could carry on for as long as eight years and that in large part his policies *were* put into practice. Moreover, inferring from the existing materials we can say that the

Emperor Shenzong's focus was more on repelling the external threats, while Wang Anshi's attention was on stabilizing the domestic situation; he wanted to build a stronger basis for the people's livelihood as the means of ensuring the foundations of state power. Shenzong had his reasons to press urgently for results, while Wang turned his efforts toward strengthening the base. Later ages have admired the degree of harmony and trust between the ruler and his chief minister throughout Shenzong's entire reign, the likes of which has rarely been seen in all of history. Yet can one be sure to what degree the ruler and his minister in fact truly shared identical goals and viewpoints?[38]

VI. NEO-CONFUCIAN PHILOSOPHICAL THOUGHT

Apart from the statecraft concerns with which the newly energized thinkers and statesmen of the eleventh century had to grapple, as discussed in the foregoing sections, the early Northern Song thinkers and scholar-bureaucrats undertook to examine a very large set of more purely philosophical problems. The need to clarify basic issues in understanding the nature of human life, and explaining the cosmos that included and sustained the real world around them, in one way or another engaged the entire community of educated persons, including those whose energies were primarily involved in serving the state and, at the other extreme, those who disdained public life but shared the commitment to their culture. The nationwide community of the educated, led by the elite of public life in or close to government, served both as the performers and as the critical audience; theirs was a broadly shared undertaking to resolve divisive and contradictory issues in their various conceptualizations of how the moral universe functioned. The resulting new age in philosophy was the central element in the new culture of the Northern Song, strongly reflected in the lives of all the Song period personalities discussed throughout this volume.

The philosophical development itself, here called Neo-Confucianism, included various strands. There remained an unresolved disagreement on what we would call epistemology, the major current proclaiming itself "rationalist" (the school of *li,* or principle), the minor branch "intuitionalist" or "idealist" (the school of *xin,* or mind). This did not become an issue that sharply divided Neo-Confucians until Southern Song times. There also was the division between those who emphasized statecraft and those who emphasized ethics, but again, there was considerable overlapping and shared concern among these groups throughout the entire Song period. There were also intellectual positions that identified with more or with less of Buddhist philosophical conceptions, or with Daoist variants in the sphere of cosmology. Doctrinal exclusiveness was not congenial to the Chinese cultural milieu; Neo-Confucian developments cannot be neatly compartmentalized and set in opposition to one another despite the intensity of the debates at many points. Historically, the School of Principle which I refer to here as Lixue became the more significant trend, encompassing many distinct thinkers and sub-schools.

Here I shall focus on its emergence and the character of its fundamental achievement in resolving the issues facing Confucian-minded thinkers of the time. These are matters having great explanatory value in history, whether or not the philosophical conceptions in themselves retain intrinsic value and interest for people in China or elsewhere in the present time.

Lixue is a movement rich in cosmological and metaphysical speculation.[39] At the same time, it explored in much depth the particularly Chinese ways of defining ethics. It probed the classical writings of Chinese preimperial antiquity: the *Classic of Poetry (Shi)*; the divination text we call the *Book of Changes (Yi)*; the *Documents (Shu)*; the historical *Annals (Chun-qiu)* from the ancient state of Lu, with their three extensive commentaries *(San-zhuan)*; the writings on ritual; and the philosophers, beginning with Confucius and his school followers. It was, in short, a learned tradition, in command of exegetical traditions and philological methods. Chinese thought drew authority from those texts representing mankind's earliest accumulation of wisdom and from the force of the arguments that could be constructed from them. Since the beginning of the imperial era more than a thousand years earlier, those writings and their traditions of learning had been the core of Chinese education. Neo-Confucianism was not "new" in the sense of having discovered or recovered them, in the way that the Renaissance in European history was new in having generated a rebirth of classical learning. It was "new" in quite another sense.

Neo-Confucianism was "new" in that it undertook its scholarly and philosophical tasks in a new intellectual milieu, and therefore had to respond to an array of new questions, challenges, and problems. The intellectual milieu of the ninth and tenth centuries, when the call to restore the primacy of Confucian values was first raised, and of the eleventh century, when the Song Neo-Confucianists worked out their new philosophical systems, had taken form well after the classical age, in the wake of alien Buddhism's naturalization in the Chinese cultural environment and the concomitant rise to broad influence of native Daoism, along with Chinese family-centered religious practices and other elements of folk religion. All of those components of the eleventh-century Chinese mentality competed with the formal reaffirmation of Confucianism in their claims on parts of Chinese people's minds.

The Neo-Confucian project was a reassertion of Chinese values. It defined those at this point in China's long cultural history as transcending Chinese ethnic identity, its thinkers believing that its truths had universal validity which made them suit the needs of all humans, especially those whose cultural levels enabled them to enter into the spheres of civilized human company. If not all humans were at present able to do so, the possibility was nevertheless open to them, even those (such as non-Chinese invaders from Inner Asia) who in present circumstances could be a danger to their fellow humans of the Middle Kingdom. Some of the ostensibly Chinese inhabitants of the realm also could become dangerous to society if they failed to acquire the civilizing norms of their tradition, or if the state failed to ensure that the conditions allowing proper life in human society were maintained. Neo-Confucianism thus faced many responsibilities: to demonstrate the superiority of the Confucian philosophical position; to correct the errors stemming from the infiltration of other ways of thought and other values; to bring all the people of whatever backgrounds into the refining ritual and social practices as set forth in the accumulated body of Confucian learning; and to guide the state (and local society) into correct practices so as to work a transforming effect on human nature. That is a very large set of tasks, met in a spirit that remained essentially intellectual, secular, egalitarian, and inclusive.

So broad a set of tasks, from clarifying all the fundamental philosophical issues to working out all the essential social applications, could scarcely have been expected to display uniformity. Thinking persons, then as now, thought for themselves, lived their individual experiences, and achieved their particular visions. It was an immense movement, full of renewed Confucian responsibility and commitment. That core of essential ideas lent a sense of shared values to the intellectual leaders and to the character of their age.

The general characteristics of Song Neo-Confucianism have been described as comprising fundamentalism, restorationism, humanism, rationalism, and historical-mindedness.[40] As W. T. de Bary uses the term in his extensive and authoritative writings on Neo-Confucianism, fundamentalism means returning to the fundamental authority of the Confucian classics. Restorationism refers to the strong spirit of revival, *fugu* (returning to antiquity), the intent to regain the essential values of early Confucian thought before Buddhism and Daoism and later developments in intellectual life clouded the pristine message of Confucius and Mencius. The other three terms (humanism, rationalism, and historical-mindedness) are used in their ordinary senses. Taken together, they aptly characterize the Confucian thought of the Northern Song in general. Those qualities are equally evident in the utilitarian political thought discussed earlier; its driving impulse too was to make practical for Song times the noble qualities found in the Confucian classics. Those same five qualities also permeate much of the literary production of the age, especially evident in the prose writings and the poetry of men such as Ouyang Xiu and Wang Anshi. And, in varying mixtures, those modes of thought are evident in the five founders of Northern Song Lixue as well. Almost 200 years later, near the end of the Song dynastic era, the synthesizer of Song Lixue, Zhu Xi (1130–1200), helped to formulate an authoritative standard view of how the movement had developed and what it had accomplished. That idealized account of Lixue was convincing; it remained the accepted version of Neo-Confucianism's emergence. We cannot explore the vast realms of the new Confucian thought through Song history, but it is instructive to see, in barest terms, what those thinkers were held to have accomplished in the fundamental task of explaining their world in its cosmic dimensions, and in linking all the parts of their ethical and social principles to that underpinning in cosmology. It is a useful, if partisan, simplification of the central story running through Neo-Confucianism's history. The five founding figures are:

1. Zhou Dunyi (1017–1073). Zhou was strongly influenced by the *Book of Changes* (the *Yijing*), his point of departure for all his metaphysical specu-

lation. He also adopted much Daoist language in the course of giving Confucian meaning to his cosmological ideas drawn from many sources, particularly his concept of the "Great Ultimate" (or "Supreme Ultimate," *taiji*). His "Explanation of the Diagram of the Great Ultimate" describes schematically the processes through which matter *(qi)* is differentiated to take form in particular things. That he was basically Confucian in outlook, despite the broad range of his thinking, is made unmistakable by his consistent commitment to humanistic ethics at the center of his thought.

2. Shao Yong (1011–1077) was a man fascinated with numerical concepts; he believed that numbers reveal (or describe) the principles underlying existence. He seems to have been both mathematician and numerologist. He too based much of his reasoning on concepts drawn from the *Book of Changes,* where numbers are used to symbolize cosmic relationships and processes. Zhu Xi excluded him from his history of Lixue's founders, finding his thought not directly relevant to the succeesive steps taken to define the new system, yet greatly respecting his mind. Zhu said that in his understanding of the *Book of Changes,* Shao was superior to Cheng Yi, and criticized Cheng Yi for having failed to learn from Shao in these matters.[41] The veneration accorded him in his own time by many of the other important thinkers and scholars has given him a place in the succession of the essential contributors to Lixue, despite Zhu Xi's having excluded him.

3. Zhang Zai (1020–1077) also was greatly inspired by the *Book of Changes,* but he made something quite different of its philosophical material. He was primarily a cosmologist seeking to define the natural process underlying material existence. He identified Zhou Dunyi's "Great Ultimate" with *qi,* "material force" or physical matter in general. Although thoroughly materialist (as was all of early Chinese thought, if unconsciously so), he believed that man's nature, endowed with the purest form of matter, is ethical. In his search for ways to help the mind achieve greater clarity he seemed to embrace Daoist quietism or Chan (Zen) Buddhist meditation, as did many persons in his time, but his objective was to achieve the moral excellence of the Confucian sage. His most influential writing is his "Western Inscription," a rhapsodic reflection on the oneness of all within the moral universe.[42]

4. Cheng Hao (1032–1085) was the elder of the two Cheng brothers. It is usually difficult to know for sure which of the two brothers said and wrote what, because in their joint collected works their authorship is not clearly differentiated. They were students of Zhou Dunyi, friends of Shao Yong, and nephews of Zhang Zai, thus part of an intimate coterie of the most important thinkers and writers of the time, based at Luoyang. Cheng Hao and his brother, Cheng Yi, shared the common ground of Neo-Confucian thought, but each developed one pole of that spectrum, Cheng Hao favoring the more idealistic pole (philosophically speaking, "idea" being the ultimate reality intuitively apprehended). Both, however, stressed the underlying concept of *li,* "principle," the central focus of Lixue, "the learning of the *li*." Cheng Hao identified *li* with heaven, *tian,* a concept more accurately translated as "Nature." His *tianli,* the principle inherent in all natural phenomena includ-

ing man's nature, was the universal truth. Typically for Neo-Confucianism, Cheng Hao and his brother sought verification of their cosmological and metaphysical ideas in the ethical content of the early Confucian classics.

5. Cheng Yi (1033–1107), the younger Cheng brother, is the most important original thinker of Northern Song Lixue. Like his brother, Cheng Hao, he stressed principle, *li,* and found the way to link it systematically with Zhang Zai's emphasis on *qi,* "material force," to produce a comprehensive metaphysical system incorporating all the ideas of his four predecessors. When the term "Cheng-Zhu" is used to designate Neo-Confucian Lixue, "Cheng" refers primarily to Cheng Yi, whose strongly rationalistic thought became its major current, while the intuitionalistic complement stemming from Cheng Hao remained the minor, but always active, counterpart. The debate between those two possibilities within Neo-Confucianism would break forth repeatedly in subsequent centuries. Wing-tsit Chan has said that Cheng Yi's famous dictum, "Principle is one but its manifestations are many," has become "one of the most celebrated philosophical statements in China. It also sums up Neo-Confucian metaphysics in brief."[43] We may read it as a statement of utmost banality, yet in the context of efforts to define the underlying unity of existence, it spoke importantly to thinking Chinese of that time.

These brief characterizations of important thinkers do not of course convey the quality of their minds. They serve, however, to focus on the historically significant central issue that faced Neo-Confucian fundamentalists 1,500 years after the death of Confucius. Song thinkers had to turn back to the Sage's thought from a culturally matured and transformed intellectual environment in which philosophical horizons had been immeasurably extended. Buddhism brought with it a highly sophisticated system of logic as well as ontological and metaphysical concepts previously unknown in China. An example of the latter is the Indian concept of "nothingness," meaning the absence of all the qualities of being. This was almost impossible for practical-minded, essentially materialist, Chinese to grasp; they had never developed philosophical doubts about the reality of material existence. They consistently confused the Indian concept of nothingness with the Daoist idea of "no thing," *wu,* meaning the absence of specifically differentiated material forms, but not absolute nothingess in the Indian sense (as in the Buddhist idea of nirvana). Similarly, the very arcane Buddhist philosophy of "mere ideation" (*wei shi,* sometimes translated "consciousness only") also proved to be both difficult and unnecessary; it made no significant impact on Chinese thought. Resistance to highly abstract issues can also be seen in the debates over Zhou Dunyi's statement that "the Non-ultimate is also the Great Ultimate" (*wuji er taiji; wuji,* translated as "Non-ultimate," more literally means "the absence of the Ultimate"). This idea, expressed in the form of a Daoist paradox such as the early philosopher Zhuang Tzu delighted in, seems to try to encompass both being and nothingness in one concept. It suggests a resolution of an implicit distinction between two forms of reality. Neo-Confucian thinkers were forced to grapple with such ideas, unknown in early Chinese civilization, and to try to imagine how Confucius and Mencius would have defended their ethical and social philosophy in light of these newer concepts. The ancient *Book of Changes* was of special importance to them, seemingly used to bridge the gap between authentically antique philosophical conceptions and the more recent metaphysical challenges to pristine Confucian conceptions that filled their eleventh-century intellectual environment.[44]

There is an analogy to Christian thought in medieval and early Renaissance Europe, where the Scholastics endeavored to maintain simpler Christian truths in an intellectual world transformed by the introduction into it of the philosophical writings of Plato and Aristotle and the full range of classical Greek and Roman thought. Saint Thomas Aquinas (1225–1274) struggled, often brilliantly, to reconcile Christian teachings with Aristotle's logic and the Aristotelian philosophical system, known fully in Europe only from the twelfth century, and seen as so powerfully rationalistic that it could not be ignored. Aquinas, facing the difficulty that Aristotle lived prior to the Christian revelation, had to conclude that he had been granted "intimations of revelation" that gave his thought a special validity. By such devices the Scholastics accommodated their fundamentalist Christian faith to the newer intellectual environment. The Chinese thinkers of the late Tang and Song, in their fervent commitment to fundamental Confucian doctrine, often adopted similar means. The sequence of Lixue thinkers can be compared with the Scholastics, and the achievement of Zhu Xi in particular is sometimes compared with that of Aquinas; each produced a great summa that, far more so in the case of Zhu Xi, dominated subsequent thought for centuries by resolving questions that a more sophisticated later age would encounter in its effort to remain faithful to an earlier and less complicated system of thought. In that centuries-long process in China, the Northern Song thinkers made the initial breakthroughs; their followers in Southern Song times brought their work to a usable state by producing a satisfying elaboration and summation, one that the age found to be overwhelmingly persuasive. Song Neo-Confucianism wholly reorganized the entire field of Chinese thought; the Cheng-Zhu school in particular, though not unchallenged from within the Confucian orbit, held sway over the civilization virtually to the end of the imperial era.

7

DIMENSIONS OF
NORTHERN SONG LIFE

The "new elite" in the early Song period is looked at here in its relation to the entire society. That elite, however defined, lived in intimate relationship with the other strata of society, to which they were linked by both kinship and community interests. They did not live in a different world from that of the beliefs and attitudes of commoners, in whose lives they provided a readily understood and pervasive model for upwardly mobile people. An unusual example of elite achievement is seen in the life of Su Shi, better known as Su Dongpo, a figure of particular interest as the exuberant genius of Song poetry. But he was much more: he believed in, and was the exemplar of, humane culture's vital continuity, and of its broad relevance for the life of the society. He looked with sympathy on all dimensions of life and all varieties of thought and of art. The dominant trends in Neo-Confucian formal philosophizing, however, interested him very little; using him as a pre-eminent example, the discussion here turns to Su Shi as observer and recorder of society. His interests in Buddhism and Daoism lead us to a discussion of religions and thought systems, and to other elements of Northern Song life that bridged the space between a man such as Su and the sub-elite culture reflected in ordinary people's daily lives. To conclude, issues of population, urbanism, economic life, and trade are briefly reviewed. All were aspects of the society from which the elite emerged, and toward which they characteristically assumed a strong Confucian sense of responsibility.

1. High Culture

Developments in the world of ideas discussed in the foregoing chapter are of paramount significance in explaining some of the large trends in Song history: they reestablished the common ground of Confucian values, led to the emer-

gence of a new kind of elite leadership in government and society, and brought
about a renewal of the guiding elements for the entire civilization. Beyond
those large issues of historical significance, we may also be interested in the
impact on individual lives and on the social fabric of the admirable qualities
encouraged by the revitalized Confucian values.[1] The new formulations of
fundamental philosophic concepts became a central element in Northern Song
high culture, and in varying degrees also permeated the entire society.

The Northern Song is famed as an age of consummate poetry and strong
belletristic and historical prose writing, of magnificent painting and calligraphy, of matchless ceramics, and of a full complement of what the Chinese
looked upon as minor arts. The scholar-official elite, men as well as some
notable women from that sector of society, themselves were the creators and
producers of the poetry and other literature, as of the painting and calligraphy, and they patronized the craftsmen who made, to their tastes, the ceramics and all the beautiful objects they collected, treasured, and used in their
daily lives. They took a direct interest in the design and printing of the books
they wrote as well as editions of the classics and other earlier writings which
they prepared. Their printed books ever thereafter set the standard, "Song
printings" being the most prized whether judged by aesthetic or by scholarly criteria.

In some fields of humanistic learning the Song saw the beginnings of quite
systematic scholarship that is strikingly modern in its methods and goals. It
was an age when the systematizing and ordering of vast fields of knowledge
in encyclopedias was a characteristic undertaking. The study of the past saw
advances in historical study, in linguistics, in the critical study of classical
texts, in the collection and study of ancient inscriptions on bronze and stone,
and in the beginnings of archaeology. The Song elite "had progressed far
beyond the 'cabinet of curiosities' stage, still current in Europe at a much later
date, and were engaged in intelligent research concerned with identification,
etymology, dating, and interpretation. Moreover, they practiced, within the
limitations imposed upon them by the advancement of science at that time,
most of the critical methods and devices used in modern archaeological
work."[2]

From among the ranks of the same scholar-official elite that produced the
artists, writers, and humanists also came the persons who delved into mathematics, science, medicine, and technology, making the Song a high point in
those fields as well. Of course there also were the unnamed non-elite persons
who designed and built ships, applied maritime technology to sailing the seas,
built the bridges, palaces, and temples, sculpted the great Buddhist figures
and impressively decorated the temples, designed and manufactured weapons
and the matériel of war, and contributed in innumerable ways to the life of
the society. The dividing line between what the elite would and could do as
distinct from what artisans did whether or not under their sponsorship and
direction is peculiar to Chinese civilization. In the West the architects and
sculptors and military engineers at least were among the famous of their age,

whereas in China these were minor arts and applied skills that existed at sub-elite levels only. They nevertheless formed a point at which elite and sub-elite pursuits came together.

Perhaps one can generalize to say that all those things done with the writing brush, from composing poetry to making paintings and doing calligraphy, to making critical studies of the classics, writing the histories, and conducting the paperwork of governing, even to writing out medical prescriptions, were proper activities for the scholars. They lived by the brush, and all that came from their brushes belonged to high culture. All other activities of mind and hand, including sculpture, ceramics, decorative arts, and other creative fields, no matter how useful and valued, were the work of artisans and craftsmen, not part of high culture. As we today look back on China's cultural heritage, we have difficulty imposing that categorizing distinction on the works we see; but to recognize it is essential to understanding Chinese high culture throughout the entire later imperial period. The Song was an age when the elite culture—essentially the scholar-bureaucrat elite as reconstituted in the early Song—produced poets, calligraphers, and painters as well as philosophers, and these remained cultural icons of the civilization well into the twentieth century.[3]

In order to focus on the elite stratum of Song society, and to explain its functional roles in relation to the government above and the rest of society ranked below them, it is useful to be reminded of what is meant by elite status. Throughout the entire 2,000 years of the imperial era, Chinese society had only two legally established social statuses: there were *guan* (officers), men of official status, and there were the *min* (people), all the rest of the people. The latter category included *jianmin* (debased people), a tiny segment of legally discriminated-against persons, but that was a less than rigorously maintained status distinction, so it does not alter the main point. As we have seen, from Northern Song times onward, *guan* or official status was acquired primarily by passing the civil service examinations to gain a degree that carried eligibility for appointment to office. It has been usual to count these persons, whether or not actually serving in office, as the "official elite." The privileges of that status extended to their immediate families, and that small upper sector of society constituted China's legally defined elite. Practically speaking, the attributes of those scholar-officials were identical with those of commoners, often well-to-do, who had acquired equivalent educational qualifications, who lived like scholar-officials but without the legal status. Alongside them were other commoners who had the wealth to acquire status in society and a measure of cultivation, or at least to assume an upper-class lifestyle; they might be looked upon as an outer fringe of the official elite. Given these considerations, some historians define the elite more broadly, to include all those whose activities, judged by various objective criteria (giving support to philanthropies, schools, public works; using one's wealth to acquire social status), gained them acceptance as members of the upper stratum of local society. Because legally defined official or *guan* status did not create a hereditary closed class, such an open definition of the elite can be justified.[4] Such issues will be discussed at a number of points throughout this volume; here my concern is with the ways in which scholar-officials of the Song functioned in relation to the rest of society.

II. THE EXAMPLE OF SU SHI

The great poet Su Shi (1037–1101) better known by his alternate name Su Dongpo, can be placed alongside the names of Ouyang Xiu and Wang Anshi: all were among the creative spirits who typify the Northern Song elite. Nevertheless, his cultural achievement took him in directions different from theirs. Su was born in Sichuan, into a family that was beginning to move into the elite of rank and officeholding only in his father's generation. His father, Su Xun (1003–1066), never achieved the *jinshi* degree, but he became a powerful essayist in the "ancient prose" *(gu wen)* style favored by Ouyang Xiu and other reformers, and that gained him acceptance in official circles at the capital, where he took his two talented sons in 1056 to sit for the Ministry examinations. Father and sons all were highly praised by Ouyang Xiu; the elder Su was the most original-minded and brilliant thinker of the three in philosophical and statecraft fields, but he left a less notable mark on his times.[5] Sponsored by Ouyang Xiu, both Su Shi and his brother, Su Che (1039–1112), passed the examinations in 1057 with high standing and began careers in government. Su Shi's official career was the more troubled, Su Che's more stable and successful. All three, father and sons, suffered from the bitter factional infighting that attended the Major Reforms of Wang Anshi in the 1070s and early 1080s, and which continued to the end of the Northern Song dynasty in 1127. Together they formed the nucleus of the so-called Sichuan Faction, one of three fiercely opposing Wang Anshi's reforms.

Su Shi is the member of his noteworthy family who has seemed the most interesting to his own and later times. He was a personality who captivated his own age and who has been idealized in later ages as the preeminent scholar-official of literary genius. A closer look at Su Shi will augment our understanding of the age in which he lived. A noted modern critic has observed: "He has always been put forth as the Song dynasty's greatest literary figure; in all the genres, whether it be the essay, the regulated verse [*shi*], or the lyric poetry [*ci*], his achievement was of the highest."[6] Another recent scholar has written: "His writings on political matters were taken as the standard by the whole nation, probably even surpassing those of [his mentor] Ouyang Xiu. But his talent was so great and his bold spirit so irrepressible that he could not help turning his writing skills occasionally to playfully ridiculing people, earning their resentment. He repeatedly suffered demotion and banishment, and not entirely because of his political alignment in the factional struggles of his time."[7]

Su Shi was a complicated man. His exuberant poetic creativity and debonair spirit made him attractive to later ages, if not to all of his contemporaries; too many of the latter had borne the sting of his sharp wit. He was an all-around man, both a devoted administrator in local government and a fearless official at the court, a favorite of an unloved empress dowager and the admired tutor to the young Emperor Zhezong during the empress dowager's regency. For all his unmatched command of rhetoric and the power of his prose style, today we might judge him a sensible if not very profound writer on political policy and classical studies, two major concerns of his milieu. His fame today rests on his literary art: in his mind, to strive for the full command of learning and literature, and to express one's mind and feelings in a profoundly compelling way, represented the highest commitment of civilized man.[8]

Su Shi's political career was interrupted and finally ended by the factional struggles over Wang Anshi's reforms and their aftermath. Sent into political exile and living under difficult conditions throughout much of his later life, he turned to Daoist and especially to Chan Buddhist thought for ways to clear his thinking and settle his nagging doubts about life, but always (in his own manner) affirming his commitment to Confucian values.[9] His personal understanding of Neo-Confucian philosophy stressed "human feelings" *(renqing)* and the immediate joy of life over abstract metaphysical concepts such as the *li* (principle) on which the entire system of Lixue was built. He scoffed at Cheng Yi, the greatest of the Lixue thinkers, with whom he served at court in the late 1080s, finding him a stodgy man devoid of human emotions. Cheng was to be sure a stiff and withdrawn person, a man who reminded his associates of his moral superiority and was loved by few. Su Shi and he in fact shared much of the common ground of Neo-Confucian humanism, though they took it in quite different directions in their own lives. Su's criticism was apt, but it was inept. Cheng Yi was the leader of the Luoyang faction of opponents to Wang Anshi, but in the complex alignments and divisions of intellectual and political life at that time, shared antagonisms did not guarantee comradeship; the hostility between the Su family's Sichuan faction and the Luoyang faction was more intense than their common disapproval of Wang and his New Policies.

Su later visited Wang Anshi at Nanjing in the early 1080s, after Wang's retirement, and apologized for having intemperately criticized him in the past. The two rather liked each other. Su also served alongside the great historian Sima Guang (1019–1086), who led a third anti-reform faction and served as Chief Councillor after Wang Anshi. Su held him to be a dull and colorless person, his usually perceptive mind failing to appreciate Sima's qualities, and again leading him to antagonize the wrong person. Subsequently, however, as a fellow anti-reform courtier, Su dutifully composed Sima's official funeral eulogy.[10]

Su was easily impatient with men of his own kind yet boundlessly understanding toward ordinary people. In his earnest discussions with Chan monks, he loved to lead them into arguments that forced them to admit the validity of human feelings, thereby denying the bases of their Buddhist philosophical beliefs. Yet he was serious in learning from them. He was also intrigued by the Daoists' vast conception of nature, and even by the notions of some less philosophical Daoist adepts (often decried as magicians and charlatans).

Throughout his public life we see Su Shi as a man of strongly individualistic thinking, a questing intellectual striving to find the answers to his deepest personal questions and doubts, and simultaneously the aesthete seeking new modes of personal expression.

Su Shi is at his most attractive in his writings from the 1080s, when he was banished from court by political intrigue among factional enemies and forced to hold a nominal military post with no real duties in Hubei, just north of the Yangzi River. Ever cheerful in hardship, and especially happy when his young concubine gave birth to a son, he wrote a poem of humorous self-mockery:

> All people wish their children to be brilliant,
> But I have suffered from "brilliance" all my life.
> May you, my son, grow up dumb and stupid,
> And, free from calamities, end up as premier![11]

Himself a new father at the time, Su was especially sensitive to the plight of children in poor rural regions. He noted that most poor farmers raised only two sons and one daughter and practiced infanticide to keep their families small. Such desperate behavior among the poor troubled him deeply; he wrote a long letter to a local official urging that the practice be stopped by offering poor parents help in caring for their newborn children. He believed that parents who practiced infanticide did so out of desperation; without thinking, they would drown the newborn immediately upon birth. If only they could be prevented for a few days from carrying out that grim practice, they would become so attached to their infants that they would never again consider doing away with them. He therefore set up a charity foundation to intervene with help when pregnant women were about to give birth; it was headed by a respected local official in retirement, and managed by a monk in the nearby Buddhist temple. Local people of means were urged to make donations. He led the way by subscribing an annual donation, and was proud of the foundation's success in saving many lives.[12] This is a small but revealing facet of Su's extraordinary life.

His distinctive calligraphy set a style that long remained influential, and his fine literatus paintings (that is, "amateur painting" as practiced by scholar-officials, which became the most honored kind of painting in Northern Song times), as well as his acute critical writings on the art of painting, have given him a leading place in the history of the arts. Everything that could be done with brush and ink he did superbly. A critical edition of his collected writings runs to eight volumes and contains belletristic works in many poetic and prose genres, as well as official writings such as memorials and reports, other kinds of official documents, and his letters and diaries—about 3,000 items, among which the poems number 2,000, not including all genres in which Su wrote poetry. He established an image of the artist-litteratus who combined the romantic conception of genius with that of the courageous man of conviction, altogether a different kind of Neo-Confucian ideal from the philosophers and statesmen who usually come to mind. His image grew. From the time he became prominent in literary and official circles in the 1050s, no individual in the scholar-official ranks cut so strong a figure, matched his flair, or superseded the ideal which he represented to his own kind and to the East Asian world.

III. THE NEW ELITE AND SONG HIGH CULTURE

Not many of the 22,000 men who were granted the highest civil service examination degree (most of them earning the *jinshi* degree) in Northern Song times were nearly as original, as creative, or as difficult as Su Shi. Su Shi's mentor, Ouyang Xiu, and his reform-minded colleagues thought that the cause of good government was best served by testing for the ability to think analytically and to display originality, albeit in relation to the Confucian classical tradition. They of course held the Confucian tradition which they had striven to reenergize to be the repository of rational human experience, relevant to the problems of their own time. They succeeded in fundamentally altering the examination system in order to apply that body of rational knowledge more efficiently. They achieved a measure of success. Wang Anshi made a further attempt to ensure the same result, but he found that when he had some of his own critical writings on the classics designated models for the kind of thinking the examinations should look for, candidates preparing for the examinations merely memorized his views and unthinkingly regurgitated them in their answers to the civil service examinations' all-important policy questions *(ce)*. As a result, the opponents of his reform charged that he was trying to force scholars into the straitjacket of his thought system. He was dismayed to discover that he could not induce originality by changing the regulations.

Long-standing criticism of the examination system had been one of the spurs to the early Northern Song reformers, even before Ouyang Xiu and his colleagues. Criticisms continued to appear, even before Wang Anshi's second phase of reform. In the later years of Emperor Renzong's reign (1022–1063) a noted statesman uttered a long sigh as he observed the makeup of the higher officialdom: "Nowadays in appointing people it can be observed that they are advanced in office mainly on the basis of their literary skills. The highest officeholders are literary men; those attending the throne are literary men; those managing fiscal matters are literary men; the chief commanders of the border defenses are literary men; all the Regional Transport Commissioners are literary men; all the Prefects in the provinces are literary men."[13] "Literary men" to him meant educated men who lacked practical knowledge. The man who wrote that, Cai Xiang (1012–1067), was himself a brilliant literatus from Fujian who received the doctor of letters degree, the *jinshi,* at age eighteen, was famed as the best calligrapher of his time, and displayed an independent and critical mind. He would seem to have been the kind of man that Ouyang Xiu was striving to bring into prominence in government. But Cai expressed a complaint that became common in mid- and later Song times, that is, that the bookish learning demanded in the examinations, even in the reformed *jinshi* examinations that from the 1050s onward stressed questions on practical statecraft, produced cultivated literati who lacked a broad range of useful skills. The growing dominance of Neo-Confucian Lixue promised even less chance that practical learning would flourish.

From the mid-eleventh century onward, intellectual life turned against the Utilitarian Thought espoused by the reformers; it focused increasingly on metaphysical speculation, and led people farther away from socially responsible thought. This was the great dilemma of Northern Song elite culture: the burst of new vitality represented by Ouyang Xiu and Wang Anshi, and even by extraordinary geniuses such as Su Shi, soon became routinized in individuals' and families' pursuit of status and advantage, deemphasizing intellectual engagement. A new elite was formed by the examination system, more open to talent, considerably more egalitarian in its tone, but in the end bound to new conventions that supported the status quo. This dilemma was clearly seen by some statesman, but they could not devise a way out of it. It continued to mark the examination system through succeeding ages, through repeated efforts to correct and reform it. The system's strengths proved to be inseparable from its weaknesses. In general, we must conclude that China was fortunate in having its examination method of recruitment and selection. With all those well-recognized shortcomings, it nevertheless demanded individual (if family- and clan-supported) achievement, and it kept alive in the consciousness of society an ideal, however attenuated, of an open society.

iv. Religion in Song Life

Religious beliefs and practices in Song times and generally throughout the centuries of the imperial era cannot be understood by trying to separate them into distinct beliefs and practices that can be called Confucianism, Buddhism, Daoism, or popular religion. Each of those to be sure existed, but not within neat boundaries. Such classifying distinctions fit our modes of thinking, but not the Chinese realities in those times. Even at high levels of intellectual understanding, thinkers were concerned about recovering the purity of pristine Confucian tradition yet not highly sensitive to all of the "impurities" produced by long-standing concurrence of religious and philosophical ideas. Confucian teachings set forth in the school's classical texts are essentially secular, but they originated in and continued to develop in a society that harbored a broad range of religious practices. Confucians acknowledged those, often unhappily, while being sympathetic to elements of popular belief that supported their higher ideals, in particular when those strengthened the family's religious duties without too much compromise of principle. The revitalized scholarly study in Song times not only accommodated to intellectual currents reflecting Buddhist and Daoist religions, but also had to recognize practices throughout society that incorporated folk religious beliefs, even when, under close scrutiny, those were incompatible with their ideals. Song Confucians in general sought to maintain the superiority of their secularist orientations in mundane affairs of families as well as in the intellectual spheres of philosophical engagement, but they lived in a changing society and often were unaware of all the discrepancies between it and China of the classical age.

Confucian Practice and Popular Culture

The one set of religious ideas and practices common to all the Chinese is the family religion of ancestor worship, or, more accurately, ancestor veneration. That core Chinese belief system dates back to before the time of Confucius. The Confucian school accepted it and defined its rules of ritual and propriety, but those rules and the elaborate practices they generated required the expenditure of significant wealth. The Confucianized forms of ancestor veneration and all the related family religious practices, especially those concerning burials and mourning, tended therefore to be fully observed only in the upper stratum of society. Nevertheless, basic elements of the universal family practices, such as the belief that the surname represented one's direct ancestors so that marriage to a person of the same surname constituted incest, were maintained by the state's laws and were generally observed at all levels of the society.

China is the society in which universal possession of surnames developed the earliest, at least by the fifth or fourth century B.C.E.; by contrast, surnames were not legally required for everybody in England and France until the sixteenth century, and were not general throughout most other European societies until still more recent times. Universal surname exogamy in a society in which the number of surnames was quite limited (approximately 100 common surnames accounted for over 90 percent of the population) created social conditions unique to China. It was a distinct inconvenience for men in poor rural villages to have to find brides of a different surname, usually in another village and sometimes at quite a distance. But it was done. That is one indication of the importance of China's universal family religion.

Moreover, that family religion held priority over all other religious practice. When Buddhism introduced its very impressive forms and institutions of mass religion into Chinese society, and as religious Daoism came to imitate Buddhism in those forms and institutions, both had to function as add-ons to the religious life centered in the Chinese family. They might even add layers of practice to some aspects of family religion, such as in the conduct of funerals, but they never threatened to displace it.

Family practice of ancestor veneration was served by no priesthood and no church. The religious acts were performed in the family, the generationally senior male heir being the only one who could properly conduct the offerings and sacrifices to the ancestors, though a near male relative might be designated to act for him. Honoring the ancestors, tending the family graves, seeking protection and guidance from the ancestors through sacrifices and offerings before their spirit tablets arranged on a family altar in the home, and all the rest of those cult practices were conducted within separate family and lineage units. They therefore tended to vary widely from family to family, community to community, region to region. The regularizing impact of the impressive models supplied by the great lineages, even though of a kind few ordinary people could afford to adopt, nevertheless helped in some measure to standardize the simpler practices of humbler families.

After the decline of the great-family stratum in the tenth century, the Northern Song witnessed what we may call the "popularization" of the great-clan family religion. In their devotion to restoring the primacy of Confucian values, the new Song elite rewrote the book on the definition of the lineage, and on how families should organize themselves, honor their ancestors, bury their dead, pay properly differentiated deference to the many hierarchical degrees of senior kin, and teach their children how to behave. The elite models, purified of accumulated excesses by reexamining the classical ritual texts, were vigorously extended to as much of the society as could afford to adopt the purer, leaner versions. The principle of "doing as much as circumstances allow" was adopted to accommodate varying degrees of practice at the different layers of society. Socially conscious reformers, reinforced by the new focus on classical learning, sought quite sincerely to include the poorer levels of the population within normative practices based on correct Confucian rites. The Northern Song thus witnessed two developments of great importance in the life of the society: regularizing elite practice of family rituals according to a better understanding of Confucian ritual norms, thereby bringing about something like a new Confucian orthodoxy (insofar as a weakly authoritarian intellectual tradition could impose anything like uniform observance of an orthodoxy); and extending those corrected ritual norms throughout the entire society with gradations at the lower strata so that the poor also could share more fully the norms of proper society. Sima Guang, the eminent Neo-Confucian statesman and historian who wrote one of the most influential manuals of family ritual, commented, "It would be no small contribution to get the common people to abandon evil customs and participate in ritual." There were many "evil customs" to be combated, where "heterodoxy and vulgarity" had long prevailed.[14]

In idealistically promoting these kinds of social improvement, the Northern Song elite were aided by the new emphasis on education. The broadened appeal of the examination system encouraged attention to base-level education throughout the society, and specific policies of the Major Reform in the later part of the eleventh century led to the creation of many schools—both government schools at lower levels and eventually private ones—in all the prefectures. The increase in schools was historically very significant.

The contributing factors were many, of which the major ones may be mentioned: in technology there was the improvement and widespread adoption of printing; in economics there was the support from cities and their flourishing trade; in politics there was the attention given the matter by the government; in society there was the scholar-official stratum, promoting it whether in office or residing in their homes at their native places and within their clans. Consequently, even in the poorest and most remote rural places there gradually appeared lower-level country schoolteachers in the smallest villages. This development was broadly and profoundly epoch-making, having truly decisive impact. The norms of the higher levels of culture, transmitted through the various kinds of local education, broadly penetrated to the level of the ordinary people. As a result, all the common people in the streets, even if they could not recognize more than a few characters, could utter a few sentences of the Sages' teachings.[15]

The combined impact of broadened literacy and the effort to purify family ritual allows us to speak of the Confucianization of the whole Chinese society. On the one hand, more children in humble households than ever before were learning to read, using primers that introduced Confucian values. On the other hand, more heads of ordinary households than ever before began to consult books and experts on how to conduct household ritual matters and thereby, they believed, make their families prosper. What had been forms of ritual practice confined to the elite now began to permeate society, normalizing its social values and standardizing significant aspects of social behavior. Such a process of thoroughgoing social change was not to be accomplished quickly, but in the eleventh century the essential change of direction and quickening of pace were firmly set in place.

Buddhism in Song Life

Intellectually, Buddhism was derided, at least on one level of engagement. Daoism and, more important, Buddhism had long held sway in the lives of most people. The origins of the Neo-Confucian reaction against that influence go back to the late Tang, to Han Yu's (768–824) stirring condemnation of all Buddhist beliefs and especially Tang imperial patronage of the Indian religion. The movement of Confucian regeneration that followed in the early Song was therefore specifically anti-Daoist and anti-Buddhist. The one was seen as an alien creed that did not share the values of China's golden age in antiquity; the other was regarded as a morally suspect and misguided native tradition that had long attempted to subordinate Confucian humanistic values to those of the Daoists' all-embracing concept of Nature. Both had come to exist at many levels, from popular religion to the most rarified philosophy. But no one could unravel the intricate tapestry of thought and consciousness, to identify its Buddhist and Daoist threads, in the attempt to separate out a purified residue of Confucian ideas and values. Learned Confucians could attempt to realign the elements of Chinese spiritual life according to early Confucian standards, but they could not step aside from ways of thinking that had thoroughly absorbed Buddhist concepts. Those included the respect for all forms of life; the uses of meditation and mental discipline; definitions of being and non-being; the perceived and the real nature of the phenomenal world; and ideas of causation, of time, of emptiness, of absolute enlightenment and ultimate truth. None of those ideas finds direct textual support in the early Confucian writings, yet they had become Chinese by Song times.

Some of the most important of them had in fact developed in China, within wholly naturalized sects and movements of Buddhism, such as the Tiantai and Huayan schools. Moreover, some Buddhist doctrines, such as compassion for all sentient beings, were intrinsically so compelling that even thinkers who recognized their alien and Buddhist origins wanted to accommodate them within their Neo-Confucian humanism.

Although many Song thinkers became fervent Neo-Confucian partisans, despite a few halfhearted attempts to limit the wealth and power of the Buddhist establishment, the Northern Song was not an age in which the state would attempt to suppress Buddhist institutions or ban its doctrines. Philosophers and many of the literati (the scholar-officialdom) believed Buddhism to be inferior, but they enjoyed discussions with learned Buddhist monks, who often were as conversant with Chinese classical texts as were the Lixue masters. Mild competition between the two ways of thought and their followers took many forms. Some Buddhist temples were secularized, becoming schools or scholars' study retreats, where Buddhist patterns of withdrawal and meditation became accepted Confucian practices. Efforts were made to supersede Buddhist primacy in philanthropy, as in the maintenance of orphanages, in providing primary education, in medical services and famine relief, in maintaining homes to care for old people who had no family, and in offering free burials for the indigent. Despite the strong urge to secularize and Confucianize those activities, the Neo-Confucian secularized counterparts to those community services did not wholly displace the Buddhists. If we were keeping score on which side in this competition was winning, we might find many of the signs quite ambivalent.

Within elite spheres of life, the Song witnessed the prominence of many Buddhist monks whose achievements were central to the general cultural development of the age. Juran, mentioned in Chapter 1 as one of the prominent painters at the court of the Southern Tang rulers in the mid-tenth century, who then lived out most of his artistic life in the early Song, is only the most eminent of the Buddhist monk painters who assumed important places in Song art. Interestingly, they were more important as landscape or still-life painters than for depicting Buddhist subjects. Other monks were important in the history of calligraphy, poetry, and music, chess, and minor arts.[16] As managers of the vast Buddhist temple complexes and of the extensive architectural projects necessary to build and repair them and to manage their finances, the business manager kind of monk also played a very important role in the life of cities and towns, and of secluded rural and mountain locations where the temples were built. The great temples of the capital and other major cities, often patronized by the rulers, housed in some cases thousands of monks. But even a small county such as Yinxian (Ningpo) in Chekiang had over 100 Buddhist temples, some of which had several hundred monks and drew annual incomes from their temple lands, from donations, and from their pawnshops, temple fairs, and other businesses that made them the richest institutions in the locality.

It is easy to see that at the level of ordinary people in society, the Buddhist temple and its complement of monks remained central to the life of the village, the market town, the city, even the national capital. Buddhism also must be credited with having introduced the role of the female religious professional, the nun, thereby giving women in China an alternate social role that, despite general social disapproval, undoubtedly opened up an avenue of relative freedom to many women. Even so, Buddhist rules kept nuns in a position of inferiority to monks.[17]

Despite its important place in the daily life of Chinese communities, the authority of Buddhism in matters of social ethics and individual behavior was challenged at every turn. Confucian morality books, often borrowing Buddhist patterns though not acknowledging that, were produced for the use of common people; they stressed filial piety, which, they pointed out, Buddhist monks violated by practicing celibacy. They emphasized deference to family and community leaders, thus bypassing Buddhist authority figures. Confucian thinkers also began to place great emphasis on the idea of loyalty to the state (zhong); in the Song period there were efforts to turn that loyalty into an overriding Confucian virtue. Buddhist temples dedicated to the protection of the state had long existed, intended to display a secular and social role that would make Buddhism more acceptable in China, but at the expense of distorting Buddhist doctrine. Yet the state's interests were in conflict with those of the Buddhist institution at many points, despite the ambiguities arising from imperial patronage of some temples and other imperial gestures showing favor to the religion.

In the Northern Song period there are signs that the Neo-Confucian secular spirit scored some important victories. Scholarly concern for Buddhist texts and doctrines definitely waned as the scholarly vigor of the age turned almost exclusively to the study and editing of and commentary on Confucian writings. As for scholastic Buddhism, better scholarly editions of the Buddhist *Tripitaka* were made in the Liao and Korean states than in China, although six printings of the complete *Tripitaka* date from the Song. No matter to what extent the Chinese mentality had in fact absorbed Buddhist ways of thinking, the conscious intellectual energy of the age was expended almost exclusively on the secular aspects of China's cultural tradition, and especially on its specifically Confucian components. At the same time, the quality of the Buddhist *sangha* (monkhood) declined; no great clerics comparable to the leading intellectual figures of Tang Buddhism appeared in the Song dynasty,[18] and even the Chan (Zen) school, the most independent and intellectually vigorous of the schools, came to be marked by formalized discipline somewhat lacking the élan and spontaneity that formerly had characterized it.

Chinese contacts with the Indian home of Buddhism came to an end in the eleventh century; the centuries-long flow of learned Indian monks into China, from northern India and Indianized Inner Asian locales, was cut off by the Muslim conquest of northern India between 1000 and 1200 and the consequent widespread destruction of Buddhism there. Accurate understanding and the work of translating the Sanskrit scriptures of Buddhism in China had always depended on those contacts. The last learned Indian scholar-monk to serve at the imperially sponsored Institute for Sutra Translation, founded at Kaifeng by Emperor Taizong in 980, died in the 1070s, but the full staffing of the institute and the bulk of its translation work had ended fifty years before. When that link to Indian learning was severed, much of the vitality of scholastic Buddhism in China came to an end.[19]

Song Daoism

The Song founder, the Emperor Taizu, elaborately patronized Buddhism, and himself took layman's vows, one of the few rulers in all of Chinese history to do so.[20] By contrast, his brother, Emperor Taizong, who succeeded him, was deeply interested in Daoism, and commenced the dynasty's imperial patronage of the Daoist religion. Innumerable stories appeared about the magical assistance given to him by mysterious Daoist adepts; whether believable or not, they established an atmosphere at the court favorable to Daoist religious practices. His son, the third emperor, Zhenzong (r. 997–1022), continued that pattern. He received Daoist adepts at court, established honors to Lao Zi, the supposed founder of Daoist thought in the sixth century B.C.E., and sponsored the building of Daoist temples in many places. One of those, the Yuqing Gong (the Palace of Jadelike Purity), built at Kaifeng, probably was the largest and most expensive imperial building project of the entire dynasty. Sadly enough, it was totally destroyed by fire in 1029, little more than ten years after it was completed.[21] It was but one of hundreds of Daoist temples built throughout the realm during Zhenzong's reign. Patronage on a lavish scale continued, reaching its highest development under the Emperor Huizong (1101–1125), who accepted the magical beliefs and practices of the vulgarized Daoist religion, but also honored the philosophical tradition within Daoism by sponsoring editions of the important Daoist writings. The previous Song emperors' consistent patronage of Daoism did not exclude imperial favors to the Buddhist establishment; much less did it interfere openly with the throne's official support of Neo-Confucian learning. Among the Northern Song rulers, only Huizong was openly inimical toward Buddhism; he ordered that its properties be converted to Daoist use and imposed other restrictive measures, but most of his efforts to limit Buddhism had no time to be fully implemented before his reign was ended by the Jurchen wars. In any event, the Northern Song emperors' private devotion to Daoism and the public munificence bestowed upon it is unmatched in Chinese history.[22]

Despite the scale of imperial favor, Daoist popular religion was not as large an element in Chinese society as was Buddhism. Even so, by Song times Daoist temples *(guan)*, with their non-celibate Daoist priests or adepts, were everywhere. On the one hand, Daoist tales of the magical, of adepts with powers to see and to know and to control nature, of fighters who had mastered the arts of *gongfu*, of all kinds of extraordinary beings, were the source of much of life's humor, imagination, and color. Philosophical Daoism, on the other hand, based on the study of the *Lao Zi* (the *Daode Jing*), the *Zhuangzi*, and a few other early texts, was a part of high culture. Daoist imagery was important in literature and art. The popular religion, in contrast, took many forms, and produced a number of sects that, especially in Southern Song times, became important movements in popular religion. The social role of Daoist religion was in most ways imitative of and complementary to that of Buddhism, although in many respects the cultural forms of Daoism were more down-to-earth, less pious, more human.[23]

V. SONG SOCIETY

The population of Northern Song China traditionally has been said to have numbered about 60 million, based on interpretations of census figures preserved in the histories. Song census figures are particularly difficult to interpret, however, because of the way individuals were counted for census purposes, and because certain categories of people were omitted from the household counts. It is now believed that the traditional estimates are too low; a figure of 100 million by the year 1100 seems more likely.[24]

Compared with that in the Tang, the distribution of the population in the Northern Song shows a further considerable shift toward the Yangzi region and farther south, but still does not show the depletion of the North China Plain that occurred from the Jin occupation of North China in the twelfth century through the Yuan in the fourteenth. Throughout the Song the population increase shows a relatively balanced growth for all of China. Much of the growth was related to drainage of marshes and land reclamation projects, along with flood-control dyking and canal building to ensure irrigation; some of those projects, which appeared in great number in Northern Song times, were sponsored by regional governments, and some were carried out under private direction.[25]

Many Song writers as well as historians writing since that time stress the growth of cities in the Song. The few systematic studies of urbanization in China bear out the facts of increased numbers of cities and towns, and of the numbers of people who can be classified as "urban."[26] Figures are rarely found for urban populations apart from the total population of the county or prefecture in which cities were located. But Song fiscal records do include figures for the amounts of commercial tax paid at market towns, county seats, and prefectural capitals, and for cities still higher in the administrative hierarchy. Methods have been found for estimating the relative size of cities, using those tax data.[27] On that basis, Gilbert Rozman has estimated that in mid-Song times China's population was 5 percent urban. He has applied a system of seven ranks of cities, based on both size and function, and finds that in the late Northern Song there was one city in the first rank, the national capital, Kaifeng, in the 1-million population range; 30 cities in the third rank, ranging in size from 40,000 to 100,000 or more; 60 cities in the fourth rank, having about 15,000 inhabitants; and perhaps 400, mostly county seats and smaller prefectural capitals, in the fifth rank, in the range from 4,000 to 5,000 inhabitants. It is interesting that there were at that time no cities in the second possible rank, having populations midway between 1 million and

100,000, although in Tang times Luoyang had been a second-rank city of about a half-million inhabitants. Rozman's figures show twice the numbers of cities in ranks three through five than had existed in the Tang dynasty. Below them were two still lower levels of central places, altogether 3,000 to 4,000 of them, those at the sixth rank having periodic markets, and those at the seventh rank having no regular markets. These were mostly large villages in which half or more of the inhabitants may have been farmers; characteristically, Chinese farmers lived in farming villages, not in isolated farmhouses scattered throughout the countryside.[28] Most farming villages were still smaller—too small to be included in these seven ranks of what can be designated "central places."

This scheme is a useful way of looking at urban growth and urban settlement patterns. Comparatively, it shows that China's total figure for persons living in urban environments, conservatively calculated to have been 5 percent of the population, was over 6 million, probably equal to the urban population of the rest of the world at that time.[29] Any consideration of the conditions in China that made possible the growth of cities and towns in the Northern Song and thereafter strongly suggests that the increasing margin in agriculture made it possible to support larger numbers of non-farmers in the society. Improvements in agricultural production were due both to advancing agricultural technology and to the larger share of the Chinese population living in agriculturally rich Central and South China. To cite an instructive example, during the Song the Chinese introduced a variety of early ripening rice from Champa (in modern Vietnam) and further developed it through selective breeding;[30] in Central China two rice crops or other grain crops per year became possible, and in South China in some places three crops were regularly harvested.

Farmers' excesses of production over their own subsistence needs could go into trade. Some farmers living close to cities and towns began to produce for the urban markets, even buying their subsistence grain on the market in order to realize greater profits from growing or making other things. Their specialized production might be fancy fruits and vegetables for urban consumers, silk floss to make yarn for urban weavers, dried and processed foods, or even craft products. The interlocking processes of secondary production, transport, money exchange, and other forms of trade are all implicitly relevant, if not in our sources made explicitly so, to the growth of towns and cities. One specialist in the Song economy has said that in the Tang the rural society was essentially self-sufficient, the urban-rural link being more political (administrative) than economic. But he considers late and post-Tang changes to have constituted a series of revolutions in agricultural methods, in commercial development, in industrial growth, and in government, which made possible the emergence of a hierarchy of urban centers whose market functions handled local and interregional trade. The Yangzi Valley, he believes, became one integral market, mediated through its many growing cities and towns.[31]

If the factor of trade is evident throughout the many market towns, county seats, and prefectural capitals of the entire country, and especially in the richer regions of Central and South China, it is even more strikingly evident in the descriptions of life in Kaifeng. This great capital, with its population of 1 million, was overwhelmingly greater in size and wealth than the next cities in size—Luoyang, Suzhou, Hangzhou, and the like—which grew greatly in Southern Song times, but in the eleventh century may have had no more than one-fifth of Kaifeng's population. As the national capital, it had large numbers of well-paid bureaucrats who preferred the metropolitan postings to those in regional and local government. Even so, they continued to look to their places of origin as their homes to which they would return. The capital also held thousands of officials-expectant, awaiting appointment to office, and every three years it drew many more thousands of examination candidates, some of whom came with family members and servants, and who stayed for months or years before and after the examinations for which they had come. Additionally, there were many military officers, the military commands being concentrated in the capital region for greater surveillance over them. There were also many other kinds of lesser functionaries, including the thousands who served and maintained the imperial court and household. The lives of all those persons tended to display high consumption levels, lavish tastes, and a fascination with exotic products that appeared in the marketplaces and in the ateliers of craftsmen.[32] Moreover, it is evident from the study of the entertainment quarters and the kinds of popular shows and performances put on for very large audiences of ordinary people that the cities also presented new cultural patterns to rural folk who flocked there to sell products, to roam the markets, and to seek amusement. In significant degree that urban mingling was capable of breaking down urban-rural differences.

Such consumption patterns were not confined to the capital, but were found throughout the larger cities and towns in all the provinces. The dimensions of Song trade are considered more fully in Chapter 15, where the entire 300 years of the Song period are considered; during the 167 years of Northern Song, however, the broader trends of development are already evident. One feature of the new urban life was that all male members of the official elite, and often their families as well, spent some time at one point or another in their official careers at the capital, and when serving as regional or local officials they resided in county seat towns and larger cities of the urban hierarchy. They did not, however, as a social stratum shift their permanent residents to a few large urban centers; they maintained their attachments to their family's often rural principal residence, and to their lineage's rural gravesite. Even when individuals among them, as in the case of Ouyang Xiu, broke that pattern, they might well choose as he did a different rural site for their new family base. The dispersion of the official elite, true at least until quite late in imperial history, and to a great extent also true of those who by other definitions can be classified with the elite, was an unusual feature of Chinese society that contributed to the integration of urban and rural sectors of life, and to the regions making up China's huge landmass.

An eminent expert on Song urbanism has made an interesting comparative assessment of the significance of trade and of urban-rural relations in Song history; it provides still another comparison of China and the West in these centuries. He finds that the high levels of trade and the styles of urban living, with the ready availability of money to support varying lifestyles, relaxed the rigid social stratification which previously had dominated Chinese life. The consequence was that an easing of social barriers took place which increasingly permeated society under the succeeding Ming and Qing dynasties. That, he believes, "distinguished China from the [world's] other medieval societies."[33] Although formulated from another perspective, this analysis corroborates my own sense of the greater openness of Song society, compared both with Tang and earlier China and with contemporary societies elsewhere in the world.

8

ORIGINS OF THE
XI XIA STATE

The Tangut people were an ethnic puzzle; they spoke a language with Tibetan affinities but shared cultural features with other peoples living on the northwestern edges of China. Long involved with the Chinese, in early Northern Song times they established the warlike state of Xia (or Xi Xia), partially within China but defiantly independent of it and of the Liao empire to their east. After being established as an independent state early in the eleventh century, the Xia state was considerably strengthened by expansion to the west (into the Gansu Corridor) and its concomitant increasing reliance on steppe methods of warfare. At the same time that it was absorbing steppe values, the Tanguts' civilization also was interacting with both Tibet and China. The Xi Xia state holds an important place in Chinese and Inner Asian history of Song times, and commands the attention of Asian historians today—in its own right as well as for comparative studies.

1. THE TANGUT PEOPLE: NAMES AND ETHNIC IDENTITIES

By the standard ethnolinguistic criteria—their speech and language-related aspects of their culture—the Tangut people are usually classified with the Tibetans. Once again, we find that such criteria are less than clear-cut in Inner Asian history. Through long interaction with other peoples, the Tanguts became an amalgam comprising both sedentary and nomadic peoples of quite diverse backgrounds. The strong affinities between their language and Tibetan may provide the most convenient way to classify and label them, but it does not do full justice to their ethnic history. That is a complex and at many points an uncertain story.

The Tibetan state's history is somewhat clearer; it emerged into the Chinese historical record in the early seventh century when the center of its population and power was the Yarlung district adjoining Lhasa, in the Himalayan upland. The Chinese at that time called that state and its people the Tufan.[1] They called themselves "Bod." A broad geographical extension of the Tibetan upland to the north and east of Tibet Proper, the Amdo (A-mdo) region, occupied the borderland between China and Tibet, in modern western Sichuan and northward to Koko Nor (Qinghai Province) and the Gansu Corridor. Since China's high antiquity, as long ago as the second millennium B.C.E., we also have historical accounts of semi-nomadic people of the Amdo high grassland who bore a distinctive name, Qiang, by which name some present-day people in the region still are known.[2] It is sometimes surmised that those earliest Qiang and the later Tufan or Tibetans of Tibet Proper were once the same people. If that is correct, one early ethnic group was spread across a vast territory, and developed into at least two fairly distinct cultures. The Tufan Tibetans became sedentary farmers and herders, while the Qiang, chiefly herders, remained somewhat more nomadic. That conjectural relationship of peoples called Qiang to Tibetan and to Chinese history has long been speculated upon in Chinese historical accounts.[3]

During the Chinese Han dynasty (second century B.C.E. to second century C.E.) and after, the Qiang frequently were depicted as fiercely warlike people, at times warring against the Chinese. Subsequently, the Tibetans also made war on the Qiang to their northeast, pushing the Qiang tribesmen farther north and east into the edges of China. Sometimes the Chinese were able, by offering various material and psychological rewards, to enlist Qiang aid in campaigns to repel Tufan, that is, Tibetan expansion, away from the borders of China. Both the Tufan intimidation and the Chinese enticement may have hastened cleavages among these Tibetan-related peoples and led to their establishment as tribal groups with independent histories.

One group of those Qiang people, living adjacent to Tang dynasty China's western borders, comprised the sprawling and loosely knit tribes who in sixth-century Chinese records came to be known as the Dangxiang, or Dangxiang Qiang. They called themselves the Minyak (Mi-nyag, or simply Mi). They created the Xi Xia state. Later on the Khitans and the Mongols, in their own languages, called them Tangut, which may be the syllable *Dang* (of Dangxiang) with a Mongolian plural, *ut,* added. But other explanations of the name abound; we do not really know where it came from.[4]

Most of the Dangxiang Qiang who were outside the Xi Xia state lived within the territories claimed by the Liao empire and considered by the Khitans to be their subjects. But there were still other peoples on China's northwest borders, living farther to the west and also outside the rule of both the Liao and the Xi Xia, who continued to be known as Qiang through this period. To simplify this use of ethnic names, we can state that historically Qiang is the largest umbrella; Dangxiang is a smaller subset of people from Tang times into the Song period living to the east of the historic Qiang homeland; and Tangut is here reserved for the Dangxiang Qiang who moved into northwest China in Tang times and were the creators of and the principal population within the Xi Xia state. Using these arbitrary labels we may be able to distinguish the ethnic elements of Xi Xia history and to understand the references to them in the Chinese historical materials.

II. EARLY HISTORY OF THE TANGUT TRIBAL PEOPLE

If the problem of what to call the Tanguts is complicated, the remnants of information about their tribal history within the borders of China are even more so. In brief, the eight main tribal divisions of the Dangxiang Qiang in the sixth and seventh centuries were dominated by the Tuoba clan, written in Chinese the same as the name of the Turkic Tuoba nation which had founded the Northern Wei dynasty (386–535 C.E.).[5] Whatever that implied, the word Tuoba as used by the Tanguts may also link them to Tibet, for it is based on the Turkic word *tubbat*. The Tangut elite regularly intermarried with leading families of certain Turkic Tuyuhun tribes, and there must have been considerable absorption of people and language and of cultural features on both sides. The Tanguts thus came to bridge the Tibetan, Chinese, and Inner Asian cultural space, and competed in all three political orbits. Yet their Tibetan-related language and their long Qiang tribal heritage remained dominant in their culture, and thus even as they eventually became "people of the steppe," they did not fully share in the sense of community recognized by all the Altaic-speaking peoples who were their steppe neighbors, whether the Turkic-speaking Uighurs, the proto-Mongol Khitans, or the other groups with whom they interacted.

As early as Sui and Tang times (sixth and seventh centuries), those Dangxiang Tanguts invited by the Chinese to bolster their border defenses were settled in several frontier prefectures in present-day Sichuan, Qinghai, and Gansu provinces. They continued to be involved in disorders stemming from the Tufan (Tibetan) expansion into China's western borders. Their loyalties constantly shifted, and at times both the Sui and the Tang emperors had to campaign against them.

A major group of those Dangxiang Qiang tribal units requested permission to move eastward, well into Chinese territory, to escape pressures coming both from the Tibetans and from the other Qiang tribes to their southwest. Late in the eighth century the Tang court granted them permission to settle in far northern Shaanxi Province, at the edge of the Ordos Desert. The Yellow River flows 400 miles northward from Lanzhou in present-day Gansu Province, then turns eastward for almost 200 miles, then southward again for 400 miles, where it finally turns eastward across the North China Plain to the sea (see Map 7). Shaanxi, the province within that "great bend" of the river, becomes less hospitable the farther north one goes; the Ordos Desert in northern Shaanxi also lies within the great bend. It is at best a region of marginal grazing. The most important prefecture of that region bore the ancient name of Xia, a hallowed name from Chinese antiquity. The Tanguts who settled there in early Tang times lent crucial military support to the Tang throne from the seventh century onward; in the 630s they had been singled out by

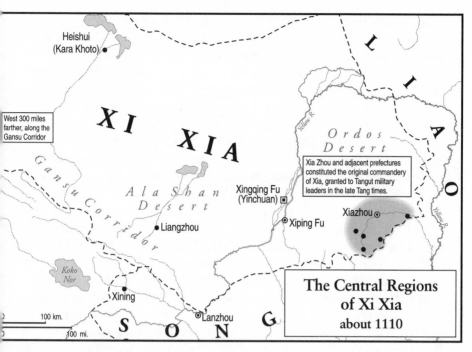

MAP 7

the second Tang emperor, who bestowed the Tang imperial surname, Li, on their ruling Tuoba clan and designated them the administrators of Xia Prefecture. Later, especially during China's internal disorders of the 870s and 880s, they gave indispensable military assistance to the weakening Tang state, as did many other border tribal peoples, including the Shatuo Turks and the Khitans. The Tuoba chieftains of the Tanguts were rewarded by being appointed Military Governors *(jiedushi)* of the region and in 883 were concurrently elevated to Dukes of Xia. Tang accounts also refer to them as the "Ping Xia tribe," that is, the "pacifiers of [the region of] Xia." Under the deteriorating political conditions of the late Tang and the Five Dynasties, the Tanguts of the Xia region gained de facto autonomy and functioned as an independent state while retaining the formalities of their nominal subservience to China.

III. THE TANGUTS COME INTO THE SONG ORBIT

In 954 a descendant of the tribal leader who bore the imperial surname Li was given a new title, King of Xiping, or "the king who pacifies the west," by the last of the Five Dynasties. In Chinese history this Tangut leader is known as Li Yixing. Through this troubled period the Chinese ever more needed Tangut military assistance, and when the Song dynasty was created in 960, it was happy to continue that relationship. When Li Yixing died in 967, the Song emperor conferred upon him the posthumous title King of Xia. That gesture, to be sure, recognized that the Xia state was politically autonomous, under no more than purely nominal Chinese suzerainty; but it also expressed the Chinese court's hopeful expectation that the Tanguts would remain peacefully submissive to the Chinese state.

As the new Song dynasty consolidated its power, its rulers worried about the few remaining border zone hereditary Military Governorships left over from late Tang times, for they possessed independent regional bases that could spawn political ambitions. The Song founder's policy was to finesse his way out of such troubles by inviting all the remaining "kings" or "military governors," whether within China or on the borders, to take high title and income at the court but relinquish their actual hold over regional power. He and his successors clearly intended to dissolve Tangut autonomy in that way, making flattering overtures to the successive Tangut leaders while simultaneously attempting to intimidate them. Some Tangut leaders resisted the Song overtures, feeling strongly that they rightfully possessed what for 350 years had been their "homeland" within the bend of the Yellow River at the edges of the Ordos Desert, and that their state had its own validity as a political entity. The weakness of China and the example of the Khitan Liao dynasty to their east encouraged them to believe they could retain those rights in perpetuity. But from 960 onward, squeezed by both the Liao and a strong new Song dynasty, the Xia leaders were under increasing pressure. The Song rulers were determined to end their autonomy by forcing the Xia to submit to subsidiary status, and to make the legitimacy of their kings dependent on investiture by the Song court. The Liao court, however, also expected that the Xia kings would acknowledge some kind of subsidiary status under them. As with Korea, caught between Liao and Song competing for their at least nominal submission, the Xia kings were forced to play a deceptive two-faced game in order to survive.

Underlying all the demands of protocol and threats of war, there also were very real issues of trade. Trade between Inner Asia and China was so lucrative for the intermediaries, and of such strategic importance for the Chinese, that much of the conflict over the control of the Xi Xia state turned on it. The commodities of greatest market value were horses, necessary for Chinese armies, and a particularly high quality salt produced in areas under direct or indirect Tangut control. At a number of border trading marts these, along with other steppe products such as furs and felt, and caravan route exotica, were traded for cereal grains and Chinese iron and craft products, as well as silks and other luxuries. The Tanguts vied with Uighurs, Tibetans, and other Qiang tribes to control the sources and the delivery routes. They steadily improved their geographic location with respect to trade and gained a near monopoly over much of it. The formidable Tangut fighting power and the Xia state's strategic position astride the Inner Asian trade routes to Central Asia gave it strong cards to play.

It fell to the Xia king Yuanhao (Li Yuanhao), who came to his throne in 1032, to play those cards with bravado and skill; he was the founder of the (Xi) Xia dynasty, the first to claim the title "emperor." The political maneuvers of the Xia leaders, from the 980s to the 1030s, created the conditions that made his dynastic enterprise possible.[6] But before taking up that story, we must first note some of the difficulties in assessing the historical record as well as the writings of recent historians; together they compound the problems of bringing the Tangut experience into focus.

Assessing Xi Xia History in Relation to China

There is no Chinese dynastic history of the Xi Xia, and no history of the Tangut people written from their own point of view, unless such a work emerges from the rich finds of recently recovered Tangut documents not yet fully known to present-day historians. We are dependent on chapters devoted to the Xi Xia in the Chinese-language dynastic histories of the Song, the Liao, and the Jin dynasties, all written by Chinese attempting to observe the official historians' obligation to write from the points of view of those states, but nonetheless writing as Chinese. The private historical writings, all by Chinese, in varying degree also present Chinese points of view. Thus we lack full information at many points; moreover, we must be very careful in interpreting the Xia leaders' purposes and motives, for we can know those only from historical records that are partisan to others' interests.

The Tangut people and their Xia state have been badly treated in the Chinese historical record, and their place in history has been further distorted by recent Chinese writers, many of whom continue to reflect Song-period hostility. Other modern scholars, also serious historians but writing about the past to make it accord with present-day political necessities, have written about the Tanguts as culturally backward "younger brothers" of the more advanced Han (i.e., Chinese) race. In this view the Tanguts, like all other peoples within and on the borders of China, had no independent history but were merely components of the process by which the larger "Chinese" history was formed. Brief passages translated from the writings of recent Chinese scholars, published in 1979, display those points of view. First, a historian in Taiwan:

> Through the 320 years during which the Song dynasty ruled (960–1279), the Liao, Xia, Jin, and Yuan one after another inflicted serious harm on China. In terms of the Northern Song, although its downfall was caused by the newly risen Jin, in point of fact it was the Xi Xia which harassed the Song the longest and debilitated China the most severely. From Li Jiqian's occupation of Yinzhou [985] and his rebellion against the Song and submission to the Liao [986] onward, the Xi Xia joined with the Liao in defying the Song. Li Jiqian's rebellious uprising was most welcome to the Liao, who strongly supported it. Consequently the Liao ruler Shengzong [in 989] married a daughter of his imperial line to the Xi Xia ruler and enfeoffed him King of Xia. Thereafter the Liao and the Xia were closely united, responding from a distance to each other's initiatives, mutually reinforcing their separate attacks, carrying out a pincers tactic to keep up pressure on the Song . . .

> The Xi Xia formed its alliance with the Liao for the sole purpose of

intimidating the Song, to which purpose it maintained friendly relations with the Liao through the years, assiduously carrying out its servile submission to them. The Liao also in successive generations bestowed the marriage relationship upon the Xia, further tying the Xia to them through grants of titles and enfeoffment, in order to solidify the Xia people's amicable submission to them. Because of the pressure exerted by the Liao, the Song fell into a diplomatic entanglement which deflected it from using its full strength against the Xia.

From the time when Li Jiqian called for his people to rebel [against the Song in 991], the incursions and attendant disorders grew steadily more severe. The Xia would first rebel, then again submit to the Song, in prolonged inconstancy. The Song court's policy was one of calling for voluntary submission and showing benevolent concern for those far away, repeatedly extending generous terms of accommodation. When Yuan-hao [in 1038] usurped the title and proclaimed himself emperor, [Song] Emperor Renzong issued an edict ordering a punitive expedition. Only at that time did the two sides formally assume the stance of enemy countries, therewith commencing a long period of violent warfare. But the Xia were men of crafty treachery and constant scheming, fiercely courageous and daring in combat, repeatedly alternating rebellion and submission, deceptive in war and deceptive in making peace, when strong invading the borders, when weak dispatching envoys to seek for accord. Through the years they constantly turned this way and that, yet through the long period of years maintained their hostile attitude toward the Song. The Song court's policies, whether of grace and trust in calling for the Tangut people to place themselves under its care, or of employing military force in punitive expeditions, encountered successive failures. During the prolonged inimical confrontation of Song and Xia, both sides used military means against the other through many decades, and their greater and lesser armed conflicts without doubt numbered in the hundreds. Although both sides knew both victories and defeats, and were alike in experiencing exhaustion, the damage done to the Song far exceeded that borne by the Xi Xia. Not only were human resources, wealth, and material goods wasted over a vast expanse of time, but also there was the loss of the [Chinese] state's prestige and authority, the decline in its international stature, the blow suffered by its people's and its officers' morale, and the shattering of the nation's self-confidence, all of which constituted even greater losses for which no value can be calculated. It induced a debilitation of spirit and a weakening of national power. "Once the problems in the West [Xi Xia] are settled, conflicts in the North [Liao] will arise." The [Jurchen] Jin then came along, and so the [Northern Song] state was overturned. The disaster worked upon the Song by the Xia must indeed be considered vast![7]

The second is from Mainland China:

From the last years of the Tang dynasty onward, some of the Dangxiang tribes came into Han territories taking up residence in prefectural cities.

The Dangxiang tribes were subject to continual division and subdivision. Those who came into prefectural cities to live among the Han people gradually accepted the Han people's feudal cultural system. Some of their nobles and tribal chieftains purchased lands and subjected the Han people to exploitation, some even going so far as to take up craft industry and commerce, acquiring extensive property. Those Dangxiang tribal households were called the "tamed" [literally the "cooked"] households by the Han people.

But the largest portion by far of the Dangxiang clans and tribes were scattered throughout the vast expanse of mountains and wilds, where they continued their nomadic herding way of life; they were called the "wild" [literally the "raw"] households. The various tribes still acknowledged no commonly recognized leader, and still had neither laws nor taxation. They believed in primitive shamanism. When someone was ill a specialist shaman called a "Si" would exorcise the demon to effect a cure. The various tribes carried on warfare and pillage against one another, and mutually sought vengeance. Those not strong enough to inflict revenge would gather their womenfolk together and go off to burn their enemies' houses. After so dispelling their anger, the two sides would then drink the blood of chickens, swine, or dogs and swear a solemn oath. One guilty of killing someone had to pay a sum in restitution for the lost life. Those circumstances clearly reveal that the Dangxiang race had achieved a system of private property; moreover, in order to seize property and slaves they carried on internal as well as external fighting for plunder. The tribes of the "wild" Dangxiang households were constantly raiding the Han people's areas in order to seize and carry off "captives" to be their slaves.

Through the Tang and the Five Dynasties period, however, the Dangxiang slave society was unable to achieve rapid development [despite their proximity to the more advanced Chinese]. Tang China and Tibet both were large and powerful states. During the Five Dynasties both the Later Liang and the Later Tang were strong enough to impose control over the Northwest. After the Khitans established their [Liao] state, they also possessed great state power and extended their control all the way into the region where the Dangxiang resided. The Dangxiang's internal and external wars for plunder could not but come under extreme limitations, which is to say that the source of their slaves was greatly limited. In the period of Song rule the Dangxiang people guadually progressed from the stage of tribal society to that of slave-owning, and simultaneously established their Dangxiang slave-owning state of Xia.

. . .

The Xia state, within our nation's northwestern area, ruled for 190 years. On its borders it had, at one time or another, the Song, the Liao, the Jin, Tibet, and the Uighurs. Among those races there occurred continuous warfare and all manner of conflict, of greater or lesser scale, but within the processes of that conflict those races also gradually increased their mutual understanding as well as economic and cultural interaction. The basic form of production of the Dangxiang people was herding and hunting, but as their relations with the Han race were strengthened and as the Xia state's territories were expanded, they gradually took up agricultural and hand-craft production, and also developed relations of commerce and trade with the various peoples. Moreover, it was the hard labor of all these people together which opened up development throughout the broad territories ruled by the Xia state, thereby enriching its people's economic livelihood. On the foundations of the Dangxiang people's traditional culture, the Xia state drew in and absorbed the culture of the Han race and that of the various other races, giving form to the racially distinctive Xia culture. In the history of the Chinese peoples' cultural development, the Xia made their own contribution.

. . .

The Xi Xia, in the midst of the many currents of interaction among the various races, created their own culture. The Tibetans, the Uighurs, and peoples of various other races also strengthened their cultural relations with all the elder- and younger-brother races through the mediation of the Xi Xia. In the process through which all the various races together were jointly creating their histories and cultures, the part played by the Xia state is one that fully merits our attention.[8]

These extracts from recent Chinese historical writing merit quoting at some length because they illustrate problems that affect all of the histories of non-Chinese peoples on the borders of historic China. The first extract, from a historian's study of exasperating Song-Xia relations, is fervently if under-standably partisan to a degree that lowers its credibility. The second, a set of three extracts from chapters on Xia history published in a college-level textbook, is so bound up in the dogmas of "scientific" historical materialism employed to support modern China's political requirements that it too loses contact with reality. Both kinds of distortion are frequently encountered. Note also that the post-1949 Mainland Chinese writings refer to the Chinese as the Han people while all other peoples who have ever lived within the borders of the present Chinese state are called "Chinese," thereby coopting them and their independent histories as mere elements in the formation of "China." In both the historic and contemporary relations, the Chinese (called the Han) are always the "elder brother." Both of the foregoing examples, representing the nationalist and the historicist (and, each in its way, equally nationalistic) mind-sets, are instructive.

Given the problems imposed by bias in the historical documents and the heavy intrusions of ideology into current academic writings, it is difficult to gain an independent view of Xia history. Nevertheless, we must strive to do so, for there is a fascinating narrative to be reconstructed of Xia relations with the Song and with the Liao courts. In particular, the half-century from 980 to 1030 is the crucial period in the emergence of the Xia state; we see it quickly developing skills to survive the changing conditions imposed by its powerful new neighbors, the Khitans in Inner Asia (toward whom the Xia were anything but "servile"), and after 960 by the Song dynasty in China, which, understandably enough, could not tolerate the insolence of yet another upstart state on its borders which refused to remain subservient to it (as the Chinese saw the problem).[9]

Song Efforts to Control the Xia

I have noted that in 967 the Xia leader Li Yixing was given the posthumous title King of Xia by the first Song emperor. His grandson Li Jiyun held the throne until his death in 980, then passed the succession as King of Xia to his younger brother Li Jipeng. This man is a puzzle for the historian, for it appears either that he was quite susceptible to the blandishments of the Song court, or that he was remarkably evasive in seeming to submit to their coercion. In 982, the Song historians tell us, he promised to relinquish the title King of Xia, confirmed to his predecessors by the Song court, in exchange for a purely nominal military governorship in the interior of China, with the understanding that he and all his clan heads would receive comparable titles and would be housed in style and comfort in the Song capital. He presented himself at the Song court at a great embassy in 982 and was invested with those benefices. He then sent out a call to his relatives to move to the Song capital at Kaifeng, to enjoy similar treatment.

Back on the home turf, his young cousin Li Jiqian, then barely twenty years old (b. 963), called together other cousins and brothers and the tribal councillors and delivered an emotional speech, the gist of which is recorded (in quite secondhand literary Chinese): "Our ancestors have been here for more than three hundred years. If all our clan should now move to the capital, living and dead we shall be under restrictions imposed by others. We would be finished." His younger brother Li Jichong spoke: "The tiger must not leave the mountain fastness; the fish must not leave the water's depths. It would be better to pounce while they are unprepared, kill the envoy from the Song court who brings these instructions, and base ourselves at [nearby] Yin and Sui prefectures. That way we can gain our victory."[10] But a cooler head advised that they were unprepared for all-out war and that there were Song garrisons close enough to strike back. It was decided instead to flee to the deserts farther north and prepare their resistance more carefully. That was early in 983.

Throughout the next three years Li Jiqian traveled among the Tangut tribes, aroused their will to resist, and led them into battles that were mostly defeats for his forces. Then he repudiated the Song imperial surname Zhao that had been bestowed on the clan. Moreover, as a further gesture of defiance he resumed the family's previously used Tang imperial surname Li (by which name I have been referring to them). In 986, when Song Taizong was engaged in his second unsuccessful invasion of the Liao, Li Jiqian submitted to the Song state's principal enemy, the Liao. He immediately gained Khitan assistance, and the course of his local war against the Song turned in his favor. In consequence he submitted tribute at the Liao court every year, was granted a Liao princess to marry, and agreed to turn all Song prisoners of war over to the Liao. Late in 990, after capturing some important Song prefectures in northern Shaanxi, he was issued a patent of enfeoffment as King of Xia by the Liao emperor. Thus he regained recognition of the royal rank on which the Song had reneged. In 991 Li Jiqian's cousin Li Jipeng was sent back from the Song court to govern his brethren at Xiazhou and to make war on his cousin and all the dissident Tanguts. The Song planned thereby to divide and rule. But throughout the next few years the two cousins, whose enigmatic relationship (as presented in the Song histories) alternated between competition and cooperation, declared loyalty variously to the Song and to the Liao. To the chagrin of the Chinese, the Tangut leaders used their dual loyalties skillfully and unpredictably to advance Tangut interests. The Liao court named Li Jipeng King of Xiping, a title some of his forebears had been granted but which was junior in rank to King of Xia.[11] In 997, when Li Jipeng seemed again to be in the service of the Song, the Liao court named his younger cousin Li Jiqian to the same title. But, like the Song court, the Liao emperor also had become suspicious about Tangut loyalties. In fact, all three sides in this struggle distrusted one another mightily. The Liao emperors alternated between sending punitive expeditions against their adoptive kin, the Tangut rulers, and continuing military assistance to them.

Liao-Song relations also grew tense in the 990s, marked by Liao raids into North China and Song defeats in local skirmishes. The Song court repeatedly sent envoys to the Khitans proposing peaceful resolution of their conflicts but were refused. All of this was leading up to the Liao invasion that approached and threatened the Song capital in 1004, and thereby produced the epochal Treaty of Shanyuan in January 1005 (see Chapter 3, Section V, and Chapter 5, Section IV). Throughout all, the Xia leaders appear to have remained in diplomatic communication with the Song yet benefited greatly from the military alliance with the Liao. They used those circumstances to enlarge and strengthen their boundaries.

On January 6, 1004, Li Jiqian died, having been wounded the previous autumn in battle with a Qiang Tibetan state lying to the west, centered at Liangzhou in the Gansu Corridor. He had moved his political base westward from Xiazhou to the city of Xiping, nearer the Yellow River, and had turned the major thrust of expansion away from the Song, against the Tibetan and Uighur states and tribes to the north and west. His cousin Li Jipeng also died in 1004, at the Song court. Li Jiqian's son Li Deming ascended the Xia throne in 1004 at age twenty-two and for almost thirty years continued the devious pattern of dual relations with the Liao and Song.

The Liao court at first confirmed Li Deming in the lesser title of King of Xiping; not until 1010 did they allow his elevation to the title King of Xia. The *Song History* claims that every year Li Deming sent envoys to the Song court declaring his submission, saying it was the dying wish of his father.[12] In 1006 the Song court also acknowledged him as king, but only with the lesser title King of Xiping, not of Xia. The *Song History* states that the Liao emperor unsuccessfully led an army against the Xia in 1020;[13] the *Liao*

History does not mention it. The *Song History*'s boast that Li Deming never missed a year in dispatching envoys to the Song court to profess his loyalty may be correct; the large gaps in the *Liao History*'s chapter on the Xi Xia and other evidence strongly suggest that throughout these years the Xia state, while still taking advantage of the Liao court's interest in it as a troublemaker to the Song, was in fact much closer to the Song than to the Liao. Song policy makers clearly saw the benefit to be gained by keeping the Xia in some kind of non-hostile relationship, and thus obtained a relatively peaceful quarter-century on their northwestern frontier. Li Deming on his part skillfully exploited the double relationship with the Song and Liao, but that changed dramatically when his son Li Yuanhao succeeded him in 1032.

IV. YUANHAO PROCLAIMS THE XIA DYNASTY

In Chinese histories (Li) Yuanhao (or Zhao Yuanhao, as Song histories call him) is described as "of virile and resolute character, a man of vast plans, a skilled painter, a man who could create and establish institutions anew. He had a round face and a high-bridged nose, and was over five feet [*chi*] tall." He liked to ride and shoot, but he was also a man of intellectual attainment: "He was knowledgeable in Buddhist studies, and had mastered both Chinese and Tibetan writing; he kept works on law on his desk."[14] He clearly was a man of many-sided culture, quite at home in both the Chinese and the Tangut spheres. That did not create problems as it did for the early Khitan Prince Bei, the son of the Liao founder, for in this stage of their history the steppe nomad values did not dominate Tangut life, and dual cultural attainment did not arouse suspicions of weakness and unworthiness. Steppe values would come to be more important under Yuanhao. Before ascending the throne, when still in his early twenties (he was born in 1003), he personally led troops to attack and defeat both the Qiang and the Uighurs at Ganzhou and Xiliang (present-day Wuwei) in the Gansu Corridor. This was a momentous turning point in the Tangut effort to dominate the previously victorious Uighurs and to expand Xia military might into the steppe. The Tanguts' adaptation to mobile warfare demanded access to richer grazing lands for cavalry horses, and the best grasslands within the sphere of Tangut expansion were those in the Gansu Corridor. The son's military successes induced his father to have this capable military leader invested as the heir apparent, adopting that Chinese institution to strengthen the throne and guarantee a smooth succession.

The young prince was independent-minded and did not always approve of his father's rule. According to the *Song History:*

> He repeatedly remonstrated against his parents' willing servitude to the Song. Once his father admonished him for that, saying: "I have long led armies, but now I am tired. Our clan for thirty years has been clothed in brocades and fine silks. That is the favor bestowed by the Song; we must not be ungrateful for it." Yuanhao responded: "To dress in skins and furs and to tend one's flocks and herds are more natural to the Tangut nature.

A bold leader's life should be that of the kings and conquerors; what does that have to do with brocades and fine silks?"[15]

It was clear that he intended to launch a new era in Tangut history.

Yuanhao's Cultural Policies

Yuanhao's intentions became evident in his cultural policies immediately upon his succession to the throne in 1032. These turned sharply away from the pattern of the recent Tangut past, as he pressed for the recovery of native elements at the expense of Chinese influences. Perhaps moved by the already century-old Khitan example, in 1037 Yuanhao ordered the adoption of a new script designed to fit the Tangut tongue but, like the Khitan scripts, using graphic elements derived from Chinese characters. It is said that he and his principal adviser, also highly educated in Chinese, helped to devise this script, or to compile a volume of writings explaining it.

That the new script was based on Chinese writing instead of on Tibetan offers an intriguing puzzle. The Tibetans in Tibet had adapted an Indian alphabetic script to their language in the seventh century. One might think that linguistic and cultural affinity would have led the Tanguts to adjust that much simpler script to their related language (as the Mongols later did in adopting Uighur alphabetic script to their language). Instead, they invented a script having about 6,000 characters with which to write their tonal, mono-syllabic language. An expert on the Inner Asian scripts has called it, "a script of great beauty and elegance, but of enormous complexity."[16] Most of its characters combine two elements, in which each element represents either an aspect of the semantic content combined with the other half to indicate meaning, or one-half of the phonetic value of the word, the two halves in combination indicating its pronunciation.[17] Most Tangut characters are written with more than ten strokes. The Chinese scholar who in 1804 was the first in recent centuries to find and identify examples of Xi Xia writing said of the script forms: "At first glance they all appear to be recognizable, but on closer scrutiny there is not a character one can read."[18]

Why did the previously illiterate Tanguts (illiterate in their own language, that is, for many of their elite were literate in Chinese and other languages), at a time when they were enlarging their independence of Chinese cultural influences, decide to create a new script derived from the none-too-facile Chinese way of writing? Chinese historians of course see this as evidence of the overwhelming power of the Chinese cultural example. But the example of the Khitans may have been the pertinent model: they had successfully created a new script (actually two new scripts) instead of relying solely on the Chinese language and its script. The Tangut script, however, came to be more widely used in the Xi Xia state than were the two Khitan scripts in the Liao realm. All official documents and national records were written in the new script exclusively, many Chinese works were translated in it, and a state printing bureau published materials in it. Communications with other states were bilingual, the Tangut text accompanied by a translation into the appropriate language where a script existed—Chinese, Khitan, Uighur, or Tibetan. The discovery in the last hundred years of such bilingual documents has aided the largely successful (if not yet widely known) decipherment of the Tangut script.[19]

Matters of State

The importance of the Chinese language in international relations and protocol was recognized in the establishment of dual secretariats, one using Tangut and the other using Chinese. That suggests the analogy of the Khitan Northern and Southern Chancelleries, but there are significant differences. For 300 years many of the Tangut tribal nobility had held Chinese appointments as officials nominally subservient to the Tang and the Five Dynasties; they included many individuals who could use Chinese in official contexts. Many Han Chinese families originally resident in regions acquired by the expanding Xia state came to serve in the Xia government. The Xia state, however, unlike the Khitan state, did not include a sedentary alien majority. According to some scholars, its sedentary population was largely Tangut, or Chinese and others who were in some degree assimilated into Tangut ways. They could readily be governed by Tanguts using their own new script, once the new emperor insisted on it.

Other efforts of the 1030s and 1040s display Yuanhao's desire to eliminate or reduce Chinese influences. He repudiated both of the imperial surnames previously bestowed on his clan, the Li surname from Tang times and the Zhao surname from the Song dynasty; he adopted a Tangut surname which, transcribed into Chinese, sounds like "Wei-ming" in modern pronunciation. Here we shall call him simply Yuanhao to avoid the confusion arising from the three surnames found in various kinds of early writings. Introducing strong cultural reform measures, he ordered, for example, that all male heads should be shaved within three days or be lopped off, and the old Tangut headress and clothing be restored. That rejection of Chinese manners was symbolically significant. At the same time, he also formally rejected Confucian humanism as unsuited for a warlike steppe people (which he hoped his people were becoming). Nevertheless, he may have found a Chinese political tradition that appealed to him. He is said to have been much interested in the study of laws, and the inference drawn from the way that is stated in Chinese is that he studied the ancient Chinese Legalist statecraft tradition, attracted to its doctrines of rigid discipline, harsh punishments, and full mobilization of society for warfare and the production of wealth to sustain warfare. The reorganization of his government seems to have consisted mainly in using Tangut names for offices and titles; if he devised more innovative approaches to governing, that is not made clear in the Chinese historical record.

Strengthening the Military

The reorganization of the military component appears to have been more thoroughgoing. As in other tribal societies, males were considered adult at the age of fourteen or fifteen and were then conscripted. Yuanhao departed from known precedents in forming new kinds of military units. One unit was an army said to have numbered 150,000 men conscripted in two categories, "regulars" and "bearers," on a one-to-one basis or, according to some accounts, two regulars to one bearer. They formed a fixed unit, were quartered together as a team, and in battle had complementary tasks. The regulars bore the brunt of fighting while the bearers systematically looted, took captives among the enemy's nonmilitary population, and seized livestock. This kind of warfare was highly effective against sedentary neighbors.

Yuanhao also enhanced the role of cavalry, organizing his enlarged personal mounted guard along new lines. Its 5,000 members were drawn from leading families in the tribal nobility. It not only formed the elite corps of the army, but also was the instrument for holding hostage the heirs of each noble clan. It is clear that he increasingly identified with the steppe interests, that is, with cavalry warfare and with expansion to the north and west instead of into China. Organizing large segments of his population more directly for mobile warfare served that cause, as did elevating warfare to the position of the state's primary activity. Such "Legalist" touches, if indeed his study of that discredited early Chinese political school explains them, are evident at a number of points in Yuanhao's new governing style.

V. THE XI XIA AS AN IMPERIAL DYNASTY

In 1038 Yuanhao proclaimed himself the head of a new dynasty called the Da Xia (the "Great Xia"). In Chinese records it usually is called the Xi Xia (Western Xia). In many ways that action parallels the Khitans' adoption of the Chinese imperial institution when Abaoji created his imperial state in 916. The rhetoric of rulership was Chinese. Adopting it and all its associated concepts and practices, especially its claims of exclusivity and universality, was a way of pointedly rejecting the concept of China as the center of the universe. By calling himself *huangdi,* or "emperor," and simultaneously adopting his own calendar and reign period names, Yuanhao was infringing on prerogatives which the Chinese emperors long had regarded as exclusively theirs. The Liao had already done the same, so that two "Sons of Heaven" heading universal empires already coexisted in close proximity. Now, with the Xi Xia also making such claims for their state, there were three "Sons of Heaven," but there were differences among them. The Song leaders had been forced to accept the Liao empire as a state on equal footing, grudgingly granting it a measure of Chinese respect, but the Xia remained in their eyes merely a "western barbarian state." The Song emperor therefore immediately rejected Yuanhao's new competing claim; the Chinese took their Heavenly Mandate to exercise universal and exclusive sovereignty more seriously than did their Khitan competitors, even when the Liao were strong enough to turn the Song claim into empty rhetoric. The Song immediately closed the borders to commerce with the Xia and made threatening gestures. The Liao, for their part, could wink at the Xia impertinence, for they had already forced the Song emperors to admit the realities of a multistate system. The Liao rulers appreciated the value of the Xi Xia as a threat to Song security, and allowed Yuanhao to call himself by any title he wished—in dealings with others. But the Liao court was no more willing than the Song to grant the Xi Xia state even symbolic equality in their bilateral relations; they continued to invest the Xi Xia "emperor" as King of Xia, a title that no emperor needed, and that no truly universal sovereign could have tolerated.

We translate the grandiose title *huangdi,* used by Chinese emperors since the third century B.C.E., as "emperor," but that is not strictly correct. It implies that the Chinese state is an "empire," which in our historic usage implies extending control over other nations and peoples. Strictly speaking, the Song state was not truly an empire, despite relatively small numbers of minority peoples within its boundaries; essentially it corresponded with the area of Chinese cultural unity, and it did not wish to go much farther. The Liao state was genuinely an empire, in that the Liao central government created by the Khitan nation was in fact extended over many other nations and peoples. The Xi Xia dynastic state was not "imperial" in that strict sense. It was, to be sure, a strong state formed around the core Tangut population, but one that never included all of its ethnic brethren under its rule. It did not have much potential for imperial expansion, and it did not impose its rule on large numbers of non-Tanguts. Its conquered Chinese population, probably fewer than 1 million, was its largest minority group; it occasionally defeated but did not govern its Inner Asian neighbors. By claiming to be a *huangdi* and establishing a Chinese-style dynasty, Yuanhao demanded for his state the highest dignity that the political vocabulary of East Asia could express, but that was largely a matter of semantic inflation, whether we think of the title as really meaning "emperor" or, more correctly, as meaning a ruling figure in the grandiose mode of the Chinese head of state.

The problem of how to translate *huangdi* complicates all our efforts to understand Chinese and other East Asian polities. Nonetheless, we are constrained by common practice to translate it "emperor" in most contexts.

Whether or not he deserved to be called *huangdi,* Yuanhao adopted all the appurtenances of the Chinese-type imperial institution even as he rejected Confucianism. He posthumously bestowed upon his grandfather Li Jiqian the temple name of Taizu ("Grand Progenitor," the standard Chinese title for a dynastic founder) and gave the title Taizong ("Grand Ancestor," the standard Chinese title for the second ruler of a new dynasty) to his father, Li Deming (Chart 3). An ancestral temple was built, and regular sacrifices on the pattern of the Chinese court were instituted. When he died, the Taizu title was therefore not available for his temple name, so he appears as Jingzong, the "Splendid Ancestor," a rather ordinary posthumous temple name that obscures his actual role in founding the dynasty.

Whether or not truly "imperial," the Xi Xia state was militarily quite powerful, and from the moment he assumed the imperial title in 1038, Yuanhao turned the might of his cavalry to the task of defending against the Song. The Song attacked almost every year, sending an army against some point on their

CHART 3. THE XI XIA SUCCESSION, 1032–1227

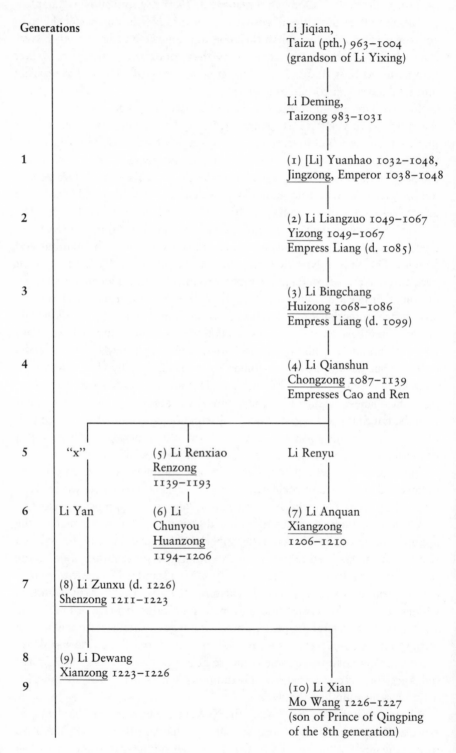

Generations

Li Jiqian,
Taizu (pth.) 963–1004
(grandson of Li Yixing)

Li Deming,
Taizong 983–1031

1   (1) [Li] Yuanhao 1032–1048,
Jingzong, Emperor 1038–1048

2   (2) Li Liangzuo 1049–1067
Yizong 1049–1067
Empress Liang (d. 1085)

3   (3) Li Bingchang
Huizong 1068–1086
Empress Liang (d. 1099)

4   (4) Li Qianshun
Chongzong 1087–1139
Empresses Cao and Ren

5   "x"   (5) Li Renxiao   Li Renyu
Renzong
1139–1193

6   Li Yan   (6) Li   (7) Li Anquan
Chunyou   Xiangzong
Huanzong   1206–1210
1194–1206

7   (8) Li Zunxu (d. 1226)
Shenzong 1211–1223

8   (9) Li Dewang
Xianzong 1223–1226

9   (10) Li Xian
Mo Wang 1226–1227
(son of Prince of Qingping
of the 8th generation)

common boundary and often suffering severe defeats. The threat from Xi Xia bore heavily on Song policy making, but the inept Chinese military actions against the Tanguts in the late 1030s and early 1040s were costly. In 1042 the Liao ruler, observing how successfully the Xi Xia were menacing the Song, joined the Xia in threatening to invade. That realized the Song rulers' worst fears of a Liao–Xi Xia alliance against them. The threat was enough for the Song to offer the Liao a large increase in the annual peace indemnity paid to them.

In granting the increased indemnities to the Liao in 1042, the Song court hoped that China had bought the assurance that the Liao would keep tight reins on their Xi Xia vassal. As for Yuanhao, he was furious that Tangut military actions against the Song throughout the preceding years had been used by the Liao to gain favorable terms in the treaty revision of 1042, while the Tanguts had gained nothing. The Song court, following these matters closely, managed to apply influences that would induce Yuanhao to make war on the Liao in 1043, and in 1044 sent an envoy to invest Yuanhao with the long-withheld title King of Xia. That led to a treaty by which the Song agreed to pay the Xi Xia an annual indemnity on the model of their annual payments to the Liao. Under the agreement worked out in 1044, the Xi Xia received annually 130,000 bolts of silk, 50,000 ounces of silver, and 20,000 catties of tea. In addition, on the three big annual festivals and on Yuanhao's birthday the Song sent "gifts" of 20,000 ounces of silver, silver vessels weighing 2,000 ounces, 23,000 bolts of various silk textiles, and 10,000 catties of tea. The Song agreed to bypass the delicate problem of whether to address the Xia ruler as "king" or as "emperor" by referring to him in interstate documents simply as the "ruler" *(zhu)* of Xia.

Xi Xia–Liao Relations

While the Song and Xi Xia were thus resolving their differences, the Liao emperor personally directed a punitive campaign against the Xia. He was angered that certain Dangxiang (that is, Tangut) tribal groups within the Liao empire's western borders had revolted, emboldened by Yuanhao's successes, and had sought support from the Xi Xia throne. The Khitan ruler led an army of 100,000 to the undefended Xia borders and defeated a Xia army quickly sent to repel the invasion. Yuanhao went in person to the Liao capital, offered apologies, and sued for peace. He acknowledged that it had been an error for him to seem to extend Xi Xia protection over brother tribes long within the Liao sphere.

At that juncture, inept Liao officials argued that since they had gone to the trouble to send so large an army into the field, they should maximize their advantage by going ahead with their offensive. Having returned to his capital, Yuanhao now called up all his nation's forces and soundly defeated the Khitan invaders. The Liao emperor set up negotiations for peace, and the two sides exchanged prisoners and agreed to resume proper diplomatic relations. The Xia had demonstrated to the Liao, and to the Song, that after over a half-century of reliance on Liao support, they now were able to stand up for themselves. Then, in 1048, Yuanhao was assassinated. The Liao invaded again in 1049, and in part because of the confusion caused by the assassination, the Liao prevailed. The Liao and Xia alternately warred and negotiated for a number of years. They did not remain in permanent hostility thereafter, yet the ever-vigilant Song manipulation can be said to have eased the threat of an effective Liao–Xi Xia military alliance against China. Complex triangular diplomacy in that pattern continued to be played out through the eleventh and twelfth centuries.

Moving the Xi Xia Capital Westward to the Yellow River

By Yuanhao's reign the Xia territories had expanded from the original five prefectures clustered around Xiazhou in north-central Shaanxi to eighteen prefectures. The boundary in the northeast was extended some two-thirds of the distance across northern Shaanxi, in the direction of both the Song and the Liao boundaries. By late in the eleventh century the Xia state's boundaries extended 300 miles to the north from Xiazhou, into the Gobi Desert, and 900 miles to the west to include all of the Gansu Corridor and beyond. That region, between 700 and 800 miles east to west and over 500 miles north to south, included vast areas of desert. The core of the state was a smaller zone of mixed agriculture and grazing centered on the portion of the Yellow River that flows northward from Lanzhou, containing important irrigation works, some dating from the Qin and Han dynasties a thousand years earlier. The original Xiazhou's prefectural city, in the present day a long-abandoned site, was just north of the Great Wall line where it cuts across Shaanxi, and south of the Ordos Desert, which makes up much of northern Shaanxi. From that political and spiritual center of the Tangut people, the actual center of military and political action had been shifting westward to the Yellow River. Li Jiqian had moved his base area westward to the strategic outpost called Lingzhou, renamed Xiping by him in 1003; it lies just east of the Yellow River. His son Li Deming subsequently walled the city of Xingzhou just west of the Yellow River when he made it his capital in 1022. In the 1030s Yuanhao enlarged the walled area of Xingzhou, gave it the alternative name of Xingqing Fu, and built new palaces and gates in anticipation of its becoming his national capital in 1038, when he proclaimed himself the emperor of a new dynasty. It was very near the site of present-day Ningxia, or Yinchuan. The two cities, Xiping on the east side of the Yellow River and Xingzhou on its west bank, remained the political centers of the Xia state (see Map 7).

Domestic Problems

Fierce factional fighting plagued Yuanhao's reign. The dissenting factions composed of members of the tribal elite who (like the Khitan tribal elite in response to Abaoji's structural changes) resented the centralizing consequences of the ruler's enhanced powers. Yuanhao took wives from four leading Tangut clans as well as a princess from the Liao imperial household. His relations with the Khitan princess were not friendly; she died without issue in 1038. He left at least two possible heirs: one, born in the 1030s to a consort from the Yeli clan, was named his heir in 1043; the other was born in 1047 to a woman of the eminent Mozang clan. This woman was belatedly elevated to the rank of empress after she had given birth to his son, Li Liangzuo. Quite unconventionally, the birth occurred in Yuanhao's traveling tent while he was on a hunt. There are hints of scandal and impropriety in this liaison. This infant son was taken to be reared by his maternal uncle, the head of the powerful Mozang clan, who was now named chief of the imperial household, tantamount to becoming head of the Tangut secretariat in charge of governmental affairs. Members of an opposing clan, supporting the other heir, forced their way into the palace early in 1048 and assassinated Yuanhao. A bloodbath followed as opposing clans warred for control of the throne by supporting rival princes.

The factional violence was not resolved until 1061. It weakened the Xi Xia state for more than a dozen years. Some scholars see in it manifestations of a deep conflict in Tangut society between forces in favor of restoring the Chinese patterns and values and those of "nativist" reaction that favored the steppe-oriented military society. The younger heir, Li Liangzuo, who was born in the hunting tent in 1047, emerged from the factional warfare as the accepted emperor, and starting in 1061 he carried out widespread reversals of his father's cultural policies. He restored the use of the imperial surname Li, dating from Tang times. He sent an embassy to the Song court announcing the restoration of Chinese rituals and protocols and asking for a gift of Chinese books. The Song emperor sent a full set of the Confucian *Nine Classics*. Border disputes with the Song were amicably settled, and long-closed border trading stations with the Song were reopened. The young emperor's consort was from a family from Xiazhou, of the surname Liang, probably originally of Chinese background. The emperor is said to have enjoyed the company of Chinese and to have had a taste for the study of Chinese literary works. There are widely varying ideological interpretations of these developments, ranging from Chinese sentimental explanations of the power and attraction of the advanced Chinese civilization in a tribal society, to Marxist ideological interpretations that see continuing dominance of slave society elements in the militarist and nativist factions opposing the more advanced feudal tendencies stemming from contacts with Chinese society.

Such irrelevancies aside, the real phenomenon here is the use made of cultural policy in factional struggles that put Tangut society, or at least its elite sector, under great stress. It points up the dilemmas of Inner Asian tribal societies under pressures to change. Some of their leaders saw opportunities to exploit the techniques of social organization that they observed among their much richer sedentary neighbors. They were challenged by others in their society, the military leaders who controlled the instruments of warfare and coercion, but whose hold on power was often insecure. The diversity of responses in different societies in this period holds great interest for the historian; the Xia experience provides one of the valuable cases for comparative study.

Emperor Yizong, as Li Liangzuo is known to history, clung to his advocacy of sinification even though a diplomatic dispute with the Song court in 1064 led to several years of border warfare. The Chinese arrogance and diplomatic bumbling (they insulted the Xia envoy to their court and refused to make apologies) led the angered Xia to respond with border raids, in turn drawing a strong punitive attack from the Song armies. The great Chinese historian Sima Guang, then head of the Remonstrance Bureau at the Song court, strongly objected to this failure to deal appropriately with the Xia and the failure to take advantage of opportunities to extend Chinese influence by peaceful means.[20]

When the Xia emperor Yizong died in 1068, he was succeeded by a seven-year-old heir, Li Bingchang, who became the Emperor Huizong. His mother, of the Liang clan and now the dowager empress, became regent. She was strongly supported by her brother, General Liang Yimai. His name as written with Chinese characters appears to be a rough approximation of a Tangut sound; this suggests that even if the Liang clan was remotely Chinese, it had been assimilated into Tangut culture. The pro-Chinese court had been humiliated by defeats at the hand of Song armies in 1064, and now, in order to strengthen their hold over the Tangut nobility, the court had to pursue a strongly anti-Chinese policy including the rejection of the late emperor's cultural program. By the time the young emperor came into his late teens, however, he declared himself in favor of his father's former policies in opposition to his Liang clan mother and uncle, who had controlled the government during his minority. He overruled them, offered to make peace with the Song, and again resumed the sinification program. In 1081 his mother and uncle placed the independent-minded young emperor (he was now twenty-one) in custody at an isolated garrison post. This again threw the country into virtual civil war.

The Song court, watching this internal struggle intently, chose this moment to invade the country in force. For several weeks in the winter of 1081–82 the Song were able to penetrate the defenses, but they did not have adequate force to hold their conquests, and in 1082 were decisively beaten and forced to withdraw in panic and disorder, suffering great losses. In the following year the empress dowager decided to restore her son to the throne in a move to reunify the warring factions. Part of the arrangement was that he marry his cousin, the daughter of General Liang Yimai, thus giving the Xia state two empresses, aunt and niece, from the same Liang clan, albeit from different generations. The Song armies still held the Xi Xia southern territory near the city of Lanzhou, and Xia attempts to dislodge them continued for several years. Then, between November 1085 and August 1086, the dowager empress, her brother General Liang Yimai, and the emperor all died within the space of a few months.

The emperor left a three-year-old son as his heir, the future Emperor Chongzong, who reigned for fifty-three years until his death in 1139. The struggle among the clans broke out anew at his succession and continued for more than a decade, as did the intermittent but often fierce border war against the Song. In 1092 we see the younger Empress Dowager Liang, the mother of the now six-year-old emperor, personally leading troops in the field against a Song army. She was badly beaten on this occasion and had to flee the field in disguise, barely escaping with her life. In 1094 an uprising of dissident Tangut nobles killed off most of the Liang clan but left the empress in charge of the government. She continued to lead armies in the field with alternating success and failure through the 1090s; after some important victories she suffered setbacks and in 1099 appealed to the Liao for assistance. According to quite plausible Chinese gossip, a Liao envoy accompanying a relief army to aid her administered poisoned wine to kill her, and arranged matters so that her many Tangut enemies received the blame. The Liao, no strangers to strong female rulers, nonetheless had found her a willful and troublesome vassal. After her death the Liao could all the more easily intervene in domestic matters to support her now fourteen-year-old son, the newly orphaned Emperor Chongzong, as he assumed direct control of throne and government. During the next decade he too returned to the earlier sinification policies. He also managed to make the tribal chieftainships appointive kingships, as the Khitans had done, and in that and other ways achieved a new measure of centralized authority.

Continuing Dilemmas of "Nativism" versus "Sinification"

The long period of struggle between "nativists" who benefited from a weak throne, and their opponents who pressed for political changes on the Chinese model and sought to strengthen the imperial institution, was drawing to a close. Under Chongzong the adoption of Chinese cultural norms reached new heights. Latent opposition to that policy, however, was not wholly eradicated. As Chinese sources report it, the leaders of the opposing factions continued to memorialize the throne, calling for resumption of the Legalist-sounding "strengthening and enriching" policies, condemning Confucian values for sapping the vitality of the fighting men, and praising the governing concepts that had been promoted by Yuanhao, the dynastic founder, during his eighteen-year pursuit of nativist policies.

Even discounting for the obvious bias in the Chinese sources, we see the curious spectacle of Tangut ethnocentrism employing the ancient Chinese statist philosophy to articulate its resentment of overrefined, militarily weak tendencies associated with Confucian learning. To the modern reader this may evoke thoughts of other times and places. It finds a late echo in Mao Zedong's glorification of Legalism and vilification of Confucius in the 1970s, in defense of his primitivist nativism that marked the era of the so-called Great Proletariat Cultural Revolution. Yet, from the point of view of the Tangut nation, an attempt at this time to cling to the qualities of preliterate militarized nomadism is not without justification. There was a real danger that the Tanguts would lose their national integrity, even though that now was maintained by the greatly expanded reliance on nomadic-style, highly mobile steppe warfare. In the Tangut case, "nativism" refers not to the pristine Tangut way of life still followed in the ninth century, but to an alternative to sinification that developed in the late tenth and early eleventh centuries when Li Jiqian and Yuanhao turned Tangut expansion toward the west to exploit the potential in cavalry warfare.

The Khitans and the Mongols both came out of the steppe into the Chinese orbit, but by quite different means in their two cases escaped the kind of internal crisis that afflicted the Tanguts. The Xia experience offers a foretaste of the Jurchen crisis, even though under different circumstances vis-à-vis China. Chinese civilization induced different responses in each of the various Inner Asian nations that bore its impact, even though they all were tribal societies at more or less the same levels of development. Those differences obviously are to be explained by the distinctive elements in their individual histories, their cultural awareness, and the particular choices different leaders made as they utilized their varying opportunities. Those problems of later Xi Xia history will be explored in Chapter 11.

PART TWO

CONQUEST DYNASTIES AND THE
SOUTHERN SONG, 1127–1279

Overleaf:

Spring Festival on the River

Zhang Zeduan (active early 12th century). Detail, handscroll, ink and color on silk. Palace Museum, Beijing. From reproduction 1958, Beijing, in the author's collection.

Famous for its lively draftmanship and close observation of ordinary life, this detail depicts life in the side streets, suburbs of Kaifeng, the Song capital.

9

THE "WILD JURCHENS"
ERUPT INTO HISTORY

In Aguda the "wild Jurchens" had a founding figure resembling the Khitans' Abaoji in legendary stature, but the circumstances of the Jurchens' rise are as different as the two leaders' personalities. Here we follow the Jurchens' sudden burst into history and their rapid destruction of the Liao empire followed immediately by their conquest of Song territories in North China. A necessary digression then continues Khitan history in the creation of the Kara Khitai offshoot of the Liao empire, far to the west of China. The Jurchen conquests are briefly narrated first as their victorious triumph over two formidable enemies; following that, the tale is twice retold from the other side, as the baffling collapse of Liao power, and as the ignominious defeat of the Song. Seeing this event from the varying points of view may aid assessment of the military conflict per se, and also amplify understanding of other contributing elements. Finally, the account returns to the background of the Jurchen people, the rise to leadership over them of the Wanyan clan, and their astounding success as a new conquest dynasty under Aguda and his brother Wuqimai.

During the more than three centuries from the end of the Tang dynasty in 907 until the Mongols completed their conquest of China in the years 1275–1279, China's history had no single center. The mainstream of the Chinese people's history, to be sure, was the history of the Song dynasty from its founding in 960 until late in the thirteenth century, when the Mongols ended all the separate currents of events and absorbed the entire realm of Chinese civilization, and much that lay beyond, into their world empire. One of the historian's, and his readers', problems with the coexisting dynasties of these centuries is that we must move back and forth in time, carrying the account of one dynasty to a reasonable stopping place only to pick up a different strand and then set forth again through the same time period, but focusing on a different sequence of events. In that way we have followed the Liao, the Northern Song, and the Xi Xia from their beginnings in the tenth century into the twelfth century. Those accounts have frequently alluded to the Jurchen nation, whose Jin dynasty coexisted in North China with the Xi Xia, and in South China with the Southern Song from the 1120s onward. Now we must go back before those twelfth-century events to search out the early history of the Jurchen people and the founding of their Jin (Gold) dynasty. The many twists and turns in the interactions among the Chinese and the conquest dynasties in these centuries reveal much that is important to an understanding of Chinese and East Asian civilizations.

I. AGUDA'S CHALLENGE

The *Liao History* records an event in 1112 that the *Jin History* curiously omits:

> In the second month the emperor [the last Liao emperor, Tianzuo], traveling into Chunzhou, stopped at the Huntong River to fish.[1] Jurchen leaders from beyond the borders for a thousand *li* around all came, as a matter of long-standing practice, to pay court to the emperor. It was on the occasion of "the feast of the emperor's first fish" when all had imbibed to the point of being half-drunk that the emperor appeared in the banquet pavilion and commanded the tribal chieftains one after the other to arise and dance. Only Aguda refused, saying he was not able to dance. He was repeatedly pressed to do so but in the end was adamant in refusing. On a later day the emperor said privately to the Military Affairs Commissioner, Xiao Fengxian: "On that occasion, during the feast, Aguda displayed a bold confidence, glaring about in an extraordinary manner. Perhaps we should have him executed on pretext of involvement in some border incident. Otherwise he is certain to be the cause of future trouble." Xiao Fengxian replied: "These ruffians simply do not understand good manners. If we were to have him killed for less than a major offense it would, I fear, harm our efforts to work our transforming influence on them. Even if he should harbor some improper intent, what could he ever do?" Aguda's younger brother Wuqimai [and nephews] Nianhan and Hushe on one later occasion accompanied the emperor on a hunt. They knew how to call deer, spear tigers, and capture bears. This so pleased the emperor that he awarded them promotions of rank and title on the spot.[2]

Never was a Liao emperor less perceptively advised; moreover, his adviser was not a Chinese civilian dedicated to promoting Confucian ideals. Xiao Fengxian was from the Liao imperial consort clan whose responsibilty to the state, as envisaged by Abaoji 200 years earlier, was to control military and northern border affairs and, more precisely, to maintain Khitan tribal interests. Had the Liao emperor in this instance followed his own instincts to do away with Aguda and his family, he might have saved his empire. Instead, while he was taking delight in the young savage chieftains' display of woodsmen's skills, simultaneously the young savages were learning all they needed to know about the organization of Liao border defenses and the weaknesses of Liao policy there. The next year, in 1113, Aguda's older brother died, and the leadership of those tribes known as the "wild" Jurchens passed to him. In 1114 he was ready for the open break. He planned a cavalry attack to test the Liao border defenses and captured an important outpost. This so emboldened the Jurchens that Aguda proclaimed his own Jin (Gold) dynasty, to begin with the lunar New Year in 1115.[3] By that time he had achieved what was a wild dream to him only two or three years earlier: he had assembled his army of 10,000, and with it he resoundingly defeated the leading column, perhaps 100,000 strong, of a Liao army in some reports said to have totaled 700,000, led by the hapless Tianzuo emperor himself.[4] Most of the large Liao force retreated without ever coming into direct combat.

This victory launched the Jurchens on an unstoppable military conquest. Their forces swelled with turncoat Khitan armies and those of other tribes rebelling against Khitan rule. Successes came faster than they could make plans for; military commanders in the field, mostly Aguda's close relatives, were ordered to "make decisions on their own discretion in the light of current circumstances." Often there was no time for careful review and coordination from a central point. The conquerors first moved southward in the Liao River valley, taking the Eastern Capital in 1116, then argued with the Khitans about terms of an armistice while solidifying their grasp on the Liao eastern territories and peoples. Angered by Khitan arrogance and duplicity, they abandoned further negotiations and made all-out war. They captured the Liao Supreme Capital (the Northern Capital) in 1120, and the Central Capital in 1122, driving the Liao emperor in flight to his Western Capital (at Datong, in present-day northern Shanxi). At the end of 1122 the Jin forces, led by Aguda, entered the Liao Southern Capital (present-day Beijing), while other Jurchen armies pursued the Liao emperor westward into the Jia Mountains on the border with the Xia state.

Aguda died in the late summer of 1123 when still only fifty-five. He was succeeded by his younger brother Wuqimai, later known as the Jin emperor Taizong, who reigned through the next dozen years of further lightning conquests, when Jin armies overturned the Northern Song. At first, the Jurchens and the Northern Song hastily made an alliance to coordinate their military actions against the Liao. Now they fell out over the terms by which they had agreed in 1120, the agreement formalized in a treaty signed by both emperors in 1123, to return to the Song at least a portion of the occupied lands on the northern frontier. The Chinese wanted, and assumed that they would get, the return of the Sixteen Prefectures, which the Khitans had held since 938. Song armies were supposed to retake the Liao Southern Capital and keep it, but the Jurchen forces under Aguda grew impatient waiting for them to meet the agreed-upon schedule. They took the city on their own. The Song armies, in fact, contributed nothing to the military collapse of the Liao.

After looting the Liao Southern Capital, a mainly Chinese city in the Chinese-populated southern zone of the Liao state, and taking much of its population off to become slaves, the Jurchens further infuriated the Song court, for although they kept their agreement to turn the city over to the Chinese, they did so only after emptying it of its residents and thoroughly looting it.

Following that, the remnant of Liao local commanders in North China surrendered first to the one side and then to the other, inviting struggles that quickly added to the open hostility between the Jurchens' new Jin dynasty and their nominal allies, the Song. The Jurchens first brought local commanders under their military control, or else forced them out of the region. Then they took two further steps to clear their flanks: they forced an alliance on the Xi Xia state in 1124, and captured the fleeing Tianzuo emperor at the edge of the Ordos Desert early in 1125. Those steps completed, the Jin emperor Taizong (Aguda's brother Wuqimai) ordered war against the Song at the beginning of November 1125. Local Jurchen-controlled forces retook the Liao Southern Capital early in 1126. One of the two main Jurchen armies rushed on southward across the open North China Plain to surround the Song capital at Kaifeng in Henan. The other worked its way more slowly south through mountainous Shanxi Province, where it was held up besieging Taiyuan, the provincial capital. The first of those two Jin armies, called the Eastern Army, crossed the Yellow River on the twenty-seventh of January, 1126. The next day the Song emperor Huizong, the politically ineffectual artist-poet who had reigned since 1100, abdicated in favor of his eldest son, known in history as the Emperor Qinzong, and fled south to the Yangzi. On January 31 this Jin army tightened its siege lines around the Song capital. The next day Emperor Qinzong sent emissaries to acknowledge Song fault and to sue for peace. Wanyan Zongwang, a son of Aguda and the reigning Jurchen emperor's nephew, was the field commander of the Eastern Army; his cousin Prince Zonghan led the Western Army, still held up by the siege in Shanxi (see Map 5).

Prince Zongwang made the decision in the field to allow the Song to sue for peace and negotiate a revised treaty setting stiffer terms: (1) a substantial increase in the indemnity previously paid to the Liao, but by prior agreement to be paid to the Jin on the defeat of the Liao; (2) cession to the Jin of three strategic prefectures that were the major Song defense bastions lying just south of the Sixteen Prefectures in Shanxi and Hebei, thereby erasing any further Chinese claim to the Sixteen Prefectures; and (3) the Song emperor's agreement to refer to himself as "nephew" and the Jin emperor as "uncle." "Oath letters" also were exchanged, in which the two sides swore to uphold all the terms and provisions; their wording was particularly humiliating to the Song. The hostages in hand, and the treaty documents' terms all signed and delivered, the Jurchen armies withdrew to the north on February 10, 1126. Despite their recent entrance into international politics, they clearly had already learned from Liao and Xi Xia experience how a northern conquest dynasty should deal with the Chinese. The treaties and letters appear to have been prepared only in Chinese, showing that the Jin had quickly taken over Chinese bureaucrats or sinicized Khitans to staff their diplomatic offices.[5]

Taiyuan in central Shanxi, which Zonghan's Western Army, in its much slower progress through the mountains, was just approaching in March 1126, was one of the three strategic prefectures that had been ceded to the Jurchens. Its Chinese commanders may not have known or believed it. In either case, it appeared to Prince Zonghan that the Chinese were not honoring the treaty. The Taiyuan defenders held out stubbornly. The invading Western Army withdraw to Datong, leaving a small Jin force to maintain the siege at Taiyuan.

The situation in Song China throughout the summer of 1126 became so unsettled, despite the treaty wrung from Emperor Qinzong in February, that the Jurchens decided at the end of summer, when the weather in the North China Plain was more to a northerner's taste, to launch the two field armies anew. The Western Army finally broke through the walls of Taiyuan on September 21 and went on south to meet the Eastern Army, which by this time had again worked its way through or around the main Song garrisons on the North China Plain. The two field armies joined forces under the walls of the Song capital in mid-September. A long siege followed. On January 16, 1127, Emperor Qinzong surrendered in person to the Jin armies, along with his imperial household and a large group of servants and retainers. The emperor's father, the abdicated Emperor Huizong, was soon captured by Jurchen armies raiding farther to the south. Several months elapsed; then in May the two captured Song emperors, their households, and their entourages were escorted under heavy guard to the Jurchen homeland in an immense baggage train of loot from the palaces. Many captives of all social ranks were also taken along. The hapless Song emperors were formally declared by the Jin to be mere commoners, denied the right to wear elite dress or to be granted courtesies of high status. They lived out their lives in bitter exile in far northern Manchuria.

Heading a Song field army that was able to remain just beyond the Jurchens' southern advance, Emperor Qinzong's younger brother claimed the Song throne and strove to maintain it from points farther south. Known in history as the Emperor Gaozong (r. 1127–1162), he was the first of the emperors who would reign for the next century and a half from Hangzhou, south of the Yangzi River, as rulers of the Southern Song.[6]

Throughout 1127 the Jin armies continued to press southward. Gaozong's retreating Song court and government of resistance, hastily put together, were forced to flee farther south to Yangzhou, then finally across the Yangzi River. Throughout 1128 and 1129 the Jin armies were busy consolidating their hold on the North China Plain, campaigning down to the Huai River. They extended their raids south to the Yangzi in search of plunder. In 1129–30 two armies were even successful in crossing the Yangzi, one of them forcing the Southern Song emperor to flee his new "temporary capital" *(xingzai)* at Hangzhou and take to the high seas to evade capture. But the Jurchens quickly learned that they had overreached. In the wet land of the Yangzi Delta, ignorant of boats and naval warfare, they were mauled by Song resistance forces; with great difficulty and heavy losses they finally made it back across the Yangzi (see Map 9).

The Jurchens' feelings about Central China were not unlike those of the Liao emperor Taizong; in 947, after spending a few late spring and summer months in Kaifeng, then the capital of the Five Dynasties' state of Jin,[7] he gave up his intent to govern North China. Now, almost two centuries later, the Jurchens were more deeply committed to holding North China as far south as the Yellow River, but were at this time unprepared to go farther. This is evident in the fact that on departing from Kaifeng early in the summer of 1127, the Jurchen Jin ruler hastily commanded a Chinese turncoat, Zhang Bangchang, to assume the throne as the emperor of a state of Chu that was expected to govern for them the rest of North China, that is, the regions lying south of the Yellow River. Little over a month after the Jin armies' departure the turncoat turned again, surrendering himself to the Southern Song emperor and begging forgiveness. The Chinese denounced him as a traitor, and soon thereafter he died in exile. This attempt to "use Chinese to govern Chinese" (a play on the ancient Chinese method of "using barbarians to govern barbarians") was a failure. But it shows that the Jurchens realized there were limits on how much they could accomplish; they knew they were not yet ready to absorb more of China. In 1130 they again resorted to the device of a puppet regime, this time called the state of Qi, to maintain an aggressive stance toward the Southern Song. This tactic was quite effective for a few years, but was abolished in 1137. Gradually the Jurchens fixed their southern boundary along the Huai River, about 200 miles south of the Yellow River but still more than 100 miles north of the Yangzi.

The new Jin dynasty vigorously consolidated its hold on that northern third of China. The invaders often had to overcome stiff resistance from Chinese regional forces and local leaders. In a landmark treaty negotiated through the winter of 1141–42, a pattern of peace was established on the model of earlier Liao and Xi Xia treaties with the Northern Song. Like those, this agreement required the Southern Song to make annual payments and submit to elaborate diplomatic courtesies. It also provided, on the Jurchens' demand, for regular border point trading stations, through which a flourishing commerce soon developed.[8]

What the Jurchens accomplished in less than fifteen years, between 1114 and 1127, is unparalleled. They defeated in war the two largest and most powerful nations in all of East Asia, the Khitans and the Chinese. The former they entirely absorbed except for the small remnant that fled west to become the Kara Khitai. The latter gave up the northern third of its territory, the China of revered antiquity, down to the Huai River boundary that separates wheat- and millet-eating North China from the South, where the ordinary man's daily fare is rice, and where rice paddies made difficult terrain for cavalry forces to maneuver. China would not be reunited for another 150 years, and then under the Mongols, another conqueror from beyond the northern frontiers. The enduring consequences of the Jin conquest would prove to be profound, but at that moment it was the suddenness of the great Song state's ignominious surrender that shocked all of China and, no doubt, all of its East Asian neighbors as well. The unfortunate Song emperor Qinzong, on coming to the throne in January 1126, changed the Chinese reign title for that year to Jingkang, which, as it turned out with his surrender exactly one year later, was applied only to that single year. To this day the Jurchen conquest and the capture of the two Song emperors is still referred to as "the disaster of Jingkang." For almost 900 years that phrase has stirred anger, frustration, shame, and sorrow in the minds of Chinese.

11. The End of the Liao Dynasty

The failures of both the Liao and the Song to survive the Jin onslaught caught all of East Asia by surprise. How could that have happened? These events must be reviewed from the point of view of Liao and Song history before we turn back to the story of the Jurchen people's abrupt rise and their ensuing place in Chinese history. First, a brief analysis of the Liao dynasty's collapse.

The Later Reigns

The Liao failure was indeed sudden, but it must be seen in light of a less perceptible decline in its rulers' effectiveness over several reigns. The long reign of the sixth Liao emperor, known by his posthumous title Emperor Shengzong, was the high point in Khitan imperial history. He came to the throne at the age of eleven in 982. At the age of fifteen he had to lead his armies south to fend off the invasion of the Song emperor Taizong in 986. He died in 1031, forty-five strenuous years later, still leading armies in the field to settle domestic disturbances and fend off external enemies. The half-century of his reign marked the peak of Liao power and influence; it was also the time when domestic governing was most effective. That was in large part because during his reign, in 1005, the pattern of Liao relationships with China was worked out, to the considerable benefit of the Khitans; the dynasty endured for a century thereafter.

With the hindsight of history, knowing that an empire was terminated at a certain date, we tend to assume that we can discover "decline and fall" symptoms leading inevitably to that terminus. Or, misusing a biological analogy, we seek in the "life history" of a nation its youth, then its maturity, followed by failing health and old age with its inexorable (hence falsely "explained") incapacity to ward off final, fatal attacks. Empires and nations are not organisms; such metaphors, while suggestive, may in fact divert us from sounder explanations of historical processes. The last three reigns of the Liao, leading to the collapse of their empire in 1125, may provide better clues to explain the collapse.

Emperor Shengzong's long reign reminds us forcefully of an essential fact about Khitan history. The most striking feature of his reign is its restlessness; the ruler was incessantly busy with military activities. After his teen-years exploits against China in 986, and indecisive warfare on that border in the years that followed, he successfully invaded the Song empire in 1004, forcing it to propose the humiliating terms of the Peace of Shanyuan early in 1005.

He intervened repeatedly in Korean affairs, finally in 1010 leading an invading army, reportedly of 400,000, that demolished the capital but left unsettled conditions that required repeated further military intervention. During the next twenty years Khitan relations with the Jurchens required constant attention. The many tribal chieftains of the latter nation regularly displayed militant tendencies that had to be suppressed at the borders. On the northwest frontier a succession of turbulent tribal uprisings had to be convincingly defeated to keep the peace in that quarter. The Dangxiang tribes were routed, and their ethnic kin, the Tanguts of the strong Xi Xia state in the west, acknowledged Liao overlordship, but only so they could make common cause in keeping up profitable pressure on the Song. Finally, in 1029 the conquered Bohai people rebelled once more, this time in force, and were only successfully suppressed a year later. The foregoing is but a selective accounting of some of the most important military actions which the Khitan emperor undertook throughout his reign.

In short, even at its height the Liao empire was surrounded by dangerous neighbors, and it included within it and on its borders many restive peoples who constantly tested the Khitans' resolve to keep them in their place. The dynasty had set itself the task of maintaining eternal vigilance, and was constantly under pressure to demonstrate its military superiority. Throughout his life Emperor Shengzong devoted himself relentlessly to that task. Incessant military activity was what sustained the Liao Inner Asian empire; it gave the imperial role focus, and kept its authority high.

Emperor Shengzong was succeeded in 1031 by his eldest surviving son, then fifteen years old, known in history as the Emperor Xingzong. He is described as tall and sturdy, skilled in riding and shooting, but also as excelling in Chinese learning. His succession once again aroused bitter struggles at court, pitting the empress dowager, who had reared him, against his natural mother, though both were of the Xiao consort clan. The emperor's indecisiveness allowed hostile factions within the imperial clan to dominate politics throughout his reign. The importance of all this is that it shows to what extent the succession issue within the imperial clan still was the source of weakness in the leadership of the state. It wasted people, diverted energies, and deflected the attention of the rulers from the tasks of governing.

The emperor died of an illness in 1055 and was succeeded by his eldest son, known as the Emperor Daozong. His was a long reign of almost forty-seven years, until his death in 1101. His reign started well but soon degenerated into favoritism and corruption, again spawning deep factional conflicts for which his personal ineptitude must be held responsible. His powerful armies had some successes in the field but were not often led by the emperor himself; he preferred to stay behind to study Buddhist sutras. Nonetheless, when Daozong died of natural causes, he was smoothly succeeded by the designated heir apparent, his grandson. This last Liao ruler is known simply as the Tianzuo ruler (di), denied the posthumous temple title zong, meaning "ancestor," because he did not succeed in transmitting the throne to a descendant. But we shall call him the Tianzuo emperor.

As this brief review suggests, none of the rulers after Shengzong was able to devote himself consistently to the tasks of empire. All were too deeply distracted by the suppression of dissidence within the ruling elite, in particular, fending off rivals within the two ruling clans of the emperors (the Yelü) and their consorts (the Xiao). Attempted palace coups, assassinations, and clumsy efforts to thwart uprisings gradually eroded what had been the cohering strength of the imperial institution. The state's attention and energies, even more than its material resources, were squandered on in-house fighting instead of being fully deployed in the military tasks of the frontier. Liao power and prestige were diminished, though vigorous leadership might still have revived it.

The story of how the Tianzuo emperor lost his throne in 1125 belongs as much to Jurchen as to Khitan history, and the Jurchen story is in many ways the more interesting, as Section I of this chapter suggests. Only a brief account from the Khitan point of view need be given here.

Failure and Collapse

As we have seen, the Liao state's Jurchen component quickly became a new kind of enemy, and that is the decisive factor in explaining the Liao collapse. In the eleventh century the numerous tribal units of the Jurchens were mostly still in the traditional Chinese historians' category of the "wild" Jurchens. Other Jurchen tribes, called the "tame" Jurchens, living closer to the Khitan heartland, were to a degree assimilated into a manner of life that combined their original farming and hunting with the mobile warfare of the Khitans. But they all resented the harsh Liao overlordship and became increasingly turbulent as they learned to adapt the Khitans' more advanced military way of life. Their defiance progressed from small raids by individual tribes to larger attacks by confederations of tribes. By the early twelfth century the wild and the tame Jurchens had found a national leader in the most successful of the tribal chieftains—Aguda. He kept up continuous military pressure on the Liao eastern border, where he absorbed turncoat Liao detachments into his armies; his tactic was to wear down important border garrisons while intercepting their supplies. In the autumn of 1115 the Tianzuo emperor, more the martial leader than his predecessor (his grandfather) had been, took to the field to lead the Liao forces against the just-proclaimed Jurchen Jin dynasty, which was obviously modeled on the Liao state. The Tianzuo emperor was forced to flee in defeat from their first major confrontation.

Defeats of that scope suffered by emperors in the field were commonplace in Liao history; the difference in this case is that the leaders of the two ruling clans, the imperial Yelü and the consort Xiao, seized upon the defeat as an excuse to discredit their emperor. They began plotting to displace him. This cabal was not successful, but it had a number of serious consequences. Some leaders, taking their military followings, deserted to the Jurchens. That defection was well within expected patterns of tribal behavior; it could have been dealt with. But in addition, Chinese forces in the Sixteen Prefectures of the

Southern Chancellery came under suspicion of contacting the Song, with the result that they were disbanded and sent home. Thereafter the throne was hesitant to rely on them. That denied the Liao state a source of possible military assistance, though one on which it had never been dependent.

Divisions and hatreds within the Khitan ruling groups were never overcome by this emperor. In 1116 the Bohai people again revolted, this time asking the Jurchens for help; that had the effect of turning the Liao Eastern Capital over to the Jurchens. In 1117 the Jurchens proposed peace negotiations. Terms in large part similar to those of the Song-Liao Treaty of Shanyuan (1005) were agreed to, but the Liao court refused to call the Jurchen upstart "older brother." The Khitans, that is, refused to put themselves in the humiliating position that they had imposed on the Chinese more than a century earlier. They had developed this pattern of diplomacy but now were unable to exploit it.

The Jurchen chieftain Aguda, less patient than the Song or the Liao had been in their negotiations, threw the peace effort aside and declared his intention to get on with the war. In 1120 he captured the Liao Supreme Capital, forcing the emperor and his court to flee to the Western Capital (at present-day Datong). Even in these severe straits, factional struggles continued unabated at the Liao court; losing factions continued to flee, joining the Jurchen enemy. In 1122 the Central Capital also fell. Shortly thereafter, Jurchen armies pursued the emperor all the way to his North China base at Datong, forcing him to take 5,000 of his cavalry and flee farther west into the mountains north of Shanxi at the edge of the Ordos Desert. That cut him off completely from the remnant of his state, now leaderless, so a faction of nobles placed the emperor's uncle on the throne in their sole remaining bastion, the Liao Southern Capital (at present-day Beijing). They called him the Tianxi emperor.

Among the prime movers in that desperate rescue effort was Yelü Dashi, a member of the imperial clan and chief of military affairs at the improvised Tianxi court. The Song state, long bound by treaty to amicable relations, now unwisely chose this moment for confrontation with the Liao, putting pressure on their common border near the Southern Capital. To their surprise, the remnant Liao forces there still had the capacity to defeat large Song invasion armies two years running, in 1122 and 1123. The Khitans were not militarily spent. After the Jurchens took and then abandoned the sacked Southern Capital in 1122, the Liao made frantic diplomatic efforts with both the Jurchens and the Song in the hope of ending the war on any terms. But the Liao side did not know that the Song and the Jurchens had secretly forged a pact under which they would join together to destroy the Liao. When the Tianxi emperor died, Jurchen forces focused on capturing the Southern Capital; they surged in via the Jurong Pass, the gateway from the north into the capital region, and surrounded the city. Some court figures, seeing the hopelessness of further resistance at the Southern Capital, and in command of some elements of the army, fled to the west in 1123 to join the fugitive Tianzuo emperor. Among those was Yelü Dashi.

The official *Liao History* records very revealing conversations between Yelü Dashi and the Tianzuo emperor. According to one of them, immediately upon Yelü's arrival the emperor charged him with treason for having supported the elevation of his uncle, the Tianxi emperor, who for three months had held that title at the Southern Capital. Yelü Dashi replied: "You, sire, when you still commanded the full strength of the state, were incapable in your one effort to resist the enemy, and then abandoned your state and fled, leaving the ordinary people to suffer ruthless suppression. Even if we had elevated to the throne ten Prince Chuns [the Tianxi emperor's personal name], they all would have been direct descendants of the Emperor Taizu [Abaoji]; isn't that better than begging others to spare one's life!" The emperor fell speechless; Yelü Dashi was pardoned. The emperor had demanded from Yelü Dashi the kind of one-sided loyalty that a Chinese emperor could command. Yelü, himself an eighth-generation descendant of the Liao founding emperor, and moreover a man of fully dual cultural attainment, was accusing his overlord not of being a bad emperor but of being a weak tribal chieftain. He sternly rebuked him for failure to demonstrate successful leadership in a time of national crisis. This leader no longer deserved a steppe warrior's loyalty.

On another occasion Yelü Dashi rebuked the emperor for faulty military thinking in planning an ill-considered offensive that would rely on using the forces Yelü had brought with him. Yelü analyzed the emperor's plans and showed them to be tactically deficient. He advised the emperor to harbor his forces until they had become strong enough to prevail. The emperor ignored the advice and ordered all the troops to follow him into battle. Yelü feigned illness and stayed behind with his units, then revolted, killed a number of courtiers, and led his small following northwest acrosss the Gobi; in that move he started a campaign to make himself the new Khitan leader.[9] Again, his behavior was that of a tribal chieftain, not that of an imperial servitor.

The Tianzuo emperor attacked the Jurchens, was defeated, and fled with his few remaining supporters to the west, but was captured early in 1125. He died a prisoner, perhaps two years later. Thus the great Liao empire came to its sorrowful end in the uncongenial sands of the Inner Mongolian deserts, far from the scene of Abaoji's spectacular early successes, far from the pleasant meadows and deep grasses on the eastern slopes of the Khingan Mountains.

How should we explain the dynasty's fall? Had the adaptation of Chinese culture compromised the Liao imperial line and sapped the vitality of the Khitan elite? Had the Liao state degenerated, becoming administratively incapacitated to the degree that it could no longer function? Was the fall of the Liao long foredoomed, or was it the result of incidents in the previous few years, incidents that might have turned out otherwise?

Despite the undoubted elements of acculturation, the Khitans remained true to their tribal values; their Chinese cultural skills were an additional attainment, not a replacement for abandoned tribal ways. The tribal commoners remained supremely able and willing to fight. They give evidence that their society was still intact. The experience of Yelü Dashi in establishing the

Western Liao (or Kara Khitai) shows that to be true: the only reason why more of the nation did not follow him westward was that at the time of his rebellion in 1124 he was too far off to the west from the Khitan homeland for most Khitans to have heard about and responded to his leadership.

As for the possible degeneration of the Liao state apparatus, despite the mismanagement of the court through the long Daozong reign (1055–1101), one cannot find signs of serious economic or fiscal breakdown that might have impoverished it or crippled its ability to respond. Nor had any of its steppe rivals acquired a stronger economic or demographic base. Much less had any threats from Song China, which might have had sufficient power to threaten the Liao, become newly significant. In fact, while it was not lacking great military resources, the Song state proved to be totally useless when it tried to join with the Jurchens to attack the Liao. Traditional, and to some degree modern, Chinese historians, wedded to their cyclical interpretations of the rise and fall of dynasties, usually stress the culpability of rulers and leading statesmen in the final reigns of a dynasty; in that way the fall of the Liao is made explainable by the cumulative failings, especially the moral failings, of emperors and prime ministers. That kind of explanation allows dynasties to fall without discrediting the ideological foundations of dynastic power. Successor dynasties, no matter how "illegitimate" in the manner of their founding, of course embrace such explanations because they demonstrate that their predecesors' fall from grace was inevitable: it was sanctioned by heaven.

In this case, the arguments which hold the late Liao emperors responsible for weakening the state have some force, but overall that explanation is inadequate. Our conclusion must be that the Liao state remained strong, capable of functioning at reasonable levels and possessing greater resources for war than any of its enemies. True, one source of its earlier strength had declined: what had been a strong imperial institution had become a deeply troubled one because tensions between its tribal and its alien cultural elements had engendered a basis for deep and crippling factional conflict. One can show that the Liao emperors always were quite exposed, that they had to perform in person in at least two cultural milieux. In the one, they did not have much support from a bureaucracy which, unlike its Chinese model, had failed to become a core of civil governing which could sustain itself through its own recruitment and staffing procedures and which generated its own standards of performance. In the other milieu, tribal interests still could be aggressively reasserted at the expense of the emperor's authority. Abaoji had elevated the Khitan Great Khan to something approaching the sacrosanct eminence of the Chinese imperial counterpart, and had endowed him with a Mandate of Heaven reinforced by overwhelming ritual and lodged in immemorial tradition. Much of that authority, however, became mere decoration back at the Supreme Capital, where Chinese ritual and tradition were in the hands of foreign experts. The bureaucratic and ideological supports, therefore, did not work for the Liao emperor the way they did for a Chinese ruler.

Less strong institutionally and culturally, the Liao emperor was therefore more at the mercy of factions, inimical relatives, and the contempt of independent-minded tribes, threats that had to be met by tribal means of demonstrating leadership. Instead of servicing the incessant demands on the empire to display its superior military might, thereby maintaining the tribal confederation's essential bases of power, the later emperors were increasingly inept in preventing the two ruling clans and the elite from fighting among themselves over the spoils of empire. The Jurchen nation was primitive by comparison, but it could be welded together by a fierce will to destroy a hated enemy that had long browbeaten and misused it. The Jurchens were able to destroy the Liao empire in part because fortuitous circumstances in particular battles favored them, in part because they were ably led at a time when the Khitans were weakly led, and in part because their raw ferocity was truly formidable. Yet such ferocity was by no means unprecedented in Khitan history. This last phase of Khitan Liao history could have turned out differently.

Khitan Epilogue: The Western Liao

When Yelü Dashi fled from the camp of the last Liao emperor at the edge of the Ordos Desert in 1124, he had no more than a few hundred followers. He traveled northwest across the Gobi and arrived at Zhenzhou, a Liao outpost on the Orchon River in what is today northern Mongolia.[10] An important border bastion of the Liao empire, it in normal times was the base for a garrison of 20,000 cavalry troops and their supporting tribal households. This base, at that moment perhaps not up to full strength, nonetheless was still unaffected by the Jurchen invasion. Yelü addressed the Khitan population and people of the associated tribes present there urging them to remain loyal to the Liao, and to assist him in taking revenge on the Jurchen invaders whose cruelties had fallen on all their tribal kin further east. He was able to convince these isolated garrison soldiers that he was a natural leader and that it would be advantageous for them to follow him. In a ceremony late in 1124 he proclaimed himself the new Khitan king. Significantly, he also took the Turkic title "Gurkhan," meaning chief of the khans. Always politically perceptive, he recognized that the Chinese institutions of the Liao dynasty needed to be buttressed by forms of authority widely acknowledged in this remote Inner Asian environment.

His following grew through absorption of local fighting units from Khitan and other garrisons in the region. Between 1124 and 1129 he remained in the vicinity of Zhenzhou and farther north, preparing to move far enough west to be out of practical reach of the Jurchens, whose expertise and interest in the problems of steppe empire were limited. When his strength permitted, he would strike back at them. In 1131 he proclaimed himself emperor, adopted a reign title and other symbols of imperial stature, and led his following northwestward through the Great Gate of Dzungaria and on into Transoxiana.[11] After obtaining the submission of several important and ancient Central Asian cities, he turned eastward again to make his capital at the old city of Belasaghun. That site is on the Cu (Chu) River, south of Lake Balkhash in present-day Kazakhstan, some forty miles southeast of Alma Ata. He was very successful in building a new state, and soon he felt that his strength was great enough to attempt the restoration of the former Liao empire. In 1134 he sent an army of 70,000 to the east, but it got bogged down in the desert sands. After suffering a few defeats it turned back. "It is not Heaven's will," Yelü Dashi concluded. He then turned his energies to building a nation of Khitan-led tribal peoples in westernmost Inner Asia and Central Asia, extending both east and west of the Pamir Mountains.

In Western Asian sources his state is called Kara Khitai (Qara-Khitay, and so on), meaning the Black Khitans, because it adopted black for symbolic and ritual purposes. In Chinese historical writings it is called the Western Liao (Xi Liao). The state extended from the Oxus 2,000 miles eastward to the borders of the Xi Xia state, and about 700 miles from north to south. That is, it stretched from the borders of Tibet northward across the Tarim Basin, the Tian Shan Mountains, and the Dzungarian Basin, all the way to Lake Balkhash. A Chinese-type household registration carried out in 1151 counted 84,500 households in the realm having adult males capable of serving in the armies; this figure suggests a tribal population of more than one-quarter million. That obviously does not include the populations of the great Central Asian cities subject to Kara Khitai rule; those cities, on the strategically important trade routes, included Samarkand, Bukhara, Balkh, Kashgar, Khotan, and Besh Balikh (Beshbaligh) among the most important. Those great trading cities were populated by sedentary Uighurs and other Turkic as well as Iranian peoples; their total population probably was in excess of 1 million.

Yelü Dashi died in 1143 and was given the posthumous Chinese temple name of Dezong, "the Virtuous Ancestor." His noteworthy command of Chinese learning was coupled with fame as a horseman and military leader. He typified the best of the culturally dual Khitan elite at the end of the Liao dynasty. There was a Chinese element of some size among his courtiers and government officials. The Chinese language continued to be one of those officially used at his court and throughout the state. Uighur administrative aides, including some who were competent in Chinese learning and statecraft, continued to function importantly as intermediaries between steppe and sedentary ways of life. Throughout the twelfth century the Western Liao, the Xi Xia, the Jin empire of the Jurchens, and the Southern Song dynasty in China were the four great mainland powers in eastern Asia, all highly conscious of one another and each affecting the concerns and policies of the others. The Northern Song court, for example, sent envoys to Yelü Dashi's court on several occasions. Exchanges with the Xi Xia were frequent. Yelü's son and grandson continued the line, and his policies, until 1211. During the early thirteenth century that multiplicity of states in mainland East Asia was reduced to one, as the Mongol empire absorbed all.[12]

III. THE NORTHERN SONG FALLS TO THE JURCHENS

The fall of the Liao to the upstart Jurchens is paralleled by the collapse of the Song, or Northern Song, as the earlier half of the dynasty came to be called after its fall in 1127, when its continuation was designated the Southern Song. Like the demise of the Liao, the fall of Northern Song also deserves further comment.

In the early Northern Song there was a widely shared endeavor to regenerate society by restoring Confucian values. An exuberant spirit of positive political involvement set the tone of eleventh-century literati (or scholar-officials) leadership. That spirit degenerated by the end of the century, following Wang Anshi's dismissal from the Prime Ministership in 1076 and the temporary reversal of his Major Reform program. Politics then turned ugly. Reform ideas as such were no longer the issue; they became mere slogans and accusations used by embittered factions in a debased struggle to control the government. In 1100 the eighth Song emperor, known as Huizong, came to the throne at the age of eighteen. He was an eager supporter of Wang's policies, but Wang had died in 1086 and the leadership of the reform faction had fallen into the hands of opportunists. So although Emperor Huizong's reign saw some of the reform measures reinstated, the atmosphere at his court was not one of high-minded commitment. Leading officials engaged in corrupt practices. They encouraged the emperor to believe that he possessed inexhaustible wealth and enjoyed unchallenged power, and they distracted him with lavish projects while maintaining their control over the government. Huizong built gardens and pleasure pavilions; he extravagantly supported Daoist building projects and religious exercises; he set up ateliers and workshops to provide luxury objects for court use, and kept hundreds or even thousands of transport barges busy moving ornate garden rocks and building materials to Kaifeng from the lower Yangzi region. His agents managed those affairs ruthlessly; eventually their rapacious behavior aroused serious revolts of people who in desperation took up arms against them.

One of those rebels was a local bravo from Shandong Province, Song Jiang, who gathered a collection of thirty-six bandits at his impregnable Liang-shan lair, successfully defied the incompetent government for two years, and finally was induced to surrender in 1121. He became the central figure in later fictional accounts based on the story of his bandit gang, the most important of which is the sixteenth-century version known as *Shuihuzhuan*, one of the four great Ming dynasty vernacular novels. It is interesting that another of those four great novels, the *Jinpingmei*, also is set in the reign of Emperor Huizong; it revolves loosely around the hated Prime Minister Cai Jing.[13] Although both of these Ming novels use the conventional device of setting their story in an earlier dynasty while in fact reflecting conditions of their own time, one must note that the reign of Huizong gave rise to much later fictionalizing of its disastrous history.

The most important of the large-scale uprisings in Huizong's reign, however, was that of Fang La in northern Zhejiang, in 1120 and 1121, in direct response to the excesses of Huizong's procurement agents. Fang's rebellion reached a large size; his armies numbered in the hundreds of thousands of common people, and controlled much of northern Zhejiang and adjoining areas. Suppressing this massive rebellion required extraordinary measures.

Huizong was kept ignorant of the uprisings as long as possible by the conniv-ance of Prime Minister Cai Jing and the eunuch Tong Guan, the Commis-sioner of Military Affairs. Eventually the emperor became aware of the seri-ousness of the Fang La rebellion and sent Tong Guan with full discretionary powers to Zhejiang to direct its suppression.[14]

The best that can be said for the Emperor Huizong is that, despite his faults as a ruler, he was wholly committed to art. He maintained an academy at his court to which many of the great painters and calligraphers of the age were attached. He was a discerning and scholarly collector of calligraphy, paintings, ancient bronzes, and other antiquities, building one of the great imperial collections in all of history. He sponsored an array of scholarly and curatorial activities. And he was himself one of the supreme calligraphers of all time as well as being a fine painter, probably the only first-rank artist ever to have occupied the throne of China. If his brother, the Emperor Zhezong, had not died at age twenty-four in 1100 and Huizong had remained merely the ruling emperor's brother, perhaps to become his unofficial caretaker of the arts, his place in history might have been that of a cultural hero untar-nished by the misadventures of governing.

As it turned out, however, this superb artist and aesthete must be held responsible for much of the policy making and the appointments of leading personnel at his court. He is even more directly culpable for establishing an atmosphere of imperious unconcern for the conditions in his nation at a time of considerable stress. That stress came to its apex with the rise of the Jur-chens, an event that could scarcely have been anticipated by the most astute statesman or ruler. The Song dynasty failed to meet the challenge. Its failure to defend the state in that emergency sprang not so much from military weakness (although most modern historians exaggerate Song military weaknesses in explaining the fall of the Northern Song) as from inept use of the dynasty's vast resources in the emergency. Above all, the crisis created by the sudden Jurchen rise was compounded by Song arrogance and incompetence in diplo-macy. Influenced by Cai Jing, the Song emperor and Tong Guan, who was in overall control of the military establishment, made unwise choices in launching what has come to be known as the "alliance conducted at sea" with the Jurchens. Yet even in that mismanaged enterprise one can see that Huizong too felt the immense pressure that all the Northern Song emperors had to bear, that of trying whatever stratagems seemed to offer hope of recov-ering the Sixteen Prefectures.

The plan was hatched soon after a Chinese subject of the Liao defected to the Song in 1115. He reported that the Liao Tianzuo emperor was incompe-tent and the Jurchens were making great headway in their uprising. The defec-tor reported this to Tong Guan, then coming into full control over the military and eager to find ways of enhancing his standing. It would indeed be a great coup if an attack on the Liao should regain some of the border strongholds, perhaps even the Liao Southern Capital (present-day Beijing). Tong Guan and the emperor decided to explore the matter by sending envoys to Aguda, but in secrecy for fear that the court would raise objections. The stable diplomatic relationship with the Liao had been maintained for over a hundred years, and thoughtful statesmen might well have had reservations about any plan to scuttle the solemnly executed treaties. Nevertheless, in secret the emperor's envoys were sent to propose to Aguda that the Song should join with him and his new Jin dynasty to construct a pincers movement that would bring the Liao state to its knees. The Jin would then return the Sixteen Prefectures to China, and the Song would transfer to the Jin the annual indemnities and other obligations owed to the Liao.

The exchanges of envoys of necessity occurred by sea, using a port on the north coast of Shandong to cross to what is now the port of Dalian on the Liaodong Peninsula, and thus to avoid crossing Liao-held territories. The so-called alliance conducted at sea at first used as a cover the pretext of purchasing horses for the Song armies. The idea of the joint military venture grew ever more attractive as the Jurchens battered the Khitans in the years 1116 and 1117. Envoys went again from Kaifeng to Aguda's camp in 1118, and other envoys came from the Jurchens to meet with Cai Jing and Tong Guan in Kaifeng in 1119. The proud Aguda, however, found the Chinese attitudes demeaning; he demanded more formal and higher-level exchanges with proper diplomatic documents addressing the Jurchens as equals. If the Chinese thought they could easily draw the Jurchens into the traditional gambit of "using barbarians to control barbarians," they failed to perceive the new realities. The rude "wild Jurchen" leader undoubtedly had well-informed advisers, and he would not be easily tricked, much less overwhelmed by the splendor of China.

The story of the diplomatic negotiations is too long and complex to be recounted in detail.[15] It must suffice to say that the two sides fixed a time, first in 1121, then changed to 1122, when they would launch their concerted attacks. The Jurchens were to drive the Liao from their Central Capital while the Chinese took the Southern Capital. But Aguda had grown increasingly angry with the Chinese for sending a succession of low-ranking envoys, failing to negotiate in sincerity, thinking they could trick the Jurchens into giving the Chinese larger gains than originally agreed upon, and generally underestimating the other side's will and sophistication.

Finally, on February 23, 1122, the Jurchens met their side of the agreement by taking the Liao Central Capital, then went on to take the Western Capital (Datong) as well, while waiting for the Song to take the Liao Southern Capital. In 1121 Tong Guan, at the head of a large Chinese army, had advanced northward into Liao territory, but he found the remnant of Liao power fiercely ready for battle. He suffered significant defeats at the hands of the Liao defenders and was forced to turn back. The next year he was badly defeated for a second time and again withdrew to Kaifeng. The Jurchens grew increasingly impatient with their Chinese allies. They drove on to the Southern Capital, easily captured it, sacked it, and emptied it, of people, then departed to turn it over to the Chinese.

This brought forth new exchanges of envoys, the Chinese going to the Jurchens, and Jurchen envoys going again to Kaifeng. They argued about the extent of the territory to be turned over to the Song, the amounts of the promised indemnity payments from the Song, and which side was responsible for breaking the agreements. These bitter negotiations produced the first Song-Jin treaty agreement in 1123, but simultaneously Aguda died quite suddenly, late in the summer. His brother Wuqimai, who succeeded him, told his generals in the field to make decisions on their own judgment without delaying to refer to the distant Jin capital. Resentful of Chinese perfidy and scornful of their former allies' incompetence on the battlefield, the generals decided against further haggling and in 1125 abandoned the troubled alliance to take up the offensive in earnest against the Song.

Meanwhile, Tong Guan's military failure brought about attacks on him at the court; early in 1126 he was dismissed and soon thereafter executed. Cai Jing also was degraded and exiled, and in the late summer of 1126 he was assassinated. At the beginning of 1126 Emperor Huizong abdicated in favor of his son, known in history as the Emperor Qinzong, and left the capital to find safer conditions in the south. As we have seen, one of two Jurchen field armies pressing southward into China surrounded Kaifeng in February, wrung costly surrender terms from Emperor Qinzong; the troops then withdrew to wait for the other Jurchen army to join them. Later in the year Kaifeng was again surrounded and besieged by the two armies. Finally, in January 1127 Qinzong surrendered unconditionally. Jurchen armies again entered Kaifeng and made captives of Qinzong and the abdicated Huizong (captured in the south before he could cross the Yangzi). In May the captive emperors and the train of prisoners and booty wagons left Kaifeng for the Jin homeland. The military action against the Song capital was followed by extensive raiding throughout North China; that brought an end to the Northern Song.

Why did the Northern Song fall so quickly? Despite their large military establishment, the Chinese were unable to gain any alternative to abject surrender. We must place the blame on political weakness. Court and central government had degenerated through the quarter-century of Huizong's rule. Huizong himself wanted nothing more than to wash his hands of any further involvement; he shrugged off all responsibility. The high civil officials at the court (among whom we must count Tong Guan, the eunuch Commissioner of Military Affairs), were thoroughly discredited by their long collaboration with Cai Jing, but they were not replaced soon enough for a new leadership to take the reins, mobilize Chinese wealth and strength, and take a determined stand. The Jurchen military force was truly awesome, but the Song never fully tested it. The Chinese were not ground down and crushed by a coordinated, systematic Jurchen offensive; they were routed by a succession of raids and adventitious campaigns.

We have seen how the Jurchen armies, in an unbelievably short time, were able to impose their will throughout North China following the defeat they inflicted on the Liao. To understand the fierce energy that impelled them through those conquests, we must now turn back to their history in the century leading up to those military triumphs.

IV. WHO WERE THESE JURCHENS?

The abrupt rise and triumph of the Jurchen state was one of the most unexpected and explosively upsetting events in all of East Asian history. From open rebellion in 1114 to the lightning-quick destruction of the Liao empire and then, by 1127, the defeat of the Song armies and the conquest of all Song territories in North China, the Jurchens did not stop to rest. The fierce rapidity of their emergence into history surpasses the rise of the Mongols a century later. Where did they come from, and how did they accomplish so much so quickly?

The Jurchens' language is Tungusic; that is, it belongs to the farthest eastern extension of the Altaic language family. The Tungusic branch of Altaic also includes Korean, Manchu, Po-hai, and, though more remotely, possibly also Japanese. Scholars speculate that the Jurchens' tribal ancestors moved eastward from the region around Lake Baikal, north of modern Outer Mongolia, perhaps in the last centuries before the Common Era. The early Chinese historians, dutifully noting down the oral traditions of Inner Asian peoples, have left us the only documentary record, but they were not scientific ethnologists. The Jurchens, like all early peoples of the region, tended to assume that they were descendants of almost any and all peoples named in earlier accounts of their home regions.

Most of the legendary history of the early Jurchens is of the same character: it is imprecisely broad and suggestive, but it is not useless. It seems to indicate the existence of a seashore culture centered in the area of modern Korea's northern boundaries with China and Russia, and of a mountain forest culture located in the the Changbo Mountains just north of the border, and extending all the way northward through eastern Manchuria to the Amur River. Yet no tribes verifiable as Jurchen ancestors in either of those culture regions are known earlier than the tenth century. The Jurchens of course had ancestors, and they probably had been living in that general area for some centuries; yet the questions *who?* and *where?* still evade clear answers.

From the tenth century onward, Abaoji's Liao empire imposed its will over many "inner" and "outer" tribal nations. In the latter category were seven subsidiary states of Jurchens, each a tribal "kingdom" located in central Manchuria east of the middle reaches of the Liao River. These were called the "tame" (in Chinese the *shu,* or "cooked") Jurchens. They practiced some agriculture; their leaders held nominal offices granted to them by the Liao government, and they formed military units under Liao direction. They were very much subject to the transforming influences of the Liao. The Jin dynasty, however, did not spring from these "tame" Jurchens.

Beyond the tame Jurchen regions loosely incorporated into the Liao administration were the "wild" (in Chinese the *sheng,* or "raw") Jurchens.[16] At that time they lived farther to the east, occupying the wet, deeply forested mountains of northern and eastern Manchuria within the zone dominated by three great rivers: the Amur, the Ussuri, and the Amur's large tributary in Manchuria, the Sungari. According to their own legends some of the Jurchens had long lived in southern Manchuria, in the Changbo (ever-white) Mountains along the Yalu River on the Korean border. By the tenth century the wild Jurchens were divided between those in the north and those still in the south. Those in the north took their identity from the Amur River (in Chinese, the "black river") and were called the "Black Jurchens," while those in the south identified with the Changbo Mountains and were called the "White Jurchens."

The White Jurchens were more advanced. They thought of themselves as kin of the Bohai people and had a long history, at least as preserved in oral tradition, of interaction with the Koreans. When the Liao conquered and absorbed the Bohai state in 926 and at the same time stabilized all of central Manchuria east of the Khitan homeland, the unassimilated Jurchens remained the dominant people on the eastern and northeastern boundaries of the Liao empire. The Khitans found them hostile and turbulent but attempted to impose a loose suzerainty on them also. Hoping gradually to attach and absorb those "wild Jurchen" tribal units, they granted titles and privileges to the best organized among them, much as the Chinese divided off segments of border peoples and in that way claimed to rule over them.

From the tenth century, when Jurchen history assumes a coherent shape, it is dominated by the Wanyan, the most successful and expansive of its "wild" tribes. No dates are known for any of the leaders of this powerful tribe before a certain Wanyan Wugunai (1021–1074), the grandfather of Wanyan Aguda, the first Jin emperor. In their oral tradition, Wugunai was held to be the sixth-generation successor to the "primal ancestor," the first leader of the Wanyan tribe whose name is preserved in legendary prehistory. As recorded much later in the official *Jin History,* the primal ancestor's story is unusually interesting. It reveals that the wild Jurchens were still at that time quite primitive, a mere six generations or little more than 100 years before the time of Wugunai. This tribal legend tells that the primal ancestor was one of three brothers. Two remained behind, one in the Korean and one in the Bohai area, when Hanpu, the primal ancestor, wandered northward into the territory of the Wanyan tribe. He was accepted as a "wise man," probably a shaman. Then sixty years old, he lived among the Wanyan for several years. Upon a severe outbreak of intertribal or interclan violence, the Wanyan elders said to him that if he could induce the people to give up blood feuds and resolve issues of tribal justice without resort to violence, they would give him a worthy maiden of their tribe—supposedly aged also about sixty. He succeeded in introducing a system of indemnities for murders and other crimes that ended the feuding, and so married the lady. She bore him two sons and a daughter. He was taken into the Wanyan tribe and became its chief. His elder son was the first of a succession of tribal chieftains descended from him.[17]

This story is seen by some scholars as encapsulating the account of a process of social change. Hanpu's two brothers, one of whom remained in Korea while the other remained with the Bohai, may represent the tribe's memory of their ancestral links to those two peoples; later, when the Jurchens were expanding to the south in the late eleventh century, they appealed to the Bohai to join them in resisting the Liao, calling them their "brother tribes." The homeless Hanpu's marrying into the Wanyan tribe by accepting their "worthy maiden" and then becoming their chieftain may reflect the era of transformation from matrilineal to patrilineal society, as well as the persistence at that time of uxorilocal marriage. At the time of Hanpu's fourth-generation descendant, the wild Jurchens are said to have first learned to build houses above ground; previously they had lived in pit dwellings. They built stockaded communities on the banks of the Anchuhu River, whose name means "gold," so called because the precious metal was found in its sands. Much later, in 1115, they adopted the Chinese words Da Jin (Great Golden) as their dynastic name.[18] A tributary of the Sungari River near modern Harbin, the Anchuhu today is called the Ashi River.

As late as the time of Wugunai, who died in 1074 and was the sixth-generation descendant of the primal ancestor, the wild Jurchens are said to have first taken up the use of iron, acquiring it in trade and, perhaps by using captive enslaved ironworkers, learning to make farming implements and weapons. They still had no writing system, no calendar, no money, and no system of appointed officials, the last being a particularly serious matter in the eyes of Chinese historians. Wugunai knew the Liao empire well and cooperated with local Liao officials in wars that were to their mutual advantage. The Liao presented him with a seal of office and named him Military Governor of all the wild Jurchens. They also wished to bring him and his people into more direct administration as subjects of the Liao empire. He accepted the title of office but had his assistants inform the Liao authorities that if he went any further toward enrolling his people into the Liao governing structure, his subjects would kill him. In this way he deviously maintained the formal independence of his nation while benefiting from Liao legitimation of his tribal leadership.

The material advances that now came to the Wanyan tribe, such as the supply of iron, allowed them to grow more powerful. They extended their hegemony over an ever-widening group of wild Jurchen tribes. Wugunai is described as a leader of remarkable personality, as generous with material things as in forgiving those who differed with him, simple in lifestyle, deeply trusted by other tribal leaders. The histories say he was "addicted to wine and women and could outdrink anyone," but he was a great fighter. He left his tribe with the preeminent position among all the wild Jurchens, and those who bore the Wanyan surname (the tribal name had become a surname) were distinguished by the hereditary right to fill the military governorship over all the Jurchens, under the Liao system of border state relations.

The second of his nine sons, named Holibo, succeeded him. Wugunai had declared that his eldest son was "of yielding and peaceable nature, well suited to the management of family affairs," whereas Holibo was "of vast capacities and knowledge; what tasks could he not bring to successful accomplishment?" Holibo, crafty in battle and diplomacy, was indeed successful in enlarging the powers of the growing Jurchen confederation. Upon his death in 1092, he was succeeded in the leadership of the Jurchens by two younger brothers; the first died in 1094 and the second in 1103 (see Chart 4). At that point the succession passed to Holibo's eldest son, Wuyashu (d. 1113), and then to his remarkable second son, Aguda, who in 1115 proclaimed himself the emperor of the new Jin dynasty. Succession through several brothers before passing to the next generation, instead of primogeniture, continued to mark the Jurchen chieftainship, and later the Jin imperial inheritance system.

The wild Jurchens' first emergence into history and more or less simultaneously into a patriarchical social system, then into the iron age, and into a state organization with a rudimentary system of offices and duties, all occurred within an amazingly short time, from about 950 to 1100. The impact of their more advanced "tame Jurchen" kin, and especially their tutelage under the Liao system, contributed greatly to their rapid advancement. Their social order was highly volatile and rapidly changing, and as we shall see, so it remained. That is a distinctive feature of Jurchen history; it is in sharp contrast with the much more stable Khitan way of life.

Aguda, during his uncle Yingge's chieftainship in 1102, was the first wild Jurchen ever to have commanded an army of more than a few hundred soldiers. Seeing the force of 1,000 mounted soldiers that his uncle, with Liao support and approval, had recruited from various tribes that year to pursue a fleeing traitor wanted by the Khitans, he said with great excitement, "With armed troops of this number, where are the limits to what we can do?" Within little more than a decade after that a saying had become general on the Liao frontier: "When a Jurchen army reaches the number of ten thousand, nothing will be able to stop it." It appears that the semi-agricultural, forest-dwelling wild Jurchens, their economy still significantly dependent on hunting and fishing, began in the late eleventh century to expand their use of horses, with all the social changes implicit in that development. They emulated the Khitan pattern of steppe mobile warfare (but not their full-scale nomadism) in order to possess armed forces consisting primarily of mounted archers. They imposed that new military element on their more typically Tungusic ways: a mixed hunting, farming, and pig-rearing economy based in fixed villages along the rivers of the Manchurian forest. The Jurchen people's explosive rise to military dominance thus required a fundamental adaptation to their society of another people's (the Khitans') basically nomadic military system, one characterized by the horse and the skills of the mounted warrior, yet without giving up their village agricultural social base. They never acquired the mobility of steppe peoples. Despite that, soon no people surpassed them in horsemanship and archery. They were, in short, an amazingly volatile, adaptable people.[19]

The Jurchens hated the Khitans, and thus learned much from them. Throughout history the interaction between oppressed subject peoples and their military oppressors has often produced a selective imitation, or acculturation, with military and technological skills passing from the overlords to their subjects. There have been border zone situations in which the Chinese themselves, under the dominance of steppe nomads, also have made that

CHART 4. THE JIN IMPERIAL SUCCESSION

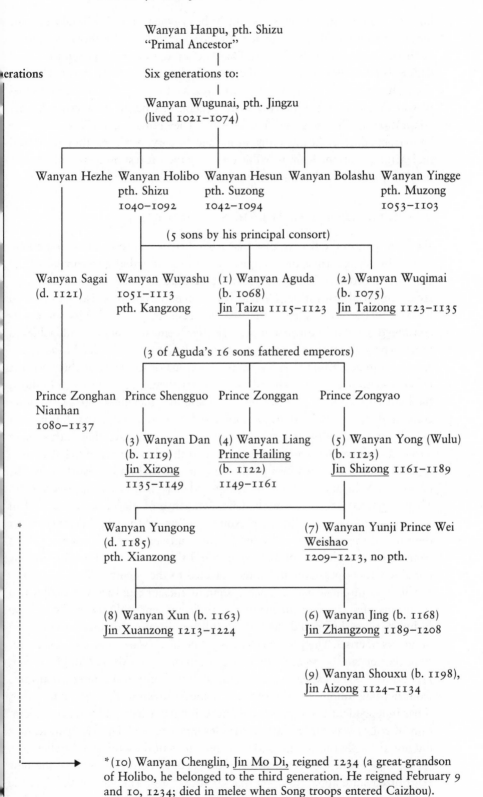

Wanyan Hanpu, pth. Shizu
"Primal Ancestor"
|
erations   Six generations to:
|
Wanyan Wugunai, pth. Jingzu
(lived 1021–1074)

Wanyan Hezhe Wanyan Holibo Wanyan Hesun Wanyan Bolashu Wanyan Yingge
           pth. Shizu   pth. Suzong   pth. Muzong
           1040–1092   1042–1094   1053–1103

(5 sons by his principal consort)

Wanyan Sagai Wanyan Wuyashu (1) Wanyan Aguda (2) Wanyan Wuqimai
(d. 1121)   1051–1113   (b. 1068)   (b. 1075)
         pth. Kangzong   Jin Taizu 1115–1123 Jin Taizong 1123–1135

(3 of Aguda's 16 sons fathered emperors)

Prince Zonghan Prince Shengguo Prince Zonggan   Prince Zongyao
Nianhan
1080–1137
           (3) Wanyan Dan (4) Wanyan Liang (5) Wanyan Yong (Wulu)
           (b. 1119)   Prince Hailing   (b. 1123)
           Jin Xizong   (b. 1122)   Jin Shizong 1161–1189
           1135–1149   1149–1161

Wanyan Yungong   (7) Wanyan Yunji Prince Wei
(d. 1185)   Weishao
pth. Xianzong   1209–1213, no pth.

(8) Wanyan Xun (b. 1163)   (6) Wanyan Jing (b. 1168)
Jin Xuanzong 1213–1224   Jin Zhangzong 1189–1208

                           (9) Wanyan Shouxu (b. 1198),
                           Jin Aizong 1124–1134

*(10) Wanyan Chenglin, Jin Mo Di, reigned 1234 (a great-grandson
of Holibo, he belonged to the third generation. He reigned February 9
and 10, 1234; died in melee when Song troops entered Caizhou).

kind of adaptation, showing that farm boys when necessary could become mounted archers able to compete with the steppe's best. But those exceptions to the normal pattern of Chinese life were limited in space and in time, and Chinese could always revert to the more traditional agrarian ways. The Jurchens, having made a very rapid adaptation to the neighboring Khitan modes of warfare, within one or two more generations began to make a further adaptation to Chinese social organization. They remained socially volatile to an extreme degree. At this moment in their history, however, they were bent on learning from the Khitans while retaining their forest hunters' proud independence and fierce hostility toward their overlords.

V. EXPLAINING THE JURCHENS' SUCCESS

We have seen in the Khitan case that Abaoji struggled to strengthen the Liao throne by reorganizing the complex, centuries-old tribal government of the Khitans in order to achieve a greater centralization of powers and a more secure imperial institution. He had been forced to compromise with the old forms and the long-established tribal interests they served. His successors continued to work toward more effective central control, and achieved much. Throughout the process, however, the Khitan tribal leadership structure remained intact; Khitan leaders were conscious of the tensions between the tribes (functionally like "fiefs" of the tribal aristocracy) and the state. In short, the Liao state had not been wholly successful in achieving a cohesive military command structure. It could be dominated by strong emperors, but institutionally it nonetheless was unable to overcome the fact that diffusion of authority is inherent in an essentially decentralized hierarchy of tribal aristocracy. Not even the members of the Khitan imperial and consort clans, the privileged Yelü and Xiao clans, always sided with the central government. They remained aristocrats with their own sense of place, of rights, and of privilege. Not overawed by the personal qualities of the reigning emperor, at the time of the crisis posed by the Jurchen uprising in 1114, many of them were at odds with current state policy and the conduct of the court; many remained uncooperative, and some defected to the enemy.

The wild Jurchens had no such system of ancient dignities and established traditions of state government of the kind that lent stability to the Liao in ordinary times but could deny them full mobilization of their strengths in moments of crisis. The Jurchens had as yet no history as a national confederation; that began to emerge only in the youth of Aguda (b. 1068). His father, Holibo (d. 1092), experienced considerable difficulty in keeping tribal units from fighting among themselves, and if the Wanyan leaders had allowed it, those independent tribal powers might well have increased as the confederation of tribes was forged late in the eleventh century. The Wanyan leaders did not allow that to occur. Under the pressures of the explosive Jurchen rise, their simpler and looser tribal institutions could be made to serve the new centralized state apparatus as it quickly took form. The idea of the dynastic state, symbolized by the adoption of the name the Great Jin Dynasty in 1114, imitated the Liao example, but of course in both cases that represented acceptance of the Chinese model for the state. In both the Liao and the Jin cases, difficult adjustments of tribal expectations to the demands of Chinese state institutions created problems for the founding emperors. But tribal institutions also could be made to contribute to the process of building the hybrid state system of the conquest dynasties. Aguda's uncle Yingge, the supreme Wanyan chieftain from 1094 to 1103, was an institutional innovator and a strong contributor to Wanyan supremacy. Among other moves, by imposing the customary law of the Wanyan tribe as a uniform law on the entire Jurchen confederation, he broadened the leaders' authority at the expense of tribal independence.

Also, during the decade of Yingge's rule, and in the following decade under Wushuya (Aguda's older brother and predecessor in leadership), traditional tribal offices were quickly and effectively transformed according to the needs of the emergent Jurchen nation. Appointments to all the tribal supreme chieftainships, called in Chinese the "Bozhi" or "Bojilie" (the Jurchen pronunciation has been reconstructed as *bogile*), came to be subject to central control, in effect causing all the highest chieftains now to function as officials of the new state government instead of as independent hereditary leaders with their own tribal power bases.

Institutionally most important was the famous Jurchen *meng'an* and *mouke* system, a traditional but not previously fully developed system of mobilizing the population in times of war and of governing in times of peace.[20] *Meng'an* in the Jurchen language means "one thousand," and *mouke* probably meant "village community."[21] The two terms developed meanings as titles of the chieftains who headed mobilized fighting units of 1,000 and 100; hence they are sometimes translated "chiliarchs" and "centurions." The groupings they headed were based on natural kinship relationships within clans and tribes. As the two terms were adapted into the military and political systems by Aguda in about 1114, they came to refer both to the military units and to the groupings of households that provided the fighting men and supported them, that is, to the natural units making up the entire Jurchen population. During Aguda's early years in power, he made of this social order an administrative system: households were registered into units of about 100, the *mouke*, ten of which formed a *meng'an*, the unit of a thousand households, loosely equivalent to a tribe. As the system was now made uniform, it served in times of war as a national system of mobilization. When the population had to be mobilized for war, the Bojilie, or tribal chieftains, then simultaneously held the rank of *meng'an*—"head of a thousand," or chiliarch.

Jurchen society lived by a rather primitive kind of agriculture supplemented by hunting and fishing. The tribal organization, however, kept all the people readied for warfare as the means to a better life. The *meng'an* and *mouke* were not just wartime units of fighting men. As I have noted, they were the basic organizational units of the entire population for all purposes. Each household in a *mouke* was required to supply one able-bodied fighting man, his weapons and armor, and two to four mounts. Other males were to serve as assistants or, in case of need, as replacements for fallen or disabled warriors. If one household was stricken with losses that prevented it from fulfilling its military obligation (and there were no taxes or other obligations to the state), other households within the *mouke* village kinship community assumed the responsibility. Beyond maintaining that self-supporting military service, the *mouke* was the baseline unit of organization for economic, religious, and ritual purposes. The head of the *mouke*, that is, the centurion, had the responsibility for governing society at the base level; he combined some of the old tribal responsibilities with the newly formalized obligations to the state. We may well use the term "*mouke* society" to refer to Jurchen social organization, for these units represented the pattern of the Jurchen extended family system and thus were the building blocks of the society.

Historically, the institutional standardization of the *meng'an* and *mouke* system at this point in Jurchen history was a very important innovation. It successfully utilized the preexisting familiar tribal organizational lines, giving the state a rational and uniform tool of organization that could be quickly extended to control the growing, increasingly diverse national society. One can surmise that it was accepted by the people as something old and familiar while being made to function to quite new ends. Some aspects of it, particularly the organization of society uniformly into military units of standard size, would exert an influence on the Mongols a century later; that is evident in their system of centurions, chiliarchs, and myriarchs (these last heading units of 10,000). Such "decimal systems" of military organization were characteristic of Inner Asian peoples from much earlier times; the Jurchen adaptation was to broaden these into a social system that guaranteed recruitment as well as support for the fighting forces and united military obligations with civil governing. This system provided the model that would later be adapted and still further expanded by the Jurchens' ethnic kin the Manchus as they created their famed Banner organization, the military machine that conquered China in the 1640s.

In 1116 Aguda enlarged the *mouke* from 100 to up to 300 households. The *meng'an* populations grew correspondingly in size. But the military units they provided and supported appear to have remained at the levels of about 100 and 1,000, respectively. Expanding the capacity of the system in this way, without increasing the numbers of leaders required to manage it, was a temporary expedient allowing the very small Jurchen population to absorb a large influx of captured and surrendered people. The fighting populations the Jurchens encountered in their rapid sweep through the Liao and Song territories, such as the Bohai population and even Han Chinese in the Liao military service, as well as surrendered or captured Khitans and their ethnic kin the Xi, could all be quickly organized, governed, and made to contribute to the Jurchens' military strength. Chinese-type local administrations, however, were left more or less intact in regions where the Liao had governed sedentary populations.

The meng'an-mouke institution continued to change rapidly through the following century of Jurchen rule in China. It can be taken as the institutional definition of the Jurchen nation, and the changes it underwent therefore define for us the transformations of the Jurchen people, particularly in relation to the Chinese. Those changes will be noted throughout Chapter 10.

One of Aguda's most interesting acts as he sought to bring his nation to greatness was his call for the invention of a Jurchen script. As in the case of Abaoji two centuries earlier, he also had a bookish distant clansman, Wanyan Xiyin, whom he called on to devise a script. Xiyin's short biography in the *Jin History* does not explain how a Jurchen of his time became literate, no doubt in Khitan and possibly also with some knowledge of Chinese writing. He could well have been one of those Jurchen chieftains' sons who had been sent to the Liao court for training. The *History* merely says that as the Jin state grew in power and importance, because it still lacked a script for its language it was forced to use the Khitan script in its diplomatic dealings with neighboring states. Aguda therefore ordered Xiyin to compose "a national script, in order to make complete our institutions. Xiyin thereupon, in imitation of the Chinese people's model script and in accord with the system of the Khitan script, and in keeping with our national language, made the Jurchen script."[22]

The new script system was completed and submitted in the late summer of 1120, to the great delight of Aguda, who ordered it adopted throughout his realm to supersede the Khitan script. The Khitan writing system, however, had become widely used by the Jurchens and other peoples, and the new script did not entirely succeed in replacing it, except in official use by the Jin government. A second script, called the Jurchen small script, was added in 1038.[23] No complete book using either script has survived; we know these scripts primarily from a few inscriptions on stone, a few pieces of wooden printing blocks, and other fragments. Although many of the Jurchen characters have been identified, the script has not been well studied. The Khitan scripts may have been technically superior, or their use may have become so well established among many peoples that they could not be displaced. As late as 1191 the Jin emperor had to command his translation bureau to no longer translate first into Khitan and then from Khitan into Chinese. From such evidence, of which there is much, we know that the Jurchen script was not as successful or as widely used as the earlier Khitan script had been; there is also much evidence, of which this is part, that the Jurchens did not retain their cultural identity in the competition with Chinese literary and cultural forms as well as had the Khitans. That, however, is to anticipate developments that lie far beyond the time of Aguda.

Where the historical record allows us glimpses of his personality, Aguda appears to have been a man of strong passions. His truculent behavior, made strikingly evident in his refusal to dance at the Liao emperor's feast in 1112, before he proclaimed himself the Jurchen emperor, displays one aspect of his character: in that situation he was courageous, stubborn, and canny in creating a politically useful effect. He knew how to play on the emotions of his fellow tribesmen, and that ability to arouse their fiercest feelings must be seen as a critical component of the Jurchens' rapid achievement of unity and commitment. There is a striking example in the crisis of 1115, when the Liao emperor declared that he personally would lead a massive army to extirpate the upstart Jurchens. Aguda's back was to the wall. He had proclaimed his new dynasty only the previous year, and his overmatched army was untried in large-scale war. News had just come that the Liao Tianzuo emperor had issued an edict declaring that his armies should totally exterminate all Jurchens they encountered. A twelfth-century Chinese account records Aguda's response to this crisis.

> Aguda assembled all the Jurchen chieftains. He grasped his knife and scored his forehead. [A Jurchen ritual to implore the sun god for assistance in extremity; as the blood ran down his face to mix with tears, the supplicant turned to the sun and wailed.] He looked up to the sun and wept. He spoke: "From the beginnings of our uprising we have all borne together the cruelties inflicted by the Khitans, our sole desire being to establish our own state. If today I were to choose to surrender, humbly and piteously, there is scant chance that we should escape disaster. They intend to exterminate us. Only if each one of us fights to the death can we turn them back. It might be better if you were to kill me and all my clan; you could then offer surrender and in that way turn disaster into good fortune for all of you." The assembled chieftains all gathered round his tent to bow down to him, saying: "Having come this far, we shall obey your every command, and resist to the death." The Liao emperor's forces included more than one hundred thousand Khitan and Chinese mounted troops, and their battle wagons stretched along for more than five hundred *li*. The sounds of drum and horn, the colors of banner and pennon, thundered and glittered through the wilderness. Approaching by separate routes from Changchun they encountered the Jurchens, who, before the Khitans had assumed battle positions, seized the chance to launch a hurried attack. The Tianzuo emperor suffered a grave defeat; his armies panicked and fled.[24]

Playing the impassioned leader, Aguda dramatized the peril that so starkly faced his people. He left his tribesmen only the two choices: to act like cowards or to fight desperately. He turned their grim situation into an asset by evoking violent emotions. The haste, passion, and desperation of that moment typify the entire rise of the Jurchens; they were driven by passionate rage. Under Aguda those emotions were all concentrated on the military tasks of their explosive rise to nationhood and conquest. The Jurchen style displays both cunning calculation and frenzied passion. The Liao rulers, and the Khitan people as a nation, by contrast seem to have been of a different temperament, more self-confident, more cool and detached. That too was a source of strength in some situations, but in this first major test of the Jurchens, Aguda held the upper hand.

Aguda died in 1123. His younger brother Wuqimai, known to history as Emperor Taizong of the Jin dynasty (Taizong is the expected Chinese posthumous designation for the second emperor in a dynastic line), succeeded smoothly to the leadership. That permitted the conquest of North China to continue without any pause or break. He appears as a less powerful personality, perhaps a less emotional leader, although an effective, flexible administrator. Aguda's and Wuqimai's cousin Sagai, the most able representative of his generation in the senior branch of the Wanyan clan, had died in 1121. Sagai's equally vigorous son Nianhan, known in history as Prince Zonghan, belonged to the next generation, that of the nephews. He was serving ably on the front in North China with siblings and other nephews (that is, his cousins), and he was not an immediate contender for supreme power. Succession to tribal leadership would trouble the Jurchen dynasty at a number of points, but at this crucial juncture potential rivals had other roles, allowing the succession to pass uncontested to the individual designated: in this case Wuqimai had been designated by having been appointed senior Bojilie in the Council of State. In the years 1124–1128 it was Wuqimai who directed the final pursuit and capture of the last Liao emperor and the negotiations that forced the Xi Xia state to accept Jurchen suzerainty, as well as the two-pronged advance across North China to the Yellow River commanded by two of his nephews. That action had led, as we have seen, to the capture of the two Song emperors and the subsequent consolidation of Jurchen control throughout North China. When Wuqimai died in 1135, the extraordinary period of the conquest came to an end. The new Jin dynasty at that point faced many problems of state-building and governing.

10

THE JURCHEN STATE
AND ITS CULTURAL POLICY

Jin dynasty political history, recounted here, reveals the circumstances in which a succession of rulers and their regimes made decisions that established the contours of the dynasty's development. During their reign of 120 years, the Jin rulers moved the Jurchen people from their Manchurian homeland southward into China. The dynasty transformed its institutions in successive phases of change, and reformulated its cultural policies from adoption to rejection of Chinese norms, while all the time becoming ever more thoroughly assimilated to Chinese ways. Yet throughout, the Jin still sought ways to remain Jurchen, ultimately struggling valiantly to survive. In 1234 they at last fell before the Mongols, but only after protracted and stubborn resistance. The Jin dynasty represents one pattern of conquest and rule within the orbit of Chinese civilization, building on yet differing from the Khitan Liao and the Tangut Xi Xia experience.

1. THE CONQUERORS TURN TO GOVERNING

The military tasks of the conquest were soon superseded in importance by two more enduring problems that were to test all of the Jurchens' capacities for rule: the continous need to adapt and expand their governing institutions, and the need to secure the Wanyan line of tribal chieftains in the Chinese-type emperorship while retaining the tribal basis of their military power. Both problems had also faced the Khitans and the Tanguts, whose solutions were well within the ken of Jurchen leaders. The Jurchens faced those problems under conditions that were new and different, peculiar to their historical situation. The narrative of Jin dynasty history alternates between these two leading themes and is embroidered by the further element of the characteristic Jurchen style, consisting of passion, haste, and violent urgency.

One can plausibly argue that the way the Jurchens went about adapting their governing institutions weakened them. That is, should one conclude that their increasing acceptance of Chinese models in government and of Confucian values in society so undermined their commitment to the tribal military bases of their dynastic power, and so corrupted the tough resilience of their social order, that their dynasty eventually collapsed? That was the stated belief in China, much debated as early as the thirteenth century, and it continues to be argued. But in fact the demise of the Jin was not brought about solely, or even principally, by such internal factors. Despite the continuous changes in the patterns of Jurchen life in China and in the workings of the Jin dynastic state throughout the twelfth and early thirteenth centuries, the immediate cause of the dynasty's extinction was external and unrelated. The Mongols' rise to sudden dominance of Inner and East Asia early in the thirteenth century cut Jurchen imperial history off before it had worked its way to any internally generated conclusion. We must therefore be wary of such arguments: history must deal with what actually happened.

What actually happened is that the Jurchen nation turned its attention away from further conquests in the steppe after it had completed its destruction of the Liao dynasty. It occupied only those Liao territories adjacent to the Jurchens' own homeland, lands that included principally Manchuria plus a relatively narrow zone extending no more than 300 miles to the west of the Greater Khingan Mountain Range.[1] The focus of Jurchen energy turned to the governing of an empire comprising its own people and a small number of Inner Asian tribal peoples remaining in Manchuria along with the large population of Chinese who resided in North China, the ancient heartland of Chinese civilization. The Jurchens themselves constituted no more than 10 percent of the total. Their Chinese subjects were densely settled across an area larger than the Jurchens' homeland in Manchuria. The Jurchen conquest of all those regions was accomplished with the greatest speed, but holding and governing the demographic mass of North China was a new, difficult, and complex task. The agent of the cataclysmic change was the widely ranging Jurchen field armies, active simultaneously on a number of fronts. They were given the on-the-scene responsibility of ensuring social order, but in fact they possessed neither the time nor the means to transform the aftermath of their blitzkrieg into a scene of settled normalcy. They brought their new dynasty's military presence to vast reaches of newly conquered territories; their field generals were in no sense prepared to deal simultaneously with alien problems of civil governing.

To meet the civil governing need, the armies in the field through the years 1115 to 1130 could do no more than make ad hoc arrangements to continue and expand the Liao pattern of dual institutions. They retained in office most local and regional civil officials, whether originally appointed by the Liao or, farther south and west, by the Song Chinese. Wherever possible they coopted military officers and their surrendered troops to assist in both their military and their civil tasks. But such hasty measures were insufficient to secure the regions through which the conquering armies had recently passed, much less to ensure stable social conditions in the aftermath of conquest. To meet the needs of this situation the Jin court took an unprecedented step.

In what has come to be known as the Great Migration, starting in the 1120s and substantially completed by the 1140s, the new Jin dynasty felt compelled to move almost the entire Jurchen population, first into newly conquered Liao territory and then on into the much larger regions wrested from the Song dynasty in North China. From the beginning this was seen as a permanent transfer of the Jurchen people, nothing less than the mass removal of the Jurchen nation, to a new setting. It could be accomplished with the efficiency of a military maneuver because the Jurchen population was organized into *meng'an* and *mouke* units, a system of organization that had been extended to other tribal peoples as they fell under Jin control. Those units were ordered to deploy at widely dispersed new locations throughout the North China provinces, to settle down and support the field armies whose soldiers were drawn from them, and to establish a permanent military presence in their new locales. We do not have population figures from this period, but estimates of the total military population of the *meng'an* (and their constituent *mouke*) units that were moved into China during these two decades are in the neighborhood of 3 million persons. Many of the individuals in those units were captives and slaves; some further were ethnic Khitans, Xi, and other surrendered Inner Asian fighting peoples newly assigned to *meng'an* and *mouke* units. Jurchens thus probably numbered half of the 3 million total figure.[2]

Once moved into North China, all were given lands and oxen for farming. Their leaders were given hereditary offices of standardized rank and salary status. Their duties at the *mouke* level were twofold: they were the responsible for training the adult males in military skills and for leading them in battle; and they also were the responsible heads of the entire population of roughly 100 Jurchen (or other) households assigned to their *mouke*, in addition to Jurchen and other individuals and households in the status of slaves or captives. (Jurchens could suffer enslavement as punishment for certain crimes but eventually could be restored to free status; most slaves were Chinese and other war captives.) As the "family head" of that kinship group, its slaves, and its other dependents, the *mouke*[3] were simultaneously the military leaders and the civil governors at the base level of the transplanted Jurchen society. Soon they also were assigned other duties (assisting with tax collection, suppressing banditry, and maintaining order in their localities), so they exerted influence over the nearby Chinese population as well. But there were many problems attendant on the Jurchens' move away from their homeland into a new environment in which they were a ruling minority.

Unlike China's other northern frontier invaders during these centuries, the Jurchens were constantly forced to adjust to the new geographic and social bases of their real power while devising and adapting structures through which to rule. During his nine-year reign Aguda gave impetus and direction to that process. After his death there seemed to be no leader with a commanding presence to unify the Jurchens' vision of their national destiny; even within the Wanyan imperial clan there were jealousies and conflicting ambitions and competing views of national policy. Not surprisingly, the Jurchens' lightning-like military successes were far ahead of their struggling attempts to deal with the stranger and more complex worlds of policy and politics.

Recent scholars have described four periods within the 120 years of the Jin dynasty. First, the two reigns from 1115 to 1135 constituted a period of rapid adaptation to dual institutions on the Liao pattern; that is, retaining or adapting native Jurchen institutions for the Jurchen population while continuing to use Chinese governing methods for Chinese and other sedentary subjects. Second, there was a period of centralizing changes, at first somewhat ad hoc, then headlong abandonment of the dual administration in order to elevate the emperor to the utmost heights of despotic power; that occupied the two reigns of Wanyan Dan and Wanyan Liang, from 1135 to 1161. Third, from 1162 until 1208, there followed a period of strongly felt but gradually diminishing reaction against what was taken to be the China-derived imperial tyranny, and the concomitant struggle to achieve a nativistic return to essential "Jurchenness." It did not succeed as an effort to revive tribal society's pristine values and sources of strength, yet it restored some balance and perspective to the Jurchens' cultural adaptation. Finally there was the fourth period, in the early decades of the thirteenth century, when the Jurchens faced their ultimate enemy, the Mongols, and the Jin state disappeared from history. This useful four-period framework will be followed here.[4]

II. THE PERIOD OF DUAL INSTITUTIONS, 1115–1135

While Aguda, in his almost nine years on the throne, was furiously busy leading the armies whose conquests created the Jin state, his younger brother Wuqimai, his designated heir, served as the chief of the Council of Bojilie (the Great Chieftains). He headed the administrative machinery being assembled at the newly founded Jin Supreme Capital (Shangjing, near present-day Harbin in the Sungari Basin of Manchuria). Throughout the first two reigns, those of Aguda himself (1115–1123) and Wuqimai (1123–1135), new political institutions took form.

From the beginning, Aguda was strongly guided by a Bohai scholar-official named Yang Pu (in the Chinese pronunciation of his name), a man who had earned the *jinshi* degree, the highest Chinese-style official degree, in the Liao civil service examinations, and who had a sound working command of Chinese classical learning. He was completely familiar with the inner workings of the Liao dual administration; in addition, he had Aguda's confidence, enhanced no doubt by the fact that the Jurchens looked upon the Bohai as kindred people. Yang Pu's involvement led to the rapid expansion of the Jin dynasty's machinery for governing its growing empire. That assistance was of crucial importance. At the beginning of each of the conquest dynasties we see such a figure, an expert in civil governing, well versed in Chinese learning, who exerts guiding influence during the transition to the new imperial order. In this case, Yang Pu's guidance eased the conquerors' takeover of the institutional structure well worked out in long practice by the Liao state. This was a dual structure of parallel administrative pyramids for the sedentary and the tribal-nomadic divisions of the state, under one overarching concentration of military-based power headed by a Supreme Chieftain/emperor. The special significance of this in the Jin dynasty's case is that the Jurchen tribal base was small, yet by 1130 the Jin had conquered territories with long-established sedentary populations vastly larger than the sedentary populations over which the Khitans had ever ruled; the Khitans' territorially larger empire was aimed at expansion into the sparsely inhabited steppe, and not so deeply into China.

One must wonder what the Jurchens might have done when they faced immense governing problems quite outside their own experience had the Liao institutional formula not been in place awaiting ready adaptation to their needs. It makes one conscious of the creative genius of the Khitans, and of their impact on a thousand years of institutional history. The case parallels technology transfers of other kinds in more recent history that have enabled countries facing new tasks to adapt quickly to a range of alien methods, from those for governing and managing economies to those for manufacturing industrial goods or for controlling epidemics. We think of these technological elements as universals of modern civilization; in a sense, the Chinese and the steppe governing methods and tools, successfully combined into one political system by the Khitans and in another modification by the Tanguts, had become a technology of statecraft capable of transcending particular cultural bases in twelfth-century East Asia. Throughout that century the Jurchens, the Tanguts, and the Khitan remnant in far-off Western Liao (or Kara Khitai) all continued to add to the store of such universal governing techniques that the Mongols would draw on in their turn in the next century.

Wuqimai, a man of administrative rather than military talent, headed the Wanyan imperial clan at a time when the various military fronts all produced generals of outstanding abilities. All of the Jurchens among the commanders—and most were Jurchens—were his cousins or nephews, some of whom considered their status in the imperial clan to be equal or even superior to Wuqimai's, and who felt that as victors at the front they had earned the right to make policy and set directions for the entire Jurchen enterprise. Wuqimai, as Aguda's younger brother and designated heir, sought to strengthen the system while responding to the vastly enlarged tasks of governing all of North China—to the south well beyond the Yellow River and to the west into Shaanxi. Nominally at least, all that region was administered centrally, on the Liao model, from a Supreme Capital, where a machinery of permanent civil government was emerging even while the territories it governed were in a state of flux in the wake of campaigns planned and guided at the discretion of powerful generals in the field. Those generals—not only the emperor's cousins and nephews but also a few powerful associates (some of them Chinese who had come over to the Jurchen side)—were designing the patterns of conquest as they progressed with it. Some indeed tried to create military fiefs as bases for their own power. They were not united in their understanding of the Jurchen purpose in North China. While campaigning and bargaining with the enemy, they sponsored the creation of two puppet regimes, one in 1127 that lasted about one year, and one in 1130 which was abolished in 1137.[5] These moves were implemented by generals in the field to create buffers between the Jin territories and the Song areas farther to the south. It is quite clear that the emperor's leading generals (and kinsmen) on the front were uncertain about how much of North China they could hold, or where the boundary between their conquests and the Song state should be drawn. The puppet states were useful shields on their southern flanks, as well as added threats to the Song, in this very uncertain phase of consolidation.

In the confusion and lack of unified action among the Jin leaders, peace negotiations with the Chinese representing the Song government were under way, off and on, throughout the entire period prior to the treaty settlement that was reached in 1141–42 under Wuqimai's successor. After that settlement was reached, the Jurchens gave up thoughts of indirect control through puppet regimes or of returning portions of the North China provinces to the Song; the treaty boundary was drawn at the Huai River, roughly halfway between the Yellow River and the Yangzi; with it, they committed themselves to direct governance over their large region of China. To greatly simplify the situation that existed from the 1120s to 1141, one can say that the generals in the field pressed for traditional tribal leaders' feudal prerogatives through their status as members of the Council of Great Chieftains (Bojilie), while at the capital a civil government faction sought to strengthen the emperor's powers through the extension of dual administration and the further adoption of Chinese forms of centralized imperial government. Despite the implications of this struggle pitting decentralizing tendencies against centralization of authority in the person of the emperor, throughout Wuqimai's eleven-year reign, until 1135, the military interests of the new dynasty remained supreme and Wuqimai acted more as a tribal chieftain than as an emperor. His personal relations with his kin remained close, and he could safely empower his chief generals on the shifting China fronts to make the basic campaign and administrative decisions on their own. To be sure, that limited his own powers as the chief executive of the central government while strengthening his generals' striking power. Yet at the same time he understood the need to strengthen his own position and to achieve a more stable pattern of government: in 1134, the year before his death, he announced a reorganization of his central government that eliminated the Council of Great Chieftains. That did not please his generals.

Doing away with the chieftains' council greatly undermined the "feudalizing" process favoring the imperial kinsmen who held high-ranking generalships; it was an action that exacerbated the divisions within the Wanyan imperial clan. Wuqimai's successor, the Emperor Xizong (Wanyan Dan, 1135–1149), took further steps in that direction, essentially pitting Chinese cultural forms (but not necessarily cultural values) against the modes of Jurchen tribal society. He continued to recognize some of the traditional rights of the military nobility, on whose power the emerging state depended, while putting into place a structure of civil governing ever closer to the Chinese model. That further deepened the tensions within the Jurchen elite and prefigured fierce struggles soon to come.

A sidelight on the tensions in cultural policy at this phase of the Jurchen conquest is seen in a proclamation issued by the Grand Marshal's office, in the field in 1126, saying that because the Jurchens had conquered all, it next would be appropriate to unify the customs of the conquered to make them conform to Jurchen norms. Thus he ordered all the Chinese inhabitants of the conquered zones to shave the hair on the front of the head and to dress only in the Jurchen style, on pain of death. It is not known how long or how thoroughly this proclamation was observed, but for a time it struck terror in the Chinese population.[6] This curiously prefigures the action of descendants of the Jurchens, the Manchus, in their conquest of Central China in 1645, when enforcement of a similarly worded decree caused riots and fierce resistance, which were put down only with intimidating massacres of whole towns. But in that case the Manchus succeeded in forcing the Chinese to submit to their cultural policy.[7] The short-lived Jurchen forehead-shaving command of 1126 probably should not be taken as evidence that the military commanders were basically hostile toward or fearful of Chinese cultural influences as such; the requirement to adopt Jurchen hairdressing and clothing styles was simply a standard Inner Asian way of forcing conquered peoples to display their subservience to their conquerors. On the other side of that cultural issue, however, neither were there many cases of the Jurchen institutional centralizers in the civil administration having been drawn to Chinese cultural values per se; they attempted to implement the Chinese imperial model because it enhanced their power, not because it elevated their culture.

During the decade of Wuqimai's reign (1123–1135), the influences of Chinese and of sinified Bohai and Khitan advisers on the forms and practices of government steadily increased. That was true at the Supreme Capital in the far northern homeland, and it was also true in the provinces of Song China that fell under full Jurchen control. As I have noted, throughout the sedentary portions of the former Liao realm many officials were recruited into service simply by being retained in the posts to which the Song or the Liao regimes had appointed them. That expedient represented the Jurchen adoption of the Liao dual administration under which Chinese subjects were to be governed in the Chinese manner. But in Jin practice it accompanied a sharp qualitative shift, from the quite limited Liao dominance over a narrow zone of sedentary, mostly Chinese society, to a situation in which the Chinese land and people constituted the major share of the Jin empire's total area and population. The Jin had become the governors of China's entire heartland. They ruled over 30 million Chinese in China north of the Huai River, while their own population stood at perhaps 2 to 3 million late in the twelfth century.[8]

If the Jin dynasty had followed the Liao pattern of state-building, it would have maintained and strengthened the Jurchen homeland. That is, had the Jin dynasty built its strength on a tribal base designed to absorb ethnically compatible tribal peoples while employing its less compatible sedentary subjects, especially the Chinese, as its subordinate associates, the primary concern would have been the management of a steppe-dominated empire. The preponderance of Chinese subjects, if so managed, might have been no more a threat to Jurchen survival than it was in the next century to China's Mongol overlords.

The Jurchens did not do that. They were not Khitans, nor were they Mongols. Uneasy about their control mechanisms in North China, they promoted the massive migration of Jurchens into China out of the nomadic "reservoir." Relocated in China, they were dispersed in the separate *meng'an* and *mouke* organizational units throughout the North China provinces, where they were given the means to settle down on lands granted to them by the state. That policy answered a lingering Jurchen popular ideal of landowning, one that the fully nomadic Khitan common warriors would have scorned.

The Great Migration brought about changes in the pattern of Jurchen social life that in time eroded both the Jurchens' cultural distinctiveness and their economic dominance. Through several generations the Jurchen household heads in those military units in their new Chinese rural setting played the roles of local landlords, and their unit heads became the local governors even as they became indebted to Chinese usurers or dependent on Chinese managers. Under their chiliarchs and centurions, the Jurchen common soldiers were expected to utilize their new Chinese land and their privileges to sustain themselves as a fighting elite, policing the conquered land. Yet they of course could sense that they had long-range interests in their alien setting, and these led them into close interactions with the society around them. They appear to have commenced to intermarry with Chinese sometime in the middle of the century (although the ban on the Jurchen nobility's intermarriage was not lifted until 1191). It also appears that many rapidly became bilingual, then rather quickly abandoned their own Jurchen language. But most important, as landowners they became involved in the shared interests and disputes of their localities. A high degree of assimilation was inevitable. Evidence of this became apparent by the 1140s even as the migration into North China was completed.

The Jurchen rulers became understandably uneasy about the foundations of their power in the rapidly changing circumstances. Seeking scapegoats for policy failures, they fell prey to factional cleavages even within their own Wanyan clan. Their struggles produced forced reversals of national policy and purges of those held responsible for failures. In consequence the Jin dynasty government was less stable than the Liao system had been, whatever the tensions we have seen in the Liao structure of power in earlier chapters.

III. THE ERA OF CENTRALIZATION, 1135–1161

Deep anomalies of the Jin political structure emerged sharply as early as the reign of Wanyan Dan (1135–1149), one of three grandsons of Aguda who successively inherited the throne in the middle decades of the twelfth century. He is known to history as the Emperor Xizong. In a succession manipulated by his uncles, he came to the throne as a boy of fifteen. Although born during

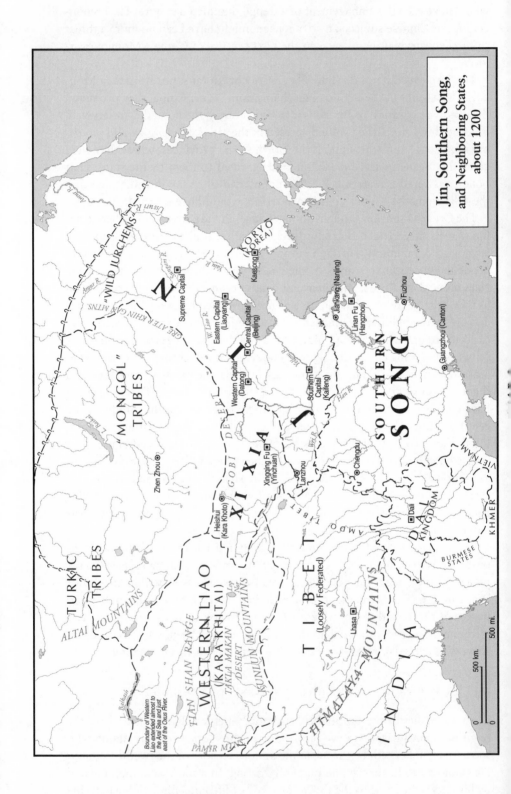

Jin, Southern Song, and Neighboring States, about 1200

the early years of the conquest, he had been reared in the home of a relative in which Chinese was spoken and Chinese lifestyles were becoming fashionable. An early account says, "He had completely lost the traditional Jurchen character."[9] In the official *Jin History* he is quoted in many conversations with his high Chinese officials in which his allusions to the classics and histories are as learned as those of most Chinese emperors in history. He not only had mastered the classics and was able to write Chinese poetry, but also adopted attitudes of scorn for his ruder Jurchen relatives.

During Emperor Xizong's fifteen-year reign, from 1135, to 1149, the deep problems which emerged within the Jurchen governing aristocracy were not simply due to his personal weaknesses and his courtiers' rivalries, though those too were extreme. More fundamentally, the anomalies of that political scene reflected the shifting bases of power. This young ruler was an inexperienced and inept leader, a mere figurehead trying to assume personal rule without strong institutional supports, either from the alienated tribal power structure or from the still superficially adapted Chinese-type administration. Several of his uncles, who in arranging his succession had improperly disinherited Wuqimai's sons, became the leading players in factional politics. They had arranged for themselves to be appointed the highest-ranking officials in the Chinese side of the dual administration. There followed an important centralizing reorganization of the civil government. The Council of Bojilie, or Great Chieftains, had already been abolished in 1134, depriving those high military tribal leaders of their voice in decision making; now the office of Great Chieftain itself was abolished. That terminated the principal remnant of tribal institutions at the level of Jin dynasty central government.

At local and regional levels in North China, the military administration remained largely in the hands of the Jurchen tribal nobility and their hereditary successors. The military commanders became the essential factor in civil government because the local military authorities still were superior to their civil counterparts in the circuits, prefectures, and counties. Their local military autonomy, however, was seen by the emperor as competing with the authority he exercised throughout the machinery of regional and local governing from his Chinese-style court and central secretariat. Everything about those shifting relationships within the appropriated structure of dual institutions was anomalous and conducive to struggles within the Jin government. The anomaly demanded some kind of rationalization.

As the young Emperor Xizong reached his maturity in the 1140s, he found himself in intense conflict with his powerful uncles at the court and with the generals controlling the base-level military government that taxed and exploited the Chinese population. For whatever reasons, the emperor became a dissolute, alcoholic, violent ruler. He wantonly executed many of his high Chinese officials in an attempt to intimidate them and silence their criticism. He also murdered many Jurchen leaders, including members of his own Wanyan clan, to suppress their opposition. The *Jin History* says of him that when he came to the throne the realm was untroubled and the forces of civil governing made notable progress. But by the end of his reign he had become a drunken tyrant and all the people were in terror.[10] He was murdered in his palace by a cabal of resentful relatives and courtiers led by his cousin Wanyan Liang, who then ascended the throne and carried out a bloody purge. That led to a brief era of ruthless centralization.

Wanyan Liang reigned from 1149 until he too was murdered in 1161.[11] In all Chinese records he is known as Prince Hailing, denied the posthumous honorific normally given to all deceased rulers, to show that he did not merit the honor due an emperor. There had been no doubt about his imperial status while he lived, but he was hated by his relatives of the imperial clan and by the Jurchen nobility; in revenge, they demoted him posthumously. So fully do all the historical records denigrate him, and so pervasive in the Chinese mind are the glorifications of his depravity, that it is difficult to take his true measure.[12] It may be true that he was uninhibited and given to excesses in his personal conduct, and he certainly was prone to violence. Those qualities do not set him apart from several other Jin dynasty emperors. Yet even today most Chinese readers of history see him as the caricature of lechery, a depiction established early in scurrilous fiction. Despite an element of truth underlying that caricature, unlike his cousin Wanyan Dan, whom he murdered to gain the throne, Prince Hailing displayed certain capacities as a ruler. He had large and perceptive ideas about governing, and he implemented (if violently) what were sound administrative reforms.

Even the moralistic Chinese histories admit that Wanyan Liang was very intelligent, and it is clear that he had a consuming drive to achieve vast plans. He was master of the Chinese literary tradition and a skilled poet, although that cultivation seems not to have deepened his humanity. His view of the problems of Jin government was very much like that of his murdered cousin, but he was more systematic and purposeful in abandoning most of the on-again, off-again remnants of dual administration in an urgent drive to eliminate the Jurchen tribal nobility's prerogatives. He continued the adoption of Chinese institutions, rituals, and forms of court behavior, and he succeeded in eliminating the autonomy of local military governors. All civil and military decision making was centralized in his hands. He sought by these moves to achieve heights of imperial might and awe that he, like other Inner Asian rulers of tribal societies, took, however incorrectly, to be the essence of the Chinese imperial institution. In his distortion of that concept and in the willfulness of his conduct, he went farther than perhaps any foreign ruler in China before him. Simultaneously, his not unreasonable fears of the enemies he created led him to brutality and murder. But such brutality, focused especially on potential rivals within the imperial clan, had all along been a feature of Jurchen politics.

In a grandiose final effort to turn attention to the external enemy and to gain imperishable fame as a Jurchen national hero, he planned and led a misconceived war to exterminate the Southern Song: in effect, he wanted to complete the conquest begun forty years earlier (and wisely abandoned) by his grandfather and granduncle, the first and second Jin emperors Aguda and Wuqimai. Prince Hailing expected that military challenge to bring him the crowning achievement of his rule. He wrote Chinese poems bragging how he would take to himself the "unsurpassed beauty of the world," personified as a woman in the Song emperor's harem; how he would ride his horse to the top of the highest mountain peak in Wu, the region adjoining the Song capital at Hangchow, and in command of a million soldiers would surround the West Lake on which the city was situated. The project obsessed him. But he also had a realistic appreciation of the populous and productive lower Yangzi region's riches. His sights were set on the greater wealth of the Chinese South.

In his attempt to lead a conquering army across the Yangzi, Prince Hailing commanded a force headed by the famed Jurchen cavalry units, but it also depended on many conscripted foot soldiers, most of whom were Chinese. A great share of his resources went to building ships to contest the Song control of the inland and coastal waterways so that he could ferry his army safely across the Yangzi. That represented a technological enlargement of military skills not previously attempted by any northern conqueror. A century later the Mongols also had to acquire a Chinese navy to follow their route of advance southward into the middle Yangzi, and then downriver, to eliminate the Song. The later Mongols' progress in enlarging their military capacity in that way was no doubt informed by the Jurchens' failure, and invites comparison with it.

The preparation for Prince Hailing's war took more than two years. The many courtiers and high officials who opposed it were brutally silenced. The expenses were crippling. The strategy was faulty. His Jurchen generals were not committed to it with the fury that had helped Aguda triumph over great odds, nor did Hailing have Aguda's charismatic power. He appointed incompetent leaders who would do his bidding. The great expedition was launched in October 1161. In early December it suffered a defeat in an unsuccessful first attempt to cross the Yangzi, at Caishi near Nanjing, a crossing point used throughout history by armies from the north. Song naval power had developed rapidly since the 1130s and could overwhelm the forces manned by the local Chinese boatmen hastily impressed into service by their northern masters. But Prince Hailing was undeterred; he drew back to Yangzhou and planned a second crossing. On December 15 his generals, frustrated by the incompetence displayed in the initial attempt, and fearing the consequences of a second defeat, murdered him at his forward military camp near Yangzhou, on the Grand Canal twenty miles north of the Yangzi. So ended this offensive against the Song. But Prince Hailing's importance in history goes beyond this failure in warfare; his reorganization measures had a lasting effect on the structure of Jin government.

First among those measures was his transfer in 1153 of the Jin capital from the old Supreme Capital (Shangjing) in northern Manchuria to the former Southern Capital (at the site of present-day Beijing), now renamed the Central Capital after its rebuilding in the grander style of a Chinese capital. That move was not unpopular with many of the Jurchen tribal leaders. The Great Migration had brought most of the Jurchen population into North China, where they held lands and followed lifestyles that caused them rapidly to lose their identification with the deep forests of their Sungari River homeland. Prince Hailing could see that except for a few princely military leaders personally opposed to him, the interests of all strata of Jurchen society lay within China. The old Supreme Capital was a distant empty city of little use or meaning. Putting the Jin capital in China closer to the *meng'an* and *mouke* settlements could be seen as an appropriate action. But as Hailing went about that task, his excesses aroused resentment.

When the government was ostentatiously moved into its new city in 1153, Hailing instituted elaborate court rituals and ceremonies symbolizing his desire to become the complete Chinese imperial despot. At the same time, he moved the imperial tombs of the Jin founding emperors and their ancestors to a new tomb park near the Central Capital. In 1157 he ordered the leveling of the nobles' residences back at the old Supreme Capital and the destruction of the former palaces and shrines; the land was returned to farming. His purpose was to cut the Jurchen nobles off from the possibility of return. In that same year he issued a decree abrogating the title of "prince" held by Jurchen nobles, demoting them to lesser titles of nobility. These were mostly members of his imperial Wanyan clan. Their denigration further distanced him from the aristocrats and the imperial relatives who thought of themselves as the founding emperors' peers and the possessors of unshakeable privilege. Their privileges and their feelings of independence were, of course, precisely the target of Hailing's larger plan. But his moves aroused fear and threatened desperate actions by his opponents. He was repeatedly forced to deal with their dissidence by ruthlessly killing off large numbers of Jurchen nobles and imperial princes. Despite their resentment, institutionally the throne was strengthened by his cold-blooded measures. The transfer of the capital successfully destabilized the aristocratic opposition to him. More important, it placed the seat of the administration in a central location and improved the functioning of government.

In the late 1150s another set of rationalizing actions was undertaken. Hailing fundamentally altered the structure of the central government, largely inherited from the Liao and further shaped by the model of the Song. His new measures simplified the system of offices and made the government much more responsive to his direction. Much of the incoherence of ill-defined offices and overlapping duties was cleared away. The measures legalized and systematized the strengthening of imperial power and rooted out all the remaining bases of competing princely prerogatives held by the old Jurchen tribal aristocracy. One of those bases of competing powers was the *meng'an-mouke* leadership, the economic basis of the military aristocracy. Certain of the *meng'an* units had become the hereditary private legions of high-ranking princes in the imperial household; they abused these positions to seize lands and slaves, to build fortunes, and to threaten the throne's centralizing measures. Hailing executed some 155 of those princes, abolished the most abused of their former privileges, and appointed his own loyal followers to many of the *meng'an-mouke* headships. At the same time, he had the few important *meng'an* remaining in the old Jurchen homeland in Manchuria transferred to

North China, in a sense completing the Great Migration. But in this instance the motive was quite different: he wanted to abolish bases of competing power located too far from the capital for his central government to control them.

Prince Hailing also lavishly reconstructed the former Song capital at Bian (Kaifeng), which he had designated the Jin Southern Capital; he planned to make it again the center of a China reunited under his rule. Such moves, further orienting the Jin dynasty geographically, institutionally, and culturally toward China, symbolized to many an insidious sinification of the Jurchen polity. The widely shared enmity toward him within the Jurchen tribal aristocracy not only took the form of rebellion leading to his murder, but also was expressed thereafter in a nativist revival that attempted to repudiate his cultural policies and to restore Jurchen ways. It did not, however, wholly undo the rationalizing and centralizing features of his political reorganization. Jin government, committed as it was to ruling a largely Chinese population within the North China Plain, remained more centralized and more effective because of his efforts, no matter how repugnant his personal style as imperial ruler had been.

The southern expedition in 1161 triggered the opposition's efforts to get rid of Prince Hailing. The military expenses and the simultaneous costs of lavishly rebuilding the old Song capital at Kaifeng had placed heavy burdens on the fiscal system. The levies of fighting men and of money were oppressive. Protests and military uprisings began to occur. One of the largest was an uprising among Khitans in their old homeland in Manchuria. Claiming to be threatened by warlike neighbors among other tribal peoples of the steppe, they requested exemption from service in the expeditionary force so that they would not have to leave their homes undefended. When that request was refused, they rose up and killed the officials who had been sent to impose Prince Hailing's will on them. Some of the rebel Khitan leaders wanted to lead their people westward to join the Western Liao (the Kara Khitai) in Central Asia, while others among them wanted to create a base of opposition at Linhuang, the old Khitan Supreme Capital. That disagreement was not resolved, and throughout 1161 the Khitan rebel movement remained disorganized but nonetheless was a serious threat to Jin control in the North. Other smaller rebellions among the Chinese in North China and among some non-Chinese peoples in Inner Asia also broke out. Sidestepping all these disturbances, Prince Hailing may have persisted in his plan to conquer the South because he thought that a great military victory would consolidate the nation in support of him, or he may have been too obsessed with that pursuit of glory to take stock of the troubles developing all about him. It was a bad time to be inattentive.

Far more significant than any of the other grave troubles was a rebellion of Jurchen nobles in southern Manchuria, at the Eastern Capital (present-day Liaoyang) in October 1161 led by Prince Wanyan Yong, whose Jurchen name was Wanyan Wulu. Wulu was proclaimed the new emperor in repudiation of Prince Hailing, and two months later, in mid-December, Hailing was assassinated by the generals in his camp at Yangzhou. His assassination encouraged leading courtiers to have Hailing's son and heir assassinated as he was awaiting his father's triumphant return to the new Central Capital. The courtiers then sent emissaries to welcome Wanyan Wulu to ascend the throne. He is known to history as the Emperor Shizong.

IV. THE PERIOD OF NATIVIST REACTION, 1161–1208

"Nativist reaction" has been seen at many times and places in human history. As we observe its manifestations in some of the conquest dynasties belonging to this phase of Chinese history, we might remind ourselves that something akin to it is present in the world today as well. African Americans in recent years have adopted African names, hairstyles, and dress, and have studied their ancestors' African languages. Many American Indians also have turned to the study of their traditional tribal rituals, their ancestral lore, their art and music. Many twentieth-century Jews of the Diaspora, in different parts of the world, have turned from the secularized lifestyles of their parents to Orthodox religious practice, study of Hebrew, and identification with the new Jewish homeland in Israel. History holds many parallel examples of the process. Such movements seldom have led to the mass displacement of the "adopted" culture and full return to the idealized "native" culture by the reacting society. But that is not the whole measure of their meaning. They can provide culturally destabilized or socially dissatisfied persons with the means to reorient their lives and regain the ability to integrate their individual needs with trends governing the larger society. The remarkable thing about the Jurchen nativist movement is that it expressed the feelings of the power-holding ruling element in the society, not those of the conquered host society; it was a movement not of oppressed Chinese seeking forms to vent their desire for freedom or their resentment against their overlords, but of the overlords reacting against the cultural norms of their subjects. But even that is not entirely without near parallels elsewhere.

We cannot recapture the workings of the Jurchens' nativist revival in the twelfth century at the level of ordinary individuals. But we can gain some sense of its importance to the Emperor Shizong (1162–1189), who sponsored the movement for his tribal elite and for all of his people at a time of great stress, and one can perhaps imagine its significance for more ordinary people as well. Even though the nativist measures had at best a limited impact on policy, and their implementation failed to stem the accommodation of the Jurchen nation to the Chinese host culture, the nativist reaction nevertheless must be assigned some weight in assessing the Jurchens' maturing adaptation to their setting.[13]

Emperor Shizong's long reign of twenty-eight years was followed by that of his grandson, the Emperor Zhangzong, who reigned for nineteen years, until 1208. These forty-seven years mark the high point of Jin history. Although dominated by the often vague and contradictory feeling of nostalgia for the old Jurchen ways, those were nonetheless years of continued adaptation to the problems of ruling China. The importance of this period does not lie in the futile attempts to undo Jurchen acculturation and return the Jurchen people to the forests of far northeastern Manchuria that marked it. This phase of Jurchen history is important for the example it offers of rapidly developing though now more stable patterns of acculturation—even when nominally decried by the leaders of the society.

During these five decades from 1162 until 1208, relations with the Song and other neighbors were mostly unthreatening, although domestic uprisings were troublesome for a few years. Domestic governing, while not without displays of political violence, nonetheless also adopted a greater reasonableness of spirit. There were, to be sure, unresolved problems in the conflict of cultural ideals and social realities. They give this period of Jin history much interest for the historian who wants to understand the Jurchens' place in the successive experiences of conquest dynasties.

The Emperor Shizong's succession to Prince Hailing in 1162 was violently imposed by rebellious Jurchen nobles in southern Manchuria. It was generally welcomed by the tribal aristocrats, the local military leaders, and the bureaucrats, except of course for Prince Hailing's immediate followers. Even so, it had occurred under difficult conditions, and the Jurchen elite were eager to regain the status and power that Hailing's policies had diminished. Their control over the machinery of state had been badly shaken by the dead emperor's policies, and were shaken again by the way in which he and his faction had been destroyed. In addition, the power of the Jin state was being challenged on several domestic fronts by rebellious uprisings. Wulu, the new emperor, was a man of thirty-eight, one year younger than his cousin whom he had displaced. He had spent most of the previous reign trying to distance himself from the vicious court in order to stay alive and did not have much administrative experience. By Jurchen concepts governing succession, he could be considered the next person in line in his generation; he was the third of that generation to reign and was accepted as the legitimate successor by most of the Wanyan clan. Like them, he had feared and hated Prince Hailing, and, while not fiercely vindictive, now shared their repudiation of all he had stood for. Those factors bore heavily on the policies that Wulu, as Emperor Shizong, adopted to deal with the Jin state's immediate difficulties.

The military uprisings were countered by transferring units of Hailing's expeditionary force, quickly brought under the new emperor's control, to the various domestic fronts, and to the steppe where the Khitan uprising was beginning to look more serious. That warfare dragged on through 1162 and was not fully eliminated until 1164. In retaliation the Khitan population was subjected to rigorous suppression, to forced mixing with remnants of the Jurchen population farther to the east in Manchuria, and forced surrender of their horses so that, like their Jurchen neighbors, they had to take up agriculture to survive. In the history of the Khitan people this became an era of grim suffering and humiliation. Emperor Shizong was ruthless in imposing military solutions, but he succeeded in restoring order throughout the realm and cohesiveness to the ruling elite.

In the traditional histories this man Wulu who had become the new emperor is given praise quite as exaggerated as the hatred expressed toward Prince Hailing. The Chinese histories honor him as a latter-day sage-emperor like those of China's antiquity. In fact, although a thoughtful and rather generous-minded man in many situations, he was less clear-headed than Hailing and was not unfailingly effectual in achieving his policy goals. The more interesting aspects of Emperor Shizong's long reign are those of his cultural policy. It embodied obvious anomalies. Prince Hailing's tyrannical rule was repudiated as much for the murdered emperor's elevation of himself as supreme ruler, and the accompanying centralization of all authority, as for his recourse to violence. His exaggerated imperial style was seen by all as displaying slavish preference for the Chinese imperial model (although, as I have noted, that model was fundamentally distorted in his emulation of it). Yet the new emperor, who denounced all that pomp and display, was by no means a steppe barbarian with no appreciation for Chinese tradition. His father, one of Aguda's sixteen sons, had taken as his consort a Bohai woman from a family with strong traditions of Chinese learning; Wulu became an accomplished student of Chinese high culture. He denounced Hailing's pretentious Chinese grandeur and criticized the luxury and degeneracy of the assimilated Jurchen aristocrats. Yet he nonetheless expressed admiration for the simple, austere ways of early China, and in doing so he adopted the Chinese cultural mode of criticizing the present by measuring it against an ideal past. He claimed that the golden age of Chinese antiquity—that is, the time of the great Zhou kings in the first millennium B.C.E. and on to the age of Confucius and Mencius—had much in common with the Jurchen ethos.

He owed a debt to the Jurchen nobles whose rebellion had placed him on the throne, but he was circumspect in repaying that debt. He restored most of their princely titles in 1163, and he reassured the elite in matters of their privileges and incomes. At the same time, he exhorted them to regain their martial spirit. He reestablished the great autumn and winter hunts, but not in Manchuria; instead they were carried on in North China, where hunting parks could be established that would not interfere too severely with agriculture. He restored the annual archery contests. He specially honored the few who could still use the Jurchen language at court, and urged broader study of the Jurchen script. For a whole year, 1184–85, near the end of his life, he resided at the somewhat refurbished Supreme Capital (near present-day Harbin), spending his days in the company of the few Jurchens who still lived there, enjoying the festivals and rituals, the hunting, banqueting, and roaming in the forests. Throughout his reign he clung to the sentiment of valuing the old ways, and undoubtedly that had some impact on the tenor of the age.

Nonetheless, the Emperor Shizong could not but recognize that Prince Hailing's institutional reforms had significantly centralized the patterns of governing. Not only was centralization more effective, but also it enhanced the ruler's authority in ways no ruler would willingly forgo. Despite his condemnation of Prince Hailing's excesses, Shizong did not abolish or even weaken his predecessor's many institutional reforms that strengthened the central government. Tribal princes got back their titles, but not an automatic place in the councils of state. The tension between them, in their unbridled ways, and the throne, with its interest in regularizing the conduct of government, remained a latent problem.

Emperor Shizong's attitude toward the central government's institutions reveals an obvious contradiction between sentiment and reality. Another anomaly is evident in the means he found to protect and favor his Jurchen people. He cared deeply about their well-being, in their *meng'an* and *mouke* units scattered throughout China's northern provinces. Like Prince Hailing before him, he also found abuses of privilege, unfair treatment of the ordinary Jurchen soldier-farmer households by their leaders, great disparity of wealth, and a trend toward impoverishment and overcrowding as the population grew. He saw faults in Jurchen attitudes—laziness, addiction to alcohol, frivolous dissipation and pleasure-seeking, and wasting of lands and resources by irresponsible household heads. Many were in debt to Chinese moneylenders and confidence tricksters. In short, the Jurchens had all too easily adapted to the Chinese social setting. Although they were conquerors able to exploit their status, many of them had quickly became entrapped, some by their own leaders' misdeeds, and many more in the indigenous society's complex patterns. In consequence they now were in danger of losing their organizational cohesion, only fifty years after the conquest and thirty years since the Great Migration into China had taken place.

Emperor Shizong introduced a broad set of reorganization measures in the years 1180–1183: the roughly 200 *meng'an* and nearly 2,000 subordinate *mouke* units were closely scrutinized to assess their problems and weaknesses. Each unit was reconstituted, and both its leadership and its member households were redefined. Tax obligations and exemptions were reformed to eliminate those abuses which interfered with the government's control, but they also were generously designed to aid ordinary Jurchens. An effort to enhance control over the *mouke* led to regulations that tightened supervision and leadership responsibility and encouraged the Jurchen warriors to hone their military skills.

Most important, many units were relocated to richer, more productive lands where *mouke* units could be sustained at full strength, for poverty had thinned the ranks and depleted family communities in many places. While this improved individual householders' economic position, a great effort also was made to restore the old communal ways of cooperative planting, plowing, and harvesting, in the hope of thereby regaining social cohesiveness and shielding ordinary Jurchens from the intrusive influences of Chinese rural society all about them. Together, the emperor hoped, these measures would reverse the obvious decline of Jurchen society and restore its military readiness. Shizong's attempt to bring about a thorough reorganization of his people's base-level society was driven by his need to ensure the loyalty of its leaders after the stresses of rebellion and civil war during Prince Hailing's last years.

When the Khitan rebellion in Manchuria was finally suppressed in the early

1160s, Shizong abandoned a long-standing policy; at first he proposed abolishing all the Khitan *meng'an* and *mouke*. As early as 1124 a Jurchen prince leading an army in the field had objected to the ad hoc creation of *meng'an* and *mouke* for the purpose of incorporating surrendered units of Chinese and Bohai soldiers into the Jurchen armies. His grounds were that "mixing together peoples of different social customs was not appropriate."[14] In 1140 all Chinese and Bohai *meng'an* and *mouke*—that is, units of the Jurchen military system composed of sedentary non-Jurchen peoples, all in Manchuria— were finally abolished and their soldiers placed on the military registers under the administration for the Chinese population. But the superb cavalry units of the Khitans, the Xi, and certain other tribal peoples formerly part of the Khitan armies were highly valued, and were retained as units of the Jurchen forces until the Khitan rebellion demonstrated their threat to Jurchen dominance. In 1163 an edict was issued abolishing them all, but a few months later it was modified to abolish only those that had rebelled between 1158 and 1163 and to retain those that had remained loyal, continuing them in their indispensable role as defenders of the northwest frontier in the steppe. Such Khitan forces still loyal to the Jurchens were, however, becoming few in number.

The *meng'an* and *mouke* were essentially of and for Jurchens, and the emperor's extensive reorganization of the system in the early 1180s granted them more generous support and greater privilege than ever before. Although the emperor's intent was to arrest a downward spiral of degeneration, historical evidence suggests that in the long run his indulgent concern induced ever greater abuses and demoralization. Moreover, the net effect of the reorganization tended to turn hereditary chieftains into landlords who exploited their opportunities to live the good life instead of competing for military advancement in the traditional manner. One can imagine that Aguda would have known better how to deal with these problems.

Still another anomaly appears in Emperor Shizong's cultural policies, such as in his sponsorship of learning. Shizong honored pristine Confucian concepts as congruent with true Jurchen ways and fostered a program to translate the ancient Confucian classics into Jurchen, to be published in the Jurchen script. That gave imperial approval to Confucian learning but it did not, as the ruler had hoped, broaden the use of Jurchen. Most literate Jurchens could by this time use the Chinese originals more easily than they could the new translations, and as an instrument of advancement they found that mastery of Chinese held more practical value.

Eventually the horrors of Prince Hailing's reign faded from people's memories and ceased to drive Jurchens so strongly toward an emotional identification with pristine Jurchen values. For many reasons they gave up the unrealistic cultural measures to which even Emperor Shizong himself could not bring clear-cut direction. With only a small fraction of the Jurchen people living in the old Jurchen environment where traditional ways still had practical meaning, the ruler could not forestall his people's continuing accommodation to the Chinese social environment. Jurchens were never more than a tiny fraction of the population of the entire realm they governed, and unlike the Khitans, they did not remain outside the line separating sedentary China from Inner Asia. There was no significant reservoir of uncontaminated Jurchens back in Manchuria, into whose company the Jurchens of the *meng'an* and *mouke* military units could be rotated, there to recover their receding "native" ways. Nor were Jurchens physically distinct from Chinese. Nothing marked them as a group apart in Chinese society; there was no irreversible core of Jurchenness. Perhaps they felt, quite consciously, that their own interests were better served by adapting to—inevitably being absorbed into—Chinese life. Emperor Shizong's nostalgia for the old Jurchen way of life was a romantic delusion, however meaningful it might have been from a military point of view had it succeeded in reversing cultural trends.

When Shizong died early in 1189, he was succeeded by his grandson, known in history as Emperor Zhangzong. Shizong had living sons, and Jurchen patterns would have indicated one of those as his successor. Shizong, however, had designated one particular son as his heir, and because that son had predeceased him, the only grandson born to that son's principal consort was next in line. This was entirely within Chinese patterns of succession, and historians have seen it as further evidence of adaptation to Chinese norms for the imperial institution. But it must also be noted that this grandson had especially pleased the emperor by his unusual and quite thorough command of Jurchen language and cultural traditions, along with his deep immersion in Chinese learning.

Throughout his reign (1189–1208), Emperor Zhangzong continued the pro forma veneration of Jurchen values, but he did even less than his grandfather to recover them. It had become all too clear that the Jurchen people had willingly abandoned most of their cultural distinctiveness, clinging of course to all legal privileges as conquerors while ever less conscientious about earning them. Jurchen statesmen themselves came to view the imperial institution wholly in Chinese terms. A modern historian who has analyzed all aspects of the cultural shift has noted in particular how the emperor's role was modified during Zhangzong's reign. On one occasion the emperor planned to leave the Central Capital (at present-day Beijing) to participate in the autumn hunt at a place just beyond the present-day Great Wall, by no means a distant journey. His Jurchen courtiers dissuaded him, using traditional Confucian arguments that "it was dangerous for an emperor to ride in the wilderness and it was detrimental to the economy of the state."[15] That advice persuaded the ruler of a state which, a mere seventy-five years earlier, had achieved its political and economic dominance through military skills based on the hunt! In the preceding reign, Zhangzong's grandfather had still encouraged the hunt as essential to military training, and because it provided the context in which the ruler could best maintain his personal relations with his own kind. Now it had become mere recreation, and of a kind considered unseemly for an emperor. By comparison, it must be noted that neither the Liao emperors nor their tribal elite ever abandoned those steppe elements of Khitan life, no matter how far they had gone in mastering Chinese learning. The Khitans retained their dual cultural world; for the Jin rulers the ancestral ways had become only a nostalgic ideal.

Zhangzong's reign became famous for the flourishing of literary culture, a golden age in the minds of some Chinese historians writing after the fall of the Jin dynasty. The Chinese-style examination system, as it came to function in these later reigns from Shizong onward, fostered a preoccupation with poetry and, some critics charged, with only superficial command of solid Chinese classical studies and historically informed statecraft. Zhangzong's Chinese empress and her relatives became central figures in a court faction that was identified with fashionable literary trends; it alienated many Jurchens and Chinese. The quality of governing was seen to decline as corruption and incompetence filled the court. Although military emergencies occurred with alarming frequency from the 1190s onward, the arts of peace held sway. The Jin dynasty cultural achievement will be more fully explored in Chapter 11.

Near the end of Zhangzong's reign, the Southern Song court authorized an ill-advised invasion of the Jin. Following an initial minor setback, the Jin response was vigorous, to the surprise of the Chinese. After repeated defeats, the Song court sued for peace. The Jin court demanded that the head of Han Tuozhou (1151–1207), who had led the war faction, be sent to the Jin capital in a box, and the Song ignominiously complied.[16] The Chinese were forced to make peace on terms that again raised the level of their annual indemnity payments. The Jin army by this time was, to be sure, largely composed of Chinese conscripts, buttressed by Jurchen cavalry units that enhanced its striking power. It was no longer the great war machine it had been a century earlier, yet on occasion it still could fight effectively, even valiantly, as was demonstrated time and again during the final harried decades of the dynasty's existence.

The *meng'an* and *mouke* units of course continued to exist, and at the end of the twelfth century could still field impressive cavalry forces. In the view of most historians, however, that famous institution created by the dynastic founder had degenerated. Its hereditary leaders had become managers of the lands granted to the people in their command, often illegally expanded at the expense of neighboring Chinese farmers; their military virtues had been compromised by the pursuit and enjoyment of wealth. The rich Jurchens became richer and the poor became poorer, as the irregularities of the system again came to the fore. The distinctive social organization that once had sustained Jurchen social cohesiveness had eroded. The soldiers in each *mouke* currently on active duty were the first to be mobilized in time of war; they retained their privileged warrior status. Except for some crack cavalry units, however, the Jurchen soldiers' fighting skills were no longer much different from or far superior to those of the Chinese conscripts who had to make up the main body of any large army.

After Zhangzong's death, as pressing emergencies increased, the Jurchen military machine was under sharply increased pressures. Yet throughout the last quarter-century of the Jin (from Zhangzong's death in 1208 until the Jin collapse in 1234), the system could still be shaken up and partly restored to fighting trim. Like so many other aspects of Jurchen life, it was by the end transformed into a hybrid, increasingly Chinese institution.

v. THE END OF THE JIN DYNASTY, 1208–1234

When Emperor Zhangzong died in the last days of 1208, the succession reverted to his father's generation even though Zhangzong had sons. His uncle Wanyan Yunji, known to history as Prince Wei (or Weishao; r. 1209–1213), came to the throne in a somewhat troubled succession. He was succeeded by an older brother of Zhangzong, known to history as Emperor Xuanzong (r. 1213–1223). Xuanzong's third son then reigned for eleven years, until the Jin collapse in 1234; as the last emperor of a fallen dynasty he is known posthumously as Aizong, "the Forlorn Emperor." All of these emperors after Zhangzong had Chinese mothers, an indication of the increasing Chinese influence at court throughout the last decades of the Jin dynasty. Also, all of the last three successions were troubled in one way or another, with factions threatening to advance the cause of contenders, or were clouded by other irregularities.

Prince Wei had the misfortune to occupy the throne at the moment when the Mongols commenced to take serious interest in the great sedentary civilization to the south. Chinggis Khan had probed the Xi Xia lands in 1205, and had come back to impose serious defeats there in 1209, but he had not yet attempted to eradicate the Xia dynasty. In 1211 he set forth against the Jin, leading one army of perhaps 50,000 mounted bowmen, each with three mounts, and coordinating its advance with another army of similar size led by three of his sons. They were essentially Mongol cavalry armies, but the Mongols were beginning to absorb Khitan and Jurchen units that had rebelled against the Jin, as well as levies from the Xia. Also, they were beginning to include units that understood siege warfare and other ways of attacking the fortified strongholds that sedentary peoples relied upon. The reduced Jin armies may still have numbered 150,000 cavalry, mostly Jurchens, plus 300,000 to 400,000 foot soldiers, mainly Chinese. Despite the social changes that had weakened it, the Jin retained a reputation as the most powerful military state in the known world. Chinggis Khan approached this enemy with tactical caution: What remnants of the famed Jurchen ferocity would he find? One is inevitably reminded of the days, just one century earlier, when very small but frenzied Jurchen armies, bursting suddenly onto the scene, overran the great Liao empire. Now a very large Jin state with a population of close to 40 million people, of whom perhaps 3 million were those same Jurchens, was being set upon by a newly formed Mongol nation numbering not much more than a million people. Mongol tactics, however, would prove to be quite different from those which Aguda had employed a century earlier.

The Mongol approach to this enemy, one of five or six great sedentary states throughout Eurasia that they were simultaneously probing and testing, was audacious but coolly methodical. Neither hatred nor a frenzied demand for revenge nor even a fierce desire to conquer and rule motivated them.

Throughout this entire campaign of 1211 and 1212 Chinggis had little interest in territory; he plundered and pillaged and then withdrew, allowing the defeated Jin armies to repossess the fallen bastions.

Late in 1211 the Mongols forced the Jin commanders to abandon the Western Capital (present-day Datong) and then laid siege for about a month to the Central Capital (present-day Beijing), where the emperor and court were residing. As the Mongols withdrew to the north early in 1212, they looted the Jin Eastern Capital (present-day Liaoyang in Manchuria). They returned in 1213 and again took the Western Capital, then again threw a heavy siege around the Central Capital, this time for several months, while Mongol field armies wandered through the Jin provinces of North China—present-day Shanxi, Hebei, and Shandong—leaving much destruction in their wake. Before withdrawing in the early months of 1214, they imposed a humiliating peace settlement on the Jin. But again they had failed to take the stoutly defended Central Capital.

Those blows to Jurchen power and prestige emboldened the Xi Xia to defy the Jin state, and encouraged still more units of the resentful Khitan population to defect to the Mongols. Within the Chinese portions of the Jin state local uprisings occurred. Defeated Jurchen commanders excused themselves and blamed one another, and statesmen at the court fell into factional bickering.

A most serious crisis arose in the fall of 1213, shortly before the Mongol armies arrived at the gates of the capital. The crisis was created by a Jurchen military leader, an irascible ruffian descended from one of the old hereditary military chieftainships, by the name of Hushahu. Prince Wei, the emperor since 1209, probably saw in Hushahu some of the military qualities of the early Jurchen heroes. "At this juncture," we can imagine him thinking, "what else can save the Jin dynasty?" Overlooking Hushahu's outrageous faults, the emperor called on him to fill strategic posts during the Mongol emergencies. In 1211 Hushahu fled his post, allowing the Mongols to capture the Western Capital at Datong. But he was not alone. The Jin supreme commander of defenses on that front, in command of armies considerably larger than those of the invaders, lost his nerve and fled, losing most of his forces and barely reaching the Central Capital; his flight allowed the Mongols to proceed through the passes without being seriously tested. A member of the Wanyan imperial clan, the commander was not censured for this failure. But the *Jin History* comments: "The army's morale is the essential element in warfare," and after these routs, "the spirit of resolution was lost and could not be regained. The collapse of the Jin was foretold in this event."[17]

As the second invasion of the Mongols drew nigh in 1213, Hushahu was given command of a garrison of 5,000 cavalry soldiers stationed just north of the Central Capital. His conduct brought fresh censure from court officials. Late in September, probably more in rage than in fear of the court's punishment, he forced his way into the palace city by a ruse, captured the emperor, who had always favored him, and ordered palace eunuchs to murder their ruler. Hushahu may have hoped to assume the throne himself but then realized that only a member of the Wanyan clan would be accepted by the Jurchen nobility. So he placed the fifty-year-old Wanyan Xun, an older brother of the Emperor Zhangzong (d. 1208), on the throne and set about to intimidate the courtiers and dominate the government. It was only two months before another military commander murdered him and restored the authority of the throne.

Wanyan Xun is known to history as Emperor Xuanzong. His ten-year reign, commenced in violence and marked by the second Mongol invasion in the winter of 1213–14, was a turning point in Jin history. After negotiating the humiliating peace with Chinggis Khan early in 1214, after which the Mongols left North China, Emperor Xuanzong decided that the Central Capital was too exposed and made the decision to abandon it. In the summer of 1214 he stealthily moved court and government to the Jin Southern Capital (present-day Kaifeng), as Prince Hailing had intended to do in 1161. Some Jurchen leaders tried to persuade the emperor to move in the other direction, to the Eastern Capital back in the old Jurchen homeland. But when the resources of the North China heartland were compared with those of Manchuria, that idea was seen to be clearly impractical to Jurchens who were committed to the Chinese way of life. They made the obvious choice: a great baggage train of 30,000 carts loaded with documents and court implements, and 3,000 camels loaded with treasure, left the capital in July. Two months later the entourage reached the Southern Capital at Kaifeng. That was, of course, the former Northern Song capital, and it is interesting to speculate that some of the treasure transported back to it at this time may have been in the baggage train that left the same city in the spring of 1127, carrying the loot of the Jin conquerors (see Chapter 9, Section I).

On hearing that the Jin capital had been moved, Chinggis was angered by what he took to be Jurchen duplicity; the Jin state was now supposed to be subordinate to the Mongol empire. Immediately he sent his armies to encircle the vacated Central Capital, placing it under siege from late in 1214. But the garrison forces left behind to defend it did not surrender easily. Finally Chinggis himself returned to supervise the action and, no doubt, to learn more about how to conduct warfare against a great walled city. It fell to him in June 1215 after a most bitter siege. The Jin empire now consisted of a province-size remnant in the central Yellow River basin, totally cut off from the Inner Asian homeland of the Jurchen people.

Perhaps Chinggis Khan's greatest prize from this campaign was a captive, a tall, bearded, impressive young man, Yelü Chucai (1189–1241), a descendant of the Khitan imperial clan. He had been employed as a high-ranking secretary in the Jin imperial government, and had experienced the Mongol siege of the Central Capital and the looting and destruction that followed its fall. He spent the next three years in intense study of Chan Buddhism and perhaps for that reason was recommended to Chinggis Khan's viceroy, General Mukhali, who, while not himself a Buddhist, had close contacts with certain Chan masters. In 1218 Mukhali sent Yelü to be interviewed by Chinggis, somewhere in Mongolia. When Yelü was brought before the

Mongol conqueror, Chinggis is said to have addressed him, "Liao and Jin have been enemies for generations; I have taken revenge for you." Yelü, committed to Confucian social ethics, replied: "My father and grandfather have both served it [i.e., Jin] respectfully. How can I, as a subject and a son, be so insincere at heart as to consider my sovereign and my father as enemies?"[18] Such courage and directness always pleased Chinggis. In addition to the young man's knowledge of China, he also saw in the Khitan the best qualities of a fellow man of the steppe. Yelü was taken into his entourage; for twenty-five years, until his death in 1243, he faithfully served the Mongol rulers as secretary, political adviser, astronomer-astrologer, and regional administrator, attempting the while to protect essential features of Chinese civilization from the destructive pressures of Mongol rule.[19]

The immediate consequence of the Jin government's move to Kaifeng in 1214 and the fall of the Central Capital in 1215 was turmoil and fighting throughout much of North China and all of the Jin territories in eastern Inner Asia and Manchuria. Chinggis himself withdrew to deal with enemies farther west, in the Western Liao state (Kara Khitai), which he absorbed in 1218, and the Turkish Muslim state of Khwarazm in Central Asia and northern Persia, which he subdued with a massive army in 1219–1223. His trusted general Mukhali, named viceroy in 1217, was left to direct continuing actions against Xi Xia and Jin. Mukhali probably commanded about 75,000 troops, of whom no more than one-third were Mongols, so successful had the Mongols been in drawing Khitans and other steppe peoples as well as Chinese to their side. He had already led the Mongols' rapidly moving campaigns through Manchuria in 1215–16. For the next several years (1217–1221) he campaigned through Shanxi, Hebei, and Shandong (to use the modern province names) then (1221–1223) west through the Xia territories and farther into Shaanxi and Qinghai. Mukhali died in Shanxi in the spring of 1223 after having done much to establish the pattern of delegated local administration in North China to prevent anti-Mongol military action there.

When Chinggis returned to the Mongolian hearthland from India in 1223, he turned next to punish the Tanguts for their inconstancy. He moved his front to Xia territory in late 1225 and campaigned against the Xia, then farther west until he died in 1227, just before the final assault on the Xia capital (see Chapter 11, Section III). During these years the Jin state lost its two capitals in Manchuria (the Eastern Capital at Liaoyang and the old Supreme Capital farther north, on the Sungari River). There, and everywhere throughout the former Jin territories in North China, uprisings and rebellions flared, both against Jin rule and against the Mongol invaders. In many places Jin and allied commanders and spontaneous associations of common people resisted the Mongols bravely. Elsewhere, disaffected local leaders fought among themselves or surrendered to the Mongols.

North China thus fell into a period of terrible destruction of lives and of the material supports of civilization. Such devastation was to recur a number of times throughout the next century and a half. Many parts of North China did not recover until the sixteenth century. Between 1220 and 1260 the disorder was aggravated by the Mongols' policy of not holding territory that had submitted to their armies, thereby assuming no responsibility to govern. In this respect the Mongols' protracted conquest of North China differed sharply from the Khitan, the Tangut, and the Jurchen modes of conquest. Those three nations were eager to hold and to govern, which they did with innovative energy. Eventually the Mongols also became institutionally more adaptive, but in the years before 1260 they had not yet focused on problems of civil government.

The story of the shrunken Jin state from 1215 until the Mongols finally absorbed it in 1234 is one of tragedy. While North China suffered the depredations of Mukhali's roaming campaigns, one faction at the Jin court believed that salvation lay in expanding to the south by warring against what it took to be a supine Southern Song state. Another faction favored alliance with the Song against their common enemy to the north. Both policies were unrealistic. At the end of 1216 the war faction won Emperor Xuanzong over. He began aggressive actions against the Song, first on the Huai River front in the east, then in 1217 also in the Han River drainage of northern Hubei and even farther west, in Sichuan. In 1219 the Jin attackers threatened to cross the Yangzi at Caishi, near present-day Nanjing, at precisely the crossing point where Prince Hailing had been defeated in 1161. They were thrown back with heavy losses. A number of other points along the frontier saw heavy but indecisive fighting. The protracted offensives with no victories induced serious conflicts among the court factions. In 1220 the peace faction persuaded the emperor to execute the war party's leader, yet the war continued. It was still in progress when Emperor Xuanzong succumbed to illness at the end of 1223.

Two of the dead emperor's sons contended briefly for the succession. The designated heir, Wanyan Shouxu, twenty-six years of age and an experienced administrator, won out. Considering the circumstances, his reign of not quite eleven years commands respect. In the unfriendly opinion of one contemporary observer, a Chinese official who served at his court in the final years, the emperor was rather too confident in his own judgment, vain about his public image, and yet dissolute in his private life. He valued associates who displayed the resolute Jurchen warrior character, but he could not always effectively discipline and lead them.[20] He was nevertheless a vigorous and in some ways an unexpectedly effective ruler. Against any enemy other than the Mongol nation he might have reestablished the Jin state.

Immediately on coming to the throne with the New Year of 1224, the new emperor tried to set new policies in motion. He drew about him a group of strong leaders and able administrators who favored turning all the shrunken state's energies to defense against the Mongols. He quickly terminated the war against the Song and drew those armies back to the capital. He also made peace with the Tanguts, who had borne the brunt of the Mongol pressure and were having second thoughts about their nominal alliance with Chinggis. Some initiatives were taken to restore Jin authority in the North China provinces following the departure of Mukhali's marauding armies in 1221; in many places local leaders were given high-sounding Jin titles and encouraged to govern as Jin surrogates. The Jin achieved a creditable improvement in their position by the time Chinggis led his main armies in the final destruction of the Xia in 1227. During that campaign the Great Khan died, and all Mongol leaders everywhere across Eurasia had to convene at the tribal council that would validate his successor. That brought at least temporary respite to all the Mongols' enemies.

The Jin were less lucky than most. In 1228, even before the *khuriltai*, or Council of Great Chieftains, in 1229 named Ögödei to succeed his father, Chinggis's youngest son, Tolui, was ordered to resume the war against the stubborn Jin. His initial success was limited. Then, late in 1229, Ögödei, as the new Great Khan, set the main arm of the Mongol military machine in motion against the Jin. Warfare seesawed. Through 1230 and 1231 the Jurchens lost some battles but won others, greatly slowing the Mongol advance. Ögödei pulled his field commanders back to reassess the situation, and in 1232 put a new war plan into action. Again the Jurchens offered stubborn resistance. The Jin emperor sought to negotiate a settlement, but there was no reason for the Mongols to grant one. The Jin then pleaded with the Southern Song court to help them for the common good, but that appeal was scorned. At the end of 1232, after the Southern Capital (Kaifeng) came under attack, the Jin emperor and his household fled south, where they sought to establish new bases for resistance. The Southern Capital fell in the spring of 1233 and was looted. Almost a year later, in February 1234 at Caizhou (present-day Ru'nan) about 125 miles south of Kaifeng, Emperor Aizong, the "Forlorn Ancestor," committed suicide to avoid imminent capture.[21] Two days later the Jin dynasty was obliterated.

The Mongols had taken twenty years to defeat the Jin—seven or eight years for the last continuous, intensive struggle. The once powerful Jin state had not disintegrated, despite its many internal problems. It has been noted that the dynasty's ineffectual statesmen, after the transfer of the capital to Kaifeng in 1214, bickered and moaned, sought excuses, and evaded responsibility for twenty years. Yet Emperor Aizong, for all his personal shortcomings, struggled valiantly to restore his civil and military authority in order to resist the Mongol invaders. At the end his armies mostly stood their ground and fought to the death against a fearsome enemy. The last remnant of the Jin dynasty was slowly ground down to final extinction. It perished with honor.

11

THE LATER
XI XIA STATE

The Xi Xia state was an important player in Inner Asian and Chinese history, all the more important to us today because it has so long been neglected or misunderstood. Its political and military history, following the displacement of the Liao by the Jin in the early twelfth century, continued to unfold in patterns important for our understanding of Chinese and of East Asian civilizations. Its social and cultural developments took very distinctive turns that command our interest today. Beyond that, the study of Tangut civilization in its own right is becoming an important field of historical knowledge bridging Chinese and Inner Asian history.

I. XI XIA IN THE ERA OF THE JIN DYNASTY, 1115–1227

The world in which the Xi Xia state existed was radically altered midway in its emperor Chongzong's long reign (1087–1139).[1] Between 1115 and 1123 the Jurchen nation threw off its Khitan overlords, destroyed the Liao empire, and in the next six or seven years absorbed Song North China far beyond the Sixteen Prefectures that the Liao had held since 938. The shrinking of Song territory in the era of the Southern Song dynasty (1127–1279) meant that Xia lost its long common boundary with the Song state. Moreover, its now helpful, now inimical neighbor and suzerain, the Liao empire, was replaced by the quite different Jin dynasty and empire of the Jurchens (see Map 8).

Late in Northern Song, the Chinese court in 1114 appointed the noted eunuch General Tong Guan to be Military Commissioner for the Shaanxi region,[2] and for the next five years the Song expended great energy in a series of invasions from various points on the borders between Shaanxi and the Xia territories. At some points they were successful in penetrating and holding fortified cities, even forcing the Xia ruler to submit to the Song briefly in 1119. In the end they lost all, weakened themselves, and caused much destruction. It was the last echo of Song warfare against the Tanguts; after that the Chinese became deeply involved in their efforts to ally themselves with the Jurchens against the Liao, and the Xi Xia was ignored in the tumult of the following years.

Xia-Liao relations had grown closer from the beginning of the twelfth century. Xia envoys were at the Liao court almost every year from 1098 to 1110, requesting that the Liao intervene in their behalf at the Song court or asking for military aid. In 1104, after repeated requests, the Liao sent an imperial princess to marry Li Qianshun, the then twenty-year-old Xi Xia ruler who would become known posthumously as the Emperor Chongzong. In 1108 the happy news that she had borne him a son was reported at the Liao court. (This child, who was not the eldest son, did not succeed his father in 1139.) The record of the two states' relations grows rather scanty after 1110, but at the very end of the Liao it is reported that in 1122, when the pursuing Jurchens forced the last Liao ruler to flee from his Western Capital (present-day Datong) into the Yinshan (Jia) Mountains at the edge of the Xi Xia state, the Xia emperor personally led an army to lend assistance. Defeated by an intercepting Jurchen force, he sent another army the following year that first was victorious over a Jurchen army, but a month later was driven from the scene in defeat. One of the grateful Liao emperor's last acts, in 1123, was to enfeoff the Xia ruler "Emperor of Xia." Up to this time the Liao had always called the Xia rulers just "King of Xia"; now the Xia founder, Yuanhao's, elevation of himself in 1038 was at last acknowledged by the head of another state, albeit by the fugitive ruler of the collapsing Khitan empire.

That late warmth between Liao and Xia did not constitute a liability when the Jin replaced the Liao, for at this time the Tanguts could not assume much importance in Jin plans. Jin armies were deeply engaged in North China for the next few years. Also, after 1124 there was the new phenomenon of the Western Liao, which became Xi Xia's neighbor off to the far northwest (see Chapter 9, Section II). Yelü Dashi's Western Liao state, or Kara Khitai, was new, unexpected, and difficult to assess. Its Khitan ruler had proclaimed that his purpose was vengeance, nothing less than destruction of the Jin dynasty. At this point the Jurchens, not wanting to force the Xi Xia into some kind of alliance with the Western Liao, granted them a respite.

In the rush of events a son of the newly proclaimed Jin emperor Aguda, Prince Zongwang, who was leading the pursuing army into the Yinshan region in 1123, apparently took no special notice of the Xia ruler's effort to help the Liao emperor. On his own discretion he issued a field decree to the Xia state saying that the Jin dynasty saw the Xia as a mere creature of the Liao, unshakably loyal to the bitter end. Such loyalty was honored in the steppe, even by one's enemies. The decree stated: "Now we have conquered the Liao. If you perform your subject duties to us as in the past to the Liao, we shall allow your tribute envoys to approach and will receive them without suspicion. If the Liao ruler should approach your territory, however, you must take him captive and turn him over to us."[3]

A bit over a year later the Xia responded by sending an envoy with declarations of fealty, offering to assume the place of a subordinate state and asking that certain border issues between the two states be settled. The Jin court agreed, confirming the Xia in possession of all their territories with only some minor losses on the southern boundaries. In 1127 it redefined the boundaries, granting the Xia some lands recently seized from the Liao and the Song. As the Jurchens pressed their offensive against the Song in the later 1120s, the Xia also took some border prefectures still in Song hands, and the Jin subsequently confirmed Xia in possession of those. The Xi Xia state thus gained in territory from the Jin conquest of Northern Song China; it also lost its most adamant enemy, the Song, against whom it had been forced to maintain strong defenses for a century and a half.

As for Xi Xia relations with the Jurchens, they were of an entirely different flavor from the Xia's earlier relations with the Khitans. The Khitan princess, the Emperor Chongzong's consort, starved herself to death when she learned of the capture in 1125 of her uncle, the last Liao emperor. The ties of actual and fictive kinship, usually strong among Inner Asian tribal peoples, were never established with the new Jurchen neighbors. In place of "family" quarrels they now experienced protocol disputes of a new kind. When the Xia first sent their tribute envoys to the Jin court, they were reproved for assuming that the former pattern still prevailed. The Jin court coolly instructed the Xia: "Xia and Liao were as nephew and uncle; therefore rituals expressing kinship were allowed. Today Xia is simply a subject state of the Great Jin; therefore rituals appropriate to lord and servitor are to be observed."[4] Despite the coolness of tone, the Jin dynasty had more important objectives than absorbing Xia, and thus had no choice but to allow it to exist so long as it remained placid.

Within the Xia state the long reign of Emperor Chongzong ended in 1139. He was succeeded by his son Li Renxiao, then fifteen, who reigned until 1193, and is known to history as the Emperor Renzong. Father and son together reigned for 107 years, from 1087 to 1193, a record perhaps unmatched in East Asian history.

The Emperor Renzong's mother was Chinese. A second consort of his father, also Chinese, was the daughter of a regional military commander of the Song, Ren Dejing, who had surrendered to the Xi Xia. With the young Renzong's accession, both his own mother and this second consort were elevated to the status of empress dowager; using that relationship to the Xia throne, Ren Dejing began to assume a dominant role in the military establishment. The young emperor took his own empress from a powerful Tangut clan that had long led in the adoption of Chinese cultural forms. The young empress, as might be expected, became a force for the observance of Chinese ritual proprieties at the court. Once again we see the emergence of a powerful faction at the Xia court favoring not a pro-China policy in the political sense, but a pro-sinification policy in cultural matters.

Chinese things represented to the Xia nobility a sophisticated international cultural mode. In addition to that mode's ritual, artistic, and philosophical components, there also grew a taste for luxurious elite living styles, with Chinese dress and furnishings, houses and gardens, food and entertainments. Within the Tangut elite, many sought to exploit Chinese forms of landlordism, and the court came to rely more heavily on Chinese methods of taxation, in order to increase incomes to pay for ornate luxury and extravagant consumption. This burden fell heavily on the Tangut population and aroused rebellious reactions. Natural disasters struck: a severe earthquake in 1143 devastated the agricultural population along the northward-flowing portion of the Yellow River, where the capital and the population concentrations were located. As far to the east as Xiazhou Prefecture, earthquakes opened deep cracks from which black sands poured forth. Tens of thousands died, and the disruption of productive activities brought on famine. Armed uprisings of desperate people ensued. They found leadership among some of the Tangut military nobility who resented the tone of the court and its high-living aristocrats. The dowager empress's father, Ren Dejing, ruthlessly suppressed the rebels and broke the back of all resistance. This time there was no Chinese enemy on the borders poised to take advantage of the domestic turmoil as there had been so many times in the past. The Jurchens were not free to intervene; thus the crisis of the 1140s passed.

It is tempting to argue that the crisis hastened the sinification of Xia government. The institutional reformers had demonstrated that Tangut tribal resistance to the court could be controlled. Some tribal leaders accepted the changes and came to support them, sharing in the benefits of association with the court. The earlier division of the central administration into separate Tangut and Han Chinese secretariats was gradually being outgrown. An amalgamation of the two services took place. We must assume that bilingualism became typical of career officials, for the paperwork of government continued to employ both languages and both scripts. From the late 1140s onward the court and government adopted a number of further changes in administrative procedures modeled on the government of Song China.

Throughout his long life the Emperor Renzong (Li Renxiao) took a personal interest in Confucian education. He enlarged the National Academy established by his father, ordered that prefectural schools be established throughout the realm, created a Chinese-style Hanlin Academy to provide literati-advisers to the throne, and set up a primary school within the palace which he occasionally visited, sometimes to assume the role of teacher. He conscientiously led the rituals to venerate Confucius at the Confucian shrine in the capital. His reign witnessed the fullest ascendancy of Chinese literary culture at the Xia court and throughout the realm. It paralleled a similar high tide of Chinese cultural forms in the Jin state in the decades from the 1130s to the 1160s. Both went beyond the levels of acculturation that the Khitan nation-state had experienced under the Liao dynasty, which, throughout its existence, had remained more selective and cautious in its adaptation of Chinese-derived elements to Khitan needs.

II. THE CRISIS OF THE "PARTITION OF THE STATE"

A curious episode in Xi Xia history occurred in 1170. A full explanation is beyond our present knowledge of that history's inner workings, yet what we know of the facts reveals intriguing information about the Xi Xia state's internal affairs as well as its foreign relations. On the surface the events are as follows. The emperor's nominal "great-uncle" Ren Dejing (the father of the late emperor's second consort, who now was one of the two dowager empresses) had advanced to the head of the civil administration in the late 1150s while continuing to dominate the military establishment, his original base of power. We must remember that he was a Chinese immigrant, a turncoat Song military official who had worked his way into Xia politics and who had ruthlessly suppressed the uprisings in the 1140s. He had been granted the title Duke of Xiping, and thus ranked second in the state only to the emperor and his heir. At Xiping, the second city of the realm, he maintained an extravagant court and entourage. He had placed his brothers and nephews in important posts in government. Throughout the 1160s he became ever more overbearing, intimidating the emperor and not bothering to conceal his ambition to usurp the imperial authority. In the early summer of 1170 he presented an ultimatum to the emperor: the state must be divided, a large southern portion to become the independent state of Chu, of which Ren Dejing would be the absolute ruler. He forced the emperor to send an envoy to the Jin court announcing the partition and requesting a patent of enfeoffment to legitimate the move.

The official *Jin History,* in its chapter on the history of the Xia state, records the Jin court's reactions. At first, leading officials advised the Jin emperor: "This is a matter internal to the affairs of another state. Why should we become involved? The best course would be simply to accept the situation and grant our approval." But the Jin emperor Shizong, leader of a Jurchen nativistic revival at that time and ever suspicious of Chinese treachery, replied: "Since when have the rulers of states willingly given away half their territories for no reason? There can be no doubt that a powerful official has intimidated the throne to force this seizure. It cannot be the real will of the Xia ruler. Moreover, the Xia state has long been our subsidiary. Now, of a sudden, it has come under the coercion of a treacherous minister. How can I, as master of all within the four seas, countenance such depravity? If the Xia cannot set their house in order, then we shall send troops to punish the evildoer. We must not acquiesce in this!"[5] Tribute had been submitted along with the request for approval of the partition; the Jin emperor ordered it returned to display his disapproval, and sent the message that an envoy would be dispatched to investigate the real circumstances.

Rebuffed, Ren Dejing then sought assistance from the Southern Song court by sending a messenger through Jin territories into Sichuan, the nearest point under Song control, to communicate with Chinese provincial officials there. He promised that when he became master of the state of Chu, he would be subservient to the Song and would assist it militarily. The Song officials were delighted; they sent back a message promising approval and help.[6] This message was intercepted by the Xia ruler. Emboldened by the Jin emperor's attitude, and possessing concrete evidence of Ren Dejing's treachery, he exposed the plot. On October 11, 1170, he had Ren Dejing and his entire party of followers publicly executed. (Ren's daughter, the emperor's "stepmother," the dowager empress, had died the preceding year.) Then he sent a memorial to the Jin court thanking his overlord for having sustained upright principles and reporting in full on the suppression of Ren Dejing's plot.

Although he was a turncoat Chinese, Ren Dejing had opposed the Confucianization of Xia government. Tangut scholar-officials, recruited through the schools and the examinations in the Chinese classics, tended to be scornful of him as a militarist who had usurped legitimate authority (and who would not be well-disposed toward them). There was a strong tendency for Confucian-trained persons to be moral fundamentalists. The Xia Confucians spurned this Chinese evildoer. Ren's fall from power and the elimination of his faction brought about a restoration of legitimate authority carried out in the spirit of the Confucianized literati's triumph over evil. That strengthened civil elements and weakened the political role of the Tangut military establishment, although that was where real Xia power lay.

After the Emperor Renzong's death in 1193 the state was ruled by a rapid succession of five weak or inept rulers.[7] Their reigns ranged from one to twelve years. Only two were father-to-son successions, and one of those was by the irregular route of forced abdication. The successions of 1206 and 1211 were by open usurpation. It appears that the institutions supporting the Xia throne had been weakened through the fifty-five years of Renzong's long reign; he had alienated his court from the sources of Tangut power, the tribal military machine. His own conduct as ruler was vacillating and timid. Even so, the military establishment he bequeathed to his successors still possessed impressive resources in the early thirteenth century. When the Xia state fell in 1227, it was to external forces that would have been irresistible at any time. We have no grounds for speculating that the Tangut state, whatever the depth of Chinese influences, had lost the capacity or the will to fight and to rule.

III. THE DESTRUCTION OF THE XI XIA STATE

The first Mongol attack on the Xi Xia state came in the spring of 1205 in a raid on the northern frontier led by Temüjin, who, a year later, would be proclaimed Chinggis Khan, the supreme leader of all the Mongols. In 1207 he again raided northern outposts, and in 1209 Mongol armies surrounded the Xia capital. The Xia ruler requested help from the Jurchens, but was insolently refused by a Jin court suddenly caught up in a misbegotten plan to conquer the Southern Song and glad to see two of its other powerful neighbors fighting among themselves. The Mongol besiegers diverted that summer's unusually high water of the Yellow River to flood Xingqing Fu, the capital city (present-day Yinchuan). The Xia ruler sent an offering of women, including a daughter, to the Mongol emperor and made other motions to sue for peace. Satisfied for the moment, the Mongols withdrew.[8]

The usurpation of 1211 brought Li Zunxu, an uncle of the previous ruler, to the throne. Known to history as the Emperor Shenzong, he was a man nearing fifty and a figure of imposing prestige. He took charge vigorously but, as it turned out, disastrously. Angered by the Jin court's refusal to send aid in 1209, he made peace with the Mongols and offered them an alliance against the Jin. Until 1217 the two nations collaborated in annual wars. The Mongols looked upon the Xia primarily as a source of good mounted warriors to be deployed at their discretion. They made annual levies for troops that the Xia found difficult to meet. In 1217 the Xia refused to supply the fighting units demanded, and the Mongols sent an army to punish them for insubordination. The capital was surrounded for several months before the Mongols withdrew. In 1218 the Xia proposed to the Jin that they resume their anti-Mongol alliance, but the Jurchens refused. In 1219 Xia sent an envoy to the Southern Song via regional officials in Sichuan Province, proposing an anti-Jin alliance with the Chinese. The Song, hard-pressed by the last great Jin offensive against them, were glad to have help, but under the pressures of the moment were unable immediately to send an army for joint operations against the Jin flank. Not until 1220 were the two states able to coordinate an attack. The Xi Xia army first took the region adjacent to Xi'an and threatened the northwest corner of the Jin state. Now the Jin court was forced to sue for peace, for it was under strong military pressure from both the Chinese and the Mongols. The Xia emperor Shenzong, remembering the Jin court's refusal to cooperate in 1218, now proudly refused to deal with the beleaguered Jurchens. That was a mistake; in subsequent fighting the Xia were repeatedly defeated by the Jin, and the alliance with the Song also crumbled. For a few years the Emperor Shenzong's vigorous actions had appeared to be making headway, but ultimately they brought total failure. He was becoming very unpopular.

In 1221 the great Mongol general Prince Mukhali, Chinggis Khan's viceroy for the China front, drove eastward across Xi Xia territory with a vast army en route to attack the Jin capital, now withdrawn to Kaifeng (the old Northern Song capital) in Henan Province. For the next two years the Mongols made themselves at home in Xia territory, constantly demanding troops to join their command, and behaving so oppressively toward the Tangut population that anger was aroused against the Emperor Shenzong, who was blamed for the disastrous consequences of the alliance with the Mongols. Late in 1223 popular resentment forced his abdication. The new emperor had little choice but to change policies. He again placed his nation in alliance with the Jurchens against the Mongols. It was in truth a situation in which all the alternatives were equally perilous. The Mongols could forgive and even admire a brave enemy but they despised an inconstant ally; they determined now to wreak full vengeance on the Tanguts.

In 1226 Chinggis Khan himself led a large army into Xia territory. Surprising him, the Xia armies fought well, inflicting defeats on wings of the Mongol forces. Nothing could have been more infuriating to the world's most dangerous opponent. He now ordered his generals to focus their might on the systematic conquest of all Xi Xia territory; they proceeded to overrun it, fortified city by fortified city, garrison outpost by garrison outpost, leaving total destruction and desolation in their wake. In the spring of 1227 Chinggis himself resumed personal direction of the final siege of the Xia capital. A valiant defense held out for more than five months. In August Chinggis died in his camp at some point near the besieged city, of unknown or at least of widely disputed causes. One rumor that the Mongols' enemies greatly savored was that the captured Xia queen, the widow of the last Xia ruler, placed sharp pieces of glass or a steel blade in her vagina, causing Chinggis to bleed to death. But that kind of rumor also appeared in other places; there is no particular reason to believe it in this case. It is more likely that Chinggis Khan fell ill of some summer fever and died, but the truth cannot be known. His death was kept secret from the besieged Xia defenders.

Shortly thereafter the last Xia ruler offered to surrender. By prearrangement he walked out of his capital with a small group of attendants into the Mongol camp to offer his surrender. He was chopped to pieces on the spot. Then the Mongol forces entered the city and, according to the accounts, slaughtered every living thing; as a further punitive step they plundered the Xia imperial tombs in the hills to the west of the city. So ended the history of the Xia state, which had existed for 190 years, since Yuanhao proclaimed himself the emperor of the Great Xia in 1038. If we count from the establishment in 881 in late Tang times of the Xiazhou Military Commission, which was tantamount to a regional government, the Xia existed as an autonomous political entity for 347 years, longer than most of the great Chinese dynasties.

The Tangut nation did not immediately disappear, yet what happened to the Tangut people of Xia is not fully known. There appears to be good evidence that some surviving members of the imperial Li or Wei-ming clan fled southwest into Tibet taking with them enough of a Minyak (or Mi-nyag, i.e., Tangut Xia) community so that their name and customs persisted in that place into modern times. The location of their small state was west of Kangding District City (about 200 miles southwest of modern Chengdu), on the upper reaches of the Yarlung River. In the early twentieth century this area was part of China's Xikang Province, but it since has been absorbed into western Sichuan. Another group, probably more sedentary, moved southeast into China and were settled in what would be modern Henan and Hebei provinces. In China, intriguing bits of information show that Tangut communities survived, with their language and forms of civilization, through the era of Mongol domination and on into the Ming period. For example, in recent years there have come to light portions of Buddhist sutras in the Tangut script, some printed with movable wooden type. It now appears that the typefaces were cut and the type was set and printed for Tangut Buddhist use almost a century after the fall of the Xi Xia state, during the Dade reign period (1297–1308) of the Mongol Yuan dynasty in China.[9] That this was done by Tangut craftsmen at Hangzhou in Central China, then a great center of printing, but under the direction of a high Tangut or Tibetan Buddhist official, and that it probably was meant for use in Tangut Buddhist communities in far-off Northwest China, where the Tanguts of Xi Xia had lived, adds to the mystery. Other evidence of the use of Xi Xia script by Tanguts in China was recovered archaeologically in Hebei Province in 1962.[10] Sculpted stone shrine columns bearing inscriptions are dated to the year 1502, in mid-Ming times. Such fragments of post-Xia Tangut history await more thorough study.

IV. THE TANGUT ACHIEVEMENT

The Xia dynasty's achievements are indeed impressive, in governing, in conquest and military prowess, in adaptations of institutions to their particular needs, and in acquiring techniques essential to the management of their complex society. For example, in the course of their movement westward out of arid northwest Shaanxi, they placed their capital first on the east bank and then on the west bank of the Yellow River, creating major population and political centers there. Early in the eleventh century this brought them into possession of a region of highly developed ancient waterworks for irrigation with hundreds of miles of canals and water control installations serving an agricultural region of high productivity. This irrigated valley of the northward-flowing section of the Yellow River was an area of 8,000 square miles, roughly the size of Massachusetts. According to figures dating from the 1260s, when the Yuan dynasty rehabilitated the irrigation works following heavy destruction in warfare, the irrigated core area may have been as large as 2 million acres, hence capable of providing food for up to 4 or 5 million persons.[11] We do not know if it in fact attained those maximum figures under the Xia, but it clearly became the core area of the Xia state, being somewhat larger and much richer than Xiazhou and the original five prefectures in northern Shaanxi. Governing it presented innumerable new kinds of management problems. Much of the Tangut population was moved there along with the relocated government. They learned to live in a new kind of environment and to interact with the resident Chinese and other sedentary peoples. They also had to acquire the technology necessary to restore and maintain the waterworks and to make the most profitable use of the water it provided. The Xia government worked out detailed regulations for the system's operation and maintenance, recognizing its importance and utilizing it efficiently.

The urban life in a half-dozen major cities of the Xia realm was varied and interesting. An artisanate, partly of Tangut and partly of subject peoples, developed a high level of skills in weaving, leather working, building techniques, and the metallurgic craft industries. By the twelfth century or earlier the society made paper; translated, compiled, and published books; practiced astronomy and devised its own calendar; minted copper coins; manufactured and distributed salt; produced wines and liquors and other commodities; built palaces, fortifications, imperial tombs, and great temples; maintained public works projects; and managed international and domestic trade of great volume which supplied its elite with luxuries and the state with revenues. The Tanguts of Xia had come a long way from the simple warrior life they had known in the ninth century. They occupy a more important niche in history than historians of the last several centuries have understood.

With the study of recent archaeologically recovered evidence, with the full decipherment of their script only since the mid-twentieth century, and especially with the excavation of Xia imperial tombs in the foothills of the Helan Mountains just west of the old Xia capital near present-day Yinchuan in China's Ningxia Hui Autonomous Region, scholars are acquiring the means to understand the Tanguts' place in Inner Asian history. They were an independent people governing their own state and creating their own history. But that history interacted significantly with Chinese and several other histories; in addition to having its own intrinsic significance, the burgeoning field of Xi Xia studies increasingly will contribute to our better understanding of China and of all Inner Asia.

As an episode in the history of Tibet-related tribal peoples, Xi Xia offers an interesting point to consider. The Xia dynastic state did not become the political organization of the entire Tangut (i.e., Dangxiang) tribal nation. To measure it against an even larger political criterion, it did not unify all the Tibetan peoples outside of Tibet Proper (e.g., the Qiang) on China's northwestern frontier. It would be ahistorical to invoke our modern sense of nationalism and presume that it should have done so or that its leaders thought of their dynastic goals in that way. We should see the Xia leaders as heirs to the regional military governorship established at Xiazhou in the late Tang dynasty. They defended and preserved and greatly enlarged those hereditary privileges. As for associating themselves more broadly with their ethnic kin, they had suffered much from the expansionist drives of the Tufan state (Tibet Proper) since mid-Tang times. Moreover, they also had been required to assist the Chinese in wars against the Qiang tribes of the Amdo borderland. They may have felt little warmth toward all their ethnic kin to the west. And they were also unable to unite the other Dangxiang tribes on their northern and northeastern borders, often unruly subjects of the Liao state. Some of those tribal peoples occupied regions directly adjacent to the Xi Xia boundaries and requested protection from the Xia rulers, who could not grant it.

The point is not to speak of the "failure" of the Xia rulers to unite their fellow tribesmen under one government, but merely to note in passing that if they had done so, they might have greatly increased the Xia potential for survival. By leaving other Dangxiang and Qiang peoples on their borders out of their sphere of concern, they were left with enemies who otherwise could have added significantly to the Xia national strength. That situation cut the Xia off from a large portion of the nomadic reservoir which might continuously have renewed the Tanguts' martial resources. We need to gain a much better understanding of Tangut history to understand why this—to us seemingly obvious—source of ethnic or national strength was not exploited.

To look at their historical accomplishment from another point of view, having set out to preserve the independence of the Tanguts of Xia, their leaders successfuly added enough territory to the original five prefectures in northern Shaanxi to make a viable territorial unit. They increased their territory many times over despite the existence of relatively firm boundaries on the east (Liao, later Jin) and on the south (Song, later Jin). The one boundary open to expansion was that on the northwest and west where Qiang Tibetans, as well as Uighurs and other Turkic groups, had formed states. The strategic advantage gained by that expansion, after Yuanhao led the successful campaigns into the Gansu Corridor and beyond, came from their having acquired some of the best grazing lands in Inner Asia. In the words of the *Jin History*'s chapter on the Xi Xia, the zone adjoining the Gansu Corridor, centering on the ancient garrison outpost of Liangzhou (present-day Wuwei), was "the best in the world for pastoralism."[12] It received ten to twenty inches of rain per year, if modern rainfall statistics can be applied to the eleventh and twelfth centuries, and twenty inches was twice the precipitation of any other part of the Xia state. The Tanguts' early eleventh-century success in securing that territory heightened the potential level of their nomadism by increasing their wealth from herds of camels and horses, and consequently their military capacity as mounted warriors. A second strategic advantage in holding the Gansu Corridor derived from their control over the trade systems and caravan routes leading from China and eastern Inner Asia into western Inner Asia and beyond.

The disadvantages of their geographic situation are perhaps more obvious. Already in the tenth century, when the Xia state took form, they were a people including both nomadic and farming subdivisions. The three dynastic histories (of the Liao, the Jin, and the Song), in their chapters on the Xi Xia, all describe the Xia's mixed economy. That in some places Tangut people were already essentially agricultural is subtly revealed in the cautious advice one of his colleagues gave Li Jiqian in 983 when he decided to lead a national revolt against the Song (see Chapter 8, Section II). "After we have killed the Song envoy and proclaimed our independence," Li said, "we can base ourselves at Yin and Sui prefectures" and continue to resist. (Yin and Sui were two of the five original Xia prefectures.) His adviser responded: "The Dangxiang Qiang [i.e., the Tanguts] of Yin Prefecture have long been unaccustomed to the practice of war; they would not be able to hold out under attack."[13] So Li took his rebel command north into the Ordos Desert and assembled a mounted fighting force. Yin Prefecture, just east of Xia Prefecture, was peopled by Tanguts, but they clearly were no longer full-time warriors. The implication is that they had become sedentary. In that arid edge-of-the-desert region there was to be sure a certain rationality in a warrior society's having a portion of its population devoted to agriculture to provide winter fodder for the herds and other support for the fighters. Tangut pastoralism specialized in the the rearing and employment of Bactrian camels in conjunction with horses, the basic form of wealth. The Khitans depended on cattle in conjunction with horses. In the richer grazing lands of the Greater Khingan Mountains, the Khitans were assured reliable winter fodder. In the arid Tangut region, a supply of winter fodder to keep the herds and thus the cavalry provisioned and in fighting trim was more difficult to ensure. It had to be a by-product of farming. The social base of Tangut life differed in this respect from that of the Khitans.

The options for combining the elements of strength to gain the greatest advantage were different in each Inner Asian nation's historical experience. Among the Tanguts of Xia, an agricultural sector within their own ranks was a valuable component, but it gave the society a divided stance with regard to farming and the ethos of the sedentary life. The course undertaken by Yuanhao ensured that the warrior and his mobile steppe life would remain the more honored way. An extreme example is seen in the various histories' comments on Chinese taken captive by the Tanguts: the strong and able were absorbed into the army; the sickly and weak were sent off to farm. Presumably they were sent off to join the mixed sedentary population of Xia, which also surely included Tanguts. But those Tanguts who had been established in cavalry units in the northwest extension of Xia territories out into the steppe had become the most honored sector of the state's population.

The Tanguts were subject to unremitting pressures—military, political, and cultural—from the sedentary Chinese on one side and from nomadic neighbors on the other. The tensions within their already divided society were intensified by the ways in which their geographic setting denied them a clear-cut choice in favor of the one or the other. This is evident in Yuanhao's rebuke to his no longer martial father (see Chapter 8, Section III). His nativist rejection of sinification early in the eleventh century was accompanied by his successes in expanding Xia territories into the steppe on the north and west. It was he who succeeded in finally securing the rich grazing lands of the central Gansu Corridor. The Xia state then reached the peak of its military power and acquired assets that kept it formidable to the end of its history. The subsequent alternations of cultural and political policy to the close of the eleventh century display the continuations of those tensions. But from the early twelfth century onward we can see a turn toward full acceptance of cultural policies and governing methods drawn from the Chinese model. That does not mark a cultural surrender. A distinct Tangut identity, essentially military, was maintained. The adoption of the more universalistic components of Chinese intellectual life, or even their adaptations of specific social management instruments such as coinage, tax systems, and laws, did not turn the Tanguts into a cultural colony of China.

Yet those cultural adaptations do seem to indicate that the later Xia state was well set on the path of adjustment to sedentary social forms and values. The Tanguts' restricted geographic setting did not permit their total commitment to the opportunities for growth of their military power that accompanied their enhanced nomadism. Their complementary accommodations to sedentary life guaranteed compensating, or perhaps even superior, sources of wealth. The only point here in arguing what "might have been" in history is to help us understand alternatives—why choices were made. In that light we can imagine that the Tangut military machine could have been transformed into one depending increasingly on term recruits drawn from Tangut and Han Chinese farming households. That would have signaled the choice not to depend on lifetime military specialization of all adult males in nomadic households. That is, the Chinese social model might have come more fully into being, following the more complete adaptation to the Chinese political model. The consequence would have been the gradual transformation of the Tangut population away from the steppe patterns of life. In comparison with the situations of the other conquest dynasties, such a transformation was not even on the distant horizon in the case of the Khitans after 200 years of managing their dual state, or of the Mongols until many centuries later when, in the sixteenth century, they began to forgo essential elements of their nomadism. Something rather like this transformation, however, occurred among the Jurchens in the twelfth century when they were only a few decades into their rule over large sections of China. And we can see parallel examples in the histories of other Inner Asian peoples, both earlier and later. If the Mongols had not wiped the slate clean and started Inner Asian history anew in the Xia case, as in so many others, the trends well established in Xia society might have continued in the direction of its transformation toward a settled society, in which its agrarian sector—originally of mixed Tangut and other peoples—would have become the dominant one. Or the two sectors might eventually have become regionally specialized and then would have developed separate histories, one of sedentary Tanguts and the other of their nomadic steppe kinsmen. That is all speculation, to be sure, but it may help us to focus on some of the issues that underlie an appreciation of the Xia achievement. Xi Xia society had the potential to go in several directions of further development.

v. Xia Buddhism

Buddhism flourished throughout Inner Asia in these centuries, accommodating easily to the presence of other religions. Confucianism eventually became the state cult of the Xi Xia, but Chinese popular Daoism also was patronized, Manichaean doctrines were becoming important in the neighboring Uighur communities despite their continuing commitment to Buddhism, and some evidence for Nestorian Christianity in the Xi Xia state also exists. Islam too was known, but it would become much more important later. Despite that spectrum of religious elements, Xi Xia society was primarily committed to Buddhism.[14]

Each of the conquest dynasties with which we are concerned in this period of Chinese history was, or became, essentially Buddhist. The process by which that happened and the roles assumed by Buddhism offer some of the most useful cross-cutting comparisons available for enlarging our understanding of the conquest dynasties. Buddhism's attraction for Inner Asian peoples was powerful and widely pervasive. Its vast ideas were appealing on any level of awareness, and in that way were not too demanding; in its initial approaches to nonbelievers, it invited them to believe on any level of understanding of which they were capable. Thus they could readily accommodate their new Buddhist belief to their pre-Buddhist faiths. Buddhism appealed further to Inner Asian rulers by offering them the ideal of becoming Cakravartin Kings, or Universal Rulers (*zhuan lun wang* in Chinese), an ideal that had attracted Indian and Inner Asian Buddhist conquerors for hundreds of years. Also

Buddhism, while known primarily in its Chinese forms, was specifically non-Chinese in its origins. For this reason it was that much more attractive to Inner Asians who worried about resisting the overwhelming impact of Chinese civilization.

The Khitans of the Liao dynasty, like the Koreans and the Japanese before them, took their Buddhism from Chinese sources. That is, they adopted the Chinese versions of Buddhist scriptures, and Chinese functioned as their language of access to the serious study of the religion, the way Latin did for early Christianity before more scholastic efforts arose that went directly to the Greek and Hebrew sources of pre-Roman Christianity. Similar Chinese scholastic efforts to command the Sanskrit and Pali sources of pre-Chinese Buddhism were in some periods important within the Chinese Buddhist establishment in China, and also at times along the Inner Asian routes to India. Direct contacts with Indian sources of Buddhist learning were sharply diminished in the eleventh century; in general, however, that kind of scholastic effort was not engaged by the mass of Buddhist believers. Buddhism transmitted through the medium of the Chinese language was seen to have a universal quality, and that sufficed for them. Only at the level of ordinary religious practice was Buddhism fully assimilated into the host cultures, their native languages supplanting the Chinese of the sutra texts in daily religious activities. The Khitans became ardent Buddhists yet produced few written religious materials in Khitan, though they undoubtedly conducted Buddhist rites in their own spoken language. Buddhism in that dress became a stronger element in their civilization than did Confucianism and other genuinely Chinese patterns of religion and thought.

Comparison with the Khitans reveals much about the special character of Tangut Buddhism in the Xi Xia state. Unlike most other Inner Asian peoples, the Tanguts were not solely dependent on the Chinese sources of Buddhism. There were three literate Buddhist traditions at hand for them to draw on: in addition to the Chinese source, there were the Uighur and the Tibetan Buddhist communities. All three were the bearers of important traditions of learning as well as popular religious practice. The Tanguts' own language had a close affinity to Tibetan. The Xi Xia state's environment, however, was one in which Chinese civilization dominated one broad range of activities and interests. The Uighur Buddhist tradition was sophisticated and cosmopolitan. Uighur translations of sutras and learned Uighur scholar-monks were known throughout the Inner Asian world, and were introduced into the Liao state and later to the Jin state by the Xi Xia. Yet there was little reason for the Tanguts to identify with Uighur civilization; the Tibetan and Chinese worlds were closer and more important to them.

An expansive phase in the history of the Tufan kingdom of Tibet in the eighth and ninth centuries is of greatest importance to our understanding of Xi Xia Buddhism's dual relationship to those two worlds. That expansion extended Tibet's borders northward and eastward for two centuries, well into the western boundaries of China. Before it withdrew, it had established a network of Buddhist institutions and traditions having great authority for the

Buddhist believers of the region. Long after that expanded Tufan military power waned, Buddhist teachers continued to serve this large region from their home monasteries in Tibet. As the Xia state was extended to the northwest in the eleventh century, it acquired territories where Qiang (i.e., Dangxiang or Tangut-related) populations were the dominant element. The eleventh century was a time of deep ferment and religious revival in Tibet; many learned monks fired with zeal for reform of their church spread out into neighboring parts of Inner Asia to teach the purified doctrines. A number of them were quite naturally drawn to the Xi Xia state to serve those Tibetan populations, made more approachable by all the Tanguts' and related peoples' linguistic and cultural affinities with Tibet. An eminent lama of the new Karma-pa order, founded at the end of the twelfth century in Tibet, was invited to the Xia court in 1221 and was still in Xi Xia territory when the state fell to the Mongols in 1227. Tibetan Lamaist Buddhism clearly had a special place in Tangut religious life, particularly in the last century of the Xi Xia state's existence.

Large-scale translation of Buddhist scriptures into Tangut, using the Tangut script, began in the late eleventh century. Some were translated from Chinese texts and some from Tibetan. Tibetan monks and Tibetan-trained Tanguts developed the habit of writing the transliteration, that is, writing out the sounds to be pronounced in chanting the texts, into the sutra texts in the Tibetan script between the lines of the printed Xi Xia script. This practice led to a kind of standardization of Tangut as written phonetically in the Tibetan alphabetic script, one that came to function as a second "national script" for Tangut. It was never officially acknowledged as such by the Xi Xia government, but its use nonetheless seems to have spread among the people. Examples of manuscript texts showing the two versions side by side are among the trove of documents discovered at Dunhuang by Sir Aurel Stein in 1907 (now in London), and by the Russian archaeologist Colonel P. K. Kozlov at the old Xi Xia city of Khara Khoto between 1907 and 1909 (his findings are now in St. Petersburg).[15]

Alongside these Buddhist relations with Tibet we find many kinds of evidence of a similarly close but qualitatively different Buddhist relationship of Xia and China. Both the Tangut "nativist" ruler Yuanhao, the founder of the Great Xia dynasty who reigned 1032–1048, and his pro-sinification successors appealed to the Song court for complete Chinese printings of the Buddhist canon, the *Tripitaka*. Upon receiving such gifts they then built great imperially sponsored temples in which to venerate and study them. The architecture of these and of all Xia Buddhist temples appears to be essentially Chinese, but with significant "international" elements derived through contacts mediated by the Liao empire with other parts of northern Inner Asia.[16] Monks from Xia regularly visited China, the Liao empire, and its successor the Jin empire, as well as places throughout the western reaches of Inner Asia. Buddhism was a great force for cosmopolitan intercultural exchange.

On the one hand, the quantities of Tangut-language materials from the Kozlov expedition held at the Hermitage Museum in St. Petersburg, far greater in bulk than all the extant remains of Khitan or Jurchen scripts, bear out the strong Buddhist orientation of Tangut civilization. More recent archaeological finds in China also are extensive, but neither group of materials has yet been fully exploited. Eventually those Tangut-language materials will add much to our understanding. On the other hand, almost all of the available extant documentation of Tangut civilization to which we have ready access is the Chinese. Fortunately, it is quite extensive, but it nonetheless was written by Chinese who probably did not appreciate and hence did not record the cosmopolitan features of Tangut life. Moreover, it has largely been studied by modern Chinese scholars who usually are not sensitive to cultural relationships other than those with the Chinese. As we have seen (Chapter 8, Section II), even very recent Chinese scholarship on the Xi Xia state tends toward sinocentric distortion.

The Buddhist record, usefully supplementing Chinese historical writings, does, however, allow us to glimpse the important presence of Tibetan culture in Xi Xia history. It also allows us to see other aspects of Tangut history such as its indigenous Buddhist religious, intellectual, and artistic developments in a more balanced light. From them we can draw inferences about the many-sided complexity of the Tangut peoples' civilization.[17]

12

TRENDS OF CHANGE
UNDER JIN ALIEN RULE

Throughout the 120 years of Jurchen rule, the large bloc of the Chinese population in North China responded in many ways to the changed circumstances of their lives. The Jurchen rulers also constantly adjusted their governing methods and altered their social policies according to their perceived interests, while their Chinese subjects adapted. The divisions in Chinese society are first examined here in relation to social cohesion and cultural change. Kept largely out of touch with trends present in the Southern Song, the Chinese under Jurchen rule carried on a bustling urban life, shared in the general growth of trade and commerce, and developed their own new forms of drama, music, poetry, and art. Of particular interest is the way Chinese literati competed with the Jurchen elite in the realm of scholar-officialdom. Concurrently, new forms of drama and popular entertainment drew much talent; those developments also offer indirect evidence for the prosperity of North Chinese society throughout Jin times. Moralizing Confucian-minded historians have mostly been critical of the Jin era, finding its cultural florescence to be indicative only of insubstantial, superficial display; it would be more accurate to label the Jin an era of vitality in which both continuities and changes inform us about the course of Chinese history.

1. Divisions: North and South, Chinese and Non-Chinese

The Jurchens ruled over a much larger portion of the Chinese area and population than did the Khitans or the Tanguts. Their Jin dynasty was the last alien regime in the more than three centuries starting in 900, a long period marked by Inner Asian conquerors' varying patterns of acculturation and of their Chinese subjects' accommodation. That distinctive era was brought to its end when the Mongol conquerors, during the mid-thirteenth century, imposed a quite different pattern of conquest and rule on both Inner Asia and China. One can best recapture the pre-Mongol period's special character by exploring some of the historically intriguing issues of fact and interpretation. Chinese cultural survival is one of those.

Late in the Jin dynasty, the Jurchens ruled over a population exceeding 40 million Chinese in North China. Their dynasty's reign, from 1115 to 1234, on that basis alone constitutes a major chapter in the history of Chinese civilization.[1] The Southern Song dynasty, which coexisted with the Jin after 1126, governed about 100 million Chinese. They were neighboring states whose underlying hostility was contained within a mutually agreed-upon pattern of civil relations, only occasionally broken by the resort to warfare. By greatly reducing all the forms of interaction between the two regions, the separation of those two massive blocs of the Chinese people for over a century deepened the gulf between North and South. The consequences for social change stemming from that long separation were many.

The depth of the North-South divide in Chinese civilization should not be overstated; North and South China in all periods have displayed far more common features than differences. Yet there are ecological differences that have led to divergent cultural forms, such as the differences between mainly dry land farming in the North versus wet paddy field agriculture in the South, with attendant differences in the basic cereal grain crops grown, in the use of human labor and of work animals, in the means and costs of transportation, in the margin of agricultural production and hence of wealth, even in the diet and the clothing of the people. Those material differences long have appeared to many observers' eyes to be associated with differing attitudes and values and, to some extent, differences in both physical and personality types. At least, the Chinese traditionally have made such associations. Local and regional traditions in learning and culture also could lead to differing emphases in elite pursuits, in manners and customs, and in the cultural practices by which the guiding strata of the society maintained the social models for all to observe and, in varying degree (according to their means), for all to follow. The resulting local and regional variations at all social levels have always contributed much to the richness of Chinese civilization.

Given that base of regional cultural differences which preexisted this era of conquest and its alien regimes governing over the North Chinese population, the question arises: As we see the underlying North-South cultural distinction being overlaid by a Chinese versus alien political division, one that endures and expands, what consequences should we look for?

But first we must take note of special elements of the situation. A telling example of Chinese cultural distinctiveness is found in the language differences within the vast Chinese population. A sense of Chineseness, shared among all the "Han" Chinese who used the Chinese languages and were aware of a common cultural heritage, transcended the many local and regional variations. That shared sense of Chineseness persisted, despite the separation into Chinese and alien states. In the minds of the time, the line between China within and the non-Chinese (or "barbarian") world without was rarely ambiguous. The fellow Chinese whose language was strange, even unintelligible, was seldom confused with the non-Chinese whose language was outlandish. That line was meaningful, but it was not fundamentally one of mutual hostility. Even in ordinary times there were of course cultural impulses that might, in stressful situations, give rise to hostility between Chinese and non-Chinese people; there were also many elements of the cultural scene which fostered Chinese acceptance of the border region peoples. Officially, those linguistic and cultural outsiders were seen as humans learning to become Chinese; however arrogant that assumption seems to us today, it helped to lower hostility.

Conquerors and Conquered

If the foregoing correctly describes the general mind-set of the Chinese people with regard to the non-Chinese all around them, one must then ask how those remarkably open-minded people reacted when they were the victims of violence, such as in the brutal initial phases of the Jin invasion? This issue is little discussed, no doubt in part because the historical record offers little direct evidence to discuss. Did the Chinese calmly observe as their cities and villages underwent rape and pillage and the mass destruction of human lives? Obviously not. Communities ravaged by cruel warfare, perhaps numbed by the scope of their losses, undoubtedly were emotionally shattered and overcome by deep resentment. Did they thereafter remain captives of their hatred, seeking ways to vent their anger against anyone they could identify with the armies of destruction? It is important to look for signals in their social psychology if we are to understand the life of Chinese society thereafter. Its capacities for change and growth under this alien regime and, by analogy, under those which followed in the subsequent phases of later imperial history turn in large part on this issue. We must assume that a captive society, smoldering with suppressed hatred, would not have been able to function in the same way as one which put the initial reaction aside and quickly regained its emotional balance. The historical record shows that the latter is what happened; we must try to understand how it happened.

The reader of history might invoke analogies found in other civilizations and in more distant places. In these same centuries there is the example of the conquest of the Eastern Roman Empire by the Seljuks, then by the Ottoman Turks, beginning in the eleventh century, and the Norman conquest of Britain in 1066. Did those conquered peoples respond in ways similar to the Chinese in the twelfth century? Or one might compare the subjugation of peoples in more recent history, such as that caused by the Japanese invasion of and rule over much of China in the 1930s and 1940s. Such comparisons inevitably raise useful questions about cultural survival and social change. We cannot digress so far as to develop those comparisons, but the reader of history undoubtedly will bring them to mind.

To return to North China under the Jin dynasty in the twelfth and early thirteenth centuries, there is little direct evidence about attitudes and emotional responses from the population at large, even from the educated elite whose observations are preserved. Indirectly, however, we can see that the society, even in regions where severe destruction occurred, displays few signs of having been obsessed with anti-Jurchen feeling as such. It shows many signs that the Chinese population responded with resilience to the presence of alien conquerors in their midst, carried on their own way of life, and found many ways to take advantage of new situations to benefit themselves, and even to exploit their Jurchen neighbors.

It may well be that war conducted by Jurchens was, in the eyes of ordinary people, little different from warfare inflicted on them by Chinese leaders and armies. It was like a natural disaster, something to flee when possible but to be survived by whatever means. Among the educated, it was possible to blame the Jin invaders for the cruelties of war, and among resistance leaders (such as Yue Fei, the Southern Song resistance leader, discussed in Chapter 13), it was useful to build the morale of their armies (in Yue Fei's case made up largely of refugees from Jurchen-conquered regions) by arousing their desire for revenge. Among the Chinese who lived on under Jurchen rule, however, we can observe very little enduring hatred or irredentist sentiment. This is not to suggest that the Chinese were passive subjects of alien conquerors; rather, they were active in adapting to changed circumstances, ready to rebuild and carry on the lives of their families and their communities.[2] The experience of war at the hands of alien intruders does not appear to have altered Chinese attitudes toward non-Chinese. Their relatively open attitudes toward other varieties of humankind probably were bolstered by a sense of unity among the Chinese themselves. Even when conquest cut one portion of the Chinese people off from the rest, and the cultural forms expressing common Chineseness may have weakened, the sense of being Chinese did not disappear. Nor, so far as we can observe, was it diverted by that experience into lasting feelings of hatred and resistance.

The Meaning of Chinese Ethnic Identity

The confident cultural attitudes derived from the sense of being Chinese should not be obscured by recent efforts to shift the terminology, to call the Chinese and their languages "Han," so that all the other peoples who have ever resided within China or on its borders can be labeled "Chinese" in the inflated usage dictated by present-day political ends. That practice forces some historians to strive to create a past that did not exist.[3] It is completely ahistorical to say that the "Han" Chinese and the Jurchens, or whatever other people, were all "Chinese." In this period when the Jin, the Xi Xia, and the Southern Song coexisted, and other non-Chinese peoples on many borders interacted profoundly with China, it is particularly important that no arbitrary new definitions of terms should confuse the issue of China's historical relations with them. Ethnic identities were important in the consciousness of the time, not as the ground of a defensive hostility, but as the ground of transcendent cultural values and the awareness of a common history.

Today, ethnic identification relies on labels taken from the languages people speak.[4] In the definitions of what was Chinese, we find some linguistic complexities that have no ready parallels elsewhere. The Chinese today speak languages, sub-languages, dialects, and sub-dialects all belonging to one very large family of Chinese languages that vary widely among themselves. These all represent the present stage of development from analogous language differences of the past. As spoken language, many of those branches of the Chinese family of languages are mutually unintelligible. Parallels exist in all families of languages. What *is* unusual, something that in fact has no parallel elsewhere, is that speakers of all those Chinese languages used (and continue to use) but one shared written form of their languages, one that does not reflect the wide differences in the sounds of the spoken varieties of Chinese. The elements of regional distinctiveness and of local variants in customs and lifestyles, even the basic linguistic differences separating the speakers of China's seven or more genetically related Chinese languages and their innumerable dialects,[5] are features of Chinese civilization that have existed throughout the ages. To what extent did those differences divide them?

Under normal conditions their divisive impact was diminished by travel and contacts, by the central government's appointing in all places regional and local officials drawn from a national pool created by standardized written civil service examinations, by the widespread dissemination of books and teachers and ideas, and, above all, by attitudes among all the people which led them readily to accept variations in the ways fellow Chinese spoke. Because local and regional language variation was not reflected in written Chinese, the literary culture remained the same for all. Without doubt, the fact that literate Chinese all wrote the same language also contributed to the large numbers of individuals who could understand and use spoken variants of Chinese languages other than their own, and who were tolerant of people whose speech might seem amusing or difficult to understand. The prevailing social-psychological attitude among the Chinese people was one of inclusiveness. The linguistic unity of China at the level of the written language was a principal element reinforcing the general sense of Chineseness, and that was evident in Liao, Jin, Song, and Yuan times despite the protracted political division lasting from 900 C.E. onward to the thirteenth century. To summarize: on the one hand, that political division did not alter people's language identity; on the other hand, the culturally non-Chinese remained non-Chinese in the general consciousness. Both kinds of distinction were culture-based and thus were mutable; moreover, they were not paralleled by corresponding physical distinctions, which would not have been mutable. All lines could be crossed, but until non-Chinese convincingly crossed the line by merging with the Chinese population, their non-Chineseness remained. (By the same measure, Chinese also could become non-Chinese, and in the border zones of interaction, many did.)

There are to be sure some contemporary reports, especially from Chinese envoys who went from the Song court to the Jin capital, about the impact of Jurchen ways on the Chinese population living under alien control. It is not surprising that they deplored the influence of the Jurchen lifestyle on their fellow Chinese (even on those whose speech they could not understand), noting in particular that Chinese in the military wore Jurchen military attire and that their manners were affected (for the worse!) by their association with Jurchen fighting men. The military had elite status in Jin society; elite modes tend to be imitated. Nevertheless, some aspects of Jurchen life such as hats and hairdresses, jewelry and decoration, food, music and dance, while seldom found to be preferable by the Chinese outsider, had an exotic quality that stirred Chinese imaginations.[6]

Other kinds of evidence, however, support the view that by the later decades of the Jin dynasty, not enough of Jurchen culture remained intact among Jurchens living in China to sustain a separate alien community within the sphere of Chinese society. In all fields of learning, thought, the arts, in literature and in entertainment, even in architecture and the crafts, distinctive modes and patterns were developed under the Jin. While it is admittedly a debatable observation, I believe that we do not see the emergence of a hybrid culture. Those period-distinctive cultural features mostly can be best understood as continuations of earlier Chinese cultural trends. To be sure, the Jin region's separation from the rest of China, plus the factor of alien rule, helped to create special conditions that encouraged differing potentialities. Except for a few superficial and ephemeral trends, however, we can see in the Jin period not an amalgamation of Jurchen and Chinese cultural elements but rather the further development of a Northern Chinese style. That is, whether or not a significant portion of the Jurchen population became "Chinese" by thoroughgoing assimilation, one can see a deepening of North Chinese regional distinctiveness. There are several explanations for that. The most important one is that few Chinese could travel across the geographic boundary separating North China from South. It now corresponded to a political boundary. That affected many aspects of official as well as private life, but the largest group of those who were unnaturally confined within the new barriers undoubtedly was that consisting of ordinary traders and traveling merchants.

Interregional trade, when unobstructed, could contribute powerfully to the homogenization of life throughout China. Traveling traders, buying and selling goods and establishing personal contacts throughout large trading areas, had become a feature of Chinese life by Song times. But once the barriers dividing the Chinese culture zone into two or three mutually hostile states were in place, the framework of commercial activity changed. Trade remained at high levels, but it was mediated through border marts and control barriers where goods were passed on while the carriers of goods stopped; the unifying impact of trade was thereby diminished. Such barriers began to be set up by the conquering Khitans and Tanguts in the tenth century, but they did not yet cut off major portions of China. When the Jin established their rule over North China in the 1120s, the new line of trade barriers cut deep into the center of China. Beyond the obviously shattered patterns of China's interregional trade, there is also evidence of a more general tendency toward regional separateness. Here the concurrent question, Was there a "Northern Chinese style" affecting many components of Chinese life? acquires special meaning. This question points to an undercurrent running through discussions of Chinese civilization; it recurs in various contexts where separation and reunification are the subject.

II. JURCHEN DOMINANCE

The conquerors' patterns of rule and control also contributed to cultural change. The Jurchen nation's leaders managed the conquered Chinese provinces to serve Jurchen interests. That was their wholly expectable stance as conquerors and rulers. They attempted to guarantee their advantages by reserving the dominant positions in military and civil government for Jurchens, and by giving privileges of various kinds—such as tax privileges, service exemptions, access to office, legal preferences, and differential standards of justice—to their own people. At first, as we have seen, the Jurchen conquerors took over the Liao dynasty's system of dual institutions and dual staffing of government offices in which the Khitan official, later the Jurchen official, remained superior to his Chinese counterpart with whom he shared the duties and, to a lesser extent, the privileges of office. As the Liao precedent was abandoned in favor of a more centralized kind of administration on the Chinese model, Chinese continued to staff much of the government, but higher offices with more power, prestige, and greater economic benefits were reserved for Jurchens. One sees few exceptions to that general rule. Few Chinese were admitted into the highest ranks of policy making, even on the civil side of government. The Jurchen Wanyan imperial clan reserved most of the top positions in all branches of government to its members, largely excluding even other Jurchens. Such hereditary privilege, long abandoned in Chinese society and counter to its ethos, discouraged talented Chinese. It became a cause of irritation even in Jurchen society.

Within the military command, not only were Chinese denied higher positions of power and trust, but also as time passed even the Khitans and the Xi and other Inner Asians who had participated in very important ways in the Jurchen conquest saw their opportunities for leadership in the Jurchen military machine sharply reduced. There also were auxiliary armed forces made up of non-Jurchens, essentially of Chinese infantrymen who were conscripts or volunteers; those units were organizationally apart from the Jurchen *meng'an* and *mouke* elite cavalry forces. Such units, of course, included Chinese officers in direct command of Chinese troops. But the higher ranks in those non-Jurchen military units were dominated by Jurchen appointees; few Chinese were trusted to hold decision-making or discretionary powers. A few exceptions to that rule began to appear quite late, almost all in the crises of the last two decades, when the situation had become desperate. By that time, ambitious Chinese military officers often saw more to gain by defecting to the Mongol invaders or to the Southern Song than by remaining loyal to Jurchen overlords who had never granted them full partnership. Curiously, the more culturally Chinese the Jurchens became, the less they trusted their Chinese subjects, especially in military roles.

As for postings in the civil administration, by late Jin times the Chinese examination degree holders achieved something close to parity in numbers with Jurchen and other non-Chinese higher officials, yet still were largely excluded from the highest ranks. For reasons that are not difficult to understand, the Jurchens were more open to participation of other non-Jurchens from among the northern tribal peoples of the former Liao empire. They tightened that access to shared power after their rule was established, yet there still were Khitans and other tribal peoples serving in the Jin civil and military establishments until the end of the dynasty. To summarize, the Chinese did not achieve parity with their Jurchen overlords or even with other Inner Asian subjects. Barriers between the two communities remained.

III. THE IMPACT OF THE CIVIL SERVICE EXAMINATIONS

Despite conditions of service that were unsatisfactory to the Chinese elite, when we turn away from the staffing of government to the inner workings of the conquered Chinese society, we find that the pre-conquest patterns by which Chinese society prepared and supported its elite stratum were essentially untouched by alien rule.[7] The twelfth-century Jurchens conquered the Northern Song dynasty and took North China. After establishing their own rule in North China, the Jin curbed the Song patterns of open recruitment of men drawn from an achieving meritocracy. That is, they adopted the system, but they did not give it full play in staffing their government. It supplied the government's staffing needs only at the lower levels of political authority. The high-minded service ideals imbedded in the system, built on education and on examinations, were not extinguished, but ambitious Chinese understood that their careers would be limited to the lower ranks of office.

In other words, the Jin system allowed Chinese subjects no more than a very limited "political presence"; in contrast, the "cultural presence" of the Chinese literati (that is, the elite of learning and of literary achievement) came to occupy an extraordinarily significant role in Jin history.[8] Traditional Chinese learning, weighted toward the Confucian classics and long-recognized genres of literary expression, continued to supply the criteria for defining the Chinese elite, even though learned Chinese did not thereby gain the full range of rewards. Interestingly, the Emperor Shizong wanted a broader segment of Jurchens also to command the kind of prestige that success in the examinations brought to Chinese, and to earn their place in government in parallel fashion. He saw that prestige as a way both to enhance Jurchen dignity and to counter the Jurchen tribal aristocracy's independence from the throne. Those considerations undoubtedly influenced the Jurchen emperor's decision in 1173, some years after regularization of the broader functioning of the Chinese system, to adapt (albeit somewhat superficially) the concept and the mechanics of the Chinese civil service recruitment system to the Jurchen elite as well.

By late in the reign of the Emperor Shizong (r. 1161–1189), the two Jin examination systems—one for Chinese and one for Jurchen candidates—had been expanded and regularized to function on a scale matching that of the Northern Song a century earlier. That is, the Jin regularly conducted examinations at qualifying and final levels, in the provinces and at the capital, to grant in large numbers the degrees that carried official rank and appointment. The examinations were supplemented by the creation of two National Academies (Guo Zi Jian) at the capital, one for scions of the higher Chinese and non-Jurchen officials using the Chinese language and classical texts, and one for Jurchens conducted at least in token degree in Jurchen. Adopting the new pattern of the late Northern Song system, they also established Confucian schools at all levels of local government, and they added some schools using Jurchen language for Jurchen students preparing for the examinations. The numbers of Chinese examinees grew rapidly.

The parallel system of academies and examinations for Jurchen scholars, using the Jurchen language and script, subjected Jurchen examination candidates to much simpler standards, and they passed at much higher rates. Moreover, even though Jurchen degree holders were fewer by far in number (never more than fifty per triennial examination), a much larger percentage of them could expect to achieve high rank, and in a shorter time. The inequities were obvious to all. Even when, in mid- and later Jin times, the two examination systems were expanded, that did not equalize opportunity in officeholding for the Chinese participants, nor can they have realistically expected that it would. But the late expansion of the Chinese examination and recruitment systems brought large numbers of Chinese into the lower official positions in government and gave them a place in society that partially satisfied Chinese desires.

Estimates based on the incomplete records show that the Jin government awarded a total of more than 16,000 *jinshi* degrees (the highest-level degree, sometimes known as "the doctorate") between 1123 (when small-scale examinations first were held for captured Liao and Song literati) and 1233.[9] Three-quarters of those were awarded late in the dynasty, the bulk falling between 1161 and 1208. In the later years of the Emperor Zhangzong's reign (1189–1208), it can be said that Jin China was awash in holders of the Chinese-type *jinshi* degree. That highest degree was awarded at an annual rate of over 200, or about 600 per triennial examination. Those figures come very close to matching the highest rates of *jinshi* production in all of Chinese history, those for the years 976–1057 in Northern Song times.

By comparison, the Liao dynasty also had started out rather tentatively to examine Chinese, Bohai, and sedentary subjects in the manner of the Tang civil service examinations. Then after a century it instituted the examinations on a more regular basis to recruit mainly subject Chinese officials to staff administrative offices in central and local government under its Southern Chancellery. In its last hundred years, from 1030 until the final Liao examination in 1123, it awarded about 2,000 *jinshi* degrees, that is, about 20 per year, fewer than one-tenth the number produced by the Jin system at its height. Late in their history, especially during the long reign of Emperor Jenzong (1139–1193), the Xi Xia also reached a high point in their adoption of Chinese cultural forms (see Chapter 11). But although they established Confucian schools and shrines throughout the state and at the capital, and created a Hanlin Academy of learned Chinese advisers, so far as we can tell they did not reach the point of instituting regular civil service examinations for recruitment and appointment of officials in their central government. This comparison with the Liao and Xi Xia experience reveals how extensively the later Jurchen rulers promoted the broad functioning in their society of what has been called China's defining social institution. Were the consequences of the Jin period examination system equally significant?

First of all, the examination system, with all its attached activities of lower schools and the National Academy, private academies and teaching traditions, teachers, editing and publishing of study texts, and the rewards of public prestige and officeholding, continued to define the elite of Chinese society under alien rule.[10] It did not, to be sure, function in that way for the Jurchen elite, whose self-identification and ideal social roles remained those of warrior society. Nonetheless, this defining Chinese social and political institution clearly had a deep impact on the later Jurchen rulers. A fascinating anecdote recorded in the *Jin History* reveals the depth of that influence on their thinking. At the beginning of the Emperor Shizong's reign (perhaps in 1162), some of his Jurchen courtiers, reflecting the general reaction against Prince Hailing's promotion of Chinese institutions, proposed that the civil service examinations be abolished. The emperor said that he would consult the Grand Preceptor Zhang Hao, an eminent senior Bohai official whose forebears had earned the *jinshi* degree under the Liao. Zhang Hao himself had earned the degree in 1130 and had held high posts in previous reigns. On an occasion when Zhang Hao came into the court, the emperor asked, "Among all the emperors and kings of the past were there any who did not employ the literati?" To all present, "the past" could only mean the Chinese historical past. Zhang answered, "Yes." The emperor asked, "Who was that?" Zhang replied, "The First Emperor of Qin." The emperor glanced back and forth at those present and said, "Would you have *me* be a First Emperor?" That resounding rhetorical question could only be answered in the negative, so the proposal to abolish the examinations was shelved.[11] The First Emperor, 1,300 years earlier, though reviled by the entire Confucian tradition, had created the Chinese imperial system by force of arms, and one might think that the Jurchen alien conquerors would have felt free to identify with his grand accomplishments. One can imagine that Aguda, after he had been told who the First Emperor was, might have expressed his admiration for a fellow military conqueror. Instead, we can see Aguda's grandson, the Emperor Shizong, shuddering as he replies to the advice of a sinified Bohai official in words that mean "What kind of a monster do you think I am?" He is completely under the influence of the Chinese view of history.

Second, from a purely practical point of view, the Jin adoption of the civil service examination and recruitment system shows us that the Jin state had urgent need for civil officials to staff its Chinese-type government structure at all levels. Without this regularized form of recruiting Chinese participants, the kind of governing the Jin wanted to implement would not have been possible. To be sure, the Jin allowed easy transfer of Jurchen officials, both hereditary and appointed, from their *meng'an* and *mouke* offices into the higher civil bureaucracy; but that source could not satisfy the need for officials in the day-to-day work of governing in the districts and prefectures and provinces or in the central government. Jing-shen Tao cites figures from the *Jin History* stating that in 1193 the number of Chinese ranked officials then in service was 6,794 (not, of course, including the thousands of clerical staff and other sub-officials), compared with 4,705 Jurchens in official posts (mostly military).[12] The reported figures do not show what ranks the Chinese reached during their careers in office, and we must assume that not many reached the highest levels of officialdom. Yet those figures may be typical of the ratio of civil service–ranked Chinese to Jurchen officials in the later Jin dynasty.

Those numbers are high. Could the Jin examination system have provided enough degree holders to meet the government's need? We cannot reconstruct the numbers of successful degree candidates in each of the triennial (or more frequent) examinations throughout the Jin dynasty. But if we estimate that they numbered about 150 to 200 per year (450 to 600 per examination) during Shizong's reign, and that the average career-life for degree holders after attaining the degree was about thirty years, the pool of regular examination-route *jinshi* that would have accumulated in the thirty years from 1161 to 1193 would number from 4,500 to 6,000. When we add in the *jinshi* degrees awarded in special examinations, by imperial grace, and by other means, the pool could come close to filling the 6,700 positions reported by Jing-shen Tao. In the thirty years after 1193 the numbers undoubtedly exceeded these figures. That is not to say that it was ever expected, under either Chinese or alien dynasties, that all civil posts in the bureaucracy would or could be filled by holders of the highest examination degree. But the *jinshi* were expected to supply the majority of appointees and to dominate the higher career patterns. The figures show that under the Jin, the numbers were sufficient to accomplish that purpose. Even though the Chinese *jinshi* were not permitted to dominate in the highest ranks of officeholding, the Jurchen Jin is nonetheless the only one among the four conquest dynasties in these centuries of Chinese history (the other three being the Liao, the Xi Xia, and the Mongol Yuan, which followed the Jin) whose civil service examination and recruitment system provided enough degree holders to meet the state's administrative needs.

The later emperors appear to have recognized that officials recruited through the Chinese and the Jurchen examination routes were better qualified and more dependable than those who achieved office through inherited status and privilege. In particular, they found that using *jinshi* as censors and investigating officials was an effective way to root out abuses and keep the higher Jurchen hereditary officials drawn from the tribal aristocracy under a useful kind of surveillance. In the ongoing contest between the Chinese imperial institution and the Jurchen tribal aristocracy's prerogatives, the Confucian-inspired examination system became a useful instrument of the throne. Although it did not operate fairly (from a Chinese point of view) in rewarding Chinese talent with full opportunity to advance into key posts high in the government, it nonetheless became an indispensable element in Jin governing.

Third, and perhaps of still greater importance, is the fact that tens of thousands of men were engaged in the regular and systematic activity of acquiring higher learning that would qualify them to pass through the local levels of the examinations and sit for the triennial *jinshi* examinations. The highest numbers recorded of men sitting for the *jinshi* examination are those for the year 1213, when 9,000 qualified candidates sat for the examinations at the capital, and over 800 were granted the degree.[13] Quite apart from those who gained official degrees, the activity of preparing for and taking the examinations occupied a very large elite sector of the society that engaged in literary and intellectual pursuits. The records show that only one-tenth to one-fourth of the qualified candidates who took the examinations were successful in any examination year. The Chinese, however, have never felt that those who failed the highest examinations, under those odds, were necessarily of inferior cultivation and intelligence. Many noted literati throughout history failed, sometimes repeatedly; they were seen not as "failed men" but as learned persons whom fate had not (yet) favored.

Those who did not receive degrees had to make their livelihoods apart from official service. They could pursue careers in teaching and writing, editing and publishing, and could fill roles in their home communities as doctors of medicine, experts on rituals, interpreters of government announcements and proclamations, specialists in religious matters, and keepers of local history. They drafted tomb inscriptions and obituaries, provided poetry for public occasions, kept watch over public and private schools, identified talent among the young, and kept the traditions of the literate elite alive. They also formed important networks of personal relationships and interaction throughout the elite, transcending their local identities. That was the norm of Chinese society during the Song and under later dynasties, but the Jin is exceptional among conquest dynasties before the Qing (1644–1911) in maintaining an educational system of such broad extent. As the Chinese saw it, the health of the society was ensured by the examination system and its many by-products.

Yet the special character of that system as implemented under the Jin has also been held responsible by later historians for some weaknesses of the period. The examinations were open to candidates in several fields of preparation, only two of which drew significant numbers. One was belles lettres, in which composition of stylized poetry was stressed. The other, which stressed memorization, was devoted to classical texts. By far the largest number, because of the emphases stressed by the government's official examiners, chose the literary or poetry specialization. A third, more rigorous field, demanding the ability to explicate classical texts including history, statecraft, and philosophy, and the capacity to analyze and formulate answers to empirical problems, drew very few applicants. During the Northern Song, as we have seen, reforming statesmen strove with some success to make the more practical topics the essential element in the examinations. The Jin examination system, even in its fuller workings of the later reigns, was not subject to such pressure for reform. It thus has been criticized for failing to produce "down to earth" intellectuals who on the one hand would have a firm ethical grounding, and on the other could serve their society in practical ways. As a result of the emphasis on belles lettres in the Jin examinations, the literature of the age has been seen as florid, formulaic, full of shallow sentiment, and lacking the firm spirit of moral commitment. To be sure, a minor "golden age" of literary achievement in the Jin (Gold) dynasty, linked to the examination system, has been recognized by all traditional historians, but in the eyes of men of that and later times, it was not without serious weaknesses.

IV. HIGH CULTURE DURING THE JIN DYNASTY

It is undoubtedly fair to say that we do not see as much outstanding intellectual or literary achievement in Jin times as its numbers of literati might suggest. Only three or four of its poets and writers are mentioned in general histories of Chinese literature or have had their collected works included in major collectanea representing the entire span of Chinese history. Perhaps the same verdict can be extended to painting and calligraphy, the other two art forms in the triad of the highest arts in the Chinese view. There were many competent artists, but few whose names remained among the best known in later ages. Yet present research may alter that view, for the field has not been thoroughly investigated in the past.

The most highly regarded literary figure born during the Jin dynasty, ironically enough, is Xin Qiji (1140–1207), who is not classed as a Jin writer. One of the supreme masters of the "lyric" *(ci)* poetry, the characteristic poetic mode of the Song dynasty, Xin was born in Shandong and studied under eminent Jin literary figures of the day. But he was a man of action. At the time of Prince Hailing's campaign against the Southern Song in 1161, after some flamboyant demonstrations of his fighting skills and upright valor in the service of the anti-Hailing cause, he crossed the Yangzi at the head of a thousand fighting men and defected to the Song. He died in Southern Song China more than forty years later and thus must be classed as a Southern Song writer. Nevertheless, it is useful to mention him in this context because in highly refined Southern Song political and literary circles, his straightforward, abrupt, and forceful "northern manner" repeatedly created difficulties for him, and frequently frustrated his political career as an adherent of the war party at the Song court. There is a double irony in the fact that his heroic northern cultural style, which would not have been out of place among Northern Song literary and political figures a century earlier, not only was somewhat jarring in Southern Song times, but also did not typify the milieu of Jin China into which he had been born.[14]

The best-known literary figure classed as a Jin literatus is Yuan Haowen (1190–1257), a *jinshi* of 1221 who was at the Jin court until the end in 1234, but who lived the last two dozen years of his life as a Jin loyalist in retirement under the Yuan dynasty. Yuan Haowen was a poet in several genres, essayist, political thinker, and informal historian. He produced well-developed critical ideas about the nature of poetry, and has drawn the attention of modern scholars both in and outside China.[15] It has been convincingly argued that Yuan and many of his kind among the abundant crop of scholar-official poets in late Jin times saw literary cultivation as an essential vehicle for preserving the core values in the heritage of Chinese civilization.[16] They believed that as a pursuit to which to devote one's life, belletristic literature was equal in its value to ethical philosophy, classical exegesis, and other intellectual pursuits that Northern Song Neo-Confucianism valued as the main concerns of scholars. That stance within the Neo-Confucian elite is identified with the image of Su Shi, the late Northern Song poet (discussed in Chapter 7). He had an extraordinary reputation during the Jin, when his cultural values are said to have held more appeal than those of the Lixue philosophers.[17]

Moreover, the literary figures at the helm of cultural developments in the Jin period saw themselves as the direct successors to the great age of Northern Song, when philosophy, history, and statecraft, as well as the literary arts, all flourished in a great reinvigoration of scholar-official intellectual and artistic pursuits. In the view of these Jin-period Chinese literati, they themselves should be considered a more valid link to Northern Song cultural achievements than was the Southern Song, Jin's contemporary state in Central and South China, which in their view had succeeded the Northern Song only politically, and even then not with unquestioned validity. The Jin literati's intense cultural commitment appears not to have included anything anticipating more recent history's nationalism. Nevertheless, among many of their Chinese contemporaries in the Southern Song, the same cultural commitment *was* linked to strongly patriotic identification with the dynasty against the obvious threats from China's (or Chinese culture's) alien enemies.

Cultural Achievement and Dynastic Legitimacy

Proud self-esteem and assertions that the Jin functioned as the valid heir to the Northern Song's cultural achievements led, by the logic of then current Chinese statecraft thinking, to the larger issue of dynastic legitimacy. The later Jin emperors, Zhangzong (1198–1208) and his immediate followers, were not without reason to wish to buttress their legitimacy vis-à-vis the Southern Song at a time when the weaknesses of the Jin state and the threats from the Mongols farther north were becoming serious. All theories concerning the legitimacy of a dynasty turned on the question of how the Mandate of Heaven had been transmitted from its previous acknowledged holder to the present dynasty. In the case of the Jin, there followed serious discussions at the court that extensively reexamined all the possible views on dynastic legitimacy, never suggesting that the Jin was not legitimate, but attempting to ascertain just how the transmission of that legitimacy had occurred. If the great florescence of Northern Song cultural vitality to which Jin literati believed themselves the heirs had demonstrated cosmic approval of the Song, then how did the further transmission of the Mandate to Jin work in relation to the symbols and the paraphernalia, all the palladia of legitimate rule? The antique Chinese political theories of the Five Agents, somewhat out of date by Jin times, were revived and minutely examined.[18] Were the safety and health of the Jin dynasty guaranteed by the Agent Metal (as the dynasty's name, "Gold," would suggest, as was argued at the Jin court when Aguda proclaimed the dynasty in 1215), or was the sequence in which the Five Agents produced and succeeded one another to be understood in a way that made the Agent Earth the protector of the Jin?[19] The emperor appointed panels of experts on three occasions over a period of eight years, between 1194 and 1202, to investigate, debate (often in his presence), and draw up reports. On each occasion the panels appear to have engaged in study and discussion for some months. One panel was made up of ten learned Chinese officials and twelve high Jurchen officials and nobles. They formed smaller groups supporting four or more different solutions; both Chinese and Jurchens appear to have been among the supporters of each proposed solution. The arguments put forth were often intricately ingenious, but seldom if ever profound. Some of the debaters even went so far as to challenge the legitimacy of the Northern Song itself, and declared the Jin to be superior to "barbarian" challengers (e.g., the Liao, from whom the Jin would seem to have derived its legitimate succession), and also to (in such eyes) pretenders to legitimacy such as the Song and the Five Dynasties.

Emperor Zhangzong ultimately decided in favor of the Agent Earth instead of Metal (gold). That decision made the Jin the successor to a legitimate Northern Song dynasty which was declared to have existed under the Agent Fire. While that decision acknowledged the Northern Song's legitimacy, the Jin claim to the successor Agent Earth implied that the power of the Song had ended with the Jin rise and that the Southern Song therefore was no longer legitimate. That intricate argument did not put the matter to rest. It was reviewed and re-argued about ten years later under Emperor Xuanzong. The determination bore upon many aspects of ritual, such as the color of the imperial robes, the forms of ritual objects, the dates on which certain ritual sacrifices were to be conducted, and the like. The importance of these arcane-seeming protracted debates lies not in their intellectual content per se but in the evidence they provide that the later Jin rulers, under the stresses of the times, "manipulated Chinese ideologies and practices, even at the expense of their native tradition."[20] They constitute an intriguing chapter in the Jin dynasty's involvement in the management of Chinese high culture, inviting comparisons with other conquest and native dynasties.

Law

Another field of cultural management in which the later Jin emperors took a hand was the study of Chinese law. The codification of penal laws, a necessity for governing, had been undertaken by most earlier dynasties. The code promulgated by the Tang dynasty in the seventh century and issued in a revised final form early in the eighth was held to be the best example of legal scholarship; it had not been recodified or replaced by succeeding dynasties. The Northern Song had issued a Unified Penal Code (Xing Tong) among its first political acts after the dynasty's founding in 960; it largely followed the Tang Code. The Liao had declared that Khitan law would be applied to Khitans; Chinese law (probably meaning the Tang Code) would apply to the sedentary population. Late in the tenth century the Liao had the "Chinese laws" translated into Khitan. But in disputes between Chinese and Khitans, legal problems arose that the Liao never resolved.[21] Similar problems became more serious under the Jurchens simply because the numbers of Chinese over whom they governed, and the complexity of the relations between Jurchens in China and the Chinese, had become so much greater.

After several earlier attempts, the Taihe Code of 1201, named for the Taihe reign period (1200–1208) of Emperor Zhangzong when it was promulgated, was completed and adopted as the law of the realm. It too was heavily influenced by the Tang Code, and is another example of Jin reliance on Chinese tradition, with certain modifications to favor Jurchen interests. The Taihe Code did not fully solve all the thorny issues arising from applying one legal standard for a population divided by two ethnic traditions; but despite some provisions favoring Jurchens, it attempted to deal with such matters in one code that applied to all, not in the spirit of dual institutions and separation on ethnic lines. It is considered a very important milestone in Chinese legal history. It remained in force through the early years of Mongol rule in North China, but was declared invalid in 1272 when Khubilai Khan announced the establishment of the Yuan dynasty.

Drama and the Social Milieu

In many ways the most interesting development in Jin culture is the emergence of Chinese drama and other forms of entertainment literature, which in Jin times began to mature into several broadly popular forms. The texts of these increasingly literary entertainments were produced by Chinese and a few non-Chinese authors, many of whom clearly were men of considerable literary cultivation.

Until the early decades of the twentieth century it was believed that before the Yuan dynasty the Chinese had neither a strong tradition of theatrical arts nor any dramatic literature. Then, suddenly in the mid-thirteenth century, there appeared full-blown masterworks of staged drama with texts of extraordinarily high literary value, particularly in the poetry of the sung parts, the arias imbedded in the dramatic texts. These lyric poems, called *qu* (or *san qu*), were a new genre of poetry, different in their musical patterns and of still more intricate prosodic features than the Song dynasty lyric poems, the *ci*. The arias from the dramas were so attractive that poets imitated them in lyric songs meant to exist apart from the dramas, and thus produced a new independent genre of lyric poetry; the resulting *qu* lyric poetry came to characterize literary achievement in the Yuan dynasty, just as the *ci* lyrics had typi-fied poetic art in the Song dynasty.

The authors of the new dramas, insofar as their names were known and their lives could be assessed, were mostly not scholar-official literati, yet the dramas, known today as Yuan *zaju*, and their related poetry were of such undeniable quality that they had to be accepted. Moreover, their sudden emergence had to be explained in a way that would somehow link it to the dominance in literature and art granted to the scholar-official elite. That tradi-tional account went roughly as follows: Amazingly, these drama texts by obscure or unknown persons indubitably are works of genius, and they reveal high literary cultivation; therefore they must have been written by highly culti-vated literati. But under what kind of circumstances would persons qualified to belong to the scholar-official elite come to write such "low culture" popu-lar works intended for common entertainment? A plausible explanation was found for this abrupt appearance of a hitherto unknown art form and the almost simultaneous apogee of its development. The conquest of Jin China by the Mongols in 1234 led in North China to a conjunction of irregular conditions: alien rule; patronage of Chinese literati in humble circumstances by an alien unlettered elite who sought tuneful but simple entertainment; loss of status by the same Chinese literati, idling them and making them desperate for income, forcing them to debase their genius and produce the dramas. Otherwise, how would the dramas, ingenious in structure but accessible to an audience of common tastes, have come to include songs whose poetic texts were often of subtle and refined excellence? The answer, this elaborate expla-nation continues, was that unlettered audiences would appreciate the action and the singing, while the frustrated geniuses creating the dramas could indulge their sensibilities by writing song lyrics pitched somewhat over the heads of the common audience.

This way of explaining the Yuan drama is deeply imbedded in the Chinese sources dating back to the fourteenth century and remained virtually unques-tioned until the twentieth. To be sure, there is indeed a certain incongruity between the refinement of the aria lyrics and the frequent low comedy effects of the action. That lends credibility to the foregoing explanation of Chinese drama's brilliant history in the thirteenth and fourteenth centuries, but it has been shown to be wrong. Many of the clichés concerning the role of theater in Chinese civilization have been totally superseded by a mass of recent schol-arship. Above all, the new scholarship assigns to the Northern Song, and especially to the Jin dynasty, an important place in a much longer develop-ment which led to the flowering of *zaju* in late Jin and Yuan times.[22]

We now are learning that the emergence of staged formal drama was pre-ceded by a thousand years of steady growth of theatrical entertainment, including puppet shows, dance and mime performances, singing to accompa-niment of new instrumental music (much of it from Inner and Central Asia), acrobatics and martial arts, magic shows, professional storytelling that often included sung interludes, and elaborate staged entertainments at religious fes-tivals. During the Northern Song dynasty, the form of such entertainments presented in theaters not only at the court but also in the pleasure quarters of the larger cities came to assume the pattern of well-developed dramatic skits in which spoken dialogue alternated with sung parts. With the Jin conquest of Northern Song, the further development of these dramas bifurcated; in the North that split led eventually to the Yuan dynasty's famed *zaju,* and in the South to what were called *xiwen,* both terms meaning drama texts. Basically similar, they differed slightly in their music and in other conventions of theatrical performance.

Under the Jin, the development toward the final product, the *zaju,* went through further stages of more elaborate and better-constructed skits with fuller attention to the sung interludes. The names of more than 600 Jin dynasty *yuanben,* or "theater guild texts," have come down to us, along with those of many *zhugongdiao,* or "medleys," but few of the texts themselves have been preserved. Nor do we know much about their authors. The most famous of the medleys, written during the reign of Emperor Zhangzong (1189–1208), the only complete Jin period text in the genre that has been preserved, has been translated under the name "The Romance of the Western Chamber." Its author is known only as "the Honorable Mr. Dong," or Dong Jieyuan. It is one of the longest poem sequences in this semi-dramatic form in all of Chinese literature; it is typical of the dramas in that it is a retelling of a famous love story from the past. It was in turn recast as a full-blown *zaju* during the Yuan dynasty.[23]

A number of the most famous early Yuan *zaju* writers were born late in the Jin and were reared in the literary atmosphere created by the emphasis on lyric poetry in the conduct of the Jin civil service examinations. These dramatic works lay beyond the accepted boundaries of high culture, and despite the obvious evidence that the writers were well educated, their personal lives probably were closely tied to the rowdy milieu of the entertainment quarters, so the proper historical records have ignored them.[24] But when it comes to the major writers of the new *zaju* dramas written by a sudden concentration of geniuses born in the late Jin and on into the early Yuan, there is more reason to believe that they were drawn to the theater because it satisfyingly employed their talents than there is to believe that they were forced by demeaning circumstances to follow a lifestyle that they would otherwise have avoided.

Most of the earlier Jin period dramas no longer exist, so their literary qualities cannot be assessed, but they have something else of importance to tell us about Jin history. That is, North China in Jin times was populous, its many cities were centers of flourishing trade, and it sustained a rich and vigorous cultural life at sub-elite as well as elite levels. Drama depended on a supply of theatergoers, and it had to compete with other forms of crowd-pleasing entertainment in an atmosphere of shops, inns, restaurants, bawdy houses, baths, temples, sporting events, and many other attractive places for recreation. These served government officials, traders, idle youths, rustics from the surrounding countryside, Buddhist monks and Daoist priests, Jurchen aristocrats, soldiers, thieves, pickpockets and more serious criminals, peddlers of snake oil, fortune-tellers, all kinds of entrepreneurs and their customers. There were crowds in the streets by day and by night, and among them were many with time and money to spend. From the social history of drama more than from any other directly relevant source we learn that the great cities such as the Jin Central Capital (at present-day Beijing) and the expanded and refurbished Southern Capital at Kaifeng, the former Northern Song capital in Henan Province, as well as a number of smaller places in Shandong, Hebei, and Shanxi—even middle-sized cities and larger market towns—offered urbane surroundings whose pleasure precincts included theaters, acting companies, and writers of dramas. The Jin conquest had not destroyed that flourishing life of the old Chinese heartland; the stark disparities between North and South China that we know from slightly later times are not yet evident.

There is good evidence about the prosperous life of society generally in Jin China, and it is important that we be reminded of it. The Mongol conquest brought long decades of disorder and anarchy in the North, more or less from the fall of the Jin Central Capital in 1215 until well into the reign of Khubilai Khan, who succeeded to the Mongol leadership of China in 1260. Little over half a century later, from the 1330s to the 1370s, North China was again subjected to destructive warfare and general chaos attendant on the rise of the Ming dynasty. Those two phases of internal disorder devastated the North, greatly reduced its population, destroyed its cities and market towns, and eliminated much of the wealth, the trade, and the margin for consumption, setting it back far behind the levels of social well-being and prosperity known in the South. The North did not begin to recover until the fifteenth century, and never did fully overcome the disparity in living standards. But in Jin times, that was not yet so.

V. Economic Life under the Jin

Up to the time when the Jurchens began their rebellion against the Liao in 1114 they had not yet governed anything corresponding to a centralized state. Yet ten years later they were in possession not only of the Liao homeland but also of much of North China. The Liao, and of course the Song, had developed sophisticated economic management systems for their states, from methods of taxation and other revenue measures to centrally managed granaries and treasuries, with accounting procedures and record keeping and regulations for disbursement of funds. Money was paid out for salaries, payment of invoices, and other allocations of the government's resources to regular (e.g., public works projects) and extraordinary purposes (e.g., famine relief, emergencies such as floods and disasters, and the preparations for war). Special sections of the government at all levels attended to those tasks with full record keeping and paper pushing, and were staffed by bureaucrats who gained specialist expertise in performing them. Such was governing on the Chinese pattern.

Money and the Management of the Economy

The Jurchens took over existing Liao, then Song, government offices and personnel, and continued the established procedures without questioning them. But they did not immediately acquire great sophistication about issues of economic management. At first, in the manner of all China's conquerors, they accepted the Chinese norms as relevant to their needs. They had never issued coinage, but they had learned to use Khitan money, and noted that Song coins also circulated in the Liao state. They had never been subject to taxation in their own society, but they quickly learned that Khitan strength depended on tax revenues to support the military machine. Within a decade they were doing all the basic things necessary to operate the economy, mostly by designating Khitans and Chinese to continue doing those things, but now to do them in their service.

The Chinese used copper coins as their basic unit of value in ordinary transactions, and they accepted the precious metals as well as bolts of silk and *shi* of grain (130 pounds) as standard units of value in larger transactions. They did not mint coins of the precious metals but used gold and silver in ingots and bars of standard weight. By Northern Song times the Chinese also had begun to use paper money issued by the government in several forms, including exchange vouchers for basic commodities in trade. Paper currency denominations were nominally equivalent to different numbers of copper cash; for example, a bill labeled equal to one string of 1,000 copper coins (copper cash) was nominally equivalent to one ounce of silver. Trade with Song China and other neighbors required that money and standardized units of value could easily circulate across national borders.

Eventually the Jin began to issue their own copper coins. This was the only dynasty since antiquity that also minted coins of silver for general circulation, but that was done only briefly, between 1197 and 1200. Throughout the dynasty the Jin continued to allow the circulation of Khitan and Song money. Their issuance of paper currency commenced in 1153 under Prince Hailing, and was fairly stable until the 1190s, when confidence in it began to wane. The coinage of silver in the late 1190s was designed to prop up the silver certificate paper notes. Confidence continued to slip as the military crises of the early thirteenth century became more serious. Runaway inflation took over, and the Jin experiment with paper currency, unlike its more successful use in Song, quickly failed. Nonetheless, by the reign of Emperor Shizong (1161–89), the Jin had become fairly adept at fiscal management. The Jurchens' record in managing their economy is quite creditable.

Treaties and Trade

The landmark Treaty of Shanyuan, imposed on the Northern Song state in 1005 by force of Khitan arms, established the pattern of interstate relations between and among the three conquest dynasties and the Chinese throughout the entire period of the Liao, the Xi Xia, and the Jin dynasties. The landmark treaties of 1005, 1041–42, and 1142 and their revisions have been discussed in terms of interstate relations at many points. Here I shall take note of their impact on people and society. In the early years of the Jurchens' conquest of the Liao, the treaty of Shanyuan (1005) as subsequently revised was still in force between the collapsing Liao and the Song; in the process of taking over from the Liao, the Jurchens invoked it in negotiations intended to establish cooperation between themselves and the Song Chinese as they sought jointly to destroy the remnants of Liao power in North China. The Chinese welcomed their acceptance of the treaty system and hoped it would maintain or improve their northern defense and boundary problems. In 1123 the Jurchens swore to return Liao-occupied areas of North China to the Song in return for their military help. They probably did not really intend to carry out those promises. They found reasons to continue to press southward into Song North China, and by early in 1127 (after first forcing a humiliating new treaty on the Song early in 1126), they had surrounded the Song capital on the Yellow River, captured two emperors, and ended Song control in China north of the Huai River (see Chapter 9, Section II). The Song, which we can now speak of as the Southern Song, had acknowledged its diplomatic inferiority to the Jin and had been forced to indemnify the peace by agreeing to further adjustments in the annual payments. The treaty system, originally a Chinese idea, continued to be used with great skill by the northern invaders to their advantage. Despite temporary breaks in the peace in the early 1140s, in 1161, and again in 1206–1208, the treaty system maintained noteworthy stability until the end of the Jin dynasty.

The treaty relations and diplomatic intercourse among these states from the tenth to the early thirteenth centuries reflect an unusual period in China's relations with its neighbors. The period is marked by the rationality of "pure power politics," unmarked by China's usual ideological stance as the center of the universe to which subservience must naturally be paid by all other peoples.[25] The Chinese continued to express scornful attitudes in private, but in their public relations with the Khitans and the Jurchens, they treated them as equals. The treaties recognized that the benefits to be gained by establishing a stable peace were mutual. Although they rewarded the militarily more powerful partner with material and psychological benefits, the very large cross-border trade, channeled through controlled trading stations, consistently returned a balance in favor of the Song. The treaties were remarkably successful in securing peace and profits for all.[26]

The Jin state benefited from its takeover of Liao assets, then again reaped an immense amount of wealth by seizing Song state treasure when it captured the Song capital in 1126–27. It plundered the Song fiscal reserves in the capital's vaults, amounting to 150 million ounces of gold and over 400 million ounces of silver, as well as the contents of its warehouses, crammed with millions of bolts of silk, weapons, and valuable manufactures and art products. In 1137, when the Jin abolished its puppet state of Qi in Honan, it again seized a vast amount of gold and silver bullion. Military conquest paid handsomely.

Throughout the remainder of the century after the conquest of North China in the 1120s, the Jin dynasty maintained a strong fiscal position. The captured wealth gave it a head start, and the annual payments continued to shore up its treasury balances. During the reign of Emperor Shizong (1161–1189), the high point of Jin peace and prosperity, it is reported that the annual grain tax, the state's principal revenue, totaled about 9 million *shi* of grain received at the capital, of which 1 million was surplus that could be added to its stored grain supplies, at that time enough for five years' consumption. That sound fiscal position did not begin to erode until early in the following century, and was not overturned until the military crises after 1208 diminished the state's income while greatly increasing its expenditures for defense.

Two elements of the Jin economic stability through its first century are noteworthy. First, the Jin inherited from the Northern Song the populous and prosperous region of North China, where there was a vigorous economic infrastructure based on high levels of coal and iron production, an extensive craft industry producing both basic necessities and exportable products, and a supporting network of cities and market towns linked in trade and distribution. Second, the Jin conquerors seized vast accumulated wealth from the Song and continued to receive large annual payments of silver bullion and valuable commodities. To these must be added a third element: international trade with the Song, made possible by the treaties, did not earn a net balance in favor of the Jin at the border control points but nonetheless helped to keep the level of economic activity high throughout the Jin state.

The Pattern of Jin-Song Trade

The Jin-Song border, drawn along the lower Huai River from the east coast westward into the center of China, and thence on to the northwest into southern Gansu, was initially quite fluid and in constant dispute until 1142. Then the new treaty succeeded in establishing a line based on possession and military control. The treaty provided for the opening of *quechang,* or "controlled trade sites." All cross-border trade was to be channeled through these, taxed, and subjected to trade controls. At first, two or three *quechang* were placed along the Huai. Then, from 1142 onward, twenty or more were opened along the entire length of the Jin-Song boundary line. Their numbers and locations varied from time to time, and they often were closed when warfare broke out or was threatened. But on the whole the officially managed trade quickly grew in volume and assumed considerable economic importance to both states.[27] Effort was made from both sides to prevent smugglers from crossing the boundary at other places, but those efforts appear to have been inadequate. At the established trading sites, traders from one side were not allowed to deal directly with their counterparts on the other side; each was required to turn his goods over to the officials, to be sold at standard market prices to the agents on the other side of the border after an ad valorem tax had been added. The inducement to smuggling was thus very great. Occasionally even the officials in charge of the *quechang* were indicted for conducting illegal trade at other nearby points used by smugglers.

The most important *quechang* were located astride water routes or main overland transport arteries which had carried trade before the conquest. Inter-regional trade in Song times had greatly expanded and was largely freed of earlier restrictive controls. Some scholars speak of a national market system that was coming into being to distribute standard commodities. The Jin-Song boundary blocked off many of the main trade and transport routes. From that point of view the tight controls on trading at the designated trade sites were a step backward, reminiscent of the tight domestic controls from which trade in China had gained freedom two or three centuries earlier. Increasingly through Jin times, the managed trade restrictions left North China out of the further growth of commerce that continued apace in Southern Song. Yet the managed interstate trade conducted across the Jin-Song border kept some of the major trade patterns open, and with the extensive smuggling and other illegal trade, some measure of the economic integration of North and South China remained in effect. In absolute terms, the cross-border trade attained considerable volume.

The principal Song exports to Jin China were led by tea. North China also could produce tea, and under Jin efforts to reduce the outflow of silver for Southern Song tea, North China's tea production was increased. But the Jin domestic tea was greatly inferior to that grown farther south, and tea remained a major element in the unfavorable balance of trade. Other impor-tant items imported from Song were medicinal products, ginger, incense, fancy silks and brocades, and luxury goods imported into Southern Song through the ports of Southeast Asia and more distant lands; among those commodities, shark's fins, betel, tortoiseshell, coral, gems, ivory, and spices all were important. Coastal merchants in South China used their cargo vessels to send large shipments of grain to landing places on the Jin coast. Some of it was legally imported but much of it was smuggled. As for the Jin, its principal exports to Southern Song were gold, pearls, ginseng, pine nuts, licorice root, and furs, mostly from Manchuria, as well as large quantities of common silk textiles made in North China that were used as ordinary clothing material. The Jin subsidized its export textile prices, keeping them low enough to increase Song purchases, thereby helping to offset the outflow of silver used to buy other imports. Most of the time the export of horses and weapons from North China to Song was forbidden, so smuggling of such items became especially profitable.

We cannot calculate the total volume of the interstate trade, but it has been estimated that the net profits to the Song more than covered the value of its annual payments to the Jin. As for its historic importance, both in relation to the Jin economy and with regard to the daily life of the people in Jin China, the system of treaties regularized the flow of money and goods which brought benefits to both sides. In strict accounting terms, the Song profited, but not to the extent of greatly harming the Jin economy. In broader social terms, the Jin learned about currency and forms of monetary management that helped its fiscal system to mature and kept its commercial entrepreneurs aware of their Southern Song counterparts. Through trade the people in Jin China remained in contact with that larger world of commerce and of cultural influences, however much the restrictive conditions both sides imposed may have diminished the volume of trade. The trading activity itself became a focus of energies involving a large segment of the population, leavening the social order and providing alternate careers for many, in cities and towns, and throughout the networks of settlements making up the entire landscape of Jin China. Above all, trade tended to turn a hostile boundary of military confrontation into a soft boundary of interaction along which it became highly desirable to maintain the peace. The people of East Asia were its beneficiaries. The growth of trade, especially the expansion of interregional commerce, was one of the significant changes affecting Chinese society during the twelfth and thirteenth centuries; the separation of Jin and Song did not slow that change, and in some ways may have advanced it.

13

THE SOUTHERN SONG
AND CHINESE SURVIVAL

The Song dynasty escaped extinction in the years 1126–1131 by the narrowest of margins. In that crisis the young Prince Kang, son and brother of the last two Northern Song emperors, grappled with sheer survival; then, as Emperor Gaozong reigning until 1162 (he died in 1187), he became the effective ruler who established the character of the Southern Song court and central government. Here his perilous path to personal and imperial survival is examined; those experiences bore heavily on his policies thereafter. The case of the all-powerful Chief Councillor Qin Gui and his murder of the hero general Yue Fei also is examined carefully, as is the subsequent pattern of powerful Chief Councillors under weaker emperors. Throughout this chapter the emphasis is on the Southern Song style in high politics, the uses and abuses of power, the politicizing of scholarly orthodoxy, and the contest between war and peace factions.

1. A Fleeing Prince—A New Emperor

Zhao Gou was the Northern Song imperial prince whose fate it would be to continue the dynasty after the crisis of Jurchen invasion in the 1120s; the first emperor of the Southern Song, he would be known posthumously as Emperor Gaozong, the "Lofty Ancestor." His early life and the chain of circumstances that brought him to the throne contribute to the understanding of his deep influence on the character of Southern Song China.

In the normal pattern of Song imperial princes' lives, when he was fourteen years old Zhao Gou was elevated to an imperial princedom, his title being Prince Kang. He was only twenty in 1127 when his older brother, the Emperor Qinzong, and their father, the retired Emperor Huizong, were taken into custody by the conquering Jurchens and, with all the imperial household, carted off as prisoners to the Northeast (Manchuria). Zhao Gou evaded the same fate, more by accident than by design, but that provided the key which would prevent the termination of the dynasty at the hands of the invaders.

The Song capital at Kaifeng was surrounded by the invading Jurchen armies in February 1126. Complex negotiations with the Song went on throughout most of that year. The invaders demanded that a Song imperial prince accompany high court officials into their camp to negotiate a peace settlement. The Emperor Qinzong asked this younger brother if he would be willing to undertake that assignment, and Prince Kang willingly agreed. In the course of that mission he was retained in the camp of Prince Zongwang, the second son of Aguda, the Jin emperor Taizu, and nephew of the reigning Jin emperor Taizong. His family status gave Zongwang the highest field command in the Jurchen forces, with the authority to make decisions at his own discretion.[1] While the Chinese delegation was in his camp, Chinese resistance forces attacked, arousing a furious retaliation. It was feared that Prince Zongwang might hold the Chinese envoys responsible and perhaps mete out fearsome revenge. The other Chinese were overcome with fright. Prince Kang, we are told, alone remained relaxed and lighthearted, arousing Zongwang's suspicions that this might not be the real prince. He sent instructions to Kaifeng that another imperial prince be sent to represent the court instead. When that prince arrived, Prince Kang was sent back to Kaifeng. In that way he escaped detention.[2]

After a long summer of inconsistent demands from the conquerors and desperate stalling by the Song court, the Jin field armies again surrounded the Song capital, and further negotiations at the Jin headquarters in North China were demanded. This time the Jurchens, now better informed, specified that Prince Kang again be sent with the negotiating delegation; he departed Kaifeng with his entourage in mid-December. En route, Chinese regional military officials who were angered by the Song court's inability to resist the invaders, and who believed that Prince Kang was being led off to become a sacrifice to the enemy, assassinated the official negotiator in Prince Kang's entourage. They then encouraged the young prince to place himself at the head of loyal resistance forces, making it clear that he should neither return to Kaifeng nor fall into the trap of again entering the Jurchen camp.[3] In this way, by no design of his own, he became at age twenty the nominal commander of Chinese resistance elements in North China, whose military leaders repudiated the court's concessions to the invaders and wished to rally the people for resistance.

Among Chinese local military leaders in North China, the savagery of the Jurchen armies had aroused much spontaneous will to resist. At heart, Prince Kang did not strongly believe in the policy option of military resistance, but he was not averse to assuming prominence among his brothers, the imperial princes. He has been much villified in modern historical writing as the weak-willed scion of a degenerate imperial line. That characterization is unfair. He was by no means a nonentity. Indeed, he appeared to many of his contemporaries to be an ideal imperial leader. He was powerfully built, and could ride and shoot; at the same time, he was noted for his quick mind and strong memory. He appeared to possess both the military and the civil virtues and to be a man of action.[4]

When the Jurchen forces again invested the capital, Prince Kang gladly remained with the hastily regrouped field armies in North China, if only for the sake of his own unexpressed intentions. During the subsequent negotiations at Kaifeng, the Jin commanders demanded that the emperor order his younger brother to return to the capital. By gathering in all members of the imperial household on whom they could lay their hands, they hoped to leave behind no potential successors around whom Song resistance might coalesce. Throughout the spring months of 1127, Zhao Gou became the focus of their efforts. He moved his headquarters from place to place in Hebei, Shandong, and Henan while the Jurchens repeatedly tried by trickery and deceit to make him return to the surrounded capital at Kaifeng, where they could detain him. When that failed, they sent special cavalry forces to seize him. Shifting bases, he evaded all their attempts.

Impatient to return to Manchuria before the onset of summer, the Jurchens could wait in Kaifeng no longer. Their immense train of carts laden with precious loot from the Song palaces, with the two captured Song emperors and their entire households, including their palace attendants and high officials of the court, totaling many thousands, finally left Kaifeng in mid-May 1127; it did not reach its destination until over a year later.[5] Those among the distinguished captives who did not die from the hardships en route would live out their lives in the cold forests of the far Northeast and never see their homes in China again.

The imperial family was a very large group of men, women, and children. The retired Emperor Huizong, then forty-five years old, had fathered his eldest son, the Emperor Qinzong, in 1100, when he was eighteen. Between that year and his capture in 1126, he produced thirty-one sons and thirty-four daughters, that is, on the average between two and three formally recognized children per year. Six of the sons and fourteen of the daughters died when still very young; the others, except for Zhao Gou, the future Emperor Gaozong, and perhaps one of the married daughters, all were carried off to live and die in captivity.[6] In 1135 Huizong himself died there; he was then fifty-three. Qinzong also died in Manchuria, in 1161, but we have extremely little information on his younger brothers and sisters. It is quite probable that other, unrecorded imperial children were born in Manchuria.

Zhao Gou's place in the imperial sibling set raised issues of great importance to him and to the Chinese. Between his eldest brother, the Emperor Qinzong, and himself there were born seven other sons, two of whom had died in infancy. But four or five other imperial princes who were senior to him were still alive; should any one of those escape capture, he would have a better claim on the Song throne. And many among the people still hoped that through negotiations the two captured emperors might be returned and Qinzong restored to the throne. In the early months of 1127 it must have seemed wildly unlikely to Zhao Gou that he would ever become the ruler, even if he should escape capture. Yet others were urging him to assume that role, and at some point he must have begun to think it possible and to scheme toward that end.

The record is filled with reports of secret messages sent to him by the senior emperor his father, or by his brother the Emperor Qinzong, naming him commander in chief of all Song resistance forces in North China and instructing him to protect the dynasty's interests, fight on, and rescue them. In the coming months he refused to follow the advice of the more aggressive military leaders who wanted an immediate attack on the Jin forces then holding Kaifeng. Prince Kang was more concerned to evade pursuit than to attack. The histories, deeply committed to the idea of legitimacy in the succession, say that eventually the captured emperors ordered him to take the throne, making his succession proper. With or without that directive, he did so on June 12, 1127, at the Song Southern Capital, the present-day county seat town of Shangqiu, some eighty-five miles southeast of Kaifeng. That site was symbolically important; it had been named one of the nominal but nonfunctional capitals of the Song by Zhao Kuangyin, the founding emperor, to commemorate his military governorship there before he became emperor, and because that site is associated with the ancient Shang dynasty from whose rulers the Song imperial clan claimed descent.

Zhao Gou and his advisers were alert to everything of symbolic meaning that might enhance the legitimacy of his succession. It is recorded that he ascended the specially erected altar to the Spirits of the Land and Grain to receive the Imperial Mandate; there he read the announcement to Heaven-on-High, stating that he was the legitimate heir, forced by circumstances to ascend the throne. Then he wept aloud bitterly, and sent his silent gratitude to "the two emperors" far away in captivity. His future nonetheless depended on their remaining captives. Following Chinese historiographic custom, I shall henceforth call Zhao Gou, or Prince Kang, by his formal imperial name, Emperor Gaozong, although that temple name was given to him posthumously.

There were at least 100,000 Song troops in North China under local leaders who were eager to resist the Jurchens, and ready to acknowledge the self-proclaimed new emperor as their legitimate leader. A large number of those troops soon came under the direct command of Gaozong's headquarters, and still larger numbers were potentially available if resistance under Song leadership could be encouraged. Throughout mid-1127 Gaozong's mobile court was under the strong management of Li Gang, who had been a prominent official, a Grand Secretary and Prefect of the capital city before the Northern Song collapse.[7] Since Li Gang was on assignment away from the capital in 1127, he therefore also escaped capture and was able to join Emperor Gaozong at the Southern Capital. He now was named Junior Grand Councillor of the Department of State Affairs and concurrently the Vice Director of the Central Secretariat, making him in effect the prime minister. He became for a crucial but brief period of two and one-half months the vigorous crisis manager of the court, directing its responses to the touch-and-go situation and attempting to ensure the survival of the Song dynasty. He guided the newly formed court while it gained strength and purpose. Although he decidedly favored the war party's aims, he realistically insisted on first strengthening the management of the state's resources, saying that more aggressive military action depended on first gaining that strength. Li Gang was nonetheless a decisive leader whose purpose clearly was to prepare the remnant Song government for full-scale counterattack. The emperor's tepid support of all aggressive policies, however, encouraged Li Gang's political enemies, and he was soon forced out of government. Yet he left his mark on politics, at least to the extent that the statesmen of Huizong's reign at the end of the Northern Song continued to be blamed for the Song failure, while the current ruler and government were not held responsible. That was Li Gang's strategy; on all sides it was agreed that the new emperor and his court should be seen as untainted by Song collapse and that Gaozong's governance would be different.

The emperor and his chief advisers began to construct a government. They appointed men to the full range of offices. At the same time, they called on the loyalty of the populace, urging them to take up military resistance, even though they did not establish a plan for doing so or provide positive leadership. Emperor and court continued to distance themselves from the policies of the end of the Northern Song. In particular, they focused on Huizong's reign (1100–1125). They said it was misguided, its faulty policies stemming from the earlier implementation of Wang Anshi's New Policies in the 1070s (see Chapter 6, Section V). By holding the entire Song experience with reform responsible for the disaster, they thoroughly discredited the idea of reform in general; both the genuine reformers and their less admirable later followers all were declared to have favored anti-Confucian principles and to have filled the government with evil men. In the political atmosphere of imperial China, one scarcely could be faulted on any policy issue without thereby also becoming morally suspect.

The discredited idea of broad institutional reform had always been associated with those who favored war against the northern invaders. The Emperor Gaozong was caught in a dilemma; he did not dare expose the extent to which he was prepared to abandon military confrontation and by all means avoid full-scale war with the Jurchens. Yet there can be no doubt that he was glad to see Li Gang replaced by adherents of the peace party.

Emperor Gaozong's new government, taking form at the Southern Capital in southeastern Henan, soon came under military pressure from the Jin field armies and was forced to move farther south. By the end of 1127 he had had to retreat as far south as Yangzhou, just north of the Yangzi River. The emperor spent 1128 and the beginning of 1129 in that beautiful and all too comfortable city, though various courtiers warned that the place was exposed to sudden attack and urged that he should move across to the south side of the river. Privately he may have wished to do that, but he was advised that he must remain north of the Yangzi in order to appear to be making preparations for a general counterattack. Soon he would regret that he had not fol-

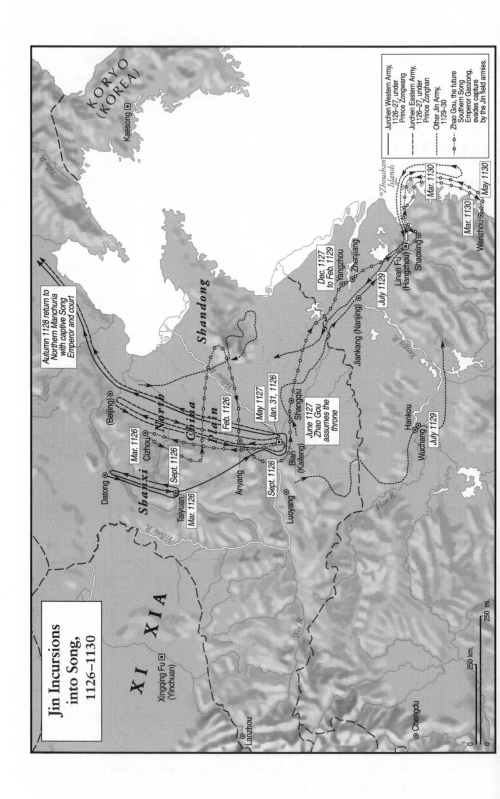

Jin Incursions into Song, 1126–1130

KORYO (KOREA)

Kaesong

Jurchen Western Army, 1126–27, under Prince Zongwang

Jurchen Eastern Army, 1126–27, under Prince Zonghan

Other Jin Army, 1129–30

Zhao Gou, the future Southern Song Emperor Gaozong, evades capture by the Jin field armies.

Zhoushan Islands

Mar. 1130

May 1130

Mar. 1130

Wenzhou

Shandong

Dec. 1127 to Feb. 1129

Yangzhou

Zhenjiang

Shaoxing

Linan Fu (Hangzhou)

July 1129

Jiankang (Nanjing)

July 1129

Autumn 1128 return to Northern Manchuria with captive Song Emperor and court

(Beijing)

Cizhou

Mar. 1126

Sept. 1126

Datong

Shanxi

Taiyuan

Mar. 1126

North China Plain

Feb. 1126

May 1127

Jan. 31, 1126

Bian (Kaifeng)

Shangqiu

June 1127 Zhao Gou assumes the throne

Anyang

Sept. 1126

Luoyang

Hankou

Wuchang

July 1129

Han R.

Yellow R.

Wei R.

XI XIA

Xingqing Fu (Yinchuan)

Lanzhou

Chengdu

Yalu R.

250 km.

250 mi.

lowed the advice to cross the Yangzi and settle his government in a safer place, behind the barrier of the great river.

February 23, 1129, must have been the most terrifying day of the young emperor's life. What follows is a straightforward account of events that subsequently were heavily intertwined with legend. The story is remarkable enough without that embellishment.

Two days before the fateful twenty-third of February, the emperor found the local people thrown into panic by news that the Jin army was approaching; he wanted to cross the Yangzi immediately, but dillydallying advisers told him to hold off until fuller reports were received from the Song defense line, just to the north of Yangzhou. They were reluctant to give up the splendid comforts of Yangzhou. Some courtiers nevertheless were ordered to proceed on south with the emperor's infant son and others of the imperial household, to take up residence at Hangzhou. On the morning of the twenty-third the emperor learned that the Song forces holding off the Jin advance had collapsed and fled the battlefront. That shocking news, which should not have been so unexpected, induced a general panic. The emperor and a few attendants now had no choice but to flee Yangzhou immediately on horseback.

As they encountered turbulent, threatening crowds of fleeing people along the way, their situation grew tense. This imperial prince, elevated to the title of emperor under irregular circumstances, was a young man of twenty-two who never before in his life had been forced to fend for himself. As he fled on horseback, galloping the dozen or more miles from Yangzhou to the crossing point on the Yangzi, it is said that only one remaining attendant, his umbrella bearer, was able to keep up with his fleet horse! No doubt nervous and terrified, but required to maintain an imperial manner, Zhao Gou at one point along the way was addressed by a soldier in an insolent and threatening tone. The emperor drew his sword and killed the man. It was but one incident in a day when many high officials were killed by the angry people crowding the roads as they all fled to the south. Thousands of people who had rallied to the court throughout the past year now were escaping on foot; crowds of them were massed at the river's edge, struggling to get into small boats to make the crossing. Thousands died there, some by drowning, some in the melee on the shore.

Two loyal officials located the emperor and guided him to a boat they had arranged to ferry him across, alone, or possibly with an aide. In that way he reached Zhenjiang on the south shore, where, unattended, he sought shelter in a small temple. It is said that at first he could only sit, somewhat dazed, all the while wiping the blood off his sword onto his felt boots while trying to regain his composure. Later that evening he went on into the city of Zhenjiang and spent the night in the prefectural offices. The city was virtually empty, abandoned by its frightened population. Without a proper entourage to care for him, or even any bedding for him to use, he spread his sable cloak out on the floor, sleeping on half of it and covering himself with the other half.[8]

We must remind ourselves that Chinese rulers (at least after the generation of each dynastic founder), and their sons the imperial princes, were not public figures in the manner of Europe's royal personages. They lived far more secluded lives. Even after they were moved out from the imperial precincts to their own palaces and assigned official entourages when still in their early teen years, they were never without their swarm of attendants who guarded them, cared for all their needs, and counseled them on all their words and actions. They were wholly unprepared to be alone in ordinary situations, much less when exposed to peril and forced to make life-and-death decisions. Emperor Gaozong was able to meet this crisis and survive it. That is testimony to his personal resilience, yet it nonetheless must have had a paralyzing effect on his psyche.

On the afternoon of February 23 a forward party of 500 Jurchen cavalry reached Yangzhou, searched for the emperor, and learning that they had just missed him, galloped on to overtake him at the Yangzi crossing point. By the time they arrived at the mighty river's edge, they were told that he had already crossed. They could only stare out over the wide river and, finally, return in frustration to Yangzhou. But they would soon cross the river in force and pursue him.

The emperor's next few days continued to be filled with tension and peril, but he managed to reach Hangzhou and reassemble the core of a central government. The Jurchens pursued, but again in small force and unsuccessfully. They would be back.

Throughout March at Hangzhou, the collection of courtiers and statesman making up the government fought among themselves, embittered by failures, dangers, and recriminations. Most of them did not know where their wives and families were; the emperor made gestures of sharing their hardship by ordering all comforts of the palace to be given up and only one plain dish to be served to him at each meal. These austerities were part of a symbolic political image that was demanded by tradition. Despite his observance of such ritual acts, he was not shown as much dignity and deference as reigning emperors expected.

He was openly criticized, especially for continuing to employ court eunuchs in important posts. In this respect his governance was not, as he promised it would be, different from that of the discredited late Northern Song. A cabal of courtiers and opponents focused on the failure to eliminate eunuch influence at the court; seizing control, they forced Gaozong to abdicate in favor of his infant son.[9] They then executed dozens of rival courtiers and still more court eunuchs. The rebels, however, were seen for what they were—ambitious conspirators, not high-minded reformers. Military leaders on the various fronts protecting the borders came quickly to the emperor's rescue. Within two months, on April 20, 1129, they were able to oust the conspirators and return Gaozong to the throne. He then made gradual headway in getting a stronger government organized. Only slowly did he recover respect and command personal authority comparable to that accorded previous Song emperors.

The military history of the next two or three years is very complex. Jin armies, several under the command of Jurchen imperial princes authorized to act on their own discretion in the field, ranged throughout North China, while in many places Chinese armies, large and small, hastily organized independent local defenses. The pursuit of the Song emperor was but one of the Jin objectives, and ensuring his safety was not within the practical reach of most of the local Song commanders. There was no center, either within the Jurchen invasion forces or within the Song resistance. Reports of continuing defeats of Song loyalist forces throughout North China continued to pour in. Many Song officials, both civil and military, responsible for defending the regions in which they served, fled to save their lives. Others defected to the enemy and were appointed to office. People debated whether the Song had the will to continue. The young emperor had to take personal responsibility for all the failures that threatened the legitimacy of his dynasty.

Throughout the summer and autumn of 1129, peril and uncertainty reigned. Early in July the emperor learned that two Jurchen armies had crossed the Yangzi. They were able to roam at will through Hunan and Jiangxi, capturing cities, pillaging, burning, killing. Government forces seemed demoralized. The emperor issued a personally drafted edict blaming himself on four counts: for having had only hazy ideas about the longer-range concerns of the state; for having lacked overall plans for dealing with all kinds of difficulties; for lacking the force of personal virtue to enable him to exercise a restraining effect on others; and for losing his grasp on the handles of power with which to control his courtiers. He ordered that this edict be made public to the court and throughout the realm, to make known that he acknowledged his faults.[10] Fear gripped the court and pervaded the lives of all. The emperor's only son, the infant who had briefly been proclaimed emperor in the spring, lay seriously ill. One day a palace servant accidentally kicked a bronze tripod in the courtyard, making a booming noise that echoed through the palace halls. It threw the child into convulsions of fright, causing his death. In grief and frustration, the emperor ordered that the attending servants be executed.[11] He continued to issue appeals and exhortations. As he received the incessant reports of hardships borne by his people throughout the realm, he repeatedly blamed himself publicly for having failed them. The lighthearted young prince sent to negotiate with the Jurchens early in 1127 had become the anxiety-beset and care-ridden emperor of 1129.

One of the two Jin armies that crossed to raid the south side of the Yangzi in 1129 turned eastward to threaten the emperor's temporary capital at Hangzhou. Among the people there were many rumors about what secret plans the emperor and court might have for dealing with the coming crisis. The low point came in the winter of 1129–30. When the Jurchens got as close as Jiankang (present-day Nanjing), the emperor and court left Hangzhou to move farther eastward in Zhejiang, nearer the coast, where large ships were being collected so that, when pressed by Jurchen advances, emperor and court could flee out to sea. In all of history no such thing had ever been heard of; but on January 26, 1130, it happened. The assembled ships were hastily boarded, and the fleet sailed for safety into the Zhoushan Archipelago, the islands lying off the coast of northeast Zhejiang Province. On that same day the Jurchen raiders, under the command of Prince Zongbi,[12] captured Hangzhou. Then they continued east to pursue the emperor. By March the imperial fleet of large ships was forced to sail all the way to the southern Zhejiang coastal city of Wenzhou to evade pursuit. But as March turned into April and the lower Yangzi summer heat and rains arrived, the Jurchens were anxious to return to the cooler north. They began to withdraw throughout April. In May they crossed the Yangzi and quickly proceeded on to North China.

The emperor's fleet sailed back north to the Zhoushan Islands in May 1130, and by June the court had come ashore, to be housed at Shaoxing, thirty-five miles southeast of Hangzhou. They waited there until early 1133, both to ensure the ready escape by sea if again necessary, and to allow for the pillaged capital city to be hastily restored.

For a number of years throughout the 1130s, the Jurchens' policies with regard to their conquests in North China remained unsettled. After concluding a treaty in 1141–42, however, they attempted to violate that arrangement only twice, once when Prince Hailing in 1161 unsuccessfully campaigned to the Yangzi, and again unsuccessfully in 1216–1220.[13] On the other side, the war party at the Song court threatened to adopt offensive policies on and off throughout the reign of Gaozong, and intermittently thereafter, until the end of Southern Song.

II. WAR VERSUS PEACE

His harrowing experiences left a deep mark on the Emperor Gaozong and affected the conduct of his governing. His narrow escape from capture or death, the rebellious behavior of his courtiers who had attempted to dethrone him, his feelings of guilt or at least of public failure on having abandoned efforts to rescue his father and older brother, and his own ambition to rule made him fearful, cautious, unwilling to take risks.[14] The Southern Song was born under a cloud of the emperor's questionable legitimacy, as had been the Northern Song. Beyond that point of similarity, however, the two situations were wholly different. The Northern Song founder possessed great self-confidence and expansive vision, and his court was marked by his scholar-officials' intense commitment and hopeful spirit. The Southern Song court in the reign of Gaozong was dominated by recriminations against those who had managed the Northern Song's last decades, by rejection of policies and modes of governing, and above all by feelings of both peril and political uncertainty, which set the tone for a quite different dynastic era, one of forced territorial contraction and diminished spiritual resources. Throughout the remaining thirty years of his reign, Emperor Gaozong continued to bend all policy "to win imperial safety at any cost," and it has been observed that there was an accompanying shift in the tone of Song civilization; one eminent historian has described the early twelfth century as the period of "China turning inward."[15]

More aggressive-minded elements within Song scholar-officialdom, and especially within the military ranks, had to be repeatedly and ruthlessly restrained. They threatened to undermine the emperor's preference for passive, negotiated accommodation with the Jin. Had Gaozong chosen to encourage militancy and irredentism, could he have restored the united Song state? Might he at least have recovered the vibrant sense of engagement that characterized the early Northern Song? Such interesting if ultimately pointless arguments have been kept alive through the centuries. At the time, the *one* course he without doubt would not support, that of determined resistance and counterattack, attracted many military and civil officials; their scattered successes against the Jurchens often made larger victory seem to be within grasp. Deeply committed to the dynasty, some military leaders continued to fight on, at many places in the still unsettled and war-ravaged regions of North China. One might have thought that the struggling dynasty was strengthened by their courageous and often quite competent military adventurism. But the emperor feared that they would merely induce a stronger Jurchen counteroffensive. He could not openly repudiate them nor could he bring himself to support them. The "public at large," meaning those elements whose views can be known to us, expected the emperor to applaud the resistance leaders' daring, as they grumbled against the high courtiers of the peace party, who were given the blame for "misleading" the young ruler.

The Yue Fei Episode

The military uncertainty of the late 1120s and 1130s produced one of the most famous heroes of all Chinese history; he is Yue Fei (1103–1142). Even today the Emperor Gaozong's reputation is marred by his vacillating relationship with Yue Fei and other proponents, both civil and military, of the war policy. This relationship echoes Northern Song political conflicts between peace and war factions at the court, but it acquired still larger dimensions thereafter, and left problems that troubled the Southern Song to its end.

The emperor himself clearly was the responsible person, but the two figures who symbolize the struggle between war and peace policies are General Yue Fei and Prime Minister Qin Gui (1090–1155), acting for the emperor. They have come to embody noble-minded loyalty on the one hand and, on the other, base treachery. Would that the facts of this historical drama were so simple! Yet, historically, the myths surrounding this stark confrontation of policies and personalities have been more important than the reality. We must consider both the truth about Yue Fei and the shaping of the myths, old and new, for they too became facts in the consciousness of Chinese.

YUE FEI'S CAREER

Yue Fei is a storybook hero. He was the only surviving son born late into a poor farmer's family in what today would be Anyang County in northeastern Henan. He typified what the Chinese regard as North Chinese characteristics: he was a bit above average height, physically strong, taciturn and of stoical temperament, endowed with an honest, direct manner that won people's confidence. He received some rudimentary education at home or, more likely, in the village "winter school," where boys who did not plan to prepare for the examinations could acquire basic literacy during the farming year's short slack season. He was early attracted to a military career. It is said that his father had lost the family's small inherited landholding, and the son hoped to avoid the only other option, that of becoming a tenant farm laborer, by preparing for a military career. When still a young boy, he was accepted as the protégé of a noted archery instructor. He soon excelled in the military arts; he could draw the strongest bow with either the right or the left hand and astounded people with his shooting skill, and learned as well to wield a pike and a battle sword. According to some traditional accounts, at about age sixteen he entered into some kind of service under the Han family, the locality's most eminent elite family.[16] He may have been merely a tenant farm laborer, or perhaps served in their family's private guard force. In any event, born in 1103, and living in Anyang County on the North China Plain, he had ample opportunity to become aware of the Liao-Jin wars that commenced in 1115 and the Jin invasions of North China throughout the early 1120s, which terminated the Liao dynasty and left the Song exposed to a new and more dangerous enemy. He was brought face to face with the ruthless mode of Jurchen warfare and the suffering it brought to the ordinary people wherever the Jin armies passed.

Early in 1122 he responded to a recruiting announcement issued by one of the regional commanders calling for daredevils who knew how to fight. By that time he appears to have acquired some ability to read classical Chinese, although the extent of his traditional Chinese learning is one of the subjects around which myth has grown. The myths have depicted him as an ideal "scholar-general" with a sword in one hand and a book of classical learning in the other. That account clearly exaggerates and idealizes. He remained essentially a fighting man of limited cultivation.

His father's death in 1123 required that he return home to manage the funeral and observe the three years' mourning, which, it is said, he did with punctilious devotion. After the mourning period he remarried and stayed another year, but at the end of 1126 he again volunteered for military service, this time under the commander of Xiangzhou near his home, and was there when Prince Kang (the future Emperor Gaozong) stopped on his way to his second mission as peace envoy to the Jin commander's camp. He undoubtedly approved of the developments which prevented Prince Kang from reaching the Jurchen camp and which led to the prince's becoming the leader of Song resistance in North China; though we have no reason to believe that Yue Fei and the prince met at that time.

Local commanders loyal to the Song in North China faced both the wide-ranging field campaigns of the marauding Jin troops and uprisings of local Chinese military leaders who sustained themselves by plunder. The latter are referred to as bandits in the Chinese records. Yue Fei saw action against such bandits, and against turncoats, and was consistently successful. He undoubtedly believed that the suppression of such disorder was necessary to consolidate the resources of the region for the more important tasks of resisting the Jurchen armies.

Some years later, dissatisfied with the machinations of the peace party, which he thought had prevented Prince Kang from organizing a general war against the invaders, Yue Fei went to join the Song forces defending the abandoned capital at Kaifeng, once again in Song hands after the departure of the Jurchens in May 1127. He remained there during 1128 and early 1129, while Prince Kang, now the self-proclaimed emperor, was based at Yangzhou. But when the Song troops withdrew to the south of the Yangzi later in 1129, Yue Fei followed and became a member of the forces stationed at Jiankang (present-day Nanjing) responsible for defending the south bank of the river. When Prince Zongbi crossed the Yangzi and pursued the Song emperor in 1129–30, driving him from his capital at Hangzhou and forcing him to take to the sea to escape, Yue Fei led a detachment that harassed the invaders and helped to drive them back across the Yangzi.

His fame as a daring leader and successful campaigner began to grow. He was given higher titles and larger assignments, and after being called to the court in 1133, he was at age 30 named commander of the main armies in the central Yangzi region. In 1134 he led a daring offensive against the Jin puppet state of Qi, which, with Jurchen military assistance, had recently expanded into the Song defense zone north of the central Yangzi.[17] He campaigned far north into the region of modern Xiangyang in Hubei, capturing that bastion and a number of important military bases. This was one of four campaigns that he led deep into Jin territories north of the Yangzi throughout the next six or seven years. Myth has it that among all the noted Song commanders of the time, Yue Fei was the only one who led offensives northward into Jin territories. That is an overstatement; a number of other generals, some genuine "scholar-generals" with elite backgrounds, also fought ably to defend the buffer zone between the Yangzi and the Huai rivers against Jin incursions, and when opportunities to be more aggressive presented themselves, they too occasionally also turned their forces northward as Yue Fei did. After returning from the Xiangyang campaign, Yue Fei in 1134 was given command of the Central China field forces based at Ezhou, present-day Wuchang in Hubei. This was his base on and off throughout the remaining years of his career.

The Song also faced both large-scale banditry and popular rebellious uprisings south of the Yangzi. The most famous is that of Yang Tai, called by the nickname Yang Yao (youngest son of the Yang family), which threatened Central China in the mid-1130s. Yang Yao and his son had long been military followers of a radical-minded religious leader, Zhong Xiang, who, through three decades at the end of the Northern Song and Gaozong's early reign, had built up a wide following in Hunan and southern Hubei. In 1132 Zhong openly rebelled, proclaiming himself King of Chu, but within two months Song forces had captured and executed him. Yang Yao then stepped into the leadership role and took over Zhong's fortified military bases.

Zhong Xiang had taught what appear to be strikingly modern revolutionary sentiments, declaring that differences of wealth and poverty should be
eliminated and high and low status should be equalized. It is easy to make
those doctrines sound like forerunners of modern class warfare and social
revolution.[18] But Zhong Xiang's doctrines also included many elements
drawn from popular religion; he proclaimed that he could make his followers miraculously rich overnight by magical means. He also had declared that
all Confucian scholars, officials, Buddhist monks, Daoists, geomancers and
fortune-tellers, and shamanistic healers—in short, all of his competitors for
authority and social leadership—should be killed. Rampaging through the
region in 1133, Yang's followers killed and plundered, declaring that they
were carrying out their late master's disruptive "equalization" measures.
They had become a large-scale threat to social order, as often happened in
Chinese history whenever central authority weakened.

In military history, Yang Yao's movement is interesting because of his reliance on inland naval forces to conduct warfare, and in particular for his adoption of armored human-powered paddle wheel ships of large size and good
maneuverability.[19] Because Yang's menacing rebel uprising was close to Yue
Fei's base at Ezhou, Yue was assigned to suppress it. He was fortunate in
capturing some of the astounding new vessels and turning them against the
rebels; within a few months, late in 1135, he had seized and executed Yang
Yao and his chief lieutenants. Then he took over Yang Yao's naval forces;
this marked a turning point in the growth of the Song inland navy. Yue Fei
absorbed some 50,000 or more of the defeated rebels' best troops into his
"Yue family army," thereby increasing his command to more than 100,000
troops. He had become one of the three or four most potent military leaders
in the Southern Song state, and clearly the most independent-minded.

Yue was a rigid disciplinarian. His soldiers were rigorously trained and
taught, and exposed to intimidating examples of his stern rules of conduct.
His soldiers were famed, no doubt correctly so, for their fighting spirit, their
obedience to command in battle, and their strict observance of rules that prevented them from stealing and looting, from imposing any kind of hardship
on the ordinary people, even from accepting gifts or offers of hospitality from
grateful residents of localities they cleared of bandits. Such qualities, rare
enough in Chinese armies throughout history, also have been enlarged in the
Yue Fei myths that grew throughout late Song times.

Yue Fei's forces were called the "Yue family army" (Yue jia jun) as certain
other armies of the time also were called the "family armies" of their noted
commanders, not because they were private armies raised and supported by
those commanders (the Song state paid for them), but because it was still
the mode of military organization for the state's various armies to take on
characteristics imposed by their leaders. Personal links between commanders
and soldiers were strong. The officers and common soldiers identified with
their commanders and expected to remain with them. The Song did not just
move generals from one command post to another; along with them often
went whole armies subordinate to those generals. Yue Fei was noted as the

one commander most ardently committed to recovering the territories lost to Jin occupation. Men from Jin-held regions of North China who could escape to the Southern Song territories all wanted to join his army, accepting his stern discipline with pride and calling themselves his men. Their mostly northern backgrounds and their special esprit de corps set them apart and contributed to the growing awe in which Yue Fei was held by the Southern Song court and government. That led inevitably to his conflict with the emperor's accommodation policies, and with Chief Councillor Qin Gui, who implemented those policies.

Openly, however, the emperor continued to reward and to praise Yue Fei, and to meet with him when Yue went to court to express, often bluntly and awkwardly, his views on state matters. It was not until 1140, during Yue Fei's fourth and most successful campaign deep into Jin territories, that he was abruptly ordered to withdraw; he was called to the court, where plans were afoot to relieve the leading soldiers among the Song generals of their posts in order to replace them with civilian commanders. Late in the summer of 1140 he went to the court at Hangzhou, protested against what he knew or suspected of the plans for change, and demanded that he be allowed to resign. He was denied that demand and reassigned, but a few months later was called again to the court to be relieved of his military command and given an administrative staff assignment. Military emergencies forced the court to give him another brief command in the summer of 1141, but on successful completion of the task set for him he was again relieved of command, this time to be jailed for insubordination and malfeasance. Peace negotiations with the Jin were on the point of producing a treaty; as a condition for agreement on the treaty of 1141 (concluded in a series of negotiations from October 1141 to October 1142), the Jin may have demanded that Yue Fei be collared. In any event, aggressive military action along the Song-Jin borders was no longer needed to protect the Southern Song.

High officials sent to interrogate Yue Fei in his prison cell were unable to prove a credible case against him, and in some instances openly sided with him. Finally, early in 1142, he was poisoned in his prison cell on the order of Chief Councillor Qin Gui. Sympathetic jailers stole his body and secretly buried it where it would not be found, but marked so that it later could be recovered and given proper burial. That had to await his rehabilitation by Gaozong's successor, the Emperor Xiaozong, after the old emperor's retirement in 1162.

YUE FEI IN HISTORY AND IN MYTH

Under the powerful Chief Councillor Qin Gui until 1155, Emperor Gaozong's court allowed very few of the documents concerning Yue Fei's official career, or about other policy issues of the time, to survive. In 1161 a grave crisis appeared to threaten the security of Southern Song when the Jin emperor known in history as Prince Hailing decided to invade the South with immense armies he had brought to the banks of the Yangzi just north of Nanjing. The Jin ruler's assassination by his underlings at the end of 1161 ended the invasion effort, but the Huai River border zone between the two states remained unsettled and subject to military action for three or four years thereafter. At the height of that crisis in 1161, Gaozong had declared that Yue Fei, along with Yue's son and a chief associate, both of whom had been executed in 1142 at the time Yue Fei was poisoned, together with a group of late Northern Song political and military figures, all should be granted posthumous pardons and their titles and confiscated properties restored to them. Those moves to rehabilitate persons and policies from recent history who all along had been denigrated by Gaozong's court were no doubt part of a desperate attempt to firm up the morale and loyalty of the generals and their troops. The Song government now faced a grave emergency in which it might again have to call on its armies to defend the Yangzi, for the Jurchens had abrogated the treaty arrangement on which the Song had come to depend. Yue Fei had acquired very large symbolic importance as a loyal and upright military leader who had suffered unjustly, it now was said, at the hands of a corrupt and evil Chief Councillor. The "deceived" emperor could now make amends for that injustice. A stark policy reversal thus was established by the emperor who, in fact, had been directly responsible for all those actions.

In the summer of 1162 Gaozong, like his father before him in the crisis of the first Jin invasions of late Northern Song in 1125, abdicated in favor of his heir, a son adopted in 1132. This stepson became the emperor known in history as Emperor Xiaozong (r. 1162–1189).[20] Residing in his retirement palace at the court, the old emperor would watch over his stepson's shoulder for a quarter-century, until his death in 1187.

The new Emperor Xiaozong found the reversal of policy toward the memory of Yue Fei entirely to his liking. Soon he took measures to rehabilitate Yue Fei's surviving widow and living son as well as to restore posthumously the titles and rights to the descendants of others who were no longer living.[21] In this way the Yue family came into considerable wealth and prestige. One of the grandsons, Yue Ke (1183–1240), became a scholar-official who devoted much of his life to restoring his grandfather's place in history. By the time he was old enough to pursue actively both official documents and informal accounts and reassemble Yue's purported literary production (consisting of a few poems of doubtful authenticity and a number of memorials and reports probably drafted for him by his literary staff assistants), more than sixty years had elapsed since Yue Fei's death. Yue Ke gathered the documents relating to his grandfather's career, collected writings in any way attributable to Yue Fei, and published them together with a life of his grandfather that is piously hagiographic.[22] It represents the first phase in the growth of the Yue Fei legend.

In the semihistorical myth, Yue Fei became the number two military hero of all Chinese history, a close second to another semihistorical, wonderfully legendary figure, Guan Yu (d. 219), one of the heroes of the Three Kingdoms era known to all in fiction, drama, and popular storytelling. Kuan Yu is also known as Duke Guan (Guan Gong), and sometimes as the God of War. The cults of Guan Yu and of Yue Fei began to take shape in Yuan times and grew to full-blown proportions during the Ming dynasty; state shrines to Yue Fei proliferated after the Mongol invasions of the Ming in 1449, when the reigning Ming emperor Yingzong became, for a brief time, the captive of the invading Mongols.[23] Whenever invasion threatened this otherwise civilian-oriented society, military heroes were resuscitated.

Many elements of the Yue Fei myth go back to Yue Ke's reconstruction of his grandfather's life. Some of the best known and most widely accepted have been shown to be suspect, and in many cases have been proved false. These include the remarkable stories about his birth and his mother's ingenious rescue of the one-month-old babe and herself in a flood, his father's instructing his son in classical and military texts, and his mother, at some unspecified moment in his life, having tattooed four large characters on his back, *jinzhong baoguo,* meaning "requite the state to the limits of loyalty." That element of the myth is particularly hard for some recent scholars to abandon; they see it as the directing theme of his entire life, having an importance that overrides his "crime" of suppressing popular uprisings, and their need to retain it overrides their commitment to verifiable history. The myth also exaggerates Yue's intellectual attainment, making him the model of the "literatus-general" who studied ancient texts as well as the accumulated military lore of his civilization, and who also wrote stirring poetry. Yue also became famous as a calligrapher, but we must note that all the extant examples attributed to him are false.[24]

At some point in his life he is said to have composed a *ci* lyric to the tune "Man jiang hong" (Full river red) containing the stirring lines: "My hair bristles in my helmet, . . . My breast is filled with violence . . . My fierce ambition is to feed on the flesh of the Huns / Laughing, I thirst for the blood of the Barbarians. / Oh, let everything begin anew. / Let all our rivers and mountains be recovered / before we pay our respects once more to the emperor."[25] Not even Yue Ke included this verse in his anthology of his grandfather's writings, and no unambiguous record of its existence dates from earlier than the fifteenth century. It has nevertheless been taken as the rallying cry of devotion to the Chinese state in times of peril. During World War II it was set to music and sung as an anthem of resistance against the Japanese invasions, and the words "recover our rivers and mountains" were written on walls everywhere. Because historically irrelevant considerations remain strong, even critical-minded recent scholars are reluctant to give up favorite aspects of the grand invention that has grown up around Yue Fei's name.[26]

Despite all the elements of exaggeration and pure fabrication, Yue's standing as a very successful general and his devotion to the cause of repelling the Jurchen invaders are nevertheless enough to give him an important place in history.

The Cause of Peace

Most modern scholars have bluntly stated that any attempt to justify the peace faction, and especially to grant any credit to the all-powerful Chief

Councillor Qin Gui's persistent pursuit of a negotiated peace with the Jurchens throughout the 1130s, is insidious and unacceptable. Qin's policy is categorically defined as a morally weak one of supine surrender; that it might have contained elements of wise trade-offs benefiting the Song, and farsighted assessment of China's ultimate advantage, is seldom admitted. Such arguments, attempting an objective assessment of the peace policy, invite denunciation as unpatriotic and treacherous, especially when raised, for example, by Chinese who favored accommodation with the Japanese in the 1930s. Similarly, that line of reasoning has been fiercely rejected by all scholars working under the government of Mainland China since 1949. Historical controversy, however, must be examined apart from such ahistorical sentiments.

Qin Gui served briefly as Chief Councillor in the crisis situation of 1131–32, was dismissed, then was recalled to that position in 1138 to serve until his death in 1155. Previously he had been captured along with the Northern Song court at Kaifeng in 1127, and the story goes that while in captivity he drew the favorable attention of high Jurchen tribal aristocrats and so was allowed to escape with his wife and family to return to Gaozong's court in 1130. His captors expected that he would gain high office and promote policies favorable to the Jurchens. The conspiracy implied in that version of the events may well be unfounded; the myth of his evil nature has grown in tandem with that of Yue Fei's nobility. It is true that Qin Gui presented himself to Emperor Gaozong as a "Jurchen expert" who could communicate effectively with high nobles close to the Jin throne. He was deeply involved in the peace negotiations from his return to high office in 1138 until their successful conclusion in 1142; his importance in the implementation of the peace policy was praised by the emperor when Qin died in 1155.

As a man, he appears to have been a self-important and mean-spirited politician, guilty of excessive nepotism and self-aggrandizement even by the standards of the time, and disliked by his fellow bureaucrats. Whether or not done with the emperor's approval, ridding the court of the prickly Yue Fei by poisoning him in his prison cell cannot under any circumstances be justified. Yet we today must try to transcend moralistic judgments to assess the pros and cons of the peace policy itself as an objective issue in Southern Song politics. The politics of the time must be seen apart from the no doubt morally flawed chief politician Qin Gui.

Emperor Gaozong had his own motives. He may have feared that the Jin would try to undermine him by returning the captive emperors, and may well have felt under pressure to appease them in order to prevent that card from being played. Yet we have no reason to believe that the weak-willed Qinzong, if restored to his throne, would have been better able to serve Chinese interests than was Gaozong. Moreover, it can be argued that Gaozong was true to the principles set down by both the founder and the second emperor at the end of the tenth century in preventing a military leader such as Yue Fei from becoming so independent of the court that he could threaten the nation's policies. Bringing the principal generals, especially Yue Fei, under civilian control in 1140 was quite reasonable in light of Song political traditions.

Gaozong also appears to have felt guilty for having failed to stand resolutely for resistance that might have regained some of the occupied territories, and simultaneously might have restored his older brother to the throne. Yet we cannot say that he had not at the same time carefully surveyed the long experience of the Northern Song in maintaining a stable peace through treaties with the Khitan Liao dynasty; he could well have concluded that peace, even under those humiliating circumstances, preserved his dynasty, and brought benefits to the Chinese people that far outweighed the costs of further warfare. Gaozong had become an able ruler; he was an intelligent man who took his role quite seriously. The sweeping denunciation of peace under the treaties as supine and unprincipled, whether made at that time by war party adherents or revived in the twentieth century in anachronistic terms of modern nationalism, is out of touch with reality. While the treaties were indeed resented by many at the time, and the anti–peace party statesmen continued to agitate for war against the Jurchens, there also were many Chinese who saw in the treaties an intelligent Chinese response to a grim situation. Gaozong could have been genuinely aware of those dimensions of the issues, apart from the fact that his personal interests also gained from the peace policy.

The historian today may not feel it is possible to come down conclusively on one side or the other, but he or she must remain open to the full range of issues. In the longer-range view, it can be strongly argued that the peace treaty solution did not diminish China's strength or curb its internal social development or harm its people, at least not more than protracted and not necessarily successful warfare might have done. A coolly detached assessment of the issues leaves Emperor Gaozong and his executive arm, Chief Councillor Qin Gui, less villainous than they usually appear in Chinese traditional and modern historiography, whether or not they emerge as sympathetic individuals.[27]

iii. Patterns of High Politics after the Treaty of 1141

The Treaty of 1141, its provisions settled by December 1141 and its further exchanges of diplomatic documents completed late in 1142, stipulated the amounts of the annual Song payments and the details of interstate protocol.[28] The relations of the Song to the Jin were defined in terms of both political subordination and fictive kinship making the Jin the generational seniors. The payments were labeled "tribute" as they crossed the border, although in China the Song tried to avoid the open use of that humiliating word. They were set at 300,000 units each of silver and silk, "units" meaning taels of silver bullion and bolts of common silk cloth. In addition, annual birthday and New Year's gifts also were required, as stipulated in the Sung-Liao Treaty of Shanyuan in 1005. Of great symbolic importance to the Song was the return of the coffins of Gaozong's father, the Emperor Huizong (who had reigned 1100–1125 and had died in captivity in 1135), and of two deceased empresses, as well as the repatriation of the living Empress Dowager Wei, Gaozong's mother.[29]

Other treaty provisions covered the pursuit of defectors across the border between the two states and the maintenance of peace and security on those borders. The Song Oath Letter sworn to the Jin is couched in extremely humble terms; one sentence gives the flavor of the whole: "If your superior state agrees to all this, our insignificant state too begs that this treaty should be jointly put into effect."[30] The very lucrative border trade was allowed to resume. Trade was desired by both, though its profits favored the Song. The treaty relations were adjusted twice, in 1165 in favor of Song after Prince Hailing's attempted invasion, and in 1208 in favor of Jin following a failed Song attempt to invade the Jin. As a result, the Song gained by somewhat reduced payments in 1165 but lost by the restoration of the higher levels in 1208. These adjustments show that the treaty system realistically reflected the changing conditions of interstate relations.

Emperor Xiaozong (r. 1162–1189), Gaozong's adopted son, was actually his remote nephew in a collateral branch of the family descended directly from the Song founder. He displayed intense devotion to his adoptive father; to mark that virtue he was given the posthumous temple name Xiaozong, "the Filial," by which I shall call him here. Traditionally his reign has been considered the high point of the Southern Song; his court regarded him as an earnest, attentive ruler.[31]

He was taken into the palace in 1132 when he was only five; Qin Gui's long control of the government corresponded with his life from age eleven to age twenty-seven. He feared and resented Qin and sought to ensure that as ruler he himself would never have to endure such a person at his court. As emperor he appointed people he thought he could trust to the two Chief Councillorships and to the posts of Assistant Grand Councillors, but also encouraged his Surveillance Censors to report on their actions and rotated the Councillors frequently in short tours of duty. For the duration of his reign no "all-powerful Chief Councillor" would again be tolerated. His court and central government functioned better than at any other time in the Southern Song.[32] Some adjustments were made in the institutions of central government, but there was no thoroughgoing overhaul. In 1189, on the model of his grandfather and father before him, Xiaozong too abdicated in favor of his forty-two-year-old son, the Emperor Guangzong (1189–1194). But he did not do so irresponsibly; he was so deeply grieved by the death of his stepfather in 1187 that he became unable to meet the court or function normally; leading courtiers had to persuade him forcefully to accept abdication in 1189; he died in 1194.

With Xiaozong's retirement, an era of Southern Song political history came to an end. The first sixty years, covering the reigns of Gaozong and Xiaozong, started uncertainly in the crisis of the Song state's collapse under the Jurchens' assault. After slow beginnings, however, those six decades became a period of strong imperial leadership over an orderly and disciplined bureaucratic establishment. It is true that Gaozong allowed himself and his court to be

CHART 5. THE SOUTHERN SONG IMPERIAL SUCCESSION
(Continued from Chart 2, Northern Song)

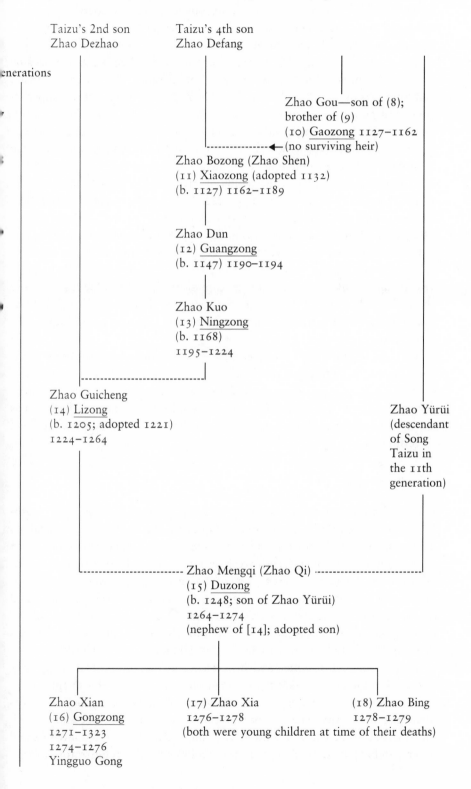

Taizu's 2nd son
Zhao Dezhao

Taizu's 4th son
Zhao Defang

enerations

Zhao Gou—son of (8);
brother of (9)
(10) Gaozong 1127–1162
(no surviving heir)

Zhao Bozong (Zhao Shen)
(11) Xiaozong (adopted 1132)
(b. 1127) 1162–1189

Zhao Dun
(12) Guangzong
(b. 1147) 1190–1194

Zhao Kuo
(13) Ningzong
(b. 1168)
1195–1224

Zhao Guicheng
(14) Lizong
(b. 1205; adopted 1221)
1224–1264

Zhao Yürüi
(descendant
of Song
Taizu in
the 11th
generation)

Zhao Mengqi (Zhao Qi)
(15) Duzong
(b. 1248; son of Zhao Yürüi)
1264–1274
(nephew of [14]; adopted son)

Zhao Xian
(16) Gongzong
1271–1323
1274–1276
Yingguo Gong

(17) Zhao Xia
1276–1278

(18) Zhao Bing
1278–1279
(both were young children at time of their deaths)

dominated by Chief Councillor Qin Gui for almost twenty years (1138–1155), but even throughout that period, when the hated and feared Qin Gui in fact carried out major policies approved by the emperor, Gaozong remained an engaged and closely informed ruler. He established the pattern of assertive imperial involvement followed by Xiaozong until 1189.

Strong imperial leadership began to break down when Xiaozong became emotionally impaired in the last two years of his reign. The pattern of strong rulership was not recovered thereafter. The reigns of the next three emperors covered a period of seventy-five years: Guangzong (r. 1189–1194), his son Ningzong (r. 1195–1224), and Ningzong's adopted nephew Lizong (r. 1224–1264). Each was, in turn, mentally or morally deficient; Lizong was one of the infamous lechers of Chinese imperial history. From 1189 onward the central government was usually in the hands of strong but often less than upright Chief Councillors. Serious flaws appeared. After Lizong's death in 1264 there would be only one more reign, that of Duzong (1264–1274), before the final phase of the Mongol invasions was under way. Forced abdications after 1274 led to a succession of three very short reigns of child emperors. The first was taken prisoner by the Mongols in 1275 and held hostage, and the younger two reigned while in flight from the capital at Hangzhou; the last of those three children, pursued to the extreme south (modern Hong Kong), died at sea in 1279. With him, the Southern Song came to a moving and unusually bitter end.

Much of the political narrative of the final century of the Southern Song, from Xiaozong's efforts to regain a strong and cohesive central government in the 1160s to the surrender of the court in Hangzhou in 1275, is a fascinating story of court politics.[33] Here we must forgo that story in order to focus on two or three episodes from that century that reveal the character of Song government.

The Political Environment

A central problem throughout the entire Song dynasty, Northern and Southern, arose from the relationship of the emperors, who had personal and family interests, to their Chief Councillors, who represented the entire bureaucracy in the running of the state. All were deeply committed to the dynasty, but for different reasons. Those two sets of divergent interests were often played out in the tensions between the Inner Court, serving the ruler directly, and the Outer Court, heading the civil bureaucracy. The essence of the problem throughout Song times is not *whether* but to what extent and by what means the emperor shared power with his advisers and bureaucrats. The central government—that is, the ruler and his court, and the administrative agencies centered in the capital—are the focus in the remainder of this chapter.

To an unprecedented degree the overriding Song dynasty policy issue was that of state security. The ever present threat posed by the succession of conquest dynasties provided a continuing point of friction between advisers and rulers, and among the different groups of advisers and administrators seeking the ruler's backing. In varying degrees all were either proponents of war or advocates of peace, earlier with the Liao, and after 1115 with the Jin dynasty. The Xi Xia, a focus of intense resentment and antagonism during the Northern Song, was more remote and of less concern in Southern Song times. The potential for dispute over war and peace was reflected in all other issues before the government, such as demands for administrative reform, the recurring need for emergency social welfare, the state's role in education and recruitment of officials, and so on.

All policy problems facing the government had to be worked out in relation to the basic issues of executive power: who should formulate state policy, who should control the use of the military, and who should manage the state's fiscal resources and allocate revenues.

The Song dynasty's political style differed from that of previous dynastic eras. Its bureaucrat administrators, the so-called scholar-official elite of Song times, achieved their privileged status through demonstrated individual skills in classical learning and understanding of the ancient texts of Confucianism. In Northern Song times, even before the implementation of Wang Anshi's New Policies in the 1070s and 1080s, the rapidly developing strands of Neo-Confucian thought provided the context within which political positions were formulated and discussed.[34] The uses of political power and the sources of its underlying authority, for that reason, came to be closely tied to the arena of learned discourse. Both the philosophical-minded scholars and their more practical-minded scholar-bureaucrat colleagues took the meaning of the ancient classical texts and the traditions of their interpretation to be the stuff of political debate.

Underlying all that debate, however, was an anomalous element: the demands of intellectual independence often were at odds with those of political loyalty. The men who staffed Song government, their intellects shaped within that context of ideas, could often be vigorously independent in their thinking, but of necessity they also were directly dependent on the ruler and his government for their official appointments. The virtue of loyalty to ruler and dynasty was stressed in Song times as never before in Chinese history.[35] Gaining office enabled a man to meet his responsibilities to his ancestors as well as to his living family, and to satisfy the family group's desires for status and wealth. Many had to resolve a conflict between the stimulus to be free spirits and the obligation to conform; it could be a vexing problem with quite practical consequences.

Most Song elite families could not afford to stay long uninvolved and apart from official careers. Of great importance to men of that background was that they looked upon governing as their enterprise; the nation's scholar-officials who were also its bureaucrats followed a high calling for which their personal achievements as society's most talented members had qualified them. Poorer families also strove, against still greater odds, to produce a son who could enter the competition and join that elite. In whatever mix of men from privileged or humble backgrounds (and the debate on that mix is not yet resolved), a broad talent pool was maintained by the examination system and supplementary recruitment devices. The interplay between what its members held to be correct Confucian ideas and what they defined as appropriate political means continued to develop throughout Song times, both in realms of more abstract learning and in those of political action. Here we are concerned with the latter dimensions, political behavior at the highest levels, illustrated in the case studies that follow.[36]

The Affair of Han Tuozhou

A new stage in the relationship of thought to politics was reached when the court was dominated by Han Tuozhou between 1195 and 1206. Han's rise to monopoly of political power fell within a pattern that can be traced back to early Southern Song, when Qin Gui, Yue Fei's nemesis, was Chief Councillor between 1138 and 1155. Qin amassed overwhelming authority by holding the powers of Chief Councillor concurrently with control over the military, and further subordinating to his position the revived State Finance Office. He could amass that combination of great powers only because of his special relationship to the imperial household.

It had been the intention of the early Northern Song rulers to keep those three functions—civil administration, military powers, and fiscal control—separated and subject to mutual checks, and separately subservient to alert emperors who kept their hands on policy. Moreover, the Chief Councillors, under whom the civil administration and the implementing ministries functioned, were supposed to be two in number, so that with their two principal Assistant Councillors they formed an executive council of four men who would each have individual access to the throne and would provide a check on one another. That separation of functions began to break down in late Northern Song times. It was in those decades that some extraordinary Chief Councillors came to hold concurrent titles of Commissioner of Military Affairs, and under one device or another also extended their grasp over the management of the state's revenues. For one man to monopolize those three handles of supreme administrative power remained an extraordinary situation in Northern Song times, but reappeared early in Southern Song, notably when Qin Gui was in charge. After him the new phenomenon, labeled the "all-powerful Chief Councillor" (quanxiang), repeatedly appeared.

The supreme powers of the emperor himself could in this way be compromised and he could be brought under strong pressures. Emperor Gaozong, for example, is said in some contemporary unofficial histories to have so feared his Chief Councillor Qin Gui that on Qin's death in 1155 he remarked privately to a courtier that he now felt he no longer needed to keep a stiletto concealed in his court boot to defend himself. That might be an unfounded or exaggerated tale, but it may express something of the way people at the time perceived things.[37] Or it may simply serve later needs to reinterpret that discredited phase of history. In Tang and earlier times such power to challenge or threaten the ruler came primarily from military men or imperial relatives outside the ranks of the civil bureaucracy; in Southern Song times those conditions could be achieved within the civil bureaucracy itself.

The reign of the Emperor Ningzong (1194–1224) provided the special circumstances permitting the concentration of executive powers in the high court bureaucracy to reach new levels. That led to an awkward situation in government. Ningzong came to the throne as a young man in his twenties when his stepfather, Emperor Guangzong, became mentally and physically incompetent and was pressured to abdicate in his heir's favor. An imperial relative, Zhao Ruyu, a man of great probity and strong connections to the most eminent scholars of the age, became the leading personality high in the court. He managed the Emperor Guangzong's abdication in 1194, and served briefly as Chief Councillor until 1195.[38] Zhao brought leading personages from the ranks of scholar-officialdom into the court, rid the government of debased officials, and began to produce an era of dynastic revival.[39] Among the intellectual figures drawn in by Zhao was the preeminent Neo-Confucian thinker Zhu Xi (1130–1200). It seemed to men of the time that Ningzong's reign might well allow the best of scholar-officialdom to serve the state and establish the reign of high ideals and energetic reform.

Not everyone was eager for such a development. Rivals for power saw an opportunity to attack the scholar-official elite, calling them bookish incompetents. Han Tuozhou was one of those critics. He had not risen to prominence via the esteemed path of classical learning and examination success. He claimed some kind of descent from the great Han clan of northeast Henan,[40] but he totally lacked their kind of distinction achieved through cultivation and public service. Han Tuozhou had gained power through an alternate route: he was related by marriage to Emperor Ningzong and used that connection to gain the important Inner Court post of head of the imperial bodyguard. Having neither the expected personal qualities nor the examination-route credentials, he was scorned by those who did. Han hated Zhao Ruyu and all the learned eminences Zhao brought into government. By manipulating the emperor, Han was able to have Zhao dismissed, and went further to denounce Zhu Xi and his followers—a very large and influential segment of scholar-officialdom—as perpetrators of "false learning," men who used their scholarly authority improperly to hoodwink the court and dominate access to official position. The emperor, a dully placid and disengaged man, upheld Han. By 1205 Han had grasped concurrently all the highest civil, military, and fiscal powers, and his underlings staffed the top layers of all branches of government.

That was not enough for Han. He knew that Emperor Ningzong, for all his placidity, privately favored the war policy and would be happy to achieve glory by regaining some of the Jin-controlled North. Han now took up the galvanizing issue of war versus peace. He had to convince the emperor that his opponents, some from within the imperial family and others constituting the majority of high court officials, were deluded, misguided, even morally delinquent. He made the particular scholarly stance of his Neo-Confucian opponents in the scholar-bureaucracy a central issue in politics.

Throughout imperial times the state, of course, always possessed the power to intimidate thinkers and curb intellectual discourse when it chose to do so, but that was not commonly done. A new factor from Song times onward is that scholar-officials were more closely identified with the central government and more dependent on their relationship with it. Han Tuozhou blundered into the error of trying to define the state's interests in scholarly orthodoxy. In the twelfth-century, as at so many points in human history, to link politics to philosophy was a dangerous move. It could only enhance trends toward absolutism, for when intellectual issues, in this case the interpretation of classical texts, are defined in exclusive and morally correct terms, it gives the holders of power an instrument for suppressing all thinking about the sources of authority, even when carried out in rather recondite scholarly ways at the margins of politics.

Han Tuozhou gained great power improperly and employed it recklessly. He attempted to bludgeon his scholar-official opponents in government by declaring that the intellectual stance then assuming dominant influence in Song elite life was politically insidious. He was no doubt quite cynical. The substance of that charge held no importance for him. He was carelessly attempting to wield a political weapon always at hand but best avoided, thus taking a step toward authoritarian control over the all-encompassing realm of discourse. His clumsy attempts to do so in fact produced a new political environment, one that he did not anticipate.

To define this issue more clearly we may look back to the case of Wang Anshi in the late Northern Song era, more than a century earlier. As Chief Councillor, Wang was a stubborn reformer whose New Policies were attacked as misguided, based on faulty learning. His contemporaries in government, however, could openly disagree with him, and among themselves, about the intellectual dimensions of such issues. That disagreement engendered intense political debate. Wang was driven from power despite the emperor's continued confidence in him. Yet he remained a respected figure. In that episode, correct thinking and sound scholarship were at issue, not "orthodoxy" as defined by the state.

Han Tuozhou, in contrast, did not possess Wang Anshi's credentials as a critical scholar. He was merely a manipulative power holder, not a participant in the arena of discourse. His denunciation of "false learning" was motivated solely by his need to strengthen his grasp on government and to devise a weapon against his enemies. He appeared to have succeeded, but his further ambitions brought about his downfall.

Han claimed to understand the Jurchens because he came from the North. He believed that Jin cultural policy had weakened the fighting capacities of the Jurchens by the late years of the Jin emperor Zhangzong's reign.[41] In 1206 Han led the Song government to declare war on the Jin. Armies stationed along the boundary at the Huai River moved northward into Jin territory, and in an initial engagement one of the Song armies won a minor victory. Han, elated, ordered that it be followed up by a full-scale offensive.

His assessment of the realities was disastrously wrong on all counts. His proscription of Zhu Xi's school was untenable. Moreover, by denigrating scholars he gained a vast network of enemies. His judgment in making appointments to military command was grievously faulty, and his evaluation of the Jin capacity for war was quickly shown to be wrong. The Jin soon mobilized and sent several columns southward, to engage Song armies in Anhwei and Henan. They won enough convincing victories to blunt whatever confidence the Song leaders might have entertained. As news of Song defeats was received at court, Han desperately sued for peace. The court now abandoned Han and turned the peace negotiations over to others. Jin negotiations included demands for restoration of the higher annual indemnity payments to the levels of the treaty of 1141, and a special levy to cover the victors' military costs, but the Jin agreed to restore the boundaries to the Huai River line as before Han's invasion. As a condition of peace, however, the Jin also asked that Han's head be sent to them in a box.

It was often said, at the time and later, that the Song never executed a high official for any reason; while not precisely true, this statement expressed a widely held faith in the dynasty's high standard of civility. (The poisoning of Yue Fei in 1142 was not looked upon as an exception because people believed it to have been an unofficial act carried out by Qin Gui.) At this juncture, the Song emperor and his new Chief Councillor, Shi Miyuan (1164–1233), not quite able to make a public case for Han's malfeasance because that would implicate the emperor, agreed instead to have Han secretly assassinated. Then, the next year they ignominiously dispatched his head off to the Jin court.[42] That debased way of dealing with the too powerful minister damaged the image of Song civil government.

Han Tuozhou came to power through the Inner Court; he did not represent the scholar-officials and was widely despised by them. Nor did the despicable manner of his death gain him the stature of Yue Fei, a proponent of war who was disgracefully assassinated to remove an obstacle to the ruler's policies. Yet the judgments on him were clouded by the issue of war versus peace. For, despite his personal deficiencies, Han Tuozhou was not more universally repudiated only because his espousal of the war policy was meaningful to many. Two eminent poets of the age are known as the best "patriotic poets" of Song. One of them, Xin Qiji (1140–1207), himself a man born in the Jin-occupied North, sided with most of the scholar-officials in rejecting Han Tuozhou.[43] The other, the aging, venerated Lu You (1125–1210), felt that the cause of regaining the North was more important than Han's personal failings, and endorsed him.[44] So the issue of war versus peace continued to be played out in many sectors of Song life.

The Career of Shi Miyuan

After the removal of Han Tuozhou, court politics followed more conventional patterns, though dominated by Ningzong's consort, the Empress Yang, until her death in 1232. She is one of the most acutely perceptive and politically able women in Song history, criticized for her assertive involvement (or meddling) in political matters but all in all a constructive influence.[45] She operated in close collaboration with Shi Miyuan, a member of one of the two or three most successful families in Southern Song politics.[46] After the dismissal of Han Tuozhou, Shi served as Chief Councillor for twenty-three years and came to hold great power.

Shi Miyuan must be ranked along with Qin Gui, Han Tuozhou, and the later Jia Sidao as one of the "all-powerful Chief Councillors" of Southern Song.[47] His rise into the higher bureaucracy was conventional. He originally entered officialdom as a teenager through "protection" (yin) on the strength of his father's having served as a Chief Councillor, but Shi Miyuan followed by taking the examinations and placing first in them when he was only seventeen. His father's status gave him initial entry, but his own extraordinary abilities made his career. He worked his way quickly up through the ranks, becoming Chief Councillor in 1208, shortly after Han Tuozhou was dismissed. He is described as having exceptional talent for politics; he was manipulative, could be dishonest, and aroused hatreds but skillfully countered his enemies, served his emperors well, and left his family's great wealth and status secure.

The succession to Ningzong, who died in 1224 without an heir having been clearly designated, was troubled and irregular; once again the imperial household turned to an adopted son from a collateral line. Shi Miyuan and Empress Yang adroitly maneuvered through that crisis. Throughout this period the briefly banned (1195–1202) school of Neo-Confucian learning identified with Zhu Xi, in reaction against Han Tuozhou's designation of it as "false learning," was favored by Chief Councillor Shi Miyuan and his successors. Zhu Xi's so-called School of Daoxue ("The Learning of the Great Way," otherwise identified as Lixue), was strengthened in its prestige and general influence for having survived Han's unprincipled attack on it.[48]

The New Issue of Confucian "Orthodoxy"

The commentaries on the classics prepared by Zhu and his followers began to be used as the basis for the examinations, giving those teachings the standing of "orthodoxy"; this pleased the elite and helped gain their support in the stressful time following the fearsome Mongols' replacement of the Jurchens as the enemy in the North after 1234. Zhu's school of thought grew ever more widely influential.

Han Tuozhou's disastrous espousal of the pro-war cause also led to the renewed dominance of the cause of peace. The appearance of the Mongols as the new enemy replacing the Jurchens led at the court to still more open support for the so-called peace party. For the first time, issues of war and peace became intertwined with the unfortunate issue of "orthodoxy," even though by no means all of those now considered to represent that orthodoxy agreed with the peace policy. Linking the two issues had at first been a political gesture toward a very important segment of the scholar-officialdom, if for the time a rather peripheral one intended to strengthen the Song dynasty against competing Mongol claims of legitimacy in dynastic succession.[49] Domestically, the new concept of a concretely defined Confucian "orthodoxy" could also become a tool of the Chief Councillors and the Outer Court, used by them to strengthen their role in politics. As sponsors of orthodoxy, they had a strong way of claiming that their guidance was essential to the running of the state. As we shall see in later history, however, this orthodoxy also could be made to serve the throne against any and all free-ranging and independent-minded tendencies in the Outer Court itself and throughout scholar-officialdom. Politically speaking, in the long-range view of history, the subsequent triumph of Lixue as orthodoxy, in reaction against Han Tuozhou's incidental attack on Zhu Xi as the perpetrator of "false learning," was far more important and, it is often argued, more to be regretted than Han's clumsy effort to suppress it. Debased politics, whether practiced in the Outer Court or in later ages in the Inner Court, had gained a new instrument.

It is worth reminding ourselves, however, that in China the concept of orthodoxy remained a secular and rationally derived notion. It meant little more than establishing a particular set of texts and exegetical commentaries for testing scholars in the civil service examinations. Although that excluded differing ideas at this one crucial point in the training of political leaders, in China the idea of orthodoxy never reached the level of binding adherence other than in the examinations; it did not demand the banning of non-orthodox texts, beliefs, or practices in general, or punishing the unorthodox. A rigorous concept of orthodoxy supported in widely consequential social measures is more typical of civilizations where a superrational religious authority was linked to state power. Nevertheless, in Neo-Confucian China from the twelfth century onward, the however limited enforcement of Confucian orthodoxy became a somewhat restricting factor in intellectual life simply because unorthodox ideas, especially when they competed within the Confucian sphere, might become a liability in public life. Nonetheless, that did not prevent the Song dynasty from being officially the patron of Daoism, nor did it prevent individuals (including members of the imperial household) from patronizing Buddhism. Much less did it eliminate the access of private scholars to any field of learning. Orthodoxy was a new instrument that potentially could enhance the powers of the authoritarian state but was not employed significantly in that way during Song times. Nor did it thereafter ever gain overall intellectual hegemony. It was orthodoxy vis-à-vis politics, not an orthodoxy defining the entire realm of personal concerns, beliefs, and practices.

The Reform Policies of Jia Sidao

The Southern Song government recognized with some unease that the fall of the Jin to the Mongols in 1234 removed the stabilizing (however resented) treaty arrangement securing its northern borders. It did not, however, attempt to replace that treaty with a new kind of arrangement with the Mongols, even though the Mongol side made some gestures signifying that an at least temporary accommodation might have been possible. It is safe to say that by the early 1200s the loss of the North had become an issue less insistently in the minds of statesmen or the public at large, and Han Tuozhou's strident effort to make it the focus of state policy, failing dismally, had only strengthened the peace party. Even those whose grandfathers had moved south to evade life under alien rule had become "southern" in their outlook and concerns. Irredentism had by no means faded from statesmen's consciousness, but other issues seemed more demanding of everyone's attention. Even in the North, before the 1250s the Mongols themselves may not have appeared to people in China to be more than marauding nomads. Thereafter, the Mongol presence in the former domains of the Jin dynasty and the Xi Xia state, both hostile polities previously important to the Song, was gradually recognized as a serious threat. The South's safety was seen to be in peril only when Möngke Khan (r. 1250–1259), a grandson of Chinggis Khan, launched invasions of the Song. After Möngke's younger brother Khubilai became the Great Khan in 1260, the government of Song realized that it faced immediate danger, yet no general plan for dealing with the threat by diplomatic or military means was formulated.

Jia Sidao (1213–1275) became Chief Councillor in 1259 and held the fullest measure of power until he was dismissed a few months before his death in 1275. His control of government coincided with the period of Mongol aggression against the Southern Song, giving him in Chinese eyes responsibility for the collapse of the dynasty. Like Han Tuozhou's, his biography in the official *Song History* appears in the section titled "Biographies of Treacherous Ministers."[50] His vilification at the hands of past and present historians is more extreme than that of Han Tuozhou. He had many personal faults, but the collapse of the Southern Song cannot be laid at his feet. His personal character affronted many of his contemporaries, and his social policies, especially the forced buying up of large private landholdings for redistribution to landless farmers, whether or not ill-advised as social policy, ran counter to the interests of members of the landholding elite. All of these factors contributed to his evil reputation and to the bias against him in historiography. His case merits independent assessment in our time. It has not received that from historians in China.[51]

In the spring of 1275, after the failure of a last-minute military expedition against the Mongols led by Jia, a high official petitioned the Empress Dowager Xie to have Jia executed. She was the widow of Emperor Lizong, who had died ten years earlier, but was not the birth mother of his son, the Emperor Duzong, who had died in 1274. This interesting woman, then in her mid-sixties, had borne the title of empress for almost half a century. She gave the Song court strong and conscientious leadership as regent for the child emperor who had succeeded in 1274, and again in the subsequent crisis of surrender to the Mongol commander who besieged the capital throughout much of the following year. Her reply to the petition for Jia's death reveals something of the civility of Song government even under stressful circumstances at the end:

"Jia Sidao has labored untiringly through the successive reins of three emperors; how, for the failure of one morning, could one bear to abandon the proprieties due to a great official?"[52] Despite her intervention, later that year after Jia was sent into banishment he was stalked and murdered by a local official, perhaps encouraged by persons at the court, but certainly not with the concurrence of this lady.

How do we evaluate this "bad last minister" of the Southern Song? Although we cannot clear him of all the character faults ascribed to him, he is more interesting than the other "all-powerful Chief Councillors" of Southern Song. The son of a mid-ranking military administrator, he gained entry into officialdom not through the more prestigious examination route, but through the less-esteemed alternate route of "protection" granted in recognition of his grandfather's official posts. Like Han Tuozhou, he had marriage links to the imperial household; his sister had been a favorite consort of Emperor Lizong but was never named empress. In any event, she had died in 1247, by which time Jia held only low to middling positions in the civil bureaucracy. His rise to high position in the 1250s was accomplished without any special favor from the Inner Court; he belonged to the Outer Court, the civil bureaucracy, and was quite typical of leading bureaucrats of his time. He was intelligent, cultivated, a sponsor of scholarly projects, and as a collector of art he displayed refined tastes. In his personal behavior he was famous for his addiction to wine and women and to enjoyment of all the fabled luxuries offered at the beautiful capital city, Hangzhou. That was behavior common to men of his social position, and to the lecherous Emperor Lizong himself, under whose reign (1224–1264) Jia's career was mostly spent. The point here is that Jia, despite his lack of the civil service examination qualification, was accepted as an insider by the scholar-official elite. He came to be hated and vilified because he controlled the government in a period of political and military failure, and because his social policies angered the elite. By Song times the elevation of emperors had reached the point where chief ministers were made to bear the blame for dynastic collapse which in earlier times was typically ascribed to "bad last rulers."[53]

When we work our way past that obstacle to fully understanding Jia Sidao, however, we see that his attempts to overhaul the administration grew from practical observation of real problems, much like those of some of the most eminent of Song period Chief Councillors, especially Wang Anshi in the 1070s of the Northern Song. Even more than Wang Anshi, Jia attempted to implement radical reforms in the state's revenue system by limiting landholdings and reallocating the tax burdens in rural society. His historical importance is to be measured by his agrarian reforms and fiscal innovation.[54] He increased the tax revenues and turned the increases to strengthening the armed forces. The late Song military problem was not one of small or weak armies and navies; the armed forces were very large. They suffered from weaknesses of leadership and training, of discipline and material support, and from poorly planned defenses. His improved financing of the army helped to strengthen the state, but given the nature of the Mongol enemy, that could not long stave off the defense crisis.

Jia Sidao's agrarian reforms are harder to understand. He set low limits on private landholding (about 100 English acres), at first applicable to families which had any kind of official status, but soon extended to all landholders. A fixed portion (usually one-third) of any owner's land over the set amount was bought by the government on terms considered to be akin to expropriation. That land was then to be rented at fair rates to landless rural households or otherwise used to produce income for the state. It long had been clearly seen by many Southern Song observers that extensive landholding by the richer sectors of society encouraged abuses of the tax exemption regulations and an increase of tax evasion among official and wealthy households. These caused severe imbalances in the revenue system, bringing about widespread hardship in rural society. Jia was unusual not in recognizing that problem but in finding the energy and will to attack it.

His plan, however, was not implemented until the mid-1260s, so close to the fall of Southern Song that its impact cannot be fully assessed. The *Song History,* written by an official commission seventy-five years later, complains bitterly about the suffering caused to the people. "The people," in traditional sources, usually means "those affected," not the masses of the ordinary population; in this case "the people" clearly designates those of the economic elite whose estates exceeded the limits set by Jia Sidao.[55] The plan sent tremors through rural life; it also left large areas of "public lands" *(gongtian)* in the hands of the government in regions closest to the capital, where implementation was most fully carried out. The use of those lands remained a problem for the Yuan and Ming governments through the next century or more. It is not possible on the basis of present information to measure the social impact. We can do little more than observe that by attempting reforms of such fundamental nature, Jia Sidao demonstrated that he was something more than the usual all-powerful Chief Councillor, even though it has remained standard to brush his reforms off as little more than the superficial meddling of a power-hungry dictator,[56] and the person responsible for the Song's downfall. The latter judgment is myopic.

To conclude, I have said that after the Emperor Xiaozong retired in 1189, the Southern Song's initial sixty-year period under the two strong managerial-minded emperors Gaozong and Xiaozong was followed by ninety years during which a succession of imperial nonentities allowed, or necessitated, the shift of leadership into the hands of very powerful Chief Councillors. This account places the focus on high politics, the realms of involvement of emperors, their consorts, and their courts, along with major players among all the statesmen and scholar-officials, eunuchs and generals, sycophants and opportunists. It is important to note that within the patterns of high power politics discussed herein, we see the emergence of new modes for the exercise of political power and the enlargement of the scope of the bureaucratic state. The Song period has been called the beginning of early modern China, meaning among other things that the character of its political life in particular belongs with the age that followed and led directly to the present day.

Through the long ninety-year final phase, the Southern Song was ruled by inconsequential emperors who defaulted in governing, yet their dynasty continued to draw the devoted service of a broadly based elite of learning. This dominant segment of the late Song elite was primarily devoted to the culture, to the civilization and its historical models, and secondarily to the dynasty and to emperors as individuals. The overriding importance of loyalty to ruler and dynasty did not deter all courageous criticism. The scholar-officials who made the governing of China their main concern were quite capable of reprimanding emperors for their ethical lapses and giving their own judgments more weight than those advanced by august imperial minds. Their emphasis on individual learning and broad cultivation as a qualification for elite status was a new characteristic of Chinese imperial government; by the Southern Song, long after the founding of the Song in 960, a stable new pattern of elite dominance had been worked out.

Their sense of themselves, new in Song China, defined for members of the scholar-officialdom their entire role in society and in government. That circumstance imparted a special character to political life. Much of that Song style within the scholar-official elite remained, surviving the changing circumstances of the following dynastic eras to become part of the civilization of later imperial China.

Through Southern Song times elite life was marked by an increasing estrangement from the North of Chinese antiquity, away from the conditions of life in that ecologically different region, and from the nostalgia for recovering the region which hitherto had dominated Chinese civilization. The South came into its own. Whether or not because the physical environment of court and government was no longer the North China of Northern Song and all earlier ages in Chinese history, the tone of elite life changed when the state was confined to the richer central and southern provinces. In Southern Song the effete scholar-official with metaphysical, literary, and artistic preoccupations became the norm, if not the ideal. The vigorous polo-playing scholar-official of earlier times who ideally displayed both the martial and the more refined qualities gave way to the physically unassertive, sedan chair–riding, soft-voiced if more elegantly expressive male ideal of Southern Song.[57] Exceptions to this generalization are too numerous to count, yet the generalization has force.

Some of these cultural changes held significance for politics: the mind-set, the lifestyle, the cultural values, and the ideal patterns of elite behavior all played a role in governing. They are noted here because they help to describe the political milieu. Nowhere else in the world of those centuries was there a political and social order much like that of Song China (unless it be the close but highly incomplete imitation of Song China in the Jin state of North China). The Mongol conquest, completed in 1279, brought a sudden end to the Song style in governing. Despite that, the Song left its mark. As James

T. C. Liu has written, "To hypothesize boldly about the culture of China through its last 800 years, it is the Southern Song that has provided the dominant model, and the Jiangsu-Zhejiang region [where the central government of Southern Song was located] that has been its center."[58] In the foregoing, the focus has been on government at the higher levels; an assessment of the more general implications of Southern Song cultural development follows in Chapter Fourteen.

14

CHINESE CIVILIZATION
AND THE
SONG ACHIEVEMENT

The intellectual vigor of the Northern Song was generated by a rediscovery of Confucian values. The Southern Song continued and deepened the philosophical, scholarly, and artistic developments, refining the cultural content of Chinese civilization. Instead of attempting to catalog the components of the Song achievement, I first introduce a few individual lives to display a range of elite interests and activities. From these one may glimpse the rich texture of Song life and the broad scope of its intellectual and artistic horizons. The focus then turns to the further development of Neo-Confucianism by Southern Song thinkers, men who belonged to the same milieu of scholar-official elite life. The dominant figure Zhu Xi receives special attention. His too was a life that exemplified the patterns of scholar-officialdom, though he has been called the most influential figure in all of later imperial history, and thus was at the same time an extraordinary person. Other kinds of elite lives and some generalizations about the Song elite follow. That elite stratum in Song society acquired a social character that endured until the end of the imperial era in 1911, albeit with continuing adaptations to the changing political and social scene in the dynastic eras that followed.

1. New Social Factors

The Song era has been summed up in a phrase: it was an age in which a "new culture"[1] took form. A development of such broad significance must be explainable in relation to the social base. It implies significant social change. We should therefore remind ourselves that during the three centuries of the Song dynasty, the social system was indeed taking on a new character that would endure for centuries, and that by the twentieth century it would be looked back on, whether in admiration or in scorn, as the paradigm for "traditional China."[2]

The term "new culture" to be sure describes primarily the lives of the Song elite, but that elite stratum in Song society was itself new in its composition and in its social values, and therefore in its relation to the rest of society. On the one hand, the newly defined Song elite stratum provided the men who staffed the central government and governed in the dynasty's name. On the other hand, that elite's relationship to the main body of society was twofold: these were the men who administered local government, but they also headed the families which, through their influence on the local population, guided and led their home communities. Neither of those social roles was wholly new, but during the Song the relationships both with the imperial throne and with the people at large were constituted in new and different ways. The quality of those relationships had become different.

Typically, men of the Song elite were dependent on their personal achievement, even when wealth and position in many cases made it relatively easy for them to acquire the education necessary for success. Elite status functioned normatively; that is, it established expectations that conditioned behavior throughout society. Members of the elite all had lineage ties to relatives at other social levels; they were models of success to be imitated within their clans and throughout society, and particularly in their home locales. It has often been noted that during the Southern Song, the scholar-official elite came to see their interests in local affairs as even more important than their careers on the national political scene. That probably is an imprecise generalization, but it calls attention to a trend of change.

A more balanced view might be that members of the Song elite were conscious leaders in government *and* in their communities, as Chinese elites usually were. In the Song, a new spirit in learning and thought, in which all of the elite were immersed, encouraged at its best strong individual self-esteem coupled with feelings of direct responsibility for the world in which they lived. They were free to make their own decisions on what constituted "correct learning," because those truths were available to all through their own powers of study and reasoning, not (as in most other premodern civilizations) as unquestionable truths attained through some kind of suprarational revelation; much less was it mediated through a surrogate for such authority in either a church or a state institution. For men of the Song, to stand stubbornly for what one felt to be right went hand in hand with the self-confidence derived from being part of an elite whose members, generally as well as ideally speaking, had *earned* their status. That combination lay at the heart of the normative component in the functioning of Song society.

Other factors also were part of the social change that marked the Song period. These included increased sources of wealth in society from developments in agriculture, industry, and commerce. The prosperity of Song life is part of the Song achievement. All the evidence indicates that China was the richest, most orderly, most culturally and technologically advanced portion of the world throughout the more than three centuries of the Song, but particularly in the two-thirds of the Chinese lands that became the Southern Song after 1127. China contained the world's largest cities, and a disproportionate share of all the world's lesser cities and large towns. It supported greater commerce, domestic and international, than all the rest of the world. It produced thousands of titles of printed books before the rest of the world (except for Korea, which shared in and contributed to China's printing technology) had printed books. Although we cannot calculate very closely, it undoubtedly had the largest share of the world's literate people, as well as a growing rate of literacy among its ordinary people. Literacy and books together meant that China could effectively accumulate, preserve, and disseminate knowledge, and because much of that knowledge had pragmatic application, it helped to improve lives. That is not, however, to overlook the inequities in the generally prosperous society or the abuses that might be suffered by the poor, for example, at the hands of local government.[3]

This age of cultural richness cannot be explored in satisfying depth here. The reader of history must also read its essays and poetry, study its philosophical and religious writings, learn to appreciate its painting and calligraphy and other arts, become familiar with its monuments of architecture and urban construction and vast public works, witness its ever-surprising inventiveness in science and technology, and sample its immense accumulation of historical records. What follows here may help to open doors into those rewarding byways, but it cannot encompass all of that historical achievement. My interest is to recognize the historical character of Song civilization and to understand how it worked, not merely to sing its praises.

II. ELITE LIVES AND SONG HIGH CULTURE

The historian has a number of possible ways to measure and assess the character of Chinese society. I will attempt to indicate some of that character impressionistically, by introducing first a few Song individuals. They are fascinating historical personages by any standard, and from their individual cases inferences can be drawn about the society in which they lived. A sense of how such unusual yet representative persons could leave their mark upon history in various fields of their endeavors may emerge.

Shen Gua and Song Science

At the beginning of his large project to record the history of science in Chinese civilization, Joseph Needham (1900–1995) wrote: "Whenever one follows up any specific piece of scientific or technological history in Chinese literature, it is always at the Sung [Song] dynasty that one finds the major focal point."[4] Needham's views are not without bias: he believed that scientific thought and practice were congenial to Daoism (especially the practices of Daoist adepts, alchemists, and elixir makers) but incompatible with Confucian values, so scientific activity declined in post-Song times as Neo-Confucianism triumphed. Also, his emphasis on the undoubted accomplishments of the Song led him and others in the new field of the history of Chinese science to underestimate continuing development in post-Song times. Both points, but especially the incompatibility of Confucian values with scientific investigation, are challenged by other historians of science.[5] Yet Needham's emphasis on the Song is justified. Important advances were made in both theoretical and applied sciences, and in humanistic studies such as history, archaeology, and philology, where scientific methods were applied.

In particular, historians of science admire Shen Gua (Shen Kua, 1031–1095); Needham calls him "perhaps the most interesting character in all of Chinese scientific history."[6] Shen was a perceptive observer of natural phenomena and one who speculated reasonably and methodically about curiosities. On travels through Shanxi he took particular note of fossilized sea creatures in the Taihang Mountains, recognized them for what they were, and theorized that land forms had changed through millennia to make mountains of what had once been seabeds. To cite but a few other representative examples: Shen developed improved instruments for making astronomical observations; invented methods for solving problems in mathematics; analyzed and explained metallurgical techniques; appears to have understood atmospheric refraction; solved the problem of how to measure the topographical contour of the land surface so as to calculate within a fraction of an inch the differences in level of the Bian Canal at points 420 kilometers apart; devised relief maps to illustrate water control techniques; made a detailed atlas of China; conducted medical experiments and compiled a work on pharmacology; was the first to write in detail and with accurate understanding about the compass, a much earlier Chinese invention that in Song times came to be applied to maritime navigation; and wrote about many aspects of applied techniques in everyday work and production processes, such as his commoner friend Bi Sheng's "invention" or technological improvement of movable type printing in the 1040s, which Shen described so fully that the methods can be reconstructed and demonstrated.[7]

Shen Gua was born into an official family of Hangzhou. As a very young man he first attained official status and a minor post through "protection," as a reward for the merit of his father. That indicates that Shen's otherwise unknown father had attained at least a modest position in the bureaucracy. Two children of his father's brother also received office in this way, yet one of those brothers as well as Shen Gua went on to take the regular civil service examinations and earned the *jinshi* degree, the highest-level examination degree, in that way becoming eligible for careers in the higher bureaucracy. The three Shen men, Shen Gua and his two cousins, all had unusual careers and displayed impressive scholarly attainment as well as highly individualistic personalities.[8]

Shen Gua greatly admired Wang Anshi, the political reformer who dominated the government in the late 1060s and 1070s. After serving at several posts in the provinces, he joined Wang at the capital and served there, eventually becoming Academician at the court of Emperor Shenzong. He was sent on a diplomatic mission to the court of the Khitan Liao dynasty, where he solved an important dispute about the border by citing his extensive geographical and military knowledge. He often advised on military matters, and accompanied a Song army sent in 1081 against the Xi Xia state of the Tanguts in the Northwest; the army was successful in 1081 but the next year suffered defeat. Although Shen was in another sector of the front at the head of a force that was successful, he was demoted. He was becoming discouraged about developments at court after Wang Anshi was dismissed in 1076 so gladly retired to live out the last nine or ten years of his life at his Dream Brook home at a site he had bought without seeing it. Later, on inspecting the place, he recognized it as a scene that he had often dreamed about through the years, so built his retirement residence there. Throughout his active life he was always surrounded by friends and fellow spirits from all walks of life, elite and commoner, with whom he explored all avenues of knowledge. In retirement he wrote his "Brush Talks from Dream Brook" not primarily as a scientist systematically recording new knowledge, but informally, to continue exchanges of knowledge and opinion among his friends. The range of those writings, in the surviving 580 short essays, goes well beyond the scientific and the technological, to include political affairs, historical subjects, literary tastes, and the like. In Song times he was known as a learned literatus, not appreciated as a scientist so much as a man of humane letters. It has taken our times and our interests to assess his achievements in science fully.

Throughout Southern Song times important figures continued to appear, especially in the fields of algebra, astronomy, medicine and pharmacology, civil engineering, and agricultural sciences. Most of those whose names we know and some of whose writings have been preserved were members of the scholar-official elite. Yet we know from remarks made by Shen Gua and many others that they were both conscious and appreciative of countless craftsmen and builders, soldiers and sailors, working men and women throughout the sub-elite, often the illiterate persons in society. Those men and women made their pragmatic discoveries and transmitted their skills. They were an indispensable element in the development of Chinese civilization, even more so than the few great and fully identified figures such as Shen Gua. Today we are more apt to find the physical evidence for their achievements in bridges and towers, city walls and tombs, canals with their locks and dams, hulls of sunken ships—in the countless artifacts of ordinary life—than we are to find written records documenting the invention and transmission of all that accumulated knowledge.

The quite practical base of ordinary Chinese life sustained the society in which the great learned discoverers lived and worked. Needham has written that "Chinese scientific humanism, though all its achievements were made before there was any modern science in China at all, rested on two main bases. It never separated man from nature, and never thought of man apart from social man."[9] He compares the origins of "scientific humanism" in China of the fifth to third centuries B.C.E. with the parallel developments among the pre-Socratics in ancient Greece; two great and enduring traditions in scientific thought followed quite different paths in Western and Chinese history, the Chinese tradition flowering particularly in the tenth through the thirteenth centuries at a time when the Western scientific tradition temporarily slumbered for several centuries. One can differ with Needham's particular point of view, but this comparison with early science in the West is nonetheless stimulating. Moreover, Shen Gua's writings give additional evidence that some of the Song intellectual elite, perhaps most, had interests and personal contacts which extended far beyond their own social stratum.

Zhao Mingcheng and Li Qingzhao

The reign of the Emperor Huizong (1101–1125) witnessed the collapse of the Northern Song under the force of the Jurchen invasions after 1120 and ushered in the calamitous withdrawal from North China as the Jin dynasty established its rule there. That disaster left deep scars on the lives of all the elite living in the occupied regions or stationed at the court at Kaifeng, as it undoubtedly also brought suffering to the ordinary people. There is no better illustration of the way that cataclysm affected elite lives than the one we find in Zhao Mingcheng and Li Qingzhao, man and wife, two real persons who embody an ideal image of the Song elite.

Zhao Mingcheng (1081–1129), from Shandong Province in the North, was the son of an eminent scholar-official family. His father, Zhao Tingzhi (1040–1107), served briefly as Chief Councillor early in the reign of Emperor Huizong.[10] Li Qingzhao (1084–1155?) also came from one of the most distinguished scholar-official families of Shandong. Her father, Li Gefei (1046?–1106?), known as a classical exegete and literary figure as well as a successful statesman, also held high office at the court. He is the author of a work called "Description of Famous Gardens in Luoyang" *(Luoyang ming yuan ji),* which is itself a study of the lifestyles of the cultured and wealthy elite of Song times, undertaken because he felt it revealed something about the political culture of Song.[11] Li Qingzhao's mother, noted for her learning and literary accomplishment, was her eldest daughter's early teacher, carrying on a family tradition of learning; her maternal grandfather was ranked first in the palace examination for new *jinshi* in 1030 and attained the high office of Minister of War before his death in 1085.[12] The marriage of Zhao Mingcheng and Li Qingzhao in 1101, when she was seventeen and he twenty, thus linked two families that, in the eyes of the time, perfectly represented the scholar elite; the two young people personified cultivation, beauty, and talent.

Their lives were in fact idyllically happy throughout the twenty-five years of Huizong's reign. When they married, Zhao was still a student in the National Academy at the capital, preparing to earn his *jinshi* degree and embark on an official career. They began collecting works of art and antiquities, especially ancient bronzes dating from the preimperial era which were from time to time accidentally uncovered and sold by art dealers. Zhao Mingcheng did not have much money in his student days, so they frequently had to pawn their belongings to acquire objects of particular interest, which they then studied and recorded. Ancient bronzes were Zhao's passion. He developed skills in authenticating genuine pieces, making rubbings of and deciphering their inscriptions, on the earliest pieces often no more than a few words, but on later Zhou bronzes sometimes quite lengthy. He used the information he gained to correct writings on early history. Later, when he held office and had more money to spend, their collection of ancient pieces and scholarly books grew. Together they prepared a catalogue called *Jinshi Lu* (Record of Inscriptions on Bronze and Stone), first published 1119–1125. It contains texts of 2,000 inscriptions with detailed critical notes. A number of important works on antiquities and archaeological subjects were written during the Song.[13] Zhao's book, written with Li's assistance, is credited with anticipating modern standards in the handling of archaeologically recovered objects.[14]

Li Qingzhao was already an accomplished scholar and writer of prose and poetry by the time of her marriage. She specialized in writing poetry in the *ci* genre, which had become the characteristic form of poetry during the Song. Unlike the then standard regulated verse *(shi)* that was written in lines of even length, the intricate prosody of *ci*, in long and short lines, required special sensitivity to musical effects. *Ci* means "song lyrics," and the melodic patterns to which they were written demanded not only adherence to the rhythm of the lines but also attention to the phonic qualities of the words. She became one of this poetic mode's important critics, helping to distinguish its generic qualities from those of regulated verse and to establish *ci* as a distinct genre. When Zhao as a government official had to travel away from home, Li wrote poems to him whose quality he struggled to match, usually unsuccessfully, in the poems he sent back in reply. When they were at home together, whether in Kaifeng or at his family home in Shandong, or at other places in Shandong where he served in local government, they spent days and nights working together on scholarly studies, playing literary games, laughing and joking, enjoying the intimate pleasures of two perfectly matched persons sharing an ideal life. When his father died in 1107, Zhao returned home to observe the mandatory twenty-seven-month mourning period, then extended it to ten years of retirement before resuming his officeholding. He was not intent on having a distinguished official career; literature and scholarship meant more to him.

That way of life changed suddenly. The couple were in Shandong when Emperor Huizong abdicated in January 1126, leaving his heir to face the invading Jurchens. Zhao Mingchen's family home was burned by the invaders; they lost much of their collection of antiquities and twelve rooms filled with books, though they still had many cartloads of books and antiquities to move south across the Yangzi, under difficult conditions, as the enemy armies roamed up and down across all of North China. They were separated, both fleeing to the South, he assigned to new posts there and she in the company of relatives trying to move their most valued possessions to safety. In that confusion lasting for more than a year, they lost the bulk of their remaining treasures and their personal belongings to plundering troops or to bandits. In 1128 Zhao was assigned to Nanjing, where he fell ill. Li, also ill, managed to reach Nanjing late in 1128, but Zhao died there, of malaria, in 1129. Li was now a childless widow, her relatives likewise impoverished and less than generous with her. She felt herself a stranger wandering desolately through a China she did not recognize. Finally she settled with her brother's family at Jinhua in northern Zhejiang. She lived on there into her early seventies.[15]

She continued to write poems, but now they were melancholy lyrics of pained memories and loss. Her poems nonetheless continued to display her daring use of words, surprisingly keen observations, unexpected turns of thought, and matchless artistry. She worked on an improved edition of her husband's *Record of Inscriptions* for which she wrote a postface in which she nostalgically recalled their happier days and their shared joys in producing the book. Most of her literary works are lost; there remain only ten or a dozen prose essays and poems in regulated verse, and sixty or seventy *ci* lyrics, perhaps a fifth of her total production, but the latter in particular are enough to display her genius. She is one of the great poets of the Song, and usually is considered the finest woman poet of Song and later times.[16]

Shi Cai

The old Chinese ideal of the poor boy who by dint of hard study and virtue becomes a high official is a topos of Chinese civilization, one realized frequently enough to have some credibility, enough to drive countless parents and inspire countless sons. Shi Cai (d. 1162) of Mingzhou (modern Ningbo in northern Zhejiang) was the first to become an official in his poor family, one that was to grow spectacularly successful thereafter. His is not quite the story of a barefoot herd boy who memorized a borrowed copy of the *Analects* while riding the family water buffalo in the fields, but his is nonetheless a remarkable enough story. In it we see another aspect of elite life in Song China.[17]

The story of Shi Cai properly begins with his remarkable grandmother, who at an early age was left a widow with one young daughter and a son born a few months after his father's death. Her husband had been a minor clerk in the prefectural magistracy, a very humble position and one not accorded respect; magistracy clerks often were hated exploiters of the common people, and this one, moreover, had died as the result of a brawl. The young widow was nevertheless a hardworking seamstress, ambitious for her children. She possessed enough basic literacy to start her son's education, then turned him over to a friend of his late father's, a schoolmaster who helped him with further studies. This son became a model youth, known for his devotion to his mother and his hard work. We are not sure how he lived or what occupation he followed, but he gained some standing in the town. At the age of about fifty, with five young sons and perhaps other children as well, he was nominated for appointment to the local school, where he could prepare for further advancement to the National Academy under the category of "men exemplifying the eight virtues of conduct," of which filial piety was deemed the most important. He refused the appointment on grounds of filial responsibility, saying he had a higher duty to care for his old mother. The virtue he accumulated thereby in the eyes of the community probably helped his two older sons to be approved for admission to the prefectural Confucian academy. Just in those years, under Emperor Huizong's short-lived reform of the school system, entrance into the prefectural school was the direct route to appointment to the National Academy and access to the *jinshi* examination. Shi Cai, the second son, entered the academy and won his *jinshi* degree in 1118. The topos of the deserving poor boy (here, a middle-aged man) of great virtue is in this case represented by Shi Zhao, Shi Cai's father. In justice, he should be seen as the progenitor of the eminent Shi family of later generations. His son and his grandchildren made the great leap from commoner status into the official elite without family wealth or influential relatives, aided somewhat by the new emphasis on broader recruitment through the government school system, but in large part because Shi Zhao and his devoted mother provided a family atmosphere that prepared for their children's success.

Shi Cai, by contrast, the first man in the family's history to become a *jinshi* and to hold official appointment, is a historical figure of tarnished repute. After becoming an official in 1118, he was appointed to local government posts in the South so was not directly involved in the collapse of the capital in 1127 and the disorderly withdrawal of the government to Hangzhou. After observing the required period of mourning for the death of his father in 1130, he again served in local government posts near the capital and may have spent some years out of office. In the early 1150s Shi Cai was recommended for appointment at the court, then under the total domination of the notorious all-powerful Chief Councillor Qin Gui (see Chapter 13, Section II). The details of his three years at the court, during which he rose quickly to the high-ranking post of Assistant Chief Councillor, have been told elsewhere.[18] It is enough here to say that he collaborated with Qin to rise in rank, then quickly was abandoned by Qin, who arranged to have him charged with improprieties and dismissed. He was seen as an opportunist under conditions that were held to be dishonorable. He returned home to live out his remaining seven or eight years, and the family's attention was turned to his nephew Shi Hao (1106–1194), whose career mainly at the capital earned him honor and respect.

Shi Hao was tutor to the heir apparent (later the Emperor Xiaozong) and twice held the top post in the bureaucracy, that of Chief Councillor. Subsequent generations of the Shi family flourished. In large part through imperial beneficence, they acquired great wealth, enabling them to produce many sons (because rich men could afford to keep secondary wives), all of whom could be educated for the examinations. A remarkable number of them earned the *jinshi* degree and held high positions. There is no more spectacular story of continued bureaucratic success in all of Song history. Despite the success of the Shi clan and a few others in producing large numbers of officials through several generations, it has been well argued that their success does not signify "entrenchment of a hereditary elite," because the element of competition meant that no family or clan could be sure of maintaining its official elite status. Although rank and wealth gave such families advantages in continuing to hold wealth and prestige, "the Sung [Song] civil service . . . functioned as a meritocracy."[19]

The civil service examinations stressed knowledge of the classical tradition and the ability to compose prose essays and poetry. The examinations were difficult. Even the best-tutored and most favored son of an elite family had to display his own genuine ability to become a *jinshi,* and the Shi clan became famous for producing men who could pass those examinations. Many Shi sons to be sure could achieve official status through the route of "protection," but even they had to pass qualifying examinations, and then were restricted to lower ranks and modest appointments. It is nonetheless surprising that many of the Shi did not depend on that less favored route to office but earned their degrees in the mainstream. In its century and a half of eminence, between 1118 and 1265, the family produced no fewer than twenty-six *jinshi,* in addition to almost twice that many who held office at lower ranks, an astounding record. Among all of those high and mid-level officials, however, there were no published scholars, no thinkers of importance in intellectual history, no men or women noted for their literary or artistic skills. They were politicians. In an elite society in which the attributes of cultivation and learning were expected to be universal, they could of course perform acceptably, but none of them appears to have been drawn to concerns other than officeholding and developing the family's mundane interests.

It is likely that the Shi family in that respect represents a large portion of the official elite. Perhaps most bureaucrats were men who in their youth worked hard to prove their qualifications for official status, and gaining that, filled conventional roles while looking to office and rank to sustain their privileged position in society. We like to think of the Confucian scholar-officials as the bearers of the high culture at its most creative and original, intellectuals who lived the life of the mind. But should it surprise us to find that many of those highly selected "scholar-officials" with all their polished ways were simply bureaucrats, men whose lives and those of most of their family members were bounded by the focus on their careers?

After achieving eminence, the Shi clan produced genealogies, claimed distinguished forebears, and performed elaborate rites venerating their ancestors. In those ways they met the expectations of the society with regard to elite patterns. Unlike many clans of the time, however, the Shi appear never to have become formally organized into a lineage association with jointly owned communal property or charitable estates to care for their poorer relatives and to make sure bright young sons could receive the best education. Under the special conditions of the succeeding Mongol Yuan dynasty, when access to office greatly changed, their still rich descendants were not prepared to weather that change in social patterns; their wealth dwindled, and they quickly faded from prominence.

III. CONFUCIAN THINKERS

The detailed study of the Shi clan drawn upon here reminds us that Song China's bureaucrats, despite their uniformly high educational level, were not all intellectuals living the life of the mind. In fact, the Southern Song's leading thinkers were almost all men who shared the aspiring bureaucrats' education and passed through the same stages of advance into public life. They too were "scholar-officials," as we usually designate the official elite.

Later imperial China came close to developing a "single-career" elite; we can find only a few variants among upper-stratum career choices. At that level all careers were truly dominated by one prestigious pattern, that of scholar-officialdom. That public career brought the largest material and psychological rewards and drew the able, the ambitious, and the merely dutiful to strive for its pattern of success. The thinkers granted leading importance in Song intellectual history virtually all come within that pattern. All were men who had received the education necessary to sit for the examinations, and in the vast majority of cases they went on to earn the *jinshi* degree. Some to be sure accepted the alternate course of gaining official status through "protection" extended to relatives of high officials. The occasional few of particularly independent mentality expressed disillusionment with the examination system and refused to submit to it, proudly remaining *bu yi* (dressed in common cloth), or "commoners." Even those men, however, did not always escape the mentality of officialdom. In some well-known cases of that kind, they still submitted memorials, or policy proposals, advising the emperor, accepted office through direct imperial appointment, or were flattered by marginal appointments as "classics lecturers" or "advisers" to the throne, and in other ways spent their lives and a good share of their energies within the orbit of officialdom, if not formally part of it.

The striking unity of the Chinese elite stemmed not from their economic status, for they represented a broad spectrum ranging from poor scholar or humble teacher to rich Chief Councillor. What they all shared was the content and the tone of their humanistic education. That gave them all command of the learning through which ultimate intellectual authority was derived, and an underlying awareness of shared values, even though the manner in which they realized those values might vary widely.

The intellectual elite of scholars, philosophers, social and political thinkers, along with the more ordinary officials, grappled throughout the Song period with the reformulation of Confucian principles taking shape against the background of Buddhist and Daoist influences.[20] The process of creating a multifaceted Neo-Confucianism continued throughout Southern Song. What was becoming the central current in Neo-Confucian thought, the Lixue of Northern Song times, still had its Confucian and its non-Confucian opponents, whether intellectual or political. If we accept that the process of its development was completed in the life and work of Zhu Xi (1130–1200), it was some decades after his death before that fact came to be generally accepted.

Throughout the Song the Confucian thinkers continued to debate fundamental issues among themselves. Much of the debate turned on their searching
examination of classical texts and their often systematic and thoroughgoing
philological and exegetical commentaries. Because those same texts were also
the basis of the education shared by all the official elite, and because many
of the leading Confucian thinkers also had careers in office, the important
thinkers were well within the "real world" of their time.

To summarize the intellectual scene in briefest fashion, we may distinguish
three principal groups of thinkers representing three intellectual positions
within the large arena of Confucian thought. The most convenient designations for the three are the utilitarians, the idealists, and the rationalists. But
as I have noted previously, these terms have somewhat different connotations
in Chinese thought from those we associate with the same words in the West
(see Chapter 6, Section VI).

Southern Song Utilitarian Thinkers

The utilitarian stance within Neo-Confucian thought stressed the nature of
political authority and the uses of government to benefit the people. The Chinese term for this school of thought, *gong li,* here translated "utilitarian,"
does not imply the subordination of ethical norms to the goal of benefit and
profit (as the word may imply in other contexts); it indicated the need for a
strong state that could "accomplish" *(gong)* its governing ends to bring real
"benefits" *(li)* to the people.[21] A benevolent social order, safety from external
threats, and material well-being at all levels in society are the practical benefits
it sought. In recent decades it has become politically correct in China to label
such social thinking "materialist" (i.e., "good" by Marxist criteria), or, in
Chinese historical terms, "Legalist," a comparison with the statism of the
ancient Legalist *(fa jia)* school of thought that triumphed in the unification
of the Chinese world under the brief Qin dynasty late in the third century
B.C.E. Although their intent is to praise, it is more accurate to ignore such
anachronistic interpretations; the content of Song period *gong li* thought is
solidly Confucian, directly derived from the thought of Mencius, the early
figure second only to Confucius in defining Confucianism. The touchstone of
Song utilitarian thought is the pronouncement in the *Mencius* that the people
are the most important element, the state subordinate in value to them, and
the ruler unimportant. Mencius went on to say that under the best circumstances, "He who gains the support of all the ordinary village people will [and
should] become the ruler."[22] The common people will support a benevolent
government; that alone gives it legitimacy. In that vein, the utilitarian thinkers
placed great stress on practical effectiveness in statecraft; theirs was but one
Confucian response to the ethical demand that government exists to benefit
the people.

In the twelfth century, that "utilitarian" Confucian stance was heir to the
activist political reform tradition of Northern Song, especially the important
attempts at institutional reforms of Fan Zhongyan (active in the 1040s) and

Wang Anshi (active in the 1070s). Like those predecessors, the Southern Song utilitarian thinkers also were strongly in favor of abandoning the peaceful accommodation with the Jurchens and their Jin dynasty, even to make war if necessary to regain occupied North China. Not all exponents of war under successive Southern Song rulers (e.g., Han Tuozhou in 1206) were thinkers of this school, but all of the half-dozen or more important Southern Song utilitarian thinkers opposed the peace policy. Two of those figures can represent for us this interesting school of thought.

Chen Liang (1143–1194) was known for his brilliance even as a child. He loved to discuss military strategy in history, and as he matured he was active in a circle of politically minded young scholars preparing for the examinations. Before sitting for the highest-level examinations, he submitted memorials to the throne. In 1162, just as Emperor Xiaozong came to the throne and, to the delight of court and officialdom, the revision of the peace treaty was settled, Chen Liang submitted a memorial attacking the peace settlement as dangerous and unwise. It startled the new emperor, unexpectedly confirming his own unspoken reservations. Some years later, still not having passed the *jinshi* examinations, Chen went to the capital and submitted two more such memorials, one calling for the recovery of the North and the other analyzing current political conditions. Again Emperor Xiaozong was moved by his ideas and wanted to give Chen a direct appointment to office. According to his biography in the *Song History,* Chen responded: "My purpose is to solidify the basis of our dynasty's strength for hundreds of years. Would I do this just to win an office?" He indignantly refused appointment and went home, where he continued to discuss politics and philosophy with a growing number of like-minded men of the learned elite.

Chen Liang's strong-willed eccentricity repeatedly got him into trouble. He was jailed on several occasions but always spared punishment when sympathetic officials appealed for the emperor's intervention. Frequently distracted by such activities, he did not get around to sitting for the triennial examinations until 1193, when at age fifty he placed first. He was assigned a position in local government but died early the next year before assuming office. Chen left collected writings in thirty chapters.

The essential thrust of Chen Liang's thought is that politics and philosophy must accept the social realities. They must describe the less than ideal men, governments, and situations as they really are and not talk vacuously about sage rulers and golden ages of the past. Although he derived his sense of political authority from the benign populism of Mencius, in other contexts he derided the vague idealism of Mencius and sought more practical terms for describing the real problems in administering government at the level of everyday human affairs. The Neo-Confucian Lixue theorists hated his unconventional behavior and his sharp criticisms of their high-flown explorations of "the nature of things"; some were quite willing to declare him a danger to society. His call for practical political skills and problem-solving human abilities nonetheless aroused a following within the elite.

Chen Liang's criticisms of Song government turned on two main issues.

First, he saw dangers in the excessive centralization that represented the Song overcorrection of Tang political weakness. He wanted to give greater discretionary authority to regional and local governing in both civil and military fields of responsibility. Second, he criticized the sense of false security encouraged by the elaborate treaty arrangements with the Jin dynasty, feeling that the earlier arrangements between Northern Song and the Liao had left China exposed to the Jin invasions. He both resented the humiliation of Chinese compromise and feared the consequences, inherent in that posture, of weakening civilization's defenses. Both were real issues in the minds of many among the Song elite, and he framed his arguments forcefully in ways that drew sustained attention to them.[23]

Ye Shi (1150–1223) came from a background very similar to Chen Liang's; like Chen, as a young man he displayed great talent for learning, and also shared Chen's interest in military strategy among the practical needs of the state. His intellectual orientations within Neo-Confucianism also were, like Chen Liang's, derived from Mencius, whose stress on benevolent government he fully adopted. Like Chen Liang, he too has been (favorably) mislabeled a Legalist by present-day writers in China under pressure to interpret China's past according to modern ideological demands. Unlike Chen, Ye Shi sat for the examinations in the normal pattern, received his *jinshi* degree at age twenty-eight, and received his first appointment to an office in local government. Through long years of service he eventually reached high regional and court positions.

Ye Shi has a more important place in Song intellectual history than any of the other Southern Song utilitarians because he lived longer and so was able to interact more significantly with other thinkers and officials, and he left more voluminous writings in a variety of fields. In those writings all the strands of Song utilitarian thought are brought together in a conspectus of the field, including broad-ranging critiques of all the sages of the past and of ideas current in intellectual life of his time.

Like all those of the elite who prepared for careers by mastering the ten or twelve basic Confucian classics, Ye Shi had to come to terms with that corpus of antique writings, to determine what their meaning for Song dynasty thinkers should be. He shared the practical-minded mode of all the utilitarians: in his view, the classics contain sound observations of human affairs in relation to the natural world and should not be studied for abstract or remote ideas. They offer realistic encouragement to undertake actions that will be constructive and beneficial. It was clear in his mind that throughout history, mankind's political performance had declined as the focus of thought became ever more abstract; it was under too strong an influence from thinkers who diverted attention away from real life to vast notions and ultimate explanations. Metaphysical speculation was to him a largely useless pursuit. He could debate the leading exponents of the other schools of thought on their ground, but he saw no great point in such debate except to turn attention toward more relevant concerns.

In political thought he focused on how the agencies and institutions of government actually functioned. He believed in strong government and wanted it to be effective in accomplishing all its tasks down to the level of villages and families, where lay his Confucian sense of ethical responsibility to better ordinary lives. Success in achieving that goal, he felt, depended on the ruler's being strong enough in his own capacities, and in the institutionalization of his authority, so that his governing produced results. When that capacity to employ power directly was fragmented in its misuse by courtiers, consort clan members, generals, and unworthy local and regional officials, or worst of all by sharing it with court eunuchs and sycophants, social upheaval and ultimate disaster were sure to ensue. That view of the ruler's authority can be traced to the early Confucian thinker Xunzi (ca. 298–238 B.C.E.) but also has echoes in the thought of the early Legalists. Nevertheless, as with Xunzi, Ye Shi's basic commitment to ethics and to the well-being of the ordinary people kept him well within the Confucian fold.

Ye Shi's greatest contributions to political thought lie in his acute attention to the way institutions function and in his strong analyses of historical examples in making judgments on institutional successes and failures. He was perceptively critical of government's faults. He examined historical failings ranging all the way from the overcentralization and abuse of power in the Legalist state of Qin, on through all the great ages of Han to the Tang and into the time of his own Song dynasty. He hoped to turn Confucian political thought away from superficial complaints about the moral failings of government toward more concrete analyses of all governing institutions. Ye Shi and the other critical-minded utilitarian thinkers of the Southern Song, by drawing on the strengths of Song historical studies, their own strong commitment to making government better serve the ordinary people's needs, and their realistic philosophical stance, came close to inaugurating a new movement in statecraft thinking. They accomplished less than that; leaders of other trends in Neo-Confucian thought were absorbed in other issues, and their concerns ultimately prevailed.[24]

Neo-Confucian Idealists and Rationalists

It is easy to discuss the so-called utilitarian school thinkers of the Song because their hardheaded and practical ideas about political and social issues are readily comprehensible across cultural boundaries. To say as much nonetheless somewhat oversimplifies the matter. They shared the intellectual milieu of the entire Song elite of education and public life. But that was a complex milieu in which Buddhist, Daoist, and Confucian ideas intermingled, new cosmology and metaphysics were emerging, and a new ground was prepared from which social and political thought could emerge.[25] The strong Chan (Zen) Buddhist component of the Song consciousness was that of a transformed Buddhism marked by a turn toward involvement in the secular world; in ironic contrast, the Confucian thinkers, consciously and unconsciously, were pulled toward acceptance of Buddhist definitions of mind and of transcendental concerns. Daoist philosophical texts, in conjunction with the ancient *Book of Changes (Yi Jing),* exerted a strong influence on the earlier northern Neo-Confucianists Zhou Dunyi and Shao Yong[26] but thereafter, despite official patronage by the Song emperors, Daoism contributed less to the mix of ideas until the end of Song. Then it was the new Daoist sectarian movements which drew large followings, mostly at sub-elite levels.

From the hindsight of history the Chinese have delineated "main lines" of development in the fields of Neo-Confucian thought that accorded with their later sense of what was most important, and we in the West have accepted much of that simplification. In fact, Song Neo-Confucian thought was a mixed and changing scene in which early Qing historians of Confucianism have been able to identify and record some eighty or more "coteries of think-ers," each with a dozen to a hundred identifiable participants along with sum-maries of their leading ideas.[27] If nothing else, that portrayal displays the rich-ness and volume of Song period intellectual life.

When attention is turned beyond the schools of utilitarian thinkers, it becomes possible to designate most of the other Confucians as thinkers who tended either toward the idealist School of Mind or toward the rationalist School of Principle. The former, emphasizing the mind as the ultimate reality and seeking to verify truth intuitively by turning the mind inward upon itself, is called Xinxue, "the learning of the mind"; because the Chinese regarded the *xin* (heart) as a seat of the knowing capacity and used the word to mean "the mind." The influence of Buddhist mental disciplines is most obvious in that emphasis on the mind, but Song and later Xinxue is solidly Confucian in its ethical grounding. The rationalist tendency, by contrast, is called Lixue, "the learning of principle," because it accepts *li* (principle, Principle of Nature, reason, in various explanations of this word's meanings) as the expla-nation of all phenomena.[28] *Li* was, moreover, one with Dao, used here in its Confucian sense of the great moral Way. In that identification of principle with the moral sense of Dao, principle not only makes things what they are but also defines the ethical norms for all human behavior.

These concepts go back to the beginnings of Neo-Confucianism in the Northern Song, especially to the brothers Cheng Hao and Cheng Yi, whose differing emphases left room for subsequent Neo-Confucian thinkers to diverge along epistemological grounds: Is truth verified by subjectively intu-itive or by objectively rationalistic means? Should we approach it intuitively or deductively? Granted those disputes about *how,* the two sides might still agree on *what* they knew, and the Cheng brothers did in fact agree on most things. The concept of *li,* or principle, was accepted by both kinds of thinkers, as were most of the values of the long Confucian tradition (see Chapter 6, Section VI).

With all their shared excitement about the rediscovered Confucian values, it was the divergence into the two schools, the School of Mind (Xinxue) and the School of Reason (Lixue), supported by two quite different ways of know-ing, that became the major dividing line in Song Confucian thought. This basic difference in thought has counterparts in earlier Chinese intellectual history, for example, in early Daoist mysticism versus early Confucian rationalism, especially that of Xun Zi. In fact, this pattern has appeared in many times and places. It finds loose parallels in Aristotelians versus Neoplatonists, Thomists versus Augustinians, Sunni Muslims versus Sufis, Berkeley versus Locke, and in many other cases in human history. Yet cultural variables also are evident; in the case of China, the competition between two quite different ways of understanding played itself out in the Chinese cultural world. That world of thought lacked a revealed religious basis for ethics as for cosmology, and in other equally important ways it was different from the worlds of thought in which the parallel epistemological problems emerged elsewhere.

As far as later Confucianism is concerned, it was in the Song that the ground of most later philosophical speculation was defined and clarified. I cannot do full justice to Neo-Confucianism's many-sided development here, but many of the Song philosophers can be read in translations and read about in critical studies. Here I can only mention Lu Xiangshan as the most influential spokesman for the idealist School of Mind. As for the rationalist thinker Zhu Xi, because of his vast significance for all later Chinese civilization, he must be discussed somewhat more fully. We have already encountered him in the realm of politics, in the political crisis engendered by Han Tuozhou at the end of the twelfth century (see Chapter 13, Section III).

Lu Xiangshan

Lu Xiangshan (formal name Lu Jiuyuan, 1139–1191) became the principal spokesman for the idealist School of Mind that developed in the Southern Song. He came from a well-to-do family of local landholders in Jiangxi. Both of his parents were very well educated. Several of his five brothers became officials and his associates in philosophy. He became a *jinshi* at age thirty-three and served long and conscientiously in office, but he found the experience of teaching his Confucian message directly to all kinds of people most congenial. Throughout his career he gave public talks on philosophical subjects, drawing large audiences. He spoke simply and directly before audiences of common people, but his recorded debates with the eminent Zhu Xi and with others reveal a subtle and profound mind.

The ideas of the School of Mind had great appeal for many people. Its adherents believed that in denying the existence of significant truths other than what one gains through his or her own subjective awareness, one becomes one's own authority on what is right and wrong, true and false. If that suggests the spiritual autonomy and mental discipline of Chan Buddhism, Lu was nonetheless strongly opposed to Buddhism, in his mind a "selfish doctrine" incompatible with Confucian ethical responsibility. His most important ideas were summarized by himself in two sentences: "The universe is my mind and my mind is the universe," and "The mind and universal principle [*li*] are one."[29] "Universal principle" in his thinking was of course moral principle. The Confucian rationalist thinkers were nonetheless suspicious of Lu's doctrine of intuitive knowledge, seeing that it could undermine all authority in thought, in ethics, and also in social behavior, and not just provide the individual with an unassailable philosophical position. Their differences, however, did not lead to fierce antagonisms in Song times; the two sides were insistent on the superiority of their own positions, but their relations were in general marked by mutual respect and considerable interaction.

Lu Xiangshan had many followers, but his writings were not extensive or systematic and could not compete in influence with those of Zhu Xi and his far more numerous followers. Yet he kept alive in the consciousness of Neo-Confucians the awareness of an alternative to Neo-Confucian rationalism, and that "minor mode" of thought was always present. It reemerged and flourished in Ming times in the thought of Wang Yangming (1472–1529; see Chapter 26, Section VI). In the intellectual history of Song through Qing times, the Lu-Wang idealist school is contrasted with the Cheng-Zhu or rationalist "major mode" in Song thought as the enduring complementary currents of Neo-Confucianism.

Zhu Xi and the "Completion of Neo-Confucianism"

Zhu Xi (1130–1200) is often spoken of as the most influential figure in Chinese intellectual history after Confucius himself;[30] this clearly implies that his impact on Chinese civilization in general also has been profound. The latter implication is based on the character of the scholar elite and their functional relationship to the entire society, especially as that relationship developed in Song and later times. In this chapter I have explored the character of the Song elite, and the remainder of this volume will in many places point to the functional relationship between elite and society. For those reasons we must attempt to come to terms with Zhu Xi's place in Chinese history, although it is not possible to set forth his philosophical ideas in appropriate detail.

Zhu Xi is of course an extraordinary figure, yet at the same time he also is in many ways a typical member of the Song elite. His grandfather was a poor scholar who did not seek advancement through the civil service examinations but carried on a family tradition of leading an exemplary life. He urged his sons to follow that example, saying, "We have accumulated virtue as Confucian scholars for five generations; among our descendants there will surely be one who achieves greatness. You all must exhort one another and conduct yourselves properly and not allow our ancestral heritage to fall by the wayside."[31] His father, Zhu Song, received his *jinshi* degree in 1118, when he was twenty-one years old, near the end of Northern Song, and held office at the capital. After the removal of the capital to the South, he was among a group of court officials who strongly opposed Qin Gui and the peace settlement of 1141 with the Jin dynasty. Qin was enraged and had Zhu Song transferred to a minor post in the provinces, where he soon died. Zhu Xi, his youngest son, was only thirteen when the elder Zhu died, but he was carefully reared by his mother, a model of Confucian propriety, who oversaw her brilliant son's education. Zhu Xi passed the *jinshi* examinations at age eighteen and was immediately posted to a minor position in a county government in Fujian. For various personal reasons he repeatedly refused higher appointments offered to him, especially those at court. He held office in local government positions for a total of only nine years. In the growing crisis at court in 1195 and 1196, when Han Tuozhou was consolidating his hold on supreme power there, Zhu's only court office lasted less than two months before his Confucian teachings were branded "false learning" and he was impeached and driven from office along with his sponsor and many high officials.[32] He died four years later, in 1200, still under a cloud that was not lifted until his complete exoneration and posthumous restoration to official rank and the award of honors in 1202 and thereafter.

Zhu came from a poor family and remained poor throughout his life, always dependent on support received from sponsors and friends as well as loyal students who flocked to his home to receive instruction. Possessing the *jinshi* degree and holding office did not enrich him or his dependents. He appears to have been survived only by his youngest son, Zhu Zai, who gained office through his father's merit and served at court, but not in a high position, and the family slipped into obscurity after that. The great eminence that Zhu Xi's grandfather had predicted must come to one in the family was fully realized in the extraordinary grandson who, by the standards of the elite, was thereafter to be the most honored figure in later Chinese history.

Does he deserve that eminence? By modern standards he may be found to have produced a philosophical system lacking intrinsic interest for thinkers today. Moreover, in the minds of many impatient modernizers in the present century, he has been roundly criticized as the prime source of backward forces in society. Especially under the Communist government since 1949, he has been denigrated at best, and at worst vilified as the most reactionary of Chinese thinkers. Much of China's failure to retain its leading role as one of the world's most advanced civilizations in later centuries has been blamed on him, and an honored name for his school of thought, Daoxue, "The Learning of the Great Way,"[33] came eventually to be used cynically; by the eighteenth century it appears in the new satirical fiction as a term of ridicule, and in the twentieth century it came to be used to describe someone stiffly proper, unthinking, and probably hypocritical.

That Zhu Xi has been the focus of so much anger and blame serves to corroborate his great importance. The modern criticisms do not state that Zhu Xi's place in history has been exaggerated, only that its consequences must be regretted. We must try to see why he has been held responsible for so much.

We may start with Zhu Xi's place in philosophy. The Neo-Confucian movement was still unformed in the mid-twelfth century when Zhu Xi reached adulthood and began his official career, a century after the vigorous flowering of cosmology in the eleventh century that got it started. Zhu put the strong stamp of his mind on the intellectual field. He selected the elements in that world of thought that could be fitted together into a consistent system meeting his philosophical requirements. The ideas all had to have a textual basis in the Confucian canon, or, if they were extraneous elements drawn into the Confucian sphere by the eleventh-century masters, their import had to be credibly explained by reference to the canon. Just as some of those elements were originally Buddhist or Daoist, so too was Zhu Xi himself apparently unaware of the extent to which his philosophical horizons had been broadened by Buddhist thought. Despite that fact, it was his exhaustive command of the Confucian textual bases for his arguments that lent them great force. He was convincing.[34]

The leading ideas of Neo-Confucianism, to be sure, came from his predecessors, most of all from Cheng Yi, but he built from them a coherent structure. He reaffirmed the ancient Chinese cosmological system shared by all the indigenous schools of thought, positing an organismic, self-generating cosmos. Zhu Xi fused into it a powerful sense of Confucian ethics and projected a vision of a new ontology. He was at his most inventive in imposing on that system the concept of the Supreme Ultimate (Taiji), drawn from Daoism but by way of the Northern Song Neo-Confucian cosmologist Zhou Dunyi. That borrowed feature functioned to mold the entire system; by identifying the Supreme Ultimate with Principle *(li)*, he found a satisfying way of linking all the parts into one whole having concreteness (to combat the Buddhist concept of emptiness) and process (to explain mankind's place in the moral cosmos). In the ever-renewing conditions of all existence he postulated a moral, benevolent process; to accomplish that, he assigned the role of its creative, harmonious, generative element to Benevolence (or humaneness, *ren*). That was the long-standing prime virtue of the Confucian system; he explained it in terms that made the abstract force of *ren,* for which the word "benevolence" is an inadequate translation, responsible for all states of being, and the force which imparts mankind's basic nature. An optimistic Confucian in the Mencian tradition, he too affirmed that the universe is good and that man's nature is to be and do good.[35]

Zhu Xi's new configuration of Neo-Confucian and other elements was given authority by his extraordinary command of classical learning. Not surprisingly, however, in view of the Chinese emphasis on history, he also provided the system with a supporting account of how its philosophical content had been transmitted from antiquity through Confucius and other early figures to the great Northern Song philosophers acknowledged by him as his masters. He called that the "Dao Tong," the "Transmission of the Way." This schematized explanation of Neo-Confucian rationalism's background convincingly claimed for his new system a venerable line of development, thereby imparting to it the authority that in the Chinese cultural setting could be sustained only by giving it a history.

Finally, Zhu Xi provided his great synthesis with a pedagogical underpinning to ensure that the future entrants into China's educated elite would grow up prepared to live, think, and make judgments within the Lixue system of thought. He grouped together four books: the *Analects* of Confucius, the *Mencius,* and two chapters called *The Great Learning (Daxue)* and *The Doctrine of the Mean (Zhongyong),* taken from the Han period compilation known as the *Book of Rites (Li ji).* These four works constituted a corpus of basic educational texts; he then provided them with interpretive commentary drawn from his meticulous textual scholarship, reinforced by his philosophical and historical reasoning. They became *The Four Books,* the foundation of Chinese education thereafter. To that basic set of texts he and persons working with him added new editions with exegetical commentaries for most of the other nine Confucian classics. He also wrote voluminously on related subjects. Presented in this way, the system was powerful and complete. No other school of thought or philosophical system could compare with it.

His pedagogical system soon dominated education. Recognizing that fact, in 1313, a little more than a century after Zhu Xi's death in 1200, his editings of the Confucian classics were officially designated the standard for the civil service examinations; they remained so through successive dynasties and successive eras of cultural growth, until the abolition of the civil service examinations in 1905. That his system of learning should become primarily identified with the pursuit of success in the examination system is a great irony; his purpose was to teach people how to enlarge their minds and their humanity through study of the classics, and he was bitterly discouraged by trends becoming evident in his time toward the debasement of learning as a mere device for gaining status and wealth.[36]

Yet that is not all of Zhu Xi. He left over 300 chapters of writings, including his collected literary works in 140 chapters and the *Classified Collection of Conversations (Zhu Zi Yu Lei),* also in 140 chapters.[37] His collected literary works, in the manner of Song and later scholar-officials' collected writings, contain almost a thousand poems in many genres; memorials, petitions, and other official writings that were by-products of officeholding; hundreds of letters, many on philosophical or scholarly subjects; a wide range of miscellaneous writings, mostly on learned subjects; prefaces and other occasional writings; ritual texts such as funerary inscriptions and the like; and biographies. The other major work, his "conversations" *(Yu Lei),* is didactic and philosophical. It is the principal record of his exchanges with his students and followers, and with thinkers within and outside his philosophical following.

He also prepared, or had prepared under his supervision, a small book that has exerted great influence on the life of Chinese society. It is his manual of ritual practices of the family, called *Family Rituals (Jia li).*[38] It told elite families how to conduct the rituals of capping (for boys at their entrance into adulthood, usually in their late teens), marriage, funerals, and regular ceremonies to venerate one's ancestors. It was a matter of great concern to many of the Neo-Confucian thinkers that elite ritual practices be standardized and performed properly to convey their underlying meaning; they were the nexus of Chinese religious observance as well as of family-centered social practices. Other manuals of this kind had appeared, but Zhu Xi's became the most widely adopted and came to exert the greatest influence on society. Later manuals, written for broader audiences beyond the elite, also based their simplified ritual instructions on Zhu Xi's manual, making its impact pervasive in an increasingly "Confucianized" society.

It also should be noted, however, that his views on the proper norms of family life were responsible in later times for increasingly restricting women to roles denying them many of the freedoms that women in Song elite society possessed. He did not think it proper for women to control financial resources or use them independently of their husband's family, to lead lives devoted to learning and literary or artistic pursuits, or to have independence of their husband and family in matters of marriage, divorce, and remarriage.[39] His ethical strictures not only limited women; they narrowed the range of action of all young people, male and female, inculcating a rigidification of deference patterns and notions of obedience that might be as painfully binding on young men as they were on young women; middle age brought a measure of relief to both, but more to men than to women. His personal responsibility for social patterns in later ages has been magnified, yet the historical impact of his family ethics was considerable, eventually contributing to features of Chinese life, particularly elite life, that draw the criticism of Chinese and non-Chinese observers today.

Another of Zhu Xi's most influential books is his *Reflections on Things at Hand (Jin si lu)*, a critical history of the development of Neo-Confucianism in the great age of his acknowledged predecessors, the Northern Song thinkers Zhou Dunyi, Zhang Zai, Cheng Hao, and his brother Cheng Yi; it is in the form of extensively quoted passages from their writings, classified by subject and provided with critical commentary.[40] It was compiled by Zhu Xi with another scholar, Lü Zuqian, a very learned thinker who visited him for ten days or more in 1175. They had corresponded for many years about scholarly matters. During this meeting they read together the important texts and discussed them. They decided to make up an anthology of the basic writings for the instruction of others, which has served as a high-level textbook for students of thought. This collaboration with Lü displays Zhu Xi's breadth of mind at his best, for Lü Zuqian was not at all a like-minded follower but was an important thinker in a competing school, an associate of Chen Liang and Ye Shi (discussed earlier among the utilitarian thinkers).[41] His occasional disagreements with Zhu Xi in the compilation of the *Reflections* clearly display their philosophical differences, but each respected the other's sincerity and specialized knowledge.

Political thought was not central to Zhu Xi's concerns; that must be held partly accountable for the weakness of Neo-Confucian political thought in the centuries during which his system of teaching and of thought prevailed. Despite that fact, he is not to be classed with the Neo-Confucians of the century before his time and most of those during the seven centuries following his death; their stale and formulaic calls for the restoration of institutions which they thought had prevailed in a remote past, coupled with varying degrees of indignation about the moral decline of later ages, constituted about all they had to offer on the topic of government.

Zhu Xi was different. We have seen that his father had opposed the infamous Chief Councillor Qin Gui and his promotion of the peace treaty in 1141, and was punished for his opposition. Like his father, Zhu Xi also favored the war party in court politics (even though he was denounced as the perpetrator of "false learning" by the war leader Han Tuozhou, and driven from his office at court in 1196). His objections to the peace settlement were precisely those of the utilitarians. He also was quite clear on the subject of the ancient "well-field system," the favorite nostrum of other rationalist as well as idealist thinkers for curing society's evils: the well-field pattern of equal landholdings and shared agricultural tasks may have worked in a distant past, he said, but he could see how time had brought changes to society that would render foolish any effort to reimpose it or other revered antique ideals. He had a much better sense of history and of cultural change than had most Confucian thinkers of his school, then and thereafter.[42] He also expressed approval of many of the reform ideas of Wang Anshi, and suggested reforms in the examinations, in local governing, and in making landholding more equitable; all those points echo the great reformer of the 1070s.

In short, despite his primary focus on ethics and metaphysics, Zhu Xi was not typical of Zhu Xi-ists in his own time, much less of those in later centuries, though he has been somewhat maligned by association with those contemporaries and with later followers. Even today it is difficult to get either his detractors or his admirers to see these other aspects of him, in large part because he himself devoted his energies mostly to other kinds of issues in thought.[43]

Above all, the consequences of Zhu Xi's life must include the completion of Neo-Confucian thought and the many facets of his work to establish that system. It endured, never excluding competing trends but lending stability and consistency to the focus of elite life. His impact is clearest on ethics as applied to family and community and in all personal relationships, and in the stress he placed on learning: a principal goal of all human life should be that of learning, not for the learner's social advancement as much as for individual growth. His "teachings of the Dao" brought a sharp definition to Neo-Confucianism, and that in turn contributed largely to the definition of Chinese life through the centuries of the later imperial era.

Yet it is precisely for that success that he is criticized in modern times. He stressed the importance of learning, and sought to solve problems by "the extension of knowledge through the investigation of things," in the words of *The Great Learning,* one of the *Four Books.* To him and his followers, however, the extension of knowledge meant the investigation of the principles of things, not the things themselves. Such investigation was more apt to generate ethical and metaphysical speculation than science. Despite his strong rationalism, it was abstract issues of human nature and moral obligations that drew his focus, a focus that displayed little of the realism of the utilitarian school's analysis of governing institutions. Most consequential is the fact that Zhu placed ethically and ritually correct interpersonal relations ahead of more objective analysis of problems. The no doubt unintended consequence of his social thought was to harden the status quo, close minds to unconventional ideas, and discourage those in government from taking any disruptive actions. There was no impulse toward the study of law, which might have induced the capacity to formulate "technical solutions" to public problems.[44] The brilliant Song dynasty was, in some respects, father to the moribund late Qing. However unfairly, Zhu Xi is often blamed for that.

IV. OTHER KINDS OF ELITE LIVES

So far I have concentrated on the scholar-official elite, but even within that sector there were men whose lives included other pursuits. For example, there were artists and calligraphers in great number. The history of art in the Song is largely one of artists who came from elite backgrounds, whether or not they themselves acquired the credentials to hold office. It was a magnificent age in art history. Song painters covered a spectrum from creators of vast Daoist-inspired landscapes in which tiny man moves insignificantly past huge mountains and rivers, to realistic portrayers of daily life, and those who expressed intimate and lyrical conceptions of idealized forms in nature. Most of the Song emperors, whether competent or disastrous as rulers, as well as some of their empresses, were themselves artists and calligraphers of some skill and were often lavish patrons and collectors.[45]

Readers familiar with European history may be surprised that so little is said about soldiers in the Song elite (or that of later ages). China, of course, lacked what was a fixture of other social systems, the professional soldier-aristocrat. Military officers, even most generals, were bureaucrats on a separate ladder of promotion, in careers that usually lacked prestige in society. The exceptions were civil bureaucrats who in the course of their government assignments took up military tasks, formed armies, and organized the defense of outposts, or even planned and led offensive campaigns. It was the expectation of Chinese society that military leadership lay, or should lie, within the generalized competence of the scholar-officials, and in earlier times there were many esteemed examples of that dual competence. One of the changes of Song elite life was that because status now depended so heavily on demonstrated competence in book learning, the elite became bookish and even effete, less apt than their predecessors to pursue physically vigorous lives.[46] During Northern Song we still find scholar-officials who wanted military command appointments and who participated in the life of the professional soldiers. In the Southern Song we find a few commoner soldiers of outstanding effectiveness, such as Yue Fei, but fewer scholar-generals of elite standing.

The elite also had close ties to the professional religious, usually learned Buddhist monks, but also Daoists. Chan (Zen) monks might seem to be the last persons in society to value book learning, the antithesis of their spontaneity and direct knowledge, but by Song times the monkhood, predominantly Chan, was full of men who were literati, as scholars on a par with the scholar-official elite with whom they associated. Many came from elite families. The official *Song History* contains a number of brief biographical notices on eminent Buddhist monks and Daoist practitioners.[47] Rulers patronized them, high officials sought their company, and members of the elite associated comfortably with them.

Medicine made great strides in Song, and was largely an activity within or on the edges of elite life. The ideal of the learned doctor of medicine had the greatest prestige; such doctors often were from elite families. Sometimes sons of elite families who had fallen on hard times by failing to achieve examination successes turned to studying the pharmacological texts, producing new works in *materia medica,* compiling prescriptions and treating patients at their own pharmacies. Even those dependent on the income from their medical practice might keep up a pretense of being altruists who treated the sick as a social responsibility; elite values carried over into sub-elite lives in this and many other ways. Medicine, or more properly pharmacology, had natural affinities for elite ideals, but its practitioners could degenerate into a caricature of the serious, learned doctor. Medical practice in fact existed on several levels; there were the highly learned doctors, and there were many varieties of their less creditable imitators. As in Renaissance Europe, medicine often became the profession of barbers; in both places the many quacks among them were ridiculed and derided, made into stock figures in popular entertainment.

As we approach the outer fringes of the true elite, we find others who aspired to that standing and took on some of the manners and lifestyles of the scholar-officials. A small number came from the military services and other professional specializations. Most important in numbers and in social significance were merchants. Life histories are frequently lacking, yet there undoubtedly were many merchants who attained affluence and could educate their sons for civil service, marry their well-dowered daughters into elite families, and themselves turn to landholding and bookish hobbies. In terms of numbers, the openness of the elite may in fact have been more evident in the entry into its ranks via the route of commerce than by the entry of poor village boys possessing great talent for study. Some in the scholar-official elite engaged in commerce somewhat covertly, fearing to lose face; many in the upper echelons of commerce aspired to achieve official status through their sons or nephews, thereby to gain great face. The trend that increasingly brought commercial wealth into the sphere of officialdom started in Song and continued past the end of the imperial era early in the twentieth century, but instead of bringing entrepreneurial vigor and brains into officialdom, it tended to deprive the commercial sector of initiative and resources, human and material. Crossing over required uneconomic employment of resources to a degree that might dilute the merchant's ability to acquire and deploy capital. Nonetheless, merchants in Song constituted an element of elite life, having a place in the elite of wealth, if less frequently in the higher scholar-official elite.

v. Some Generalizations about the Song Elite

China's elite in imperial times can be defined in different ways. Here the term is taken in a broadly descriptive sense to include, first, the households of all who had gained scholar-official status through the civil service examination system, which was both the route of greatest prestige and that which dominated the higher ranks of office, and second, the households of those who attained official status through "protection" *(yin)* granted to relatives, heirs, and in some cases non-kin protégés of higher-ranking officials, and to a small number of others granted official rank through the direct intervention of the emperor. "Official" *(guan)* status, the key element in both of these categories, was legally defined and was privileged; it applied to the male individual, but its benefits extended to his household and immediate family; it was not inherited, but through imperial grace, official status could be extended, in a diminished form, to the persons to whom "protection" was granted.[48] We may also include in the elite a third group of persons who did not gain "official" standing but in other respects resembled scholar-officials; that is, persons of comparable education who did not take or did not pass the official examinations but who lived like and associated with the scholar-official elite. In many cases they had recent forebears or other relatives who were scholar-officials, which allowed them to carry on in a reflected aura of honored status. The poorer among them might earn their living as teachers; many followed literary or artistic lives. A fourth and final elite group were the rich, including both large landholders and large-scale merchants. Many of these had sons or nephews or grandsons who would attempt the civil service examinations. They devoted a share of their wealth to imitating the lifestyles of scholar-officialdom and preparing their heirs to enter into that status.

The first and second categories define the official elite. They were not of one economic stratum, but most were at least moderately rich. The third and fourth categories were designated *bu yi*, or "commoners," along with the mass of the population, but they lived an elite lifestyle. The latter two groups overlapped somewhat, especially the large-scale landlords among them. To be a "farmer" was an honored status, and that is how they usually identified themselves, though their hands may never have touched a plow. To be a rich merchant was not an honored status per se, but the rich could deploy their assets in ways that brought them into proximity with others of the elite. It was quite standard for members of the first three categories to intermarry, and in Song times the daughters of men in the fourth category also began to be seen as desirable daughters-in-law by the heads of the other kinds of households. The principal element of unity among the four categories of the elite was that the demeanor, the manners, and the proclaimed ideals of the first category dominated the lifestyles of all the others. That was most evident in their adherence to ritual proprieties, a major focus of scholar-official concern in Song times.

There were two other elements of the elite in Song times, as in other periods of later imperial history. First, there were the lineal descendants of the imperial household and their rapidly multiplying offspring. The immediate lineal descendants of an emperor, male and female, bore titles in the nearer generations, but the Song allowed these titles to diminish in rank with each successive generation; in particular, the descendants of collateral lines held only nominal honorific designations, and though granted some preference in access to the examinations, they were little different from commoners. Still, they became a large group in Southern Song times, and because of their privileged access to the examinations, they formed a disproportionately large bloc of the Song *jinshi,* the holders of the highest civil service degree. They were an important element in the Song elite; even those without a degree or inherited rank might be deferred to with a measure of respect. Second, there were meritorious individuals, civil and military, to whom ranks in the nobility were awarded; these might be heritable, but on a declining scale as generations passed. Such individuals were not analogous to titled members of European nobility in numbers, in social position, or in political power. Confusion arises because we often translate their titles—*gong, hou, bo,* and the like—with the English terms "duke," "marquis," "earl," in that way giving the impression that China had an aristocracy like Europe's. It did not. These titles carried with them no fiefs and no rights to office or power, only stipends and a certain amount of prestige. They were nonfunctional and purely decorative. Nonetheless, the bearers of these awards in Song society were members of the elite.

The early Northern Song ideal of an elite broadly open to talent from all levels of society was no sooner realized in significant measure than its members as well as the state found ways of diminishing the ideal. The state found it useful to reward its most distinguished civil servants with the privilege of "protection" for their sons and others dependent on them; that preferment provided a supply of men who had knowledge of governing and of official norms, and it helped keep the families of the most powerful men in the society loyal to the dynasty. There was a tension between that state interest and the advantages the state gained from maintaining an open elite. Officials by "protection" were confined to the lower-ranking offices, and as the "protection" privilege came to be abused, the state increasingly restricted it.

As in all societies, Song families that had achieved prestige, wealth, and power found strategies for aiding their children to cling to those advantages. Young men had to be certified in their home communities as qualified for the entry-level civil service examinations, and that certification was dominated by the locally prominent families. Genuine competence still was required to pass the examinations. Nevertheless, while new talent could not be excluded entirely from admission to the examinations, the oversight function allowed the already privileged to narrow the competition for their kin. How far that strategy went in restoring the pre-Song pattern of a self-perpetuating elite stratum is a matter of dispute among those who study the issue, but it did not eliminate the factor of meritocracy in defining Song elite society, and significant upward mobility is evident in society at large.[49]

Other strategies for securing elite status within one's larger network of kin, that is, the clan or the lineage as those terms are commonly if loosely used by historians,[50] took on new forms under the new conditions of the Song dynasty. Organizations of various kinds were devised to strengthen lineages. The most important invention of Song times in this regard is the "charitable estate," the first of which was founded by Fan Zhongyan (989–1052).[51] The Fan clan's charitable estate consisted of property held jointly in the name of the clan to benefit all its members and give them a corporate base; it was the influential model for a pattern that grew in later Song times, and became the defining feature of clan organization in some regions of China.[52]

Other aspects of clan organization, with or without the feature of joint property, also developed in Song times. Rituals of reverence for ancestors were formalized and standardized; clan genealogies were prepared and often printed so that all members of the clan could possess them; ceremonies of veneration (sometimes called, and in fact sometimes practiced in ways making it "worship") at ancestral graves drew the members of a clan together at least once a year and often allowed one senior clan member to function as a leader and arbiter of disputes; family naming patterns were adopted which revealed a person's generational place in his or her lineage; and endowed schools might be set up to educate talented clan males in preparation for the civil service examinations, or educate the less talented ones along with ordinary village boys for lesser careers. By such measures, gradually emergent in Song times, well-to-do clans, and to a large extent less affluent clans as well, assumed patterns of social action that became standard for Chinese society thereafter, within considerable regional variations. Some eminent Song scholars devoted much concern to the standardization of family and clan behavior as a means of rectifying social faults and extending Confucian values to the entire society; in that process, elite family patterns became the model for the entire population.

These patterns of action strengthened the Chinese family's millennial emphasis on the surname, the male descent line, and the primacy of males in society. Yet it has been pointed out that organizing clans successfully for continued preeminence in local society also involved women in many roles: strategies for clan success emphasized marriage relations among clans; wives and mothers, hence daughters, were seen to make contributions to the fortunes of the clan and were taken into the calculations for ensuring family success.[53] Many women in elite families were given some education, sometimes quite high-level education. There are a few noted female poets in Song times, and many a successful man's life story includes an account of receiving his basic literacy at his mother's knee. Women were deferred to, if not often as authorities in matters of clan ritual and organization, then not infrequently as managers of the clan's household and estate affairs. The roles of women in Song society appear to have grown, both in elite families and among the common people. The poet Li Qingzhao, discussed earlier, was an extraordinary person and a gifted writer; hence we know a great deal about her. Unfortunately, we can get only glimpses of most women, extraordinary or ordinary, whether as key figures in the development of elite clans or as brave, chaste, or devoted exemplary figures in the narrowing Neo-Confucian definitions of female virtues, of the kinds found in the brief notices of forty such women in the "Biographies of Women" tucked into one section near the end of the official *Song History*.[54] In the next chapter, however, we shall find that recent researches on the place of women in Song society have given us considerably more, and more interesting, information.

15

SOUTHERN SONG LIFE –
A BROADER VIEW

The historical record seldom focuses on the lives of ordinary people in the distant past, making such information difficult to recapture. One would like to know how many people there were, how their towns and villages were governed, what their government cost them, what careers were open to them, how relations of men and women in family situations and in local society were conducted, what they believed, and how they lived their hardworking lives at sub-elite and commoner levels. Seeking the broader view of the whole society, one must attempt to gain insights indirectly by looking at the functions of government and society at local levels; clues also can be taken from what we know about the elite sector in their daily life, and their occasional records of their interactions with relatives, neighbors, and others in non-elite society. Occasionally we are fortunate to find someone like the Southern Song poet Lu You, a large portion of whose poetry records his observations of the daily life of ordinary villagers among whom he lived; it is quoted in the final section of this chapter. Although we cannot quantify and analyze such information as scientific data, it is nonetheless illuminating. And it reminds us that all the strata of Chinese society shared one arena of social interaction.

1. CALCULATING SONG CHINA'S POPULATION

The world's population, calculated at about 200 million in the first year of the Common Era, did not reach the 1 billion mark until 1800. Then it climbed to 2 billion by 1930, and in the next seventy years surged to over 6 billion. It has been calculated to reach 10 billion by the year 2050.[1] That may well be the most important fact in contemporary world history, a matter of direct impact on the life of every individual everywhere.

Demographic historians considered Europe (including European Russia) and China to have contained the globe's two main population masses throughout history, at least until very recently. In the tenth century, when the Song dynasty began, Europe had only about 35 million people, but by 1300, or just about the end of Song, that number had grown to 70 million. Thereafter, in the aftermath of the Black Death in Europe, 1347–1350, Europe's population may have fallen as low as 50 million and did not make substantial recovery for a century.

It has customarily been said that China's population was roughly equal to Europe's in those centuries, estimates running to about 65 or 70 million in all of China by the end of the Song dynasty in 1279. We now think those figures, based on inadequately critical acceptance of the Chinese government's traditional census records, are too low. A brief look at the ways by which total population estimates are derived from traditional census records can help to explain.

In Roman times in the West, population counts were made, as they were in China from the beginnings of the imperial age in the third century B.C.E. In both cases those were registration figures for special categories of the population needed for specific administrative purposes. Full counts of all individuals were not attempted. Even in small segments of nations, full counts did not begin in the West until the eighteenth century. The new United States in 1790 carried out the first national count anywhere of all its people of both sexes and all ages, in order to meet the requirement for equal representation demanded by the Constitution. England held its first national census in 1801, and other European states did the same in subsequent decades of the nineteenth century. No modern state could govern without reference to regularly updated and highly detailed censuses. Historically, China counted households, and some or all of the people constituting them, but it did not attempt a complete registration and count by modern methods of all individuals until 1953, when it found 600 million people, half as many as censuses reported in the 1990s.

A population census in traditional societies, as in Roman times or in China before the twentieth century, was a limited tool for specific purposes, such as levying troops from sectors of the population or, most commonly, allocating tax burdens and managing collection and transport of taxes paid in kind. In China the census count of taxpaying households (and of individuals, whether to register all of them or only the taxpaying adult males) was combined with registration of cultivated land, because some portions of the tax burden borne by the entire population were based on land and its productivity. The reported relationship of people to productive land provides a corroborating kind of information. Historical demographers have used a few landmark censuses among all those reported, those taken to be most reliable, to estimate the population of China through the early imperial centuries prior to the Song.

Population estimates for the Song, however, are especially complicated. The Song government used administrative procedures different from those used in other dynastic eras, and therefore counted its people differently. Demographers trying to estimate the population of China have generally assumed that the numbers for households are closer to being accurate than those for individuals. In some cases women, or the very young, or the aged, were omitted because they were not relevant to taxation, and other categories of persons might also escape registration. The Song records appear to report no more than 40 percent of individuals; these are assumed to be adult males liable to labor service, but the figures do not run in consistent series, and they are difficult to interpret. By studying the organization and functions of households, however, the historical demographers have established sound hypotheses about the average number of persons per household. That figure, more or less stable throughout Chinese history, is calculated to be about 5.5 persons per "small family" household. Household figures from all ages appear to be more consistent and more reliable than figures for individuals, so by multiplying them by 5.5, a total population estimate is produced.

But are the household figures recorded in the Chinese histories complete? Demographers have never assumed they are, but have judged that because the state had an interest in using good figures, they probably did not fall far short of the total numbers. More recently the assumption that the state's administrative needs would have guaranteed full counting of households has been questioned. One calculation, now widely accepted, is that the combined total for Southern Song and Jin China, shortly before the fall of Jin in 1234, was in excess of 120 million persons. Of those perhaps 40 million were in Jin-held North China, and well over 70 million were in territories governed by the Southern Song.[2] This figure for Southern Song alone equals that for all of Europe at the time and, together with the Chinese population in the Jin-held North, raises China's share of the world's population from about one-fourth to a bit more than one-third.

At the same time when the Black Death dramatically lowered Europe's population in the fourteenth century, China's population also suffered a significant decrease, but not a decrease caused by pandemic disease; China's losses were caused by invasion and warfare coupled with the consequent destruction of the economy. China's losses, however, were suffered principally in the northern regions, where the population decreases were proportionately as large as those throughout Europe. Like Europe, the distressed regions of North China also did not recover until the fifteenth century or later. Yet overall, China's population was much more stable; wide drops in the numbers probably reflect failures to record—that is, administrative failures in troubled times—much more than actual decreases. China's share of the slowly growing world population remained at about one-third until the nineteenth century; that share has now fallen to one-fifth.

Population is the basic reality of all social history. China's place in the world's population throughout history suggests significant facts about the level of China's material well-being, its social stability, and the quality of living conditions for all the people. The existence of an affluent elite does not significantly affect population figures; only an economically sound society that provides reasonably secure conditions for all people can sustain a population and produce margins that allow for its steady growth. Those necessary conditions varied regionally throughout Song China, but were at their most favorable in the regions of Central and southern China making up the Southern Song's territories.

II. GOVERNING AT THE LOCAL LEVEL

The enduring units of traditional China's administrative geography are the counties or districts *(xian)*. Many of the approximately 1,500 of these at the beginning of the Song dynasty had already been in existence for a thousand years, their names occasionally changing and their boundaries somewhat modified from time to time, but their identification with a particular locality remaining. Above them were regional administrations called *zhou* or *fu,* supervising from three to eight counties (in most cases); to simplify, both names are here translated as "prefecture." The names and boundaries of prefectures were less permanent than those of counties, yet they too were remarkably stable elements of the administrative structure of government. There were roughly 300 of them, that is, on average five counties per prefecture, at the beginning of the Song. After the fall of Northern Song in 1127 until the end of the dynasty in 1279, the reduced territories of Southern Song included about 900 counties and close to 200 prefectures. They were the basic building blocks of Southern Song local government.

The prefecture and county levels of local and regional governing were directly responsible to the central government, yet there was an intervening layer of administrative offices, based on earlier models but modified by the Song founding emperor. His concern was to ensure that heads of regional military garrisons would not go undetected if they began to usurp authority, control finances, and start on an all too familiar path toward autonomy. The Song offices designed to provide that intermediate-level oversight were called circuits *(lu)*. All of China had been divided into twenty-three circuits in Northern Song, but with the loss of the North the number remaining in Southern Song was initially fifteen, subsequently sixteen (Map 10).[3] They were smaller than the provinces of later dynasties, and they were not integrated regional governments. The circuits supervised certain activities at lower levels; they investigated, and they provided a communications link between localities and the center. The circuit offices were based in the more important prefectural cities within each circuit. The three or four major components of circuit level supervision were often physically separated and located at two or more cities. The officials staffing these offices traveled throughout the prefectures and counties making up the circuit.

Four main functions were guided and supervised at circuit level: carrying out military and police actions to maintain social order; transporting tax grains and collecting other revenues; administering law and justice and investigating breaches of the laws; and maintaining granaries and emergency provisions and distributing relief in disasters. Eventually two further functions were added briefly: supervising the schools and the conduct of local examinations,[4] and overseeing the community organization of households in mutual responsibility and community self-defense corps called the *baojia*.[5] Other offices also were added from time to time as needed at circuit level in particular regions; they might manage the procurement of military horses, build and operate transport boats, supervise customs collections on commercial goods in transit, and the like. There was no integrating structure of lateral interaction among the four regular offices within each circuit; each dealt with counterpart organs in the capital, while the prefectures and counties below them had to deal separately with each circuit-level office.

Among the circuit offices, the Transport Commissioner who collected and transported taxes was considered the most important; his office had a larger staff than the others. The idea of establishing the circuit level of administration goes back to the important military support functions assigned to Transport Commissioners of high rank who accompanied the early Song armies charged with bringing the Ten States under Song control. They provided logistical support and provisions to the armies in the field, and they also served to investigate and report on local conditions. As time went on, they were assigned direct responsibility for planning and supervising the transfer of tax grains and other revenues to the capital. Collecting the revenues and concentrating those material resources in the capital region had a high priority. It was part of the early Song plan to centralize governing. The entire Song governing structure was designed to reduce initiative and discretion at all levels below the center, something all the political reformers and statecraft thinkers saw as a weakness.[6] In sum, the Song period circuit level of administration did not develop into a strong component of government, yet its functions were held to be of strategic importance.[7] The Song circuit anticipated the creation of provinces *(sheng)* in Yuan and later times.

The significant action in local governing took place at the government offices, the prefectural and county *yamen,* where the magistrate headed his small staff of officials appointed by the central government, and much larger numbers of clerks and office helpers. The county magistrate had the responsibility of dealing directly with the people. His duties are described in the official *Song History* in these words:

He held overall responsibility for governing the people, promoting and taxing agriculture and sericulture, settling and resolving penal and judicial matters, and when there were acts of imperial grace or commands and prohibitions [i.e., all communications from the central government], he was to make those known throughout his jurisdiction. He was responsible for handling in person all matters of population registration, levying taxes and labor service [corvée], monies and tax grains, distribution of relief, receipts and disbursements, and seasonally to manage the regular registration of households and supervise the collection of summer and autumn grain taxes [i.e., the magistrate was required to assemble and account for the revenues in preparation for their transport to the higher levels of administration]. When in times of floods or droughts there were reports of damage and suffering, he was to allocate and distribute relief supplies; when because

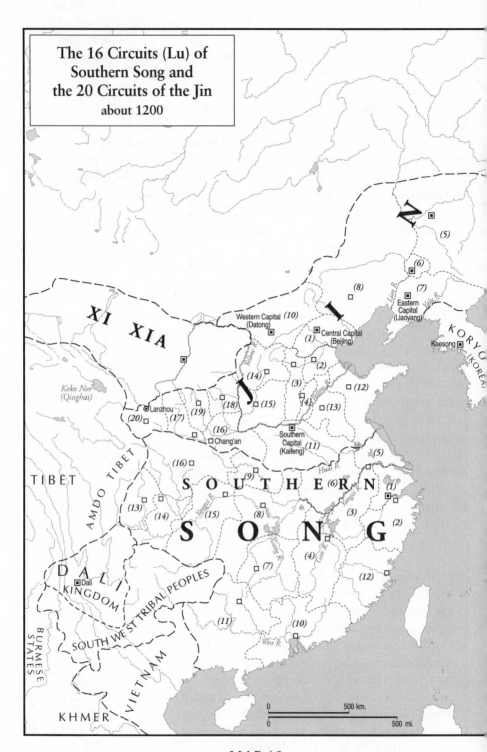

The 16 Circuits (Lu) of
Southern Song and
the 20 Circuits of the Jin
about 1200

MAP 10

MAP 10

Southern Song:

Circuit name	Administrative seat
1 Liangzhe Xi	1 Lin'an (Hangzhou)
2 Liangzhe Dong	2 Shaoxing
3 Jiangnan Dong	3 Jiankang (Nanjing)
4 Jiangnan Xi	4 Longxing Fu (Nanchang)
5 Huainan Dong	5 Yangzhou
6 Huainan Xi	6 Luzhou
7 Jinghu Nan	7 Tanzhou (Changsha)
8 Jinghu Bei	8 Jiangling
9 Jingxi (Nan)	9 Xiangyang
10 Guangnan Dong	10 Guangzhou (Canton)
11 Guangnan Xi	11 Jingjiang Fu (Guilin)
12 Fujian	12 Fuzhou
13 Chengdu	13 Chengdu
14 Tongchuan	14 Tongchuan (Santai)
15 Kuizhou	15 Kuizhou
16 Lizhou	16 Xingyuan (Hanzhong)

The Jin Empire:

Circuit name	Administrative seat
1 Zhongdu	1 Zhongjing (Beijing)
2 Hebei Dong	2 Hejian
3 Hebei Xi	3 Zhending
4 Daming	4 Daming
5 Shangjing	5 Shangjing (Supreme Capital, not on map)
6 Xianping	6 Xianping
7 Dongjing	7 Liaoyang (Eastern Capital)
8 Beijing	8 Beijing (Dading, Northern Capital)
9 Linhuang Fu	9 Linhuang (not on map)
10 Xijing	10 Datong (Western Capital)
11 Nanjing	11 Kaifeng (Southern Capital)
12 Shandong Dong	12 Yidu
13 Shandong Xi	13 Dongping
14 Hedong Bei	14 Taiyuan
15 Hedong Nan	15 Pingyang (Linfen)
16 Jingzhao	16 Jingzhao (Chang'an, Xi'an)
17 Fengxiang	17 Fengxiang
18 Fuyan	18 Yan'an
19 Qingyuan	19 Qingyang Fu
20 Lintao	20 Lintao

Present-day names are given in parentheses; all the circuits are separately mapped in Tan Xixiang (1991), vol. 6, pp. 58–69.

of floods or droughts the people fled or became homeless, he was required to reassemble and comfort them, assuring that they would not lose their means of livelihood. When notable examples of filial and fraternal conduct and righteous deeds were talked about in countryside and humble lanes, he was to report those in truthful detail to the prefecture, by that means to exhort the people to follow upright ways.[8]

Serving as a county magistrate was a large job; some officials did it well and conscientiously and were happy to remain in such posts, to which they were ordinarily appointed for three-year terms. It is likely that most new entrants to the ranks of officialdom, however, looked upon the lowly county-level appointments as their initial testing for higher office, hoping to do well enough to be promoted to court and central government positions.

The county magistrate's staff of officials (guan) minimally consisted of himself, a vice magistrate in the larger counties, an assistant magistrate or recorder, and the captain of the militia or guard unit. The rest of his staff all were locally hired commoners, not men of guan rank and status. In very large and important counties, or in those exposed to military dangers, other officials might be appointed. Prefectures had somewhat larger staffs. Yet the grassroots level of governing was accomplished parsimoniously, using very few officials, if not economically in terms of costs to the locality.

Concrete examples show how government was structured at the lower levels—in the circuits and their subordinate prefectures and counties in the Southern Song period. The two circuits called Zhe East and Zhe West (Zhexi Lu, Zhedong Lu), divided by the Zhe River which bisects the region, corresponded to present-day Zhejiang Province together with most of present-day Jiangsu Province south of the Yangzi. That was the richest and most densely populated region of China at the time. Together the two circuits had an area of about 50,000 square miles. Zhe East circuit contained seven prefectures having under them forty-one counties; Zhe West circuit had eight prefectures with thirty-nine counties, including the national capital, Linan (Hangzhou). The eighty counties averaged about 600 square miles each in area, roughly 25 miles square. The registered population of the two circuits together in the year 1162 gives figures of over 12 million, or an average of 150,000 per county.[9] But "Sung [Song] population figures are very much below the truth";[10] we probably can add 20 percent to those figures.

For one comparison with a somewhat poorer region of similar size, we may look at Fujian circuit, approximately the same area as the modern province of Fujian (Fukien). Its 46,000 square miles were divided into eight prefectures having a total of forty-seven counties, averaging almost 1,000 square miles in area. Fujian circuit's registered population in 1162 is reported at 7.65 million, averaging about 160,000 people per county. Again, those figures for registered population are much too low. Zhejiang and Fujian, both on the southeast China coast, despite their differences in population and wealth were ahead of most regions of China in the twelfth century; elsewhere populations were less dense and counties were apt to be larger in area.

For another comparison we may look at England, which (without Wales and Scotland) also is about 50,000 square miles in area. The population of England has been estimated (on the basis of figures in the Domesday Book, compiled in 1086) to have been at that time between 1.1 and 1.5 million; it was growing rapidly and may have reached 2 million in 1162, the year from which the Chinese population figures are derived.[11] Local government in England was then based in its shires, later called counties, roughly forty in number in the twelfth century. They therefore averaged over 1,200 square miles each but had average populations of only 50,000. The most important administrative official of the shire was the king's sheriff, but locally based members of the aristocracy and of the clergy also contributed to governing.

Comparing the structure of local government in twelfth-century China and England shows that in both cases the country was divided into manageable units that could be administered from a center interested in revenues, stability, and social well-being. Beyond that, they display striking differences stemming from their entirely different social and political systems. The comparison with twelfth-century England could be more fully developed, and other such comparisons also are well worth pursuing to gain perspective on the structures and scope of governing, but they cannot be carried further here.

III. PAYING FOR GOVERNMENT

Like most premodernized countries, China in imperial times assumed a limited range of governing responsibilities. From the state's point of view, chief among those were collecting revenues and defending dynasty and territory. On a different plane, there was another set of primary governing acts: nominally, if not so in practical reality, maintaining ritual correctness at the court, in the dynastic and state ritual observances, and throughout the government was a most significant duty of the Chinese emperor and his appointees. Scholar-advisers and ritual specialists prescribed the forms, justified them by the study of their history, prepared the handbooks, and operated the Ministry of Rites. Correct ritual demonstrated that the ruler merited the Mandate of Heaven. It was more than a matter of the elaborate forms such ritual assumed, or the official and sub-official participation it required, or the profusion of accouterments it employed; it symbolized in profoundly compelling manner the entire ordering of mankind's place in the human and natural worlds. And it cost a great deal in money and resources, drawn primarily from the immediate locality, the *xian*.

Beyond these chief concerns, Chinese government in Song times performed other functions as well: it proclaimed norms of social behavior by defining crimes and administering punishments; it anticipated crop failures and natural disasters by providing grain reserves and relief measures; it encouraged public medicine, hygiene, and associated philanthropies; it set standards for higher education and testing to recruit civil officials; it carried out a program of public works including construction and repair of roads, canals, bridges, dikes, ports, transport and communications facilities, manufacture of military matériel and armaments, and building of walls, palaces, and imperially sponsored projects; and it managed state monopolies and mines and supervised trade. All those activities and the lesser ones not listed were carried out bureaucratically, with officials *(guan)* and their clerical staffs supervising, keeping accounts, and compiling documentary records in several copies for distribution to other offices. Governing the Song state required many minds, hands, bodies; it cost the governed large sums of their money and products to pay for it all, as well as much of their labor to service it. Money, cereal grains, textiles and other products, and labor service all were elements of Song period taxation. Yet it usually is said that, in comparison with other premodernized societies, tax rates were low in China, and much of the tax revenue was retained in the county to contribute to the local economy.

Precise counts are not possible, but the best estimates are that the central government in late Northern Song times, when the Song state was still intact, employed about 10,000 civil officials at the capital, with another 10,000 in the regional and local governments. The 1,500 counties each employed three to six appointed officials *(guan)*, and the 300 prefectures each had six to ten such officials. Together with the staffs of the circuits, those figures total about 10,000. After the loss of the North at the end of the 1120s, Southern Song, as I have noted, had about one-third fewer of those offices of regional and local governance, but it appears that the total number of officials assigned to the reduced number of local units and to the central government did not decrease. We also can estimate that there were ten to twenty clerical posts for each official post in the central government, and somewhat more than that for each centrally appointed official in local offices at county and prefecture levels. If we count all the lowliest office servants and *yamen* aides along with the skilled clerks, it seems possible that the Song government supported between 200,000 and 300,000 civil employees, of whom 20,000 were ranked officials *(guan)*.

In addition, the size of the military forces of late Northern Song surpassed 1 million men, and those numbers did not decrease in Southern Song times. All historians have complained that Song armies were too large, swollen with men who did not and often could not fight. In addition to its fighting duties, the army also provided a labor force used for building projects, transport services, manufacturing arms, and other needs. The presence of many military incompetents in the armed services wasted money and lowered fighting efficiency. The officer corps lacked prestige and was at best on the margins of elite status. Yet the Song forces were by no means militarily inconsequential.

Official salaries in Song times, after niggardly beginnings, soon reached quite generous levels. Monthly salaries were calculated in strings of cash (nominally 1,000, more often 800 copper coins, called "cash," making up one "string" that was roughly equivalent to an ounce of silver or a picul, i.e., 130 pounds of rice, but those values varied).[12] High officials also received annual allotments of grain and grants of revenues from designated lands (but no administrative control over those lands), and in many cases favored Chief Councillors and others received direct gifts of great value—gold and silver, gems, houses and estates, lavish garments, books and works of arts, decorative items—from the ruler in appreciation for their services.

In amounts varying according to their rank, officials also were given exemptions from taxation and labor service, and from most kinds of punishments for violations of law, preferment in access to the lower-level examinations for their sons and other relatives, and the possibility of direct appointment to *guan* status through "protection" *(yin)* for sons or younger male relatives. We think of these as defects in the open merit system of advancement because they were readily overused and abused. Some conscientious Song statesmen and thinkers also were critical of these aspects of official life, especially when flagrantly abused. In fact, however, those all were elements of the salary system; no less than their actual salaries, those too were rewards which officials received for their services. The costs of hiring and paying all the civil and military employees of the state, those in official rank and status *(guan)* and all the lower-ranking ones throughout much of the Song period, used up virtually all the annual revenues. At least, that is what the fragmentary fiscal records appear to indicate. The Song imperial government usually was short of funds.[13]

Fiscal shortages could inflict pain on emperor and imperial household, too, for unlike royal figures in Western history, China's emperors were "bureaucrats" in the sense that they were dependent on disbursements to them through the appropriate fiscal agencies. They could command that disbursements from the general revenues be made for whatever purposes they wished, but they did not have significant independent incomes from inherited lands and estates, and whatever funds went to their support were subject to bureaucratic procedures. In times of fiscal stringency, profligate emperors or members of their households had to find ways of bypassing or ignoring their ministries' planning and control, although to do so earned them criticism and subjected their personal agents to bureaucratic attacks.

Present information does not permit us to carry an analysis of the Chinese government's fiscal operations to a more satisfactory level of detail. For our purposes here it is sufficient to note that the Song government annually collected and disbursed what seem to be very large sums of money, by some measures larger sums than were available to later dynasties when the population had grown much larger. Differences in accounting methods may explain such seeming anomalies; we do not know. There is better descriptive information (and evidence of much complaining) about the kinds and amounts of taxation and other sources of the government's revenues.

The Song government kept in place the system of taxation inherited from the Tang dynasty. One of the landmarks of Chinese fiscal history is the adoption of the so-called "two-tax method" *(liang shui fa)* designed by the eminent Tang financial expert Yang Yan and fully adopted in 780. That method of levying the "summer tax" and "fall grains" taxes on agricultural production remained the basic component of the Chinese tax system not just through Song times but until the nineteenth century. It was, however, managed somewhat differently in each succeeding dynasty. The Song agrarian taxes were levied not on the basis of households but on the land they owned or farmed. Land was classed into three grades according to its productivity, and a share of the expected (not the actual) produce was collected as tax-in-kind. In years of calamitous harvests or disasters, the central government could authorize reductions or total exemptions.

An often cited set of figures from the year 1077 indicates that the summer tax provided about one-fourth of the annual agrarian tax revenues of the state, and the autumn grains levies, collected when the principal crops of the major cereal grains had been harvested (whatever combination of cereals was produced in any region), provided about three-fourths of the agrarian tax revenues of the state. Wheat was the major grain product north of the Huai River, which in Southern Song times served as the boundary with the Jin state. Rice dominated south of that line, but in both parts of China those and many other cereals were grown, including different varieties of millet, barley, beans, and peas. Other agricultural products also were part of the summer and autumn taxes: silk floss, bolts of ordinary cloth, lacquer, fodder grasses and hay, tea, and reeds for fuel or other uses also are listed. Some levies of silver and gold were included, as was salt.

Apart from the "two-tax" system levies, there were many other forms of taxation. In towns and cities, land and buildings were taxed. Oxen for plowing, leather products, iron and iron goods, farm implements, wine and wine yeasts, alum, forest products, and many others were either government production monopolies producing revenues for the state or were taxed as private forms of wealth.

Commercial taxes on goods in the market and goods in transit to markets began to be a major element in taxation only in Song times. Tariffs were collected at seaports and at the customs barriers operated all along the land boundaries between China and its northern neighbors, the Xi Xia, the Liao, and later the Jin. Shops were taxed on the volume of sales. Goods in transport within the country were taxed at the rate of 2 to 3 percent of their value every time they passed a tax barrier, often several times in the course of a hundred miles. Smuggling was rife. Taxes were a burden, yet commerce flourished as never before, and it is difficult to argue that taxation discouraged it.[14]

Government production and distribution monopolies also were a form of taxation. Salt was by far the most important; it produced revenues of the greatest volume, and because it was a necessity of life, it was distributed to every household. It had been a government monopoly since long before the beginnings of the imperial era in the third century B.C.E. It came from dry salt beds in the Inner Asian deserts, from deep salt wells in Sichuan, and from coastal salterns where seawater was sun-dried or boiled dry to produce the salt. The government subsidized the production costs then gained those back tenfold through its sale, handled through franchises on which salt merchants could bid. The methods of bidding for distribution rights, and controlling distribution from certain production areas to designated distribution areas, were highly developed in Song, and anticipated the systems that would continue into later times.

The same monopoly agencies frequently managed other consumption monopolies such as those for wine and liquors, for wine yeasts, for vinegar, for tea, and for alum, incense fragrances, and other items used in the preparation of commercial goods. Salt and other products were often transported back to the consumption areas on boats and barges which had delivered the tax grains from those areas. The organization of production and distribution took large steps forward. We see highly integrated systems that supported both the government's revenue collection and the distribution of commercial products. During the Song, the historian can observe a complex economic system under rapid development.

A basic measure of that economy has been based on its industrial sector. How much iron and steel did Song China produce, and was its consumption relevant to further productive activity; that is, was it used for agriculture and other constructive purposes, or mostly consumed wastefully, for example, in warfare? The mining, smelting, and fabricating of iron, steel, copper, tin, lead, mercury, and other minerals (in addition to gold and silver, which were not primarily for industrial use) were government monopolies or were under strict government management. Also controlled were production of charcoal and coke made from coal because of their use in the manufacture of industrial metals. Coal was not known as a fuel elsewhere in the world until several centuries later. Wrought iron, cast iron, and steel of various kinds have long been used in China.[15] Ox-drawn cast iron plows and other agricultural implements began to be used as early as the mid-first millennium B.C.E., and deep plowing with improved plows greatly increased productivity during the Han dynasty, a thousand years before the Song. While these advances went hand in hand with improvements in the use of steel for arrowheads, swords, spears, and armor, it seems clear that a large share of the iron and steel China produced went into agricultural uses. A pioneering study of coal and iron production in Northern Song times has established very high levels of ferrous industry activity centered on the region surrounding Kaifeng, certainly the highest absolute as well as per capita quantities of iron production in the world at that time, and high by any pre–industrial revolution standards of later centuries in the West.[16] This activity contributed to the Song state's revenues both because the production of metals was taxed and because the use of metals increased productivity in other sectors.

Much of Song taxation was paid in kind, but taxes paid in money, particularly the commercial taxes, grew rapidly throughout Song times and probably accounted for one-fourth to one-third of the government's revenues. Everybody in Song society used money. The round copper alloy coins with a hole in the middle for stringing on cords or thongs were commonly used loose— five cash for a bowl of wine, a hundred cash plus the daily rice allowance for a day's wages[17]—or as whole strings of standard number. In larger transactions unbroken strings were the unit of account. Their equivalents in unminted silver ingots, bolts of common silk cloth, or other commodities also were recognized as standard units of value.

With the rapid growth of commerce and large transactions ever more common, those bulky forms of "money" became too clumsy to transport, and too inconvenient for arranging trading activities. During the Song the Chinese began to use "credit currency," notes of credit or paper currency, at first privately issued and soon taken up by the government. About the year 1000 the government recognized the issuance of paper notes called *jiaozi* (exchange medium) by licensed merchant associations in West China, and soon thereafter took that activity over as a government monopoly like the minting of coins. From that beginning various forms of official paper bills (most commonly called *huizi*) developed, all denominated in equivalents of strings of cash for which they were expected to be redeemable. They were printed on high-quality paper from brass printing plates, often in two or three colors to discourage counterfeiting. Their use spread throughout the entire country. Inflationary pressures weakened their value; they might ultimately be redeemed at only one-fourth or less the amount in which they were issued. Paper currency worked well, then as now, only when fiscal management was sound.

The need for a more convenient currency illustrates the growing importance of commerce in the daily lives of the entire population.[18] The experiments with paper money were successful enough that they established a pattern for Yuan and Ming times, but paper currency was abandoned in later centuries and did not lead to the regular substitution of paper for precious metals until the twentieth century. A curious anomaly of Chinese economic history is that minting of silver and gold coins was not practiced, although the level of the economy and the needs of commerce could have sustained it by Song times; the explanation undoubtedly lies beyond economic history.

The great wealth of Song society was heavily drawn upon to pay for its highly elaborated structure of governing. We must look at the organization of society and the lives of ordinary people to see whether the costs of government were repaid in the quality of their lives.

IV. STATUS IN THE CHINESE POPULATION

In European history of the centuries that correspond to the Song dynasty, that is, the tenth through thirteenth centuries (and beyond, into early modern times), we think of rural and urban populations as having little in common, with quite distinct life patterns in which elite modes consisted of the aristocratic lifestyles of a closed upper class. As European towns became cities in the later Middle Ages, their leading citizens were the new burghers, or bourgeoisie, town folk whose commerce-derived wealth allowed some of them to develop new kinds of lifestyles that competed in luxury and comfort with those of the aristocracy. Rural-based aristocrats, too, increasingly moved into towns and cities, and their modes of life merged with those in the richer commercial sector of city life. They might intermarry; they might share some activities of governing their cities. Both of these components of the urban population, while not necessarily fond of each other, shared the separation from the countryside and a scorn for the rural population. "Peasant" in feudal and post-feudal Europe did not just mean *paysan* in the sense of a rural or rustic person, but also carried connotations ranging from that of "villein" (cognate with "villain") in bond service, to that of "serf," and by extension could mean a base person, in contrast both to the nobly born and to persons of noble character.[19] People who worked the land, especially those bound to it or to a landowning master, given the heritage of European feudal society, were thought of as crude rustics at best, and basely deficient in the finer human qualities at worst.

Readers of history often expect that words such as "peasant," "bondsman," "villein," or "serf," indicating social status, should be interchangeable with counterparts in other languages, and thereby should indicate parallels with other social systems. In the broadest sense they do, but they also may convey misunderstanding. In the West we have had a strong tendency to generalize about all societies from what we know about the European past. Words used to translate descriptions of the social order are particularly subject to such misunderstanding. The actual status of persons in Chinese history, both at the highest echelons of traditional society and in the lower strata, became the subject of fierce debate in twentieth-century China, when non-Chinese ideas about society became important elements in historical study. Japanese and Western historians also have become heavily involved in such debates. Much of that focus has turned on later centuries. The subject will be discussed in subsequent chapters as an issue of dispute among historians when Ming and Qing social history is the topic.

Here, without wishing to foreclose such discussion, I adopt the view that most of the people in Song and later China were farmers who owned their land and could freely buy and sell it, could bequeath it to their children and grandchildren or other persons, and could leave the land for other occupations or for other localities more or less as they chose. Despite some regional variations in the number who owned all or part of their land and those who rented all or part of the land they worked, and despite the existence of some who, temporarily at least, were tenant farmers or hired laborers, a farming population of private landowners was the norm.[20] Those conditions had developed over a very long span of time.

In ancient China, before the beginning of the imperial era in the third century B.C.E., the vast majority of all people already had become free landowning farmers, just as they all had acquired surnames and belonged to relationship groups beyond their immediate families. The Chinese mentality, unlike the European, displayed no carryovers from a feudal present or from a recent feudal past.[21] The Chinese word *nong,* "farmer," is often translated "peasant," but in English that word is quite misleading; in the present work it is not used. Ordinary Chinese people of all occupations were most commonly referred to en masse as *liang min,* or "the good people," people who pursued orderly lives and caused no problems to their communities. That term, or simply *min* (ordinary people), designated village farmers as well as town folk and city dwellers, and they might be of any economic status. Some *min* households were specially designated "military," "artisan," "salt-field worker," and the like, but the vast majority were farmers or villagers of whatever economic status. Only men in the individually attained status of *guan,* meaning "official" (and kin in their immediate households), were not included in the category of *min,* or "ordinary people."

The exceptions to the general categorization of all persons as *liang min* were so few as to be statistically insignificant. China indeed had bond servants, but they were not necessarily rural or agricultural, and they were not legally confined to that status; they could work their way out of it. There were also still poorer people; the very poor in China might become so desperate in times of famine or disorder that they would "sell" children, even occasionally adults, to richer neighbors who would take them into their families as servants or, in some cases, as wives, or even (usually by deceiving the parents) to be reared in houses of prostitution. In neither the Chinese legal definition nor the popular consciousness, however, were such miserable humans chattel; they were not mere property.[22] Their status is sometimes translated as "slave," but that misrepresents the situation. They had some basic rights as humans, and they might quite realistically hold out the hope that they or their children would work their way out of that status. Additionally, there also were the *jian min,* or "base people," those who followed certain "debased" occupations, defined differently in different ages but often including prostitutes, barbers, actors, and, under the impact of Buddhist beliefs, sometimes also butchers. Legally designated "base people" probably were no more than 3 to 5 percent of the population. They and their children were discriminated against in some contexts—they were supposed to be ineligible for the civil service examinations—but that discrimination was often evaded. These poorest of the poor in China, including some for whom derogatory names were used, did not in the Chinese view have any necessary connection with farming or with rural life.

The purpose of this digression into the statuses of the poor in China is to show why the word "farmer" *(nong)* did not designate a humble segment at the lower edge of society. In China the word "farmer" was used for the largest portion of the population; moreover, it included individuals and their households who ranged in economic status from rich gentleman-farmers to independent self-owning households (the largest portion), to lower economic statuses including partial owner–partial renter families, to tenant farmers and hired farm laborers. Because all of those statuses were fluid, not fixed in law or in popular expectations, and the category called *nong* ranked second in prestige among the four traditionally defined occupations in society, it is an obvious error to translate *nong* as "peasant" on analogy to the use of the word in Western history, where its meaning is often derogatory, and where it in any case carries overtones of that occupational group's historical background in serfdom. Chinese farmers were often called, or called themselves, *xiangxia ren,* "people of the rural countryside," meaning that they lacked sophistication and might be laughable; the simple villagers who came to the city and were overwhelmed by urban ways were stock figures in Chinese humor.[23] But that is another matter. It was always possible, if only barely so, that the rustics' sons or grandsons might prosper enough to educate a son, and he might even become an official, attaining the highest status in society. That possibility made a difference in many of their lives. It engendered a measure of optimism that helped to make China an "achieving society," in which economic and social status remained fluid.

v. Urban and Rural

A counterpart to the openness of Chinese society is the open relation of towns and cities to their rural hinterlands. There was a high degree of interaction between urban and rural, in contrast to the separation of city and countryside in medieval Europe. The contrast starts with the ways they were governed. Chinese towns and cities possessed nothing resembling city charters, which in Europe often granted rights and privileges to burghers organized for self-rule. Chinese cities and towns were not incorporated; they did not have urban administrations, Lord Mayors, town councils. They were governed in the name of the dynasty by the same magistrates and other appointed officials who governed the counties and prefectures in which they were located. Their inhabitants were organized (if loosely) into the same kinds of household groupings as for rural people, although different names were used for urban wards, suburban wards, and rural subdistricts. One uniform, centrally controlled administration served all.

Cities and their surrounding countryside were open for the people from one to come and go in the other. Both the urban and the rural settings were relatively safe and stable; Marco Polo, who lived in China immediately after the end of Southern Song, remarked on the safety of city streets, although he also expressed admiration for the skill of Chinese thieves, pickpockets, swindlers, and burglars. Rural travel to famous sites and scenic places began to develop as a form of elite recreation. A literature of scenic description had long existed; to that genre now was added that of the practical tour guide, telling where comfortable facilities were to be found and what sights and smells were to be enjoyed. The region around Hangzhou, the Southern Song capital, was the subject of several of them.

The two capitals, Kaifeng in Northern Song and Hangzhou, called Linan as the Southern Song capital, are the most fully described.[24] They were cities of great wealth, ostentation, cultivated pastimes, and the fullest array of entertainments.[25] They did not, however, monopolize those forms of urban development, much less did they concentrate in one city all the learning, the arts, the literary life and high culture of the age. China was very large, and it never was dominated by one great capital city in any respect other than the political. In Northern Song times Luoyang, for example, was close to Kaifeng in size and rivaled it in its cultural life. Throughout the Southern Song many cities, especially those in the lower Yangzi region, were almost as important as the capital for art and literature and for commerce. For many of the elite, to be away from the capital made it possible to live a more ideal life.

In many ways the rural sector took precedence over the urban. The calendar of the agricultural year set the pulse of the entire society. In addition to the periods named for the two solstices and the two equinoxes, the other twenty of the twenty-four solar periods of fifteen days each bore names such as spring begins, excited insects, grain rains, grain in ear, great heat, white dew, little snow, great snow, severe cold. That agricultural year calendar set the cycle of greater and lesser festivals and observances: the New Year; the "Clear and Bright" *(qing-ming)*, when graves were visited; the Fifth of the Fifth *(duanwu)*, when boat races were held; Mid-autumn, when the harvest moon was admired and families gathered together; the Ninth of the Ninth, when people ascended heights; and many others.[26] For each there were special foods and particular activities; most centered on family and home. The great Buddhist and Daoist temples, whether in urban or remote rural locations, also played a major role in the cycle of festivals. At those times the streets of cities and towns would be filled with the bustle of people buying and hawking, making preparations, and incidentally enjoying theatricals, fireworks, and displays.

Especially at those times, rural people streamed into the larger towns to sell the special foods and products necessary for the festival activities. During some, urban people also went into the countryside, as when the annual cycle prescribed attention to the family graves and rituals of veneration to the ancestors. Grave plots were always rural and were family owned, not managed by an arm of the government. Families had to care for them, therefore were drawn regularly back to those rural settings to contemplate the family's origins and to consult together on its present problems. In addition, pilgrimages to famous mountain temples and shrines drew crowds of the faithful, among whom were also many out for the recreation, coming from both towns and rural villages. The rich, many of the officials out of office (as they were for half their careers, on average), or others having the means or the personal taste, might own rural homes where they lived part of the time. These comings and goings went on at all levels of society, keeping the links between city and rural village strong. In these respects, the Song period established patterns that would develop fully in the later dynasties. They too were part of what Saeki Tomi calls "the new culture of the Song."

VI. FAMILIES, WOMEN, AND CHILDREN

Large families, with multiple wives and concubines and many children, constituted an ideal of Chinese life that was rarely realized. We have detailed information on only some elite families in this period of Chinese social history, but analysis of overall population patterns shows that it was demographically impossible for there to have been a surplus of females necessary to allow more than a statistically insignificant number of males to have more than one spouse, or for the average family to have had more than two, at most three surviving children. The *ideal* of the large family was so strong, however, that countless sources refer to it as if it were the *actual* family structure; it is a classic example of the discrepancy between ideal and actual patterns.[27]

During the Song, as frequently noted here, many leading figures in the scholar-official elite were concerned about the ritual life of families; they sought to standardize and purify ritual practices by preparing manuals to guide practice. As elite families adopted these norms and emphasized ritual practices, sub-elite families imitated them, if usually with less elaborate forms and at lower cost; in an upwardly mobile society the modes of the elite have a downwardly pervasive influence. We have little information about commoner households so must draw inferences from elite models.

Marriage was looked upon as a matter of greater importance to families than to individuals; the interests of the bride and groom might be considered by parents on their children's behalf, but the marriage couple did not make personal choices.[28] Propriety was of great importance in arranging marriages. Professional go-betweens might be hired to handle elaborate details; among the rich the dowry was carefully negotiated. Among the sub-elite dowries might be little more than wedding gifts, and the poor probably dispensed with all beyond the simplest of token gifts. Commoner families might dispense with the services of a professional go-between or matchmaker, but parents nonetheless arranged marriages for their children. Some formalities were observed at most levels in society. Among the poor it was more likely that bride and groom would have met before marriage, unless the bride came from another village. It was often necessary to go to a different village to find a bride of another surname from the groom's, an absolute requirement in marriage even among the poor. It was still common in Song elite life for widows to remarry, so we must assume that it was the norm in poorer sectors of the society as well. Adoption of children usually was confined to children of relatives having the same surname, or to children of the mother's surname to whom the adoptive father's surname would be given, but only temporarily. Adopted children from another surname normally resumed their own family name before marriage to ensure that persons of the same surname would not accidentally marry and thereby offend against the incest taboo. That requirement, of course, could complicate the marriage of foundlings, whose parentage was unclear.

Ideally, marriage was between families of similar status. Yet well-to-do families might seek husbands for their daughters among talented young men of lesser means in a strategy of coopting talent to build the future success of both families. Marriage is a favorite subject of entertainment literature; the element of romantic love between the bride and groom is by no means absent, yet it often is the hidden dividend, not the principal feature driving the plot. Companionate marriage as an elite phenomenon is noted in some Song examples (such as the marriage of Zhao Mingcheng and Li Qingzhao, discussed in Chapter 14); it is not unlikely that something like that often developed among the ordinary people as well. In plays and stories, however, romantic love often is found outside marriage, condoned for males, condemned for females.

Elite brides coming into their husband's family retained control of their dowry and could make what use of their material assets they wished. We must assume that all women in Song times could own property and control the uses of money. That was an aspect of marriage that Zhu Xi sought to change; he thought that a woman's resources should become the property of her husband, or at least should be devoted entirely to his family interests.[29] The Neo-Confucian stress on the subordination of women became more pervasive in post-Song times.

It has been observed that marriages were a key element in the strategies of upper-stratum families to enhance their wealth and success in the localities where they lived;[30] among the ordinary people such planning undoubtedly also went on, but within the more limited range of options open to them. The family was the unit of ownership and production, the locus of basic religious beliefs and practices, the vehicle for achieving human success now and in the future, and the agency for attaining the state's as well as the individual's social goals; in those senses, the family played the same roles at all social levels, but with more resources and more options the higher its place in society.

VII. A POET'S OBSERVATIONS

One can describe the patterns in local government and rural social organization and infer much about the circumstances under which ordinary people, whether urban or rural, pursued their individual and family interests in Song times. Yet in China, for all its massive documentation of past history, the actual qualities of ordinary lives, as in all premodern societies, remain largely beyond our clear vision. Much more could be done to overcome that. An effective way to gain a sense of having come into contact with the real people among those tens of millions of Chinese who populated the Southern Song is to look beyond the bare-bones descriptions of governmental structures, taxation, social organization, and all the topics touched upon in this chapter. To see what lives were really like, one must borrow the clear and informed vision of those in the Song dynasty elite who observed and described the ordinary people among whom they lived. The mundane facts of humble lives did not attract many writers; who needed to be told about those things? There were, however, some who wrote about the patterns of ordinary life, not to compile a record for history, but incidentally, as the background against which they expressed other thoughts and sentiments. The best example in the later Song period is the poet Lu You (1125–1210).

Lu You is considered by most anthologists and historians from Song times to the present to have been one of the half-dozen greatest Song poets. He also has left the largest body of poems by one writer from the dynasty, more than 9,000. He is known as a "patriotic poet," one whose obsession with the need to destroy the Jin dynasty and restore Song rule over all of China is evident in much of his poetry. He even went so far, long after he had retired and left the world of politics, as to associate himself with the all-powerful Chief

Councillor Han Tuozhou, a widely despised figure who launched the unsuccessful war against the Jurchens in 1206. He displayed a "lack of realism, which was peculiar to his obsession," apparent also in his "wishful thinking" about the ease with which the Song might invade and defeat the Jin dynasty.[31]

His travel diary of his journey from Hangzhou up the Yangzi into Sichuan in 1170, from which I quote in this section, gives observations on ordinary life and mundane affairs. To most later readers of his vast poetic output, of greater interest are the poems written in the last twenty years of his life, when he had retired to a tiny village near Shanyin, his family's old home in northern Zhejiang. His was a humble retirement, generously supported at first by his salary from minor official duties and his pension, but later at times without those sources of income. Better off than his farming neighbors, he nevertheless lived very simply, happy in the rustic environment of a farming village. There he became not just an elite observer but an actual participant in the daily activities of his village. Among all the many "pastoral poets" of the Song period, he was the rare man who did not distantly observe the hardships of poor farmers to write in clichéd sympathy or indignation about them. Lu You wrote from his immediate involvement as a participant. Thus, this poet's descriptions more truly convey the texture of humble lives. His other observations of Song conditions possess a similar immediacy. Some of his writings to which we can turn in English translation are drawn upon to conclude this chapter.

None among the contemporary observers appears to have been conscious of the population increase as such. People of that time did not think demographically. They reported grievous losses caused by warfare and famine, or noted with satisfaction the bustling crowds in urban marketplaces; they mourned the former and took pleasure in the latter. Lu You, however, at times reported with greater specificity, as when in his travel diary (October 4, 1170) he took special note of the size and commercial prosperity of Wuchang, the large city of the central Yangzi which is part of the present-day metropolitan center of Wuhan in Hubei. He wrote about seeing peddlers' and merchants' "countless boats" tied up in the river on the city's north side in a line stretching for miles along the riverbank. He saw "rows of shops packed together" inside the city walls, and a huge market area extending for a long distance outside the walls on the south or inland side. Calling Wuchang a major metropolis, he says that not even the national capital at Hangzhou or Nanjing (or presumably other great cities of the lower Yangzi that he also knew well) could compare with it. This evidence for general prosperity and urban growth supports the upward revision of Song population figures proposed here.[32] Two days later (October 6, twenty-fifth day) Lu reported a crowd of "several tens of thousands" who flocked to the river's edge to watch a naval exercise involving more than 700 large vessels, each 200 to 300 feet in length, that flew bright flags from their many masts and cut through huge waves as if soaring through the air. That is impressive evidence for the size of the Song dynasty's inland river naval forces, which, a century later, offered stiff resistance to the invading Mongol armies in a series of battles from

Wuchang downriver all the way to Nanjing. We know from recent archaeo-logical evidence and other studies that Song naval technology made great strides. Official reports from naval commanders of the time might not be as credible as this midlevel civil official's responses both to the size of the crowds onshore and to the unexpected display of naval might, "surely a grand specta-cle rare in this world."

Lu You's entire travel diary offers glimpses of village and river life that are not found elsewhere. One can travel with him to learn how a government transport boat operated, what kinds of travelers it carried, what and how they ate, how they went ashore to amuse themselves and visit famed sites after the boat tied up at dusk each day. One also sees how Lu You related to the other officials he encountered along the way and learns the small details of official courtesies and friendships.

After 160 days of travel from the Song capital (Hangzhou) to Kuizhou, his initial posting in Sichuan, Lu You and his family spent almost nine years in that western province (1170–1178). His diary ends with his arrival there, but from his numerous poems and other writings from those years, one can learn much about the life of a midlevel official. At times he was very busy with administrative duties such as repairing dikes, building bridges, preparing for the annual review of the militia, supervising the prefectural examinations, and the like. Those busy months and years alternated with long periods of idleness and boredom when he was assigned to nonsubstantive posts; he passed those times drinking with friends, visiting scenic places, and writing poetry. Unfortunately, little of the material from Lu You's Sichuan years has been translated.[33]

Lu You's poems about rural north Zhejiang require more careful reading; a vivid mosaic of village life can be assembled from them. He wrote several thousand poems over the span of twenty years that corresponded to the last phase of his vigorous, hearty old age. He describes the house he built and expanded over the years, at the edge of Mirror Lake, near the county seat town of Shanyin in Shaoxing Prefecture of northern Zhejiang. We see him talking to his neighbors, attending their parties and celebrations, stuffing his pockets with sweets to take home for his grandchildren, arriving home a bit tipsy from too much wine. From his neighbors he says he learned the humble skills of planting and caring for his garden, and he shared with them their anxieties in years of bad harvest and their joys in plentiful seasons.[34] He does not record as much about his six sons and their beginning careers in govern-ment, their families, or his grandchildren.

His comments on village activities, however, are full of detail. They con-firm, for example, the bits of information from other sources telling of the existence of primary schools for village boys who were not from families affluent enough to start them in classical education that might lead to the civil service examinations. The students he observed, and may also have taught, were ordinary village boys who probably could attend school only during the slack winter months of the agricultural year. "It's late; the children come home from school; / braids unplaited, they ramble the fields; / . . . Father sternly calls them to lessons; / grandfather indulgently feeds them candy. / We don't ask you to become rich and famous, / but when the time comes, work hard in the fields!"[35] Most of them probably acquired little more than basic literacy, but other evidence suggests that such schools were found in most villages. That helps to explain how, as some scholars believe, the rate of literacy throughout the population was higher in Song and later dynastic eras than in other societies in those centuries. There is no way to develop quantified data to prove or disprove that. Careful use of inference from scattered information can lead to useful assumptions.

There are many poems and other writings showing that Lu You, like most Neo-Confucian intellectuals, read the Daoist classics and associated with learned Buddhist monks; he wrote a number of commemorative stele inscription texts for Buddhist and Daoist temples. Yet we also find him very disapproving of lavish rural temples built and supported by the "weary people," whose pittances were given willingly, but under pressure of common beliefs. He found that improper. It was all right for the rich to donate heavily, but not the poor villagers. Until there is an end to these costly activities, he wondered, how will the little people, "muddled and bemused," ever escape hunger and death?[36]

Mention of the government is almost totally lacking. The lack of direct evidence cannot be given too much weight, but it seems to imply that in the villages people seldom gave a thought to the magistrate and the other officials in the county *yamen*. From the more conventional historical materials we know many stories about good magistrates who earned the gratitude of the people, to the extent that when good officials were assigned to another posting, the ordinary people crowded into the roadway to hold back the departing magistrate's carriage, hoping he could be persuaded to continue on in the post. Some local officials were famed for upholding justice, others for providing famine relief, still others for promoting welfare services and building schools for the poor. Do these stories represent no more than topoi created by the elite? That seems unlikely; some of those stories about the people's affection for good officials must have had basis in fact. Yet such good, or bad, county magistrates do not appear in these poems, and much less do we hear of higher-level government officials. Did the common subjects of the realm have no awareness of the vast structure through which the emperor, far away and unreal to the ordinary people, appointed the thousands of officials and managed the affairs of state? They of course knew that there was an emperor, but they appear to have concerned themselves seldom about even his lowliest appointed civil servants in their own counties, much less of the more powerful ones off at the capital.

The only agents of local government who are mentioned, and those frequently, are the sub–official level tax collectors. When the county clerks came pounding at the gates, the villagers within trembled in fear, knowing they might be beaten, have money extorted from them, or be taken away to the county jail. At a village festival described in one of Lu You's poems, the joyous people fancifully appeal to spirit mediums in mock seriousness, expressing the wishes they most wanted answered. Among those is the wish that all taxes will be remitted, whips no longer be used, and prisons all be emptied.[37] But no one expects that to happen. A more realistic hope is that a year of good harvests will ease their tax burden.[38] Lu You himself knew that better officials could ameliorate conditions in the countryside by taking initiatives to carry out improvements, but he explained that most were too busy trying to get ahead in their careers to be concerned about practical matters.

If Lu You was discouraged at times by some of his own kind, the scholar-officials who did not live up to the Neo-Confucian high ideals of office, he nevertheless loved the countryside and the simple, generous people who dwelled there. He shared his humble neighbors' lives by choice, delighting in the good he found among them. Allowing us also to view that life, he tells us about it in ways that realistically supplement the formal historical records, and in words more often expressing joy and contentment than complaint and fear.

16

A MID-THIRTEENTH-
CENTURY OVERVIEW

In the almost four hundred years from the end of the Tang dynasty in 907 until the Mongols completed their conquest of China in 1279, China and Inner Asia shared a new phase of closely interactive histories, each contributing much to change and growth in the other. Under Mongol rule in the fourteenth century, profound transformations occurred which ended that era, and which have obscured our view of it. The reader of history might well at this point reflect on some of the circumstances which prevailed before the rise of the Mongols, and bring together for a closer view some elements of that previous international scene that have appeared in scattered fashion throughout the foregoing chapters. In this chapter we look at several of those elements: the underlying bases of interstate relations, ritualized diplomacy as an international system, related aspects of ritual compared with international law, issues in interstate as well as domestic trade, and some final thoughts on cultural interaction in these centuries. Through such an overview of this period, important dimensions of Chinese and Inner Asian history may be brought to light.

I. THE HERITAGE OF THE LIAO, XI XIA, AND JIN PERIODS

At the beginning of the thirteenth century the Mongols were militantly on the scene in Inner and East Asia; by midcentury they at last had prepared for the final showdown, to become China's greatest peril. That had taken them half a century. The reasons for their hesitation to engage China fully are not entirely clear. Following the death of Chinggis Khan in 1227, his successors did not focus attention directly on Song China again until Chinggis's grandson Möngke held the Grand Khanate (1251–1259). After 1234 the militarily powerful Xi Xia and Jin states no longer shielded China against the steppe, but the Mongols' return to East Asian conquests temporarily took second place to their extension of their world empire into Western Asia and Europe in the 1240s. Their invasion of the Southern Song began in earnest in the 1250s. Khubilai Khan, who succeeded his brother Möngke, finally completed that conquest in the 1270s. These events are the subject of the following chapters.

Before we proceed to the Mongol conquests and the reunification of China under Khubilai Khan, some reflections on the centuries of a divided China are in order. Those centuries witnessed increasingly successful alien incursion into North China, starting with the rise of the Khitans and their Liao dynasty at the beginning of the tenth century. The Khitans fundamentally altered the international scene in East Asia. To acknowledge that fact, the histories of those Inner Asian dynasties have been presented here not just as prelude to an inexorable Mongol conquest, but as forming a period having its own special significance in Chinese and Inner Asian history. The long period from Abaoji's rise at the beginning of the tenth century until the Mongols' termination of the Kara Khitai in 1218, of the Xi Xia in 1227, of the Jin in 1234, and finally of the Southern Song in 1275–1279 is rich in historical interest.

Up to this point, the chronological accounts of those alien and Chinese dynastic histories have followed lines of political development made complex by the region's division into states and the sequence of coexisting dynasties. An overview of the period may enable us to find some simplifying patterns. It also may prepare us to understand how the Mongol invasions that ensued were not just another wave of alien conquest but something new and different in history. No aspect of the following era shows that difference more starkly than the conduct of interstate relations.

China's relations with non-Chinese peoples and governments did not adhere to an unchanging pattern through all of imperial history. From the sixteenth century onward, the European newcomers to the region, resenting the rigidities of the "Chinese world order," eventually came to scoff at what they regarded as its myopic delusions. Moreover, they were made to believe that the Qing dynasty's tribute system, under which they chafed, represented the pattern of all earlier Chinese history. To be sure, on the level of ideal patterns, that kind of world order is both solidly grounded in some, not all ancient experience, and justified in classical texts. The Europeans accepted that situation as part of "unchanging China," in itself a myth that still lingers in some writings. China has never been "unchanging," and the rigid tribute system format of China's foreign relations has not always been in place. The actual pattern of China's relations with non-Chinese states during the centuries of the conquest dynasties leading up to the Mongol conquest has been largely ignored until quite recently. The founders of the Ming dynasty after 1368, following their expulsion of the Mongols, then reconstructed a much earlier tribute system and vigorously reimposed a sinocentric world order. Their restoration was so successful that by the time the European maritime powers began to enter the East Asian shipping lanes in the sixteenth century, they had little reason not to believe what they were told about it. Both they and the Chinese with whom they dealt believed that it had "always" been so; in proof, ancient writings in abundance were cited.

Convinced, after two or three centuries of butting heads against established patterns, that Chinese thinking on the subject was impregnable (and by that time it truly seemed to be), in the nineteenth century the Europeans resorted to war and force to impose their modes of international behavior unilaterally on the disintegrating Chinese imperial system. It is intriguing to think that a better sense of history might have helped the Chinese to adjust more pragmatically to their world at that time.

It has now come to be recognized that, in the period covered by the foregoing chapters of this volume, the relations among states were quite different from those under the later Ming and Qing tribute system. This most historical-minded of peoples, preservers of the documents of their own and their neighbors' histories, venerators of historical study, could nevertheless impose myths on themselves even about relatively recent and fully historical phases of their past. Modern historians, Chinese and others, have come to examine the interstate relations of the Liao, Xia, Jin, and Song dynasties, from the tenth into the thirteenth centuries, and have revealed that the Chinese in those centuries adapted pragmatically to less than ideal international circumstances. To borrow the title of an iconoclastic collection of studies, those centuries have been called an era of "China among equals."[1]

Diplomatic equality with the Liao then the Jin dynasties, as we have seen in the foregoing chapters, was to the Chinese a matter of national shame. China's statesmen and historians glossed over the mass of facts and hoped to forget them, but they did not expunge them from the record. Fortunately, their culture demanded that they be responsible historians, in recording if not always in interpreting. The facts are there.

Through those centuries of interstate equality, the Chinese among themselves continued to express their sense of China's cultural superiority. There is a particular irony in the fact that Chinese of the conquest dynasty era, like some Chinese of recent times, considered it a matter of "national shame" that China sank into a condition of mere "equality" with neighboring states. Through much of the period since the late nineteenth century, it has been one of the great struggles of a modernizing China to be admitted *into equality* as a modern nation, to be on equal footing with others in the worldwide system of modern nation-states.[2] China's goal in recent times has been to free itself from the "unequal treaties" to which it had been subjected in an era of still more painful humiliation, from the 1840s until the 1940s. Yet modern China has not characteristically looked back on its own Ming and Qing period tribute system, the institutionalized basis of the so-called Chinese world order (to borrow the title of another influential book),[3] as a period in which it was China that demanded unequal relations with all its East Asian neighbors. And in truth, there are enough differences in those two kinds of unequal situations to complicate any easy analogies: during the Ming and Qing periods China asked only for essentially voluntary[4] participation in the take-it-or-leave-it tribute system, while under the system of modern international law the Western powers, and subsequently also Japan, imposed unequal treaties on China after 1840 by force. But the flavor of irony in these long-range comparisons persists.

The newer view of China's historic international relations, based on a more careful look at the Liao, Xia, and Jin periods, allows us to put both the recent century and a half of interaction with the West as well as the preceding five centuries of the Ming-Qing tribute system into a useful perspective. From the 920s to the 1230s, China perforce displayed a remarkable capacity to adapt flexibly and pragmatically to unfavorable conditions imposed by the powerful steppe empires, conditions implied by the phrase "China among equals." Although that phrase somewhat overstates the extent to which "equality" prevailed among all the states that then existed on the borders of China, it is an important historical fact that China for some centuries did accept its equality with at least the Khitan Liao and the Jurchen Jin dynasties.

By the late fourteenth century, when the founding of the native Ming dynasty led to a spirit of national revival, China was happy to believe that it had put the shame of equality with barbarians[5] forever behind itself. Today we are unwilling to relegate that phase of the Chinese experience to obscurity. Not least important, it reveals something of the underestimated capacity of Chinese society to adapt. Even under its traditional cultural norms, China was quite capable of flexibility and pragmatism. Once we see that the Chinese, even while undeviating in their commitment to hallowed models and ideal forms, could nonetheless adjust quite realistically to painful circumstances, it becomes easier for us to recognize discrepancies of ideal and actual patterns in all Chinese political behavior, both international and domestic. We should therefore be prepared to look for analogues elsewhere in China's historical experience.

II. THE SYSTEM OF RITUALIZED INTERSTATE RELATIONS

One might first ask what "being equal" with its "barbarian" neighbors meant to the Chinese, and especially to the statesmen and rulers who were most directly involved. What it meant to the ordinary people, if it meant anything, is much harder to know.

To ask whether the Chinese genuinely accepted the idea of equality when forced to coexist with a diplomatic equal that was militarily superior is to pose an intriguing but not very important question, because the answer should be obvious. We know, for example, that in private court discussions about foreign relations, the officials in the Chinese court and political observers throughout the society characteristically adopted the rhetoric of intense resentment against, and of smug superiority to, the "barbarians." Yet those same internal court conferences also produced documents for external use that adopted all the polite language used to convey mutual respect and courtesy. The "barbarians" were neither wholly unaware of nor deeply affected by these discrepancies; their own sense of self-confidence, even superiority, was not a gift conferred by the Chinese in diplomatic contexts.

Even while remaining true to their Confucianism in acknowledging the often admirable "noble savage" qualities of the "wild Jurchens" of the early twelfth century, the Song Chinese felt vastly superior to them. Within a decade they were forced to accept the by this time fiercely hated new Jurchen Jin dynastic state into a structure of international relations in which its parity with China, continuing that with the Khitans, again had to be openly acknowledged. Before the Jin ruler Chinese envoys from the Song would humbly prostrate themselves in full conformance with Confucian ritual etiquette, as they conveyed the felicitations of their Song dynasty Son of Heaven to his fictive nephew or brother or even generationally senior uncle who occupied the barbarian throne. The Chinese had learned to do these things and to pay heavily in money and goods for the privilege. Adherents of the war party at the Chinese court were enraged and sought to undermine a policy so treacherous that it could permit such servile behavior. The peace party, however, could argue with convincing plausibility that it was China which had fashioned these cultural restraints accepted by a dangerous enemy, and that all parties benefited. As we have seen, throughout these centuries the peace party mostly prevailed.

"Being equal," it becomes clear, had at that time a limited yet quite practical meaning. The special circumstances of the period entailed adherence to well worked-out diplomatic procedures which, in essence, embodied genuine reciprocity based on mutually acknowledged principles. In bringing violent disputes to a peaceful resolution, the parties negotiated settlements, bargained by making offers and counteroffers, and worked out the settlements to their interstate problems in the form of written, sworn, signed and sealed treaties. They established elaborate protocols governing embassies and other diplomatic missions, guaranteed special status to envoys and their entourages; and although they did not establish permanent resident embassies on one another's soil, they carefully specified the times of the several annual diplomatic missions along with other details of their conduct. Chinese ritual and etiquette provided the principles and the outward forms of diplomatic behavior. That demonstrated to the Chinese that ultimately it was Chinese cultural values that dominated. Their partners in interstate relations might at times display some measure of practical respect, or even awe, for the ancient sources of Chinese ritualized state behavior, but by and large the applied norms came to function as universals, not as Chinese achievements per se. Much as the culturally particular norms of international law came to function widely in the West from the Renaissance onward, the East Asian and Inner Asian world's ways of defining and ordering relationships through ritual, with or without all the age-old Chinese ethical and philosophical underpinnings, provided the international society of the major states in this period with a system, a "technology" for resolving problems. Violators of its norms, whether Chinese or other, might be subjected to the same forms of indignation, disparagement, and political redress. The system prevailed because it was useful and practical.

That is understandable. One can think of the mentality of modern lawyers in their practice of the law; how often do philosophical concerns for truth or abstract concepts of justice enter their minds, let alone prevail over a purely practical commitment to the clients' and the lawyers' own interests, as they use the legal system in the resolution of conflicts? We depend on the higher judges and their understanding of transcendent constitutional principles to maintain the spirit of the law. The Chinese depended on their classical scholars and statecraft thinkers to maintain the correctness of the rites. So, too, we might observe that Khitan or Jurchen rulers and statesmen did not have to read and revere Confucius and Mencius (although some of them did) in order to commit themselves to the norms of ritualized Chinese diplomacy. In the same way, litigants at the World Court in The Hague do not have to be aware of, let alone hold in reverence, classical philosophers or the Judeo-Christian Bible, on which Hugo Grotius and the other conceptualizers of modern international law based their legal thought. In both cases, without necessarily being committed to the deeper cultural sources of the regularizing systems of international relations, the participants accept it because it works. It works at a lower and more pragmatic level, perhaps more smoothly than might be the case if its philosophical underpinnings had to be deeply engaged in all instances of its application. That analogy should be kept in mind as we look at examples of how the normative system of ritualized interstate relations functioned in Song times.

When the Khitan leader Abaoji, later known as Emperor Taizu, declared his state an empire on the Chinese model early in the tenth century, his people had already experienced more than two centuries of close interaction with Chinese imperial governments, first with that of the Tang dynasty (until 907), and then at the capitals of the Five Dynasties. After 960 the Liao empire continued that pattern of interstate relations with China, now with the newly unified China of the Northern Song. Until 916 the Khitans had claimed to be not a "state" in the orbit of China, but merely a client vassal to which the Tang had granted some authority for local military matters. Appearing often at the Tang capital, Khitan chieftains became very familiar with the claims and pretensions of the Chinese imperial court and the forms to be adopted by non-Chinese taking their places within the Chinese imperial system.

After declaring the existence of their own imperial state in 916 (when they could militarily enforce their claim to be equal or even superior to the state in China), they simultaneously backed up that claim by assuming the Chinese imperial manner, adopting the ritual forms which they understood to be appropriate to an empire headed by a Son of Heaven. They easily fell into those established patterns and extended them to *their* client states, such as the Xi Xia state, the Uighurs, and Korea. The ultimate triumph of the Chinese world system as utilized by militarily powerful non-Chinese states is seen in the imposition on the Song, in 1005, of the landmark Treaty of Shanyuan, which set the pattern for centuries of indemnified peace.

The Chinese did not spend much time formulating general statements of principle regarding interstate relations. Instead we find innumerable references to the implementation of ritual niceties in the forms of communications between states, in exchanges of ceremonial gifts, in such courtesies as announcing imperial deaths and dispatching mourning envoys, in the adherence to sworn oaths of submission and allegiance, as well as in other details of ritual. After the treaty of 1005 came into effect, and through subsequent revisions and additional treaties, we see clear evidence on all sides of the widespread acceptance of formalized protocol and ritualized proprieties. Herbert Franke sees this as signifying "full-scale absorption of the non-Chinese northerners into the Sinitic ritual orbit."[6] That is true, but the acceptance of form should not be taken to signify the simultaneous acceptance of substance; the non-Chinese northerners mostly remained true to their own cultural values.

The example of Korea illustrates the play of cultural nuances. Korea was an old civilization long favored in its relations with China. It scorned the Khitans as latecomers to civilization. The new unified Korean polity of Koryô was established in 918, just as the Khitans were becoming an "empire" with a strong interest in conquering their Bohai neighbors. Koryô immediately established relations with the courts in China, first with those of the Five Dynasties (907–960) and then with the Song, spurning the Khitans at that level of interstate relations. When, however, when the Treaty of Shanyuan in 1005 clearly revealed that the Song was not able to play the expected dominant hand on its northern borders, Koryô accepted formal subordination to the Liao empire, hoping to maintain that relationship in the long-established Chinese pattern.[7] Both the Liao and Koryô relied on the system of ritualized diplomacy, although the Koreans felt themselves to be quite superior to their new Khitan overlords by reason of the distinctively Korean mastery of that system's classical foundations and historical precedents. They participated actively as experts on the details of international ritual and precedent, arguing their case in terms of the system's universalistic norms. The system did not fully protect Koryô from subsequent Khitan depredations, but it still gave a pattern to their interactions that served both their interests and those of the Liao.

When the Jurchens rose in sudden fury to conquer the Khitans and take most of North China from the Song in the decade after 1115, in the eyes of their East and Inner Asian neighbors they were viewed as primitive savages coming upon these old established forms and proprieties. Yet the newcomer Jurchens too immediately perceived the advantages of taking their place within the system and of using it in their interests as new dynasts and claimants to universal rulership. As early as 1121, the sixth year of the new Jin state, the Jin emperor Aguda sent envoys to Koryô demanding that the Koreans assume a subservient relationship to the Jurchens. The Koreans had suffered greatly from the Khitans, who, despite both sides' acceptance of the standard diplomatic proprieties, had invaded and sacked the Korean capital in the 1030s. The Koreans now hoped for a distantly proper relationship with the Jin and probably did not at first respond warmly.

Late in the year 1123 the Jin sent a formal embassy, entirely within the modes of the system; they were met at the Korean border on the Yalu River but went no farther because in the Koreans' reception of them "the rituals of receiving and entertaining envoys were not respectfully observed." Or so the Jurchen envoys reported to their government. At that time in mourning for Aguda, who had died in the fall of 1123, the Jin court instructed the delayed embassy waiting at the border: "Koryô has through successive generations displayed its subservience to the Liao. It therefore is appropriate that it should serve us by the same rituals as those with which it formerly served the Liao. But in our country we are newly in mourning, and moreover we have not yet captured the fleeing Liao ruler, so we should not press them too precipitately."[8] The Jin armies were fully occupied at that moment in the campaigns in North China; in addition, the death of their emperor distracted them with succession formalities. Nevertheless, the Jin armies needed to secure their flank against possible Song-Korean activity, and they found in the prevailing system of interstate relations an instrument for accomplishing that goal without diverting their strength. In invoking the system they were forced to acknowledge, quite contrary to their normal modus operandi, that patience was appropriate. Also, they had to recognize that under this system, Koryô's relationship with its former ritual overlord, the Liao ruler, was still somewhat ambiguous since their own armies had not yet terminated all Liao claims to suzerainty. They could not use the system and at the same time ignore so important a component of it. The records show, however, that within a year or two Jin and Koryô had established full diplomatic relations, the Jin accepting Koryô's sworn oaths of submission, ritual exchanges of envoys for the New Year as well as on royal Korean and imperial Jurchen birthdays, a negotiated border settlement, and all the other components of full diplomatic relations. Each side used the system to its advantage, and subsequent Jin-Korean relations were fairly stable.

In 1124 the Xi Xia also observed the same formula used by the Jin court in its instructions to its envoys at the Koryô border: the Xia "declared itself a border dependency adopting the same rites with which it previously had served the Liao," and its relations with the new Jin state too were in that way quickly stabilized.[9]

For a particularly interesting example of how two parties, both lying well beyond the boundaries of China, invoked the system of ritualized interstate relations, refer to the earlier discussion of the partition crisis in the Xia state in 1170 (Chapter 11, Section II). In brief, the Xia ruler requested that his imperial overlord, the Jin emperor, give his approval to the Xia ruler's intent (under duress) to divide his state, giving half of it to his treacherous chief minister Ren Dejing. The Jin emperor Shizong in that instance responded with a question framed in typical Chinese imperial rhetoric: "How can I, as master of all within the four seas, countenance this act?" Then he went on to note that "Xia has long and conscientiously maintained the ritual proprieties of a border subordinate." Consequently, expressing Confucian responsibility to uphold the norms of (Chinese) civilization, the Jin ruler denounced the treachery in Xia. After the affair had been concluded and Ren Dejing had been executed by the Xia ruler (emboldened by Jin support), the Xia ruler apologized for having allowed the treacherous Ren to seek improper enfeoffment from the Jin Son of Heaven. The Xia ruler's apology turned on the phrase: "The State of Xia has outrageously troubled the [Jin] court, deceitfully seeking the enfeoffment of a treacherous minister; that profoundly impairs the norms of ritual."[10]

Examples of this kind abound in the historical records of these centuries. The system of ritualized interstate relations functioned very broadly among participants who were in some degree aware of its foundations in Chinese tradition, but not necessarily committed to the full range of Chinese philosophical values underpinning it. Again to invoke the comparison, our understanding of today's universalistic systems, within which our personal lives and our modern nations' affairs are conducted, may often be superficial. So also it was with the workings of the ritual-based system in East Asian and Inner Asian interstate relations.

In such cases involving two non-Chinese states, we see a system that could function beyond China, independent of profound knowledge about or genuine commitment to the full range of the values from which the system had grown. Nevertheless, we must not underestimate how deep and how important ritual was *in Chinese society* in these middle centuries dominated by the conquest dynasties. Ritual was a general feature of Chinese life, not something primarily focused on interstate relations. Its provisions for the individual and the family, and for defining and ordering all social relationships, were extended by analogy to relations among heads of states, clearly implying that all humans belong to one order of being. That basic issue of values probably held more meaning for all aspects of human relationships throughout traditional Chinese society than the somewhat abstract universality, or cultural neutrality, which the system of modern law holds for most of us today.

In contrast with China, however, north of the Chinese border the rituals defined a system that functioned almost solely in the narrow range of interstate relations. Gradually, among those neighboring peoples, ritual proprieties were also in some cases extended to affect the social behavior of their elite strata, especially in contexts of education, and in funerals and other family rites. That kind of social practice was not necessarily linked thereby to Chinese ideals of a fully ritualized society. Korea was the outstanding exception; otherwise, such spillovers of the rites outside Chinese society were distinctly limited to the highest strata in any non-Chinese state and society. There the observance of elaborate ritual was (as in aristocratic preimperial China) a mark of status. The rites were fashionable. They conferred dignity. Beyond China proper, however, they held little other meaning.

Ritual in Chinese Society

In Song China, under the impulse in these centuries of a reinvigorated Neo-Confucianism, the Chinese were attempting to realize the fullest permeation of the entire society to the grassroots level of standardized and classically correct ritual behavior. That was a major concern of Song philosophers and statesmen; it would remain a major concern to the end of the imperial era. In these respects, ritual was the systematizing element serving essential state needs in diplomacy; but simultaneously, and far more basically, ritualized behavior held a significance among the Chinese far different from that which it held in those non-Chinese neighboring states. Among the Chinese, the commitment to ritual rectitude was not thought of primarily as a matter of interstate protocol; it pervaded all aspects of social life. When the Chinese observed that the essentially Chinese ritual norms of family existence, and hence of all social behavior, were in some measure universally recognized and punctiliously applied at the highest levels in interstate contexts (e.g., in maintaining kinship proprieties between the Chinese rulers and those of the conquest dynasties), it quite naturally reinforced Chinese confidence in the superiority of their civilization. It showed that theirs was in point of fact the world's only civilization. In their eyes, maintaining the universal (i.e., Chinese) civilization was not at all a matter of honoring ethnic pluralism by allowing the not yet fully civilized border peoples to retain their customs so long as they conducted interstate relations properly. They had a grander notion: no humans were in principle excluded from the prospect of becoming civilized—that is, becoming Chinese. Despite the cultural arrogance of that view, its foundations were thoroughly humanistic, and deeply imbedded in the rich intellectual life of China during those centuries. China's ritualized patterns of social behavior were the touchstone of all civilization; that they also provided a practical system for handling affairs among the barbarian powers must have seemed to the new intellectual elite of Song times entirely within the realm of reasonable expectations.

Whose Interests Were Served?

Chinese *forms* prevailed; but Chinese *interests* did not dominate the ritualized relationships among states. The treaties were forced upon China by the military circumstances and other very real pressures. In such emergencies it usually was the Chinese who sought a treaty as an alternative to continuing unpromising warfare; and it was also usually the Chinese who, with their backs to the wall, proposed the indemnities they would pay, or at least indicated a willingness to seek such a settlement. Their offers frequently were used as bargaining chips against demands for territory or for marriage alliances or other concessions that would have been viewed as still more humiliating. In desperate circumstances, the Chinese learned to negotiate very skillfully. (Late in the nineteenth century, they also quickly mastered the intricacies of the international law then being forcibly imposed upon them and used it to salvage some elements of Chinese interest where possible.)[11] The treaties with the conquest dynasties, to be sure, cost the Chinese vast sums and also exacted a high cost in "face," yet there were still deeper issues: in particular, for the Chinese ruler to acknowledge his counterparts in the steppe states as his equals or seniors within a fictive pattern of imperial kinship exacted a very high symbolic price. The Chinese emperors' family rituals were central to dynasty and state, much more than mere diplomatic trappings. They expressed the state's definition of itself.

Nevertheless, the Chinese knew that the psychological price, and more immediately the cost in treasure and goods, *did* resolve conflicts with the northern enemies. The barbarians could be bought off. Should the Chinese then not have believed that their neighbors to the north were incurably avaricious, were simple, impoverished peoples who lusted for glittering treasure and thus effectively open to manipulation by the richer, more sophisticated state? That unattractive view of the Xi Xia, the Khitans, the Jin, and later of the Mongols was not without a basis in fact. The northern barbarians *did* in fact live lives of rigorous austerity often under conditions close to a bare subsistence-level economy, and their tribal leaders *did* indeed covet the wealth of all the sedentary societies located on the oasis islands and along the littoral of their Inner Asian desert sea.[12] The Inner Asian peoples' material well-being was in fact dependent on riches to be acquired through raiding, intimidation, or conquest. Their relationship with China (as with other sedentary societies) was that of an unbalanced symbiosis; the pressing material need lay all to the one side, the side which in these centuries possessed the means to coerce. Yet to explain the centuries-long process of that symbiosis primarily in terms of the barbarian nations' being poor and greedy is a faulty simplification of the motives which drove those peoples to confront China, and to work out so perceptively the patterns of their coexistence with their vast and rich neighbor.

As for the Chinese, who also engaged the problem of coexistence by drawing to the full on both their cultural and their material resources, they were willing to pay the high price of indemnified peace only when they had to conclude that it was their best choice. They were not characteristically averse to wars they could win, nor did they wholeheartedly accept their own comforting observation that within a spreading Sinitic orbit a *better* world was emerging. Events of the Five Dynasties period (906–960) gave the Liao dynasty the opening wedge to play a leading role in a divided China. Song China, after 960, was never able to erase the heritage of that alien presence within China and finally, in 1005, had to acknowledge full diplomatic parity with the Liao in the landmark Treaty of Shanyuan. Subsequently, the displaced Southern Song continued the same pattern of diplomacy with the Jin court until 1234, but no other states or peoples were ever granted full diplomatic parity. The Xia, the Korean state of Koryô, and the Annamese were granted the much-valued high recognition as states *(guo),* the Xia because they too could apply military and strategic pressures, the Koreans and the Annamese because their levels of sinification earned them that privilege. All other "subordinate" peoples were graded according to the Chinese perceptions of their power, cultural attainment, and strategic importance. The traditional style of unequal tribute relations thus continued to apply most of the time in these less consequential interstate relations.

The Chinese Pattern in Non-Chinese Hands

Song China's relations with the Liao and thereafter with the Jin broke long-standing patterns; the new system extended mutuality in protocol with China and parallel changes in treaty relations among all the other states. The Liao court, for example, not only attained a formal equality with China by being a major power, which allowed it to negotiate from a position of strength in its relations with the Song, but also simultaneously could play the previously unique role of a superior China in its further networks of relations with other neighbors. Some of those other states had no direct relations with China; others, such as Korea and Xia, had to balance their relations with two power centers, often with intricately contrived and intentionally ambiguous diplomatics. Thus for a time, a multistate system formed around two central states, Northern Song with Liao, and Southern Song with Jin. China's claim to be the Middle Kingdom was effectively compromised.

Chinese civilization nevertheless continued to influence political processes well beyond China's geographic borders. The spreading system of international relations emanated from Chinese concepts of human relations and of social values. Those norms became internationalized: the principles they invoked were taken as appropriate, in some contexts at least, to all human behavior and were not regarded by the non-Chinese participants as the cultural property of the Chinese alone. When non-Chinese states then carried those patterns over into their further bilateral relations, as when the Liao entered into treaty relationships with the Xia, or the Jin with the Koreans, they in effect demonstrated that the Chinese patterns possessed a universal validity, or at least a transnational validity within the nearer horizons of China's world. I have said that on the level of day-to-day practice, the conceptual underpinnings of China's cultural norms seldom entered the consciousness of the players. It is not inconsistent with that observation to note, however, that the spread of Chinese ideals and forms, albeit under those limiting conditions, deeply affected a very broad zone of human history.

On a more commonplace level, those Chinese who were well enough informed to feel involved were sorely strained as they observed the diminution of China's political centrality, but they could be assuaged by believing that civilized norms ultimately must prevail. Throughout this long period the Chinese relinquished the comfortable idea that China could dominate a world that extended outward from its proper center to all its neighbors and beyond. Diminished by the hard facts, many Chinese statesmen found it temporarily adequate to gain from their diplomacy whatever measure of comfort can come from rejecting the unattainable. Some rare statecraft thinkers were even able to convert that cold comfort into a feeling of triumph.[13]

Ultimately it was the Mongols' raw new order, not a restoration of China's earlier military dominance and cultural intransigence, which brought this phase of spreading siniticism to its end. The Mongols would do things very differently. The operational precedents for ritualized interstate relations that had emerged during the preceding two or three centuries no longer mattered.

Ritual versus Law in Interstate Relations

The reader coming to this discussion from the vantage point of European history, especially one who compares the emergence of this East Asian interstate system with that of Renaissance Europe (which provided the foundations for modern international law), will be struck by the absence here of an element then dominant in the European case. That element is the various concepts of law itself, whether in the category of divine, natural, or national law *(jus divinum, jus naturae, jus gentium)*. Concepts of legality were central to the authority of European rulers and to the relations among their states. The sources and derivations of law simultaneously constituted a major focus of philosophy. Law in Renaissance European civilizations was the dual heritage of the Judeo-Christian concept of divinely ordained law (giving the Christian church in premodern Europe ultimate authority over jurisprudence), and of the Greco-Roman tradition of secular, rational legal authority and legal practice as the Romans had extended it throughout their multinational empire. Both of those sources of legal tradition imparted a universalistic quality (even though Roman law applied somewhat differently to Roman citizens than to others). In short, in all those concepts of law, whatever their historic roots, law possessed transcendent authority rising above temporal and local political and cultural differences. From the Middle Ages onward, within the ideally universal realm of Christendom, law was rooted in divinely ordained precepts to which all mankind could only adhere. We might observe that in its origins, the secular, rational character of Roman jurisprudence was somewhat akin to the defining norms of practical Chinese laws and statecraft, even though in post-Roman times that component of law in the West also was perceived in medieval and Renaissance Europe as being dignified by and subject to religious authority. In short, the overarching grand idea that law must transcend the human nexus of affairs possessed an unassailably high position in Europeans' minds. In defining kingship, sovereignty, and especially the rights of states and individuals in international conflicts, the transcendence of law was and has remained the major concept underpinning everything, even though a continuously redefined one, until our time.

In contrast, the China-centered world of East Asian civilizations did not have that concept of law. Here it is useful to distinguish between the concept of the rule of law and that of governing by laws. Historically, the latter practice was the norm in Chinese statecraft. "Laws" *(fa)* in Chinese political thought and practice referred to current administrative enactments. All the rules and regulations, even the penal codes, were perceived as no more than instruments of governing, not "law" as in the West, meaning the codified embodiment of a transcendent authority to which all kings and states, at least ideally, should be eternally subject.[14]

Some observers have argued that at least two elements of Chinese civilization were in some respects similar to "law" in that higher sense. One of those is the rites *(li)*, to which I have ascribed great importance here in talking about the ritualized aspects of interstate protocol. It is sometimes said that China employed *li,* the highly articulated and widely acknowledged body of rituals and proprieties, in much the way that law was used in the West. Ritualized behavior as prescribed in the ancient classics on ritual has seemed to some scholars to be functionally analogous to the Western ideal of law. That analogy overlooks the essential differences between law and rites: the Chinese rites claimed no transcendent authority. Ritual behavior was a crystallization of Chinese man's historical experience, codified by wise men who commanded a full, rational knowledge of that history. *Li* (ritual) was thus a culture-bound thing, ideally universal, to be sure, when all mankind adopted the one higher civilization, which the Chinese believed was inevitable. To be taken seriously as the basis of all social life and activity, this mind-set required that all persons of other cultures eventually abandon their own civilizations and adopt Chinese ways. States that could meet the Chinese standards for the observance of *li* would then have no reason, in their people's minds or in the minds of Chinese, to remain apart, nor would they wish to do so. Although the rites, broadly defined, played the basic role in regularizing the norms of interstate behavior at a very high level, in analyzing interstate relations they must be seen as both conceptually and functionally different from international law in the West.

A more philosophical discussion of this issue has centered on whether there existed within Chinese concepts of the organismic natural world a set of principles that functioned like natural law in the West.[15] Regardless of those continuing debates, in China concepts of nature did not contribute significantly to theories of justice which might thereby reinforce the concept of transcendent law, as did the philosophical theories of natural law in the West. In the search for loose functional analogues within Chinese civilization, we do not find much that matches the role of law in defining the principles on which both social norms and interstate relations have been grounded in the West.

The point of the foregoing comparisons is that the international relations of China and its East Asian neighbors during the Liao, the Xi Xia, and the Jin dynasties were built on elements distinctive to those civilizations in that time. Assumptions about the nature of interstate relations quite naturally come to mind from our knowledge of more familiar European precedents. Such assumptions must be used with great care. They will mostly be wrong, although they can help us ask penetrating questions.

That is not, of course, to say that international politics had no theoretical underpinnings in the China-centered world of the tenth through the twelfth centuries. On the contrary, abstract concepts of sovereignty and compelling beliefs about the behavior appropriate to monarchs, statesmen, and generals in their conduct of interstate relations gained ever wider acceptance. We have seen how the impressive Chinese model of the imperial institution, which was perceived by steppe rulers in a grandiose distortion of its actual character, appealed to them all, and all chose to adopt it. Along with that went an acceptance of rules of conduct which all humans must ideally observe. As those rules took on international force, disorder gradually gave way to a shared sense of interstate propriety.

Something like an international system was coming into being; it operated across national boundaries and set limits within which states-as-actors should, ideally, confine their behavior.

The underpinnings of this system, however, were not new, nor were they significantly amplified and analyzed in these centuries, even though they were being put to fundamentally new uses. The widespread reliance on Chinese norms in interstate relations in these centuries generated no new ideas. There were no great formulations of novel theoretical bases for the new kinds of political behavior demanded by the real and largely unprecedented conditions of this period. The same historical precedents and classical allusions continued to be invoked in these extraordinary times, with no apparent sense of disjunction. Antique models continued to be employed as the culture's (not the state's) sources of authority, even during the following century, when the Mongols swept the board clean and set up their own ways of managing interstate relations. Likewise, no reexamined and refurbished concepts were invoked when, late in the fourteenth century, the Ming tribute system transformed the conduct of interstate relations back into what the Chinese considered more appropriate patterns. Perhaps this continuity of ideal patterns that overlay all the changes in actual circumstances obscures much, and may explain the failure to discern the historical features unique to each age. While political behavior was highly adaptive, political theory remained more or less constant: this has been the case in very recent periods of Chinese political life as well.

To summarize these reflections on the conduct of international relations from the tenth through the twelfth centuries, an East Asian community of shared procedures and common cultural patterns was enlarged. If we cannot identify a Chinese Hugo Grotius on the scene, ready to produce an East Asian *On the Law of War and Peace,*[16] we can nonetheless see an important phase in the growth and adaptation of Chinese cultural patterns to the conduct of interstate affairs. To some degree, but in ways not yet precisely definable, those Chinese elements interacted with steppe cultural forms. Under pressures demanding considerable give and take, the ways in which interstate relations worked themselves out during this period hold much interest for the historian. It is possible to surmise that they held greater promise for cultural growth than did the subsequent rigidities of the tribute system when, after the Ming dynasty came into being in 1368, that system's less adaptive patterns were again imposed on all international behavior involving China. Moreover, the flexibilities observed in the Chinese adaptations to the conquest dynasties help us to perceive and to appreciate the fact that considerable latitude, in actual practice, also existed throughout the following period of formal diplomatic intransigence.

III. THE GROWING SCOPE OF INTERNATIONAL TRADE

In exchange for Chinese goods, the Chinese world has drawn to itself exotic objects of trade from very distant places since prehistoric times. By historic times, well-traveled trade routes radiated outward in all directions not only from the North China Plain (which we think of much too exclusively as the place where all early Chinese civilization originated) but from other regions as well. Trade within and beyond China's borders has existed as an element of Chinese life for millennia, complementing the other supports of material life and incidentally bringing along with it ideas, religions, materials, and techniques. All the great civilizations have participated in and benefited from the existence of trade and traders. Despite early China's relative physical isolation from the other ancient high civilizations, since prehistoric times the opportunities for benefiting from far-flung trade have not been less important in China than in other early civilizations.

Although trade has always been important to China, it is just as true that quite early on China acquired distinctively negative attitudes toward commerce. Early social thinkers, especially the Confucians, spoke of the "Four Social Classes." Ranked downward in prestige and status, those were the scholars (or scholar-officials), the farmers, the craftsmen, and the merchants. That ideal ranking is notable for lacking both a hereditary aristocratic class and a class of hereditary knights or professional military men.[17] It also is distinctive in placing merchants, despite the fact that they might be wealthy, at the bottom of the social system.

It is understandable that a class of professional administrators in early imperial times, the scholar-officials, molding a social order to their ideals, should have wished for a civilian environment in government that they could more easily dominate; thus they would relegate the conduct of war to farmer-recruit armies led by professional soldiers of low status who could be kept under civilian authority. Themselves men of acquired more often than of inherited status, they could not easily coexist with a military aristocracy. And we can imagine why they also would fear the power of money in competition with the civil governors' authority, so would try to exclude merchants from easy entry into high status. They were also strongly inclined toward physiocratic notions: believing that the land was the source of all true wealth, they consequently acknowledged that farmers were indispensable to human life (and to the state), while denigrating trade as "parasitic." Their open society therefore allotted to farmers (at least in theory) a dignity and station above that bestowed elsewhere on farmers ("peasants")[18] in most other early societies. And because it was an open society in which 80 or 90 percent of the people were farmers, it was from the more prosperous layers of that socially fluid farming base that scholar-bureaucrats would most commonly be recruited. The scholar-officials' alliance with the land and with its farming population is easy enough to understand. Add to that the fact that craftsmen were seen as only "secondary producers" allied with trade and traders in many ways, and that petty traders especially seemed to be an ungovernable, floating element in society, and the prejudices of the Chinese social order all become understandable.

Despite those understandable attitudes, the ideal social order fashioned by the early thinkers has always been at odds with reality. In some periods, the command of the military forces did not remain under the control of civil bureaucrats. Military leaders usurped the power to govern and to transmit that power to their heirs as a hereditary privilege. If that situation occurred only occasionally among the Chinese, it was the norm among the tribal aristocracies of the conquest dynasties. As for traders and commercial entrepreneurs, as society developed greater complexity and generated more wealth, the importance of craft products grew. Productive labor became more specialized, and the distribution of products by merchants was a powerful integrating factor in the economy. The demand for goods and services, previously limited to the upper echelons, increasingly spread throughout society; opportunities to acquire wealth through commerce grew rapidly. At the same time, the governors began to recognize in commerce a significant source of state revenues. Commerce was gradually accepted by official society, even if not with warm approval from its most conservative thinkers.

By the ninth century, the legal barriers erected against merchants in early imperial times, especially against their right to live sumptuously, to marry into the ranks of the officials, and to enter those ranks by educating their sons to compete with the sons of bureaucrats or of rich farmers for official careers, simply could no longer be maintained. Denis Twitchett has written of a "commercial revolution" commencing in the ninth century that transformed social patterns, spreading from economically more advanced regions to the entire realm of Chinese civilization.[19] By Song times the attitudes underlying the anti-merchant bias of an earlier social ideal still lingered (as indeed they did until the end of the imperial era), but the legal restrictions were largely abolished. The exclusion of sons of merchants from the civil service examinations in Song times was something of an anachronism; and among the richer and more successful merchants it was a rather easily avoided form of lingering discrimination. Even though low in *ideal* terms, the *actual* social status of merchants was high. While petty traders were still held in disrepute, it was largely because they were not wealthy enough to establish the kind of lifestyle that would command respect. Rich merchants, many of whom had risen from backgrounds in petty trade, constituted an element of the social elite. The old ideal patterns still affected their lives, most directly by inducing them to imitate the patterns of scholar-officials' lives, to invest family talent in official careers and to invest family wealth in land, even though neither paid the maximum in economic returns.[20] Successful merchants thus tended to dissipate wealth rather than to accumulate it, and in so doing adopted the prevailing pattern of the bureaucratic social elite.

The point of reviewing these well-known facts here is that both domestic and international trade came to assume an unprecedented importance in China by the end of the Tang dynasty, early in the tenth century, just as my account of the conquest dynasties begins. Commerce was driving the change to a money economy: it was becoming an important element in the management of the Chinese state revenues; it was bringing about the creation of instruments of credit and making new demands on the currency system; it was generating a vastly expanded network of markets with important new market towns; and it was forcing changes in elite attitudes and government policy.

Those expanding roles of commerce also brought about far-reaching changes in the lives of most farmers. There were regional variations in levels of economic development, but by Song times few farmers did *not* produce things that entered the market, and few did *not* purchase or barter items for daily life in the market. The market systems were rapidly becoming crucial structures of social interaction in ordinary persons' lives. That change can be more easily discerned in the historical materials of Ming and Qing times, but the process of social change stimulated by commerce was clearly well advanced by Song times.

This commercial transformation took place alongside the new pattern of interstate relations. The non-Chinese conquest dynasties and other border peoples such as the Uighurs whose states lay northwest from that of the Xi Xia engaged in large-scale commerce with China on the one side, and on the other with regions of Asia still farther west. Those non-Chinese states were created by militarized tribal societies whose leaders were unconstrained by any reservations about the value of trade. Even though trade was often conducted by traders mostly from outside their tribal communities, it was of great importance to them. Through it they became deeply involved in the changing Chinese economy. Their territories gave some of them profitable control over regions through which the overland caravans had long passed on their journeys to and from the West. On their eastern frontiers, the Liao and subsequently the Jin empires also held coasts and ports opening on the Sea of Japan, the Gulf of Bohai, and the Yellow Sea, which gave them access to the maritime trade of East Asia. Coastal zones of Central and South China began to engage in regular maritime trade with North China, Korea, Japan, and Southeast Asia. In the tenth century the northern dynasties in particular encouraged merchants to bring trade to their borders by land or by sea and to conduct it through their territories. Their expansive attitudes toward trade undoubtedly contributed to the speed and scale of commercial development throughout Asia, centered in large part on the wealth-producing society of China.

The large annual indemnities fixed by the treaties, to be paid to the Liao, the Xia, and the Jin by the Song state, had to be recovered in some way. With that in mind, the Song established supervised trading emporiums on the borders, many of them located at those fortified passes along the frontier which best suited their purposes, and granted merchants from both sides the right to carry on trade at those points. Members of embassies were also allowed fixed numbers of days on which to conduct private and unsupervised trade while at the Chinese capital. Profits from the officially supervised trade and the tariff dues levied on it are reckoned to have covered China's annual outlays for the various indemnities and ceremonial gifts. The Song state's interest in the revenues it collected from long-range domestic trade and even more from the international trade was a major stimulus to the growth of that kind of trade in this period.

One could go so far as to say that the enforced outflow of Chinese treasure under the treaties not only helped finance the luxurious lifestyles of the tribal aristocrats, thereby enabling them to maintain both their military readiness and their loyalty to their governments, but also financed their participation in the China trade. The profits earned by the Chinese in that trade in turn helped to finance the growth of commerce throughout Chinese society. Some examples illustrate the way that process worked itself out. International trade paid for China's development of special tea plantations in Sichuan and Shaanxi in West China, which provided the export tea needed to trade for steppe horses, China's one essential import item. Its profits also helped to pay for the maintenance of China's canals, roads, and border trading entrepôts. It helped finance private shipbuilding within China's merchant community. It spurred China's participation in the rich carrying trade that took Chinese merchants and products abroad and brought back exotic luxuries, a large part of which was then sold across the landbound frontiers. Seen in this way, the military pressures on China were converted into stimuli for the expansion of China's domestic economy while at the same time broadening China's horizons and increasing the growth of China's place in world trade.

There is no doubt that China had the most advanced economy in the entire world during this period when its military power vis-à-vis its nearer neighbors was at its lowest ebb. While that circumstance does not imply a direct cause-and-effect relationship, it nonetheless shows that military weakness in these centuries did not have a stultifying impact on Chinese civilization, and in certain ways it generated constructive stimuli.

China's principal exports across its northern land borders were silk, including silk floss for spinning and weaving, woven finished silks, and especially the heavy brocaded luxury silks; some gold and silver bullion (but not large amounts) and coined copper in large volume; porcelains and lacquer wares; rice and other grains; such processed food products as tea, ginger, preserved fruits, and spices; the innumerable items constituting China's vast production and processing of medicines; paper and printed books; rare products of the tropics brought in by Song maritime trade with Southeast Asia and beyond; and other manufactured objects ranging from ironwares to fine jewelry.

In addition to horses, sheep, and camels, the northern and northwestern trade routes brought back to China the same precious metals that China had paid out for its imports or had offered as tribute payments. Differing gold-to-silver ratios between East and West Asia made the trade in bullion profitable to the Inner Asian middleman. But horses were the item of greatest value and of highest strategic importance to both sides. The Liao recognized this and attempted to prevent the sale of horses to China, especially by the upstart Jurchens to the Song state late in the Liao dynasty. The Xi Xia control over the far northwestern source of fine horses, and over high-quality table salt, also gave them a particular advantage in trade.

Although China was not functionally dependent on any particular import items (a partial exception being its military's urgent demands for fine Inner Asian horses to supplement limited domestic supplies), the Song Chinese nevertheless bought great quantities of exotic goods, whether imported across the northern boundaries or from other directions. The most important import trade items were furs and pelts; carpets; exotic Indian and Persian cotton cloth and silks that were different from those produced in the homeland of silk; precious gems and jewelry; armor, swords, and saddles; incense and perfumes; rare medicines and pharmaceuticals; and such precious materials as ivory, amber, coral, rare woods, tortoiseshell, and horn to be worked by Chinese craftsmen. The presence of objects made from exotic materials must have increased Chinese awareness of faraway places.

In sum, trade became important in international relations during this period owing to a conjunction of factors. Internally, Chinese society had reached a stage of development in which trade suddenly assumed far greater importance and acceptance than previously known; externally, China at this time had powerful new neighbors eager for Chinese products and also ready to play the intermediary's role in linking China to international trade across Eurasia. Commerce thus came to impart its particular kind of rationality to widespread social growth. This was a fortuitous conjunction of new elements, some of which would not long survive the end of this exceptional period. Through these three or more centuries, however, the special circumstance under which conquest dynasties controlled all of China's northern borders contributed markedly to the integration of East and Inner Asia, turning what previously were boundaries into zones of enhanced interaction. Whether assessed in economic and fiscal terms or in terms of the social awareness of the wider world and acceptance of ideas and such cultural forms as music and dance, industrial crafts and artistic skills, foods and cuisine, and no doubt others as well, trade enriched Chinese culture and simultaneously made China's legendary wealth known to distant parts of Eurasia.

IV. CULTURAL INTERACTION

As important vehicles of cultural contact, diplomacy and trade have always served to stimulate change at all levels of social interaction. Whether by diffusing ideas or by transmitting techniques and products, travelers who cross cultural boundaries whether as envoys, traders, members of armies, religious teachers, indeed in whatever capacity, have incrementally and largely unwittingly transformed civilizations.

Other forms of cultural interaction result from less benign aspects of interstate relations. Strong states inevitably provoke competition and defensive (or admiring) imitation, which hasten the processes of social change. One example is dramatically evident in the Jurchens' aggressive imitation of their Khitan overlords. Earlier, the Bohai (Parhae) nation, which extended from Korea into northeast China, had more or less disappeared in the tenth century under the Khitan onslaught. In that deadly competition a nation disappeared; but in the same process the conquering Khitans of the Liao empire absorbed a broad range of valuable skills—in agriculture, in industry, and in the techniques of managing societies—from those Bohai people who survived and were made to serve them. Some tribal groups in the steppe also appear to have lost their independent identity when the Khitans made them subservient components of their confederation. Still more was that true in the subsequent Mongol period, when many distinct peoples disappeared as separate nations. In this earlier period of steppe history, tribal entities were for the most part retained intact in the larger empires, and under the stimulus of interstate relations new levels of cultural growth were attained. That is true above all of the Mongols themselves.

During these centuries of heightened cultural interaction, did culture flow in one direction only, from the more advanced societies to the less advanced, as the Chinese implicitly believed? It is easy to generalize that such was the case, and there is much evidence to support that view, but the matter is not that simple. A few examples might help to refine the generalization.

The three states with which we have been most concerned, the Liao, the Xia, and the Jin, all moved quickly from illiteracy in their own languages at the time they established their states to the creation and adoption of writing systems that were based on the forms of Chinese script. Those new writing systems were deliberately designed to be distinctive. Although at first glance they might appear to resemble Chinese characters, they remained unintelligible to literate Chinese. The ability to record speech in writing was seen by the ruling elites in all three states as an indispensable tool. Nevertheless, the wholesale adoption of the Chinese writing system, which would have necessitated simultaneously adopting literary Chinese as their nations' official written language (as medieval European states used Latin and as Chinese was used at this time in Korea, Japan, and Annam), was pointedly rejected by all the three northern border states. The Liao even created a second script, its so-called small script, which still used linear elements borrowed from the Chinese script but incorporated phonetic spelling principles influenced by their knowledge of Uighur, which itself used an alphabetic writing system derived from Western Asian Semitic scripts. The Xia also used unofficially the Tibetan alphabetic script as an alternative way of writing their Tangut language, especially in religious contexts.

The importance of literacy, a fundamental tool of civilization, was most fully demonstrated to these border zone peoples by the inescapable example of a literate, bureaucratic Chinese state which kept records, used official documents, accumulated archives, and thereby regularized its governing procedures. That model of overwhelming cultural prestige was drawn upon in ways that were intended to maintain the borrowers' sense of cultural independence and distinctiveness. The spread of literacy thus provides an example of how the outward flow of a Chinese cultural element, one of supreme importance to the civilization of the borrower, could be borrowed in a defiant spirit of independence from China.

Yet there are in that example two curious anomalies. One is that we see in the influence of Uighur script on the Khitans, and of Tibetan script on the Tanguts of Xi Xia,[21] that non-Chinese peoples on the edges of China were brought into contact with the other major system of writing that Eurasian man had invented, the single if widely divergent family of alphabetic scripts of Western Asia and the ancient Mediterranean world. Those simple, phonetically adaptable systems of writing might seem to us to be preferable to the clumsy way in which the Chinese wrote their own language (one for which alphabetic simplicity offered a less obvious advantage), yet they nevertheless were not preferred by the Khitans or the Tanguts despite their awareness of the alternative. They, like the Jurchens at the same time, were moved by the near-at-hand example of Chinese civilization to adopt scripts that imitated the complex characters of the Chinese writing system.

The other noteworthy point in this context is that after having invented and successfully applied their own scripts, large numbers of the literate members of all three societies, the Liao, the Xi Xia, and the Jin, also became fully literate in Chinese and masters of its literary heritage. Even though the Khitan small script in particular proved quite popular and was widely adopted beyond the Khitan nation, Khitans appear to have produced no body of literature composed in Khitan using that script. Nor did the Jurchens produce a corpus of Jurchen-language writings. The Tanguts, to be sure, created a large body of writings, mostly Buddhist texts and administrative manuals, but they too became increasingly dependent on the Chinese world of letters in their later dynastic history.

The literary heritage of China, including its classics, its histories, its statecraft writings, scientific and technological compilations such as medical works, and its vast corpus of belletristic works, was accessible to anyone who learned the Chinese script, and it offered vast treasures to a person with such interests. In these centuries, when the Chinese state was militarily inferior to its northern neighbors and subject to their coercion, the pull of Chinese culture still had great power. It could not coerce, but it could enrich, and in that process subvert.

When we look to the spread of political institutions, the evidence reveals a different and perhaps somewhat more ambiguous pattern. On the one hand, as we have repeatedly seen in the foregoing chapters, the Chinese emperor was regarded by all the states whose envoys came to the Chinese capital as a supremely elevated and theoretically omnipotent monarch. It was not easy for such visitors to perceive the subtleties of that imperial institution in relation to the sources of its authority and the interplay of responsibilities among officials and ruler. It was enough that at ceremonial convocations of the court, replete with all the pageantry of supreme power and universal dominion, they saw the highest and most powerful nobles and officials—even the leading generals of the world's largest and richest state—prostrate themselves before the Son of Heaven, displaying in that way the Chinese emperor's extravagant luxury of imperial power. Their own tribal societies did not afford them a similar luxury of power. Moreover, the Chinese ruler's succession was securely determined. He enjoyed stability in inherited and transmitted powers and was in addition able to appoint and dismiss at will all of his servitors (actually his associates) in governing. We have seen that the northern societies were more volatile. Their leaders were forced to demonstrate their capacities for leadership in an unending process of contest and competition. Although it is our sense that the steppe pattern of leadership was far better suited to their tribal governing needs, their leaders did not always see it that way. It is not surprising that those leaders who had been successful in building great personal power within their own states looked enviously upon an institution capable of guaranteeing that their leader's (the emperor's) power would pass unopposed to firstborn sons, and which in so many other ways also seemed to make life easier for the Chinese heads of state.

Each of the three conquest dynasties we have considered here made its own responses to the Chinese model. In differing degrees, each also kept some of the instruments of power native to its own traditions. In particular, in order to maintain and preserve their highly efficient hierarchies of military organization, the steppe leaders possessed instruments of power they could not easily abandon. The Liao rulers were the most adept at being Chinese-style emperors in some contexts and gaining the potent aura that went with that, while continuing to be Supreme Chieftains to their own people. At the same time, the administrative forms which were borrowed from the Chinese bureaucratic model, and which utilized literacy and paperwork as tools for governing, also pervaded their system of tribal governing and strengthened it. Yet in the end the last Liao rulers failed as Khitan Supreme Chieftains: having lost their credibility with their own tribal aristocracy, they were unable to command either the institutionalized obedience of the Chinese system or personal loyalty to a tribal leader. They failed in the steppe pattern of failure.

The Jurchen Jin dynasty went much further in adopting Chinese institutions. The Jin rulers were despots in the Chinese style but with differences; many contradictions between their tribal military institutions and the civil governing modes borrowed in the Chinese pattern remained unresolved. We cannot say that their institutional system failed; it collapsed under the incursion of a greater steppe power, that of the Mongols, much as other states, both in China Proper and in the steppe, collapsed before that same power. It is nonetheless apparent that the Jin rulers had not fully worked out the fundamental incompatibilities between two very different institutional systems.

The Xia state of the Tanguts exhibits yet another pattern of adaptation that incorporated elements from both sedentary Chinese-style and nomadic steppe institutions. It appears that those based on Chinese models were beginning to gain importance under the later Xia rulers, shortly before their expansive and successful state also fell to the Mongols. There is a suggestion in that history, too, that their military power base in the rich grazing lands acquired in the northwest constantly grew in importance. Their institutions developed in two simultaneous but mutually contradictory directions, a pattern forced on them by the limited options offered by their geographic setting. Eventually they might have experienced destructive tensions between the bureaucratized southern pole of their state, close to China, and the northwest extension of it that had expanded into the steppe. But to say as much would be to speculate on the outcome of matters still inchoate when the Mongols terminated their history.

In sum, the Chinese imperial model held a great attraction for states throughout East Asia in this period, not only in these three states but in Korea, Annam, and Japan as well. There is an easily identifiable outward flow of political forms and ideas, as well as a broad spectrum of concomitant cultural elements disseminated from the Chinese center. At the same time, it is not surprising that some outside institutions came into China, leading to Chinese adaptations of steppe models. This is most clearly evident in military organization and leadership. Especially in the case of the military, superiority clearly lay with the steppe, and the Chinese were not opposed to imitating what clearly worked. In the pre-Mongol period, the intriguing phenomenon, however, is the steppe societies' different patterns of resistance to Chinese cultural models. Their resistance varied widely and often was resolved by creating amalgams of native and Chinese styles and forms in governing.

An altogether different mode of cultural interaction can be seen in the history of Buddhism in this period. Steppe peoples all were highly conscious of the fact that Buddhism was not a native Chinese religion. Especially in these centuries of the Neo-Confucian revival in Song China, nominally at least Buddhism was somewhat denigrated there, since it lacked the kind of official support and veneration that the Inner Asian societies accorded it. That undoubtedly contributed to the favor the Inner Asian peoples lavished on the Indian religion. Even so, the Buddhism that they so quickly and enthusiastically adopted was known to them in its Chinese forms. Their Buddhisms used the sacred texts as transmitted in the Chinese language, and favored Chinese adaptations of the liturgy, of the arts and architecture, the ancillary crafts, and the evangelizing methods. Despite these massive links to the Chinese cultural base, Buddhism transcended cultural particularisms and created its own world of universal truths and practices. Only Tibetan Buddhism ever had an equal or even superior authority, but in this period its influence had not yet extended to the steppe, having made a great impact only in the Xi Xia state at the edge of Tibet Proper. Even there it was not exclusively dominant, but shared authority with texts, practices, and teachers from the Chinese Buddhist community.

The vast role that Buddhism played in cultural interaction displays its truly international character. The movement of Buddhist teachers across national boundaries and throughout East Asia at this time provides one clear item of evidence. Royal and imperial patrons of Buddhism throughout the regions on all of China's boundaries convened gatherings of learned teachers to discuss doctrines, practices, and philosophical tenets. Even though some of those learned Buddhist teachers knew Tibetan or Sanskrit, in this period Buddhist scholasticism was overwhelmingly within the Chinese tradition. Buddhist scholarship using Chinese appears to have been more active and its achievements more distinguished in the non-Chinese states than in Song China. New editings of the Buddhist canon and scholarly commentaries on it were produced first in the Liao state. The Liao *Tripitaka* (produced nonetheless in the Liao Southern Capital, modern Beijing, primarily by Chinese scholars and printers), the finest yet produced, was taken as the basis for further editions subsequently produced in Korea and in Japan. All were, of course, in the Chinese language. Buddhism was thus, ironically enough, an important vehicle for carrying Chinese cultural influences in religion, in art, in literature, and in other related fields far beyond the borders of China. Buddhism also was, at the same time, a vehicle for carrying non-Chinese Buddhist teachings into China. Tibetan Tantric Buddhism, with its related philosophical and social ideas, is particularly significant as an example of the two-way flow of cultural elements facilitated by Buddhism. This exchange became more important in Mongol and post-Mongol times, both in China and in the steppe. Here we see a particularly significant long-range mode of cultural interaction growing out of developments in this period.

The rich cultural history of these centuries demands our attention. It is all too little studied, but it provides a focus for expanding the understanding of both Chinese and Inner Asian histories and for correcting the imbalance that encumbers sinocentric history. Diplomacy, trade, and the more comprehensive issues of cultural interchange all can be seen as facets of one problem: the mechanisms of social change. The Inner Asian dimension of Chinese history—to remind ourselves of the present work's limited objective—is in no period more interesting or more important than in these pre-Mongol centuries. And although the Mongols truly did begin a new era, they did not emerge from nowhere, nor did they interact with their historical and social environment less than did other peoples.

PART THREE

CHINA AND THE
MONGOL WORLD

Overleaf:

Khubilai Khan Hunting

Attributed to Liu Guandao, active 1275–1300; dated 1280. Detail from hanging scroll, ink and color on silk. Collection of the National Palace Museum, Taiwan, Republic of China; used with permission.

The aging, overweight Khubilai Khan, sixty-five years old in 1280, had his Chinese court painter show him at the hunt with his falconers somewhere in the nearer expanses of Inner Mongolia. In this detail, the artist depicts him with a secondary consort, richly robed, and on horseback, showing that he was still competent in the skills of Mongol life. To our present-day view, the scene is perhaps "exotic" in an oriental manner; to Chinese of that time and now, it is opulently alien, Inner Asian, strikingly un-Chinese.

17

THE CAREER OF THE
GREAT KHAN CHINGGIS

The Mongol period in Chinese and in Inner Asian history was created by the extraordinary man Temüjin, born probably in 1162, who by the time he was given the title Chinggis Khan in 1206 had forged a Mongol nation and set it on the path to world empire. Here the Inner Asian setting of his rise to power, the ethnic elements in his background, and the nature of nomadic society are set forth, and the remarkable saga of his youth and early manhood are related, borrowing from the poetry of the *Secret History of the Mongols*.

1. Backgrounds of Mongol History

Nothing in world history is readily comparable to the achievement of the Mongols in the first half of the thirteenth century. Their spectacular rise from a minor tribal group to their creation of the Mongol nation and leadership of the greatest empire, in territorial extent, that the world had yet seen was accomplished under the leadership of one man. He was Temüjin (Temuchin) of the Borjigin lineage, an aristocratic descent line of chieftains in the relatively small and at that time fragmented and powerless tribe called Mongol. He was born in the mid-1160s, probably in 1162 but possibly in 1167; the Mongols attached little importance to the precise recording of birthdates. He was confirmed in the title Chinggis Khan, or "Universal Ruler," in 1206.[1] By the time of his death in the field in 1227, when he was campaigning in northwest China against the Tanguts of the Xi Xia state, he had permanently transformed the ethnography and the political geography of Inner Asia, and had established in his sons and grandsons a line of rulers, the Chinggisids, who dominated much of Eurasian history for two centuries and who continued to lead the Mongol nation into modern times. The full impact of his accomplishment was to be worked out in Russia and eastern Europe, in the Levant, in Persia, in India, in Transoxiana, in China and Korea, and especially in the vast Inner Asian region of which his new nation of Mongolia became the center. That history involves us in a score of national histories and takes us far beyond the sphere of China. I can do no more than suggest its full scope here. Yet we must take full note of the fact that in the century or more following Chinggis's death, China was an appendage—albeit the most populous and the richest part—of the Mongol world empire. In that way, China became a participant, however peripheral, in world history to an extent not realized again until recent times.

Who were the Mongols, and where had they come from? The answers, until the tenth or eleventh century, are shadowy at best. They did not have a long history as a prominent nation at the edges of the Chinese realm, as had the Khitans, the Tanguts, and the Uighurs, among other nations discussed here. Their name does not appear in the Chinese records until quite late. That undoubtedly means that they were small in number, backward in their cultural development, and unimportant in the lives of their more advanced neighbors. Still, the larger history of the steppe peoples, from among whom they acquired their distinct identity, provides some important clues.

All the tribal steppe peoples had their oral traditions, and a surprising amount of material bearing on their histories and traditions is preserved in the Chinese documents. In those records we find references to a tribal name, rendered Meng-wu in modern Chinese, but at the time pronounced perhaps something like "Mung-nguet," designating a people in the eighth century C.E. living in the Manchurian forests. Two or three centuries later people bearing that tribal name lived in the grasslands of the eastern steppe, west of the Greater Khingan (Xing'an) Mountains and southeast of Lake Baikal. These people are somewhat more clearly identified in historical documents, and it is assumed that there was a continuity of identity from the earlier Manchurian forest dwellers to these steppe pastoral nomads, but that is no more than an assumption. There was at the time a general movement of peoples out of the forests, south and westward into the steppe, away from the life of very rudimentary agriculture supplemented by hunting, fishing, and food gathering to that of advanced pastoral nomadism in the open grasslands. Among their varied patterns of adaptation to the environment, we see the Jurchens and other speakers of the Tungusic branch of the Altaic languages remaining in the wet forests to the east. The Khitans were among those who, many centuries before they founded their Great Liao empire, had moved southward as far as the slopes of the Greater Khingan Mountains, where horses and herding came to dominate their lives. After the Khitans established their vast multitribal empire in the early tenth century, the name Meng-wu or Meng-gu, for Mongol, does not appear among the names of tribes brought under their hegemony, although there is a single record of a visit to their court, in 1084, by people so identifying themselves.[2] By the succeeding Jin period, however, Mongols are clearly and repeatedly identified as a tribal people who figured in Jin border wars in the northern steppe, importantly from the 1140s onward.

All of the tribal peoples identified in the Chinese records going back to the fifth and sixth centuries, occupying parts of the vast region stretching from the eastern rim of the forests along the Pacific coasts across the steppes of Inner Asia and far beyond to the west, spoke languages belonging to one of the three divisions of Altaic.[3] Those who moved out of the forests and into the eastern steppe the earliest spoke Turkic languages. The great empire of the Uighurs who contested with the Chinese Tang dynasty in the eighth and ninth centuries for control of Inner Asia was located in what we now loosely call Mongolia. It represented the most advanced Turkic civilization of that time, although other Turkic speakers had founded states farther west at least two centuries earlier. When another Turkic-speaking people living to their north, the Kirghiz, destroyed the Uighur empire in the mid-ninth century and drove the Uighurs westward into the region we now call Chinese Turkestan, or Xinjiang, that left a vacuum in the eastern steppe into which the Khitans and other nomadic peoples extended their power. As we have seen, the Khitan language seems to have been basically "Mongol" but with heavy borrowings from the Uighurs and other Turkic speakers. Many of those peoples became more independent, advancing politically and militarily after the fall of the Liao empire as their Jurchen Jin dynasty successors turned their attention to China, leaving the peoples of the steppe freer to go their own ways.

When the Mongols emerged as a tribal people with a fairly distinct history in the early twelfth century, they were but one among the many nomadic tribal confederations in the region. Those included the Tatars (more frequently identified in historical records of the time as the Zubu), the Merkits, the Keraits (Kereyits), the Ongüts, the Ongirats, and still farther west the Naimans. Some of these peoples appear to have been more Turkic—that is, more like the Uighurs—linguistically and culturally, and others were more like the Mongols.

In consequence of his conquests and the imposition of Mongol ways, Chinggis Khan in the early thirteenth century absorbed most of those peoples, expanding the meaning of Mongol to include many previously distinct tribes and nations impressed into the core population of the new Mongol nation. A century earlier it may be more correct to call all of the languages showing some affinity with what was to become the Mongol language simply "proto-Mongol." One could go so far as to speculate that if the Uighurs, for example, had achieved a great resurgence of their former military power and had created a new empire reaching all across the eastern steppe, many of these peoples could have become speakers of Turkic; if so, proto-Mongol might never have become fully differentiated as a distinct language family within Altaic. Or if the Tatars or the Merkits or another proto-Mongol–speaking confederation had played the role of the unifier of the steppe instead of the Mongols, the proto-Mongol languages might have evolved into what we would today call Tatar or Merkit. In short, these ethnolinguistic criteria were quite fluid at that time, greatly subject to the fortunes of peoples in their historic developments.

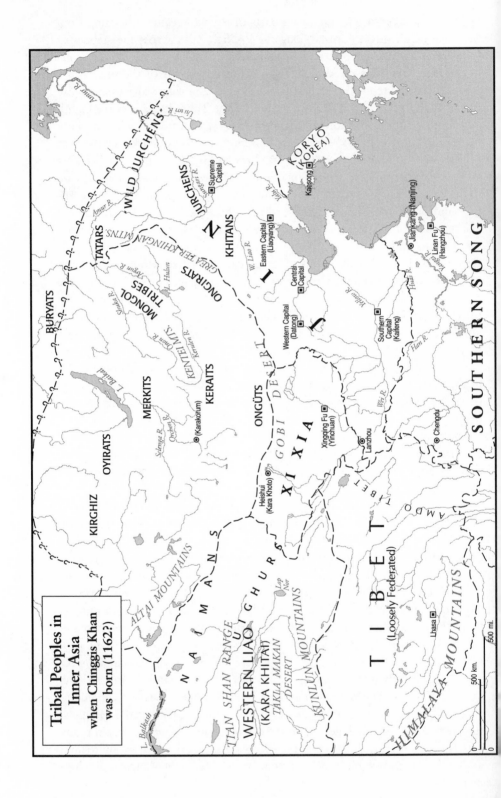

Tribal Peoples in
Inner Asia
when Chinggis Khan
was born (1162?)

11. The Ethnic Geography of Inner Asia in the Late Twelfth Century

Chinggis Khan was born into the very complex multiethnic world of Inner Asia. It was one of uneven cultural and political development. The Mongol tribes occupied a small corner of that world, centering on the upper reaches of the Onon (Onan) and Kerulen rivers, which flowed northeast on the borders of the present boundaries of the Mongolian Republic and Russian Siberia. From there the Mongol-dominated grazing and hunting lands extended westward to the Kentei Mountains, within which was located their sacred ancestral site on Mount Burkhan. That region lies north of the present city of Ulaanbaatar (Ulan Bator), the capital of the Mongolian Republic, and 200 to 300 miles south of Lake Baikal. It is not the region of sandy wastes that we often associate with Mongolia, but one of rich grasslands and rolling, almost treeless hills, well drained by rivers and adjacent to the southern rim of the Siberian forests.

To the north in the transitional zone between the steppe and the Siberian forests were kindred Mongol and Turkic-speaking peoples such as the Oyirats (Oirats Kalmucks), the Buriats (Buryats), and the Kirghiz (Map 11). At that time they were still weakly organized and dependent more on hunting and gathering than on herds, but they also used horses and were marginally nomadic. Later they would be drawn fully into the sphere of Mongol activity; the Oyirats and Buriats in particular would become major components of the Mongol world.

Immediately to the west of the Mongols were several confederations that were stronger and, by cultural indices, more advanced. The Merkits, just northwest of the Mongols, occupied a region that was part steppe, part forest, on the lower Orkhon and Selenga rivers, which flow northward into Lake Baikal. The Merkits were a confederation of four tribes that had advanced rapidly in the eleventh century. Probably under Uighur influence they had adopted Nestorian Christianity. To their south, also adjoining the Mongols on their western front, was the Ke200 (Kereyit) confederation, a strong union of six tribes whose people also were Nestorians. The Mongols enjoyed friendly relations with the Keraits but were hostile to the Merkits. To the west of both these confederations lay the domain of the Naimans, extending from the southern slopes of the Altai Range in the north to the northern slopes of the Tianshan Mountains, giving them possession of much of the rich Dzungarian Basin. The Naimans displayed strong Turkic characteristics and had adapted the Uighur Turkic script to their language, making them one of the few literate peoples among steppe nomads at that time. They too were largely Nestorians, like many among their Uighur neighbors to the south.

Farther to the west from the Naimans and the Uighurs was the domain of Kara Khitai or the Western Liao, a centrally organized state of Khitan rulers and Turkic subjects; it was an offshoot of the Khitan Liao dynasty that was terminated by the Jurchens in 1125. The Kara Khitai territories straddled the

Pamir Mountains and reached far west into Transoxiana. Refugees from the Jurchen conquest, the Khitans who founded the Kara Khitai state in the 1130s brought their dynastic adaptations of Chinese institutions with them. They then came into contact with Persian high civilization in Transoxiana. The Uighur states based on the oasis cities of central Turkestan (modern Xinjiang) came over to Chinggis in the first decade of the thirteenth century. Kara Khitai was absorbed by Chinggis in the second decade. This succession of contacts brought to the Mongols human resources of great importance, steppe kin who nonetheless were in command of administrative and organizational skills that they had acquired through their contacts with the great sedentary civilizations.

The Turkic-speaking Uighurs had the most advanced culture in western Inner Asia at this time, but they were no longer a nomadic people as they had been in the heyday of their great empire in the eighth and ninth centuries. Their empire had been located in the center of the region now forming the Mongolian Republic. When it collapsed under Kirghiz attack in the 840s, most of the Uighurs then moved westward into the Gansu Corridor of northwest China and to Turkestan beyond. In the eleventh century the Tanguts pushed them farther to the northwest, out of the Gansu Corridor, depriving them of their best grazing lands. They became increasingly dependent on the intensive agriculture of the oases strung out across the Tarim Basin, and on the valuable trade that passed along its caravan routes, the fabled Silk Roads connecting China to Western Asia. The Uighurs did not have a strongly unified state at this time; their various oasis-based communities acknowledged the loose suzerainty of Kara Khitai.

The Uighurs played a very important role in advancing the civilization of western Inner Asia. They had been the agency for introducing the Syrian form of Nestorian Christianity to several neighboring tribal groups, although still earlier they had been strongly influenced by Manichaeism from Persia. By the thirteenth century Buddhism was slowly superseding Nestorian Christianity throughout the Uighur population. Somewhat later they would be Islamicized. Their broad cultural experience and elements of the several literate high traditions with which they had at one time or another been familiar, as well as their acceptance by nomadic peoples as kindred "people of the steppe," meant that they could mediate to others a wide range of religious and intellectual ideas and practical governing techniques.

To the south of the Mongol homeland and across the Gobi Desert, along the Yinshan Mountains at the north of the Yellow River's big bend, there was a confederation of Turkic tribes called the Ongüts. They too were Nestorians and considered themselves to be descendants of Shatuo Turks important in that region during Tang times, the same group who later had founded three of China's Five Dynasties which ruled in North China in the years 923–950 (see Chapter 1).

Just to the north of the Ongüt confederation along the western slopes of the Greater Khingan Mountains, the Ongirats were the dominant group. They were a small but well-consolidated tribal group having a long-standing affin-

ity with the Mongols. As we shall see, the Borjigin lineage of Mongol chieftains regularly sought brides among the Ongirats. We presume that their languages were similar or the same.

To the east, immediately adjacent to the Mongols' territories, lay the
domains of the Tatars, the last important group to be mentioned in this discussion of human geography in the Inner Asian steppe in the late twelfth
century. The Tatars were the Mongols' most powerful neighbors and their
most hated enemies. The Liao and Jin histories call them the Zubu, possibly
to avoid the loose and pejorative way the name Tatar had long been used in
Song and Jin times, as also more recently in Western history. The earliest
descriptions of the Mongols, for example, two small accounts written in the
second and third decades of the twelfth century in Song China, use the name
Tatar for the Mongols. In later history the name Tatar (or, as vulgarized by
confusion with another word, Tartar) has been used by Europeans for the
Manchus of the Qing dynasty and for many other peoples in history. Tatar
is also the official name for a Turkic people within Russia in the former so-
called Tatar Autonomous S.S.R. in the central Volga Basin and other Tatar
groups in the Crimea and elsewhere, all said (somewhat contradictorily) to
be descended from the Mongols of the Golden Horde.[4] It is not possible,
however, to establish any specific historical links with those Tatars, or others
in history called by that name, and the proto-Mongol–speaking Tatars of the
eastern steppe in the twelfth century, who were the most powerful confederation in the steppe at that time. The Jin dynasty aligned itself with the Tatar
confederation in the attempt to divide and control. The confederation's central homeland was the very rich grazing lands on the lower Kerulen River
and around Lake Hulun, and including also the lower Onon and Argun rivers.

East of the steppe, across the Greater Khingan Mountains in what
would be present-day Manchuria, considerable concentrations of Khitans still
resided in their original homeland along the Shira Muren or Western Liao
River, which drained the eastern slopes of the range. They were bitterly resentful of Jurchen rule, and many of them looked to join any group antagonistic
toward the Jin dynasty. The old Jurchen homeland along the Sungari River
in northern Manchuria held but a remnant of the Jurchen people. The Jin
dynasty attempted to maintain control or influence throughout much of
Manchuria and north of China in Inner Mongolia. The Jin maintained strong
garrisons at many points, especially in places closer to their territories in
North China, which had become the principal base of the Jurchen population.
Throughout the period of their rise, the Mongols knew the Jin dynasty as the
government of China; they of course knew little or nothing of the Southern
Song lying much farther south.

Still to be mentioned is the Tangut state of Xi Xia, with its capital at
present-day Yinchuan on the Yellow River. From that base the Tanguts had
greatly expanded to their northwest against the Uighurs early in the eleventh
century, and by the late twelfth century their possession of lands astride trade
routes leading into and out of China gave their territories high strategic
importance. The Mongols under Chinggis would regard them as a source of

mounted warriors for use against the Jin dynasty. Tibet, farther to the south-west beyond the Tangut state, played no role in steppe politics at this time.

The Mongols before Chinggis were aware of the Jin dynasty not only as the rulers of North China but also, of more importance to them, as allies of their enemy the Tatar confederation. They also knew about the Tanguts and their Xi Xia state. China, by whatever name, was known to all as the legendary land of riches. But the Mongols were not yet thinking about China; their immediate attention was focused on their own internal consolidation, and to contests with powerful enemies on their borders. In Temüjin's youth the Mongols must have seemed, to all people then aware of conditions in the steppe, to be the least likely agents for powerful expansion of any nomad confederation.

III. MONGOL NOMADIC ECONOMY AND SOCIAL LIFE

The basic features of nomadic life in the Inner Asian steppe, described in foregoing chapters on the Khitans and others, also apply to the Mongols. Yet their culture remained distinctive in many respects because they lived under circumstances in which they developed some of those features more inten-sively than others.

Of most importance in understanding them is their total mobility. While they made hereditary claims to the use of certain good grazing areas and used those regularly, they had no property that was not mobile. For several centuries, from their emergence in the twelfth century until their second and decisive conversion to Lamaist Buddhism beginning in the sixteenth, they allowed no compromise with that mobility. When they at last compromised it, they lost their comparative advantage in warfare and gradually became a governable component of the last great Inner Asian empire, the Manchu Qing realm, into which they were coopted in the seventeenth century. But that would occur far into later history.

The mobility of the steppe nomads was defined by the horse. Steppe horses were sturdy, small, agile, and able to flourish on minimal pasture. Throughout his or her entire life, all members of a steppe tribe were as accustomed to riding as Chinese farmers were to walking. Troops went into battle with three to five mounts for each rider, and by alternating them could stay in the saddle, awake or asleep, for days on end. In an extremity, when it was not possible to stop to find food and take rest, the mounted warrior would open a vein in the neck of the horse and drink the blood as he rode. The horse, and the tribes that had best mastered the use of the horse, ruled the grasslands from the eastern steppe on westward, wherever grass was available. That was true all the way west to the plains of the Volga and the Danube and into the Anatolian plateau. Altaic peoples moving on horseback throughout that vast region created a wide variety of nations and civilizations; they claim it as their homeland today, although no longer as nomads.

Even the less fully nomadic peoples on the forest rim of Siberia north of the steppe used the horse and thus were available for absorption into the nomadic hordes. We have seen that the Jurchens, from the deep Manchurian forests, also acquired horses and the skills of mounted warfare, making them invincible against the Khitans and the Song Chinese in the early twelfth century, even though they remained farmers and did not become fully nomadic steppe warriors. Along the southern rim of the steppe, especially in the west, where the Gobi, the Ordos, the Alashan, and the Takla Makan deserts limited the use of horses, people depended on the great two-humped Bactrian camels to cross expanses that horses could not cope with on their own. Yet even there the horse was the basis of the superior nomadic military power that brought mastery over the large and culturally advanced sedentary societies. In the case of the Tanguts, that was illustrated in the shift to incorporate grazing lands and to adapt more fully to mobile warfare. Although sheep, goats, oxen, and donkeys also were necessary to the economy of the nomad, the horse was key to his mobility and to his superior striking power, essential to the strategy and tactics of warfare by which he lived. This was generally true of all the nomadic peoples of Inner Asian history. The mobility of mounted nomads was nonetheless realized to a greater degree by the Mongols than by any other people in history.

With horses, herds of sheep and goats, oxen to pull their wagons, and camels to carry logistical support for traveling armies where necessary, the Mongols could supply most of their needs. They ate the flesh of their animals and drank their milk, even making their fermented liquor, koumiss (khumis), from mare's milk.[5] They made garments from the leather of their animals and from the felt made of their fur. They made various products from the horns and bones, and they burned the dried droppings as their basic fuel in the essentially treeless steppe. But they also fished in the rivers and hunted in the mountain forests. They did not, however, practice any kind of agriculture except in the most straitened circumstances, yet they needed grains and textiles, which had to be procured from other sources. They also needed iron and other metals which they could not mine or smelt, but they could forge stirrups and bits and knives and could make the cocking devices for their crossbows from iron obtained by trade or raid. Expert smiths were their most valued artisans; they also had tanners and carpenters. These three trades were practiced by specialists who also served as soldiers and accompanied armies in the field, but to some degree these crafts were practiced by almost everyone. Tanners also cured furs, a valuable item in trade and tribute, and made leather goods of all kinds, from armor and quivers to saddles and harnesses. Carpenters made bows and arrows, saddle frames, wagons, and yurt (or, more properly, *ger*) staves to hold up the felt tents that were the identifying mark of the nomad.

When lineages (extended families) prospered and tribes (large lineages or groupings of lineages) were successful in warfare, plundered goods made life more comfortable, and enslaved captives performed many of the supporting tasks. When confederations of tribes encountered damaging defeats and dissolved, and when large lineages fell apart because of unsuccessful leadership or upon the unexpected death of a charismatic leader, the standard of living fell. Each person then would be forced to work at the most basic tasks of survival in one of the world's harshest environments. Multi-competent persons with strength and daring were most apt to survive those low points of social organization.

Under the special conditions of that way of life, social grouping was designed to support and improve life's prospects in the most basic ways. Isolated families lived in great peril, so families would join together in "circles" to enlarge the working group. Lineage cohesion, sustained by legends about common ancestors, tied families into still larger groups when a convincing leader appeared who could accomplish that. Yet lineages could subdivide when their leaders went their separate ways. Or they could enlarge and become tribes on their own, or when they could assemble collateral lineages to accomplish the next level of social organization. We may think of a multitiered social structure of families, circles, lineages, tribes, and confederations in which lineages and tribes are the basic building blocks. But these were fluid structures, and it is often difficult to know whether a large group at a particular place and time should be considered a single lineage or a tribe. Marriage was not permitted within the tribe because the tribe recognized a single founding ancestor, and tribe endogamy would therefore be incestuous—even though most tribes also included families and individuals not recognized as kin, such as captives who had been freed and taken in. Tribal exogamy thus led tribes inevitably to form marriage ties to other tribes, and those ties could serve to enhance the relationships among tribes, leading to cooperation in warfare or even to confederation among tribes. We might think of confederations as "nations" even though they lacked the enduring, consolidated territorial definition that some theorists consider necessary to the definition of the state. As such definitions gradually transcend Western cultural parochialism, the case for considering the political form achieved by the nomadic nation-builders to have been "states" becomes stronger.[6]

Although they differed in the degree of their commitment to mobility, and in the details of their social organization as well as in the history of their respective power buildups, the predecessors of the Mongols whom they most resemble are the Khitans. To be sure, the overall tone of Khitan elite life as we see it demonstrated in the activities and attitudes of rulers and aristocratic elite was more sophisticated, displaying far greater interest in the civilizing arts of their sedentary neighbors than the Mongols had evidenced before the fall of their Yuan dynasty in China in 1368. But in their ultimate commitment to the steppe and its nomadic life, and their ability to remain apart from Chinese entanglements that might threaten that independence, the Khitans most interestingly foreshadow the later Mongols.

In the story of Mongol origins found in their *Secret History,* we see a curious parallel with the founding legends of the Khitans. The Mongol story begins with the mating of a blue-gray wolf and a fallow doe who traveled together to Mount Burkhan, in the present-day Mongolian Republic north of its capital at Ulaanbaatar, northeast from the site of Chinggis Khan's eventual capital at Karakorum. There the union of the pair produced a human male who was to become the primal ancestor of the Mongols. In the Khitan national legend, a horse and an ox united to produce the primal ancestor. In both stories the animals probably are totems of two distinct tribal groups that combined, followed by the birth of the ancestor at a mountain that would become sacred to the lineage, later to the nation.

The Khitans and the early Mongols also shared the pattern of tribal exogamy, in both cases leading to regular continuing intermarriage between leading clans of two tribal groups. That pattern was far more fully institutionalized in the case of the Khitan royal Yelü clan's systematic intermarriage with its Xiao consort clan. In the Mongol case, we see a looser pattern of intermarriage with women from various lineages in the Ongirat confederation; that pattern was loosely maintained after Chinggis Khan's consolidation of ethnic and tribal groupings in the new Mongol nation.

We also see parallels in the place of women in the two societies. There are many examples of women who not only possessed high intelligence and energy (which is true in any society), but also were free to display publicly their great force of character, strong will, and independence of action. Some of those women wielded considerable political power. Nomadic life demanded that women associate freely with men in all the circumstances of daily life. When necessary, they had to be competent to perform under their own leadership most of the tasks that men performed. Their lives entailed grim hardship and endurance, but they were essentially the same hardships borne by men, except that women usually did not have to assume the specialized duties of military life. To be sure, they could fight alongside the men in extreme circumstances, as when their encampments were under attack. But even when royal women had military units of large size attached to their names as perquisites of their rank, they did not have careers as soldiers or as generals. And although their advice was often sought or given without being sought, and usually respected, it was exceptional for them to be invited into tribal councils or hold governing posts. Women were not equal with men, but neither were they mere household servants or laborers, virtual slaves serving nonproductive males. That phenomenon is characteristic of neither East Asian nomadic nor sedentary societies. Ordinary women in Mongol society, however, had a far wider range of roles and were freer in the manner of their lives as partners with men in most essential life activities than were women in most of East Asia's sedentary societies.

Khitan royal women accompanied their ruler sons into battle and made strategic decisions about war and peace. That level of involvement is less evident among elite women in Mongol history, but the dominance of strong mothers and wives over their sons, and their influential if less direct impact on policy, is nonetheless evident, most clearly before the time of Chinggis Khan, but also through the earlier generations of his descendants.[7]

IV. THE MONGOLS EMERGE INTO HISTORY

The earliest history of Chinggis Khan and his forebears is the so-called *Secret History of the Mongols.* It was composed within a few years after the death of Chinggis Khan in 1227, then some decades later committed to various kinds of writing, one imperfect Mongol-Chinese version of which has been preserved.[8] Fortunately it has been possible for modern linguists to reconstitute the original Mongol text. The *Secret History* is our most important source for the Mongols' own view of their legendary origins and gradual emergence into history; it is also the Mongol epic, one of the great literary monuments of East Asian civilizations, and the source of the story about the mating of the blue-gray wolf and the fallow doe who traveled together to Mount Burkhan near the headwaters of the Onon River, where they gave birth to the Mongols' primal ancestor, named Batichikhan. Some dozen generations later Dobun and his heroic wife, Alan (Ah-lan) the Fair, gave birth to two sons, and after Dobun's death she produced three more sons fathered by a mysterious being "as yellow as the sun" who entered her tent by the light of moonbeams coming through the smoke hole, rubbed her belly with his hands, and caused the light emanating from him to enter her womb; then he crawled away again on the shafts of light in the smoke hole. Each of these five sons prospered and became the head of a clan. The youngest, Bodonchar, became the head of the Borjigin clan. His great-great-grandson was Khaidu, "the first to rule all the Mongols." In the fifth generation after Khaidu was born Yesugei[9] the Brave, the father of Temüjin.

At some point that legendary account must link up with verifiable history, but at present it seems impossible to go back farther than Khaidu, who may have lived about 1050 to 1100. The official *Yuan History* (compiled in 1369–1370) states that under him the clan greatly prospered and its numbers grew.[10] His great-grandson, Kabul Khan, is described in other sources as having "ruled over all the Mongols." He clearly is a historical figure who may even have appeared at the Jin court in the reign of Emperor Xizong (r. 1135–1149).[11] Kabul Khan subsequently, throughout the 1140s, made war on the Jin border garrisons to the northwest of the Jin Supreme Capital, inflicting serious defeats.[12] That led to cooperation between the Jin armies and those of the Tatars to combat the now troublesome new Mongol confederation. By the 1160s, when Temüjin's father, Yesugei the Brave, the grandson of Kabul Khan, was a young man, the retaliatory warfare against the Mongols conducted jointly by the hated Jin and the even more hated traditional enemy, the Tatars, had undermined the Mongols' tribal unity and reduced the family of the Borjigin clan leader to destitution.

v. The Youth of Temüjin

Yesugei never achieved the title of khan, but he was an active leader who, contesting for authority within his lineage, had been successful in taking captives, amassing herds, and winning the adherence of a growing number of Mongols. He showed all the marks of being a rising steppe leader. Temüjin, the future Chinggis Khan, was only eight or nine when Yesugei took him eastward, through Tatar-occupied areas to the Ongirat homeland of his wife, to find a bride for his eldest son. At that moment his lineage's prospects were not auspicious, but Yesugei could appeal to the long intermarriage relation-

CHART 6. CHINGGIS KHAN'S LINEAGE TO 1294

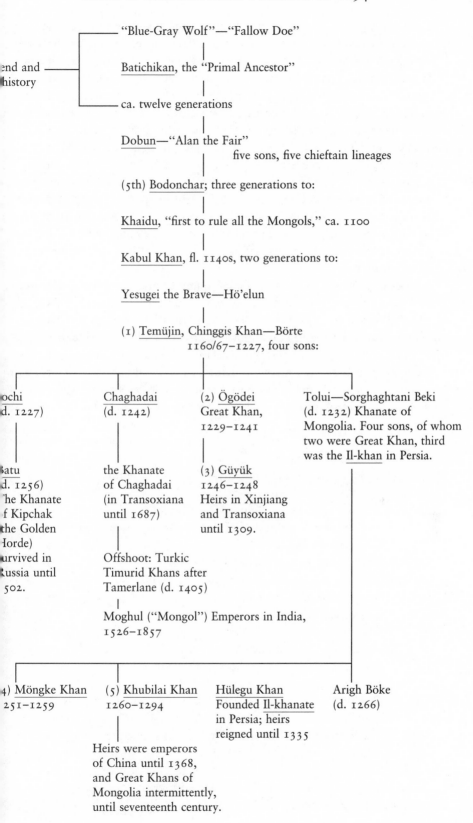

"Blue-Gray Wolf"—"Fallow Doe"

legend and history

Batichikan, the "Primal Ancestor"

ca. twelve generations

Dobun—"Alan the Fair"
five sons, five chieftain lineages

(5th) Bodonchar; three generations to:

Khaidu, "first to rule all the Mongols," ca. 1100

Kabul Khan, fl. 1140s, two generations to:

Yesugei the Brave—Hö'elun

(1) Temüjin, Chinggis Khan—Börte
1160/67–1227, four sons:

Jochi
(d. 1227)

Batu
(d. 1256)
the Khanate
of Kipchak
(the Golden
Horde)
survived in
Russia until
1502.

Chaghadai
(d. 1242)

the Khanate
of Chaghadai
(in Transoxiana
until 1687)

Offshoot: Turkic
Timurid Khans after
Tamerlane (d. 1405)

Moghul ("Mongol") Emperors in India,
1526–1857

(2) Ögödei
Great Khan,
1229–1241

(3) Güyük
1246–1248
Heirs in Xinjiang
and Transoxiana
until 1309.

Tolui—Sorghaghtani Beki
(d. 1232) Khanate of
Mongolia. Four sons, of whom
two were Great Khan, third
was the Il-khan in Persia.

(4) Möngke Khan
1251–1259

(5) Khubilai Khan
1260–1294

Heirs were emperors
of China until 1368,
and Great Khans of
Mongolia intermittently,
until seventeenth century.

Hülegu Khan
Founded Il-khanate
in Persia; heirs
reigned until 1335

Arigh Böke
(d. 1266)

ship with the Ongirats. It is true that Hö'elun, his Ongirat wife, had been
acquired by abduction from a Merkit husband, but the abduction had been
considered justified by the regular pattern of intermarriage with the Ongirats.
Among Yesugei's male kin were others who also had Ongirat wives. The
Ongirat chieftain's little daughter Börte (Bortei) was only nine, but already
noted for her alertness and beauty. In the custom of the time, Temüjin was
left to live in his future father-in-law's house so he could become acquainted
with the family. Yesugei concluded a future marriage arrangement for his
young son. As he journeyed home alone, well satisfied with his new daughter-
in-law, he met a small hunting party of Tatars. Despite the intense hatred
between Mongols and Tatars, they offered him steppe hospitality, and he ate
with them. But he was given a slow-acting poison, causing his death three or
four days later when he arrived back at his camp. Temüjin had been sent for,
but arrived too late to see his father alive; Börte had been left behind in her
father's family.

Despite Yesugei's powerful personal qualities and his status as a *baatur*
(a hero, a brave), there was but a flimsy organizational base for his newly
achieved leadership. Lineage members and other followers, in typical steppe
fashion, now scattered to find another chief who could guarantee their interests by successfully leading them in warfare. Hö'elun, widowed and deserted,
was left to rear four sons and one daughter, including the children of Yesugei's
second wife. They were left alone to starve; at that low point in the family's
history they were in genuine peril. The *Secret History* describes their plight:

> When Hö'elun Ujin [i.e., "the Lady"] saw the people
>   were leaving her
> She grabbed up the standard of Yesugei the Brave
> and rode into the travelling camp.
> Just the sight of her holding the banner
> and shouting caused half of the people to stop and turn
>   back with her.
> But the ones who turned back couldn't stay.
> They were forced to return with the others . . .
> and told to move on . . .
> leaving only Hö'elun Ujin,
> her sons and her little ones, . . .
> leaving only the mothers[13] and sons.
> Hö'elun Ujin, a woman born with great power,
> took care of her sons.
> Proudly she put on her headdress and gathered the folds
>   of her skirt.
> She went up and down the banks of the Onon
> and gathered pears and wild fruit.
> Day and night she found food for their mouths.
> Mother Hö'elun, a woman born with great courage,
> took care of her sons.[14]

Her four boys were too young and too few to raid, or even to hunt, and they were vulnerable to any attacking group looking for captives to enslave. With remarkable intelligence and force of will, she took her family westward into the Kentei Mountains, where steppe enemies might be less apt to find them. She kept them alive by fishing, hunting for small game, and grubbing for berries and roots. Thus they survived for several years, keeping alive the image of Yesugei's leadership. That became a charge upon the young Temüjin. He grew to an early manhood under these most difficult circumstances. In the steppe a male child was an adult warrior by his mid-teens. By that age Temüjin excelled in riding and shooting, and displayed uncommon willpower. Once he was captured in a raid by his father's former followers, but he managed an ingenious escape and returned to his family, the more aware of the need for vengeance. In the hunt and the small raids that he and his maturing brothers began to undertake, he became the mainstay of his family, sharing his mother's responsibilities. He suffered other captures and escapes, raids, and horse rustlings. He formed bonds of sworn brotherhood with other young men encountered in these escapades and established himself as a powerfully ambitious man, brave but not foolhardy, and above all as a magnanimous and trusted leader.

At some point in his teens he rode off to claim his wife, Börte. His father-in-law, hailing him as a future Mongol chieftain, gave him Börte along with her dowry—a rich black sable cloak worth a fortune in that society. The support of his father-in-law was important to his growing stature as a young brave. Temüjin appealed at several points to other chieftains who had been in close personal relationships with his father. Using all the possibilities in the tribal social system, he gradually began to reconstitute, in small beginnings, the clan following formerly built up by his father. To do that, he had to prove in daring actions that he was a leader who could be trusted to make war successfully and thereby provide for his followers. Börte shared fully in these events. Her dowry, the fabulously valuable black sable cloak, was used to gain the favor of Toghril, the leader of the Keraits. Toghril was called the Ongkhan (Prince Khan). Temüjin reminded the Ongkhan that because Yesugei had been his sworn brother, he, the son, looked up to the Ongkhan as a stepfather. That reaffirmed an obligation of friendship and loyalty between Temüjin and the Keraits. The Ongkhan had to assess Temüjin and decide whether to commit his tribe's fortunes to this alliance. He accepted the relationship and offered help. Temüjin's fortunes were rising.

But soon he encountered a humiliating setback. The old enemy, the Merkits, raided and abducted Börte in revenge for Yesugei's having abducted Hö'elun twenty years earlier. To be able to fight another day, Temüjin had to flee. That humiliation had to be avenged. Börte was in captivity for several months; the paternity of her eldest son, Jochi, was later held to be in some doubt, although legitimacy in the strict sense was not a matter of great concern among the Mongols. Temüjin again went to the Keraits to claim the special relationship with the Ongkhan Toghril, who once more was forthcoming with support. A night raid was planned with Toghril's military assistance to free Börte. By this time Temüjin could assemble a force of 10,000 of his own Mongols, and the Kerait leader brought a similar force. Temüjin's sworn brother, or *anda,* whose name was Jamukha, from a rival branch of the Mongol chieftainship, also somewhat reluctantly joined in this raid. It was a great success, and markedly advanced Temüjin's status as a future leader. The *Secret History* tells:

> As our soldiers rode out of the night capturing and
>   killing the Merkit,
> Temüjin rode through the retreating camp shouting out:
>   "Börte! Börte!"
> Börte Ujin was among the Merkit who ran in the darkness
> and when she heard his voice,
> when she recognized Temüjin's voice,
> Börte leaped from her cart.
> Börte Ujin and Old Woman Khogaghchin saw Temüjin charge
>   through the crowd
> and they ran to him,
> finally seizing the reins of his horse.
> All about them was moonlight.
> As Temüjin looked down to see who had stopped him
> he recognized Börte Ujin.
> In a moment he was down from his horse
> and they were in each other's arms, embracing.
> There and then Temüjin sent off a messenger
> to find Toghril Khan and Anda Jamukha, saying:
> "I've found what I came for.
> Let's go no further and make our camp here."
> When the Merkit who ran from us in the night saw our army
>   had halted
> they halted as well and spent the night where they'd stopped.
> This is how Temüjin found Börte Ujin,
> saving her from the Merkit.[15]

The *Secret History* stresses these colorful personal events in Temüjin's life; it makes the rescue of Börte seem somewhat more romantic than it probably was. Here we see Temüjin as an ardent young hero of twenty-two (or possibly only seventeen) being reunited with his beloved under the light of a bright moon during the chaos of a night attack. She is twenty-three (or eighteen), eight or nine months pregnant, and the child she carries, his firstborn son, probably although not certainly was fathered by him. From the point of view of his standing in the eyes of the steppe, his victory in this clash was of immense importance, hence deeply satisfying to him and to Börte. The moving tales about the heroic deeds of the young Temüjin aside, there is no evidence that Chinggis was susceptible to passionate commitments to the many women who shared his bed.

Romantic tales aside, it is clear from his life as recorded in the *Secret History* that Temüjin's rise to power started from a much lower point in his clan's history than did the rise of the Khitan dynastic founder Abaoji or the Jurchen Aguda or the Tangut Yuanhao, all of whose families were well established in leadership and who inherited considerable military and political force. Temüjin's attack against the Merkits to rescue Börte probably occurred in 1184. Up to that time, throughout his late teens and early twenties, he was no more than one among several minor Mongol chieftains who were fiercely ambitious to acquire status and power. But in those years his noted generosity toward his own followers and toward the leaders of other Mongol groups caused many of them to join him. His wealth in herds and spoils grew. He encouraged shamans who predicted his future greatness, and legends began to develop around him. Although nowhere is the event dated, at some time in the late 1180s a number of his Mongol tribal leader associates, fearing the ascendancy of Jamukha and other less congenial leaders, assembled at sacred Mount Burkhan to confer the title of khan on the young Temüjin, and gave him the name Chinggis, meaning the "boundless" or universal leader. That "coronation" was to be repeated, with more widespread significance, in 1206. At this moment he had exceeded his father's achievement, and had begun a dramatic rise to power. From this time onward, it is appropriate to call him by this new name.

VI. CHINGGIS KHAN AS NATION BUILDER

In the 1190s Chinggis allied himself with the Ongirats to make large-scale war on the Tatars, defeating them and greatly reducing their impact on events thereafter. At this time Jamukha, both a kinsman from a related Mongol lineage and Temüjin's sworn brother, became his open enemy. Jamukha was unwilling to acknowledge Temüjin as Chinggis Khan, leader over all the Mongols, so now decided on open war against him. He led a large army drawn from other Mongol tribes to attack; his force may have numbered 30,000 cavalrymen. Chinggis had been warned. He hastily assembled all the tribal leaders of clans and lineages whose loyalty he could command, with all the manpower they controlled. Chinggis's army was organized into thirteen wings, each headed by a person in a traditional leadership position. The first wing was made up of his family members, their subordinates and adoptees, servants, and slaves, and belonged to his mother, Hö'elun. The second wing was made up of Chinggis's own sons, personal guard members and household staff, captives, and other affiliated households. Each of the other eleven was led by associated nobles and other lineage heads and their various categories of subordinates. Their total numbers were roughly equivalent to Jamukha's force. These forces were well deployed to give battle, although there were some command tensions and hints of insubordination. While some Mongol sources claim total victory for Chinggis in the fateful Battle of the Thirteen Wings, the fighting did not go well and the results were at best indecisive. He withdrew and reassembled his battered forces, all still loyal to him. Jamukha's behavior toward other Mongol nobles was notoriously rash and vindictive. Chinggis, for all his ruthlessness in certain circumstances, nonetheless was noted for fairness. That reputation now served him well. Following Jamukha's indecisive attack, Chinggis's forces grew and Jamukha's waned.

Chinggis was discovering that a tighter and better-regularized leadership and command structure was needed. He was an innovator, not bound by conventional ways of acting. He began to reorganize his armies into decimal units of tens, hundreds, and thousands. As earlier in the case of the Jin dynasty, there came a time when Chinggis too realized that the tribal authority pattern of voluntary cooperation from fellow chieftains was too dependent on interpersonal relations. He could not yet afford to displace those bonds, but he recognized the need to supplement them with a more tightly structured command system.

In the years that followed, the wily Jamukha repeatedly joined forces with Chinggis in attacks against outside enemies but then would betray him and violate alliances, attempting to wrest from Chinggis the leadership within the Mongol confederation. Chinggis repeatedly forgave him, taking him back as sworn brother and ally. There are many things about the dynamics of Mongol behavior that are not clear to us today, but throughout these years Chinggis was a leader of growing stature and power.

In 1203 he made successful war on his former allies the Keraits, whose leader, the Ongkhan, had befriended him. Chinggis felt forced into that act by the serious military rivalry that had developed between him and the Ongkhan's son. The *Secret History* tells us:

> Then the two messengers reported to Chinggis Khan,
>   saying:
> "The Ongkhan doesn't suspect we're here.
> He's set up his golden tent and he's holding a feast.
> If we assemble our army and ride through the night
> we can surround his camp and attack by surprise."
> Chinggis Khan agreed with this plan . . .
> For three days and three nights they fought,
> until on the third day Ongkhan's army surrendered.
> . . .
> Then they took all the Kerait people
> and dispersed them among us,
> taking all their possessions as spoils.
> Among them was Ongkhan's younger brother,
>   Jakha Gambu,
> and his two daughters.
> Chinggis took the eldest daughter, Ibagha Beki, for himself
> and gave the younger, Sorghaghtani Beki,
> to his youngest son, Tolui . . .[16]
> So they took away the possessions of all the Kerait people

and divided them among us so that everyone had what they
   wanted . . .
. . .
The Kerait people were disbanded.[17]

Shortly thereafter a similar fate befell the Merkits. The *Secret History* uses
similar language:

> This time Chinggis Khan made a decree, saying:
> "In the past we've said,
> Let them live as a tribe.
> But these people continue to resist us."
> He ordered that the Merkit be disbanded,
> distributing their people among all the other divisions,
> so that they ceased to exist as a people.[18]

The remaining leaders of all the Mongol and Turco-Mongol nations in
the steppe, seeing Chinggis's intentions clearly revealed, banded together to
eliminate him and retain their independence. By a combination of tactical
genius, skill in undermining alliances, and good fortune, Chinggis defeated
them in serious warfare occupying most of the years from 1201 until 1206.
A second war of extermination against the Tatars in 1202 had allowed
Chinggis to destroy their men of fighting age and absorb much of their
remaining population. The last enemy to stand against him was the Naiman
nation, which dominated the western steppe. They had drawn to them the
remnants of the Keraits, the Merkits, the Tatars, and other nations, and also
Jamukha, Chinggis's sworn brother, now his fiercest rival and enemy, who
led a diehard collection of Mongol holdouts.

Chinggis prepared carefully for this great campaign against the Naimans.
During the previous two or three years he had completed the reorganization
of the Mongol armies; he had abandoned the traditional chain of command
through tribal unit leaders and formed his armies into the decimal units of
ten, a hundred, and a thousand mounted soldiers, on the model of the Jurchen
army which the Mongols had come to know. Chinggis now sharpened this
tool of control, giving command over the various wings of his armies to his
most trusted and able personal associates without regard to position in the
tribal hierarchy. He led his armies westward from the Kerulen, where they
had wintered, into Naiman territory in the spring of 1204. He commanded his
forward column, forcing back the leading elements of the combined Naiman
forces, with great losses to them.

At last the full battle was engaged on a steep peak of the Manggai Range
on the southern slopes of the Altai Mountains, in what is the western portion
of the Mongolian Republic today. The Naimans held high ground, but were
encircled by three advancing columns of the Mongol armies, which pushed
relentlessly upward, trapping most of the enemy at the top. It was a decisive
victory, although some leaders, including the Merkit chieftains and Jamukha,

escaped the encirclement and fled. Even though widely scattered portions of the large Naiman population had not been involved, the Naiman confederation had been shattered.

The Merkit leaders and Jamukha, with a dwindling following, fled northward into the Altai Mountains. Chinggis pursued them through the fall of 1204, camped there for the winter, and resumed the pursuit in the spring. Within a few months, leaders of all four tribes of the remnant Merkit confederation had been subdued. Those Merkit people still under their own command were broken up into their smallest units and widely distributed among the Mongol tribesmen to serve them as slaves. Shortly thereafter some of his forward troops encountered the fleeing Jamukha. This time Chinggis did not again forgive him, but he was persuaded to allow Jamukha his wish to be executed without spilling his blood, in a last recognition of his noble status and their long relationship. From this moment onward no rivals again contested his claim on the Mongol leadership.

Chinggis had become the unquestioned leader of all the peoples of the steppe, from the western boundaries of Manchuria to the Dzungarian Basin. His new steppe confederation, unlike the Liao empire of his Khitan predecessors, however, was not an assemblage of dozens of distinct tribes. By the forced absorption of conquered peoples, disbanding and dispersing them so that they "ceased to exist as a people," he was creating a unitary and vastly expanded Mongol nation. There is an apparent anomaly in the fact that the names of the absorbed states or confederations, such as the Tatar, Ongirat, Naiman, Kerait, and the like, were retained in some contexts, at least in the families of the old chieftains, to function as clan surnames. For instance, we see that the vast majority of the empresses whose brief biographies appear in the *Yuan History* are identified as "of the Ongirat clan [*shi*]."[19] This shows the continuing preponderance of intermarriage between Borjigin males and Ongirat women, although women identified as from other clans also are found. The fact that they are now seen as "clans" and not as national entities is significant of the change Chinggis had wrought in Mongol society. In any event, it is unlikely that the use of old tribal-nation names as clan surnames, an aristocratic holdover, was paralleled in social practice among ordinary Mongol people; they called themselves simply "Mongols" so far as we know, and later subdivisions among them were identified by geographic designations.

We do not see much evidence that Chinggis was attentive to governing. True, he organized his "companions" (Mongol, *nököd*), who served the camp needs of daily life around him, into a formally structured body of managers of his household. Most of them had come to volunteer their service to him in a personal capacity, many from other tribes. Their well-differentiated service roles gave to the mobile center of his governing—wherever his tents were pitched—some semblance of order, and eventually would develop into something like a central government with functionally specific subdivisions. And in 1203 he began to organize an elite military guard (Mongol, *keshigten*) into a corps of braves from which would come many of the most trusted of his military lieutenants. Some of these also were chosen from among his "companions." His new decimal-pattern military organization was roughly equivalent to a government, although the prime characteristic of the Mongol military was its total and constant mobility. Little thought was given to creating stable political organs identified with geographic boundaries within which to govern his own or conquered peoples.

Nor do we see much direct evidence about Chinggis's military leadership. He fought at the head of his armies until his death in the field in 1227, but we do not learn much about his strategic planning or about how he formulated his usually successful tactical measures. He deputed authority to his sons and to his leading generals, punishing them for failure and rewarding them handsomely for success. He was magnanimous toward a brave and upright opponent, often taking such persons from among defeated enemies and giving them high position in his armies, because in his mind their loyalty to fallen leaders showed that they could be trusted. He was unforgiving, however, toward treacherous persons or cities or states that broke their word to him. He did not kill such despised enemies out of delight in killing, but he unsentimentally ordered the annihilation of entire populations when that appeared to be appropriate according to his standards. Whatever his own sense of those standards, his armies slaughtered millions of people across Eurasia and caused destruction of the means of livelihood, bringing many more millions to destitution, disease, and death.

Was he a military genius? He lost many battles but no wars. His ability to draw the most courageous and devoted service from his military associates, as well as the long-perfected tactics of mobile steppe warfare, made his armies virtually irresistible in the field. He imposed the most rigorous discipline on them, something new to Mongol military life. Tribal leaders lost their traditional power to detach themselves from a higher leader and go their own way; they were locked into an exacting military organization that had complete power to assign and deploy them and punish them ruthlessly for failure to perform. But he also instilled a spirit of total commitment. Under his command they would travel farther and more rapidly, endure more hardship without complaint, and fight longer and more fiercely than any of their opponents. They were well provided with arms, horses, and supplies. They knew that if they fell in battle, they would be honored and their descendants would be provided for. They also knew that the spoils of war and plunder would be equitably divided among them. He kept their loyalty by fair and generous treatment. His noted magnanimity toward his own people was not typical of Mongol leaders; it became his strongest personal asset.

One of his most original and far-reaching moves was to create a body of his decrees, dealing with all aspects of the nomadic warrior life, assuring his people that rigorously maintained standards would be impartially applied. It is usually said that starting about 1204 he made an assistant responsible for judicial matters and ordered him to write down and preserve all of his decrees.

Those included his judgments on particular crimes and offenses brought before him. The resulting body of legally binding pronouncements came to be known as the Mongol Jasagh (or Yasa). It was based upon, and came to function as, an enlarged version of Mongolian customary law, but was not a systematically worked-out legal code. No text of the Jasagh written in Mongolian is known to have survived, but that it existed is beyond doubt, for extensive quotations from it were recorded by contemporary Western Asian historians.[20] The formulation and implementation of this uniform law, however it occurred, must be considered a central feature of Chinggis Khan's and his successors' achievements. It was an important tool of governing. Most notably, it reinforced uniform standards of Mongol behavior, in that way solidifying Mongol identity at a time when the Mongols were absorbing large blocs of other tribal peoples. And it became one of the enduring Mongol contributions to the life of Eurasia, for it was widely influential throughout the subsequent four divisions of the Mongol empire, from which it shaped law and administrative practice in a still wider geographic sphere.

Also in these years, probably in 1204, Chinggis accepted the voluntary submission of the Uighurs and the Ongüts, two literate, Turkic-speaking Nestorian Christian tribal confederations with long experience in governing by Chinese-influenced methods. He appointed leading figures from among these peoples to teach his sons, hence also many of his elite, to write Mongolian in the Uighur script, and to manage the bureau of non-Mongol affairs in his growing government apparatus.[21] From this point onward, the keeping of records, the transmission of orders and instructions in writing, and a range of applications to governing were instituted. The new tool of literacy was quickly and indispensably utilized, yet at no time does it appear that many of the Mongols themselves became literate. A small service corps, at this time made up largely of Turkic subordinates, seems to have sufficed.

These various steps, unprecedented in Mongol history, indicate that Chinggis Khan was building something more than a typical steppe confederation. By the time the consolidation of the steppe was completed in 1206, Chinggis and his thriving Mongol nation were ready for a new phase of conquest—for the creation of an empire. In fact, further conquest to keep all the Mongols focused on a single set of military goals may have seemed necessary to maintain the new unity of the Mongol nation.

18

FORGING THE
MONGOL WORLD EMPIRE,
1206–1260

Waves of Mongol conquest swept west from the Mongol homeland into Central Asia and beyond, to what are today Afghanistan, Pakistan, Iran, Ukraine, Russia, and into eastern Europe; farther south they crossed Anatolia to reach as far as the Levant. The three great campaigns between 1218 and 1260 drew the full energies of the Mongol nation; they were amazing displays of stamina, tactical genius, and military resourcefulness. The character and personality of Chinggis Khan and his immediate successors, the changing impulses that drove their conquests, the size and organization of the Mongol forces, and the establishment of the four khanates that existed as separate states after 1260 are briefly reviewed here. The Mongol world empire is not part of Chinese history, but China was part of its history. Events as vast in scope as any in world history impinge on the story, but can receive no more than cursory attention, largely from the ground of Chinese history.

1. THE NEARER HORIZONS OF EMPIRE, 1206–1217

In keeping with steppe practice, all the principal Mongol lineage and tribal leaders were gathered into a great assemblage called a *khuriltai,* or conference of tribal leaders, to validate Chinggis's claim to be the khan, that is, to be their supreme chieftain, or in Chinese usage, their emperor. It confirmed him in the grandiose Mongol title Chinggis, meaning "Universal Ruler." The *khuriltai* was held in the spring of 1206 on the banks of the Onon River, in the heartland of the Mongol nation. It did not elect but rather acclaimed Chinggis, in conciliar fashion. There was no challenge to his claim on this occasion, nor was the name of any competitor put forward. Yet the process effectively validated his accession in the eyes of the Mongol world. Each time a succession occurred from his death in 1227 until the succession of Khubilai in 1260 (after which the Mongol world no longer acknowledged a single overlord), a *khuriltai* was assembled to approve the successor. They were also held from time to time to consult on and approve important policy decisions, such as the beginning of a major campaign to conquer a new region. Such gatherings of chieftains to consult on leadership and policy were, as we have seen in the case of the Khitans and the Jurchens, central to the pattern of the tribal governing traditions.

The new Mongol nation which conducted the momentous *khuriltai* in 1206 was different from its steppe predecessors, especially the Khitans. The Khitan Liao empire had at its core an amalgamation of all the closer Khitan tribes, but beyond that it was a multi-tribal world of great racial, linguistic, and cultural diversity held together by constant displays of military intimidation, necessary to maintain subservience to the Khitan overlords. Somewhat differently, Chinggis Khan from the later stages of his rise to power insisted on the ethnic, linguistic, and cultural unification of "all the people of the felt tents," that is, all the steppe nomads. From the time of the *khuriltai* of 1206, we can speak of the existence of Mongolia, a new creation that included all the absorbed Turco-Mongol tribal nations, and occupied a much larger core homeland than had ever previously been established by any people in Inner Asia. Through the next half-century the empire was extended beyond the Mongolian homeland by imposing suzerainty over the periphery of mostly sedentary cultures, eventually including Korea, China, the oases of Inner and Central Asia, Persia, and Russia. That larger outlying empire would crumble, but its collapse did not threaten the integrity of the newly defined Mongol homeland. That is an important difference from all the previous steppe empires. Mongolia existed from the fourteenth century into the early twentieth century as the consolidated geographic base of an ethnically unitary new nation.[1]

Before disbanding the *khuriltai* in 1206, Chinggis dispensed rewards to his principal associates and gave out many hereditary appointments to positions of high rank and power to men who did not already possess that status. His military associates included men of humble birth, blacksmiths, horse herders, carpenters, and others of common Mongol stock whose individual bravery, leadership, and loyalty had been notably demonstrated. Elevating such men into the tribal aristocracy was an important step in a status-conscious society. Chinggis continued to devote his principal energies to ensuring full loyalty to his command by weeding out potentially dissident persons and improving the organization of his military forces. As we have seen, he campaigned repeatedly across and into Tangut (Xi Xia) territory and led attacks against the Jurchens that drove the Jin emperor to abandon his Central Capital (present-day Beijing) in 1215, to flee to the Jin Southern Capital at Kaifeng. Starting soon after 1206, Chinggis also began to turn his attention to the west. The half-century of Mongol expansion in that direction which followed belongs to world history. I can do no more than outline it in briefest form here.

The Mongols' human resources were quite limited. Their armies in 1206 numbered 95 units of 1,000 men each, usually called the chiliarchies (Chinese, *qianhu*). These organizational units accounted not only for the 1,000 fighting men in each, but also for their families and dependents (including slaves and other captives who might not be Mongols and who in any event are not counted in the figures that follow); thus they represented the entire Mongol nation. Only by the roughest estimate can we calculate the size of that population. Because all Mongol adult males to the age of sixty were assigned to a chiliarchy of 1,000 fighting men, and because it may not be far wrong to assume that each fighting man belonged to a family of five or six persons, that would give a figure of slightly over one-half million for the entire Mongol population in 1206. By the time of Chinggis's death in 1227, the number of chiliarchies had grown to 129, nominally at least representing 129,000 fighting men, thus perhaps close to 700,000 people. But in those years certain numbers of Khitans and Jurchens as well as Central and Western Asian Turkic fighters had been added to the war machine and organized into Mongol-led chiliarchies, at least some of which were counted among the 129 chiliarchies. Thus, not all of that growth represents Mongol population increase. There were even a few Chinese warlords who came over to the Mongol side with their troops after the Jin abandoned their control over North China in 1215; initially those too were granted status as regular chiliarchies alongside the Mongol forces, but their numbers were not large. Later, in the 1220s and thereafter, the Chinese auxiliaries mostly were organized separately. Apart from the figures for the essentially Mongol military units, we have no other indications of the size of the Mongol nation in these centuries, although the calculation for average household size (in addition to males between fifteen and sixty) may be too low. It was by any estimate a remarkably small army and supporting population that built the Mongol empire.[2]

The Mongols were able to augment their own forces significantly and could not have achieved their broader conquests without having done so. We see the role of the Mongol chiliarchies in the light of two factors: on the one hand, they undoubtedly were the elite cavalry units that formed the awesome core of Mongol military might. On the other hand, they exerted the power to intimidate and coerce other peoples of significant fighting capacity to serve as subordinates or allies in war. The chiliarchies were grouped in myriarchies (Chinese, *wanhu*), units of 10,000, called in Mongolian the *tümen*. A *tümen* was somewhat comparable to a division in modern Western armies, large enough to form an independent field army; it also could become the territorial administration for a conquered area.[3]

After the initial period of fighting in Mongolia and on the edges of China, Chinese and other soldiers impressed from the various conquered sedentary populations usually were organized separately, therefore not counted among the 129 Mongol chiliarchies. And as the Mongols, especially in their western campaigns, conquered other Turco-Mongol nations such as Kharlukhs, Khanglis, Kipchaks, and Crimean Tatars, as well as some Persians, Georgians, Armenians, and various Slavs, nations that were not to be consolidated ethnically into Mongolia, they compelled those conquered armies to be organized into *tümen* to fight alongside them. When soldiers were drawn from sedentary

populations, they formed infantry units used to supplement the nomads' cavalry; such auxiliaries often outnumbered the Mongol forces under which they
served. In these ways the Mongol armies could achieve field forces of great
size.

Chinggis gave primary responsibilities to the four among his sons whose
status as legitimate heirs made them superior to all others. But he also
assigned to his sons a handful of truly remarkable generals to whom he
granted princely status with discretionary powers to act in the field, as in the
case of the great general Prince Mukhali, who conducted warfare as his viceroy on the China front from 1216 until Mukhali's death there in 1223. Only
the four sons born to his primary wife, Börte, were accepted as his heirs and
lineal descendants possessing the almost magical aura of Chinggisid legitimacy, but among the many sons born to his secondary wives and their heirs,
some were given high positions of trust according to their individual merits,
as generals in his forces and as administrators. The eldest of the four principal
sons, Jochi, must have been born in 1184, for his birth took place during the
return from Börte's captivity among the Merkits. On one occasion, Chaghadai (Jagatai), the second son, born probably in 1185, referred to Jochi as "that
Merkit bastard."[4] The bad blood between Jochi and his younger brothers is
a fact of Chinggisid history. Ögödei, the third son, was almost certainly born
in 1186, and the youngest, Tolui, two or three years later, before the end of
the 1180s. By 1206 they had been active at Chinggis's side for some years,
the three older ones at that time in their early twenties; Tolui, who was to
become the most renowned warrior among them, was in his late teens—
already an adult by steppe reckoning. Soon they would be dispatched on field
expeditions on their own.

II. THE FIRST CAMPAIGN TO THE WEST, 1218–1225

The leaders of the Naiman confederation in the western steppe had been thoroughly defeated in the campaign of 1204–5, but remnants of the Naiman
nation threatened to reassemble and resist. Also, the heir to the last Naiman
khan had entered the state of Kara Khitai and seized control over it, to use
it as the geographic base of a new power buildup. Kara Khitai, the Western
Liao state, extended from western Turkestan (modern Xinjiang) across the
Pamir Mountain Range farther to the west into Central Asia. There it came
into direct contact with the powerful Islamic state of Khwarazm (Khorezm,
Khwarizm), with its Turkic population. It was an expansive military state
extending across much of Transoxiana and south into modern Afghanistan,
eastern Iran, and as far as northern India. This was the first Islamic state to
face the Mongols. They were heirs to several centuries of Turkic states in
the region founded successively by the Ghazni Turks, the Seljuks (Saljuqs,
Seldjuks), and the Turkmens, and like them the Khwarazmians too were
under strong cultural influences from Persia.

Jochi, as Chinggis Khan's eldest son, was expected to establish himself in
the regions farthest from the homeland. Chinggis now sent him with the great

general Jebe to capture and execute the Naiman chieftain who defied the Mongols from his base in Kara Khitai. This they accomplished in 1218, but as they pursued fleeing Naiman forces farther southwest, they came into conflict with Ala al-Din Muhammad II, the shah of Khwarazm. The Mongols did not intend to seek war with the Khwarazmian shah, and in fact offered to divide the world with him and to promote the caravan trade between their two domains. The proud shah bridled under such patronage, and while he allowed a truce to take effect, he clearly intended to follow his own designs. In 1218 or 1219 he created a famous incident, the massacre of the merchants and envoys at Otrar (Utrar). A trading caravan with Mongol envoys among the traders reached the Central Asian city of Otrar, northwest of Tashkent. The local governor, a relative of the shah, ignored their diplomatic status and ordered them all killed. This was a declaration of war. The conflict that followed drew the Mongols into Western Asia and generated the three great campaigns that over the next forty years led to the establishment of the Mongol khanates in Central Asia, Persia, and Russia.

Chinggis assembled a *khuriltai* to plan the 1219 campaign. The generals Jebe and Sübötei (Subotai, Subedei) were assigned to assist Jochi in the field; in fact it was they who planned and led the military operations. Chinggis accompanied the great army westward beyond the Dzungarian Basin into what would be modern Kazakhstan, where they camped and engaged in great hunts as training for the field maneuvers to come. Modern scholarship provides no acceptable estimates of the size of this and other field armies utilized in the three western campaigns. While they probably were larger than armies known in Europe up to that time, they were not as large as the armies available to the shah of Khwarazm, nor could they match in numbers those which were fielded by the Song Chinese or by the Jin dynasty in North China, all of which could conscript from large sedentary populations. Military historians generally conclude that the Mongols' unparalleled successes in the western campaigns were achieved by brilliant field tactics, not by overwhelming numbers.

In the autumn the army turned south to invade the northern part of Transoxiana with its many rich cities, then at the height of their Islamic cultural development. Chinggis employed all the deceits and feints in his repertory, trying to win as much by psychological warfare as possible. Cities were threatened, informed that they would be spared if they did not resist and obliterated if they did. Unfortunately, many were obliterated, whole populations massacred except for some categories of artisans whom Chinggis and later khans shrewdly spared. Some of these were attached to his field army, others sent back to Mongolia. The rich cultural and intellectual life of Central Asia was destroyed by the war; the loss to the region was incalculable. But militarily it was a great success. Western Asia's strongest state was routed and its shah driven into flight; he died on an island refuge in the Caspian Sea in 1221. The numerically superior Khwarazmian forces never were brought together to face the Mongol enemy. The shah's own son denounced him as a coward for failing to pit his full force against the invaders.

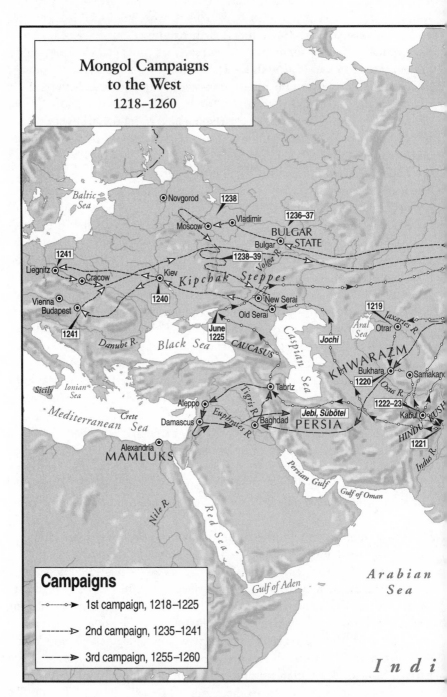

MAP 12

1st Campaign, 1218–1225. Chinggis Khan led this campaign in person to enter Central Asia where he conquered all its great cities, and then went on to the Indus River (1221). At that point, he turned back with a small force to spend a year in the Hindukush, and thence returned by leisurely stages to Mongolia 1222–1224. But his main forces were sent on from western India in two large armies in 1222–1224, by separate routes into the Caucasus and the Kipchak Steppe; one under generals Jebe and Sübötei, the other under his eldest son Jochi. All forces returned to Mongolia 1224–1225.

2nd Campaign, 1235–1241. Led by Great Khan Ögödei's general Sübötei and Jochi's son Batu, Khan of the Golden Horde, this campaign first destroyed the Bulgar state on the Volga 1236–1237, thence went on west to sack Vladimir and Moscow; it headed farther west toward Novgorod in the spring of 1238, but turned abruptly south to conquer the Kipchak Steppe; the Mongol forces destroyed Kiev 1240 and then turned northward into Poland, to defeat a European army at Liegnitz, April 1241; simultaneously part of the Mongol army invaded and conquered Hungary. All forces received a call in December 1241 to return to Mongolia.

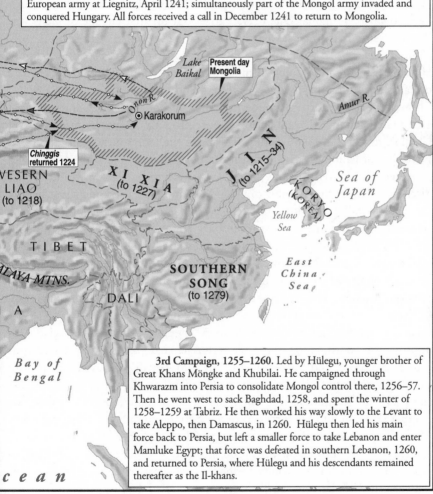

3rd Campaign, 1255–1260. Led by Hülegu, younger brother of Great Khans Möngke and Khubilai. He campaigned through Khwarazm into Persia to consolidate Mongol control there, 1256–57. Then he went west to sack Baghdad, 1258, and spent the winter of 1258–1259 at Tabriz. He then worked his way slowly to the Levant to take Aleppo, then Damascus, in 1260. Hülegu then led his main force back to Persia, but left a smaller force to take Lebanon and enter Mamluke Egypt; that force was defeated in southern Lebanon, 1260, and returned to Persia, where Hülegu and his descendants remained thereafter as the Il-khans.

In the spring of 1220 Bukhara (Bokhara), the region's greatest center of learning and wealth, was plundered and burned; Samarkand followed soon thereafter. As for the size of the forces that took these two cities, Persian sources give figures of 12,000 to 20,000 for that portion of the field army that Chinggis himself led to besiege and then massacre Bukhara, and which then went on to take Samarkand. Samarkand is said to have been defended by an elite garrison of 110,000 Turks and (ethnically Persian) Tadjikhs, but it fell easily. Khwarazmian resistance collapsed. The armies pushed on south-ward through Afghanistan and reached the Indus River in what would be modern Pakistan, south of Peshawar. In 1221, receiving unfavorable omens and concerned about disease and morale among his overstretched forces (and urged to turn back by his Khitan adviser Yelü Chucai), Chinggis withdrew back toward Mongolia. One reason given out for that change of plans was that messages had come saying the Tanguts had rebelled against him.

En route back to Mongolia, Chinggis spent part of 1222 camped in the Hindu Kush, the mountains forming the upland along the modern borders of Pakistan, Afghanistan, and the western end of China's Xinjiang Province. There, at a place north of modern Kabul, he first met the Chinese Daoist called Changchun, "Eternal Spring," more properly known by his name Qiu Chuji. Qiu, then in his seventies, had made the long journey on the urgent invitation of Chinggis, who had heard reports that the old Daoist adept had mastered the mystery of long life; he was held to be 300 years old.[5] Their discussions about the meaning of life in May and June 1222 and subsequently through the fall and winter of 1222–23, as the old Daoist accompanied the returning Mongol army on its route back to Mongolia, reveal much about Chinggis Khan. It is a curious episode of his late years, showing his exagger-ated respect and kindness toward the old man, his earnest desire to learn from him, his openness to beliefs of all kinds, and his respect for all manner of religious teachers. The meetings also had consequences for the administration of the religious communities of China (see Chapter 19).

Before starting his return back to Mongolia, Chinggis had given his approval for continuation of the Western Asian campaign, led by his generals Jebe and Sübötei and his son Jochi. The two generals received approval to push on westward to the south of the Caspian Sea, then turn north to cross the Caucasus Mountains and enter the Kipchak steppe of southern Russia (Map 12). Jochi and his forces were to continue to the west by going north of the Caspian Sea, and were to meet up with the others somewhere in south-ern Russia. The formidable operation included a winter crossing of the Cau-casus Mountain Range, which formed a high barrier running east to west between the Caspian and the Black seas. It occupied the two generals from the early winter of 1221 until June 1223, when they met and defeated a combined Russian-Polovtsy army at the Kalka River, on the northern shores of the Sea of Azov, delivering the most serious blow the Russians suffered in this first western campaign. Some historians see this entire campaign as one of the greatest military accomplishments of all time.[6]

Later in 1223 or early the next year they met up with Jochi. They then obtained from Chinggis Khan permission to create a permanent Mongol garrison to hold the region against the Kipchak Turks. In 1225 Chinggis, who had been lingering throughout 1224 in the region north of Lake Balkhash, ordered his own forces and all the field armies to return to Mongolia to take up the problem of the rebellious Tanguts. So ended the first of the three Mongol western campaigns.

III. CHINGGIS KHAN, THE MAN

Chinggis, as we have seen, died in the late summer of 1227 in northwest China during the final phase of the war to exterminate the Tangut state of Xi Xia. We should pause here to reflect on his personal characteristics and on the measure of his achievement. What kind of a man was this Temüjin who became the conqueror of the world? The best portrait of Chinggis is offered by his biographer Paul Ratchnevsky:

> Genghis was an imposing figure. The Chinese, Zhao Hong,[7] writes: "The ruler of the Tatars [sic], Temuchin, is of tall and majestic stature, his brow is broad and his beard is long. His courage and strength are extraordinary." Genghis' eyes bespoke a lively spirit. "Your son has flashing eyes and a lively face," Dai-sechen [Börte's father] said to Yisugei [Yesugei] when he saw the eight-year-old Temuchin for the first time. Despite the strains of the wars which he fought throughout his whole life, Genghis Khan kept his robust health even in old age. Juzjani comments that, according to the evidence of witnesses who saw him during the fighting in Khorasan [in northwest Persia, in 1220, when he was in his late fifties] Genghis Khan was distinguished by his height, his powerful build, strong constitution, his lack of grey hair and his cat's eyes.[8]

He had, adds Ratchnevsky, strong personal powers of attraction. Many of his important companions were so struck by him on first meeting that they gave up whatever they were doing to become his followers. His appeal was magnified by his lack of pomposity, rashness, or arrogance, and by his magnanimity. He was unusually generous with material goods, keeping little of the plunder of battle for himself; although that was the principal source of Mongol wealth, he distributed it generously to others. He disliked luxury and saw it as evidence of weakness in others. Ratchnevsky quotes from a letter Chinggis dictated to the Chinese Daoist sage Qiu Chuji, called Changchun: "Heaven grew weary of the excessive pride and luxury in China . . . I am from the barbaric North . . . I wear the same clothing and eat the same food as the cowherds and the horse-herders. We make the same sacrifices and we share the same riches. I look upon the nation as a new-born child and I care for my soldiers as if they were my brothers."[9]

Yet that side of him is matched by his undoubted ruthlessness and ferocity. Vengeance was important to his sense of mission. Ratchnevsky says he "was as merciless and cruel towards his enemies as he was generous and liberal with his friends and his comrades-in-arms." He explains, "The idea of vengeance was the basis of the nomads' sense of justice; the duty to avenge was handed down from generation to generation."[10] Chinggis never forgot those who had mistreated him or his family, and given opportunity he slaughtered them to the last living person. Thus he destroyed the nation of Tatars, and virtually exterminated the Merkits.

As for women, Chinggis is said by the *Yuan History* to have had "four *ordos* [camps, households], each with more than forty women; their clan identities are not recorded; their names are all listed in the Tables."[11] Mongol law prescribed the death penalty for both parties in adultery, the man as well as the woman, and was unusually strict in all matters of socially disruptive sexual misbehavior within Mongol society. Nevertheless, women taken from conquered peoples were looked upon as legitimate booty. Chinggis often ordered that large numbers of the most attractive young captive women, after the best were selected for his use, be awarded in groups of thirty or fifty to meritorious associates. It was an effective way of increasing the Mongol population. His field armies were reported to have been followed by troops of captive women, for his personal use and that of his army. Yet he is said not to have been subject to passionately emotional commitments to any particular women.

When his destructive wars and ferocious acts of vengeance are judged by the standards of our time (and by the standards of many in his time), he can be depicted as a monster. But in the eyes of his people he attained godlike stature; he remained the integrating historical personality from whom Mongols thereafter derived their identity. From the historian's point of view, Chinggis Khan did not merely fulfill the highest expectations of the people he led; he in fact transformed those expectations and in the process transformed the Mongol people, defining their new level of social norms through the workings of his institutions such as the Jasagh, and by the consciousness that he instilled in them of being Mongol. He was, for Mongol history, a new kind of national leader, one who created his own role and then played it out, bringing the Mongol people's consciousness of themselves along with him. He was truly the founding figure in Mongol history.

iv. The Second Campaign to the West, 1236–1241

At the *khuriltai* of 1219 that authorized the western campaign, Chinggis had reluctantly designated his third son, Ögödei, to succeed him, having been rebuffed by his other sons in his desire to make Jochi his heir. Ögödei was subsequently confirmed at a *khuriltai* in 1229. At the same time, Chinggis's division of his conquests among his four sons was implemented. By now Jochi, the eldest, had died, probably also in 1227, and Jochi's second son, Batu, became the Khan of the Golden Horde, based in southern Russia. Chinggis's second son, Chaghadai, became the khan of Chaghadai, holding the Central Asian lands wrested from the shah of Khwarazm and extending northward to include most of the former state of Kara Khitai. Tolui, the youngest, in keeping with Mongol custom, inherited the Mongols' homeland, their "hearthland." Ögödei bore responsibility over the administration of the entire empire, and shared occupancy of the hearthland with Tolui. To distinguish himself from the other khans, Ögödei now took the more elevated title of Great Khan, or in Mongolian Khaghan (Ka'an, Qa'an).[12] Here I shall continue to refer to Ögödei and his successors as "Great Khan," or simply as "khan." Subsequently, Ögödei's heirs also received a geographic base in the northeastern part of the Chaghadaid territories. The four khanates thus came into being; they still acknowledged a common overlord in the Great Khan and the guidance derived from their joint participation in their nation's *khuriltai,* but their boundaries and the relations among them were to remain unsettled. Holding and governing territories was becoming more important to them.

The new khan first turned his attention to the borders of China. Ögödei campaigned through Sichuan on the western borders of the Southern Song in 1231 and 1232 and left field armies that actively carried on destructive warfare in Sichuan until the end of his reign. The intent was to soften up the western approaches to an invasion of the Song. He also completed the conquest of the Jin in 1233 and 1234. At the same time, on the other edge of China, Korea was invaded, commencing a long phase of repeated Mongol incursions, leading to the submission of Korea in 1259.[13] In 1235 Ögödei convened a *khuriltai* to approve plans for a new western campaign intended to secure the claims to the Kipchak steppe and Russia that had devolved on Jochi's sons and heirs.

The second campaign to the west was largely dominated by the great general Sübötei, whose feats in the next five years excelled even the extraordinary achievements of the early 1220s in the Caucasus, during the first campaign to the west. The scope of this campaign is well-nigh incredible. The airline distance from Karakorum to Hungary and back is over 8,000 miles; the actual routes followed on the ground must have been several times that. Many tens of thousands of Mongol cavalry with at least five mounts for each soldier, plus herds, wagon trains, support units, and auxiliary forces pressed into service along the way, had to be kept provisioned, disciplined, and under tight tactical command for a period of five years, while they acquired local intelligence, formulated strategy, and won countless battles. There is nothing similar to these immense feats in all of military history.[14]

Sübötei, the senior commander of the entire operation, was accompanied by Batu, who had succeeded his father, Jochi, as Khan of the Golden Horde in Russia. Batu, who would be a dominant personality among Chinggis Khan's grandsons, was still at odds with his uncles and cousins at many points, as his father had always been. Ögödei did not take to the field but remained in Karakorum, where he was engaged in building a somewhat more permanent Mongol capital city. That in itself reflects a change in Mongol modes of behavior.

The armies this time proceeded to the west through Dzungaria and into Central Asia, staying north of the Aral Sea, and on to the middle Volga. There, in 1237, they destroyed the old Bulgar state, occupying its two or three large trading cities (near the modern city of Kazan).[15] Then the armies followed the Volga farther west, to take the Russian cities of Ryazan and Vladimir (on the upper Volga) in the winter of 1237–38. They also took Moscow, then a less important citadel, and headed for the great city of Novgorod, but an unexpectedly early spring thaw made the crossing of the Pripet marshes impossible, so they turned south again and spent 1238 and 1239 consolidating their hold on the Kipchak steppe and taking other Russian cities. In 1240 they commenced a campaign through the Ukraine, to destroy the old state of Rus, with its capital at Kiev. In December 1240 Kiev was taken and reduced to rubble, ending the early phase of Russian political and ecclesiastical history with its links to Byzantium. That defeat made it possible for Moscow in northern Russia to emerge two centuries later as the center of a realigned Russian nation.

The armies went quickly on to Poland, where they defeated Polish and German armies repeatedly, most significantly at the famous Battle of Liegnitz in April 1241. The army had divided, and at almost the same time a southern field force entered Hungary, defeating the Hungarian king in April. The fronts continued to expand in several directions; the Mongols seemed poised to follow the Danube all the way to Vienna and to bring much of Europe under attack. But in December 1241 the Great Khan Ögödei died at Karakorum, and the famous Mongol post relay brought the command to return to Mongolia. Thus ended the second western campaign.

v. Mongol Adaptations to China under Chinggis and Ögödei

While their attention was often focused on the possibilities for expanding their empire to the west, the first two Mongol khans were nonetheless aware of the importance of their newly conquered territories in China; they began the long process of adapting the Mongol nation's interests to the arena in which their steppe predecessors had coexisted with the great sedentary society to the south. All the rulers of the conquest dynasties in these middle centuries of Chinese imperial history faced the problems of governing sedentary societies whose level of civilization and of material well-being far exceeded their own. All sought to draw wealth from China's productive society, first by raiding and plundering, eventually by ruling over and taxing its farming people, making its craftsmen produce on demand for them, and drawing profits from its commerce. As we have seen in the cases of the Liao, the Xi Xia, and the Jin, exploitation of the conquest dynasties' military superiority is the common theme of their separate histories. Yet, despite their similar purposes and needs with regard to China, they developed widely varying patterns of adaptation to their roles as conquerors and exploiters.

The Mongols came to this set of problems with their own quite different attitudes and values. Through the reigns of Chinggis and Ögödei they did not formulate any specific political goals with regard to their conquered territories. They were not even much concerned to maintain social order in the wake of their invasions and conquests; later, when they began to take an interest in such matters, it was only for military reasons, as when they coopted local Chinese military leaders and gave them responsibility for maintaining security in newly conquered regions of North China. In so doing they created local Chinese armies supported by their localities. They kept those armies in place, to be drawn upon as the Mongols needed reinforcements. In the 1210s and 1220s the Chinese local military leaders who were given high hereditary titles as associates in the Mongols' conquest, the so-called "hereditary lords" *(shi hou)*, were often much more concerned about effectively governing their base areas than were their new Mongol overlords. But together they controlled only a small portion of the conquered territories in North China.

In interstate relations, through the middle of the thirteenth century the Mongols recognized no alternatives to domination by military force; they had their own rules for accomplishing that, based on their sense of justice and right as practiced in nomadic steppe settings. They did not acknowledge any usefulness in participating in the by that time well-established international system of treaties and agreements that was governed by Chinese ritual norms, although it was their steppe predecessors who had helped to create that system, and had used it to their benefit. It is true that the Mongols regarded envoys as specially protected persons and that they felt agreements between states, especially when those had been gained by Mongol intimidation or coercion (as in their alliance with the Tanguts, whose inconstancy brought Chinggis Khan's wrath down on the Xi Xia state), should be fully carried out, but solely on Mongol terms. They did not recognize anything approaching the system of equality and reciprocity in interstate relations that had long and successfully maintained the peace among the Song, the Liao, and the Jin. Despite that system's imperfections, their predecessors in conquest had found it to be useful. Not so the Mongols. Nor did the Mongols, not too surprisingly, accept Chinese norms of social rectitude and propriety as applicable to themselves, or even as something it would be socially useful to uphold among their Chinese subjects. Their lack of cultural sophistication kept them from becoming aware of and competent to assess such features of other peoples' ways. Quite understandably, we might say, they extended their Mongol view of life into all situations. Apt learners in some aspects of their lives, in others they were not open to new ideas. From the time of Chinggis Khan's early conquests of the Jin onward, the Mongols recruited non-Mongol advisers and listened to their arguments, but often they were not swayed by them.

Chinggis Khan interviewed the captured Khitan statesman Yelü Chucai in 1218, was impressed by his combination of Khitan virtues and command of Chinese learning, and retained him on his advisory staff as a highly honored personage. But for twenty-five years, under Chinggis and his successor, Ögödei, Yelü struggled to exert what he considered to be a civilizing influence on his Mongol masters, to make them appreciate the benefits to themselves from ruling their Chinese subjects in established Chinese ways. He was mostly frustrated in that lifelong effort.[16]

We have also seen that Chinggis in 1222–23 had invited the Daoist leader Qiu Chuji, known as Changchun (Everlasting Spring), to visit him in Central

Asia and had inquired at length about Daoist religious beliefs and practices, displaying the greatest respect and humility toward him. He also made full inquiry about the religious situation in China, learning about Buddhist-Daoist rivalries, and about Confucian social roles as well. Qiu was the leader of the then-powerful Quanzhen sect of Daoism, which had great social influence in North China. Chinggis shrewdly calculated that benefits could accrue from favoring Daoism and granting privileges to this sectarian leader to help build support for his Mongol forces in China. He thus gave Qiu Chuji an edict exempting all clergy in China from taxes and labor service obligations, and appointed Qiu the administrator of all the religious communities, so that on his return to China he could exercise control over large segments of the population and guarantee cooperation with the Mongol cause. Nevertheless, Chinggis's concern in so doing was to aid the short-term exploitation of the Chinese population; he was not much interested in how the other society worked, or in adopting Chinese ways of governing it.

The numbers of non-Mongol advisers grew under Ögödei, but the situation did not greatly change, because Mongol policy toward conquered regions continued to develop on an ad hoc basis. This is not to deny the significance of several administrative innovations achieved by Yelü Chucai in the early 1230s. Arguing against Mongol proposals to clear large portions of North China of its agrarian population in order to turn it into unbroken grazing lands for Mongol horses and herds, Yelü devised a system for revenue collection and gained the khan's approval for trying it out. In the first year of implementing the new measures, Yelü demonstrated that the tax revenues that could be equitably and systematically collected could exceed the random and rapacious extortion previously practiced by Mongol managers. Without these resources provided by the Chinese farming population, he asked the khan, how will you support your future invasions of Song China? The khan, impressed, named Yelü chief of the Secretariat in charge of administration for the several provinces then under Mongol military control. Yelü already had held the title of scribe or secretary at the khan's court; now the Secretariat was divided into two sections, one using Uighur and Mongol (both written in the same script), and the other using Chinese in the daily paperwork of governing. Yelü employed mostly former Jin dynasty administrators, Khitans like himself, as well as Jurchens and Chinese. In addition to making the tax burdens more bearable, Yelü and his civil governing aides did much to curb the abuses of the Daoist and Buddhist monasteries, which, under the edict of exemption from taxation and obligations granted by Chinggis Khan to Qiu Chuji, had come to engage in many forms of improper economic activities. Further, Yelü sought with some success to restrain the Mongol heads of appanages (fiefs) or their managers in North China from enslaving and misusing the Chinese population, and especially to free Confucian scholar households from slave status.

Yelü Chucai's reforms, in short, began to put in place the kind of governing mechanisms previously employed by the Khitans and the Jurchens. Their significance for the well-being of the Chinese can scarcely be overestimated. But Yelü's administrative practices aroused suspicion and dissent among the Mongol nobles around the khan. They attacked him with rumors and false charges, and gained the khan's ear at least to the extent of being able to undo much of what Yelü had accomplished. The Mongols' objectives at this early stage remained what they always had been: the greater exploitation of the conquered Chinese population, not the establishment of a peaceful, orderly, productive society per se. Their views of how to achieve that exploitation were shortsighted, and they were not yet close to accepting a longer-range view of things. In brief, their original view of the purposes underlying nomads' control of sedentary peoples had not changed. Much less had they acquired any appreciation of the Confucian values and the humanistic traditions of Chinese civilization, the things that Yelü and his associates strove valiantly to preserve through this period of crisis. When Yelü died in 1243, two years after the death of Ögödei, at a time when the khan's widow, Töregene, ruled as regent, Turks and Central Asians intent on undermining Yelü's policies were brought into positions of power. This initial phase of the Mongols' adaptation to Chinese modes of governing had come to an end. Despite some important accomplishments, the adaptation had been at best superficial.

VI. Möngke Khan and the Third Campaign to the West

The succession to Ögödei after his death in 1241 displayed the extent to which disputes among the four Chinggisid lineages threatened the unity of the Mongol world. Batu, his nephew, refused to attend the *khuriltai,* making it difficult to achieve consensus. Hoping to benefit her son by feeding the disagreements, Ögödei's widow, Töregene, managed to have herself named regent in 1242 until a decision could be reached. One of the famous strong women of Mongol history, she was determined to gain the succession for her son Güyük. He was finally elected at a postponed *khuriltai* in 1246, but died two years later. Then his own widow was named regent while political factions again struggled to advance their candidates. At this point Tolui's widow, Sorghaghtani Beki, equally wily in her own way, managed to gain the support of Batu and to bring about the election of her eldest son, Möngke, at the *khuriltai* of 1249, but objections from the other lines delayed his formal accession until 1251.

Möngke Khan was an intelligent, sober-minded upholder of Mongol tradition and an able administrator. He was consumed by the desire to achieve strict adherence by all Mongols to his grandfather Chinggis Khan's Jasagh (Yasa), to eliminate slackness and corruption, and to regain the élan of the earlier phase of Mongol world conquest. As a manager of the empire, he was the best of the great khans.[17] His succession had been opposed by members of the Ögödeid and Chaghadaid lines who, it was said, had gone so far as to plan to assassinate him. He spent his first year or more rooting out all such disloyalty, purging the Mongol elite, greatly weakening the house of Chaghadai and almost eliminating that of Ögödei, where opposition to him was strongest. Then he strengthened the hold of his Toluid line by assigning large responsibilities to his three brothers. Khubilai, the second, was given responsibility for supporting the Mongol homeland on the east by developing a strong position from which to complete the conquest of China. Arigh Böke, his youngest brother, very much in the pattern of their father, Tolui, became his military assistant in Mongolia. And Hülegu (Hulagu, Huleku), the third of the four, was made responsible for developing a subordinate khanate, the Il-khanate in Persia, where he was sent to reconquer the region and establish a strong government that would protect against any dissidence from the Golden Horde, farther away in Russia. As defined at this time, the four khanates were the Golden Horde, the khanate of Chaghadai, the Il-khanate in Persia, and the khanate of Mongolia. The khanate of China, established by Khubilai after 1260, was at first subordinate to Mongolia; subsequently, throughout the Yuan dynasty, that relationship was reversed. The line of Ögödei, greatly weakened in stature after the purges of 1251, passed from the scene after 1309.

Hülegu in 1253 launched his western campaign with a force of 75,000 troops.[18] He crossed Khwarazm, which was now the domain of the Chaghadai khanate, and pushed on into Persia, where his first objective was to put down the secret order of the Assassins, associated with the Isma'ili sect of Shiite Islam. The Assassins had long been active in the region and were regarded as a general threat to political stability, and in the eyes of all the Islamic states in the region were the bane of their existence. Hülegu captured and executed their feared leaders at their previously impregnable stronghold in the Elburz Mountains on the southern shores of the Caspian Sea and virtually extinguished the order. Then he took over all the provinces of Persia, restoring what had been a fragile Mongol presence remaining only in the plains of far northwest Persia since the first western campaign in the 1220s. Following that, he pressed on to the west toward the seat of the 500-year-old Abbasid caliphate in Baghdad. He took and sacked the city in February 1258, killing perhaps as many as several hundred thousand people, and executed the caliph, thus ending a phase of Islamic history. Hülegu then turned northward into Azerbaijan, took Tabriz, and wintered in the region before going on west into Syria. There, where the Seventh Crusade under King (Saint) Louis IX of France had recently reinforced the Frankish establishment in the Holy Land, he in some measure appeared to align himself with the Christians, sparing their bastions and attacking those of the Muslims. He first occupied Edessa, then besieged Aleppo, capturing it in February 1260. After that he moved quickly on Damascus, took the terrified city in April without a fight, and went on to take other cities in the Levant.

Pasturage for his cavalry was scarce in the Levant. He withdrew to Persia, leaving behind a force of between 10,000 and 20,000 cavalry under the command of a Naiman Nestorian Christian commander named Ked Bukha (Kitbuqa). In a landmark battle in southern Palestine in September 1260, Ked

Bukha was badly defeated, captured, and executed by a Mamluk (Mameluke) army, thereby turning back a planned Mongol invasion of Egypt. The setback also caused the Mongols to withdraw from further involvement in Syria and the Levant.[19] Hülegu settled himself in Persia as the Il-khan, and remained there without returning to Mongolia for the *khuriltai* convened in 1260 following the death, in the late summer of 1259, of his elder brother, Möngke Khan. So ended the third and last great Mongol campaign from Mongolia to Western Asia and Europe.

Möngke had busied himself with China while his third brother, Hülegu, was conducting the western campaign. He ordered his second brother, Khubilai, to invade western China in 1253, launching the campaign that skirted the Tibetan upland all the way south to Yunnan, where Khubilai defeated the Dali kingdom in 1254 and brought Yunnan under Mongol administration. Yunnan was seen as a base from which to launch one prong of an eventual multipronged invasion of Song China. The campaign was a test in which Khubilai, not previously seen as a Mongol warrior, was able to win his spurs. Möngke then turned responsibility for governing North China over to Khubilai, granting him much discretion, but often suspicious of his growing accommodation with Chinese governing means and with Chinese cultural interests. In the mid-1250s Möngke determined to lead the conquest of Song China himself, preparing for it carefully for more than a year. Then in 1258, with Khubilai in attendance, he led yet another army south to attack the Song. He personally commanded the main force which went south into central Sichuan; another column paralleled his main army on a route farther west, and Khubilai headed a third column that traveled farther east of the main army, assigned to enter Hubei and the central Yangzi region. Khubilai had left his principal field commander in Yunnan in 1254; that man was now ordered to bring a fourth column from Yunnan to attack in the Song southwest.

While in the field in the summer of 1259, Möngke contracted an illness (or suffered from an injury inflicted by projectiles fired from a Chinese walled city), and died in Sichuan in August. Whether this invasion of China could have succeeded had Möngke not died is an intriguing question. Song, while averse to war as a matter of policy, was by no means militarily weak. Much of the Mongol military resources were deployed in Persia, denying adequate striking power to Möngke. And Möngke's strategy of attacking Song China from the west has been held up to criticism. There is also the question whether more farsighted and realistic diplomacy on the part of the Song court might have forestalled the Song-Mongol conflict, allowing a protracted peace on the pattern of Song-Jin relations in the century and a half after 1127. But these questions, while not meaningless, are nonetheless somewhat academic, for that phase of Mongol-Song relations had ended.

Möngke's body was taken home to Mongolia, and further campaigning against China was called off for several years. One enduring result of Möngke's reign was the orientation of the khanate of Mongolia toward primary engagement with China.

VII. RELATIONS AMONG THE FOUR KHANATES

Hülegu's older brother Khubilai succeeded Möngke in 1260 by simply declaring himself the successor before a small and unrepresentative *khuriltai*. There appears to have been an agreement between Hülegu and Khubilai that Hülegu would remain in Persia as a buffer against the Golden Horde. In any event, Hülegu heard of Khubilai's elevation before he could have traveled all the way to Mongolia, and then he was almost immediately tied up in a war with the Golden Horde over disputed claims to parts of Azerbaijan.

The Golden Horde was particularly susceptible to centrifugal forces within the Mongol imperial clan from the time their far western sub-khanate was created. Jochi was constantly at odds with his brothers, as we have seen. Chinggis was chagrined that his other sons would not accept Jochi as his heir in 1219, but before both father and eldest son died in 1227, a deep hatred had developed between them.[20] Ögödei had planned the second western campaign to secure Jochi's line in possession of the farther western conquests making up the Golden Horde, but relations between Ögödei's line and Batu had deteriorated by 1241. Batu was originally granted four chiliarchies of Mongol cavalry and their dependents, perhaps 25,000 persons in all, and he settled down to rule over his khanate from the first of two Golden Horde capitals, Old and New Sarai, built successively on the lower Volga. The critical mass of Mongols in his realm was inadequate to long preserve a Mongol identity; his khanate came to be known as the Kipchak Horde as its Turkic population gradually absorbed its Mongols, turning it into a Turkic-speaking realm. When Batu died in 1256, his brother Berke succeeded him as khan and led his people in a conversion to Islam in the 1270s, thereby erasing a major distinction between Mongols and the Turkic nomads of the region. That was the first bloc of Mongols to adopt the religion that eventually would claim all the Mongols outside of Mongolia. Batu's successors maintained their indirect rule over the Russians (the "Tatar Yoke," as the Golden Horde's power to coerce and collect taxes was called) until late in the fifteenth century.

Berke, heading the Golden Horde when Möngke died in 1259, did not accept Khubilai's irregular succession and seemed on the point of throwing his support to Arigh Böke, the youngest brother of Möngke, who also claimed to have been validated by a sparsely attended *khuriltai* held in western Mongolia in 1260, and who then declared war on Khubilai. Arigh Böke was much more the model Mongol warrior chieftain than was Khubilai, and for that reason probably had considerable support throughout the Chinggisid lineages and among the tribal nobility. A civil war lasting four years ensued before Khubilai prevailed. The threats to the stability of Mongolia gave the alliance between the other two brothers, Khubilai and Hülegu, great strategic importance. Hülegu died in Persia in 1265; his son and heir Abakha ruled ably until his death in 1282. Struggles between Buddhist and Muslim elements were already developing among the Il-khans, and in 1295 that branch of the Chinggisid line also converted to Islam. The Mongol element in the population was overwhelmed by the Persian, and Persian culture and language reigned.

The khanate of Chaghadai sprawled across a large area that lacked natural boundaries and unifying cultural traditions. It consisted of Khwarazm plus the territories of the former Kara Khitai state that extended in the northeast across the Pamir Mountains to include the important oasis cities of what is today western Xinjiang in China. Political warfare and instability plagued the region for decades. Descendants of Chaghadai struggled to regain something of the region's former prosperity, but without success. In the 1330s the Chinggisid khans of Chaghadai converted to Islam, as the khans of the Golden Horde and the Il-khans previously had done. At the same time, the Mongol element there was overwhelmed by the Turkic population and, as in Russia, the khanate of Chaghadai also became a Turkic state during the fourteenth century.[21] After the conversion of the Chaghadaid khans in the 1330s, all the Mongols outside Mongolia were Muslims.

To look ahead, the khanate of Chaghadai is of special interest as the home region of Tamerlane (Temür the Lame). He was born into an insignificant Turco-Mongol tribe in the 1330s and flashed onto the scene almost as a new Chinggis Khan in the latter decades of the fourteenth century. Using the Chaghadai khanate as his base, and trying to take on something of the Chinggisid legitimacy by marrying a Chinggisid wife (thereby making his sons descendants of Chinggis Khan), he determined to become a world conqueror.[22] After subduing Persia and Iraq and invading India, he established a Timurid line of successors and future rulers of the various parts of his realm, sometimes called Moghulistan (Mongol state), where they ruled until 1687. Tamerlane himself died in 1405 at the head of an army on the western approaches to China, fully intending to add China to his domains. Notable among his successors was Babur, who conquered India in 1524–1526, and whose heirs ruled as the Moghul (Mogul, Mongol) emperors of India until 1857. But, of course, they were in fact ethnic Turks of largely Persian cultural identity.

With Khubilai's unrecognized succession to the Great Khanate in 1260, all pretenses of unity within the Mongol empire disappeared; the four khanates went their separate ways. Nevertheless, the Mongolian core of the Mongol nation remained intact, even though the civil war between Khubilai and Arigh Böke for control of the Mongol hearthland disrupted the harmony for some four years, until Khubilai's armies prevailed, in 1264; Arigh Böke died in captivity in 1266. Khubilai's disruptive succession in one sense caused, in another sense coincided with, the final breaking apart of the empire created by Chinggis Khan. Yet all the four parts remained important and grew still more powerful for shorter or longer periods of time following the breakup in 1260. The most important example is the khanate of China, which brought under Mongol rule the largest and richest state in the world. When he turned his energies to completing the conquest of China in the 1270s, Khubilai accomplished the reunification of China after more than 400 years of division, and for a century Mongol history was fully merged with Chinese history.

19

KHUBILAI KHAN BECOMES
EMPEROR OF CHINA

Chinggis Khan's grandson Khubilai is an equally fabled historical person in history; Marco Polo reported on him, on himself as a resident in the Great Khan's realm, and on the unbelievable riches and splendors of "Cathay," the name Polo used for China. Europe's earliest images of China derived mainly from the book which Marco Polo dictated to a literate Italian associate after his return from China, a book long believed to be too fabulous to merit credibility. The book is not without basis in fact, but today we can write about the Yuan dynasty from more credible historical sources. They reveal a Khubilai who struggled militarily and politically to gain the khanate of Mongolia, then the throne of China, combining them to create a new phase in the histories of each. The emphasis here is on the new pattern of foreign rule over China which Khubilai Khan worked out, an impressive political achievement. The reigns of his nine successors on the throne of China in the remaining seventy-five years of the Yuan dynasty constitute an epilogue to Khubilai's life; those reigns reveal that the balance Khubilai had struggled to create between the Mongols' commitment to the khanate of Mongolia and their interests in their Chinese dynastic state could no longer be maintained. Unresolved conflicts undermined the conquerors' power, leaving China vulnerable to political decay.

> In Xanadu did Kubla Khan
>   A stately pleasure-dome decree:
> Where Alph, the sacred river, ran
> Through caverns measureless to man
>   Down to a sunless sea.
>   . . .
>
> And there were gardens bright with sinuous rills,
> Where blossomed many an incense-bearing tree;

444

And here were forests ancient as the hills,
Enfolding sunny spots of greenery.
. . .

> The shadow of the dome of pleasure
> Floated midway on the waves;
> Where was heard the mingled measure
> From the fountain and the caves.
> It was a miracle of rare device,
> A sunny pleasure-dome with caves of ice!
>
> from "Kubla Khan," Samuel Taylor Coleridge, 1797

Coleridge's poem, known to every reader of English poetry, makes of Khubilai Khan (Kubla Khan) a magical figure in a realm of fantasy, richly perceived through Coleridge's opium dreams as a land of opulence and refined splendor. Those images of Khubilai no doubt were derived from Marco Polo, whose book of travels reported on the things he had seen during the years he lived in Khubilai Khan's China, 1275–1291.[1] Polo's glittering account of the land's fabulous wealth, its sophistication, and its emperor's great capacities deeply marked the European consciousness. On the one hand, his reports drove Columbus and his contemporaries to find the way to "Cathay"; on the other, they led into mythical realms generated by European imagination. Coleridge's poem is only the best known among the romantic imaginings about lands of the East that colored the West's consciousness, quite apart from the many solid travel accounts.

In sharp contrast with those images, Khubilai's grandfather Chinggis Khan, the "scourge of God," had become well known throughout the world because of the fierce destruction his and his successors' armies visited on Central Asia, eastern Europe, and the Levant during the Mongols' western campaigns, and by the knowledge of him spread through the direct contacts between the papacy and the Mongols at the time of the Crusades.[2] In both their cases, the contrasting Western images of these great Mongol khans, one envisaged as an inexplicable monster and the other as the great and wise prince of an exotic realm, are more myth than history. Yet there are elements of truth in both. In the preceding chapter I attempted to reveal the true Chinggis Khan. With Khubilai, the task may be more difficult. He was an impressive figure, handsome, physically favored, mentally alert, ambitious, yet an enigmatic, contradictory, at times quite puzzling ruler. Whatever else we may conclude, Khubilai Khan is a historical personage of immense significance for Mongol, for Chinese, and for all of East Asian history. We must try to walk slowly around him, seeing him from different sides, in order to understand his place in Chinese history.

1. The Early Life of Khubilai

Khubilai was born in 1215, the year in which his father, Tolui, in the company of Chinggis Khan and Tolui's brothers, besieged and captured the Jin dynasty's Central Capital at the site of modern Beijing. Tolui was the quintessential Mongol warrior chieftain, at his father's side in innumerable campaigns. In the ultimate arrangements for dividing responsibilities, he as the youngest son was to inherit the Mongol "hearthland" and to assume charge over the army, in service to the successor Great Khan. Earlier, when Chinggis finally made war on his former ally the Ongkhan of the Kerait confederation, he had taken the vanquished Ongkhan's two nieces as war booty; he kept the older one for himself, and bestowed the younger one on Tolui to be his principal wife. That was in 1203, when Tolui was in his mid-teens. Bringing this Kerait princess into the family was to be of special significance for the Chinggisid line, for the wife Tolui gained in this way, Sorghaghtani Beki, was to become an influential figure in Mongol history. We do not know when she was born, but her first son, the future Great Khan Möngke, was born six years after she was given to Tolui, in 1209, suggesting that she was younger than Tolui and consequently their marriage was not consummated for several years. Then she bore Khubilai in 1215, Hülegu in 1217, and the youngest of her four sons, Arigh Böke, some time after that.

We know almost nothing about Khubilai's life until the mid-1240s, when he approached the age of thirty. It has been noted that Sorghaghtani Beki made sure her sons were taught to read Mongol, that is, in the script adapted from Uighur, the script by which Nestorian Christianity had been transmitted to East Asia.[3] She, as a Kerait, was a Nestorian. She also made sure that Khubilai and all her sons learned to ride and shoot and acquired a taste for the hunt so that they would be competent Mongol leaders. In addition, she is credited with imparting to her sons, and especially to Khubilai, who remained closest to her, a broad and inquisitive outlook, a benign attitude toward all religions, and an awareness of the need for sound administration. When her husband died in 1232, his older brother Ögödei was the Great Khan. She firmly refused to become the wife of her husband's surviving brother or nephew in the pattern of the levirate, saying her responsibilities to her young sons were of greater importance. She had the further assertiveness to request from Ögödei an appanage, or fief, in China, to ensure her livelihood; in 1236 he granted her the district of Zhending (now Zhengding) in what would be present-day southwestern Hebei. She took its administration quite seriously and sought advice about its proper management.

Khubilai also was granted an appanage at that time, receiving the district of Xingzhou,[4] just south of Zhending. At first he ignored the administration of the district, allowing alien managers to exploit the population ruthlessly, with the result that a large number of the inhabitants fled. Under his mother's influence, and because of her interest in seeing that their appanages were better managed, Khubilai began to investigate and to take a hand in supervising them. He is said to have begun to recruit Chinese advisers as early as 1239, when he was twenty-four years old.[5] That was the beginning of his personal involvement with the problems of governing in the Chinese conquered territories. At the same time, he must have been an intensely interested observer of the factionalism and deadly infighting at the Mongol court.

When Ögödei ordered the second great campaign to the west in 1236, he commanded the senior grandsons of Chinggis to lead portions of the invading armies, under the generalship of Sübötei and the nominal command of Batu, the most senior grandson. It therefore fell to Sorghaghtani Beki's eldest son, Möngke, at age twenty-seven, to join that campaign. In the course of it Möngke pleased his cousin Batu with his respectful manner and efficient leadership. Ögödei's son Güyük, however, developed at that time an intense hatred for his cousin Batu. Khubilai was twenty-one, quite old enough to fight in the field, but he was not ordered to do so and remained behind, no doubt in close association with his mother and two younger brothers.

Succession disputes emerged in 1241 when Ögödei died. Over much opposition, his strong-minded widow, Töregene, demanded that her son Güyük should succeed. After several years' delay during which she acted as regent, Güyük finally was acknowledged Great Khan in 1246, but he lived only two years after that. Another succession struggle took place. This time the Ögödeids and the Chaghadaids struggled against Batu, the Khan of the Golden Horde far off in Russia. The house of Tolui remained on the sidelines during this factional struggle, but Sorghaghtani Beki carefully monitored the developments from her residence in Karakorum, the capital.

On becoming Great Khan in 1246, Güyük had plans for a surprise attack against Batu. Sorghaghtani Beki learned of his plan and secretly sent a warning to Batu, at great risk to herself and her family. Fortunately Güyük died in 1248, before his offensive got well under way and before he learned about her role. In the succession struggle that followed, Sorghaghtani Beki was well positioned to take advantage of the political currents and to gain Batu's support for her eldest son, Möngke. Thanks to her adroit maneuvering Möngke was named the fourth Great Khan at the *khuriltai,* and after a delay caused by further factional bickering, was proclaimed khan in 1251. His mother lived just long enough to see that event, then died early in 1252. Khubilai survived those years, learning about the uncertainties of Mongol politics but without being deeply involved. His brother now had become the Great Khan, and the house of Tolui was in the strongest position to retain the Grand Khanate. Was Khubilai still destined for a peripheral role, or did he begin to see himself as one day succeeding his brother?

It was in those same years that Khubilai began to become deeply involved in the management of his own appanage in North China, and because of that, he commenced seeking out Chinese advisers with whom to discuss statecraft, philosophy, and history. Living in the Mongol capital at Karakorum, he had opportunities to meet prominent persons called to the court. He began to look to them as sources of information and advice. There was something in his mentality, perhaps to be credited to the influence of his remarkable mother, that guided him toward a search for other means of maintaining Mongol interests in China. That quest came to dominate his life and his governing. It set him and some members of his generation of Mongol leaders apart from their predecessors. The way in which he came to pursue that course demands our attention.

II. KHUBILAI AND HIS CHINESE ADVISERS BEFORE 1260

Khubilai began to cultivate the company of Chinese advisers when he was still in his mid-twenties. By that age his father had already become a seasoned warrior, and in 1236 his elder brother Möngke, six years his senior, joined the second western campaign, where he won acclaim as a field commander.[6] So far as we know, Khubilai was not ill suited for or averse to that traditional Mongol path to power and success, but he was merely one among several young Chinggisid princes, and he was not given that role. He found other ways of nurturing his ambitions.

The first prominent Chinese he sought out, so far as we know, was the Chan (Zen) Buddhist monk Haiyun (1203–1257). A brilliant man of compelling personality, Haiyun at an early age had served as abbot of prominent temples and monasteries, one at Zhending, Sorghaghtani Beki's appanage in Hebei Province. His principal base, however, was a famous temple and teaching monastery at Yanjing, as the former Jin Central Capital on the site of present-day Beijing was then called. Haiyun had become well known for intervening with Mongol officials in the regional government there, using his standing as a man recognized for his spiritual powers to urge better treatment of the people, to restore status and privilege to Confucian scholars who had been enslaved by Mongol captors, and to introduce capable Chinese scholars for official appointment.

Haiyun's reputation, both as a spiritual master of Buddhist doctrine and as a social activist, spread throughout high Mongol circles, reaching all the way to the capital at Karakorum, where Khubilai heard about him. Haiyun received Khubilai's summons and traveled to Karakorum, where they held long talks about current problems in which the Buddhist monk explained Confucian principles of governing. Haiyun represented the syncretic movement in thought, increasingly important from Southern Song times onward, which stressed the ultimate convergence, or unity, of the "Three Teachings"—Confucianism, Daoism, and Buddhism. At the higher levels of intellectual concern and spiritual enlightenment this syncretist movement transcended sectarian squabbles and rivalries. Haiyun was, of course, ultimately loyal to Buddhism as the highest level of truth, but he fully appreciated the great legacy of Daoist and Confucian thought, and he believed that civilization depended on the proper functioning of Confucian social values. Khubilai apparently found this Buddhist outlook highly attractive; he formed a lasting relationship with Haiyun and introduced him to others in the court. Both Ögödei and later his widow, the regent Töregene, bestowed high honors on the monk. When Khubilai's second son was born in 1243, Haiyun conducted Buddhist services and gave the infant his Chinese name, Zhenjin, pronounced "Jingim" in Mongolian, meaning "True Gold," a name with overtones of Buddhist allusion.[7]

Haiyun introduced a number of Chinese to Khubilai. Traveling to Karakorum for that first meeting, he encountered en route a young Chinese scholar then studying at a famed teaching monastery where Haiyun and his party had stopped for lodgings. Struck by his unusual appearance and intellectual force, he invited this man to join him for the trip to Karakorum, and once there introduced him to Khubilai. This was Liu Bingzhong (1216–1274). Liu also was a Three Teachings syncretist. He studied Daoist philosophy as well as Chan Buddhism but at heart was basically a Confucian savant. Despite the unconventional range of his interests and his serious pursuit of both Daoist and Buddhist practices, he was deeply committed to Confucian governing methods and social values. He became one of Khubilai's principal advisers. For thirty years until his death in 1274, Liu served as a source of practical advice on all manner of affairs, from staffing offices of government, to determining by geomancy the best location for a new capital city, to making taxation more equitable. He was an intellectual who engaged the most basic problems of philosophy, classical learning, religion, and the sciences—astronomy, mathematics, calendrics—as well as the proto- or pseudosciences of the time such as astrology, geomancy, prognostication, and divination. He introduced a very large number of Confucian scholars to Khubilai's circle of advisers and largely left it to them to be the political activists while he remained on the sidelines, pursuing his studies and his contemplations. He is one of the great figures of the age, one whose name will reappear hereafter in many connections.[8]

The young Khubilai's advisers also included Lian Xixian (1231–1280), an Uighur whose father was the administrator of Sorghaghtani Beki's appanages in North China. Although the father was not educated in Chinese, he had his sons taught by expert tutors so that they grew up with a sound command of Chinese traditional learning. Lian Xixian was both a civil affairs adviser and a military leader of great courage and incisive judgment.

Still another was Shi Tianze (1202–1275), named one of the Chinese "hereditary lords" *(shi-hou)*, regional warlords who had surrendered to the Mongols in the 1210s and 1220s and received appointments as hereditary local military commanders. Prior to that, Shih Tianze's father had turned his native district, Zhending in southwestern Hebei, into his family's power base. He organized militia from among the local farming families, protected his district, and created there a well-governed, well-defended base which he headed as a self-proclaimed but popularly supported leader. He was able to maintain the region's stability and prosperity in a time of general breakdown caused by the collapse of the Jin dynasty under the initial Mongol incursions.

After the early Mongol attacks on the Jin, Chinggis Khan left his great general Mukhali behind to serve as his viceroy for North China in the years 1217–1223. Facing a shortage of manpower for the armed forces, Mukhali systematically induced a number of local and regional military leaders to surrender on terms granting them hereditary control of their forces. Then he placed their armies under the larger Mongol army system. That is how the "hereditary lords" became an important group of local power holders early in Khubilai's reign. The Shi family was one of the earliest and most important; several of the family members were granted the hereditary title of myriarch, or head of an army of 10,000. Shih Tianze, the third son of the man who surrendered to Mukhali in 1213, was a born soldier but also had an interest in Chinese traditional learning; he was the most prominent member of his large and important family, and a loyal supporter of Khubilai at several crucial turns.

Finally, one must mention Yao Shu (1203–1280) and Xu Heng (1209–1281), the most important of the more orthodox Confucian scholar-officials who were close to Khubilai in these years. They were not Three Teachings syncretists but Neo-Confucian fundamentalists, classical exegetes, and scholar-officials of high moral commitment. Their names will occur frequently in what follows. They fill out the full spectrum of adviser types who made up Khubilai's Chinese-oriented brain trust, men of varied social and ethnic backgrounds who had in common their fervent devotion to traditional means of governing Chinese society, and to the preservation of Chinese cultural values. Whatever the differences among them, they all thought those goals could be achieved by putting their trust in Khubilai as the vehicle for the transformation of the conquest into a regime that would meet China's needs.[9]

Khubilai came to see that two problems faced the Mongols in North China. One was the depth of the destruction, loss of population, economic disaster, and rending of the fabric of Chinese society caused by the invasions and the many years of civil disorder that the early pattern of conquest had allowed to ensue in the wake of the Mongols' plundering armies. By comparison, the Khitans in taking over the Sixteen Prefectures of North China in 938 had annexed a small but intact strip of China, where the society was undisturbed, with its rural villages, markets, cities, and networks of trade. They very quickly turned that zone of 5 or 6 million Chinese into a stable asset, providing taxes and labor, professional skills and cultural resources. Almost 200 years later, when the Jurchens destroyed the Liao dynasty and went on to invade North China in the years 1115–1125, they acquired a much larger piece of China. Their wars, and their initial uncertainty about how to deal with civil governing, caused some destruction and dislocation, but on the whole, Chinese patterns of life were able to recover very quickly. Soon the Jurchens were governing 30 or 40 million productive Chinese, who provided the material basis of the Jin dynasty's existence. In sharp contrast, the Mongol invasions had reduced the registered population of what had been Jin North China to perhaps one-third of what it had been before 1215. The Mongols' conquest had given them at best a rapidly diminishing asset, with severe problems of order and governance.

The second problem facing Khubilai as he investigated the conditions in North China was that centralized governing was undermined by the Mongol practice of giving grants of land, complete with their inhabitants, to Mongol nobles and high officials as their *fen di* (allotted lands), or appanages. The people living on those lands, no matter of what class or status or occupation, became their *qu kou* (captives), that is, their slaves. They assigned managers, usually non-Chinese from Inner Asia, to administer their lands for them, encouraging their agents to exploit them mercilessly for short-term gains. The regular local civil administration could not intervene. This system atomized the governing, prevented any kind of general supervision and planning, and quickly impoverished the entire society. People fled to escape their enslaved status; human resources were wasted, cultural norms were destroyed, and society was rendered well-nigh ungovernable. North China was in deep economic decline, yet few of the Mongol elite were fully aware of the crisis that had overtaken their conquests. Khubilai was one of the few who seemed genuinely concerned to engage these problems.[10]

Khubilai drew about him at least sixty notable talents, mostly Chinese, but also including some Khitans, Uighurs, and others, with whom seriously to explore those problems and devise courses of action. He treated his advisers with unusual respect and kindness, displaying none of the arrogance or impatience of the conqueror; on the contrary, he associated with them as a colleague who shared their purpose. In the 1240s he began to experiment with the implementation of new ideas, on a small scale within his own appanages, but after 1251, when Möngke came to the throne, he was assigned by his brother full administrative responsibility for all of North China. At this point he set up what amounted to Chinese-style central government agencies to engage in all aspects of civil governing, made some progress in taking management of the appanages away from their owners and placing them under his civil officials, and attempted to regularize the many aspects of tax collection, labor service imposts, and other obligations to the government. He had become the Mongols' expert on China, and it became for him the way of realizing his ambitions. He would use China to build up a power base, then he would be ready to contest for the position of Great Khan after Möngke.

I do not mean to suggest that Khubilai had become a benevolent Confucian ruler, or that he was intellectually or emotionally won over to the humanistic foundations of Chinese civilization. Rather, he had come to recognize the rationality of governing the Chinese population by Chinese methods in order to maximize the long-range benefits to himself as ruler. He never learned Chinese (beyond a possible smattering of spoken Chinese), never read a book in Chinese, much less composed a Chinese poem, never identified with the values of the Chinese cultural legacy other than to recognize the utility of systematic and reasoned exploitation in the Chinese pattern. He probably gained some understanding of the wholeness of the civilization, however, and indulged his Chinese advisers as they sought to restore the full range of China's cultural patterns.

In 1252, after initial successes in improving the governing at selected test locations in North China, Khubilai then went on to put in place a broad plan for governing. It was drawn up for him by Liu Bingzhong and other advisers. The plans won immediate improvements in social conditions, but also began to encounter opposition from Mongol interests. Nevertheless, his plans went ahead, even though he was in that year ordered to lead a military campaign through the western borders of Song China into the southwest region of Yunnan. This was part of Möngke Khan's larger plan to complete the conquest of China in eastern Asia while building a strong base of Mongol power in western Asia; Hülegu would be ordered into Persia the next year to do the latter, just as Khubilai was departing in September 1253 for the southwest frontier of China.

III. MÖNGKE'S FIELD GENERAL IN CHINA

Khubilai established a staging base in southern Gansu for his Yunnan campaign. Then he moved forth at the head of his army. His military chief of staff was Uriangkhadai, son of the great general Sübötei (d. 1248), who had masterminded the field tactics of the first two western campaigns. Other advisers who accompanied Khubilai on this campaign included Liu Bing-zhong, Yao Shu, and the sinicized Uighur Lian Xixian. Two anecdotes reveal something of the way Khubilai was depicted by his advisers during this campaign. The *Yuan History* reports:

> In the summer of the year *renzi* [1252] Khubilai presented himself at court where he received the command to conquer Dali. On reaching Quxian-nao'er [perhaps Güsen No'er, in Gansu] he was entertaining his staff one evening. Yao Shu told the story of how the Song dynasty founder had sent [General] Cao Bin to conquer the Southern Tang kingdom (in 975), issuing to him a command that he was not to take as his model [General] Pan Mei, who in attacking the state of Shu had indulged in needless slaughter. In consequence, when Cao Bin captured [the Southern Tang capital at Jinling, or Nanjing], he did not kill so much as a single person; the markets did not alter their openings, and it was as if the proper overlord had returned. On the next morning as they were setting off, Khubilai, leaning on his saddle, called out: "What you told me yesterday about Cao Bin not killing people, that is something I can do." Yao immediately congratulated him saying: "The mind of the Sage, benevolent and enlightened to this degree, is indeed the good fortune of the people, a blessing for the state."[11]

Another scholar among the advisers also lectured Khubilai on a passage in the *Mencius,* in which a ruler asked Mencius how the realm could achieve stability. Mencius replied that it would be stabilized by being united under one leader. "And who can accomplish that?" Mencius was asked. He answered, "He who takes no pleasure in killing people can accomplish that."[12] The adviser went on to press the comparison with Khubilai, saying that he now had the opportunity to unify the realm by showing that he would not allow needless killing. Subsequently, when his forces took the capital of the Dali kingdom in Yunnan, Khubilai was enraged that the king and his military advisers had violated an understanding about the surrender and continued to resist. Khubilai was about to order the slaughter of the city in retribution. But Yao Shu and the other Confucian-minded advisers argued that the faults of the leaders should not be blamed on the common people, who had no choice but to follow their duplicitous leaders; the punishment should be limited to the king and his military advisers. Eventually, even the king was spared and retained in place to help the Mongols set up a successor regime under their control.[13] These anecdotes, probably enlarged in the telling, show how Khubilai's Chinese advisers hopefully built up the image of a humane and educable Mongol leader, and perhaps exerted some kind of influence over him, if not as much as they led themselves to believe.

A digression concerning Khubilai's Yunnan campaign in relation to Southeast Asian history is warranted here. That event was made a central feature of a Thai national myth developed in Siam, later Thailand, from the late nineteenth century onward. According to this myth, China was once all Thai, the homeland of the early Thai people. The Chinese at that time, it was said, were steppe barbarians who, through the centuries corresponding with Chinese imperial history, pushed the more advanced, peace-loving Thais ever farther to the south. For some centuries that pressure concentrated the Thais in what we now call Yunnan, where they formed in the seventh century C.E. a great kingdom called Nanzhao. When Khubilai Khan's armies invaded Yunnan in 1253–54, they were seen by the Thais there as "Chinese" barbarians from the north again warring on the peaceful Thais, destroying their kingdom of Nanzhao, and again driving the Thai people south, this time into modern Thailand, where they have maintained their national entity ever since.

Starting in the late nineteenth century, this legend was widely disseminated by Thai and Western scholars alike, and still occasionally finds its way into Western academic writings. Within recent times the Thai scholarly world has abandoned it, seeing in it a total misunderstanding of history. The Nanzhao kingdom was not Thai but was dominated by the people today known as the Baizu, and they continued to rule from the city of Dali in Nanzhao's successor Dali kingdom, which Khubilai conquered. Khubilai and the Mongol invasions had nothing to do with Thai history, which, in any event, does not reveal any forced expulsion of the Thai people from China. The Thais acquired writing only in the thirteenth century, and there is therefore little documentation bearing on their early history. A small minority of Thai-related people now living in the southernmost edge of modern Yunnan on the Laotian border, in a locality called the Sibsong Banna (in modern Chinese, Shishuang Banna), may however be descended from such a peripheral community already living there in the thirteenth century.

To return to Khubilai's campaign, the Dali kingdom surrendered to his invasion forces and was placed under the management of a succession of resident Mongol princes, some of whom began to foster important cultural development. Yunnan's very gradual absorption into China commenced at this time.

Also misleading are the anecdotes telling how Yao Shu and others persuaded Khubilai to accept Confucian values. The strategy of encouraging surrender by promising to spare the lives of opponents for not resisting, seen in these anecdotes as having been practiced by Khubilai in conquering Yunnan, had long been a strategy on all fronts of the Mongols' far-flung conquests, with or without Confucian-minded advice. It was used by them along with the intimidating slaughter of whole populations which resisted or failed to observe terms of agreements. In Mongol eyes the two sides of this intimidation-enticement policy reinforced each other. Khubilai did not need to be reminded of this often employed stratagem, although the urgent pleadings of Yao Shu to spare the residents of Dali may indeed have occurred. The other anecdote has Confucian advisers fervently preaching the theme of benevolence, wanting the reader to believe that this incident displays a triumph of Confucian humanism over the savagery of Mongol culture. But at the same time, they also were preaching utility: the promise of benevolent treatment of the enemy could hasten low-cost victories. Even if his Confucian advisers were sure that Khubilai would at least be impressed by that pragmatic advice, they also could hope that his awareness of the larger ideal was strengthened by their praising him for displaying enlightened, sagelike attitudes. In this campaign, and in the subsequent campaigns against the Southern Song, the presence of advisers arguing strongly for the rightness of their moral statecraft probably did have some effect, saving many lives and preventing even greater destruction of the Chinese heritage. Was Khubilai in fact succumbing to their "civilizing influences," as they no doubt believed? This is one of the enigmas of his career. For whatever reasons, in these years he indeed sought Chinese assistance and enlarged the application of Chinese methods in governing.

In 1257 Khubilai's association with Chinese advisers appeared to have brought deep trouble down on him. The Mongol elements in the government at Karakorum complained to Möngke that Khubilai's devotion to Mongol interests was being subverted by his Chinese advisers (who undoubtedly *were* interfering with the Mongol-appointed managers' exploitation of appanages in North China). They cast dark hints about Khubilai's ambitions, his growing prominence after his successful military campaign in Yunnan, and the power dangerously concentrated in the hands of Chinese military leaders such as Shi Tianze's family and the other Chinese "hereditary lords." They claimed that revenues from North China were being improperly collected and put to illicit uses.

Möngke appears to have had his own suspicions of his brother. He ordered a thorough audit and review of the government in certain places where Khubilai's North China experiments had gone the farthest. Khubilai and his Chinese advisers recognized the threat; would he be eliminated by a jealous brother, cast aside, cut off from all future importance in the Mongol world, or even killed? Such things had happened. They consulted, reinforcing Khubilai's will to resist this attack on his integrity and loyalty. They advised him to take his family to Karakorum to see his brother, showing that he was willing to place himself at Möngke's disposal. At the same time, some of them who had been responsible for administration in North China, such as Shi Tianze, courageously took responsibility for any irregularities that might have occurred and invited thorough inspection of the records.

Möngke met Khubilai in Karakorum, embraced him emotionally, and restored his brother to his good graces. The audits and investigations found no evidence of malfeasance. Yet Möngke ordered some of Khubilai's principal administrative aides removed from their offices in North China, to be replaced by Central Asians who not only would be, he thought, more loyal to him but who also would revert to old governing measures, thereby pleasing the Mongol nobility. It was a setback for Chinese governing and a distinct rebuff to Khubilai.[14]

In the next year, however, Möngke launched the long-awaited campaign against the Southern Song and assigned Khubilai an important role in that military undertaking. Khubilai would lead an eastern column across Central China to the Yangzi, to take the Song bastion of Ezhou (Wuchang, on the south bank of the Yangzi, part of the present-day city of Wuhan), while Möngke himself would lead the main force through Sichuan and then, it was planned, turn eastward to join forces with Khubilai in Central China. But, as we have seen, Möngke died in Sichuan in the summer of 1259.

IV. MANEUVERING TO BECOME THE GREAT KHAN

Khubilai, at Ezhou on the Yangzi deep in Central China, heard that Möngke was dead. At first he was reluctant to break off a successful campaign without achieving some decisive victory. Then word came that his youngest brother, Arigh Böke, with the support of the Mongol traditionalists, was about to call a *khuriltai* to have himself proclaimed Möngke's successor. Khubilai seemed uncertain about what to do. At this point his Chinese advisers played several crucial roles. First, they persuaded him to break off his campaign and return at once to his own base in Mongolia to contest Arigh Böke by all political and military means. That Khubilai should become the next Great Khan was absolutely fundamental to their interests and, as they believed, to those of Chinese civilization. Second, they persuaded Khubilai to preempt his brother by calling his own *khuriltai* early in 1260 and having himself proclaimed the next Great Khan. Khubilai did that, although his *khuriltai* was held away from the traditional meeting sites in the Mongolian hearthland, and attended by so small and unrepresentative a group of Mongol nobles that it was of unconvincing validity. Arigh Böke convened a more substantial *khuriltai* with participants from the other khanates, and after being declared the proper successor, he called for war. Third, at this juncture the Chinese advisers (including the able Uighur Lian Xixian) led the troops that fought Khubilai's war for him in its most dangerous sectors, depriving Arigh Böke of access to the resources of China in the northwest provinces, closest to his supply routes, where Lian and others had been administering the regional government.

The civil war went badly for Arigh Böke. By 1262 his offensive had been blunted and his efforts to align himself with Mongol supporters farther west were deflected. By 1263 Khubilai could feel reasonably confident of having won this contest, and in 1264 Arigh Böke surrendered, eventually to throw himself on Khubilai's mercy; he died in 1266, perhaps unnaturally, while under Khubilai's supervision.

It is clear that in the succession crisis Khubilai triumphed because he could call up the resources of China with which to mount bold action. China provided not only material resources that no other Mongol leader or sector could match, but also political advice, tactical thinking, military leadership, and moral support. Khubilai's career would be China-centered from this point onward.

Giving priority to ways of strengthening his China base, however, did not guarantee a free hand for his Chinese advisers. They in fact suffered a serious setback. In 1262, at the height of his involvement with the war against Arigh Böke, Li Tan, the regional commander of western Shandong, revolted and proclaimed allegiance to the Southern Song court. Li Tan had succeeded his father, who, on surrendering to the Mongols in 1227, had been rewarded with the military governorship of his home region. Li Tan's father-in-law, Wang Wentong, was one of the important Confucian advisers to Khubilai, an expert in administration and fiscal management who had contributed much to the strengthening of the Yuan central administration. Khubilai survived this quite threatening revolt by transferring Shi Tianze from the northwest China front in the civil war to combat Li Tan in Shandong. Shi captured and executed Li Tan late in 1262 and uncovered evidence that seriously implicated Wang Wentong; Khubilai then had Wang summarily executed as well.[15]

Reflecting on the Li Tan rebellion, Khubilai concluded that the Chinese warlords in his service might at any time turn to the Song. They should no longer be so fully trusted. He revoked the military commands of all the "hereditary lords," including Shi Tianze and all his family. Shi cooperated fully; some have said that it was his idea to have Khubilai remove all Chinese military leaders from their hereditary commands in order to allay Mongol suspicions and simplify Khubilai's problems.

Khubilai also drew ominous conclusions from the involvement in this treason of Li Tan's father-in-law, one of his trusted Chinese advisory group. Perhaps he should no longer grant them such full trust. He recognized the import of their ideological commitment: these Confucian-minded advisers were not as apt as military leaders to shift their loyalty opportunistically to the Song. But he also recognized that their real loyalty was to Chinese culture even more than to Mongol interests. He had given them a virtual monopoly on policy and administrative posts; perhaps he should create a counterpoise to their powers. As Li Tan's rebellion had led Khubilai to remove leading Chinese from control over military forces, now he simultaneously began to demote leading Chinese administrators and replace them with men from Central Asia, especially from the Islamic lands. He gave to this group opportunities to reverse policy, alter Chinese methods, and institute harsh exploitation in fiscal and economic matters in Western Asian patterns of administration. This commenced an era of competition and hard feelings between these two blocs of his officials which persisted to the end of Mongol rule in China.

v. THE GREAT KHAN KHUBILAI BECOMES EMPEROR OF CHINA

Having been assigned governing oversight of China, Khubilai decided to move the seat of his government away from Karakorum in 1256 to the eastern steppe, closer to China, in the region where he had long maintained a base camp. His justification was that given his responsibilities toward the conquered regions of North China, he needed to be nearer at hand to maintain control and communication. He asked Liu Bingzhong to select an auspicious site and plan the layout of a new capital, to be called Kaiping. It was located about 200 miles almost directly north of modern Beijing on the Luan River. Later, in 1263, when he had become the Great Khan and was planning to move his capital city still deeper into China to Yan, the site of the former Jin Central Capital (at present-day Beijing), he changed the name Kaiping to Supreme Capital—in Chinese, Shangdu—Marco Polo's and Coleridge's "Xanadu," with its "miracles of rare device." It would remain the Mongol emperors' summer capital during the five or six months each year when, like all the steppe nomads, they found the heat of North China oppressive.

At Shangdu, Khubilai regularly met with Mongol and other Inner Asian nobles and envoys in a steppe setting, and there he had the traditional Mongol rites and religious ceremonies performed. Marco Polo could well have been present at one or more of those gatherings, yet there is no reason to believe that he was close to Khubilai personally. Shangdu was a large and well-constructed city with open parks and hunting grounds where imperial tents could be placed and the oppressive urban atmosphere of sedentary society could be escaped.[16] Only eight years after building Shangdu, in 1264 he proclaimed that another new capital would be created at Yan. He retained Shangdu as a secondary capital of empire, in that way establishing a dual capital system suggestive of the Khitan system, under which the same city, Yan, was designated the Liao Southern Capital, site of the Liao dynasty's Southern Chancellery, which administered the Chinese portion of the Liao state through a separate set of governing institutions. In that case, however, the Southern Capital was the Liao secondary capital, while in the Yuan case, Dadu (Beijing) not only was to become the principal capital of China, but also would supersede Karakorum as the seat of Khubilai's khanate which claimed to head the entire Mongol world of the four khanates. Khubilai would assume that fading role as an emperor residing in China, not from the forty-year-old Mongol capital which the Great Khan Ögödei had built at Karakorum, far off in Mongolia.

Within a few months of becoming the Great Khan in 1260, Khubilai commenced using the Chinese system of reign period names. It is often difficult to know what the Chinese reign titles meant to the rulers and advisers who chose them. In this case they chose the reign name "Zhongtong." On the level of rather abstract philosophy it could mean "pivotal succession"; on a more mundane level it might have meant to ordinary people that Khubilai's government now "controlled the center" of China. Regardless of its semantic import, the practical significance is that 1260 became the "first year of Zhongtong," 1261 the second year, and so on, until a new reign period title was adopted. This was a significant departure from Mongol norms. To proclaim a calendar was the prerogative of the Chinese emperor, one that each of the conquest dynasties also had claimed when they announced that their ruler was the founder of a new Chinese-style dynasty. Khubilai was moving in the direction of doing that, but by quite deliberate steps.

Moving the Great Khan's capital from Karakorum to China in 1264 was the next step in the process. At that point he also changed his reign period title to Zhiyuan, probably intended to mean something like "achieving the proper beginning." He would retain this reign title to the year Zhiyuan thirty-one (1294), the last year of his long reign. Changing the reign period name traditionally marked a new phase in a Chinese reign; in this case it was the phase of Khubilai's ruling both as heir to Chinggis Khan and as the successor to imperial dynastic rule in China, symbolized by moving the capital. When the Jin dynasty abandoned its Central Capital in 1214 under the assault of Chinggis Khan's armies, the city resumed its old Chinese name: Yan, or Yanjing. As Yanjing, it had become the seat of Khubilai's Branch Secretariat, through which up to this time he had administered all of North China. By making it the site of his great imperial capital, he recognized the city's long-standing importance in the governing of North China.

The new city at Yan was rebuilt to grander specifications beginning in 1267. This project again was placed under the aegis of Liu Bingzhong. He shifted the site slightly to the northeast so that only a small portion of the former Jin city was incorporated within the new city walls. The ground plan of the capital, reflected especially in the way its layout embodied ancient Chinese symbolism, probably meant much more to the Confucian-minded advisers than to Khubilai himself. For whatever reason, the city plan is closer to those antique ideals than are other capitals built during China's imperial era.[17] The area enclosed within its massive walls was larger than that of the Ming capital which a century and a half later would incorporate much of Yuan Dadu in another rebuilding of the city, completed in the 1420s. That is the Ming and Qing Beijing, which still existed into the twentieth century, before the extensive modifications of the city after 1950.

The construction of the city, basically completed in 1276 after nine years of intensive effort, was carried out largely by Chinese conscripted military labor. In area Yan was one of the largest cities in the world; its population, at about one-half million by the year 1300, also made it one of the largest cities in the world of its time in population, although not as large as Chinese capitals before and after. It dwarfed all the cities that Marco Polo saw in Europe and Asia en route to Cambulac (Khan Baligh), "the city of the Khan," as he called it.

The enigmatic qualities of Khubilai are evident in some of the other steps he took early in his reign to conform at least outwardly to the formalities of China's imperial institution. The imposing pattern of Chinese imperial majesty and awe had attracted the rulers of all earlier conquest dynasties, but that does not appear to have been an issue among the Mongol rulers. They did not covet the power of Chinese monarchs or seek to borrow their formulas for manifesting power. They had no doubts, it would seem, about the nature of their power, which was derived directly from military performance and was sustained by their own religious and ritual sanctions. When Khubilai, therefore, in the 1260s and 1270s adopted the Chinese imperial Ancestral Temple (Tai Miao) and a schedule of ancestral and state sacrifices, and allowed his advisers to design regalia and accouterments for the conduct of his court—and all the immense further proliferation of prescribed ritual forms and behavior extending throughout official life—his intent was not at all like that of Prince Hailing (r. 1149–1161) in the Jin dynasty. As we have seen, by adopting similar measures, Hailing elevated himself above the competing holders of authority in Jurchen tribal society, thereby gaining absolute power.

On the contrary, Khubilai seems, on the one hand, to have accepted the concept of the wholeness of the Chinese imperial system in which the symbolism surrounding the emperor had functional significance. He would accede to that because his advisers persuaded him of it. And, on the other hand, it is quite possible that, accepting the essential validity of all religious and philosophical systems, he was unwilling to cut himself and his dynasty off from any potential sources of spiritual power. Much of the Chinese imperial ritual was at least formally religious in nature where it focused on Heaven, Earth, ancestral spirits, spirits of rivers and mountains, and the like. We see the Mongol rulers in all the khanates similarly responding to locally prevailing definitions of supreme religious authority—be they any of the varieties of Islamic or Buddhist teachings—adding those on to their own Mongol shamanistic and pantheistic beliefs. Herbert Franke has speculated, "Had the Mongols stayed in Hungary after 1241, they would have as easily become converts to Christianity and their *tengri* [absolute Heaven] amalgamated with Christian *deus* (or Hungarian *Isten*)."[18]

In China the Mongols, and especially Khubilai, tried to take account of Chinese Buddhist and Daoist currents of thought in proclamations and governing actions. Khubilai's mother, a devout Nestorian Christian, piously extended her concerns to all religions, patronizing the building of mosques, temples, and churches. Khubilai authorized the building and rebuilding of the Tai Miao at the ritually correct location in his palace city, allowed imperial temple names and titles to be posthumously bestowed on his predecessors from Chinggis Khan to his own father, allowed ritual sacrifices to them on the days his Chinese advisers told him were appropriate (but disappointed them by refusing to conduct the sacrifices in person), and ordered the building of Confucian temples throughout the realm. The Chinese record covers all these things in detail, with intent to show Chinese successes in sinicizing the rulers and their government. They barely hint at the fact that at Shangdu the traditional ("barbarian") Mongol rituals also were carefully maintained. What, then, were Khubilai Khan's own personal beliefs? How is his mentality reflected in the newly adopted Chinese formalities of imperial conduct? We cannot draw many helpful hints from the historical record.

In 1272, in the midst of the capital building project, when the palaces were being readied for occupancy and the enlarged offices of government were beginning to function, Khubilai at last took the biggest step of all: he announced not just that he was moving the seat of Mongol central governing, but that the city would serve as the seat of a new dynasty within the Chinese succession of dynasties, claiming the transfer of the Mandate of Heaven to himself as emperor of China. On the advice of Chinese advisers, and incorporating their knowledge of history and precedents, he proclaimed that his new dynasty would be called Da Yuan, "the Great Yuan," and the Central Capital would now be called Dadu, "the Great Capital."[19] The Southern Song emperor also claimed that he alone held the legitimate transmission of the Mandate which his dynasty had possessed since it was founded in 960. The threat implicit in Khubilai's claims troubled the Song. To be sure, Song had coexisted with a second "Son of Heaven" throughout three centuries of the Liao and Jin eras and had worked out reasonable arrangements for getting by under those humiliating circumstances. But it was clear that Khubilai had no intention of going the route of coexistence. The Song would be eliminated, as the Mongols had intended since the time of Chinggis Khan.

VI. THE CONQUEST OF THE SOUTHERN SONG, 1267–1279

The conquest of China had been begun by Chinggis Khan in his attacks on the Jin dynasty after 1210. The further conquest of the Southern Song had been pressed by Ögödei Khan in border attacks from the west, in Sichuan, throughout the 1230s. A new phase of conquest was begun by Möngke in 1258, when Khubilai had led an army as far as the middle Yangzi. Now that task was taken up again after a fifteen-year interlude.

This time the military operation was planned differently from all earlier Mongol offensives in China. It would follow a different route into the Song state, and it would employ different military means, notably inland navies, and more sophisticated techniques for besieging and capturing walled cities. And it would rely much more heavily on Chinese foot soldiers, sailors, and specialists in other aspects of military technology. It would take six years to open the Han River invasion route by capturing the Song stronghold in northern Hubei at the twin cities of Fancheng and Xiangyang on the Han River early in 1273. Then it would require another year and a half, beginning late in 1274, to move down the Han River to the Yangzi, and then eastward the length of it and then go on to capture the Song capital, Linan, at the site of modern Hangzhou. After that success in 1276, it would take three more years to consolidate, mop up lingering resistance, and bring about the death of the last Song claimant to the throne. The Mongols' conquest of China thus took three generations, much longer than they had needed to reduce any other enemy.

Although he did not in person lead troops in the field at any point during the nine-year final campaign against the Song, this great military victory allowed Khubilai to take his place among the renowned Mongol conquerors, a matter of political and probably also psychological significance to him and to the Mongol world. There was widespread resistance to him, even after the defeat of Arigh Böke in 1264, from within the Mongol imperial clan and throughout the military establishment in the other khanates. His rivals charged that he had surrendered Mongol values to become an effete Chinese. He would prove his military prowess by adding territory, wealth, and glory to the Mongol nation.

The Southern Song dynasty, Khubilai's Chinese enemy in the great campaign of conquest, governed about 100 million people in the southern two-thirds of China that lay below the old Jin-Song boundary. The Southern Song emperor who had reigned from 1225 until 1264, the Emperor Lizong, had been one of the dynasty's weakest and most unsympathetic rulers. The *Song History* says of him, "From middle life onward his addiction to sensual pleasures ever grew; he neglected the governing and turned his powers over to treacherous ministers."[20] He and his adopted son, the Emperor Duzong, who succeeded him (r. 1265–1274), were served for sixteen years (1259–1275) by a Chief Councillor named Jia Sidao, who traditionally is depicted as the very model of a treacherous minister and the worst in a succession of bad ministers.[21] Such depictions have been exaggerated by historians seeking face-saving explanations for the fall of the revered Song dynasty. At its end the Song was politically weakened, yet it still was militarily strong, defended by a number of intensely loyal and deeply committed military leaders, and it was sustained by a wealthy society. Its ordinary people showed more will to resist the Mongols than did its government, and its elite of scholar-officialdom maintained a more deeply felt, morally charged passive resistance to Mongol rule after 1279 than China had yet seen.[22]

The Southern Song capital at modern Hangzhou was a city of art and culture, learning and scholarship. Although seen as only a temporary capital when the first Southern Song emperor fled there in 1129, in the meantime it had grown prodigiously. "In less than two centuries, this town of medium size and provincial character was to become the richest and most populous city in the world. The animation, the luxury and the beauty of Hangchow [Hangzhou] at the end of the thirteenth century was a kind of revelation to Marco Polo." Other travelers from Europe who, like Polo, did not see it until after the end of the Song, agreed that "this city is greater than any in the world."[23] Yet all the contemporary Chinese observers said it had declined noticeably after the Mongol takeover. What Marco Polo and other European visitors commented on in such extravagant terms was already a diminished city and region when they saw it.

The fabled glories of Hangzhou exemplified the wealth of Southern Song China. It is understandable that, like a powerful magnet, it drew the Mongols to it. Khubilai had been preparing for the invasion for a number of years, collecting intelligence, assembling specialists, and building up military supplies. He recognized that his Mongol cavalry, supreme in most settings, nonetheless when campaigning across the terrain, climate, and settlement patterns of China suffered from the lack of naval support. The Mongols, of course, knew nothing about building or sailing boats, and after expanding outside Mongolia, they always coopted others to assist them in providing and manning boats for ferrying armies across rivers or seas. Now Khubilai decided that in order to follow the best route into the Song territories, down the river from Hubei to the middle Yangzi, his armies would need their own supporting naval forces. He was not prepared to make sailors of Mongols, but he was ready to put Mongol cavalrymen on boats built and manned by Chinese or Koreans, to move armies through enemy territory, going ashore to fight wherever necessary. This would become the basic strategy of the conquest.

On opposite banks of the Han River in northern Hubei, the important bastion cities of Xiangyang and Fancheng had to fall before the Mongols could invade. The siege of these two cities is an epic of Chinese and of Mongol military history, full of heroism and spectacular deeds, particularly among the Chinese defenders. But the invaders also were superbly prepared and led. Khubilai chose Aju, the son of Uriyangkhadai, who had been his chief of staff in the Dali campaign of 1253–54, to be his field commander for the siege. Aju was the grandson of Sübötei, the greatest of Mongol generals in the western campaigns. Khubilai had come to know Aju when he was only nineteen, then a very junior captain attached to his father's forces in 1253. In the Yunnan campaign Aju was in command of one myriarch (10,000 men), and in small engagements had won outstanding victories; he was known as an invincible leader. In 1267, given full command of a major military undertaking at age 31, Aju represented the best of the Mongol military tradition.

The Song Chinese were convinced that their great bastion on the Han River could hold out for ten years if necessary. It almost did that. Aju had to solve the problem of how to bring it down. He led an advance party to the scene, surveyed it carefully, and decided on siege tactics. He would have to blockade the cities by land and by water, prevent their communication with each other across the river separating them, and cut off Song supplies and reinforcements coming up the river. The siege became a landmark in the history of warfare in China.[24] In 1268, after a year in the field, Aju sent word to Khubilai: "The forces I am leading consist entirely of Mongol military units [cavalry]; encountering barriers of mountains and rivers, stockades and forts, without Chinese army forces I can do nothing. It would be appropriate to send [General] Shi Shu in command of Chinese army units to assist me in this advance."[25] Khubilai gave his approval. When the Chinese reinforcements arrived on the scene, they began to capture enemy boats, build their own vessels, and imitate Song inland naval tactics. This proved of basic importance to the conduct of the entire campaign until the end of Song resistance in 1279.

Encircled by the Mongols in 1268, the twin cities did not fall until February 1273, fully demonstrating that neither military abilities nor will to resist was lacking on the Chinese side. But the two cities were isolated outposts on the outer edge of the Song realm. A crucial element in the fall of Fancheng, the first of the two to be taken, was the Mongol use of *hui-hui pao,* or "Muslim trebuchets," catapults capable of throwing heavy projectiles against the walls and gates of fortified cities, or propelling shells over walls and dropping gunpowder-filled explosive charges into the streets and on buildings. The Chinese had long used such catapults, but at this time an improved version, counterweighted to increase the force and velocity of the projectiles, appears to have come from the Muslim lands.[26] Soon after Fancheng fell in January 1273, the officers commanding the defenses of Xiangyang surrendered.

Aju went urgently to the court at the beginning of 1274, a year after the fall of the two cities, to urge Khubilai to delay no longer with the invasion of the South. After cautious deliberations, the Chinese advisers agreed, and Khubilai set the preparations in motion. But the invasion did not get under way until late in 1274. Khubilai called in the trusted Mongol statesman-general Bayan (1237–1295) to assume overall control, and assigned Aju and others to the command headquarters. Bayan had been born into the family of a high Mongol noble attached to the court of Khubilai's brother, the Il-khan Hülegü in Persia; he did not come to China until he was twenty-eight years old, yet at that age he nonetheless learned to speak Chinese well and could also write and read. He served in the Secretarial Council as a civilian administrator for five years before being appointed in 1274 to head the invasion army; he clearly was a man of unusual intelligence and temperament, well suited to this command.[27]

Song forces were very strongly entrenched along the entire Han River route down to the Yangzi. Heavy garrisons guarded the points at which the Mongol forces might enter the Yangzi River. A Mongol diversionary force was sent overland to the southeast across Anhui. Bayan, following the Han River route, led the main force, made up of large Chinese units including the naval complement and an elite corps of Mongol cavalry. His forces were said to total 200,000, mainly Chinese. It may have been the largest army the Mongols had ever assembled. Nonetheless, they did not outnumber the Song forces. The invasion army won important engagements all along the way, and by early 1275 had entered the Yangzi and were ready to go downriver across Central China.

Much of the warfare was conducted by political means: turncoat generals were sent ahead to persuade Song defenders to surrender, and many did. But the Mongols did not hesitate to engage the enemy directly and win the big battles, especially against massed naval forces on the Yangzi that greatly outnumbered their naval units. In March 1275 the Song chief minister Jia Sidao was forced by public anger to lead an army of 130,000 into the central Yangzi (where other large Song forces were already in place) to oppose Bayan's rapid approach to the capital. He was supported by a naval force of 2,500 ships blocking the Yangzi. The opposing forces met in March 1275 on the middle Yangzi in Anhui.[28] Bayan attacked with Mongol cavalry put ashore on both banks of the river, and he bombarded the massed enemy fleet with his catapults. Jia and the Song generals fled in disorder. The Song court in desperation sent out an emergency appeal for all Chinese local leaders and people to make the ultimate sacrifice to preserve the state.

The Dowager Empress Xie, Emperor Lizong's widow, took charge at the court. She ordered that Jia Sidao be removed from office and placed under detention, in banishment, but did not order his execution. That was done by local Chinese officials acting on their own.[29] On the Song side, it would have been acceptable at this point to negotiate a peace settlement that would have divided the country, leaving a rump Song state in a diminished South, but neither Bayan nor the Mongol court would consider any such offers. They demanded total victory.

Reaching Nanjing, then called Jiankang, in August, Bayan felt compelled to pause long enough to set up civilian governing institutions to cope with the problems of order in the newly conquered territories. This shows how far the Mongols had evolved as conquerors since their initial conquests in North China sixty years earlier: under Khubilai, to conquer had come to mean to hold and govern. But lest we think of this difference as entirely due to the influence of his Chinese advisers, we should note that a similar evolution had occurred in the 1260s under Hülegu in Persia, although that too was quite possibly influenced by the general development of governing modes within the Mongol world, in which Chinese and Central Asian governing assistants played their parts.

After pausing a few weeks, Bayan planned to push on rapidly toward Hangzhou despite the stifling late summer heat of the region, from which his northern Chinese and Mongol soldiers suffered greatly. But Khubilai had to call him to the court to discuss the serious turn of events in Mongolia, where Khubilai's grand-nephew Khaidu, grandson of the late Great Khan Ögödei, had been leading a civil war against Khubilai since 1268. Bayan left for Shangdu late in August, made plans with Khubilai for dealing with the crisis in the northwest, then returned to the Yangzi in November.

The conclusion of the conquest went very rapidly, despite fierce resistance at several of the lower Yangzi regional cities. Two or three major battles still remained to be fought, the most important at Changzhou on the Yangzi east of Nanjing in December. There a stubbornly loyal Chinese defense force held out; Bayan stormed the city, captured it, and had the entire garrison and civilian population killed to intimidate other would-be holdouts. That was the last large military confrontation of the campaign. It was one of at least two occasions during the campaign when Bayan reverted to Mongol military practice, ignoring the instructions from Khubilai to act in the manner of Cao Bin, who had conquered Nanjing for the Song at the end of the tenth century "without killing a single person."

The fall of Hangzhou two months later was bloodless, and without too much exaggeration the Yuan tried to project that as the characteristic mode of their entire conquest of the Song. Bayan could be patient in appropriate circumstances. He took time to work out a format for the surrender with the Empress Dowager Xie. He entered the city on February 10, 1276. On February 21 the boy emperor, her grandson, led the high officials of the court to bow deferentially to Bayan and turn over the documents of surrender. Then they were sent off to Dadu, where they were treated with dignity and respect; Khubilai's consort, Empress Chabi, showed particular concern for the exiled Song empress dowager's comfort.[30] The boy emperor was granted a ducal title but meager support; he lived out his life in China, later becoming a Buddhist monk. The Song dynasty had come to its formal end.

Song loyalists organized resistance and held out fiercely until a final showdown three years later on the coast in what would be present-day Hong Kong. Eminent Song officials attending the last boy emperor were forced to board Song warships and take to sea to escape the enclosing Mongol forces. The seven-year-old younger brother of the boy emperor who had surrendered at Hangzhou in 1276 had been proclaimed emperor by the loyalist resistance movement, the third such hapless child to fill that role. He was nominal head of the resistance government now facing a Mongol army that pushed them off the soil of China and out to sea. One venerated old official of the court took the boy on his back and leaped into the sea, committing suicide to avoid capture. There was now no longer a center around which to organize military resistance, but passive resistance by a significant portion of the entire generation of scholar-officials continued until they died out. Their high-minded loyalism was not politically, much less militarily, significant; the Mongols could afford to ignore it.

VII. THE WAR AGAINST KHAIDU

Resistance to Khubilai in China after 1279 was not militarily significant, but continuing Mongol resistance to him is quite another story. As I have noted, this antipathy toward him was based among the western princes, the Chinggisids within the other three khanates, and found its leader in a grandson of Ögödei called Khaidu (1235?–1301). The house of Tolui had been resented since Möngke became Great Khan in 1251, after which he purged the opposing Ögödeid and Chaghadaid lines, greatly weakening them. They had sided with Arigh Böke in his civil war against Khubilai in 1260, and they now induced their cousins in the Golden Horde to support them. As the Great Khan, Khubilai claimed but could not enforce seniority and executive power over all of them. He had sent them orders in 1264 to attend a *khuriltai* to be held in 1267, at which they all should help settle on the punishment to be imposed on Arigh Böke and decide on other matters in the central governance of the Mongolian Great Khanate. Before it could be convened, not only Arigh Böke but the three heads of the other khanates as well all had died and were succeeded by younger heirs. No further meeting was called. Khubilai, however, repeatedly summoned Khaidu, hoping to talk out their differences. Khaidu avoided the meetings, saying that his horses were lean, but when they had been fattened he would be able to make the long journey.

Instead he led his cavalry on their fat horses to make war on Khubilai in Mongolia, trying to capture and restore the abandoned capital at Karakorum as prelude to reestablishing that center of the Mongol empire; then, it was clear, he would invade China. Khubilai was surprised to discover inimical Mongols still on the scene within Mongolia; he believed that they had been driven out and the borders made secure before he commenced the last phase of the war against the Song in 1274. In fact they were only waiting to take advantage of his involvement there to resume their attacks. In 1276 they managed to get some of the eastern princes from Khubilai's own khanate based in eastern Mongolia and Manchuria to join them. Among these were two nephews, sons of Möngke and Arigh Böke, along with others of Khubilai's near kin. They opposed him on the very serious grounds that he had become too strongly identified with the Chinese.

Khubilai had the material resources of China and many loyal and able military and policy assistants. He had to fight on two Mongolian fronts, one in the east and one in the far west, as the fighting rose and fell sporadically over a period of many years. Both Bayan and Aju were assigned to the Mongolian front after their return from Hangzhou in 1276, and they were generally successful in all major confrontations. The resistance among the eastern princes was fully overcome. Yet the dissident Chinggisid princes in the other three khanates of the west were always ready to abandon the offensive, withdraw, and wait to attack again in the future. Khaidu did not die until 1301, seven years after the death of Khubilai. His cause had failed, and the Chinese khanate was able to hold the western boundaries of Mongolia securely enough after that, but the wars had devastated the region causing much loss of life and property. As Karakorum dwindled in importance, the center of Mongolian life shifted to the east. Relations among the four khanates were reduced to insignificance. But all that belongs to an ever more distant periphery of Chinese history.

VIII. KHUBILAI'S LATER YEARS

The uncertainties in his relations with the Mongol world, and his failure to assume so dominant a stature that his will would prevail, probably had a great deal to do with Khubilai's decisions to embark on other military conquests.[31] Finding the Japanese replies to his diplomatic overtures in the 1270s insolent and ill-mannered (the feeling was mutual), he had sent a small army supported by Korean naval forces to invade Japan in 1274. The invasion, which landed in November 1274 in remote Kyushu, a poor region with small military forces, was an initial success. While the Japanese defenders were able fighters, the Mongol military formations and tactics were new to them. They were unable to repel the invaders. But then a great storm arose. The Korean naval commanders, who understood the urgent need to sail their ships away from the coastal rocks, ordered the Mongol armies to board ship and depart. Not all made it aboard; isolated, those left behind on the shore were easily slaughtered. The ensuing storm caused great destruction to the flotilla; of some 300 large and 500 smaller ships, most sank, with losses of over 10,000 Mongol soldiers. Remnants of the army escaped back to China to report to Khubilai, who at that moment was unable to detach other forces to punish the insolent Japanese.

With reckless self-confidence after their heaven-aided escape, Japanese leaders executed envoys sent by Khubilai in the ensuing years. In short, Khubilai thought he had full reason to return to Japan in 1281. This time he made more thorough preparations, and had fuller cooperation from the Korean king, who sent an admiral and 900 ships. Khubilai had raised an army of 140,000, most of them Chinese, Khitans, and Jurchens, in addition to the

Korean navy, but he also had sent along a sizable Mongol cavalry unit. This time the forces sailed simultaneously from Korea and from Fujian on the southeast China coast to rendezvous at their destination in Kyushu in June 1281. They landed and fought for two months without making much headway against the stiff and well-directed Japanese resistance. The Chinese soldiers in particular had little heart for this adventure. Then again, in August, a typhoon which the Japanese designated a *kamikaze,* or "divine wind," blew in. Many of the soldiers onshore did not make it back to their ships and were slaughtered by the Japanese, and many of the ships sank in the storm. Again, remnants of a failed expeditionary force returned home to report to Khubilai. The impact on Japan was significant; the Japanese felt they had again been rescued by their gods and made of the event a revitalizing national epic. Khubilai at first thought of trying a third time but eventually accepted military and civilian advice to let the Japan matter rest.

His desire for further military conquests remained strong. In the 1280s he made repeated war against Burma from his southwest China base in Yunnan, and against Annam from South China. He also ordered an invasion of Java in 1292–93, but this also turned out to be a fiasco. All of these wars of the 1280s and early 1290s appear to have been devised as diversions from the increasingly unhappy personal life of the old ruler's later years. They were costly diversions, and they accomplished nothing. Despondent, he became addicted to strong drink and ate to the point of gross obesity, undermining his health and his mental alertness.[32]

One source of his unhappiness in later life was the death of his principal wife, Empress Chabi, in 1281, followed by that of his favorite son and designated heir, Prince Zhenjin (Jingim), in 1285. Chabi had been an important helpmate and companion throughout his life. Her son Zhenjin as a young man was educated in Chinese and worked warmly with the often beleaguered Chinese advisers at his father's court. Had he not died, the Yuan dynasty would have had in its second emperor a ruler somewhat assimilated into Chinese culture, fully literate if not profoundly educated, able to discuss affairs with his Chinese associates in their language. This might have deeply affected the conduct and tone of Yuan government. But it did not happen.

IX. KHUBILAI KHAN'S SUCCESSORS, 1294–1370

Counting Khubilai Khan as the first Mongol khan who concurrently claimed the title emperor of China, there were altogether ten Mongol emperors who came to the throne of the Yuan dynasty before it was driven out by the succeeding native Chinese Ming dynasty in 1368 (see Dynastic Succession Chart 7). In addition to Zhenjin, his second son, Khubilai had three other surviving sons by his two principal consorts and at least seven others by lesser wives. None of them was considered a contender for the succession because Khubilai had made it clear that the throne should pass to sons of Zhenjin, and he had chosen the youngest of Zhenjin's three sons to succeed him. Those three lines of descent from Zhenjin, however, all produced heirs among whom subse-

CHART 7. MONGOL EMPERORS OF THE YUAN DYNASTY

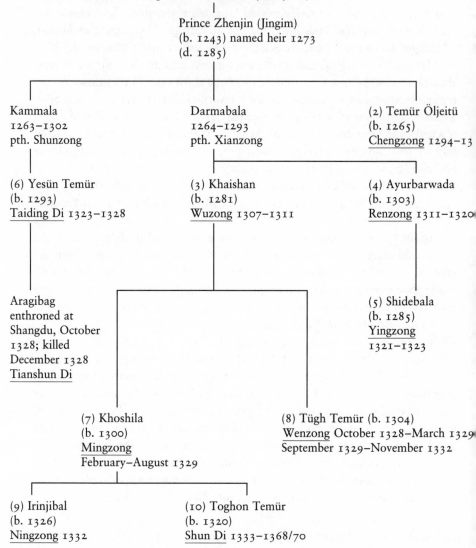

(1) Khubilai Khan, Fifth Great Khan and First Emperor of Yuan, pth. Shizu, 1260–1294. Succeeded to Khanate 1260; proclaimed Yuan Dynasty 1272

Prince Zhenjin (Jingim)
(b. 1243) named heir 1273
(d. 1285)

Kammala
1263–1302
pth. Shunzong

Darmabala
1264–1293
pth. Xianzong

(2) Temür Öljeitü
(b. 1265)
Chengzong 1294–13

(6) Yesün Temür
(b. 1293)
Taiding Di 1323–1328

(3) Khaishan
(b. 1281)
Wuzong 1307–1311

(4) Ayurbarwada
(b. 1303)
Renzong 1311–1320

Aragibag
enthroned at
Shangdu, October
1328; killed
December 1328
Tianshun Di

(5) Shidebala
(b. 1285)
Yingzong
1321–1323

(7) Khoshila
(b. 1300)
Mingzong
February–August 1329

(8) Tügh Temür (b. 1304)
Wenzong October 1328–March 1329
September 1329–November 1332

(9) Irinjibal
(b. 1326)
Ningzong 1332

(10) Toghon Temür
(b. 1320)
Shun Di 1333–1368/70

( ) Sequence as emperor

Note: Aragibag, son of (6), is sometimes placed in the succession as (7), with the temple na
Tianshun Di.

quent rulers were chosen, and jockeying for position among potential heirs in those three lines produced struggles and uncertainties which came to turn not on legitimacy to succeed per se but on fundamental policy disputes over the direction that the Yuan dynasty should take.

Of the nine emperors who followed Khubilai, most came to the throne in their twenties or thirties, as mature adults; only the ninth and tenth succeeded to the throne as children. Yet all were figureheads for cliques of Mongol nobles and political leaders whose policy differences for several decades turned on the single issue of furthering steppe military interests versus a commitment to the advantages the Mongols gained from tending the Chinese base of their power. This underlying policy divergence was already evident in the relations between Khubilai Khan as a young man and his older brother Möngke, who was the last Mongol Great Khan to reign (1251–1259) over the entire Mongol Eurasian empire. Möngke Khan looked upon China as an appendage of the Mongolian steppe-based empire, while Khubilai, who could not assert his authority over the three western khanates, came to regard China as the base of Mongol power exercised through his creation, the Yuan dynasty. Unlike the Jurchens in the management of their Jin dynasty, most of the Mongol population remained in the Mongolian steppe and continued to seek outlets for their ambitions in the pattern of steppe-based military expansion. Many of them resented Khubilai's failure to continue that focus of their expansionist energies. As Khubilai discovered, that resentment and sense of thwarted ambition continued to plague his rule to the end of his life.

For thirty-five years after Khubilai's death in 1294, those conflicts were evident but not explosive. Chengzong, the second emperor, who came to the throne in 1294 despite some opposition on those grounds, reigned in relative peace until his death in 1307. He had received a smattering of Chinese education. He retained most of Khubilai's leading courtiers and continued his grandfather's cautious domestic policies. Chengzong called off preparations left in place by Khubilai for further military campaigns in Vietnam and against Japan, and called for peaceful relations with the Mongol khanates to the west, where hostility toward Khubilai had always threatened to link up with the smoldering resentment in Khubilai's Mongolian hearthland. Chengzong was a man of passive temperament; he was happy to carry on with few changes and to limit his day-to-day involvement. Chinese patterns in statecraft were not disturbed, and the commitment to governing over the huge Chinese population remained the main focus of his governing.

On his death, Mongol activists who rejected the pro-China focus of rule engaged in fierce factional struggles to bring Chengzong's nephew Khaishan (or Qaishan) to the throne. Posthumously designated Wuzong, "the Martial Emperor," the twenty-six-year-old Khaishan had spent a number of years absorbing the military traditions of the steppe, after receiving the beginnings of a Chinese education. Even though not untainted by the influences of sedentary life in China, he was looked to as a future Mongol warrior ruler because his uncle, Emperor Chengzong, had given him large military responsibilities in the steppe in which he had performed well. His Mongol relatives with whom he had associated in the steppe believed that by turning the khanate of China's resources toward expansion in Mongolia, the whole Mongol world of the four khanates might again be reunited. Bringing Khaishan to the throne encouraged those ambitions. But instead of providing forceful leadership in pursuit of military expansion in the steppe, he became a self-indulgent and extravagant tyrant who squandered the state's resources, emptied the treasury, and spent his days in dissolute diversions. He died before he had reigned five years, bringing his younger brother Ayurbarwada, whom he had previously named his heir, to the throne in 1311. He is known in history by his posthumous title, the Emperor Renzong; as the fourth Yuan emperor, he reigned 1311–1320.

The brothers had received quite different educations. Renzong had remained in China and had been exposed to Chinese education. He was under the influence of leading officials who looked first to managing the Chinese realm. Among the few Yuan emperors who could read as well as speak some Chinese,[33] Renzong was the first who had mastered classical texts; he also enjoyed the study of Buddhist sutras written in Chinese. After the administrative chaos ushered in by Khaishan, he saw the benefit to be gained by restoring what has been called "Confucian" politics, meaning a focus on China as the basis of Yuan power. A reversion to those modes in governing prevailed for the next dozen years.[34] Immediately on being named the successor he ordered a roundup of his late brother's chief officials; he executed or banished many of them, and cowed others who might openly oppose him. A state council was established, staffed by senior officials from Khubilai's time, mostly learned Chinese, along with some Mongols who were competent in Chinese statecraft. It was Emperor Renzong who, in 1313, took the major step of restoring the Chinese examination system, providing that the first examinations for the *jinshi* degree would be held in 1315. In the eyes of his Chinese subjects that was a landmark event. He also attempted to tighten up the administration and raise standards in education, but undercurrents of opposition, even from the surviving empresses dowager and others in his imperial household, denied him free exercise of his authority. He did not have a strong personality and was forced to yield at many points. When he died early in 1320, his eighteen-year-old son succeeded him, to become known as Yingzong, the fifth Mongol emperor of China.

Yingzong also had received some Chinese education and in general shared his father's outlook. But before he had formally ascended the throne, enemies within the imperial clan and their associates took charge of the court, slaughtered a number of Renzong's chief ministers, and threatened the young emperor's life. An opposing faction of powerful courtiers came to his support and made a battleground of the offices of government. For a time they prevailed in an atmosphere of tension. Yingzong bravely announced a full program of "Confucian" governing changes, including some of the most important political measures promulgated in the decades following Khubilai's death. The high Mongol nobility and Central Asian contingent of the government felt that their interests were directly threatened. The struggles grew bloody, with assassinations and counterattacks becoming frequent. In the autumn of 1323 the opposing factions intercepted the emperor on his way back to Dadu (Beijing) from the summer capital at Shangdu and assassinated him; Yingzong was only twenty years old, a victim of the unresolved policy conflicts that increasingly dominated Yuan governing.

Yingzong's enemies found an heir to the third line of descendants of Prince Zhenjin, a son of his eldest son, Kammala, and made him the sixth Mongol ruler; he was posthumously given the title Taiding Di.[35] He had been party to the assassination of Yingzong, and he was close to the Mongol lords who advocated the steppe policies, but on coming to the throne he did not pursue those policies. To distance himself from the assassination, he turned on his co-plotters, arresting and executing many of them, while at the same time bringing back some of Yingzong's courtiers to staff his court. His reign was marked by growing hostility between the two camps, and his death five years later at Shangdu, the summer capital in Mongolia, brought on a period of fierce civil war among the sponsors of various contestants for the succession. The Taiding emperor's followers tried to place his young son on the throne there; two months later, in October 1328, the nine-year-old boy is said to have "disappeared," evidently murdered. At the same time, at the capital a powerful minister, who twenty years earlier had served Emperor Wuzong (Khaishan), took command of the court and demanded that the sons of Wuzong should now inherit the throne. There were two sons, neither of whom was near the capital. The elder was declared the new emperor in the spring of 1329, while the younger one, who had been given the title late in 1328, now deferred to his older brother. In fact he was planning to have his brother brought to the capital where he could be taken captive and murdered; that happened late in the summer of 1329, after he had held the title of emperor for only a few months. He is known in history as Emperor Mingzong, the seventh Yuan emperor. The younger brother, who then reigned until 1332, is known as Emperor Wenzong, the eighth Yuan emperor. Not above fratricide, he nevertheless was highly educated in Chinese, the only Yuan emperor who achieved a measure of genuine cultivation; his posthumous title Wenzong, means "the Cultivated Ancestor." He sponsored many cultural activities, wrote poetry, painted, and read the classical texts. Examples of his quite competent calligraphy have survived. But his reign was brief, state policy was in the hands of powerful ministers, and his personal qualities had few consequences for history.

The civil wars and factional violence during the years following the death of the Taiding emperor in 1328 marked a turning point in long struggle between the "Confucian" policies and those oriented toward the steppe; from that point on, Yuan governing was entirely in the China-centered mode, and the factional struggles which continued as fiercely as before now were between competing factions of power-hungry ministers for control of the throne. The ninth emperor, Ningzong, was only six when he came to the throne in 1332, followed the next year by the tenth and last Yuan emperor, who came to the throne at the age of thirteen. By name Toghon Temür, he was driven out of China thirty-five years later by the conquering Ming armies in 1368, and died in Mongolia in 1370.

The tenth (counting from Khubilai Khan) and last Mongol emperor to reign in China, Toghon Temür, is known in history as the Emperor Shun, or Shundi. His reign, considered as lasting until his death in 1370, was the longest of all the Mongol rulers since Chinggis Khan. As a young boy he was educated by a Chinese monk who taught him to read and write Chinese and to memorize some classical texts used for primary education. He appears to have been extremely bright. Even as a boy he produced Chinese calligraphy that was remarkable. But he became a self-indulgent emperor, interested in religious and cultic practices taught to him by Tibetan monks. The Chinese looked askance upon that, considering Tibetan Tantric arts to be degenerate. Perhaps they were in this instance; they were in any event quite distracting. The young ruler paid very little attention to governing. He was largely a figurehead of the political factions which successively controlled his court and government. On the few important occasions when he asserted himself to impose a political decision, the results were disastrous. His reign saw the total breakdown of the dynasty's ability to rule beyond the capital region. For much of his reign his court and government were dominated by an able Chief Councillor, a Mongol nobleman named Toghto who worked well with high Chinese officials and who concentrated on strengthening the fiscal and military position of the dynasty.[36] Despite Toghto's strong hand at the helm for some fifteen years, the Emperor Shun's court was constantly subject to factional warfare and political dispute.

The long last reign of the Yuan dynasty appeared to many Chinese to demonstrate that the Mongols had lost the ability to retain control. Emperor Shun has been vilified in the Chinese historical record, in large measure somewhat unjustly. If he was personally irrelevant to the fate of the dynasty, he was nevertheless an interestingly intelligent if quite unconventional occupant of the throne. In the longer view of history he is easily disregarded; the story shifts from the Mongol court to the rebellions in the provinces. Yet both he and his reign deserve more serious consideration than we find in the contemptuous verbiage that has been lavished upon him in Chinese historiography in the stereotype of the "bad last ruler." His fate as the last Mongol ruler of China was ignominious, to be sure, yet his descendants in Mongolia claimed that title for many decades. Mongolia, Chinggis Khan's creation, remained a potentially powerful state, an ever-present threat to the northern border defenses throughout the following Ming dynasty.

Khubilai Khan's successors on the Yuan dynasty throne can be looked upon as a dismal procession of incompetent rulers and failed policies, but their history is more important than such an image suggests. It is also the account of a failure to resolve an underlying problem: Did the Mongol nation want to remain a steppe power, as the Khitans decided to do, or was it in their greater interest to shift the basis of their state power decisively to China, as the Jurchens (and the later Manchus) did? Their Chinese subjects decided that issue for them by returning them to their steppe homeland and by succeeding to their dynastic aspirations, adopting some of their political and military means, and much of their view of "Confucian" state policy, with many of the anomalies implicit in that designation. After a survey of the life of the Chinese people under Mongol rule in the next chapter, the story of Yuan state failure and descent into military regionalization, leading to the creation of the successor dynasty, will be taken up in Chapter 21.

20

CHINA UNDER
MONGOL RULE

The experience of being under Mongol rule, lasting well over a century in the northern regions and almost a century in Central and South China, deeply affected Chinese society. Positively, the entire country was again unified after a long period of division between conquest dynasties in the North and Chinese dynasties in the South. That reintegration affected many aspects of life; it also brought a measure of satisfaction to many of the elite, and perhaps also to the people at large. Negatively, the impact of Mongol rule on China's political heritage and on many aspects of social life was disruptive and deeply felt. The Mongols' management of society, hence the lives of people, differed in many ways from previous history. In this chapter, two dimensions of those problems are explored. Sections I and II describe the formal structures of governing over the Chinese population of Yuan China, which, in part, were without precedent in Chinese history. Sections III, IV, and V discuss some of the broader social realities, showing how different sectors of the population adapted to the special conditions of Mongol overlordship. The conclusion is that despite the intrusive elements and social disturbances, Chinese civilization through Yuan times displays more continuities than discontinuities with its Chinese past.

I. YUAN GOVERNMENT

When the Mongols turned from conquering to governing, as they did in all the parts of their world empire in the second half of the thirteenth century, they did so in China without having formulated any large plans about how government should function, what the scope of its responsibilities should be, or how conquered peoples should be dealt with apart from being put under some kind of military administration. Nor did their mindset allow facile adaptations of the existing patterns available for borrowing. One can surmise that their hesitancy about reaching out to political solutions arose from the fact that in the lifetime of Chinggis Khan, they still were working out the means for governing themselves through a rapidly enlarged tribal confederation—essentially a military structure being stretched to meet pressing needs within their own expanding nation. How they should govern conquered peoples had not yet come to be an immediate concern.

The situation in which the Mongols found themselves differed sharply from that of their conquest dynasty predecessors: they did not have the Khitans' long experience in observing China's Tang dynasty, nor the Jurchens' readiness to assume the Khitans' role in managing a dual empire. The Mongols began by improvising ways to extend the khan's authority as a tribal chieftain. Beginning about 1200, as we have seen, Chinggis Khan took the initial steps toward authorizing a small corps of trusted associates to manage his expanding household, to form his personal guard, to record his decrees, and to serve other functions in the daily operations of his camp, which, wherever it was situated, constituted all there was of his court and his government. Simultaneously, he also undertook the difficult process of reorganizing his army into decimal units of 10, 100, 1,000, and eventually 10,000 men, and of imposing on those units a chain of command that brought his military subordinates under strict discipline. These measures were new to Mongol experience and were in themselves major alterations of authority patterns, demanding accompanying changes in Mongol self-awareness and cultural style.

Taken all together, those were bold steps toward forging a new Mongol nation; they accomplished no less than a basic restructuring of tribal society. While that process was under way, we can hardly expect that Chinggis and his Mongol leadership could have simultaneously done much more. His new means for extending strong authority from his reorganized Mongol tribes to all the steppe populations so as to exercise systematic command over their military manpower and resources functioned as the main vehicle for Mongol governing in that early period. In brief, the khan's military chain of command *was* the government. Regularized and developed, those institutions became the government of a historically new Mongolia that successfully consolidated its steppe homeland. China and other sedentary parts of the empire, however, were peripheral to those concerns, and Mongol governing in all the outer khanates remained less stable.

It is useful to compare the Mongols in that early phase of their history with the Khitans three centuries earlier. Under Abaoji early in the tenth century, the Khitan nation also faced the problem of strengthening its ruler's authority to meet enlarged demands and improve the structure of governing. By that time the Khitans had accumulated several centuries of experience with their tribal confederation under its councils of chieftains, all in a context of intimate coexistence with the "other world" of Chinese government. They had a good sense of how the two worlds interacted. They could make choices among familiar alternatives in governing. That is how their system of dual institutions emerged. Moreover, the Khitans' well-defined and successful pattern of governing was one that the Jurchens, as successors to the Khitans two centuries later, could quickly comprehend; through a transitional period they could simply commandeer Liao institutions as they existed on the ground. The further step of taking over Song offices of government in North China as their conquest continued, often retaining the current officeholders, was all of a piece with that.

After 1217, in the wake of the their first attacks on the Jin, when Prince General Mukhali served as Chinggis's viceroy for North China, the Mongol conquerors' efforts to impose order on the massive Chinese population presented new and unfamiliar problems. The Mongols had an urgent need for military manpower. Most of the Chinese males were not soldiers; from a Mongol point of view they were not even potential soldiers. They could not just be conscripted and organized into military units, as had all other newly subjugated peoples in the Mongols' experience up to that time. Faced with large conquered populations that could not be absorbed en bloc, they did not quite know what to do. Some localities were then under de facto rule by Chinese warlords; they were gratefully taken over as easy solutions to the problem, their leaders coopted into the Mongol system and given high titles as "hereditary lords" *(shi hou)*. But most of China could not be managed in that way. It was still under the remnants of the highly sinified Jin dynasty's government, which, until the Jin was eliminated in 1234, was the immediate enemy. The Mongols appear not to have made the psychological preparation to slip into the enemy's shoes and use those remnant forms, as the Jurchens had done when they so quickly conquered the Liao in the early twelfth century.

Their long-range goals in conquest not yet worked out, the Mongols allowed an interregnum of twenty-five years to pass. North China was only one sector of Mongol engagement, which extended from Korea to Russia. Strictly military concerns dominated their actions.

At that stage, advice from Yelü Chucai (d. 1243) led to the initial steps toward putting into place a general system for civilian governing of the Chinese population. A highly sinicized Khitan, Yelü understood both worlds and could lend a measure of "psychic mobility"[1] to his Mongol overlords, especially Chinggis and Ögödei. Yet, despite their respect for him as a man from their steppe world who also understood the other world, they could not quite grant him the full trust that the founding emperors of the Liao and the Jin had granted their sinicized advisers. Yelü therefore had to bear responsibility while lacking full authority. Frustrated, he nevertheless persisted, and accomplished some basic steps. A decade after Yelü's death in the 1250s, and building on his hopeful initiatives, a much fuller approximation of civil governing began to take form under Möngke and Khubilai. It was extended throughout North China, with responsibilities toward collecting revenues and maintaining the social order. Not even the large pool of Khubilai's Chinese and Chinese-minded advisers, however, succeeded in convincing this fifth Mongol khan that in one systematic transition he could achieve a comprehensive plan for meeting all the diverse needs of governing his rapidly growing Chinese subject nation. Nor did Khubilai accept the concept of complete but separate dual institutions, one set for the steppe and another for China, as had the Khitans and the first rulers of the Jurchens. Neither could he envision a wholesale takeover of Chinese institutions, as the later Jurchen rulers had done. Instead, as emperor of China (both when anticipating that role, 1260–1271, and in realizing it, 1272–1294), Khubilai built his Chinese-style government by making innumerable ad hoc decisions, some adopting existing features of Jin or Song administration, some modifying or undermining those, some imposing measures advocated by Central Asians who derived them from experience in other societies far distant from China. An eminent authority has written: "Before the Yuan dynasty was formally proclaimed in 1271, the framework for a central government modeled on the Chinese pattern was thus already in place. The next decades witnessed an enormous growth in agencies derived from the Chin [Jin], Sung [Song], and even the T'ang [Tang] governments, producing one of the most complex imperial governments in Chinese history. Along with these developments at the center came the adoption of a system of successive local administrative units of a Chinese type."[2]

The complex imperial regime that took form in the thirteenth century continued to undergo minor changes throughout the entire Yuan dynasty until its end in 1368, but here the focus is on the political decisions made during Khubilai's long reign, when it functioned at its best. The Yuan dynasty rulers' selective adaptations of older Chinese institutions influenced the conduct of Chinese government in the succeeding Ming and Qing dynasties. Yuan government also invites comparisons (lying outside the scope of this volume) with the ways in which Mongol modes of governing altered institutions and influenced post-Mongol political developments in Inner Asia, Central Asia, Persia, and Russia.

The Central Government

The leading organ of the Yuan bureaucracy was its Central Secretariat, the Zhongshu Sheng. Yelü Chucai had held the title Chief of the Central Secretariat, Zongshu Ling, as early as the 1230s, but at that time it was no more than a somewhat exaggerated Chinese translation of his Mongol title, which meant only that he was "principal secretary" among the khan's many scribes and secretaries. This was a motley group of wielders of the pen in the various languages then used at the Mongol court. By the 1270s Khubilai intended something different. His Central Secretariat was to be given charge over all civil governing affairs throughout the realm. He wanted a centralized executive agency. Models for it had long been part of Chinese imperial government, but now it was to function in a new context. In Tang times the Zhongshu Sheng was one of three principal divisions of a differentiated set of secretarial functions, distributed among a Chancellery (Shangshu Sheng), a Department of State Affairs (Zhongshu Sheng), and a Central Secretariat (Menxia Sheng). The Song modified that tripartite division of executive agencies in the central government. Under the Song, as also under the Liao and Jin, those organs had exercised much of the executive authority for the emperor.[3] Now under the Yuan, the Central Secretariat with enlarged functions stood alone as the sole organ to lead the civil administration of Khubilai's realm.

The Mongols adopted the Chinese civil service system of nine ranks, each divided into A and B (senior and junior), making a total of eighteen levels of rank that assigned status and determined precedence, deference, salary, and other perquisites.[4] Khubilai's Central Secretariat was headed by a Secretary General, a post normally left unfilled unless the designated heir apparent held it. Otherwise it was headed by one Senior and one Junior Chief Councillor (or, at times, up to five Chief Councillors), ranked 1.A; four Privy Councillors, ranked 1.B; Senior and Junior Vice Councillors, ranked 2.A; and an array of lesser assistants. The agency included as many as 210 ranked civil officials and hundreds of subofficials at clerical levels.

Next in importance to the Central Secretariat were the Six Ministries (Liu Bu): Personnel, Revenues, Rites, War, Punishments, and Works. Those were the traditional Chinese executive ministries. Ministers were ranked 3.A. Under each of them were many service posts and supporting agencies created for specific functions. For example, the Ministry of Revenues had superintendencies for copper currency; for incense and paper; for satins; for textiles; for gold and silver; for paper currency; for various livestock markets; for fruit, fish, coal, wood, and alcohol; for grain transport (because taxes were paid in kind); for granaries (where tax grains were stored); for salt production and distribution (because after agrarian taxes, salt was the second most important source of revenues); and many others. Under the Ministry of War there were directorates or superintendencies for grain transport (because soldiers were used for transport labor, as for many other kinds of labor); for hunters, falconers, and artisans; for weaving and dyeing (to supply army uniforms); and so on. Under the Ministry of Works was a particularly long list of such subagencies, some of which handled "several classes of artisans," one for Buddhist icons (to supply temples patronized by the imperial household); one for lost-wax casting; also a bronze foundry; offices for working agate and jade, and for masonry, woodworking, paint, materials, felt, weaving and dyeing, carpets, miscellaneous manufacturing, tents, embroidery, patterned satins, wood turning, kilns, leatherwork—in all a total of fifty-three specialized suboffices under this one ministry.[5] There were Song dynasty and earlier precedents for many of these subagencies but not for others. Their proliferation in Yuan times reached unprecedented complexity.

The central government also included surveillance and justice agencies. Most important among these was the traditional Chinese Censorate, Yushitai. The Yuan established administrative offices with regional oversight of the Censorate in three locations: one provided surveillance over agencies of the central government, including the capital city and immediately adjacent regions; the other two were situated one in the Northwest and one in the Yangzi South, each responsible for regions comprising several provinces. That was a new element of decentralization in the supervisory and investigative organs of government, matching the decentralization seen in the case of other central functions.

The Yuan Military Establishment

The central government's management of military affairs was accomplished through a separate hierarchy of offices quite apart from the Ministry of War among the Six Ministries, which in Yuan times functioned as no more than a civilian support agency for military undertakings. Under the Song the Ministry of War had functioned in tandem with a Bureau of Military Affairs (Shumiyuan, literally "office for confidential matters of supreme importance"). The Yuan state attached extraordinary importance to the conduct of war and was extremely sensitive to military security; that gave the Yuan period's military administration its quite special character. The actual conduct of war, the management of military households and conscription matters, and many aspects of support for the military units constituting the total armed force were administered under the enlarged Yuan Bureau of Military Affairs.

The Yuan Bureau of Military Affairs, or Shumiyuan, was first established in 1263 as part of the reorganization of the military following the Li Tan rebellion in 1262, which seemed to Khubilai to demonstrate the need for a complete institutional separation of civil and military government. Anticipating its establishment, an edict issued early in 1263 proclaimed: "In all circuits the officials responsible for the ordinary people are to take charge only of civil affairs, while officials responsible for the troops shall handle only military matters; each shall have his separate duties and they shall not exercise any control over one another."[6] They feared the possible exposure of military secrets to the civilian agencies of government. The creation of the Bureau of Military Affairs followed a few months later.

The bureau was headed by six Overseers, each of rank 1.B, with many categories of assistants ranging down to rank 9.B. This bureau controlled the guard units, the command units, and the myriarchies and chiliarchies constituting the armed forces, whether Mongol, Chinese, or other. It also managed the production and storage of armaments and military supplies. The Bureau of Military Affairs was an extremely large, spreading agency. Its heads nominally were one rank lower than the heads of the Central Secretariat, a formal nod to the Chinese principle of military subordination to the civilian. In reality it was an essentially Mongol agency, highly secret, set apart from ordinary civilian government and often regarded by the Chinese as being of more direct importance to the throne than was the civilian side of governing. (Some writers translate Shumiyuan, the title of this agency, "Privy Council," suggesting its character as an office that controlled state secrets.) Chinese officials were not to be appointed to any positions in it, not even to the purely administrative posts responsible for paperwork, and were not permitted to join in the bureau's deliberations.

The Yuan dynasty's fate was closely tied to the capacities of its military establishment. The great challenge facing Khubilai Khan was to transform the Mongol army into a national army of the Chinese state in which the pre-ponderant manpower would be non-Mongol, while maintaining Mongol superiority and control. Large numbers of Central Asian Turkic soldiers had been taken over during the western campaigns and in North China, where not only Khitans and Jurchens but also Chinese soldiers in large numbers had been coopted, often by the expedient of taking over existing local armies and incorporating them into the Mongol military administration.

With the press into Song China from the 1260s onward, Chinese military manpower was essential in providing the large numbers needed to face the massive armies of the Song. Chinese soldiers also were needed to supplement Mongol military skills when situations did not permit sole reliance on cavalry, that is, in situations where cavalry lost its comparative advantage in fighting (as when walled cities were besieged) so that other means had to be adopted to win battles and establish control. As Song armies surrendered in large num-bers, they were given the designation "newly adhered armies" (Xin fu jun). With them came enlarged administrative problems. Some of those had been anticipated. When creating his Bureau of Military Affairs in 1263, Khubilai had made the decision to bureaucratize the management of his military estab-lishment, to make it operate according to the uniform methods of keeping records, following standards for testing and advancement of personnel, creat-ing a hierarchy of ranked military officials parallel to that for civil officials, and placing the support given to military households under bureaucratic con-trol.

That was a further remove from the tribal system out of which Chinggis had forged a new kind of national army half a century earlier. To a certain extent Khubilai's changes in the management of the military simply continued the rationalizing of the command structure begun by Chinggis Khan almost a century earlier. Chinggis had found it necessary to replace inherited tribal command privilege with a disciplined system of merit appointments, given to persons of proven loyalty and ability. Chinggis nevertheless continued to stress the personal factor in his relationships with his commanders. Khubilai, in new and different circumstances, bureaucratized military leadership in a way that depersonalized the relationships. Previously it was precisely the per-sonal factors that had made the Mongol military system work so well. Chang-ing it to meet new conditions in a larger empire composed mainly of a non-Mongol population was not an easy set of tasks. One can argue that the changes undermined the basis of traditional Mongol military effectiveness; but Khubilai's management decisions were taken at a time when sole reliance on the Mongol military machine was no longer adequate to maintain a state consisting of a small conquering nation ruling over a vastly larger sedentary population. During his conquest of Southern Song, the "newly adhered armies" could be quickly taken over and used to enforce his control over more than 100 million Chinese subjects. Khubilai had been percipient enough to see that he had no alternative to experimenting with boldly different solu-tions influenced by Chinese models even in the realm of the military.[7]

Other changes were required in the management of the Mongol military establishment. The Chinese practice for well over a thousand years had been to recruit mainly infantry to be trained as soldiers. They were recruited as individuals, not as households; they were paid salaries and were expected to return to rural civilian life after a period of service. The Mongols, by contrast, were a nation of military households which expected to be supported, governed, and retained in lifetime status; all the adults males were expected to serve, and their families were expected to support them. As they moved into North China after 1215, the Mongols gave "allotted lands" or appanages to the hereditary heads of their military units; those were geographically intact areas (often a Chinese district or county) containing Chinese village farming communities whose tax revenues and productive capacities belonged to the appanage holder. They extended the practice of giving such tracts of territory to Khitan and other surrendered fighting forces, and eventually to some Chinese as well. In addition, large tracts in North China with their village farming population also were bestowed on Mongols of the imperial clan, and on many nobles who had fought in Mongolia and in the Central and Western Asian campaigns but who had never been in China; they gained those rewards by the Mongol practice of apportioning the fruits of conquest to successful military units. Appanage holders' interests were solely in the revenues produced, not in living on the allotted lands and governing their inhabitants. That steppe system of appanages was incompatible with the workings of Chinese society.

Khubilai understood that. He had to undo much of the system, thereby depriving his military forces of their earned rewards. He accomplished a great deal, but he did not completely succeed in reconstructing the support basis of his military. Some appanages survived all the efforts made throughout his reign to rationalize the system according to principles more suited to the Chinese setting. A national army emerged of which Mongol cavalry units were the elite core, still an important striking force and still bearing the invincible reputation of the steppe armies.

As time passed, throughout the fourteenth century the economic foundations of the Mongol units steadily eroded. Mongolia itself had been impoverished by the century-long wars which, no matter how successful, had exhausted the manpower and the material foundations of the steppe economy. In China the military units (chiliarchies and myriarchies) were given appanage lands to sustain them, but Mongols themselves could not easily make the transition to holding and managing farms (as the Jurchens had done), for they had neither experience in nor taste for that way of life. Legally they could keep slaves to farm for them, but their Chinese captives would do anything to escape that status, and most of them succeeded. Eventually many Mongols sold their allotted lands and quickly used up the proceeds; then they soon could become underprivileged people, even homeless beggars, or be forced to take work as servants of Chinese. Mongol poverty in later Yuan China was common. Some of it came about because of the corruption which riddled all ranks of government but was particularly flagrant within the military; military chiefs did not always show concern for their common soldiers. By the middle of the fourteenth century the Yuan armies, whether the Chinese units of conscriptees or the elite Mongol hereditary soldiery, had become almost useless. Khubilai's farsighted efforts to construct a new basis for Mongol military power in China were undone by the incompetence of his successors, it usually is said. Yet those problems would perhaps have proved insoluble even if he had been succeeded by the most competent heirs.

Other Components of Central Government

In addition to those principal civilian and military components of the central government, the central administration also included many other kinds of bureaucratic organs. The imperial court and the court of the heir apparent both demanded many service agencies, as well as ritual or protocol offices. These included an elaborate structure of offices charged with provisioning the imperial household, having special kitchens, granaries, warehouses for wines and beverages, and places where things were specially made, from garments to rare foods. They also required artisans to work gold and silver, to care for porcelains and utensils, for gems and precious materials, for rare textiles and items of imperial dress, for the emperor's hunting facilities, the imperial stud and the horse farms, and for the slaves and servants to staff all the agencies of the imperial household and inner imperial palace city. The life of the court also demanded a staff of majordomos, managers of all the special events conducted around the imperial family, specialists in entertainments, and supervisors for all the manufactures required by the court. The agencies, again, were not wholly new in Yuan times, but their bureaucratic forms were particularly complicated and unnecessarily duplicative.

The more elevated services to the court demanded the ritual masters, advisers on religious affairs, and specialists in higher kinds of paperwork, such as the keepers of the imperial diaries, the historians, the specialists in drafting edicts and other imperial documents, translators and interpreters, experts in astronomy and calendrical studies, doctors of medicine and pharmacologists, directors of imperial libraries, and the specialists who maintained imperial shrines at the capital, supervised the Altars of Heaven and Earth and the Imperial Ancestral Shrine (the chief shrines of the state), provided ritual music, and constructed and maintained the imperially patronized temples and shrines elsewhere throughout the realm.

We might well think it more rational for the central government to have supplied the court and administrative offices simply by purchasing goods and hiring special services. But in China the long-honored way of standardizing an activity was to bureaucratize. Offices of government were set up and staffed with ranked officials as well as subofficial clerks, managers, and workers. Especially under the Yuan we see that one way the battered Chinese bureaucrat could find a secure role in an alien regime was by filling minor official posts of this kind. The Chinese cooperated. That did not, however, signify an increase in the power and importance of the civil government, for it did not enlarge the role of Chinese at levels where power resided.

We find among the Yuan offices of administration certain agencies that are not found in other dynastic periods, such as the Mongolian Hanlin Academy and the Mongolian National Institute (Menggu guozijian) and College (Guozixue). There also was created a Muslim Bureau of Astronomy (Hui-hui Sitian Jian), to which astronomers from Western Asia, mainly Persians, were assigned to practice their scientifically different tradition in competition with Chinese astronomers. This special agency gives testimony to the important scientific and cultural exchanges that developed between the eastern and western Asian ends of the Mongol world empire.

Tibet

The most important of the unprecedented special agencies was the Commission for Tibetan and Buddhist Affairs, the Xuanzhengyuan, rank 1.B. It managed the entire Buddhist clergy throughout the realm, and supervised all temples, monasteries, and other Buddhist properties, at least in name. It also was responsible in a curious way for administering Tibet. That is, this office was given responsibility for administering the Buddhist establishment in Tibet, which was tantamount to giving the persons in charge of that office the dominant role in local governing. During his reign Khubilai's interest shifted away from Chan Buddhism, then the dominant trend in Chinese Buddhist teachings (but not a separate sect, as was Chan, or Zen, in Japan). Lamaist Buddhism from Tibet came to supersede Chan in his religious life. The Tibetan monk Phagspa (P'ags-pa, 1235–1280) was named the National Preceptor, subsequently elevated to the title of Imperial Preceptor by Khubilai in the 1260s.[8] He was concurrently named the director of the Bureau of Buddhist and Tibetan Affairs.

Phagspa is one of the more remarkable figures in Yuan history; he was an intellectual figure of undoubted genius, an administrator, and a spiritual leader and writer of great influence. After his death he became something of a Buddhist patron saint of the Yuan government.[9] He used his very close relationship with the emperor not only to promote Tibetan Buddhism in China but also to advance the interests of his sect of Lamaism in Tibet. His close relatives and other leaders of the Sa-skya sect were appointed, on his advice, either to act as the khan's viceroy or to staff the crucial Pacification Commission for Tibet. In this way the Yuan court found eager surrogates to govern Tibet for them. Those measures, however, clearly did not bring Tibet under Beijing's rule. The Mongol army did not invade and conquer that country, nor did it maintain any regular military presence there, although on a few occasions it did attempt to coerce dissidents and rebels by limited military actions or by stationing intimidating forces on the borders.

Phagspa's quite extraordinary contribution to East Asian linguistics merits a digression here. The Mongols in 1204, on Chinggis Khan's command, had adapted the Uighur alphabetic script to their language. It worked well enough; in fact, it is the script that, with subsequent improvements, has remained in use for Mongolian up to the present, and from which the script for Manchu also was derived early in the seventeenth century. Khubilai, however, asked

Phagspa to devise a script that would function universally, with one set of phonetic symbols for all the languages of the Mongol empire. That is a most interesting idea, comparable to using the Latin alphabet, if somewhat clumsily and with variations, for all modern Western languages; it might better be compared to the International Phonetic Alphabet (IPA), which linguists can use with absolute uniformity to transcribe all the sounds of human speech.

The task facing Phagspa was of similar complexity. He devised a system known as "square writing," or more commonly "the Phagspa script." He drew on his knowledge of Tibetan, possibly of some Indian languages, and his apparently perfect command of Chinese, and consulted with Uighur assistants. With what might be described as a professional linguist's capacity to analyze the phonetics of the other languages, he produced a script that beautifully meets the demands of phonetic accuracy and graphic simplicity. It was officially adopted, taught in government schools, and used during Khubilai's reign but in fewer contexts thereafter. The Mongols who were literate (no doubt a small minority of the population) were already in possession of a script they had used for more than half a century, and they did not convert to the use of Phagspa script in their daily lives. Some scraps of other languages of the time transcribed in Phagspa, still extant, are phonetically so precise that modern linguists treasure them as the only accurate evidence for the sounds of those languages as then spoken. This monument to Phagspa's intellectual acuity and precision shows us that the young Tibetan monk was a man of remarkable attainments.[10]

To return to the Yuan government's supervision of religions, this did not include any supervising agency for the Daoist religion in parallel with the superintendency for Buddhism. Much earlier, Chinggis Khan had assigned full responsibility for both Buddhism and Daoism in North China to Qiu Chuji, the old Daoist sectarian leader also known as Changchun, "Everlasting Spring," summoned to meet with Chinggis in Central Asia in 1222. After Qiu's return to North China, he used the power granted to him in the khan's edict to favor the Daoists. That imperial favor, much misused at the time, was not continued by later rulers. Nevertheless, important new sects of Daoism flourished among the people throughout late Jin and Yuan times.

The Nestorian Christians, thanks to the patronage of both Khubilai's mother and his principal consort, Empress Chabi, were regarded more favorably. An Office for Christian Clergy (Chongfu Si) was established in Khubilai's reign, headed by four Commissioners of Religious Affairs at rank 2.B and assisted by other officials. Nestorian communities persisted in several parts of China at least until the end of the Yuan period. The succeeding Ming dynasty ignored them, so they disappeared from the official records. The most interesting Nestorian monk of the time, one Rabban Sauma (ca. 1225–1294) traveled to Europe, where he met the pope and the kings of France and England; he was a counterpart to Marco Polo, traversing Central Asia at about the same time but in the opposite direction. Unfortunately he did not return to inform China about the West.[11]

Communities of Jews were also reported in China at this time, probably transplanted from Central and Western Asian lands, but no special administrative measures for fitting them into Chinese society are recorded.[12] There is interesting nonofficial evidence for the existence of Jewish communities in Yuan China.

Regional and Local Governing

The Yuan dynasty introduced several new elements into the structure, staffing, and operation of government at middle and local levels. The most important was the creation of a provincial level of administration, the *xingsheng*, which in Ming and Qing times became the provinces, or *sheng*. This system came about through the Mongols' practice of dividing off a portion of the Central Secretariat, or Zhongshu Sheng, to function as a branch secretariat in regions where their armies were engaged in conquest. The temporary expedient became a permanent fixture; those branches were then retained as permanent organs of regional government with their own regularly assigned staffs, thus creating the provinces, larger units of regional administrative geography than the Chinese had previously demarcated.

There were Jin dynasty precedents for this administrative device, but as a permanent institution the province is a Yuan innovation. In all, China acquired ten of these regional divisions, each headed by a branch secretariat, with the Metropolitan Province, comprising the capital at Dadu along with adjacent territories of considerable extent, counted as the eleventh province (Map 13). Having a nexus of governing authority at the regional level was useful; the eleven Yuan provinces as somewhat redrawn became the fifteen provinces of the Ming, and from these in turn were formed the eighteen provinces of Qing China. Since 1949 China's provinces have again been redefined, but elements of the eighteen Qing provinces are apparent in Chinese administrative geography today.

The central administrative organs also were divided to create branches that functioned at the *xingsheng* level. That was true of the Six Ministries, which set up counterpart bureaus at the provincial level, and of the Bureau of Military Affairs, which established provincial-level Pacification Commissions, or Xuanweisi, to control the garrisons stationed in each of the provinces. The Censorate, the surveillance arm of government, also had province-level offices, as did the Bureau of Buddhist and Tibetan Affairs, nominally to oversee the Buddhist establishment in each province. This new pattern was extended to almost all the executive agencies of the central government.

Despite the presence at province level of so many branches of central agencies, they were not united into integrated provincial governments. On the contrary, there was little lateral integration; all the offices communicated vertically, whether upwards with their counterparts in the capital or downwards with subordinate agencies at prefectural and district levels. This was meant to ensure that no powerful provincial governors wielding great regional power would emerge to contest the authority of the center. But neither did the Yuan central government exercise the degree of control that should have

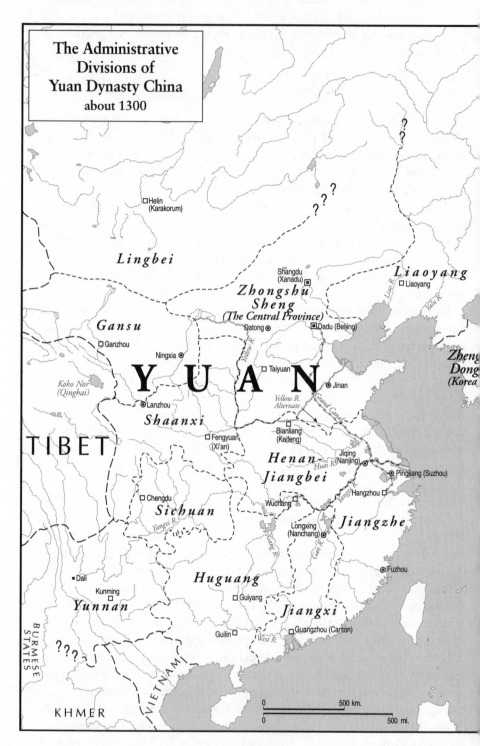

The Administrative
Divisions of
Yuan Dynasty China
about 1300

Helin
(Karakorum)

Lingbei

Shangdu
(Xanadu)

Liaoyang

Liaoyang

Zhongshu
Sheng
(The Central Province)

Gansu

Datong

Dadu (Beijing)

Ganzhou

Ningxia

Zheng
Dong
(Korea)

Taiyuan

Koko Nor
(Qinghai)

YUAN

Jinan

Lanzhou

Yellow R.
Alternate

Shaanxi

TIBET

Fengyuan
(Xi'an)

Bianliang
(Kaifeng)

Jiqing
(Nanjing)

Henan-
Jiangbei

Pingjiang (Suzhou)

Chengdu

Wuchang

Hangzhou

Sichuan

Longxing
(Nanchang)

Jiangzhe

Dali

Fuzhou

Kunming

Huguang

Yunnan

Guiyang

Jiangxi

BURMESE
STATES

Guilin

West R.

Guangzhou (Canton)

KHMER

VIETNAM

0   500 km.
0   500 mi.

MAP 13

been possible through its system of vertical communications. Affairs in the provinces were not closely supervised by the center. In consequence, with the weakening of central authority in the final decades of the dynasty, regional warlords emerged to assume control over whole provinces, making of them private kingdoms using the governing apparatus in place at that level. Yuan government demanded a strong center. It was unable to maintain that in the decades following the death of Khubilai Khan, its only strong emperor.

Yuan government included four further levels of local administration below the provinces. They were called circuits *lu* (also called routes), prefectures *(fu)*, sub-prefectures *(zhou),* and the basic building blocks of administrative geography, the counties or districts *(xian).* The designation of both the circuit and the route is peculiar to the Yuan; taken together the Yuan circuits and routes corresponded to the later Ming and Qing prefectures, and it seems reasonable in functional terms to call them prefectures.[13] If we adopt this terminology, there were 217 prefectures (*lu* and *fu*) throughout the Yuan state, 393 sub-prefectures, and 1,125 counties.[14]

The prefectures were staffed with chief officials at ranks 3.A or 4.A, and were of two classes: first class with over 100,000 households, and second class with fewer than 100,000 households. In each case those figures included the populations of all the subordinate sub-prefectures and counties. Supporting staffs of prefectures could vary, some having two or three dozen ranked officials in ten or twelve specific duty assignments, but most, especially those in poorer and less densely occupied regions, had only four or five centrally appointed ranked officials. Large staffs of clerical help, bailiffs, and workmen could run to hundreds. There also were military officers, myriarchs or chiliarchs or their subordinates, assigned to each prefectural unit of local government but in a direct line of control extending upward to the Bureau of Military Affairs at the capital.

Sub-prefectures *(zhou)* of the first class had over 50,000 households, second class between 50,000 and 30,000, and third class under 30,000 households. They were headed by officials at ranks 4.B to 5.B, and had smaller supporting staffs.

Early in Khubilai's reign the counties *(xian)* of the first class were those which had more than 6,000 households, second class from 2,000 to 6,000 households, and third class under 2,000 households. After the conquest of the much more populous Southern Song regions of China, new standards were applied there: first-class counties were those with over 30,000 households, second class had between 10,000 and 30,000 households, and third class had under 10,000. Heads of counties were ranked at 6.B to 7.B. The difference in criteria for North and South China is evidence for the impoverishment and loss of registered population in the North in Yuan times. A third-class county in North China, with 1,000 households, or perhaps 6,000 inhabitants, having an area of perhaps 800 square miles, would have had three or four ranked officials and a clerical staff including bailiffs, menials, and the like of perhaps forty; a first-class county in the lower Yangzi might have a population of 250,000 in an area often smaller than the typical county in the

North, five or six ranked officials, and a clerical and work staff of 200 or more. The disparities are obvious, but in all cases the scope of governing was limited, so the costs of officialdom in relation to population were low. It is clear that the actual base-level governing depended largely on a layer of sub-official communal organization and on normative controls.

The focus therefore turns to those subofficial levels of social organization: they were the families and lineages residing in rural villages (Chinese society in almost all regions did not have isolated rural families; farmers lived in villages and walked to their fields adjacent to the villages), or in larger settlements ranging through market towns on up to major cities. Throughout much of North China and in some other regions, rural people formed "communities," called *sheh*,[15] seen as natural groupings (often essentially the natural villages) that were united in support of religious activities, and acquired certain other kinds of social involvement. Governments for centuries had looked to these natural social groupings to extend the work of government, especially for collecting taxes, maintaining law and order, and dispensing relief in times of emergency. In the 1270s the Yuan government issued several decrees requiring that the system of sub-county *sheh* community organization should be implemented uniformly throughout all of North China. The leaders, nominally chosen by acclamation and unpaid, were charged with supervisory obligations, particularly to guide the communities in the rehabilitation and improvement of agriculture following the destruction of warfare. But maintaining local order also was stressed in their instructions. The county officials then imposed wards *(fang)* with ward captains on urban and suburban households. In short, the government attempted to impose a gridwork of subofficial authority on the entire population, urban or rural, using existing organizations and retaining their local names when possible.[16] That they remained the focus of community religious life is likely; nevertheless, their leaders had essentially secular qualifications: age, probity, and relative economic position (however humble), not spiritual powers or priestly functions. Yet it should be remembered that the basic meaning of the word *sheh* is "shrine to the spirits of land and grain," and community loyalty to a commonly maintained shrine undoubtedly underlay this simple social organization.

As the Yuan took over the Song dynasty with its much larger and denser population, the community system was extended to much of South China. The government's standard for its administrative communities in the South was much larger; as many as 400 or 500 households might constitute one such community. Throughout the breadth of the country, existing local names for the community units were used. There appears to have been much organizational variation in the subofficial systems and in the success with which the government was able to use them. They were expected to extend the basic tasks of governing beyond the minimal framework of official posts at the county *(xian)* level, the lowest level of governing staffed by ranked officials. Without this infra-county base level of social organization, the formal structures of regional and local government could not have functioned. Also, we must note, without the pervasive normative controls that they maintained and transmitted, local society would have been less orderly, even ungovernable. When war destroyed the communities in their village settings, as happened at the end of the dynasty, violence and disorder became widespread.

II. MANAGING SOCIETY AND STAFFING THE GOVERNMENT

The structure of governing under the Yuan dynasty described up to this point does not seem very different from what we would expect; it combined Yuan innovations with features of Liao and Jin and Song government in a somewhat ad hoc manner, forming a sprawling bureaucratic system. While much of it had some kind of precedent in the near past, other features of Mongol local governing were unprecedented. For example, when we turn to the way in which the Mongols chose to *staff* their government, we find that they introduced radically different notions about the way the conquered society should be managed. It should be stated at the outset that they did not thereby transform Chinese society, but for the duration of their rule they intervened forcibly in what had long been the "natural order of things," giving a quite special character to the period. I refer to their four-tiered ranking of people by ethnic and geographic identity, and to the dual staffing of government offices, the Mongols' functional substitute for the earlier Khitan (and, briefly, the Jurchen) system of dual institutions.

In China, as elsewhere in their empire, the Mongols were beset by shortages of manpower, both military and civilian. Their means of meeting military manpower needs have been discussed. As for the need to supply civilian administrators, by the end of Khubilai's reign in the 1290s, the Yuan government had about 20,000 ranked official posts to fill in the many agencies of civil governing at all of the central and local levels. Those posts normally were filled on a rotation basis for terms of three or four years. A large pool of qualified replacements was required to maintain staffing needs. Under a Chinese dynasty, all of those persons of course had to be competent to do the paperwork of a complex bureaucracy, and under the Mongols, too, most were required to be more or less literate and skilled. Within China Proper those tasks had to be done in the Chinese language, therefore by educated Chinese. After the rebellion of the Shandong warlord Li Tan in 1262, Khubilai devised ways of lessening Chinese dominance of his administration by giving preference to appointees of non-Chinese identity. The idea was not new; in various ways the conquest dynasties all favored their own people; after their own kind, they preferred to use steppe associates of non-Chinese identity. Khubilai went further. He established permanent legal definitions of status based on ethnic identity, to be applied to the entire population of his empire. The highest-level group were the Mongols themselves. Although none of the implementing decrees have survived, the historical record is full of references to the kinds of legally established privileges they enjoyed. They were given preference in appointment to office; many high posts were to be filled only by Mongols. There were privileges under the law; for example, punishments for Mongols were lighter than for others committing the same offenses.

In disputes between Mongols and non-Mongols, the courts allowed Mongols exemptions that were denied to others. Also, non-Mongol civilians were forbidden (at least nominally) to own or to bear arms of any kind.

A second tier of privilege was granted to Western Asians and Central Asians of all kinds, and to some Inner Asians: they were called Semu, or "people of varied categories." Numerically, the Uighurs were the most important members of this group, but it also included all other Turkic peoples as well as Persians and Arabs and even Europeans; Marco Polo probably held some minor nominal posts in the Yuan government. This Semu group was drawn upon most heavily to fill civil administrative posts. Their favored status under the law, vis-à-vis the Chinese, was similar to that granted to Mongols. The Mongols and the Semu were the two privileged groups within Yuan society, the Mongols holding power and the Semu exercising both policy making and day-to-day supervision in the interests of their employers.

The rest of the population was divided into two further subdivisions. First were the Han, a word usually meaning the ethnic Chinese but in Yuan usage designating the population of the conquered Jin territories of North China and Manchuria, thereby including not only the Chinese who lived there but also the rather substantial numbers of Khitans and Jurchens, even Koreans. Finally, at the bottom of the privilege ladder were the Chinese inhabitants of the Southern Song territories conquered after 1273; they were called the Nanren, or "southerners." They of course were by far the largest element in the population of the Yuan state. The Chinese, particularly the southerners, bitterly resented their debasement and created exaggerated accounts of their sufferings under this unfair system. Without taking those at face value, one can see that serious inequities existed, in particular in appointments to government posts, but also in the treatment of individuals throughout society. Even when the civil service examinations were at last established in 1315, the regulations for the conduct of the examinations, and the postings earned by examination success, favored the non-Chinese candidates.

Filling Offices

Most civil posts under the Yuan were filled not by open recruitment through the examinations or by other established measures such as recommendation or advancement from the sub-official ranks. They were filled by the workings of the inherited preference principle, the so-called yin privilege (elsewhere translated "protection"). That is, sons or other male relatives of high officials had the privilege of automatic eligibility for direct appointment by inheritance. Since the Mongols favored closed social classes, that system suited their concept of how social status and privilege should be awarded: on the merit of fathers and grandfathers. The yin system for confining rewards to persons born to a recognized status in society (one earned by the merit of their forebears) was vastly extended to all the subject peoples, including the occasional Chinese, because it matched the Mongols' sense of how societies should work. The irony is that the yin preference system was of course an old Chinese institution; it had been used somewhat excessively in later Song times but had never overtaken in numbers, much less in prestige, the importance of status earned through the *jinshi* examinations. In China it ran counter to the Chinese ideal of individual merit. By contrast, the Mongols at first were suspicious of the *jinshi* route to official status. Examination winners gained individual prestige, hence authority in the eyes of society, quite apart from the rulers' power to bestow and thereby to control. Might that not make them potentially troublesome? When the Emperor Renzong (r. 1312–1320), the first Mongol emperor literate in Chinese, finally acceded to the persistent demand of Chinese advisers to reestablish the abandoned Chinese civil service examination system, he did so on such a small scale, and allowed so many abuses, that it was of little more than psychological importance to his Chinese subjects; they rejoiced that a fundamental cornerstone of their civilization had been restored, but it did not create a significant flow of Chinese examination degree holders into the government. It held out a weak promise to would-be Chinese scholar-officials, but it did not grant them substantive relief.

The *yin* system, and increasingly the promotion into official ranks of sub-official clerks, which also was decried by some Confucian-minded literati, remained the main ways of filling the routine lower and mid-level ranks of government. By these "irregular" means the Yuan government found bureaucrats competent enough in Chinese to prepare documents, submit reports, interpret laws and regulations, and maintain the uniform paperwork of the traditional administration.

The problem of how Yuan government should be staffed was thus but an aspect of how the entire society should be managed in order to secure the conquerors' interests. We do not know much about the staffing or, indeed, the structure of government in the Lingbei Xingsheng (Lingbei means "north of the mountains," that is, the line of hills that demarcated China Proper from Mongolia), nor do we know much more about the Liaoyang Xingsheng specially set up for Manchuria, which did however have a substantial Chinese and other sedentary population in its southern zone. It is nevertheless clear that even in those Inner Asian regions adjacent to China, the Mongols did not establish clear-cut parallel structures of regional governing (like the Khitans' Northern Chancellery) to match their vastly larger central government in China administered from Dadu. One difference, of course, is that the Khitans retained their Supreme Capital in the North, where the base of their military force lay. Their Southern Chancellery was apart from that main center of their power at a secondary capital down in North China.

The Mongols, however, had moved their principal capital into China, leaving both their Mongolian homeland and the larger Mongolian empire without a major administrative center in the steppe.[17] The balance of governing responsibilities (like the ultimate source of their power) had shifted so overwhelmingly to China that they did not have the luxury of the Khitan choice. The necessity of managing the immense Chinese social base in a way that would protect the Mongols from being submerged in that human sea was of the greatest political importance.

Khubilai Khan proved to be a ruler capable of penetrating and understanding that problem. It was no mean feat to work out the institutional solutions while implementing safeguards that would protect his regime's interests. Some of his Chinese advisers recognized the breadth of his achievement and praised him for it. The brief "Encomium" appended to the "Basic Annals" of his reign in the official *Yuan History,* written by Chinese Ming dynasty official historians seventy-five years after his death, says of him: "The Emperor Shizu [Khubilai's posthumous title] was a man of broadest capacity for judgment. He knew men and was skilled in employing them. He had deep confidence in Confucian methods, and was able to utilize them so that Chinese ways transformed alien practices. He established the basic principles and set forth ruling norms in such a way that the institutions of the age were of vastly encompassing scope."[18] Those Confucian historians to be sure exaggerated Khubilai's surrender to Chinese civilization; all learned Chinese of the time were committed to that view. Adjusting for that mindset, we nonetheless see in this ritually correct expression of appraisal, formulated here for the ages, an appreciation of Khubilai's broad understanding and judgment and for his great achievement in working out usable institutional solutions for his hybrid dynasty.

Problems of Dual Staffing

That assessment of Khubilai Khan offers a way of understanding the dual staffing of offices and the other patterns of rule that he imposed. His departures from the models that Chinese advisers held up for him were reasonable attempts, from his point of view, even when they ultimately failed to serve him well. Even the much maligned and truly unworkable four-tiered status system that he imposed on the entire population should be seen in that light. It clearly should *not* be seen as a system of four "social classes," as they have been called.[19] Recent Chinese scholars no longer use the term "social classes" to describe the system, calling it instead one of "four ranks" or "four levels" *(sidengren zhi).* The four-tiered Yuan system obviously was not one of social classes as the post-Marxian world usually understands the term. The four tiers described certain kinds of legally and institutionally differentiated degrees of privilege, not economic status or social power. In fact, despite the benefits it bestowed on some Mongols, there were more poor, exploited Mongols and Semu than there were rich and powerful ones. And among the denigrated Chinese population, whether of the Han or the Nanren categories, there continued to exist a stratification of wealth and status that more or less resembled that of pre-Mongol Chinese society. It is true that the Yuan system made rich, upper-stratum Chinese who had enjoyed prestige and authority within their own society much less secure about retaining their high status. Many of them in fact, especially in the early years of Mongol conquest and rule in the North, were ruined by being taken captive and forced into servitude. Despite those examples, however, the pre-conquest structure of Chinese society was temporarily inconvenienced, not permanently transformed, by the Mongols' inept social engineering.

The impact on officeholding of the four-tiered system and all the benefits that should have accrued from it were nonetheless profound. A large number of the favored Mongols and Semu were illiterate, at least in Chinese. Through the thirteenth century, the Semu probably conversed and communicated mostly in Turkic (especially Uighur) and Persian, but as a group they were dependents, and as such they became insecure, and thus more susceptible to cultural assimilation. We see them steadily accommodating to their environment, not standing apart from Chinese society. To be educated in Chinese became the rule among them, especially after the time of Khubilai. The Mongols, in contrast, were showing only the first signs of a similar cultural accommodation by the end of the dynasty, and still in very small numbers.[20]

Until the end of the dynasty, the top echelon of officials in the Central Secretariat were Mongols or Semu. Chinese occasionally appeared in the second echelon, but dominated in numbers only in the middle and lower ranks. Most Chief Councillors and Vice Chief Councillors in the Branch Secretariats (Xingsheng) in the provinces were Mongols or Semu. Throughout the entire dynasty no Chinese was ever allowed to hold substantive office in the entire structure of military administration; it was feared they might gain access to classified information on troop strength, disposition, and armaments. The Censorate and other surveillance and investigative agencies also were off-limits to Chinese, at least as a matter of standing regulations, if not always in practice.

Dual staffing of government offices at all levels led to the creation of a distinctive Yuan dynasty phenomenon, that of the Mongol or Semu senior co-incumbent of offices, called in Mongolian Darughachi (Chinese, Daluhua-chi).[21] Darughachi were appointed to virtually all administrative offices to serve alongside the responsible officeholder, outranking him by one or more steps, and to be in the position to oversee and authorize all actions of governing. It would appear that the Chinese did the work while the Mongol or Semu senior counterparts merely controlled for narrow Mongol interests. The real situation in local government was somewhat different. It has been convincingly demonstrated that Darughachi posts in local governing were often filled by Chinese, not infrequently in posts senior to Mongols or Semu serving in lower-ranked offices. In practical terms it was impossible to carry out the regulations forbidding that. Moreover, especially in the later Yuan period, the Mongols and their alien allies could be as able and as concerned about good governing as their Chinese counterparts. Generalizations notwithstanding, their characteristic mode of acting was not necessarily arbitrary and authoritarian; they often brought to their tasks the typical Mongol tribal government spirit of consultation and consensus, preferring to conduct affairs of office in conciliar fashion. They held meetings (endless and too numerous, the Chinese sometimes complained), discussed options, and often exerted their influence reasonably, seeking agreement with the entire staff of officials in a prefecture or a district, perhaps even to the extent of lacking decisiveness.[22]

Still, contemporary Chinese writings are full of abuse and scorn for the Daru-ghachi for being ignorant, illiterate, eager to profit from officeholding, often acting in collusion with clerks and other subofficial types who, not being learned gentlemen, were readily debased. Where the truth lies is not entirely clear, but the research cited here clearly shows that the typical Chinese complaints are exaggerated and misleading. Yet even if we demand fairer consideration of the Mongol and Semu role in governing, as we should, the conduct of government under the Yuan cannot be counted highly successful. It was an imperfect, deteriorating system, for whatever reasons, throughout much of the dynasty's history.

Financial Wizards and Scoundrels

The problems of Yuan administration can be powerfully illustrated by a series of fiscal administrators appointed by Khubilai. The first, a Muslim from Central Asia, is known in Chinese history simply as Ahmad. His family had been retainers of the family of Khubilai's empress, Chabi, and on her recommendation he came into the central government in the early 1260s. He became an able administrator who specialized in ways of enhancing revenues, often by ruthless means. Khubilai badly needed revenues in the 1270s as the expansion of government into the Song South was under way, and when he also was planning the second expedition to Japan and other overseas military ventures. Ahmad's methods were opposed by many of the senior Chinese advisers and by some prominent Mongols such as the great general Bayan, the conqueror of the Song. But Ahmad was a wily politician who managed to win Khubilai's complete confidence. By the mid-1270s he had become the dictator of the central government, in sole charge of all taxation and revenue-related matters. His personal life was disreputable. His power to wreak vengeance on those who opposed him was greatly feared. Many officials were murdered or imprisoned and executed. Eventually even Khubilai's son, the heir apparent Prince Zhenjin, developed strong opposition to him, but Khubilai still trusted Ahmad. The central government was polarized: Ahmad's partisans (including a number of highly placed Chinese, later denounced as opportunists) on one side, and his opponents on the other.

In 1282, while Khubilai was away at his summer palace at Shangdu, plotters managed to assassinate Ahmad and, using the follow-up inventory of his personal belongings, they proved to Khubilai that he had been a corrupt schemer. He was posthumously denounced; several hundred of the associates with whom he had packed the important offices of government were dismissed, and many were executed. Ahmad's methods, while ruthless, were nonetheless effective, and it has been argued that he represented not villainy so much as a different political tradition, that of the typical Grand Vizier in the Muslim courts of Central and Western Asia. The political disarray into which he plunged Khubilai's court and government resulted from a clash of disparate cultures.

After the fall of Ahmad the management of revenue collection fell to a

Chinese who had served under him, Lu Shirong. Lu had a sharp eye for ways to increase revenues. He too was able to convince Khubilai that he should be given unlimited powers. Again, Khubilai was drawn to the policies of a ruthless if coldly efficient manager; the emperor decreed organizational changes in the central government, ignored charges that Lu was corrupt, and gave him full rein until Lu's excesses quickly brought him down. He was executed in 1285, little more than a year after achieving full authority in the Central Secretariat.

At that point the third "treacherous minister" of Khubilai's reign began to come to the fore in the same path to dictatorial power—as manager of revenue policies. This was Sangha, a Tibetan who may have been an ordained Lamaist monk, and who had been an official in the Commission for Buddhist and Tibetan Affairs. He had initially introduced Lu Shirong for appointment, and in the disorder caused by Lu's execution, he offered himself to Khubilai as someone who understood financial matters, proposing to issue a new form of the Yuan state's paper currency. Again Khubilai was readily convinced and accepted Sangha's plans; he ordered administrative changes in accord with Sangha's wishes and ignored the criticisms of his long-standing advisers, whether Mongol, Semu, or Chinese. Sangha was an intelligent man with an analytical mind and a good understanding of the inefficiencies in civil administration as those affected revenue collection. The new paper currency issuance was well planned and proved strikingly successful. But he was ruthless, corrupt, and power hungry. In 1291, after four years in power, the evidence against him mounted, and his enemies were able to convince Khubilai that he too was a debased official. He was executed. He had aroused popular discontent on all sides, as well as deep opposition from the "upright" faction of Confucian-minded civil officials at court.[23]

In these three instances we see not a conflict between Chinese and alien officials, as the Chinese record presents the matter; all three of these notorious officials appointed associates from all the ethnic and religious categories, and the opposition to them likewise was spread throughout the entire officialdom. Rather, we see in their briefly spectacular careers a conflict between traditional Chinese and alien methods of managing the state, and we see an emperor who found it so necessary to increase revenues that he would give a free hand to officials who could produce quick results even if that entailed overturning all procedures and principles. Under such circumstances it was difficult for the Yuan state to achieve institutional stability, or to retain its elite sector's confidence that it truly was capable of governing. Khubilai was justly praised for his understanding of human capacities and his ability to work out usable institutional solutions. That assessment is essentially correct, but he also must bear responsibility for occasional spectacular failures.

The Household Registration System and Base-Level Governing

A third aspect of social management that deeply affected society in Yuan times is the system of household registration imposed on the entire population. The Chinese had long based their taxation on households, or on adult males, and on their property holdings, in different mixes of those components at different times. That required the maintenance of census figures on which to base the levies and collect taxes directly from the taxpayers. It had been standard practice to register households in a few basic occupational categories. By far the largest number were "common people," most of whom were village-dwelling farmers; other categories were military families, saltern workers, artisans, and the like.

In all parts of the expanding empire, the Mongol rulers began to take a great interest in ways of guaranteeing steady economic support levied on the conquered populations, using methods native to the different parts of the empire. In China they seized on the traditional Chinese census registration procedures and fashioned from them an instrument for placing all households in highly specific, differentiated categories. There were some ethnic or geographic categories, but most were occupational. Under the Yuan dynasty system, those newly defined household registration categories then became hereditary classifications from which individuals were not allowed to escape. Sons were required to carry on the occupations of their fathers, and to pay to the tax collectors every year the specified amount of the particular product or labor service.

This was strictly a Mongol way of making societies produce revenues in regular, consistent, reliable ways. By the time of Chinggis Khan, it has been shown on evidence from the *Secret History* that the Mongols had as many as twenty-six specifically differentiated occupational categories in their own society.[24] Most of those were military specializations, but they also included carpenters; blacksmiths; herdsmen as broken down for cattle, horses, sheep, camels, and lambs; as well as fishermen; sable hunters; servants and dependent persons; and shamans. Of course, all the males among them also bore arms, but specific kinds of service to the tribal society also were provided for in these officially recognized occupations.

When they came to managing the much more complex Chinese society, the Mongols extended the concept and defined eighty or ninety such categories to cover all aspects of production and occupation. Not all were found everywhere; for example, gold panners and pearl fishers were specific to certain geographic settings. Moreover, some were ethnic, such as the household categories for Khitans and Jurchens, and some were not obviously productive in the economic sense, for example, those for representatives of various religions such as the Muslim Imams, the Christians, Buddhist monks, Daoist priests, Confucians ("Confucian household" was a new category established by the Mongols on analogy to the professional religious), and so on, although in the eyes of the Mongols these too were providers of specific services to society. The basic rationale of the system lay in its control over all productive activities, from farming to the craft industries, mining, ceramics, weaving and other phases of textile production, the smelting and forging of metals, manufacture of weapons and armaments, transport of grain, merchant activities of several kinds, medicine and pharmacology, and dozens of other more narrowly differentiated categories.

This system had its own logic. It probably seemed to secure the benefits of conquest to the conquerors. But in fact it ran contrary to the ethos of Chinese society, as did the four-tiered ranking of ethnic and geographic subsets of the population. China's was an open society, by that time having accumulated more than a thousand years' experience with free ownership of land and high degrees of social as well as geographic mobility. There may have been a strong tendency for sons to follow the trades and occupations of their fathers, but they were under no legal and little social pressure to do so. Hereditary status was resisted, not only among the elite who denigrated the *yin* preference system in access to official appointment, but also among the ordinary people. For example, several Chinese as well as alien dynasties tried to make military service hereditary, but none could prevent Chinese soldiers and sons of soldiers from fleeing that life. The Yuan household registration system restricted ordinary people in many ways in making their fundamental life choices; in so doing it denied individuals access to the small steps that might lead toward bettering themselves. It was thus contrary to the spirit of the achieving society, and it was resisted. The Mongol government maintained all of its social engineering regulations until the end but could not effectively enforce them. Anything so widely resisted becomes counterproductive.

III. Religions

In the remaining sections of this chapter we turn from the Yuan dynasty's formal structures for governing the Chinese people to the lives of people in society. Mongol government's special character is particularly evident in its position on religions, seen here in the state's attempts to manage and use religious activities for its own purposes. The attitude toward religions was largely benign, yet much of the story concerns the ways in which the religious groups misused or evaded the state's attempts to manage them. The highly unusual religious situation throughout the century of Yuan rule, which had consequences for subsequent ages, is the subject of this section; here I discuss the special features of that situation at some length in the hope of casting light on the period's social environment. Other features of Chinese life distinctive to this age are discussed in the following sections.

The New Daoist Sects

The long history of Daoism began in the preimperial "golden age" of Chinese philosophy, the sixth through the third centuries B.C.E. That period produced Confucius and Mencius and the "Hundred Schools" of thought; it also is the period when the *Daodejing* attributed to the philosopher Laozi was written and when the great fourth-century B.C.E. philosopher Zhuangzi wrote the essential core of the book that bears his name. By Han times (second century B.C.E. to second century C.E.), a popular religion had appeared which included veneration of Laozi (to a lesser extent of Zhuangzi) and the mythical Yellow Emperor, Huangdi, but had little to do with the philosophical thought of

Daoism. In fact, it was often a caricature of that philosophy, diametrically opposed to its passivism, its acceptance of nature and death, and its scorn for government and all forms of organized social action. In tandem with the newer Daoist popular religion, Daoism as philosophy continued to interest some philosophers, was often admired by scholars, and worked a profound influence on artists and literary people among the elite.

The Daoist popular religion, by contrast, was often typified by individuals who are difficult to categorize because they present an almost incongruous combination of what we today might call the profound and the debased, the serious and the ridiculous. The religion took on institutional forms largely in imitation of Buddhism, which, in the early centuries of the Common Era, was becoming the religion of the Chinese people. Daoist priests built and occupied temples (Dao Guan), conducted rites, foretold events, aided in funerals by, among other things, performing geomantic exercises to locate graves properly, cured the sick and the possessed, and at the same time shared some of the ground of scholastic activities with the elite of scholar-officialdom. The professional Daoists, often called "adepts," commanded esoteric learning and practiced occult skills.

The "organized" Daoist church was much more loosely constituted than organized religions in the West. It did not impose uniform discipline or over-riding authority on professional Daoist priests and adepts, much less so on ordinary believers. They, in any event, might also simultaneously observe Buddhist and other practices, and universally honored and maintained the ancestral rites and practices of the family religion which Confucian teachings strongly upheld. Despite its at best loosely organized character, the Daoist church nonetheless acquired a family of hereditary leaders, the Tianshi ("Celestial Masters") of the Zhang family, sometimes called the Daoist popes. Their base was at Dragon-Tiger Mountain (Longhu shan) in Jiangsi, where they claimed descent from a late Han dynasty historical figure called Zhang (Dao-) Ling, who had led a popular religious uprising. That sect of popular Daoism was reduced to obscurity for centuries; it was not until the Northern Song emperors discovered and patronized the Zhang clan leaders that their fame and hence authority were enhanced. Their sect, called Zhengyi Tianshi Dao (the Celestial Masters of the Way of Correct Oneness),[25] in Song times became the most important Daoist sect in China south of the Yangzi River. Despite that, the Zhang Celestial Masters never gained anything approaching jurisdictional authority over Daoist priests or believers. Daoism as popular religion was a pervasive presence throughout Chinese society, but as a religion it did not have distinct boundaries and usually lacked sectarian cohesion.

Daoism was, however, capable of producing leaders (usually addressed as "teachers") who could lead sectarian movements, even armed uprisings, although they tended to appear in abnormal times when the usual forms of social authority were temporarily weakened. In such circumstances the successful leaders of Daoist popular sects claimed some kind of extraordinary authority by reason of their own spiritual discoveries, their interpretations of omens, the efficacy of their communal prayer ceremonies, their magic talismans, or other such demonstrations of extraordinary powers. They could take over social disturbances and make mass disorders of them, as in the late Han cases and subsequently in later history. Or they could launch sectarian movements, acknowledge a particular doctrine or doctrinal founder, and preach new teachings to arouse a following. Three or four such new sects in North China, and the newly important Celestial Master sect in the South, appeared in Jin and Yuan times.

The Northern Song emperors' patronage of Daoism at all levels led to the strengthening of the Daoist presence at court, and throughout society. Chinggis Khan was attracted to the Daoist teacher Qiu Chuji because he thought Qiu had achieved the secret of long life. Chinggis gave him authority over all religious organizations and personnel in China, greatly strengthening the influence of Daoism thereby. In an atmosphere of imperial favor, of social insecurity caused by alien rule, of diminished influence in local society of the Confucian-minded elite, and of disruptive social change, the so-called new sects of Daoism appeared, starting in late Song and Jin times, to become larger and more important in the Yuan dynasty.

Qiu Chuji's sect, called Quanzhen Jiao, "The Teachings of Perfected Truth," stemmed from a founding teacher, Wang Chongyang (or Wang Zhe, 1113–1170), who was born in Shaanxi near the old Tang dynasty capital of Chang'an (present-day Xi'an) just before the Jurchen conquest, and grew up under the Jin dynasty. A Three Teachings syncretist, he was intent on combining the best of Confucian, Buddhist, and Daoist doctrines to make a new religion. Hence the name *quan* (perfected, all-encompassing) and *zhen* (truth, reality), together suggesting its syncretic character. Wang may have held Song loyalist sentiments, as traditionally believed, though that seems unclear. He taught withdrawal from public life and concentration on perfecting the individual's mental state. After moving to Shandong late in his life, he accepted ten disciples (one of whom was a woman) and allowed an association of his followers ("believers") to take form.[26]

His immediate followers among the ten disciples stressed the Daoist components of his teachings and turned his doctrines into a more purely Daoist religious mold. They also transformed the sect's character, leading the believers into public and social roles, in that way finding favor in the elite sector of Jin dynasty society. The second generation of followers, that is, the younger persons among his immediate disciples, included Qiu Chuji (1148–1227), who was only twenty-two when Wang Chongyang died. Qiu subsequently became the most important leader of the sect. He attracted the favorable attention of the Jin emperor Shizong (r. 1161–1189), and the sect soon had followers throughout North China. But Shizong's successor, the Jin emperor Zhangzong (r. 1189–1208), initially was suspicious of the sect and its potentially rebellious following, so attempted to limit its growth. Later Zhangzong came to terms with the sect, which appeared to be strong enough to be useful to the state. After Zhangzong's death, in the disorders of the last decades of the Jin, the Quanzhen sect prospered. Late in the failing dynasty, Qiu Chuji rejected the overtures of the Jin emperor and also the envoy sent to invite him to the Song court. He was readying himself to be patronized by the Jin's successors. He could play a strong hand because his following within North China society was widespread and large enough to be significant in maintaining social order. When Qiu finally, in 1222, accepted Chinggis Khan's imperial command-invitation to visit him in the Hindu Kush, that signaled Qiu's prophecy that the Mongols would triumph in China. When they did, he was rewarded with personal honors and political powers.

The account of his travels to visit Chinggis in Central Asia, written by one of his disciples who traveled there with him and who later succeeded Qiu as head of the Quanzhen sect, provides a record of Qiu's first conversation with Chinggis Khan. After Qiu arrived at the khan's camp and was provided with tents for his small party, he presented himself. Chinggis thanked the old master for traveling so far in response to his invitation, noting that other rulers (the emperors of Jin and Song) also had invited him but had been refused. Qiu deferentially responded that his doing so was the will of Heaven. Pleased by that response, Chinggis showered Qiu with further courtesies and then asked the all-important question: What magic medicine of long life have you brought to me? Qiu answered quite simply that he did indeed know ways of protecting life, but had no elixir that would prolong it. The emperor was favorably impressed by that frankness.[27] The two got on famously thereafter.

In addition to giving advice to Chinggis on matters spiritual and hygienic, Qiu also proved to be quite canny about practical issues of government. It was as a politician that he was sent back to Yanjing (Beijing) to take control of all religious activities in Mongol-controlled regions of North China. He had gained tax exemptions and favored status for the recognized religious groups—Buddhists, Daoists, Nestorian Christians, and Muslims—and made a contribution to the survival of those religions in the ungoverned conditions left by the initial phase of Mongol conquests. In the main, however, it was the members of his own Quanzhen sect that benefited from his status in the eyes of the Mongol authorities, and people flocked to join the sect in great numbers to receive that protection.[28] As a politician he (and his successors) abused the powers given to him. That abuse of power, to profiteer, and especially to help Daoist sects benefit at the expense of their Buddhist rivals, soon had to be corrected. Yelü Chucai was able to defend Buddhist interests to Chinggis's successor, Ögödei Khan, and the leaders of the Quanzhen sect lost their superintendency of all religions. The Daoist-Buddhist rivalry had also led to doctrinal competition, so open debates were sponsored by the Mongol khans to determine which set of doctrines had the greater validity. The Buddhists regularly won those debates. The triumph of Daoism through the success of Qiu Chuji and his Quanzhen sect in the 1220s was greatly diminished by the 1240s.

Nevertheless, the four more important new Daoist sects in the North,[29] together with their offshoots, brought a lively sense of involvement in community religious practice to North China. Later, when the Southern Song was conquered, the Zhang Celestial Masters in the South were acknowledged by the Mongol government. Some of the new northern sects also spread to the

Yangzi Valley and beyond. At the same time, Yuan period contacts with Western Asia introduced elements of Catholic Christianity, Judaism, Zoroastrianism, and Manichaeism into the already complex mix of Chinese popular religion. Thus the stage was set for new and potentially explosive constituents of religious sectarian activity to be folded into the mix. A body of organized sectarian teaching was in place, to be drawn upon by the desperate people who were driven to rebel against their government's ruling authority at the end of the Yuan a century later. People rose up in arms in response to doctrines that appear to have Buddhist identity, but in fact were popular religion in the true sense of the word, combining elements of many kinds. The special conditions of Jin and Yuan permitted the capacity for fervent religious expression, always latent in Chinese society, to take form in sub-elite community activities. Those religion-motivated movements could test the government's means to control them. Thereafter, a residue of experience and belief remained in the common awareness of the Chinese people, ready to be reactivated, and against which the more effective governments of Ming and Qing China had at all times to remain vigilant. At the same time, some of the more formally organized Daoist religious activities also found a new lease on life.[30]

Yuan Period Buddhism

Khubilai's youthful interest in Chan Buddhism, then strongly present among the Chinese elite, was superseded by his turning to Tibetan Lamaist Buddhism, introduced to him by the learned Tibetan monk Phagspa, whom he subsequently designated the Imperial Preceptor. It became his personal faith. He was followed in that by his successors to the end of the dynasty, but (contrary to widely held views) he did not declare it to be the sole religion of the Mongol nation, nor was it the only religion to receive support from the Yuan state. He did not make a thorough effort to have all the Mongolian people converted to Buddhism. Most Mongols remained faithful to their steppe shamanism at this time; their effective conversion to Lamaism as a people did not occur until the sixteenth and seventeenth centuries.[31]

Two aspects of Chinese Buddhism in the Yuan period should be noted: Chan was the strongest element within the native Chinese practice of the religion, and Tibetan Lamaism received the bulk of imperial patronage and favor from the time of Khubilai to the end of the dynasty. The latter point is of particular importance in the history of the dynasty.

Tibetan monks in China enjoyed two kinds of favored status. As Tibetans they were classed with the Semu, the aliens of "varied categories" who were given privileged status and access to political appointments. And as monks representing the favored religion of the rulers, they enjoyed many further privileges, high status, exemptions from legal obligations, and inviolable protection. Large numbers of them came into China, especially following the Mongol conquest of the Southern Song in the 1270s. Special temples and lamaseries were erected for them at a number of places; these were lavishly supported by the throne.[32] The "foreign monks" flocked especially to

Hangzhou, the former Southern Song capital city noted for its scenic beauty and cultural refinement, with its many large Buddhist temple complexes.

Chinese writers of the Yuan expressed virtually unanimous condemnation of Tibetan monks for abuses of their privileged status. In those writings they are depicted as crude, grasping, lascivious, violent, and overbearing. That undoubtedly is unfair to many among them, who were men of deep learning and spiritual cultivation. Modern historians of Chinese Buddhism, acknowledging that the Tibetans' behavior was regrettable, see little impact on Chinese Buddhist doctrine and practice from the Tibetan religious presence in China at that time.[33] There was, however, extensive scholarly translation of Chinese and Tibetan Buddhist texts into Mongolian, some of which were printed under the auspices of the state. The quality of much of this work was high. It remained important to the later development of Buddhism in Mongolia.[34]

Quite apart from the issue of Tibetan Lamaism in China, Buddhism was strong both in Chinese elite society and as the religion of the common people. There was much temple building; the numbers of monks and nuns increased. Among the people adherence to clandestine Buddhist sects also was widespread. The Maitreya Society, clinging to a form of popular Buddhism that was much influenced by Manichaean doctrines, preached that the Maitreya Buddha would descend to earth bringing paradise here and now; all suffering would be eliminated. As the times grew darker and more desperate, which they did indeed in the fourteenth century, his coming was more certain and more imminent. It was a doctrine well suited to arouse insurrection. Other secret movements in Buddhism were the new White Lotus Society[35] and the White Cloud Society. All three stemmed from Song dynasty beginnings, were suppressed, and continued to be covertly transmitted, waiting for more opportune times to come forth again. Both the Maitreya Society and the White Lotus Society were deeply involved in the late Yuan popular uprisings.[36] They shared many features of the new Daoist sects, making it difficult to classify them as the one or the other.

The Yuan was a period of important contacts between Chinese and Japanese Buddhists. A number of Japanese monks traveled to China in a new wave of contacts that started during the Southern Song and continued significantly through the Yuan. Japanese interest was spurred chiefly by a desire to experience direct contact with the great masters of Chinese Chan (Zen) and the teachings and disciplines at the famed Chinese centers. After years of travel and study in China, most returned to Japan, where they significantly influenced the development especially of the Rinzai Zen sect. A number of Chinese monks responded to invitations to come to Japan, where some of them remained to serve prominently in the Japanese Sangha.[37] Even though the Mongols attempted two invasions of Japan from bases in China, in 1274 and 1281, the travels to and from Japan by monks actually increased in the second half of the thirteenth century.[38] The Buddhist contacts also had implications for trade between the two countries, and for the two civilizations' awareness of each other, evident particularly in the spheres of their arts and literature.

IV. CHINA'S PEOPLE UNDER MONGOL RULE

It is difficult to make meaningful generalizations about the lives of ordinary Chinese people, whether rural or urban, whether civilians or those in military households, whether residing in the rich Yangzi provinces or struggling to survive in the poorer northwest. The voluminous Chinese record does not always provide all the material necessary to answer many questions that present-day historians seek. Yet some generalities can be established about the people at commoner levels, and in the elite.

Ordinary People

In the foregoing it has been shown that the Mongols at first looked upon people as chattel attached to the land, and as conquerors they felt free to bestow the land and its owner-tillers or its tenants on their victorious commanders as the proper spoils of conquest. This policy undoubtedly imposed misery on millions of people of all social statuses, but particularly on the humble farmers, craftsmen, and petty traders. Later the Mongols began to modify that policy, not for humanitarian reasons (although their Confucian-minded advisers argued the matter both in altruistic and in practical terms) but because, as the Mongols created a central state apparatus for China, they wanted more centralized control over revenues and resources than their bestowal of autonomous appanages allowed them. They also began to apply throughout the entire population the system of household registration categories (discussed in Section II), confining all heads of households and adult males to occupations declared to be their hereditary obligations, in order to regularize production of goods and services. That elaborately differentiated system of categories was in its way a rational management idea, but one that ran counter to the ethos of Chinese society; it produced hardships and resentment. Moreover, it does not appear to have been fiscally efficient, because the Mongols also felt the need to introduce the Western Asian idea of tax farming in order to enhance the state's revenues. That method of tax collection allowed abuses, caused suffering, and contributed further to the deterioration of ordinary lives as well as to the morale of government.

The conquest of Southern Song in the 1270s brought to Khubilai, the second ruler in the third generation of Chinggisid khans and the first to call himself emperor of China, the vast territories, population, and wealth of Central and South China. The Mongols' governing policies toward their now more than 100 million Chinese subjects continued to evolve, to adapt to new realities. While the rulers did not openly repudiate their earlier governing modes, they adjusted them in ways that the Chinese of the time looked upon as improvements. The ordinary people in Central and South China in general did not undergo the extremes of stresses and disruptions that had accompanied the conquest of the North China Plain a half-century earlier. Most of them remained in their homes and on their land, paid taxes to the same tax collectors, and in most cases may have felt little impact from the newly imposed household registration categories, under which most of them remained farmers as they always had been. True, their sons were now legally bound to continue as farmers, but those who so wished usually could find ways of evading that requirement. The complaints of the elite in their localities about the quality of governing probably did not arouse the ordinary farmers' concern. Their lives went on in much the same way in the more remote rural areas, although the ordinary people living in and around the larger cities may have noted more change where the alien presence, and abuses of power, were apt to be evident.

As for trends of change affecting the ordinary people, the general social stability of Khubilai's reign in the central and southern regions lasted until early in the fourteenth century, after which the authority of the central government in the provinces began to break down. Demographic trends should be most basic to our understanding of social history, but it is impossible to speak with certainty about them. Southern Song plus Jin China had a combined population of at least 110 million in 1200, perhaps well over that figure.[39] By 1300 the official records (compiled for tax collection but not for genuine census purposes) showed a registered population of less than 70 million, and when counted again for the same purposes under the relatively more effective government of the early Ming (in 1392–1394), some quarter-century after the end of Yuan rule, the count still showed a registered population of under 70 million. Does that indicate a great loss of population owing to killings in war, plus further deaths from disease, malnutrition, and hardship occasioned by the disruptions of warfare, plus the forestalled births that otherwise would have occurred? Or does it merely reflect the deteriorating Yuan administration's inability to compile tax records? Or does it reflect the flight of people to avoid war and chaos—people who left their ancestral homes probably never to return, and who remained "transients" in the eyes of the new communities into which they migrated and hence were not counted in the tax censuses? The present level of our knowledge does not allow us to solve this demographic puzzle. We might hypothesize that the population of Yuan China hovered in the range of 85 million or more, a decrease to be sure from the estimate of 110 to 120 million in 1200, but not a reduction by almost half. Moreover, whatever actual decrease occurred, it was not evenly distributed; it was far greater in China north of the Huai River (the old Jin–Southern Song boundary), in the northwest, and in Sichuan than it was in central and southern areas, where most of the Chinese people lived by the fourteenth century.

The Elite

The lives of people in the several strata of what we may call China's elite are of course much more fully documented than those of ordinary people. The elite produced the documentation, and they produced it in great volume. In addition to the voluminous *Yuan History* compiled in 1369 and 1370 in the first years of the succeeding Ming dynasty, we also have the "collected writings" *(wenji)* of well over 200 literati and scholar-officials (more than two such collections for each year of Yuan history), and a hundred other titles of often large works belonging to other categories, such as collections of notes and sketches, historical writings, geographies, and many others.[40] There also have been preserved more than 100 Yuan dramas; although directed to audiences of ordinary people, they all reflect the times and the feelings of their well-educated upper-strata authors.[41]

Later Chinese writers from Ming and Qing times wrote at length on the Yuan period, often having access to materials no longer available to us. That vast documentation of Yuan society has not all been thoroughly studied, yet the quantity of information stemming from and reflecting conditions among the Yuan elite is very great. An interesting example of such little-noted information bears on the practice of foot binding, a subject of much interest among social historians. A scholar writing at the end of the Yuan (ca. 1367) included in his collection of "notes and sketches" *(bi ji)* a brief study of the custom, noting that it is not mentioned in any historical materials prior to the Five Dynasties. The earliest evidence he cites dates from the reign of Li Yu, the last ruler of the Southern Tang, whose reign (961–975) was noted for opulence and frivolity (see Chapter 1). He is said to have had a dancer at his court for whom a six-foot-high lotus flower was made of gold; she performed her dance on it, "her feet wrapped in strips of silk to make them small, curved upward in the shape of a new moon. This lent to her dancing the effect of walking on the clouds as she turned and twisted, as if reaching up into the sky." The late Yuan writer concludes his brief account: "From this we can ascertain that binding the feet is something that has been done only since the Five Dynasties. Moreover, it was still practiced by very few before the [Northern Song] Xining and Yuanfeng reign periods [1068–1079]. In recent times, however, everyone imitates this mode, and those who do not do so are shamed." But the practice still was not universal: in another place the same writer, describing a popular style of slipper woven from straw, observes, "Women whose feet have not been bound all wear them."[42] This is useful if fragmentary information about an inadequately understood social phenomenon; the challenge to social historians is to make systematic use of such materials, however fragmentary, to draw clearer pictures of social life.

The Yuan period writings reveal curiously contradictory feelings about the dynasty. In general, writers were euphoric about the reunification of China after almost 400 years of political separation of North and South. The embittered Song loyalists who lived on into Yuan times did not express that euphoria, but undoubtedly they too felt some satisfaction. The generation of Chinese who survived the end of Song soon passed, and most Chinese who read history and wrote about society began to take pride in the vast extent of the "Chinese" Yuan empire as they encountered the reports about the Mongols' exploits in Central and Western Asia. They looked for positive aspects of the Mongol conquest with which they might identify.

Yet their attitudes toward current circumstances in Yuan China are contradictory. On the one hand, they were deeply critical of many aspects of life:

the governing, while carried out by a government of approved traditional form, was often seen as faulty in practice; the governors included many Mongols and Semu (Central and Western Asians of the "various categories") who were their social superiors but cultural inferiors. Among their complaints: the elite in those alien categories often lacked the educational qualifications for the offices they held; the Chinese were not allowed to take fair examinations and advance in public service according to their merits; the administration of justice was haphazard and biased against the Chinese; and corruption was rife. On the other hand, the Confucian-minded elite on the whole accepted the Mongols as legitimate bearers of the Mandate to rule; they acknowledged that Mongols and Semu often were "good people," even superior to some Chinese in their honesty, generosity, and straightforward (if childlike) naïveté; the imperial government at its best was sincere and on the right track even though still far from perfect; and so on. The Chinese of that time were fully committed to an ideal of legitimacy. That commitment, along with unshakeable faith that civilization inevitably would transform the aliens, made them eager to find evidence that the transforming impact of Chinese civilization was working. They noted with satisfaction that the Yuan government incorporated traditional Chinese models. Its alien rulers honored the ritual proprieties, or at least allowed the forms. In service to that regime there were some notably learned and reputable Chinese; even though they were not in leading positions of power, their presence nonetheless showed that the Great Way was being recognized. The Chinese elite therefore tended to stress the examples of Yuan conformance with Chinese patterns and to underplay the significance of contrary evidence. They truly believed that civilization must triumph, and as often as not they were optimistic in the face of discouraging facts.

Those contradictory attitudes leave us with unresolved issues of interpretation. For example, was the entire structure of civil (i.e., Chinese) governing in fact the essential government of Yuan China, or was it merely a facade, a concession to Chinese interests, masking the fact that the parallel structure of Mongol military force was the real government? Was the government powerful and centralized as a chain of military command should have been, or was it as ineffectual and decentralized as the civilian structure usually appeared to be? It probably was a bit of both, stronger and militarily more effective in the reign of Khubilai, but with the features of weakness and decentralization steadily becoming more evident after 1300.

That problematic government denied Chinese of the elite strata the place they felt was properly theirs; but did the elite truly suffer humiliation, poverty, lack of opportunity for self-realization? Again, in some measure they did. Especially early in the conquest (1215–1270), there are stories about dispossessed and destitute members of the old elite who had to struggle to live, or who failed to survive their hardships. But gradually such cases appear in ever smaller numbers. Many of the elite whose education and personal cultivation under more normal circumstances would have led them to serve in public life turned away from the usual careers to seek compensatory roles in private life.

Many withdrew into what, for that society, constituted eremitism—turning one's back to the world (whether or not out of lingering loyalty to the overturned Song dynasty) to live out more obscure lives.[43] Many who might have been ministers of state in normal times found meaning in lives devoted to the arts, especially those who painted endless variations on the allegorical themes of withdrawing to retain one's purity, and wrote enigmatic poems on their paintings to communicate their rarified sentiments to others of comparable cultivation.[44] Others, while still refusing to serve in public office, sought lives of greater involvement and social responsibility—as teachers, as directors of Confucian academies built and financed by themselves and their kind, or as scholars trying to ensure that Confucian learning was engaged with the essential issues of ethics and history, the sources of moral man's authority. The elite were denied the place in society that they most valued, but they still had a range of choices in planning their lives.

V. THE YUAN CULTURAL ACHIEVEMENT

The Yuan became one of the great ages for art—for poetry, painting, and calligraphy. It was an age when the institutions of Confucian education, the academies, the publishing of books, the scholarly attention to exegetical texts, philosophical and political writing all displayed significant achievement. By all relevant criteria it was an age of high cultural attainment. By some measures those dimensions of elite life in fact fared better than they were to fare in the opening decades of the Ming dynasty which followed. That the high levels of cultural attainment in the Song were not lost during the Yuan is evident in this brief survey.

The Intellectual Tradition

Two important trends stand out in Yuan intellectual history: the summation of Neo-Confucian thought achieved by Zhu Xi (1130–1200), based on critical scholarship in the Confucian classics and expressed in convincing affirmations of Confucian ethical and metaphysical superiority, achieved a dominant place in the intellectual life of Chinese civilization during the Yuan period; and the debates within that Neo-Confucian intellectual sphere between the idealist and the rationalist positions continued, while tending strongly toward compromise and harmonious resolution of the differences.[45]

First, the more sophisticated learning carried on in Southern Song, in which scholars in the Jin North were unable to participate, quickly spread throughout the North in the first decades of Yuan rule after the reunification of North and South in the 1270s.[46] Knowledge of Southern Song intellectual and scholarly developments was not entirely lacking in the Jin dynasty's North China, but unification made possible direct contacts and a flow of published works. That aroused a high degree of intellectual excitement among classical scholars who either accepted Zhu Xi and his synthesis, or were stimulated to disagree with aspects of the Zhu Xi school tradition. In general, the Zhu Xi stance prevailed, and when the civil service examinations were finally reinstituted under the Yuan in 1315, the Zhu Xi school's critical editions of the classics were designated the official texts for purposes of the examinations. They remained the "orthodoxy," in that limited but significant sense, through the remainder of Chinese imperial history to the early twentieth century.

The model figure among those Confucian scholars who were eager to serve the Yuan government under Khubilai Khan was Xu Heng (1209–1281), an earnest and capable scholar and official who reached high positions of influence in the government.[47] From a poor farming family in Henan, he suffered greatly through the years of the Jin collapse and Mongol campaigns that ravaged North China. He persisted in his studies and made his living as a teacher in Confucian schools, several times declining appointments out of reluctance to serve a regime whose character was not yet clear. In 1261 he finally accepted an appointment at the court, impressed by Khubilai's determination to establish a government in which Chinese values were to be protected; after that he progressed quickly to high offices, reaching Assistant Chief Councillor in the Central Secretariat and then Director of the National Academy. He advised on institutions and had much influence on Khubilai's political decisions.

Xu Heng ardently maintained the superiority of Zhu Xi's teachings, but he was not of philosophical bent and probably did not have extensive knowledge of Zhu's highly refined scholarship. He was important more as a promoter of Confucian education than as an intellectual figure in his own right. He typifies the fundamentalist-minded Neo-Confucian committed to social responsibility and public service. But he was important above all for his effective promotion of the basic Confucian education as a defining element of elite life in the long-occupied North. His message, in his philosophically uncomplicated and direct style, had enormous impact on the recovery of Confucian norms in North China. It made Confucian activists of his followers, most of whom were northerners rediscovering their Confucian heritage, and non-Chinese drawn to the values of cultural accommodation.

The breadth of his influence is illustrated in the intriguing life of Guan Yunshi (1286–1324), a sinicized Uighur whose distinguished family's traditions included the model of the warrior-scholar. Xu Heng died five years before Guan was born, but his influence on the younger man was exerted through Guan's great-uncle, an ardent student of Xu who, like a number of highly cultured Uighurs, was personally devoted to Xu and his teachings. The young Guan Yunshi began his studies in that mold: in his early twenties he produced his own annotated text of the *Classic of Filial Piety,* modeled on Xu Heng's annotations of other Confucian texts.[48] Because of that orthodox Confucian alignment, Guan was appointed to high offices in the early fourteenth century, when the pro-Confucian forces were strong. At heart, however, he was a poet, a man powerfully drawn to the Chinese literary tradition. He subsequently became one of the finest lyric poets of the age; yet he also retained his devotion to classical studies and the writing of classical prose, bridging the more popular fields of lyric poetry and those more rarified traditions of classical learning. It is his poetry, especially his *san-qu* lyrics written to the prosodic models drawn from the songs of the Yuan drama, for which he has remained best known to the present time. He can be accepted both as a Chinese literary figure of the first rank and as an example of achievement in Chinese high culture by a non-Chinese. His interesting life tells us much about the milieu of elite life in mid-Yuan times.

Xu Heng, a model of Neo-Confucian commitment as one of the most influential Confucian advisers to Khubilai Khan, is often compared with Liu Yin (1247–1293), also a northerner who came to Confucian studies by a route much like that which Xu Heng had followed some years earlier. He too was deeply impressed by Zhu Xi's great synthesis of Neo-Confucian thought but was far broader in his philosophical interests than was Xu Heng, and more independent-minded. The Yuan government sought persistently to appoint Liu Yin to office, but he steadfastly declined. In the minds of many at that time, his refusal to take office appeared to rebuke those, including Xu Heng, who were eager to serve despite conditions of compromise and undignified servility. Because it was not solely a matter of loyalty to a dynasty, the question whether to serve continued to be important to thinking people even after the generation of Song loyalists had died off; Liu Yin's response added substance to the debate because his command of learning was impressive and his credentials were unblemished. His contribution to intellectual life included efforts to clarify and correct the understanding of Zhu Xi's commentaries on the Confucian *Four Books,* as well as to probe the profound thought of the Northern Song cosmologist Shao Yong, about whom Zhu Xi had expressed reservations.[49] Liu Yin typifies the Neo-Confucian tradition of scholarly breadth and philosophical endeavor.

In the judgment of many, however, the most important philosophical thinker in the Yuan period was Wu Cheng (1249–1333), a southerner from Jiangxi whose home region was conquered by the Yuan armies in 1279, when he was thirty years old. He thus grew up in the richer intellectual atmosphere of late Southern Song China and had to adjust to being a scholar and professional teacher under the newly imposed Mongol regime. He was a deeply introspective man, strongly attracted to the intuitionist idealism of Zhu Xi's debating opponent Lu Jiuyuan (1139–1193).[50] Yet he also appreciated the practical importance of the Zhu Xi school's powerful synthesis of Neo-Confucian thought as well as that school's impact on education. He accepted the Zhu Xi tradition, yet sought to enlarge it by including within its horizons some of the epistemological range of the radical idealists. Called three times to serve at the court, each time he resigned after short periods in office to return to the quiet life of the teacher and scholar in Jiangxi. Classical scholarship was the activity that thinkers drew on to define issues and give authority to their ideas; in this field, Wu Cheng was without peer in Yuan times as a profound and meticulous master of classical texts. His contribution was to maintain high standards in learning and to impart the stimulus of authoritative criticism to intellectual life.

The Yuan period forms a continuation of Song intellectual life, albeit under conditions of particular difficulties for the elite of learning. In Confucian thought as in other kinds of cultural activity, the Yuan dynasty displays the afterglow of Song greatness.

Other Fields of Learning

Historians of the Yuan period faced the obligation to produce a history of the preceding Song dynasty, a task that the Yuan government was expected to bear, but which private historians also could assume. Compiling that history was complicated by the fact that the Jin dynasty had failed to produce an official history of its predecessor, the Liao dynasty, and that the history of the Jin now also had to be written. The Jin had in fact begun the process of writing a Liao history, but it was never completed and authorized for publication because scholars and statesmen of the time could not agree on how the Liao and Jin successions should be explained. How had the Mandate been transmitted? Which dynasties had been principal bearers of the legitimate succession and which ones were subsidiary? Which of the Five Agents *(wu-xing)* governed each of those dynasties? Such issues suddenly assumed great import among Jin period scholars (see Chapter 12, Section IV). Theories about dynastic succession had a curious revival of importance in Jin times.[51] Before the work on the three histories of Liao, Jin, and Song could be brought to a conclusion, those attendant questions first had to be answered.

Official efforts to compile the histories were started at several points, but only in 1343, more than seventy years after Khubilai proclaimed his new Yuan dynasty, were commissions at last established that would quickly bring these projects to completion. The Mongol Chief Councillor Toghto, named to head the effort, himself proposed that the histories be compiled simultaneously as three separate works, that is, not combined into one integrated account of the long period from 906 to 1379. Toghto had received some Chinese education and was a promoter of Confucian policies; his general editorship of the historiographic project, however, was purely honorary.[52] The three histories, brought to conclusion in a very short time in 1344 and 1345, are a major accomplishment of Chinese historical scholarship. They are numbered among the period's several significant achievements in that field.[53]

In the sciences, the Yuan period benefited greatly from contacts with Western Asia, particularly with Persia, in fields of mathematics, astronomy, medicine, hydraulics, and others. An Institute of Muslim Astronomy (Hui-hui sitian jian) was set up in 1271, alongside the (Chinese) Institute of Astronomy; the two worked closely with the Academy of Calendrical Studies in observing astronomical phenomena and preparing the imperial calendars and almanacs that were sold each year in great numbers and used throughout the empire.[54] These institutions were paralleled by the Imperial Academy of Medicine and its counterpart, the Office of Muslim Medicine, and their pharmaceutical bureaus. Medicine, astronomy, mathematics, and horology all had flourished during the Song. In that atmosphere the outside contacts were of large importance for all concerned. There were exchanges of personnel and diffusion of instruments and techniques between China and its so-called Muslim (Hui-hui) counterparts who represented Arab science transmitted via Persia. The Institute of Muslim Astronomy, established to accommodate a major focus of the state's interest, remained a permanent fixture of the Chinese government thereafter.

The most interesting figure in Chinese science during the Yuan period was Guo Shoujing (1231–1316), from a scholarly family of North China having a family tradition in classical studies as well as specialized learning in mathematics and hydraulics. Guo added his own studies in astronomy, calendrical science, and the practical application of hydraulic engineering in water control projects. As an astronomer he contributed to the design and fabrication of instruments for astronomical observation, supervising their manufacture by expert bronze casting techniques. Although he drew on Chinese traditions in these fields, it is clear that he also was greatly stimulated by the knowledge introduced from Western Asia; he and others interacted with counterparts from Persia, leading to important advances in Chinese science.

There were also notable achievements in historical geography and in cartography. The *Comprehensive Atlas of the Great Yuan* was completed and published in 1303 in 1,300 chapters after twenty years of work by a government commission. Private scholars also were active in cartography and geography. Government sponsorship led to a series of works on agricultural technology, and on water control methods—diking, draining swamps, and building canals for irrigation and transport. Medical science in Yuan times included dietetics, pharmacology, and the diagnosis and treatment of major diseases, continuing important lines of development from Song and Jin times. In all of these fields, important works were published and widely disseminated. The quality of books printed in the Yuan is almost on a par with that of the Song in both their artistic and technological aspects.

The Major and the Minor Arts

Poetry, calligraphy, and painting traditionally are held to be the major arts of Chinese civilization; here all the forms of literary expression will be included along with poetry. Literary figures—and most educated men and some women—continued to write poetry and prose in the honored genres of the past. In particular, poets wrote the standard "regulated verse" *(shi)*, brought to its highest perfection during the Tang, and many added to their repertory the "lyric poems" *(ci)*, developed late in Tang, that became the representative genre of poetry under the Song. During the Yuan, the new form of lyric poetry was called *qu* or *sanqu*, referring to the aria form of the Yuan dramas. Despite its intricate prosody, during the Yuan that song form took on a life independent of drama to become the representative poetic form of the age; highly emotive lyrical poetry, it rivaled the Song period's *ci*. But the development in literature for which the Yuan is most noted is the drama.

Yuan drama *(zaju)* flourished within a short space of time from the later Jin dynasty through the fourteenth century. It was valued by cultivated Chinese at the time, but thereafter the dramas were denigrated by Ming and Qing aesthetes. The special circumstances of Yuan period society undoubtedly brought about the special relationship of dramatic authors to their popular audiences. That explains how this new dramatic form was at one time performance literature to entertain the broadest popular audience and dramatic texts incorporating sung passages that appealed to the most cultivated tastes. Yuan drama's value was recognized within the literary establishment of the time. Subsequently denigrated, it nonetheless exerted a strong influence on later dramatic art. Early in the twentieth century, scholars in China and Japan commenced a fundamental reevaluation of the Yuan drama; it has now become a major field of literary scholarship.[55]

Calligraphy and painting in the Yuan continued lines of development that had seemed to peak in late Song times, yet the Yuan achievement is in no way inferior to Song; some indeed say that the Four Masters of the Late Yuan are among the supreme painters of all Chinese history.[56] They are among a very large contingent of calligraphers and painters who made the Yuan one of the most important ages in the history of Chinese art. The reunification of China in the 1270s produced as profound a stimulus to artists of that time as it did to thinkers, writers, and statesmen. The impact of reunification has been described as "a revelation" in the lives of calligraphers and painters in particular. Southerners who could travel to the North and see pre–Southern Song works of art previously unknown to them, and northerners who could come into contact with the quite different cultural ambience of the South, all were transformed by the experience. Much of the period's great cultural flourishing, otherwise not easily explained, must be attributed to the heady new environment of a reunified China.[57]

Sometimes called by traditional Chinese writers the last of the "Eight Princes of Calligraphy," Zhao Mengfu (1254–1322) exerted a powerful influence on the historical development of calligraphy styles. He also was one of the most influential and highly valued painters of his age, an at least competent poet in several genres, and a voluminous writer on many subjects. He had, moreover, a reputable career as a civil official. Thus he met all the criteria for distinction in the minds of the scholar elite—all except one. He was born near the Southern Song capital at Hangzhou in a family descended from the early Song emperors and was in his twenties when the region fell to the invading Yuan armies. For ten years thereafter he withdrew from the world, apparently observing the ideal of the scholar under one dynasty who will not serve the successor dynasty. Then, in his mid-thirties, he came forth and took service at the strong urgings of eminent Chinese of the time. He was much favored by Khubilai Khan and high figures at the Mongol court. Still, he was a turncoat. The blemish of "disloyalty" as that was then understood could be forgiven by many, but could not be erased. It brought him scornful rejection by many relatives and early associates.

Zhao Mengfu nonetheless appears to us as one of the exuberant talents of Chinese high culture, a man in his time compared to the greatest of the Northern Song literary figures, Su Shi (Su Dongpo, 1037–1101), as a man of all-around genius. The point of the comparison is that genius is irrepressible, and those who possess it must be expected to express it in remarkable, even unconventional ways. Zhao's admirers hoped to draw attention away from his failure to remain loyal to the Song dynasty. In fact, in his painting Zhao Mengfu broke through limits of convention much as Su Shi had done in his *ci* lyric poetry. It has been said that by using techniques and concepts drawn from calligraphy, Zhao transformed painting into a new art form; in that way he "created a startling prefiguration of Western modernism."[58]

Zhao Mengfu's public life illustrates the kinds of problems encountered by many Chinese who maintained the high culture. In his private life, he was married to Guan Daosheng (1232–1319), an accomplished painter and poet and a woman of intriguing personal qualities.[59] Theirs was a stirring example of the ideal companionate marriage, an ideal of growing importance in later Chinese elite society. They married late, when he was thirty-six and she twenty-eight. She traveled with him throughout his postings in many places during his official career, and bore him several children; their eldest son, Zhao Yong (ca. 1290–after 1360), also became a noted painter, as did their grandson Zhao Lin.

In the minor arts, to adopt the Chinese view of the highly valued but secondary lines of artistic activity carried on by craftsmen, the Yuan is most noted for its ceramics. Many of the great kilns of Song times no longer held their previous importance in Yuan, but others flourished. Best known are the celadon wares of the Longquan kilns in southern Zhejiang Province. This center of ceramic production was patronized by the Yuan government; tens of thousands of pieces were exported by sea to Korea and Japan, and to Western Asia via the Inner Asian land routes. Thousands of pieces have been recovered archaeologically, some found as cargo in ships that sank off the Korean coast. The Longquan glazes, ranging from pale to dark green, have never been excelled. The great center of porcelain production at Jingdezhen in Jiangsi Province, best known for the elegant blue-and-white wares produced from Ming times to the present day, also began production in Yuan times. Yuan period pieces are among the prized holdings of museums throughout the world.

The arts of Yuan China attest to the continuity of Chinese civilization through the long era of alien rule under the conquest dynasties. The Yuan contribution to that ever-renewing civilization can be measured in many ways as foreign rule drew to a close in 1368. The elements of that contribution mentioned briefly here can do no more than hint at the richness and complexity of Chinese life in the fourteenth century.

PART FOUR

THE RESTORATION OF NATIVE
RULE UNDER THE MING, 1368–1644

Overleaf:

Viewing the Palace Examination Results

Qiu Ying, ca. 1495–1552. Detail, handscroll, ink and color on silk. Collection of the National Palace Museum, Taiwan, Republic of China; used with permission.

Qiu Ying was a revered professional painter who spent his life in Suzhou and nearby places, creating masterpieces for gentry patrons. He never traveled to Beijing, the setting depicted here, where a crowd gathers at the palace wall to see the large sheets of paper on which the triennial examination winners' names were posted under a temporary awning. This event announced the new *jinshi,* the latest entrants into Ming China's elite, to the capital and to the Chinese world. If one image can be taken to epitomize scholar-official ideals, this might well be it.

21

FROM CHAOS TOWARD
A NEW CHINESE ORDER

The Yuan dynasty was Khubilai Khan's ambitiously conceived instrument for merging Mongol and Chinese, steppe and sedentary patterns of rule; after his death in 1294 the flaws in his hybrid system of power began to reveal themselves, and through the following half-century his Mongol dynasty's hold on power weakened. Successor movements came into being, some from within the dynasty's forces, but most in open hostility to it. Those took form as regional power bases that nullified the political dominance of the central government and displayed a full spectrum of political and ideological characteristics. A general crisis ensued. After 1350, six or eight "rival contenders" had grown powerful enough to contest the Yuan dynasty's mandate, but their energies were focused on fighting one another more than on attacking the center. The Yuan dynasty's disintegration and the gradual emergence of a dominant claimant to successor dynasty legitimacy was a long process that reveals structural features of Chinese society and capacities for organization and military leadership latent in the Chinese population. A major element of the period is the role played by the so-called sectarian religious movements; they dominated the civil wars and were the matrix from which the new Ming dynasty emerged. One of those sectarian rebellions was led by an unlikely future emperor, a man from the poorest of the poor in a plague- and famine-ravaged rural village. A colorful account of his youth, translated from a recent biography, concludes this chapter.

I. DISINTEGRATION

The Yuan dynasty's central government faltered badly early in the fourteenth century. By the 1330s its political weaknesses were obvious to all, and by the 1350s rival rebellions had cut the country into province-size and smaller local regimes that fought one another more fiercely than they warred on the Yuan central government. The still potent government armies based at Dadu, the capital city on the site of modern Beijing, became almost irrelevant.

Descent into chaos occupied close to half a century.[1] As general disorder came to prevail, there were leading actors of several kinds, some within the government, others generated by circumstances over which the government no longer could exert direct control. The most potent of the actors, those who gave form to the next phase of history, were men who rose to power through popular rebellions. Mass rejection of the fading imperial government among the people, susceptible in their desperation to leaders who promised them the means of survival, is precisely what Chinese dynastic cycle theory stipulates should normally bring down tired old regimes and give birth to vigorous young ones. That has almost never happened in history; the metaphors of age and youth work far better in biology than in social history, and cycles tend to flourish most convincingly in the eye of the beholder.

How, then, should one understand the chaos of the mid-fourteenth century? The last decades of the Yuan dynasty were an era in which the center squandered the means to impose control, and because the regularly constituted regional and local governments were unable to hold firm without the authority and credibility that the center should have provided, general disorder ensued. Most of the men who rose to regional military leadership in that chaotic period were not from elite backgrounds. They led armies of untrained farmers and rural bandits, ordinary people who were in large part moved by millenarian doctrines that people of education scorned. The insurgent leaders, like their supporters, mostly came from the lowest social stratum. Successful leaders were men who could win ever larger followings, take decisive command, and gain military victories—mostly over rival forces of similar origins. In short, the character of all the rebellious movements was inconstant and difficult to categorize, but "class warfare" it clearly was not. How that state of affairs came into being, and how China emerged from that unprecedented degree of social disorder, is one of the most interesting stories in history. It is different from all the other dynastic beginnings dealt with in this volume and has no close analogue anywhere in Chinese history.

Many recent scholars have attempted to fit the Mongol collapse and the rise of the Ming into a general formula for mass rebellion; those efforts, however interesting, have not been successful.[2] Yet the late Yuan rebellions indeed merit our special attention. Here we shall start with the dissolution of Yuan imperial governing at the center.[3]

The last Mongol emperor is called in the Chinese records the Emperor Shun, or Shun Di, "the emperor who complied" (with the change of the Mandate); that is a not very complimentary title granted him by the founding emperor of the Ming dynasty, whose armies drove the Mongols out of China and back into the Mongolian steppe in 1368. Emperor Shun's Mongol name was Toghon Temür. Like all the later Mongol rulers of the Yuan dynasty, he came to the throne through factional intrigue; that was in 1333, when he was a boy of thirteen. The previous forty years had been relatively free of wars and external threats, and few serious challenges to the state's authority had yet arisen among the Chinese population. The court and imperial house-hold, however, marked by extremes of conflict and stress, had witnessed regicide and violent factional struggles. Manipulated by a powerful factional leader, Emperor Shun was a figurehead ruler who remained a pawn of Mongol political leaders throughout the thirty-five years of his reign, while competing factions rose and fell.

In Mongol politics, factions were led by often ruthless men who lusted for personal power; but they also were driven by conceptions of what the Mongol state based in China should be. Since the days of Chinggis Khan and the great founders of Mongol history, the khanate of China had become a hybrid state combining three distinct elements: there were features drawn from Mongol experience; there were practices taken over from Inner Asian—especially Turkic and Persian—administrative modes; and there was the Chinese institutional base coupled with its traditions and governing norms. The political offices were staffed by men from all three backgrounds, among whom the Mongols alone held the ultimate authority. The population and its traditions were, however, Chinese.

The Mongol leaders of Yuan dynasty political factions disagreed about the ways to use China's resources to best serve Mongol interests. Should Yuan China strive to become a stronger and richer Chinese state, the better thereby to sustain its (Mongol) governors in the stable pattern of Chinese politics? Or should it function as an inexhaustible treasury to pay for more glory days of Mongol exploits based in the steppe? Among the Mongols themselves opinions varied, while the Chinese, of course, but also an increasing fringe of Inner Asian administrators, believed that traditional Chinese priorities must be maintained. Policies of the latter kind have been called "Confucian," not because of any specific philosophical orientation but because they shared the practical objectives of traditional Chinese statecraft.[4]

There was little altruism in any of the competing calculations. The rulers and the governors all realized that they gained the most when Chinese society worked well. The purposes behind the China-centered policies were security, control, and to a lesser extent economic exploitation. It was widely seen that agriculture should be rehabilitated in the wake of war's destruction, that commerce should be encouraged, and eventually that people in local society should not be prevented from continuing their ordinary ways, so far as possible under the administrative measures already imposed.

Chinese at many levels had come to accept limiting circumstances and could go along with the system. For the elite group of Chinese officials and scholars among whom issues of legitimacy were paramount, the dynasty had come to be regarded as legitimate. Regardless of their feelings about how the Mongols had terminated the venerated Song dynasty, the Mandate of Heaven had been transferred, making the Yuan their dynasty. Yet it became increasingly difficult to serve. The government was ineffective. It was widely held to be corrupt, and it allowed the abuse and mistreatment of people in many circumstances. When its ever-shifting policies veered toward Chinese interests, Chinese officials gladly put aside doubts and suspicions and went off to serve in it; when its policies swung back again, they left in frustration. In many cases they concluded that they could do better things at the local level, especially by encouraging the establishment of schools and by teaching. By the final decades of Yuan, such attitudes had become widespread among the Chinese scholar-official element in Yuan society.

The failures of governing went far beyond court and central government; they had direct consequences for local society. When the system of paper currency was mismanaged, its collapse brought widespread hardship. The court's demands for costly things was excessive, and they were wrung from the goods and the labor of ordinary people. Protection given to non-Chinese aroused anger: for example, there was a large influx of Tibetan monks who enjoyed the protection of the imperial household and who were notorious for riding roughshod over cities where they acquired special interests through the Buddhist establishment, such as at Hangzhou.

Add to such complaints the things for which the government was not responsible. The fourteenth century was a cold period in the world's climate history; growing seasons were briefer, and the need for protection against winter weather was heightened. Perhaps for that reason, severe epidemics occurred. Summer floods repeatedly destroyed much good farmland, and genuine distress became widespread. The first half of the fourteenth century would have been a difficult age with or without the inept Mongol government.

During the 1330s minor social disturbances began to break out; country people here, canal workers there, disgruntled soldiers in some other place, all created little uprisings of the kind that Chinese sources traditionally called "banditry." Then strange religious doctrines spread among the rural people. Predictions circulated widely that calamities were imminent. Clandestine leaders appeared who claimed spiritual powers and stirred their followings to defy convention and the usual sources of authority. Popular religious movements with messianic doctrines took root among the people at large; some, indeed, had long been there and after some decades now blossomed forth in an environment where the usual constraints were weakened. Many accounts report that bandits were able to bribe local officials to ignore their banditry, or to release them when caught. We also have much anecdotal evidence that underlying suspicions led Mongol and other non-Chinese officials to charge their Chinese co-workers with covertly aiding and excusing dissident Chinese. Defense against such charges was difficult. From all the evidence one must conclude that the tone of government at middle working levels greatly deteriorated, exacerbated by the flagrant lawlessness in society that no one knew how to control. Many satirical ditties like the following example circulated among the common people in late Yuan times:

> Last year the edict forbidding us to ride horseback;
> This year another edict saying we cannot carry a bow.
> Yet we still hear about all those robbers who by the light of day
> Ride their horses and shoot people on the empire's highway.[5]

The government issued ever stricter laws and set ever fiercer punishments in an effort to prop up the forces of order; this ditty ridicules it for those efforts. Social order normally was not maintained by direct coercion but by the much less intrusive reliance on society at large to uphold the norms of appropriate behavior. When that no longer worked and the government's failures could be openly ridiculed, it was in deep trouble. Moreover, disorder itself created a willingness to accept surrogate leaders such as religious agitators who promised to restore peace and safety.

In the 1340s some towns were attacked by bands of "rabble bandits," meaning ordinary people who had been made desperate by worsening conditions and had been organized for action by ambitious leaders. In many places people loyal to the government also found emerging leaders, occasionally among the educated elite, to organize them for community self-protection where the government's forces were shown to be incompetent. In other places no specific loyalty either to the government or to an anti-government cause was proclaimed, but autonomous military defenses were organized and led by anyone who proved to be competent. A broad spectrum of uncontrollable local dissident movements was spawned. Some proclaimed secret society doctrines and predicted ominous events. Some posed as defenders of the public interest, and for that service expropriated the people's goods, grain stores, and valuables. Some pillaged and looted and caused the people to flee. Those homeless refugees were all the more susceptible to recruitment by ambitious leaders.

By the 1350s Chinese society was rent by disorder on a scale that had not been seen for centuries. It deserves to be described here because it was not just some recurring feature of cyclical history, as has often been claimed. In this mid–fourteenth-century breakdown of social order, the central government was ineffectual for several decades. It attempted to meet the military challenges by sending armies against uprisings near the capital; but those efforts, at first promising, quickly failed. Rebels were emboldened to take even more aggressive action. In the face of general chaos, powerful regional movements developed; some merely defended their local interests, while others were ambitious to bring down the imperial government. We have here a rare case study of what could happen in China when a society long accustomed to being ruled by a coherent centralized governing authority found itself without one.

II. COMPETITORS FOR POWER EMERGE

The foregoing discussion has indicated some of the ways devised in localities for maintaining social order when the state gradually lost its capacity to govern. All of them necessitated the direct recourse to violence, to the use of force by armed people.

China was not normally an armed society. Here we see a steady process of militarization in which social action was accomplished by force, employing violence on an ever-widening scale. It could end only when one armed political movement would win out over its competitors, succeed to uncompromised rule, and then demilitarize the society, allowing it to regain the patterns of normative social order sustained by civil institutions. In this epoch of four-teenth-century history, the alien regime, which initially had risen to power by perfecting its own people's total commitment to warfare, had to be expelled militarily. Only that would allow the society over which it ruled, also abnor-mally militarized in a brief late phase of that conquest dynasty's reign, to be restored to its normal working patterns. That is in fact what happened. But let us not anticipate the larger story; first we must look into the components of the mid–fourteenth-century scene in which Yuan loyalists, local self-defense organizations, and bandit gangs turned into local and regional governments, and sectarian movements warred among themselves. The competitors for power can be loosely classified as belonging to one of these types.

Yuan Loyalists

Chaghan Temür was a Turkic (probably Uighur) Inner Asian whose family had settled down in Henan three generations earlier after assisting Chinggis Khan's armies complete their conquest of the Jin dynasty in 1234. On the one hand, his family continued to be fighting men fully assimilated into Mon-gol culture, and as provincials were little interested in court politics. On the other, Chaghan's father had added to those qualities an interest in Chinese learning, and Chaghan himself had sat for the civil service examinations but had not progressed to the highest level. As Mongol military power in North China contracted, Chaghan took it upon himself to raise and lead militia forces to supplement the fading Henan provincial garrisons. His power grew rapidly. Hoping to retain his loyalty, the court encouraged him to expand his provincial forces and maintain order.

Chaghan's sister had married a Chinese by the name of Wang; when wid-owed, she brought her only son to live in Chaghan's household. Having no surviving heirs of his own, Chaghan adopted the boy, Wang Baobao, who, despite that informal childhood name meaning "little darling," grew into a commanding figure, a powerful warrior much resembling his stepfather. His Chinese enemies liked to taunt him about his Chinese baby name and accused him of being a traitor to his ancestors. He became even more the model Mon-gol warrior than Chaghan himself, universally feared by his Chinese oppo-nents. In 1361, when sent to deliver a grain shipment to the straitened capital, he was received at court. The Emperor Shun, seeing the very martial-looking young man, bestowed the Mongol name Kökö Temür on him, accepting him as a Mongol.

In an interesting example of assimilation, his special background and the need to prove himself undoubtedly contributed to the fierceness with which he professed loyalty to the Mongol cause. Yet in his career he never placed the court's needs ahead of his own regional interests; he appears to have scorned the rebels as scum more than he loved the Mongol ruler. He neverthe-less remained on the government's side, fought its enemies when he chose to do so, and at the end turned out to be the strongest military supporter left to the dynasty.

When his stepfather was assassinated in 1362, Kökö Temür was confirmed in Chaghan's titles and offices, to which Prince of Henan was soon added. He expanded his territories beyond Henan to the north into Shanxi at the expense of the Mongol military governor there, who happened also to be the emperor's father-in-law. He inevitably became entrapped in the dangerous factionalism of the court and had to fight the government's other regional commanders both to defend the court and to secure his own territories. The weakness of a court whose military supporters were forced to engage in internecine wars instead of cooperating to defend their imperiled dynasty was made all too clear.

Chaghan Temür and his formidable stepson Kökö Temür developed the most powerful of the several regional organizations nominally loyal to the Yuan cause to the end. After the removal of Chief Councillor Toghto in 1355, there was no Mongol prince or general who played a major role, no great army in the steppe waiting to rush in and defend the khan-emperor's court. There were, however, some Chinese who, like Chaghan and Kökö, became regional warlords, fought against the various uprisings, and supported the fading government through the final decades.

One was Chen Youding, the illiterate son of a poor farmer in Fujian on the Southeast China coast. Born about 1330, he knew only troubled times throughout his entire life. Because he was tall and strong and quick to learn, he attracted the attention of minor local officials who recruited him into the constabulary, and as the provincial government was pressed to defend the region against the Red Turbans (discussed later in this chapter) who invaded from Jiangsi in the west in 1352, he repeatedly proved himself in battle and was rapidly promoted. He served under the Mongol commander of provincial forces, and for his exceptional bravery he was promoted to the office of county magistrate, despite being scarcely literate. Thus were careers made in those troubled times; but his career was extraordinary even for the age. He was further promoted, into the provincial government, and by the mid-1360s he headed it. He ran the province like a private empire, commandeered all its resources for his own use, and ruthlessly eliminated enemies, but nominally at least he remained loyal to the dynasty. When he was captured by the Ming armies in 1368 and taken to the capital at Nanjing, the Ming founder, an admirer of raw courage, offered him titles and rewards. Chen Youding would have none of it. He reviled the newly proclaimed Chinese emperor, said that he would accept no alternative to death, and was executed.

In neighboring Guangdong (Canton) at the same time, a man named He Zhen had a somewhat similar career, rising from an obscure background to become military governor and warlord of the region by 1362. He Zhen, however, was not an illiterate farm boy; he came from a well-to-do family and was highly educated, in addition to being a swashbuckling soldier by choice. After ruling the region for seven years, when the Ming armies approached in 1369 he quickly surrendered, was taken to the capital, and was granted titles and rewards. He served very capably in high office on and off for the next twenty years, and when he died was honored by the Ming founder.

Local Self-Defense Leaders

In addition to Chen and He, who rose rapidly and whose names are recorded in history, there were many other Chinese, both men of education and status and men of humbler backgrounds, who responded to the chaotic times by trying to defend home and community against the rising perils of daily life. In countless villages and towns, as it became obvious that the Yuan government could not be relied on to maintain public safety, people organized their own defense corps. They often turned to senior persons of higher standing, though not necessarily members of the official elite, to head up their hastily assembled militias, thus to validate them by their participation and to help plan their tactics. Stockades were built and gates manned, crude arms were assembled, and young men were formed into defense units. In many cases the actual leadership would soon fall to younger men who proved under fire that they possessed some military skills and leadership qualities. In this time of troubles, talents not usually valued rose quickly to the surface. Chen Youding, as we have seen, skyrocketed to prominence in that way; most, however, did not rise so high, and remain unrecorded in history. Commenting on those conditions, the *Ming History* notes: "At the end of the Yuan, banditry sprang up everywhere. Among the common people volunteer forces were formed to protect village and locality. Those who called themselves commanders of such forces were too numerous to count. The Yuan government granted them official ranks and titles at the drop of a hat. Thereafter, some would go off to become bandits; others served the Yuan cause but without resolve."[6]

Organizing ad hoc local defenses was dangerous work, and typically it was unsuccessful. China lacked the traditions of a hereditary knighthood or a professional fighting class, and it lacked the infrastructure of castles, armories, and defended bastions. It had a few walled county seat towns scattered across an open countryside (far fewer than would be walled three centuries later), but those were not impregnable. The struggle to protect lives and property could draw on little beyond desperate initiatives and makeshift ingenuity. Despite the learned elite's insistence that force and violence provided no path to honor, their high-minded code could not prepare people for the extremes of social breakdown which they now faced. When arms became widely present and all people were made subject to the use of force, everyone had to adjust to that unthinkable situation. Many men proved to be more than merely adjustable. "Heroes" emerged from among the burned villages, corpse-strewn fields, and camps of fleeing people. New modes of behavior were formed, and new kinds of leaders were found to take charge. With normative means no longer dominant, alternate social controls came to the fore. Local leaders of ad hoc militia forces became a prominent if temporary phenomenon in the late Yuan.

Bandits and Smugglers

Anyone who became socially disruptive and defied authority might be called a "bandit" in China, but as used here the term refers to the often sophisticated leaders of illicit activities who built organizations to support their schemes. It is easy to see how persons who in normal times engaged in small-scale crime in conjunction with their regular activities could quickly expand their operations to take advantage of the breakdown of authority. Two examples were very important in the last decades of the Yuan; both rose through the salt distribution systems on the Central China coast.

Salt was produced from seawater in salterns located along the coast north of the Yangzi River in Jiangsu and farther south in Zhejiang. Its production and distribution were under government controls, the profits providing a major source of revenues for the state. The barge workers who moved the salt from production sites to distribution centers had many opportunities to profit from the transport of illegally produced or untaxed salt, or more simply, to engage in smuggling, characteristically in collusion with corrupt salt tax officials. Their clandestine organizations were in place, ready to be exploited for larger purposes, and the collapse of authority in the late Yuan gave them new opportunities.

Zhang Shicheng was a salt transport worker in what would today be northern Jiangsu, on the coast north of the Yangzi in the region dominated by the great city of Yangzhou. In 1353, when he was thirty-two years old, Zhang grew tired of being cheated by the corrupt officials for whom he transported illegal salt. He killed one such man and set fire to his home, then fled with his three younger brothers and a number of toughs who were personally loyal to him. Soon he had a large following which he organized into an army, taking over the hierarchy of leaders and sub-leaders that already existed among the salt workers. He plundered the important county and prefectural seats in the region and in 1353 captured the city of Gaoyou, strategically astride the Grand Canal just north of Yangzhou.

Zhang was an ambitious and imaginative man, able to profit from the abnormal times. He immediately declared himself to be the founder of a new dynasty, the Great Zhou, and adopted a reign name in defiance of the Yuan government. He dared attempt that bold stroke because much of the territory between his base and the Yuan court at Dadu had been thrown into turmoil by the outbreak of sectarian rebellion since 1351. The court tried at first to win him over by granting him high titles and office; he negotiated with the court's envoys as if considering the offer, then murdered them. Zhang's resources were limited, but his location on the canal gave him high cards to play. The court was then under the dominance of Chief Councillor Toghto, long its most able and energetic high official. Toghto himself took to the field in 1354 with the last great Yuan dynasty field army, and in 1355 had cut a swathe across North China, clearing away all opponents. In November he surrounded Zhang Shicheng's base at Gaoyou and laid siege to the stoutly walled city.

Zhang Shicheng should have disappeared from history at that point, but to the amazement of all, the court suddenly demanded that Toghto withdraw to the capital and turn over his command. He was banished and died soon thereafter, at one blow depriving the Yuan dynasty of its last able Chief Councillor while saving the fortunes of Zhang Shicheng. In 1356 Zhang crossed to the south side of the Yangzi, captured Suzhou, and made it the seat of his rebel government, then extended his territories farther to the south toward Hangzhou. Controlling northern Jiangsu with its large salt revenues, and southern Jiangsu–northern Zhejiang with its abundant agricultural resources, Zhang quickly became the richest of all the final contenders to replace the Yuan dynasty. He was a ruffian who liked to play the scholar-king, a man not far advanced beyond basic literacy who cultivated the elite of learning and the arts. He is one of the most interesting figures of the age, an example of the way in which turbulent times created opportunities for the daring to reach great heights. After Zhu Yuanzhang, the future Ming founder, destroyed the threat from the southern Red Turbans under Chen Youliang in 1363, Zhang remained his strongest rival for mastery of Central China. Success in that rivalry would bring victory in the war against the Yuan. Zhu's better-organized forces slowly ground Zhang down, reduced his territories, and finally placed his capital at Suzhou under a protracted siege in 1367–68 before its starving defenders at last surrendered.

Fang Guozhen also was a salt smuggler, but based on the coast in northern Zhejiang. His family's fleet of seagoing vessels not only allowed him to be a transporter of legal and illegal salt, grain, and other commodities, but also gave him the means to practice piracy against coastal shipping and to plunder coastal towns. Although he was illiterate, he was tall and powerfully built, a natural leader of fighting men. He was not ambitious to create a viable state on land, but used his control over three coastal prefectures of Zhejiang to support his seafaring activities. He became very important to the Yuan court at Dadu for a few years when his ships transported the urgently needed grain supplies to the capital by sea after the Grand Canal became inoperable in the 1350s. Fang alternately took titles and honors from the court and openly rebelled against it. He remained apart from the Ming founder's spheres of interest but maintained diplomatic contacts with him, so when the tide finally turned in favor of the new Ming dynasty in 1368, Fang could surrender and live out his days as a guest of the Ming. His fleet significantly augmented the early Ming navy. He died in 1374. In him we see still another pattern of success built on canny use of resources acquired through force by a man of action.

The Sectarian Rebels

A "sect" can be defined as "a religious following; adherence to a particular religious teaching or faith," and "sectarian" as "confined to a particular sect." In the West those terms have often been used by mainstream leaders to disparage schismatics: we have the truth; they are benighted sectarians. Within the

Asian religious traditions of nonexclusive truth, where people of different religions, and of different "followings" within a particular religion, freely adopted doctrines and forms from one another, the word "sectarian" takes on a somewhat different meaning. The sects discussed here are religious followings, each having a particular focus of beliefs drawn from various sources and using particularized rituals, forms, titles, and names of the deities to whom special veneration was shown. Their followers were not, however, consciously "confined to a particular sect." That is, many of them ardently believed the teachings promoted by their sect leaders but might simultaneously accept many other familiar features of the popular religious landscape.

That religious landscape had undergone great change during the Southern Song dynasty.[7] Many new cults had appeared. In most cases they were cults that venerated recent historical figures who had been elevated in the popular imagination to the status of local deities.[8] The actions their followers sought from them might be within established Buddhist or Daoist patterns in popular religion, or their characteristics might be less clearly differentiated, partaking of diverse elements in a new mix. One caveat must be noted in passing: one must not rush to assumptions about the implications of "popular" in describing religion in later imperial times. It is convenient, and largely accurate, to think of undifferentiated, undiscriminating religious practice as typical of "popular religion." The highly learned, philosophically oriented study of thought and religion that carefully distinguished between historical traditions and separate schools of thought was indeed an elite undertaking and expressed elite attitudes. Certain figures within the elite, to be sure, assumed that analytical attitude. Yet many members of elite families, men and women, participated in the cultic and sectarian practices of "popular religion." Even the great Zhu Xi, intellectual leader par excellence of Southern Song Neo-Confucianism, who often told his students that he disdained the religious practices of his time, nonetheless visited a cultic shrine patronized by his relatives and commented humorously on the experience of doing so to please his family.[9] Many scholar-officials did not share his disdain. The life of the entire society was involved in many aspects of the popular religious beliefs and practices, not just the lives of people at the lower levels.

During the Southern Song and on into the Yuan, the new Daoist sects grew, spread throughout the country, and became an important element in the life of society. Those movements often had a threatening political dimension for which they were at times banned by the Song and Yuan governments; their potential for fomenting dissidence was feared in official circles. Banning them simply drove them underground, however, forcing them to avoid public attention but permitting base-level organizations among their followers to continue, even to spread. If nothing else, the new Daoist sects gave religious movements new models for action.

Coming into the Yuan, political conditions encouraged the Chinese to draw together in defense of their common heritage. Thoughtful people encouraged syncretic tendencies, offering the view that the Three Teachings, meaning

Confucianism, Buddhism, and Daoism, shared a "single origin" or "one source." Under that influence, and with ingenious schematizations designed to show the complementary nature of the three sets of doctrines, broad approval developed within the elite for the idea that all the great systems of ethical and spiritual teachings are inherently compatible.[10] In Chinese, the word meaning "teachings" traditionally was used for what we call "religion," thereby blurring the distinction between the religious and the secular that someone from the West is predisposed to look for. Moreover, none of those three was a "revealed" system of absolute and exclusive truth; aspects of all three might contribute to any person's beliefs. Most syncretists having Buddhist or Daoist affiliations, for example, stressed that the system of Chinese social ethics (usually identified with Confucian teachings) was necessary for state and society to function properly, even while insisting that Buddhism or Daoism had other points of superiority.

Syncretist ideas changed elite attitudes, and by so doing they also relaxed the atmosphere, aiding the sub-elite religious practices to thrive in the thirteenth and fourteenth centuries. Among the several elements within the popular religions of Yuan times that acquired new importance were doctrines previously imported from Western Asia. Long present in China, they were new in the fourteenth century in the uses to which they were put and the influence they gained. Two deserve special mention.

First is the element of popularized Manichaean doctrine. Mani, a third-century C.E. Persian born in Babylonia, traveled into India and other regions adjacent to the Persian empire of that time. Important elements of many religions have come from that time and that region, including components of later Christianity and Mahayana Buddhism. Mani was influenced by the earlier Persian religion of Zoroaster among the many strands of religious thought that he encountered, but he believed that all were only partially true and that a universal system transcending them all had been revealed to him. As partially understood and popularized in the course of being carried into eastern Asia, the central tenet of Mani's teaching was that forces of light and darkness, good and evil, struggled for mastery of the world. Light, the sun, fire, the color red all symbolized the agency of good in a rigid dualism in which day and night, light and dark, are incompatible and by nature wholly antagonistic. From that derives our use of "manichaean" to describe rigidly dualistic, reductionist patterns in thought. Mani's teachings, however, were elaborated in a subtle mythology and well-worked-out social doctrines that merit fuller understanding. His followers brought his ideas into China via the Silk Roads in Tang times. By the fourteenth century they had lost their distinct identity, having merged with Buddhist and other elements of Chinese popular religion.

Second is the transformation, in the Inner Asian and Chinese settings, of the Buddha Maitreya into the bearer of messianic teachings. Belief in Maitreya goes back to early Buddhism in India, but only when his cult was carried to China in the fourth or fifth century C.E. did his role become defined as that of the Future Buddha who reigns in the Tushita Heaven, the "realm of wonderful joy." In the thirteenth century that role was enlarged; Maitreya became the Buddha who could descend from the Tushita Heaven at any time, bringing all its features to earth to relieve the sufferings of mankind. The message of this messianic doctrine was one of relieving humans from the strictures of normal life as they prepared for the imminent descent into their midst of the transforming savior, for his reign would make the superficial details of daily life irrelevant. At the least, such a doctrine could give great hope to humble people that their miseries might soon end and make them eager to follow leaders who would deliver them into the care of Maitreya.

What most troubled many Chinese observers of these phenomena at that time, however, was that as such doctrines were widely popularized, they could lead crowds of their believers into highly improper social behavior. That concern aroused anxieties about the threat to social morality; Manichaean and Maitreyan doctrines were therefore not sympathetically received by the leaders of society.

In the middle of the fourteenth century we see a profusion of popular sectarian movements led by men and women who taught an amalgam of traditional Buddhist and Daoist beliefs with additions of Manichaean and Maitreyan Buddhist doctrines. The state often condemned them, making their followers practice them in secret. Large gatherings of men, women, and children met at night to conduct their rituals, venerate Maitreya, light fires signaling the Manichaean triumph of light over darkness, perform penances, invite Daoist adepts to cast spells and read the future. That future usually predicted the demise of the dynasty and its replacement by kings having transforming powers. When the state intervened with force to break up those meetings, leaders were captured and executed for treason. All means were tried to suppress them. By the 1340s, sectarian leaders were often emboldened to arm their movements so they could defend themselves. They might further invoke the arts of alchemy and spells to make their warriors invincible, set up secret infrastructures among the people to keep leaders informed, and protect them when forced to flee. They became "secret societies," dangerous sects, in a word, "sectarian bandits."

The largest and most consequential of those movements was called the White Lotus Society. Confusion about it has long existed because it used the name of a much earlier elite Buddhist study organization dating back to the fourth century C.E. In fact, the Yuan period White Lotus secret society historically had nothing in common with the earlier elite association. In the form in which it existed in the Yuan period, it dated from a twelfth-century founder who instituted "radical" practices such as full vegetarianism and other dietary restrictions, penance sessions, and ritual performances at which the sexes mingled freely, and it spread doctrines drawn from both Manichaean and Maitreyan backgrounds. It taught that the disorder into which the world had fallen was proof that Maitreya's coming could happen any day. Several leading teachers appeared across a large area, extending from south of the Yangzi in Central China to north of the Yellow River in northeast China and on into Manchuria. The White Lotus doctrines and religious observances, particularly their "incense burning" ceremonies which in the popular mind came to typify them, merged with the doctrines and rituals of the Mai-treyan sectarians; that produced a cohering ideology among rebel groups, uniting them in common purpose and supplying discipline with which to build a broad movement, recruit armies, and establish civil governing.[11] Their color symbolism switched from white to the more auspicious Manichaean red. Their soldiers wore red headbands *(hong jin)*, from which the movement acquired its popular name, usually translated "Red Turbans."[12]

This Red Turban movement is identified in historical records first in the late 1330s in Jiangsi under a leader who in recent decades has been promoted to mythic importance as a true revolutionary leader of the people.[13] His name was Peng Yingyu, also called "Monk Peng," for he had started out as a monk in a Buddhist temple in Jiangxi. There he actively studied and promoted Maitreyan doctrines and eventually led an unsuccessful uprising. When the authorities attempted to arrest him, he fled and hid among sympathetic sup-porters north of the Yangzi, in the Huai River drainage in central Anhui, then one of the poorest regions in China. Later he resurfaced, back in the southern Red Turban areas, where he led field armies. He appears to have been cap-tured and killed in Jiangxi in 1353. His stirring teachings spread from the regions in Anhui where he had lived and preached in the 1340s farther north into northern Jiangsu and Shandong and beyond.

Peng Yingyu's followers, left behind after his secretive activities in the Huai River region of North China in the early 1340s, apparently merged forces with a cult leader called Han Shantong of the clandestine White Lotus Society. Han's forebears, who for several generations had been identified by the gov-ernment as active leaders of White Lotus associations, had been captured and relocated in southern Hobei, where, as known troublemakers, they were kept under surveillance. Han's White Lotus Society, long active as a seditious movement, now openly took on the Red Turban identity. The two geographic extremities of the Red Turban movement, one eventually scattered through-out the North China Plain and the other solidly based on the central Yangzi in southern Hubei, went their separate ways. No leader appeared who could unite them across that great distance. They acknowledged a common sectar-ian identity, but their leaders were more concerned with their own immediate interests than in cooperating for any larger cause.

Zhu Yuanzhang, as we shall see, through small steps eventually inherited leadership of all the northern Red Turbans, but soon relocated to present-day Nanjing in the lower Yangzi region. The southern branch, upriver in Hubei, quickly became militarily powerful, under better-centralized manage-ment. Its first "emperor," a simple figurehead leader by the name of Xu Shou-hui, was murdered and replaced by a ruthless and able military leader, Chen Youliang, who changed the movement's dynastic name to Han. Chen's Red Turban "Han dynasty" spread its control over a large portion of the central Yangzi, planning to move aggressively against Zhu Yuanzhang's Nanjing base farther down the river (Map 14).[14]

An offshoot of Chen Youliang's "Han dynasty" emerged still farther west on the Yangzi when the organizer of a local self-defense militia named Ming

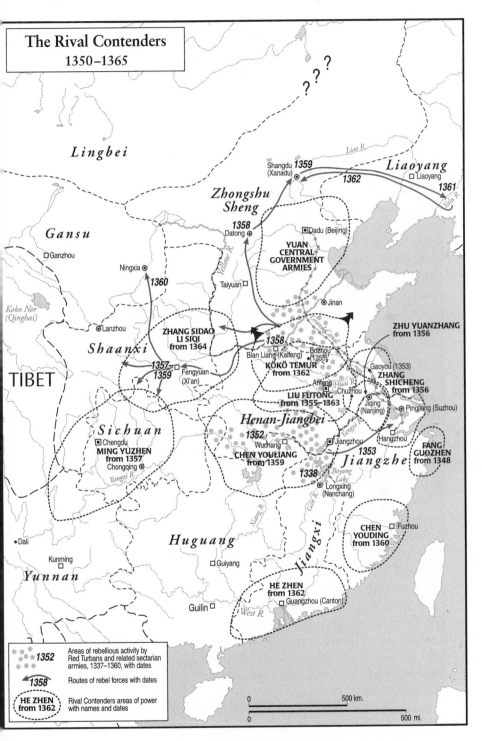

The Rival Contenders
1350–1365

MAP 14

Yuzhen was forced to place himself under Chen's expanding leadership. He split off from the rebel Han state in 1357 and entered Sichuan; there Ming Yuzhen set up his independent Red Turban state, which he called the Xia dynasty. Somewhat isolated from events central to the demise of the Yuan, Ming's rebel state attempted to expand both into Shaanxi in the north and into Yunnan to its south. Conquering it and absorbing Western China back into the Chinese state became an urgent task after 1368, early in Zhu Yuanzhang's reign as emperor of the Ming dynasty.

In North China, Han Shantong, the White Lotus leader, had long plotted to lead a rebellion. For several months in 1351 a major engineering project was undertaken by the Yuan central government to rechannel 100 miles of the Yellow River east of Kaifeng. The work site was about fifty miles south of Han Shantong's home. Large numbers of laborers were recruited from the farming population of that region, perhaps as many as 200,000. The canal project's supervisors badly mistreated the workers, who became disgruntled. Han Shantong decided that if this fortuitously assembled mass of angry farmers could be aroused by a prophetic omen to create a disturbance, that would distract the government's attention. He spread a rumor that when a stone figure of a man with one eye appeared to those who were digging the new Yellow River channel, it would signify that the whole empire would be plunged into revolt. He had such a stone figure planted in the path of the work where the laborers would uncover it, and made sure that his followers would be present, masking as fellow workers, when it was found, to fan the turbulence. Han was prepared simultaneously to make a diversionary attack on the government forces nearby, calculating that the restive mass of workers plus his military diversion would give him freedom from surveillance long enough to launch an uprising from his home base. But he was preempted. The local county magistrate learned of his preparations and raided his headquarters. Han was captured and executed; his chief of staff, Liu Futong, escaped in the melee, as did Han's wife with their infant son. She changed her name and hid out in a mountainous region; Liu went farther south into Anhui to stir up other revolts.

Han had earlier claimed that he was the descendant of the Emperor Huizong of Northern Song (r. 1100–1126). Leaders of various earlier minor outbreaks scattered across various provinces had proclaimed their intention to restore the Song dynasty. The idea was capable of arousing some response seventy-five years after the fall of the Song, just as Ming restorationism still persisted in rebellious sentiment at the end of the Qing dynasty, 250 years after the fall of the Ming in 1644. Han's claim to be a descendant of Song emperors was ridiculous, but its credibility was not apt to be challenged in that environment.

Liu Futong, with several counties in the Huai River region of Anhui under his control, retrieved Han's widow and young son, symbols of his sectarian authority, and brought them to a new base located at the county seat town of Bozhou in present-day Anhui. There, in 1355, after four years during which the Yuan court's counteroffensives and the Red Turbans' quickly spreading insurrection kept the North China Plain in turmoil, Liu announced that he had restored the Song dynasty. For a number of years before his death, Han Shantong had let it be known that he also carried the Manichaean-sounding title Prince of Radiance (Ming Wang). At this time, Liu therefore proclaimed Han's heir, the child Han Lin'er, the "Young Prince of Radiance," implying that he was the manifestation of the Manichaean King of Light, who, guided by the Maitreya Buddha, was preparing for the imminent descent of Maitreya to reign in a Tushita heaven on earth. That gave the figurehead leader of the movement dual legitimacy, as a Song heir and as an anointed religious figure. Both were intended to gain him broad sympathy among the people.[15] A wily and ambitious leader, Liu transformed the earlier armed White Lotus movement of "incense burners" into a broadly spreading if weakly organized Red Turban military uprising. His northern Red Turbans lacked a secure and enduring base area; their several branches held widely scattered regions, and their ranks were filled with ambitious leaders who proclaimed themselves independent "commanders in chief," fought among themselves, and pursued opportunities where they could find them. The movement was strongest in the Ying and Huai River drainages extending east from Henan across Anhui, while subordinate armies were active in Shandong and Hebei, still farther to the east. The future Ming dynasty evolved out of one of its allied branches.

The Red Turban movement thus controlled the largest areas and produced three of the late Yuan regional powers. These competed with the several Yuan loyalist regional regimes and the two states organized by the bandit leaders Zhang Shicheng and Fang Guozhen. The 1350s and the 1360s are referred to as the era of the "rival contenders" *(qunxiong)*, a time when no fewer than twelve regional warlords kept the entire nation in a state of many-sided civil war. I shall attempt to simplify that complex story here.

III. RIVAL CONTENDERS, 1351–1368

There were two kinds of contenders for mastery over all of China in the last two decades of Yuan rule. First was the Yuan government, which exerted direct rule over a dwindling area around the capital at Dadu (modern Beijing), together with those regional regimes that continued to acknowledge it by using its calendar and reign year dating, accepting officials appointed from the court, and sending tax revenues and grains to it when possible. Kökö Temür, the Prince of Henan, was the most important of the regional powers. Yet wherever rebel movements had not overrun and occupied a region, Yuan court-appointed local officials, having the all-important quality of being "legitimate," were still nominally in charge, if not in fact fully able to carry out their duties. In some places local self-defense militia leaders were in actual control and cooperated in varying degrees with the government's officials. This group of regional and local leaders committed to resisting rebellion under the Yuan dynasty's banner held essentially all of the country in 1351, but soon thereafter could control only a rapidly diminishing portion of it. The second group of contenders was the wide spectrum of openly rebellious leaders and unreliable allies of the court (some shifted back and forth as best served their own interests); these included the three principal branches of the Red Turban sectarian uprisings as well as the bandit rebels, salt smugglers Zhang Shicheng based at Suzhou and Fang Guozhen in coastal Zhejiang. To simplify the very complex political and military history of the period, these two groups will be discussed separately.

The Yuan Government, Its Allies and Defenders

There is not much precise information about the strength and disposition of the Yuan armies at any point in the dynasty's history. In the general preface to the "Treatise on the Military," the official *Yuan History,* compiled in 1369 and 1370 by scholars who had lived under and some of whom had held office under the Yuan, the lack of such information is apologetically explained by reference to the Mongol government's insistence on military secrecy; it explains that no one at the time, even the highest officials close to the emperor in the Bureau of Military Affairs, with the exception of one or two most senior figures, ever had any knowledge of the troop strength numbers and disposition.[16] Modern scholars, lacking details, have had to deal with Yuan dynasty military strength in very general terms.

THE CENTER

All agree that the size, quality, and effectiveness of the Yuan dynasty's military forces seriously declined in the fourteenth century. The dynasty's principal forces were its Mongol cavalry, to which were added some cavalry units made up of Inner Asian soldiers incorporated into the Yuan armies, and armies of Chinese foot soldiers who were supplied by the hereditary military households, made up from conquered Chinese armies. The largest numbers were taken over following the conquest of the Southern Song in the 1270s, and by the 1330s, two or three generations later, they provided ample evidence that hereditary occupational status did not work well in Chinese society. Many had deserted to find other ways of surviving. Those who remained were derided at the time for being incompetent, untrained, undisciplined, and wholly unreliable. Most such Chinese units had Mongol or Inner Asian commanding officers, who made halfhearted efforts to recruit replacements and train them for combat. Chaghan Temür in Henan, discussed earlier, was a rare example of success in rebuilding a province's regional armies after the widespread rebellion starting in 1351 made that necessary. Chief Councillor Toghto at the court also succeeded in revitalizing some of the capital garrisons in that way. But in most places the inequities and rampant exploitation of the soldiery had gone too far, not only in the Chinese units but also in the Mongol cavalry. There too the common soldier families garrisoned in China had been impoverished by corrupt officers; weapons were lacking, training was seldom given, and whole units were found to be incapable of fighting.

What troops the Mongols could rely on after 1340 were mostly concentrated in the garrisons near the capital and in Henan. Those eight or ten garrisons normally might have had as many as 100,000 cavalry soldiers but probably were undermanned. It was normal to use those crack forces to spearhead larger armies of Chinese foot soldiers, but even in the capital region such Chinese armies were not kept fully ready for battle. The capital garrisons and imperial guard units could protect the emperor, but they did not have the capacity to campaign far afield to defend the vast Chinese component of the Mongol khanate. The unified command structure created by Chinggis Khan a century earlier no longer functioned; the commands were divided among rival generals among whom cooperation seldom served their perceived interests.

The beginnings of widespread disturbances in the 1340s spurred Chief Councillor Toghto to restore the military effectiveness of the capital garrisons. An energetic and able man, Toghto achieved some notable successes, but fell victim to factional quarrels and left the court. He returned in 1349 following five years' absence. The shock of the 1351 uprisings made the need for military rebuilding even more urgent. In 1352 he hastily put together a strong force, said to have numbered 100,000, to counterattack against the North China Plain uprisings, and was briefly successful. When the Grand Canal was cut by Zhang Shicheng's capture of Gaoyou in 1354, he assembled an even larger and more potent force, said to have numbered 1 million, probably a conventional exaggeration. But, we have seen, when enemies at court again engineered his dismissal early in 1355, his staff officers were moved to tears of rage and chagrin; many deserted, and a large share of the soldiers in that huge field force defected to the rebels. The Yuan court was still able to field generals in command of armies, but there was no figure strong enough to impose overall direction. "Yuan resistance, often fierce, was ineffective because it was uncoordinated."[17] That sentence, describing the final defense of Yuan China against the Ming in 1368, can be applied to the entire final phase of Mongol rule in China.

THE DYNASTY'S FAILING STRENGTH IN THE PROVINCES

From what has been said of Chaghan Temür's rise to prominence as military governor in Henan, it is already clear that he, and later his stepson and successor, Kökö Temür, were to become the most powerful counterforce in North China against the northern sectarian uprisings. At times they also defended the emperor and the heir apparent against threats within the Mongol establishment, as when other military leaders warred among themselves to determine who would dominate the capital and the government. But throughout, Chaghan's and Kökö's interests were primarily those of regional power holders, not those of devoted servants of the throne.[18] While in the field leading his army eastward into Shandong in 1362, Chaghan was assassinated by a pair of dissatisfied subordinates; the court quickly appointed Kökö to succeed him. He avenged his stepfather's death by capturing and executing the assassins, and then brought most of Shandong under his control while finding excuses not to campaign farther afield at the court's direction. His personal obligation to his adopted Mongol warrior image seems to have meant more to him than obedience to the Yuan court. The court accordingly demoted and restricted him.

Thereafter Kökö was deeply enmeshed in wars against other Mongols, particularly against Bolod Temür, the empress's father, whose military base in Shanxi impinged on Kökö's regional interests in adjacent Henan. Shanxi at that time was the North's richest producer of grains, necessary both to Kökö and to the court. Kökö's military pressure against Shanxi forced Bolod in 1364 to withdraw his armies to the capital; there he commanded the court and the capital region, threatened the heir apparent, and made war on Kökö in Henan. A year later the emperor's courtiers contrived to have Bolod assassinated, then restored Kökö to his former powers and positions, adding the title Prince of Henan. That position allowed Kökö to set up an enlarged provincial administration, strengthening his base. His rise to new heights, however, made former associates and present subordinates resentful and jealous. A league of regional generals in the northwest, mostly Chinese in the Yuan service, was formed against him, and some of his own subordinates also rebelled. A court faction again took shape to oppose him, under those other influences and calculations of probable outcome. In 1367 the emperor again turned openly against him, dismissing him from his titles and commands, just as the new Ming dynasty (proclaimed late in 1367, to begin with the New Year in 1368) was setting in motion its final push to expel the Mongols forever from China.

It was not until mid-1368 that the court awakened to its plight and hastily turned back to Kökö for help. He continued to resist the Chinese Ming armies. He certainly did not feel strong personal devotion to the emperor and court, but he remained firmly on the side of the Mongol dynasty. Sometimes he won major engagements and sometimes he was routed and forced to flee. By 1370 the fighting was mainly in Mongolia. Kökö suffered a grave defeat in the fall of 1370, when the Ming forces, in total numbering perhaps 150,000, captured 85,000 men of Kökö's army and 15,000 of his cavalry's horses. Those are among the few recorded figures that give us some idea of the numbers involved in the major actions. Kökö still had opportunities to fight on, even after the death in Mongolia in 1372 of Emperor Shun, the last of the Yuan dynasty's rulers to have reigned from Beijing. He went with the Yuan court (as it continued to call itself) west from the old Mongolian capital at Karakorum, and died in western Mongolia in 1375. On hearing the news, the Ming founder praised Kökö Temür as his fiercest and most admired enemy.

Kökö, like Chief Councillor Toghto before him, was dismissed just when he was most needed by a confused and bumbling emperor in a faction-ridden court. His career illustrates the larger story of Mongol collapse. His dismissal in 1367 may not have changed history in the longer range, but it hastened the dynasty's demise.

The other Yuan loyalists, especially the regional warlords Chen Youding in Fujian and He Zhen in Guangdong, created problems for the rebels, slowing down their conquests of Central and southern China. Their role, however, was not decisive for the history of the era. Yet they too represent a failed opportunity on the part of the Yuan court. Strategically, if the court had been able to build political alignments between them and the two most important bandit-rebels in the same part of China, Zhang Shicheng in Suzhou and Fang Guozhen in Zhejiang, bringing them all into closer cooperation with the still powerful provincial government based at Hangzhou (the former Southern Song capital), they might have accomplished much. Both of those rebel leaders, having no ideological commitment to sectarian rebellion, accepted titles and honors from the court in the 1360s and nominally at least became legitimate holders of regional power in the eyes of many of their subjects. Hangzhou had remained a particularly strong and important base of Yuan power, second only to the capital region, and the provincial officials there were given the intermediary role in negotiations among all the parties. Such an idea, if ever clearly conceived in Dadu, was in any event not skillfully followed through; both Zhang Shicheng and Fang Guozhen shifted their postures back to open rebellion. They soon lost out to the Ming forces nearby. Again, the Yuan government had failed to use its resources effectively and, after decades of such failure, allowed its domestic enemies to overtake it.

Sectarian Rebels Fragment the Yuan Dynasty

The outbreak of sectarian revolt in 1351 triggered widespread rebellion in several provinces a dozen years after the first emergence of minor social disorders caused by clandestine religious movements. The Red Turban movement, whose beginnings are described in Section II, does not account for all incidents of sectarian rebellion, but it was by far the largest element among those outbreaks. The roles played by its three geographically separated major divisions displayed distinct characteristics and had their separate histories; those will be briefly recounted here.

Undeterred by the capture and execution of Han Shantong in 1351, in 1355 his reassembled followers under the leadership of Liu Futong declared that they had restored the Song dynasty (defunct for three-quarters of a century). From that point onward, the story of the northern Red Turbans is essentially the story of Liu Futong. Liu was wildly ambitious, a decisive field commander but not an effective organizer. He made himself the chief minister to the "Young Prince of Radiance," who now doubled as the lineal descendant of the Song emperors and the spiritually anointed successor to his father's sectarian movement.

A fairly elaborate governing structure was set up at the new Red Turban capital, at Anfeng in Anhui; coins were minted, military commands were authorized, and officials appointed.[19] Nonetheless, it remained a weakly organized base on which to build a successor state, and it included many second-tier military leaders who remained virtually autonomous and would not subordinate themselves to an overall policy. Their potent armies roamed across the countryside, throughout much of North China and even into Manchuria, where one branch sacked the Yuan summer capital at Shangdu and sought alliance with forces in Korea. All the Red Turban field armies relied on pillaging and looting to support their forces, and their rapid successes thoroughly upset the Yuan governments' regional order.

Their depredations provoked Chaghan Temür in neighboring Henan to assume command of his province's defenses, and eventually also to combat the rebels in the east, in Shandong. In 1357 Liu Futong took the step of laying siege to Kaifeng, the provincial capital of Henan, then to capture it in 1358 to relocate his figurehead boy "Song Emperor" there. The potent symbolism of a rebel emperor sitting on a throne in an imperial palace in the former Song capital became too ominous for Chaghan's comfort. In 1359 he raised a large army to attack and capture Kaifeng, but Liu and the boy emperor, along with most of their government, escaped and returned to Anfeng.

Liu Futong made little further progress after that, although he continued to control a significant base region. In 1363 Zhang Shicheng, temporarily cooperating with the Yuan court and trying to embarrass the future Ming founder, sent his leading field commander to surround Anfeng and destroy the Song rebel state. It is likely that Liu Futong was killed in that fighting, but Zhang's army took the Young Prince of Radiance to nearby Luzhou, an important prefectural city a hundred miles to the south, to be held captive there. That forced Zhu Yuanzhang, for reasons I shall explain, to go to the rescue. The following month Zhu in person led a rescue force, accompanied by his two leading field generals, captured Luzhou, and took the boy emperor and his mother and other family members to Chuzhou, a city near the Yangzi not far from Zhu's base at Nanjing. With Liu Futong eliminated, Zhu Yuanzhang became the protector of the northern Red Turban rebellious movement's symbolic head, and its most important figure. Apart from Zhu and his Nanjing base area, little else of the northern Red Turbans remained by the mid-1360s.

The southern Red Turbans, based in Hubei on the central Yangzi, followed quite a different course of development. Once news of Han Shantong's and Liu Futong's 1351 uprising in Anhui reached Peng Yingyu (Monk Peng) and his followers, they too rose up in rebellion; before the end of 1351 they had named as their emperor Xu Shouhui, an impressive-appearing cloth peddler with no significant abilities other than to impersonate an imperial figure. His dynasty was called Tianwan and its first capital was at Qishui, near the Yangzi and fifty miles or so east of Hankou. That rebellion too spread like wildfire. In the spring of the following year its armies attacked Hanyang and Wuchang (components of the present-day city of Wuhan) on opposite banks of the Yangzi and soon controlled much of Central China. The armies extended through Hunan and Jiangsi eastward into the coastal provinces, where for a few months they occupied Hangzhou. They were soon driven out as the local Yuan government armies regained the city, but they remained a very strong force with a large base.

At the beginning, the southern Red Turbans were more zealous in support of their religious doctrines than were their northern counterpart, and at the same time were more tightly organized, but as in all of the contenders' organizations, dissidence appeared among the leading figures. In 1357 one of them tried to murder Xu Shouhui and was in turn murdered by another general, Chen Youliang, who quickly made himself the master of the movement. Chen was the son of a poor fisherman, but he had acquired enough literacy to serve as a government clerk. In 1359 Chen moved the Tianwan capital to Jiangzhou on the Yangzi (the present-day city of Jiujiang in Jiangxi), well downriver from Hankou, the better to prepare for the showdown with the other rebel movements in the lower Yangzi. The following year he murdered the useless Xu Shouhui, changed the dynastic name to Han, and proclaimed himself its emperor.

This new rebel Han dynasty, with large naval forces on the Yangzi and its tributaries and strong land forces on both banks of the Yangzi, became a very powerful state. Chen Youliang was an able administrator and a formidable strategist; his serious fault was that he had an impatient temperament and undertook his moves in haste. He pressed relentlessly downriver to the east against his main rival, Zhu Yuanzhang, based at Nanjing.

Zhu's territories were not as large or as rich, and Zhu was squeezed between two strong opponents, Chen Youliang to his west and Zhang Shicheng, with whom he shared a common boundary to his east. The fact that both Chen and Zhu represented parts of the larger Red Turban movement, and thus were brothers in religion, meant little to either. The religious zeal of the earlier phase of southern Red Turban history disappeared with Chen Youliang's rise, and Zhu appears to have easily shaken off his earlier commitment to the Red Turban doctrines. At the level of their leadership these two sectarian rebellions had become secular, even while they continued to keep up appearances of religious devotion to avoid alienating a large bloc of their followers.

For some years the three rivals, based on segments of the Yangzi drainage—Zhu at Nanjing, Chen in the central Yangzi, and Zhang downriver at Suzhou—concentrated on building up their three base areas. They planned and plotted, watched for opportunities to enhance their positions, and prepared for their inevitable showdown. The Yuan court still held the legitimacy card, and there was a possibility that Kökö Temür, though at this time very busy with his war against Bolod in Shanxi, also might at some point take a hand. Yet it appeared unlikely that a real challenge would come from a fourth player.

The turning point was a great naval battle between Zhu and Chen fought on Boyang Lake in Jiangxi, near Jiujiang, in 1363.[20] Victory could have gone to either side, although Chen's stronger forces and his aggressive stance employing more daring and impetuous tactics might seem to have favored him. Zhu Yuanzhang nonetheless won the battle and captured or destroyed most of the enemies' forces; in doing so he terminated the rival Han dynasty and with it the southern Red Turban movement.

The third Red Turban base of military significance was that of Ming Yuzhen, who broke off from the Tianwan dynasty after hearing that Chen Youliang had gained controlling power there. He had been assigned to extend Tianwan power upriver into Sichuan. He occupied Chongqing in 1357, and in

1359, on learning that Chen Youliang had murdered Xu Shouhui, he declared himself an independent king, then in 1361 elevated himself to emperor, calling his new state the Xia dynasty. He gained control over all of the large province of Sichuan and extended his boundaries into Shaanxi in the North, and into Yunnan to the South. He refused all contact with Chen and the Central China Han dynasty of the Red Turbans, and maintained diplomatic relations with Zhu Yuanzhang, but he was not a player in the contest for mastery of China in the years that followed. He died in 1366 and was succeeded by a son, but his movement fell prey to leadership struggles and, after valiant defense efforts, had to surrender to invading Ming forces in 1371.

Ming Yuzhen is nonetheless one of the period's most interesting figures. The son of a farmer in central Hubei, he had received a little education. When the disorders attendant on the outbreaks in 1351 came to Hubei, his village elders appealed to him to head their hastily organized self-defense militia. A sturdy and resolute young man of twenty, he well deserved the confidence of his village neighbors, for he proved to be a natural leader who quickly displayed military skills of a high order. His original intent was merely to defend his home community from the disorders, but when the Tianwan emperor sent him word that he must take sides, he joined the Red Turban movement and moved rapidly up the ladder of military promotions. Boatmen coming downriver from Sichuan told him about the sad state of affairs in that once-rich province, badly damaged by warfare and poor governing in Yuan times, and now suffering from local wars among rival gangs. They told him that Chongqing was undefended and could easily be taken; probably they served as his guides in the campaign to conquer Sichuan for the Tianwan dynasty in the late 1350s.

In Sichuan he proved himself to be a man with interesting ideas about social and ethical issues. He banned the Buddhist and Daoist establishments and made a state religion of the Maitreya worship, ordering shrines built in all counties. It is likely that his surname was not Ming, the same word that is translated "radiance" in the Manichaean title of the northern Red Turban Little Prince of Radiance (Xiao Ming Wang); originally it was probably the more standard surname Min. He apparently changed his name to express his commitment to what was, in his understanding, Maitreyan doctrine about the imminent triumph of light over darkness. At the same time, he was quite susceptible to guidance in statecraft from Confucian scholar-official advisers; he set up examinations, changed official titles to correspond to antique models, encouraged frugality, lowered taxes, and sought to restore security to the ordinary people's lives.[21] He was a self-proclaimed man of humble farming background who explained that he had been forced into a leadership role to aid the suffering people; in many ways his responses to the challenges of leadership paralleled Zhu Yuanzhang's serious acceptance of responsibility in the early years of his rise to power. His efforts to rehabilitate Sichuan, although peripheral to the main flow of history, deserve further study.[22] His Xia state is one additional example of the varieties of political leadership that emerged from the lowest levels of fourteenth-century Chinese society.

Zhu Yuanzhang, the future Ming emperor, offers a still more striking example.

iv. Zhu Yuanzhang, Boy to Young Man

I have briefly introduced Zhu Yuanzhang in his role as Red Turban regional leader and contender for the role of new dynastic founder who would bring Mongol rule to an end. He will be the focus of succeeding chapters on the creation of the Ming dynasty. But first, an account of his boyhood, in the form of excerpts translated from an outstanding work of historical writing, may bring us closer to the lives of ordinary people at the end of the Yuan dynasty. The excerpts that follow are translated from the first three chapters of Wu Han's 1965 *Biography of Zhu Yuanzhang (Zhu Yuanzhang zhuan)*.[23]

Chapter One: The Young Buddhist Novice

Through the first half of the fourth year of the Zhizheng reign period of the Yuan emperor Shun [1344, the Yuan emperor Shun, Toghon Temür's twelfth year on the throne], the people of the Huai River drainage suffered grave disasters: drought, locusts, and on top of all that, plague.

For many months there had been no rain. Grain seedlings were scorched dry and yellowed; fields showed cracks like the patterns on a tortoise's shell. It was obvious that there would be no harvest, and no one could think of any way to manage. Everywhere people were beseeching the gods to make it rain, urging the Dragon King to manifest his divine powers. Old people wearing white linen shirts, barefoot, knelt ever so reverently in the hot sun, kowtowing to the Dragon King to grant their wish. Children wearing on their heads crowns of twisted dry willow twigs were running in and out of the Buddhist temple; the blowing of high-pitched horns and the beating of gongs and drums shook the heavens, and all the monks wore wide-eyed smiles [to see all the donations brought them]. After days upon days of such supplications, the sun still blazed fiery hot and not even a tiny trace of cloud appeared. The farming people were like ants frantically twirling in a hot pan. And then came the locusts filling the skies. They quickly devoured the tiny heads trying to form on the millet stalks. All those in the locality who had lived the longest said they had survived to their great age without ever having seen such a year. There seemed no way to live through times like these . . .

Without warning, in the way that disasters never come singly, in the wake of the drought next came the plague. In Haozhou County (today's Fengyang in Anhui) the people living in Zhongli village of Taiping township were taken sick in droves. People who had already been subsisting on grass and tree bark for days collapsed as soon as they contracted the disease. At first they felt their bodies weakening, then developed high fevers coupled with vomiting and diarrhea, and in no more than two or three days they stopped breathing. At first people couldn't understand it. But when it spread into a village and in one day a dozen or several dozen people would die, people dying in every household, continuing on with more dying every day, they realized that it was a contagious epidemic. Terror began to overtake them. Never mind that old saying, "When your time is up there is no escape"; it was imperative to flee, and in every village people carrying and leading their little ones fled like streams of ants, going to the homes of relatives and friends farther away. In no more than ten days' time all the ten or so villages in Taiping township were virtually deserted; no smoke came from the chimneys, all the crowing of chickens and barking of dogs stilled—a scene of chilling desolation.

In Guzhuang village, in the house of Zhu Wusi, in less than half a month three persons died. Zhu Wusi, the father, was sixty-four years old; he died on the sixth day of the fourth month. On the ninth his eldest son, Zhu Chongsi, also died, and on the twenty-second Zhu Wusi's wife, Chen Erniang, died too. Their second son, called Chongliu, and the youngest son, Yuanzhang (also called Chongba, later changed to Xingzhong), saw their elders die one after the other before their eyes. They couldn't afford to call in a doctor, nor could they lay their hands on any medicines; all the two could do was shed their bitter tears together. The worst thing was that the corpses were still lying there in the house; they didn't have so much as a single paper note or a crumb of silver, so couldn't afford coffins, and yet just to leave them there was unthinkable. No matter what, they simply had to come by a plot of ground where the dead could be buried.

But a plot of ground? They didn't own so much as one hand-spread of land. They thought about it, back and forth, again and again; the only way was to go and plaintively beg their landlord, Liu De. They reminded him that for a number of years the family had been in the landlord-tenant relationship with him, had never been late with rent, nor ever had been in any kind of trouble; now that it had come to this pressing need for a bit of ground, shouldn't he be able to grant a small favor? Who would have guessed that not only would he say no, but they would have to bear his vicious cursing as well. They were totally at a loss. What should they do next?

Then their neighbors, the elderly couple Liu Daxiu and his wife, Lou Daniang, came to the door complaining that when the two brothers needed help, how was it they had not come to old Uncle Liu but had first gone to seek out someone else? And all for nothing! The fact was that Liu Daxiu's youngest son, Liu Ying, was a playmate of Zhu Yuanzhang's, his good friend, and he had just been at Liu De's house, where he saw Zhu Yuanzhang and his brother wailing and weeping. It made him so sad that he went home and told his parents. Liu Daxiu and Zhu Wusi had been next-door neighbors and members of the same tithing community [i.e., the agrarian tax organization]; moreover they were about the same age, got along well, exchanged small talk. So when their son Liu Ying came to tell them what had happened, the couple put their heads together and came right over to look in on the two boys. Zhu Yuanzhang and his brother immediately knelt down to kowtow to them and express their gratitude; it appeared that the problem of a grave plot had been solved.

But as for burial garments, as for coffins, there still was no solution in sight, and there would be no other place to turn for help. They would simply have to wrap the bodies in a few worn-out old garments, get a carrying pole, and transport the bodies over to the Liu's field for burial. The two brothers with the carrying pole, weeping as they shouldered the load, struggled with great effort to get the bodies moved to the foot of the hillock. Then suddenly a strong storm blew up. Thunder flashed and lightening roared. It seemed as if the whole sky was falling down upon them. The two brothers crouched under a tree, shivering. After a short time the rain passed and the sky cleared. When they went back to the foot of the hill to look, they were startled by what they saw: the corpses had disappeared. The soil on the hillside was loose, and the sudden downpour had washed it down in a rush of water and mud. Just at the place where the bodies had lain waiting, a thick mound of earth had been formed. In everyday speech that went by the name "Heaven burial." Thirty-five years later, when Zhu Yuanzhang composed his "Imperial Tombs Inscription," he still felt grieved at heart remembering that day: "Buried without inner or outer coffins, the bodies wrapped in worn old garments, placed in a scant three-foot grave, and what ceremonial offerings could we make?"

For some days more Zhu Yuanzhang survived on grass and tree bark. A neighbor woman, Wang Daniang, and her son saw how alone and pitiable he was and often invited him in for meals, and so he scraped by for a time. But he realized this could not go on much longer and decided to try going door to door seeking odd jobs; but of course the better-off families all had fled the drought and plague, while all the poor households were, like him, also starving, so how could they hire anyone? He hustled that way for several more days and everywhere ran into blank walls. One day, returning from the neighboring village where he had been looking for work, he was coming home along the road that ran past his parents' graves. He didn't need to hurry on home, so sat down beside the graves to give serious thought to his problems and think how to meet the insistent demands of the stomach.

He was a tall and husky fellow with a dark complexion, high skull ridge and large nose, big ears and bushy eyebrows over large eyes. His chin protruded quite a bit farther out than his forehead. His face, overall, resembled a three-dimensional *shan* (mountain) character lying on its side, while a prominent bulge on his skull rose up like a small hill. Although his appearance was anything but handsome it was quite compelling, giving the impression that he was both awesome and profound. Anyone who met him once would never forget his odd features . . . (pp. 1–5)

When he was small he had once attended the class of a primary school teacher for a few months. On the one hand, he was fond of play, and on the other, at busy times he had to work in the fields, so he had never really spent a full day properly studying. Yet he had a good memory and had been able to learn a few hundred characters, but even so he was not prepared to take on any kind of clerical work, nor could he write letters or contracts. His father had moved to this village in the first place because there was so much unused land in the locality and a shortage of human labor. It seemed one might be able to make a somewhat better living there. He had not counted on the truism that "all the world's ravens are equally black"; the more land a land-owner possessed, the harder his heart and the stingier his treatment of his tenant farmers. On the three major festivals they had to make gifts, and the rents had to be paid on schedule, while he smilingly manipulated the weights and measures to his advantage, all the time complaining that the moisture content of the grain was too high and that his share of the crop was not enough. In a year like the present one it was an extraordinary act of grace to be granted a small temporary reduction in the amount owed; how would one dare to utter a word requesting a loan to get through the crisis? . . . (pp. 7–8)

As for members of his own more immediate family, all the nearer and far-ther ones, no matter how hard he thought it over, there was no one to whose home he could now go. So, were there any other places to which he might turn? . . . (p. 8)

[Zhu Yuanzhang recollected the vivid impressions gained when he was very young of his maternal grandfather, then a very old man, apparently somewhat literate, who had been a professional fortune-teller and seer, and who had told him stories about his experiences with the Song armies fleeing the Mongols in 1279, all the way to the end; he had been with the fleet carrying the last boy emperor, who perished when pursued out to sea, off the coast of present-day Hong Kong, by the Mongol army and navy, and himself had narrowly escaped drowning. Zhu grew up hearing his mother's frequent retelling of the story of the Mongol conquest, and the spirit of Song loyalism made a deep impression on the young Zhu. The old grandfather, who lived to the age of ninety-nine, had long been dead. There was no possibility of seeking help now from his mother's family, if any still survived.]

The wife in the neighboring Wang family knew that Zhu Chongliu [the elder of the two surviving brothers] worried about his younger brother, so reminded them that some years earlier [Zhu's father] Zhu Wusi had made a pledge at Huangjue Temple, offering his young son to Monk Gao Bin to serve him as his novice. Why not go there now and take up the life of a monk? That would, on the one hand, repay the pledge once made, and on the other, it would provide a daily meal, if only a bowl of plain rice. Wouldn't that be preferable to starving? Zhu's older brother agreed.

As a baby Zhu Yuanzhang had frequently been ill. In the first three or four days after he was born he couldn't take his mother's milk, and his distended stomach had swelled up to look like a tightly stretched drum. He was close to being beyond help. Zhu Wusi was distraught, thinking of all possible ways to save the child. Then he had a dream in which he saw the child slipping away beyond all help, and thinking that only a Bodhisattva could save him, he decided to give the child to a temple. He instantly picked up the baby and ran off with it, entering a large temple where, curiously, not a single monk was to be found. Unable to make any contact, he had no choice but to take the child back home. Then, hearing a child crying, Zhu Wusi awakened from the dream. His child truly was crying and its mother was nursing it; it now was able to take the milk, and in a few days its swollen belly was cured. But as the child grew, he was continually afflicted by ailments that were never overcome. His worried parents, remembering the dream, really took him off to the temple and made a pledge to give him up, eventually, to become a monk.

The Wangs, husband and wife, got together for Zhu Yuanzhang some incense, candles, some other small offerings, and approached Monk Gao Bin about the matter. Consequently, in the ninth month, the Huangjue Temple gained a new young novice. Zhu's head was shaved clean like a gourd. A worn cassock discarded by an older novice was given to him to wear. Whenever he met anyone he learned to press his palms together and bow. He had truly become a disciple of the Lord Buddha. He swept floors, set up the incense for lighting, rang the bells, beat the drums, cooked the rice, and washed the robes; those were his daily lessons. On meeting persons from within the temple, he would address them "master teacher," "teacher older brother," or "teacher mother" [implying cynically that the monks were not necessarily celibate], and when he encountered persons from outside, he addressed them "gracious donor"; all his ways of addressing people had to be learned anew. Morning and night, when he heard the bells and the drums and the "wooden fish" [the wooden cadence drum struck while chanting sutras] and the sounds of chanting, his thoughts turned to himself and to the lively household in which he had lived only a short time before, and he thought about his bereaved and sole surviving next-elder brother and about his group of young friends, all of whom had been forced to go away to seek some means of livelihood, and in his heart he was deeply uneasy. (p. 10)

Chapter Two: The Wandering Monk

Huangjue Temple was dependent on its rents to maintain itself. This year the scale of the natural disasters was too great. It collected no rents, though the monks went constantly to their tenants' houses to try to collect, arguing, threatening, saying that if they were not paid, the debtors would be taken off to the magistrate's office to be punished, even beaten; but that was of no avail. The temple's stocks of rice, one could clearly see, would not last many more days. The more mouths, the greater the outlay; the head monk's wife [!] suggested a plan: first send out all the single monks to wander abroad, then send out all the senior monks of the temple to roam about, depending on voluntary offerings. Zhu Yuanzhang had served as a novice a scant fifty days, but finally he too was sent out, the last to go. He had no choice. Unable to chant sutras and conduct Buddhist ceremonies, he could only pose as a monk. Wearing a tattered bamboo hat, carrying a "wooden fish" and an earthenware bowl, a small pack on his back, he bid farewell to his master and to the temple's head monk and, trying to firm up his resolve, took grim leave of his home village.

What was called "wandering about" or "roaming everywhere" was a monk's term; it was also called "seeking donations." In the language of ordinary people, however, it was just begging. It meant asking for food, finding a rich household and asking for money or for something to eat . . . (p. 13)

Zhu Yuanzhang had lived in the temple for only a few weeks, but he had heard the daily conversations about the business of begging, and he had observed it being done, so even if he did not know how, he understood how to go about it. And since he had no choice but to do it, he sought out people for advice, where it would be best to go. Hearing that conditions this year were somewhat better to the south and the west, so because his only objective was to get enough food to survive, it did not matter much to him just where he went. Nor did he have any schedule. He walked as long as he wanted to walk, went as far as he wanted to go . . . He learned all the tricks of begging, how to sleep in the mountains and in the wilds and to bear all the discomforts of wind and cold. He walked all through the Huaixi region [today's eastern Henan and western Anhui], seeing its famous capitals and great towns, becoming intimately familiar with this region's rivers and streams, its mountain ranges, its geographic features. Most important, he got close to the population of the area, understood the feelings of the people, learned about products, customs, beliefs. He encountered the face of life, he broadened his mental horizons, he came to understand and to learn about innumerable things. It enriched his knowledge of society and at the same time it tested and toughened him physically . . . (pp. 13–14)

The Huaixi region through which Zhu Yuanzhang roamed for several years was precisely the region in which the subsequent founding figure of the western [or southern] Red Turbans, Peng Yingyu, lived secretly at this time, actively propagating the teachings about the Maitreya Buddha's imminent descent to earth and organizing his revolutionary [sic; "rebellious"] forces. Peng Yingyu also was a wandering monk, and even if Zhu Yuanzhang may never have met him in person, he certainly must have encountered some of Monk Peng's followers. Some years later this same region would become the eastern [or northern] Red Turban army's base area; those seeds also were sown by Monk Peng. Zhu Yuanzhang wandered widely for three or four years throughout the entire region, living with the lowest stratum of society; he accepted the new sectarian teachings, the new ways of thought, the new political education, and became a member of their secret organization. He was a novice who had matured both in mind and in body. After his return to Huangjue Temple, as he began to form friendships, he made a point of seeking out those of strong will and courage, stout fellows who dared to take action. He frequently went into Haozhou city [the county seat, very close by] to ferret out information. At the same time, he determined to improve his literacy, to read some books, to understand more of how things work, preparing to go forth eventually to do great things. (pp. 14–15)

Chapter Three: The Red Turban Uprising

In the fifth month of the eleventh year of Yuan emperor Shun's Zhizheng reign period (1351), throughout the whole region of the Yangzi and Huai river drainages the poor farming folk . . . in their short coats and straw sandals, wearing their red headbands and carrying red banners, shouldering their bamboo staves and their hoes, and with long spears and axes, killed the officials, occupied the cities, opened granaries to distribute the stored grain, battered down jails and freed prisoners, set up their own names and titles—they sounded the death knell of the Yuan dynasty. All this is what was done by the historic Red Turban armies' uprisings . . . (p. 22)

At the temple [in 1351] Zhu Yuanzhang continually received news from the outside. "A few days earlier the Red Turban armies had occupied Xiangyang [in northern Hubei] and the Yuan forces suffered large losses." "Another field force occupied Nankang [in Jiangxi, south of the Yangzi], and the Yuan forces fled without fighting." " 'Sesame Seed' Li and Community Chief Zhao, in a group of eight men, all dressed up like workers on the Yellow River dredging project; in one evening's effort they captured Xuzhou [the important city of northern Jiangsu]." The persons delivering these news items reported them with great excitement . . . A few days later came the news that Xu Shouhui had set up his capital at Qishui [in southern Hubei], where he was now the emperor of a dynasty called Tianwan, with the reign period name "Zhiping." He had appointed Zou Pusheng his Grand Preceptor, while armies under Monk Peng and Xiang Nu'er were fighting their way eastward into Jiangxi. Yuan armies were being defeated everywhere; with difficulty the government had mobilized 6,000 Muslim Asud cavalry [units of the Yuan armies from Inner Asia] along with a few units of Chinese soldiers to advance against the Red Turban army based at Yingshang [in the Huaixi region]. The Asud were known for their ferocity and their skills as mounted archers; their discipline was bad, however, and everywhere they went they looted and robbed. A number of their generals overindulged in wine and women; so their minds were clouded as they were on the point of drawing up their ranks to oppose the Red Turbans. Then they saw how large the Red Turban army's deployment was and were overcome with fear. Their chief general raised his whip and turned his horse to the rear, shouting: "Abu, abu!" "Abu" means "Run for it!" The whole army immediately turned and retreated. The Red Turbans pressed forward, and the Yuan army was ground up. Throughout the Huai region the people all told about that battle as a great joke; everywhere people all knew about it . . . (p. 45)

In the second month of 1352 Zhu Yuanzhang heard that nearby Haozhou also had been occupied by the Red Turban army; the leaders there were Guo Zixing, Sun Deyai, and a group including men named Yu, Zeng, and Pan.

Guo Zixing was a famous local bravo from Dingyuan County [in Anhui]. The family originally had come from Caozhou [in Shandong]. Guo's father had come to Haozhou as a fortune-teller and seer. There was a landlord there who had a blind daughter with no prospects for getting married. Guo Zixing's father had married her, gained a rich dowry, and had three sons by her, of whom Guo Zixing was the second. The three bothers were clever at calculations, buying goods when cheap and selling dear, buying land, and opening shops. Within the space of ten or twenty years they were among, if not the wealthiest landlords in the locality . . . Angered [by officials' constant slights and demands for money], Guo Zixing joined the Maitreya sectarians, freely dispersed his riches to gain an armed following, took in all the toughs and roughnecks, burned incense and held secret meetings, and waited for the day when he could take the big step toward getting even. After the great Red Turban uprisings, the farmers from Zhongli, Dingyuan, and other nearby places shouldered their hoes and mattocks, and in one sudden wave men gathered by the tens of thousands. Local officials who ordinarily were concerned only about demanding money were now faced with a situation they could not handle, so pretended they were not aware of anything, couldn't be bothered, and in any event need not meddle. On the twenty-seventh of the second month, Guo Zixing, leading several thousand men, under cover of darkness and by prearranged signal from cohorts within, stealthily entered Haozhou; in the middle of the night, when a signal cannon was fired, they burst through the gates of the county office, killed the magistrate, and with previously negotiated orders from Du Zundao [a higher-level Red Turban leader] the five leaders of this insurrection all received titles of Haozhou Defense Commanders . . . (pp. 46–47)

[One day when Zhu Yuanzhang was away, government troops, suspecting links between the temple's monks and the Maitreya sectarian rebels, burned the temple. On returning and finding the smoldering ruins, he at last decided to run off and join the rebels at Haozhou under Guo Zixing, from which place one of his childhood friends recently had written to urge Zhu to join them.]

The next day he left Huangjue Temple and went to join the Red Turbans. This year [1352] Zhu Yuanzhang was twenty-four years old. (pp. 48–49)

22

ZHU YUANZHANG BUILDS
HIS MING DYNASTY

The momentous founding of the Ming dynasty is intimately bound up in the personal history and the changing character of Zhu Yuanzhang, known formally as Ming Taizu, its founding emperor. Coming from the lower depths of destitute rural society, he had unusual physical and mental capacities that led to his rapid rise to leadership in the Red Turban rebel movement, then to his transformation of his role into that of an emperor on the model of the Han dynasty founder 1,500 years earlier. For reasons variously explained, under the great stresses of the imperial role he was further transformed into a tyrannical despot. It is the transformed ruler who is reflected in the enduring form and style of Ming dynasty government. The enigma of Zhu Yuanzhang, probed at the end of this chapter, remains one of the intriguing puzzles of Chinese history.

1. LEARNING TO BE AN EMPEROR

He had still not passed his twenty-fourth birthday when, in the second month of 1352, Zhu Yuanzhang fled the burned-out monastery where he had been preparing to become a monk, to join the rebels at nearby Haozhou. It is said that his unusual appearance and demeanor attracted Guo Zixing, the first of the Red Turban commanders who saw him, when Zhu appeared at the gates of Haozhou saying that he had come to join the rebellion. He was immediately assigned to serve as a squad leader, a humble corporal in charge of ten soldiers doing the bidding of Guo, a rebel defense commander who gladly became his sponsor. Guo was then hard-pressed by the discord among the five defense commanders heading the base's unwieldy administration. He had need of reliable men.

Zhu found a number of his former village friends serving there in the rebel army. He soon was able to form a military unit under his leadership around a group of twenty-four of them, and made that his personal army corps. It quickly expanded because he proved to be an able leader. Within a year he was a rising star, frequently leading attacks on neighboring strongholds and often winning engagements through his sharp sense of battlefield tactics. Equally adept, it would seem, at domestic tactics, he married Guo Zixing's adopted daughter, whose own surname was Ma. Becoming the son-in-law reinforced Guo's support of Zhu, as well as Zhu's loyalty to Commander Guo. Such considerations aside, the bond of affection between Zhu Yuanzhang and his bride appears to have been genuine. Years later, as the Empress Ma, she played an important role in the imperial household.

Zhu soon found that the strife-ridden atmosphere of the Haozhou base was too troublesome for comfort. While loyally supporting Guo Zixing in his conflicts with the other commanders, he increasingly struck out on his own in more distant raids that gained stores and drew in soldier recruits personally loyal to himself. Late in 1353 Zhu took his personal band of troops off to the southeast, his objective being to capture the walled administrative town of Chuzhou, not far north of the Yangzi. His force soon would number between 20,000 and 30,000 men, many recruited or captured and trained by himself.

Zhu's First Elite Advisers

When he struck out on his own early in the summer of 1353, Zhu headed a force still numbering only a few hundred men. His progress southward toward Chuzhou brought him first into Dingyuan County. There a local man named Li Shanchang (1314–1390) called on him. Zhu had been told about Li, an educated man who studied the writings of the ancient Legalist statecraft thinkers and dealt in prognostication theories. That made him a somewhat marginal figure in the eyes of the local scholars and officials.[1] Zhu and Li hit it off very well. Zhu invited Li to take over the secretarial and staff management duties of his field command, and found him an energetic and able assistant.

On their first meeting Zhu had asked Li Shanchang when their long-troubled world might again be at peace. Li is said to have delivered a short lecture on history, summarized in his official biography in the *Ming History*. The purport was that the founder of the Han dynasty, Emperor Gaozu, like Zhu, had risen up from commoner status *(buyi)*, but had been magnanimous, quick to learn, wise in selecting aides, and humane in avoiding killing. Zhu, he said, had those fine qualities and could do the same.[2] In Li Shanchang, Zhu had found the first of his preceptors, and he was given the potent historical precedent of the great Han dynasty's founding emperor on which to model himself. Comparisons of himself with the Han founder and of the new Ming dynasty with the glorious Han (206 B.C.E.–220 C.E.) subsequently became a theme of the court and its historians.

At about the same time Zhu also met the Feng brothers, Feng Sheng and Feng Guoyong, a small landowner's sons who had received some schooling. They too became part of his entourage and won his full trust. Their advice also stressed that Zhu was different from the other rebel leaders in that his goals were higher than mere plunder. Feng advised Zhu: "Jinling [present-day Nanjing] is at the place where the dragon coils and the tiger crouches, a past capital of kings and emperors; if you capture it as your base, you can then go forth in conquest from it in all directions, and championing benevolence and righteousness you will capture the hearts of the people. If you display no avarice for plunder, the realm can be readily pacified."[3] This was typical of Confucian-minded advice in its stress on "benevolence and righteousness," yet it also planted in Zhu's mind the concept of capturing Nanjing in order to identify with all the historical symbolism of "coiling dragon and crouching tiger," symbolism very close to the popular imagination, as well as pointing out to Zhu the strategic advantages of its location.

Late in 1353 Zhu's rapidly growing forces enabled him to attack and capture the small walled town of Chuzhou. This became his staging base. His forces continued to grow rapidly. He remained at Chuzhou through 1354 and 1355, bringing his father-in-law, the embattled Guo Zixing, there to ensure his safety. Before dying there in 1355, Guo named Zhu his chief of staff. No doubt on Guo's recommendation, from its base at Anfeng the Red Turban court also gave its young field commander high titles and honors. Zhu continued to expand his territories north of the Yangzi.

Then, near the end of 1355, he undertook the daring step of crossing the Yangzi to attack the metropolis of Nanjing, the largest city in the region and a bastion of Yuan power. He was unsuccessful in that first attack; but, remaining on the south bank, he withdrew to the prefectural town of Taiping, a short distance to the southwest. There he wintered while preparing for a renewed attempt. A local eminence named Tao An led several Confucian scholar-officials to greet him, and Zhu was pleased by their cordial gesture of welcome.

Tao An had passed the Yuan *jinshi* examinations fifteen years earlier and had served in local government but had been forced by the worsening social conditions of late Yuan to retire from office. He talked to Zhu about the real problems of local government as seen from the administrator's side, and he too praised Zhu for being different from the other rebel leaders in disciplining his troops and in genuinely winning the support of the populace. He also urged Zhu to seize Nanjing and make it his base. Zhu took him into his growing secretariat of literati advisers.[4]

The official record, on which the foregoing is based, probably has embroidered the topic of Zhu's earnest attentiveness to Confucian advisers, and in particular has perhaps overstated the degree to which his troops were well disciplined and forbidden to steal from or abuse the people. That became the official image of Zhu that his dynasty's historians were encouraged to promote. Even discounting for such exaggeration, the larger record makes it clear that his good reputation was in significant measure deserved. Scholar-officials who praised his genuine concern for the people's well-being hoped this was so. They were assuming a role expected of Confucian scholars—to guide the holder of power toward socially responsible governing. They saw in Zhu a leader who had become important in the developing scheme of things and who, they may well have felt, was susceptible to their guidance.

In the spring of 1356 the second attack on Nanjing, accompanied by fierce fighting, was successful. One of Guo Zixing's two remaining sons, and Guo's brother-in-law, with both of whom some rivalry had developed, conveniently died in the fighting. That left Zhu Yuanzhang the unchallenged leader.[5] He changed Nanjing's name to Yingtian, meaning "In response to Heaven." He had acquired a growing corps of scholarly advisers. He regularly sought their advice, and they enthusiastically laid out the model of the Han founding emperor for him to follow.

Guo Zixing had remained a loyal supporter of the umbrella government of the northern Red Turbans, that is, the so-called restored "Song" dynasty under Han Shantong, the "Little Prince of Radiance," and of Liu Futong, Han's chief minister. Zhu supported those pretensions, and received ever higher titles and appointments from the "Song" court. But he was in fact increasingly independent of the Red Turban hierarchy; he professed loyalty to their rebellious doctrines while building a political movement of his own. Changing the Yuan name for Nanjing (then called Jiqing) to Yingtian, "In response to Heaven," was clearly a rebellious act, displaying his intention to claim the Mandate of Heaven. For the time, he was content to do that in the name of the Red Turban "Song" dynasty.

Zhu's elite advisers found that allegiance a continuing point of awkwardness in their support of him, and urged him to make a clean break with doctrines and modes of behavior to which few members of the elite could grant credence or respect. Zhu's problem with such elite disdain was not that it offended his personal sense of piety, although he probably was more genuinely in awe of the sectarians' religious claims than most present-day historians acknowledge.[6] Zhu's problem was that he knew that his soldiers and many of his officers accepted those doctrines and were loyal to Zhu because in their eyes he was the agent of the Little Prince of Radiance. It took Zhu a long time to establish a different claim on their loyalty; the Little Prince was in his direct care from 1363 onward (after Liu Futong was killed), and only in 1366, after the Little Prince was drowned in an "accident" while crossing the Yangzi to join Zhu in Nanjing, did Zhu believe that he could put his youthful sectarian affiliations behind him. His elite advisers, with whom he was ever more closely associated, were pleased by this development, but he was never sure that some of them did not slyly mock him for his lack of refinement.

The Military Component

It was the young Zhu Yuanzhang's nature to be serious; he pondered life's choices carefully and took action cautiously. At a time when a dozen upstarts like himself were claiming the title of emperor or were being pushed into it by their ambitious handlers, he began quite early on to examine the options. He set about to raise himself from low-ranking military captain in an ad hoc rebel organization into the ranks of the contenders fighting to found a new dynasty and become the real emperor of China.

One of the more interesting questions in fourteenth-century political history—some would say the most significant question—is how this untutored young man, with only the slightest exposure to the high cultural tradition, could develop the self-awareness to imagine himself as anything more than a rough-and-ready rebel captain, or at most a Red Turban commander. Personal ambition and the promise of immediate rewards of course motivated everybody in that situation. Zhu, however, began very early in his military career to set goals well beyond the desire for immediate rewards. He was significantly different from others among the "rival contenders" *(qunxiong)* who dominated the scene throughout the third quarter of the fourteenth century. He somehow found within himself the vision and the discipline that enabled him to cross the great distance separating the highest reaches attainable by a rebel mock emperor, and the vastly more elevated summit on which the Mandate of Heaven might come to rest. The questions about the means, the capacities, and the tools by which he accomplished that transformation continue to intrigue all who read history. The vision of imperial governing that he made his own in the process of growing into that role came to have very far-reaching significance: Zhu Yuanzhang established a strong and long-enduring dynasty—his Great Ming—that set the parameters of Chinese state politics from his time onward, well beyond the life of his dynasty. His elite civil advisers gave indispensable help as he worked out his vision of dynastic rule, but through the 1360s warfare continued to occupy most of Zhu Yuanzhang's time and his vast energy. His methodical rise to power was based entirely on his military successes; a historian who has led in the study of the military has summarized the situation: "Between 1352 and 1368 the Ming grew from a small rebel band to a new Chinese empire as a result of military victories against rival regimes of similar composition . . . [M]ilitary victory . . . alone could ensure the survival of the regime or permit territorial expansion or army reorganization."[7]

That well describes the essential fact about the beginnings of Ming history: Zhu Yuanzhang was a young warlord in the making, in competition with many others whose success in all cases was a consequence of their ability to attract followers, enlarge their armies by warfare or negotiation, plan strategies, and win victories in the field. Regrettably, the full historical account of battles and campaigns lies beyond our focus here.

We have no more than a few clues to explain Zhu Yuanzhang's success as a military leader. The Red Turban doctrines provided an appealing popular ideology and gave his soldiers a strong incentive to win. He drew heavily on that source of power in the beginning and, without alienating those to whom the doctrines continued to be important, gradually allowed his own purposes to take precedence. In his role as a military leader, he had a commanding physical presence. He was both courageous and calculating. He was a good judge of men. And he drew from a talent pool that was able to provide a remarkable number of skilled and eager associates. His rivals also had some of those qualities and benefited from similar conditions. Was he simply the luckiest of them, or is his success over all the rival contenders to be explained in some other way? The traditional sources, of course, read into this phase of history a preordained success, whether preternaturally interpreted or explained by extraordinary personal qualities. Now, more than six centuries later, how should we assess those issues?

China's normally unarmed, civilian-led society, as we have seen, underwent a process of militarization through the last half-century of the Yuan dynasty. "Militarization" as used here means that arms became widely present, and direct recourse to force came to be a norm in a society whose established patterns were quite different.[8] The militarization of the population had occurred only a few times in the past and would not again occur in the same degree in imperial history. It points to interesting facts about the latent capacities of Chinese society. China had lost most of its memory of having once had a warrior elite. More recent warrior heroes such as Yue Fei (1103–1142) had been mythologized to give them the qualities of scholar-officials, and the valiant leaders of Southern Song resistance at the time of the Mongol conquest, who provided the most recent images of Chinese military leaders, were indeed scholar-officials doubling as war leaders. Ideally, war was a sideline of civilian leaders.

In short, there was on the scene in mid–fourteenth-century China no proper element in society through which the skills to make war were transmitted; there was no European-style knighthood, no Japanese-style samurai class, no aristocratic warriors at court or high in society, no pattern of young men winning their spurs and going on to gain fame and glory and the love of a beautiful princess. That is the stuff of medieval European feudal society, and of its romantic carryovers in the later post-feudal institutions of upper-class military aristocrats. In China the elite were civilians who might temporarily double as defense commanders in times of extreme need. Normally they did not carry swords or own expensive suits of armor; they had other marks of status. They were expected at most to know a little about archery, which was learned as an adjunct to their preparation for the civil service examinations; but their careers did not depend on it.

One must ask, therefore, where the military skills resided in that society and how they were transmitted. Strategy was a field of learned study; there was a well-maintained tradition of bringing out new editions of the old military classics with the accumulation of later scholars' commentaries, but they were recondite books that soldiers may not have valued. Yue Fei himself, when chided by a learned superior for not studying them, said that they offered nothing he could use to win battles. He came from a background much like Zhu Yuanzhang's. Where had he acquired his unquestionable military skills? His biography says that in his teens, having decided he did not want to be a poor tenant farmer, he was taken in by a famed teacher of archery, probably an old soldier, and soon surpassed his teacher in archery and other modes of fighting. Some instruction in weapons and fighting techniques existed at sub-elite levels, dependent not on literacy but on old retired sergeants who knew how to do everything from using weapons in hand-to-hand combat to scaling walls and firing trebuchets and mortars. In times of disorder such persons might find themselves with many disciples from among the ordinary people. (For Yue Fei, see Chapter 13, Section II.)

In addition, there were the traditions of the stylized martial arts—known to us today by Asian names such as *taiji, taekwando,* and *karate*—often transmitted by teachers who may have been Buddhist monks or priests in the new Daoist sects. Skills in physical combat techniques associated with secret doctrines and hierarchies of master-disciple relationships grew in importance during periods of protracted lawlessness and disorder. The new Daoist sects that originated during Jin and late Song times, spread throughout China during the Yuan; they appear to have had links to the sectarian uprisings of the 1350s. Were they responsible for the emergence of so many first-class fighting men at that time? There is little evidence one way or the other.

As we examine the three possible sources of military knowledge and practical combat skills in Chinese society in the mid-fourteenth century—the scholarly study of the military classics; the teaching of combat skills by professional teachers, perhaps mostly retired common soldiers in the lower ranks of society; and the transmission of the martial arts in connection with secret doctrines—we do not find an adequate explanation for the sudden appearance of so many men from humble backgrounds who became brilliant generals and field marshals, or for the many thousands more who served as their very competent staff and field officers. How did a civilian farming society generate those individual skills and the military capacity to organize and use them effectively?

An obvious answer might seem to lie in the presence of the totally militarized Mongol conquerors. To be sure, the Yuan government attempted to keep the Mongol military establishment rigorously separate to prevent Chinese from gaining knowledge of how it functioned. Garrisons of Mongol cavalry were, however, present in many parts of the country, and officers drawn from them often commanded units of Chinese foot soldiers who fought with the Mongol cavalry. As the answer to our question, however, that does not bear up well under scrutiny: the Chinese armies of this period were led by men whose early careers show little or no interaction with the Mongol armies. There were exceptions such as Kökö Temür, who was part of the Mongol military system, and Chen Youding, who as a very young man served in a Mongol-led militia unit in Fujian; but both were on the Mongol side. There is no clear evidence that either the sectarian rebels or the bandit warlords adopted Mongol cavalry tactics or other Mongolian military techniques. Moreover, using their own military means, they repeatedly met and defeated the government's armies.

We have seen how the Jurchens within the space of a generation or two completely mastered the more advanced methods of warfare of the Khitans and then went on to obliterate the Khitan Liao state. The case in late Yuan China bears no significant resemblances to that. Most telling of all, after building the largest and most effective military machine and riding to imperial power on its back, Zhu Yuanzhang did not then create a military regime on the Inner Asian model; from the beginning he was determined to build the basis for a civilian government in which the military would be subordinate. The Mongol presence in China thus may explain something about sources of specific military skills, but it cannot count for much toward answering the large question about how China could so quickly produce a generation of highly skilled military leaders.

Zhu Yuanzhang's military associates all came out of the Huai region; most were from poor farming families like his own, and many were close to being illiterate. Tang He (1326–1395) had been a boyhood companion of Zhu's in their native village. Two years the elder, Tang left their village a year earlier to join Guo Zixing's uprising at Haozhou and welcomed Zhu when he arrived there in 1352. Zhu, who had achieved a kind of seniority by marrying Guo's stepdaughter, chose Tang to become one of his twenty-four military associates or staff officers as he began to organize his own independent force. Tang served capably and loyally and rose to positions of great responsibility on Zhu's staff. As Zhu's small but rapidly growing force moved south from Haozhou in 1353, along the way he encountered Xu Da (1332–1385), a soldier in an allied Red Turban army. Zhu immediately recognized Xu's extraordinary qualities and brought him under his command to become another member of the core group of twenty-four and eventually the preeminent military figure of the early Ming.[9]

Feng Sheng (1330–1395), rare among Zhu's command staff for having received some higher education, and his brother Feng Guoyong (1324–1359) had organized a local self-defense militia in their home community in response to the disorderly times. These two also joined Zhu when he passed through their locality in 1353. Feng Sheng had a long career as one of the new dynasty's leading generals. Although he initially served as one of Zhu's educated yet only marginally elite advisers, his military expertise appears to have evolved without benefit of any previous military experience—though he was considered an excellent archer.

As Zhu's forces moved farther to the south on the way to Chuzhou in 1353, other potential military leaders flocked to join him, all from poor farming households in his native region. Chang Yuchun (1330–1369) was the most brilliant general of all, feared for his aggressive attacks and as a superior tactician. He also came from a destitute village family in the Huai region, was forced into banditry to survive, but came over to Zhu voluntarily in 1355, seeing greater opportunities in serving under a rising leader.

In Anhui an area of marshes and lakes opening onto the Yangzi in the region called Lake Chao had long sheltered gangs of fishermen who also practiced piracy. Two of their leaders, the brothers Liao Yong'an (1320–1366) and Liao Yongzhong (1323–1375) also joined Zhu; they provided him with boats and crews for crossing the Yangzi. In the subsequent attack on Nanjing they planned and led successful forays using their small boats against the large ships of the government's river fleet. Liao Yongzhong later became the principal naval commander in the Ming forces.

Within the space of a decade these men all became Zhu's leading generals and admirals. At a minimum they all possessed a sound sense of tactics, and some displayed a genuine talent for the larger issues of strategy. They were men who could lead field campaigns, organize support and logistics, govern garrison cities, plan great campaigns, and pursue the fleeing Mongols and associated Chinese armies across the Mongolian deserts. They devised the means that wore down the besieged Zhang Shicheng at Suzhou in 1367–68, ascended the defiles of the Yangzi gorges in 1370 to conquer the Red Turban Xia state and add Sichuan to the Ming empire, employed naval tactics against superior forces in the Battle of Boyang Lake in 1363, breached the walls of Beijing in 1368, devised and led the naval attack on the holdout regions of the southeast coast in 1368–69, and added Yunnan to the realm in 1382.

Zhu Yuanzhang did not lead armies into the field himself after the Boyang campaign in 1363. His armies had grown enormous, and his motley array of amateur commanders had become professional generals equal to any in Chinese history, which reveals to us that the knowledge and skills needed for such a feat were within the reach of poor, uneducated men who had no military background. It is a striking demonstration of the high quality of the human resources available to a political leader. Most important, it demonstrates the social significance of this society's wide access to upward mobility, uninhibited by attitudes and constraints which a closed social order would have imposed. If a man could perform, the upward path was open to him in the military arena just as it was at the more refined levels of engagement for examination success.

The Military Phase Completed

Having considered the sources of Zhu Yuanzhang's military power, we can better understand the task that faced him at the end of the 1350s as he expanded his base beyond Nanjing. After occupying Nanjing in 1356, his troops soon moved downriver to take Zhenjiang, the important city controlling the point at which shipping on the Grand Canal crosses the Yangzi, and then points farther east; that fixed the battle lines between himself and Zhang Shicheng's rebel state, which held the lower Yangzi Delta. Then his forces fanned out to the south to take county after county in southern Jiangsu, northern Zhejiang, and parts of Jiangxi lying just to the west (to use the present-day province names).

After his armies had penetrated northern Zhejiang in 1358, Zhu went in person to lead the continuing attack from the important prefectural city of Jinhua. He was concerned that failures of troop discipline in the field had aroused negative feelings against him. His generals were absorbing troops so rapidly from conquered areas—in this case units taken over from surrendered Yuan local officials—that they did not have time to sort out the best among them and train them. Zhu was anxious to restore his standards of military discipline. While he was there for several months in 1358 and 1359, he had some of his most important encounters, taking time out from managing the campaign to sit and talk with eminent scholars. Jinhua was a center of Confucian studies, one of the most vigorous in China at the time, where Yuan failures and the need for social correctives were being analyzed. Zhu recruited a number of the leading figures in Confucian learning; they subsequently began appearing at Nanjing in 1360. The best-known names among them are Song Lian (1310–1381) and Liu Ji (1311–1375), who became the most important advisers and officials in the early years of Zhu's government, and who contributed directly to his plans to establish the Ming dynasty in 1368.[10]

These new scholar-advisers continued to press Zhu Yuanzhang to detach himself from his identity as a Red Turban leader. Zhu was not difficult to move on that subject, his only concern, as we have noted, being not to alienate the ardent religious believers within his following of officers and soldiers or among the people in regions of strategic importance. As early as 1358 Zhu's armies in southern Jiangsu and northern Zhejiang were carrying yellow banners, not the former red ones. No proclamations denouncing the Red Turban practices appeared for another decade, but careful reading of the record reveals that this change was under way.[11]

Competition with Chen Youliang (1320–1363) provided strong reasons for Zhu to delay any overtly anti–Red Turban action. Chen had consolidated all the southern (or western) branch of the Red Turban forces under his command. Although he was not openly religious, as the heir to the movement founded in the 1330s by the hallowed Monk Peng, Chen in the minds of some sect followers was a legitimate sectarian rival to Zhu Yuanzhang. Zhu had to avoid doing anything that might drive wavering Red Turban local leaders into Chen's camp. Chen was a very powerful warrior with great resources at his command, a rash risk taker, clearly Zhu's most dangerous enemy. His threat was brought to an end and his regime terminated after Zhu led his armies and naval forces to defeat Chen in the Battle of Boyang Lake in 1363. Thereafter, Zhu himself was the sole remaining Red Turban leader, and the only other enemy able to pose a grave threat was Zhang Shicheng, who from his base at Suzhou on Zhu's eastern flank controlled the wealth of the Yangzi Delta.

As the Red Turban movement diminished, and especially after he had defeated Chen Youliang in 1363, Zhu worried less about losing sectarian believers to rivals. Finally, after the Young Prince of Radiance died in 1366, the last figure of great symbolic significance for the sectarian camp was gone, and Zhu was freed from further need to maintain his now outgrown identification with the Red Turbans. From that time forward his proclamations to the people in regions coming under his attack denounced the violent actions of the Red Turbans and disassociated himself from them. He had made the full and open break with that aspect of his past.

He was nevertheless conscious of latent sympathies among the people, and it is acknowledged that he chose the name Ming (radiance) for his new dynasty in 1367 because he felt the need to retain some appeal to those people.[12] The Manichaean concept of the "radiant king" in its popular form was strong enough that even his Confucian adviser Liu Ji may have participated in selecting Ming as the dynastic name. But other associations of his surname Zhu, meaning "red," with ancient Chinese historical legends also could be invoked to justify the choice of Ming (and to mask his early sectarian affinities when Red Turban associations later became a tabooed subject). The Red Turban movement went underground when the Ming government began to suppress it, and it lost much of its organizational base. Yet it persisted and reappeared from time to time thereafter throughout the course of the dynasty, if only in nonthreatening minor uprisings.

The other influential component of the Red Turban doctrines was their anti-Mongol content. The indignities forced upon the conquered Chinese by their Mongol overlords were bitterly resented by many among the elite as well as by foot soldiers in Zhu's commoner armies. This issue was not clear-cut in either its ideological foundations or its practical ramifications for Zhu Yuanzhang and his scholar-advisers. There is no possible Confucian basis for ethnic hostility per se, yet a suffering people turned their resentment quite naturally on their non-Chinese rulers. Zhu wished to invoke that resentment as a mobilizing force, but without alienating the Mongols and Inner Asians who might defect to his side and come under the protection of his new dynasty. After railing against Mongol abuses for some years, he finally worked out his government's official statement on the subject in the proclamation he issued to the people of the northern regions just before his expeditionary force took to the field in 1367 to capture Dadu (present-day Beijing) and expel the Mongols from China. Drafted by Song Lian, it reads in part:

> Ever since our rulers in antiquity assumed governance over the realm, China occupying the center has extended its control over the Yi and Di [barbarians] while the Yi and the Di have resided on the outside and acknowledged China. Never has it been heard that the Yi and Di resided in China and governed the realm from there. When however the right to rule shifted away from the Song, the Yuan Dynasty as Northern Di [barbarians] entered and has ruled over China. Within the four seas and beyond there are none who have not submitted to it. How could this be the consequence of human powers? It was in truth bestowed by heaven. At that time their ruler was enlightened and their officials good, quite capable of upholding the norms of the realm. Yet even so, knowledgeable men and scholars of firm purpose still sighed that "caps and sandals had traded places" [higher and lower had traded places]. Thereafter, the Yuan officials failed to observe their rulers' "Ancestral Instructions"; they abandoned and destroyed the norms of conduct . . . and [their rulers] shockingly despoiled the principles of father and son, ruler and servitor, husband and wife, senior and junior. For the ruler of men must set the standard for his people; the court is the basis of the realm; Rites and Principles form the great defense [of civilization] in governing the world. Committing deeds like that [as described in incidents from Yuan imperial behavior, omitted here], how could they maintain the standards for later generations? . . . And so the people's hearts turned against them. Warfare broke out throughout the realm, causing the despoiled bodies of our Chinese dead to be strewn across the land, and the living to be unable to keep safe their own flesh and blood.

And although that was brought about by the misdeeds of men, in fact the time had come when heaven despised them and no longer sustained their right to rule. The ancient saying: "The Hu [barbarian] caitiffs' fortunes can never last out a hundred years" is today again proved true, assuredly and beyond any doubt.[13]

The proclamation goes on to denounce those who still served the Yuan cause; but it also denounces the destructive actions of the Red Turbans. It says that time has come for one born in China to rise up among the people and drive out the Yuan, to restore the proper order among the people, and to rid China of its shame. It nonetheless accepts the original legitimacy of the heaven-assisted Mongol conquest of China, and blames the failures of Yuan governing on human misconduct, whether that of the alien rulers or of their Chinese associates.

In this document Zhu and his court articulated elements of Chinese ethnic consciousness that were still important to the Red Turban ideology; but in stressing the Yuan dynasty's original right to rule (which incidentally affirmed the eventual transfer of that legitimacy to themselves as the Mongols' successors), they stood firmly on the side of Confucian-minded legitimacy, their resentment focused on the decay of ethical norms.

In his general amnesty issued a year later, after the success of the northern expedition, Zhu included this statement: "Those Mongols and Inner Asians who live on our land also are our children, and those among them who possess talent and ability also shall be selected and appointed to office by us." Further proclamations in the early years of his reign continued to stress that "there are no [immutable] differences that should separate Chinese and Yi [barbarians]." At meetings of the court he upbraided his chief officials for continuing to employ derogatory language when discussing the Mongols, reminding them that his and all their parents had been born under and were nourished by the legitimate Yuan dynasty.[14] Zhu also made a point of honoring some notable Mongols and Inner Asians, even granting posthumous titles to some who displayed Confucian righteousness by remaining loyal to their Yuan sovereign in the face of his own forces. It had become more useful to honor the exemplars of conspicuous loyalty than to denigrate those whose loyalty was to the vanquished side. That was always the case in the wake of dynastic change.

Despite that apparently broad-minded acceptance of the Mongols and Inner Asians as subjects of his realm, Zhu Yuanzhang's rhetoric continued to display a visceral indignation about the evidences in daily Chinese life of lingering Mongol customs, in dress, hairstyles, manners, and modes of speech and etiquette. To the literati, all that signified cultural loss. Zhu's pronouncements focused on lingering Mongol customs and modes in life as evidence for the weakening of the moral order. He repeatedly stressed his dynasty's need to restore upright old Chinese ways. There is nevertheless much evidence that he himself and members of the imperial clan wore Mongolian military dress and did not abstain from following some Mongol practices. North

China had been under non-Chinese rule for over four centuries, and the entire country had been ruled by Mongols and their Inner Asian associates for almost a century. In the new atmosphere of that time, when northerners and southerners once again could mix together, it must have been difficult to sort out the genuinely Chinese from the recently borrowed. Where issues of "cultural taint" could be identified, the southern literati in particular demanded reform, and Zhu Yuanzhang found it appropriate to lend his voice to their cause.[15]

He was genuinely attentive to rehabilitating rural life. The child of destitute victims of the decaying social order, he knew the problems firsthand. As he strove quite realistically to improve the economic foundations of the farming people's livelihood, he also struggled more idealistically to correct the corrupt behavior of some members of the upper strata that had led to sufferings and abuses among humble people. Those were not abstract ideals; he saw the problems as basic to the stability of his rule. Some of his scholar-advisers shared his concern over such fundamental problems.

Through the years from his rise in the 1350s until his reign was solidly established in the 1370s, we see the broadening of Zhu Yuanzhang's mentality. It is also possible to discern the traces of suspicion and intolerance toward his scholarly advisers and his fear of potential subversion within the ranks of his political and military officials. As a young man in his late twenties and thirties, however, he appears to us, on the whole, as intelligent, reasonable, and infinitely educable.

Zhu Yuanzhang's personal qualities contributed decisively to his success in the ultimate struggle. From 1356 onward, his base at Nanjing controlled smaller territories and produced smaller revenues than those of his rivals. His strength lay instead in his attention to organization, to management, and to careful planning. The destitute village orphan lad vividly portrayed by Wu Han (in the biography quoted extensively at the end of Chapter 21), who spent more than seven years preparing to become a monk, subsequently underwent several remarkable transformations, from eager field captain to serious student of political traditions, and then to imperial aspirant and architect of dynastic institutions. There is no other personal success story quite like this in all of Chinese history.

The Alternative to Zhu Yuanzhang

If Zhu Yuanzhang's story in these years is a sympathetic one, so too is Zhang Shicheng's. The record is highly partisan; to understand Zhu Yuanzhang's success against this potent rival, we must look more closely at him. Understanding Zhang Shicheng is important because he had become the alternative to Zhu as the likely victor in the final contest to create a new native dynasty. Practically speaking, after Zhu's victory over Chen Youliang in 1363, they were the principal remaining contenders. Zhu had to analyze Zhang's strengths and strive to prevail over those. Civil and military leaders throughout society had to make the choice whether to serve either one of them. And the common people were not a passive mass; their feelings about the two potential rulers also played a distinct role in the outcome.

Zhang Shicheng was an entirely different kind of contender for rule; the differences between them and the use he made of his assets help us better understand the age as well as Zhu's ultimate triumph. Zhang too had come from north of the Yangzi, had been reared in humble circumstances, and had crossed the river in 1356, like Zhu, to base his rebel regime in the rich lower Yangzi Delta region. Zhu and Zhang competed for the support of elite adherents and advisers without whom they could not govern, though each bore certain liabilities in the eyes of the elite. Zhu's was his association with the Red Turbans.

Zhang Shicheng's liability in the eyes of potential elite advisers and political associates was that he was a smuggler and a bandit, a ruffian whose career had given little evidence that he could become more than that. Like Zhu he had become literate, although not highly so. Far more than Zhu, he treated men of cultivation and learning with humble deference and with extravagant generosity; he was, after all, exceedingly rich. Many responded with ill-disguised scorn. Zhu Yuanzhang took great pleasure in a literati joke played on Zhang Shicheng by some of his early scholar-advisers. In devising elegant-sounding formal names for Zhang and his brothers, they had given Zhang the name Shicheng, not telling him that in the book of *Mencius* there is a well-known line where those two words appear in sequence. With a slight adjustment in the punctuation the line in *Mencius* can be made to read: "Shicheng is a cad."[16] This ingenious display of contempt toward Zhang Shicheng made Zhu laugh, until he grew suspicious that his literati advisers in all likelihood had similarly ingenious ways of denigrating him.

In addition to Zhang Shicheng's lack of cultivation, made the more obvious by his love of playing the gentleman ruler and patronizing all who would pay him court, he also suffered from a fault that Zhu Yuanzhang did not have: Zhang displayed no commitment or consistency in the way he went back and forth between service to and betrayal of the Yuan, first accepting appointments and titles, then repudiating the dynasty. That made him seem unreliable in all things. Even so, men of cultivation flocked to his generally peaceful and abundant territories to escape the disorders of the age, though many avoided direct association with him. Later, some wrote nostalgic reminiscences of the opulent life that his regime had made it possible for them to enjoy for fifteen years, while the rest of the country was frighteningly unsafe. After Zhang's capture and death, in the suspicious mind of Zhu Yuanzhang the most insidious aspect of Zhang Shicheng's career was that the people of Suzhou revered his memory, gave him a place in a hierarchy of potent local spirits, and secretly maintained shrines to him. Zhu and his more austere Nanjing regime were compared unfavorably with Zhang.[17] People of the time were sharply aware that the two ruled in quite different ways. That Zhu would ultimately triumph was, we now say, inevitable; at the time the outcome appeared to be far less certain, almost up to the final year of the struggle.

Nor were the signs then clear that Zhu Yuanzhang subsequently would undergo the changes in temperament for which his reign is known. He was forty in 1368, the first year of his reign as the dynastic founder. He soon became a violently paranoid ruler capable of monstrous acts. After describing the design of his new imperial government, I shall come back to the enigma of his later years.

II. SETTING THE PATTERN OF HIS DYNASTY

Symbolically at least, the fourteenth of September 1368 should be the most important day of Zhu Yuanzhang's life. Five weeks before the emperor's fortieth birthday, in the first year of his new Ming dynasty, his general Xu Da led the Great Ming northern expeditionary army into the Yuan capital at Dadu (present day Beijing) and took the city.[18] On the ninth, the Yuan emperor Shun, after stressful all-night meetings with his court and his generals, had overruled their pleas that he stay and defend his capital to the death; he had a gate on the northern wall opened, allowing him to flee in the night, northward into the steppe, with his family and household and some guard units. Five days later Xu Da thus easily entered a lightly defended city, and other than having to execute a few military leaders who refused to surrender, took it without bloodshed, disorder, or destruction. Its government offices and palaces were sealed and guarded, and all documents and archives were moved to Nanjing. That was 104 years after Khubilai had moved his capital to the site, 432 years since the Khitan emperor Abaoji's son, the Liao emperor Taizong (Deguang), in 936 took the Sixteen Prefectures of the North China frontier that included the bastion of Yan; Yan later became the Liao and Jin Southern Capitals, and Khubilai Khan's Dadu. The long era of the conquest dynasties had at last ended.

The proclamation of the new dynasty at the beginning of the year that corresponds with 1368 had anticipated this victory; Dadu's capture was marked by its name being changed to Beiping, "the North pacified," and the event was celebrated amidst preparations for further conquests in the North and in the South to complete the consolidation of the Ming state. The cautious Zhu Yuanzhang scarcely paused over this symbolic victory in his tireless pursuit of the larger goals, yet it truly was a turning point in his life.

Naming Zhu Yuanzhang as Emperor

What should historical writings call Zhu Yuanzhang once he had proclaimed himself the emperor of the Ming dynasty? In all traditional Chinese sources he is accorded the retroactive deference of being called at all stages of his life "the emperor," even as a sickly baby whose destitute parents strove to save his life. After he ascended the throne, those records more often call him by the titles granted to him posthumously, usually using either the first two words in that twenty-five-word title, Taizu, meaning "Grand Progenitor," the usual title for a dynastic founder, or else the long title's last three words, Gao Huangdi, the "Lofty Emperor." The latter title undoubtedly was meant to remind readers of the parallels between Zhu Yuanzhang and the founding emperor of the Han dynasty, whose posthumous title was Gaozu, the "Lofty Ancestor." Writers in China before the twentieth century might identify him by giving his personal name, called his "tabooed name," but after its first appearance would not continue to call him Zhu Yuanzhang. Only in the twentieth century, under contemporary inclinations to look upon emperors as like other humans, has that become a common if not the universal practice.[19]

In historical writings in Chinese we also find him referred to as "the Hongwu emperor," that name sometimes translated "Abundantly Martial," but that is in no sense his name. It is the name of his reign period, his "era name," and while we may call him "the Hongwu emperor" (the one who reigned during the era named Hongwu) it is incorrect to call him "the Emperor Hongwu." The latter is often done, not only with this emperor but with all rulers in the last two dynasties, because Zhu Yuanzhang established the practice of not changing reign period names during a reign. He used the reign name Hongwu from the year of his accession in 1368 through 1398, the year in which he died. That pattern endured. From 1368 onward to 1911, for the first time in Chinese history one era name consistently corresponded with the reign of one emperor. That practice made the era name a convenient alternate designation. Although writers frequently avail themselves of that convenience, it has the drawback of being inaccurate and misleading and so will not be used in this book. In keeping with Chinese historiographic practice, his posthumous temple name Taizu is used anachronistically to refer to him throughout his life here; he will be called that, or Zhu Yuanzhang, or occasionally the Hongwu emperor.

Changing Implications of "Dynasty" in Later Chinese History

"Dynasty" as used in Chinese history has three levels of meaning. At the core of those meanings is the essential one: the emperor, his immediate family, and his lineal descendants. Dynasty means the continuous rule within successive generations of males in one patriline.[20] (In some circumstances one generation may provide more than one ruler, as when a younger brother or a cousin succeeds.) A second level of meaning derived from the first is the period in history in which that succession of rulers holds the throne. The third level of meaning is the country, the nation, the territory under those rulers. A Chinese of the time usually would identify his native country as Da Ming, "the Great Ming," but in some situations the name Zhongguo, the "Central Country" or "Middle Kingdom," also was used. (Today, of course, Zhongguo is the standard name for China.)

In short, "the Ming dynasty" means Zhu Yuanzhang and his imperial successors; it means the period in history from 1368 to 1644; and it means the country and people of China during those years. In the Ming period, the ambiguity inherent in these overlapping senses of the word had serious political consequences, especially when Zhu Yuanzhang's fourth son, Zhu Di, usurped the throne in 1402 (see Chapter 23, Section I). Was the government to be answerable to the head of the imperial clan or to the people of the land? Could loyal servants of the dynasty-as-the-state charge the emperor with usurpation, or was that beyond their powers? Is the government an instrument of the imperial household, or does the state belong to the people, the nation? Were the high civil officials of the court servitors of the dynasty as the government of the nation or of the dynasty as the imperial clan? Where did their prime responsibility lie? Such questions were prefigured by changes in the relations of throne and court since Song times; by the Ming, the ambiguity was thrust into the open.

The founders of dynasties have always taken to themselves the authority to determine the dynasty's style of governance. Ming Taizu took that implicit authority a step further: in 1369, the second year of his reign, he asked his scholar-advisers to study and draw up a set of regulations outlining the powers and duties that would be given to his sons and daughters and their heirs. At the age of puberty, emperors' sons moved out of the imperial residence quarters to establishments of their own on the outside, staffed with tutors and aides. Taizu was preparing to take the next step, to grant them "fiefs" throughout the empire, locating in particular his older sons on the sensitive northern border, where they would be responsible for maintaining the empire's, that is, the dynasty's safety. Along with such princely titles as Prince of Jin, based in Shanxi, and Prince of Yan, based at the old Yuan capital, now renamed Beiping, they were to receive princely incomes and some supervisory duties in local governing, at least in respect of maintaining law and order. But their "princedoms" were titular and did not carry decentralizing privileges and powers that would have made them princes with hereditary rights to territorial fiefs, as in the European feudal system. Zhu decided to formulate precise regulations governing all aspects of their lives. When he and his advisers had worked out an initial text in 1373, he referred to it as his "family law," giving it the character of the Ming dynasty's "house law." There was little or no precedent in earlier Chinese imperial practice; in the past a dynasty's promulgation of its codified laws and punishments, the "state law," had sufficed.

The Ming dynastic "house law" bore the title Zu Xun, meaning "Ancestral Injunctions." In the early versions of the text, and through its repeated revisions up to 1395, the date of his final rethinking of its many problems, the Ming founder showed that he conceived the role of his imperial family quite differently than any previous founder of a dynasty.[21] He stipulated that none of his sons or their descendants should live in society, follow careers, study and take examinations for office, or ever hold any offices other than certain specified military assignments. Although for most the ranks and stipends decreased with each successive generation's increasing distance from the original imperial ancestors, they would have to remain confined in princely establishments scattered throughout the country and could never pursue any kinds of gainful or useful careers in society. That requirement was unprecedented. Taizu probably never attempted to calculate how many descendants his twenty-six sons and sixteen daughters might produce over time. Later Ming historians calculated that by the mid-sixteenth century they numbered more than 100,000.[22] Their support became one of the great burdens on the state's fiscal system. Not counting those who reached the throne, no more than a dozen of them are noted for any personal achievements.

Ming Taizu's earlier thoughts on the ways in which his sons and their descendants would function in maintaining the dynasty changed over time. In the earlier versions of the Ancestral Injunctions, the princes were to control large garrisons, receive lavish annual stipends, and exercise a measure of sovereignty within their princedoms. His court advisers told him that there was no good precedent in history for creating such decentralization of powers, and the experience of the Han dynasty should indicate how dangerous that could be; its princedoms proved to be dangerously rebellious and eventually had to be eliminated. Taizu's early inclination was to believe that family solidarity would ensure the defense of the realm and ready support of the throne should treacherous ministers ever come to dominate the court. Eventually he realized that the powers given to his sons were too great: in the final version of the Injunctions issued in 1395, three years before his death, he cut their annual stipends to one-fifth, and he took away their unilateral control over military forces in their regions, putting the major garrisons under court-appointed officers and allowing the princes to retain control only over their personal guards, thus implying that the civil government should check the abuses of the imperial clan's powers. He also restricted the princes' rights to visit one another and to come to the court; and to diminish their aura of status and authority, he reduced their privileges when at court. All those measures failed to prevent his own sons, and again his grandsons, from plotting against the throne. Further reductions in the powers of princes were made administratively (without challenging the wording in the Injunctions) during the reign of his son the Yongle emperor (r. 1402–1424). With those corrections, the imperial institution became a fairly stable and secure pivot of government. Sadly, however, other provisions of the dynastic house law could not be altered; it created a system that squandered vast amounts of the imperial clan's human and material resources over a span of two and one-half centuries. Like many of Ming Taizu's enactments, it went through repeated changes and reversals of policy and in the end imposed shortsighted regulations that were inflexible. In later reigns no attempts to revise and improve the Ancestral Injunctions could ever be openly discussed. A man who changed his own policies constantly throughout his reign left open no provision for his heirs to do the same. Perceptive statesmen and rulers throughout the later Ming were always seeking ways to bypass that stultifying institutional rigidity.

III. CONSTRUCTING A CAPITAL AND A GOVERNMENT

The city of Nanjing on the south bank of the Yangzi River, which Zhu Yuanzhang occupied in 1356, was a large and well-constructed walled city built in the first half of the tenth century to serve as the capital of the Southern

Tang dynasty, one of the short-lived Ten States.[23] The city was dominated by its massive walls and imposing gates. By the early fourteenth century it had become one of the more impressive cities in Central China. While not as large in population or as rich in its hinterland as Suzhou and Hangzhou to its southeast, it had served as the capital of successive dynasties holding South China during the post-Han era in the third through sixth centuries, and again during the Five Dynasties. Its historical associations contributed to its "imperial" aura, in the popular mind a place where "the dragon coiled and the tiger crouched."

The Capital

Zhu Yuanzhang was still not certain that Nanjing should serve as the capital of his dynasty. It concerned him that no previous ruler of the entire country had ruled from a point so far south as the Yangzi River; to control all the regions, perhaps his capital should be located on the North China Plain. There was, however, the immediate practical need for a walled palace compound within the city that could at least temporarily accommodate both the imperial residential quarters and halls to house court agencies; in 1366 he ordered the Nanjing city wall extended to the east so his new "palace city" could be auspiciously placed to the south of Mount Zhong (in English also called Purple Mountain). To have a guardian mountain rising on the north was geomantically desirable. Both at the Northern Song capital at Kaifeng and at the later Ming capital at Beijing, artificial "mountains" were built north of the palaces to achieve that effect. Nanjing had the beautiful Mount Zhong rising impressively in the correct position. Simply designed and quickly built, this palace city was ready for occupancy a year later.

Zhu continued to consider other sites as future dynastic capitals. In 1368 he went with his northern expeditionary armies as far north as Kaifeng, the former Song capital, to inspect the site, then turned back to Nanjing (Yingtian) via Fengyang, the new prefectural designation given to Haozhou, his birthplace. The previous year he had decided to designate Fengyang his Central Capital (Zhongdu) and named an official to assume responsibility for designing and constructing an imperial city there. In 1370 he also designated Kaifeng his "Northern Capital" (Beijing) but did not initiate any building projects there to make it ready for use, despite the fact that the city had been repeatedly plundered since the Northern Song departed from it in 1127.

Construction got under way at Fengyang in 1369. Zhu wanted to make the Central Capital in the locality of his birthplace a splendid and imposing city with high walls and gates and lavishly adorned palaces and ritual buildings. Skilled workmen by the thousands were sent there, and luxurious materials were gathered from many distant places. He went to inspect the progress in 1375, as the Central Capital was nearing completion. It appears that he was somewhat appalled by the evidence of expense and waste, and he called a halt to the building. Later in the year he ordered that the layout of Yingtian

(Nanjing) should be reconsidered, the plans enlarged, and the palaces in particular rebuilt on a larger scale, but in a less ornate style than he had found in the new Fengyang palaces.

Construction on the palaces in Nanjing was completed in 1377. The next year he ordered that the city be designated Jingshi, "the Capital," and withdrew the designation "Northern Capital" for Kaifeng. He seems to have resigned himself to making Nanjing his principal capital in a traditional two-capital system, as was the case in the Han and Tang dynasties. Zhongdu remained his Central Capital at Fengyang, but it was scarcely used; within decades its buildings were being cannibalized for materials, and it fell into a state of disrepair. People forgot that it had been the premier capital building project of the early Ming and had become a splendid city, at least for a short time.[24]

Some building continued at Nanjing throughout Taizu's reign. In the course of rethinking the city's layout in the early 1370s, a decision was made to rebuild the city's northern wall much farther to the north, almost all the way to the edge of the Yangzi, where a defensible mound called Lion Hill could be incorporated into the city wall. This height provided a site from which to look down on the river's edge and the defense installations placed there. The city wall was irregular, incorporating parts of the old Southern Tang city wall but bulging and turning at several points to take advantage of hills and heights.

Nanjing's city wall became the longest city wall in Ming China. Although not as long as the walls of the Tang dynasty capital Chang'an had been, it remained China's longest existing city wall for the rest of imperial history. It measured almost twenty-four miles in total length, averaged forty feet in height depending on the contours of the land, was twenty-five feet broad at the top, and had thirteen gates with immense, defensible multiple portcullis gate enclosures. It was a rubble-filled wall built on foundations made of huge slabs of stone to prevent enemies from breaching it by placing gunpowder charges underneath it—a recent addition to the technology of warfare. The lower part was faced with huge blocks of stone and above that very large fired bricks. Several of the gates were double, a land gate alongside a water gate which permitted entry by boats bringing freight from the Yangzi. About half of the wall and some of the gates escaped the general destruction of city walls carried out throughout China in the 1960s and 1970s.[25]

Despite the vast investment of resources to build his capital, Ming Taizu still had doubts about the symbolic and geopolitical aspects of the Nanjing site. In 1391 he sent his eldest son, the heir-designate Zhu Biao, to study the site of ancient Han and Tang capitals at Xi'an in Shaanxi in the far northwest. Zhu Biao returned, submitted a brief report setting forth no definite conclusions, and then fell ill. He died the next year, and the idea of establishing another capital died with him. This vacillation again reveals Zhu Yuanzhang's lingering uncertainties about the correctness of his imperial actions, his nagging doubts about whether he had done all he could to secure his dynasty and transmit his power to his successors.

The Structure of Central Government

Zhu Yuanzhang (who usually will be called Ming Taizu, or the Hongwu emperor, from this point on) was somewhat uncertain about what would be the most suitable structure for his new central government. Like most of the rebel leaders, at first he simply took over the previous regime's local and regional offices of government, sometimes even retaining their former incumbents, as new territories came under his rule. In 1361 the Little Prince of Radiance had bestowed on him the title State Duke of Wu (Wu being the regional name for present-day Jiangsu south of the Yangzi and adjacent parts of Zhejiang). When Zhang Shicheng, his rival based at Suzhou, declared himself the Prince of Wu in 1363, Zhu elevated himself to the same title in the following year, but continued to use the Red Turban "Song" dynasty's reign period name, to show he had not repudiated that regime. As a "prince" of the "Song," he had no right to a government organization on a scale higher than would be found at the provincial level. With the convenient death of the Little Prince in 1366, that obstacle was removed.

On the first day of the following year he promulgated his own calendar, calling 1367 the "first year of Wu." That was an awkward stopgap measure; he surely had already determined to proclaim his own dynasty, take the title of emperor, and name his own reign period. He did so on the first day of the new year in 1368 (January 19, 1368). Four days later he ascended the throne, observing all the rituals and ceremonies punctiliously. His reasons for calling his dynasty the Great Ming (Da Ming) have been discussed; his reign name, Hongwu, reminded the world of his martial qualities at a time when his conquest was not yet complete. He had raised his status from army commander to duke to prince and now to emperor quite cautiously, with careful, deliberate steps.[26]

His first imperial acts on coming to the throne were to designate his eldest son his heir, to name his principal wife, née Ma, empress, and to name Li Shanchang and his old comrade in arms General Xu Da his Chief Councillors of the left and the right. Reversing Mongol practice, he restored the priority of the left over the right, thus making Li the senior Chief Councillor and the head of his court. General Xu Da in any event was constantly in the field enlarging the Ming territories. Both men had already held those titles and appointments, but they were now renewed in the name of the Great Ming dynasty. Many other civil officials and generals also had their appointments confirmed, and promotions were passed out in large number. In short, the formal announcement creating the new dynasty continued a structure already in place, based on earlier Chinese models. A functioning if still incomplete system was given a name and a face as the Great Ming.

The Yuan dynasty did not create a comprehensive law code on the model of earlier dynasties. Instead, the Mongol government of Khubilai Khan and his successors produced partial codes and bodies of legal precedents that on the one hand made a symbolic gesture of reducing punishments, and on the other incorporated elements of Mongol customary law. Zhu Yuanzhang was disturbed by the Mongols' laxity in implementing laws, and determined to overcome their slipshod practices by thoroughly reworking the Tang Code, the most influential of earlier dynastic law codes, and rigorously observing a system of punishments.

A preliminary version of his new Ming code was issued in 1368. He then established commissions to reconsider and expand it, through five revisions between 1374 and 1397, the year before his death. Every item in the earlier code was reviewed along with the Tang Code's parallel items, in his presence, by a team of experts, the final determinations coming directly from him. Thus the Great Ming Code (Da Minglü) came into being.[27] Its 460 articles (compared with the Tang Code's 502) were arranged in six main categories, corresponding to the administrative concerns of the Six Ministries, plus an introductory section of "General Principles." While the emperor was determined to produce a universal code that could be minutely followed, he undermined that intent by constantly issuing laws which met immediate needs and which often contradicted his Great Ming Code, thereby producing the anomaly of a Code that all officials were required to follow, and a body of his edicts (typically ordering much harsher, often cruel punishments that his Code specifically abolished) which transcended the Code's authority; that would prove to be typical of his imperial style.

All these were transitional measures. A full array of imperial governing offices was sorely needed and was gradually brought into being. To cite one important example, the pre-1368 government did not have the Six Ministries, the executive agencies called the Ministries of Personnel, Revenue, Rites, Punishments (or Justice), War, and Public Works. Some of these essential administrative functions had been loosely organized under four departments, for tax grains, ritual, punishments, and construction. In September 1368 the traditional Six Ministries were formally instituted and the full range of offices and officials was created under each of them. And so it went, in establishing all the other components of a central government, during the first years of the dynasty.

Finding qualified administrators to staff the full complement of new offices emerged early on as a major problem. Taizu was a military man, close to his military cronies from his home district, many of whom were illiterate or scarcely literate. They were not able to function as civil officials. A regime dominated by such men would not have been widely attractive to the literate elite. Taizu understood the issues and discussed solutions with his most trusted literati associates, especially men of the caliber of Liu Ji and Song Lian. In November 1368 he issued a decree, no doubt formulated with their advice, which read:

> The empire is of vast extent; because it most certainly cannot be governed by [my] solitary self,[28] it is essential that all the worthy men of the realm now join in bringing order into it. Heretofore the disorders of war and conflicts over boundaries [among the rival contenders] have prevailed, with the consequence that the Great Way of gathering in the worthy men to

care for all the people has not yet received full attention. Even though We have temporarily depended on assistants to guide and rectify Our great enterprise, it is still the case that many men of exceptional talent and virtue live as recluses in remote places. Can it be said that the responsible offices have failed to earnestly encourage them to come forth [and serve]? Or that Our court has been deficient in according them honorable treatment? Or that We are so unenlightened that the worthy would disdain Our service? Or that those now holding positions would block worthy persons from receiving Our notice? Not at all! Why should all the worthy men and scholar-officials, or young scholars and stalwart men of action, who long for the rule of a sage-king such as Yao or Shun [paragons of high antiquity], just go on wasting away their lives waiting [for the millennium]? For the realm is now at last stabilized and We are eager to discuss and clarify with all learned men the Great Way of governing, to enrich Our mind and thereby to attain more perfect rule. As for all the scholars still in the wilderness who have the capacity to give Us worthy assistance, who by their virtue can bring succor to all the people, let the responsible offices courteously dispatch them here, where We shall select from among them for appointment.[29]

During the first few years of his reign, Ming Taizu repeatedly issued edicts and proclamations similarly worded and in similarly earnest, humble tone. He frequently explained who he was: I am a man of the poor people born in the impoverished Huai River region, forced by difficult circumstances into alliance with bad sectarian bandits, who has now been made aware of the Great Way of our civilization. With Heaven's approval my invincible military force has conquered the realm, and I have become the legitimate ruler, to help the suffering people, so I now need and merit your assistance (or, in hortatory edicts, I now command you to do such and such). Despite his humble tone and studied decorum of such pronouncements and the high rewards of prestige and advancement he offered, many who had the qualifications to join the new scholar-official element of his government questioned his legitimacy, or remained suspicious of him. Men of talent were reluctant to come forth.

His most successful strategem for dealing with the staffing needs of his rapidly growing government establishment was to found a Confucian school system through which to create a talent pool of potential appointees. As early as 1365 he had set up a school in the capital with a teaching staff of "Erudites" *(bo shi)*, who were charged with maintaining high standards of instruction in the classical texts. In 1368 that school became the National Academy, a large residential campus occupying some of the vast expanse of empty space inside the new city wall's northern extension. The next year he ordered that Confucian schools be set up in all prefectures and counties, each headed by a civil service–appointed Director of Confucian Studies. Local Confucian schools tested the students officially assigned to them for a basic command of the elementary Confucian teaching texts, the *Four Books*,[30] and certified them for advancement to the National Academy.

Taizu may at first have had the idea that the schools' training could standardize qualifications among sons of high officials (especially the sons of his military officers) to provide junior officials from their trustworthy ranks. It soon became apparent that the talent would have to be drawn from a much wider social base, to include the people at large. In the fourth year of his reign (1371), the academy had 3,728 registered students; a few years later the number had grown to almost 10,000. The students were exposed to disciplined study, which often was not completed, for the emperor made it clear that he would raid the student body at any time to obtain large numbers of junior appointees. Many students entered with the expectation that they would quickly gain office, but not by ignoring their academic records. It was essentially a merit system; by recognizing talent that had lain unused since the late Yuan, it could quickly upgrade many well-prepared students to its standards. Throughout the first emperor's reign this approach worked quite well. Abuses were rare, and despite the tensions springing from his unpredictable temperament, morale was high. The government could not have been fully staffed without this source of qualified men.[31]

Taizu also turned to the hallowed civil service examinations to supplement the readier source of appointees offered by his school system. As early as 1367, before he had even assumed the title of emperor, he had announced that triennial civil service examinations would be held, but he did not in fact authorize an examination until 1370. Another examination was conducted in 1373, and the impatient emperor was so dissatisfied with the results that he suspended further examinations for some years. They were not held again until 1385, with results this time that pleased the emperor. He believed that by conducting the final stage, the palace examination himself, he might inculcate a bond of personal loyalty. He was always seeking ways to assure himself of the loyalty of educated men. The highest-ranked graduates in 1385 were immediately given substantial offices. But the system pleased him less in subsequent examination years. It continued to function, but overall it failed during his reign to supplant the National Academy as the main source of candidates for office. The civil service examinations did not assume that importance until early in the fifteenth century under the Yongle emperor. Thereafter the National Academy took on a different character, becoming little more than a way station on the path to the *jinshi* examinations for most of the students admitted to it.

During the 1370s Ming Taizu both expanded the structure of his government and staffed it in ways designed to overcome the inequities of the Yuan period. A new elite emerged under conditions of great openness to talent that permitted high rates of upward mobility for a number of decades. The system continued to function well during the succeeding reigns. Early Ming society came back onto the track laid down in Northern Song times; it shared some of that age's commitment and high idealism, notwithstanding the stresses imposed by an increasingly imponderable and enigmatic emperor.[32]

Radical alterations to the structure of the central government were yet to come. In 1380 Taizu's Chief Councillor, Hu Weiyong, plotted to assassinate him. Hu and many officials were deeply disturbed by the unbelievable ferocity with which Taizu had punished a large contingent of admired and honorable officials found guilty in 1376 of technical faults in administration. It was the infamous "Case of the Pre-stamped Documents," in which hundreds of officials were found to have adopted a facilitating procedure for handling the paperwork of grain tax revenues that was technically improper.[33] Without investigating or reviewing the quite reasonable shortcut which the responsible officials had worked out, Taizu concluded that they had all connived and colluded to cheat him. He flew into a rage and ordered all those officials and many others connected to them in various ways to be summarily executed. Thousands were killed. Fear of the volatile emperor was growing. That his rage could be aroused by the most unexpected things was revealed in a number of incidents dating from the first years of his reign. As early as 1374 he ordered the summary execution of several prominent scholars in Suzhou on the ridiculous grounds that they still were loyal to the memory of Zhang Shicheng. Ridiculous or not, that incident added to Taizu's growing power to intimidate his officialdom, and that no doubt was his real motive.

Despite those ominous signs, the general mood was nonetheless one of highly committed loyal support for a ruler who was seen to be restoring the norms of Chinese society; even the young Fang Xiaoru (1357–1402), whose revered father was unjustly killed in the Case of the Pre-stamped Documents in 1376, still wanted to believe in the new dynasty and did not blame the emperor personally for that tragedy.[34] Yet there also was an undercurrent of apprehension that led many scholars to try to avoid service at the court. Others were willing to think about more extreme solutions.

The ambitious Chief Councillor Hu Weiyong was one of them; he was aware that officials of his rank could at any moment arouse the ruler's irrational anger, and he believed that he had to take desperate measures. Apparently a number of his associates shared both his ambitions and his fears. One perhaps exaggerated version of the story recounts that Taizu received last-minute warning from a palace eunuch not to attend a festival celebrated in the gardens of Hu's mansion, which was situated so close to the palace walls that the wary emperor was able to climb up on the wall overlooking Hu's residence and see the armed men concealed there, ready to spring an ambush. Hu and his fellow plotters were arrested and executed along with all their family members. But that was not enough. Taizu's suspicions led him to believe that many others were part of the plot or were tainted by some tenuous relationship to Hu. All such connections were ferreted out, and those who by any stretch of the imagination could be implicated also were executed. The initial phase of this purge lasted one year, but investigations and executions continued to be carried out for almost a decade. Some reports sat that 15,000 people were slaughtered. The emperor's policy of control by intimidation reached new heights of wanton ferocity.

The Hu Weiyong case had far-reaching consequences for the structure of the central government. The emperor concluded that the Central Secretariat (Zhongshu sheng), in which Hu Weiyong had served as Chief Councillor (Zuo chengxiang), had become a locus of power that threatened the throne. The one or two Chief Councillors with their assistants and a large staff of subordinates and secretarial aides had constituted the administrative leadership of the Outer Court and all its subordinate executive agencies, except for the Chief Military Command (which functioned like the Song and Yuan period Military Affairs Commission in command of all the military forces of the realm) and the Censorate (which maintained surveillance, investigation, and some supervisory responsibilities). Those three equal divisions of the central government were expected to check one another, but the head of the Central Secretariat exercised the powers of a chief minister, mediating between the throne and the government. We have seen that in Southern Song times the Chief Councillors could become all-powerful chief ministers who sometimes abused their positions. It is unlikely that Ming Taizu was well acquainted with the details of Song history or that his scholar-official advisers would have given him an unfavorable overview of scholar-official behavior in Song history, but he had become shrewdly aware of the tensions between the bureaucracy and the throne. His suspicions aroused, he took immediate action, no longer restrained by the caution that marked his earlier rise to power. He abolished the Central Secretariat and the position of Chief Councillor.

With one imperious command he redesigned the structure of central governing that had been developing for a millennium. In the words of a recent writer, "The imperial power annexed the ministerial powers."[35] Those ministerial powers functioned to integrate and coordinate all political action throughout the empire; that entire management level of administrative responsibility was abolished. The emperor was left alone with his principal executive agencies, chief of which were the Six Ministries, separately and individually reporting to him and receiving their instructions from him. Taizu also divided the Chief Military Command into five separate and equal Chief Military Commissions (Wujun dudufu), each individually responsible for a cluster of geographically non-integrated garrisons and military establishments. He also abolished the Censorate, then quickly reestablished it under a new structure of divided powers designed to make the Censorate more responsive to the interests of the throne. His intent was clear: all executive authority had to rest exclusively with him. All Chinese emperors ruled as well as reigned, but no emperor since the First Emperor of Qin (r. 247–210 B.C.E.) had borne a burden of daily hard work comparable to that which Ming Taizu took upon his shoulders in this fundamental restructuring of 1380. It was a formula for certain disaster when a less able and less energetic ruler came to the throne; even for a person with Zhu Yuanzhang's extraordinary drive and ability it was wildly impractical, as he soon discovered.

At first he established Four Assisting Offices (Sifu guan), headed by senior officials of recognized probity, to take over the supervisory tasks and to form a kind of "cabinet" in which problems could be discussed. Just two years later, before the duties of this office had been carefully worked out, he abolished that institution and in 1382 in its place set up offices for senior secretaries (Da xueshi), each office being attached to a hall or palace building within the Inner Court where the literary work of government—the drafting, compiling, and editing of documents—was carried on. Initially there were four senior secretaries. Although under subsequent reigns they gained a stature that justifies the usual translation of their title as "Grand Secretary," during Taizu's reign their position was less grand. They were not expected to act as a coordinated group of advisers able to integrate the imperial administration. That ultimate responsibility still lay with the emperor; they could only lessen that burden by tracking the flow of documents for him and advising him on technical matters.

He employed ever more the palace eunuchs to serve as his eyes, ears, and arms, through them to encompass the whole arena of governing activity. The senior secretaries worked in the Inner Court, but their affinities were with the scholar officials on the outside, whose backgrounds and values they shared. The eunuchs were totally dependent on the person of the emperor for whatever authority they might have; they were intended to be servants to the members of the imperial household who resided in the inner palaces, and the scholar-officials scorned them. For that reason the emperor placed trust in them and used them to check and intimidate his officials. Later their expanding roles would take them well beyond the palaces and the capital city, to postings and responsibilities throughout the empire.

The structure of the Ming central government, tortuously reached only in the middle years of Taizu's reign, was set rigidly in place. His successors could make only relatively superficial adjustments within the framework of that structure; for example, Taizu left an edict stating that any official who thereafter proposed reestablishing the Central Secretariat or the office of Chief Councillor was to be immediately executed. Yet in later reigns the real and ever-changing demands on the system required continuous attempts to modify its actual functioning.[36]

IV. THE ENIGMA OF ZHU YUANZHANG

The personality of a Chinese emperor, while never irrelevant to the understanding of his reign, usually becomes less important when he has passed into history. A founding emperor's personality and mentality, however, often have borne more directly on history, because founders influenced the forms of governing in ways that were institutionalized, sometimes for centuries. The first Ming emperor's personal impact on the subsequent character of his dynasty was profound.[37] The enigma of his personality therefore becomes an issue that historians must address, and they have, guardedly in Ming times to avoid charges of lese majesty, much more openly in the succeeding Qing dynasty, and without restraint, from all points of view, since the early twentieth century. And still we find the many efforts to explain this one man's behavior less than satisfying.

His principal modern biographer has been Wu Han (1909–1969).[38] The two versions of Wu's biography, dating from 1949 and 1965, constitute the most important attempt to come to terms with the baffling character of Zhu Yuanzhang. In his first version Wu Han closes with a description of the many anxieties and fears that beset Zhu Yuanzhang after he became emperor— "He felt that everyone was trying to destroy him, everyone was ridiculing him, mocking him"—and concludes that after supreme power came into his hands, "he suffered from intense stress, paranoia, and pathological fears." In discussing the brutality of the punishments he inflicted on people and the cruel methods he prescribed to prolong the agony of those suffering execution, Wu adds: "The disease that afflicted him was a form of compulsive sadism that drove him to use the sufferings of others to lessen his own sense of terror."[39] As amateur psychiatry, that analysis may well be too imprecise to be acceptable, but it recognizes Zhu's progress into some kind of pathological compulsion that explains his extremes of behavior. Wu also notes, convincingly, that despite those symptoms, Zhu's mind remained clear to the end.

Wu's revised version of 1965 omits all of these original observations about Zhu Yuanzhang's tormented psyche. He instead suggests that many of Zhu's victims deserved their punishments and finds the key to explaining his actions in the stresses caused by class conflict. Zhu himself is not above Wu's criticism: he sold out his class and joined his interests to the "Mongol-Chinese landlord class" [sic], yet he was "a man of many accomplishments; his merits outweigh his faults." He is "a historical figure whom we should assess positively."[40]

When we attempt to go beyond Wu Han's labored efforts to define Ming Taizu's character traits, to relate his personal qualities to the patterns he established in Ming governing, several things emerge. One is his need to be obeyed without question; disobedience triggered his rage and violence. That need is already seen in an incident of 1358, when he was only thirty years old. He was with the main column of his forces progressing south from Nanjing into northern Zhejiang. A strong army of his rival, Zhang Shicheng, also was pushing south toward Hangzhou, just to Zhu's east. There was a possibility that Zhang's army might attack Zhu's forces, or that some of the Yuan forces which recently had surrendered to Zhu might defect to Zhang. The military tension was exacerbated by civil unrest in the region, compounded by food shortages. Zhu was concerned about discipline and issued stern warnings forbidding his troops to plunder, to take supplies from the common people, or to behave in a disorderly manner. Because of the grain shortage, he also issued a prohibition against using rice to make rice wine. Hu Dahai was a senior general (and Zhu's longtime follower from the Huai region in Anhui) leading another column of Zhu's army just a short distance farther south. Zhu discovered that Hu's son and two other young officers had disobeyed his order forbidding the use of rice to make wine. In accordance with military law, Zhu ordered their immediate execution. According to the *Ming History,* a civil official advised him, "Better lighten up a bit, otherwise you might drive young Hu's father to defect to Zhang Shicheng." Zhu flew into a rage. He roared, "I would rather have Hu Dahai defect than have my discipline violated!" With that he drew his sword and executed young Hu on the spot.

The *Ming History* comments that the fearful people of the region took heart, knowing discipline was to be enforced; senior general Hu did not defect, and the lesson was not lost on the army. Perhaps this dramatic gesture was part of a well-planned scheme designed to strengthen the emperor's authority, yet the rage he displayed was terrifying, and as the years went by any infraction, even the most inconsequential oversight, might bring that rage to the surface.

Another thing that emerges is that he exhibited a strong strain of self-righteously indignant puritanism. A certain austerity was indeed authentically present in Confucian ethics and was reflected in popular values: ostentation and frivolous consumption were to be avoided. Zhu carried that proscription much further, perhaps because his youthful deprivations made him hate waste. He often condemned his enemies, especially Zhang Shicheng, who carelessly dissipated the great wealth of the Suzhou-Hangzhou region, and the Mongol emperor Shun Di in the Yuan capital, whose self-indulgence was a favorite topic for the scurrilous gossipmongers of the time. An entry in the *Veritable Record* of the first year of the Hongwu reign period (1368), usually overlooked, is of unusual interest in this regard:

> [Tenth month] the day *jiawu* [December 7] . . . Fourteen men [from the Yuan Bureau of Astronomy in Dadu] arrived at the capital . . . The Bureau of Astronomy submitted a palace clock of crystal made by [for] the Yuan ruler. It was intricate and ingenious in the highest degree. Inside it was one [or two?] human figure[s] that moved to strike chimes according to the time. The emperor looked at it and said to his attendants: "To disregard matters of supreme importance and devote one's mind to the likes of this is what is called 'to do what is useless thereby to harm what is useful.' If he [the Yuan emperor Shun] had turned his mind to governing his state, would it have been brought to downfall and extinction?!" He ordered his attendants to smash the clock.[41]

The beautiful and ingenious mechanical clock he destroyed must have been the same one described in the official *Yuan History* as having been built for Emperor Shun in 1354: a clepsydra whose mechanical moving parts were activated by water falling on a waterwheel hidden within it, it stood "six or seven feet tall."[42] The last Yuan emperor, Shun was known to have enjoyed tinkering with mechanical devices, and sometimes even helping with their construction. Earlier, to make a public show of his disapproval of such ostentation, Taizu had ordered the Ming armies on entering the Yuan capital to save all the books and government records, but commanded them to destroy the architectural embellishments and ornamental contents of the more luxurious palaces. That relates to this entry of 1368, which incidentally also reveals that members of both the Chinese and the Muslim Astronomy Bureaus in the Yuan capital formed the party that brought the clock to Nanjing.

Clockmaking demanded the same kind of engineering skills that were employed in the manufacture of astronomical instruments. Taizu had been fully advised about the importance that astronomy held for the legitimacy of his imperial regime. Calendrical studies were grounded in astronomical observation; the precision of the measurements directly affected the accuracy of the imperial calendar. It was both an emperor's responsibility and his sole prerogative to promulgate a calendar; the accuracy of that calendar was in turn seen as confirming his legitimacy in succession to the former dynasty. The Muslim Bureau of Astronomy dated from the time of Khubilai Khan, who in 1271 added it to the imperial Yuan government under the influence of scientific exchange between Mongol-ruled Persia and Mongol-ruled China.[43] Both it and the older Chinese bureau were thereafter maintained throughout the Ming.[44] Although the clepsydra was smashed to bits, the astronomers who arrived at Ming Taizu's new court with it in the autumn of 1368 were rewarded, retained at Nanjing, and appointed to astronomical posts in the Ming government.

To the puritanical first Ming emperor, the mechanical marvel these astronomers proudly—or hopefully—brought as evidence of their technological skills symbolized only ostentatious display. His uncultivated mind did not perceive its intrinsic value. Its engineering design represented a high point in the centuries-long development of Chinese horological science, which had all manner of other useful applications. His indignation may have conveyed a useful message to his military establishment and to all the new officials: austerity was to be the watchword of his reign. Soon, however, he despaired of making either frugal or honest men of them. That failure gnawed at him.

Ming Taizu's mind was "uncultivated," but he was by no means unintelligent. He was a very quick learner. Notwithstanding his late start in education, under the guidance of eminent scholars in the 1350s, he learned to read the hundreds of documents that came before him every week, perhaps thousands of them after his reorganization of the government in 1380, and to draft responses to them. His drafts were often revised by highly cultured assistants, but some drafts directly from his hand remain; they reveal that his literary competence had reached a level allowing him to supervise the paperwork of his government. Still, he felt embarrassingly inadequate, knowing that he lacked their level of literary cultivation and suspecting they would always despise him.

In fact, they were in most cases much more likely to praise him for his intellect and his hard-won achievement. Distrust between them arose not so much from their evaluation of him as from his inability to believe in their sincerity. His growing ability to read their literary works provided him a tool to spy on them, to discover their hidden attitudes, and to pry open the intricate literary double-talk they used to denigrate him. Or so he thought. From the first years of his reign he began to scrutinize every single document they submitted, even purely conventional memorials thanking the ruler (as protocol demanded) for appointments or congratulating him on festival occasions. When those, innocently and inevitably, contained words that sounded somewhat like the words for "bandit," "monk," "baldpate" (a derisive word for a monk), or made references to the color red, or included any other elements that could be construed as having a double or hidden meaning, he assumed they must be denigrating references to his past. He also tried to analyze the poems they wrote for private circulation to discover additional evidence of sedition or disrespect. A literary inquisition followed which led to the death or banishment of many literary figures and virtually eradicated what had been a flourishing generation of poets reared under the last years of the Yuan. Officials at court became so terrified that they begged him to designate the standard language which would be acceptable in conventional memorial submissions. He complied, but his suspicions only increased, and the literary inquisition continued unabated. The dangers of serving in his government, or even of living under it if one were a writer, drove people out of government and into hiding.

Seeing that the scholarly sector of society, necessary to run his bureaucracy, was boycotting official life, he issued edicts making it culpable to turn down appointments or seek to resign. Life became very difficult for educated men, sudden death common.

Ming Taizu felt that his efforts to instruct and intimidate his scholar-officials had all been in vain. They were hopelessly corruptible, constantly being caught up in peculation, or worse, in sedition. A new side to his personality began to emerge in the 1370s: instead of humbly consulting with able scholars and learned advisers about how to act like a true emperor, he grew obsessively suspicious and hostile. Having gained the ultimate prize, he became irrationally fearful that he would lose it. He began falling into uncontrollable rages in which only his wife of many years, the Empress Ma, dared to restrain him. After her death in 1382, there was no other restraining hand. His tangled involvements with many secondary wives and female palace attendants probably only added to the tensions and suspicions under which he lived.

The foregoing account has emphasized the nonrational aspects of Ming Taizu's behavior, but he also had a highly rational side: he clearly saw the possibility that his associates who had served with him since his Red Turban bandit days might resent him for painstakingly excluding them from real power and might have ambitions to replace him. He also could see that cabals of his scholar-officials might wish to acquire influence with his sons and possible heirs in order to overthrow the patterns of his rule once he was entombed. Corruption and misuse of authority could pose a genuine threat to the quality of his government and undermine its stability. All of those were substantive issues: as the saying goes, even paranoiacs can have real enemies, and he undoubtedly had many. In the midst of this apparent decline into an erratic state of paranoia, one must also take into account the rational elements driving his behavior. Is it possible that his violent displays of imperial despotism reflected a misguided understanding of Confucian statecraft gone awry?

In 1358–59 Zhu Yuanzhang came into contact with leading figures in the northern Zhejiang school of Confucian social thought—called the Jinhua school, from the name of the prefecture where their studies were centered. That encounter has been looked upon as one of the momentous events of Zhu's rise to power.[45] The political thought generated at Jinhua stressed both the expected primacy of ethical issues and an unusual Confucian concern with specific governing skills and legal thinking.[46] In terms of subsequent influence on the new Ming regime, Song Lian and Liu Ji, among the several scholars recruited there in 1359 by Taizu, came to be the most important. Song Lian was considered the most broadly learned savant of the new court, while Liu Ji acquired an awesome if exaggerated reputation as a strategist, diviner, and master of occult learning, without losing his credibility as an excellent classical scholar.[47]

Liu Ji's political thought has been described as essentially derived from *Mencius;* that is apparent in his stress on the primary obligation of the ruler to serve the well-being of the people.[48] While out of office in the late Yuan, after service in the government had proved too frustrating, Liu wrote a collection of political parables that set forth his ideas on government. They reflected his observations on why the late Yuan collapse of the political system had been inevitable. The book is called *Yuli zi.* In it he stresses a need to eliminate corruption and abusive behavior, and to provide stronger and more clear-minded rule if social disaster is to be avoided. He believed that mistreatment of the people would cause them to rise up and overturn the dynasty, for while the ordinary people may be ignorant, they cannot be deceived.[49] The sage ruler therefore has the crucial role to play in warding off chaos and establishing order. Did those Jinhua scholars, deeply troubled about the conditions of late Yuan society, define Zhu Yuanzhang's subsequent behavior?

The entire issue of Liu Ji's and other learned Jinhua Confucians' influence on Zhu Yuanzhang, and through him, on early Ming governing turns on the age-long problem of heaven, often meaning simply nature or the natural order of the cosmos, in relation to the life of mankind. Is heaven sublimely inattentive to mankind's problems, or is it a caring upholder of the moral order? Are natural disasters sent down to warn rulers and their people about the consequences of misdeeds, or would they happen in any event? If heaven embodies the moral order, do its workings directly uphold that order among humans, or does heaven wait for a sage (or a sage-like ruler) to carry out the natural order's objectives? These problems were debated throughout history, from the time of Confucius and Mencius, their answers ranging from Xun Zi's (d. 238 B.C.E.) and others' highly rational rejection of heaven's involvement, to those of Dong Zhongshu (ca. 179–ca. 104 B.C.E.), who strove to restrain rulers by making them aware of the cosmic consequences of their behavior.

In his book of political parables, the *Yuli zi,* Liu Ji blamed the laxity of Yuan governing, its lack of system and of standards, even its failure to have produced a codification of its laws, for the general breakdown of social order and the consequent danger to the dynasty. Did Zhu Yuanzhang, at that time still impressionable and eager to master the art of ruling, come under the dominating influence of Liu's political analysis of the Yuan failure? If in his own eyes he functioned as the agent of a distant and perhaps unfeeling cosmic order once the Mandate had passed to him, was it then Zhu's purely rational decision to wield his great power in an awesome and ruthless way, pursuing what he took to be a Jinhua path to the good society?

Or, as seems more likely, are the extremes of his subsequent behavior to be explained as in part nonrational, or even erratically irrational? The argument has been made that "the patent tyranny that the early Ming state became was no mere result of autocratic caprice. It was certainly foreshadowed in late Yuan Confucian writing, and it can surely be understood to have emerged from the emperor's sincere effort to put Confucian theory as he understood it into concrete effect."[50]

That hypothesis holds the Jinhua scholars such as Liu Ji and Song Lian, and their colleagues in Neo-Confucian statecraft, at least indirectly responsible for Zhu Yuanzhang's ruthless modes of ruling. While it offers one way to explain much of his behavior, if correct it forces us to believe that Zhu Yuanzhang quite failed to understand the intent of Liu Ji and the other late Yuan political thinkers. They themselves held widely varying views on governing, and Zhu did not feel bound to follow closely the advice of any of them. As early as 1371, Zhu wrote a letter in his own hand to Liu Ji (then living at home in Zhejiang) asking for Liu's view on policy following the successful conquest of Sichuan. He noted in particular that because the Yuan had failed through overly lax governing, he had countered the consequent social disorder by employing harsh laws, and asked for Liu's response. Liu's benign reply was, "After the harsh winter the warm spring sun must shine." To paraphrase his further explanation of how the ruler should govern, Liu Ji said that the urgency had passed; the time had now come to relax harsh penalties and exercise more lenient governance.[51] Liu Ji here and elsewhere is seen as one who tempered rather than reinforced the emperor's severe measures.

None of the Jinhua advisers long survived; most died directly or indirectly as a result of the emperor's actions. Possibly because their serious concern for social order had impressed him, it is clear that Ming Taizu earnestly endeavored, indeed drove himself, to meet the overwhelming responsibilities of his office, sincerely wishing to better the condition of the ordinary people. He was anguished when he observed that his guidance repeatedly failed to bring about upright government. His anguish, however, also appears to have stemmed in large part from the fear that his dynastic enterprise was being undermined and his personal power was in danger of being stripped from his grasp. His fears were in part rational; his responses were simultaneously both rational and quite beyond reasonable explanation.

The enigma of this Ming despot centers on why his character underwent such profound change. It is difficult to believe that his violent rule was induced by a Confucian-guided learning process. Nor does it suffice to say that he was reared in the late Yuan atmosphere of political brutality, so in crises he fell back on violent modes of behavior that had come to be commonplace.[52] He delighted in cruel methods of punishment not practiced under the Song or earlier dynasties; he brutally humiliated officials at court in ways unthinkable during the refined age of Song. That alone suggests that the conduct of politics had undergone a sea change during the Yuan, between 1279 and 1368. In the final analysis, however, the Ming founder's personal addiction to brutality must be seen as the mark of an insane mind, not basically a reflection of a violent era. Time after time he succumbed to violent outbursts and then emerged to express regret that all the bloodshed had been "necessary." Throughout his life he never lost his shrewd and calculating grasp of the immediate political scene, yet he was often incapable of controlling his rage and fear.

That is the tragic enigma of Zhu Yuanzhang, one that was played out at the center of his world's stage and that shaped the subsequent long history of the dynasty he had so assiduously created. He was even able to see the dysfunctional consequences of his ruling style. After his last great series of purges in the early 1390s, carried out when he saw that his tender-minded young grandson would succeed him, he said that he hoped he had slaughtered enough to ensure a stable succession. He issued a decree in the summer of 1395 explaining that a turbulent age had brought out all manner of evil persons, which required him to use extralegal punishments in order to intimidate them. But, he added, such methods would not be appropriate for his successors. They must observe his Great Ming Code and his Great Proclamations; they could not employ any of the ancient and long-discarded forms of corporal punishment such as branding and tattooing, cutting off noses and limbs, and castration (tame though those were in comparison with the cruel means he had regularly employed to destroy people). "Should any official ever memorialize the throne to propose their use, the civil and military officials shall immediately all impeach him and he shall be executed."[53] Ironically, that late comment on his own career can be read, in effect: Should any one else ever kill and injure as I have long done, kill him! His descendants, unfortunately, imitated him more than they heeded that late injunction.

23

CIVIL WAR AND
USURPATION, 1399–1402

When Ming Taizu died in the summer of 1398, he left the Ming throne to his grandson, the Jianwen emperor, who conscientiously determined to be a reforming ruler but whose chances of retaining his throne were made precarious by Taizu's ill-considered measures. The civil war that ensued exposed elements of a revealing historical confrontation: what "might have happened" reveals other directions history could have taken, hence a latent but enduring potential for redefining political elements and cultural values. For the suppression of those other directions in this political crisis did not eliminate them from the realm of political thought. The civil war and usurpation of Jianwen's throne by his uncle the Prince of Yan did, however, lead to the installation of a powerful pattern of imperial rule, one that strongly marked the course of the dynasty's remaining two and one-half centuries. Here we glimpse a spectrum of possibilities; the chapters that follow focus on developing patterns in the usurper's reestablished Ming rule.

1. THE NEW ERA

With the death of Ming Taizu, an era in Ming history ended. He had founded a dynasty, but in his manner of accomplishing that he created conditions which could not be long sustained. Thorough revamping of the manner in which governing was conducted was hoped for by all those who were essential to it. They were waiting for the next phase of the dynasty's existence, in most cases committed in loyalty to waiting out the founder's passing. They were by no means waiting to repudiate his reign openly, yet everybody knew that present conditions were both intolerable and counterproductive. The dynasty had raised great hopes. The primacy of Chinese values had been restored. Vigorously pursued civil governing helped foster an economic recovery. An elite of learning once again found access to appropriate careers, and their intense satisfaction—and probably a degree of that also among the population at large—for the time made the Ming founding "right" no matter how wrong its governing became. Throughout the Hongwu reign, had the governing elite not become resigned to enduring the numbing experience of surviving under the founder's harsh rule, they might have more openly planned for the next phase. As it was, they simply waited.

The old emperor, who had scarcely ever known illness in his adult life, lay ill for a month before he died on June 24, 1398, four months short of his seventieth birthday. No succeeding Ming ruler lived so long. He was buried at a large tomb complex in a mausoleum park stretching upward from the level plain, on the south-facing slopes of Mount Zhong, the Purple Mountain, in Nanjing's northeastern suburbs. Today his partially restored mausoleum lies near that of Sun Yat-sen (1866–1925), the father of Republican China, buried there in 1929. The layout of Sun's mausoleum, the primary shrine of Nationalist China, was consciously modeled on the Ming founder's tomb. Sun Yat-sen was honored by his Nationalist Party (Guomindang) as a modernizing Chinese leader who, like the Ming founder, also restored native Chinese rule. The image of Zhu Yuanzhang and his Ming dynasty resonated powerfully with anti-Qing sentiment in the nineteenth and early twentieth centuries. Little else about the Ming founder mattered to the early Republican movement five and one-half centuries later.

In 1398 when the old emperor died, however, his awesome image remained all-powerful. The new emperor was his grandson, Prince Yunwen, who had been designated the heir in 1392, a few months after the death of his father, Zhu Biao, Prince Yiwen. Tutored in the classics and history, Zhu Biao was a gentle and unassertive man, fond of literature, devoted to the Confucian proprieties. The old emperor thought him to be a bit too soft to rule vigorously but nonetheless was exceedingly proud of him.

The New Emperor

Zhu Biao's son, young Prince Yunwen, like his father was strongly drawn to learning, but he was nevertheless eager to assume the large burden of governing. When he came to the throne in 1398 he was twenty-one, married, already the father of one infant son, a mature and well-prepared young ruler. On coming to the throne he took the era name Jianwen (Establishing the Civil), matching Taizu's era name Hongwu (Abundantly Martial). That was meant to signal a change of style.

The Jianwen emperor (also known in history by a posthumous title, Hui Di) faced the problem of combating the oppressive atmosphere lingering from his grandfather's reign. He not only had to establish a prevailing civility but also needed to reenergize his associates in governing, the scholar-official elite. He made it clear that he did not intend to govern without their close collaboration when he raised some of his most trusted scholar-advisers to positions of prominence and gave them a looser rein than any Ming officials had previously enjoyed. The most important of them, Qi Tai (d. 1402), Huang Zicheng

(1353?–1402), and Lian Zining (d. 1402), had all earned their *jinshi* degrees in the palace examinations in 1385. Lian and Huang had placed second and third among the more than 500 winners of *jinshi* degrees in that examination, and all three had drawn Ming Taizu's approval after some years of able service at his court. Lian, in particular, had boldly spoken out in criticism of the emperor's policies but, in the unpredictable manner of Taizu's responses, had earned his respect.[1] All three now were given high substantive posts and were asked to formulate policy on pressing issues. A fourth scholar-official, Fang Xiaoru (1357–1402), is usually classed with them as the "four outstanding martyrs" of the usurpation; all four were executed in 1402.

Two grave institutional problems immediately faced the Jianwen emperor and his advisers in 1398. Both problems were the direct legacy of the Hongwu reign. One was the institutional weakness, more precisely the unworkable structure of the central government stemming from Taizu's ill-considered reorganization in 1380 when he abolished the Central Secretariat, its leading officials the Chief Councillors of the Left and the Right, and all their assistants. Yet the new emperor believed that he must work out a system for turning supervisory responsibility and coordinating functions over to regularly instituted assistants. How could he do that without running afoul of the very explicit wording of the Ancestral Injunctions saying that anyone who might ever propose reestablishing the Central Secretariat should be beheaded? Fang Xiaoru was noted as a profound student of institutions. The new emperor turned to him for guidance in resolving this dilemma.

The other grave problem facing the emperor was the excessive decentralization of military power implicit in the princedoms created for Taizu's many sons. How to regulate their powers and duties was a central focus of the founder's Ancestral Injunctions, and it has been noted that Taizu repeatedly revised that "house law" document almost up to the year of his death. The large grant of military and supervisory powers and lavish annual stipends initially set forth in the earliest versions of the Injunctions were sharply reduced in the 1380s under advice from officials who could see the dangers in that degree of decentralization. In particular, Taizu removed the princes' control over all the military garrisons that were adjacent to the princedoms on the northern borders. He placed them under command of military and civil officials directly appointed from the central government, leaving the princes in charge only of their personal guard units. That perceptive change was, however, insufficient; he had failed to forestall the possibility that a strong prince might yet dominate and coopt such officials. From the moment the young Jianwen emperor came to the throne, he knew that the princes might challenge his succession. Most to be feared was the Prince of Yan, his uncle Zhu Di, of the princedom based at Yan (present-day Beijing; after the fall of the Yuan it had been renamed Beiping). The Prince of Yan, stealthily and by long design, was getting ready to challenge his nephew and emperor.

The emperor turned for advice with this problem to Qi Tai and Huang Zicheng. Qi was Minister of War, a post given to him because he had made himself the best-informed expert on the northern military garrisons and the empire's defenses. The old emperor, before his death in 1398, had become aware of Qi's expertise and had charged him with responsibility to protect his grandson when the latter came to the throne. Qi and Huang Zicheng began to work out an overall plan to "reduce the feudatories" *(xiao fan),* as the term for radically limiting the powers of the princes is usually (though incorrectly) translated; the princedoms were not feudatories in the sense of Western feudalism, but by taking to themselves illegal powers to control appointments and local revenues and expand their military powers, they could become something similar.

The dangers in that possibility were clearly seen; Qi Tai and Huang Zicheng, their eyes on the Prince of Yan, acted as if to bring about a general reduction to safe levels of all those independent princely powers, without seeming to put the ambitious prince in such peril that he would take preemptive action. They failed. Agents of the court arrested officials posted in Beiping who were clearly disobeying the laws and secretly conniving with the prince. It was reported also that he had violated explicit restrictions in the Ancestral Injunctions by visiting other princedoms on the northern frontier. The prince went especially to consult with his younger half-brother, the Prince of Ning, whose princedom lay on his eastern flank and who controlled large numbers of surrendered Mongol cavalrymen in the Ming service. Eventually he was able, through trickery or coercion, to gain control over units of those Mongol warriors and add them to the garrisons under his own control. In the war that soon followed, those troops were led by the Prince of Yan's second son, the martial princeling Zhu Gaoxu, and were of crucial importance. The Prince of Yan also had begun to organize a quasi-government at Beiping with his own brain trust of conspiratorial advisers who laid plans, gathered intelligence from Nanjing, and plotted.

In the summer of 1399 the Prince of Yan, with totally hypocritical indignation, denounced the evil goings-on at the court in Nanjing and proclaimed a military campaign to "rescue his nephew" from perverse officials dominating the court. The Ancestral Injunctions provided that, under circumstances of a ruler being improperly coerced, the princes should assume such a responsibility, but left the definition of those circumstances vague. The scene was set for a conflagration.

The civil war that broke out in the summer of 1399 lasted until Nanjing fell to the Prince of Yan on July 13, 1402. It is reasonable to assume, although not proven, that the Jianwen emperor and his empress and elder son died in the burning of the palace. The Prince of Yan ordered an honorable burial for three badly burned bodies. He took the throne, declared the new reign name, Yongle (everlasting happiness), and demanded that the Jianwen emperor's leading officials acknowledge his accession. Their heroic display of fidelity to the presumed-to-be dead emperor made a deep impression on the public. As these events unfolded, the Ming emperors' definition of how their dynasty in the sense of the imperial family and household related to their dynasty in the sense of the government also emerged as a new element in imperial politics.

The Usurper

The Prince of Yan was both ruthlessly ambitious and psychologically quite insecure about committing the act of usurpation. If this were early English history, Shakespeare surely would have probed his psyche in a profound historical drama. We see Zhu Di as a highly rational man, but rational within the terms of his time. What did he at heart really believe about the cosmic forces that in theory had given his dynasty the Mandate to rule? Must he reassure those cosmic forces by gaining popular support? The ancient classics say that heaven sees and hears as the people see and hear. What did he believe about his father's powerful spirit, and the spirits of all his forebears to whom veneration was rendered at the Zhu family shrine? Was that magic, or was it ritual propriety, or was it hollow convention? What must he do to protect himself from baleful consequences of his wrongdoing? It is difficult to reconstruct those aspects of his consciousness.

He had spun out the lengthy recital of abuses at the court and invoked the Ancestral Injunctions to show that it was his duty to "Clear Out the Disorders, in Response to Heaven" *(Fengtian jingnan)*, as his subsequent white paper on the subject was titled.[2] He knew that was not convincing. And knowing to what extent the Injunctions perpetrated a charade (as we shall see in the following section), he may have felt less guilty about violating his father's rules. Quite rationally, he could calculate the political impact of his treachery and know that he should mask it. Great benefits would accrue to his cause if he could be spared the name of usurper.

In the several irregular dynastic changes of the Five Dynasties and the early Song, there had always been the authority of an empress dowager to validate the usurping act in the name of the legitimate ruler, always a child, who lost the throne. In the Yongle emperor's situation, there was no member of the imperial family to whom he could turn. Instead, some of the Jianwen emperor's prominent and publicly respected officials, men who also had been praised by the Ming founder, would have to recognize that the change was inevitable. Some of those men would have to come forth to accept his claim that he was the only legitimate successor to his father—overlooking the line of his older brother, who had died in 1392, and his nephew, who, he said, had set fire to the palaces as a desperate act of suicide. He refused to mention that the Jianwen emperor's three younger sons, infants to be sure, were still alive, as were two or three of his younger brothers. As (or so he asserted) the "senior surviving son of Empress Ma," and thus claiming that he was directly inheriting his father's dynastic position, not that of his older brother's heirs, was he not legitimately the next in line of succession? Legitimacy in the role of the successor could only mean legitimacy by the norms of Chinese family rules, that is, to be senior in the line of the eldest son by a proper consort. That is what the Ancestral Injunctions specified. How could he lay claim to being that? It could be sustained only if the Jianwen emperor had died leaving no acceptable male heir.

Defiant Loyalists

The Prince of Yan's claim would remain an unconvincing fiction unless leading public figures of stature accepted it. He could scarcely expect Qi Tai or Huang Zicheng to provide him with that kind of respectability; he had targeted them as the principal villains for having "misled the young emperor" to "reduce the feudatories," and had marked them for death. Indeed, they were caught and killed before the prince's eyes, valiantly denouncing him until they dropped dead.

Two other officials at the Jianwen court had the reputation for integrity and high public reputation that could give the prince's usurpation respectability. They were Fang Xiaoru and Lian Zining. When they were brought before him he tried to induce their cooperation. Lian, in chains, stood before him and refused to listen to his self-justification. Zhu Di told Lian he had come to protect his nephew, comparing himself to the venerated Duke of Zhou, of high antiquity, whom Confucius had lauded as the greatest man of all time. The duke had gone from his fief to the Zhou capital to protect his nephew, the young King Cheng, on the death of the Zhou founder (the duke's older brother King Wu). This exemplary deed by an uncle who might have usurped but instead protected the rightful heir is traditionally dated to 1116 B.C.E.[3]

Lian Zining, whose courage in criticizing Ming Taizu became legendary, sneered at the Prince of Yan's self-serving comparison. He was struck down. He continued to berate Zhu Di, the Prince of Yan, who ordered the guards to cut out his tongue to silence him. Lian, prostrate, used his finger to write on the floor, using the blood streaming from his mouth: "And where is King Cheng?"[4] He was taken away to be executed by dismemberment. According to popular legend, the words written in blood on the palace's stone floor could not be scrubbed away, and gave off a luminescent glow in the dark. Such legends immediately began to take form.

Zhu Di's last and best hope was Fang Xiaoru. It is said that the chief of Zhu Di's brain trust, the Monk Daoyan, had forewarned the prince: "When Nanjing falls he is certain not to surrender to you. It would be best, however, if he is not killed. If Fang Xiaoru is killed, the realm's seeds of [future] scholarship perish with him."[5] Daoyan, a learned monk, earlier had served for some years at a temple in Nanjing and was familiar with the intellectual milieu. He knew that Fang Xiaoru was irreplaceable and that the entire scholar-elite of Central China would deeply resent his loss. Zhu Di replied to Daoyan that he would not forget that admonition. After the fall of Nanjing, therefore, Zhu Di desperately wanted Fang to draft the accession proclamation.

He had Fang brought before him from his prison cell soon after the scene with Lian Zining. Fang's wails of grief echoed through the hall as he was brought in. The prince came down from his dais and spoke comfortingly to Fang: "You must not grieve. I have come in the manner of the Duke of Zhou when he supported King Cheng." The following dialogue was carried on using the historical analogy. Fang retorted, "Where then is King Cheng?" The prince replied, "He has committed suicide by fire." Fang said, "Then why not place the son of King Cheng on the throne?" The prince responded, "The dynasty needs a mature ruler." Fang again retorted, "Then why not enthrone King Cheng's younger brother?" At that point the prince made a statement of special significance: *"This is my family matter."* That is to say, my dynasty is not a matter of state in which officials such as you should have a say; it is my private matter on which you may not express an opinion. Then he ordered attendants to bring brush, ink, and paper, saying politely to Fang, "My proclamation to the realm must be drafted by you, sir." Fang threw the brush to the floor, and both wailing and cursing him, said, "If I must die then let me die; I will not draft your proclamation." The prince realized that there was no hope of persuading Fang. Flying into a rage, he ordered that Fang too be taken away and executed by dismemberment.[6]

Fang's relatives and associates "to the tenth degree of relationship" were sought out and exterminated. He had several times conducted the civil service examinations; by long convention, the successful candidate must thereafter address the principal examiner as his teacher, a relationship of great weight in Chinese society. For that reason many of those who passed when he was supervisor of the examinations were located and killed, along with all persons in various degrees of relationship to them. In the ensuing purge to root out lingering support for the dead emperor, the prince's underlings went through all the documents in the palace offices to find the names of men who had been appointed, promoted, or honored by the Jianwen emperor during the four years of his reign, and then executed hundreds of them who were suspected of feeling personal devotion to him.[7] In its viciousness his purge exceeded even those of Ming Taizu; tens of thousands were killed. Once again a great swathe was cut through the ranks of the scholar-official elite. Most affected were the regions nearest the capital in Jiangsu and Zhejiang, which supplied the largest number of the early Ming officials. Their writings were proscribed, and all documents relating to the Jianwen reign were destroyed or altered; the years numbered one to four under the era name Jianwen were stricken from the records (*ge chu,* "expunged"), and those years were artificially added to the Hongwu years, as if that reign had lasted four more years after Taizu's death. The Prince of Yan hoped that, other than his contrived accounts justifying the civil war, officially written and rewritten at his direction, the entire episode of the Jianwen reign would be forgotten.

The response in Chinese society denied him that hope. Legends grew about it: the Jianwen emperor's body was not among the three unrecognizable ones officially buried, for he had escaped and survived; sons of all the loyal martyrs miraculously survived and produced heirs to continue their family lines; the associates of the Prince of Yan all suffered appropriate disgrace; and a direct descendant of the Jianwen emperor, more than 200 years later, rose up in the disguise of a bandit leader (Li Zicheng) to bring down the descendant of the Prince of Yan, the last Ming emperor, whose reign ended with his suicide in 1644. So the popular imagination avenged the cruel usurpation.[8] The legends became ever more precise and detailed, as legends do the longer the time that separates them from the event. Some later Ming historians were willing to entertain the possibility that they might contain a kernel of truth. And thus an enduring "mystery" was created: What became of Hui Di, the Jianwen emperor? Attempts to answer that question produced a spate of late Ming writings.

Implications of the Usurpation

Zhu Di's revealing statement to Fang Xiaoru, "This is my family matter," is one among several items of evidence which show that the Ming emperors looked upon their dynasty in a somewhat new manner. In discussing the three levels of meaning conveyed by the word "dynasty" in the previous chapter, I stressed the ambiguities. In particular, how does the governing structure of the state relate to the concept of dynasty? It is clear that Ming Taizu saw the dynasty as a private possession not to be fully shared with the heads of his government. They worked for him; the dynasty was not their common enterprise. Among the several state shrines at the capital, the shrine to the imperial ancestors, Tai Miao, located at the front of the palaces, was where the emperor, under ritual supervision of his Ministry of Rites, conducted observances to his forebears. That had always been so; even Khubilai Khan had permitted his Chinese officials to persuade him to build such a shrine at Dadu, and usually dispatched Chinese civil officials to conduct the dynasty's great rites there in his name. The new Ming dynasty's Tai Miao was set up promptly in 1368, but soon thereafter Taizu broke with precedent and in 1370 established a second shrine to his ancestors inside the private residence quarters of the inner palace, which he called the Fengxiandian, or "Temple for Offerings to the Imperial Forebears." He ordered that daily offerings of food items commonly eaten in ordinary homes, quite different from the list of offerings his high ritual experts prescribed for the Tai Miao, be made by members of the imperial family in person. He commented to his rites officials who found this innovation difficult to justify, "The Tai Miao symbolizes the Outer Court; the Fengxiandian symbolizes the Inner Court."[9] In other words, I will not share with the officials of the realm my family's ritual observances to my ancestors; they are my family matter.

We also have noted that after promulgating the Da Ming Lü (the Great Ming Code), the laws for the people of his realm,[10] Taizu also compiled a separate code of laws and regulations for his family and their descendants, that is, for the "dynasty" in the first of the term's three meanings. No previous dynasty had ever taken that step. The enforcement of those regulations, or Ancestral Injunctions, was a responsibility not primarily of the government but of his imperial clan members themselves.

This privatizing of the "dynasty," in the sense of the imperial family and lineage, enhanced by the great gulf that developed under Ming rule between the Inner and the Outer Courts, made it difficult for officials to know where the boundaries of their official duties should lie. That attitude is reflected in Zhu Di's response to Fang Xiaoru, "This [issue over the succession] is my family matter." The state, represented by the scholar-officials at the court, had an interest in matters affecting the stability of the throne, such as succession and the designation of the heir apparent; what should the civil government's role be? Into what issues could officials not inquire? About what issues should they not express opinions? In fact, dynasty and government were two faces of an indivisible entity. That is clear in Zhu Di's need for Fang to draft his accession proclamation; his family enterprise needed validation by the scholar-officials to be workable.

The old distinction between an ideal of Gong tianxia, "the realm open for all to share," and Jia tianxia, "the realm as one family's (dynasty's) private interest," one ancient formula for expressing the problem, took on new meaning in Ming times.[11] That led to many further conflicts between the ruler and his government throughout the remainder of the Ming dynastic era. It probably is not coincidental that the new attitude partook of the way the Mongols and their conquest dynasty predecessors (as well as the later Manchus) felt about their dynastic interests vis-à-vis their Chinese subjects.

As opposition to the usurpation was suppressed, the brutality with which it was carried out shows that Ming Taizu's unrestrained recourse to violence in ruling was not to end with his death. The Prince of Yan did not have Taizu's unfathomable temperament, but brutal force had become institutionalized. One cannot imagine the gruesome scenes I have described occurring in Song times. Nor were the great purges of Taizu's and Chengzu's reigns repeated in subsequent Ming reigns; but the pattern of brutality in the treatment of officials at the court was to remain a feature of the dynasty's political life, a feature characteristic of post-Yuan history in general.

II. THE THOUGHT OF FANG XIAORU: WHAT MIGHT HAVE BEEN

Fang Xiaoru is central to the brief Jianwen reign's rethinking of the dynasty's institutional arrangements and possible improvements. He aroused the young emperor's great enthusiasm for a return to antique models described in ancient texts, especially the *Institutes of Zhou (Zhou Li)*, the classic text purportedly describing the ideal forms of government instituted by the founders of the Zhou dynasty about 1100 B.C.E. This work has always intrigued political reformers; Wang Anshi in the Northern Song studied it and was influenced by it in the reforms he tried to bring about when serving as Chief Councillor to the reform-minded Emperor Shenzong in the 1070s.

Fang Xiaoru (1357–1402) was the son of an earnest and upright official who had been executed by the Ming founder in 1376, quite unjustly, in the infamous "Case of the Pre-stamped Documents." Prior to that the young Fang, already noted as a prodigy in his mastery of classical learning, spent about four years in Shandong when his father served there as Prefect of Jining. He assisted his father, took a deep interest in local government, and explored the region, which was home to Confucius, Mencius, and other great figures of antiquity.

Previously at the capital Fang had met Song Lian (1310–1381), the man he admired as the pivotal figure in early Ming intellectual life and scholarship. When Song retired from office at the beginning of 1377, Fang, then twenty years old, was in mourning for his father, executed in 1376. Shortly before that Fang had presented himself to Song at the capital and asked to become his student; now he went to Song's retirement home at Jinhua to assume that relationship in earnest. The old man was pleased; he had found a disciple worthy of him. Fang lived and studied at Jinhua for most of the next three or four years. He was temporarily back at his own home at the end of 1380 when Song Lian was arrested and sent into exile in Sichuan, one of the thousands of victims of Taizu's great purge following the exposure of Hu Weiyong's treason that year. Song Lian died the next year, in exile. Fang Xiaoru had lost first his father, then his teacher, to the senseless brutality of the Ming emperor. Why did he remain loyal and eager to serve the new government? Its achievement in expelling the Mongols and ending their threat to Chinese civilization held the greatest significance for Fang. For all its blind violence, the new dynasty was the only hope, the vessel which must be preserved.

When the Jianwen emperor called him to the court in 1399, Fang was very hopeful; now the time was ripe for great achievements. He exemplifies the high morale and optimism of Confucian scholar-officials that was to remain quite typical of Ming officialdom at its best, despite the often discouraging political environment of the court.

The mature political thought that Fang Xiaoru in his mid-forties brought to bear on the Jianwen emperor's institutional reforms was not confined to the conventional Neo-Confucian mold. It has been criticized as unrealistic; he at times promoted antique ideals such as the ancient "well-field" *(jingtian)* system, described by the philosopher Mencius in the fourth century B.C.E. as at that time already having long passed into a remote past. The sometimes foolishly idealistic Mencius nonetheless saw in it an ideal pattern of rural village life, in which neighboring families shared labor and benefits and upheld the norms of behavior. That kind of Mencian idealism still formed a main current in Neo-Confucian political thought, especially in the rather empty political ideas of the Lixue thinkers.

Fang, however, was a realist in the tradition of the Song dynasty Neo-Confucian utilitarian school. The record of his political thinking has been largely destroyed, but we can assume that he used the well-field idea as a symbol, a way of referring to a pattern for communal cooperation in village-level society. He described a hypothetical local interclan organization, which village family units would spontaneously and voluntarily join, to be guided by local elders acceptable to them and not appointed by the government. That, he thought, could take up the fundamental task of restoring the ethical norms indispensable to a healthy society. In his mind this plan incorporated Ming Taizu's laudable focus on the well-being of village society and his stress on local schools and village elders and on choosing locally selected men to serve as tax captains to ensure equitable collection of the grain taxes.

Departing radically from conventional theorizing, Fang believed that imperial government was not omnicompetent, that in local governing especially it could not accomplish much, and that the ordinary people had the means to take over basic responsibilities quite apart from official acts of governing. He was not proposing democracy in the modern sense, nor was he proposing that the formal structure of governing was unnecessary; he was proposing that local families and clans should establish their moral authority and assume responsibilities toward mutual assistance, social welfare, disaster relief, and other aspects of base-level social life. The importance of his thinking does not lie in any practical applications of it; that never happened. Its importance lies in the fact that Fang Xiaoru was able to hypothesize about political solutions to social problems that did not assign all governing functions to the system of imperial government. This was not unprecedented in the Neo-Confucian era, but for his time it was different. He perceived government's limitations, accepted them, and looked beyond them for solutions lying with the people. An undercurrent of such thinking would continue to surface from time to time thereafter, as in the thought of the sixteenth-century Confucian thinker Wang Yangming (see Chapter 26, Section VI).

Those views had their counterpart in his understanding of central government's weaknesses. As the well-field concept was his symbol for ways to revive the health of communal life at village level, so his focus on the *Institutes of Zhou* offered a formula for rethinking the structure of imperial governing at high levels. He reached out boldly for concrete measures by which to supplement what he openly recognized as imperial power's inadequacy, on its own, to effect good governing. Drawing on that ancient book's ideal patterns, he first proposed what seemed to many to be unrealistic concern with superficialities. He suggested to the emperor that he change the names of offices, replace official titles, alter names of palaces and of the gates in the imperial capital's walls, and in other such ways reconstitute ancient forms of royal government. All that apparently was done. In these changes the outward and visible forms were expected to symbolize profound internal renewal. Fang Xiaoru appears to have used those formal changes to put in place institutionalized advisory and executive functions that, not in name but in essence, were to overcome Taizu's abolition of the Central Secretariat twenty years earlier. Fang was deeply committed to enlarging the responsibilities of scholar-officials and instituting broad cooperation between them and the ruler.[12]

The originality of Fang Xiaoru's political thinking and surviving items of information about political changes attempted under the Jianwen emperor suggest the possibility that if the civil war had not succeeded, the character of Ming governing might have been profoundly altered. It was one of those rare occasions in Chinese history when a ruler was prepared to give his trust to a group of learned advisers, to produce structural changes of potentially far-reaching consequences.[13]

Fang's intent in service to the Jianwen emperor offers an intriguing prospect of what might have been. All it in fact accomplished was to give a pretext to the Prince of Yan, who indignantly decried the defilement of his father's inviolable institutions and proclaimed it his duty to rescue the dynasty from evil ministers exerting undue influence on a young ruler. Zhu Di, the Prince of Yan, subsequently became the very strong ruler who then also faced the same set of problems. He too saw that adjustments must be made in the way Ming central government worked, but his alterations took quite a different direction from the Jianwen emperor's. Zhu Di is an equally interesting figure in Ming history, and because he succeeded, he is the more important ruler. His treacherous route to imperial power and his reinstatement of despotism in a rationalized and more effective form are not the entire story of his place in history.

III. FROM PRINCE TO EMPEROR

Seen from Zhu Di's point of view, his treachery, the civil war, and his usurpation of the throne are quite understandable. His usurpation succeeded; that contributed to its gradual acceptance in the minds of his subjects, for to succeed is to be validated. He too became a man of destiny. From any point of view, his reign accomplished some very good things. It also had its failures, and it did not escape the notice of later Ming historians and critical thinkers that he inaugurated certain destructive developments, but few would say such things openly and clearly. Scholars' implicit, and occasionally explicit, criticisms of him will be encountered in later chapters. Here one must try to see Zhu Di's difficult choices from his point of view.

Born at Nanjing in 1360, he is identified in the official accounts as the fourth of Ming Taizu's twenty-six sons and the fourth of five sons who were born to Empress Ma. The Ancestral Injunctions stipulated that only sons born to her, the only imperial spouse elevated by Taizu to the rank of empress, were to be in the line of succession. But were they her sons? In particular, was Zhu Di her son? This became a defining issue in politics of the time, and merits a digression here to explain it.

One of the anomalies of Ming Taizu's mentality is the fact that his Ancestral Injunctions, to which he devoted much thought in making repeated revisions, specifies unequivocally that only sons born to the empress, that is, to the ruler's principal spouse, could succeed to the throne. Yet it must have been known to at least a few officials of the time, as it has long been known to historians, that Zhu Di was not Empress Ma's son. Recently it also has been concluded that she bore no children.[14] According to Ming Taizu's meticulously prepared regulations, if that suspicion is correct (and it appears to be well founded), none of his sons could legitimately succeed him!

Was it simply not possible to admit that the revered Empress Ma had borne no sons? Taizu acknowledged seven sons born before the first version of the Injunctions was promulgated. He knew from the beginning that he was perpetrating a charade. One can argue that in Chinese law and custom the senior wife was the principal mother of all her husband's children whether or not borne by her; she was owed deference by all the husband's children, superseding that owed to the biological mothers. Sons, however, also owed ritual responsibilities to their birth mothers as well, so could not be kept ignorant of the facts. Zhu Di's mother probably was a Korean woman, a secondary consort who also bore one of Zhu Di's younger brothers, the Prince of Zhou. Zhu Di and his brothers clearly knew the truth but were forced to act out the charade, possibly because the first five sons were turned over to Empress Ma to be reared and had a special bond of affection with her. Perhaps Ming Taizu saw in that special relationship the basis for declaring those five to be "her sons" in a metaphorical sense strong enough to become an acceptable substitute for the biological truth. Yet it is the biological truth that the Injunctions explicitly demand. For whatever reasons, the charade of the princes' maternity was set in stone, and its consequences for Zhu Di's subsequent behavior were very great.

Of Zhu Di's three older brothers, the designated heir, Zhu Biao, died in 1392. The second and third sons also died before Taizu.[15] When the Jianwen emperor came to the throne in 1398, therefore, the Prince of Yan, Zhu Di, was his senior uncle and the oldest surviving son of Taizu. That gave Zhu Di great authority over his brothers and made him the generational although not the ritually senior member of the imperial clan; that is, in imperial clan affairs, as in Chinese family rules generally, and independent of his being the ruler, the Jianwen emperor as eldest son of the eldest son outranked his fourth uncle, as would also the Jianwen emperor's brothers and sons.

Zhu Di, however, had long been seen as the most able of all Taizu's sons and had been given special recognition by his father. He grew to be tall, powerfully built, and athletic like his father, and if the official portraits can be believed, he was a much more handsome and regal-looking figure than his father. In 1376 he was betrothed to the daughter of Xu Da, the preeminent military figure of the early Ming and the closest of all in personal relationship to the emperor. The marriage was carried out in 1367, when he was seventeen and she fifteen. In addition to that mark of his father's favor, Zhu Di was given the most important of the princedoms, Yan, based at the former Yuan capital, its name changed to Beiping (the North pacified) when the Ming armies drove the Mongols out in 1368. He took up residence there in 1380.

Xu Da had been stationed at Beiping more or less continuously since 1371 and used it as the base of all military operations against the Mongols in defense of the entire northern border. After Zhu Di and his bride took up official residence there, he came under the tutelage of the old general, his father-in-law, who taught him about war, military organization, Mongol tactics, and the strategic issues of defense. Zhu Di accompanied him every year on maneuvers. Xu Da became very ill late in 1384, but when he returned to Nanjing to report (and very favorably) on the Prince of Yan's development as a soldier, he left behind seventeen guard units with half a million soldiers. Personally loyal to General Xu, those officers and soldiers readily transferred that loyalty to the old general's son-in-law. Xu Da died the following spring in Nanjing. Thereafter other generals were sent to head the northern defense armies, but Zhu Di's influence among those forces remained strong.

Zhu Di, Prince of Yan, probably had been encouraged to think that he might inherit the throne. He spent nineteen years at Beiping, living in the palaces of the Mongol emperors (a bit run-down but nonetheless of grandiose scale), enough to make a man think about living the life of an emperor. Had his father not encouraged him to think like that by appointing him to this most important of the princedoms, ahead of his two older brothers? There were occasional hints that Taizu too had such thoughts. Zhu Di continued to scheme and to hope through the long years, aided by his strong-willed and intelligent wife and a brain trust of wily plotters. He was extremely careful not to arouse the old emperor's suspicions, for he could not be sure about the response: Could he push his father into recognizing his superior credentials and get the succession changed, or would the old man go into one of his rages and destroy him? That was the great imponderable. But as soon as the old emperor was off the scene, he would be ready. Within the year thereafter he struck.

The Jianwen emperor lost the war because he did not take personal command of it. He had superior forces and could take the war to the Prince of Yan's doorstep, driving him into a defensive stance on his own ground. The emperor also had the powerful element of legitimacy on his side. Yet he allowed his immersion in reform of his government to deflect him from direct involvement in defending his state. He let his generals fight the war. Several of them were highly competent and loyal; several were less competent, and some ultimately were disloyal. Had he been personally in charge and on the scene, the incompetence and disloyalty might have been overcome.

The Prince of Yan saw himself in the image of the warrior-emperor. He led his troops in battle and was constantly in the field, while his wife and eldest son, physically impaired but intelligent and highly committed, maintained the home base. Once when the prince was in the field Beiping was surrounded by the government's forces. The future Empress Xu mounted the walls, shouted brave encouragement to her forces, and hurled rocks down on the enemy. The city held. Her example reminded people of Empress Ma's feats when in the early years she had given similar help to Zhu Yuanzhang. The two vigorous empresses had been personally close; they set an admirable standard for Ming imperial women.[16] Empress Xu's other sons were at their father's side, audacious commanders leading troops in daring actions. The martial vigor of the usurper and his family had no counterpart in the emperor's camp.

At first the war went well for the emperor. He could field immense armies, often exceeding 200,000 men, though the prince also had large field armies. Both sides had excellent cavalry units that used Mongol tactics, but the prince's cavalrymen were in large part real Mongols, surrendered forces long in the Ming service, who added fearsome striking force to his side. The war see-sawed through 1399 and 1400 into 1401. Then the prince adopted a new strategy, bypassing the defended areas along the Grand Canal to strike overland farther west, and had significant successes through the spring of 1402. By late June he was approaching the banks of the Yangzi.

A peace faction at court urged negotiations. A delegation was sent out from Nanjing, headed by an imperial relative who made a secret pact with the prince to betray the emperor; when the rebel armies crossed the Yangzi and approached Nanjing's impregnable walls, he had one of the massive gates opened to admit the prince's army. A naval commander, part of the same plot, defected with his fleet to the prince, assuring him unimpeded crossing of the river. On July 13 the rebel armies approached Nanjing's walls, and as secretly agreed, a gate on the northeast side was opened to them. In the melee that followed, the palaces were set afire and the civil war was ended. We have already seen Zhu Di's first acts in the aftermath of his armies' entry into Nanjing. His reign and the patterns in Ming governing that ensued from it are the subject of the next chapter.

24

THE "SECOND FOUNDING" OF THE MING DYNASTY

The Jianwen emperor's efforts to reform the Ming dynasty's institutions and governing methods were quickly overturned, leaving the new ruler of China, the Emperor Chengzu, the task of realigning his government while proclaiming his fidelity to the Ming founder's intentions. He sought many ways of establishing his state domestically and in foreign relations, using the great maritime expeditions of Admiral Zheng He to Southeast Asia, India, Western Asia, and Africa to proclaim his legitimacy and the centrality of China. His principal efforts were devoted to devising ways to strengthen the imperial institution, defending China's northern borders, and repeatedly leading armies into Mongolia to war on those Mongols who could not be restrained by his diplomacy. That preoccupation led him to transfer the Ming capital from Nanjing to Beijing and to build there the great city of which we still can see impressive remnants.

I. MING CHENGZU'S IMPRINT ON MING GOVERNING

If the usurper had not won the civil war of 1399–1402, we might now read about the "metamorphosis" of the early Ming dynasty under the innovative Jianwen emperor; instead historians today often speak of the "second founding" of the dynasty under the strong rule of Zhu Di. From the moment of his claiming the throne in July 1402, he must no longer be called the Prince of Yan but, as is the custom, by his eventual posthumous temple name, Chengzu.[1] His reign from that year until his death in 1424 was a very busy period of political changes, wide foreign contacts, war, and domestic rehabilitation. Chengzu set his course in some new directions, but at the same time affirmed many features of Taizu's rule. His decision to move the capital from Nanjing (Yingtian) to Beiping, its name in consequence of that move changed to Jingshi (the capital) but usually called Beijing ("the northern capital," as it is called today), and formally known as Shuntian (Obedient to Heaven), marks a disjunction from the Nanjing period. The shift of the capital along with the other changes he effected justify the idea that the Ming dynasty underwent a second founding.

There is reason enough to look upon him as a co-founder of the dynasty, as the Jiajing emperor thought when he changed Zhu Di's posthumous title from Taizong, an expected temple name for the second ruler of a dynasty, to Chengzu. The final syllable *zu* in imperial titles is usually translated "progenitor," and shows that the ruler who bears that title is more important to the creation of the dynasty than is implied by the syllable *zong*, a mere "ancestor." To be sure, the Jiajing emperor's reasons were a bit more complicated than that, but we may take it as a justified elevation of Chengzu's status within the succession of Ming emperors. Insofar as it suggests the idea of a second founding, it calls attention to his importance in both interrupting and then refocusing Ming history. The content of those changes can be noted only briefly in what follows.

On coming to power under such disruptive circumstances, the usurper's first need was to stabilize the scene. He rewarded his military accomplices with high titles, creating a new "nobility of merit" to replace the leadership that in the previous decades had suffered first Ming Taizu's systematic purge of his old associates, and then the destruction of many military and civil officials who had remained loyal to the Jianwen emperor.[2] He also sought out men who, despite having served under his predecessor, were judged not to be of seditious mind, and appointed them to solid posts, in that way reassuring officialdom about his intentions. He soon ordered the rebuilding of the fire-destroyed palace buildings and settled into the regimen of ruling.

Uncomfortable in the role of overseer and manager of a large bureaucracy, he quickly began to seek ways to make governing suit his temperament. His chosen role for himself was that of the warrior-emperor; but to be that, he could not emulate his father as emperor. Taizu had given up leading his armies in person in 1363, five years before he took the throne, to devote himself to the arduous labors of minutely supervising his administration. Chengzu had little patience for that task; he much preferred the arduous labors of campaigning. To indulge that preference, he sought ways to delegate greater authority for day-to-day decisions to scholar-officials. He began immediately to build up a pool of qualified officials, announcing the resumption of the triennial civil service examinations to begin in the second year of his Yongle reign period (1404).

His attention also fell on the Hanlin Academy, established under Taizu to provide a body of scholar-officials for literary services to the Inner Court. They drafted proclamations and edicts, processed documents, supplied specialists for the highest-level clerical supports needed by the emperor. Chengzu turned the Hanlin Academy into a prestige assignment for the best-qualified and most ambitious young *jinshi* degree winners. Those who won their degrees at the top of the ranked lists were given the newly created status of Hanlin Bachelors (Shuji shi). In several of the earlier triennial examinations in his reign, starting with the first in 1404, as many as fifty or sixty *jinshi* might be selected for assignment to the Hanlin Academy.[3] Thereafter the numbers were much smaller. The Bachelors received further in-service training, took special examinations, and were guaranteed access to careers at high levels in central government. These measures gave reassuring importance and stability to civil service careers and greatly enhanced the esprit of his government.

While building strength in the civil service, he went further toward devising ways of turning day-to-day administrative management over to his high officials. He created a cabinet (Neige) of scholar-advisers based in the Inner Court, since his father's reign called Grand Secretaries (Daxueshi). In 1402 he appointed seven young officials to the low-ranking but newly prestigious posts of Grand Secretaries. They constituted a remarkable set of appointees, men of unusual talent for administration. Most of them served for many years, even after the end of his reign.[4] He formed very close personal relations with them, saw them frequently in formal and informal settings, and even took some of them along with him on his field campaigns to manage policy and administrative tasks that could not be left behind. In all that he displayed a sharp political intelligence; he knew how to delegate authority and use men wisely.

These central governing adjustments created what became the fixed patterns in Ming bureaucratic life. While at first Chengzu could choose men who did not yet have career service credentials for posting in the Hanlin Academy or elsewhere, procedures soon became fixed; by the mid-fifteenth century, only men with earned *jinshi* degrees (and normally only those who ranked among the highest) could serve in the Hanlin, and only men from the Hanlin could become Grand Secretaries.

More effective relations with the leaders of his Outer Court also grew out of Chengzu's changes. After Taizu's reorganization of the central government in 1380, the senior officials in the Outer Court were the six ministers heading the ministries of Personnel, Revenues, Rites, War, Punishments, and Public Works, plus the Left and Right Censors-in-Chief. Chengzu selected relatively young men of high promise for those eight leading positions and kept them in office for very long terms. A number of great figures emerged from these high career posts. Their interaction with Grand Secretaries often was close and congenial; it became customary to grant Grand Secretaries concurrent nonsubstantive titles as ministers, giving them higher rank than their Inner Court posts carried, and allowing them limited concurrent presence in the Outer Court. All of those measures induced a greater spirit of collegiality than had been the norm.

In the first decades of the fifteenth century, under Chengzu and his successors the central government took on a dignified and serious tone. Deep rivalries and animosities were not wholly eliminated, but government acquired an atmosphere of able and serious men devoted to a high calling. At times that could degenerate into an atmosphere of stodgy, conventional-minded men pursuing personal aggrandizement, even to one of petty-minded rivalry and hypocrisy, but through most of the Ming that was not a serious problem.

The examination system functioned to send a broadly selected cohort of talent into the public service stream, which tended to uphold morale and commitment. That the brutality which began the Yongle reign could be so quickly succeeded by an atmosphere of collegiality and common purpose is in itself remarkable; it reflects a redirection of the invigorating sense of purpose which was widely shared throughout the decades of the dynasty's founding. The quality of Ming governing was at high levels in the fifteenth century, maintained even after the quality of the emperors sharply declined.

Ming Chengzu, the warrior emperor, was also a man of thorough education. He wrote a few philosophical essays, knew history, and had strong tastes in calligraphy, particularly evident in the elegant "palace editions" in large format produced by his state publishing office.[5] Taking up proposals from his scholar-officials, he diverted much of the best talent joining the growing pool of examination graduates into work on several extraordinary undertakings, of which he was proud to be the patron. One of those became a vast project of literary compilation. He ordered that the existing literature, no doubt including more printed works (a half-century before Gutenberg's first printed book) than all the manuscript books then in existence throughout the rest of the world, be drawn upon to create an encyclopedia of accumulated knowledge in all fields. It was called the *Yongle Dadian,* bearing the name of his reign period. Whole works or extensive portions of works were copied into it under a comprehensive analytical scheme that arranged materials by subject. More than 2,000 scholars worked for more than five years to produce a work in 22,938 chapters *(juan)* bound in half that number of large volumes. Its content was drawn from more than 7,000 works, and it contained over 50 million words.[6] It was so vast that it was not practical to engrave blocks and print it. The beautifully written manuscript was placed in the palace for use by the emperor and his scholar-officials, but that set disappeared before the end of the Ming. Some think the Jiajing emperor, who died in 1567, had it placed in his tomb, which is still intact, so that original may someday be recovered. One identical copy had been made. Only 700 or so volumes from that copy still exist; some had long been scattered, but the largest number were destroyed when the British and French forces sacked the Summer Palace in 1860.

Other large literary projects also were undertaken in the effort to identify the Yongle reign with intellectual life, something not true of his father's reign. His scholars put together two *Great Compendia (Da Quan)* of learning essential for the civil service examinations. One was made up of extracts from the *Five Classics* and *Four Books* with the Zhu Xi commentaries. The other was called *The Great Compendium of the Principles of Human Nature (Xing li da quan),* a basic introduction to Neo-Confucian Lixue philosophy. Both *Compendia* were printed in large numbers for distribution to county and prefectural Confucian schools, to assist students preparing for the examinations. They also were reprinted in a number of privately sponsored editions, and in others brought out by local offices of government. Like the Yuan, the Ming also used the Zhu Xi versions of the classics for the examinations, giving them that limited but important measure of "orthodoxy."[7] The intent behind this project was to help students by making standard editings of the basic Confucian texts available everywhere. Later in the dynasty these were roundly condemned as shortcuts for lazy students: they narrowed the scope of study, discouraged philosophical debate, and diverted budding scholars away from the practice of making their own intellectual inquiry into the full texts. The decline of classical scholarship in the later Ming was decried by many scholars who laid the blame for it at the feet of a meddling emperor—although most would not make that charge in unambiguous language until after the fall of the Ming.

It is probable that the emperor sponsored the various literary projects of his reign to gain the participation of scholars and earn elite goodwill when many people were still critical of the usurpation and the purges. The emperor was treading a narrow and difficult path between enticement and intimidation, as all successful despots must.

II. THE EUNUCH ESTABLISHMENT AND THE IMPERIAL BODYGUARD

Eunuchs were a part of all imperial Chinese courts, considered indispensable to the life of the ruler's household and necessary to guarantee that the imperial succession would not be tainted by scandal. Other people in society were forbidden to employ eunuchs, so they were also a mark of sumptuary privilege reserved to royalty. Today it is difficult to understand how such a practice could have been so long tolerated in a civilization which held up ideals of rationality and humanistic cultivation, but such anomalies are not unknown in other civilizations. It is not at all difficult to see how eunuchs, given their role in the imperial household, would then infiltrate the workings of the court and all aspects of governing in which the emperors took a direct interest. These extended roles given to, or appropriated by, eunuchs are what have made them so resented, so unreasonably vilified, by most officials, historians, and writers. The hatred directed toward them also had some foundation in fact. Some periods of history are particularly marked by "eunuch disasters" when unscrupulous eunuch officials ran amok. The Ming dynasty witnessed several such episodes. Yet the greater number of the thousands of eunuchs who worked in Ming government were no doubt faithful, competent servitors of the emperor.

As men who had been castrated in their boyhood, by early Ming preference drawn so far as possible (but by no means exclusively) from non-Chinese populations in border areas, and reared in the palaces with little or no family contact, the eunuchs were true unfortunates. They were confined mostly to base roles, ridiculed and scorned in most contexts. They could, however, be close to the occasional member of the imperial household, a prince or empress or young ruler, for whom they were personal servants and companions, even favored confidants. It was all too easy for those favored ones then to abuse their status, seize unwarranted powers, and exercise authority improperly in the name of the ruler who favored them. Some, however, especially those who made careers in the military service outside the palace, became respected figures of importance to the state. The most unusual among the latter is the sinified Turkic Muslim eunuch Admiral Zheng He, who commanded Cheng-zu's great fleets on voyages into the Indian Ocean throughout much of the Yongle reign. We shall come back to those voyages later.[8]

Ming Taizu employed eunuchs in his household service from the mid-1360s onward and established a bureau for eunuchs in his Nanjing palace in 1367, the year before he declared himself the emperor of the new Ming dynasty. Later on he reorganized the eunuch establishment in twelve functionally distinct supervisory offices *(jian)*, each to handle a service needed within the inner palaces where adult males other than the emperor were forbidden to go. In the beginning, palace women were expected to provide most of the services of preparing food, caring for clothing and equipment, and attending the emperor and his growing harem of secondary spouses and their young children. But from the beginning the need for stronger-bodied males was supplied by eunuchs, probably fewer than 100 in the early Hongwu years, many hundreds by the end of his reign. Eunuchs displaced palace women in many of those roles, and their numbers grew. There is a widely accepted misunderstanding that Taizu forbade eunuchs to perform secretarial and management services which required them to be literate. That has been shown to be inaccurate.[9] According to that erroneous view, it was Chengzu who first employed eunuchs in roles paralleling those given to junior scholar-officials or clerical assistants in the palace, and entrusted them with many tasks requiring the ability to read the flow of documents which kept the government working. Chengzu indeed established the first regular training school in literacy for eunuchs, a rationalization demanded by the very large role already well established for them in the founder's reign.

An oft-quoted statistic on the volume of paperwork needed to make Ming government function is found in the *Veritable Record* of Ming Taizu's reign: "On the day *jiwei* of the ninth month of the seventeenth year of the Hongwu reign [October 9, 1384] the Supervising Secretary Zhang Wenfu reported: from the fourteenth day of the ninth month through the twenty-first day, a span of eight days, the various inner and outer offices [i.e., those in the capital and those in the provinces] submitted memorials numbering 1660, dealing with 3391 separate matters."[10] The emperor used the occasion to complain that one man could not infallibly oversee such a volume of work in which errors on his part could have grave consequences. He therefore demanded that all the officials perform their tasks diligently. Those officials of course read the memorials and attached summaries with their suggestions for handling the problems, saving him the necessity to do all the work by himself. It has been shown, however, that from the beginning some of that work was done by eunuchs who at least read the officials' summaries and sorted stacks of documents according to the branch of government that would implement the ruler's decisions. It seems likely that with many of the documents they wrote out the emperor's response, or even anticipated it, applied his seal, and sent the matter on for handling by others. In later reigns they read memorials, prepared summaries, and processed other documents. Ming Taizu frequently warned about the loss of control over governmental action implicit in giving such tasks to eunuchs, but that warning contradicts his own actions in explicitly setting up such a system. In later reigns, officials who rightly perceived those eunuch roles as in competition with their own muddied the history of Ming court procedures by stressing the founder's statements warning against the employment of eunuchs in secretarial duties.

Chengzu carried the delegation of executive authority much farther, both in the assisting roles given to Grand Secretaries and members of his high-level secretarial pool, the Hanlin Academy, and in still further enlarging the roles of eunuchs. A full-fledged eunuch bureaucracy grew from the earlier beginnings. It consisted of the Twelve Directorates, plus Four Agencies, and Eight Bureaus, together known as the Twenty-four Offices. In Chengzu's reign the Directorate of Palace Eunuchs (Neiguan jian) functioned as a ministry of personnel for the entire eunuch establishment; its director was comparable to a chief minister, responsible for the careers of all eunuchs.

Later, and for the remainder of imperial history the Directorate of Ceremonial (Sili jian) came to hold the higher position, its director being the head of all the eunuchs and an official of great power. That was the post usually held by the infamous eunuch dictators to whom we shall return in later chapters. The Directorate of Ceremonial's duties acquired an ever broader range. Starting out with responsibilities for attending the emperor at all times, making all arrangements for and supervising all meetings of the court, maintaining security, and overseeing the other eunuch directorates in providing for all the imperial household, it later came to be responsible also for the eunuch school, for the emperor's collections of books and artworks, for the palace publishing enterprise where many books were printed, for the management of the imperial tombs, and for handling all the documents that came before the emperor for his, or just as likely for their, attention. Its director could reward and punish all other eunuchs, could assign, promote, banish, even execute them. He was closest to the ruler himself both in daily contact and in personal relationship, so could exercise imperial power by proxy in many situations.

The names of some of the other Twenty-four Offices will give a sense of the scope of other eunuch functions: there were directorates of manufactories, palace maintenance, imperial seals, imperial regalia, imperial horses, imperial temples and shrines; the Four Agencies took care of providing firewood, paper, bells and drums, and administering the baths; the Eight Bureaus were responsible for such services as making arms, crafting jewelry, weaving and dyeing, sewing, caring for the gardens, and the like. Many of those activities also were served by parallel agencies outside the palace administration that were not staffed by eunuchs. Duplication and waste grew in the eunuch bureaucracy as in that of the regular government; all bureaucrats gain from the growth of their staffs and the expansion of their duties.

The eunuch bureaucrats were ranked and paid on the model of officialdom, but their ranks were supposed to range downward from rank four, thus comprising only the lower six ranks instead of the officials' nine, and their salaries were minuscule. Nonetheless, some of the notorious eunuch directors of ceremonial and their more important colleagues acquired fabulous wealth. They also had an insidious kind of power because they were not persons in their own right but were mere extensions of the ruler's person, and like him, they could attain authority that regular civil officials could not easily check.

The most insidious form of power gained by eunuchs was that granted to them by Emperor Chengzu in 1420 when he established the Eastern Depot and placed it under the direction of his chief eunuch. The Eastern Depot (Dongchang) was the ruler's principal extralegal investigative agency, staffed and operated by eunuchs who specialized in intelligence work against officials, prying into all aspects of their behavior from malfeasance and corruption to disloyalty and sedition. Arrests could be made at any time without warrants. Suspects were imprisoned, interrogated, forced under torture to make confessions.

The Eastern Depot (and its later counterpart, the Western Depot, or Xichang) functioned in tandem with the Embroidered Uniform Guard (Jinyi wei), one of the emperor's personal bodyguard units at the capital, which was a prestige assignment for certain kinds of appointees. It also, however, included mostly men of military training who worked as military police. The Embroidered Uniform Guard had existed since the reign of the founder but gained new duties in the Yongle period's reorganization of institutions. Under Chengzu it was given responsibility for a notorious prison at which the eunuchs of the Eastern Depot conducted their punishments. It was the place where many who entered gave up hope of ever again seeing the light of day.

The infamous practice of beating offending officials at the court, a practice begun at the Yuan court and continued under the Ming, also was jointly carried out by the eunuchs and the Guard. Under eunuch supervision, the Guards administered the beatings, often in the court in the presence of emperor and officials. The beatings were sometimes fatal, but their main purpose was to humiliate and demean the best representatives of the scholar-official elite so that they would not forget they were servitors *(chen)* of an almighty ruler. After the Ming founder's reign the beatings at court were less frequent, but the practice was not ended.

The Eastern Depot and the Embroidered Uniform Guard together formed the core of the Emperor Chengzu's (and his successors') private surveillance machinery, to differentiate them from the openly official, bureaucratically managed offices of the Censorate. On the one hand, Emperor Chengzu enhanced scholar-officials' careers and enlarged their role in administering the nation and making policy. On the other, he balanced that positive approach with the negative one of intimidation. The blunt instrument of his father's rage and fury was replaced by Chengzu's much more focused and efficient security system. After the initial fury spent defending the usurpation, violence came to be less frighteningly unpredictable, less irrational, but it remained.

III. DEFENDING THRONE AND STATE

Only eight years old when his father, Ming Taizu, announced the establishment of his new Ming dynasty, Zhu Di was reared in the heady atmosphere of successful warfare; arms won the empire. During his twenty years as Prince of Yan on the northern borders, he was surrounded by military men engaged in fighting the remnants of Mongol power and planning Ming northern defenses. As the emperor after 1402, he continued to give his attention largely to his empire's and his throne's defense. Those were problems that he understood. Solving them required actions of kinds he himself could perform; they were problems of guarding and strengthening the throne against internal challenges and defending the borders against external enemies.

From the beginning he faced the same problem of defending his throne that his unfortunate nephew had faced: other imperial princes were an unreliable lot. They too might use the resources of their "fiefs," that is, their princedoms, to build up regional military power. Having that, they might invoke the Ancestral Injunctions precisely as he had, finding there the excuses for rebellion. Among his early acts in 1402 and 1403, after rewarding and praising the remaining princes, and restoring to their ranks and titles the princes who had been demoted by the Jianwen emperor, he set out to "reduce the feudatories" in his own more devious way. His younger brothers, and in some cases his nephews who had already succeeded to the first generation of princes, were in general a loutish collection of arrogant and violent men, fond of high living and low scheming. There were one or two exceptions, princes such as the Prince of Shu in Sichuan, who devoted themselves to learning and to useful lives, striving to bring credit to the dynasty. There was, however, little pressure on any of them to so bestir themselves, and most of them indulged in the kinds of activities that frequently got them into trouble.

Chengzu did not announce an overall plan of reorganizing the princedoms. He allowed them one by one to come before him to answer charges of grave misbehavior and punished them in all cases by removing their command of garrison units and leaving them only insignificant personal guard detachments, in some cases by demoting them to the status of commoners, thereby cutting off the state's support. When his punishment was not that drastic, he nonetheless reduced their revenues, reassigned them to less important princedoms, and imposed restrictions on their activities. That was an astute way of handling the problem. Within ten years, the consequences were that all the incumbents of the crucial northern border princedoms had been reassigned to out-of-the-way locations in the interior; all were relieved of their military commands, and their personal guard units were reduced to insignificance; their ability to interfere in the local governments where their princedoms were located was abolished, and central government officials were assigned with increased powers to manage all aspects of their lives. Later emperors continued to add restrictions. Their descendants were forbidden to engage in any of the normal productive activities of ordinary people in society, and were confined to the walled compounds of their princely estates to survive on dwindling resources, leading dreary and useless lives. After a prince's challenge to the succession in 1425, when usurpation was again attempted, the prince-doms threatened national security in only two other (and readily suppressed) attempts to overturn the throne throughout the remaining two centuries of Ming history.[11] Chengzu's policies did not attempt to alter the enforced isolation and uselessness which the founding emperor's Ancestral Injunctions imposed on all imperial clan members. It was too early in the dynasty to see how their numbers would grow, or to calculate the fiscal burden they would in time create. His only concern was the security of the throne vis-à-vis the princes.

External Relations

In Ming times China was thought of, by its own people and by their neighbors, as the territorial extent of the Chinese (Han)[12] people, where the Chinese languages and culture were dominant. That culturally defined China was loosely identical with politically defined China; its ethnic and cultural boundaries coincided with the administrative reach of the Ming state. Ming China did not exercise rule over any substantial portions of Inner Asia, the one exception being the narrow coastal strip of long-standing Chinese settlement in southern Manchuria called Liaodong. Otherwise it governed none of Manchuria or Mongolia (Inner or Outer) on its northern borders, or Xinjiang in the farther northwest, and of course did not hold or govern Tibet. In the southwest the Ming state pushed its boundaries outward in the 1380s when it succeeded in conquering and holding the region making up the modern province of Yunnan and then reorganized adjoining marginal areas into the new province of Guizhou. In other parts of the southern frontier also the Ming imposed various forms of control, mostly indirect, over many non-Chinese peoples within what are its present-day southern boundaries, and during the brief period 1407–1427 extended its presence still farther south into Annam (northern Vietnam). That was a misguided move from which it soon had to extricate itself by abandoning the annexation effort.

The history of the Ming state's borders is important, because myths about China's historic claims to territories lying far beyond the boundaries of Chinese administration appear regularly in writings on China's past relations with its neighbors. In fact, all such territories beyond China Proper remained autonomous, and the Ming government was able to exert essentially no influence over them, even when it granted leaders of non-Chinese peoples titles and honors. Those leaders warred for or against China as suited their own purposes. Yet in many instances, the award of titles to their chieftains and princes could entail significant gifts of material things as well as high-sounding titles, and many leaders were eager to obtain them. When those leaders died, their sons or other heirs might then come to the Ming court asking to be confirmed in inheritance of the titles and to receive a further outlay of gifts. In some situations, having the empty Ming titles enhanced a chieftain's prestige among his people and aided him to fight off rivals. On both sides the maneuverings were intricate, but on neither side was there any sense that sovereignty was at stake.[13]

One interesting example may be cited: Chengzu is praised by some recent historians for his foresight in sending envoys among the Jurchens in far northern Manchuria as early as 1403, to gain information about those potential allies of the Mongols as he planned ways of eliminating the Mongol threat. This usefully illustrates the character of such relationships. In 1411 he sent as his envoy a Jurchen eunuch, Isiha, who spoke both Jurchen and Chinese and had family ties to Jurchen chieftains. He was an effective diplomat.[14] He led an expedition of twenty-five vessels by the sea route, around the eastern coast of Korea and north to the mouth of the Amur (the Heilongjiang River), opposite the northern part of Sakhalin Island. The Chinese ships entered the mouth of the Amur and sailed inland for a few miles, where they met their Jurchen counterparts and signed some agreements bestowing the title of Regional Military Commissioner on the chieftain, and to mark the event they erected a preinscribed stele they had brought along from China. Subsequent visits by Isiha led to the building of a Buddhist temple and the erection of a second stele. The text of that stele is today taken as proof that "this vast region was in Ming times incorporated into the territory of China. The Nu'ergan Military Affairs Commission established by Ming Chengzu was the agency through which to administer this region's highest regional military government institutions."[15] The "administrative region" called Nu'ergan, that is, of the Nurkal Jurchen tribesmen, is shown on recent maps as being almost as large as China Proper! Any claim that it was then part of China is wholly groundless.

The Warrior Emperor's Mongolian Campaigns

Ming Chengzu was not subject to any such delusions. He knew he could not appoint any civil or military officials in such regions, could not register households so as to levy and collect taxes, and could not establish any institutions that might influence their people's lives. The northern frontier was of great strategic importance to him, and diplomacy was applied to the problem of gaining cooperation of regional leaders from one end of it to the other. His purpose in granting titles and gifts and awarding trading privileges was to isolate groups of Mongols, tie their leaders to his side by offering them rewards, and keep them in competition with one another so they would not coalesce into leagues of tribal peoples capable of warring on China.

The Uriyangkhad tribes had links to Mongols who had surrendered to the Ming in the 1360s. The leaders of three groups of them, called the Three Eastern Commanderies of the Uriyangkhad, were granted rights to settle in southern Manchuria. They had fairly close ties to the Chinese court; in order to come to court and receive gifts and honors, they submitted "tribute" so frequently that the Ming court had to restrict the number and times of their embassies. They remained an important element in Ming relations with tribal peoples in Manchuria, including groups of Jurchens who lived among them.

By trying to build a relationship with the Nurkal Jurchens to their east and north, Chengzu hoped he could apply additional pressure on the Three Eastern Commanderies to remain docile, or at least might divide their attention.

On the farthest northwest borders of Mongolia, the Oyirat Mongols also were granted titles acknowledging their control of that region in the hope of driving a wedge between them and their Mongol cousins in what we today call Mongolia. In none of those cases did the titles and privileges granted by the Ming court imply that Mongol chieftains accepted any measure of Chinese sovereignty.[16]

By the serious effort to acquire intelligence and to intervene diplomatically, Chengzu was preparing to make war on those Mongols close enough to China's northern borders to be of present risk. The problem he faced there was genuinely one of security; Chinggis Khan had welded the Mongols into a large nation with Eurasia-wide territories and a powerful sense of being the heirs of an invincible conqueror. Subsequent to Chinggis Khan's death, internal struggles left the Mongol empire divided into four separate khanates, but three of them gradually ceased to be Mongolian in population and culture. The essential Mongolia was the enlarged hearthland, a new creation including all of what we today know as Inner and Outer Mongolia. Ensuing Mongol civil wars weakened Mongolia, yet there remained a real possibility that the divided and weakly led Mongols in Mongolia would find a new leader capable of restoring their unity and strength. Even before that might happen, some Mongol leaders were able to raid along China's northern borders. The Ming emperors Taizu and Chengzu understood their Mongol problem in these terms.

Throughout Ming Taizu's reign, the Ming court treated the Mongol heirs to the Yuan dynasty with respect and sought favorable diplomatic relations with them in the hope of inducing them to surrender and give up their pursuit of military resurgence. There was reason for this Chinese circumspection: the Chinese military establishment battled the Mongols on Mongolian ground through the thirty years of Taizu's reign and held the Mongol fighting man in awe. The Chinese court clearly recognized that the Mongols had the potential for again becoming powerful and aggressive neighbors. They did not know that Tamerlane, the greatest conqueror of the age, also was planning an invasion of China. While heading a large invasion force, in 1405 he fell sick and died at Utrar, north of Samarkand, on his way into western China. His less bellicose successors in the Chaghadai khanate developed friendly relations with the Ming court and the Chinese were never made aware of Tamerlane's ambitions. Chengzu's northern border problems all would have become insignificant compared with an invasion from that quarter; as it was, the Mongol threat fully occupied him for the next twenty years.

When Chengzu came to the throne in 1402, there were three cohesive groupings of Mongols to be dealt with. First, the Uriyangkhad Mongols in southeastern Mongolia, mentioned earlier, were in closest contact with the Ming, and were the most closely related to the thousands of Mongols who had surrendered, to serve in their own separate units within the Ming armed forces. The Ming princedom that was designed to function as a bastion against Mongol incursions from southeast Mongolia on the Manchurian border was that of the Prince of Ning, one of the more able and martial princes. While still Prince of Yan, Chengzu in 1399 had forced the Prince of Ning to turn over to him units of Mongol cavalry. As emperor after 1402 he did not relish the idea of having a strong princedom there with the capacity to draw on the military resources of Mongolia. In 1403 he therefore deposed his younger brother and transferred him to a safer location in Jiangsi, perhaps making China's throne more secure but leaving a serious gap in the northern defense line. To fill it, he located the Uriyangkhad Mongols of the Three Commanderies in southern Manchuria, and attempted to keep them dependent on China by granting titles and material rewards, including the right to send delegations more than once a year, when they could both trade and receive further gifts. Yet that lavish treatment could not guarantee their performance, as he would soon learn.

Second, the bulk of the Mongol population scattered throughout Mongolia and regions farther west was nominally under the descendants of the Yuan emperors at Karakorum, whom many Mongols regarded as failed leaders despite all the symbolic power of their Chinggisid legitimacy. In 1403 a Mongol chieftain, not of that imperial line, assassinated the last claimant to the Yuan dynastic title (but not the last to claim Chinggisid legitimacy), and tried to proclaim himself the successor Great Khan, but could not quite achieve that goal; he therefore repudiated the imperial line and took the title of "Tatar Khan" (Dada Kehan) to replace the name "Mongol."[17] He was in turn assassinated and replaced two years later by Mongol dissidents led by an ambitious Mongol (now Tatar) general named Arughtai. Arughtai was to remain China's principal opponent in Mongolia until he was killed in 1434 by his sometime allies, sometime enemies, the Oyirat Mongols.

The third group, the Oyirat confederation, were known as the Western Mongols, living at the northwestern edges of Mongolia. They too were ambitious to lead a reunified Mongol nation and took advantage of all opportunities to attack the Uriyangkhad and the Tatar "Eastern Mongols" or to ally with one against the other, all for the sake of putting pressure on the Chinese border. They also warred on China's nominal allies in Hami and other places and tried to take over the Inner Asian trade routes. Later in the century they would invade China.[18]

The Ming founder had sent his armies repeatedly into Mongolia to break up concentrations of Mongol power, destroy armies, and capture the steppe resources of people and animals. He established some forward garrison points many miles north of what would become the future Great Wall line. Chengzu tried to continue that policy but found that the forward defense garrisons in Mongolia were too exposed, and impossible to maintain. He led five campaigns into Mongolia between 1410 and 1424, each time to take advantage of a perceived weakness among his enemies or to forestall the formation of a coalition that would produce a serious attack on the Ming borders. Each time he met the Mongol armies in battle he could trumpet those engagements as great victories; but he did not drive the enemy back or forestall their future offensives. Each time he failed to capture Arughtai or to leave the enemy incapable of reorganizing and fighting again. His campaigns occupied most of the months from spring into late autumn in 1410, 1414, 1422, 1423, and 1424. He led large and well-provisioned armies at great expense; they probably exceeded 250,000 troops, many of them cavalry, on each of the campaigns.[19] In 1414 he proudly took his fifteen-year-old grandson, Zhu Zhanji, the future Emperor Xuanzong, along with him to inure him to the realities of warfare. On the last campaign, in August 1424, he fell ill and died, far up in Eastern Mongolia, exhausted at age sixty-four, the decisive victory over the Mongol enemy still eluding him. As a warrior emperor he clearly did not achieve his own goals.

Following his death the situation on the northern border changed; the Ming outer defense line, intended to support an interventionist Ming role in controlling the Mongols, was gradually abandoned; the outer garrisons were pulled back in favor of a static defense line nearer to the border of Chinese settlement. Those nearer defense points then came to constitute the Nine Defense Areas of the garrisoned border zone. That withdrawal from forward positions left nothing to prevent the Mongols from forming strong regional groupings, and eventually filling in the entire fringe zone between China and the steppe. Moreover, the initiative now lay with them to accept Ming diplomatic controls or reject them and assume an offensive posture. It led to the debacle of Mongol invasion and capture of the Ming emperor Yingzong in 1449, after which the boundary of actual Ming military involvement shrank still further. The situation remained unsettled, hence unpredictable and dangerous. Defense of the northern border remained the continuing military focus of the Ming state, greatly limiting its capacity to maintain its interests elsewhere.

War in Annam

The southern frontier truly presented no threats to the security of Ming China, but troublesome disputes among unruly peoples along that boundary often led to requests for Chinese intervention, or were used by Chinese regional military commanders there as pretexts for taking military action.

The kingdom of Annam, roughly equivalent to present-day northern Vietnam, existed in territory that had been governed as a province of China, on and off, from Qin and Han times (third century B.C.E.) until the Tang dynasty (ninth century). After that it existed as an independent kingdom in close relationship to China, looked upon by the Chinese as a region under strong Chinese cultural influence. Its people wrote their language in the Chinese script, honored the Chinese classics, and, like the Koreans, requested envoys from the Chinese court to conduct formal ceremonies of investiture for their kings, in that way granting them prestige and validity in conflicts with rivals. Theirs had become a special relationship with China.

In 1400 a usurper killed off the Annamese king and many members of the royal Tran family, named himself king, and sent the usual delegation to the

Ming court to request investiture, claiming that the Tran royal line had "died out." The Chinese did not know the circumstances but accepted the envoy's request, only to learn four years later that a member of the Tran family was alive and was asking for Chinese help to restore his dynasty. On receiving that news, Ming Chengzu sent an envoy to intervene, but was told by the usurper that he regretted his act and would restore the Tran king. In 1405 a Chinese delegation with an armed guard unit entered the country but was ambushed; the Tran claimant and the Chinese envoy were killed, and the unrepetant usurper claimed victory. Angered by this defiance and worried about Annamese warlike activity in other areas, Chengzu sent a large army in 1406 that crushed the Annamese forces and occupied Annam's two capitals, reporting complete victory to the Chinese court at Nanjing in 1407. On the advice of the Ming general in command of the invasion force at Hanoi, Chengzu, who knew little about the Annamese, decided to annex the country and reestablish it as a province, as it was several hundred years earlier.

That commenced a long war. The Annamese were tenacious, were fighting on their own ground, and stubbornly continued to resist for twenty years. The region had no particular value to China; it was not necessary for defense of the Chinese borders, nor did China's control over it benefit any other Chinese interests. At the court in Nanjing the Yongle emperor's civil officials urged total withdrawal. They reminded him that his father, Ming Taizu, had included Annam on his list of benign border states that China should never invade. But Chengzu was stubborn, responding to his courtiers with his own reminders: the usurpers had deceived the Chinese, had attacked a Chinese diplomatic mission and killed diplomats and soldier-escorts, and had boasted about their crimes. The war stalemated. Finally, in 1427, three years after Chengzu's death, the Annamese usurper found a way to restore a semblance of the pre-1400 legitimacy, pretending to restore an heir of the Tran royal house; the Ming court gratefully accepted that as reason for breaking the stalemate, knowing that the supposed heir would soon be executed and the usurper would again take the Annamese throne. The Ming armies withdrew, Annam again became an independent kingdom, and within a few years China recognized the heir of the usurper as the legitimate king of Annam. His name was Lê Lo'i; he is remembered as a great figure in Annamese history.[20] It had been a painful and costly experience for both sides.

IV. SECURING CHINA'S PLACE IN THE ASIAN WORLD

Preoccupied with the Mongol problem, frustrated by his dead-end policy in Annam, the Yongle emperor still had time for other issues in China's external relations.

Korea and Japan

In Korea the new Yi dynasty was founded in 1392 and immediately sought and received Ming Taizu's formal recognition. The name of the country was changed to Chôson in the following year. Ming-Yi interstate relations developed in the long-established pattern. Envoys came and went with great frequency between Chôson Korea and Ming China; in consequence of those frequent visits, the Korean court records, written in a slightly eccentric style of classical Chinese, have preserved extensive reports of their observations, and are thus a major source of often unflattering information on Ming court politics in particular.

In Japan the Ashikaga shogun sent his envoys to Nanjing, first in 1399, when the Jianwen emperor received them cordially, and again in 1403, when as the first foreign envoys to Chengzu's court they were given a most friendly reception.[21] The Shogun Yoshimitsu was an ardent Zen (Chan) Buddhist; he surrounded himself with both Chinese monks and Japanese monks who had been in China, and who taught him to revere that home of Zen Buddhism. The shogun also needed money and was determined to place the trade between the two countries in his own hands. It was a sure source of great riches. Yoshimitsu's unnecessarily fawning letter to Chengzu acknowledged China's suzerainty and was signed "the King of Japan." That title is of course fraudulent; as shogun he was the Japanese emperor's chief military officer, not a king. On both counts—in acknowledging China's suzerainty and in his claim to royalty—it was an erratic act, controversial ever after. Chengzu was not aware of those delicate dimensions of the situation; he welcomed the shogun's friendly overtures and granted the Japanese official trading status. A trade of great volume immediately ensued, lasting until 1410, two years after Yoshimitsu's death.

His son and heir, Ashikaga Yoshimochi, was cool toward Buddhism, detested China, and rejected his spendthrift father's policies. He refused to accept any more envoys or trade officials. A brief episode in Sino-Japanese relations came to an end, but unofficially the trade carried by merchant sailors on both sides continued to flourish. Later in the dynasty issues in the management of what had become multilateral private trading in and out of China's coastal ports led to the so-called Japanese pirate problem.

The Maritime Expeditions of Zheng He

By far the most remarkable foreign relations initiative in Ming Chengzu's reign was his promotion of China's contacts with many of the maritime polities of Southeast and South Asia. He chose, for whatever reasons—and these have been the subject of speculation from that time to the present—to make his reign known throughout the sea lanes and all the countries on their shores, to tell all of them that he was now the legitimate ruler of China, and to invite their rulers to visit his court to offer tribute in the old Chinese pattern of interstate relations. In seven stupendous maritime expeditions his envoy in chief was the famed Admiral Zheng He (1371–1433).

Zheng He was a boy of ten when Ming armies entered the region of Yunnan in 1381 to conquer it and bring that southwestern frontier region under China's direct administration. Earlier, Khubilai Khan had conquered the region in 1253–54; thereafter it was governed as a Yuan dynasty province with a Mongol prince at the head of its government. When the Ming general Fu Youde got to Yunnan, one of his tasks was to gather a number of boys to be castrated and sent to the court for service as eunuchs. One of the Ming officers saw the young Zheng He in the street and asked him a question; the answer displayed such alertness and courage that the general took the boy captive and sent him with the group, marked as a candidate of exceptional qualities. His original family name was Ma; his family were well-placed Muslims whose ancestors may have come to the region a century earlier in the retinue of Sayid Ajall (1211–1279), a Turkic Muslim governor from Bukhara in Central Asia who served with high distinction under several Mongol rulers. As governor in Yunnan from 1273 to 1279, he introduced Islam and a Muslim population into the region; from that beginning a sizeable community of Mongol, Turkic, and Chinese Muslims came into being, and still exists in Yunnan.[22]

The young eunuch was first assigned to the retinue of the Prince of Yan at Nanjing, and later remained in his service at Beiping. He was trained for military service, for which his height, powerful build, and imposing presence suited him. He served the prince well, gaining notable merit when he accompanied the prince in maneuvers on the border and later in battles of the civil war. The emperor gave him the name Zheng He. When the prince came to the throne in 1402, the eunuch was one of his most trusted associates. Possibly for that reason Chengzu chose him to head the fleets that would carry him into places where Zheng's awesome presence would serve him well. Also, it may have seemed wise to send a Muslim to lead expeditions into sea lanes then dominated by Arab merchant sailors and into countries that were in many cases Muslim.

Preparing the fleets required huge expenditures. Two shipyards in the river adjacent to Nanjing were enlarged and stocked with materials. Chinese shipbuilding technology had made great strides in Song times, incorporating many features of advanced design such as compartmentalized hulls divided by waterproof bulkheads so that the hull could be breached in two or more places but the ship would not sink. They also had external stern-post rudders moved by mechanical steering devices, making the ships easy to control in tight navigation circumstances. Those features were not known in Western marine technology until many centuries later.[23] The largest of the ships specially built for these voyages, called the "Treasure Ships," were as large as 440 feet in length and carried nine masts. For the first of Zheng He's seven voyages, his fleet included 317 ships of which 62 were of the "Treasure Ship" class. His smaller ships ranged in size down to 200 feet in length. The personnel carried on each expedition numbered from 20,000 to 32,000 men. The Chinese ships and their men made a display of maritime strength unknown elsewhere until much later in history. Zheng He's larger ships had 2,500 tons cargo capacity and 3,100 tons displacement; by comparison, the largest of the three ships which brought Columbus to the New World in 1492 was 125 feet long and had a capacity of only 280 tons. The Spanish Armada, the greatest fleet up to its time (1588) in European history, included 137 ships, of which only 7 were as large as 1,000 tons burden.

The seven expeditions each occupied two or more years, sailing with the monsoon winds as they reversed direction from summer to winter. The Chinese fleets visited Vietnam, the Straits of Malacca, and the many states of the Indonesian islands, the coasts of India, Sri Lanka, and on to Hormuz and the Persian Gulf, the coast of Arabia (modern Oman and Yemen), and into the Red Sea, south to the coast of Africa in the region between Mogadishu and Mombasa. On some voyages the fleet split up, sections of it going to different places. The seven voyages took place in 1405–1407, 1407–1409, 1409–1411, 1413–1415, 1417–1419, 1421–22, and the final one, after Chengzu's death, in 1431–1433. Zheng He died in 1433 and was buried at Nanjing, near the great shipyards where the ships were built.[24]

No further voyages were sent. Officials of the court objected that they were too expensive and produced nothing of value. The state ceased its building of the largest ships and thereafter built only smaller war and transport vessels needed for its coastal and inland waterways naval operations. Chinese merchants had visited all of the destinations of Zheng He's voyages long before his time; they continued to ply those trade routes in their smaller and more economical vessels. Their trade thereafter undoubtedly benefited from the early fifteenth-century demonstration of China's power and magnificence.

The voyages induced a spurt in diplomatic activity. Everywhere the great fleets went, Zheng He played the diplomat, going ashore to visit rulers, transmit proclamations of China's peaceful intentions, and bestow lavish gifts. Rulers were invited to go in person or to send envoys, often with the fleet, to China, where they had to engage in the ritual courtesies of kowtowing to the emperor and being feted in appropriate manner. The voyages often carried kings and sultans and ambassadors back home on the next voyage. Chengzu may have found it adequate return for his large investment in the expeditions to have so many heads of states and statelets acknowledge him as the Son of Heaven and center of the universe. He also delighted in the treasures the fleets brought back, but their value was offset by the ceremonial gifts he had to make to all the rulers and their envoys, so there was no direct economic return for China from its huge investment. The exotic things the expeditions brought back included rare and precious materials as well as plants and animals: giraffes and lions from Africa; parrots and singing birds from Southeast Asia; Indian cottons finer than silk; gems and fragrances and spices from many points. These were not seized, nor were they marketed when brought back to China; they all went into the imperial household.

It was rumored at the time and speculated on thereafter that the real motive of these expeditions was to locate the Jianwen emperor, suspected of having fled to the southern oceans, where he was protected by Chinese merchants. It seems most unlikely that Chengzu could have believed that, or if he did at first, that it would have taken seven huge expeditions to prove it wrong.

The ships carried soldiers, cannons, all the means of making war, but their purpose was not to engage in warlike activities. At most they would put down a local rebellion to restore a legitimate ruler to his throne, suppress pirates, and the like. It cannot be denied that the show of Chinese military force was expected to overawe and intimidate, and thereby to encourage submission to China, yet no single square mile of territory was added to the Chinese realm as a consequence of the expeditions, nor were claims for territory or of suzerainty made—except for the politically hollow Chinese claim to be acknowledged the superiors of all rulers in the world. The ritual obeisance required of any state entering into "tribute relations" cost nothing in terms of territory, authority, or wealth, and could in fact help protect the first of these and augment the other two. In short, the ritual behavior that the Chinese demanded, in a relationship that was urged on all states with no small pressure, nonetheless remained voluntary; that meant much to the Chinese and very little to anyone else. Zheng He's voyages were in these ways quite different from the expeditions of the European states commencing with the Portuguese and the Spanish at the end of the fifteenth century.[25]

The great voyages showed that the Chinese early in the fifteenth century had the technology, the organizational capacity, the wealth, in short, all the means of becoming a great maritime empire builder. They could have preempted the Europeans in that regard had they wished to do so. But they did not attempt to expand by force the territories ruled by the Chinese state. They had no conception of a Chinese maritime empire created by the powerful instrument of their naval strength. The idea that they might have been in competition, for advantage or status, with other states would have been incomprehensible to them: Who could compete with China? The Europeans of the time were driven to create their mercantile empires largely by competition for survival with other states. They could scarcely comprehend the vastly different Chinese mentality.

Chinese interests lay at home. These voyages are the great anomaly. Their abandonment soon after the Yongle emperor died reflects the regularity of Chinese foreign relations.

The anomaly is that it was Emperor Chengzu who launched them. He was the emperor most obsessed with China's Inner Asian land frontiers and, one might think, the least aware of China's great potential for maritime expansion. Part of the explanation must lie in the fact that Chengzu was extremely independent-minded, anxious to cultivate support from the scholar-elite but equally anxious not to become their captive. The expeditions reflected his curiosity, his personal desire for all that they brought to his court, from kowtowing kings to marvelous things. It was his high ministers and advisers who from the beginning resisted the project, and with his death they prevailed.

As they prevailed, even to the point of recommending in later times that the very records of Zheng He's accomplishments be burned so that later rulers would not be drawn to make the same mistake, an important feature of Chinese imperial history is brought to our attention. In recent times Chinese scholars have theorized about the conflict between "yellow China" and "blue China." Yellow China refers to the Yellow River, the yellow loess soil of North China, to canal and irrigation projects and the vast bureaucratic apparatus for managing them. It stands for cultural conservatism, wasteful use of manpower, uneconomic investment in public works that officials could plan and direct and keep under their control. Blue China refers to the blue waters of the ocean and its doorways to the outside world, to entrepreneurship and individualism supported by the private mercantile activity that could not be bureaucratized and controlled. Some historians have come to see China's dilemmas in very recent times as stemming from the dominance of yellow China over the undeveloped potential of blue China. The idea is not new, nor has it been very convincingly developed by recent writers, yet the point has undoubted force.[26]

Zheng He's voyages were a rare example of maritime China's latent force coming to the fore. The argument over abandoning all government-sponsored seafaring reveals the tension between seafaring interests and the stronger landward-oriented interests. It was a one-sided argument after the Emperor Chengzu was gone from the scene. We shall return to this theme when the great projects to reconstruct and maintain the Grand Canal are discussed in the next chapter.

v. The New Capital

Despite his fascination with his great fleets' maritime adventures, Ming Chengzu's real orientation was to the Inner Asian land frontier and China's enemies in the steppe. Nothing makes that clearer than his decision, early in his reign, to move the capital to Beijing, the site of his former princedom, and the Jin and Yuan dynasty capitals before that. He renamed the capital prefecture Shuntian, "Obedient to Heaven," in keeping with his efforts to justify the civil war, undertaken "on the command of Heaven" to rescue the dynasty. Here I use the more common name for the city, Beijing.

Yingtian (Nanjing) became the secondary capital after the move to Beijing. Before leaving the city, Ming Chengzu started the building of one of his great architectural monuments, an imperial project dedicated to the memory of the Empress Ma, claimed by him as his mother. This was the Bao'en Temple with its commanding pagoda, a tower rising to 240 feet capped with a wrought iron finial rising another sixty feet. The tower was of masonry construction entirely sheathed in tiles of gleaming white porcelain specially manufactured near the site for that purpose. The construction of the "porcelain pagoda" required nineteen years; it was not completed until six years after Chengzu's death, in 1431. It became known in the West by travelers from the time of Matteo Ricci, the Italian Jesuit who lived in Nanjing in the 1590s, among many Europeans who wrote about it up to the early nineteenth century. A circular staircase occupied the central core of the structure, opening to balconies at each of its nine stories. Hundreds of oil lamps hung from the eaves were lighted each evening, and bells tinkled in the breeze. It was a magical sight, famous throughout China and much admired by non-Chinese visitors as well.[27]

Nanjing was the Taiping Rebellion's "Heavenly Capital" from 1853 to

1864. The tower, outside the city walls and immediately adjacent to the main south gate of Nanjing, provided an observation point giving full view of the entire city. Fearing that the Qing armies would use it for that purpose, the Taiping leadership ordered its destruction in 1856, without regrets for the loss of a revered cultural monument. Because of their fanatical form of Christian belief, it was in their eyes a monument to monstrous idolatry. It was in all likelihood a monument to the Emperor Chengzu's birth mother as well, although that was a closely guarded secret. One or two officials who served the Ming loyalist government at Nanjing in the mid-1640s (after Beijing had fallen to the Manchus) gained access to the locked memorial hall in the pagoda's ground floor and discovered that in addition to the main altar table where the spirit tablets of the Ming founder and the Empress Ma were kept, in a locked and closely guarded side chamber was an altar table where the spirit tablet of "Consort Gong" was displayed in a manner showing that she was honored as the mother of Zhu Di, the Emperor Chengzu. Publicly the temple was constructed to *bao'en* (requite the benevolence of) his mother, the Empress Ma, while secretly it also acknowledged his debt to his real mother.

Chengzu was a great builder. He is said to have contributed more than a million ounces of silver to construct an immense Daoist temple complex at Wudang Mountain in northwestern Hubei. It became a state shrine, guarded by an army garrison, to which each emperor on ascending the throne was to dispatch officials to perform special ceremonies asking for the blessings of the "True Martial Ruler," a Daoist divinity whose cult was associated with the martial arts.[28] It became a flourishing pilgrimage site in Ming and Qing times, with rooms for thousands of visitors. Chengzu also selected the magnificent site north of Beijing for the Ming imperial tombs and supervised the construction of his own tomb complex, started in 1409 to prepare a tomb for his Empress Xu, who died in Nanjing two years earlier; his decision to move the capital away from Nanjing is implicit in the choice of this site for his family's tombs. The construction of his own tomb, the grandest of those at the Ming tomb park, was completed in 1418.

His finest monument as a builder was his comprehensive rebuilding of Beijing. He piously ordered that it should replicate the palace city at Nanjing, but in fact it was built to more expansive plans. Imperial Nanjing was destroyed during the Taiping Rebellion in the mid-nineteenth century, and Hangzhou and Kaifeng retain no material evidence from their years as Song dynasty capitals, so Beijing is the only remaining example of an imperial Chinese capital city. Chengzu got the project started in 1407, collecting materials from all over the country and assembling the work force. It was complete enough in 1420 to allow the announcement that the formal transfer would take place with the beginning of the following year. The building continued for a generation.

Justifications for the move included the idea that had troubled Ming Taizu, the dynasty's founder: the capital of a united China had always been in the North. That is in itself weak reasoning, we might think, but a civilization for which history and precedent weighed so heavily found it a strong consideration. Moreover, it usefully reinforced Chengzu's more immediate reasons: Nanjing was his displaced predecessor's city and the center of the region which had felt the usurpation and the purges most deeply, and as the scene of his crime, it was a place of unpleasant associations. Equally important in his mind, however, was the fact that in his chosen role as warrior emperor he was obsessed with the northern borders. By placing his capital within the zone exposed to the steppe, he could at all times oversee its problems and take immediate action against them.

The immense area enclosed within Beijing's Yuan dynasty walls had been reduced in 1370 or 1371 when general Xu Da, then responsible for the defense of the newly conquered North, built a new north wall almost a mile to the south of the Yuan wall, reducing the enclosed area by one-fourth. As the new construction got under way after 1407, the south wall was moved a third of a mile farther south, slightly enlarging the city and providing more room for the main entrance into the imperial city. The city had three walled enclosures, one inside the other. Inside the outer city walls of the capital was the walled imperial city *(huangcheng)*, and inside its walls was the walled and moated palace city *(zijincheng)*, the latter often called the (Purple) Forbidden City.[29] It was not until 1553, under threat of Mongol incursions, that the new south wall was added, enclosing what had been a dense commercial and residential buildup outside the main south gate.[30] Within the physical boundaries of those walls the grand plan of Ming Beijing was realized, creating a city that was little affected by the Qing dynasty's conquest of the Ming in 1644, and which was inherited almost intact by post-imperial China in 1911.

Now, however, that city has been radically altered; it is difficult today to see or even to imagine the imposing city that still existed into the middle of the twentieth century. Its walls and all but two or three of its massive gate towers have been razed. Those walls and gates once defined the city, imparting the character which oriented all the parts to the whole, managed all the movement on the wide boulevards serving the gates, and made the plan of the city immediately comprehensible to people in its streets and lanes. The central palace city toward which the streets formerly were oriented, and whose roofs were the highest in the city, no longer dominates the entire urban complex. The handsome arches *(pailou)* crossing main boulevards at strategic locations have been torn down as traffic hazards. The main entrance approach to the south gate of the palace city disappeared in the 1920s, and in the 1950s a vast new space was created there by razing other buildings. That allowed the creation of Tian'an Men Square, a new city center where, in a new kind of social and political order, the overwhelming setting of the palace city's entrance could be used by the leaders of the present-day Chinese nation for reviewing mass parades and demonstrations, a form of political activity not known in imperial China. Today the city is an undefined sprawl, crowded with high-rise buildings and busy traffic arteries, very much a bustling modern metropolis. It may be excessive to label the physical changes made there as vandalism, yet one must observe that the Beijing of Ming and

Qing times, one of the world's most distinctive and ingratiating cities, no longer exists.[31]

Fortunately the palace city has remained more or less intact, parts of it "restored" with not entirely happy results, but much of it retaining the original appearance. The great front courts, more than 400 yards on a side, and the main palace halls onto which they open, still have their white marble terraces and carved railings, their golden-colored glazed tile roofs, and their reddish walls. Behind those front halls are government offices and residence quarters of the Inner Court, many of the rooms now used to house the National Palace Museum. An inventory made in 1955 showed that of more than 9,000 rooms (jian) in the original Ming palaces, 8,662 were still intact and usable. Outside the enclosed palace city Chengzu also constructed palace compounds called the residences of the ten princes (some accounts say fifteen princes), with more than 8,000 rooms. The "Street of the Wells of the Princely Residences," Wangfujing Street, is today a principal section of the city center.

Chengzu's capital was more than a grandiose imperial residence; it functioned as the nerve center of Ming governing. Ming China was highly integrated for a premodern state. All the officials posted throughout the entire state were appointed by the emperor according to procedures managed by the Ministry of Personnel; all civil officials and all military officers went to Beijing to receive their appointments, and came back to Beijing at the end of their terms to be reappointed or retired. They had all taken civil service examinations administered under the auspices of the Ministry of Rites, first in their prefectures, at the second level in their provincial capitals, and finally at the jinshi level in the capital, with a final examination conducted at the palace to rank the winners. Except for a portion of those whose careers were confined to the capital, most officials did not make permanent residence there, but by the continuous flow of persons into and out of the capital, a regularizing influence combatted local particularisms and helped to integrate the country.

The language of the capital became the standard spoken Chinese, the guanhua or "officialese" to which Europeans in the sixteenth century gave the name "Mandarin." At some levels of society that metropolitan speech coexisted with the regional languages and local dialects. On the level of spoken Chinese it significantly reinforced the universalizing impact of the written language, in which differences of pronunciation and usage are not reflected. The capital never dominated the country the way Paris and London have dominated France and the United Kingdom through the more recent centuries of their history; culturally China was always polycentric, its many other great and small cities not only contributing in very large ways to intellectual and cultural life but also often providing desirable living milieux for the elite. Despite that, the capital functioned importantly in many aspects of Chinese life. In Ming and Qing times, Beijing served those functions splendidly.

The fiscal system of Ming China, requiring the delivery of taxes in kind, supplies of many kinds, and money to the capital, demanded a transport system with Beijing at its hub. At Nanjing most of the transport moved by water routes. To service Beijing, a network of roads and post relays had to be created to supplement the single system of water arteries, the Grand Canal, the artificial waterway connecting the lower Yangzi with its northern terminus at Tongzhou, in Beijing's eastern suburbs.

In the early Ming, as all the building projects of walls, palaces, government offices, and state shrines as well as canals and roadways were brought to completion, it is possible to think of Beijing as a funnel gathering in the revenues and human resources of the state and focusing them on the capital, especially on the northern defenses and their military garrisons. The military portion of the Ming state's budget was its largest element. The great city was perched on the rim of potentially hostile lands which commanded the primary attention of rulers and statesmen. Underneath all the comforts and pleasures of the city's refined elite and the vigorous life of its common people there was a sense that Beijing's reason for existing was the confrontation of sedentary civilization with the ever more sophisticated nomads of the steppe. The city both radiated what the Chinese thought of as "civilizing influences" and was the command center for all of China's military resources.

25

MING CHINA IN THE
FIFTEENTH CENTURY

After Emperor Chengzu died in 1424, six successors held the throne in the remaining eight decades of the fifteenth century. The period's largely overlooked political history cannot be understood apart from their individual personalities and their widely varying modes of political behavior. After a brief survey of their reigns, we will examine as case studies two issues that reflect the Ming state's evolving character in the fifteenth-century: the mechanics of governing through the institutions of the court and the central agencies where policy was made and responses were formulated to conditions throughout the realm; and the challenges faced by government and society in the necessity to maintain the Grand Canal and channel the Yellow River.

I. SUCCESSORS TO THE YONGLE EMPEROR

The usurpation settled Chengzu's lineal descendants on the Ming throne to the end of the dynasty. Very few of those thirteen subsequent rulers were more than barely competent, although several of the worst were perversely intelligent. All directly influenced the conduct of government, thus are central to the history of the centuries from 1424 until 1644. Here I briefly examine the reigns of six who ruled over a steadily recovering society through the fifteenth century.

The Renzong and Xuanzong Reigns, 1425–1435

Ming Chengzu died in the Mongolian steppe in mid-August 1424. His son Zhu Gaozhi announced that beginning with the New Year (January 20, 1425), the Yongle reign period would be succeeded by the era name Hongxi. This new emperor's posthumous temple name, by which he is known in history, is Renzong, "the Benevolent Ancestor." The Hongxi reign was brief; the sickly Zhu Gaozhi died in May 1425, bringing his son Zhu Zhanji to the throne. This young ruler's succession was contested by his uncle, echoing the Yongle usurpation in 1399–1402. This time, however, the attempt quickly failed.

With the New Year of 1426, the new emperor's Xuande reign period commenced, to last only ten years until his death early in 1435. Despite its troubled beginning, the Xuande reign has been considered by historians to mark a high point of Ming rule.[1]

Zhu Zhanji is known in history as the Emperor Xuanzong. He was the young grandson who accompanied the Emperor Chengzu's Mongolian campaign in 1414; at the age of fifteen then, he was his grandfather's pride and joy. The old emperor frequently took him along on field maneuvers and other military activities and encouraged him to be a martial emperor, on his model. When Zhu Zhanji's very unmilitary father the Emperor Renzong died, perhaps not unexpectedly, in May 1425, Renzong's younger brother failed to assess his nephew's mettle. In the pattern of Chengzu, who made war on a nephew in 1399, this uncle, named Zhu Gaoxu, also thought he had been improperly denied the succession; he saw himself as the one who should have succeeded in 1424 instead of his sickly older brother, and he became even more ambitious when that brother's untested son came to the throne less than a year later.

The would-be usurper Zhu Gaoxu had proved himself an able and courageous if somewhat rash military commander in his father's service throughout the civil war (1399–1402). An unruly and arrogant man, he had always treated his obese and physically impaired older brother with contempt; he was quite unable to appreciate the great contribution to the civil war, and thereafter to the government, made by his brother's steady hand at the helm of central administration during Emperor Chengzu's many absences from the court. Now Zhu Gaoxu turned the same contempt on his nephew. But Chengzu's success in systematically reducing the powers of the imperial princes had changed the circumstances; Zhu Gaoxu found himself in a much weaker situation than his father had faced in 1399. The young emperor, ably advised by his father's and his grandfather's Grand Secretaries and other senior officials, led the imperial forces in person against his rebellious uncle and quickly forced him to surrender.[2] Zhu Gaoxu, his spouses and children, and a few of his advisers were arrested and eventually put to death.

Following the usual pattern, the Emperor Xuanzong's reign period, called Xuande, began on the Chinese New Year following his accession, that is, February 8, 1426, and continued in force until January 17, 1436 (the New Year following his death), a mere ten years later. It was a decade of unusual stability and good feeling. The young emperor saw himself as a warrior, as his grandfather had encouraged him to do, and he did indeed quite competently lead some minor skirmishes into the steppe. On one occasion he killed several Mongol soldiers in battle with arrows from his own bow, thus proving himself. The Mongol problem, however, appeared to be nonthreatening during his reign, giving him no great opportunities to display military prowess. Civil governing too made no unusual demands on him. He was well

CHART 8. THE MING IMPERIAL SUCCESSION
(Dating follows DMB, p. xxi)

Generations

1 | Zhu Yuanzhang 1328–June 1398
(1) Taizu
"Hongwu" 1368–June 24, 1398

2 | Zhu Biao
1355–1392   Zhu Di 1360–Aug. 1424
(3) Taizong (Chengzu)
"Yongle" Jan. 23, 1403–Jan. 19, 142

3 | Zhu Yunwen 1377–July 1402?
(2) Huidi   Zhu Gaozhi 1378–May 1425
"Jianwen" Feb. 1399–July 1402   (4) Renzong
"Hongxi" Jan. 1425–Feb. 1426

4 | Zhu Zhanji 1399–Jan. 1435
(5) Xuanzong
"Xuande" Feb. 1426–Jan. 1436

5 | Zhu Qiyu 1428–March 1457   Zhu Qizhen 1427–Feb. 1465
(7) Daizong Jing Di   (6) Yingzong
"Jingtai" Jan. 1450–Feb. 1457   "Zhengtong" Jan. 1436–Jan. 1450

"Tianshun" Feb. 1457–Jan. 1465

6 | Zhu Jianshen 1447–Sept. 1487
(8) Xianzong
"Chenghua" Jan. 1465–Jan. 1488

7 | Zhu Youguan 1476–1519   Zhu Youtang 1470–Jun. 1505
Son of (8)   (9) Xiaozong
Prince Xingxian   "Hongzhi" Jan. 1488–Jan. 1506

8 | Zhu Houcong 1507–Jan. 1567   Zhu Houzhao 1491–Apr. 1521
(11) Shizong   (10) Wuzong
"Jiajing" 1522–Feb. 1567   "Zhengde" 1506–Jan. 1522

9 | Zhu Zaihou 1537–Jul. 1572
(12) Muzong
"Longqing" Feb. 1567–Feb. 1573

10 | Zhu Yijun 1563–Aug. 1620
(13) Shenzong
"Wanli" Feb. 1573–1620

11 | Zhu Changluo 1582–Sept. 1620
(14) Guangzong
"Taichang" Aug. 1620–Jan. 1621

12 | Zhu Youjiao 1605–Sept. 1627   Zhu Youjian 1611–Apr. 1644
(15) Xizong   (16) Sizong
"Tianqi" Jan. 1621–Feb. 1628   "Chongzhen" Feb. 1628–Jan. 1645

The Southern Ming Resistance: three rulers, 1645–1661 (see Chapter 31)

Note: Reign period names, in quotation marks, are frequently (albeit incorrectly) used as the emperor's personal name.

served at court by a corps of Grand Secretaries and other senior officials who had served for many years, some since his grandfather's reign. Notable among them were three men, not related though all of the surname Yang. At the head of the government the "Three Yangs" provided a degree of continuity and confidence that was unmatched in any other period of Ming history. They came to symbolize the proper style in governing—wise and mature leadership by scholar-officials whose rulers gave them a strong voice. In the minds of the elite the ideal norm had at last been achieved after the painful first four decades of the Ming, when scholar-officials were often at hazard.[3]

Xuanzong was a man of exceptional talent. He was a skilled painter, especially fond of painting dogs and other animals; he has been called the most accomplished painter emperor in Chinese history after Emperor Huizong at the end of Northern Song. He also was a good calligrapher and a competent poet and writer. Genuinely a man of cultivation, he displayed the ideal combination of civil and military virtues more fully than any other Chinese ruler in the later dynasties. Like Emperor Huizong, he too sponsored painting and calligraphy at his court. He did not go so far as to create a painting academy to which artists were given official appointments, but he did appoint a few painters and calligraphers to honorific posts in his bodyguard, the Embroidered Uniform Guard, giving them stipends and court patronage, though that did not institutionalize Ming imperial patronage of the arts.[4] His reign is particularly noted for the high quality of its ceramics, especially the famed Ming blue-and-white porcelains from the imperial kilns at Jingdezhen bearing the Xuande reign mark. Other decorative arts, notably fine manufactures of small objects such as incense burners made of bronze and other alloys, unmatched in quality, also were produced at this time.

Under Xuanzong, the last military-minded ruler until the following century, the arts of both war and peace flourished. The practical adjustments in modes of governing started by his grandfather and father were continued. His reign is praised for significant efforts to better the common people's livelihood, for reversing Chengzu's disastrous policy of annexing Annam, and for tightening up the management of the government bureaucracy. Yet it is noted that he also had his faults, if not of kinds that seriously affected governing. He was sometimes harsh with his civil officials and overly protective of military personnel, but was genuinely concerned about the well-being of common garrison soldier families.

Life in his Inner Court took on a tone of luxury and waste in contrast with previous reigns. He was licentious. He sent his eunuchs on frequent missions to southern provinces to recruit virgins for his harem and for the troupes of musicians and entertainers kept in the palace. He also made heavy demands on the Korean kings for tribute offerings of suitable virgins. When he died, fifty-three such Korean women received permission to return to their families in Korea, and several thousand palace women asked for and received permission to leave the palace service. His temper occasionally flared, as when court officials criticized him for such excesses, but his mind was not closed to stern advice. If the Ming dynasty was to have vigorous, intelligent, highly active rulers, it was not to be expected that it would find any who better suited that criterion, and no subsequent Ming ruler would measure up to it. In view of the events of the next decades, it is much to be regretted that he did not live longer. Yet his actions contributed to the events that troubled the succeeding reigns.

For example, he dismayed his civil officials by giving great latitude to his high court eunuchs. He enhanced their role by regularizing the status of the palace school for eunuchs. A eunuch there named Wang Zhen came to his favorable attention. Wang Zhen had received a Confucian education, and although he never received a higher civil service examination degree, he had held minor office, married, and fathered one or more sons before entering the eunuch ranks. Emperor Chengzu at one time had made a special effort to recruit such men, still young but with male heirs (to satisfy a point of Chinese family values), who were willing to be castrated so as to be permitted to teach the palace women. Wang Zhen was in that way recruited into the eunuch bureaucracy, where his abilities stood out. Xuanzong took Wang Zhen into the Directorate of Ceremonial, promoted him to serve as the tutor to his elder son, and entrusted him with some aspects of the boy's supervision. That was to lead to a crisis in governing in the next reign.

The Yingzong and Jingtai Reigns, 1436–1465

Xuanzong's early death at age thirty-seven, of some unspecified illness that lasted less than two months, brought his eight-year-old son to the throne, to be known as the emperor Yingzong. The boy's name was Zhu Qizhen. Xuanzong had not had much time to prepare for his young son's accession. There was no provision in the founder's Ancestral Injunctions for the accession of a minor, no provision for establishing a regency. Senior officials consulted with the boy emperor's grandmother, Grand Dowager Empress Zhang, about what to do. It was decided that she, as the senior figure in the emperor's immediate family, would "attend the governing from behind a screen," that is, she would not formally assume the powers of a regent, but would in fact consult with the court in making important decisions until the heir was mature. His mother, Empress Dowager Sun, also occasionally sat in on deliberations, but her personality and her junior status did not allow her a large role. Although she had borne a son who had become the emperor, she was, after all, a daughter-in-law, often the most difficult role for any Chinese woman to fill.

The Grand Dowager Empress, by contrast, was a wise and noble-minded woman of very strong personality. She was perceptive enough to see the danger in the eunuch Wang Zhen's overweening influence on her young grandson and did her best to curb it, even threatening his life if he did not cease his meddling in the emperor's affairs. She also berated the senior figures in the Inner Court for not preventing the eunuch's improper activities. On one occasion she said to them: "The emperor is still but a boy. How can he know that throughout all history it is precisely creatures of this kind who have so often brought harm to persons and to states?"[5]

She could not forestall all of Wang Zhen's transgressions. She was growing old. Wang Zhen was patient. After she died in 1442, when Emperor Yingzong was still only fifteen, the course was set for a new pattern in Ming government, although one not unknown in earlier history: a eunuch who was favored by an immature and foolish ruler used his influence to become a virtual dictator.

Within a short time after his grandmother's death, the emperor appointed Wang Zhen to one of the three leading posts in the Directorate of Ceremonial, allowing him in fact to control the entire eunuch bureaucracy.[6] He also was given personal direction of the Western Depot, making him the head of the secret service agencies as well. He began very quickly to intimidate all opposition at the court, dividing it into sycophants who served his purposes, and terrorized officials who remained silent. He anticipated the young emperor's wishes and sought to please his every fancy.

In particular, the emperor had been taught by his father to play soldier. As he grew older, he was ambitious to make his mark as a military leader. Wang Zhen looked for problems demanding military solutions; that made work for generals, earned them great rewards, and allowed Wang Zhen's eunuch agents accompanying the armed forces to rake off large profits. Two large campaigns took to the field in the years 1441–1449 against the Shan chieftain Thonganbwa, known in Chinese as Sirenfa, in Yunnan. They were reported to the throne as great victories.[7] Rebellious activity among exploited silver miners in Fujian and Zhejiang in the late 1440s also were suppressed by armies sent from Beijing. The emperor's soldiers were winning glory for him.

In 1449 a larger opportunity for military glory presented itself. Under Wang Zhen's guidance the emperor, now twenty-one years old, was ready to lead armies in the field as his father and great-grandfather had done. The Oyirat or Western Mongols, briefly inactive following Chengzu's last campaigns in the steppe, now had a new leader with great ambitions. He was Esen, whose father (Arughtai) had extended Oyirat influence to the east; he soon came to control most of Mongolia. Esen thirsted to be acknowledged the Great Khan of all the Mongols, but he needed impressive military victories to achieve that. He would defy China.

Wang Zhen's plan was to preempt the Oyirats by striking at them first. He convinced the emperor that by leading a large Chinese army northwest into the southern rim of the steppe, to Datong in northern Shanxi, he could overawe the Mongols; then in glory Wang would guide the emperor and all the Chinese military leaders back to Beijing via a more southerly route that would take them through his native place (Yuzhou, in northeastern Shanxi). There he could display his power and dispense favor to his relatives. The plan was fatally misconceived; most of the court, except for his sycophants, bitterly opposed it.

Wang Zhen overawed the protesting officials, forced many to accompany the army, and set out on August 4, 1449. The armies were ill-prepared and disorganized. They reached Datong on August 18 after a journey in which many things had gone wrong. At Datong another eunuch posted with the army there convinced Wang Zhen that there was genuine danger of falling into Esen's trap. Beginning to sense peril, Wang Zhen gave up the glory of parading through his home district, reluctantly deciding instead to return to Beijing by the most direct route. Esen's forces harassed the forward units and waylaid the rear guard. The Chinese generals grew very concerned. On September 1, while they were camped for the night at a small military guard station called Tumu, Esen attacked. In fierce fighting the entire army of 50,000 was destroyed. The emperor, miraculously unharmed though sitting quietly in the thick of the fighting, was taken prisoner. Wang Zhen was killed, probably by one of the Chinese.

It had been centuries since a Chinese emperor had been captured by an enemy army. What would Esen do with a captive emperor? That problem appears to have left him without a ready answer.[8]

Back at Beijing, where the emperor's younger brother Prince Cheng had been left in charge, news of the debacle brought panic. Some officials urged fleeing to the south, to Nanjing, where the court would be safe and a counter-offensive could be planned. A courageous minister of war, Yu Qian (1398–1457), emerged as the strong man in the government. He insisted that Prince Cheng take the throne and that the government remain in Beijing to defend it. China thus had two emperors—one in captivity, and his younger brother, newly enthroned in the capital. This dilemma, and the responses to it by members of the imperial family and by officials debating policy at the court, reveals much to us about the character of the Chinese imperial institution.

Prince Cheng as interim emperor is known in history as the Jingtai emperor (his reign period name), or by his posthumous temple name Jing Di; he and the resolute Yu Qian, who had become the actual head of the government, firmly held their ground: the emperor of China who mattered was the one in his capital, not the one being held in a Mongol yurt in the steppe.

The Mongols, after long negotiations in which they attempted to realize great gain from the captive Ming emperor, at last decided that Yingzong was not a strong bargaining chip. Esen returned his captive in 1450. During the year's captivity he had been treated with great ceremonial politeness. Back in his capital city he found himself a discarded emperor, granted a modest palace and barely enough to live on, sealed off from all contacts with officials and the public, and ignored.

Prince Cheng, the "Caretaker Emperor," reigned ably, with good counsel from several outstanding high officials. He was particularly attentive to floods on the Yellow River (repairs to the system made during his seven-year reign will be discussed in Section III in relation to the Grand Canal). His unexpected way of coming to the throne awakened ambitions; having attained the great prize, he did not want to lose it. He made no efforts to secure Yingzong's release from the Oyirats or to intervene when his brother was shabbily treated after his return to the capital. The successor emperor earned some criticism among officials when he removed Yingzong's son's title as designated heir in order to give that title to his own infant son. Then his son died, and there was no other heir to designate. When he fell seriously ill in the winter of 1456–57, officials tried to force him to name an heir but without result. The gravity of his illness aroused all manner of speculation and opportunistic scheming at the court.[9] A group of officials who were in the failing emperor Jing Di's service plotted to restore the discarded emperor Yingzong. They stormed into his retirement palace and took him in a palanquin to the main entrance of the Forbidden City, where they battered down a gate and delivered him to the great throne hall. That was just before dawn on February 11, 1457, a day when the court was expected to meet at dawn. When the officials arrived, they were astounded to see Yingzong sitting on the throne to receive their homage and to hear him announce that because his brother, Emperor Jing, was ill, he had been called back to the throne. He generously ordered that the sick Jing Di be well cared for, but he died a month later; it is most likely that he was smothered in his bed by an attending eunuch, probably on orders from someone other than his brother the restored emperor. His death resolved the problem of what to do about two legitimate Sons of Heaven simultaneously living in the same imperial palace. That problem did not arise again.

Yingzong thus resumed his reign. He was the only Ming emperor to have two reign names, one for each of the two parts of his interrupted reign. The first phase of his reign, from the New Year of 1436 until that of 1450, was the Zhengtong reign period; the second, from February 1457 until early in 1465, a year after his death, is called the Tianshun era. Because he had two era names, it is more convenient to call him by his temple name, Yingzong, "the Heroic"; today one would like to think the name was posthumously granted to him with ironic intent, though that is unlikely.

Yingzong apparently learned nothing from his experience. He remained attached to the memory of Wang Zhen and awarded him elaborate posthumous honors. He fell under the control of those who had plotted his restoration; they bitterly resented the vigorous actions by Yu Qian in the crisis of 1449, when he had called them cowards for urging that Beijing be abandoned to the Mongols. They had been made to look quite bad. In revenge, they now charged Yu Qian with planning to place some other member of the imperial clan on the throne to prevent Yingzong from coming back. That accusation was groundless. The savior of the dynasty in the crisis of 1449 was now charged with treason, one of the great cases of injustice in Ming history. Yu was executed five days after Yingzong's restoration, along with others who had served high in Jing Di's government. The illicit and in fact unnecessary plot to "seize the palace gate" *(duo men)* and restore Yingzong could, the plotters calculated, be justified only by charging the officials who had placed Jing Di on the throne with some form of treachery. These tarnished officials now gained full control of the government and were able to manipulate the grateful emperor. Yingzong was not personally vengeful, but he was still a prisoner of court politics. His second reign was brief. After eight years in the role of restored emperor, he died of a sudden illness in 1464 at age thirty-seven, leaving a sixteen-year-old son to succeed him.

The Chenghua and Hongzhi Reigns, 1465–1506

The two reigns that filled out the remaining years of the fifteenth century are made interesting by the sharp contrasts in the personalities and ruling styles of the emperors who presided over them. Both came to the throne in their late teen years, one dying at age forty and the second at age thirty-five.

Yingzong's son Zhu Jianshen came to the throne upon his father's death early in 1464 and died in 1487; his reign period, Chenghua, thus covered the years from 1465 into January 1488. His posthumous temple name is Emperor Xianzong. He was only two years old when his father was captured by the Oyirat Mongols, and during the seven years thereafter when his father languished as a deposed emperor, the boy was reared in another part of the palace city by the mean-spirited deposed empress, not by his real mother. Mother and son both suffered great hardship and deprivation in those years before his father returned to the throne; his serious speech defect may have been caused by that experience.

Emperor Xianzong grew to be a stolid, somewhat doltish man, broad of face and frame, willfully independent but slow to act. He was easily misled by his consort, by his eunuchs, by charlatans claiming to have spiritual powers, and by innumerable sycophants. He is nonetheless praised by historians from his own time onward for his utter lack of vindictiveness. His lack of guile tended to randomize his behavior, making him the more difficult to deal with.[10]

His grandmother had in her service a palace woman who came to be called the Lady Wan. When Xianzong was still a boy, Lady Wan came to him as a gift from his grandmother. By the time he succeeded to the throne at sixteen, she had become his favorite consort, although she was then thirty-five, more than twice his age. She was a shrewish, manipulative, highly jealous woman with a brassy voice and a mannish appearance. His mother once asked him how he could be attracted to such a woman; his reply was that what she did for him had nothing to do with her appearance.[11] We can only imagine the rest; one is tempted to surmise that the attraction had much to do with his emotional deprivation as a child. In 1464 Lady Wan bore him one son who died in infancy. She never again became pregnant, and for the next decade she tried to prevent any other woman from bearing an heir. She kept close watch on the harem and had her eunuchs administer drugs to induce abortions when any of them was reported to be pregnant, or if a birth occurred, she would have the baby and its mother poisoned.

The emperor remained in her thrall for many years. In 1475 he learned that he had a son, born in 1470 to a palace woman with whom he had had only one chance encounter; the palace attendant sent to induce an abortion had taken pity on the woman and returned to report to Lady Wan that the pregnant woman was at death's door. The eunuch subsequently sent to drown the newborn baby also felt pity, or as he later told the emperor, he shared the court's concern that the emperor still had no son, so had secreted the woman off to the quarters of the former empress, Lady Wu, where child and mother could be protected in secrecy. Five years later, delighted to learn that he had a son, the emperor ordered that the boy be brought from the remote quarters of the Lady Wu, his initial consort who had been banished to the rear apartments shortly after their marriage because of Lady Wan's jealousy. Lady Wu must have gained much satisfaction from hearing about the emperor's emotional encounter with the boy, his first son, kept alive by her determination to spite her rival. Within a month the boy's mother died suddenly and suspiciously; the histories suggest that she was poisoned.[12] The emperor, now realizing that the child was in danger from Lady Wan, sent his son to the palace quarters of his own mother, Dowager Empress Zhou, to be reared in safety. He also began to distance himself from the Lady Wan. In quick succession thereafter he fathered eleven other children, but it was the eldest child, called Zhu Youtang, the later Emperor Xiaozong, who was named his heir and who came to the throne when Xianzong died at age forty in 1487.

Zhu Youtang's mother, a palace woman whom Xianzong had encountered one day in a palace storehouse and who had charmed him by her manner, was a Yao tribal woman from Guangxi Province in the south, brought to the capital by a eunuch commander with the armies fighting the Yao in the 1460s.[13] When Zhu Youtang came to the throne in 1487, he made exhaustive attempts to locate his mother's family among the Yao tribesmen but never succeeded. Nevertheless, he established a monument to her in Guangxi and also made offerings to her spirit at a shrine in his palace. He himself took as his empress a Lady Zhang a few months before he ascended the throne. Thereafter he remained completely devoted to her. He has been called perhaps the only monogamous emperor in all of China's history.[14] Empress Zhang bore him two sons and three daughters; he apparently had no other liaisons, despite the many opportunities afforded by inner palace life.

These desultory details of the two emperors' private lives are not unimportant, although they may seem frivolous. The emperors' quite different personalities bore directly on their relations with their eunuchs and with their consort clans, and on their attitudes toward their fathers—in each case repudiating them—and deeply influenced relations with their Grand Secretaries and other leading officials. Ming dynasty emperors could govern badly, but government could not function without their acts, whether they performed those acts directly (conscientiously or lazily) or delegated them to their chosen surrogates. Our understanding of each reign's character may well start with a sense of the emperor as a person trapped in the very consequential and burdensome imperial role.

The Emperors Xianzong and Xiaozong were mediocre rulers and impaired personalities, but were opposites in their personal qualities. A very brief account of their reigns will display that fact.[15] Xianzong came to the throne in 1464 having suffered much because of his foolish father's dependence on the eunuch Wang Zhen; he detested the squabbling that went on among political factions following his father's restoration. At the beginning he swept the court clean of persons he did not like and in general gave prominence to a few very good scholar-officials. Those senior figures, however, soon died, and he appointed no more competent, high-minded Grand Secretaries. He also greatly curbed the eunuchs, dismissing many and limiting their postings outside the palace, particularly those in military supervisory positions. That was a promising beginning, but it did not last long. He was himself much inclined toward Daoist and Buddhist beliefs, especially the more credulous forms of vulgarized religious practice, and in this was encouraged by Lady Wan. She virtually ruled in his name for the first ten or more years. She gained appointments for her relatives, for seers, geomancers, and Daoist adepts, and for sycophantic officials of all kinds.

Lady Wan introduced the eunuch Wang Zhi into the emperor's personal service in 1476. He was a Yao tribesman taken for eunuch service by the armies in Guangxi. He was a man of exceptional intelligence and a taste for power. The emperor first ordered him to disguise himself in ordinary dress and prowl about the city investigating suspicious persons. Wang Zhi was so successful that the emperor ordered the establishment of the Western Depot, a new police organ duplicating the functions of the infamous Eastern Depot but soon outstripping it. For five years, until sent away from the capital in 1481, Wang Zhi intimidated the court and terrorized officialdom, bringing many to their deaths, confiscating the accumulated wealth of many prominent families, and exerting unprincipled influence on all acts of governing. Courageous officials repeatedly submitted bills of impeachment against him, but the emperor always sided with his eunuch and punished the remonstrators. Even so, the emperor began to realize that Wang Zhi was drawing too much anger from officialdom.

After Wang Zhi was temporarily sent away from court in 1481, courtiers began to suspect that he was losing the emperor's favor. Thus they dared to expose his crimes. Another eunuch impeached him for improper conduct. This eunuch, a scoundrel protecting his arena of power, showed evidence that Wang Zhi had misused confidential information about the emperor himself. At last, in 1482, Xianzong reluctantly disbanded the Western Depot and cashiered certain commanders of the Embroidered Uniform Guard whose behavior had been the most flagrant. Wang Zhi waited impatiently to return to the capital. Finally the emperor, reluctantly, punished him lightly by transferring him in 1483 to the humble post of keeper of the stables in Nanjing.

It was widely noted at the time that all the courageous protests of high officials against eunuch abuses accomplished little, but once another eunuch, in this case one no better than Wang Zhi, denounced Wang for all the wrong reasons, it brought the desired results. The emperor was slow to comprehend the full nature of the abuses, but at this time he began to turn away from reliance on the "bad" eunuchs and their cohorts. The "good" officials who had suffered were in time restored to their offices and gradually regained their dominance of the court, but there were no outstanding figures among them. Nor was the swollen scope of eunuchs' roles substantially reduced.

A complicating element in this problem is that there also were "good" eunuchs. In Xianzong's reign there is one notable example, the eunuch Huai En, famous for his moral authority and strict adherence to principle. In his role as Director of Ceremonial he headed the entire eunuch bureaucracy, and was looked upon with awe within the palace service as one who always opposed impropriety. He intervened with the emperor to calm his wrath and to prevent punishment of officials who had aroused the imperial anger. Huai En indignantly returned bribes from Outer Court officials wanting his intervention and upbraided them for their moral deficiencies. Eventually, by convincing the emperor that he should not deny the succession to his elder son, he earned the hatred of Lady Wan. Xianzong sadly transferred him to the Central Capital, Zhongdu in Anhui, a demotion signifying punishment. He was called back to serve in the succeeding reign and was responsible for introducing several excellent high officials to the new court, but died shortly thereafter.[16]

Another "good" eunuch associated with Huai En, Tan Ji, tutored the future emperor Zhu Youtang in the basic Confucian texts and is praised in the histories for exerting that good influence. Officials were always eager to identify and praise the "good" eunuchs because they understood that they must have allies inside the palace. They welcomed cooperation with eunuchs who were congenial to the officials' values, as many of them were.

The ongoing competition between the two bureaucracies—the proper court bureaucracy of the scholar officials and the disdained eunuch bureaucracy—reached destructive heights only under the few so-called eunuch dictators, and when that happened, the scholar-elite suffered humiliation, imprisonment, expropriation, and not infrequently death. That officials would tolerate the situation and not fight back more effectively is difficult to understand. They of course wanted to fight back. They constantly reminded emperors of the evils that eunuchs had brought down on their predecessors in history. Yet no matter how badly their emperor and his attendants misused them, most officials remained loyal and committed to service. In their view of the world, of society, and of the state, the ruler was indispensable; his political, ritual, and symbolic roles had to be fulfilled. His judgment did not have to be respected, but there was no alternate source of the authority in the sphere of politics that was his alone to wield. One historian has observed very perceptively that the "pervasive tyranny" of the earlier Ming emperors by this time had been reduced to a petty despotism, ugly, dysfunctional, and dangerous; it was something against which the officials should be ever vigilant, but which they could regard as an inevitable aspect of imperial rule. Through their constant vigilance and remonstration, imperial misbehavior must at least be confined to the private life of the ruler within his palace walls. It must not imperil his person or his heir; otherwise it was of no consequence to officialdom and the state. The emperor's indispensable role outside his palace enclosure was all that mattered to the functioning of their society, so even when intolerable behavior spilled out in ways that imperiled them personally, it simply had to be borne, resisted, and eventually corrected by them.[17]

It has often been observed that when monarchy is subject to rigid rules confining the succession to one family, and more particularly when succession is confined to the eldest son by the principal consort, the odds are that quite ordinary persons will occupy the throne much of the time, and occasionally the totally unfit will inherit. In a closed society having an aristocratic elite, unlike China's, the discrepancies between rulers and their close associates may be less extreme, for the aristocracy is governed by the same laws of biological chance and also produces its share of ordinary and unfit aristocrats. Mediocrity is endemic to closed aristocracies under kings. In China, by contrast, there was a particular dilemma in the situation whereby an elite selected for individual talent and merit had to sustain an imperial institution filled much of the time by incompetents. Chinese scholar-officials had to learn to rationalize the situation, to survive, and to make their ideals prevail. Throughout the later Ming dynasty their capacity to do so was tested more severely than in most other periods of China's imperial history. Alternatives to relying heavily on the indispensable functions of the ruler and his central government to solve all political and social problems began to be considered.[18]

Xianzong's reign faced real problems both of defense and of domestic order; the borders were repeatedly threatened by the growing organizational success of the Mongols (at the time often called Tatars). Several rebellions of Chinese and of minority peoples reached serious proportions. The government's ability to respond was impaired by the misbehavior of his consort Lady Wan, then by the uninhibited violence perpetrated by the eunuch dictator Wang Zhi and his lesser cohorts. Xianzong's mediocrity encouraged such inroads.

The seventeen-year reign of his son Zhu Youtang, who as the Hongzhi emperor reigned until 1505, was entirely different in tone and atmosphere. The two rulers, though father and son, could scarcely have been more different. Zhu Youtang was small and dark, probably like the Yao mother he lost when he was only five. As a young boy he was thoroughly tutored in the *Four Books* and remained genuinely devoted to the Confucian verities. His alert eyes revealed a quick mind; he had a mild demeanor and yet could be stubborn and mildly difficult in matters of his small private world inside the palace. In all the larger concerns of state, he was invariably earnest in striving to meet the high standards of his Confucian-minded advisers. He promoted the best persons to the high posts in the Inner and Outer Courts; a renewed spirit of optimism marked the tone of his government, encouraging vigorous attention to duty in the interests of the state and dynasty.

Only seventeen when he came to the throne, Zhu Youtang, the Emperor Xiaozong, quickly asserted himself to make his Hongzhi reign period different from that of his father. He dismissed the disreputable sycophantic hangers-on of his father's court, demoted and (advised by the noble-minded eunuch paragon Huai En) punished many of the higher-ranking eunuchs, rid the court of his father's spurious spiritual advisers masking as Daoist and Buddhist wise men, and gave full support to a tightening-up of administrative practices, especially in those cases where eunuchs had superseded the responsible civil service appointees.

Ming Xiaozong's devotion to Confucian teachings was, by all accounts, genuine, and it was quite unprecedented in the Ming dynasty. He restored the Classics Mat lectures *(jingyan),* a traditional institution that normally was maintained only as a formality. In his reign, eminent scholar-officials in his government were assigned in regular rotation to discuss sections of the classics with him and others of the court, to analyze current problems in relation to the classical precedents, and in those ways to guide his governing. He tirelessly attended these lectures, assuming the role of the diligent and self-effacing student. He was not feigning an attitude of seriousness. He was in fact like his great-grandfather Xuanzong (r. 1425–1435) in having acquired some cultivation; he was interested in scholarship and literary matters, and even had some modest abilities as a painter and calligrapher. But above all, he sincerely accepted his Confucian obligations. The high officials of the court could scarcely believe what was happening; they were so delighted that they forgave him his minor faults. Yet they also could not refrain from making ever greater demands on his patience and his willingness to submit to their often impractical Neo-Confucian fundamentalism. We must sympathize with him; at times driven to respond, he adopted evasive humility, saying that their advice was correct and he would hold it in mind. He was frail, sickly, often able to meet his court and perform his duties only with difficulty. His officials may have contributed to his early demise by keeping him under incessant pressure to be the perfect ruler. When would they again have such an opportunity?

Because of his compliant and sincere manner, he has been praised by the official historians from the moment of his death in 1505 as the model emperor. He was given the posthumous temple name Xiaozong, "the Filial," the first among the Confucian virtues. In fact, he allowed his empress to demand favors for her avaricious brothers and through them to exploit her position outrageously; he stubbornly supported her and them. Thanks also to her influence, the court indulged in luxury and extravagance to a new degree. He would not reprove her. Because of his own forgiving nature, his reforms often were not rigorously pursued.

His were minor faults, faults of the inner palace and his private life; officials were happy to overlook them while praising his model behavior as head of state. His improvements in governing led to strengthened border defenses, better-managed revenues, and an upright tone at the court. The official *Ming History* says of his reign:

> The Ming held the realm throughout a succession of sixteen rulers. Other than Emperors Taizu and Chengzu, those worthy of commendation are only Renzong, Xuanzong, Xiaozong, and no others . . . Xiaozong was alone in having the ability to maintain his governing in humility and modesty, to be diligent in governing and to have deep concern for the people, ever vigilant to uphold the Great Way of guarding the realm's riches and not abusing his powers, maintaining the purity and uprightness of his court, and assuring that the people would enjoy abundance.[19]

That is a bit excessive, but it displays the honor that the scholar-officialdom felt was his due.

Historians today also must consider other factors. During this period of the late fifteenth century, the eunuch bureaucracy grew to equal the entire civil service bureaucracy in size, each at roughly 12,000 persons. In the next 150 years, until the end of the dynasty, the civil service posts less than doubled while the eunuch bureaucracy grew to six or seven times its size in 1500. The tendency has been to focus on a few eunuch dictators, the notoriously bad examples of eunuch misappropriation of power. Of far greater significance, however, is the regularizing of eunuch roles that spread into all branches of governing. One can see why. Emperors preferred these often very competent, always compliant agents of their authority to the high-minded, principled, moralizing scholar-officials. The growth in the eunuch bureaucracy produced a systemic or structural change in the exercise of government, one that threatened the traditional scope of scholar-official bureaucracy. It was a threat that the officials could combat only by gaining the confidence of the erratic individuals who occupied the imperial throne, and through them to curb that growth. It was a problem that the Ming dynasty never solved.

The foregoing account covers almost a century of political history linked to emperors and their courts. It shows that many problems of the entire government and society were deeply affected by what might at first glance appear to be superficial details of individual rulers' lives. That context of governing must be kept in mind when other kinds of issues are examined.

II. THE MECHANICS OF GOVERNMENT

The Hongzhi reign, 1488–1506, is a good point at which to look at the mechanics of governmental operations under the Ming dynasty because Emperor Xiaozong's court and governmental apparatus were able to work with less distortion than in most other periods. Improper eunuch influence was lessened, the emperor's relations with his officials were excellent, the quality of the leading tier of officialdom was high, and the minor blemishes such as consort clan interference were not allowed to go too far.

Legal and Statutory Foundations

The emperor was the sole source of law in China. There was no legislative organ within his government. Any statement he made on any subject had the force of law when it was issued in writing to which he fixed his signature or seal (or allowed that to be done by others in his name) and then was distributed in the proper fashion through the relevant offices of government. In practice, however, the important bodies of law and regulations were not formulated in an ad hoc manner. The ruler set up commissions of scholar-experts in the pertinent subjects—law, ritual, institutions, historical precedent—to draft the larger items. He then read and approved the final versions and authorized their promulgation to make them the law of the land. That is how the Great Ming Code, the Ancestral Injunctions, all the basic statutory enactments became law. Those statutory compilations mostly appeared during the founder's reign.[20] As the formally constructed laws and regulations approved by the founder of a new dynasty, they established the governing institutions, defined infractions and fixed penalties, and assigned responsibilities at all levels in society. Some large items continued to be added to that corpus, which became the largest body of statutory codes and institutional regulations produced by any dynasty in Chinese history.

Laws, however, were no more than instruments of the dynasty's governing; they were not bodies of transcendent law founded on a higher authority or principle, making them binding on everyone, including the emperor. Ming Taizu regularly violated the laws and legal procedures he himself had established. He explained that he was forced to adopt harsh "penalties beyond the law" to deal with extraordinary problems of his reign, but ordered that imperial successors, having no further need to do so, should adhere strictly to his laws. In fact, later emperors did not feel closely bound by that command, whether in penal law, in administrative procedures, or in ritual practice. They of course made a show of following their predecessors' models, but as a matter of filial propriety; that was the binding principle. Meanwhile, they altered and freely added to the dynasty's laws and regulations. No "higher law" prevented that. Statesmen could not appeal to a higher law to which an emperor's dynastic authority should be subject. The Chinese political and philosophical traditions did not include a conceptual basis for claiming that laws possess a transcendent validity.

Operational Modes

Each ruler's individual enactments might be directed to an immediate personal whim and be highly erratic. There were to be sure checks on his legislating: both the force of precedent and the critical assessments of his scholar-officials could be appealed to for that purpose. They could invoke strong arguments based on human reason, historical experience, and especially on the society's shared ethical values. Those were effective in some situations but did not curb all the Ming emperors. Some of the worst emperors were foolishly credulous, believing in the crudest charlatans and all manner of persons who claimed to wield divine powers. The scholar elite usually would not stoop to applying countermeasures on that level of vulgar belief. Even in the interest of bettering government, they mostly scorned such methods.

They did, however, do something that to our modern minds appears to come close to invoking magic, as when they reported signs of heaven's displeasure—earthquakes, disasters, astral phenomena—and interpreted them on the plane of ancient imperial Confucian theory about correlative interactions between man and the cosmos.[21] When emperors were informed of unnatural events, they customarily asked for criticisms of themselves, issued amnesties, and took other measure to restore cosmic harmony. Two examples from the reign of Xianzong illustrate the ways such influences might be brought to bear.

At one point his Confucian advisers worried that he did not produce an heir after two sons died in infancy and he confined his attentions to Lady Wan. They thought she was too old to conceive again. In the autumn of 1468 a number of comets were sighted; a Grand Secretary and the Minister of Rites (among whose duties it was to record and interpret astral phenomena and other prodigies) repeated their advice to Xianzong that he should spend more time with other consorts in order to ease the state's concerns about the lack of an heir.[22] Angry, Xianzong replied, "This is a domestic matter in which I will make the decisions." The comets did not worry him.

On a second occasion some years later, however, when Zhu Youtang, the future Xiaozong, was growing up and other sons also had been produced, the Lady Wan and her crowd of unsavory associates began to worry that Zhu Youtang would someday come to the throne and would want to settle scores with them. Represented by the "bad" eunuch Liang Fang, they began to insinuate that Zhu Youtang exhibited such inferior qualities that it would be wise to designate another son the heir.[23] Xianzong appeared to give the matter some thought. The famous "good" eunuch Huai En sternly opposed interfering in the legitimate succession, warning about the threat to dynastic stability. For that he was sent away from the court to a post at the Central Capital, a form of banishment. Then an earthquake at Mount Tai in Shandong, the Eastern Peak, was reported. The Eastern Peak was from antiquity taken as a symbol of the heir apparent and as the protector of the dynasty. Court officials interpreted the earthquake to the emperor as a warning from heaven. Frightened, he denied that he might name a different heir.[24] An earthquake frightened the emperor more than the anger of the Lady Wan, from whom he had somewhat distanced himself but who still dominated the Inner Court. The court officials must have known how far they could go in threatening the ruler with such signs, and may have done so with a measure of cynicism mixed with their own feelings of awe toward the vast cosmos.

Cynical manipulation of the concept of imperial responsibility to an ever watchful heaven with the intent to intimidate an errant ruler was not, however, congenial to the worldview of most scholar-officials of the time. The appropriate curbs on willful rule were pragmatic, not theoretical. When a despotic ruler was shown that his mistakes exposed himself to loss or peril, that he was being cheated and robbed, he could be expected to change. The upright Ming officials who struggled to rescue the state from the misdeeds of bad rulers mostly sought to do so in that way, relying on material evidence more than on cosmic signs.

Officials were committed to helping emperors, good or bad, to perform the necessary tasks. We might think that all good officials did so conscientiously, even bravely, while the bad ones quickly exposed themselves as frauds and earned the condemnation of their peers. Many situations, however, remained ambiguous; the officials' roles were essentially those of compromise with political realities, and their Confucian ethics demanded that each person make his own judgments according to his own sense of the situation. The life of politics was one of subtle nuances and shaded judgments.

In the ruler's daily work, in each of his proclamations and edicts, and in each memorialized proposal to which he gave his nod, he added the force of his exclusive lawmaking prerogative. No one else could do that. Such was the legal basis of Ming government. In practical terms, if he did not use that power wisely the dynasty suffered. Xiaozong was fully aware that, more by default than by purposeful actions, his father had used the imperial power very unwisely, and that the state was fiscally and operationally weakened. Xiaozong sought earnestly to correct those weaknesses. He did so by carefully responding (with sound advice from wise senior officials and the upright eunuch Huai En) to the memorials urgently submitted in the spirit of reform that swept the court immediately upon his accession in 1487.

Court Audiences and Governmental Procedures

All governing was centered in and transmitted from the court in Beijing. The capital cities of the thirteen Ming provinces and the southern metropolitan district (the province-size region centered on Nanjing) were the seats of government offices separately responsible to counterpart agencies in the central government for their oversight of fiscal, judicial, and military matters within the provinces; the provinces nevertheless did not form an integrated level of governing with significant discretionary powers. Investigative and supervisory activities of the government also emanated from the capital, but through an independent hierarchy of offices (Map 15).

Below the provincial level the prefectures, sub-prefectures, and counties (districts), little changed from Song and Yuan times, were responsible to the provincial level of supervision but were staffed by appointments made directly at the capital. The entire structure of governing down to the county level was highly centralized. The emperor in Beijing was supposed to be kept informed about all the issues, to understand the reports and memorials received from all levels throughout the realm and from all the ministries, bureaus and agencies in the two capitals, and to respond with decisions in all cases brought before him.

In his daily attendance to governing, the emperor's most demanding responsibilities were to attend court, to issue edicts and decrees, and to formulate his rescripts or responses to all incoming memorials, reports, and proposals. Those duties were so burdensome that even the hyperactive Ming Taizu complained about being unable to meet the full scale of his responsibilities. He precipitately reorganized the central government in 1380 in a way that denied him the highly rational and effective form of assistance that all earlier dynasties had employed: a strong Outer Court led by Chief Councillors based in a Central Secretariat. To review briefly here the state of the problem in mid-Ming times, Taizu imposed on himself and all his successors the practical necessity to make ad hoc arrangements in order to keep government working. Emperors also had a heavy schedule of ritual acts, some of which could be assigned to others to perform in the ruler's name. Many routine tasks in the daily work of central government also had to be assigned to others. Chengzu

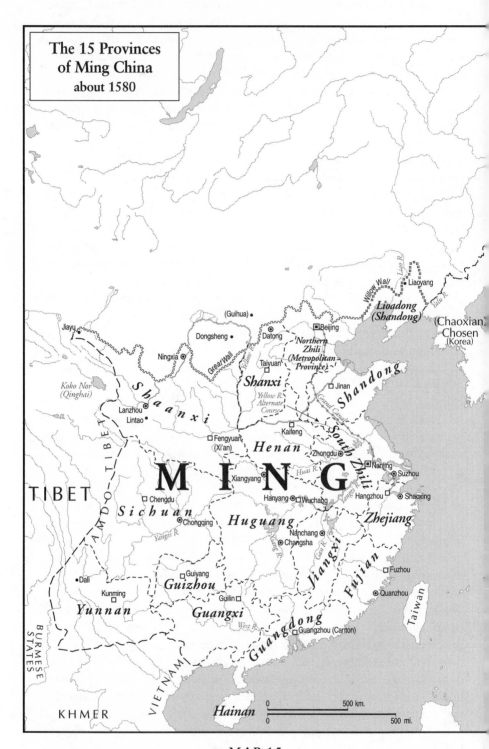

The 15 Provinces of Ming China about 1580

MAP 15

established an Inner Court cabinet of his Grand Secretaries based in the Hanlin Academy, and turned a large share of the workload over to them. He also gave routine tasks to eunuch secretaries. Those elements of the political structure evolved through the fifteenth century, but during the reign of Xianzong (1465–1487) the procedures of regular governing at the center degenerated under abuses initiated by or tolerated by this ruler. His conscientious son Xiaozong, in contrast with his father and most mid-Ming emperors, worked hard to govern and to improve the conditions he had inherited from his errant father.

Presiding over (or at least being present at) the audiences of the court was any emperor's central formal obligation. Meetings of the court were of two kinds, with different ritual formalities. There were the Great Audiences held on holidays and commemorative occasions, such as the New Year, the solstices and equinoxes, and the emperor's birthday. On the New Year the emperor also received ambassadors and heads of states. At Great Audiences he accepted congratulatory memorials and issued hortatory decrees but dealt with no regular business. These audiences took place in the great throne hall, the largest building within the imperial city, in earlier Ming times called the Fengtian Dian, The Hall of Serving Heaven, known today by the new name given it by the Qing rulers, Taihe Dian (Hall of Grand Harmony).[25] Court dress was at its most formal, and the procedures were highly ritualized.

There were also the Regular Audiences, at two levels of formality: those held on the first and fifteenth of each month also were held in the great throne hall, and regular business usually was not conducted. Otherwise the Regular Audiences were held daily, before the dawn, in Ming Taizu's time. After Chengzu came to the throne, and especially after he moved the capital to Beijing, it was felt that in coldest winter the dawn audience in unheated throne rooms was too difficult for aged courtiers; they might have to stand, kneel, bow, and kowtow over a period of many hours. Chengzu ordered that in cold weather the court would meet briefly to go through the formalities then would adjourn to a heated side hall; only those officials with specific business would attend, while all the others went back to their offices. We can imagine them plodding stiffly to and from the audiences, with padded or fur-lined robes under their formal court gowns, eager to draw a bit of warmth into their frozen hands by holding a hot cup of tea as the early sun rose. The life of a courtier was at times austere; meeting the dawn court audiences was its most trying duty.

Chengzu also added the noonday audience, held in still more informal settings with smaller numbers in attendance, where only officials directly involved might engage in fuller discussion. The accession in 1435 of Emperor Yingzong, then only eight years old, called for changes. Worried that the boy's health would be affected, his senior officials and his grandmother decided that no more than eight items of business would be conducted at the dawn audience and that summaries prepared by the Grand Secretaries would be submitted in writing on the previous afternoon in order to shorten the presentation and discussion. The noonday audiences were canceled. Those changes became permanent; noonday audiences were only rarely held thereafter, and yellow slips with the summaries were regularly attached to all documents requiring action, written by responsible officials or, later on, by eunuchs in the Palace Secretariat, an agency of the eunuch Directorate of Ceremonial. Those summaries guided the emperor in making his vermilion rescripts, his decisions concerning implementation written in his hand, using a brush with red ink. Later some rulers allowed eunuchs to write these for them and apply the imperial seal that made them legal.

Eventually the business of the court came to be carried on more or less apart from the audiences. That was decried by purists as signifying decline, but it must also have been seen by others as rational. When the nine-year-old Emperor Shenzong (the Wanli emperor) came to the throne in 1572, with regard for his tender years the dawn audience was held only on the third, sixth, ninth, thirteenth, sixteenth, nineteenth, twenty-third, twenty-sixth, and twenty-ninth days (the Chinese would say, the days with three, six, and nine). An emperor notoriously fond of defying precedents and conventions and hating the formalities of court, he made that reduced schedule the standard for his reign, and it was retained in later reigns. He also simplified the circulation of memorials by asking that no originals be sent to him, only brief summaries. The complete texts were used only by his advisers and by the implementing agencies. Those changes were looked upon by most not as rationalization but as dereliction of imperial duty.

There was no danger that Ming Xiaozong, a century earlier, would ever become willful or indolent. He faithfully attended the Great and Regular Audiences and took his responsibilities very seriously. His court officials and many of those stationed in the capital agencies and throughout the provinces had the duty to submit memorials to the throne, and others could do so by right even if not in the course of performing their specific duties. Memorials were statements drawn up by officials to inform the government or to propose action by it. There were ten forms or categories of communications from officials (occasionally also from non-officials) sent upward to court and emperor. Translations of the technical terms for them are not standardized; loosely they might be called proposals, information memorials, reports, discussions, impeachments, petitions, manifests, and the like.[26] The formalities of presentation were meticulously observed. They were written on paper of prescribed size and quality, in calligraphy of approved style, folded in a particular way, enclosed in a stiff paper wrapper, addressed, and sealed.

The Office of Transmission

Whether coming from the capital or from the provinces by official post, all memorials were sent to the Office of Transmission (Tongzheng si), the central nexus of the government's paper flow. Along with the ministers of the Six Ministries (Personnel, Revenues, Rites, War, Punishments, and Works), the heads of the Censorate, and the Chief Minister of the Court of Judicial Review, the Commissioner of the Office of Transmission was known as one of the "Nine Chief Ministers" of the government. Holding an office of high dignity, he was supposed to be autonomous and protected from all political influence. His work was indispensable to the regular functioning of the government.

All the documents constituting the paper flow, both in and out, were expected to pass through this single office. Because paper was power, this office controlled the flow of power. All incoming memorials were scrutinized: Were they properly framed and presented? Were the persons submitting them acting within regulation and precedent? Did they contain any improper content? The Office of Transmission exercised at least the nominal power to "reseal and send back" or to "correct and forward" as necessary, although the next stage of processing was to send all memorials on to the Six Offices of Scrutiny, staffed with supervising censors, where the Office of Transmission's discretionary power to receive or to reject documents was duplicated by the censors. The Six Offices (one office exercising supervisory powers over one of each of the Six Ministries) then sent them on to the Palace Secretariat for the use of the emperor and his Grand Secretaries.

The Office of Transmission's most important function was to register each incoming document, note a precise count of the number of its words, and keep a record identifying each incoming and outgoing document with a notation on how it was handled. All the incoming documents that were accepted were copied by scribes—enough copies for the Six Offices, the relevant ministries and implementing agencies, and the Palace Secretariat for the emperor's use. At some point soon thereafter the emperor and his attendants would receive advice from the ministry or other relevant agency on how the matters set forth in each document should be handled. Eventually the imperial response would be added; that might take the form of a mere notation "accepted," "noted," or "tabled," or there would be a lengthier response detailing the action that should follow.

The ruler's responses would take any of six or eight prescribed forms, which are translated "edict," "rescript," "proclamation," "decree," and the like. Those were sent back to the Office of Transmission with the original incoming memorial. It was again recorded, and copies of the imperial response were made for the implementing agencies, with a copy for the archives. In times of good government the Office of Transmission served well to coordinate and keep a record of all the government's actions. It was nonetheless not immune to corruption; nothing so crucial to the exercise of political power could be. When a powerful Grand Secretary or a eunuch dictator dominated the government, he might try to place an accomplice in the post of Commissioner of the Office of Transmission, where their collusion could lead to suppression of incoming memorials, or to identifying so as to silence officials who might submit impeachments of their actions, or to gain improper information about operations from which they might benefit. Interference of that kind could not be lightly attempted, but there were officials who at times gained enough power to do so.

In mid- and later Ming times there also developed another kind of more informal memorial (called *ti ben*) that certain officials in the capital were permitted to submit directly to a collection point in the Inner Court, bypassing the Office of Transmission. These never superseded the regular flow of memorials through the proper channels, but they detracted from the system by diffusing power. Strong rulers recognized that their access to regular information was essential to their control, and thus protected the Office of Transmission as the agency serving that need.

The first few months after Ming Xiaozong's accession offer interesting examples of the way memorials initiated important political action. His father, Xianzong, died on September 9, 1487, when Zhu Youtang, the future Xiaozong, was only seventeen years old. He was inexperienced, but quite alert to the corruption and rampant abuses that marked his father's reign. The formalities of putting the court in mourning, ascending the throne, issuing the accession proclamation, working out a posthumous temple name for the old emperor, and sending his funeral catafalque off to his tomb occupied two and one-half weeks. On September 28, when the Regular Audiences resumed, the court was flooded with memorials demanding punishment of the scoundrels (who all still held their ill-gotten positions and were in attendance at the court), and requesting personnel changes to clear away the stench, so as to start a new era. The new emperor quickly established the principles that would guide his reign, defining himself as a ruling personality.

He of course expressed his grief in elaborate conventional rhetoric and praised his late father's sagelike qualities. It is quite interesting that the first of the impeachment memorials, in listing the worst of the criminals who must now be expelled and punished, names first of all the man who, as a Vice Minister of Rites, had been given concurrent command of the Office of Transmission. Within a few days he and the holders of that office's three or four other chief positions also were stripped of their offices and punished in various ways, mostly by demotion. Xiaozong indulged in no purges of the kinds carried out earlier in the dynasty. When subsequent memorials urged, virtually demanded, that he take sterner measures, he replied: "These persons have indeed employed treacherous and insidious means and have done violence to standards of upright behavior, and they deserve to be held guilty of severe crimes, but because my house is now in mourning I have proposed leniency."[27]

Some of the incoming memorials reviewed the later years of Xianzong's reign. A particularly sensitive issue was the misbehavior of Lady Wan, the emperor's favorite consort (but never named his empress), who had dominated the court throughout his reign. She was thoroughly hated; her sudden death a few months before the emperor's death (she was nineteen years his senior) had been a cause for relief and rejoicing in court circles. Xiaozong had grown up in fear of her. When he was a small boy his grandmother had warned him never to eat or drink anything she might offer him, for fear of being poisoned, and he knew that she had been responsible for the death of his mother by poisoning. Yet he discouraged the official circles from speculating on private affairs within the imperial household; he said that those matters would be properly investigated and proper action taken to right all wrongs. He did not wish for the officials to keep up the pressure on him to expose such facts in court. Even these matters concerning a hated woman and a father for whom he could have felt no warmth were "my family matters," not issues of state.[28] Lady Wan's three dissolute and arrogant brothers were nonetheless stripped of their offices and banished, their property confiscated. The message was clear that there would be a thorough purge, albeit a bloodless one.

The most important matter of administrative procedures that the memorial writers demanded be corrected was that of improper appointments. Xianzong had made thousands of appointments to persons whom the Ministry of Personnel would not have considered qualified for any official post. They included specialists in aphrodisiacs and sex techniques, illustrators of erotic manuals, 789 Buddhist monks and nuns and Tibetan lamas, 253 Daoist "True Masters," and many craftsmen and entertainers who were irregularly appointed to official posts in reward for their services. Instead of going through the usual bureaucratic procedures, these persons had been appointed by direct command of the emperor, usually meaning that the Lady Wan or chief eunuchs wrote out patents of appointment and sealed them with the emperor's official seals. Those were called *chuanfeng* officials, or "officials by direct appointment." The procedure could not be called illegal because the emperor could do whatever he wished, but it was seriously in violation of precedents and regulations. The memorial writers could not effectively oppose it during Xianzong's reign, but now they protested vigorously, calling attention to the irregularity of it all. One Supervising Censor in Yunnan submitted a memorial that declared in part: "Of late the direct appointments have been egregiously made, so that persons having no command of literacy have been appointed to civil [i.e., "literary"] offices, while persons of no military accomplishment whatsoever have been made military officers, and artisans and persons doing ordinary crafts have been given official advancement." A flood of such memorials stressed the evils of direct appointment and recommended that all holders of such offices be stripped of their improper official titles and sent back to their home communities to rid the capital of their presence. The emperor agreed. He slashed thousands from the payrolls and confirmed that the practice would be abolished.[29]

We see in the actions of the emperor and his counsellors in these last months of 1487 the beginnings of an imperial reign in which a young emperor and a group of upright senior officials began a partnership in governing. It reflected a tone that is rare in Ming history, perhaps matched only in the Xuanzong (1425–1435) reign of this emperor's grandfather, but the imperial personality in this case was far less assertive that the martial Xuanzong. Nevertheless, Xiaozong and his trusted officials conscientiously analyzed the perilously corrupted operations of government under the previous reign and set about to make the system work again. That process of thorough correction undoubtedly strengthened governing procedures for the duration of his reign. Under his successors, however, those procedures were again strained, until conditions in the 1570s provided justification for the powerful Chief Grand

Secretary Zhang Juzheng, in the years 1572–1582, to again impose discipline and strong management on the machinery of governing.

III. THE GRAND CANAL IN MING TIMES

The Grand Canal and the linked problems of Yellow River flood control constituted a major concern of government throughout the entire Ming dynasty. The way that concern was handled reveals to us both the capacities of Ming government and some characteristics of Chinese civilization at this period in late imperial history.

In this connection, the end of the fifteenth century is important for one event: in 1495 the main course of the Yellow River was turned from its path where it flowed northeast to enter the sea north of the Shandong Peninsula, to run south and exit to the sea through the channel of the Huai River. That would remain its principal course until 1852. The event of 1495 is reason enough for examining at this point the larger problems of the Grand Canal and the Yellow River in Ming times. These were problems first of politics, then of technology, and throughout of cultural values.

Ming China's Grand Canal, connecting Hangzhou south of the Yangzi to Beijing north of the Yellow River, was a major investment of the central government, a major support of its fiscal and economic systems, and a major expression of its ruling philosophy. It deeply affected countless aspects of Ming life.

From antiquity the Chinese were great designers and builders of canals for flood control and land reclamation by drainage, for irrigation, and for transport. Efforts to connect the Yangzi drainage with the political and military power centers of North China commenced long before the imperial era. Under the early imperial dynasties (from the third century B.C.E.) on through the Sui and Tang dynasties (to the ninth century C.E.), those efforts were largely confined to Western China. Especially important were linkages made between the middle Yangzi and the Wei River in the northwest; the Han and Tang capitals at Chang'an (present-day Xi'an) became in that way the northern terminus of routes leading south via the Han River in Hubei and its tributaries.[30] The Sui dynasty (581–619 C.E.) added the important Bian Canal, which extended southeast from the Yellow River in northwest Henan to reach the Huai River, from which point water transport was possible on to the lower Yangzi. That inland waterway became so important that it influenced the further eastward shift of North China's political center, influencing the choice of Luoyang as the secondary Tang capital (see Chapter 1, Section III). Subsequently Kaifeng, still farther to the east, became the principal capital of the Northern Song. After the Mongols absorbed all of China late in the thirteenth century, there was a need for a shorter north-south water link lying farther to the east to connect the Yuan capital at Dadu (present-day Beijing) in a more direct north-south line to the nation's economic center in the lower Yangzi drainage. Portions of existing canals were joined together, new sections were built, and a transport system was set up that later became the Grand Canal *(yun he)* of Ming and Qing times (Map 16).

During the Ming dynasty that canal was broadened, deepened where necessary, supplied with more locks and dams, and made much more usable. It incorporated eight major segments, each having its own name and maintained by separate regional bureaucratic agencies. Labor forces numbering from 50,000 to 250,000 might be called up from the civilian population for specific repair projects usually lasting five or six months at a time, in addition to the regular use of military labor. Costs were enormous, as was the diversion of bureaucratic resources to manage the project. Two chapters of the official *Ming History* are devoted to the details of maintaining and repairing the Grand Canal in the Ming period.[31] A large body of specialized writings on the canal, on hydraulics, and on the related problem of Yellow River water conservancy also dates from Ming times. It was a principal preoccupation of the Ming state and society.

As it emerged in early Ming and was maintained through the Qing, the Grand Canal was slightly more than 1,000 miles long and from 10 to 50 feet deep, and varied in width from 50 to 150 feet. It crossed five major rivers and opened onto numerous spurs and side canals, with extensions at the northern terminus serving the border garrisons north of Beijing.

The technical information on the design of the canal and its engineering problems is of forbidding complexity.[32] Two of those problems will illustrate the point.

First, the Grand Canal is of the type called a "summit canal." Midway in its northern half, as it passes through Shandong Province, it must cross a summit 138 feet above its mean level where it crosses the Yangzi. Its southern terminus at Hangzhou is roughly at sea level; the canal is about 25 feet above sea level at Zhenjiang on the Yangzi, then rises to 138 feet above that level 400 miles farther north in Shandong near the point where it crosses the Yellow River; it then falls to 40 feet above mean level near Tianjin, and rises again to 118 feet above that level in the final segment of 100 miles to reach Beijing.

It was not the first summit canal that the Chinese had built, but it had its own quite special problems. Crossing the high points required the diversion of rivers to supply the canal with water in dry North China, and in order to retain that water it was necessary to construct an elaborate system of locks, dams, sluice gates, and slipways; those devices held the water back while permitting boats to pass. Mechanical devices, great capstans and pulleys driven by animal or human labor, were necessary to pull the boats through the sluice gates and slips. For these needs and for other kinds of maintenance, labor crews, mostly of military conscripts, had to be kept in readiness all along the canal; they might double as guards for security purposes. Roads paved with stone and planted with willows were maintained on the banks of the canal so that the human and animal towing crews could move easily, and bridges were built with high central spans so that boats could pass underneath, although some might have to lower their masts. In the late Ming, when

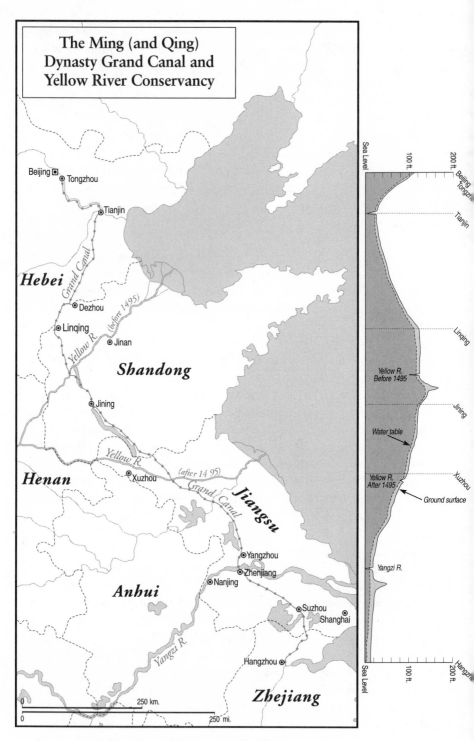

The Ming (and Qing) Dynasty Grand Canal and Yellow River Conservancy

Beijing
Tongzhou
Tianjin
Hebei
Grand Canal
Dezhou
Linqing
Yellow R. (before 1495)
Jinan
Shandong
Jining
Yellow R. (after 1495)
Henan
Xuzhou
Grand Canal
Jiangsu
Yangzhou
Zhenjiang
Nanjing
Anhui
Suzhou
Shanghai
Yangzi R.
Hangzhou
Zhejiang

0   250 km.
0   250 mi.

Sea Level
100 ft.
200 ft.
Beijing/Tongzhou
Tianjin
Linqing
Yellow R. Before 1495
Jining
Water table
Yellow R. After 1495
Xuzhou
Ground surface
Yangzi R.
Sea Level
100 ft.
200 ft.
Hangzhou

MAP 16

the first Europeans traveled on the canal, they described it as one of the marvels of the world.

A second set of problems were those caused by the Yellow River. This subject can scarcely be brought up at less than full book length. Here the briefest outline must suffice. The Yellow River is often known as China's sorrow, and for good reason. No river in the world has caused more floods, famines, and deaths among the millions who have lived within its drainage and who have been dependent on it. China's two greatest rivers, the Yangzi, running through Central China, and the Yellow River, which enters from Inner Asia and winds through North China, are of quite different character. The headwaters of both are very close together in the northeast extension of the Tibetan Plateau, in present-day Qinghai Province. The Yangzi, 3,500 miles long, flows to the southeast from that point, crosses Sichuan Province and through the famed Yangzi Gorges (where a giant dam is being constructed), and on east to the sea near Shanghai. It is a deep and fast-moving stream, confined most of its way between hills and high land, and its flow is steady enough that silt deposits along its channel are not excessive.

The Yellow River is 2,900 miles long, flows northeast from Qinghai into Inner Mongolia, then south to form the boundary between Shaanxi and Shanxi provinces but then turns abruptly to the east again through the Tong Pass and the Sanmen Gorges, finally reaching the flat North China Plain in northern Henan. When it reaches Kaifeng it is no longer confined by hills. In late prehistoric times, from that point on to the sea it flowed into innumerable meandering channels, creating vast marshlands, the bulk of its water eventually forced to turn aside at the base of Shandong's mountains. There the water could either turn to the northeast, entering the sea north of the Shandong Peninsula, or travel southeast to join with the Huai River in its eastward progress, to enter the sea south of the Shandong Peninsula. In historic times, from the second millennium B.C.E. onward, the Chinese have channeled and diked this last 800 miles of the Yellow River, confining it and draining the vast marshland and floodplain from which North China was formed.

Confining the Yellow River to one of a few artificial channels never worked for long. The river reached northern Henan after flowing for 2,000 miles through the loess soils of northwestern China, the "yellow earth" of fine dust that through the millennia has blown in from the Takla Makan and Gobi and other Inner Asian deserts, covering North China's ground to a depth up to 100 feet, making the friable, easily worked, rich soil that sustained what the Chinese have traditionally regarded as the birthplace of Chinese civilization 4,000 years ago. That early high civilization, as its people multiplied, denuded the hills of their forest and brush covering, subjecting the region to the most serious erosion. With the summer rains, the yellow earth washed into streams to be carried to the rivers and to end up in the Yellow River. Its silt content has been measured at more than 50 percent in some places. The river carries its silt burden well enough until it reaches the flat plain in northern Henan; then the speed of the river's flow decreases. From Kaifeng on to the east the flow is too slow to keep the silt moving, much less to scour out the channel; deposits build up so that the riverbed, within its confining dikes, soon becomes higher than the surrounding land surface. In summers of heavy rains (in North China the precipitation comes almost entirely in the summer), dikes break and the plain becomes an inland sea. From time to time the diking must be reengineered all over again.

The Grand Canal of necessity made use of some sections of the Yellow River channel east of Kaifeng or in northern Jiangsu, depending on where the river found its main channel at any time. The canal also depended on the water supplied by the river to fill its nearer sections. When major floods occurred, the Grand Canal could disappear in a summer sea, and when the waters receded it might be lost in the newest silt deposits. River control was thus inseparable from canal management. The two together created problems that could not be fundamentally solved despite all the hydraulic engineering skills that the Chinese developed over time to deal with them. Were there no alternatives?

Late imperial China invested in the Grand Canal for one overriding reason: to move the tax grains. They could be moved at a cost commensurate with their value only if water transport was available. The canal was designed for one-way traffic, from the lower Yangzi region of rice and grain surpluses to Beijing and the northern defense garrisons. The million or more residents of the capital, then the world's largest city, depended for their food supply on the grain brought from the south. Official salaries were paid in large part in grain. The northern border garrison forces and other large military establishments in the capital region needed grain both for salaries and for food. Even when, as happened during the Ming, official salaries came to be paid in silver and taxes were commuted to payment in cash, the cereal grains still had to be transported to meet the need for food. I will discuss the many other uses of the canal and the two-way flow of people and goods that it carried, but those factors are quite secondary to the single purpose for which it was built. So the question remains: Were there no alternatives?

The possible alternatives were the use of land transport and the sea route from the mouth of the Yangzi or other southeast ports to the port (at modern Tianjin) serving Beijing. Both had been used in recent history. Before the rebuilding of the canal was completed in early Yuan, grain and other goods were transported on canals where they existed, with overland portages used as necessary. Much of China's canal building in earlier history was done to connect sections of waterways that otherwise utilized land transport for the intervening distances. Because of its high costs, however, land transport had to be considered a temporary expedient, so it need not be further considered.

The truly interesting alternative—interesting both as technology and for its conceptual elements—is the sea route. From the time Khubilai Khan conquered the Southern Song in the 1270s, he relied on seagoing ships to assist his imperial efforts. The surrendered naval forces of South China's merchants provided him with a navy to pursue the Song to its final demise off the coast of Hong Kong, and helped with the second invasion of Japan in 1281. The Mongols were not hesitant to use naval forces, even though they were totally dependent on Chinese and Koreans to build and man their ships. Khubilai also coopted two leading Chinese pirates to transport grains from Central and South China to Dadu. They used their fleets and their seagoing crews to move large amounts of grain from 1282 until they were executed for corrupt practices in 1303. The sailors at first explored the coastal route rather tentatively, clinging close to shore, but soon learned to strike out around the Shandong Peninsula and on to Tianjin (or Dagu, the port on the Bai River closest to Beijing). Their small seagoing junks, ranging in capacity from 300 to 1,000 piculs (*shi;* 20 to 150 tons), could make the voyage in ten days or two weeks by sailing in the late spring and summer when winds were most favorable; losses were very small. Freights reached 3.5 million catties (more than 200,000 tons) in the 1320s, the last years for which annual figures are given in the *Yuan History*.[33] The maritime transport continued to the end of the Yuan dynasty, supplementing the use of the newly constructed canal after the 1290s.

Late in the Yuan the Mongols, their canal intercepted by rebellions and their maritime transport system failing along with all operations of late Yuan government, again found a pirate to make emergency shipments. Fang Guo-zhen[34] was willing to ship grain from the Shanghai area only in return for the court's legitimization of his pirate status, and then only in niggardly amounts when it pleased him to do so. It did not help the Yuan government appreciably, but it again pointed out the connection between maritime and illegal activities: the sea routes were manned by pirates and scoundrels, to the Chinese mind.

At the beginning of the Ming the need for cereal grains in Dadu, now renamed Beiping, was on a smaller scale. The city was the base from which the northern defenses were maintained, with garrisons to feed, but the annual shipments did not exceed 700,000 piculs (about 50,000 tons). To ship that grain after 1368, Ming Taizu turned the responsibility to his naval commanders, who succeeded in making the reduced deliveries, and who also turned their attention to the suppression of piracy. Chinese, Korean, and Japanese seafarers were then troubling the waters between Korea and Shandong in an early phase of what became known in the sixteenth century as the *wokou*, or "Japanese pirate" menace. With Korean help, maritime security was reestablished. In short, Ming Taizu possessed naval capacity adequate both to ship grain and to deal with piracy, but he did not associate it in his mind with the domestic problem of how to supply the North on a permanent basis. In 1397, near the end of his reign, he abolished the sea transport altogether.[35]

After Chengzu usurped the throne in 1402, he began immediately to show concern for the Grand Canal. He had previously been based at Beiping and soon would move the Nanjing government there, changing the name to Beijing.[36] As he began to think about building the new capital, moving supplies in anticipation for eventually shifting the government, and all the other factors involved in reorienting the country to its northern border provinces, he asked that the Grand Canal be surveyed and reconstructed. The curious anomaly of his reign is that while he on the one hand built and deployed the greatest deep-water navy yet known in world history, on the other hand he accepted the non-maritime solution to the problem of supplying Beijing. The great fleets of his eunuch admiral Zheng He, which made their seven voyages all the way to India, Persia, and Africa in the years 1405–1433, were nothing if not a dramatic demonstration of Ming China's mastery of maritime skills. In some of those voyages his fleet had 300 vessels, of which 62 were the great 440-foot "Treasure Ships," each with a cargo capacity of 2,500 tons. One two-week voyage by 62 such vessels could have delivered 150,000 tons of grain.[37] In brief, the Ming dynasty clearly had an alternative to dependence on the canal for the transport of rice and other commodities.

That Ming Chengzu chose instead to invest in the canal was a decision that his officials could all understand, and in fact probably was prompted by them. Reasons were given that the sea journey was hazardous and sometimes cost the lives of sailors, that the seas were subject to pirate raids and the like. It is far more likely that the kind of entrepreneurship carried on by merchant seamen and freebooters made agrarian-minded, land-oriented officials uneasy. Building canals was an ancient activity in which China excelled, and it had the safe and well-proven bureaucratic means for organizing the labor and supervising the management of the great canal system. Within Ming times coastal shipping developed rapidly; Fujian became a grain deficit region dependent on coastal shipping from Guangdong and Zhejiang to meet its needs, to cite one major example. In fact, coastal shipping grew throughout the dynasty. It carried both import products that originated overseas and local specialties such as sugar, metalwares, textiles, and food items, but that was all private trade, very imperfectly controlled by maritime customs agencies. Unlike canal transport, all such maritime activity operated in a gray area between legal and prohibited commerce.

The Grand Canal too came to serve many purposes in addition to the transport of tax grains. It soon functioned as a major artery of travel and transport. Most uses of it other than as the government's official transport service also existed at the fringes of legitimacy. All procurement for the imperial household was in the hands of eunuchs who could high-handedly commandeer priorities for rapid shipment of ice-packed delicacies supposedly for the emperor's table, but in fact often for the luxury markets of the capital. Eunuchs and officials also might be in league with merchants who bribed boatmen to carry them and their cargoes. Nor was all private traffic illegal; the hundreds of one- and two-masted canal boats, commonly fifty feet long and narrow enough to get through the twelve-foot lock gates, with comfortable quarters for travelers and cargo capacity of thirty to fifty tons, plied the canal constantly. Crowds of the boats stopped in the docking areas underneath the walls of great canal cities such as Yangzhou, Gaoyou, Linqing, and Jining north of the Yangzi, and the even larger and richer cities such as Suzhou, Changzhou, Wuxi, and Jiaxing that crowded the 200 miles of the canal south of the Yangzi. There it was the main artery in a spreading network of canals and rivers giving access to much of Central China. North of the

Yangzi, the farther north one went on the canal, the more the supporting networks of transport had to travel by land.

Ming Chengzu's choice is seen by us today as enigmatic—because it did not launch China on a path toward a more efficient solution to problems of transportation, nor did it encourage the further development of technology. Ming Taizu smashed the fabulous mechanical clock built for the last Yuan emperor; Taizu's son Chengzu built a great fleet to sail the world's distant oceans, but he neither founded an overseas empire nor used the great navy in a new way for practical purposes at home. Were these rulers obscurantists using their imperial power to block China's exploitation of its own capacities? Or were they wisely attentive to voices from the people who conveyed the authentic ethos of their civilization? Perhaps both questions raise more grandiose issues than the specific situations justify, yet the second question points to the answer that the scholar elite of that time would have found the more pertinent: appropriate solutions to China's problems were to be found elsewhere than in privateering activities at sea.

Having chosen to depend on the Grand Canal, the Ming government was constantly faced with problems of restraining and rechanneling the Yellow River. Yellow River floods would have occurred periodically anyway, but when they interrupted traffic on the canal, as they usually did, the urgency was much greater. Through Yuan and early Ming, the main course of the lower Yellow River might take any of half a dozen channels entering the sea north of the Shandong Peninsula. That course began to break down, some of the water escaping to flow south to the Huai River in northern Jiangsu. During the 1450s, Xu Youzhen, a brilliant but somewhat tarnished talent, was given the task of dealing with broken dikes in western Shandong that caused damaging floods and interrupted the canal.[38] Xu studied the history of canal repairs, organized a work force of 60,000 civilians and soldiers, and in 550 days dug a diversion canal taking the waters from the point where the dikes would no longer hold to a new channel. Then he rebuilt and reinforced the dikes, and solved the problem. His work was praised as so successful that it held for thirty-four years! In Xiaozong's reign, in the 1490s, the dikes again failed at nearly the same place. This time it was decided to cut off the course flowing to the north of the Shandong Peninsula entirely, turning it into one main channel flowing to the south. The water was successfully diverted in 1495, and continued to take the southern route until 1852, when it was again turned to flow north of Shandong, as it does today.[39] Breaks in the dikes continued to occur regularly, often blocking the canal. In the 1560s and 1570s there was another protracted effort to make repairs in both the canal and the river's dikes.[40] Those are but the major efforts; between repairing failed dikes and dredging the canal or rebuilding locks and dams, work projects were undertaken on the average every four or five years throughout the dynasty.[41] The question whether its vast projects of hydraulic engineering should be counted successes or failures of Ming governing can be argued in many ways.

26

THE CHANGING WORLD OF
THE SIXTEENTH CENTURY

Under the Emperors Wuzong (1505–1521) and Shizong (1521–1567), the personal eccentricities of these imperial cousins brought about deep changes in the tone and manner of governing the Chinese state. Wuzong, the Zhengde emperor, flaunted his defiance of imperial norms and ignored political responsibilities in a personal quest for freedom and self-gratification. The angry response of Chinese officials was to deprecate him in their historical writings. Shizong, the Jiajing emperor, came to the throne from a collateral branch of the imperial lineage; he made destructively egocentric demands for validation of his status. He brought about the deeply disturbing conflict known as the Great Rites Controversy, which induced further change in the relationship that had come to characterize the way the throne shared responsibilities with officialdom. The consequences for state and society were great. His personal characteristics brought new stresses to the political order at a time when China's place in the larger world was undergoing shifts and challenges. Finally, a profoundly transforming change in the realm of thought and social action also dates from the reigns of these two emperors: the statesman-philosopher Wang Yangming (1472–1529) launched a movement in Neo-Confucian thought that profoundly challenged long-dominant assumptions, provided a powerful alternative to Neo-Confucian rationalism (Lixue), and led to a realignment of Neo-Confucian thought.

1. EMPEROR WUZONG, 1505–1521

The 276 years of the Ming, from 1368 to 1644, are remembered principally for the dynasty's dramatic beginnings and its emotionally stirring fall. Between the powerful events of the first three or four reigns and the "cataclysm"[1] of the protracted Southern Ming resistance at the end, the mid-Ming centuries have been neglected, but they are far too interesting to be overlooked. Throughout these two centuries one can trace society's steady recovery following the long age of division and alien rule; and we find a rich new growth of cultural expression within the expanding capacities of Chinese civilization.[2] In this chapter and Chapter 28, the story of the imperial court and government is carried forward from the death of Emperor Xiaozong in 1505 through the reigns of his immediate successors in the sixteenth century, with the focus, however, on broader developments in society.

The often bizarre imperial extravaganza, like a canopy under which Ming political history was acted out, was at no point stranger than during the reign of Emperor Wuzong. He was Emperor Xiaozong's only surviving son. Because he came to the throne in the summer of 1505, his Zhengde reign period extended from the New Year, January 24, 1506, until January 27, 1522, which was the date of the New Year following his death in the late spring of 1521. He left no heir, so was succeeded by a cousin whom he had never met. By coincidence, both of these imperial boys ascended the throne just four months shy of their fourteenth birthdays. Both were grandsons of the Emperor Xianzong, whose Chenghua reign, from 1465 to 1488, had produced its share of anomalies and curious events. Their names were Zhu Houzhao and Zhu Houcong, the shared "hou" syllable in their given names indicating that they belonged to the same generation of the Ming founder's male lineal descendants.

The mid-Ming rulers were often strong-willed, perverse, and inattentive to their governing and ritual responsibilities. Zhu Houzhao, the Emperor Wuzong, indulged in flagrant willfulness, as if to flaunt his rejection of his decorous, obedient father, the Ming emperor most attentive to his Confucian councillors' advice and direction. We can sympathize with his desire for freedom from oppressive restrictions on his daily life, but his officials and advisers could not: a ruler who so conspicuously defied procedures, willfully ignored duties, scoffed at expectations, and squandered resources threatened the stability of the dynasty, and with it the orderly management of Chinese society. He created a crisis in government.[3]

Zhu Houzhao's reign began well enough, but there were telltale signs that the fourteen-year-old boy emperor would become a stubbornly independent and self-directed adult. In the first year of his reign he began the practice of canceling the Classics Mat lectures, which his father had so dutifully attended. Senior officials presiding at them droned on endlessly, he thought (and we probably would think so too), about the lessons to be drawn from the ancient classics. He liked to play kickball and practice military drills in which he commanded troops of his palace eunuchs and guards. They were much more amusing company than the scholars and high officials of his Inner Court, serious old men burdened with his late father's charge to lead him into proper ways and make a good emperor of him. He would have none of it.

His eunuchs of course saw a golden opportunity. One of them, Liu Jin, was responsible for music and entertainment in the palaces, and thus easily gained the favor of the entertainment-loving young emperor. In 1506 he put Liu Jin in charge of the imperial household and also gave him responsibility to inspect military garrisons in the capital region. Seven other eunuch favorites also were promoted and assigned to the imperial household staff; they became known as the "eight tigers" or the "eight companions." Alarmed officials quickly submitted petitions to have all eight sent away from the court, punished, even executed. Learning of this, the eight met the emperor to plead that they were victims of official prejudice. To the officials' amazement, the now fifteen-year-old ruler coolly dismissed their petitions and said that the matter was one for him to decide on his own. The eight tigers stayed. Thereafter, the officials had to become accustomed to having their warnings, cajolings, threats, and pleas ignored.

From 1506 Liu Jin became the emperor's closest confidant and the agent of his will. Liu placed his eunuch subordinates and cooperating officials strategically; within a year he had become the master of court and central government and extended his powers into the provinces. Much of this was accomplished by using the Embroidered Uniform Guard and the Eastern and Western Depots, police agencies which were the instruments of surveillance and intimidation. A reign of terror was imposed on officialdom. Liu Jin orchestrated it, but he also depended on a completely subservient emperor whose wishes were law. In history Liu is known as one of the four "eunuch dictators" of the Ming, probably the most intelligent and able of the four. For example, when the state faced serious fiscal difficulties, Liu Jin devised administrative improvements to help raise revenues, then abetted the emperor in squandering the increased funds on palaces, war games, and extravagant pleasures. It was his plan to put all revenue collection throughout the realm in the hands of eunuchs under his control. He conceived plans for broad structural changes in the administration.

Liu Jin grew ever more confident, then wildly ambitious. If we believe the charges, he intended to assassinate the emperor and replace him with his own grandnephew; in that way he would have become the only eunuch founder of a Chinese dynasty in all history. First, however, an imperial prince based in Shanxi by the name of Zhu Zhifan,[4] noting the widespread feelings of resentment, even several small revolts of local military commanders, against the ever-higher taxes and surcharges on taxes that Liu Jin's agents imposed, decided he could rebel successfully against the unpopular emperor. In May 1510 he killed a number of officials representing the throne in Shanxi and raised the banner of righteous rebellion against a deviant ruler dominated by an evil eunuch.

Before the army sent by the court could reach Shanxi, the rebellion had been put down by military commanders on the scene and the rebel prince sent to the capital for execution. But the rebellious prince's detailed charges against Liu Jin could not be brushed aside. Zhang Yong, a eunuch of the group called the eight tigers, resented Liu Jin's overbearing treatment of them all; he agreed to cooperate with court officials to expose Liu Jin's crimes. This disaffection within eunuch ranks made Liu Jin's downfall possible. The eunuchs succeeded in raising the emperor's suspicions; he gave an order to arrest Liu Jin and search his residence. Evidence found there not only amply confirmed the plot but also uncovered immense stores of silver and valuables, deeds to estates, and other treasure. Liu Jin was executed in September 1510.

That experience did not teach the Zhengde emperor much; he gave his favor to Zhang Yong and others of the eight tigers, and to new favorites, including a cavalry officer by the name of Jiang Bin. This man, a genuine military hero who drew the young emperor's unqualified admiration, turned out to be as ambitious and unscrupulous as Liu Jin had been. Soon he was devising military diversions for the emperor, taking him off to the northern garrison commands, where they played at war and indulged in riotous excesses. The emperor appears to have grown fond of exotic women from the border areas who were of Mongol, Uighur, or other non-Chinese background.

As early as 1507, within the palace city in Beijing the emperor built a separate residential palace with its own military exercise ground and a zoo holding animals for the hunt. He called it his "new residence"; for reasons not known, it came to be called the Leopard Quarter.[5] He refused to reside in the usual palaces specially reserved for the emperor's household within the Forbidden City, thereby again flouting convention and expressing his will to be free. Now he also he had new palaces and temporary residences built at Datong, Xuanfu, and other sites on the northern defense line where, in between elaborate parties and entertainments, he could observe skirmishes with raiding Mongols. Much of the time he was drunk.

There is no need to set forth at greater length the unending details of his disorderly reign.[6] The story was brought to its conclusion by a more serious revolt, the armed uprising of the imperial prince Zhu Chenhao, the Prince of Ning in southern Jiangxi Province, in the summer of 1519. The revolt was at first successful in capturing some prefectures along the rebel army's route north to the Yangzi, but was stopped by the able military intervention of the preeminent Ming Neo-Confucian philosopher Wang Yangming,[7] then serving in local government in Jiangsi. Wang captured the prince in late August and sent a report to the capital that he was holding the rebel. The emperor, however, saw in the situation a great opportunity to lead an expeditionary army to the Yangzi south, visit the secondary capital at Nanjing, which he had never seen, and taste the fabled pleasures of the richest region of China. Wang implored the emperor not to venture forth into a region where the rebel had placed assassins, but the emperor was not deterred. Jiang Bin got an expeditionary force under way, and they set out on the march to the south, following the route of the Grand Canal.

Emperor Wuzong spent the first eight months of 1520 in Nanjing, drinking, going on hunting excursions, and enjoying the scenery. A squabble developed over the way to punish the rebel prince; Jiang Bin wanted to gratify the emperor by staging a battle in which the emperor could lead a force that would "capture" the already captive prince, but Wang Yangming frustrated that foolishness by proceeding directly to Nanjing with his captive. The emperor received the rebel and reviewed the captives in a triumphal procession held at the Nanjing palaces, then began the return march to Beijing in the fall of 1520. In October, during one of the rest stops along the march, the emperor went fishing; probably drunk, in a small boat by himself, he fell into the lake and was rescued only after he had nearly drowned. He fell ill. The return to Beijing went slowly forward, the sick emperor being carried in a palanquin, or for some parts of the journey transported on a canal barge.

He entered Beijing in mid-January 1521, seriously ill, but able to enjoy a mock victory parade with bound captives marched along the way to the palace gate. He did not recover his strength, and by March he knew he was dying. He may have issued a final edict blaming himself for the state's many problems and suggesting that an heir be selected from within the imperial line, but it is not certain that that edict was in fact dictated by him. He died in April, with only two eunuchs in attendance, at the age of just twenty-nine. His cavalry commander companion Jiang Bin appears to have been planning to revolt and capture the capital, but that effort was thwarted. The long-suffering court officials were at last free to arrange the succession and try to restore normal governing. For them, the Zhengde reign had been a very long sixteen years.

The reign of Zhu Houzhao, the Zhengde emperor, encouraged the worst varieties of official misconduct and courtier malfeasance, yet the civil officials were committed both to obeying his theoretically unlimited power to command them and to acting on their own shared sense of responsibility to keep the system functioning. That defines the underlying conflict between the ruler and his administrators. Events of the early Ming had heightened the tension between a strong throne and a strong bureaucracy. Among the later Ming rulers, Emperor Wuzong stretched to the limits the Chinese political order's capacity to accommodate both the strong-willed, often nonrational behavior of emperors and the highly committed service of strong-minded scholar-officials. When his uninhibited way of life led to his premature death, his court officials breathed a sigh of relief. Their jaundiced evaluation of him is the one subsequently preserved in the official history and their other writings.

Despite his exasperating behavior, the Zhengde emperor may deserve a more sympathetic press than he has received at the hands of traditional as well as modern Chinese historians. His love of pleasure and excitement surely signals immaturity. As for his good qualities, it is fair to conclude that he was very bright, highly energetic, courageous in danger. Nor was he devoid of all conscience about his imperial role; he simply so hated the bondage of rulership that he defied all its formalities and obligations in impetuous and self-defeating ways. As the ruler, he was indeed a disaster. Yet historians disagree in their assessments of the man and his reign.

II. EMPEROR SHIZONG'S ACCESSION

Yang Tinghe (1459–1529) was the senior Grand Secretary when Emperor Wuzong died in April 1521. From a scholar-official family of Sichuan, he passed the provincial (*juren*) examinations at the precocious age of eleven and went on to earn the highest (that is, the *jinshi*) examination degree at only nineteen. At Wuzong's court he had held a number of the senior Outer and Inner Court offices, including that of Grand Secretary since 1507. He repeatedly rebuked the errant emperor and courageously blocked, or at least voiced opposition to, the improper actions of the imperial favorites. Yet Emperor Wuzong would not allow Yang to resign and withdraw from the court. He trusted him as a conscientious and honest man even though he would not accept Yang's guidance.

Yang is counted one of the three or four strong Grand Secretaries of the Ming, men whose actions approximated those of a Chief Councillor of pre-Ming times—that is, a prime minister, the office that Ming Taizu had abolished in 1380 and said could never be reestablished because its powers threatened the throne. Yang's reputation as a statesman comes from his frustrating years of highly principled and courageous service to the Emperor Wuzong, and especially from his powerful leadership immediately following Wuzong's death. Within the officialdom he was particularly appreciated as the one who in fact had kept things going during Wuzong's erratic reign.

While directing the preparations for the imperial funeral, drafting the late emperor's posthumous edict to the government and nation, and forestalling a series of crises, he faced three immediate tasks: to purge the government of unworthy appointees, some of whom might attempt a coup; to undo the administrative changes introduced during the Zhengde reign so as to restore the normal procedures of governing; and to solve the crisis caused by the death of an emperor who had left no heir. Working closely with a small coterie of untainted Grand Secretaries and able ministers, but quite dominating their deliberations, he immediately set to work.

One incipient coup (by Jiang Bin) was blocked, whole categories of appointees were summarily dismissed, some under criminal charges, and the restoration of administrative normalcy began. But most pressing was the problem of designating an heir, an action that had to be worked out in concert with the highest officials and then validated by Wuzong's mother, the Empress Dowager Zhang, as the senior member of the imperial clan.

The Emperor Xianzong, whose reign is dated 1465–1488, was Wuzong's grandfather. He had left several male heirs in addition to Wuzong's father. Without much consideration, Yang Tinghe and the others settled on the eldest of these, Xianzong's fourth son; he was the half-brother of Emperor Xiaozong, Wuzong's father, who had died in 1505. The item in the Ancestral Injunction that Yang invoked to justify the decision was the sentence, "If the elder brother dies, he shall be succeeded by his younger brother." That of course was meant to apply when there was no properly accredited son to succeed, and in this case, because the late emperor had neither son nor younger brother, they could only go back to the preceding generation. This brought them to Xianzong's fourth son, uncle of the deceased Emperor Wuzong, whose title was Prince Xian of Xing (Xing Xianwang). He was rare among imperial princes for being a learned and deeply cultivated man. It was felt therefore that among the possible heirs, his line was worthy. Moreover, although he had died in 1519, his only son, Zhu Houcong, was reported to have inherited his father's good qualities. Speculation about who would be

Wuzong's successor had already included this prince, as he himself undoubtedly was aware. He was in any event the eldest imperial grandson in direct line of descent from Emperor Xianzong. True, his mother was not a principal wife but a mere concubine, making his choice contrary to a stipulation of the Ancestral Injunction, but that was not held to be an insurmountable bar, for the Ancestral Injunction failed to anticipate a number of quite likely circumstances in these irregular succession situations. The prince's seniority within his generation was taken to be the essential fact. In the urgent press of the moment's business, this young cousin of the dead emperor was hastily summoned to the capital to assume the throne. In the meantime, through the thirty-seven days of the interregnum, Yang Tinghe single-handedly decided all issues and directed all political actions.

Ming imperial history having provided no closely fitting precedent to apply in this particular set of circumstances, Yang Tinghe and the Empress Dowager Zhang invoked precedents from earlier dynasties in which a reigning emperor who had no heir selected one from a collateral branch of the imperial family, made that person his adopted son, then at some suitable time designated him his heir apparent. None of those earlier cases closely matched this situation, but no better argument was found, nor was any difficulty anticipated. Would not any imperial relative be happy to be designated the new emperor, whether by reason of one kind of relationship or another?

Zhu Houcong Ascends the Throne

After twenty days' travel from Hubei, the prince's entourage arrived at the capital, where he was received by officials of the Ministry of Rites. They gave him the carefully worked-out schedule for entering the palace city (the Forbidden City) by its eastern gate and taking up temporary residence in one of the front palace complexes, not in the emperor's residence palace. He would first be ritually adopted, that is, made the adoptive heir apparent, then later would be elevated from that status to the imperial position. The eastern gate symbolized the heir apparent, and avoiding the imperial residence further recognized the ritual procedures for first acquiring imperial legitimacy as his uncle's heir. The young Zhu Houcong, still four months short of his fourteenth birthday, boldly sent the Ministry of Rites officials back to Yang Tinghe to report that he would not do it that way. The succession, he insisted, had already passed to him because of his own credentials as the son of an emperor's younger brother. That is, he regarded himself as the legitimate emperor in his own right, not a prince coming to the throne as a previous emperor's adopted son (and adopted sixteen years after that emperor's death).

When drafting the accession documents summoning him to the capital, Yang Tinghe had simply addressed him as the successor without defining the issue. Yang expected him, with appropriate filial sentiment, to take on the role of the adopted son of Empress Dowager Zhang, to address her as his "mother" and refer to the Emperor Xiaozong (who had died in 1505, sixteen months before his birth in 1507) as his "father." The crucial point in Yang

Tinghe's mind (and no doubt in the minds of officials generally) was that Zhu Houcong, as the late Emperor Xiaozong's nephew, belonged to a collateral or junior branch of the imperial lineage. In the minds of people at the time, an important issue was at stake here: if he would simply conform to the general expectation, it would signify that he had been grafted onto the senior imperial line, making him more directly the heir of Ming Taizu and all the succeeding rulers down to Xiaozong. In that way the ritually senior branch of the imperial lineage would continue to reign, and its established traditions would continue to prevail.

In the impasse over just getting the arriving prince into the palace complex, compromises had to be worked out anew to allow him to enter the palace city by its main south entrance, proceed through several ceremonial stops and, as the designated heir apparent, do obeisance to the spirit of Wuzong, then ascend the throne in the main throne hall and receive the entire court's obeisance to him as the new emperor.[8] He continued to object to other of Yang's arrangements: he refused to accept the wording of the accession edict prepared by Yang Tinghe, refused Yang's and the court's choice of a reign period name linking him to the Hongzhi reign period of his uncle, and raised troublesome problems with innumerable details of his accession. All that defiance was to display his contention that he was not the heir of Emperor Xiaozong, but was the direct heir of his grandfather through his father, Prince Xian of Xing. No doubt advised by his tutor and other officials brought from the princely court in Hubei, he insisted that he would address only his biological father and mother as his parents; he would refer to the living Empress Dowager Zhang and his late uncle the Emperor Xiaozong as his aunt and uncle. That not only displayed his strong will but shocked Yang Tinghe and the entire court as well. When shortly thereafter he indicated that he wished to bestow on his father a posthumous title of "emperor" as if he had reigned, and demanded that his mother be given the ritual status and courtesies of an empress, something more than decorum had been destroyed: his demands altered the rites by which an emperor acknowledged his predecessors, thus challenging the ritual foundations of imperial legitimacy. He finally came to the throne in the summer of 1521 to reign under the Jiajing reign period name (1522–1567), and eventually received the posthumous title Emperor Shizong. Here he will usually be addressed by that title, occasionally as the Jiajing emperor.

His willful defiance of his court's expectations was strongly resisted; under Yang Tinghe's powerful leadership the court struck back by simply refusing to act on his requests regarding the change of rituals affecting his place in the imperial lineage; four times his proposals to the court were returned to him "unopened." That was an unprecedented display of senior Grand Secretary audacity. From the court and throughout government, arguments for accepting the court's arrangements were sent to him, worded in highly charged moralistic language.

Knowing he could not immediately prevail, he dropped the issue and changed tactics. He made a show of cooperating with Yang and the court on all matters of their common interest—purging the government of Wuzong's appointees and erratic administrative innovations. Great progress was made, and by the end of the year Shizong conspicuously rewarded Yang Tinghe with high honors, even granting him the grandly symbolic title (Senior) Pillar of the State. If that gesture was designed to coopt his enemy, it soon became apparent that he had not succeeded. Old Yang and most of officialdom throughout the realm were not mollified. The latent hostility on both sides intensified.

Making Government Work Again

The years 1521–1524 nonetheless saw a genuine transformation of the atmosphere in Beijing. The late Emperor Wuzong had crammed the capital with thousands of ad hoc appointees, most with no proper civil service qualifications, to perform tasks that in any event did not fall within the patterns of the civil service. They were cashiered and dispersed. Many irregular as well as regular civil service officials had improperly acquired lands, mansions, and valuables; a motive for dismissing them under charges of graft was to confiscate those possessions and transfer their wealth to the nation's depleted coffers. Construction projects were canceled. The young emperor made austerity an important issue.

Shizong brought four or five leading eunuchs from his princely establishment with him to the capital. He had a reputation for enforcing rigid discipline on his eunuchs. As those he brought with him took over major posts in the "Twenty-four Offices," the eunuch establishment's bureaucratic structure, there was hope that a new day had dawned, and indeed hundreds of eunuchs were punished, retired, or transferred to positions having no power, such as tending the Ming ancestral graves at Nanjing and Zhongdu. Within a few years the massive growth in the eunuch bureaucracy was curbed. The practices of appointing eunuch supervisors to all the regional military commands, to special tax- and revenue-collecting positions, and to oversee customs and mints were all abandoned. Under the influence of the eunuch dictator Liu Jin, the late Emperor Wuzong had issued instructions that regional and local officials were to be subservient to eunuchs posted in their regions in many important matters from fiscal to judicial and military. That was ended. Unlike his predecessors for a century, Shizong to the end of his reign allowed eunuchs, even when appointed to important provincial posts, no discretionary powers to act in his name.

Eunuchs did not regain the previous scope of their powers and governmental activities, and their numbers to be sure declined for a time, but the new eunuchs soon discovered the same interests as the former ones. For example, the throne was put under pressure from court officials to abolish the Imperial Estates (huang zhuang) and other landed estates (zhuangtian) awarded to high officials and imperial relatives and to eunuchs. Shizong's eunuchs for a time succeeded in delaying decisive action on this matter, much to the disappointment of Yang Tinghe and the court officials. A survey of Imperial Estates was nonetheless successfully and energetically carried out by a young supervising secretary in the Censorate, Xia Yan (1482–1548). For this he earned the emperor's trust and later became a Grand Secretary. His survey temporarily brought about significant decreases in the amount of improperly acquired land in the various categories of landed estates, but the emperor's zeal for this reform was not sustained. Soon the old practices returned. Dispossessed farmers continued to be a serious cause of social instability throughout the North China Plain (see Chapter 28).

Despite the promising beginnings through the years 1521–1524, and even thereafter in some fields of action, the strong-willed young Shizong soon began to display signs of changing his focus. Initially he was poised to bring about a midterm dynastic revival *(zhongxing)*. But his health was bad, he had no real flair for governing or strength to devote to its endless details, and he became focused on ways (in a crude combination of medical, alchemical, and magical arts) of ensuring his own physical well-being. His governing role deteriorated, and so did the conduct of government, despite the continuing flow into office of highly committed scholars who were eager to succeed in their roles as the appointed governors.

Yang Tinghe and the "ritual purists" of the court came to recognize that the underlying tension between himself and the ruler would not go away. He severely criticized the emperor for proposing to conduct Daoist sacrifices, for appointing his eunuchs to executive positions in the provinces, and for other lapses of behavior. In these and other instances he was ignored. He therefore retired in March 1524 and returned to his home in distant Sichuan, where he maintained no further contact with court and government. Some years later, in 1528, the vengeful emperor punished all who had opposed him in what would be called the Great Rites Controversy; of Yang it was concluded that the reasons he had advanced for opposing the emperor's wishes were so improper that he deserved the death penalty, but because of his service in bringing the emperor to the throne, he suffered only reduction in rank to the status of a commoner. Yang died in 1529.

III. THE RITES CONTROVERSY

The bitter dispute between the Emperor Shizong and his entire court had smoldered throughout Yang Tinghe's years as senior Grand Secretary; when it broke out into the open in 1524, it became known as the Great Rites Controversy (Da liyi), because the immediate focus of the dispute was the rituals for legitimating Shizong as heir to the throne. It completely dominated politics for several years, and its lingering consequences troubled the conduct of governing for the remainder of Zhu Houcong's Jiajing reign period (1522–1567). The great hopes that attended his reign up to this point soon withered.

The Rites Controversy pitted the stubborn young emperor against the vast majority of the empire's officials; they continued to follow Yang Tinghe's standard in the matter. The controversy affords us a window on the way in which political and moral issues (turning on ritual correctness) could bring

his parents and grandparents were elevated in rank within the imperial lineage and made recipients of all the previously requested ritual observances in the state shrines; in all documents they were to be addressed as "the imperial parents," while the empress dowager should now be called only "the imperial aunt."

Shizong of course had always possessed the absolute power to issue any edict. But in the eyes of the elite who staffed his government, he lacked the moral authority to take this action, and up to this point their judgment had constrained him.

The court immediately raised the most serious protests, but with Yang Tinghe gone, Shizong was more sure of himself. He ordered their leaders imprisoned. Three days later, as the morning court dispersed, some 200 officials commenced a protest. It was high noon of a hot August day. They knelt in the courtyard before the throne hall, wailing and chanting the names of Ming Taizu and the emperor's grandfather, the revered, docile Emperor Xiaozong, that is, the founder who was the source of the dynasty's legitimacy and the emperor who best represented the ideal of cooperation between throne and officialdom. By dusk they still would not disperse, and at one point rose in a group to pound noisily on the door of the throne hall. Emperor Shizong, inside his palace quarters, heard the distant commotion and sent eunuchs to investigate. When told of the affair, he flew into a temper. When they still would not desist, he ordered the entire group seized. Their names were recorded and they were sent to the dreaded prison run by his imperial bodyguard. Five days later they were brought before the court and flogged so severely that seventeen died and others were crippled. All were dismissed from office, and the survivors were punished by banishment to border region military posts with ranks of noncommissioned common soldiers.

Chinese historians writing today have difficulty explaining to modern Chinese readers why this event—and the entire controversy underlying it—could assume such importance. A major element in the profoundly destructive dispute is that it challenged established ritual, the underpinning of the social order. But disagreement over ritual forms had seldom if ever aroused such passions. Commissions of scholarly ritualists regularly dealt with such matters, always with deeply learned command of historical traditions; experts might debate, but violence between partisan factions never ensued. On the surface, the issues scarcely justified such extreme behavior.

Beyond the issue of ritualized family proprieties, there were of course political dimensions to the dispute. Political interests of the senior officialdom were genuinely threatened by a newly rising faction wishing to gain the emperor's support in order to achieve control over personnel and policies and the power to receive and grant favors. But there was far more at stake than personal and immediate interests. In the officials' view, their own higher loyalty was to the dynasty and the cultural values it embodied, not to any particular emperor. One historian has written: "It seems that the majority of Ming officials still believed that respect for the dynastic institutions rather than for imperial preferences was a higher form of loyalty. One can therefore say that the Great Ritual Controversy, though appearing to concern ethical issues, was ultimately a political struggle, albeit a subtle one: it was a contest over what constituted loyalty, who should define it, and whether loyalty or filiality had priority in dynastic government."[13] Their loyalty to the dynasty's institutions, or his filial gestures: which professed virtue would prevail?

That well explains the deeper issues underlying the extreme behavior of both the emperor and his hundreds of opponents in officialdom. The emperor, young, isolated, and insecure, needed to assert himself, to discover that "being the emperor is the whole game."[14] It was just as clear that the officials opposing Emperor Shizong also were reacting to an equally basic awareness: they could lose the whole game. They mourned Yang Tinghe's passing from government, not out of loyalty to him personally but regretting the loss of a grand leader of the bureaucratic establishment vis-à-vis the throne. The preceding emperor, Wuzong, had not explicitly granted Yang the high powers that he exercised as chief Grand Secretary during that chaotic reign, but nonetheless had allowed him to manage the routines of daily governing in a responsible, broadly competent manner, even when arrogant eunuchs and despised imperial favorites made the task almost impossible. Yang's exercise of that governing role represented a halcyon ideal of scholar-official preeminence. That ideal seemed to have been undermined by Ming Taizu when he reconstructed the central administration in 1380.[15] Yet in fact the strong advisory and administrative role of the officials, led by the Grand Secretaries, had been slowly recovering since the time of the Yongle emperor. Patterns of accommodation with eunuchs and ways of maneuvering around difficult emperors had been worked out.

The new Emperor Shizong's disturbing behavior not only exposed his peevish obsession with the imperial family ritual issue. He also had revealed himself to be unconcerned about institutional values and the weight of traditional statecraft, the special province of the scholar-officials and the instruments by which they maintained their roles. Yang Tinghe's retirement under pressure exposed the conflicting definitions of imperial power; it undermined the bases of bureaucratic resistance to the throne and threatened to mark the end of an era. Such gloomy thoughts drove sophisticated, resolutely committed officials to protest, inconsequentially to be sure, but with deepest pain. The grief they displayed before the doors of the throne hall conveyed their sense of both political and moral loss, which reverberated throughout officialdom and elite society. This young emperor's attitudes ominously echoed the Yongle emperor's assertion, at the time of his usurpation in 1402, that "this is my family's affair," removing thereby from the purview of officialdom all responsibility toward the state's ruling institution.

Yang Tinghe's son Yang Shen (1488–1559), who had won the highest rank (*zhuangyuan* or optimus) in the *jinshi* examinations in 1511, was a Hanlin Academy official. He was among the leaders of the protest. In their agitated discussions he had proclaimed, "The state has nourished scholar-officials for 150 years; this moment now is the time to speak out for righteousness and die for principle."[16] His sense of urgency had gripped the leading figures of the court, and their understanding of the realities turned out to be prophetic.[17] It was clear who would prevail, yet they had to hold their ground.

Yang Shen was among those who were severely beaten and then banished; he drew a common soldier's assignment in the malarial wastes of the Yunnan-Burma border, where he lived out the remaining thirty-five years of his life in exile. Shizong bore him and his father an intense hatred. From time to time he would inquire of men at court about Yang Shen, always to be told (protectively) that Yang displayed signs of mental instability so was harmless in far-off Yunnan. Despite that, every time Shizong issued a general amnesty he specified that it did not extend to Yang Shen.

Shizong would reign for almost forty-six years, cautiously in the early years but becoming increasingly willful as time passed. His triumph in the confrontation with officialdom had strengthened his resolve, and the imperial power. The court was purged of his predecessor's eunuch and sycophant cohorts, and he concentrated administrative authority in his own hands, although a new crowd of sycophants soon became his agents. He was the opposite of the impetuous and undisciplined Wuzong; Shizong's course was not to ignore the expected modes in governing in order to become the "counteremperor," as his reckless cousin had done. In his quite different way, nevertheless, he became one of the most perverse and unpleasant men ever to occupy the Chinese throne. With him the long procession of delinquent Ming emperors gained another exemplar.

IV. EMPEROR SHIZONG AND DAOISM

Many of Shizong's deficiencies as ruler are related to his fervent belief in magical Daoism; he was the most ardently Daoist ruler since Emperor Huizong of Northern Song, who reigned 1100–1125. For all his faults, however, Huizong was a cultivated and philosophical-minded ruler who venerated the early Daoist philosophers and valued the learned traditions of their teachings. His more questionable sponsorship of Daoist church institutions and avid pursuit of the magic promised by Daoist adepts was the less praiseworthy side of his Daoism. Ming Shizong's Daoism displayed only that less attractive side. His interests were narrowly focused on the pursuit of magical means to fertility and longevity, whether those relied on mysteriously compounded elixirs or on strengthening his *yang* essence through sex techniques that, among other things, ruthlessly exploited and discarded hundreds of young girls. His preoccupation with Daoist magic grew steadily from the early years of his reign, and by the 1530s it led him to withdraw from most direct participation in the conduct of the court. Ignoring many of the routine and symbolic imperial activities, he lived out his fantasies in the inner palaces. But he did not lose interest in power. He kept tight control over the government by dealing through intermediaries.

It appears quite likely that Emperor Shizong's use of elixirs made with the elements lead, arsenic, and even mercury affected his health, unbalanced his personality, and made him subject to fits of rage. It probably caused his death.[18] Those around him found him moody and irascible. Many palace women feared and hated him; in 1542 a group of them tried to murder him in his sleep and almost succeeded. He became ever more secluded, more ruthless in his treatment of opponents, more temperamental.

The special mark of Ming Shizong's domestic governing is his reliance on a succession of chief Grand Secretaries who by their subservience to his whims and peculiar interests functioned as his agents. He was not an awesome tyrant on the model of the first Ming emperor, the closely engaged, hands-on manager Ming Taizu; he was a self-indulgent petty despot who did not care much about the details but wanted to know that his commands were the law of the land. He had no flair for administration and was not drawn to the day-to-day management of court and government. Moreover, from his early twenties onward he displayed signs of a weak constitution; sickly and asthmatic in the cold Beijing winters, he had neither the patience nor the strength to be a managerial emperor. He was satisfied to be an imperious one, granting his uncertain favor to those who would do his bidding.

Throughout officialdom it became apparent that those who gave in to his Daoist fervor and aided him in conducting religious ceremonies could gain his trust and be given the highest positions. That was distasteful to most Confucian-minded officials; some turned away, but some perceived that it was the price to pay for the opportunity to realize good—or base—political and personal goals. Willingness to assist the emperor in his Daoist religious observances became a defining nexus of political careers throughout the Jiajing reign.

v. The Emperor Shizong and His Officials

A succession of men held the position of *shoufu*, "senior Grand Secretary," for relatively long periods under Shizong's reign. An informal designation, not a post defined in the civil service, the title indicated the one among the Grand Secretaries (usually numbering four to seven) who had held his position the longest, although the emperor could (if rarely) intervene and shift the senior position to another.[19] The chief or senior Grand Secretary was accepted as the leader of the government; specifically, by mid-Ming times (unless the Inner Court functions were preempted by an emperor's favorite eunuchs, as during the reign of Emperor Wuzong), the chief Grand Secretary alone had primary responsibility for proposing responses to or passing judgment on the documents that went to the throne for action. Yang Tinghe had enlarged the powers of the position, and after him the other chief Grand Secretaries under Shizong, one after another, sought to retain and further enlarge those powers.[20]

First among them was Zhang Fujing, already encountered as the first of the Emperor Shizong's "disruptive" supporters when still a relatively minor official in Nanjing in 1521. He was quickly promoted through a series of high offices at Beijing but did not become a Grand Secretary until 1527, when the emperor at last defied precedent and court pressures to give him a direct appointment by fiat, without court approval. He was elevated to *shoufu* in 1530.[21] He became important because he had helped forge the theoretical grounds for the emperor's stand in the Rites Controversy, but he was not successful as a political leader of the court. Even among the emperor's new appointees he was widely despised. Moreover, he lacked personal skills: he was stubbornly straightforward, uncompromisingly honest, and yet jealous of his high position and unable to work with colleagues. The emperor needed a more adroit political operator and thought he had found one in Xia Yan.

Xia Yan had first come to the emperor's attention when, as a very junior supervising secretary in the Censorate, he carried out the survey of imperial estates in 1522–23. A fine poet and articulate speaker, he made a strong impression in court discussions. What drew the emperor's interest, however, was his literary skill: he could compose elegantly worded Daoist "green prayers," intercessory prayers written on green paper to be burned in prayer ceremonies so that their message would be carried to the deities in the smoke. Xia Yan was inordinately ambitious. He was not sympathetic to the emperor's obsession with Daoist magic but was quite willing to lend his writing brush to the task of composing prayers. After being Minister of Rites, he became a Grand Secretary in 1536 and was named senior Grand Secretary, or *shoufu*, in 1539. That lasted only three and a half years; in 1542 he was dismissed and returned to private life. Then he was recalled in 1545, and for three years he and Yan Song were the only Grand Secretaries, a most unusual situation. The emperor played one off against the other until 1548, when Yan Song trapped Xia Yan in serious-sounding if groundless charges, leading to his execution for treason. Xia was the wily politician that the ruler wanted, but his pride and ambition got in the way, and he fought ruthlessly with his competitors. Emperor Shizong understood that and could have tolerated it, but Xia Yan also began to reveal his disapproval of the emperor's Daoist practices; as a Confucian high official he found it distasteful to wear a Daoist cap when accompanying the emperor at Daoist ceremonies. He refused, saying somewhat too arrogantly that it did not conform to standard court etiquette. This led to the withdrawal of the ruler's support, leaving him vulnerable in the game of court politics that could grow deadly under an unprincipled ruler. Although Xia Yan was in many eyes a debased figure, he did not see himself as an opportunist; he chose to be stiff-necked where otherwise he would draw further criticism from the ranks of scholars. That was foolish, because the kind of high officials whose approval he sought had lost real power twenty years earlier, in the confrontation following Yang Tinghe's resignation.

The man who succeeded Xia as Minister of Rites in 1536, Yan Song (1480–1565), was named Grand Secretary in 1542. Originally friends, equally famous as literary figures, the fellow Jiangsi natives Xia Yan and Yan Song might have been expected to cooperate in sharing high power. But Xia Yan was much too jealous for that. He also had grown very self-confident. Yan Song deftly accommodated himself to the ruler's whims and demands and to fellow officials. His "green prayers" were at least the equal of Xia Yan's, and he was not greatly troubled by Confucian niceties. The emperor watched the amusing spectacle of struggle among his highest appointees, and in 1544, two years after cashiering Xia Yan, he named Yan Song his senior Grand Secretary, a position Yan Song held for only a year before Xia Yan was recalled; three years later he had maneuvered Xia Yan's downfall and was again named senior Grand Secretary, holding the post until 1562. Throughout twenty years as a Grand Secretary, fifteen as *shoufu,* he parried frequent attacks and criticisms, impeachments and rumors, until the accumulation of animosities finally brought him down.

Yan Song is one of the most interesting political leaders of Ming times, a man almost impossible to assess today because he has been so totally vilified. He held power through the years when the emperor was performing ever more erratically, making the Grand Secretaries' tasks in heading the government burdensome. As Yan Song grew old and ill and his eyesight faded, his son Yan Shifan became his indispensable assistant in meeting the demands of his position. The two labored mightily to carry on the heavy duties of the position, all the time engaging in peculation and intrigue, fending off enemies in often ruthless fashion, heading a government that functioned according to the standards of a degenerating emperor. The middle and late years of the Jiajing reign became a time when serious problems faced the state. The performance of Yan Song and his perhaps loutish but nonetheless competent son in handling grave problems of state may deserve more credit than any historians until very recent times have been willing to grant.[22]

Political enemies used the channel of the professional Daoists at court to convey rumors that aroused Shizong's suspicions, and the emperor finally turned away from Yan Song. Yan was removed from office at age eighty-two, in 1562, and sent to his home in retirement, still enjoying some lingering feelings of favor from the ruler. But his enemies continued to attack, trumping up charges of Yan Shifan's and his son's collusion with the Japanese pirates, leading to their execution and confiscation of the Yan family's properties in 1565. Yan Song himself, nearly blind, unattended, impoverished, died later that year at age eighty-five.

The Jiajing reign's last senior Grand Secretary was Xu Jie (1505–1583), another man of exceptional literary and scholarly brilliance but also of tarnished reputation. He was appointed a Grand Secretary in 1552 and served alongside Yan Song for ten years until, in 1562, he replaced Yan as senior Grand Secretary. Then he served until the end of the reign and on into the first two years of the succeeding one.

A famous incident of the late Jiajing reign occurred in 1565 when a junior official, Hai Rui (1513–1587), submitted a memorial strongly criticizing the emperor for twenty years of neglect of his duties, saying he had failed as a man, as a father, and as the ruler, and had brought disaster to the entire country. The emperor was deeply disturbed and had Hai investigated. He discovered not only that Hai Rui had a reputation for integrity, but also that before submitting this memorial he had sent his family back to their home in the South, had purchased a coffin, and had made his funeral arrangements. In deep agitation and indecision about how to deal with such an attack on his person, especially troubled by Hai Rui's probing analysis of governmental and social problems, early in 1566 the emperor had Hai sent to the imperial bodyguard prison. There, under torture to find out if there was a plot involving co-conspirators, Hai Rui almost died. The emperor's death in late January 1567 was followed by Hai Rui's release and restoration to office. By that time his reputation for fearlessly speaking out in the people's interests had made him a popular hero. Among high officials at court he was considered an impractical reformer but a man of rare honesty; Xu Jie had intervened on his behalf to delay an order of execution and in that way probably saved Hai Rui's life.

Hai Rui became nationally famous again in the 1960s, when the Ming historian Wu Han wrote essays and a play about him. They were at first enthusiastically received but later censored as an indirect attack on Mao Zedong by making Hai Rui–type heroes of those who criticized an errant ruler.[23] To many the incident seemed to replay events of the mid-sixteenth century.

The forty-six years of Emperor Shizong's reign witnessed a decline in the capacity of government to deal with an increasing array of domestic and international problems: a Mongol invasion in 1550; a crisis in coastal defense under raids from the so-called Japanese pirates; arrival of the Portuguese, the first European power to conduct trade from Chinese soil; and domestic disorders and economic problems related to weaknesses in local governing. In fact, though not as well recognized, many of the problems were already present when he came to the throne. They continued to plague China in the remaining decades of the sixteenth century, Wuzong's and Shizong's personal modes of governing further intensifying them.

Was the imperial institution as it had come to function by mid-Ming times itself the problem? From our present-day point of view, we might think that social critics and political thinkers would begin to ask that question. None went that far, nor should we be surprised when we reflect on the almost 2,000-year history of the imperial order as the only political system with which Ming dynasty Chinese had any knowledge or experience. Yet starting most notably with Wang Yangming, and continuing among his followers in the later sixteenth century and among a wider spectrum of thinkers in the seventeenth century, serious questions about the conduct of government were raised. That led to more penetrating criticisms of politics than had come forth for many centuries. The consequent far-reaching reconsideration of Neo-Confucian thought and values sprang, of course, from purely philosophical considerations, but it also reflected dissatisfaction with the conditions of Ming imperial governing.

We must turn to the philosopher Wang Yangming, the leader of the new thought movement, to see how his radical rejection of Neo-Confucian orthodoxy led to a broad reaction throughout the world of thought. Political criticism was not central to his concerns, but his profound questioning of established values inevitably generated new ways of looking at many kinds of social and political issues.

VI. WANG YANGMING AND SIXTEENTH-CENTURY CONFUCIAN THOUGHT

A noted statesman and civilian general as well as a profound thinker, Wang Yangming does not conform to our usual expectations about philosophers, especially those whose thought has stressed intuitively validated paths to self-cultivation. Such a philosophical stance usually suggests quietism. Wang Yangming, however, was a thinker to whom Confucianism demanded a commitment to action. Although a man of the civilian official career, he ranks among the most successful generals of Ming history, and he was an administrator who seriously engaged the practical problems of governing Chinese and non-Chinese people in backward border zone regions of the Ming state. He would seem to have been much too busy with the affairs of the moment to have had time to probe the mysteries of how the reflective mind works or to question the established traditions in the understanding of ancient Confucian classical writings. His purely philosophical undertakings in fact drew his intense concentration on both.

Already in his teen years he was famous as a precocious student and formidable literary talent. Expected by all to triumph at an early age in the triennial *jinshi* examinations, young Wang set himself higher goals. He would indeed attain loftly positions in officialdom in the well-established career pattern of later imperial elite life, but he would do more than that: he would encompass the broadest realms of thought and of action and unite them in a larger field of engagement. He would strive to become a sage.[24]

His early years are a window on the lives of families in the leading stratum of mid-Ming society. He was born in the wealthy region of northern Zhejiang in 1472. When he was six or seven his grandfather proposed changing his formal name to Shouren, "to maintain benevolence," as a charge to him. Later Wang himself took the secondary name Yangming, by which Confucian scholars addressed him and by which name he is more commonly known in Western writings. His family did not possess great wealth, but since the beginning of the dynasty it had produced a succession of men who pursued scholarship while leading ideally independent lives in the nonofficial elite. One of his forebears six generations earlier had held an appointment briefly about 1370, but was killed by dissident Miao tribesmen whom he had been sent to govern. For more than a century thereafter no member of his line again held official rank or position; most indeed were avowed recluses. The family was close to losing its dwindling economic security when Wang's father won the *jinshi* degree and made a civil service career. The father, Wang Hua (1453–1522), not only won the *jinshi* degree but won it as the optimus *(zhuangyuan)* in 1481, the number one scholar of the realm as designated every third year when the highest-level examinations were held.[25]

As the optimus, Wang Hua was guaranteed selection for the preferred career in the Hanlin Academy at the court; in 1482 he took his wife and children to Beijing to live with him in the capital, and young Wang Yangming grew up there in the milieu of court officials, poets and writers, thinkers and artists. His brilliance, especially in composing youthful poetry of startling spontaneity combined with classical depth, suggested to many that this scion of genius might eventually outshine even his father.

Wang Yangming's unconventional interests appeared early. As a teenager, feeling there was little more he could learn from the Confucian classics, he turned his mind to other fields. He became deeply interested in military strategy, studied archery and horsemanship, and despite frequent health problems became an archer who could contest with Chinese soldiers and Mongol marksmen when he roamed about on horseback to explore the nearby border zone. He passed the provincial-level examinations to receive the second, or *juren,* degree in 1492, then took the *jinshi* examinations in 1493 and 1496, both times failing. That failure was by no means unusual even for young men of proven abilities, nor was it in any sense a disgrace, but he was discouraged; expectations had been too high among the circle of his father's associates. He went back to the family home in northern Zhejiang, where he studied such unconventional subjects as Daoist and Buddhist writings, practiced meditation, and grappled with philosophical issues. In 1499 he again sat for the examinations and received the *jinshi* degree, placing sixth among the 297 degree winners ranked below the top three. That was distinguished enough, but it did not fulfill the widespread expectation that he would match his father's spectacular success.

Assigned to routine entry-level posts at the capital, Wang found them uninteresting, and retired after three years in 1502 to return home to recover from health problems, possibly tuberculosis. He built a retreat at the famous Yangming scenic gorge a few miles from the family residence in Shaoxing; there he followed Daoist therapies and studied philosophy. He valued and identified with this experience; it was at this time that he adopted the name Yangming. When he returned to the capital in 1504, he became acquainted with Zhan Ruoshui (1466–1560), a Hanlin Academy associate of his father's, and a man whose intellectual friendship was at that time of great importance to the young Wang.[26] Wang shared the resentment felt throughout officialdom against the eunuch Liu Jin's domination of the young new emperor, Wuzong, who came to the throne in the summer of 1505. He vigorously defended the motives of two officials who had submitted memorials severely condemning Liu Jin. For that Wang was arrested late in 1506 and sent to the secret service prison to be interrogated and severely beaten; then, recuperating, he was banished to a punishment post in an aboriginal region of Guizhou Province. He narrowly escaped assassination at the hands of Liu's agents in 1507 while en route to Guizhou, but eventually arrived at that forlorn place. He devoted himself conscientiously to understanding the problems facing the Miao tribesmen.[27] It was in those circumstances, under conditions of great physical deprivation and daily hardship, that Wang Yangming experienced his philosophical breakthrough, his spiritual "enlightenment," in 1508. His radically distinct understanding of Neo-Confucian thought dates from that experience, but he continued his career as an official.

Wang Yangming was among many officials whose careers resumed normal patterns after Liu Jin fell from power and was executed in 1510. He received appointment to high-ranking posts first at the secondary capital, Nanjing, and subsequently at Beijing. He began to develop his emergent philosophic views, becoming known as a teacher who lectured to gatherings of the interested and who conducted discourses with fellow officials. Antagonism against him also was aroused among some conservative-minded high officials; they would gladly have seen him sent away from the capital. That happened when he was given an important promotion and assignment as governor of a special military district based in southern Jiangsi. The post also carried responsibilities in adjoining regions where unrest among the native (i.e., non-Chinese) peoples posed threats to local security. It was considered an unpromising assignment.

A civilian administrator, Wang Yangming also assumed the responsibility to lead the regional armies in battle, devised tactics, and set up civil procedures for dealing with the unruly if much-abused people. As a military governor and administrator over regions of non-Chinese minority peoples, Wang was firm in his insistence on their subordination to government authority and yet sympathetic to their complaints. In battle he was noted for his tactical sense, responding unpredictably to shifting circumstances and employing psychological means as well as the force to coerce. He won important victories. When the Prince of Ning rebelled in Jiangxi in 1519, Wang's military command was nearby. The prince hoped that Wang might join him in the rebellion, in protest against the willful young emperor. Loyal to throne and dynasty, if not an admirer of the current ruler, Wang himself devised the offensive strategy and led a large force of provincial troops to capture the rebel prince, ending the rebellion. Later he insisted on delivering the prince to the court, then at Nanjing, where Emperor Wuzong had come with an expeditionary force ostensibly to suppress the rebellion. Wang delivered the captive prince to Nanjing to prevent those around the emperor from bringing the ruler and his army into Jiangxi and turning their mock-military action into a circus.

Wang Yangming's civil governing in Jiangxi won him plaudits and rewards. The complete scholar-official, he could look forward to a highly successful political career. In 1521, called to the capital to receive a new appointment, he requested permission to visit his family en route, and was still at home early in 1522 when his father died. He of course resigned to observe the prescribed mourning, which lasted until the autumn of 1525. In these years he concentrated on his philosophical investigations and writings, avoiding the uproar at court in 1521 when Wuzong died and Shizong was brought in to succeed him, and to reign thereafter for forty-five years as the Jiajing emperor. Thus Wang Yangming was able to remain apart from the Rites Controversy and the political struggles which Shizong's early reign generated.

The originality of his philosophical thought attracted an ever-larger following. He might have lived out his life in Zhejiang as a retired official-turned-teacher had a military crisis not arisen in Guangxi and adjoining parts of several other southern provinces. As the expert on both the military and the political handling of the minority peoples, he was brought out of retirement to head the government's special operations. He received the appointment in the summer of 1527 and immediately submitted his resignation, but it was not accepted. Departing from the family home in Shaoxing at the beginning of October, he arrived at Wuzhou in Guangxi in the middle of December. He campaigned broadly throughout the region for a year, winning military victories and inducing surrenders and settlements by personal intervention with tribal leaders. His health was fading, however, and the exertions of his work speeded his physical collapse. Forced to leave his post to seek medical care, he died en route to his home in January 1529.[28] His stature as a thinker and teacher had come to outstrip his nationwide fame as general and governor. Despite the rise of strong criticism, rejection, even ridicule from many in officialdom and the elite, it soon became clear that he had indeed become the great sage of Ming Confucian thought. His compelling ideas stirred debate and engagement, to the extent that the more than 200 years from the early sixteenth well into the eighteenth century have been called "the age of Wang Yangming."[29]

Wang Yangming Finds His Philosophical Path

We must go back to Wang's early life to learn how he discovered his distinctive philosophical stance within Neo-Confucianism. It has become usual to see him as the continuer of the idealist trend, called Xinxue, "the learning of the [intuitive] mind," in Song Neo-Confucianism that reached a high point of development in the thought of Lu Xiangshan (Lu Jiuyuan, 1139–1193). Lu was a contemporary of Zhu Xi, the master of Song Lixue, "the school of principle." Lu had debated Zhu on issues of mind and of human nature. "Idealist" as used here to designate Lu's and Wang Yangming's thought does not of course mean "idealistic" in the ordinary sense of that word, but refers to the technical philosophical problem in epistemology, that is, the problem of how we know and how we verify what we know. That problem lies at the heart of early Chinese differences between Confucianism and Daoism, between Mencius and Xunzi among the early followers of Confucius, later between Chan (Zen) and the other schools of Buddhist thought, between subitist (sudden enlightenment) and gradualist techniques in attaining knowledge of all kinds. It is the perennial problem in the Chinese as in many philosophical traditions: Is truth verified objectively, by rational argument and demonstration, or is truth attained subjectively, by intuitive means that may not be explainable to others? Is truth to be sought inside the knower by examining the mind introspectively, ultimately by receiving sudden enlightenment, or is it to be found outside the knower by showing proof for one's ideas, aggregating the evidence, and demonstrating the points until the whole becomes rationally convincing? Some would say that, strictly speaking, each of these epistemological modes may be "rational," but the intuitive mode of knowing acknowledges no authority, ultimately, beyond the knower himself or herself. And because characteristically his or her understanding cannot be demonstrated to the satisfaction of others, the objectifying epistemologists claim for themselves the value of "reason" as the opposite of their opponents' "intuition." That usage is well established; I shall defer to it.

However irrelevant philosophically, it must be admitted that the self-derived inner authority to declare what is right and wrong, true and false, good and bad, has often led to wildly eccentric behavior among followers of radically idealist teachings in many cultures at many times. In sixteenth-century China, followers of the school of reason (often meaning little more than the school of convention) therefore have sometimes tried to establish that the epistemology of reason really implies the social values of reasonableness—although philosophically speaking that is, as noted, beside the point. The real philosophers, whether rationalist or idealist, seldom worry about this level of argument, but their followers, especially when the movement becomes one of broad social impact, may indulge in conventional-minded attacks on non-conventional behavior; or if on the opposite side, they may indulge in self-satisfied, all-wise intuitionalist ridicule of conventional-minded rationalists. Hostility between Wang Yangming's Xinxue followers and those of mainline Lixue rationalists assumed some of this character in the generations immediately following Wang Yangming's death in 1529. Within Chinese Chan Buddhism a distinction had long been drawn between other Buddhists and "wild" *(kuang)* Chan Buddhists; within the spreading sixteenth-century trends of post–Wang Yangming thought, that unflattering term long used to deprecate Chan was carried over to the denunciation of Wang's followers, implying that in addition to being in a grave state of delusion, they had been unduly influenced by Buddhism and had strayed from a true Confucian path. While Wang's thought, and even more that of his followers, was always subject to such criticism, his forceful philosophical teaching led to a century or two of wide-ranging, freethinking, often boisterous, and indeed unconventional Neo-Confucianism. As those ideas spilled over into the arts and literary expression, and into the lifestyles of many in society, they gave the mid- and later Ming era much of its imagination, color, and interest.

While his mind was taking boldly radical turns, Wang Yangming's own behavior remained thoroughly conventional. As for his philosophical system, initially it was not his intention to challenge Zhu Xi's great synthesis of Neo-Confucian Lixue. It was simply that when he probed issues seeming to require further explanation, that inevitably led him onto different ground. He felt forced, on the one hand, to part company with Zhu Xi, yet on the other hand, the entire system of his thought, even though radically different in some essentials, can be seen as a response to Zhu Xi, sharing many concerns and most of the fundamental Confucian values. Like all Ming thinkers, Wang Yangming was overwhelmed by the imposing scope and the vast authority of Zhu Xi's scholasticism. Wang broke openly with the Zhu Xi tradition only after his sudden enlightenment in 1508, following years of struggle with Zhu Xi's doctrine that "the extension of knowledge lies in the investigation of things [*gewu zhizhi*]."[30] Ultimately, he found Zhu Xi and the Neo-Confucian mainstream disturbingly inadequate. It was not easy to step aside from it, let alone to formulate ideas that ran counter to it. Where did Wang Yangming get the intellectual tools with which to do that?

He appears not to have been consciously influenced by those among his near contemporaries who also had staked out other philosophical positions. His intellectual friend Zhan Ruoshui openly identified himself with the Neo-Confucian idealist tradition; Zhan had attained that understanding from his teacher, one of the important earlier Ming idealist thinkers.[31] Wang and Zhan must have discussed those currents of thought and their relation to the Song period idealism of Lu Xiangshan, yet Wang Yangming appears to have found his own way to his new understanding. There can be no doubt that his sympathetic study of both Buddhism and Daoism, the thinking person's main sources of alternatives to orthodox Confucianism, contributed to his intellectual development. Both were inescapable in the milieu of mid-Ming life. He reached out to study their texts and to learn from living masters of those traditions. Yet that does not set Wang apart from most Ming figures, conventional or otherwise, who thought of themselves as heirs to the great Neo-Confucian ethical Way (Dao). Wang Yangming's philosophical originality must be traced to his own experiences as a restless seeker after truth while carrying on a life of fullest involvement in the world's affairs. He said that his doctrines "were achieved from a hundred deaths and a thousand sufferings."[32] "One must always be doing something," he insisted, in order to realize truth through personal experience. That is strongly reminiscent of the spirit of early Chinese Chan practice.

Our concern here with Wang Yangming's extensive philosophical thought system is with its general historical significance, not its possible intrinsic value as philosophy. To characterize his philosophy in brief, its best-known feature is his epistemological breakthrough: his sudden enlightenment came in 1508, when (in a time of great personal stress and physical hardship) he awoke from a dream to the awareness that Zhu Xi's explanation of "the investigation of things" did not lead the mind to understanding. He had struggled with the problem of knowledge for more than fifteen years. There is a story that previously, when still in his early twenties, he sat for seven days and nights in front of some growing bamboo, trying to extend his mind outwardly to encompass all features of the bamboo, to investigate the principles (li) of its existence. He fell ill from the intense concentration expended on that effort. Eventually, after years of further attempts to extend the knowing process outward and envelop the object of knowledge, in 1508 his sudden vision said to him, "Search within your own mind." Further experience led him to enunciate his doctrine of "innate knowledge" (liang zhi).[33] The doctrine that every individual possesses innate knowledge has been called "Wang's supreme philosophical achievement."[34] He wrote: "The faculty of innate knowledge is to know good and evil. The investigation of things is to do good and remove evil."[35]

That is to say, the solution to the problem of knowledge leads directly to a second point that defined Wang's thought: the unity of knowledge and action. Action stems inevitably from knowledge, and knowledge is not complete until it has taken form in action. That kind of knowledge is not compounded from factual observations or bookish learning, but springs from within one's knowing moral mind.

To sustain these defining principles of his thought system, Wang Yangming was forced to repudiate one of the textual bases of Zhu Xi's thought, Zhu's rearrangement of the ancient Confucian school text *The Great Learning (Daxue)*. Zhu Xi added extensive commentary in the course of editing the text to justify the rearrangement and to explain his use of it. Here Wang found the nub of his disagreement with Zhu Xi. He rejected Zhu Xi's use of the book, and produced his own edition of the text as traditionally transmitted prior to Zhu Xi's time, along with his own new commentary. The *Great Learning* was one of the *Four Books* which Zhu Xi had established as the core of Confucian learning. Zhu's version of it was central to every literate person's formal studies and to preparation for the civil service examinations. That Wang would dare to tamper with (he would say "restore") this text, a basic element of orthodox learning, aroused the outrage of many; they saw him as undermining the ethical norms of Neo-Confucianism and threatening state and society. While growing throngs of scholars flocked to learn from Wang Yangming, many more were offended and deeply resentful; some carried their feelings over into political reprisals. But the appeal of Wang's fresh ideas was too great for this reaction to suppress them, and the raging controversy itself added to the public's awareness of him.

Throughout his life Wang continued to broaden the scope of his thought, exploring its implications for many basic issues in philosophy such as the explanation of good and evil. He discoursed at length on the "extension of innate knowledge," meaning the ways of fully utilizing the mind's capacity to know the good. He stressed the importance of personal involvement in life's duties and obligations as the means for gaining self-awareness and deeper understanding. He analyzed the differences between Zhu Xi and Lu Xiangshan, explained his own disillusionment with Buddhism and Daoism, and spoke with subtle nuance about many practical problems facing ethical men and women. His system still draws the critics who even now, as then, find in it logical weaknesses as well as license for freethinking individuals to commit excesses; it nevertheless became a credible and widely attractive system of thought and learning. It was sufficiently impressive to profoundly challenge orthodox Neo-Confucianism of the time. Challenge contributed to the vigor of intellectual life in general, in the process stimulating many new kinds of intellectual and artistic involvement throughout elite society. Its impact, however, was not limited to the elite strata of Ming society; some of Wang's followers took their sense of Wang's message into the lives of China's ordinary people as well.

Wang Yangming's Followers and the Later Wang Schools

During the years from the summer of 1521, when he returned to the family home in northern Zhejiang, until October 1527, when he was forced to depart for the unwanted post in Guangxi, Wang Yangming spent six years concentrating entirely on developing his philosophical ideas and teaching about them. The numbers of students in Shaoxing became so great that he trained some of his best disciples to assist him. Every time he gave lectures at the study gatherings that met two or more times a year, hundreds came to listen, among them numbers of eminent senior scholars and officials. A recognized movement in thought and learning thus was under way before his death, allowing him to give it guidance and form.

He was fortunate in the first generation of his followers. They included a distant relative from Shaoxing, the very cultivated and intellectually forceful Wang Ji (1498–1583), who, after Wang Yangming's death in 1527, devoted the remaining fifty years of his life to collecting and editing the writings and records of conversations, and to carrying on the teaching at the Shaoxing base. He was assisted by several devoted senior disciples. They established the main line of transmission of his philosophical ideas.[36]

Another who came to study with him in those years was Wang Gen (1483–1541), not a relative, but a man born to a salt-field worker's family at Taizhou, near Yangzhou just north of the Yangzi in Jiangsu Province. Wang Gen's family was poor; he had to leave primary school at the age of ten to work, but continued to read and to learn. His independence of mind was clearly displayed in his unconventional behavior as a professed disciple of the historic Confucius: he dressed in what he took to be ancient garments and visited the tomb of Confucius in Shandong to recite Confucian texts, expounding on them in ways that ignored the traditional scholastic commentaries. When he heard about Wang Yangming's doctrine of innate knowledge, he was both delighted and skeptical. In 1521 he betook himself to Wang's home to test him, to determine whether Wang was genuine or merely a startling phrasemaker. Despite Wang Gen's impertinent manner and his intellectual arrogance, he formed warm relations with Wang Yangming and with Wang's senior followers such as the deeply cultivated Wang Ji. Wang Yangming recognized in this rude fellow a man of true commitment to the truth; he felt it his duty to both chasten and indulge him, eventually growing fond of him.

That conjunction of disparate personal qualities became very important for history. Wang Gen was totally converted to Wang Yangming's thought, served diligently in the community of disciples, and advanced greatly in learning. Yet he did not lose his independent spirit. After Wang Yangming died, he returned to his family home at Taizhou to teach. Soon he had flocks of students coming to him, and he traveled through the region lecturing to audiences that included poor common folk as well as officials and literati. A compelling and persuasive speaker, he focused on the simple issues in the lives of ordinary people, showed sympathy for the poor, and encouraged literacy education to improve their lot.[37] In his presentation of Wang Yangming's ideas, the doctrine of innate knowledge was taken as proof that every individual has the same access to the truth, while he concurred in Wang Yangming's stress on self-cultivation as a prerequisite for gaining enlightenment. Wang Gen's teachings took on a strong flavor of populism, but at the same time broadened and clarified Wang Yangming's teachings.[38]

It was the second, third, and fourth generations of Wang Yangming's followers, especially those who belonged to the "Taizhou school," as the transmission through Wang Gen's followers was called, who extended Wang Yangming's ideas to their limits. Some had an impact primarily on social thought; others took radical positions on the importance of the individual's spiritual attainment and artistic expression. He Xinyin (1517–1579) was harassed by senior Grand Secretary Yan Song (see Section VI) and later by the great Zhang Juzheng for challenging the moral authority of officialdom while urging the need for more compassionate social policies.[39] He Xinyin died of mistreatment in prison. Li Zhi, better known as Li Zhuowu (1527–1602), has been called "the most independent and courageous thinker of his day."[40] He discovered Wang Yangming's philosophy only in midlife; it reinforced his growing dissatisfaction with the Zhu Xi system of Neo-Confucian rationalism (Lixue) and his contempt for the conventional paragons of scholar-official life, both those of Ming times and those from all earlier times. His nonconformist personal behavior, his revision of history in which some of the great villains were presented as heroes, and shocking ideas such as his belief that women were the intellectual equals of men and should be fully educated in order to realize their equality of course moved most of the elite to denounce him. He was arrested for spreading false doctrines, and eventually committed suicide in prison. These, however, are extreme cases. Some Wang school adherents reached high positions in government; one example is the powerful senior Grand Secretary Xu Jie, who preceded Zhang Juzheng in that office (see Section V and Chapter 28, Section I).

Many other figures representing divergent strands of the later Wang Yangming school could be cited. The ferment aroused by Wang's thought often took form as the impulse to seek individual freedom in ways not consonant with Wang's own stress on personal obligation and social responsibility. The most noticed consequence of Wang Yangming's radical idealism was thought and behavior among large numbers of his school's later followers that went far beyond anything he might have anticipated. The individual's freedom to make unconventional choices, however, was clearly implicit in his philosophy. The possibility of justifying nonconformism too was part of his philosophical legacy.

The Reorientation of Neo-Confucian Thought

The foregoing discussion reveals the potential for Wang Yangming's new doctrines to be socially disruptive and intellectually unsettling. In that connection, historians have long stressed the radical social values of Wang Gen, the leader of the Taizhou school of Wang's followers, and other Wang school followers who took a strong reformist message to the ordinary people. Among the often-cited social consequences are the emphasis on the broadening of educational opportunity among the common people, a consequent rise in popular literacy, support for women as the intellectual peers of men, emphasis on communal social welfare activities, and the like. Those later waves of the

Wang school's social message have attracted much attention among recent scholars.

Although not as widely recognized, of still larger historical significance may be Wang's ultimate disillusionment with the state and its imperial institution as the agency for achieving any effective amelioration of social problems. That represents a sharp break with Confucian political thought, but Wang did not choose to convey it in his writings that formally set forth his analysis of political theory. In those he states positively what the elements of good governing should be, and they are straightforward reaffirmations of the ideals of Mencius. Government exists for the good of the people, not for the good of the governors or of the throne. He discounted the notions of a "correct transmission of the Way" that had dominated thought from Han times onward, and urged students to learn broadly from all aspects of tradition, without any limiting preconceptions of where truth might be found. For when a person strives to gain understanding on his own, even though he may make some mistakes, he is far better off than if he merely accepts unthinkingly whatever bits and pieces of the established orthodoxy conventional schooling may offer him. "For in learning, what is to be valued is what one gains through his own mind."[41] That does not mean that there is no criterion for what is true or false; it means that one's "innate knowledge" provides an infallible criterion. In developing this point, Wang explicitly denies the exclusive validity of Zhu Xi's "extension of knowledge through the investigation of things." The highest values in his political thought are consonant with the altruism and humane concern for the people set forth in the *Mencius,* and in that respect are not original; but this provided Wang an authentically traditional standard for criticizing the failings of rulers and of self-satisfied scholar-bureaucrats. He did not go further in his political writings to bring that standard to bear on the specific faults of Ming governing. He could have been confident that his readers would go on to do that "with their own minds."

Beyond reaffirming Mencian altruism, however, and as a quietly under-stated adjunct to his political thought, Wang Yangming encouraged a reorientation of the political focus away from emperor, state, and government. He turned that focus to the people who led and who made up the small community. He turned away from the traditional leadership role of the high elite in central government offices to the local context of social life in which elite and commoners shared in the responsibility for themselves and to one another. He had come to see this as the most hopeful arena of Confucian social action.

The traditional approach to politics stressed that better circumstances for society had to be achieved through the agency of the ruler, whose moral leadership of his court and the state's entire machinery of governing would work a transforming effect from the top down. In that process the scholar-official was to exert his mind and moral energy to effect guidance in government at the top. Neo-Confucian Lixue from Song times onward, although not much concerned with the mechanics and the means of governing, had never departed from that ideal of effecting transformation through the agency of the sage ruler. Wang had begun to perceive that those means to social betterment were not realistically workable. We may assume that his observations of government under the two willful and erratic despots he had served influenced that conclusion, but as a clear-minded student of the classics and of history, he also saw that the trend in government increasingly had produced layers of bureaucracy—both the proper bureaucracy in which he served and the improper bureaucracy of eunuchs and court favorites. Both kinds of bureaucratic excess effectively blocked the conscientious scholar-official's attempts to assume his Confucian responsibilities. That interpretation of Wang's political stance is not merely implicit in his political thought; it has also been pointed out that he explicitly discouraged Wang Gen and others from hoping to affect governing through influencing the conscience of the ruler. He advised them that at this later day in Chinese history, they could not realistically hope to transform an emperor into a sage by reminding him of the glorious models of good rulership in antiquity. Without developing any theoretical exposition of a new thesis on government, his message was simply to encourage each person to develop his own "innate knowledge" *(liang zhi)*, so that he or she would discover the sageliness within each person and give it free rein to work its beneficial way in society. To hope for sageliness in emperors was unrealistic, while the challenge to enlightened action before each individual was a practical reality. One's energies and commitment therefore should be turned to human problems in the closer focus of family, village, and local community, where meaningful gains could be realized.[42]

This view of Wang Yangming's impact on historical trends goes far toward explaining the tone of later Ming life, where an increased attention to the locality and the community has been widely observed. Some have seen this as a focus of new patterns in elite behavior, in some particulars going back to Southern Song times.[43] Other scholars have noted the increasing concern among Ming scholar-officials with strengthening the local community's well-being and devising ways of replicating the ethical society through community organizations.[44] A further part of Wang's new social attitudes was his recognition that merchants too have a place in Confucian society, and as individuals can realize Confucian norms in their personal lives while adding valuable components to the life of the whole society. All of these were potentially radical revisions of the social philosophy of Neo-Confucianism. Wang Yangming did not carry them all into full philosophical exposition, but he clearly was responsible for giving them a place in his own system of ideas, and in that way influencing critical thought thereafter.

To conclude this brief discussion of Wang Yangming's place in Ming history, one can say that his response to deteriorating political circumstances of imperial rule turned him and some of his followers toward alternate paths of elite behavior. That held the potential for deeply affecting the structure of Chinese life. It did not in fact lead to consequences of that magnitude, perhaps because Wang's vision of a different society was tied to a philosophical system that came under strong attack, and did not in the end retain its high standing in intellectual life. Countervailing trends were to come from both the philosophical-minded sector of the elite and the strong state established under the succeeding dynasty. Yet even among seventeenth-century thinkers who had become strongly anti-Wang in their philosophical orientations, still stronger criticism of the imperial institution and demands for changes in the conduct of governing were expressed. Wang's attacks on the sterility of Neo-Confucian patterns and his call for a higher political conscience in government may have contributed to the atmosphere which made that later phase of political thought possible. At the least, Wang Yangming effectively turned away from the traditional focus on the imperial head of the Chinese state and denied the primary relevance of his imperial government for guiding and improving man's life in society. In doing so he displayed a vision of a potentially different China and provided the basis for new kinds of criticism of the present. Various echoes of his ideas would be heard in subsequent generations.

27

MING CHINA'S BORDERS

During mid- and late Ming times, the tribute system pattern of Chinese relations with nearer peoples and more distant states (restored at the beginning of Ming after almost five centuries) produced quite different sets of problems on the various borders across which those relations were conducted. In the north, the Mongols continued to dominate the entire Chinese defense strategy until early in the seventeenth century, when the Manchus superseded them in the role of China's principal enemy. In the west, the Tibetans maintained their detachment from China while coming into a strategic relationship with Mongolia. In the south, the Chinese continued their centuries-long infiltration into sub-tropical Southeast Asia, adapting older institutions to current local needs. As for the eastern coasts, after their withdrawal from Annam, and after concluding the great seagoing expeditions of Admiral Zheng He, both in the 1420s to 1430s, for over a century the Chinese government tried to ignore the far-reaching implications of maritime trade. Only in the 1560s was the ban on Chinese seagoing traffic lifted to allow licit Chinese participation in trade with other Asian and now European traders as well. Understanding the frontiers on all the four sides helps us to define China as it existed under the last native dynasty of its imperial era.

I. BORDER ZONES, ZONES OF INTERACTION

In 1371 the founder of the Ming dynasty, Zhu Yuanzhang, made a statement that he intended would set a clear pattern for the conduct of his dynasty's foreign relations; he said that those countries which bring calamity to China must not be spared strong military punishment, but those that do no harm must never be invaded. He named the "barbarians of the northwest," meaning of course the Mongols, as the enemies who had long brought harm to China, and said that his state must always remain vigilant against them; otherwise China should not lightly take up arms against any other neighboring state. "The ancients," he said, "had a saying that extending the territories is not a way to achieve lasting peace; belaboring the people [to support war] provides a ready cause of disorder."[1] Ming Taizu clearly did not command his successors to build an empire; on the contrary, he warned them against imperialist expansion policies. They applied that advice in varying fashion, but in general Ming China represented the governing of Chinese populations; it comprised the Chinese culture zone and very little beyond.

The exceptions, to be discussed in this chapter, are found in the fringe areas on China's south and southwest, a region then occupied by mostly small polities within or partly within the Ming provinces, such as the Zhuang and the Yi, the Yao and the Miao, the Shan and the Karen, and many others, in varying degrees subjected to Chinese expansive pressures. In those border zones also, however, were well-established states such as Siam (Thailand), Annam, Zhenla (Cambodia), and Ava Burma, across whose borders Chinese local civil and military authorities frequently encroached. China attempted to impose its governing on the former small polities but claimed only a theoretical suzerainty over the latter group of states. Its relations with both kinds of polities to its south generated many small wars and some major campaigns, all conducted in the name of border defense. The tribal peoples then within and near China could be turbulent: they often warred among themselves and occasionally attacked the Chinese settlements that had advanced into their midst. None of those conflicts, however, threatened the safety or stability of the dynasty. As with most of the much larger and more dangerous wars on the northern frontier, wiser policies might have averted conflicts and prevented a large share of the warfare.

Beyond the adjacent regions in which China might on occasion be militarily active was a more distant world of less direct contacts. Admiral Zheng He's extraordinary exploits in the first third of the fifteenth century brought China into expanded diplomatic contacts with many states and statelets from the coasts of Southeast Asia to India, the Persian Gulf, and Africa. Whatever potential that kind of state-sponsored maritime activity might have had for broadening China's international horizons, after the 1430s the government abandoned those great maritime expeditions, although it continued to send envoys to the nearer states, often by sea. In the sixteenth century the sea lanes Zheng He had explored a century earlier now began to bring Europeans into South and East Asia and to China; more important, goods and products and ideas from distant places came to affect the lives of the Chinese in new ways. Modern China's dramatically changing place in the world can be dated from this century. Ming China had to make the first adjustments to that larger world without knowing, or having a way to know, that the world around it would never be the same again. Two centuries later the Qianlong emperor, who reigned 1736–1795, began to sense the full significance of that changing world, but he remained uncertain how to deal with it and ineffectual in his attempts.

Here Ming China's land frontiers on three sides will first be surveyed. Then the maritime frontier on the east will complete this tour of Ming China's horizons.

11. Tension and Peril on the Northern Borders

Relations with the Mongols dominated Ming China's northern frontiers throughout the dynasty until its last thirty years; then the Jurchens, only slowly recognized as a more immediate source of danger, superseded the threat long associated exclusively with the Mongols. In 1635 the Jurchen khan officially changed his people's name to Manchu. With much Mongol assistance, a group of newly united Manchu tribes then subjugated both the Mongols and the Chinese to create a vast empire of Inner Asian and Chinese extent; we know it as the Qing dynasty. As will become clear in subsequent chapters, groups of Jurchens and certain Mongol tribes had lived side by side in the Northeast (which we usually call Manchuria) and in adjoining portions of Mongolia throughout the Ming period; both participated in the tribute system pattern of Chinese foreign relations, were deeply involved with China, and were eager for the trade and other benefits which that system made possible. Until the early seventeenth century, however, we can discuss the northern border problems exclusively as a Mongol-Chinese problem.

To understand Ming-Mongol relations it is necessary to look at the problems from the quite different points of view of all the participants. That is consistent with the attempt I have made throughout this book when discussing non-Chinese peoples who have played important roles in Chinese history; the other side of such problems, seldom given much consideration by Chinese of the time, and often quite distorted by present-day Chinese and other historians, must be brought within our awareness. It is nowhere more important than in the history of Ming relations with the Mongols.

The expulsion of the Mongols from China in 1368 left the Mongol nation, the heritage of Chinggis Khan's brilliant exploits, in fragile condition. Having lost Dadu, their new great city on the site of present-day Beijing, where the capitals of three conquering dynasties from beyond the northern borders had been located, the expelled Mongol emperor went back to the capital of his pre-1260 forebears, Karakorum (Helun) in Outer Mongolia.[2] Still claiming to be both the Great Khan of the Mongols (as a direct lineal descendant of Chinggis Khan) and the emperor of the Chinese Yuan dynasty (established by Khubilai Khan), he and his heirs in fact found themselves discredited among their people and unable to maintain hegemony. The Mongols of the other three khanates—the Golden Horde in Russia, the Il-khans in Persia, and Khwarazm, the khanate of Chaghadai in Central Asia—had lost their Mongol language and cultural identity and no longer counted as part of Mongol history. The vast region of Mongolia, however, shared a common language (with some dialect variations) and, more important, a common sense of nationhood dominated by the image of Chinggis Khan. There was a strong expectation among the Mongols that a Chinggisid would emerge who would be capable of reuniting them and regaining their rightful place in the life of Inner Asia.

Legend colored their sense of their own history and of China's history in relation to them. They firmly believed that the Yongle emperor (who reigned

advantages vis-à-vis China were weakened, resulted in large part from their adoption of Tibetan Buddhism under Altan Khan in the 1570s. That drew them under Tibet's overriding religious authority and led to duplication in Mongolia of features of Tibetan religious and political forms. The Tibetans of Tibet Proper were not nomads. They had herds, but they also held land and grew cereal grains. Lamaism, the term referring to the special role in Tibetan Buddhism of certain monks (lamas) who were spiritual teachers,[9] introduced a new element into the Mongols' nomadic life: the monastery. Monasteries were fixed in place, attachment to them endured in time, and they offered a male role starkly new to nomad life. Through this institution the religious profession came to absorb 30 percent or more of Mongol males. In the monkish life they found an alternative to the warrior model of achievement, although it was not unknown for Mongol (or Tibetan) monks to bear arms. Monasteries for the first time gave Mongol society a large number of fixed locations, and because of their stability in the otherwise fluid pattern of steppe life, towns, market fairs, and new forms of settlement could develop around them. Lamaism also spawned literacy and the study of texts, as well as travel to study in Tibet and get closer to the authentic traditions of its distinctive Buddhism.

The adoption of Tibetan Buddhism (Lamaism) also drew Mongol manpower into wars within Tibet for mastery over the region's governing by one monastic sect there or another. Tibet's great monastic institutions had long replaced its earlier secular government, and networks of monasteries under one or another sectarian leader competed in the political sphere. Once the Mongols adhered to Tibet's religious authority, some Tibetan social patterns also were brought into Mongolian society. In accord with Tibetan Buddhism's way of designating the successor to the highest religious and political authority—transmission through reincarnation of "Living Buddhas" (Khutughtu, Hutuku, Qutuqtu, and so on)—the Mongols also began to designate many Living Buddhas, so many that later, under early Qing state direction, they settled on one chief Living Buddha each for Inner and Outer Mongolia, to centralize religious control. All of these features new to the Mongols cut deeply into previous attitudes and patterns; above all, they slowly undermined the mobility of nomad life, and thereby the mobility factor in Mongol warfare, their principal comparative advantage over their sedentary neighbors.[10]

These changes did not occur quickly. Many groups of Mongols resisted them, and all of them retained their pre-Buddhist shamanist religious beliefs and practices, accommodating the imported Tibetan Buddhism to them. From Tibetan Buddhist monasticism Mongols gained a great increase in literacy, a tool that was extended from religion to other social uses. In some measure compensating for their loss of nomadic mobility, they gained other sources of wealth through coopting the industrial and craftsmanship skills of sedentary peoples who increasingly lived in their midst, especially Chinese. Some of these Chinese immigrants into the steppe became business entrepreneurs residing in the towns built adjacent to leading monasteries, while others were farmers at locales in Inner Mongolia suitable for cultivation. These changes came slowly, but they marked a sea change in Mongol culture.[11] As for warfare, their military traditions remained strong; the Mongols continued to be Inner Asia's most fearsome warriors, well into the nineteenth century—so long as military success turned on steppe cavalry tactics.

Civilian Interaction along the Northern Border

The boundary between sedentary China and nomadic Mongolia was in fact a zone of intense interaction. Population groups from each resided in the other and came to serve as important agents of the social interplay. Some Mongol tribal groups chose to remain behind in China when the Yuan dynasty was expelled in 1368, and others later entered China to reside under conditions that appeared to them to be rewarding. These Mongol groups were particularly important in Gansu,[12] but were found throughout the northern regions, some even in Central and South China. Most were invited to remain and given a place in the system of Ming military garrisons. Some chieftains were ennobled for achievements; most rather quickly took Chinese names and disappeared into the Chinese population, but some retained their linguistic skills and were used as interpreters, served as sources of information (actually as scouts and spies, sometimes as double agents), and kept open the lines of information between the two peoples. The number of those remaining in China may have surpassed 250,000.

A still larger number of Chinese lived in Mongolia; estimates for the sixteenth century range up to 1 million. Some took on a Mongol identity, but that was not the usual pattern. Many in the sixteenth century fled to Mongolia to farm, to get away from the impoverished and troubled northern military zone along the Chinese side of the border, where they often were badly treated by Chinese garrison soldiers. Some were induced to immigrate by Mongol princes wanting to benefit from their skills as farmers, traders, and craftsmen. This was not new; Chinese have struck out to penetrate the steppe from earliest times, and as noted in earlier chapters, were particularly sought—even made prisoners and forced to migrate—by the Khitan, Jurchen, and Mongol rulers. Some Chinese have always been susceptible to assimilation into steppe society. Most of those who settled there in Ming (as in earlier) times, however, clung to their Chinese identity. At the beginning of Ming the generals pursuing the fleeing Mongols encountered such communities of Chinese along the way in Mongolia and forced their repatriation to deprive the Mongols of their skills.[13] By the early fifteenth century, many Chinese were again going into Mongolia to form agricultural settlements and commercial towns. They made significant contributions to Mongol life.[14] Some of these culturally dual Chinese, designated "barbarians" in Chinese records of the time, passed back and forth, maintaining links to both societies. Demeaned in China and not recognized as a potential asset, however, they did not greatly enhance the general understanding of Mongolia and steppe culture within Ming society and government.

To the Ming Chinese the Mongol scene remained opaque. Self-serving Chinese officials posted on the boundaries regularly reported gross distortions, in part from ignorance, but mainly to cover their peculation and malfeasance. Ignorance served their interests; they wanted the court to remain credulous and ready to believe their assessments of the border situation. It is remarkable how ignorant the Ming Chinese government remained about politics, leadership, organization, and other realities of Mongolia.[15] They perceived the Mongols as deprived people desperate for opportunities to receive Chinese imperial favors and gifts. They interpreted the Mongols' genuine need for trade as their duplicitous effort to pawn off third-rate offerings to the Chinese court, so as to qualify under the rules of the tribute system and thereby gain the right to profiteer in trade or insidiously acquire Chinese goods that would strengthen them militarily. Moreover, their innumerable tribal leaders, their identities usually unclear to the Chinese, were seen as tricksters ever eager to disavow their proper tribute relationship and make war.

Scarcely controlled confusion reigned much of the time. It was common for Mongol tribute delegations to come to the borders and even be sent on to the capital in the midst of open warfare with the same groups. The Chinese had to pretend that their ritually defined supremacy throughout the universe was acknowledged by all, and kept up the pretenses of correct diplomatic usage under the tribute system. Most Chinese who were involved knew it was a sham, but it was a satisfying sham that maintained their sense of themselves while also giving pattern and stability to foreign relations. Mongols' and Jurchens' obvious misuse of tribute for trade could be allowed as but a minor distortion of civilization's great norms by backward peoples the Chinese disdainfully labeled the "Northern Caitiffs" *(bei lu)*.

The Issue of Trade

The place of trade in the entire northern boundary relationship (as also on the maritime eastern boundary in these same centuries) is one of the most complex issues in all of Ming history. There were strong historical precedents for encouraging such trade. As noted in earlier chapters, border zone trade throughout Northern and Southern Song times, whether conducted under the state's monopoly or carried on beyond its controls, had helped to stabilize the Song state's relations with its strong northern neighbors, and had contributed significantly to Song fiscal solvency. That period in China's foreign relations was well understood by Ming Chinese.

The connotations of that period, however, were those of humiliating treaty relationships imposed by alien force. The Ming had reinstituted the pre-Song tribute system and broadened it. Ideally, the system projected an unequal relationship in which China's formally acknowledged superiority signified the restoration of the proper cosmic order. The Chinese would cling to it into the late nineteenth century, almost to the end of the imperial era, although the elements of that situation of course changed significantly under the Manchus after 1644. In mid- and later Ming times, a few perceptive statesmen, recognizing the value of allowing unhampered trading relations with steppe peoples, could do no more than propose partial steps in that direction, and with greatest care, while at the same time proclaiming the correctness of the Chinese stance.

As the Mongols saw it, the Chinese owed them the right to conduct trade; they persisted in demanding the opening of border trading stations. Their leaders repeatedly and persistently insisted that a fair commerce could resolve their conflicts. If steppe livestock and products, especially horses, for which the Chinese army had great need, could be exchanged for all manner of Chinese manufactures and raw materials (especially iron, cereal grains, and textiles), both sides would benefit, and the grounds for conflict would be diminished. Some farsighted Chinese with experience on the borders agreed with them. But the courtiers and eunuchs who both directed Mongol relations from Beijing and carried out the lucrative management at the borders, had competing interests of their own; they remained myopically fixed on nonaccommodating policies. The larger issues did not particularly concern them. They allowed the entire relationship with Mongolia to be reduced to a static border defense policy—costly, inefficient, mismanaged, and destructive of the texture of Chinese life in the border zones. It was the greatest failure of Ming statesmanship. Yet from that unresolved conflict came the Great Wall of China, today, quite ironically, the very symbol of Chinese historical greatness.[16]

The Military Posture

The Nine Defense Areas (Jiu bian) occupy an enormous amount of Ming documentation and discussion. Today we can see that on all of its other borders the Ming state had great opportunities for constructive engagement, but its obsession with defending the northern frontier against the threat of Mongol incursions seriously limited its capacity to respond to opportunities elsewhere. The system of Nine Defense Areas was an administrative device; it divided into nine sections the defense line that stretched from the Shanhai Pass, the eastern terminus of the defended line of passes and garrisons (eventually it became the Great Wall line), and extended westward for 1,500 miles, ending in the desert sands of northwest China (Map 17). The Ming capital at Beijing was close to that line, only a day's ride from it at some points. Within the low mountains to the north and west of the capital, and all the way to the sea in the east, were more than a hundred strategic passes or barriers (*guan*), defended defiles through which invading armies would have to pass. At some of these, monumental defensive gateways and bastions had long existed, and military emplacements along the line connecting them were capable of sending smoke signals to maintain communications. As it extended farther on to the west from the capital region, across the northern boundary of Shanxi to cross midway through Shaanxi south of the great bend of the Yellow River, the defense line divided the Ordos Desert region off from the

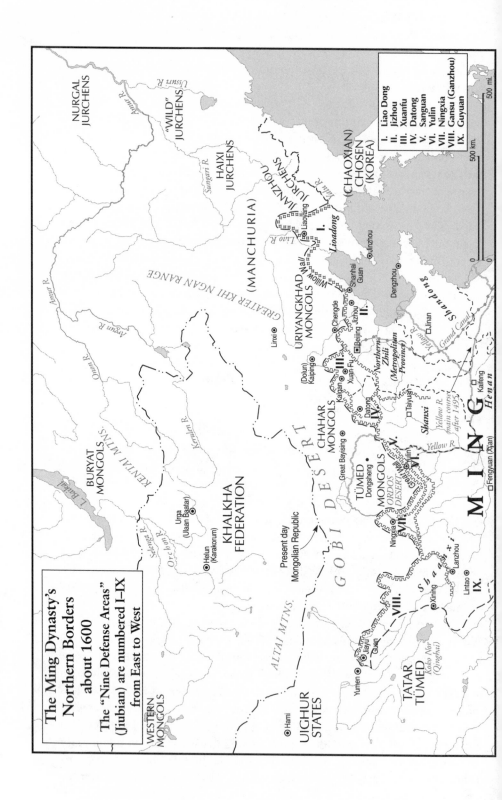

The Ming Dynasty's
Northern Borders
about 1600

The "Nine Defense Areas"
(Jiubian) are numbered I–IX
from East to West

I.   Liao Dong
II.   Jizhou
III. Xuanfu
IV.   Datong
V.   Sanguan
VI.   Yulin
VII. Ningxia
VIII. Gansu (Ganzhou)
IX.   Guyuan

sedentary life of China. Beyond Shaanxi the line extended farther west through the Gansu Corridor, the starting point of the Silk Roads which traversed the deserts of present-day Xinjiang, crossed the Pamirs, and led on west. The Great Wall, however, ended at Jiayuguan, an imposing fortress near the town of Suzhou Wei at the northwestern tip of Gansu,[17] built in the first years of the Ming to secure the western end of China's defense line. For all practical purposes this marked the limit of Ming administration in the northwest.[18]

Each of the nine areas into which the northern boundary line was divided held a major military garrison *(bian zhen)* from which it took its name as a military administrative region. Those were headed by Regional Military Commissioners (Dusi), with the high rank of 3A, usually from the civilian bureaucracy and often holding concurrent court titles of Surveillance Commissioner; these nine border zone posts paralleled the chief military commands in each of the provinces throughout the empire. In fact, the Regional Commissioners of the Nine Defense Areas sometimes concurrently held the military command position in the adjacent province. In short, they were at the top of the military-administrative hierarchy of Ming China.

Through much of Ming, the most sensitive of the Nine Defense Areas was that based at Datong; it was grouped with that of Xuanfu to its east, just north of Beijing, and sometimes with the next defense zone farther west, and placed under a supreme commander with overall responsibility for border and provincial military matters. That section of the defense line had become the point of greatest danger because of the enigmatic Ming withdrawal to the Great Wall line from the previous outer line of defense garrisons set up in early Ming times. A half-century later, after repeated and inconclusive campaigns into Mongolia, the Yongle emperor made the decision not to maintain a Chinese military presence on the nearer steppe, but to withdraw to "inner" bases from which to project Ming power into Inner Asia. By abandoning a strong defense of those outer garrisons, he ensured their loss in the early fifteenth century.

The most significant of those early Ming outposts in the nearer steppe, abandoned after the 1420s, was Dongsheng, north of the Yellow River to the west of Datong. Its loss allowed the entire inner zone of the steppe, from Dongsheng at the west to Kaiping north of Beijing, to be infiltrated and ultimately occupied by the Chahar Mongols after Esen's invasion in 1449. Dongsheng had been designed to protect the Big Bend of the Yellow River (He tao), the northern loop enclosing the Ordos Desert, before the river turns south to form the Shaanxi-Shanxi border. In the nearer steppe, just north of the Big Bend, there was (and is) a fertile zone, irrigated by the river and capable of sustaining agriculture and grazing for horses. The Chahar Mongols, previously residing farther north, then moved southward into the zone directly adjacent to China, where they could benefit from that region's strategic and economic advantages. The Yongle emperor's decision has thus been held responsible for breaking the back of the original Ming defense strategy and forcing impractical choices on the later Ming border defense system.[19] In the mid-sixteenth century Altan Khan built a large city, its Chinese population possibly as large as 100,000, fifty miles north of Dongsheng on the (Da) Heihe tributary of the Yellow River. He called it Great Bayising. It thrived on its nearness to China and on the capacity of the immediate area to sustain agriculture, crafts, and commerce. It was one of the largest and most important Mongol cities of Ming times, and a source of considerable strength to Altan Khan's military position.[20]

Building the Great Wall

In the mid-fifteenth century, administrators of the western segments of the Nine Defense Areas conceived the idea of building "long walls" to connect the principal garrison points; sometimes they built two or three more or less parallel sections of such walls. Some initial successes in trapping and defeating Mongol cavalry contingents led to the adoption of the wall strategy all across the northern border. The result, starting in the latter half of the sixteenth century, became the Great Wall of China. It was an imposing achievement. Where stone was available, it was used for lower courses and gates, and for facing and paving the rubble-filled higher courses. Where there was no supply of stone within convenient distance, brick kilns were set up to fire large bricks. In most places the higher courses of the stone walls, the crenelations, and the towers are constructed of such bricks. The new walls varied in their dimensions, but in the eastern 500 miles they may have averaged thirty-five feet in height and twenty in breadth at the top, with towers each half-mile or so sometimes reaching to fifty feet. The far western portions, sometimes built of rammed or pounded earth, sometimes later faced with brick, are smaller, probably averaging fifteen feet in height.[21] Visually, the Ming Great Wall, snaking across the crests of ridges and low mountains, crossing defiles and valleys where great defensible gateways blocked the roadways, is a familiar image in the modern world's consciousness; it is one that struck awe in the minds of travelers in the past.

The Ming walls enhanced the means for maintaining secure communications, and provided more defended points at which garrison soldiers under attack could group themselves and resist the nomad cavalry. Throughout the sixteenth century, many sections of such "long walls" (changcheng) were built, eventually connecting the entire earlier defensive system of the Nine Garrisons with their hundreds of barriers and passes. From the 1550s until the end of the dynasty in 1644, wall building continued at a great pace; it constantly filled in gaps, adding defended towers and small forts, inner walls, and secondary walls. As one historian has stated, the Wall incorporated sophisticated tactical conceptions.[22] But it was, he adds, based on strategic miscalculations; the Mongols often breached it or bypassed it, much as the Germans outflanked France's Maginot Line in World War II. China's Great Wall wasted vast amounts of treasure, and it defined a foreign policy that was shortsighted and doomed to failure.

Altan Khan and Wang Chonggu Reach a Settlement

The most potent Mongol leader in the sixteenth century was Altan Khan, Great Khan of the Chahar Mongols and leader of the coalition that invaded the capital region in 1550, surrounding Beijing for several days and creating a crisis in Ming government. Altan Khan used that military pressure to obtain from the Chinese a settlement, temporary to be sure, giving in to some Mongol requests for better treatment. Limited trading of Mongol horses for Chinese textiles was permitted, but though Altan Khan was prepared to offer a resolution of all military conflict in return for such trading rights, the Chinese agreed only under pressure and were quite insincere in their commitment. After two years they abolished the border trading fairs and did not permit their resumption.

Twenty years later the garrison commander at Datong, northwest of Beijing, had a golden opportunity to resume negotiations with Altan Khan. The Great Khan's grandson, angry at his grandfather over a family matter, defected to the Datong commander Wang Chonggu (1515–1589), asking for protection. A *jinshi* of 1541, Wang had long experience as a civil administrator involved in military responsibilities. After participating in defenses against the Wakô pirates (see Section V), he served for seven years in the 1560s at the Ningxia Defense Area in the westerly extension of the Great Wall line. There he came to know leading Mongol personalities and gained a realistic appreciation of their problems, yet was committed to a strong military defense. Appointed the Regional Military Commissioner and concurrently Governor at Datong, he was in a position to benefit from his knowledge, and at a crucial moment to understand and sympathize with the Mongols' demands. He believed them when they insisted that in trade the Chinese possessed an instrument that could unlock the Chinese-Mongol impasse.

Instead of looking upon Altan Khan's grandson as a hostage, Wang Chonggu treated him as a royal guest, informing the young man's grandfather that he would not be harmed and that they should exchange ideas about releasing him. He proposed a general negotiation in which the Mongols would take a solemn oath never again to attack China. It was a rare opportunity: one of the few Chinese officials of enough understanding to deal with the problem and enough stature to succeed was the responsible official on the scene when this opening presented itself.[23] The Emperor Shizong (r. 1521–1567) detested the Mongols and was ever suspicious of them; he would never have allowed the settlement had he still been alive.

The settlement that was reached in 1570–71 led at last to regular trading facilities for the Mongols at a number of Great Wall points, and Ming-Mongol relations remained basically peaceful until the end of the dynasty. It could have been done a century or more earlier. The Mongol demands were basically consistent, as was the Chinese response, until this breakthrough near the end of Altan Khan's long life.[24] Statesmanship could well have spared China the expense and sacrifice of building its fabled Great Wall!

III. TIBET AND THE WESTERN BORDERS

China's western frontier in Ming times extended from the arid loess region of Gansu in the northwest, southward along the edges of the Himalayan upland, then into the subtropical jungles of western Yunnan and Burma.

The northwest was administered under a sprawling Shaanxi Province that included much of later Gansu and supervised the military government of the Gansu Corridor that then lay beyond the provincial boundaries. That northwest extension of Ming local administration was surrounded by autonomous Mongol tribal federations whose leaders had been given the honorific Ming titles of Pacification Commissioners. Important among them were groups called Dada (Tatar), and some known as constituents of the Oyirat Mongol federation (e.g., the Khoshut tribe), along with other tribal groups. During Ming times the northwest thus contained a broad array of Chinese, Mongol, and Turkic peoples that included some Uighur and other Islamic communities.[25] And there were Tibetans.

Most of the western border zone, from the northwest corner of China southward, was dominated by a range of peoples usually identified as Tibetans. They were the most numerous and historically the most important of China's western neighbors. In Ming times we can think of them as the Tibetans of central Tibet, or Tibet Proper (Xizang), with its capital at Lhasa, and the Tibetans of the eastern extension of the Himalayan upland along the western border of China (Amdo and the Kham region adjacent to western Sichuan) (Map 18).[26] These northern and eastern Tibetans were often called the Qiang people in history.[27]

Tibet developed a literate high culture in the sixth and seventh centuries C.E. (about the same time as Japan and Korea). That also is when it acquired both Buddhism and literacy through its southwestern borders with Indian civilizations. The still earlier culture is now thought to have arisen in far western Tibet, in Central Asia. The first well-organized state in Tibet Proper, however, controlling central Tibet where present-day Lhasa is located, took form in the seventh century. That was a vigorously expansive period; Tibetan armies pushed out to conquer widely in all directions. On their east and northeast they made serious incursions into Tang China's western boundaries.[28] We know a great deal about this formative period in Tibet's history because Chinese historical records clearly document the Tang involvement with the Tibetan kingdom of that time. Cultural relations with Tang China began to develop, and in 641 the Tang emperor acceded to the demand of the Tibetan king to formalize their relationship by sending him an imperial princess to wed. The power of that secular kingdom subsequently disintegrated; after the ninth century, Tibet gradually came to be ruled by local leaders of its Buddhist church. Cultural links with China were greatly diminished thereafter while Tibet turned its attention to its southern and eastern borders.[29] Profound involvement with Indian culture through several centuries produced the great age of Tibetan religious and philosophical writing and of religious poetry. When the Muslim conquest of northern India took place about the year 1200,

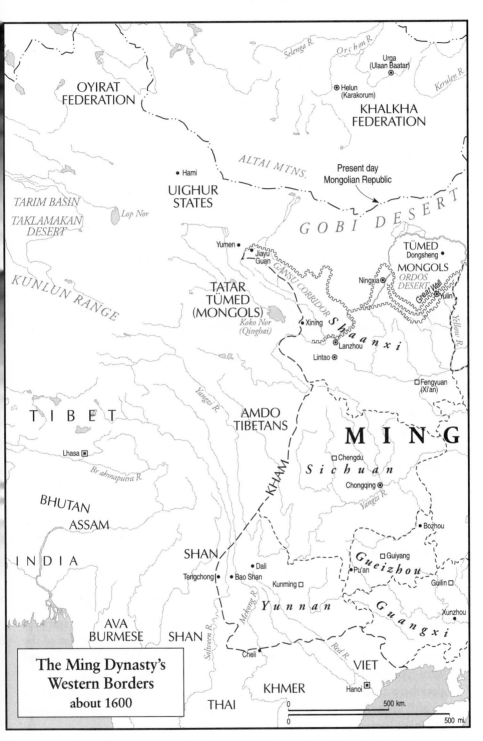

The Ming Dynasty's
Western Borders
about 1600

MAP 18

gol adventurers, especially from among the Western Mongols, frequently sallied through Tibet on visits that took on the character of raids.

The Ming state recognized the potential harm to its interests in the alliances between Tibet and Mongolia yet could do little to forestall them. It strove to control the movement of Mongols across the Ordos and the Gansu Corridor, the two countries' lines of direct communication, and sought to impose influence on the Ordos and Tümed Mongol federations in the strategic northwest region. Despite Chinese efforts, the Mongol-Tibetan axis became a fixed element of Inner Asian politics thereafter.

Yellow Hat sect leadership faltered briefly after the death of the Fourth Dalai Lama in 1617, but with Mongol military assistance it recovered triumphantly during the reign of "the Great Fifth" Dalai Lama (1617–1682), as he is known in Tibetan history.[38] One of the most important figures in Tibetan history, he gradually consolidated the Yellow Hat sect's hold on all of Tibet and played a key role in subsequent Manchu involvement there. The Fifth Dalai Lama built the Potala, the huge fortress-palace overlooking Lhasa, which symbolized the power of the Gelug-pa sect.

In Mongolia after 1577 (when Altan Khan declared Tibetan Buddhism the official religion of the Mongol nation), the Mongol princes and their subject tribesmen did not all immediately accept Tibetan Buddhism, nor were all of those who did so subservient to the Yellow Hat sect. Gradually, however, it prevailed. Its institutions and its religious authority took hold throughout Mongolia, with the consequences discussed earlier (see Section II). In fact, the religion's growing impact on the Mongols incidentally made them more amenable to coexistence with sedentary civilization.

To follow the story forward for a century or two, the early Manchu emperors of the Qing dynasty after 1644 were successful in taking over the Mongols' special relationship with Tibet. Their security in Inner Asia depended on that. The Great Fifth Dalai Lama accepted the invitation of the new Qing court at Beijing to visit China in 1652–53; that visit had something to do with the youthful Shunzhi emperor's turning away from the Jesuit missionaries at his court to devote himself ardently to Buddhism. The visit led to the lavish patronage of Tibetan church leaders by the Qing court and paved the way for the direct intervention by the Kangxi emperor (r. 1662–1722) in seating the Seventh Dalai Lama (1708–1757). That phase of Tibet's relations with China will be discussed in Chapter 33, Section III.

IV. THE "SOFT BORDER" OF THE CHINESE SOUTH

The southward movement of the Chinese people throughout their history is a well-known fact. It has never been easy to draw on a map a southern boundary line separating Chinese from non-Chinese people, yet as late as the Song dynasty (960–1279), such a line would have been much closer to the Yangzi drainage of Central China than it is today.

In Ming times the entire tier of southern provinces from parts of Guangdong in the east to all of Guangxi, Guizhou, and westward into Yunnan and

Sichuan was still largely non-Chinese in population. Yunnan became a province only in 1382, putting it under direct Chinese regional governance for the first time in history. Guizhou was created as a province in 1413 from less developed regions previously on the edges of the three adjoining provinces. These were the last two parts of what we now call China Proper to be given province-level administrations (Map 19).

In the four southern provinces of Guangdong, Guangxi, Guizhou, and Yunnan, and also in the westernmost of the next tier of provinces, that is, Huguang (Hunan and Hubei) and Sichuan, the Ming state did not attempt to set up in all places regular offices of local administration. It continued a practice begun under the Yuan of establishing regular county *(xian)* governments only where there was sufficient Chinese farming and taxpaying population to support them.[39] Many of the "native peoples" *(tu ren)* were not registered as Chinese subjects and hence were not carried on census and taxation lists.[40] Instead, their chieftains were confirmed in their right to rule their own people in traditional ways, under authority granted by the Chinese government. They were called *tuguan* or *tusi,* that is, "native officials" heading "native offices," in localities where non-Chinese people were a majority. They were given offices analogous to those in the Chinese system of ranked civil service posts, their titles usually prefixed by the word *tu,* meaning "local" or "native," that is, "non-Chinese." Commonly encountered in the civil branch of government were designations such as *tu*-prefectures and sub-prefectures and *tu*-counties, headed by *tu*-magistrates. In the military branch they might range from several high titles designating *tu*-pacification commissioners to *tu*–local commanders, down to lowly *tu*–squad leaders. Civil government *tusi* were established in more advanced regions, and might include a minority Chinese population living alongside the majority non-Chinese, under an office of non–civil service local government. Military *tusi* tended to be found in economically and culturally less advanced regions.

There were in Ming times altogether some 800 military *tusi* posts and about 650 civil posts.[41] The appointees were given formal attire, official seals, and patents of their offices. Unlike Chinese civil office, all native offices were expected to be hereditary. In another departure from Chinese practice, they might be given to women in places where it was the custom of the people to have female leaders.[42] The numbers of native offices increased at the beginning of the Qing but were sharply reduced from the eighteenth century onward. The last few remaining were abolished in the early years of the Republic, after 1911.

The native peoples governed under *tusi* were not subject to the standard forms of Ming and Qing taxation imposed on individuals and households. Those "native offices" were subject to levies of goods and labor, and of soldiers when military emergencies arose. The Ming government took the collection of those levies quite seriously, both because they had economic value and because compliance signified continued "loyalty" or subservience. In general, however, the revenues from a *tusi,* while often felt to be an oppressive burden by the native peoples, were less than the taxes and service levies from a com-

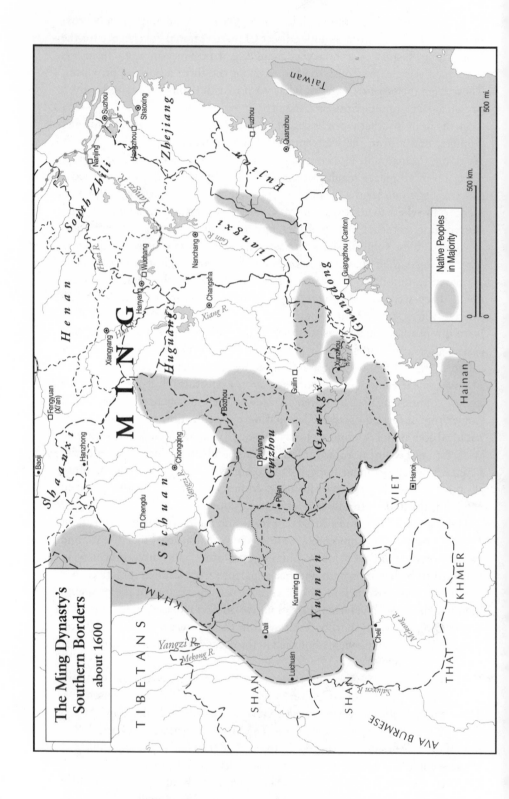

The Ming Dynasty's Southern Borders about 1600

Native Peoples in Majority

parable Chinese unit of local administration. If that was not a major consideration, other considerations made the Chinese realize that the system did not work well and should be replaced by regular Chinese-type administration. The native officials were often unruly, resisted Chinese controls, were corrupt and exploitative, did not maintain peaceful and stable conditions among their people, and at times threatened to rebel. After establishing the native offices early in the Ming, the government adopted the policy of converting them to regularly appointed Chinese offices, a policy called *gaitu guiliu,* "changing local native offices to regular civil service appointments." That meant abolishing the semiautonomous native (i.e., "non-Chinese") governments and making them counties or prefectures in the uniform structure of Chinese local government. In most cases the native peoples resisted that change, at times fiercely, for they thereby lost their claims to being distinct ethnic entities retaining their traditional forms of self-government. Also important in resistance to the changeover must be counted the simple fact that when native leaders lost their hereditary offices, they lost opportunities to enrich themselves.

The Ming *tusi* were absorbed into the Chinese system most readily where the in-migration of Chinese settlers occurred the most rapidly. In some southern provinces, notably Fujian and Jiangxi, significant numbers of non-Chinese native peoples had been administratively absorbed before the Ming dynasty began, but were still distinguishable as non-Chinese peoples. The in-migration of Chinese dated from the Tang or earlier times, and continued through Ming and Qing and since. The Chinese migrants were protected by provincial military authorities. They took over the fertile river valleys to farm the best lands by their more productive methods. That could produce a welcome increase in a province's tax base. The native peoples were reduced in status, were absorbed into the Chinese population, or were driven out to occupy less desirable hill regions or more remote border areas.[43] It was a centuries-long process of continued Chinese movement into the regions of South China in which the Chinese gradually became the locally dominant population group and then displaced the native peoples or made them an inferior stratum within local society. The potential for friction and local violence often endured.

Cultural assimilation of the non-Chinese people was the expected consequence of the process. The Chinese sublimely assumed that their cultural superiority would be recognized. For centuries they had made that assumption in all their dealings with other peoples. Sometimes that was in fact what happened. The Chinese authorities shrewdly coupled cultural programs to their other control measures. They established superintendencies of Confucian studies in the *tu*-counties and prefectures under civil management, appointed teachers, and invited sons of important native officials to attend the National Academy in the capital, and had books published (in Chinese) for the edification of native peoples. In affirming rights of succession to a deceased or displaced native official, the Ming government promulgated the principle that those who had failed to become competent in Chinese literacy and traditions were not eligible to inherit their family chieftainships.[44] In

leaders, over the span of several generations, assimilating into the native people's culture while retaining their Chinese surnames and identities. Altogether
there were some 340 *tusi* spread throughout most of Guangxi's 113 administrative civilian and military subdivisions: of civil offices, five of eleven prefectures had *tu*-prefects, and forty-two of the forty-eight sub-prefectures had *tu*-
magistrates, as did ten of the fifty counties. A still higher proportion of the
military posts was held by native officers.[46]

The four prefectures with the largest populations were among the six that
had regularly constituted Chinese administrations, yet they included some of
the areas most difficult to control. One of those was Xunzhou Fu in central Guangxi, famous for its Great Rattan Gorge (Da Teng Xia) on the Xun
River. This prefecture held thirty-two native offices, which included one
tu-magistrate, four district *tu*–police chiefs, twenty-two *tu*–assistant police
chiefs, two *tu*–district jailers, two *tu*–postal relay heads, and two *tu*–militia
chiefs. Although most were relatively low in rank, they accounted for about
one-third of the official posts in the prefecture. In prefectures and counties
that had not been changed over to regular Chinese governing (i.e., had not
undergone *gaitu guiliu*), most of the higher posts were held by native chieftains as their hereditary right. The example of Xunzhou is particularly interesting because a Yao uprising there in 1465–66 was China's largest rebellion
of native peoples in the latter half of the fifteenth century. Chinese troops
had never before penetrated the Yao strongholds; in this all-out campaign
they were aided by Mongol archers from the north and local Zhuang fighters
called "wolf soldiers" *(langbing);* both were feared for their ferocity.[47] After
the uprising was suppressed, new Yao commanders were appointed on condition that they be held responsible for any subsequent disturbances, and Zhuang chieftains were placed alongside them to guarantee their docility.[48] Such
guarantees often were unreliable, at best of brief duration.

Guizhou Province. Taking shape as a new province created forty-five years
after the founding of the Ming dynasty, Guizhou was a patchwork of many
smaller polities. Among those were communities of Tujia, Miao, and Gelao
in the northeast; in the west there were many tribes of the Yi people (previously known as the Lolo) adjacent to Yi districts in Yunnan; in the south
there were Buyi and Miao; and in the southeast there were groups of Miao,
Kam (whom the Chinese today call the Dong), and Sui. Culturally the most
advanced of those were the Yi, who had a writing system at least as early as
the Ming period. It was perhaps not capable of fully writing Yi speech, but
was used for divination and religious texts.[49] The vast majority of the native
officials in central and western Guizhou whose ethnic identity can be established were Yi. The native people whom the Ming governors found the most
fractious in the early Ming decades were the Tujia, about whose ethnic identity very little is known. They controlled much of eastern Guizhou through
the family bearing the Chinese surname Tian. Branches of the Tian clan had
been confirmed as *tu*–Pacification Commissioners in the 1360s, when the
region first came into the orbit of Zhu Yuanzhang, the Ming founder. Leaders

of the Tian family who controlled the two large prefectures making up eastern Guizhou warred incessantly on one another and caused destruction over a large area. The Ming government was able to suppress them in the early fifteenth century and subdivide their two prefectures into eight smaller ones, confirming some members of the Tian family in native offices there, but also installing native leaders of the Miao, Kam, and other groups alongside them. Guizhou remained relatively stable thereafter, except in the west, where its ethnic problems spilled over provincial lines. One example is the serious Miao rebellion that spread into Sichuan in the 1470s and 1480s, finally suppressed by heavy military involvement from the provincial governments of Sichuan and Guizhou.

More interesting perhaps is the case of a fierce female rebel leader, one Mi-lu of Pu'an *tu*–sub-prefecture on the western border that Guizhou shared with Yunnan. From a prominent Yi family of native officers, married to the *tu*–vice magistrate, she murdered her husband and other family members to make room for a lover, and the two then stirred up a major disturbance that lasted four years (1499–1502). She, not her lover, had the family status to be a chieftain, and the revolt appears to have been entirely under her direction. It was finally put down with provincial army units from four provinces and 80,000 local native troops. The record reveals no indication that social injustice or Chinese oppression had much if anything to do with this outbreak, or with many others, but such information may simply have been suppressed. This woman appears simply to have been an ambitious and effective person who fought ruthlessly for her own interests.[50] Yet the record is clearly one-sided. In the Chinese view, many of the native peoples were by their natures warlike and difficult to restrain. Despite little evidence for that in this case, mistreatment by the Chinese also was a major cause of unrest and vengeful spirit. That was noted by some officials, but their attempts to analyze the social causes of native people's turbulence and propose more enlightened governing had little effect on Ming policy.

Yunnan Province. Today's Yunnan is an ethnographer's challenge, so complex is its ethnic makeup. During the Ming it appears to have been even more so. Some of the peoples now resident in Yunnan have not yet been fully identified in ethno-linguistic terms, and we are much less clear about the Ming period ethnography of the region, especially about the many links to peoples then as now beyond the boundaries of China.[51]

The southern and western borders of Yunnan are international boundaries. The concept of an international boundary existed in Ming China, but it then had quite a different meaning from the one it has had since the nineteenth century, when the western powers imposed a new kind of international law upon China. The French, who were developing an East Asian empire in Indochina, and the British, with imperial interests in India and Burma that extended into Tibet, surveyed and defined the southern and southwestern borders of China during the late nineteenth century, hardening a line that until that time had remained soft and subject to frequent change. On recent Chinese historical maps, Yunnan's "international" boundaries are shown in early Ming as having been quite different from those in late Ming, in Qing, and in the twentieth century. While the Ming and Qing boundaries were indeed fluid, the maps mislead in their attempt to draw lines that did not in fact function as meaningful boundaries at the time.[52]

An examination of Ming behavior in Yunnan (and on the southern boundary generally) reveals that military force frequently was used well in advance of infiltrating Chinese settlement to expand the zone of Chinese interest at the expense of many native groups. Most of those existed as polities—that is, they were "politically organized entities" if not countries—and were independent of China. China's efforts to "transform" them to its cultural norms and bring them under a uniform pattern of Chinese governance was not widely welcomed among these peoples. Some fought hard to preserve their separateness; others more passively accepted the Chinese overlordship while seeking to retain features of their own ways of life.

These Southeast Asian polities in the main represented cultures more advanced than those found in the New World by the European colonizers, yet it may well remind us of the way the United States and Canada in North America and the various successor states to the European colonies in Latin America absorbed their native populations, placing a subjective sense of national interest (or "national destiny") ahead of those peoples' rights. If we compare that process with China's absorption of its southern borders, the analogy fails only when we remind ourselves that, unlike those other examples, China's advance into Southeast Asia was not completed when the process was interrupted. The successor states to the European empires—Vietnam, Laos, Cambodia, Burma, Malaysia (and Thailand or Siam, which alone remained independent throughout the period of European empire)—inherited the consequences of the firm international boundaries imposed by force in the nineteenth century. Legally defined boundaries came to protect those states against China, if not against the Europeans.[53] The infiltration of Chinese population and the enhancement of Chinese communities throughout Southeast Asia continued, but successive Chinese governments have had to adapt to the concept of sovereign borders, and to the notion that Chinese people can be subjects of other governments, concepts unknown to Ming and to more recent China. We must attempt to go back to a world in which different rules applied, in order to understand the place of native peoples in Ming dynasty Yunnan.[54]

The Yuan conquered Yunnan in 1253–54, making it the princedom of Liang, headed by princes from the Yuan imperial line. The Mongol conquest terminated Yunnan's Dali kingdom but retained Dali's deeply entrenched Duan princely family as *tu*–vice magistrates in their home sub-prefecture at Dali, and in many other military and civil offices. The Duan family, though claiming Chinese ancestry going back several centuries, were of the Bai ethnic group, probably the most advanced of the non-Chinese peoples of Yunnan then and now. The Dali kingdom dated from 937, as the successor to the powerful Nanzhao state (649–902).[55] Nanzhao was capable of invading

Sichuan and threatening the security of the entire southwest, as well as alternately making war upon and aligning itself with the Tibetans. The Dali kingdom was less aggressive but militarily powerful; its leaders wisely surrendered to the Mongols in 1253 in order to preserve their place in Yunnan society. The Bai people's tribal organization and the Duan family's leadership remained intact under the ensuing Yuan period rule.

In 1381 the Ming court determined it must invade Yunnan to end the continuing Mongol presence there, and to incorporate this region of great strategic importance into the direct administration of the Chinese state. The conquest, under General Fu Youde,[56] proceeded quite smoothly. He commanded an army of 300,000 drawn from the garrison forces stationed around Nanjing, men of the Anhui-Jiangsu region. They gained a conclusive victory early in 1382. The large army was assigned to remain in Yunnan after the conquest to form the core of Chinese population in the new province. Its soldiers brought with them their families; in consequence, their children grew up speaking their parents' southern Mandarin dialect. That form of "official speech" became standard Chinese for the province. This socially cohesive bloc of Chinese in-migrants also imparted strong cultural influences, evident in Yunnanese society thereafter.

General Fu's junior vice commander of the great expeditionary army in 1381 was General Mu Ying, one of the Ming founder's adopted sons who had proved himself a very able soldier. After the victory in Yunnan, Mu Ying was granted the hereditary title of Duke of Qian'guo, a kind of special military governorship of the region that was to exist alongside the regular civilian and military arms of provincial government. His heirs continued in that role until the end of the Ming dynasty. The Mu family greatly enriched itself in Yunnan, reportedly acquiring 360 great estates, one for each day of the year, it was said. They became the satraps of Yunnan, holding both official titles and positions as well as concrete regional responsibilities for which there is no parallel in all of Ming history. That they were given that role in itself shows how special the circumstances in Yunnan were held to be in Ming times.

Among the many important native groups, several may be singled out for special notice. The best lands of central and northern Yunnan were held by the Yi (Lolo) people. Sinified Muslims occupied a number of strategic places where they had been located by the Central Asian Muslim leaders who, as civil governors under the princes of Liang, carried on very vigorous governing during the Yuan dynasty.[57] The continuing presence of the strong Islamic community contributed to the special circumstances of Yunnan. In the western part of the province, around Er Lake, on which the city of Dali is situated, the Bai people were numerous, prosperous, and well organized. In the west and northwest there also were communities of Lisu, Naxi, and Jingpo, while farther west in the uplands there were Tibetans, Dulong, and Nu peoples. In the southernmost parts of the province there were Tai-speaking Dai peoples concentrated in the region they called the Sipsong Banna, designated by the Ming Chinese the Cheli Regional Pacification District. Cheli's cultural links were to Laos and Thailand. Other Tai-speaking peoples populated or gov-

erned most of the southwest half of the entire province; they were an important ethnic element in Ming Yunnan. Also found in the south were significant
numbers of less advanced native peoples. On the eastern borders were sizeable
communities of Zhuang, along with Miao and Yao, the latter two dominating
the mountainous areas. Within the disputed and shifting western borders
were the strong states of the Shan, with Mon and Kachin states to their north.
The Shan had interests within Yunnan but also were linked to political bases
farther west and south in what is present-day Myanmar (Burma). The foregoing list includes only the most prominent of the native peoples; a dozen more
could be named.[58]

The Yongle emperor's unfortunate decision in 1407 to annex Annam (then
called Jiaozhi, present-day northern Vietnam) led to much warfare in the
southwest, for Yunnan frequently served as the staging area for invasions of
Annam. When the Ming withdrew in the 1420s calling it a mistake, unsettled
conditions persisted along the entire southern border for some decades. Uprisings of native peoples on several occasions called for large-scale expeditionary
forces to suppress them. Yunnan was deeply involved.

The most interesting of the consequent fifteenth-century wars is that against
the Shan (or Maw Shan) peoples, Tai-related, whose state in upper Burma
extended into the disputed border zone of western Yunnan. A sequence of
very able Shan kings challenged Chinese control. In 1437 it was Sirenfa who,
as the Shan king, elevated himself from the native chieftainship granted him
by the Chinese government to calling himself king of Dian (Burma); he was
in competition with the Burmese kingdom of Ava, and with other states in
upper Burma, yet at times was forced to ally himself with them. Sirenfa incited
widespread uprisings. It took the Chinese court two years to recognize the
danger and plan a counterattack, which began in 1441. The war, known in
Chinese records as the Luchuan Campaigns, lasted for eight years. Large Chinese armies sent in from neighboring provinces were defeated a number of
times but eventually pursued the Maw Shan armies into Ava Burma. That
aroused still larger Burmese regional resistance to the Chinese. But Chinese
military pressure was unrelenting. Eventually Sirenfa (known also by his Burmese name, Thonganbwa) committed suicide and his body was turned over
to the Chinese, but that did not end China's difficult relations with the Shan
peoples and their state.

In military history the Luchuan Campaigns are noted for the successful
Chinese use of gunpowder-fired metal-barreled cannon, used against the
Shan's elephant corps.[59] That was among the earliest documented uses of true
cannon in Chinese warfare. It may serve as a reminder of how vicious and
costly these wars were, causing heavy losses on both sides. Long after the
settlement in 1448, relations with the Shan remained unsettled. Sirenfa's sons
and grandsons remained prominent in the region until the middle of the sixteenth century.[60] The Luchuan Campaigns were the largest-scale military
operations invoked to keep the peace in Yunnan, but there were many lesser
conflicts. Notwithstanding, the process of absorption into China was solidly
started. Notorious as a place to which political offenders long had been sent

to die in the poisonous miasmas, Yunnan began to be known as a beautiful region of mountains, lakes, and fertile valleys. Some Chinese of scholarly bent even began to write admiringly about its non-Chinese peoples, recognizing that they too had histories and cultures that Chinese should know about.

Huguang Province. In Qing (after 1644) and later times, Ming Huguang was divided into the separate provinces of Hubei and Hunan; it is easier for us to think of this very large region extending both north and south of the Yangzi in Central China, dominated by the great Yangzi port city of Wuhan (combining the three Ming cities of Hankou, Hanyang, and Wuchang), as two provinces instead of as one. For our purposes here, however, it is sufficient to note in briefest fashion that this central region, including some localities north of the Yangzi, had communities of non-Chinese population that were administered under the *tusi* system. Most were Tujia or Miao, and their locations were at the western edges of Hunan and Hubei, close to adjoining minority districts in eastern Sichuan and Guizhou. Many of these peoples had become culturally dual during Ming times, when, especially in Hunan, Chinese education was stressed. The *tusi* in Hunan continued to be important because their native peoples were famed soldiers who were often called up by the Ming and Qing governments. The native offices in Hubei all were abolished in the eighteenth century, but distinct communities of no longer self-governing Miao and perhaps of others existed into the twentieth century in several parts of what was Ming Huguang.

Sichuan Province. The heart of vast Sichuan Province is the Chengdu Basin, one of the oldest centers of Chinese civilization. It is about half river plain and half low hills, stretching 200 miles from north to south and more than 150 miles from east to west. The very old city of Chengdu lies near its northwestern edge and Chongqing at its southeast corner. It is protected by the mountains of the Himalayan upland to the west and is ringed by low mountains on the north and east, making it a favored place of subtropical climate and substantial rainfall. Famed for its oranges and lychees, the province was productive enough to sustain a high standard of living. The rich soils of its rice paddies produced two crops each season, wooded hillsides supplied timber and bamboo, and its many rivers and ponds yielded large harvests of fish. It was, however, repeatedly ravaged by Mongol invasions in the thirteenth century and by bandit warlord struggles in the mid-fourteenth, and so entered the Ming period with a great need for peace and reconstruction.

The province is ringed by mountains that in the past cut it off from the main centers of Chinese development, except for two entry routes. One was northern route from Baoji in southern Shaanxi (west of Chang'an, the Tang dynasty capital) to Chengdu, sections of which were the famed *zhandao*, roadways supported on timbers cantilevered into cliffsides, making them subject to some dangers in travel though easily defended against invaders. Alternate entry routes from the north (notably via Hanzhong in southern Shaanxi) also were possible but less direct. As the political center of China shifted eastward away from Chang'an in the centuries covered in this volume, the routes of entry from the north became less important. The other main route into the province was through the Yangzi gorges from Central China to Chongqing; this too was a difficult route, but as demand for communication increased, both land and river travel were improved and made more practical. Ming armies entered by both routes in the early 1370s; their experiences with the non-Chinese minority peoples they encountered are typical of the dynasty's initial responses to governing in the southwest, setting the pattern for Ming rule to follow.

As the victorious Ming armies entered the province, ending the rule set up by rival Red Turban warlord Ming Yuzhen in the era of the Rival Contenders (1350–1370) and bringing peace again to a troubled region, Ming officials gladly accepted the surrender of all the native chieftains who had been given official status under the Yuan dynasty.[61] Some of those, indeed, claimed that their families had held their titles as regional governors over their own people since the Tang dynasty. Sichuan was thus similar to Yunnan (and the other southwest provinces) in having in place a structure of regional and local governing controlling large areas of non-Chinese settlement.

In other ways it is the contrasts between Yunnan and Sichuan that are significant. They shared a long common border, but they were strikingly different in Ming times. Despite myths about an earlier Chinese presence, Yunnan had no historic core area of Chinese settlement going back into Chinese antiquity. It was entirely a new frontier zone: the Ming army that occupied it in the 1380s was forced to settle down there to become the anchor of its Chinese life. In contrast, among all the southwest provinces, Ming Sichuan was the one with the oldest and deepest experience as a center of Chinese civilization. That experience included much interaction with non-Chinese peoples who at times were strong enough to invade, making Sichuan a bastion of defense against warlike incursions from the west, the north, and the south at many points in earlier imperial history.

Geographically, Ming Sichuan can be described as a central region of long-established Chinese civilization surrounded on all sides by a fringe of non-Chinese local majorities. That fringe was narrow in the north and northeast but very wide in the west, south, and southeast, totaling half the area of the province. To impose firm control over those large areas that could not be governed by the usual Chinese civil service officials on three- or four-year term appointments, the Ming retained more than 100 native offices inherited from the Yuan and added over 200 more, for a total of well over 300 civil and military *tusi* hereditary offices in 90 territorial jurisdictions. In some of those, Chinese and native officials were appointed to serve side by side; in others the governing was entirely in the hands of non-Chinese.

Ming Sichuan included within its western borders jurisdiction over the Kham region of eastern Tibetan peoples.[62] The several large military *tusi* in that region were headed by men designated as Tibetans (Zang) or by Qiang (perhaps Amdo Tibetans), and in one case by Mongols. Some of them were at least nominally responsible for supervising Tibetan populations lying still farther west. On its west Sichuan, like Yunnan, thus had an international boundary, but one (unlike Yunnan's southern and western borders) that did not come to be defined by European-imposed international law in the nineteenth century. The consequence is that Sichuan's western boundary has continued to be defined by traditional Chinese border zone attitudes and political strategies until the present day. Provinces could and can be added or abolished, boundaries pushed far out or drawn sharply back in; governing can be civil or military, direct or tenuously delegated, all as the Chinese central government of the time finds appropriate. Because the definitions it imposes (since 1950) make all of the affected people "Chinese," their status becomes an issue strictly of domestic policy—just as the status of American Indian nations is in reality a matter of United States domestic governing. The historical difference is that as late as the 1950s some of the larger minority polities within the boundaries of modern China still possessed a significant measure of genuine self-rule. That was notably true on Sichuan's western borders.

On the east Sichuan's most important minority groups were Tujia and Miao (related to those in neighboring Guizhou and Huguang provinces), while on the south the principal groups were the Yi (Lolo), Bai, and Chinese Muslims, all related to such groups in Yunnan. Not all of them remained fixed in those locations, however. Leaders of the minority group in Long'an Prefecture who rushed to welcome the entering Ming armies on the northern border in 1371, and accordingly were confirmed in their local *tusi* offices, appear to have disappeared from the maps in later times; today we cannot ascertain their ethnic identity. Like some others in Sichuan and elsewhere, they appear to have been completely assimilated into the Chinese population.

An extreme example of the way native offices functioned in Ming Sichuan is the Yang family of hereditary Pacification Commissioners who controlled the very large region of Bozhou, then in southeastern Sichuan, centering on the present-day prefectures of Zunyi and Pingyue in central and northwestern Guizhou. In 1573 Yang Yinglong inherited the post from his father; he was the twenty-ninth–generation descendant of the original holder of that office, one Yang Duan, said to have been a Chinese, who had been appointed by the Tang emperor in the late ninth century. By Ming times the Yang family appears to have long intermarried with local "aboriginal" people under their jurisdiction, perhaps of Tujia identity, but their power came from their very widespread authority over the Miao people in Sichuan, Huguang, and Guizhou.

In all the Chinese accounts Yang Yinglong is seen as a thoroughly degenerate person, given to intricate cruelties, guilty of many murders including those of close relatives, a sly and unreliable political trickster. In the 1590s his own associates in the *tusi* government of Bozhou began to complain about his behavior to the Chinese provincial authorities. His family, however, had a long record of loyal service. Yang Yinglong personally had contributed materials of great value to the throne,[63] and he was seen as a supplier of military forces available to be used against a Qiang uprising in western Sichuan, and later against the Japanese when they invaded Korea in 1595. For such reasons the punishments proposed by provincial authorities were vetoed by the court in favor of a negotiated resolution. Matters dragged on for several years while Yang slyly watched for opportunities to make himself indispensable, all the while militantly pursuing his personal advantage within Bozhou. The court and the provincial officials offered many negotiated alternatives to war to settle the problems; Yang always pretended to comply, then regained his freedom and resumed his depredations.

By 1599 it had become clear to all that Yang had to be captured and his control of Bozhou ended. A vigorous provincial official, Li Hualong (1554–1612), drew the attention of the court; he was given a specially created position of supreme commander over the military forces of the three provinces—Sichuan, Huguang, and Guizhou—on whose territories the conflict impinged. A precocious *jinshi* degree winner at the age of twenty, Li was one of several civil officials of the mid- and late Ming who distinguished themselves in the management of military affairs. After serving on the Liaodong front at the time of the Japanese invasion of Korea in the 1590s, he was recognized for his expertise when he was called to organize the defeat of Yang Yinglong.[64] The Miao people over whom Yang had influence were spread throughout the three provinces, and the task of suppressing him required the combined resources of all three. Li Hualong organized a composite force totaling a quarter-million soldiers, 30 percent Chinese government forces and 70 percent non-Chinese from various *tusi* in neighboring provinces. It was one of the largest and most successful of the entire dynasty's domestic military undertakings. Armies drove on Yang Yinglong's base simultaneously from the three provinces adjacent to Bozhou, and after almost four months succeeded in forcing his suicide, capturing his family and staff officers, and eradicating the Yang family's power. Bozhou was transferred to Guizhou Province, divided into two regular prefectural units, and its native offices abolished; a kind of peace was thus brought to the region.[65]

The case of Yang Yinglong is extreme because of the size of the region he controlled and the length of time that he was able to prevail in his destructive behavior. One can be certain that the accounts are one-sided, but even so it is difficult to discern any mitigating circumstances, any sense of righteousness in his defiance of the Ming authority, any justice in his claims against the state. It is likely that the Miao people over whom he was absolute ruler had claims of injustice against him as well as against the Chinese, but that could not explain his insurrection. Whether we blame the native leaders or their Chinese overlords, the *tusi* system often brought disaster to the communities of native people.

To summarize some points made evident by the history of southwest China under the Ming, the Chinese government's interest in the *tusi* system was control, not governing per se. Because of that, few questions were asked about abuses, nor was political effectiveness itself much discussed. Some of the worst cases of misgoverning to be sure involved collusion with Chinese officials, and some of the suffering of native peoples in the minority regions resulted from the protected status of Chinese settlers, merchants, and soldiers. But much of the ruthless exploitation of the native peoples also was imposed by their chieftains, whose tenure in office was dependent *not* on how much goodwill they earned from their own people but on how few problems they caused the Chinese government. By emphasizing control over governing, the Chinese encouraged the degeneration of native leadership institutions. And all too often, Chinese leaders in the border areas also misused their power and, like military officers and eunuchs on the northern borders, earned the contempt of the local people.

Most modern scholars emphasize that the *tusi* system greatly enhanced the Ming government's authority and security in the southwest. That, however, appears to be a superficial assessment. Although the system was useful in effecting the transition from the Yuan to the Ming in the late fourteenth century, it is difficult to argue that it worked well enough thereafter to justify its retention through Ming and Qing and into the twentieth century. Yet it is one of the most intriguing aspects of traditional Chinese government, one that should be understood in relation to the realities of that time.

v. The Maritime Borders of Eastern China

Physically, half of the 4,000-mile coast that forms China's eastern boundary is not hospitable to shipping; good natural harbors are found where rugged mountains come down to the coast, making inlets and promontories and deep-water bays where ships can anchor and receive some protection from storms, and where ports can be built. Coastal configurations of that kind are found from the Vietnamese border north through Guangdong, Fujian, and Zhejiang provinces as far as Hangzhou Bay. North of that, they are found only on the Shandong Peninsula and, in the Northeast (Manchuria), on the Liaodong Peninsula. Otherwise, where the Yangzi, the Huai, and the Yellow rivers (and the smaller rivers in between) flow into the sea, accumulations of their heavy silt loads have built up new alluvial coastal plains bordering shallow seas with shifting sandbars. Navigation is difficult, and access to coastal places, even into the mouths of the rivers, is also rendered difficult.

The silt deposits that have steadily extended the east coast into the shallow offshore seas and clogged river channels near their mouths have in those ways brought very significant alterations to the earth's surface during historical times. Former ports have become inland cities, transport routes have been altered, offshore islands and shifting sandbars have appeared, and large new coastal plains have been created (Map 20).

An enduring misconception of Chinese history must be scuttled: China has a very long and successful history as a maritime power. Many Chinese do not understand that, nor do many in the West.[66] To be sure, China's was not much like the more familiar histories of other maritime peoples, in that the Chinese state and its official policy relegated the seafaring activities of China's coastal population to a third-rate place in the nation's life. China did not think of those activities as offering a seaborne extension of state power, unless

MAP 20

Zheng He's great voyages in the early fifteenth century provide a brief exception. Nor did any Chinese government compete with neighboring nations and commit its energies to naval warfare over issues of dominance at sea. China recognized seaborne international trade as a source of revenues, but it rarely attempted to rationalize or maximize tariff income, and was quite willing to forgo that source of state revenue entirely when attendant issues intervened. All of those negative observations bear on the role of the state in maritime warfare and commerce.

When we look past the state's role, all the other features of China's history as a seagoing people are highly positive. China contributed importantly to the technology of seafaring. It built large ships, sailed them long distances by using an increasingly sophisticated navigational science and technology, created ports and facilities, and handled impressive amounts of goods from distant places. During Tang and Song times, when Chinese vessels reached lengths of from 200 to 300 feet and had cargo capacities of from 600 to 1,000 tons, those were the largest seagoing ships in the world. By early Ming times the size of Chinese ships had reached 400 feet in length and more than 3,000 tons burden, again the largest in the world. Chinese ships regularly sailed up and down the coast of China to Korea, Japan, and the Philippines, through the islands of Southeast Asia, and on to India.[67] China's ports, particularly its most important port cities in Guangdong and Fujian provinces on the southeast coast, were filled with ships from India, the Arab states, Persian Gulf ports, and the nearer nations of the western Pacific.

China, then, was a maritime power. The Chinese state became directly involved in promoting and expanding China's maritime activities only once, in the first third of the fifteenth century, when Admiral Zheng He's famed voyages to the "Western Oceans" took vast fleets of immense vessels to India, the Persian Gulf, and East Africa (see Chapter 24, Section IV). At other times the Chinese government regularly maintained a more modest fleet of seagoing military vessels, used for moving troops and in naval battles against coastal pirates.

What is not generally noted is that Chinese private merchant shipping had preceded Zheng He by centuries, and continued after the government abandoned its sponsorship of the great expeditions in the 1430s. Privately built merchant ships were not as large as Zheng He's 400-foot-plus "Treasure Ships"; they had to be more economical, but they were capacious, seaworthy, and numerous. They kept the Chinese naval tradition alive and well throughout Ming times. Private junks of 600–800 tons cargo capacity probably were the standard for large private merchant ships in Ming times, but most cargo was carried in smaller ships that could serve coastal routes as well as enter the major rivers.[68]

Why then is pre–nineteenth-century China described as a land-oriented continental power that turned all its attention to its inland borders? Quite simply because that was true. Most Ming dynasty Chinese would have accepted that characterization as accurate, even as ideally appropriate. Seafaring to the Chinese was associated with piracy and implied unruly, uncontrollable behavior. Commerce was not idealized in China as a proper route to wealth and social standing (although in fact it was that), and the motives of merchants out on the seas, free of the Chinese bureaucracy's oversight, were assumed to be nefarious. Much of Ming China's historical experience reinforced those prejudicial views.

As the East Asian economies matured and technology advanced, peoples in Korea, Japan, China, and the coasts of peninsular and insular Southeast Asia all found that the sea could supplement livelihoods when opportunities on land failed. From modest fishing industries to coastal movement of goods, they improved their technology, built larger ships, and expanded to more ambitious searches for wealth in international trade. By the fourteenth century, when the Ming dynasty was founded, seagoing freebooters based in Japanese and Chinese coastal ports and offshore islands practiced forms of maritime commerce that increasingly became indistinguishable from piracy. The Chinese preferred to call the participants "Wokou" (Japanese, Wakô), by which they meant "Japanese pirates." It was recognized that they colluded with Chinese merchant seamen and that they were privately, or at least locally, organized in Japan. It was largely in order to work with "the King of Japan," as the Yongle emperor addressed the Ashikaga shoguns, that he sought to formalize relations and secure official cooperation in suppressing the freebooters. That effort was fairly successful in the early decades of the fifteenth century. And it again demonstrated to the Chinese that bureaucratic controls were the appropriate way to deal with the troublesome irregularities of international commerce, something in any event better discouraged than utilized as an instrument of state. Chinese who insisted on building ships and going abroad in pursuit of trade were outlawed. When initiated by non-Chinese, such trade was either put under elaborate controls or banned altogether. Subsumed under the tribute system of international relations, its economic dimensions were officially regarded as being secondary to the rituals of interstate diplomacy.

That response to trade at sea exactly paralleled the response to Mongol demands for overland trade on the northern borders. In both cases the unrealistic Chinese response failed to control the problem. At sea, the international pressure for trade grew explosively and led to the serious incursions of "Japanese pirates" in the decades of the 1550s and 1560s.[69] The Wokou raids led to grave depredations of the Jiangsu and Zhejiang coasts. The Chinese were hard-pressed to defend against them, for many of the participants were Chinese traders-become-pirates who knew the terrain, colluded with Chinese on shore to conduct their raids, then fled to the safety of their island strongholds, or even to their permanently established bases in Japanese ports such as Hirada and Sakai. Some of the leading Chinese pirates were born in Japan of mixed marriages.[70] Some built safe-haven bases in Taiwan and the Pescadores.[71] Some were beginning to understand how to work with the new entrants into the field—the Dutch seafarers based in what we now call Indonesia, and their rivals the Portuguese, based in that nation's new empire in India and the Straits of Malacca.

The pirate entrepreneurs were truly international in their attitudes, in their polylingual skills, and in sharing the techniques of commerce and seafaring brought into the region by their Asian and European counterparts. The Chinese quickly became important actors in the new enterprise, analogous to the European adventurers who were then building the Portuguese, Spanish, Dutch, and English mercantile empires in Asia. These Chinese maritime entrepreneurs represent the vigor and imagination, the capacity for organization and the freewheeling enterprise latent in late Ming China. Official China, serene in its certainty about the Great Way of civilization, ignored the potential they represented. Shizong, the Jiajing emperor, was particularly hostile to any changes in the Ming restrictions on foreign trade. During his reign from 1522 to 1567, the pirate raids intensified, reaching crisis proportions in the 1550s. They were put down with very great effort and cost to the rich coastal regions of eastern China, but the potential for their resumption remained high. It was in the year after Shizong's death that the court at last lifted the ban on Chinese participation in overseas trade, shifting the energies of the seafarers into other modes. It is no coincidence that in the decade following Emperor Shizong's death, trading opportunities for Mongols also were broadened, bringing peace to what had been a century of increasingly turbulent relations on the northern border.

The Portuguese Asian empire was of more direct significance to Ming China than the other European activities in East Asia. Its founder was Afonso de Albuquerque (1453–1515). Named the viceroy of Portuguese India, he captured the trading entrepôt of Hormuz in the Persian Gulf, built the main base of the new empire at Goa on the west coast of India in 1510, and in 1511 sent a fleet to capture Malacca on the Malayan Peninsula. In those places his navy found many Chinese vessels in the ports, and noted that valuable products from China were a major element in trade. Malacca became the outpost from which the Portuguese would attempt to penetrate China.

Portuguese from Malacca reached China as early as 1514, and in 1517 the first group of ships sailed into the harbor of Canton.[72] There were misunderstandings with the Chinese, probably caused by inadequate interpreting. These led to what the Chinese considered criminal behavior not to be excused even among barbarians: the Portuguese sailors fired cannons into the harbor, and once on shore beat and mistreated Chinese in the streets. The ships were forced to withdraw before negotiations about trade could take place, but they had left on shore in Canton the first European ambassador sent to China since Mongol times. He was Tomé Pirez, who spent two years in Canton before being allowed to make the overland journey northward. He never saw the Chinese emperor, either at Nanjing (where Emperor Wuzong happened to be in 1520) or subsequently in Beijing, where the same emperor died the following spring. Pirez was ordered to return to Canton to depart the country, but there local officials imprisoned him, holding him responsible for the earlier misbehavior of the Portuguese. He appears to have died in prison in 1524.[73] It was a most inauspicious beginning for Sino-European diplomatic contacts.

The Portuguese continued to seek out other ports on the southeast coast and tried other devices for being granted access to trade, but kept coming back to the estuary of the Pearl River, today dominated by Hong Kong. They found a small peninsula on the southwest side of the estuary and there conducted trade fairs when their ships arrived, buying rich Chinese goods, mainly silks, to trade throughout the region or to take back to Europe. The lively carrying trade within East Asian waters brought rich returns and helped pay for the new mercantile empires. In the 1540s an understanding was worked out with Chinese on the scene in Guangdong to allow the Portuguese to build a permanent town at the end of the peninsula, sealed off from China by a fortified wall and a gate across its narrowest point. This small site with its reasonably good harbor was only about two square miles in area. The Portuguese called it the City of the Name of God of Macao in China. As Macao it soon became a substantial international city; its harbor was improved, docks and service facilities were built and factories, churches, and schools set up. The Portuguese paid the Chinese government an annual rent for it until the mid-nineteenth century, then repudiated that relationship and unilaterally declared it a Portuguese colony under international law.

Macao sustained a growing European presence in late Ming China and greatly facilitated the access to China by Europeans of all nations. Until the opening of China after the Opium War in 1840–1842, all envoys, missionaries, businessmen, and adventurers coming from elsewhere on their way to China used it as their first destination, their place to prepare, to study the Chinese language and to hire bilingual Chinese assistants, and to become acclimated to East Asia.

Macao was above all the base from which the European Jesuits managed their penetration of China. Here individual Jesuit missionaries prepared for their work among the Chinese, printed books for that use, trained Chinese to assist them, and sent supplies needed by the Jesuits at the court in Beijing. Macao developed a large arsenal utilizing the best European science in the design and manufacture of weapons, especially cannons. Artillery pieces from Macao, and experts trained there, served the Ming court from the 1640s to the dynasty's end, and found themselves performing the same services for the Manchus after 1644. The story of Macao, one of the most colorful chapters in Asian history, fully repays further reading.[74]

By the end of the Ming dynasty, the Dutch, the English, the Spanish in the Philippines, and other Europeans had joined the Portuguese in building mercantile empires in Asia. Much of the inducement for that effort was China: it had countless souls to be saved, and a fabulous potential for trade. A final chapter in the present volume explores ways those sometimes competing but more often reinforcing motives brought the European powers and China into the first phase of a new relationship of profound interaction. The long-disregarded eastern or maritime frontier soon would outpace all of China's other borders in significance for Chinese history, although that fact would not be widely recognized in China until the nineteenth century.

28

LATE MING
POLITICAL DECLINE,
1567–1627

After the death of Emperor Shizong, the Jiajing emperor, who died in 1567, the four reigns that followed in the sixty years until 1627 were dominated by the longest Ming reign, that of Shenzong, the Wanli emperor. The Chinese government and people endured him for forty-eight of those sixty years. In the histories of each of those four reigns, we see patterns of political decline, showing how imperial incompetence triumphed over the best efforts of many dedicated public servants to bring about lasting reversal of the degenerating patterns. The problem was larger than simply the personalities of individual emperors, and there is much in this history of rulers and their courts that helps us to understand the course of Chinese civilization. A different story of China in later Ming times lies outside the palaces and the halls of government; it is the larger story of a vigorously growing and changing society, the focus of Chapter 29. In this chapter, however, along with evidence for the political decline, we see a concomitant feature of political life: an unbroken flow, from all manner of families, of men intent on the renovation of the entire social order. If they did not succeed in accomplishing that, even as dynastic crises multiplied, neither did they lose confidence in their civilization.

I. THE BRIEF REIGN OF EMPEROR MUZONG, 1567–1572

The unloved Emperor Shizong died at the beginning of 1567, leaving his court in the strong hands of Xu Jie (1503–1583), a senior Grand Secretary of undoubted talent if one less than scrupulous in his personal affairs. He is a most interesting case: the son of a clerk who had made his way into the lowest ranks of officialdom, Xu Jie placed third in the *jinshi* examinations of 1523. His rapid career advancement thereafter enabled his family in one generation to become among the richest landholders of Songjiang Prefecture, near Shanghai. That of course aroused rumors of impropriety, and brought impeachment charges from the crusading censor, Hai Rui (see Chapter 26, Section V). Xu Jie had succeeded Yan Song as chief Grand Secretary in 1562, but he was forced into retirement in 1568, having lasted long enough in that position to do little more than help launch the new reign that began in February 1567. Jockeying for leadership of the Neige (cabinet) by a strong *shoufu* (chief Grand Secretary) and competing with other Grand Secretaries for the emperor's approval had become the pattern in the Jiajing reign and would continue. To his credit, Emperor Shizong weakened what for a century had been the growing influence of chief eunuchs, who at many times achieved greater power than the cabinet officials. While weakening eunuch power, the emperor maintained his obsessively suspicious-minded personal control over appointments and policies at the court; he was the master, if not the leader, of his government.

Emperor Shizong's successor in February 1567 was his third son, Zhu Zaihou, the Emperor Muzong, whose reign of five and one-half years bears the reign period name Longqing.[1] It was common knowledge at court that Shizong despised this eldest living son, deeply regretting that his second son, born five months earlier than Zhu Zaihou, had died in 1547, and that a fourth son, born one month later than Zhu Zaihou, could not be named the heir. Zhu Zaihou was reared in shabby circumstances, had little or no contact with his father, and was never named heir apparent or allowed to believe that he actually would succeed to the throne. In the end, however, Shizong's posthumous edict named Zhu Zaihou the successor to the Jiajing reign, much to the relief of both the conservative-minded officialdom and the thirty-year-old heir himself.

The Longqing emperor, to use Zhu Zaihou's reign period name, was an affable, relatively serious man who had long been intimidated and subjected to restraints by his father. On coming to the throne he took pleasure in approving a number of important changes long resisted by Shizong. His short reign is often overlooked. He had no extraordinary qualities and came to be disdained by his high officials for his unseemly pursuit of pleasure, once he was released from the restrictions and humiliations of his long waiting period. The important changes, however, merit our attention.

As was customary, Xu Jie, who was *shoufu* at the time of the previous emperor's death, in conjunction with Zhang Juzheng, whom both Xu and the new emperor trusted as a statesman of undoubted intellectual ability, drafted the deceased emperor's "last edict," in effect his will (confirming Zhu Zaihou's succession), and then further drafted the new emperor's accession edict. The new emperor of course acted on his own as an adult in approving these essential documents, and their content no doubt reflects conversations Zhang had held with Muzong when he was still the prince impatiently awaiting his turn to rule. The two documents promised to "eradicate abuses" (referring to getting rid of the Daoist adepts at the court and terminating the lavish support of their religious activities) and to "implement the new" (fiscal and management reforms aiming to reduce expenditures and tighten up the fiscal system). These reforms were widely welcomed, and Zhu Zaihou became something of an instant popular hero.

The most interesting event in the conduct of the central government of the time is surely the entrance into the cabinet of Zhang Juzheng (1525–1582), who first became a Grand Secretary at the time of Emperor Muzong's enthronement in early 1567. Zhang (like others in the cabinet at that time) had previously served as the emperor's tutor in the years following 1563 when the future emperor was already a man in his late twenties. Muzong recognized Zhang's extraordinary qualities and the force of his original ideas on governing. Zhang's influence grew throughout the Longqing reign, and when the emperor died in 1572, Zhang's political adroitness enabled him to become chief Grand Secretary within a month, able to dominate the court through the transition into the reign of Muzong's nine-year-old son, the Wanli emperor. He exerted total mastery over the government through the next ten years; expanding the scope of the chief Grand Secretary's powers to make him the effective head of both Inner and Outer Courts and of the entire bureaucratic establishment. He was the most able administrator of the later Ming.

While there is general agreement on Zhang Juzheng's extraordinary abilities, historians give quite different assessments of the emperor's personal qualities. Zhu Zaihou often sat through meetings of the court without uttering more than a few grunts because he suffered from a speech impairment that made him stutter and stammer. It was so severe that he was forced to delegate court officials to speak and read for him, even the most important ritual pronouncements that normally the emperor himself should utter. At best he probably had only ordinary intelligence, yet he was intent on improving the conduct of government and therefore was an unfailing supporter of the strong men in his cabinet. That in itself was a rare circumstance in Ming times. In part, to be sure, he supported the reformers in the spirit of revenge for the despicable way his father had treated him, yet there is good evidence that he wanted to be taken seriously. The traditional sources have overpraised him because he was susceptible to scholar-officials' advice, and the truth lies somewhere in between his having been at most an earnest ruler and having been a perceptive leader of governmental reform. The former probably comes closer to the truth.[2]

The one dimension of rulership to which he was vigorously, even obsessively devoted, all his courtiers would agree, was his reign over the women's quarters of the inner palaces; there he single-mindedly gave his all—to the point of engaging more fields of conquest than even his robust physique could long sustain.

His reign of five and one-half years nevertheless should be remembered for the impulses set forth in the accession edict and the actions which followed from it. As emperor, he shared Xu Jie's distaste for his father's Daoist religious excesses, and he also reacted against Shizong's harshly vindictive, manipulative style. Even when attacks from political rivals forced Xu Jie to retire within the year, the Neige, or cabinet, was left in the hands of other able Grand

Secretaries, among whom Zhang Juzheng quickly became the most influential. They kept the government on a steady course through these years, while Zhang Juzheng was quietly launching his well-worked-out plans to reform the central administration and meet the severe fiscal crisis that dogged later Ming government.

Many who had been punished for opposing Shizong in his later years were released from prison, or posthumously rehabilitated, in special amnesties. Widespread tax remissions helped to relieve conditions among the farming population, then beset by natural calamities made more difficult by Shizong's irregular increases in tax quotas. Steps also were taken to curb improper land seizures by imperial relatives and favorites; "imperial estates" once again had to be returned to their rightful owners, and examples were made of those whose abuses were particularly flagrant.

Muzong also appears to have held less restrictive views of commerce than his predecessors. In 1567, following Shizong's death and soon after the most severe phase of the "Japanese pirate" incursions had been overcome, he took the bold step (under Zhang Juzheng's influence) of lifting the long-standing ban on Chinese participation in maritime trade. That was a landmark change of policy; it contributed much to the prosperity of the entire trading community and especially the southeast coastal region. He also eased restrictions on domestic commerce, a progressive step that contributed to growth in the economy.

Emperor Muzong's reign also saw important developments in China's relations with the resurgent Mongols; he supported the reasonable alternatives to the unproductive confrontations of his father's reign. He restored and greatly broadened the open trading policy and, in 1571, took the step of enfeoffing the Mongol leader Altan Khan with the title Prince Shunyi ("compliant and righteous"). Altan Khan was the same leader who directed the incursions into China in the late 1540s and early 1550s, including the attack on Beijing in October 1550, of which Muzong, then a thirteen-year-old boy, had fearful memories. Twenty years later, both the Mongol khan and Muzong were inclined to be more accommodating; the Chinese took steps that met some principal Mongol grievances and reversed the long-standing failed policies.

A number of domestic policies were of similar novelty and significance. Emperor Shizong had intimidated the censorial and investigative officials, blocking the "avenue of words" that was expected to function as a check on the governors, including the ruler himself. Muzong encouraged these officials to regain their expected roles. Performance in governing at all levels, from the Grand Secretaries and ministers at the center to lowly magistrates in the provinces, were made subject to performance reviews and ratings; these for the first time also included a rigorous examination of the way officials assigned to administer the princely establishments performed. Thus a major source of corruption and malfeasance in the provinces was curbed. Those measures revealed all manner of entrenched malpractice, and led to the Ministry of Personnel being charged with making more careful selection of men for appointment.

Military morale also became the subject of attention. Zhang Juzheng, probably to amuse Muzong and make him feel important, called for an imperial review of the troops, an elaborate affair only once previously conducted in Ming times. The units to be reviewed by the emperor in person in the autumn of 1569 were required to weed out all overaged and incompetent men. The rest were carefully drilled and trained and given new uniforms. Their commanders then were allowed to parade them under the ruler's intent gaze, to the delight of the entire court and a cheering mass audience. It was a costly and impressive spectacle, but it had profound impact on the morale of the usually denigrated military.

Despite these hopeful beginnings, Emperor Muzong quickly degenerated; on coming to the throne he began to make up for lost time in the inner quarters of his palaces, insatiably seeking pleasures. High officials who had advised him when he was a prince became shocked and dismayed by reports of his profligacy; those who submitted memorials outlining the consequences for his health, his dignity, and the proper functioning of his government were punished. Zhang Juzheng took no stand, observing the rapid decline into physical exhaustion and mental distraction, perhaps resigned to a change of rule in which he was well positioned with the heir to continue his constructive changes. That opportunity came when Muzong fell ill, lingered for a few months, and died in July 1572.

II. Zhang Juzheng's Leadership and the Wanli Reign

The Wanli emperor, named Zhu Yijun, was born on September 4, 1563, when his father was still the expectant heir; he came to the throne at age nine in July 1572, so his Wanli reign period, which began with the new year of 1573, ran until his death in the summer of 1620, making it the longest reign of the Ming dynasty. His posthumous temple name is Shenzong.[3] Zhu Yijun was quite different from his father; he was exceptionally, even precociously intelligent, as a boy interested on the one hand in horseback riding and archery, on the other in calligraphy and poetry. It appeared he might become a model emperor, well informed, perceptive, and conscientious, but circumstances turned him into a cynical, suspicious, lazy, and self-indulgent ruler who refused to bear the burdens of active participation in his government. Those "circumstances" were both the particular conditions of his early years and the general character of bureaucratic governing in his time. Both those sets of conditions help to explain the larger contours of later Ming history.

The particular circumstances that dominated his early years were those peculiar to his palace upbringing. As men whose boyhood had been spent in that unnatural environment, no Ming emperors ever knew what might be called "normal" family relationships. All had to learn how to be adult males without experiencing the close guidance of fathers and other male relatives; from puberty onward they were estranged even from their brothers. The Wanli emperor's deeply pious Buddhist "senior mother" (the Longqing

hypocrisies in mouthing all the while their formulaic ethical maxims. He went so far as to praise the firm standards maintained by the First Emperor of Qin in the third century B.C.E., the Legalist monster of early imperial history who was vilified ever thereafter.[6]

Zhang was not beguiled by ancient Legalist doctrines as such, but in the firmness of the Qin dynasty's commitment to laws and standards he saw a means to stabilize governing and achieve a peaceful realm. Qin's First Emperor, in contrast, had glorified war as the essential activity of the state and harshness as an indispensable tool of government. Zhang favored neither. In praising the unbridled despotism of the Ming founder, Zhang did not display a very profound understanding of early Ming government. Also disturbing is his praise of the Yongle emperor's usurpation as something made necessary by vague and softheaded altruism on the part of the Jianwen emperor and his bookish if courageous advisers. The tenor of his age perhaps drove him to exaggerate this point, but it does not show his thinking at its best. He did not in fact subscribe to political ideas matching those of the despots he praised: he did not value harshness and rigidity, much less the use of terror.

Zhang Juzheng did, however, believe in the strong state and wished to bring laxity and underperformance to an end. Yet while he expressed firm support for the Mencian tenet that the good of the people is the sole reason for the state to exist, we cannot imagine that he would have tolerated a meddling personality like Mencius, who 2,000 years earlier had pestered the ruler with abrupt questions and offered sententious advice. If Zhang was not a profound analyst of government or of the political lessons of past history, he was nevertheless a vigorous doer with a great sense of responsibility to govern effectively. The Ming dynasty produced no other Grand Secretary of similar qualities or of comparable achievement.

Zhang Juzheng's importance in Ming government is that he effected a broad range of administrative changes. Some were timely restorations of proper standards in administering and governing; some were thoroughly implemented innovations in managing the state. In the former category were his continuations of the bureaucratic reforms instituted under the Longqing emperor between 1567 and 1572, many of which he had initiated even though at that time he was not yet the senior Grand Secretary. Throughout the ten years of his incumbency as the *shoufu*, from July 1572 until his death in July 1582, the atmosphere clearly remained that of Confucian-style government of men rather than a more fully rationalized government of laws and methods, but it became better regulated and more efficient. It regained its long-dissipated morale.

As in civil governing, so also in the military sphere Zhang is credited with having eliminated many flagrant abuses. In particular, he appointed a group of genuinely competent men to military government posts on the borders. The most famous of them was the military tactician Qi Jiguang (1528–1588), appointed on Zhang's insistence to the command of Jizhou, the strategic bastion to the east of Beijing responsible for guarding that doorway to the capital.[7] With Zhang's encouragement to half a dozen commanders of that caliber, military performance was restored to levels not known for a century. At the same time, Zhang, who had supported at the court Wang Chonggu's rapprochement with Altan Khan in 1570, continued to further the new era of understanding with the Mongols by facilitating the growth of trade in which they could more freely participate.[8]

Through his strenuous supervisory measures, Zhang Juzheng greatly enhanced performance in governing, but he is best remembered for his administrative innovations. The broadest in scope was the nationwide cadastral survey which he undertook starting in 1578. He ordered that all the landholdings recorded in all the survey registers in local government offices be remeasured, using new mathematics and more precise calculation, and clearing out all the accumulated data that bore no relation to actual conditions. That was accompanied by a remeasuring of all lands registered under military households; these registers were held by the Ministry of War and not subject to local civil government. More than 7 million *qing* of unregistered or fraudulently concealed private landholdings (one *qing* equaled about seventeen English acres) were uncovered, some confiscated, and all returned to the tax registers. It was an immense task requiring several years.

In 1581, even before the survey could be completed, but seeing that it had reached a substantial level of accomplishment, he then led the government to adopt the so-called Single Whip method of allocating tax and labor service obligations on the farming and landholding population. This was the first major alteration of the taxation system since the great reforms of Yang Yan in 780, 800 years earlier, in the late Tang period. Yang Yan's system, a momentous step forward for its time, was called the *liangshui fa,* or "system of two taxes," meaning the "summer tax" on the early grain harvest and the "autumn tax," the principal source of revenue, levied on the main harvest. It also included levies of labor and other service obligations.[9] By late Ming times the system had acquired many complications and inefficiencies; it was badly in need of rationalizing reform, and that had caused prefectural and county-level administrators to begin to innovate early in the sixteenth century. In simplest terms, the basic system of "two taxes" on harvests was retained, but the complex array of service levies and grain taxes was almost entirely commuted to payment in silver; all the tax obligations were listed together into "one registry" *(yitiaobian)* and calculated as one tax. Because *yitiaobian* sounds like the word meaning "one whip," the Chinese name was often written as "Single Whip," an apt description of the way the new system worked.

The impulse for land tax reform was strong. The innovating experiments in the provinces varied in detail but agreed in essentials. Eventually the change was recognized by the center, to be uniformly implemented thereafter. All the payments in all categories of taxation were commuted to payment in silver and paid to the government in several installments over the course of a year.[10]

Zhang Juzheng's role was not to conceive the change, for it arose quite pragmatically at the local level, but to recognize its utility and ensure its implementation by the central government, against all the inertia and countervailing interests that had grown up around the old system. The effort probably could not have succeeded under any other leadership or at any other time during the Ming dynasty. Had Zhang lived a few years longer, the registration of the new cadastral surveys would have been completed throughout the land, and the uniform application of the new tax system undoubtedly would have been more successfully carried out. Without the integrating force of his continued leadership, those reforms remained somewhat ad hoc, but nonetheless had broad and deep impact, despite resistance from the court, the imperial household, and many in the scholar-official elite.

Ten years is a very long time in the leadership of the Inner Court and the government. Zhang's influence began to be challenged before his death. In 1577 his father died, at a time when if he had withdrawn from his official posts to observe the mandatory twenty-seven months of mourning at his father's graveside, all his reform measures would have been imperiled. The fourteen-year-old Wanli emperor immediately drafted an edict of condolence in his own hand, gave Zhang lavish gifts, and requested that he not return immediately to his native place in Hubei but "set aside his feelings" *(duo qing)* in order to remain on the job. The request of course was made with Zhang's concurrence; everyone recognized that he was willing to ignore his ethical duty so that he could remain at his post. This was not a minor issue. Precedents for bypassing the mourning obligation were few, and mostly involved genuine state emergencies in which it could be said that the bereaved son sacrificed his primary interest (his obligation to his ancestors) in order to serve his sovereign. It was difficult to argue that this was such a circumstance, but Zhang's son and a representative of the emperor were sent to conduct the mourning ceremonies while he remained in Beijing.

The pressures on him to forgo the usual mourning formalities, however, were not fabricated. The emperor's wedding arrangements were under way, and the empress dowager told Zhang that she was quite dependent on him to supervise the lavish affair. Early the following year, after the imperial wedding had been conducted, Zhang himself received permission to go in person to supervise the burial, but not to remain for the required mourning period. Throughout the four-month sojourn local officials, under instructions from the court, gave Zhang the most devoted attention and luxurious hospitality. That too became the subject of sniping criticism.

There followed an opportunistic hue and cry over Zhang's moral lapse. The emperor issued a decree ordering that the criticism be silenced, but like wolves baying at a wounded stag, political enemies continued to harry Zhang. It became an issue in the academies *(shuyuan)*, many of which had been organized privately during the mid-sixteenth century as gathering places where scholars shared ideas, urged one another on in the pursuit of political careers, and formed groups of like-minded men. Most academies were not hotbeds of political agitation; but the growth of academies broadened the environment in which young men preparing for careers in public life formed personal associations that later on often shaped their lives.[11] It has been noted in Chapter 26 that reforming impulses in the world of thought and learning had been greatly stimulated by the followers of the most important Ming period Neo-Confucian thinker, Wang Yangming (1472–1529). There was a proliferation of post-Wang sub-schools, some of them displaying socially radical tendencies. Other intellectual camps were opposed to Wang school radical idealism and struggled to restore the more conservative ideas of the orthodox Zhu Xi tradition. Court and government were beginning to be filled with partisans of the movements stemming from the academies, in which many scholar-officials had been trained before sitting for their civil service examinations.

Zhang Juzheng was not partisan to any of these factional stances and had little sympathy for their ideas. Seeing that the academies at this juncture pounced on his moral lapse in failing to observe proper mourning, in 1579 he issued a broad-ranging ban on the academies, especially the privately founded ones, and had them closed or their properties put to other uses. This clearly was an attempt to quell opposition.[12] Tensions between the government and the associations of scholars within officialdom would recur to the end of the dynasty. Opposition from the academies did not weaken Zhang's governing while he remained alive, but it left a heritage of political dissension that took many forms in the decades following his death.

Zhang died in 1582 after an incapacitating illness, at age fifty-seven. He was richly rewarded with posthumous honors and gifts, but almost immediately his enemies began to submit articles of impeachment against his sons, implicating Zhang himself in charges such as improperly enriching himself, misusing his authority, mistreating imperial relatives, being guilty of licentious behavior in his private life, and all manner of issues. The emperor, now going on twenty years old and happy to be free of Zhang's supervision, had the charges investigated, in his mind willing to believe them. Some of them appeared to have merit: Zhang was found to have left vast wealth. The emperor remembered Zhang's constant appeals to frugality in the imperial household and to his personal austerity, and felt he had been defrauded. His long-latent resentment came to the fore, and he made it his personal vendetta to take posthumous revenge. Zhang's family were destroyed and his influence weeded out. The old eunuch Feng Bao, in service to the court for more than fifty years and Zhang's associate through the early Wanli years, was demoted to a menial post at Nanjing, where he soon died. An anti-Zhang mood filled the court even as the old statesman's powerful image lingered on in the consciousness of officialdom.

Many of Zhang Juzheng's administrative improvements remained in place, if not vigorously maintained after his death. The principal cause of political change thereafter came not from vigorous and able successors attempting either to exceed or to reverse Zhang's achievements, for none did. The altered manner of governing that followed Zhang Juzheng's outstanding career was brought about by a young emperor who at this point adopted a totally negative attitude toward officialdom, toward policy issues, and toward his personal responsibility. He was disillusioned about the failings of bureaucrats, and his scorn led him to ignore them. Simultaneously he grew into a most perverse ruler, addicted to alcohol and sex, infinitely avaricious, and petulantly defiant toward his courtiers. His mother, who previously had relied on Zhang Juzheng, became wholly immersed in Buddhist pieties and gave no further attention to her responsibilities; in fact, the emperor in 1583 convinced her that by confiscating Zhang's family wealth, he could donate large funds to her Buddhist causes. She happily intervened no further in state and dynastic matters.

No one on the scene reminded court and government that Zhang had been the great servant of the state, a man to whom gratitude was owed. Not until forty years later, under succeeding rulers, were moves initiated within officialdom to restore Zhang's good name, return his titles and honors, and rehabilitate surviving members of his family. In the crises of the dynasty's last decades, his kind of strong leadership was looked back upon with admiration. But in the still confident 1580s, the imperial family regarded him in much the same way as they did the faithful eunuch Feng Bao—as their personal servant, and the state as their personal realm. Throughout the Ming we have seen how earlier emperors demanded the independence of the imperial household from the court's oversight. At this time, ruler and imperial family were incapable of assessing a vigorous, reform-minded Grand Secretary as an asset to the state; to them he was but a private nuisance.

Zhang's successors not surprisingly relinquished his governing through firmness and replaced it with the time-honored, infinitely nuanced modes of compromise. His encompassing vision took second place to high officials' private considerations of precedent, propriety, and social convention. Among the elite, the sense of public obligation remained strong, but it was defined by other concerns, political to be sure, but seldom innovative or politically constructive.

That a man of Zhang's immense stature and power could be so quickly brought down became an object lesson for other officials. After Zhang, Grand Secretaries and other ambitious public figures sought first to guard their career interests, only thereafter to meet the challenges of governing. The quality of Ming rule, after sharply improving in reaction to the death of Emperor Shizong in 1567 and especially during Zhang's decade in power, 1572–1582, now again declined.

The Wanli Reign after Zhang Juzheng

The reign of the Wanli emperor, who was but nineteen years old when Zhang Juzheng died in 1582, would last another thirty-eight years, until his death in the summer of 1620. Those long decades were an interminable prolongation of an absurd situation: a very intelligent and well-educated ruler spent those thirty-eight years alternately fighting the system of imperial rule and civil government and ignoring both. He made a mockery of the grand ideal of the sage emperor. For years at a time he refused even to attend the meetings of his court or preside over rituals of state. He allowed thousands of memorials and reports to pile up in his study unopened, or if read, unacknowledged. He seldom met with his Inner Court officials and often refused to fill vacant offices. When he died he was granted the posthumous temple name Shenzong, the "Divine Ancestor," thereby capping the irony of his misspent rule.

His principal fault was avarice. He constantly demanded money from his government, wasted public funds for his personal purposes, and refused to draw on his privy purse to meet state needs even in times of greatest national emergency. He constantly demanded that taxes be increased, special surtaxes be added, and new areas of exploitation be opened. Most damaging to his reputation and to the people's well-being was his use of eunuch supervisors sent to the provinces to oversee mining operations. This led to spectacular abuses. It was popularly said that whether or not there were actual mines to operate, a "mine" would be opened wherever his agents felt they could extort profits. The people's productivity—whether in farming, crafts, or trade—constituted the "ore" he coveted. Mining became just a cover for extortion. Throughout his reign officials begged that the special mining superintendencies be abolished, but he always angrily rejected their pleas, punishing the petitioners. Since he was neither ignorant nor stupid, his behavior can be explained only as perversity; he knew precisely how dysfunctional his role in governing had become. He simply allowed his personal interests to prevail, yet not entirely without occasional pangs of conscience and responsibility.

The last decades of the sixteenth century and the first two of the seventeenth were not untroubled. North of the new Ming Great Wall, the Manchus under Nurhaci were set on conquest and had begun incursions into China. The Japanese under the formidable military leader Toyotomi Hideyoshi (1535–1598) invaded Korea in the 1590s; he boasted that he would go on from there to conquer China. To drive him back, large and expensive Chinese expeditionary forces were sent to Korea via the land route across southern Manchuria (see Chapter 30). The suppression of the aboriginal uprising led by Yang Yinglong in Sichuan at the end of the 1590s also required large expenditures and a major military effort. More directly pressing were the fiscal crises of the later Wanli period, and local discontent in many places where efforts to increase revenues aroused resistance. Finally, for twenty years the emperor was engaged in a tense struggle with his bureaucracy over the issue of naming his successor; not until 1601 did they at last force him to designate his eldest son, in accord with the house law of the dynasty. Yet that did not end the tension because the younger son favored by the emperor continued to live in the capital, improperly, for a dozen more years, leading to doubts about the final outcome.[13] From military challenges threatening the nation's security, to fiscal woes causing social unrest, to the struggle with morally aroused bureaucrats who once again sought to test the perennial issue of the court's role in ensuring stable dynastic succession, an unending spate of urgent problems fed partisan conflicts within the bureaucracy. Political life fell prey to the many stresses, as intense as any the dynasty had known.

The Donglin "Party"

Among all the associations of officials and candidates for officialdom, the one formed around the Donglin Academy at Wuxi in southern Jiangsu (on the Grand Canal just west of Suzhou) came to have the largest political role in late Ming times. The academy was founded in 1604. A group of thinkers and political activists, loyal to the orthodox teachings of Zhu Xi and opposed to the socially disruptive movements instigated by the later followers of Wang Yangming, received local permission to rebuild a private academy of Song times that had fallen into disuse. It was located in a willow grove on the eastern edge (*donglin* means "eastern grove") of Wuxi, in the prosperous and populous lower Yangzi region. Even before the academy was formally reestablished in 1604, advocates of moral causes had for some decades followed the pattern of forming study associations, ostensibly to investigate and discuss philosophical dimensions of important social issues, simultaneously to build political support for their concerted action. The new Donglin Academy prospered. Thousands were drawn to its lectures, and branches were formed in other cities of the region. However genuine its commitment to moral philosophy, it was a political movement. It focused directly on getting its members into government by influencing the standards that were applied in conducting the *jinshi* examinations and by lobbying for appointment of its members to high offices.[14]

The thinker who led the Donglin movement in that formative stage was Gu Xiancheng (1550–1612). In frustration he left his appointment at the capital in 1583, returned to Wuxi, his native place, and became a leader of what its practitioners liked to call "pure criticism." He and his fellow thinkers had opposed Zhang Juzheng (who died in 1582) for being a strong man of ambiguous ethical stance, and later opposed all powerful chief officials at court who did not espouse their particular mode of critical thinking. Gu was not an original thinker of importance, but he was a public figure of great presence and force, sincerely committed to reform ideas.[15] The younger members of the elite in particular flocked to hear his lectures and to discuss current politics with him.

The Donglin movement contributed very significantly to the recharged moral atmosphere of politics in the Wanli reign. Generally speaking, we can accept the "upright people" label which the Donglin partisans took for themselves; they were genuinely opposed to corruption and debased practices. As more of their associates won *jinshi* degrees, and as they reached high capital office including posts in the Grand Secretariat, they identified other members of the government as either friend or foe. In particular they opposed those routine politicians who were not ideologically committed but wished only to carry on in the established ways, tolerating malpractice in the interests of "social harmony." They opposed some unfairly; their moral fervor, as might be expected, made them awkward participants in practical governing. Yet to many, their forthright stance within the political arena seemed to offer an appropriate corrective.

The Donglin associates' moral cohesion earned them their designation *dang,* or "party." That was a term of reproach in late imperial China; the concept of "party" had been resoundingly rejected by the throne in the eleventh century.[16] Rulers then and thereafter always distrusted associations of officials pressing for their group goals. The throne repudiated the idea of officials serving group interests whenever that activity threatened to take political form, and used the label "party" to discredit it on moralistic grounds: to join in such factions and cliques was not something that the superior man would do, for his overriding loyalty to the ruler above should take precedence over lateral loyalty to his peers. Chinese officials were not feudal barons; they had no power base apart from the throne's control. Neither, however, could the throne attempt to govern without them.

In their disagreement over what constituted proper political behavior, both sides emphasized the purely moralistic issues. That had become the hallmark of later imperial political engagement, especially under the state's sponsorship of the Neo-Confucian Lixue scholarly ground of discourse, and diverted attention away from more rational analyses of governing. It can be argued that this profoundly characteristic feature of Chinese political culture had both positive and negative consequences. In any event, they were defining consequences.

The Donglin group came as close to functioning as a true party as any such movement in later imperial history. As partisans in group behavior, however, they were denied legitimacy in politics. They could not transcend the existing political context. In that atmosphere of debased infighting and personal attack, "to disagree with me is to be morally deficient." They remained a movement of diffused energies and ineffectual behavior, for all their capacity to expose the faults of their enemies. Hope for Chinese government does not seem to us today to have lain in that direction, yet that was the basic direction of politics for the remainder of the imperial era.

Hope, however, is what truly drove much of late Ming political behavior. Thousands of families at the lower fringes of elite status made sacrifices to educate a son or a nephew so he might sit for the examinations, and thousands more of still lower economic status worked toward achieving that same goal a generation or two farther down the road. Drawing on midlevel social strata as well as on the comfortable elite who without undue sacrifice could consign sons to preparation for civil service careers, the examination system continued to produce large numbers of able men who were deeply committed to government. And in the larger context, that hopeful commitment to individual and family achievement leavened the entire society.

The tone of irony is strong in the intellectual life of late Ming.[17] But it did not give way to a generalized cynicism—not yet in the Ming period. Able to laugh at flawed heroes, sophisticated later Ming intellectuals were still moved by ideals. Decade after decade, the triennial cohorts of new *jinshi* graduates came into government service, bringing many who wanted to serve as upright, loyal officials. The admired model of the honest, vigorous, and politically effective official remained fixed in the popular consciousness. To the end of the Ming dynasty, a surprising number were prepared to defy corrupt officials and abusive eunuchs, to sacrifice their well-being, even their lives, in service of a dynasty headed by rulers as frustrating to their ideals as the Wanli emperor, or as ineffectual as his miserable successors. That is one of the great anomalies of late imperial history. The strength of Ming government did not lie in the quality of its rulers, in the perfection of its vast and complex structure, or in the scope of its responsibilities. As political decline overtook it, the enduring strengths of Ming governing lay in the constant renewal of its human resources.

III. THE WANLI EMPEROR'S SUCCESSORS

Zhu Yijun, posthumously designated the "Divine Ancestor" Shenzong,[18] took particular pleasure in planning and supervising the construction of his tomb, the Ding Mausoleum (Dingling), located in the magnificent Ming imperial tomb park about twenty-five miles northwest of Beijing. He went in person to select the site and frequently thereafter to observe the progress of construction. Work began in 1584 and was not completed until 1601. It is said to have cost 80 million taels of silver—some accounts say 800 million, in any event a very large sum. Above the ground the tomb consists of a sequence of walls, gates, halls, and towers, the last on a mound directly over the marble underground chambers. The actual tomb includes a long entrance passage leading to high barrel-arched throne and coffin chambers for himself and his two principal empresses. This tomb was scientifically excavated in 1958, bringing to light more than 2,600 burial objects of great richness, many made of gold and precious stones, carved jade and marble, and other valuable materials. The only tomb of a Ming emperor that has been excavated,[19] it is well known to visitors to Beijing and through published archaeological reports. The fabled wealth of Ming China, then becoming known throughout the world, is well attested by the contents of this tomb. Except for the intrusion of garish taste in some of the imperial regalia, most of the objects are more or less typical of those used in the homes of the elite throughout the country. These items convey the sense of discriminating appreciation for elegant objects that supported refined modes of life.[20]

When the emperor fell seriously ill in the spring of 1620, he further curtailed his already minimal involvement in governing. His Grand Secretaries pressed him to take action on many pending administrative measures, but he did not follow through after promising orally that he would do so. The death of his mother in May occupied him with many decisions concerning her funeral, burial, and posthumous rites, throughout which he complained that his health prevented him from carrying out his duties; it probably made him more aware of his own mortality. By August, it is reported, he had "greatly declined," and was making preparations for dying. On August 18 he assembled a group of officials at his bedside. Those included his chief Grand Secretary, a nonentity named Fang Congzhe, and the Duke of Ying, who was the senior figure among the honorific nobility of merit,[21] among half a dozen other leading figures. One of those was Zhou Jiamo, a man of impressive personal qualities then serving as Minister of Personnel.[22] The emperor urged all to be conscientious in carrying out their duties, and they respectfully extended their wishes for his good health. Zhou Jiamo further inquired about issues of appointments and personnel changes, to which the emperor gave his assent. They then performed the kowtow and withdrew.

In his statement to them the dying emperor is reported to have said:

> We have continued Our ancestors' great rule for forty-eight years. Affairs of state have belabored Us to the point of inducing disease of the spleen, and I am suddenly unable to rise from my bed. I have failed to uphold the trust bequeathed to me by the former emperors. The heir has been installed in that position for a number of years. Favored by your support and that of the [eunuch] Directorate of Ceremonial working in harmony to maintain and assist him, following the ancestral institutes and making firm the dynasty's grand design, your merit to the Shrines of State shall endure forever. That same day the emperor died.

Immediately following this entry in the *Veritable Record* of the Shenzong reign is the text of the emperor's oral testament, sometimes cited in later works as his "posthumous edict."[23] It is likely that this document was based on Zhou Jiamo's conversations with the emperor and thus reflects accurately his final thoughts; it shows him to have been conscious of the evils induced by his avarice, his years of misgoverning, and his irresponsible conduct of his office. He admitted that he had long ignored meetings of the court, failed to consult with his high officials, let memorials accumulate unopened, and left many high offices unfilled, and most tellingly, that his taxes and special levies, such as the hated mining tax, had made life difficult for the people. All of those taxes and procurements were ordered stopped immediately, all persons who had been punished in the past for opposing them were to be rehabilitated, and good officials were to be appointed to fill all offices so that government might again function normally. That document was promulgated on August 20, the second day following Shenzong's death. Great sighs of relief filled the court and the halls of government.

Everyone no doubt remembered that in 1602, when the emperor was overtaken by a painful illness and thought he was dying, he had gone through these motions only to awake the next morning feeling much better. He sent eunuchs urgently to the cabinet to recover his edict terminating taxes and restoring unfairly punished officials to their offices. The entire statement was revoked, and things went on as before.[24] This time he was safely dead, and the final testament could not be revoked. The nation prepared to recover as from a long illness.[25]

And indeed such a process of recovery began. But from the beginning it was troubled by events. The heir, the long-suffering Zhu Changluo (somewhat like his grandfather, the Longqing emperor, who died in 1572), had borne his father's dislike, made evident in Shenzong's reluctance to name him the heir. It had always seemed that the emperor would heed the demand of his favorite concubine, the Lady Zheng, and in defiance of the Ancestral Injunction and all tradition, she still might succeed in having her son named the heir.

Lady Zheng had remained his favorite to the end and still clamored for favor and preferment.[26] Her reputation had long been under suspicion. In 1615 an assailant had entered the palace of the heir and attacked attendants with a club, apparently intending to kill Zhu Changluo. The mysterious affair was settled without any announcement of the results of the court's investigations; the would-be assassin was quickly executed, along with two eunuchs, and it was hoped that no further questions would be asked. But the widespread belief was that Lady Zheng had engineered this attack with the intention of bringing her son to the throne.

Lady Zheng knew that Zhu Changluo, thirty-eight years old and long restrained by the insecurity of his position as the heir, had survived to that point in frustration, isolation from his father and the court, boredom, and even fear for his life. His response to being the new emperor was to plunge immediately into a totally undisciplined way of life. Lady Zheng is said to have presented him with eight beautiful serving girls from her staff of palace attendants, hoping they would further contribute to his decline, but he was, in any event, already well supplied.

We cannot reconstruct the medical facts of Zhu Changluo's illness through the next few weeks; the Chinese records tell only that he was stricken by the disease of sexual exhaustion. He had been installed on the throne on August 28, and on September 26 he died, quite suddenly, after being given a medicine known only as "red pills." These were administered not by his court physician but by a eunuch with connections to Lady Zheng. There is no proof that she was involved or, indeed, that the mysterious medicine killed him. Rumor nevertheless fixed the blame on her. The first of the "Three Cases" of late Ming had been the attack on Zhu Changluo in 1615; this "Case of the Red Pills" now became the second item of palace intrigue associated with her.

The third of the notorious late Ming "Three Cases" was caused by Zhu Changluo's favorite concubine's refusal to move out of the deceased emperor's principal residence in the imperial palace city, where she lingered, thinking that she might still be named empress dowager. The Lady Zheng also had schemed to be named empress following the Wanli emperor's death a month earlier, but without success. In neither case would the traditional norms allow that, for neither had been elevated during her husband's life, nor had either borne the son who succeeded to the throne. In this case, the problem of forcing this strong-willed imperial favorite, known as the consort Li, to move to another residence, a small, shabby place isolated from the life of the court, became the third case involving imperial household intrigue. There was well-grounded concern that she intended to control the boy emperor and through him usurp power. The ensuing contretemps caused much consternation as the reign of the Wanli emperor's young grandson began, but strong-minded courtiers associated with the Donglin movement forced her removal from the palace and from the young emperor's environment.[27]

The reign title Taichang adopted by Zhu Changluo might have been simply expunged from the record, so short a time did he live as emperor (dying before it had even come into effect), but the court deliberated and accepted the suggestion to apply it to the eighth through the twelfth months of 1620, and begin the following year with the Tianqi reign period, the new reign name adopted for his son and heir. This boy, named Zhu Youjiao, was not yet fifteen when he was enthroned on October 1, 1620; his reign period name, Tianqi, was in effect from the New Year in early 1621 until the New Year of 1628, following his death late in 1627. Once again, a new reign opened in an aura of hope and determination to overcome the long process of political decline. His weak health and short life seemed to symbolize the fragility of that hope.

The reforms called for in the Wanli emperor's posthumous testament of August 1620 provided great impulse toward reconstruction. Once again, ever hopeful officials took command of the court to implement change. The Donglin party, together with reform-minded men from other intellectual associations and literary societies, gave direction to the effort.

The Tianqi reign is important because of the further advances made by the Manchus north of the Great Wall, the deterioration of the Ming military position in Liaodong (see Chapter 30), and the fierce political struggles at the court as the last of the infamous eunuch dictators achieved control of the government. This was Wei Zhongxian, the most vicious of the four notorious chief eunuchs in Ming history, who in Western writings often are given the designation "dictator."[28] He came gradually into control of the government by capturing the emperor's favor, through the mediation of his accomplice, a palace woman called Lady Ke, who had served as the boy emperor's nurse. By 1623 the eunuch and his nursemaid accomplice were well entrenched within the palace. They turned viciously against their critics among the reform factions in the court. Wei's principal opponents were men of the Donglin party; he pursued them relentlessly, killed many, filled the jails operated by his secret services, and banned academies in order to break up the organizational base of his literati opponents in the provinces. The political conflicts over control of the court and government deflected energies away from all other aspects of governing. From hopeful beginnings, the Tianqi reign soon fell into utter disarray.

The nature of Zhu Youjiao's physical deterioration and the illness that caused his death in the autumn of 1627, still three months short of his twenty-second birthday, are not clearly indicated. He was pale and sickly yet hyperactive and fond of all manner of outings, theatricals, and entertainments. A thoroughly frivolous young man, he gave little thought to matters of state and allowed the worst elements to govern in his name. His three sons and two daughters all died in infancy. Before his death he gave his approval to the naming of his younger brother, Zhu Youjian, to be his successor. This was the Chongzhen emperor, who reigned until the capital fell to bandits in 1644. He was a more earnest ruler, but ultimately ineffectual.

The conduct of the later Ming emperors reveals an impaired imperial institution. The reader of history might well wonder why the elite, and to some extent the general population of Ming China, remained dedicated to the dynasty even when many of its most able statesmen were driven away from service to it. "The dynasty," in the sense of the emperors and the imperial lineage, clearly functioned more powerfully as a cultural symbol than as a political institution. Chinese civilization demanded its existence as the capstone of a social order that made civilization possible. The Chinese were not blind to these emperors' flaws, but they had to remain hopeful that mundane faults could always be overcome, and that government would again be made to function adequately. Recovery of that kind was always theoretically within reach. In their eyes the collapse of the dynasty was a disaster that had to be prevented. The legitimate dynasty was to be preferred to all rebel upstart enemies, while *any* institutional alternative to the imperial system was literally unthinkable.

The Chinese bureaucracy needed a strong imperial institution, but the corps of high officials at the capital in mid- and later Ming times often found a strong, independent-minded incumbent of the throne to be an awkward disturbance. That is not as anomalous as it seems at first glance. The later Ming period's imperial institution was often ineffectual not just because of an unfortunate run of emperors, but also because the scholars and officials neither needed nor wanted a strong imperial personage who might act erratically. A docile if not a weak ruler was preferable. The founding emperor, Ming Taizu, thought that by abolishing the position of the Chief Councillor, he had ended the throne's competition with prime ministerial government exercised through a strong Outer Court. After 1435, under less vigorous and less able successors who became dependent on an Inner Court cabinet, the Grand Secretaries came to master the throne's incumbents in practical ways of their designing: they caged their emperors, allowing them to be little more than frustrated ritual figures whose political lives bored most of them. There still remained fields of action in which rulers could indulge in excesses, even commit tyrannical acts, and these were dutifully deplored by the corps of high officials whose responsibility it was to keep government working in spite of uncooperative rulers.

Emperors intelligent enough to know how circumscribed they were, and to resist, often turned to their chief eunuchs for a counterweight to bureaucratic pressure. Able eunuchs (whether or not devoted to the dynasty's interests) at times helped emperors to successfully defy convention and precedent. They especially encouraged rulers to pursue the many seductive alternatives to burdensome imperial responsibility which were at hand in their inner palaces. That a strong throne and a strong emperor could mean vastly different things is one of the facts Ming history makes most clear.[29] Too great a separation between the attributes of the throne and those of its incumbents, however, could in time impair the imperial institution; this also is a profound lesson to be drawn from later Ming history. As the story of the Ming dynasty draws near its close here, these wider-ranging interpretations of its history inevitably command a share of our attention.

29

THE LIVELY SOCIETY
OF THE LATE MING

During the 150 years of the sixteenth and early seventeenth centuries, Chinese society underwent growth and change; the civilization of the late Ming astounds us with its general prosperity, vitality, and capacity for cultural expression. Here we examine the issues of population increase, the conditions of rural life and organization, the changes affecting merchants' place in a burgeoning economy, the life of towns and cities, and finally the vigor and range of elite life at a time when many choices were becoming available to men and women of unusual talent. Here, if with no more than unsatisfying brevity, a broad array of issues can be probed on which scholarship is at present suggestive more often than it can be definitive. Even so, we can see why the late Ming raises arguments about the course of later Chinese history, and offers rich fare for thought.

1. THE POPULATION OF MING CHINA

Earlier chapters have noted that Chinese society has always been the largest bloc of the human race, its population larger than that of any other ethnically, culturally, or politically defined unit in world history. That continued to be true to the end of the twentieth century, although the absolute population figures for China and other parts of the world, as well as China's relative share of the world total, have until recent times been based on estimates (however carefully arrived at) that experts dispute and that continue to be revised. This is a field of historical research in which recent scholarship provides new conclusions, however tentative, that lead toward a more accurate understanding and therefore must be given serious attention.

Changes in the estimates of China's population are important both for Chinese and for world history because the Chinese constituted between one-quarter and one-third of the world total throughout history, through the

Ming and into the Qing period. The world's population is usually estimated to have hovered at about 750 million in the middle of the seventeenth century, at the end of the Ming, when China's population was at least one-third of that total.[1] World population is usually calculated to have passed the 1 billion mark for the first time in history about 1830, the 2 billion mark a century later, and reached 3 billion in the next thirty years, by 1960. By the end of the twentieth century, China's population of 1.2 billion constituted a fraction under one-fifth of the world total of 6.3 billion, though China's share of the world's total steadily shrank in the nineteenth and twentieth centuries.

For China, one can speak of a steady if slow growth reflecting a generally stable society. China experienced no nationwide epidemics, and the consequences of warfare and social turmoil also usually affected particular regions, not the whole society. Internal migration from distressed areas to safer ones allowed escape from deteriorating conditions. The sheer mass of China was an important factor in its stability: it was less affected than many others by rapid decreases in times of disaster, and, at least until the twentieth century, it was less subject to spurts of rapid increase in response to eras of peace, advances in public health, and the introduction of industrialized production with its diversified economic growth.

In the second half of the twentieth century China's population roughly doubled. For the entire twentieth century it achieved a growth rate similar to that of the United States and western Europe in the same period, and slower than that of other parts of Asia, Africa, and Latin America. Wide swings in China's total population in the centuries from 900 to 1800 are, to be sure, posited in some of the studies in China's historical demography; more recent researches give those wide variations less credence and provide a picture of even, sustained growth. Studies of the Ming population reflect this, and by raising the estimates for Ming, they cast doubt on the earlier, widely held view of a "population explosion" in Qing times.[2] Removing the likelihood of a sudden population increase in the eighteenth century changes our understanding of the dynamics of Qing history; it eliminates factors previously given high explanatory power, such as social dislocations and disruptions of economic factors, and forces us to reevaluate the entire course of later Ming and early Qing.

While this altered view, adopted here, of demographic history must yet remain a hypothesis, it is a sound working hypothesis based on improved methods, and it possesses the convincing feature of providing a long-range view of population growth that fits well with other aspects of social history from Song times onward. Moreover, insofar as more accurate statistics for a few of the administrative subdivisions of Ming China have recently been reconstructed and analyzed, these are congruent with the estimates for the whole presented here.

A groundbreaking modern study of Ming and Qing population history concluded in 1959 that late in the first reign of the Ming, when a careful revision of the census figures was made in 1393, the population "probably exceeded 65,000,000 to an unknown degree" and "increased . . . to the neighborhood of 150,000,000 by 1600." The same scholar wrote that the population then more than doubled in the next two centuries, reaching 313 million in 1794.[3] That study did not contradict the idea of a Qing dynasty population explosion, an idea that has since been called into question. Almost thirty years later, in 1987, there appeared an overview of China's population history covering the entire 2,000 years of the imperial and contemporary eras. This study usefully places Ming and Qing population history in long-range trends, and by using different methods comes to different conclusions, giving estimates that far exceed the officially recorded data and earlier estimates based on them. A simplified growth pattern is projected in a line graph that reduces fluctuations and depicts a more or less steady upward growth through the last thousand years. Only in the nineteenth century does it show a sudden doubling of the population. Utilizing its quite different methods, this study denies a "population explosion" in the early and mid-Qing.[4]

A third study of this problem makes a very convincing case for quite different projections of population growth through Ming and early Qing times. It agrees with both of the earlier studies in increasing the estimates, but raises them much more, while corroborating the second of those studies in positing long and steady growth over a period of centuries. This most recent study's figures are accepted here as convincing in general outline, and thus are adopted as a strong working hypothesis about Ming and Qing population history.[5]

To summarize this study's findings, it uses an upwardly revised figure of 85 million for the early Ming dynasty base year 1393, then projects growth from that year forward to 1500, 1600, and 1650. Having established that there was a "steady slow decrease in the *rate* of population growth" from 1500 to 1800 (but not a decline in the absolute growth), it uses three hypotheses about the rate of annual growth.[6] If we set aside its high and low projections to adopt its medium-range projected growth estimates, halfway between the other two possibilities, we arrive at population estimates that the Ming historian can reasonably work with: 155 million in 1500, 231 million in 1600, and 268 million in 1650. Strong arguments are made to show that these figures are, if anything, too conservative. The same study's accompanying figures for the growth of the area under cultivation support the credibility of its population estimates.

The implications are many. For one thing, increasing the figures for China's population raises significantly the total world population figures and increases the Chinese share of world population to something over one-third throughout this period. This makes the loss of China's share of humankind—or, to state it differently, the increases in populations elsewhere—a more recent and more dramatic development. The implications for domestic Chinese history, however, are of much greater import. The institutional lag between the census figures used for taxation purposes and the realities of the social base became very great during the Ming. We must try to understand why a government fully capable of collecting better figures did not find it necessary to do so, but based its tax system and much of its social management effort on what appear to us incongruous discrepancies between demographic fact and institutional facade.

The Census Registers and Fiscal Management

To review, the official census data for 1393 report a total Chinese registered population of 60,545,812.[7] In those data the annual and decennial figures fluctuated thereafter between 53 and 62 million, essentially remaining stationary until the end of the dynasty 250 years later. Ming local officials recognized clearly that the annual figures which they reported to higher levels of the administration, as well as the decennial "revisions" submitted to the Ministry of Revenue, bore no direct relation to actual population numbers.[8] There were many reasons why they nevertheless regularly used those figures. Some local officials, rather than take credit for population increases, feared that upward revisions would cause the court to increase tax levies on their counties, making their jobs more difficult. In local society, patterns for handling the registers and adjusting the tax levies had become established, and no one wanted suddenly to displace working arrangements to start anew. Other social pressures and cultural norms worked together to maintain the status quo. Because the system dated from the time of the founding emperor, who left stern instructions not to alter his founding acts, it was regarded as untouchable even while it was constantly undergoing unproclaimed changes. For many kinds of reasons, the unreal figures were manipulated to maintain an apparent continuity of procedures that delivered the taxes. In administrative terms, how "non-rational" was that? (It certainly was not irrational.) Could the state have implemented a more "rational" system of managing its fiscal base? What might it have gained from so doing?

We have seen that under the vigorous statesman Zhang Juzheng, senior Grand Secretary from 1572 to 1582, the later Ming government demonstrated that a rigorous reregistration of landholdings for tax purposes could be carried out, a task far more complex than revising the household registers to show the actual population.[9] In being willing to attempt a fundamental change in fiscal management, Zhang Juzheng was an exception among Ming statesmen. He died too soon to carry out his other ambitious reforms of the state system, which undoubtedly would have included a new and more accurate census as well. The statesmen who followed him sidestepped that problem. China had a very strong tradition in the study of various branches of mathematics; it certainly did not lack practical skills in calculating and reckoning.[10] Yet most Ming statecraft thinkers and officeholders did not place much weight on using accurate statistical databases as practical tools for managing society.[11] There is considerable force in the argument that their commitment to the Confucian humanistic "government of men" prevailed, implying a restrictive view of the state's proper role in managing society. Ethical considerations and interpersonal relations held precedence over administrative efficiency. As an instrument of fiscal management, the incomplete, out-of-date official census records could be made to serve as a basis for allocating tax quotas, without requiring an accurate numerical reflection of a constantly changing and growing society. That does not mean that officials were unaware of social change, or of the institutional inadequacies. Many could see that the system functioned very imperfectly, and in some other periods fundamental reforms might have been demanded. Yet in the later Ming stage in the development of Chinese civilization, this anomalous system suited perceived needs.

Ming officials sought ways to make the system function without correcting the statistical records on which it nominally was based, but that should not lead us to believe that Chinese administrators were incapable of or unwilling to deal in numbers. Of course they did, and quite effectively; there was no other way to carry out their duties. Making their calculations to achieve practical solutions to the routine problems of governing required that they also know something about the actual figures. We can surmise that they were forced to keep two sets of accounts, for a few sets have been found of the "real" figures for population, landholding, and tax exemptions from which Ming officials in a particular locality calculated tax allocations.

Throughout the Ming dynasty, county-level officials struggled to modify and reform the system, constantly changing it in practical ways. Some of their locally generated improvements were absorbed into the periodic nationwide revisions of the system, but the way of reporting census figures remained unchanged well into the succeeding dynasty.

Changes in the Distribution of the Population

The demographic center of Ming China continued to shift toward the Yangzi drainage and the provinces farther south, a trend already well established by Song times, and one that continued to the twentieth century. Countertrends, however, also developed despite that general shift to the south. The *registered* population of the North China Plain, devastated repeatedly starting with the Jin dynasty's collapse in the early thirteenth century, continued to decrease through much of the Yuan and on through the half-century of warfare accompanying the Ming founding in the fourteenth century. The *actual* population also must have fallen, either because disorder because it caused deaths and forestalled births, or because it caused out-migration to other regions. The reduced demographic base slowly began to rebuild during the fifteenth century, and areas of sparse population in the North continued to fill in throughout the Ming period.

The capital's transfer from Nanjing to Beijing in 1420 contributed to recovery on the North China Plain. The new capital became a great city where a broad cross-section of the national elite resided for parts of their careers; indeed, some successful bureaucrats settled down there, making it their second place of residence even when keeping their registration (and their lineage base) in their native district. The city became a center of consumption, demanding the services of the transport systems, stimulating crafts and commerce. The Grand Canal effectively linked agriculturally abundant Central

Finally, in relation to agriculture and economic growth, the new crops introduced to East Asia and the world from the Americas began to be known in China in the third quarter of the sixteenth century. Their impact was limited during the Ming but not unimportant, and they steadily became significant additions to the Chinese diet in the early Qing. Of the several new food crops that found their way into China at this time, Indian corn (maize), the true sweet potato, the white or Irish potato, peanuts (groundnuts), the various red and sweet peppers (capsicum), and tomatoes were economically most important, and tobacco soon became a significant cash crop.[12] The Chinese adapted readily to most of these foods; poorer people in particular came to rely heavily on them for daily fare. The white potato is the exception; the Chinese, unlike the Europeans, found it uninteresting and never used it as a staple. Corn could be grown on upland fields that would not produce other cereals; sweet potatoes flourished under poor growing conditions and could be sun-dried and saved for off-season consumption; peanuts, which could be grown on the poorest sandy soils, became an important oil crop and rich source of nutrients. With these diet substitutes, and without lowering the quality of nutrition, farmers could use the principal fields for rice or wheat grown for the market. By the seventeenth and eighteenth centuries these new crops had exerted a transforming effect, allowing the steady population growth to continue despite the greater crowding and pressure on the land.

The New World crops affected only the final decades of the Ming; even without considering their impact, it is nonetheless possible to support the hypotheses adopted here about the higher population estimates for the Ming.

II. THE ORGANIZATION OF RURAL SOCIETY

The formal structure of Ming local government changed in its details but remained much the same in its larger outlines as that of Song and Yuan times.[13] The new province-level *(sheng)* unit of administration was the interesting innovation of Ming. To be sure, it derived from the Yuan "branch secretariat" *(xingsheng),* but the Ming quickly regularized it as a new level of regional governing. The name of this new territorial unit is translated "province," yet the structure strengthened central authority; it did not imply a significant transfer of discretionary powers from center to region (see Map 15 in Chapter 25). The province in Ming and Qing times thus does not signal decentralization, nor did Ming innovations bring greater autonomy at the base level—the level of the prefectures *(fu),* sub-prefectures *(zhou),* and counties (or "districts," *xian*). At that base level, there were in the entire country 159 prefectures, 234 sub-prefectures, and 1,171 counties.[14] Each had a small staff of civil service officials appointed by the Ministry of Personnel in the capital, and those officials were directly subordinate to the center while also under the supervision of the three agencies that constituted province-level governing. Those were the provincial administrative commissions (their heads sometimes called "governor," they were responsible principally for fiscal matters); the provincial surveillance commissions (responsible for judicial and investigative matters); and the regional military commissions.

Sub-prefectures functioned as superior counties, had slightly larger staffs of civil service appointed officials, and because they often were located at strategically important places, had larger military and police components. For our purposes, however, the sub-prefectures may be considered together with the counties to make a total of about 1,400 base-level units of local administration in the Ming state.[15] They were territorially included in and were under the jurisdiction of the prefectures. If the middle-range population estimates discussed earlier are accurate, each of those 1,400 units of base-level administration comprised on average 110,000 people in 1500, 165,000 in 1600, and 190,000 in 1650. In fact, however, they varied widely. The Ming government classified them in three ranks according to *registered* population (hence tax revenues), but also taking into consideration the complexity of their administrative problems and their strategic significance. A number of upper-level counties in mid- and later Ming times, particularly those in the lower Yangzi drainage, had well over 1 million inhabitants.

The county *yamen* or "magistrate's office" was often the most elaborate complex of buildings in a county seat town, and because of its presence there, county seats were allowed (or required) to be walled. Impressive walls, moats, and gate towers were added to most Ming county seats where they had not previously existed; this was the great age of wall-building. The city walls can be seen as both guarding and dignifying the presence of the central government throughout the land. The magistrate's *yamen* had five to seven civil service appointed officials—the magistrate at rank seven, vice magistrate at rank eight, assistant magistrate (or "recorder") at rank nine, and sometimes a military officer or two also at rank nine. Those local representatives of the imperial majesty were at the three lowest ranks of the nine-tiered system (or eighteen-tiered ranking system, since each of the nine was divided into "full" and "secondary," e.g., 1A and 1B sub-rankings). Appointed from outside the province within which they served, all these local officials served terms usually of three years and then moved on to other assignments. They might earn the genuine respect of the local society, and gain notice from the central authorities who evaluated them for transfers and promotions. Or they might be seen as lazy, corrupt, or inept officials whose interests lay in advancing their bureaucratic careers. Many undoubtedly gave no better than routine service in humdrum postings. Yet the county magistrates were popularly known as "father-and-mother officials" and were expected to treat the local population with the earnest concern they might devote to children under their care. They were under social pressure to fulfill that image. The quality of their governing varied widely.[16]

Villages as Communities

The numbers I have given for the average population of Ming counties, and the small numbers of civil service officials appointed to administer them, show office. The rotation among the ten heads remained fixed within their ten families, substitutions being made only when a family could no longer supply a responsible male. His job lent him status and prestige, but also was onerous. He had to cope with emergencies, and many irregular procurements and tax levies also fell to his supervision. The position's prestige and other advantages in early Ming soon paled before the burdens to be borne. The system nonetheless functioned through the end of the dynasty and into the Qing dynastic period.

Although the Ming administrative community heads were "of the people," they were not a manifestation of "village democracy." They belonged to a politically imposed authority structure, but they had to work within and with the community. Below them in the villages there was a large measure of spontaneous community involvement and a recognition of some individual rights (e.g., if a villager had to sell land, another family of the same village usually had the right to buy before any outsider) as well as responsibilities. As for the tone of rural life, there was a general sense that human life rested on ethical foundations and that justice should prevail. Because "human rights" were not legally codified, we should not conclude that they did not exist, as some historians have erroneously assumed.[24] The processes by which individual rights were to be protected and maintained, however, were not those of incipient democracy or of constitutional law on the Western model.

The village community in Ming times was the base-level organization of a lively society. To generalize quite broadly, landownership was general. No great status distinctions existed among the rural population beyond the fluid ones reflecting family wealth. There were no legally established social distinctions in society other than those of "official" (*guan*) and "commoner" (*min*), both of which were open social statuses.[25] Both rich and poor were found in both statuses. It was not proto-democracy, but it was a society ruled by an egalitarian spirit in which individual achievement was encouraged, was honored, and brought genuine rewards. That is not to say Chinese society was not "hierarchical," but all known societies were and are hierarchical. The elaborately worked-out deference patterns sustained aspects of the social hierarchy, but they did not in themselves imply oppression. Chinese rural society displayed many examples of social injustice and exploitation, but it was not without recourse to cultural means for coping with them. The dynamics of village society merit much further study.[26]

Village Life

Ming period rural people, about 90 percent of the population, lived in villages most of which held from ten to fifty households. Villages were smaller in the North and larger in the South as a general rule. Almost no Chinese lived as single families on isolated farms.[27] Villages were true communities, small centers of participatory activity. While most of the actions of most people were played out at that level, villagers' lives were not confined to their village streets and the adjacent fields where they toiled. Villages functioned within larger systems of social interaction. For example, many villages contained residents of only one surname. People sharing surnames were looked upon as kin, if often very remote kin. By law and by custom the married women in such villages, to avoid kin incest taboos, would have come from a different surname, hence a different village. Even families in multi-surname villages tended to seek wives in other villages. There were thus close family ties that transcended the villages and led to visiting back and forth and shared activities.

Commerce also was important in intervillage activities, although it was still moving from barter to money transactions in many parts of China in mid-Ming times. Small villages might have no permanent stores and shops but would have a market that conducted business on a regular schedule, commonly one or more days in ten, as on the second, twelfth, and twenty-second days of the lunar month, or on the second and seventh, the twelfth and seventeenth, and the twenty-second and twenty-seventh days. The sellers in such periodic markets traveled through a region with their wares, their gossip, their news, communicating their awareness of the outside. In larger villages and towns and in more prosperous regions the scheduled markets might meet as often as every other day; more often than that and they became permanent stores, a process of commercial development evident in the changing market day patterns of Ming China. When a village was too small to support any schedule of regular markets, its inhabitants would walk to nearby villages on their market days to participate as buyers or sellers, or merely as sightseers out for the excitement. Larger villages in more prosperous locales had a central street with both a marketplace and some permanent stores, craftsmen's shops with storefronts to sell their products, and stalls where services of doctors, fortune-tellers, barbers, letter writers, and others could be found.

Most villages had small votive shrines to the tutelary spirits of the place, as well as Buddhist and Daoist shrines and temples. Many monks (also some nuns) traveled widely; they too provided links to the outside. And they often fostered village group pilgrimages to religious sites, perhaps famous temples several days' walk away. These could become joyous holidays as well as spiritual experiences.[28] Most villages had a village school which might operate on temple premises. At teashops the men of farming and crafts households gathered for refreshments, conversation, and business negotiations. Where commerce flourished there would be inns and restaurants, brothels, and entertainments of many kinds; crowds gathered to listen to professional storytellers; actors and acrobats performed on temporary portable stages or in the courtyards of temples. Many of the regional great fairs held on annual schedules were hosted by Buddhist temples; they drew buyers from large distances. Most villagers got to see touring theater troupes perform at least once a year. The life of rural China was one of bustling and at times exuberant activity.

For most ordinary Chinese in the villages, however, work prevailed and entertainment was peripheral. The simple pleasures focused on holiday meals with special foods in the home, or centered on the religious events of the temples and shrines. The home, not a temple or shrine shared with the community, was the locus of the family's primary religious duties—those to its ancestors. Rituals of veneration were performed there on the first and fifteenth days of the lunar month, and on birthdays and special occasions, conducted by the eldest male heir or a near-kin surrogate, and at the family graves during outings in the spring. Buddhist and Daoist religious observances and those of local cults were colorful, popular, and widely supported, but they could not take precedence over family religious duties.

Among the popular religions, sectarian lines were vague or nonexistent, especially at lower levels of society where the distinctions between Buddhism and Daoism and local cults blurred. In all villages people no matter how poor tried to observe the three big holidays of the year: the lunar New Year, the festival of Duanwu (the Dragon Boat Festival) on the fifth of the fifth lunar month, and the mid-autumn festival after the harvests, celebrated on the full moon, that is, the fifteenth day of the eighth lunar month. Holidays were observed differently in different places, but at a minimum those three were nationwide holidays. The solar-lunar calendar marked the annual round of seasons and festivals. The sun's passage measured by solstices and equinoxes defined the year; the moon's phases numbered the days of the month. The passage of the seasons was marked off in a sequence of twenty-four fortnightly (actually fifteen-day) periods of the year, named for seasonal phenomena of importance to the schedules of farming folk. A table of those periods follows.[29]

Approximate dates (Western calendar)	Period names
February 5	Spring Begins
February 19	Rain Waters
March 5	Stirring Insects
March 20	Vernal Equinox
April 5	Clear and Bright
April 20	Grain Rains
May 5	Summer Begins
May 21	Grain Fills
June 6	Grain Forms Ears
June 21	Summer Solstice
July 7	Slight Heat
July 23	Great Heat
August 7	Autumn Begins
August 23	Limit of Heat
September 8	White Dew
September 23	Autumnal Equinox
October 8	Cold Dew
October 23	Hoar Frost Descends
November 7	Winter Begins
November 22	Little Snow
December 7	Heavy Snow
December 21	Winter Solstice
January 6	Little Cold
January 21	Severe Cold

That calendar was observed by urban as well as rural people. Poets reflected on its seasonal changes; poor farmers turned to it to add small bits of color to their down-to-earth lives. It was this agricultural year that punctuated all Chinese life. Across the vast regional variations in the settings of rural villages, village life was both scoffed at for its rusticity and idealized for its harmonious simplicity. It was in many ways the measure of Chinese customs, social patterns, and values.

Social Order

Rural China, village China, in the sixteenth and seventeenth centuries, as for most of the later imperial era, was stable, safe, a secure environment within which most people most of the time lived uneventful lives. It was healthy by premodern standards; the Chinese of all economic levels typically ate a wholesome diet of hot cooked foods, drank boiled water or hot tea, and observed some basic principles of community hygiene. Their native traditions in medicine were able to respond to many of the epidemic diseases, such as typhoid and typhus, and by Ming times they regularly practiced variolation for the prevention of smallpox.[30] The population was mostly well housed and warmly dressed. Even the quite simple standard of living of the poorer farming households probably was better than that of ordinary people in most parts of the world at that time. All that stability and order could be thrown into chaos by war and banditry, or by extraordinary regional or local conditions caused by drought, flood, earthquakes, and consequent epidemic disease. Most Chinese probably lived their lives without experiencing those conditions, yet social disorder was a potential hazard in Chinese life, and its causes and cures inform us about the nature of Ming society.

The generalizations about safety and stability in daily life break down somewhat when the northern frontier is considered, or when one looks into the frequently disturbed relations of Chinese and minority peoples, often local majorities, in the South and Southwest (see Chapter 27). Even there, however, the expectation was that the Chinese population should not be (nor needed to be) armed, and that the local representatives of the central government would maintain the peace. Throughout the realm, where no special border hazards existed, armed conflict was held to be evidence of political failure. Local authorities faced the dilemma of recognizing a threat and dealing with it quickly, or withholding the military response in the hope it would go away. A county magistrate who failed to restore order quickly would be held responsible, his merit rating would suffer, and his career might be thwarted. The military response might nevertheless be seen as an admission of failure, and in the hands of civilian administrators who did not have much experience in directing armed conflict, it might turn into a debacle. It therefore was often seen as better to underreport disturbances while trying to resolve them by indirect means— negotiating with bandit leaders, bribing or cajoling through intermediaries, even employing rival bandit leaders to take action. Those were essentially civilian responses to the prickly problems of maintaining local order.

Occasionally, however, social disorders grew to dimensions that threatened more than a few rural districts of one county, and the intervention of the central government was required. In such cases the bandits or disorderly people (sometimes desperately poor refugees from a disaster) might acquire leaders who proclaimed political goals going beyond mere plunder and loot; they then would be recognized as a different level of danger, and in the government's eyes they would no longer be bandits: they were "rebels." But the terminology was used loosely; the taxonomy of social disorder was imprecise. "Bandit" and "rebel" were terms of contempt and outrage more than they were precise legal categories. The bandits and rebels themselves were often soldiers, guards, militiamen, and others who had access to arms and military training, and it is not unusual to see their names appearing as employees of the proper authorities in one context, and soon thereafter as lawbreakers defying the government and despoiling the people. That appears to have happened most readily on the North China Plain, the region surrounding the capital at Beijing, where opportunities for collusion with corrupt officials, eunuchs, and the agents of imperial relatives were the greatest.[31] The bandit identity could be very ambiguous under those circumstances.

An example of recurrent banditry of regional scale was seen in the fifteenth century in what had once been a prosperous and stable region on the boundaries of Huguang (Hubei) and Shaanxi provinces, then called the prefectures of Jingzhou and Xiangyang (Jing-Xiang). Utterly despoiled by warfare through much of the fourteenth century, after the armies of the Ming founding emperor conquered it in the 1370s the region was declared closed to habitation, and the people who had fled into the region to escape the consequences of warfare were ordered to return to their homes. That unrealistic policy solved no problems. When armies dispersed the settlers, they would simply wait a short time and infiltrate back into the region in ever larger numbers. Leaders appeared among them who used popular religious doctrines to reinforce their authority. Those leaders organized the unregistered and technically unlawful residents into communities to support bandit army units, then deployed them to plunder neighboring districts. The problem, which had festered for many years, eventually drew a series of very large-scale military responses from the Ming court in the years 1465–1476. No military solution was long-lasting; new leaders always appeared who quickly reorganized the social base and commenced warfare all over again. Finally in 1476 a civilian administrator took charge, offering the settlers the right to claim their land and register as proper residents of the region, by those means undercutting the authority of the insurgent leaders. A new prefecture (Yunyang) was established to oversee the area, and the problem was solved.[32]

The new Ming state in the mid-fifteenth century was slow to solve that problem of displaced farming people who needed only to be resettled on the land and registered as proper taxpaying subjects. At a number of places the government successfully resettled rural people and more quickly restored order to war-ravaged regions. Yet at the end of the dynasty, circumstances similar to those that had spawned the Jing-Xiang Rebellion in the 1470s appeared again in the northwest, this time farther north in Shaanxi and along the Great Wall defense line, where garrison armies regularly engaged the marauding Mongols. Many former soldiers, ignored by the government, had been left to survive as best they could. That created a regional social problem and a pool of disaffected former soldiers who were susceptible to the call of new bandit leaders. Two of those, Li Zicheng (1605?–1645) and Zhang Xianzhong (1605?–1647), became the most powerful leaders of the "roaming bandits" who brought down the Ming dynasty; more on them in the succeeding chapter.

These are spectacular examples of very large-scale banditry and/or rebellion in Ming times. Innumerable accounts of smaller-scale "collective violence" in the Ming period also have been chronicled.[33] The potential for it always existed, and particular conditions in some regions enabled such violence to grow to large scale and affect many people. Yet for most of the people in most regions of Ming China, the civilian society was the norm; the level of danger was low enough that communities normally were open and undefended, and military values were irrelevant to most lives.

One startling event demonstrates the force of that generalization. In the summer of 1555, during the height of the so-called Japanese pirate incursions on the Central China coast, a group of about sixty pirates (probably in fact Chinese, or a group made up of both Chinese and Japanese) came ashore to raid and pillage near Hangzhou. Cut off from their ships, they turned inland, going west across northern Zhejiang, then into southern Anhui, back along the Yangzi to the east, past Wuhu and into the suburbs of Nanjing, and on east past Changzhou and Wuxi into Changshu County, where at last they were surrounded and exterminated by a large provincial military force. Near the end they were joined by other pirates, but their numbers remained very small. For almost three months this tiny force of marauders roamed at will through the open countryside in parts of three provinces, attacked towns and walled cities, dared the military establishment of the secondary capital (Nanjing) to stop them, burned and looted more or less unopposed. They killed between 5,000 and 6,000 Chinese civilians. This event is sometimes cited as evidence for the uselessness of the Ming armed forces; it is better evidence for the fact that normally no defense of town and cities, no policing of the countryside was necessary. A small but totally unexpected band of desperados could move at will and encounter nothing to stop them.[34]

The more ordinary problems of social order included the range of civil and criminal offenses known in all societies but defined in relation to Chinese custom and social ethics. The Great Ming Code promulgated by the dynasty's founder in the 1390s focuses special attention on the misbehavior of officials, but in its 460 articles it defines the crimes and misdeeds of all persons in society and prescribes their punishment. The county magistrates acted as judge and jury in all cases brought before them, and practiced a kind of penal law that appears to us to be quite harsh, but at its best was fair in maintaining the traditional morality. Persons under arrest were not assumed to be innocent, and mistreatment of prisoners in jails tested their hardiness. Humble people looked on the law more as an affliction than as their protector; it was to be avoided.

More important than penal law and judicial procedures in maintaining order in the community were the methods of arbitration and compromise. That route to resolving disputes allowed the parties to retain their dignity, utilized social pressures as understood by all, and gave problem-solving roles to senior figures acting as arbitrators. That reinforced the community's recognition of its shared ethical norms.[35] Some regions of China were known to be more litigious, more quarrelsome, less placid than others, but throughout their observations of ordinary Chinese life from the sixteenth century onward, the early European travelers remarked on the manneriness, good humor, and social graces of the common people.

III. Ming Cities, Towns, and Urban People: The Question of Capitalism

Cities and civilization (*cité*, from *civitatem, civilitas, civilizzato, ziviliziert*), urbanism and urbanity (from *urbs, urbanitas*), the burg or borough *(bourg)* and the bourgeoisie, a word that implies the *droit de bourgeoisie,* or the rights of those who lived in chartered towns and cities, and the popular saying in medieval Germany "Stadtluft macht frei," loosely "the urban atmosphere makes one free": our Western languages constantly remind us of the place of cities in the development of Western civilization.[36] The more important towns and cities in medieval Europe often demanded, and gained, from their kings charters granting them local self-governance, setting them apart from the rural countryside and small villages all around them, and giving them a special relationship to the state within whose boundaries they existed.

In the West there was a sequence of steps by which townspeople, led by the craft and merchant guilds in their midst, demanded rights to carry on their activities free of intervention by the feudal lords, to gain exemption from some taxes, and to defend themselves against piracy and other threats to their security. After gaining a measure of those rights, they created ever stronger urban-based political authority distinct from that which prevailed in the countryside. In time the great towns and cities came to rival the hereditary landed aristocracy in wealth and power. They attracted in-migrants, first feudal serfs escaping their land-bound status, who went into towns when they could manage that, often illegally, and provided an urban labor force. Gradually they became fully free townspeople with a variety of new career options as apprentices in the crafts, shop assistants, soldiers and armorers in the city's pay, boat builders and sailors, producers of special products on the suburban land controlled by the city, barbers, musicians, entertainers, and many others. As medieval European towns grew in size and wealth, they began to attract a second wave of in-migrants, the aristocracy, who found the new amenities of city life irresistible, so built their great town houses and palaces in which they resided for increasingly longer periods of the year. It clearly was the urban burghers, or bourgeoisie, who created a special environment that attracted both the top and the bottom levels of society into cities, where they gradually came to form one urban community, but one still legally stratified into hereditary aristocrats and ordinary citizens, whether freemen or bond-servants. Together they could participate in ways of life that would not otherwise have been accessible to them, whether they originally came from the higher or the lower strata of society.

That highly schematic description of the functions of cities in the development of Western civilizations, with all its overgeneralization and omission of particularizing detail, is nevertheless worth holding in mind as we turn to examine the functions of towns and the lives of townspeople in Ming China. The Ming dynasty, from the late fourteenth century to the seventeenth, corresponds with the centuries in Western history during which many modernizing changes took place, mostly emanating from urban settings. As we compare the functions of cities in the West and in China, it becomes obvious that some of the differences are as important as the similarities. Yardsticks used to measure social change in the West help us to understand Chinese social history, but they may also mask differences. Throughout this work it has been noted that formulaic history typically leads to generalizations that are not general. Comparative history, by contrast, may enable us to perceive the ways in which China was different, thereby to comprehend its distinctiveness. This is particularly true in Chinese urban history.

Administrative and economic functions have been intertwined in the histories of Chinese cities. It was unusual to see a large and bustling market center that did not also function as a seat of local administration, usually at least as the seat of a county *(xian)*. It was so unusual that the most prominent of those flourishing market towns in Ming times that were not simultaneously the seats of local administration were grouped together as the "four great *zhen*" (market towns).[37] While there were in fact more than four that would qualify as major *zhen*, they clearly were exceptions to the usual expectation.

That indicates a further fact about the governing of Chinese towns and cities. China's great towns and cities developed through 2,000 years of the imperial era without having witnessed the emergence of urban governments as such; they were not governed differently or separately from their immediate hinterland, the county in which they were located.[38] In almost all cases the county bore the same name as the city in which the county *yamen* was located, and the entire county was governed by the same staff of centrally appointed civil service officials. Only rarely were statistics preserved showing the numbers and conditions of urban residents apart from those for the entire county, where the great majority were rural village people. It is thus difficult for historians to calculate the size of urban populations.

The city had nothing like a city charter, and no independent administration, that is, no mayor or town council; no laws or privileges that applied especially to its inhabitants; and no indigenous social groups that would have thought of demanding city dwellers' "rights" from the central government. In short, Chinese cities had no separate legal or political status; they were not corporate entities and had none of the organizational features that set European cities apart.[39] Those Chinese characteristics come close to denying Chinese cities the designation "city" as defined in Western history, but of course they were cities, however different they were from cities elsewhere in these legal and organizational aspects.

Chinese cities often were bounded by city walls, gates, towers over the gates, moats, and other defense installations. They might give the impression that urban residents lived in a state of siege, but quite the opposite was true. Walls could be built not at the option of a city's inhabitants, but only on permission from the central government. Walls of course had defensive capabilities, but equally significant, city walls were powerful visual symbols of the imperial authority present within them—the *yamen* of the local magistrate and his imperially appointed staff. The Ming was a great age of wall building. Most county seat and higher-level administrative cities acquired walls for the first time, or rebuilt and enlarged older walls.

Enigmatically, the massive and imposing city walls with their gate towers and moats did not bound and differentiate the urban settlement; many large cities had areas of specialized agricultural production within them and in the near suburbs, while large urban concentrations were often adjacent to the walls but outside them. The Chinese insistence on the freshness of food supplies made the use of city land for commercial gardening profitable; at the same time, generally peaceful conditions made the protection provided by walls unnecessary, even for the commercial and moneylending activities that tended to cluster just outside city walls where main transport routes entered and left. Only in unusual times of very general disorder did people in smaller outlying towns and from the rural villages crowd into the cities for protection and, with the people of the immediate suburbs, take refuge within the walls.

The Chinese city thus was in many ways different, yet also functioned in many ways as did cities elsewhere. If Chinese city air did not make people free in specific political and legal senses, it nonetheless gave urban residents some kinds of social freedoms. The concentration of many people in a limited space produced attitudes that were distinctly urban; city dwellers were accustomed to seeing and interacting with strangers, and the ability to remain a stranger to others among whom one lived gave city dwellers the joys or pains of anonymity. Anonymity allowed the individual to escape some of the social supervision from which persons in small communities could not escape; town dwellers therefore could behave more freely than villagers. Cities also consumed special goods and services, and there were always people who could pay for them. A person (whether man or woman) would be more apt to find some way of earning money in that environment than in a small rural village. For those with a bit more money to spend, the city of course offered a vastly wider range of things to spend it on. In short, the urban environment in China contributed some elements of daily life and opportunities for individual advancement that we associate with cities everywhere in premodern times.

The number as well as the size of cities grew significantly during the Ming dynasty; there were more and larger cities than in Europe at that time. Marco Polo, who left China to return to Venice at the end of the thirteenth century, found Chinese cities larger and more splendid than any he had seen elsewhere, and he had seen much of the advanced world of that time. Near the end of the Ming dynasty, around 1600, the Italian Jesuit missionary Matteo Ricci stayed in Nanjing, about which he wrote: "In the judgment of the Chinese this city surpasses all others in the world in beauty and in grandeur, and in this respect there are probably very few others superior or equal to it. It is literally filled with palaces and temples and towers and bridges, and those are scarcely surpassed by similar structures in Europe . . . There is a gaiety of spirit among the people, who are well-mannered and nicely spoken, and the dense population is made up of all classes, of hoi-polloi, of the lettered aristocracy and the Magistrates."[40] The Chinese of the time could not make such comparisons, because almost none of them had traveled outside China. Private historians and literary figures nonetheless have left a vast treasury of writings on Ming cities and the life within them. They give the modern reader images of a life that was rich, comfortable, elegant in the taste of the elite, occasionally vulgar in the ostentation of the very rich, and above all an urban life that was varied and lively almost beyond description. The capital at Beijing had a population of more than 1 million in the sixteenth and seventeenth centuries.[41] Nanjing, the former capital and later the secondary capital, had close to a million residents. There may have been half a dozen cities in the range of one-half million, and scores of urban places with 100,000 or more residents.[42] The networks of urban places filled out during the Ming, to complete the premodernized system of cities at different size-levels and with interlocking political and economic functions.

Clearly, no single city dominated China except in the political sense; the national capital was the center of all governing, and all the large and important decisions concerning the use of military force also emanated from it. Yet the capital did not set elite lifestyles, nor did it come close to monopolizing the cultural life of the nation. Literature and scholarship, book publishing and book collecting, art and drama, music and entertainment, and the indulgence in rich elite modes all were at least as well represented in many regions of the nation as at its capital.

At the same time, cities, as the places where such cultivated modes of life could be sustained, were not cut off from the non-urban settings. There were several reasons for this. Chinese family patterns as codified and regularized in later imperial times stressed the lineage's links to its "founding" ancestors. Those were not remote "primal ancestors" but the clearly historic heads of the lineage venerated in annual rituals and usually representing six, seldom more than eight, generations. Their graves (usually located at a rural setting near the recognized clan head's home) tended to tie the descendants to that place. Many successful families that moved their residences temporarily to the capital, or to provincial places where their bureaucrat elders were assigned, maintained a branch of the family at their rural point of origin. They continued to own land there, and maintained family shrines and lineage properties (often including endowed schools) at those sites, thereby perpetuating their close links to a rural village or town. Every individual's identity, as given in official and in ordinary social contexts, included the name of his or her lineage's place of census registration. The ties of that shared "native place" (whether or not the individual had actually been born there) were fundamental to social relationships. It was still common in Ming times for successful scholar-officials to build retirement villas and gardens at or near those places, and to idealize them as places where the life of reflection and artistic activity could best be lived.

It was moreover the norm, not the exception, for Ming elite families to have relatives of modest or even poor means within their immediate lineages; the lineage functioned as the achievement group within which some measure of responsibility for poor (and especially for poor and talented) relatives had to be met. The elite in these ways remained cognizant of and involved with life in other economic strata, and with life in non-urban settings. It is these social factors that have given rise to the description of a "rural-urban continuum" in traditional China. That is reflected also in physical elements of the open city and the extension in space of its architectural modes and lifestyles, allowing some observable continuities from the city to the countryside.

Merchants

Another interesting facet of Ming and early Qing urban life is seen in the social roles of merchants. A changing merchant ethos became particularly obvious from mid-Ming times onward. Merchants began to have a distinct voice within the elite of scholars and officials, an elite with which they acquired important links of kinship and of collaboration. Sons and daughters of merchants married sons and daughters of officials and local landowning great families in greater numbers than before, and with a new impact on the makeup of the elite. What ideally had been occupationally separated elements of the economic upper layers of society thus in Ming times became one elite stratum, and social values accommodated to this change. The intellectual currency at the time when simultaneously the later school followers of Wang Yangming aroused so much ferment and broad social debate also began to reflect new ideas concerning merchants and the ethical foundations of their social roles.[43] Thinkers emerged who were sympathetic to them, in itself a novel element in social attitudes; they defined the Dao, the Confucian "Great Way," to include the special Dao of merchants as one among the patterns appropriate to responsible human affairs. Some even went so far as to equate the functions of merchant roles with those of the scholar-officials, and to rank them at the head of society instead of in the traditionally defined lowest tier.[44] They thus recognized that the great merchants possessed wealth equal to that of anyone in the elite, but also recognized that their social functions often merged with those of the elite.

The new "merchant spirit," however, was not one which would produce rebellious, authority-defying, incipiently antiestablishment revolutionaries.

That is, it is a commonplace mistake to equate the intellectual atmosphere in which China's new thought currents emerged in the sixteenth to eighteenth centuries with the bourgeois enlightenment that fostered radical thought and revolution in eighteenth-century Europe.[45] The vigorous new merchant ethos in China claimed for men of merchant background a valid role in the traditional social elite. Chinese merchants took their place in the leading social stratum and strengthened it; unlike the eighteenth-century European Enlightenment thinkers, they did not make war on the establishment. Yet it also has been noted that the rich merchants of this period occupied the social space between the established elite and the next strata of economically better-off commoners, and they retained some of the latter's mentality; as they eagerly adopted scholar-elite lifestyles and social goals, they broadened the horizons of officialdom.[46]

The "Buds of Capitalism" Arguments

It has been argued that a kind of "state capitalism" in fact characterized the later imperial centuries of Chinese early modern history. According to that argument, the state accumulated capital and performed some entrepreneurial functions, limiting the scope of private capital to do the same.[47] In quite another vein, however, historians in Mainland China after 1949 sought to establish the emergence in Ming China of a capitalist stage in the Marxist unilinear development of universal history, to which they perforce subscribed. With that purpose in mind, they discern "buds of capitalism" getting ready to bloom in late Ming society, but which failed to realize that promise under the succeeding Qing dynasty.[48] Their researches have forced us to examine anew how "capitalism" should be defined, and to look critically at those phenomena in economic and social history of the sixteenth through the eighteenth centuries that can be somehow associated with the idea of capitalism.

The standard arguments are that new forms of money and instruments of credit accompanied a great growth in commerce. The impact is to be seen both in craft production and in agriculture, where workers and farmers came to produce for the market. In particular there was a growing commercialization of agriculture, seen in the development of agricultural commodity markets that extended across provinces and became almost nationwide in scope; in some forms of craft production, complex industrial processes (e.g., textiles, ceramics, ironwares) utilized highly differentiated labor specialization; there was an improvement of machines used in some kinds of production; and a labor market appeared that is held to have signaled the beginnings of a proletariat. Some historians have attempted to add other features, such as the beginnings of an urban (often absentee landlord) class of owner-managers, bankers, and bureaucrats in league with their ideological spokesmen in the scholar-bureaucrat elite. Such efforts to find emergent capitalism in Ming society have been a major preoccupation of many recent historians; their findings must be assessed here.

Money

Among the features of Ming life bearing on those arguments, the monetary system merits a brief review. There was a significant change in the forms and uses of money in later Ming times.

At the beginning of the dynasty in the fourteenth century a decision was made to restore the paper currency system that had originated in the Song. The fullest development of paper currency took place under the succeeding Yuan dynasty, starting in 1260. Yuan paper money was highly successful, remaining fairly stable for twenty years, then was subject to mild inflation for half a century, and finally was so discredited by serious inflation after 1350 that no one would willingly take paper in exchange. Yuan paper currency was denominated in copper cash equivalents ranging from ten cash to large bills called a "string" (*guan,* or 1,000 cash) or two strings (2 *guan,* or 2,000 cash); in value, a "string" of 1,000 copper cash or the new bill named after it was equivalent to half an ounce of silver. The largest bills were denominated in silver equivalents, up to fifty ounces of silver, called one "ingot" (*ding*). Yuan paper currency was secured by silver and gold deposits, or by silk floss (also a medium of exchange) in government warehouses; the government was careful to keep it convertible, making it widely acceptable within China and throughout bordering countries. The use of paper currency also spread to Mongol-controlled Persia, which issued its own bills on the Chinese pattern.

With that historical experience to draw upon, Chinese fiscal managers of the early Ming, noting severe shortages of both domestically produced silver and copper, turned again to the idea of using a national paper currency. The "Da Ming baochao" (precious note of the Great Ming) was first issued in 1374, in equivalents of from 100 to 500 cash, and of one string of coins (nominally 1,000 cash), the last fixed as equivalent to one ounce of silver or one-quarter ounce of gold. From the beginning, Ming paper currency was not convertible. To keep it in circulation, the government attempted to forbid the use of gold, silver, or other valuables as mediums of exchange, and for a time an effort was even made to ban the use of copper cash in making small purchases. Some taxes had to be paid at a fixed percentage in paper notes, and official salaries were paid in a regulated proportion of grain and paper. The Ming statesmen, however, proved to be quite inept fiscal managers. Within twenty-five years an ounce of silver, nominally equivalent to a 1,000 cash paper note, could be exchanged for thirty-five such notes, and by 1450 an ounce of silver could buy 1,000 of those one-string notes. Finally acknowledging that the paper was useless and that silver had replaced it, the government announced that it too would pay salaries and collect taxes in silver or its equivalents.[49] Silver wholly superseded paper as the standard currency for larger transactions, while copper cash continued to circulate for ordinary expenditures when it was available; at times a severe shortage of copper increased its value and drove it out of circulation.[50]

Silver ingots weighing fifty ounces had been a standard of value for many centuries, but smaller ingots also were used. During the Ming, following earlier practice, silver circulated by weight; it was not minted into coins, but ingots of varying sizes were used in all manner of transactions in which the ingot would be assessed for quality and the appropriate amount of metal shaved or cut off. That continued to be true until the nineteenth century.

By Ming times, mines that earlier had produced larger amounts of silver and copper were difficult to work or were exhausted. China's exports of its copper coins served the commerce of all neighboring countries, especially Japan. Trade thus drained much of China's copper off to neighboring countries; in consequence, debased copper cash and counterfeit cash circulated widely. Late in the fifteenth century Japan began to buy Chinese copper cash and other Chinese exports with raw copper, and with silver from its newly developed mines, and in the sixteenth century Japanese silver in particular flowed into China in amounts greatly in excess of China's domestic production. Midway in the sixteenth century the silver of New World mines also began to flow into China in exchange for Chinese manufactures, especially silks and porcelains. One must speak of "flowing *in*" because the movement of silver was one-way; it was exchanged for Chinese goods, whether through Chinese businessmen in Manila and Macao or onshore, and it remained to accumulate and be circulated in China. Chinese importers bought virtually nothing for which they spent silver. China began to be the great repository of the early modern world's newly discovered wealth in silver.

A main trade route across the Pacific Ocean from Acapulco (then the "City of Mexico's" main west coast port) to Manila was opened by the Spanish. Spain, attempting to enter the spice islands of Southeast Asia and rebuffed by Portugal, explored the Philippines through the mid-sixteenth century. The first trading galleon was sent to Manila in 1565, and Spain's colonial base there was established in 1571. The other principal new trade route connecting Asia to the more distant world's markets was that established by the Portuguese, who after the 1540s held Macao on China's southeast coast (see Chapter 36). The traditional land routes of trade through Inner Asia to Central and Western Asia also continued to function, stimulated by the growing commerce of Renaissance Europe. Through the exchanges of New World precious metals for Chinese products, in volumes that far exceeded China's previous foreign trade, Ming China was becoming part of an economically interactive if not yet economically unified world.[51] Long a participant in international maritime trade, China at this time experienced the consequences of the greatly enlarged patterns in world trade. In that commerce China was essentially a seller of high-quality craft manufactures. Other countries could not compete either in quality or in price. The colonies of the New World and the entire Mediterranean sphere of trade, from Portugal and Spain to the Ottoman Empire, began to complain that the influx of Chinese goods undermined their economies.

Here, however, we are concerned with the domestic impact of that trade. The vast increase in the amount of silver in circulation in China, although not evenly distributed throughout the country, made money more readily available, lowered the value of silver in relation both to copper cash and to commodities, and greatly stimulated certain sectors of the economy, especially those supplying and serving the export of goods for the world market. At the same time, China became subject to wide variations in the flow of silver out of Mexico and Peru; its ultimate transfer to China in exchange for Chinese manufactures was dependent on conditions in markets as distant as Manila, Mexico, Macao, and Madrid. Sudden shifts in factors quite beyond China's control or understanding could cause temporary crises in its economy; something like that appears to have happened in the 1630s, weakening China just when it was beset by domestic disasters at the end of the Ming.[52]

Other Economic Factors

The foregoing discussion of money in the late Ming economy has introduced aspects of domestic as well as international trade; these issues too are relevant to the question of whether Ming China was witnessing the transition into a capitalist economy. The monetization of domestic commerce is said to imply that money played an ever larger role in the lives of China's people. For one example, the largest number of those, the farmers, increasingly received cash for their products, shifted from subsistence farming to growing special crops for the market (e.g., cotton for textile manufactures), and used the profits to buy not only their own food but also draft animals, tools, and fertilizers, and to hire additional labor.[53] Or some rural people fell into the condition of hired agricultural laborers who owned neither enough land to work nor, in extreme cases, the homes they lived in. Those debased conditions were not necessarily permanent, but they became a threat in the minds of farmers. Craft industries also are said to have absorbed growing amounts of hired labor, men and women who did not own their workshops or their tools but depended on their employers. In all of these economic changes, merchants played controlling roles.

Such are some of the arguments formulated to show that China was making the change to a semicapitalist economy. While they are not factually in error, in themselves they do not sustain that point of historical interpretation. For one important example, they usually posit an instrumental role for absentee landlords, but the usual arguments about the extent and character of absentee landlordism are not well founded. There were indeed absentee landlords in increasing number from mid-Ming times onward; they were most typically farmers who invested in land in a different administrative jurisdiction from the one in which they were registered because that allowed some tax advantages. Such "absentee landlords" usually still lived on and worked their own land at the place where their family was registered. One careful estimate concludes that the extent of landlordism was quite small and that the landholdings of most landlords remained small.[54] The idea, therefore, that an urban-based entrepreneurial "class" of rapacious absentee landlords who no longer had personal or family ties to the land, accumulated capital from rents, and invested it in craft industries and commerce in league with degenerate bureau-

crats whose political protection was necessary to their success is a hypothetical invention that cannot be demonstrated. Yet it is a view, formulaically
derived, that has been granted a large measure of credibility in many Chinese
and other writings.

Another part of the argument is that great disparities in wealth, especially
urban wealth, in the later Ming caused hostility between the economic classes.
The sharpening of such urban class contradictions is held to be a feature of
emergent capitalism. There is indeed much evidence for great wealth in the
later Ming, as well as for general prosperity in most regions of the country;
there is, however, little evidence for the beginnings of fundamental structural
changes of the kind necessary either to produce cohesive lateral bonds that
might become class hostilities or, more important, to generate capitalism.

The definition of capitalism in all such arguments about historical processes
is drawn from the experience of Renaissance Europe, particularly Italy, the
Low Countries, and England. That historical model implies necessary structural changes both in the economy and in the conditions under which capital
is used: it demands the wide extension of credit, legal guarantees of loans and
contracts, the regularization of services that support wider organization of
business, impersonal management in private and public business activities,
and monetary management extended to embrace all aspects of the national
economy. The emergence of capitalism necessarily also depended on the
expansion of the judiciary system to define the conditions under which private
enterprise can grow; it has also required that economic interests be given
relatively free rein to develop and that government allow rational implementation of business operations free of excessive interference. None of these
conditions was being met in the late Ming and early Qing; there is no visible
trend in that direction. The economy was growing, to be sure, but it was not
sprouting "buds of capitalism" per se.[55] Should one in fact expect it to have
done so? If the historian is not seeking one invariable succession of precisely
defined stages in the development of a "universal" human history, economic
growth and concomitant social change in China can be compared with that
in other parts of the world without making assumptions about the relevance
of the West's particular historical experience. China's growth and social
change might more reasonably be expected to take forms conditioned by circumstances peculiar to China.

IV. LATE MING ELITE CULTURE

The decline in the effectiveness of the Ming dynasty's governing by no means
signaled a general decline in the quality of Ming civilization. The government
was close to bankruptcy for decades, but that was a fiscal, not an economic
problem. After Grand Secretary Zhang Juzheng's death in 1582, for sixty
years the administrators and the rulers competed for inefficiently collected
and wastefully disbursed revenues while the society prospered, great wealth
appeared, and thought, literature, and the arts all flourished. It might even
be argued that the political failures contributed to the cultural flowering in

several ways. Political weakness stimulated the examination of politics in relation to cultural values, giving rise to the "literary associations" *(wen she)* that
became active in social and political debate. Those political failures provided
grist for the intellectual debates among the widely divergent offshoots of
Wang Yangming's teaching and their philosophical opponents. The political
atmosphere discouraged many of the most talented about active careers in
government, making them prefer alternatives to the demanding and uncertain
official careers by seeking the relatively idle postings at places such as the
secondary capital at Nanjing, where cultural life reached great new heights.[56]
Or in some cases the political atmosphere led them, after winning their
degrees and serving briefly, to retire altogether from office to live in congenial
environments in the provinces where they could devote their full energies to
the life of the spirit. Many talented men of the later Ming did not even go
so far as to gain official status at all; they dropped out of the ever more
crowded race for the competitive *jinshi* examination degree to live by other
means and follow other pursuits. The sixteenth and seventeenth centuries
became one of those rare periods in Chinese imperial history when a significant portion (though not a majority) of the literati found the attractions of
life outside the political arena greater than those within. After the fall of the
Ming in 1644, that continued for some decades to be true, but for other reasons. Those new factors included the dislocations in officialdom and throughout elite society caused by the change of dynasty. These circumstances will
be discussed in Chapter 32.

The extraordinary century and a half of the later Ming dynasty offers a
kaleidoscope of brilliant form and color, ever shifting and ever new. At the
end of the Qing dynasty and in the early twentieth century, in retrospect the
late Ming appeared to modernizing Chinese intellectuals to have prefigured
many of the changes they sought for their time.[57] Expressionism took form
in the new poetry and literary essay; eroticism found a place in expression;
trends toward abstraction appeared in the graphic arts; social freedoms were
championed in radical thought; companionate marriage could be idealized
over Confucian convention; humor and pathos filled the new dramatic literature of human feelings; and a broadly ironic rhetoric marked the profoundly
imaginative reworking of popular themes in the great works of Ming fiction.[58]
All these were aspects of the cultural life that burgeoned in this extraordinary
time.

The tone of that cultural life strongly indicates that private lives of people
in the elite and higher sub-elite social strata, about which we can know the
most, were deeply affected. What appear to be (and at the time were described
as) new and more varied patterns in family and community life are reflected
in such things as entertainment literature and travel writings, in changing
religious organization and practices, in the expanded market for cheaply produced books, and in more extravagant modes in consumption and entertainment. Of particular interest, there appear to have emerged new features in
the opportunities for women in upper-level society to express themselves and
to broaden the patterns of their lives. The newness of all that may simply

reflect the increase in informal writings being produced, and preserved, from the sixteenth century onward, but in considerable measure too the content of private lives was qualitatively new. It becomes possible to describe much more closely than heretofore the mundane existence of many families and individuals who were not among the most prominent figures of their age, because the existing written evidence for those kinds of lives is richer and fuller than for earlier times.

Scholars combing these materials in recent decades have found much information to fill out our knowledge about social welfare and philanthropy; about child rearing, orphanages and adoption; about nutrition and disease; and about the people who promoted broad social goals. Especially important are the efforts to understand the lives of women in elite society.[59] Late Ming women achieved unprecedented prominence as published writers, particularly of poetry in traditional genres. The preservation of their writings enables us to gain an appreciation of their roles in educating their sons and daughters, in supporting and sharing the lives of their husbands and the larger circle of family associations, and in maintaining literary friendships and intellectual exchanges with other women beyond their families. The exploration of the rich veins of ore in such materials is only beginning. Closer study of late Ming lives—men's as well as women's—may well lead to the emergence of a new social history.

Despite its vitality and impressive achievements, however, the age traditionally has not been highly valued. Its excesses were blamed by some for the downfall of the dynasty, and the succeeding Manchu dynasty, once again a conquest dynasty of questioned legitimacy, denigrated the late Ming in order to justify its invasion and conquest. The Qing dynasty fostered a tightening of orthodoxy. Proclaiming itself the defender of traditional values, however cynical and self-serving that stance was, it succeeded in discouraging free-ranging thought and unconventional lifestyles. For that reason some late Qing revolutionary movements throughout the nineteenth century looked to the Ming for their inspiration, holding up the slogan "Restore the Ming" as a way to arouse public resentment. That revolutionary identification with the Ming did not long endure in the early twentieth century; in the confused politics of modern China, more compelling foreign models commanded broader respect within activist circles than did any restoration of traditional ideals. In short, the late Ming's cultural florescence has not brought it much favorable attention in modern China, and probably never will. We must look at it for its own sake, not to validate any current social or political agendas.

Looked at for its own sake, nevertheless, it offers endlessly intriguing avenues of exploration. Those might well commence with the material life of a society enjoying general prosperity. Despite the undeniable regional impoverishment of the northwest, the anomaly of increasing urban poverty in the richest cities, and an expanding population always narrowing the margin in agriculture, most of Ming society experienced an unprecedented level of consumption and enjoyment. Yet many late Ming writers were fully (and often sadly) aware of this, seeing that earlier norms of orderly social behavior no longer prevailed. They cited at length specific examples of lavish waste and uninhibited consumption. Extravagant late Ming lifestyles seemed to them quite contrary to fondly recorded models drawn from earlier and purer generations. The details they offer us about degenerating social practices help us understand a time of broad change even when we do not share their dismay— and may suspect that they themselves were in fact ambivalent about it. The prevailing social conservatism, and the ever-present element of Confucian "puritanism," made their criticism conventionally obligatory. How the elite in fact participated in their changing world must be measured in many ways. The most accessible evidence comes from the world of thought.

Literary Thought

The Ming dynasty is one of the great ages in literary theory and criticism. It is often compared with the post-Han centuries of division into the Northern and Southern dynasties (third through seventh centuries C.E.) as one of China's two great periods when extensive literary thought took form in a wide variety of writings. Some modern historians have suggested that literary thought in both ages became an alternate vehicle for social and political criticism: people wrote about the current state of literature when they really were drawing attention to lapsed political and philosophical ideals. There is much substance in that interpretation, but it should not distract our attention from the creativity and force of their ideas on literature per se; in the mind of the time there was a causal link between the two, but literary criticism was no mere metaphor for social criticism. From its early beginnings it had attempted to define the purely artistic elements of literary creation.[60]

Poetry was the premier arena of literary development, the true measure of an age, and certain genres of expository prose were closely linked to poetry as keys to the worth of an age. All agreed that the ancient *Book of Odes* (*Shi Jing*, or "Classic of Poetry," thought already to have been a venerated ancient text in the time of Confucius) was the fountainhead of literary cultivation, and that the subsequently established genres of poetic writing in Han, Tang, and Song times provided models of poetic expression to which later ages must aspire. All poets, that is, virtually all educated men and growing numbers of women, produced prose-poems *(fu)* on Han models, ancient lyrics *(gu yuefu)* in the post-Han mode, regulated verse *(shi)* on the Tang and Song model, perhaps also lyrics *(ci, qu)* in the Song and post-Song styles, to display their literary mastery. Along with that poetizing they produced prose writings in a succession of historically established forms. Such was the tradition within which Ming writers lived and wrote.

Early in the Ming, both lyrical and expository writing modes took on a resonant and ornately sculpted manner associated with court and chancellery; that mode came to be called the *taige* style of writing, *tai* and *ge* being allusions to high office in the central government. That court style symbolized the "restoration" of leadership in society by scholars who found their "proper" place in a government staffed by learned men after centuries of compromise with alien power holders. It conveyed an aura of self-satisfaction. By the late fifteenth century a reaction set in which ridiculed that literary manner as stuffy and contrived. There was a call for vigor and simpler elegance, put forth under the slogan "Prose writing must adhere to Qin and Han; poetry must be that of High Tang." That meant restoring archaic models, but it was an archaism of a reforming, almost a revolutionary kind. Within that cultural milieu of unquestioned veneration of the past, one could effectively justify dissatisfaction with and reaction against the present most effectively by proposing correctives that appeared to have antique validity. The reformers called for a return to the prose of the early imperial era, when the great historian Sima Qian (145?–90? B.C.E.) wrote his *Records of the Grand Historian (Shi Ji)* in strong, uncomplicated prose, and to the unmatched *shi* poetry of the high Tang, when Li Bai (701–762) and Du Fu (712–770) lived. That was an irreproachable way of rejecting present styles in favor of a new literary voice. Such archaism in the name of reform had been employed before, notably in the *gu wen* (ancient styles) movement of the early Northern Song. Everyone understood that this was, once again, both a literary movement and a call for broader change, but its strictly literary and aesthetic significance must not be overlooked.

In early sixteenth-century Ming China, that wish for literary revival did not produce a new golden age in literature. Yet it held great meaning for the entire intellectual arena, where everyone wrote poetry and prose in those styles and, as concerned insiders, followed the related political and social controversies. During the sixteenth century, two waves of reforming influences were headed by the "Seven Early Masters," who dominated its first thirty years, then by the "Seven Later Masters," who were active throughout the second half of the century. Most of those writers are more important today for their literary thought than for their literary production per se. They debated and quarreled among themselves, and sparred with other writers of slightly different standards who also joined in the fray. Eventually the literary world of the sixteenth century concluded that the archaists' calls for reform were to be sure necessary, but that their own writing seldom transcended shallow imitativeness. The search to find a more compelling guiding spirit went on.

Within the mainstream of regulated verse *(shi)* poetry, as well as in the arena of the informal essay, there emerged powerful pleas for a literature of deeper human feelings that responded to the inner voice of intuitive inspiration. That no doubt reflected the ongoing and ever more spirited philosophical conflicts over Wang Yangming's philosophy, as carried forward in divergent ways by several schools claiming to be his true followers. Wang's philosophy of radical idealism was deeply influential throughout the worlds of literary and artistic expression. While the venerable poetry and prose genres continued to be regarded as the mainstream of intellectual and artistic life, many writers also experimented with the peripheral genres of drama and fiction. One of the greatest dramatists of all Chinese history, Tang Xianzu (1550–1616), wrote many plays, of which the four best known are constructed on the theme of dreams, thus focusing on the capacities of the mind.[61] A contemporary of William Shakespeare (1564–1616), Tang Xianzu has been called "China's Shakespeare," although similarities in their lives or in their dramas are not readily apparent. Tang was, however, a supreme master among a number of literary dramatists who brought new life to the theater in late Ming times, perhaps in that way justifying the comparison, though his particular dramatic style has not retained the broad, vivid impact in later times that we find in Shakespeare.

Drama, having some links to the refined art of poetry, was granted a high place in late Ming literary history. Fiction, by contrast, flourished without that kind of formal recognition. Four of what are called China's "five great novels" were written (or rewritten) during the sixteenth century, although two of those are reworkings of long storytellers' tales dating from 200 years earlier. The four great Ming novels are *Jinpingmei (Golden Lotus, The Plum in the Golden Vase), Xiyou Ji (Journey to the West, Monkey), Shuihu Zhuan (All Men Are Brothers, The Water Margins, Outlaws of the Marsh)*, and *Sanguo Zhi (The Romance of the Three Kingdoms)*.[62] Novels mostly appeared anonymously or under pseudonyms. Immensely popular and much reprinted, they are the works of Ming literature most valued in modern China. They were written in a semicolloquial style by members of the elite of high education who did not want their reputations to be associated with such "vulgar" entertainment literature. Short fiction also flowered in the late Ming, the colloquial short story supplementing and superseding the much older literary (or classical language) short story. Several hundred Ming colloquial short stories exist, from which a number have been effectively translated.[63] Fascinating as entertainment literature, they also can be taken to reveal daily lives of ordinary people.

The Examination Essay

The infamous "eight-legged essay" *(bagu wen)*, also called "timely prose" or "the prose of our time" *(shi wen)*, must be discussed in relation both to Ming literature and to social and political developments. This intricately constructed form of the essay came in the late fifteenth century to be prescribed for the main section of the civil service examinations, and continued to be used until that system was at last abolished at the beginning of the twentieth century. Some leading Ming literary figures wrote essays in this form, valuing it as an important genre of literary expression. By the end of the Ming, however, many reform-minded critics condemned the eight-legged essay as the villain in what they perceived to be China's intellectual decline, calling it an imposed form that discouraged originality and stifled creativity. By the end of the imperial era it had come to symbolize reactionary obfuscation and classical-minded incompetence to deal with the world's real needs.

That is ironic, for the examination essay was designed as a tool for making classically educated scholars demonstrate how classical Confucian writings were directly relevant to contemporary problems. Given a phrase from one of the classics, the examinee was required to elaborate on it in prescribed steps of development to make intellectually dazzling arguments about the timely relevance of the deepest ideas embedded in ancient texts. The exercise can be seen as an extended intelligence test, requiring almost total memorization of the classical sources and their extensive commentaries, but also demanding extreme ingenuity in penetrating the topic to arrive at a perfectly balanced and powerful conclusion. That is why some Ming writers took the eight-legged essay seriously as a genre of literature. To be sure, so complex an exercise could degenerate into one of stifling boredom and mechanically contrived effects, and that indeed often happened. Yet, simply as a test of both learning and intellectual acuity, it probably served as well as any other formal device might have for selecting Ming bureaucrats.[64]

The late Ming was a great age for painting and calligraphy, after poetry the other two major arts of the elite. Major trends in sixteenth-century painting have been interpreted as evidence for "the formation of a new literati attitude."[65] "Book culture" too flourished, both in the editing and printing of books, and in the collecting of rare and important editions.[66] Connoisseurship in all the arts reached high levels in the Ming. The elite of education (who might be persons of little wealth) developed refined lives, pursued their private activities in leisurely and cultivated fashion, gathered about them objects of beauty and of historical associations, developed innumerable specialized branches of practical learning (e.g., medicine and pharmacology, music, mathematics, geography, botany, and many more) and of antiquarian lore, and at their best led lives of both vigor and refinement. China in the last century and a half of the Ming undoubtedly had the highest levels of literacy in the world, in a population quite generally devoted to getting ahead, to achieving a better life. From its farming villages and rural markets to the urban or rural gardens and courtyards of the elite, it bustled with activity.

30

THE COURSE
OF MING FAILURE

The fall of the Ming dynasty in 1644 followed a long period of political stagnation and administrative failure, but those accumulated weaknesses need not have foredoomed the dynasty. It might have overcome those problems, to survive and perhaps even to flourish again. That did not happen, principally because poor choices were made throughout the reign of the Chongzhen emperor, the fifteenth and last of Ming Taizu's successors, who reigned over the realm from the capital at Beijing in the years 1627–1644. He and his government, further weakened by his indecisive and inept leadership, had to face three grave problems: the crippling effects of fiscal mismanagement, a new military threat from Inner Asia, and the domestic turmoil caused by the bandit-rebel armies arising in the northwest, in Shaanxi Province. The way in which the dynasty succumbed to those problems is briefly recounted here. To answer the much larger question of *why* this dynasty fell, unable to withstand perils that were in themselves neither unprecedented nor insurmountable, calls for an effort to reassess the fundamental interpretations of Chinese imperial history.

1. Launching the Chongzhen Reign: Random Inadequacies, Persistent Hopes

After the protracted failures to govern during the long Wanli reign, followed by the vicious eunuch Wei Zhongxian's dictatorship under the Tianqi emperor, the late Ming political nightmare appeared to have come to a most satisfying end in 1627. The right people won out after all, and the new emperor gave hopeful signs of being committed to vigorous and upright rule. What happened, we must ask, to bring all those initial hopes and energies to naught a short seventeen years later?

Some historians argue that the political decline apparent already in the early years of the Wanli reign period foretold the inevitable downturn in a "dynastic cycle."[1] Throughout this book the concept of successive phases in the history of a dynastic epoch, likened, on biological analogy, to birth, youth, maturity, and the decline of old age, is rejected as irrelevant to the processes of history. The only relevance that might apply in the Chinese case is that because the Chinese believed in something like that cyclical view of history, they expected to see the signs of it as they observed the course of a dynasty's development; it was thus in some degree a self-fulfilling prophecy. Yet a Chinese counterpart to that way of explaining a dynasty's life history was the concept of the midpoint revival, or *zhongxing*. The Chinese also saw examples of that phenomenon, going back initially to the venerated Zhou dynasty (ca. 1100–256 B.C.E.), and repeated at several times in later history. That "revival" idea allowed human effort to reverse the biological life process of dynasties and make them flourish anew. Quite reasonably, the Chinese avoided rigid formulas that would leave them no human way out of their problems.

In October 1627, when the sixteen-year-old Zhu Youjian ascended the throne, there immediately ensued one of those gratifying housecleanings, such as people remembered when in 1521, for example, Emperor Shizong succeeded the errant Emperor Wuzong, or earlier, when Emperor Xiaozong in 1487 got rid of the degenerate elements that his father, the Emperor Xianzong, had allowed to dominate the court. Zhu Youjian's first actions as emperor again lifted spirits and released energies. Officialdom once again drew men imbued with a reforming spirit. With the cooperation of a clearminded young ruler, how long would it take them to make the Ming dynasty flourish anew? The Chongzhen reign period, which began with the New Year in 1628, did not become the bright age in history then envisioned. We must seek to understand why, without however falling back on either the traditional or the newer formulaic devices for fitting this period of history into preconceived patterns.

The new emperor's task was formidable. None among even the most powerful eunuch dictators before Wei Zhongxian had created a network of agents and underlings so extensive or so tightly controlled as was Wei's. Eunuchs and civil officials, military officers and police under his domination held the most important positions at the capital and throughout the provinces. Their power was so pervasive that the Chongzhen emperor himself had good reason to fear that he might be poisoned, attacked by an assassin, or abducted and done away with. As in some of the previous accessions during the 260-year-old Ming dynasty, this earnest young ruler had a good sense of where the immediate problems lay; he wanted only to clear them away and bring back orderly governing. That meant first of all eliminating eunuch power and turning the tasks of governing back to qualified civil service officials.

To eliminate Wei Zhongxian, he was forced to adopt subterfuge. He was unsure of support at court. A large share of civil officials, palace eunuchs, and military men were compromised by their relationships with Wei; now they joined ranks to protect themselves. Zhu Youjian felt his way carefully, revealed no feelings, and carefully feigned acceptance of the status quo. He even turned down Wei's formalistic request to retire, to reassure him that no hostile actions were being contemplated. One by one he managed to bring in some new eunuchs loyal to himself to attend his daily needs and thereby distance himself from Wei's underlings. He made a few innocent-appearing appointments in the Outer Court. When Wei's principal military supporter, the Minister of War, was forced to retire to mourn the death of a parent, the eunuch's supporters were weakened. When lengthy impeachment documents were then received outlining Wei's many crimes, the ruler had acquired enough confidence to summon Wei to listen while the documents were read aloud. Wei was deeply shaken. He could make no defense on his own, and the emperor would not allow another eunuch to plead for him. Wei was ignominiously transferred to humble guard duty at the tombs of the founding emperor's parents at Zhongdu in Anhwei.

The old eunuch had ruled with unrestrained ferocity as a compliant emperor's alter ego; now he was but an empty shell. En route to the most humble of eunuch positions, he received a report that the emperor was planning to arrest him and many others. Defenseless and terrified of what was to come, he hanged himself. On receiving that news, the emperor ordered Wei's body shredded and exposed, an extreme measure intended to indicate the depth of his hostility to the dictator and his entire political faction. A dozen or more leading associates of Wei's were executed.[2]

That did not solve the problem. The extensive network of men throughout officialdom who were tainted by recent association with Wei during the Tianqi reign (1621–February 1628) was strongly entrenched; they fought back aggressively to protect themselves. They submitted impeachments of the new men appointed by the emperor, attempting to impugn them and alienate them from the emperor's favor. They browbeat other officials wherever they could, trying to keep a solid faction together to oppose the emperor's sweeping changes. A thoroughgoing political showdown began to take form. The emperor gained support from a younger generation of leaders in intellectual, political, and literary fields. The intellectual scene, however, was extremely fragmented. The young emperor did not possess enough presence, enough force of character, to harness all those reforming factions under his leadership.

Factional Alignments

The Donglin group, in the recent past the eunuch faction's most determined opponents and principal victims, had been reduced to a remnant by Wei's suppression in the years of his total control, 1623–1627. A new wave of reform-minded men now quickly took their place, continuing some of their ideals but organizing for more effective political action. A special feature of the time is that young officials and would-be candidates for the *jinshi* examinations expressed their commitment to purifying politics and restoring the country by forming "literary societies" *(wen she),* loosely modeled on the earlier Donglin Society. Once again in Chinese history a reinvigoration of the ways people expressed themselves in literature was linked directly to the regeneration of society and government and provided the arena of discourse for launching their reform ideas.

The most important of the many new societies was the Fu she, or Restoration Society, whose members dominated the lists of the successful candidates in the *jinshi* examinations held in 1628 and 1631, the first two examinations of the Chongzhen reign. Many of the best minds of the late Ming belonged to or associated with the Fu she. They might have become "the emperor's men" had he but been capable of trusting and deploying them. It is tempting to believe that they could have generated a thoroughgoing administrative reform. One of their outstanding leaders, Chen Zilong (1608–1647), led a group of like-minded scholars to produce the *Huang Ming jingshi wenbian* (Imperial Ming Documentary Compilation on Statecraft) which drew together an immense assemblage of memorials and other documents, covering in historical depth statecraft issues from the beginning of the dynasty to their own time. It was published in 1638 and widely disseminated. Chen Zilong and his group of compilers turned their focus away from ideology to "practical statesmanship,"[3] suggesting that in more stable times they might have accomplished a rationalization of governmental practices. Whether so large a step truly was within their intellectual grasp we cannot know; they either died with the fall of the Ming or were coopted into the new Qing dynasty political scene that allowed no such deep probing of political realities.

Still other members of the official elite and the literati were, however, neither Fu she sympathizers nor associates of the pro-eunuch faction. Many stood on different philosophical grounds. Among those, persons influenced by the Wang Yangming school of Neo-Confucian idealism that had arisen a century earlier were particularly active. The Donglin ideologues, by contrast, were Neo-Confucian conservatives; their society, dating from 1604, had been founded on support for orthodoxy and indignant hostility to the later developments in the Wang school.[4] Drawing strength from the shared experience of closely supporting one another when under Wei Zhongxian's attack, and having a moral zeal for reform, the Donglin group had been labeled the "Donglin party" by their enemies, "party" *(dang)* being a bad word in the Chinese political vocabulary.[5] Some survivors from the earlier phase of Donglin history now also made a comeback; they gained positions in the central government, but they did not dominate it. The Fu she or Restoration Society members had felt great sympathy for the Donglin martyrs of the 1620s and shared aspects of their intellectual heritage, but they were a new generation of political thinkers and activists. The Fu she group drew on a broader spectrum of philosophical positions; they placed high value on literary accomplishment and the command of history, seeing in that kind of personal cultivation the tools for analyzing the political problems facing the dynasty.

Throughout the breadth of the realm, the intellectual and literary life of the elite at the end of the Ming was as fragmented as it was vibrant.[6] At the court, however, those qualities were not always helpful; leading figures from

majority of their princely estates were located, the proportion of the local revenues needed to sustain them had become larger than could be met from the tax revenues of the local county governments responsible for them. Would the inexorably increasing weight of this fiscal burden break the back of the Ming state? Probably not.

The senior imperial heirs in each generation[10] continued to be well-maintained, but among the collateral lines, automatic reduction in rank with each passing generation rendered many of them pitifully insignificant. Local governments simply ignored the responsibility to provide them with living stipends. Many were forced to sell belongings, take out loans from usurers, suffer hardships and indignities. They could not leave their assigned estates, they could not work or earn money, and they could only petition the throne for compassion which seldom was forthcoming.[11]

This element in late Ming social history alone qualifies as a problem that inevitably intensified throughout the course of this dynasty. It alone represents the kind of growing difficulty that was supposed to foretell the state's fatal inability to cope. Further examination, however, shows that it did not possess that much significance. The status of imperial descendants might have been changed to take them off the public tax rolls; it had been proposed in the late sixteenth century that, on the model of earlier dynasties, Ming princes should be allowed to sit for the examinations and fill public offices and, if unsuccessful, then fare for themselves. That plan was never fully implemented, but in some statesmen's minds at least it opened up the option of changing the status of imperial heirs. Local officials quite generally resented the diversion of their resources to support imperial drones; alternatives, including the de facto option already in effect of simply not paying, had become thinkable. In any event, the problem was susceptible to management, and as it intensified, it clearly could have been better managed.

Such a thoroughgoing management reform did not emerge, and the number of imperial dependents was allowed to grow. But counted together with all the other persons supported by the government through salaries or other disbursements, China's seventeenth-century complement of princely heirs, officials and their families, eunuchs and their dependents, garrison soldiers and imperial guards and their families, probably numbered fewer than 5 million, less than 3 percent of the total population, which at that time was well over 200 million.[12] They were to be sure a serious fiscal burden, in large part because of the general weaknesses in fiscal management, but for the state to support 3 or even 5 percent of the population should not have become a crushing economic weight.

One must conclude, therefore, that while the steadily increasing numbers of imperial clan dependents presented an administrative embarrassment, the financial burden they created does not lend significant support to the dynastic cycle interpretation of the Ming fall. All the other problems that weakened the late Ming state were susceptible to reversal through intelligent and forceful management. That did not happen. However unlikely the chances of its happening, neither was the dynasty's collapse inevitable.

The late Ming state was administered in an inefficiently organized, purposely diffuse manner, but not significantly more so in the late Ming than at the beginning. The Ming system was structurally less rational (especially after the founder's changes of 1380) and administration was less rigorous (particularly in fiscal matters) than it needed to be; moreover, Ming statesmen were not granted much encouragement to tinker with the system, much less to revise it substantially. Yet it has been argued that precisely for those reasons, its widely accepted low performance under normal conditions lent it resiliency under extreme conditions.[13] The Ming did not collapse from its society's internal disabilities; it was the external blows, coupled with imperial failure to lead, that ultimately destroyed the dynasty.

To look at the problem from the other side, how could any rival challenge the Ming state? An enemy from without faced the largest, richest, and most populous society in the world at that time. It had one-third of the world's people; it was moreover economically the most advanced civilization, in command of traditions in practical learning and indigenous technology that enriched its people's productive capacities. Its court and its rulers to be sure often faltered, and its central government could be demoralized, but away from the center the system of governing continued to work: it ensured local social order, collected revenues, and reinforced the normative system which maintained the people's expectations. How could any enemy challenge a structure of such weight and stability?

An enemy from without had to have a base in the nearer steppe (for that time, no other enemies need be considered) from which to utilize the comparative advantages of mobile warfare over positional warfare of fixed battle lines and fortifications, defended largely by civilian farmer-soldiers. The external enemy also would need to have in place a system for governing sedentary subjects, as it acquired them, in order to take full advantage of its superior striking force. If it could not do that, it would remain a raiding, plundering force but would not become a conquering power. We have seen the brilliant examples of the Khitans, the Tanguts, the Jurchens, and above all the Mongols; those examples were still vivid in the minds of steppe leaders. Could their success be repeated in the seventeenth century?

An enemy from within, by contrast, would need to give the people, particularly the local governors and elite strata, credible reasons why they merited the Mandate to rule, and then to prove it by winning on the battlefield. The expectation that dynasties will fall is implicit in the theory about how they arise; the conceptual problems surrounding succession are not in themselves a bar to challenging a legitimate regime. The practical problems were more difficult. Any challenger from within also would have to acquire a base area, one within the Chinese world, an area with manpower and fiscal resources capable of sustaining warfare while the rebel conducted his conquest of the vast Chinese territory. The structure of the Ming state made that difficult: there were no regional armies large enough to succeed, waiting to be taken over by rebel leaders, and the fiscal support of the provinces was so fragmented that it could not be readily commandeered by a regional upstart.[14]

During the Ming, the serious challenges to the reigning emperor came from within the imperial line; in 1402 one such challenger succeeded, but his success led to measures which prevented the three subsequent imperial rebels from succeeding.[15] Otherwise, internal rebellions with the potential to construct a successor dynasty did not occur during the Ming, although one or two at the very end, in the 1630s, might have gained that potential; and the most potent of those did in fact cause the fall of the Ming, if adventitiously. Politically and militarily the Ming dynasty was very stable for 250 years.

That stability was not seriously shaken until late in the unhappy Chongzhen emperor's reign; he faced grave military challenges from both within and without, from the Manchus north of the new Great Wall, and from mass armies of Chinese "roving bandits" *(liu kou)* pouring in from the northwest provinces. Their histories will repay our brief review.

II. THE MANCHU INVADERS

The Manchus were Jurchens, direct heirs of the Jurchens whose Jin dynasty ruled over most of North China between 1115 and 1234. They did not officially adopt the new ethnic name "Manchu" until 1635.[16] The success of those earlier Jurchens under their great founding ruler Aguda, the Jin dynasty's Emperor Taizu who reigned 1115–1123, was marked by the explosive suddenness of their rise to military domination, first destroying the Khitans' Liao dynasty, then terminating the Northern Song. In the following century the Mongol armies, after completing their destruction of the Jin dynasty in 1234, absorbed the Jurchen fighting forces. After the fall of the Yuan dynasty in 1368, much of that Jurchen population appears to have resettled in southeastern Manchuria close to the Korean border, but other scattered elements of Jurchen population occupied most of eastern Manchuria north to the Amur River and beyond into Siberia.

Even after the fall of their Yuan dynasty in China, in 1368 the Mongols remained the great threat to Ming security; in the fourteenth and fifteenth centuries Ming policy was to divide and control the Mongol population throughout Mongolia. Titles and special privileges were granted to the Eastern Mongols, called the tribes of the Uriyangkhad, in the so-called Three Eastern Commanderies that were located in western Manchuria and eastern Mongolia.[17] The pivot of Ming border defense was the court's special link to these favored (but by no means trusted) Mongols, to whose chieftains they granted titles as heads of commanderies *(wei)* and as regional commanders *(dusi)*, as in the Ming military system. The granting of such titles, however, was a diplomatic gesture, not an administrative reality. The Ming court would occasionally make demands on them for military cooperation but could not dictate compliance; the Mongols responded as they saw their interests being served. Mongol policy was to draw as much benefit from their privileged trading and political relations to the Ming court as possible while occasionally attempting to reunify all the Mongols to resist Chinese domination.

Ming strategists saw the Jurchens as a counterweight to Mongol military potential; they were looked on as being equally susceptible to manipulation through trade. They granted hundreds of titles to Jurchen tribal leaders, almost 400 of whom were called heads of commanderies, but in these instances there was still less pretense of operational linkage to the Ming military system.[18] The exception was the Jianzhou Commandery in southern central Manchuria, actually a complex system of four or five adjacent commanderies here referred to collectively as Jianzhou, where the culturally most advanced Jurchens had settled.[19] Like the Mongols, these Jurchen tribal groups were entirely independent of China in all aspects of their domestic governing; they found benefits in the special diplomatic relationship to the Ming court and used them to their advantage vis-à-vis the nearer Mongol tribes, as well as with other Jurchens. The Three Eastern Commanderies (set up especially for the Uriyangkhad Mongols) gave those three Mongol tribal groups a strategic place in Manchurian power struggles. The nominal Jianzhou Jurchen commanderies incidentally served as a basis for Jurchen-Mongol interaction. Much in the shadow of the Mongols, the Jurchens too struggled for advantage at the edge of the steppe.

More than two centuries of Jurchen-Mongol interaction as well as the Jurchen-Chinese relationship bore on the rise of Manchu power in the early seventeenth century. These struggles echo the conditions in late Tang and Song times when the Khitans and Jurchens rose to great power in the same region; in other ways these circumstances had a new character in the seventeenth century. Their leaders were acutely aware of the long history going back to the tenth century; their awareness made that accumulation of history and legend a strong factor in strategic thinking on all sides.

The Jianzhou Jurchens were farming people, but also hunters and livestock breeders, as had been the Jurchens in the twelfth century before they founded their Jin dynasty. They were not steppe nomads like the Mongols, but they had lived as neighbors to the Eastern Mongols, whose cavalry warfare deeply impressed them. They imitated and borrowed from the Mongols, but not in wholesale fashion as their ancestors had imitated the Khitans four centuries earlier. In that prior phase of history, the "wild" Jurchens emerged from the deep forests of Manchuria to come under Khitan domination; they hated their Khitan masters but knew little else of the world. By the mid-sixteenth century the Jianzhou Jurchens had long lived in close relationship with both the Mongols and the Chinese, under conditions quite different from those in the twelfth century. They too constantly borrowed and imitated, but sought gains through strategic maneuvers in the multisided power game; they were proud warriors, but they were led by men who employed craft in preference to the rage and fury of revenge which had served Aguda so well. Their situation, and their tactics, were far more like Abaoji's in the rise of the Khitans (see Chapter 2) than they were like Aguda's in 1115.

Nurhaci

The founder of Manchu power was Nurhaci (1559–1626), known also by his posthumous title as the Emperor Taizu of the Qing dynasty. The official history of the Qing offers very little information about his background; it names six of his immediate forebears but gives no substantial information about their lives, and no dates for them, other than telling how his father and grandfather, while serving the Ming as scouts, were killed in 1583 in a Ming attack on other Jurchen leaders.[20] Nurhaci's birthdate, 1559, is the earliest date in the history of the Qing imperial line supplied by any of the official writings. His Aisin Gioro clan was an obscure line of minor tribal chieftains among the Jianzhou Jurchens. Like so many others, the clan leaders bore low-ranking titles granted by the Ming court. They regularly carried tribute to Beijing, traded there, and were well acquainted with the operations of Ming policy toward its northern neighbors.

Nurhaci distinguished himself as a warrior chieftain and strategist; he began by conducting wars of modest scale against other Jurchen tribal leaders to elevate his standing among the many chieftains. By the time he was thirty he had consolidated his control over most of the Jianzhou Jurchens and was awarded a high Ming title, Assistant Commissioner-in-Chief of the Jianzhou garrison forces.[21] He continued to war successfully against holdout Jurchen tribes, and he also offered to join with Ming armies then fighting in Korea to resist the Japanese invasions of the 1590s under Toyotomi Hideyoshi. For this the Ming court, though not able to accept his offer, granted him the splendid title of Dragon-Tiger Generalissimo. He consistently courted the Mongols. In 1607 an important confederation of Khalkha Mongols in central Mongolia dispatched a prince to bestow on Nurhaci the title of khan and accept him on equal grounds.

In his letter of reply to the Khalkha Mongol khan Nurhaci wrote, "We are different in language to be sure, but in the clothes we wear and the kind of life we lead we are the same."[22] The grant of the title "khan," equivalent to "emperor" in Chinese, first of all recognized Nurhaci's military leadership, but it also reflects the growing range of Jurchen cultural affinities with the Mongols, acknowledged in Nurhaci's response. A large number of Nurhaci's sons and grandsons married Mongol wives; the elite families of the two peoples formed close associations.

One other example provides further illustration. Most Jurchens had perhaps long forgotten that their ancestors once had developed their own writing system. In the fifteenth century Jurchen leaders requested that the Ming court's written communications should not attempt to use the old Jurchen script but be in Mongolian because that was easier for them to read. The shift to Mongolian was only slowly carried out, but eventually its use prevailed.[23] Only in 1599 did Nurhaci take the step, paralleling events in all the earlier conquest dynasties' histories, of ordering that a script be devised for writing his people's Manchu language, and in this case (like the Mongol decision to write Mongolian in a script derived from Uighur writing) he decreed that the

Uighur-Mongol script should now be further adapted to write the Manchu language.[24] He did not choose to invent a Chinese-type script, as his Jurchen forebears had done.

The Mongols had begun a century earlier to forgo their undiluted nomadism; they had converted to Lamaist Buddhism, built permanent monastery settlements and adjacent towns for actively recruiting Chinese settlers, who were welcomed among them to engage in crafts and commerce. They also were adapting in some measure to forms of social organization practiced among their sedentary neighbors.[25] Yet they still were the masters of mounted archery and cavalry tactics, the most formidable military opponents in Asia. Nurhaci observed how the Mongols had absorbed and governed Chinese settlers north of the Great Wall; he too encouraged trade, favored commerce conducted by the Chinese, encouraged their iron smelting and weapons manufacture, and began to enlist leading Chinese from their settlements in Manchuria for help both in military services and in civil governing. But most ordinary Chinese farmers, craftsmen, and petty traders in Liaodong who came under Jurchen rule at this time were not considered free men; they were placed in categories of compulsory service, their status sometimes translated as that of slaves. Despite that treatment of the ordinary Chinese population, many local Chinese military and political leaders, seeing an opportunity to gain higher positions, voluntarily offered their services to Nurhaci and his Jurchen nobles.

Nurhaci's attitude toward the Ming dynasty began to change. He had a vantage point from which to observe the Ming ineptitude in defense, the corrupt administration of its garrisons and trading entrepôts, and the dishonest dealings of the eunuchs who were regarded by the Mongols as China's real masters. His growing sense of Chinese ineptitude could well have encouraged him to believe that he could build a strong Jurchen state without fearing Chinese intervention. The first step was to construct an effective organization and control system over the Jurchen tribes. Despite the cultural closeness developing between the Manchus and their Mongol mentors, Manchu society remained "Jurchen," quite different from Mongol social structure and its distinctive ethos.

In the early twelfth century Aguda and his successors had organized the Jurchen tribal population into an effective system combining military and civil governing. All adult males were subject to military service for which their households supported them by providing mounts, armor, weapons, and other supplies. Those households were grouped into units of 100 (subsequently enlarged to 300) and of 1,000 that corresponded roughly to tribes and small tribal confederations.[26] The system also allowed for easy absorption of surrendered populations and captive fighters, could be expanded as needed, and gave the government an administrative means for deploying fighting units, along with the farming families who provided their social support. It differed from the Mongols' decimal organization of their cavalry forces into units of 100, 1,000 and 10,000; the Mongols were not linked to land or to place, scorned farming, and were (with their families) wholly mobile.

The Jurchen system acknowledged its people's basic values. Its fighting men were farmers, serving in some kind of rotation while retaining their links to the land.[27] This fact lies at the base of much of the historical Mongol-Jurchen difference, a difference that persisted as the Jurchens of the late sixteenth century, by a tribal name change, became the Manchus of the early seventeenth.

The basic fighting unit among these latterday Jurchen/Manchu tribes was called the *niru*, literally "arrow," and as recorded in the 1580s it was a unit of ten men, that is, a squad. Forces personally loyal to Nurhaci grew rapidly in the 1580s and 1590s, and his adaptation to that organizational need was to expand the *niru*'s size; it grew from a squad to a full company, that is, eventually to 300 men by 1601. It remained at that size thereafter. His *niru* were grouped under four "banners," *gusan* in Manchu, translated *qi* in Chinese, a word for a military flag.[28] The four banners were differentiated by color: there were the yellow, red, blue, and white banners. Heads of banners bore the Manchu title *beile*, translated *wang* in Chinese and "prince" in English. Thus the famous Manchu banner system came into being.

It is said that by 1615 Nurhaci had acquired 300 *niru*, but they probably were not all at full strength of 300 men each. At that time he expanded the number of banners from four to eight, adding four in the original colors but with borders added to distinguish them. Three of the banners had red borders, and the red banner bore a white border. At first, fighting men who surrendered to the Manchus were formed into *niru* made up of one ethnic group—whether Manchu, Mongol, or Chinese (Han)—and those *niru* were taken indiscriminately into the banners. As Nurhaci's state grew, ethnic relations became more complicated. It was an old problem. In the twelfth century, Jurchen fighting men had objected to the intrusion of non-Jurchens into their privileged sphere, forcing a reorganization of the Jin armies that relegated Chinese, Khitans, and others to a secondary form of army organization.[29] Nurhaci's tribesmen developed similar antagonisms. Eventually, as the numbers of Mongol and Han Chinese *niru* grew, separate single-ethnic banners (using the same eight flags to distinguish them) were therefore set up for Mongols and for Chinese, called the "Mongol banners" and the "Han banners." In 1615 there appear to have been only seventy-six Mongol *niru* and sixteen Han *niru*, numbers that would grow in the next half-century.[30] The first separate Chinese banner under its own Chinese officers was established in 1630; the full complement of eight "Han" banners was reached in 1642.[31] As Manchu armies invaded China, the small Manchu nation came to depend on the Chinese for military manpower, but throughout Manchu history their dependence on the Mongols for awesome striking force was still more crucial to their success.

In 1616 Nurhaci revealed greater ambitions when he declared himself the founding emperor of a new dynasty he called the Jin, or "gold," the name of the Jurchen dynasty (1115–1234) of his forebears. He started using reign period names of his own instead of acknowledging the Ming calendar. In Chinese eyes that was the most serious kind of rebellion. Did it mean that Nurhaci hoped to force the Ming to share China with him, as their predecessors had done in the third decade of the twelfth century? Would two "Sons of Heaven" again coexist, and would a treaty arrangement be worked out by which a diminished Ming state would then indemnify the Manchus to buy peace? It is difficult to know the scope of his ambitions at that time.

Nurhaci, now the khan (emperor) of the reconstituted Jin dynasty, very quickly adopted an aggressive stance, attacking Chinese bases in southern Manchuria, simultaneously trying to force the last holdout Manchu tribes to accept his leadership. He announced "Seven Great Grievances" against Ming China, including the charge that his father and grandfather had been killed in a Ming attack on a base in Manchuria, that Chinese settlers were infiltrating the Manchu homeland on the Manchurian plain, that the Chinese had aided two Jurchen tribes to resist his overlordship,[32] and the like. He invoked these fabricated grievances as his reason to attack China.

Attack he did, in 1618, at the city of Fushun in southern Manchuria. The southern coastal part of Manchuria, including the Liaodong Peninsula and the lower Liao River drainage, was settled by Chinese farmers and had been part of China on and off since the beginning of the imperial era in the third century B.C.E. In Ming times it was organized into a Regional Military Commission (Dusi), called Liaodong, administered as part of Shandong Province. Divided by the Liao River, the portion lying to the west of the river, a narrow strip of land extending southwest to the Great Wall at Shanhai Guan, was sometimes called Liaoxi, meaning "west of the Liao River."

The Bay of Liaodong lying between the Shandong Peninsula and the Liaodong Peninsula was almost a Chinese inland sea, and the larger Gulf of Bohai carried much Korean and Japanese as well as Chinese maritime traffic. Most of the Chinese in Manchuria, then as later, came by sea from Shandong Province, and the links by sea from the Shandong Peninsula to the Liaodong Peninsula were very strong. Liaoyang and Shenyang were the leading Chinese cities among the region's garrison towns and administrative cities. The Regional Military Commission of Liaodong protected the Chinese population against the Jurchens of Jianzhou. Subordinate garrison commands in Liaoxi guarded China's northern border against the Mongols, all the way to Shanhai Guan, the eastern terminus of the Great Wall. When Nurhaci captured Fushun in northern Liaodong in 1618 and threatened to push on to the southwest into Liaoxi, Ming China was seriously imperiled.

In 1618, near the end of the do-nothing Wanli reign, the court was ill-prepared to respond, yet also afraid not to strike back in some fashion. In 1619 the court sent a large expeditionary force to link up with Chinese garrisons in the Liaoxi area; from there it attempted to drive Nurhaci back, across Liaodong, into his military base in the Jianzhou Commandery. The Chinese campaign was a fiasco; Nurhaci managed to destroy the Chinese forces. He not only gained eastern Liaodong and took over most of Liaoxi, but also forced dissident Jurchen tribes, their alliance with China now rendered useless, to join him.[33] He was now the khan of all the Jianzhou Jurchens and the master of most Chinese areas north and east of the Great Wall. His sons and nephews were the eight "great *beile*," the princes who commanded the eight Manchu banners. In a mere twenty-five years Nurhaci had created a new and powerful Jurchen-Manchu confederation and had made it the principal enemy of China; his Manchus had superseded the Mongols as the prime external threat to the Ming dynasty.

In 1625 Nurhaci built a new imperial capital of his (Latter) Jin dynasty at Shenyang (Mukden) in lower Manchuria; its layout, modeled on Beijing, signaled his imperial designs. In 1636, his son and successor, Hung Taiji, named it the capital of a new Qing dynasty that was intended to contest the Ming for the Mandate. Shenyang remained the Manchu capital until 1644, and was the nominal secondary capital of the Qing dynasty thereafter.

Nurhaci had an impressive career as a military leader. His only serious defeat took place in February 1626 at the hands of Ming armies. He attacked the stronghold of Ningyuan, some fifty miles farther up the coast above the terminus of the Great Wall. He evidently intended to push on into China Proper. The defending Chinese commander at Ningyuan was Yuan Chonghuan. He deployed the new cannons of Western design which Ming China had obtained from Europeans at Macao, and with that technical edge he successfully defended the stoutly walled city and forced the Manchu armies to withdraw. Nurhaci was slightly wounded; more important, he was enraged and humiliated by the inauspicious defeat. He took sick, slowly weakened, and died on September 30, perhaps (it was rumored) of a lingering infection caused by his wound. Just one year later, on September 30, 1627, the Tianqi emperor died, bringing the Chongzhen emperor to the throne.

The Chinese-Manchu contest that followed was led on the Chinese side by Zhu Youjian, the enigmatic Chongzhen emperor, and on the other by Hung Taiji, Nurhaci's able son. They died within months of each other, Hung Taiji in September 1643 of a lingering illness, and the Ming emperor in April 1644 by suicide in Beijing.

Hung Taiji

Hung Taiji is also known in many historical works as Abahai. He was the eighth among Nurhaci's sixteen sons recorded in the official works, where his name is rendered in Chinese as Huang Taiji, meaning "imperial heir apparent."[34] That is a distortion; Nurhaci had named no heir, and Hung Taiji was a usurper who forced his selection as the successor. The Manchu meaning of his name has not been established.[35]

If that sounds like a somewhat shady beginning, Hung Taiji in fact performed very ably. Among Nurhaci's sons he had the most outstanding record as military field commander, and was the only one who controlled two of the eight Manchu banners, giving him greater leverage than his brothers and cousins possessed. Some among the Manchu nobility probably sided with him in his plot to gain the throne because he was judged to be very able. He soon faced military problems that demanded his full attention.

The Case of Yuan Chonghuan

Yuan Chonghuan (1584–1630), the official who had repulsed Nurhaci at Ningyuan in 1626, was for that success immediately named Grand Coordinator (that is, military governor) of Liaodong. His career through the next three or four years represents the entire military history of the Chongzhen era in microcosm; it is worth examining briefly here.

Yuan was a civilian scholar-official, not from the military officer corps, yet he was deeply committed to overcoming the dynasty's military weakness. His biography in the official *Ming History* begins:

> Yuan Chonghuan, courtesy name Yuansu, was a native of Dongguan [County in Guangdong Province].[36] He received the *jinshi* degree in the forty-seventh year of the Wanli reign [1619]. He was appointed magistrate of Shaowu County [in Fujian]. He was a man of large spirit and high courage who had a mind for strategy. He was much given to discussing military affairs. Whenever he encountered any old officers or retired common soldiers, he would always engage them in discussions of the northern border defense problems. With the knowledge he gained about conditions of the exposed border bastions, he regarded himself as an authority on the border zone.[37]

When Yuan was visiting Beijing on business in 1622, a senior official who knew him requested a deviation from normal patterns to give Yuan an appointment as secretary in the Bureau of Military Operations of the Ministry of War. Shortly thereafter, responding to a defense crisis in Liaoxi north of Shanhai Guan, the eastern terminus of the Great Wall, he went unaccompanied on horseback to inspect the region. Upon returning he announced that with sufficient infantry and horse, money and rations, on his own he could defend the region. That led to appointments on the defense line, and to his being put in charge of defenses at Ningyuan in 1626, when Nurhaci met his only serious defeat at the hands of Ming armies.

As the senior Ming administrator in Liaodong (1623–1626), Yuan was given the privilege of acting on his own discretion in the rapidly changing conditions. In keeping with established protocol (Nurhaci still held a high Chinese title of office), Yuan sent envoys to express condolences to Hung Taiji in the autumn of 1626 when he learned of Nurhaci's death. The mission of course was also used to gather information on the new situation at the Latter Jin court following the founding emperor's death, and to learn more about the Manchus' intentions. The Manchu armies were busily engaged in a war on the Korean front. Chinese field commanders under Yuan continued to push up the Liaoxi coast, driving the Manchus out of several strongholds and turning Hung Taiji back. The Manchu leader had not consolidated his grasp on power, was in severe financial straits, and had inherited the setback on the Chinese front; he was eager to negotiate with Yuan, if only to relieve the military pressures by shifting to other modes for dealing with China.

Hung Taiji, on receiving Yuan's formal letter expressing condolences, responded late in 1626 with a letter that opened up the idea of reaching a negotiated peace. He demanded very high payments, offering meager gifts in exchange.[38] Yuan replied that he could not forward Hung Taiji's documents to the Ming court because they did not conform to proper interstate usage— they addressed Ming China as an equal, and used language that was ritually (i.e., diplomatically) inappropriate—but Yuan too was willing to employ negotiation to strengthen his position on the ground. He told Hung Taiji that the omniscient Ming ruler knew about their exchange of letters, though it would not be appropriate for him to respond directly. Yuan proposed different terms for settling the wars between them and retaining the Chinese interests north of the Great Wall. Both sides were stalling for time while hoping to find some grounds for a settlement, but neither took the bargaining at face value. The negotiations broke off after several such exchanges, and the state of war resumed.

At the Ming court the eunuch Wei Zhongxian resented Yuan, as he did any successful and potentially influential official; Wei ordered him transferred and replaced with generals of his own. That encouraged sycophant courtiers to impeach Yuan on various trumped-up charges, principally the accusation of improperly associating with the enemy. He was forced to resign all posts and leave the government. The hero of Liaodong and victor at Ningyuan had become a criminal; the rewards for his military victories were bestowed on others.

Eunuch Wei had already granted himself and all his relatives special rewards for the victory at Ningyuan, as if his domination of the government at Beijing allowed him to assume credit for Yuan's achievement in the field. That had become a standard perversion of court procedures. Wei's further purpose in getting rid of Yuan was to prevent the buildup of a powerful military official not of his party. It was charged that Yuan's diplomatic exchanges with the Manchus were tantamount to consorting with the enemy; suspicion was cast on his loyalty.

That was the situation when the Tianqi emperor died in September 1627. The only successful commander China had sent against the Manchus had won rare victories that made him famous throughout the country and feared by the enemy; for that he was punished and sidelined.

The new emperor, in the course of rooting out and rectifying Wei Zhongxian's malpractices, determined to take vigorous action in Liaodong. In the late summer of 1628, less than a year after coming to the throne, he called Yuan Chonghuan back to the court and invited the disgraced hero to meet him at a pavilion within the palace where he often visited informally with advisers; there the two spent an afternoon in earnest discussion of the military situation. Yuan impressed the emperor very favorably. After searching discussions, he told the Chongzhen emperor that if given troops, funds, and logistical support, he would clear all Liaodong of the Manchus within five years. His plan was that of a governor, not a military campaigner; he said that the people of Liaodong should be enabled to defend the land of Liaodong, and the land of Liaodong should sustain the people of Liaodong. Defense should be the norm and warfare the exception; success would come about gradually, not in a sudden action.[39] The emperor enthusiastically approved Yuan's ideas; he presented him with a precious sword from the palace armory, again gave him full power to act on his own discretion, and pledged his full support. He probably could not have made a better decision; many at the time expressed full confidence in Yuan, and historians have called him the most able military figure of the late Ming.

Returning to Liaodong, Yuan Chonghuan immediately had to attend to a crisis developing on the border between Korea and Manchuria. A Chinese general named Mao Wenlong, acting as an independent local warlord, was raiding on all sides, keeping the border in turmoil. In Manchuria for almost a decade, Mao had been an effective fighter in the past, but at this time appeared to be acting entirely for his own advantage; he was a "loose cannon" in the unstable relations of China, Korea, and the Manchus. Mao's ungovernable behavior, Yuan thought, undermined the Ming position in Liaodong. Proclaiming that he was undertaking a general military inspection, Yuan went by sea from the coast in Liaoxi to the tip of the Liaodong Peninsula, where he had arranged that Mao Wenlong would come from his base at the mouth of the Yalu River to meet with him in July 1629.[40]

Yuan presented rewards of cash to a large number of Mao's soldiers, most of whom were refugees from the Manchus' aggression against Liaodong. Then, in a carefully arranged meeting at which Yuan's crack archery regiment screened Mao from his own troops, Yuan upbraided Mao for his twelve serious crimes against the Ming state and asked if he did not deserve death. Yuan turned to Mao's lieutenants and told them that Mao must die, inviting them to execute their general. When they, in consternation and confusion, were unable either to speak or to act, Yuan then ordered one of his officers to take the precious sword bestowed by the emperor and behead Mao. All of this was acted out in consideration of the psychology of Mao's officers and men; Yuan understood their feelings and could not afford to transform them into defectors or rebels. Seeking Mao's punishment, he stressed the legality of his charges, and emphasized that he was acting on the discretion given him by the emperor. His action was nevertheless bold and unexpected.

Yuan gave Mao an honorable military burial, then took over Mao's best troops and naval forces, put them under his command, and returned to his base in Liaoxi. He had resolved a delicate problem in a way that invited criticism. It also created turmoil in Liaodong among all the Chinese settlers there; they had thought of Mao as a protector. When Yuan's report reached the capital, the emperor was flabbergasted that Yuan had eliminated a cause of so much pain to the Manchus, but had to announce that he fully supported Yuan's action.

The Manchus, however, seized the moment to create an incident. Taking advantage of Yuan's temporary distraction with the reactions to the Mao Wenlong affair, they sent an army farther west, through the territories of friendly Mongols, to breach the Great Wall north of Beijing. Their invasion force raided and plundered in the region around the capital. Yuan had to send troops hastily to help defend Beijing. It was the first time the Manchus had crossed the Great Wall to penetrate China Proper. They raided for several months in the fall of 1629 before being driven off. A sense of extreme urgency had been created. Yuan Chonghuan's credentials began to be questioned. Had he not allowed this to take place?

That led to Yuan's rapid downfall and destruction. One of the pitfalls of being a military commander in imperial China was that one survived totally at the whim of the ruler: at any moment one could be promoted to the heights and lavishly rewarded for a victory, or demoted, cashiered, even executed for a defeat. Both victory and defeat could be falsified. There were no standardized procedures for dealing fairly with the men who bore the grave responsibilities in war. The generals at the front, or the civilian commander in charge when a defeat was suffered or, as in this case, when the imperial capital was placed in danger by marauders, could be held guilty of crimes. The highest penalties might be imposed. Once Yuan's invincible position of favor with the emperor was breached, he found innumerable enemies snapping at his heels. Their dissonance was enough to unnerve this emperor who, in any event, did not want any commander or civil official to gain too much power.

Yuan's earlier victory and sudden elevation to overall command on the war front may have made him arrogant, as was charged, or it may simply have forced him to take a strong hand on the scene in Liaodong in order to centralize his authority and bring all his field commanders into line. Was his execution of Mao Wenlong justified?[41] Was he jealous of his subordinate field commanders' successes and fearful he would be overshadowed by them? Such charges would always arise because political rather than military concerns drove the defense system. Those who could benefit by diminishing Yuan Chonghuan all had their supporters at court, striving to gain the ear of a high official or of a eunuch accomplice. All were part of a fluid political competition in which the ablest commander might be lightly sacrificed for his rivals' immediate advantage. The situation was no different in late Ming than at any other time. The difference lay with the ruler: when he or his surrogates in the court were weak and vacillating, corrupt, indifferent, absorbed in their own idiosyncrasies, the system suffered a corresponding loss of direction.[42] The Chongzhen emperor's weak character began to show itself in his responses to this crisis.

Charges were brought that Yuan Chonghuan was in secret conspiracy with the Manchus to create military emergencies that would make him indispensable, or even that he planned to defect to them. We now can show that those rumors were planted by the Manchus themselves and disseminated at the court by eunuchs still loyal to the fallen Wei Zhongxian. Innumerable other charges also were brought, arising from competing interests that favored other generals, other political appointees. The emperor who had been so favorably impressed by Yuan when they spent an afternoon in the fall of 1628 discussing the military emergency now wavered only a year later. He allowed his suspicions to be played upon by the very claque of courtiers and eunuch attendants who had been indicted by him for treacherous acts under the previous ruler. Incapable of firmly trusting anyone, he withdrew his support, and Yuan's fate was sealed. Charged with treason in January 1630, he was punished by being dismembered in the marketplace a few months later, and all his family was exterminated or banished.[43]

Hung Taiji won a great victory in the fall of Yuan Chonghuan. The Ming front in Liaodong collapsed, and through the remaining thirteen years of the Chongzhen reign, no aggressive military action there was again possible. The continuing struggle, however, came to be vastly complicated by events arising in other quarters of the realm.

III. THE "ROVING BANDITS"

The western extension of the Ming dynasty's new Great Wall ran through Shaanxi and Gansu, to use the modern province names; in Ming times they were administered, with some adjoining territories, as one province called Shaanxi. Its provincial capital at Xi'an had been called Chang'an when it served as the famed Tang dynasty's national capital. In area Ming Shaanxi was a very large province, but it held only about 5 percent of the Ming population and between 6 and 7 percent of its cultivated area.[44] This once fertile and populous center of the Chinese state of 700 or 800 years earlier by Ming times had long failed to keep up with the nation's growth, and from the sixteenth century onward became an increasingly troubled province. Decline in this very large area did not have a great impact on national population figures,[45] yet the spillover consequences of its protracted social disorder were extremely grave: as the incubator of large-scale banditry and rebellion, the northwest brought disaster to the Ming dynasty and grief to many provinces.

The regional decline had been apparent for many decades. No single cause such as protracted drought, epidemic, or natural disaster can be held chiefly responsible, but adverse weather conditions were a significant factor aggravating poverty in a region much of which had become at best agriculturally marginal. Such factors, however, appear to have been secondary; more directly relevant overall in explaining the northwest's regional decline was administrative failure and its attendant social problems. That is particularly clear in the matter of military administration; the pattern of Ming ineptitude and corruption in maintaining the northern border defense zone, particularly in that zone's western extension across Shaanxi (remote from the defense of the capital region), can be taken as the paradigm of late Ming political weakness.

The court of the Wanli emperor from the 1590s onward began to recognize the military threat to Liaodong (the Ming-held southern portion of Manchuria), posed first by the Japanese invasions of Korea in the 1590s, and thereafter by the Manchus. Very broad if clumsy efforts were made to mobilize armies of recruits, deploy forces from existing border defense zone garrisons, and provision the field armies. Surtaxes were added to taxes, increasing the people's resentment, especially in the regions closest to the northern defense northern Hubei, lost all of his army but for a few hundred close followers, and was forced to take refuge in a mountain fastness. The field commander on the scene and the Minister of War in Beijing disagreed on policy; the emperor supported the Minister of War, who favored a policy of inducing rebels to surrender instead of committing a force adequate to exterminate them.[49] Thus Zhang was able to find safety in Sichuan and survive. In 1641 he turned back into Huguang, surprised the Ming commanders, and won a series of victories. Soon he was again in possession of a vast army, with which he again campaigned to the east through Anhui. At this juncture the Ming court's concentration on the threat from Li Zicheng in northern Henan protected Zhang. Finding his opportunities in Anhui and Jiangsu not promising, he returned to the west, in 1643 bringing the great Central China bastion of Wuchang under siege.

The principal Ming officials at Wuchang fled, leaving the city in the hands of an imperial prince and some local elite figures; they opened the gates to him, only to be rewarded by being executed and all their possessions confiscated. Zhang and Li Zicheng both liked to make grandiose gestures of robbing the rich to distribute their wealth among the very poor; this he did when he proclaimed Wuchang his new capital in mid-July 1643. He called his regime the "Da Xi," and took for himself the title Great King of Da Xi (the Great Western King). A reign period name was adopted and a government on the model of the Ming central government was established. Very elementary examinations were given to recruit literate men to staff it. Moving by such steps from banditry to rebellious rule, however simple and preliminary, clearly indicated his ambition to govern as a rival of the legitimate dynasty. Zhang continued to expand his territories by sending armies into Hunan and Jiangxi, much to the annoyance of both the Ming court and Li Zicheng, whose newly established rebel government at Xi'an sent an army southward to pressure Zhang. The feared Ming commander in Anhui[50] also threatened, so Zhang Xianzhong abandoned the central Yangzi and took his Da Xi state farther west into Sichuan. Throughout the summer of 1644 he captured Chongqing, then Chengdu, and had all of Sichuan in his hands.

Li Zicheng

The story of Li Zicheng is at many points interlocked with that of Zhang Xianzhong. From the same region of northern Shaanxi, and experiencing quite similar circumstances as a youth, Li also took up the military life in the late 1620s. In 1631 he led a small band of soldiers to invade the Shanxi border, had some successes, and by 1633 was in charge of the military force that held Hanzhong, a large prefecture of strategic importance on the southern edge of Shaanxi; by the next year his forces are said to have numbered between 30,000 and 40,000. He led his army back into northern Shaanxi, his home region, where relatives and old neighbors by the hundreds came forth to join him. He joined the rebel army that ravaged Henan and Anhui in 1635, then through 1636–37 he campaigned on his own to the northwest, plundering a number of important towns in the Gansu Corridor, gathering smaller rebel bands into his army as he went. Back at Hanzhong at the end of 1637 he was defeated by a Ming army, so turned southwest into Sichuan and planned to attack the provincial capital, Chengdu. A Ming commander rushed in to save the city, defeated Li, and forced him to return northward. He spent 1638 regrouping his forces in Shaanxi.

The Ming commander who forced Li out of Sichuan was none other than Hong Chengchou (1593–1665), about whom much of the next quarter-century's history revolves. More about him later. At this point Hong Chengchou followed the retreating Li Zicheng northward. In 1638 he again confronted Li at Tongguan, where the provinces of Shaanxi, Henan, and Shanxi meet. In this encounter Hong completely destroyed Li's army. Li and a few companions escaped on horseback to the east into Henan. It was the low point in Li Zicheng's career.

He scrambled for cover, going first into northern Sichuan again, barely surviving. In 1639 Hong Chengchou was removed from Shaanxi after more than ten years of vigorous anti-bandit activity in the northwest and was reassigned to defend the capital region. That greatly changed the circumstances in the northwest. In 1640 Li Zicheng again crossed into Henan, where a year of famine was causing great suffering. People flocked to his camp, begging to join his army. His forces expanded rapidly. At the end of 1640 he again was in command of 40,000 or more soldiers. He took county after county, killed the local officials, took all the valuables, and moved on. His army numbered more than 100,000 by the end of 1641.

At this point Li Zicheng's success began to draw lower-ranking Ming officials and members of the elite to his service. One who joined him at this time had gone as far as the second-level or *juren* examinations, and held a civil service appointment in local government. Having run into trouble with the law, he joined Li's forces to escape punishment. This was Niu Jinxing. He served as chief of Li Zicheng's secretariat, which he organized into what might become the core element of a future central government. Another who joined Li at this time was a fortune-teller reputed to possess psychic powers; this was Song Xiance. He gained influence over Li and his captains, guiding their strategic decisions. A third such associate was the enigmatic Li Yan, a man of myth and legend. He was said to have come from a scholarly family of the elite and is described as a man with great compassion for the poor who distributed his private means to aid starving people. Did such a person actually exist, or is Li Yan a composite image pieced together by those who observed Li Zicheng's rise and sought to explain his extraordinary deeds?[51] That such members of the literate strata of late Ming society should have opted to throw in their lot with this rude rebel commander is, however, not too surprising; up to this point Li Zicheng's career looks much like that of the Ming founding emperor, Zhu Yuanzhang. Who would not have liked to help found a new dynasty? The strictures of Confucian morality were of course supposed to keep persons already in service to the Ming from changing their allegiance, but a surprising number found reasons to do so.

that criterion which holds him in large measure responsible for the final crisis of the Ming dynasty.

To emphasize the element of individual choices in daily lives therefore seems necessary as one assesses the life of the man whose choices through the final phase of Ming history accounted for so much of what happened. That man is, inescapably, the Chongzhen emperor.

A careful reading of that history makes it clear that the circumstances of the Ming collapse—the capital's finding itself suddenly defenseless against a foreseeable and far from invincible military attack—were not brought about by any general disintegration of government and society. Far from it. Those fatal circumstances were brought about carelessly, by an administration that simply could no longer manage its resources, utilize its strengths, and maintain its focus. The fall of the Ming was, in short, caused by an accumulation of political errors, not by the underlying element of the system's inadequacies. It obviously could survive the latter; the subsequent centuries of Qing continuation of the basic Ming structure shows that the inherited structure, for all its faults, could still sustain vigorous governing.

The Chongzhen reign was beset by the accumulation of unending, deepening political mistakes. At the center of all the government's wrong decisions, all its alienation of the civil and military leaders who failed to perform their governing tasks, all its toleration of incompetence and complaisance about corruption, was the emperor himself. It could not be otherwise, given his activist personality and fervent commitment to succeeding. He insisted on both reigning and ruling, and he ruled disastrously.

The Chongzhen emperor drove himself; he worked at being the ruler as hard as any Ming emperor after the founder, Zhu Yuanzhang, and was as unpredictable. The Ming founder's unfathomable judgments and monstrous excesses, however, did not annul his leadership. He set his dynasty on an unfortunate course of political development, to be sure, but he drew the best from his governing elite, and he fixed their shared consciousness on achieving his grand design. The Chongzhen emperor came to his throne amidst a surge of goodwill and eagerness to assist him, but, in contrast, his confusion and indecision, haste and bad judgment, and especially his susceptibility to sycophancy and deceit soon cost him everyone's confidence. His poor choices forced his most important associates and most crucial appointees into negative circumstances that deprived them of both the conditions for performing well and the confidence to do so. The atmosphere he created rendered his administration ineffectual.

There was a popular belief in the late Ming that Li Zicheng was descended from the deposed Jianwen emperor, who in 1402 was driven from the throne by his uncle Zhu Di, the Yongle emperor. The ruthless bandit Li was sent, so the credulous believed, to work the ultimate revenge on the Yongle emperor by terminating the rule of his heirs. Today, as we reconsider that history, it might seem a more fitting judgment to take Zhu Youjian, the Chongzhen emperor, as the agent of that revenge.

A recent biographer, after giving lengthy details of the emperor's many faulty choices and impetuous decisions, adds the factor of "class prejudice" as an unquestionable contributing element in the Chongzhen emperor's political failure. The dismaying examples of hasty, immature, cruelly vindictive, and inexplicably foolish acts over the seventeen years of this ruler's reign, set forth so extensively by that biographer, are more than ample to explain his failure.[56] Grand theorizing about "feudal class interests" as determinants of social process adds little and obfuscates much. Today it would seem a more incisive judgment on this history to regard the Chongzhen emperor as an individual with no clear sense of his own or his dynasty's interests.[57]

Let us look again at Zhu Youjian, the thirty-three-year-old Chongzhen emperor, who frenetically paced the immense Forbidden City's palaces and courtyards in the spring of 1644, desperately trying to decide what to do. For all his deficiencies, this young man must be seen as a sympathetic character. He was a lonely man. His principal consort, the Empress Zhou, was frail and bad-tempered; there was no warmth between them. His favorite consort was the Honored Consort Tian,[58] a cultivated beauty from the South who knew poetry and music and whose company he enjoyed. Empress Zhou was the mother of his heir, then sixteen, and of another son. Consort Tian bore another two of his seven sons, four of whom died when very young. The emperor doted on her younger son, but he died at age four in 1640, after which his mother then sickened and also soon died. The young ruler was wracked by grief, and expressed it in pained and enigmatic gestures. While no emperor ever knew normal family life, this one's existence was particularly bleak.

He felt keenly the pressures of failure. When the roving bandits despoiled his distant ancestors' tombs in 1635, he was deeply and personally humiliated. Dressed in mourning garments, he went on his knees before the spirit tablets in the Ancestral Shrine (Tai miao) in Beijing to report the disgrace, weeping and holding himself, their unworthy successor, to blame. Through all the trials of his failing reign he had no faithful, experienced senior counsellor who could reassure him and give sound avuncular advice—largely because he had grown suspicious of all the possible candidates for that role and had driven them out of office. He changed the makeup of his cabinet more frequently than any other Ming emperor, appointing and dismissing, usually in disgrace and under punishment, at an unheard-of rate; of 160 Grand Secretaries appointed through more than two centuries, he appointed 50 in his seventeen-year reign.[59] Few of them were men of ability and integrity; his judgment on men was at best erratic. That of course is evidence of his political ineptitude, but it also reflects his isolation and loneliness in an atmosphere poisoned by suspicion.

He had little time for governing between emergency measures demanded by the three constant problems: the lack of money, the defense of the realm against the Manchu invaders, and the domestic threat from the roving bandits. The bandits, he believed, were the lesser military threat. They were, as reported by his officials, always just on the point of being eliminated. In fact, that might have been so; it was within the normal military capacities of his

The Last Act

The emperor was distraught, alternately impatient and earnest in seeking advice. Throughout February and March the routine work of government continued as appointments, ritual acts, meetings with ministers and Grand Secretaries all went on as usual. The people in the streets knew that the government was running out of time, and the officials of the court and government went through the motions, their minds on the unthinkable possibilities.

Money was the aspect of the crisis that could be talked about. The emperor entreated and commanded his officials to find funds to pay the soldiers at the front, to hasten the flow of taxes into the treasury when no remittances were forthcoming, even to make private contributions to an emergency defense fund. Moving the seat of government to Nanjing was brought up, with the experience of the Southern Song in mind. When the Jurchen ancestors of the Manchus had invaded in the 1120s, the fortuitous escape of an imperial prince allowed the dynasty to survive, to establish a capital south of the Yangzi from which to reign over a reduced territory, but preserving the dynasty. The Ming had a relatively safe secondary capital. Should not the emperor and imperial family go to Nanjing while it was still possible to leave the North? Or should not the sixteen-year-old heir and his mother the empress, perhaps all the imperial children, be sent there to safety, where they could rally support in the rich and populous South? One day the emperor would listen and seem about to agree; the next day he would denounce the suggestions as betrayal of the dynasty. Nothing was done.

As Li Zicheng's progress across Shanxi toward Beijing was seen to be unstoppable in February and March 1644, it suddenly became clear that the military defense of the capital region had taken on entirely new urgency. That could not be guaranteed by Ming armies in the provinces; the defense of the dynasty could well be decided within the inner perimeter, only thirty or forty miles from the city's gates. Desperate minds turned to the defense line against the Manchus in western Liaodong: Might it not be necessary to abandon the forward outposts and draw the remaining Ming garrisons south to the pass (*guan*) where the Great Wall meets the sea at Shanhai Guan, only 175 miles east of Beijing? If Beijing's defenses could not be firmly garrisoned and stoutly held, the contemptible bandits might raid to the very walls of the city; but that had happened before, and Beijing's massive walls and gates would protect it. The Manchus were still seen as the more serious threat, but Wu Sangui, if ordered to withdraw to the strong bastion of Shanhai Pass, could still deter their incursion into China Proper. Or so the Ming court was forced to believe. In essence, the war against the Manchus was to be totally redesigned.

How could the capital have been left so exposed? In early March the emperor called a number of high officials together to discuss the military situation, as he had done repeatedly in the months before. Among them was an official named Jiang Dejing, noted for his firm and direct speech and for his practical knowledge. He had been appointed a Grand Secretary in 1642, and shortly thereafter had presented an analysis of the northern defense system in which he pointed out the shocking extent of waste and inefficiency. The emperor listened respectfully. Subsequently he summoned Jiang again for further discussions of military training. Jiang again pointed out the inordinate rise in the costs of supplying the troops despite the great reduction in their numbers. The clear implication was corruption if not treason. He reviewed the history of the capital region's defenses from the time the Yongle emperor moved the capital to Beijing from Nanjing at the beginning of the fifteenth century. The permanent capital guard units manned by hereditary military families had numbered 400,000, and the metropolitan province held another 280,000 well into the sixteenth century. Every year they were joined by troops from elsewhere, in rotation, to participate in intense training exercises. Now those guard units were "empty." Since the 1560s the state had ceased to maintain or depend on them, relying instead on impressed civilian soldiers whose pay and logistical support was managed by eunuch superintendents and incompetents in the civilian Ministry of War. Jiang strongly urged a return to the early Ming system, not a very practical suggestion in itself, but an opening wedge for more realistic efforts to reform the corrupt management system. The emperor made approving motions, but nothing was done.

All that was background to the urgent meeting called on March 30 to discuss a plan that had been submitted by other officials for paying military expenses by issuing a new paper currency. Paper currency, used when the new dynasty was strong, had not lasted long; it had not been well managed, and soon people refused to use it. Jiang Dejing snorted in exasperation at the dim-wittedness of officials who would think a bankrupt and imperiled regime could now succeed in making people accept unsecured paper. "The common people have simple minds, but who would be willing to exchange his hard cash for a piece of paper?" he demanded.[62] He had previously submitted in writing his sharp dissent against a plan to extract new taxes from the farming households of the capital province and some other regions, but the emperor tabled that memorial. No action was taken.

A few days later Jiang Dejing further angered the emperor by strongly approving a proposal to move the imperial heir to Nanjing. Finally, he entered into an acrimonious discussion of the immediate need to bring some efficiency into the manner of funding military operations. The emperor, under great strain, sharply rebuked Jiang and would have ordered severe punishment; many high officials had brought the emperor's wrath down on themselves within the past few months, to be stripped of rank, imprisoned, some of them executed. This time other officials intervened and barely saved Jiang from that outcome. The next day he submitted his resignation, and ignoring the pleas of fellow officials, he left office on April 8, moved out of the city into the suburbs because travel away from the capital was no longer possible, and so managed to survive the disaster of the next few weeks.[63]

Jiang Dejing's efforts to restore military effectiveness first gained the Chongzhen emperor's attention, then ultimately roused his anger and came to naught. His discussions of the problem reveal the severity of the capital's military weakness in 1644. The regular guard units *(wei suo)* in the metropolitan province existed only on paper. There were no funds to support the armies of recruits. The provincial armies were unable to stop the roving bandits that now bore down on the capital. The nearest effective Ming forces were north of the Great Wall in southwestern Liaodong, more than 200 miles away.

Those armies defending the Northeast against the Manchu encroachment enjoyed a very brief respite when Hung Taiji, the Manchu emperor of the Qing dynasty, died in September 1643. There was a pause of a few months while his five-year-old son was placed on the throne and a regency of his uncles was established. The regents were mature military figures, eager to press on against the Ming, and they did not long delay.

The most highly regarded Ming commander on the Manchu front in Liaoxi was Wu Sangui, then thirty-two years old, who had grown up in a Manchurian Chinese military family and had accompanied his father in the field since he was a boy. Both his father, a retired general, and Wu Sangui's own family, including a famed beauty, Chen Yuanyuan, who was his concubine, were in Beijing. On April 6 Wu Sangui was ordered by the court in Beijing to move his garrison army, about 80,000 strong, 100 miles south to Shanhai Guan. That was done by boat from a Liaoxi port, the transport boats making many trips back and forth over a period of ten days. It was mid-April before Wu's army was in place just south of the Great Wall, where he could more quickly respond to Beijing's call when needed. By mid-April, however, Li Zicheng's armies had captured Xuanfu, less than 100 miles northwest of Beijing, only half the distance that Wu Sangui would have had to march his army to reach the city. Wu was not called upon to do so; the depth of the crisis still had not penetrated the minds of the Chongzhen emperor's advisers. Nervously, on April 11, as Wu's evacuation was under way, the court bestowed an earldom, the title given for military merit, on him and three other generals. The court was fully aware that Wu was of Manchurian background, and that others of that background served the Manchus in growing numbers. They wanted to firm up his commitment to the Ming.

Only one of the other three new earls was in Beijing. This man, Tang Tong, took charge of the city's defenses, redeployed the small military units at hand, organized eunuch guard commanders to defend each of the city wall's sixteen gates,[64] and stationed himself at the last important barrier, the Jurong Pass, protecting the northern approach to the capital. When Li Zicheng got there on April 21, the new earl Tang Tong and his staff on duty at the Jurong Pass surrendered without a fight. The emperor was speechless when he heard that news; for a day he hid himself within the palaces and would talk to no one.

Li led his army on through the pass to Changping, the city adjoining the Ming imperial tomb park, on April 22, and the next day reached Beijing's outskirts. He did not immediately attack the walls and gates, waiting for his intelligence agents to infiltrate the city and learn what defense plans might have been prepared. It took a very short time for him to conclude that he could directly attack the more than twenty-one miles of the city walls and their thirteen outer gates. Their defenders were no more than a few companies of soldiers and 3,000 or 4,000 eunuchs. On April 24 the rebel army brought

up its scaling ladders and crews of sappers. The soldiers on the walls abandoned their posts and the eunuchs plotted ways to communicate with Li's
forces, to offer to open the gates from within. The first gate to be opened,
ironically, was called the Gate of Manifest Righteousness,[65] located on the
southwest side of the "southern city," the enlargement of Beijing's walls
added in the 1550s. The rebel soldiers poured in through that gate and quickly
overran the populous southern city, but were separated from the imperial
palace city by the wall that prior to 1552 had been Beijing's southern wall,
with its three massive gates controlling passage from the southern city to the
northern or main city.

That was the situation when the emperor went out from his palace into
the imperial park to climb the hill there, the highest point within the city,
and from that height to survey the scene. He could see the smoke rising from
the southern city where the invaders were looting and burning. After long
hesitation and indecision, he returned to the palace. He ordered the imperial
princes to go to the homes of their maternal grandfathers, to be concealed
there by being passed off as members of those two households.[66] That night
Empress Zhou, obeying the emperor's command, committed suicide. The
emperor ordered wine; he hastily drank several goblets of it, then attempted
to perform a further duty to his ancestors by trying to kill his daughters and
concubines to prevent their being dishonored by the bandits. He stabbed furiously but blindly at them, wounding them all; two survived. During the night
the wall separating the south city was breached, and only the palace city walls
remained to prevent the rebels from invading the emperor's residence.

At dawn of the following day, April 25, the emperor, accompanied by an
old and faithful eunuch attendant, again climbed the hill in the imperial park,
where he hanged himself from the beams of a beautiful new pavilion. The
hill was called Wansui shan, meaning the "Hill of Ten Thousand Years," a
felicitation allowed only for the emperor, and the pavilion was called Huang-
shou ting, the "Pavilion of Imperial Longevity." So, at age thirty-three, died
the last Ming emperor to reign from Beijing, effectively ending the dynasty's
rule over China. He had dressed as for a formal audience, and on the golden
silk of his robes he is said to have written his last testament, in which he
blamed his unworthy officials for the fall of the dynasty.

When it was learned that the palaces had been searched and the emperor
not found there, it was widely believed that he had escaped from the city to
flee to Nanjing. Many officials, high and humble, committed suicide.[67] On
April 26, Li Zicheng rode into the city, entered the main palace hall, and
seated himself beside the throne to receive the obeisances of Ming officials
who sought thereby to protect themselves; many of them were promptly executed by Li within the next few days. Li ordered a search for the emperor's
body, which was not found until the twenty-eighth, concealed in shrubbery
on the sides of the Hill of Ten Thousand Years. Perhaps other eunuchs had
cut the body down and concealed it. The three imperial princes disappeared
and probably died within a few days, though rumors about their survival
were many, and in the following months several impostors came forth at

Nanjing, where a resistance government was formed to continue the struggle for a Ming revival. That struggle was long and unavailing, but it makes another chapter in seventeenth-century history. Li Zicheng's short occupation of Beijing and his demise shortly thereafter also belong to another story. Wu Sangui, to become an important player in the immediately succeeding months, also belongs to the next phase of events. With the emperor's suicide the Ming dynasty perished. Concluding the account of Ming history at this point recognizes the full measure of the event's historical meaning.

PART FIVE

CHINA AND THE WORLD
IN EARLY QING TIMES

Overleaf:

The Kangxi Emperor's Southern Tour (Nanxuntu)

Wang Hui (1632–1717) and assistants. Detail from the seventh scroll, ink and color on silk, painted 1691–1698. CEMAC Ltd., Alberta, Canada; used with permission.

Depicting the emperor's second (Spring 1689) tour, this detail from the seventh of twelve scrolls shows the imperial party arriving via the Grand Canal at a canalside gate of Suzhou, one of the largest and richest cities of the realm. The emperor is a tiny figure in the boat approaching the landing at the bottom of this scene, where a red carpet is in place and officials are lined up to greet him. After being received there his party will turn to the right and pass through the decorated gateway into the city.

31

ALIEN RULE RETURNS

Manchu armies under Prince Regent Dorgon marched through the Shanhai Guan (the Pass at Mountains by Sea) and occupied Beijing, vacated by the roving bandit chieftain Li Zicheng, in June 1644. Most of China remained under Ming regional and local governing. Manchu leaders had no worked-out plans for what to do next; their conquest of China was decided upon, and carried out, with Chinese guidance offered by Ming officials who had surrendered to them. Simultaneously, a succession of Ming imperial princes led resistance governments at Nanjing, at Fuzhou, then at points in the southern tier of provinces. Why were they unsuccessful? Comparisons with earlier conquests from Inner Asia do not provide ready answers from the conqueror's side; the vibrant society of the late Ming, coupled with the deteriorating political order, imparted a special legacy to the Ming resistance. The deeply troubled two decades discussed in this chapter encompass a complex narrative, related here in barest outline. The focus is on aspects of this history that reveal important issues for understanding the long period of Qing dynasty rule that came into being under extraordinary circumstances in the middle of the seventeenth century. As it took form under alien rule throughout this last phase of imperial history, Qing society became the base from which modernizing change subsequently took place.

I. BEIJING: THE CITY RAVAGED

In the preceding chapter it was said that the Ming dynasty ended on April 25, 1644, when the Chongzhen emperor hanged himself in the Pavilion of Imperial Longevity on the hill overlooking the Forbidden City. He could not escape that act, yet neither could he have intended for his suicide to terminate the imperial lineage or, thereby, the dynasty. Filial responsibility could not have allowed such a thought. It was simply that in the chaos of those two or three final days, when no court could be assembled and orderly procedures had broken down, his imperial will no longer led to action. It probably was on the night of the twenty-fourth that he took up his brush and drafted an edict in vermilion ink (usual for the emperor) ordering all civil and military officials to attend his eldest son, the fifteen-year-old heir apparent, at his *xing-gong,* or "auxiliary palace," implying that he expected that the Ming court under his heir might for a time be located away from Beijing. The edict was left on his writing desk in the Inner Court hall where the Grand Secretaries normally assembled, but on the following morning no Grand Secretaries came to their offices, and thus it was not found and acted upon. Nor could it have been, as matters turned out.

The dashing prince Li Zicheng, whose bandit rebel army had gained entrance to the southern quarter of the capital in the night of the twenty-fourth, waited until the twenty-sixth to enter the palace city. Wearing a broad felt hat and pale blue robes, riding a black battle charger at the head of a procession of mounted military and civil aides, he led the triumphal procession. Hundreds of palace attendants and officials had committed suicide to express their loyalty to the fallen emperor. Hundreds more, however, including many palace eunuchs, military captains, and high civil officials, awaited his arrival at the gate on the northern city wall; there they welcomed him with fearful deference, and escorted him through the northwest quarter of the capital to the central gate on the south side of the Forbidden City.[1] He entered the main throne hall but seems not to have mounted the throne; instead, he gave orders that the emperor should be sought, that the imperial princes should be arrested, and that it should be determined whether the emperor had escaped and fled to the South. Then he commanded the court to assemble on the following day.

When that happened, on the twenty-seventh, it became a raucous scene, with solemn-faced Ming officials kneeling in ranks while a crowd of Li's bandit soldiers stood behind them, clapping and guffawing and behaving in a disorderly manner. A large number of Ming officials are said to have joined in urging Li to take the throne and declare a new dynasty, but he was not yet ready. Among those was the leading military official on the scene, one Zhu Chunchen, the Duke of Chengguo. Of the same surname and from the same locality as the Ming founding emperor, Zhu Chunchen was not of the imperial lineage but was heir to one of the most illustrious titles in the nobility of merit. Ironically, the next day, when the dead emperor's final vermilion edict turned up in the Grand Secretaries' offices, it was found to have named Zhu Chunchen the caretaker of the interim government to be headed by the Ming heir apparent. Li Zicheng immediately ordered Zhu arrested and executed, along with a number of high-ranking Ming turncoats. Whether Zhu truly had led the abject surrender to Li is not entirely clear, nor is it certain whether the imperial princes were located and executed at this time, as seems likely. Many accounts say the three princes were held by Li for some weeks to be used as hostages. There is no evidence that any of the three survived the month of May.[2]

On the following day, April 28, the body of the dead emperor was found on the hill overlooking the palace city in shrubbery surrounding the pavilion where he had hanged himself. Li went to examine the corpse and assure himself that the Ming emperor was indeed dead. He still hesitated to declare a new dynasty, although the name Da Shun, "the Great Shun," the name by which his rebel movement had been known since the beginning of the year, began to appear in public places as a replacement for Da Ming, "the Great Ming."

Within a few days, whatever discipline had accompanied Li's first entrance into the capital showed signs of breaking down. Li himself began to purge the Ming officialdom of many higher-ranking persons; they were arrested, in many cases tortured, and eventually executed or killed by mistreatment in prison. His captains also on their own discretion arrested high Ming officials or members of families that once had held high official position, tortured them to make them reveal concealed treasure, and then killed them. Li himself was astounded to find that so much wealth could be extorted from the capital's population. He appears to have been caught between the need to establish some kind of political authority and the lure of plunder.

Beijing quickly degenerated into chaos. People of all stations in life sought by whatever means to flee, but brigandage made the roads dangerous. Li Zicheng's second army, approaching from the southwest to join his main army at Beijing, was devastating the countryside, adding to the perils.[3] It was becoming one of those rare times in Chinese history when the open countryside offered no safety, while the great walled cities also became traps for their helpless inhabitants.

II. THE DRAMA AT SHANHAI GUAN, APRIL–MAY 1644

Li Zicheng soon was seen to be a failed leader. He could not seize the moment to make it serve some larger purpose. His performance showed that, despite his explosive entrance, he would offer no more than a curious sideshow act in the great drama of the Ming-Qing transition. If he thought of himself as its central figure, he would quickly be disillusioned. The defining events were taking form 170 miles to the northeast, at the Shanhai Guan (the famous pass where the mountains come down to the sea, the eastern terminus of the Ming Great Wall), where northeast China meets Manchuria. Wu Sangui, the young commander of the last powerful Ming army in the North, had been ordered to bring his forces southward to this strategic barrier, evacuating the last Ming bastion farther up on the seaside corridor leading into Liaoning. That left all the former Ming territory of Liaoning in the hands of the Manchus. The Manchu leader Hung Taiji, who styled himself the emperor of the Great Qing dynasty and clearly planned to invade China, died of an illness in September 1643, causing a brief pause in the Manchus' forward movement. A regency for his six-year-old heir soon was set up under Hung Taiji's younger brother, Prince Dorgon. Dorgon was a formidable man; he would dominate Manchu—and Chinese—history for the next six years.

At the end of April, General Wu Sangui received further orders, sent from Beijing before Li Zicheng captured the city, urgent instructions to come to the defense of the capital. He left Shanhai Guan and started south but soon learned that Beijing had fallen. He turned back to his defensible garrison headquarters at the pass to await further word: Was the emperor in flight and awaiting his protection, or would there be other needs for his forces? His father, a retired general, and his family, including his beloved concubine Chen Yuanyuan, were in the capital. He was very apprehensive for their safety; personal and family obligations pressed on him, forcing him to face a wider spectrum of choices than just loyal service to a collapsing dynasty.

A forward detachment of the roving bandits' armies was sent out from Beijing to attack Wu Sangui at Shanhai Guan; Wu responded, totally routing the bandits. Angered, on May 18 Li Zicheng set forth from Beijing with an army of more than 100,000 to destroy Wu Sangui. Wu had to reckon with two dangers: Li's army advancing from the southwest, and the Manchu forces poised to attack from the north. Wu Sangui was a native of Liaodong with many personal connections among Chinese who had gone over to serve the Manchus. He himself had in the recent past received probing offers from Hung Taiji. At this juncture he was unable to move against the bandit rebels unless he first made some kind of accommodation with the other enemy. Had there been another strong Ming army driving toward the capital from the south or the east, he might have had tactical flexibility to hold his ground against the Manchus while others took care of the roving bandits. He knew there was no hope of that, and he could not just wait to be attacked simultaneously on two flanks. He turned to the diplomatic alternative.

Wu dispatched messengers with a letter to Dorgon. That began a curious shift in relationships. A new direction in Chinese history was to emerge. We cannot know to what extent Wu Sangui himself anticipated the consequences of his action.

His letter, received by Dorgon on May 20, is described in later Manchu records as an offer of surrender and an appeal for help from a terrified Wu Sangui, who, without Manchu assistance, would be unable to face the bandits' armies. That is part of an elaborate later fabrication. If the text as preserved in the early draft version of the Qing *Veritable Record* is correct, those later historical writings do not accurately describe the situation.[4] Wu's "surrender" was actually was an offer of temporary cooperation in a matter where interests converged. Saying that he truly needed help to accomplish what must be done in the name of "righteousness," Wu Sangui reminded the Manchus (whom he addressed as the "northern state," not as the "Great Qing") that for 200 years they had enjoyed good relations with their Ming overlords (from whom they had received titles and ranks of office); so now, seeing the Ming for no fault of its own suffer disaster, the "northern state" should be moved to sympathy; moreover, those treacherous servitors and bandits (now in control in Beijing) at whose hands the Ming had suffered were not the sort whom the "northern state" should tolerate. His letter continues:

I beg you to consider the loyal and righteous words of a lone surviving servitor of the fallen dynasty, and with all speed select crack troops who can press strongly forward, together with the force under my command, so that our combined forces will be able to strike all the way to the gates of the capital, exterminate the roving bandits who are in the very palace precincts, in that way to make a show of great righteousness in China. Then my country's reward to your northern state will not merely be in the form of wealth and valuables, but is certain to lead to a grant of territory as well.

Knowing that the Manchus' economy was strained, and convinced by their previous behavior of their cupidity, Wu Sangui stressed the gains to be realized: "The gold and treasure accumulated by the bandits are beyond calculation. As soon as your righteous troops arrive it will all be theirs . . . No other opportunity so promising is apt to come about."

We have no information on Dorgon's response, perhaps never committed to writing, but Wu must have received oral assurances of cooperation. The details of Wu's and Dorgon's relationship are not clear, and no doubt were not yet fully understood by either party. Nevertheless, Wu Sangui had aligned himself with the Manchus and opened the door through which they could march unopposed into North China, where, in Wu's expectation, they would be his invited associates in suppressing the bandit rebellion. Dorgon was under no illusions; he saw that the Manchu interest could only gain from this alliance.

In late April 1644, however, Wu Sangui was focused only on the immediate military confrontation. Contrary to the story as later told by the Manchus' historians, he was not terrified by the roving bandits. He did not wait for Manchu forces to arrive. Li Zicheng's army approached on May 25; Wu engaged it repeatedly throughout the day on May 26 and won an overwhelming victory. Chinese volunteer forces in the region came, unsolicited, to his assistance with 20,000 or 30,000 militia troops; they fought valiantly alongside Wu on the twenty-sixth, then dissolved back into the local population. With Li's bandit army routed and in flight, Wu's armies were joined by the first detachments of the Manchu forces on May 27, and shortly thereafter the two armies set off to pursue Li Zicheng on the road leading back to Beijing.[5]

On the last day of May, Li Zicheng returned to Beijing with the remnants of his destroyed field army. His behavior became that of a man out of control. Expropriations, beheadings, and torture were meted out in an orgy of rage and revenge. On June 3 he entered the main throne hall of the palace and ascended the throne,[6] proclaiming himself the emperor of his Great Shun dynasty. This curious act on the eve of retreating in defeat has been explained in many different ways; perhaps he thought it would enhance his standing among rival rebel groups to have sat on the imperial throne in the capital. His calculations were those of a roving bandit, not those of a dynastic founder. Nor did he wish to remain and fight the pursuing armies of Wu Sangui and the Manchus. He set fire to palaces and gate towers, hastily collected valuables, melted down all the silver and gold he could find, the more easily to transport it, and on June 4 led his armies in hasty retreat to the west, back toward Shaanxi.

III. BEIJING BECOMES THE NEW QING CAPITAL

The Manchu court's calculations in May and June 1644 centered on how to realize the most from the opportunity that had come unexpectedly to them. For more than a year they had been in communication with Li Zicheng, encouraging him to attack the Ming capital, holding out suggestions that they would divide China with him.[7] They had not expected the roving bandit armies to have such a rapid success; now they began to worry that Li might become the obstacle to their expansion into North China. When the opportunity to cooperate with Wu Sangui arose, they therefore quickly altered their stance, publicly decried the rude bandits who had so cruelly terminated the venerated Ming dynasty (acknowledging that they had once owed it allegiance), and piously declared that they must help to restore order, and above all ensure that the last Ming ruler be buried in ritually proper fashion. That concern for the Ming did not prevent Prince Regent Dorgon from issuing an order that anyone claiming to be an heir of the last Ming emperor be arrested and executed, along with all who accepted him as genuine.[8]

Dorgon's blatant hypocrisy is matched in all of later imperial history only by that of the Yongle emperor when he usurped the Ming throne in 1402, but the Ming usurper's hypocrisy in stealing the throne, while leaving deep scars, was designed to benefit one member of the established imperial clan. The Manchu hypocrisy in this situation had the effect of establishing the Qing dynastic style. A public stance of being more Chinese than the Chinese became, from this earliest moment, the hallmark of Qing imperial politics. Among the earlier conquest dynasties whose histories are included in this volume—the Liao, the Xia, the Jin, and the Yuan—none had justified its presence in China in that way. Those alien peoples all presented themselves simply as what they were: conquerors whose military might and other abilities gave them the power to rule. To be sure, they recognized in varying ways the practical necessity to rule over Chinese by using Chinese means, and again in their different ways became enmeshed in the process of accommodating to Chinese society. The Manchu situation was quite different. From the beginning the Manchus did not have overwhelming military superiority and thus were heavily dependent on Mongol and Chinese participation in the tasks of conquering and, subsequently, of governing. Their ways of utilizing Mongol military power are discussed in Chapter 33; the larger issue in 1644 was how to absorb China by inducing large numbers of Chinese, both military leaders like Wu Sangui and civil administrators like Hong Chengchou, to accept and sustain the Qing dynastic claims in China. In this we see another pattern of the conquest dynasty. It was to be the last and, for modern Chinese history, the most significant of all those patterns.

Just as the Manchus were putting Hung Taiji's six-year-old son on the throne of their Qing dynasty at Shenyang, their capital in Manchuria, Prince Dorgon accompanied Wu Sangui on the march to Beijing. They reached the city on June 6, the second day after Li Zicheng's hasty departure. Wu learned that his father and most of his extended family (but not his concubine Chen

Yuanyuan) had been cruelly tortured and murdered within the past few days. He was eager for revenge against Li; he was not focused on other problems created by his sudden alliance with the Manchus, who in any event ordered him to pursue the retreating Li without even entering the capital city. The official Manchu pronouncements about righteousness and benevolence, honoring Confucian values, and restoring the people's safety and well-being made it easier for Wu to maintain his role in that alliance, postponing the ultimate clarification: Was he a turncoat or a heroic savior of the Ming cause?

In Beijing the people expected Wu Sangui to arrive escorting the Ming heir and to restore the dynasty. True, they had no direct information to support that hope. Nobody knew for sure what had happened to the three Ming princes; there were extravagant hopes that Wu had captured them from Li Zicheng and brought them with him. Instead of Wu Sangui, however, it was Dorgon who appeared on June 6 where Wu was to have been welcomed. Dorgon rode in the imperial palanquin into the palace grounds and there addressed the courtiers and assembled people, describing himself as the regent representing the Manchu boy heir. The Qing dynasty, he declared, by driving out the hated bandits, had inherited the Mandate of Heaven, forfeited on April 25 when the last Ming emperor, abandoned and powerless, was forced to commit suicide. It was thus by acts of others—the roving bandits—that the Manchus had become heaven's agents, and they were guiltless of any crimes against the fallen Ming. "None in history have ever more properly succeeded to the Mandate," they declared, appropriating an old phrase (previously applied to the Ming for having driven out an alien conqueror), and immediately commenced the elaborate public portrayal of the new Qing dynasty as the defender of principle and bearer of legitimacy. It was announced that the government would transfer its capital from Manchuria to Beijing, which it did in October of that year.

A month earlier Wu Sangui had offered the Manchus a grant of lands and unlimited treasure for their assistance; had he believed he could retain his independence in that relationship? Now he was on his way to the west in pursuit of Li Zicheng's fleeing forces, and they, in their haste to escape him, were forced to abandon all along their route great quantities of the treasure they had extorted from Beijing's population and vast amounts of military gear. The Manchus had invaded China for plunder several times in the past twenty years; they now found that gaining this strategic Chinese territory was even more profitable than they had imagined. Wu Sangui, compensated for his strenuous efforts with little more than the grandiose new title "Prince Pacifier of the West," would have to work hard for his new masters. No doubts remained: Wu Sangui was a traitor to the Ming.

Dorgon issued a succession of proclamations to the people. He was not himself capable of having conceived and worded them; they were clearly the work of his Chinese associates, among whom the most important was Hong Chengchou. Hong was the Ming civil governor who had excelled in tactics for suppressing bandits and in 1641 was transferred to the Manchurian front.[9] After being captured there in 1642 by Hung Taiji, the Manchu ruler, Hong

Chengchou contemplated suicide, the appropriate action by an official who had failed his ruler. Hung Taiji, anticipating Hong's future usefulness, secretly kept him alive by treating him with great courtesy and understanding, eventually inducing his surrender. Although that was not openly acknowledged in Ming China, we can assume that by early 1644 Wu Sangui knew it; he may also have known that Dorgon's responses to his letters offering cooperation were designed by Hong Chengchou. The Manchu coup at Shanhai Pass was thus brought about in large part by Hong Chengchou; so too would be the subsequent success in extending Manchu control over all of China.

In a report responding to Dorgon's request for an analysis of the situation facing the Manchus in 1644, Hong Chengchou wrote:

> At this moment the plan should be first to send officials to proclaim the ruler's commands [i.e., to establish the basis of Manchu authority], directed especially toward eliminating rebellion and disorder and exterminating the roving bandits; should Chinese soldiers resist, they too must be punished [killed]. The ordinary people must not be killed or harmed, their houses must not be burned, their belongings must not be taken; if it is done in this way, far and near the word will spread, and on hearing it people will submit . . . Make it known in all prefectures and counties that the law will be strictly enforced; this is of the greatest importance.[10]

A pattern of the Manchus' response to their great opportunity was taking form. We can see that Wu Sangui's initial approach to Dorgon reflected solely his personal and family interests, not a sense of duty to the Ming. Dorgon's decision to move his forces into Ming China in tandem with Wu Sangui's army, in a quick turn against the previous Manchu strategy of cultivating Li Zicheng and other rebels, was entirely opportunistic and had nothing whatsoever to do with noble sentiments, although it contained a shrewd calculation of the political realities.

At this stage the Manchus were in dire economic straits. Their need to exploit the wealth of sedentary China was far greater than anything experienced by the Khitans in the tenth century, even more pressing than that of the Mongols in the thirteenth; their limited base in Manchuria, extended westward into the steppe only by co-opting Mongol fighting power, was smaller and far less soundly organized than the bases from which previous conquerors had launched their conquests. Consequently the Manchus were more inclined to devise artful compromises, to adapt with considerable ingenuity while projecting the appearance of greater power than they in fact commanded. It was a skilled performance, commenced by Dorgon and continued by his eminent successors through the next century and a half. It was marked by initial dissidence within the Manchu nobility aroused by the lack of consensus about their goals in China: some wanted greater economic exploitation enforced by ruthless intimidation; others proposed more moderate methods of gaining longer-range goals. The latter position ultimately prevailed, yet not without much unnecessary violence masked by ever more elaborate posturing. In consequence, a poisonous and unprecedented cynicism weakened the relations of the alien rulers with the Chinese elite through whom they governed. Manchu rule also aroused serious resistance from the Chinese population at large. But the Qing prevailed and soon governed all of China. The new dynasty had an early succession of able rulers who took fullest advantage of their opportunities. Their dynasty endured. Qing society, as it developed through two centuries under those special circumstances, became the base from which modernizing change has taken place since the mid-nineteenth century.

IV. THE SHUNZHI EMPEROR, 1644–1662

When Nurhaci died in 1626, he expected his strong one-man rule would be followed by a sharing of power among the four great *beile,* or imperial princes; instead, one of his younger sons, Hung Taiji, managed by ruthless means to draw executive authority to himself, favoring those among his brothers and cousins who accepted his authority and eliminating those who resisted it. He adopted the dynastic name Qing in 1636, and when he died in 1643, he left his new Qing dynasty in the hands of a co-regency of two great princes: his younger brother Dorgon and his nephew Jirgalang. They were charged to cooperate with each other and with the other imperial Manchu princes, to hold power until his five-year-old son, Fulin, would come into his majority and assume direct rule both as emperor in China and as Great Khan outside the Great Wall.

Smooth cooperation among the princes was a vain hope; factions developed, and infighting among imperial clansmen and other Manchu nobles was intense. The situation was quite similar to that during the first fifty years of Jurchen rule under the Jin dynasty in the twelfth century. Among the early Manchu rulers, uncertainty about the succession and factional struggles over power sharing continued for thirty years, until the Kangxi emperor came into his majority in the 1670s. The fundamental conflict between tribal authority patterns and the Chinese-type imperial institution had to be resolved in all the conquest dynasties; the Qing was no exception. Among Nurhaci's descendants and the Manchu nobles aligned with them in forming the Qing dynasty, cooperation to maintain their common dynastic goals was often difficult to achieve.

Prince Dorgon, who quickly outmaneuvered his cousin and co-regent Prince Jirgalang, acted as the unquestioned ruler of China until his death on the last day of 1650, when he was only thirty-eight. He acted like an emperor, took imperial prerogatives to himself, and may have had the intention to become something more than a regent for his nephew. He was a very able statesman and warrior. His statecraft well served the Manchu dynastic interest in China, yet his overbearing behavior aroused hatred and dissension among the Manchu nobility. Long-suppressed resentment brought about his posthumous degradation and led to vindictive punishment of Manchu nobles who had been associated with him.

The young emperor Fulin, on becoming thirteen years old in March 1651, announced that the regency was ended and assumed direct rule. His reign

CHART 9. THE QING IMPERIAL SUCCESSION TO 1800
(Dating follows DMB, p. xxi)

Generations

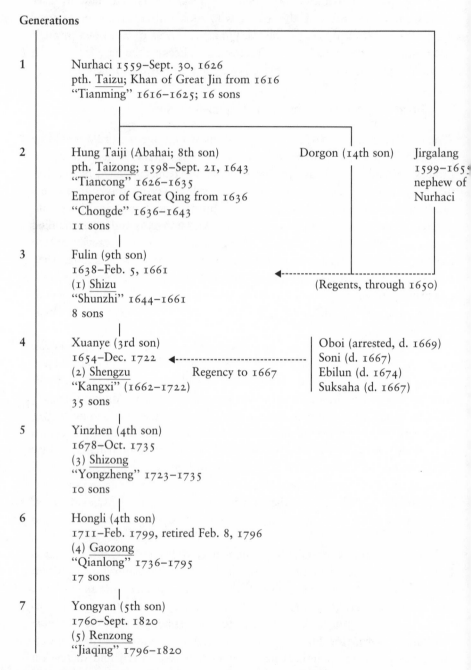

1   Nurhaci 1559–Sept. 30, 1626
pth. <u>Taizu</u>; Khan of Great Jin from 1616
"Tianming" 1616–1625; 16 sons

2   Hung Taiji (Abahai; 8th son)   Dorgon (14th son)   Jirgalang
pth. <u>Taizong</u>; 1598–Sept. 21, 1643   1599–165.
"Tiancong" 1626–1635   nephew of
Emperor of Great Qing from 1636   Nurhaci
"Chongde" 1636–1643
11 sons

3   Fulin (9th son)
1638–Feb. 5, 1661
(1) <u>Shizu</u>
"Shunzhi" 1644–1661   (Regents, through 1650)
8 sons

4   Xuanye (3rd son)   Oboi (arrested, d. 1669)
1654–Dec. 1722 ◄------------------------------ Soni (d. 1667)
(2) <u>Shengzu</u>   Regency to 1667   Ebilun (d. 1674)
"Kangxi" (1662–1722)   Suksaha (d. 1667)
35 sons

5   Yinzhen (4th son)
1678–Oct. 1735
(3) <u>Shizong</u>
"Yongzheng" 1723–1735
10 sons

6   Hongli (4th son)
1711–Feb. 1799, retired Feb. 8, 1796
(4) <u>Gaozong</u>
"Qianlong" 1736–1795
17 sons

7   Yongyan (5th son)
1760–Sept. 1820
(5) <u>Renzong</u>
"Jiaqing" 1796–1820

Note: Reign period names, in quotation marks, are frequently (albeit incorrectly) used as the emperor's personal name.

title, in effect from 1644 through 1661, was Shunzhi; as the first Manchu emperor to rule over China, he was given the posthumous temple name Shizu.[11]

Throughout the Shunzhi reign, the young emperor, as the heir selected by the revered Hung Taiji, commanded enough loyalty to keep his throne in spite of the hostile princely factions. Fulin was an active and conscientious ruler despite a weak constitution and frequent bad health. He was somewhat given to sexual excesses and was resentful of criticism. In the seven years following his marriage at age fifteen he had eight sons by as many mothers, as well as a number of daughters.

The Shunzhi reign was brief; in his twenty-third year, in January 1661, the emperor died of smallpox, a disease to which Inner Asian peoples were particularly susceptible after they came to reside within the Great Wall; they lived in great fear of contracting it from the Chinese, among whom there was a higher acquired immunity. As he lay dying, the emperor made the unexpected decision to name as his heir his third son, born to a minor concubine and not considered to be in line for the succession. This was Xuanye, then seven years old, chosen because he had survived smallpox and would thereby remain immune to any recurrence of it.[12] The dying Shunzhi emperor's ad hoc decision was of greatest consequence: Xuanye became the Kangxi emperor, whose able reign, from February 1661 through the end of 1722, was the high point of the Qing dynasty.

The young Shunzhi emperor worked hard to master Chinese so that he could handle the heavy load of government work. He continued Dorgon's practice of heeding the advice of senior Chinese advisers. As ruler he issued many politically astute humane pronouncements prepared by them. His principal characteristic was a strongly religious temperament. He was drawn to the German Jesuit Johann Adam Schall von Bell (1591–1666), one of the most eminent successors of Matteo Ricci (d. 1610), as head of the Jesuit mission in China. Schall had come to the Ming court in 1622 and remained in Beijing throughout the change of dynasty in 1644. He was appointed director of the Western Astronomy Bureau in 1644 by Dorgon, with whom he had very warm relations. As an official of the court, Schall was able to become friendly with several of Nurhaci's sons and their families. He dispensed medicines and cured a number of illnesses among members of the imperial family, including Fulin's mother. As a young boy the emperor called him "Grandpapa" and sought his company, frequently visiting his house and the Catholic church nearby. As he grew older, Fulin summoned the aging German priest to the palace for discussions of religion, philosophy, and current problems of statecraft. It appeared quite likely that he would become Christian, but in 1657 he had a sudden conversion to Chan Buddhism and remained a devout follower thereafter.[13] This most favorable opportunity to convert a ruler of China to Christianity, eagerly sought by the early Jesuits, had passed.

The Shunzhi emperor's governing, under the vigorous direction of Prince Regent Dorgon in the years 1643–1650 and thereafter under his direct rule, pointedly adhered to the institutional structure of the Ming dynasty. No major changes were made, although a few faults of late Ming practice were corrected. The hated surcharges added to the land tax from Wanli times (1583–1620) onward to pay for rising military costs were rescinded, and fiscal management was improved. This relieved a principal complaint of the people at large and eased the popular acceptance of the new rulers. At the court, steps were taken to curb the power and influence of eunuchs; new regulations limited them to positions carrying ranks no higher than midlevel (4A), and their numbers were sharply reduced. This measure won the hearty support of officialdom, as did others that curbed the abusive roles of the former Ming police and secret investigative agencies.[14] The quick resumption of the civil service examination process also was designed to win elite approval. The *jinshi* examinations were held at the capital in 1646 and again in 1647, and on a regular triennial basis from 1649 onward. Little more need be said about Qing civil government at this stage; meaningful adaptations were carried out under the Kangxi and Yongzheng emperors in the following two reigns.

The principal element of Qing military administration was, of course, the Manchu banner system created by Nurhaci, through which the eight Manchu banners and the bannermen's households—the entire Manchu population— were managed. During the Shunzhi reign the banners were brought into China, placed at strategic garrison locations, and given extensive grants of lands to support them, mostly by expropriating the best farmlands in the capital region. The banner system defined Manchu society; its adaptation to the environment of China commenced at this time, a time of constant military involvement. The "roving bandits" still controlled much of Western and Central China; independent warlord regimes held other areas; and, of far greater import, a Ming resistance government was taking form in the rich and populous South, in its capital at Nanjing, the former Ming secondary capital. The Ming loyalist regimes are known in history as the Southern Ming. They hoped to be as successful as Southern Song had been in resisting the invading Jin dynasty, created by the Manchus' Jurchen ancestors in the twelfth century. The Manchus had reason enough to think that the Ming loyalists might succeed; averting that possibility demanded their intense efforts through the next eighteen years.

V. THE SOUTHERN MING CHALLENGE TO QING HEGEMONY, 1644–1662

Away from the capital region, the rest of China had been slipping into increasingly abnormal circumstances from about 1640 onward. Cut off from Beijing by the wide-ranging depredations of the roving bandit rebels, several regions as far south as the Yangzi River drainage were despoiled, causing masses of refugees to flee the land and seek safety, carrying hunger and disease with them. Regional and local officials had in many instances been killed or had committed suicide defending their responsibilities, and had not been replaced. The nation cannot be said to have sunk into widespread turmoil, but orderly governing procedures, and normal social patterns in many private lives, had been interrupted or threatened. Communications in particular had suffered, leaving information gaps that were quickly filled by rumors. When reliable information about the rebels' occupation of Beijing and the emperor's suicide on April 25 finally reached Central China in mid-May, the news "caused great consternation among officials and members of the elite, especially at Nanking [Nanjing] . . . but also as it spread throughout the south, [it] set in motion new waves on the sea of late Ming social unrest—urban riots, revolts of tenants and indentured persons, strikes by factory and mine workers, outlaw raids, insurrections by local armed groups of various stripes—waves that did not settle in many areas for decades."[15] Loss of a national government thus added grave uncertainties to a social situation that had long been deteriorating, reflecting the failings of Ming administration from the Wanli reign (1573–1620) onward.

Without waiting to determine if perhaps the heir or one of the younger imperial sons had survived, high officials at Nanjing were under pressure to install some other prince as "caretaker of the state" *(jianguo)*, if not immediately as emperor, so as to provide their resistance government with a legitimating authority figure. Several princes of the imperial lineage had been forced to leave their princely estates in North and Central China to escape Li Zicheng's bandit raids, and were near Nanjing. None of them had significant leadership qualities; all were being put forward by competing factions within the Ming civil and military services who hoped to profit from controlling the ruler. The situation was unpromising from the beginning.

One of the princes was a first cousin of the dead emperor; their fathers were brothers, sons of the Wanli emperor. No other prince whose whereabouts were known was as close in the line of succession. This prince, unfortunately, was a disreputable individual known to bear many grudges against the "upright faction" in government, and clearly was being manipulated by a claque of scoundrels. A reluctant consensus emerged, acknowledging him as the appropriate successor. He was Zhu Yousong, the Prince of Fu.[16]

Those who stepped forward in the early summer of 1644 to create a successor Ming regime included many opportunists like the Prince of Fu's backers. There were also, however, many well-meaning if not highly effective persons who joined the effort because of their sense of duty; this virtue did not guarantee leadership skills. In the late Ming, more than in earlier times, there also was a third component of elite society, made up of individualists who pursued their private obsessions, whether in literature and drama, the arts and aesthetic experience, love, or other distractions; they neither contributed to nor sought to exploit the patriotic cause, but allowed the political drama to unfold around them without becoming deeply involved. Some were destroyed by its attendant violence; others recorded their feelings and observations in, or became the subjects of, poetry, story, and drama.[17]

Finally, there was a scattering of persons—those known to us are mostly men—who represented the best of Chinese civilization in the seventeenth century. They were thoroughly educated, ethically committed to high political and social ideals, uncompromising in their standards of performance, and competent in the tasks demanded of them. A few persons of that caliber had perished in Beijing in the wake of the Chongzhen emperor's suicide, and a few such men were on the scene in Nanjing in June, when the Southern Ming resistance government was being formed. The most notable of those was Shi Kefa (1601?–1645).

Shi's family was from Henan Province, but he was born and reared at the capital. He received the *jinshi* degree in 1628, after which he served with notable success in a number of posts.[18] In 1643 he was named Minister of War in the duplicate government at the secondary capital, Nanjing, and thus was on the scene in a high-ranking post when fragments of the news from Beijing began to filter in between May 17 and 23. When it was clearly established that not only had the capital fallen but the emperor was dead, shock gave way to the need for action. The secondary capital was declared the primary capital, its supernumerary offices normally of little administrative importance becoming the principal offices of state. With that change Shi became in fact, and was soon confirmed in name also, the Minister of War. In that capacity, and having no taste for the debased goings-on at the Nanjing court, he spent much time across the Yangzi River from Nanjing, where at Pukou on the north bank there were military garrison headquarters.

In late May 1644 Shi Kefa was sent a communication from other ministers at Nanjing. It said a consensus was forming that supported naming the Prince of Fu as emperor. But, they added, "although he is nearest in line of descent, there are seven bars to enthroning him: He is avaricious, he is licentious, he is besotted with wine, he is unfilial, he is cruel to his underlings, he will not pursue learning, and he has a record of improperly interfering with offices of government. The Prince of Luh, nephew of Emperor Shenzong [Wanli], is worthy and intelligent, and should be enthroned." Shi Kefa strongly agreed; he immediately crossed back to the Nanjing side to make his opposition known. "But," the history adds, "the Supreme Commander at Fengyang [Anhui], Ma Shiying, seeing the benefit he would gain by the Prince of Fu's incompetence, wanted to enthrone him."[19] Ma Shiying, who came onto the Nanjing scene at this time, is perhaps not too unfairly villainized by all traditional historians for the failings of the Nanjing resistance regime.

Largely because of Ma Shiying's manipulations, Shi Kefa's principled opposition to the Prince of Fu did not prevail. The legitimacy of the prince's right to succeed made a powerful argument, and Shi recognized that in addition to Ma Shiying and his faction, many men of goodwill wanted the question settled so they could get on with matters of state. Reluctantly, Shi compromised. The Prince of Fu, himself far from enthusiastic about becoming the ruler, was welcomed into the city on June 2, on June 7 was invested with the title "Caretaker of the State," and on June 19 was installed as emperor. It was announced that the present year would remain the seventeenth year of the Chongzhen reign, but a new reign period name, Hongguang, would be used starting from New Year's Day (January 28, 1645). The prince was subsequently awarded a posthumous title, Anzong, but he is commonly known in history as the Hongguang emperor.

Defense was of course the prime concern of all in the Nanjing government. An effort was made to buy off the Manchus, the way the Song had offered annual payments first to the Liao, then to the Jin, to establish a way of coexisting. Dorgon's ambitions had been raised by the ease with which he took over the Ming capital and by advice he received from turncoat Chinese. He spurned the Nanjing government's offer, undoubtedly feeling that he could come back to it if his military offensives should falter. Meanwhile, he demanded unconditional surrender.

The Southern Ming therefore had to prepare immediately to fend off a full-scale attack. In court discussions it was decided to divide the defense zone lying just north of the Yangzi and upriver to the west into four sectors, each headed by a commanding general, and to appoint Shi Kefa the overall coordinator of all defense activities, to be based at Yangzhou. Although he was a Minister of State and concurrently a Grand Secretary, these military duties meant that he could not be present to participate in the day-to-day governing and policy decisions. The scheming manipulators of the Southern Ming court, led by Ma Shiying (now dominant at the court as chief Grand Secretary), wanted the bookish men of principle like Shi Kefa out of the way; Shi was a leader of the "upright faction" in government and was a thorn in their side, if no more than that, as they took complete control to pursue their own interests.

Yangzhou, only twenty miles north of the Yangzi and just to the east of Nanjing, was the richest city, the principal center of trade and wealth, on the lower Grand Canal north of the river. It was famed for the beauty and grace of its women, for its elegant gardens and mansions and its cultivated life. The generals heading the four defense sectors were a quarrelsome lot; each wanted to make Yangzhou his base. Shi Kefa preempted them in order to avoid conflict among them, but not without the necessity to make compromises. In the interest of their common purpose, he won his way by patient negotiation, but that revealed the weakness of his position and cost him some confidence of the local people.

It soon became clear that there was no figure of preeminent authority in the Southern Ming government, and that Shi Kefa himself, although of the highest personal prestige, would not plunge into the crisis-ridden scene to impose his will on it.[20] Instead, his temperament and sense of duty cast him as a faithful and competent servant of the supreme leader—but there was no such leader in Nanjing in 1644–45. Nonetheless, he settled firmly into his Yangzhou base, strengthened it, and prepared for the Manchu assault.

VI. THE MANCHU OFFENSIVE

At Beijing in the early summer of 1644, the Manchu Qing government busily assessed its newly acquired resources and turned to its policy options for the next phase of expansion into China. Prince Regent Dorgon sought to thrown into prison for reasons unrelated to his performance in Sichuan; he soon died under prison conditions, and his coveted principal consort was taken into Dorgon's harem. The Manchu imperial line spawned continuing internal conflicts.

At Beijing, Dorgon's pressing concern was no longer how to eliminate the remnants of the roving bandits; it was to concentrate the Manchus' main energy on Nanjing and the Southern Ming resistance government. In October, Dodo was ordered to return to the capital from the joint operation against Li Zicheng; he would head the army then being assembled for the southern campaign.

All these actions appear to have been planned and coordinated for Dorgon by Hong Chengchou, whom Hung Taiji (before his death in September 1643) had described as the one person capable of guiding future Manchu operations against China. Hong undoubtedly drafted the letter Dorgon sent to Shi Kefa, the Southern Ming Minister of War and overall commander of the Ming defense forces north of the Yangzi. That letter was sent at the end of August 1644, couched in the most respectful terms and echoing all the elaborate posturing that had become the essence of the Qing self-defining propaganda. Shi Kefa's equally careful reply was dated October 15; in it Shi simply told Dorgon he was mistaken about the character of Ming resistance and about Shi's own feelings, firmly closing the door on further exchanges.[22]

Strenuous efforts were made simultaneously to persuade other Ming leaders to surrender. Hong Chengchou, by his own example, and using his extensive web of personal connections among officials dating from his career at the end of the Ming before his capture by the Manchus in 1642, was able to bring about the defection of many military men, if far fewer civil officials. The insinuating tone of these efforts is evident in Dorgon's letter to Shi Kefa: it mentions that Shi Kefa's younger brother was in Beijing and was "held in high regard there," meaning he would be held hostage for Shi Kefa's behavior; Shi Kefa was unmoved by both that intimidation and the accompanying inducements.

Dodo's field army was made up of about 100,000 banner troops, including perhaps equal numbers of Manchus, Mongols, and Chinese from Manchuria. To that number were added 130,000 troops brought over to the Qing side by a defecting general from Shi Kefa's command. The army set forth from Beijing in late November 1644. Along the route of its progress to the South, local officials mostly opened the gates of their walled cities and indicated their surrender by offering large donations of money and valuables. Many more surrendered Chinese troops were taken in along the way; they would be deployed in the front line of attack wherever battles had to be fought. The Manchu conquest of Central and South China thus employed mostly Chinese manpower, and was paid for by "voluntary" contributions from the people.

In early May the Qing armies took Xuzhou, south of the Yellow River in northern Jiangsu, and ten days later reached the outskirts of Yangzhou, where Shi Kefa commanded the Ming defenses. Dodo's agents had in fact arrived in the vicinity two or three days earlier and had gathered boats on the Grand

Canal both north and south of the city for use in storming the walls and gates. The attack began on May 20. A fierce battle raged throughout the following five days; on the twenty-fifth the gates were breached and Shi Kefa, badly wounded, was taken into Dodo's presence. Dodo had been told to treat him with dignity and concern, and to induce his surrender if at all possible. Shi Kefa would have none of it; he excoriated Dodo and was killed, although the exact circumstances of his death are not clear. In anger Dodo then unleashed his army to take revenge on the captured city. For ten days the troops slaughtered, raped, burned, and pillaged, destroying a large part of the population and leaving a charred and smoking ruin where the magnificent city had been. This notorious event of early Qing history is known as the "Ten Days' Massacre of Yangzhou," one of a half-dozen equally bloodthirsty massacres of lower Yangzi urban populations in the course of the Qing conquest.[23]

As the fighting at Yangzhou ended and the main forces moved on to cross the Yangzi River, men loyal to Shi Kefa sought his body to give it proper burial. It was never found. Some items of his armor and personal belongings were buried at Mei-hua Ling (Plum Blossom Ridge) outside the western walls of Yangzhou. The site soon became a shrine to his memory. In the minds of the people he was a noble man of heroic stature, and he has remained one of Chinese history's model figures. In the eighteenth century Shi Kefa was even honored by the Qianlong emperor as part of the Manchu conquerors' continuing effort to be more Chinese than the Chinese. Yet discussions of him, and of the entire subject of Ming resistance to the Qing conquest, remained sensitive, capable of bringing about a writer's imprisonment or banishment.[24]

On June 1 forward units of the Manchus' army crossed the Yangzi near Nanjing; the Prince of Fu fled to the west, while Ma Shiying led a small detachment that escorted the rest of the imperial family to the southeast into Zhejiang. Dodo himself did not cross the river that day but led the major units of his army farther east to cross on the seventh of June, then proceeded to enter Nanjing on June 8. As at every place the Manchu armies captured, at Nanjing a large number of loyalists committed suicide rather than surrender, while another large contingent, in this case several hundred high civil and military officials, waited respectfully at the city gates to welcome the conqueror and offer their submission. Ten days later the fleeing Prince of Fu was captured and brought to Dodo, who held him until he could personally deliver the prince to Beijing in October.[25]

As the Manchu armies then fanned out through July and August to take the large and important cities east of Nanjing and south into Zhejiang, including Changzhou, Suzhou, Jiangyin, Jiaxing, Jiading, Hangzhou, and Shaoxing, the tragedies of warfare, compounded by the moral dilemmas attending the dynasty's collapse, were repeated endlessly. Fathers and sons swore to resist to the death, organized militia counterattacks, were defeated, and took their own lives; their brave wives, mothers, and daughters watched in horror, and before they might be "dishonored" also committed suicide, usually by hanging or drowning.

tige flocked to support the Prince of Lu, inviting him to come to the important city of Shaoxing in northeastern Zhejiang in August, and persuading him to assume the title "Caretaker of the State." They assumed that he soon would be declared the emperor. Armed forces loyal to him grew in size, and won important initial victories over the thinly spread Manchu armies then just beginning to penetrate northern Zhejiang.

At the same time, and unknown to the Prince of Lu, another Ming prince was put forth as the appropriate leader of the Southern Ming resistance, at Fuzhou, the provincial capital of Fujian farther south. This was Zhu Yujian (1602–1646), the Prince of Tang, whose family had fled to the South from their princely estates in Henan. At Fuzhou in July he also was declared "Caretaker of the State," and on August 18 was named emperor. He adopted the reign period name Longwu, and is known in history as the Longwu emperor. When these two competing princes learned of each other's existence in October, the two courts, one at Shaoxing and one at Fuzhou 300 miles to the south, established a flimsy pretense of cooperation. Despite elements of rivalry and mutual suspicion, they appeared to have better prospects for success than had the Hongguang court at Nanjing. Yet they suffered some of the same problems, especially a lack of cohesion among their supporters, and dependence on military leaders whose interests diverged from those of the courts and officials composing the civil governments. Most important, no individual emerged—whether one of the imperial princes or any of their civil or military subordinates—who could establish a commanding presence and monopolize decisive leadership.[29]

The Manchu forces, continuing to expand eastward through the rich and populous region between Nanjing and the sea, then south into Zhejiang, were given a new leader in April 1646; he was Prince Bolo (1611–1652), who previously had been second in command to his uncle, Prince General Dodo. Speeding up the pace of the operation, he took Hangzhou, the premier city of northern Zhejiang, in early July, and went on to seize nearby Shaoxing on July 13, dispersing the court of the Prince of Lu but not capturing him. The prince fled, eventually basing himself for a time on the Zhoushan Islands lying off the northern Zhejiang coast, then fled to Amoy in southern Fujian, where he lived until his death in 1662. He was of no military and little political significance after the end of 1646.

At Fuzhou in northern Fujian, the Prince of Tang, now the Longwu emperor, was a capable man and energetic leader; he was ambitious and militarily active. But his resources were limited, and he was dependent on the uncertain cooperation of local warlords. The most important of these was Zheng Zhilong (1604–1661), a seafaring adventurer whose family estate near Amoy, the leading seaport of southern Fujian, was the freebooter's stronghold, the base of both his military and his far-flung maritime commercial operations.

In 1644 the Prince of Fu (at Nanjing) had named Zheng Zhilong Earl of Nan'an and Military Commissioner for the region, hoping for his military support against the region's (other) bandits. Zheng's brothers, sons, and nephews, all active in his spreading sphere of power and influence, among them controlled all of southern Fujian and, through the actions of their large fleets, dominated the entire southeast China coast from Hangzhou south to Canton. Despite the family's wealth and power, they were not of great help to the Ming cause; unwilling to squander his military resources on the court's risky adventures, Zheng Zhilong stood by and watched, all the time secretly keeping his lines open to Hong Chengchou and the Qing court.

His young son Zheng Shen (1624–1662), however, was of quite a different disposition. On April 16, 1646, the Longwu emperor, moved by the young man's fervent expressions of loyalty and desire to serve, bestowed on him the title "Loyal and Filial Earl" (Zhongxiao Bo) and commissioned him a general in his armed forces. He also bestowed on him the imperial surname Zhu and the given name Chenggong, meaning "achieve merit," and later elevated him to Prince of Yanping. Young Zheng was addressed thereafter by the polite form "gentleman of the imperial surname," *guoxing ye,* from which is derived the spelling "Koxinga,"[30] used in many Western-language sources. His mother was a Japanese woman Zheng Zhilong had married at Hirado, near Nagasaki, then a freetrade port in Japan, where he also maintained a base of operations. Zheng Chenggong (to use the name by which he is known in Chinese history) was born there, and was particularly devoted to his Japanese mother. He became a fabled figure in Japanese popular literature. He also has become the dominant figure in the early history of Chinese settlement in Taiwan, for as we shall see, he eventually moved the base of Zheng family power there, after ousting the Dutch in 1662 from their fortress at Zeelandia Castle (built by the Dutch in 1624) on the site of present-day Tainan. From Amoy, and later from Taiwan, he and his successors continued to mount military resistance against the Qing dynasty. Zheng family power in Taiwan was not eliminated until the Manchus invaded the island in 1683 and made it administratively a prefecture subordinate to the provincial government of Fujian.

The energetic Prince of Tang, the Longwu emperor, realized that his Chinese resistance forces were marginalized by being pushed ever farther south, thus diminishing their ability to influence events and claim the loyalty of Chinese in the central regions. He therefore sought ways of escaping that isolation. By sending armies westward into Jiangsi and northward to the coast of Zhejiang, he hoped to threaten the Manchu hold on the lower Yangzi and perhaps regain Nanjing. Some of the more eminent Chinese men of learning at that time, especially men such as Huang Daozhou (1585–1646) and Huang Zongxi (1610–1695), had attempted to serve the Hongguang court at Nanjing, later were associated with the Prince of Lu, and finally came into the government of the Longwu emperor. They participated actively in the military efforts to bring Southern Ming military operations back into Central China.

Huang Daozhou, a member of the late Ming Donglin party persecuted by the eunuch faction in the 1620s, later served under the Chongzhen emperor at Beijing in the 1630s; he was nationally known as a high-minded man of integrate the military campaigns. That person, not unexpectedly, was Hong Chengchou, fifty-nine in 1652, aging, infirm, and losing his eyesight, but still the most competent person available. He was named governor general (sometimes translated "viceroy") of the five southwest provinces: Huguang (that is, Hubei and Hunan), Guizhou, Yunnan, Guangxi, and Guangdong.[33] He established his base at Changsha in Hunan, arriving there in the summer of 1653, and served uninterruptedly in the governor general's post until he was at last allowed to retire in April 1662. During that period the direction of the entire southwest problem was in his hands, and the lingering Ming resistance was brought to an end. Even as historians past and present vilify him for his treacherous service to the conquerors, they reveal their admiration for his unfailing skill as strategist and manager. It is difficult to imagine how the Manchu conquest of China would have proceeded without, first, his ability to conceptualize the issues for the Manchu leadership in 1644–45, then his oversight of the campaigns to invade and govern the southeast from Nanjing in 1645–1648, and finally his direction of the remaining stages of the conquest in the southwest between 1653 and 1662. No one made a larger practical contribution to the Qing conquest.

The military situation along China's southern borders was indeed complex. Much of the region was still unassimilated, populated largely by ethnically distinct native non-Chinese peoples who governed themselves under "native chieftainships" *(tusi)* recognized by the Ming government. After the fall of the Longwu regime at Fuzhou in October 1646, Dorgon dispatched to the region three Chinese bannermen from Manchuria who had gone over to the Manchus in the early 1630s. Leading their Chinese banner troops, they had participated in the conquest of North China and had joined the pursuit of Li Zicheng and other roving bandits in the west. They were Kong Yude (d. 1652), Geng Zhongming (d. 1649), and Shang Kexi (1604–1673). All three had been associates of Mao Wenlong, the Chinese warlord in Liaodong executed by the Ming general Yuan Chonghuan in 1629. All three were ruffians, soldiers accustomed to independence from civil controls and to exploiting to the full the rewards of military success. After their leader was killed by the Ming general in 1629 for insubordination, they felt no warmth for the Ming cause; within two or three years each offered his services to Nurhaci, and then was incorporated into the new structure of the Chinese banners by his son Hung Taiji. They had little in common with Wu Sangui, who, although also a native of Liaodong in Manchuria, belonged to the main career pattern of the Ming military. The Manchus considered the three reliably unlikely to defect but nonetheless difficult to manage.

They fought well for the Qing in Guangdong and Guangxi in 1647 and 1648 against the Yongli emperor's resistance; in 1648 all three were called back to Beijing, given high honors and new titles, and sent back to the southern borders to hold permanent hereditary princedoms of province size there. Kong Yude was named Dingnan Wang, "Prince Stabilizer of the South," and granted overlordship of Guangxi Province; Geng Zhongming became Jingnan Wang, "Prince Pacifier of the South," with responsibilities for Fujian Province; and in 1649 the third, Shang Kexi, was named Zhishun Wang, "Prince Wisely Compliant," and based in Guangdong Province. These were prince-doms of the first rank, normally expected to be awarded only to nobles in the imperial lineage. Because of their exceptional status the three came to be known as the "Three Feudatories"; use of that term recognized that heredi-tary princedoms such as theirs, with local governing responsibilities, were not within the pattern of Chinese imperial government.

Wu Sangui had set the pattern for Chinese military leaders being named princes of the first rank; in 1645 he was rewarded for his services at Shanhai Pass and in helping to destroy Li Zicheng's armies by being given the title of prince (*qin wang,* usually "prince of the blood," but here more correctly translated "prince of the first rank"). His full title was Pingxi Wang, "Prince Pacifier of the West." He was not sent to the southern borders in 1648 when the Three Feudatories received their permanent assignments there, but served in Shaanxi and Sichuan for some years. In 1659, when the situation in the southwest had grown tense, Hong Chengchou advised that Wu Sangui be given full civil and military governing power over the entire province of Yun-nan, paralleling and even exceeding the roles assigned a decade earlier to the Three Feudatories in the other southern border provinces. That advice was accepted, and Wu developed the large province of Yunnan into an immensely profitable princedom within which he reigned almost as an absolute monarch from his capital at Yunnanfu, present-day Kunming.

To greatly simplify the very complicated story, as Hong Chengchou focused Manchu resources on the southwestern provinces in the 1650s, the Yongli court of Prince Gui, the Ming pretender, was forced to withdraw still farther west, while still not abandoning the hope that he could send field armies eastward to Guangdong and northward into Jiangxi to keep the Southern Ming resistance movement alive. Finally, in 1656 the prince set up court and government at Kunming in Yunnan, from which he reigned over a steadily shrinking territory until early in 1659 (shortly before Wu Shangui's arrival), then to be driven still farther west to the edges of Burma. After arranging to be accepted as a guest of the Burmese king, he went on to Bhamo in northern Burma. Two years later Wu Sangui, now prince-commander in Yunnan, led an army into Burma, forced the king to turn the Yongli emperor and his household over to him, and then took his captives back to Kunming, where, on April 30, 1662, Wu had the emperor and his heir, a fourteen-year-old boy, executed by strangulation.

To go back to the parallel account of Zheng Chenggong, in the militarily tense year of 1658 Zheng attempted a very large and nearly successful opera-tion to invade Central China. He was responding to an appeal sent to him by the Yongli emperor from Kunming to come to his aid by diverting the Manchu forces away from the southwest. Zheng amassed a fleet of perhaps a thousand boats carrying as many as 130,000 troops; in the autumn of 1658 he began to raid cities in northern Zhejiang and the Zhoushan Islands just below the mouth of the Yangzi, but was forced back temporarily by losses suffered in a typhoon. In the summer of the following year he resumed the operation from Zhoushan, sailed his large fleet into the Yangzi in August 1659, took important garrison points below Nanjing, and (against the advice of his captains) launched a full-scale ground attack on Nanjing in early September. He hoped that Chinese would everywhere rise up in rebellion in concert with his invasion.

Had they done so, Zheng might have succeeded. But everywhere Ming loyalists, largely driven underground and grown cautious, waited to see how successful Zheng's attack on Nanjing would be. Zheng's troop strength, however, was not sufficient to win important engagements on shore, and he was forced by his losses to return to his ships and sail downriver to the coast, thence on to his base on the island of Jinmen (Quemoy) in Amoy harbor. Facing strong Qing counterattack there, he abandoned that base and withdrew all his ships, treasure, and army to Taiwan, where it was not difficult to lay siege to the Dutch at Castle Zeelandia. The Dutch agreed to withdraw in 1661, leaving Taiwan in Zheng's hands. Zheng died, perhaps a suicide and in unstable mental condition, in 1662, but his heirs continued their control of the maritime activity and the island base for another twenty years. In Beijing, Zheng's father, Zheng Zhilong, who had surrendered to the Manchus in 1646, was held responsible for failing to restrain his son. After several years of imprisonment, he was executed along with his two other sons in 1661.

The Yongli emperor's death and Zheng Chenggong's, both in 1662, came eighteen years after the momentous events of Shanhai Pass in April 1644, and a year after the death in Beijing from smallpox of the Qing emperor Shizu (Fulin) early in 1661. No hope remained that any Ming heir might again attempt to revive the long-fallen dynasty. Southern Ming history had ended. The military conquest was complete, except for Zheng Chenggong and his heirs, now no longer based on the China mainland. Hong Chengchou was allowed to retire, blind and ill, shortly after Wu Sangui reported the death of the Yongli emperor; Hong lived out the remaining three years of his life, a widely hated and officially not greatly rewarded old servant of the new dynasty.

The Qing conquest was complete, in a sense, but the entire enterprise of taking China and constituting a new dynasty through which to govern needed to be carefully thought through; it was time to lay military tasks aside and begin to govern in earnest. Fortunately for the Qing, the death of the Emperor Shizu in February 1661 brought to the throne one of the most remarkable rulers of any conquest dynasty in China, the man known in history as Xuanye, the Kangxi emperor. On the throne for sixty-one years, he brought a stable pattern of governing to the Manchu Qing dynasty by integrating Manchu and Chinese interests and making traditional Chinese institutions function again, albeit under alien rule.

32

THE KANGXI EMPEROR: COMING OF AGE

The Kangxi emperor's long reign, from the death of his father, the Shun-zhi emperor, in 1661 until his own death at the end of 1722, is the crucial period during which Manchu rule took form. Here the focus is on his earliest years, from his boyhood under an oppressive regency to his assertion of independence to rule in his own right; then his success in suppressing massive rebellion against Manchu rule; and finally the invasion and annexation of Taiwan, all before his thirtieth birthday. These youthful accomplishments secured the future of the Qing dynasty. Yet many problems remained. With vigor and insight he faced the fundamental difficulty of making alien rule acceptable to the Chinese elite of learning and social status, among whom feelings of lingering loyalty to the Ming remained strong. Within that learned sector, new currents of thought and modes of scholarship initiated in the late Ming, and reflecting the milieu of continuing Ming loyalism, became an important component of Qing intellectual life. As background to discussions of the Kangxi emperor's mature rule in the next chapter, these circumstances of early Qing life are introduced here.

1. DIFFICULT BEGINNINGS

When the boy Xuanye was designated the successor in the days before his father, the Shunzhi emperor, died on February 5, 1661, he was still three months shy of his seventh birthday.[1] Twelve days later he ascended the throne and was proclaimed the new ruler, the second Qing emperor to reign from Beijing. He was then at an age comparable to that of his father when he came to the throne in 1643; for quite practical reasons both these boy emperors were initially controlled by powerful regencies put in place by their fathers.[2] Xuanye's Kangxi reign period name, often (but incorrectly) used as his personal name, was adopted with the beginning of the New Year in 1662 and remained in effect for sixty-one years, through 1722. Posthumously he was awarded the temple name Shengzu, the "Sagacious Progenitor," a title that, despite his reign's difficult beginnings, was fully merited by the time of his death. He is a great figure in Chinese and in Inner Asian history, even though uncritical praise throughout Qing times and since has blurred the image of the historical man.

In the last days before his premature death, Xuanye's father, the Shunzhi emperor, decided on four high Manchu nobles to serve as a council of regents until the boy should achieve his majority.[3] At the time it seemed surprising that neither his mother nor any members of the imperial clan were included, but the four eminent non-imperial princes had aided the late emperor in his assumption of direct rule in 1652 after the death of Prince Regent Dorgon, and had become trusted aides. They were eager to correct Dorgon's personal excesses, but more significantly, they also rejected Dorgon's accommodative policies and identified with the reassertion of Manchu rights and privileges. For most of the decade that followed, until Xuanye gained control at the end of the 1660s, senior Manchu leaders appealed to nativist reaction, that is, to a reaction against accommodating to the norms of Chinese culture or sharing power so as to enhance cooperation with the conquered Chinese.

The general assumption that Chinese civilization was superior to their own, although difficult to ignore, was something most Manchu warriors could do without. That the wealth of China was rightly theirs to enjoy simply expressed the ethos of tribal peoples who lived by war. Such feelings echoed emotions, and policies, seen sporadically in all the earlier conquest dynasties, especially in Liao, Xia, and Jin times. This phase of Manchu history calls to mind that of their tribal forebears, the Jurchens, especially in the reigns of the Jurchen Jin dynasty emperors Shizong and Zhangzong from 1161 to 1208.[4] Manchu nativist policies in the early Kangxi years were informed by past conquest dynasty practice but worked out in distinctive Manchu fashion.

Eventually the Kangxi emperor would become the integrating figure in the Qing dynasty's solutions to these problems, but for seven or eight years he would remain a peripheral observer, increasingly (and precociously) aware of the situation as he grew into his early teen years. He was forced to play a cunning game, watching and waiting as he prepared himself to assume direct rule. Until that should happen, Xuanye's will would count for very little in the conduct of Qing government.

Among the four Manchu regents, only one really mattered. Prince Oboi, although the most junior among them, soon outpaced the other three. One (Soni) died of natural causes in 1667, soon after submitting a memorial noting that the emperor was thirteen (fourteen *sui* by Chinese reckoning, the age at which northern tribal males were considered to be adults) and urging him to assume direct rule, ending the regency. In August of that year Xuanye did so, modestly noting his youth and inexperience, and asking for his seniors' continued advice. Oboi used his position as chief of the council of advisers to continue his dictatorial control over the government. One of the other two (Suksaha), long at odds with Oboi, asked to be allowed to retire, to live out his remaining years guarding the tombs of the Manchu founding rulers. Like

Soni's final memorial, that also implied criticism. It aroused Oboi's fury; he moved to have this elderly noble impeached for treason and put to death. Xuanye understood quite well the personal antagonisms between the two but did not have the power to act; and perhaps he so resented all four regents that he was willing to see them destroy one another. The remaining regent (Ebilun) lacked the force of will or the interest to seriously oppose Oboi, who thoroughly despised him. Oboi drew power into his hands by all manner of devious means. He filled the high posts at court with his followers, browbeat the entire central government, and overawed the young emperor, watching him suspiciously to determine whether the maturing boy might be planning to declare his independence and do away with his services.

Oboi has been painted the blackest of villains by all later historians. He was to be sure quite ruthless in his pursuit of power, which to him necessarily included consolidating Manchu tribal interests. Those were, nevertheless, valid interests, if not of a kind that Chinese of the time (or historians since then) have readily recognized. Oboi's ruthless conduct draws our attention away from other dimensions of his behavior. He helped the previous emperor come out from under the shadow of the all-powerful Prince Regent Dorgon in the 1650s. Yet it must be acknowledged that ten years later he came to head a far more oppressive regency than Dorgon's had been. His anti-Dorgon stance led him to oppose Dorgon's accommodation policies, allowing Oboi to make a national cause of what was in fact his private vendetta. More tyrannical than Dorgon had been, he maintained a relentless oversight of the boy Xuanye, which forced the young emperor to feel sympathy with Oboi's enemies and potential victims. When brave courtiers, mostly but not exclusively Chinese, reported in detail on the dictatorial regent's transgressions, Xuanye could only store away the facts and attempt to protect those who dared Oboi's vengeance, but he could do nothing to arouse reprisals against himself. The informal histories are full of stories showing how Xuanye cleverly masked his awareness and survived these difficult years. From an early age he was thus schooled in ruthless court politics.

The boy emperor's hatred for Oboi grew intense. Many high-ranking Manchus secretly sided with him. He may have believed his life was endangered. It is said that he developed a corps of young Manchu men loyal to him who played war games in the palace grounds, all the time making Oboi believe that they were too distracted by boyish sport to have any serious political purpose. Songgotu, a son of the regent Soni, who had died in 1667, and uncle of the emperor's new empress,[5] helped him plot Oboi's downfall, assuring Xuanye privately that he would have widespread Manchu support. In June 1669 Oboi was called to court to answer charges that he had committed lese majesty. The corps of young Manchu guardsmen obeyed Xuanye's command; to Oboi's astonishment, they seized him in the court and took him directly to prison. An elaborate indictment on thirty serious criminal charges was made public. Oboi soon died under the conditions of his imprisonment and interrogation. Many of his supporters, accused of participating in his crimes, were imprisoned and executed. At age fifteen Xuanye, the Kangxi emperor, military forces were small in comparison, and their personal talents were not of a kind to arouse serious concern. By the late 1660s, however, as the Kangxi emperor was gaining his full independence, Wu and the other two came to be recognized as anomalies within the system of Qing government, understandable in terms of the special circumstances of the conquest years but now arousing much discussion at court about how to resolve the anomaly.

In April 1673 old Shang Kexi in Guangdong, fearful that his sons and grandsons wanted to get rid of him, petitioned the court to be allowed to return to his former home in Liaodong to pass the final years of his life. This unexpected development triggered the most intense debate among Xuanye and his court advisers; the emperor decided that this provided the excuse to eliminate the remaining three border princedoms *(san fan)*, require the princes to move their families and the troops personally loyal to them out of the provinces, and surrender their hereditary governorships. He called on the other two princes to follow Shang Kexi's lead, and offered them all innocuous rewards and honors.

Testing the emperor's resolve, Wu Sangui joined with Geng Jingzhong (in Fujian) in a joint memorial in which they accepted the order to resign their offices and titles, but expressed their acceptance with an undertone of threat. Wu noted how difficult it had been to move his headquarters to Yunnan on command of the court, how long it had taken, and how long it would now take to move out with his entire household and full complement of officers and troops after nine years there; he further noted all their hardships and their great service to the throne, of which, he was sure, the emperor was benevolently aware. Wu was proud and extremely self-confident, and he calculated that the court would be afraid to arouse his dissatisfaction. The Kangxi emperor's advisers warned of an explosion, clearly understanding that Wu Sangui was not truly willing to abandon his power base. Doubtful that the Qing armies were a match for the formidable Wu, they urged various compromises and half-measures.

Neither the emperor's advisers nor Wu Sangui had taken the measure of Xuanye. The decisive young emperor, impatient with timorous courtiers, prevailed. The three border zone princes were ordered to resign their hereditary governorships.

There was shock in Yunnan when the emperor's reply was received. Backed into a corner, Wu Sangui could only rebel. After having captured the last Southern Ming emperor in Burma and then executing him, he could not credibly raise the banner of "Restore the Ming," though that would have been the tactic most likely to win him widespread support. Instead, he declared himself the emperor of a new dynasty, to be called Zhou, to commence with the New Year in 1674. But he nevertheless tried to capture Ming loyalist feelings by claiming that his purpose was "revenge for the fallen Ming dynasty." He issued a long proclamation to the people of China, recounting how the Manchus had deceived him when in the spring of 1644 he in righteous anger had sought military assistance to drive Li Zicheng from the capital and give the last Ming ruler a proper burial. He recounted many other examples of Manchu perfidy, and announced that in his Zhou empire men could again let their hair grow naturally and would no longer wear Manchu dress. Having harbored his resources for thirty years in preparation for this day, he said that the time had now come to turn his weapons against the Manchus, march his armies northward, and "sweep the land clear of their stench."[9] As his armies prepared to drive northward from Yunnan, he first made ceremonial obeisance at the tomb of the Yongli emperor, whom he had captured and executed eleven years earlier.

Despite the inconsistencies in his record, his was a powerful message. Coupled with the awe in which he was popularly held as a military strategist, and the speed with which he assumed the offensive, his proclamation was surprisingly effective. Within six months in early 1674, defections to his cause had put him in possession of six provinces in the south and southwest. He was poised to move through Sichuan into the northwest, and simultaneously, by another route, through Jiangxi into the lower Yangzi region. Manchu forces were assembled in Hubei just north of the Yangzi, but hesitated to move aggressively into Hunan, Wu's main forward base. At this moment Wu too hesitated, hoping to enter into negotiations that would save the life of his son held hostage in Beijing. The Kangxi emperor, seeing that as a source of ambiguity, ordered the son (his nephew) executed. Wu Sangui was disbelieving, and deeply grief-stricken. He named his teenage grandson Wu Shifan the heir apparent of his rebel Zhou dynasty, and after some delay again assumed the offensive. Chinese generals and civil officials continued to come over to him, and by 1675 China south of the Yangzi was virtually all under his control. Yet the momentum of his initial push began to lag, and the Qing forces began to find ways of counterattacking.

It is usually said that if Wu Sangui in 1674 had pushed directly on to the Yangzi, and then without delay had marched on to the north against Beijing, he would have toppled the Kangxi emperor and driven the Qing back beyond the Great Wall. Early in 1674 Geng Jingzhong joined him and brought Fujian over to the rebellion, and the third feudatory, that under Shang Kexi's heirs in Guangdong, also responded, if not very effectively.

The Manchus did not have prepossessing military superiority. They tried many generals in various places before they found a few who could win in the field. But as the war dragged on, Geng Jingzhong in Fujian and the Shang heirs in Guangdong surrendered to the Qing in 1677, and the next year Wu Sangui died of dysentery in Hunan, leaving his throne to his young grandson, Wu Shifan. In 1679 his Zhou court was forced to withdraw back to Yunnan from its capital in Hunan; thereafter it controlled only that province, adjacent Guizhou, and the nearer portions of Hunan, Sichuan, and Guangxi. The rebellion lingered, stubborn if no longer potent, its territories shrinking, until Wu Shifan committed suicide at Kunming in Yunnan in December 1681. The Qing armies quickly moved in to seize and execute all those who had served Wu or had expressed any measure of sympathy for his cause. The southern border region was brought under direct provincial administration. The anom-

IV. MING LOYALISM AND INTELLECTUAL CURRENTS IN THE EARLY QING

Qing control of China was constantly challenged through the dynasty's first forty years. Only after the final failure of Wu Sangui's rebellion in 1681, and the conquest of the Ming loyalist outpost in Taiwan in 1683, did it become clear to most of the Chinese who still harbored feelings of loyalty that there was scant hope of ever restoring the former dynasty. At the level of secret society activity and popular sentiment among the less well educated, the slogan "Overthrow the Qing and restore the Ming" retained currency, at times boldly taken up by dissident movements until the early twentieth century. Only near the end of the dynasty, among late Qing rebel groups, was that vague sentiment transformed into a potent image of the Ming; its impact on the Revolution of 1911 is another story, to be told elsewhere. A different kind of challenge to the Manchus, however, came from a pervasive disaffection among the educated, and perhaps also echoed more broadly in society as well; that problem continued to demand the alien dynasty's attention and to affect its policies for an extraordinarily long time thereafter.

The Quality of Ming Loyalism

During the Kangxi reign, by the 1680s and 1690s the elite of education and social standing in the generation that had come of age under the Ming began to grow thin. Even so, the Qing emperors and Manchu leaders remained suspicious of Chinese (Han) attitudes. The Kangxi emperor's grandson, the Qianlong emperor who reigned for much of the eighteenth century (1736–1796), was ever watchful against surreptitious expressions of anti-Manchu feeling, slyly concealed insults, even obscure allusions that by far-fetched imagination might be so taken. Anti-Qing feelings, to be sure, were not necessarily pro-Ming, but Qing rulers remained especially sensitive both to generalized anti-Manchu feelings and to Ming loyalism long after either presented any likely threat to Qing rule. The conquerors' political insecurity played a larger and more constant role in Qing times than under any other conquest dynasty.

In seventeenth-century people's imaginations, that lingering sentiment may truly reflect some kind of attachment to the Ming dynasty as such, although, curiously, it included virtually no idealization of Ming emperors and political heroes. Its focus was elsewhere. Before the old dynasty's fall in 1644, many of those who subsequently typified the anti-Qing sentiment had been the most critical of Ming governing, and continued to be angered by the debased political behavior they encountered in the Southern Ming regimes. The political weaknesses of the later Ming were all too well recognized, but in many minds the values that made them loyal to the Ming transcended its shoddy politics. They had been committed to fundamental political reforms within the framework of the dynasty's continued legitimacy; their disillusionment had not made them its enemies, and their commitment to it outlived their political criticisms of it. In a number of prominent cases, their behavior after 1644 displayed their continuing commitment to the causes they associated with the previous dynastic era.

Beyond that, for several specific reasons the age of Ming could be looked back upon with nostalgia by seventeenth-century Chinese: they remembered (or heard their seniors tell) that it had been an age of great promise, when cities grew, trade expanded, and all the arts of peace flourished. From the time of Wang Yangming (d. 1529) to the end of the dynasty in 1644 there was vigorous intellectual activity, whether seen in disputatious Confucian debates, in a revitalized Buddhism, or, above all, in literary and artistic realms. Books were edited and published in greater number than ever before. Entertainment literature flooded the bookstalls. Travel for sightseeing was in great vogue. A prosperous urban environment was found in the dozens of large cities throughout the realm. Life held excitement and a sense of engagement for many. All manner of memorable events could be recalled by those who remembered the Ming.

Perhaps most striking to us today is the extent to which the late Ming was a romantic period, marked by imagination, humor, and passion. Many people took advantage of growing social freedoms to lead unconventional lives. For the large sector of Chinese who were highly educated and who established the tone of elite life, a sybaritic milieu offered challenges and choices that tested men's capacities—for indulgence, but also for intellectual growth.[12]

The new Qing rulers would proclaim the late Ming modes "decadent" and denounce the age's "license." It was in their interest to discredit the previous dynasty, and thereby justify their own. But, apart from that posturing, the tenor of life under Qing rule truly changed. Some of the latent Chinese disdain for the Qing was infused with romantic color as artists, musicians, performers, and entertainers mourned the passing of an era. They in turn were recorded by writers who produced, in their discontent, a literature of nostalgia. Poets and writers idealized many who had suffered the stresses of the Qing conquest. In such works the self-indulgent excesses of the late Ming might be portrayed as the purest expressions of true feeling and noble suffering. In some cases they were. But that atmosphere disappeared early in the Qing.

An interesting example is Wu Weiye (1609–1672), one of the best poets of the seventeenth century. He was active in his youth in the progressive-minded literary associations of that time, and he placed among the top three in the *jinshi* examinations of 1631. Recognized as an outstanding talent, in 1644 he had just been transferred from the court at Beijing to an office at Nanjing. In his brief career as a Ming court official before 1644 he was in constant trouble for his strong criticism of political abuses, yet the fall of the dynasty brought him to severe despondency; but for his mother's pleadings he would have committed suicide in loyalty to it. He was appointed to the corrupt government of the Southern Ming Hongguang emperor at Nanjing in 1644–45, but left in disgust after two months. In the years that followed he wrote many poems in an ancient song style in which he recounted the affairs of contemporary persons, often persons such as concubines of famous men, courtesans famed for their artistic accomplishments, and others whose humble lives were twisted out of shape by the unexpected events accompanying war and subjugation. His poetry was never purposively subversive, but it kept alive the feeling that before the cataclysm of the mid-1640s, life had been richer and nobler. He lived for ten years into the Kangxi reign, even serving the Qing government for a few years at the Imperial Academy (again, on the insistence of parents and family, and much to his own shame), but spent the remaining years of his life in retirement, a man unable to find a place in the Qing order of things.[13]

There were many like Wu Weiye. A recent historian has compiled an anthology of more than 2,000 poems by 600 poets from the first eighty years of Qing, chosen because they inform us about historical events and social conditions.[14] Many of these poets were Ming loyalists, if not stridently so; many reported in credible detail on Qing misuses of power in the small events of ordinary life as well as in the high conduct of governing. From the few historians who have drawn perceptively upon this literary heritage to reconstruct the early Qing social milieu, we discover that the Manchus' suspicions about Chinese disaffection were often justified.[15] China did not remain on the brink of rebellion, to be sure, but genuine feelings of loyalty to the Qing were slow to develop, and throughout elite society attitudes characteristically were tinged with cynicism.

The Formative Period in Early Qing Thought

From an environment of late Ming social freedoms[16] and intellectual searching, coupled at the end with the stresses of Ming collapse, emerged thinkers whose dissatisfactions with their world led them into systematic questioning of their philosophical beliefs. Huang Zongxi (1610–1695), Gu Yanwu (1613–1682), and Fang Yizhi (1611–1671) have been called the representative figures in the " 'first generation' of what came to be known loosely as 'Ch'ing (Qing) thought.' "[17] They were also of the same generation as the poet Wu Weiye, and of many others prominent in the fields of scholarship, literature, and art.

The most important name among those "first generation" thinkers is Gu Yanwu; he has been called the "founding father" of the Qing school of learning, so powerful was his influence on his age and on critical thinking in succeeding generations.[18] At several points he came close to suffering imprisonment or death on charges of fomenting loyalist action; in 1650 he shaved his forehead in the style demanded by the Qing regulations, but as late as 1658 he was tried for treason and barely escaped punishment through the intervention of influential friends. He associated with many of the eminent Ming loyalists, but also with former Ming officials who chose to serve the Qing, as well as with a wide circle of younger scholars and officials who were not bound by the moral obligation to avoid service under the new dynasty by reason of having acquired official status under the Ming.[19] Through the years after 1657, when Gu moved to North China, he traveled very widely for months and years at a time, investigating geography, geopolitical components of governing, military history, and other kinds of practical knowledge about the real world. He also wrote profound investigations of ancient philology and phonology in conjunction with his critical study of early texts, helping to fix the methods and standards of that kind of learning. In his disillusionment with late Ming imperial governing, a stance he shared with Wang Yangming and his school, he called for fundamental structural changes, but he was not sympathetic to Wang's philosophy. He is often criticized for having said that the extreme followers of Wang Yangming (1472–1529) should be held responsible for the moral decline that brought down the Ming dynasty. He was, to be sure, contemptuous of their subjective intuitionalism, but he was equally scornful of the Neo-Confucian rationalist orthodoxy that stemmed from Zhu Xi (1130–1200), and of standards in education that led most students away from independent thinking; Gu felt that they could only mouth the platitudes that their narrow preparation for the civil service examinations served up to them. The Qing government in the early Kangxi years tried its best to make Gu take office, or to serve unofficially with the commission charged to write the history of the Ming dynasty. He steadfastly refused and, luckier than some others who refused to be co-opted, was able to evade that compromise of his principles.

Another great name from that generation is Wang Fuzhi (1619–1692). Wang's philosophical and historical writings were proscribed as treasonous. They could not be published and made known until the nineteenth century; thus his impact on early Qing intellectual life was limited. His life, however, shows another example of the critical-minded thinker who rejected some aspects of late Ming life yet was an ardent Ming loyalist. He despised the moral decline of officialdom, yet he risked his life raising and leading a resistance army in his native Hunan in 1648, and after its defeat served briefly at the court of Emperor Yongli, the last Southern Ming ruler, in the years 1650–1652. He finally gave up hope for a Ming revival, returned home, and spent the remaining forty years of his life studying, teaching, and writing voluminously. He stubbornly refused to cut his hair or comply with Qing regulations, which he successfully evaded only by living dangerously in remote places at the edges of Chinese society. He was a great classicist and original scholar; his thought has been characterized as "realistic pragmatism," even as "utilitarianism" in the tradition of Song utilitarian Confucian statecraft.[20]

Qing thought acquired its special character in the minds of these born near the end of the Ming, men whose lives were all in some measure affected by Ming loyalism. Huang Zongxi, Fang Yizhi, and Wang Fuzhi all served the Southern Ming courts, and all three refused to take service under the Qing; Fang Yizhi in fact shaved his head completely to become a Buddhist monk rather than submit to the Manchu hair and dress code. He encountered Wang Fuzhi when both were trying to help the hopeless cause of Ming resistance; they became close friends and continued to correspond and exchange ideas until Fang's death in 1671. Huang's and Gu Yanwu's lives took quite different courses, Huang's in dismayed seclusion and Gu's ostensibly quite public, but both achieved reputations for being among the greatest scholars and critical thinkers of their time while remaining (in their different ways) steadfastly loyal to the Ming.

The "special character" of Qing thought that these men and their contemporaries succeeded in establishing came from their rigorous methods and from their focus on rational, systematic analysis of meaning in the classical texts, including especially the writings of the early Confucian thinkers. If, despite its brilliance in Song times, Confucian thought had become metaphysically overextended, these thinkers would bring systematic thinking back to the roots of its authority in the texts, and would show that the texts' correct meaning led to practical understanding of human moral life. Theirs was "the unambiguously Confucian aim of deriving guidance from history for moral conduct that has a social effect."[21] That had always been the responsibility of China's scholars and thinkers, but in the 1630s it came to demand of these unusual scholars (it was not yet a prevailing mode) a new commitment to rigorous investigation of the textual evidence that sustained their beliefs and values. The spirit of painstaking analysis of meaning could also spill over into other intellectual activities, such as the study of medicines and medical treatment, or the study of institutions and historical circumstances, or the study of hydrology and water control and other branches of useful knowledge. Whatever their capacity to deal with the present world, it was the texts and the transmission of classical teachings that drew their main effort.

What is referred to as the special character of Qing thought is summed up in the term "evidential learning," primarily a mode of studying, of thinking, and of reaching solutions to ethical and social issues through textually rigorous scholarship. "Evidential learning" *(kaoju xue, kaozheng xue)*, taking form in the late Ming, came to be the characteristic mode of Qing period thought.[22] The formation of "evidential learning" cannot, of course, be traced to any outside influences. Yet Fang Yizhi's contributions to this development may nonetheless have been strengthened by his interest in Western scientific thought, recently introduced into Ming China by the European Jesuits.[23]

The new critical mode in Chinese thinking drew its character from the detached and critical stance of late Ming political and social thinkers; they were deeply disapproving observers of faulty performance all about them, while remaining loyal to their dynasty. They spurned the attractions (and airy grandeur) of metaphysical speculation, while turning to an emphasis on more purely intellectual concerns and away from the dominant focus on moral philosophizing. Their powerful ideas helped turn thinkers in Qing times to the careful search for sound philological and historical evidence that could come from more accurately determining the meaning of texts. In their minds that was to turn away from "Song learning," or what I have referred to as Song (and Ming dynasty) Neo-Confucianism, although that remained the "orthodoxy" supported by the Qing state; they invoked in its stead the more forthright manner of "Han learning."[24] Their use of the two dynastic names, Song and Han, to designate methods and goals in learning was to make a symbolic characterization of their new stance. The name "Han learning" (Han xue) became fixed in later Qing usage, meaning roughly the same as "evidential learning." By either name, this dominant focus in Qing thought retained the late Ming spirit of ethical commitment, political detachment, and individual independence—from politics as also from current scholarly authority.

Throughout the Kangxi reign (1662–1722), as a second generation whose members became adults after 1644 came to the fore and engaged the problems of life under the alien dynasty, they did not face the troubling dilemmas of whether or not to display, or how to conceal, their loyalty to the fallen dynasty, but neither was it the mood of the times for them to be simply the compliant subjects of the Qing. This "second generation" of scholars who were active throughout the mid- and later Kangxi period have been described as displaying "an uncomfortable ambivalence toward conventions of public service, scholarship, and personal conduct . . . which must be understood in relation to late Ming trends in politics, philosophy, and scholarship."[25] The Kangxi period's younger thinkers, scholars, and learned men in political life were the link between the forerunners of the new modes in thought and the maturing of those modes in the great figures of the eighteenth century, when "evidential learning" came into full flower (see Chapter 35). The fundamental circumstances of seventeenth-century and later intellectual life briefly described here must constitute an essential element in the mature Kangxi emperor's political leadership of his Qing dynasty.

33

THE KANGXI REIGN:
THE EMPEROR AND
HIS EMPIRE

The sixty-one-year reign of the Kangxi emperor is heralded as one of the glorious ages in late Chinese history, reflecting the ruler's many accomplishments. He understood the necessity to reintegrate state and society: he was able to induce much of the Chinese elite to accept an approximation of their traditional role in government while maintaining Manchu power prerogatives. He extended Manchu/Chinese rule over vast tracts of Mongol and Turkic Inner Asia, launching thereby the Qing empire, which, as further enlarged in the eighteenth century, gave present-day China its boundaries. He intervened in Tibetan affairs in the effort to sustain Manchu interests vis-à-vis the Mongols. Domestically, in the middle years of his reign he displayed skill in surmounting factional politics. When issues contingent on naming his successor arose after 1700, however, orderly governing suffered setbacks and his reign ended in agonizing turmoil. Yet he bequeathed to his successor a strong monarchy and a vastly larger realm than he inherited.

The courageous, intelligent boy named Xuanye, the Kangxi emperor, survived all the difficult early tests of his mettle and, as he approached his thirtieth birthday in 1684, he had become an astute ruler. He did not just reign but engaged fully and directly in ruling over the world's most populous country. His grasp of the large issues in governing was unfailingly acute; he made the Qing political system cohere, at a time when the necessary working relations between rulers and their civil governors—between Manchus and Chinese— might have disintegrated.[1] He deserves to be called a wise ruler through the middle years of his reign.

His armies, moreover, with himself occasionally supervising in the field, were adding to the territory of China a new Inner Asian empire that has endured into the present time. China has accepted this legacy of geographically extended Qing rule as if it inhered in the geopolitical facts of Chinese history. It does not. The Inner Asian empire was grafted onto the Chinese culture zone in the process of meeting Manchu power needs and interests. Securing and retaining the Qing empire is thus a Manchu achievement that added a vast realm to the historic China only because China's alien rulers at that time had need of it. The Kangxi emperor did not initiate the process of incorporating it, but he carried the process forward with vigor and skill.

This emperor's guile and craft, buttressing his many other strengths in statesmanship, were essential to Manchu success. Much of Inner Asia, from Manchuria in the east to the westernmost extremities of Xinkiang, peopled by many groups and nations of non-Chinese, was made subject to the Manchu government in China,[2] while within China several kinds of administrative and social problems were at least temporarily resolved.

What kind of man was he? In the decades from the end of the last Southern Ming resistance in 1662 until the end of that century, we see him as an earnest, indefatigable problem solver. He was immensely curious and eager to learn about all manner of things from all manner of teachers, from European Jesuit priests who taught him about astronomy and mathematics, to Chinese tutors who imparted in him a respect for Chinese history and traditions, to Manchus and Mongols who taught him about the hunt, war games, and field maneuvers. He seems to have had a reasonable cast of temper, was willing to listen to dissent, and displayed a humane concern for the well-being of his subjects, albeit not to the extent that he would compromise Manchu interests (see, for example, his handling of Manchu banner lands in North China, discussed in the following section). He is reported to have had a great appetite for sex, yet he was not distracted by that from his ever-disciplined devotion to his imperial responsibilities.[3] His family life was the one arena in which his judgment failed most grievously; emotionally blinded, he made disastrous decisions, and they were seriously consequential. After 1700, factions developed around several of his many sons who were considered to be his possible successors. The destructive politics of the ensuing succession struggle imperiled his very life, amidst the ever-worsening political circumstances of his reign's final years.[4]

The disheartening mishaps at the end of the Kangxi reign, however, should not distract attention from the emperor's impressive accomplishments. Early in each of the conquest dynasties there was one ruler who gained the kind of empathy and understanding, coupled with a capacity for ruling, that enabled him to work out practical ways for making alien interests coincide with the patterns of Chinese society. In the Qing, the last and most important of all the alien conquest dynasties, that leader was Xuanye, who, as the mature Kangxi emperor, had many years of rule in which to build his dynasty.[5] Here we shall examine several of the difficult governing issues that faced him.

1. BANNER LANDS AND THE MANCHU MIGRATION INTO CHINA

Nurhaci, the founder of the Manchu dynasty, before his death in Manchuria in 1626 created the banner system as an instrument for governing and simultaneously for mobilizing the Manchu people. He looked upon the bannermen as farmer-soldiers who would feed the military machine, supply its fighting men, contribute various kinds of labor service, and hold the tribal population uniformly subject to his governing.[6] From the time when his son Hung Taiji succeeded him in 1626 and took the new dynastic name Qing, the Manchu population (less than 1 million) was engaged in constant warfare, completing the takeover (begun in 1620–1622) of Chinese Liaodong, outside the Great Wall in Manchuria, and daring to make ever more extensive incursions across the Wall into China. In that period the soldier-farmer model became impractical. The standing regulation that one adult male in three should be on active military service was regularly extended to two out of three, greatly increasing the pressure on the Manchu adult male population. Banner lands were enlarged through expropriation to include all the agricultural land in Manchuria that was owned and worked by the non-Manchu population, principally Chinese farmer-settlers. Some of those had long been resident there. Tens of thousands of civilian Chinese were added to the Liaodong population during the several major incursions in the 1630s and 1640s, when whole villages and towns in the nearer parts of North China were made captive and herded into Liaodong by returning Manchu armies. Whether long-settled residents working their own lands or North China's rural folk brought in as recent captives, the Chinese were attached to banner lands and made to serve on them as farm laborers: in substance, they became production slaves.

Chinese society had previously known some forms of tenant labor and bond servant statuses, but there was no precedent for the enslavement of an entire segment of the population, in this case the largest segment, its farming households. Nor was there precedent in Jurchen history, that is, in the history of the Manchu forebears' Jin dynasty, which conquered North China in the twelfth century.[7] The nearest model for this pattern of Manchu rule is found in Mongol history: the Mongol fighting forces expected to take possession of lands and inhabitants as spoils of war. They called captured people *qu kou,* "impressed" or "enslaved" people, and the expropriated lands were called their *fen di,* "allotted lands" or fiefs.[8] The first phase of Mongol takeover in thirteenth-century North China was as disorderly and as destructive as that of the Manchus 400 years later.

As the new banner organization expanded and came to include all the Manchu population in the years of Hung Taiji's reign (1626–1643), Manchu fighting men became economically dependent on the enslaved farm households, which not only grew the crops and herded the livestock, but also produced textiles, made garments and craft objects, and served as household slaves. Shortly after the Manchu banner armies (and their associated Mongol and Han Chinese banner units) invaded China through the Shanhai Guan (Pass) in 1644, they brought their own families as well as their Chinese slave households with them. Some of their Chinese slaves were to accompany their military units as servants and orderlies; most, however, were to be settled on the newly allotted banner lands in North China.

The wholesale expropriation of Chinese farming lands in the metropolitan province and enslavement of a large portion of its farming population created a deeply disruptive process of change. These new lands were very extensive, and usually were conveyed to the banners along with whatever Chinese people were living on them, whether or not the Chinese had considered themselves free landowning farmers.[9]

Starting from the time of Prince Regent Dorgon (1643–1650), and thereafter through the remaining years of the Shunzhi emperor's reign (to 1661), the Qing regime continued to urge all Manchus to migrate into North China and settled them on banner lands allotted to them. These were concentrated in the prefectures nearest to the capital at Beijing. At first the Qing government took over ownership of former Ming "imperial estates" and all empty lands where Ming officials had fled, and allotted those lands to the banners. But very soon they had to expropriate privately owned and farmed lands to meet the need, and by the early years of the succeeding Kangxi reign, those expropriated (quanzhan) lands accounted for half the cultivated acreage of Zhili, the Northern Metropolitan Province inside the Great Wall, including all its most productive lands.[10] Manchuria's loss not only of its Manchus (who in any event had moved into Chinese Liaodong from farther east in Manchuria only two or three decades earlier) but also of their newly enslaved Chinese households virtually depopulated southern Manchuria. What occurred was something like the "great migration" of the Jurchens in the first half of the twelfth century. While promoting the exodus, the Qing government also recognized that it weakened the Manchu homeland. To replace the productive population there, permanent banishment to Manchuria was adopted as the punishment to be meted out to Chinese convicted of all manner of crimes.[11]

Much suffering was caused by the disorderly influx of Manchus and their expropriation of huge tracts of Chinese rural farmlands, as well as residences in the capital and other cities. It also created potentially destabilizing problems for the Qing rulers. The Manchu overlords treated their Chinese slaves very harshly. Chinese officials reported that suicides were common and that escapes depleted the agricultural work force. Chinese were unaccustomed to slavery and serfdom. Their response was to flee the harsh conditions to seek better lives elsewhere. Stern laws were issued through the Shunzhi reign (1644–1661) to punish escapees and all who might befriend or protect them. A first offense brought severe beatings and tattooing of the face, a second attempt brought more of the same, and on a third attempt the penalty was summary execution, without waiting for the autumn reviews of death penalties when there might be an amnesty. Anyone harboring or assisting fugitives was subject to even more severe penalties, and those punishments were extended to neighbors and relatives.

Other social consequences also arose. False charges of harboring fugitives were made against the more prosperous Chinese landowners by persons who coveted their lands. Endless disputes and resentments were aroused. Chinese whose ancestral graves were located on the expropriated lands were often forbidden access to them to perform rites of veneration; that could arouse great bitterness and drive the Chinese former owners to rash reprisals. Manchu bannermen made unlawful use of their slaves to extort and to conduct illicit trade; the Manchu rulers worried that such diversions were displacing the orderly modes of Manchu life and weakening their soldiers' fighting spirit. Among Chinese rural households in the region that were not granted to the banners, the practice arose of offering themselves and their lands to bannermen to avoid paying taxes, sharing the gains with their new masters, but also envisaging opportunities for further exploitation of the relationship. In short, wherever banner lands existed, the banners' grip broke up the mutual assistance and community welfare patterns normally found in North China's rural villages. The quality of rural life was quickly debased. Linked to that was a startling increase in banditry; it might be banditry of desperation or simply banditry of opportunism. In either case, the sharp increase signified the erosion of orderly society. All of these phenomena were indicators of the conquest's social disruptiveness.

During the first Qing reign (Shunzhi, 1643–1661) the court's response to these problems was to issue ill-tempered decrees. It was proclaimed, in the name of the Shunzhi emperor, that he cared equally for both his Chinese and his Manchu subjects, but stated that it was only right for the Manchu soldiers, who had after all sacrificed so much in the conquest of China, to be guaranteed the reward of perpetual support by the Chinese population. It was decreed that no Manchu bannerman should ever labor at farming, work at crafts, or engage in commerce. The strong Manchu work ethic of previous generations was undermined. The Manchus were encouraged to become parasites, while Chinese complaints were rejected.

Early in the Kangxi reign it was announced that further allotments of banner lands would cease, but that announcement was repeated on several occasions, the last time in 1685; we can assume therefore that the emperor understood the dysfunctional consequences but was only slowly able to ameliorate them. As the situation stabilized, the Chinese began to devise ways of escaping their plight by taking advantage of their Manchu masters, hiring out to work as sharecroppers, lending money and taking liens on the land, trapping the Manchus in debt. The emperor issued frequent exhortations to his people to be less addicted to expensive pleasures and idle pursuits, and blamed their officers for failing to give them sympathetic counseling that would guide them into healthier ways. But of course the officers were no different from ordinary soldiers in these regards. The government repeatedly created special funds to help Manchus pay off their debts and recover their homes and belongings. The results were always short-lived. The conditions that undermined the health of Manchu society in China could not be reversed. As long as the Manchus were led to think that apart from fighting they need not work to earn their livelihoods, they were in danger from their hardworking subjects and slaves, who quickly learned how to profit at their masters' expense.[12]

By the end of the Kangxi reign, the impoverishment of the ordinary Manchu soldiers was well under way. The Manchu banner armies, essentially cavalry forces, were still the basis of Manchu power, but grew less reliable as time went by. The eight banners of Mongol cavalry, however, numbering between 25,000 and 35,000 mounted archers on military duty at any time, kept their populations in Mongolia, where their way of life was less significantly affected; they became ever more important, relied on to provide the cutting edge of Qing military successes. The new provincial armies of Chinese recruits, called the Armies of the Green Standard *(lü ying),* were largely foot soldiers and specialists in auxiliary services, such as artillery and military transport. They were paid salaries, not given grants of land. Based throughout the provinces and recruited locally, they grew in numbers to the point where they accounted for 75 percent of the Qing state's armed manpower through most of the dynasty. Those units were under the control of Manchu provincial military authorities, and their garrisons always had Manchu or Mongol commanding officers. They were supplemented in mid-Qing times and later by new local militia-type forces.[13] The changes and adaptations show that the Qing was little more successful than earlier dynasties in creating strong, stable military institutions in an essentially civilian-minded host population.

Throughout his long reign the Kangxi emperor faced serious military crises and managed to survive them. At first his armies of bannermen still had much of the vitality that had marked their rise to power in Manchuria before they settled among the conquered and became deeply involved in day-to-day life of Chinese society. But the ruler was forced to recognize that, in the Chinese setting, his fellow Manchus were unsophisticated and vulnerable. He strove to implement measures that might protect them from their own foolishness, about which he often chided them. Perhaps he also foresaw the degenerative trends that someday would weaken the dynasty's power, but even if he was that prescient, he could not have changed the basic circumstances of Manchu overlordship. He could, however, do a great deal in the arena of traditional Chinese civil governing. If he lacked means to keep the Chinese in awe of steppe military might, it then became all the more important that he cultivate the civilian bases of Manchu domination. Xuanye's responses to that set of problems reveal a thoughtful emperor working hard to broaden his grasp of governing.

II. RECRUITMENT AND THE EXAMINATION SYSTEM

A conquest dynasty, especially one that did not have overwhelming military superiority, faced difficulties that a native dynasty did not. Its claims to possess the Mandate would be tested by members of the educated elite who felt it their responsibility to be the judge of such matters. Its rulers feared that elite dissidence might be accompanied by resentment among the common people against alien overlordship, a dangerous combination. It is true that the fall of the Ming did not bring forth an outpouring of elite anger and resistance to the conquerors like that which swept China after the fall of the Southern Song to the Mongols in 1275–1279. In the 1640s many Chinese accepted the view (assiduously promoted by the Manchus) that the roving bandits, not the Manchu invaders, had terminated the Ming claim to the Mandate. That explanation of how the Ming fell, together with the widespread dissatisfaction with late Ming misgoverning, may have made it easier for Chinese to accept the change, and for some to take service under the new rulers. But even so, there were many among the elite who, as we saw in the previous chapter, were firm in their moral commitment to loyalty. The Kangxi emperor had good reason to suspect that in their hearts, many men of education rejected Manchu rule and could invoke a higher morality that sustained their potential for dissidence. Four centuries earlier, Khubilai Khan, with Mongol self-confidence in his military superiority, could be indifferent to widespread Southern Song disaffection; it was politically irrelevant. In contrast, the Kangxi emperor lacked that self-confidence; he had to assume that bookish Chinese troublemakers still had the capacity to foment further revolt against his Qing dynasty. His successors would continue to fear that. Thus, a problem that should have dissolved after at most twenty or thirty years, once the take-over generation died off, was perpetuated by a Manchu obsession that in turn helped to keep the issue alive in Chinese minds. The rulers' focus on rooting out anti-Manchu sentiment became a distinguishing mark of Qing rule through the eighteenth century, to be somewhat relaxed only in the nineteenth.

I argued in Chapter 31 that the early Qing leaders were fully aware of the high risks in attempting to conquer and rule over so vast and populous a nation as China; they undertook the attempt in a conscious gamble that they could dominate the conquered Chinese by maximizing the limited Manchu military resources while manipulating the cultural elements. Dorgon, it is said, on learning that Wu Sangui in April 1644 was about to offer him the unanticipated opportunity to turn the pattern of Manchu border incursions into one of full-scale invasion, hastily ordered the mobilization of all Manchu males between the ages of ten and seventy, ready to risk all in that crucial moment. Later, after taking Beijing, he announced that the Manchus would never return to the Northeast, and their permanent migration into China began. He planned to turn the entire capital region, the former Ming Zhili Province, into an impregnable Manchu military base, and so commenced the ruthless confiscations that provided the system of banner lands. The declaration that Manchus should never engage in other than military careers and must therefore be fully supported by the Chinese was intended to forestall (and prolonged for a century) the gradual dissipation of Manchu military force. It would prevent Manchu officers and soldiers from acquiring other means of supporting themselves, and becoming assimilated in the process. According to this analysis, the Qing government's suspicion of Chinese, and the repeated intimidation of the elite, were all consciously designed cultural devices for keeping the Chinese in fear of Manchu reprisal; for maximum effect, these were alternated with displays of admiration for Chinese culture and of favor to learned and loyal Chinese.[14] This analysis probably gives a succession of Manchu leaders too much credit for being more profound strategists and in greater control of events than they actually were. Yet certain elements of it match the historical facts.

There is no doubt that from the moment the Manchus took Beijing, they recognized an urgent need for large numbers of Chinese trained to do the work of governing. The new Qing dynasty was by no means institutionally innovative. The structure of government continued that of the Ming in almost all ways. In staffing the government, the Manchus made one modification: dual staffing was used for high and important positions, such as Grand Secretaries, heads of the Six Ministries, chief censors, and provincial governors, where a Manchu (or Mongol) official always held the higher ranked of two positions, or outnumbered the Chinese (Han) officials within any group of co-incumbents. In military commands and coordinating posts, as in all postings to the strategic border regions, only Manchus and Mongols were appointed at any level. To staff its civil government, the Qing relied on the civil service examinations, conducted as in the Ming.

The Qing moved with haste to implement its civil service examinations, holding *jinshi* examinations in 1646, 1647, 1649, and triennially thereafter, with special examination years "by grace" added from time to time. Those special examinations commemorated notable events and made a display of the imperial favor toward the Chinese elite. A separate system was not fully implemented for Manchus and Mongols, although special preparatory schools were established in the banners to aid their candidates, and on two occasions early in the dynasty separate examinations were given at the capital for Manchu *jinshi,* in 1652 and 1655; at those, the candidates could use either Chinese or Manchu, and at each, fifty Manchu *jinshi* degrees were awarded. The purpose was to encourage more Manchus to enter the competition, but thereafter the *jinshi* degree examinations were open to all, and only the Chinese language was used at that level. It was always an embarrassment that large numbers of Manchus had to be appointed to the highest posts despite lacking the *jinshi* degree; it became routine to cite "other qualifications" in making such appointments.

The number of new Chinese *jinshi* degrees awarded every three years was about 240, not as many as in the Song or the Ming, but enough to accumulate a large pool of civil service appointees-expectant.[15] As in the Ming, that pool was supplemented by the much larger number of those who had got only as far as the second-level or *juren* examinations that qualified them for appointment to lower-ranked posts. Overall, the system satisfied Chinese expectations and functioned as a main instrument for keeping the elite sector of society linked to the dynasty. Steps also were taken to maintain a high level of intimidation over that sector of society, and in the early years, before the Kangxi emperor came into direct rule in the late 1660s, those steps produced frightening incidents when thousands suffered sudden and harsh punishments.

In 1657 a series of disclosures of cheating in the provincial-level examinations (for the *juren* degree that made candidates eligible to sit for the *jinshi* examinations at the capital in the following spring) led to ferocious punishments, first in the capital province and soon thereafter in several Central China provinces. Cheating in the examinations, always regarded as a most serious crime, had grown more frequent in the late Ming; it usually took the form of bribing the examiners with money or doing substantial favors for them to ensure success to persons who were in any case highly qualified but unsure of succeeding because the quotas for degrees were set very low in relation to the ever-growing number of candidates. There is no reason to doubt that cases of bribery were detected in the provincial examinations in 1657, and it is possible that the Chinese sons of the elite had come to think that Manchus and their Chinese examiner colleagues would in slipshod fashion go along with illicit but common practices from which they also benefited.

They were wrong; once the malpractice was reported, the government saw in it an important opportunity to intimidate a strategic sector of society. The ferocity of the punishment was out of proportion to the crime. Hundreds were summarily beheaded, hundreds more given the second most serious punishment of death by strangulation; their families' property was confiscated, and thousands of family members were banished to slavery in Manchuria.

In 1661–1663 another infamous instance of intimidation was carried out, this time in the four richest prefectures of Jiangsu. A provincial governor, a Chinese trying to gain favor at court, conducted a minute inspection of taxation records and made up a list of 13,500 names of men held to be delinquent in paying their land taxes. Most were from the well-to-do families of the region. Another 240 names of county government clerks were added to intimidate those low-ranking sub-officials often accused of being in collusion with the rich gentry households. Rigorous investigations were ordered, and more than 3,000 of the accused were found to be guilty in a degree meriting severe punishment, although the actual discrepancies might be of insignificant amounts, or might be explained by procedural technicalities. In this famous case of the "Jiangnan tax defaulters," punishments were similar to those in the examination cheating scandal. In addition, implicated members of the 13,500 families, regardless of the degree of their punishment, were removed from the student rolls and denied future access to the civil service examinations. Many careers were blighted, or at least interrupted. It was widely believed that the court followed through so fiercely on the sycophantic governor's original charges because it resented the widespread support given to Zheng Chenggong when he invaded this same region in 1659, attempting to overthrow the regime. Deep tremors spread shock everywhere throughout the self-satisfied and proud elite.

Also in the years 1661–1663 there occurred what was declared to be a treason case, and the punishment was aimed directly at Ming loyalists. It is known in history as the Zhuang Tinglong case, the case of an unauthorized history of the Ming dynasty. Zhuang Tinglong was a rich merchant in northern Zhejiang who had the ambition to make his name by sponsoring the compilation of a large history. He hired scholars to cooperate in preparing a Ming history based on a work originally published in the last years of the Ming.[16] Even so famous a scholar as Gu Yanwu was invited to collaborate, but declined because he did not think those in charge were competent. Others, some quite competent, eventually were associated with it. When the book appeared, it was reported to the court that it contained passages defamatory to the Manchus. Those reports, vigorously investigated, turned up supporting evidence, although it was mainly evidence of unintentional mistakes, such as the failure to edit out Ming titles and forms of address carried over from the late Ming original version. The careless retention of Ming proprieties was to be sure no longer appropriate, but it was taken as evidence of a scholars' plot to defame the Qing dynasty.

The bungled history was turned into a truly frightening campaign to intimidate all who might want to write about the history of the former dynasty: such history, on pain of death, was to be written from the point of view of the Qing, down to the smallest details. The collaborators were arrested, as were the printers and all persons known to have acquired copies of the work, even local officials who had failed to report it to the court. All the principals were executed, other male members of their families were annihilated, and the females were made slaves in Manchu households. The corpses of those who were implicated but had died (among them Zhuang Tinglong) were disinterred and burned. Again, the impact on intellectual circles was deep and enduring.

Xuanye, on achieving his majority and taking over direct rule, repudiated those harsh actions as excesses committed when Oboi still dominated the government. He tried to mask the harsh tone of Manchu imperial governing by sponsoring more accommodating attitudes toward Chinese traditional values. He strove to project the image of the Chinese sage-ruler, although on the annual visits to the Manchurian homeland he also had to perform as the Manchu warrior-hunter among his tribal chieftains. He was the last of the Manchu rulers who still had to be culturally dual in that demanding manner, even though there was a measure of pretense in both of his cultural identities. With regard to his "Chinese sage" role, he established a study within the palace called the Southern Study (Nan shufang), to which respected Chinese men of learning were appointed, to guide his continuing education, and to consult with him on issues of government. He practiced calligraphy, and although the publicly displayed examples of his brushwork often were written for him by surrogates (his handwriting, while strong, remained somewhat crude), as were the texts of his proclamations, book prefaces, and stele inscriptions, he eagerly adopted that venerated method of presenting himself in the world of learning.[17] He sponsored the compilation of what became the standard dictionary of the Chinese language, the *Kangxi Dictionary*, and of a much vaster dictionary of literary phrases and allusions, the *Peiwen yunfu*, and of other scholarly works.

His most important effort as a sponsor of learning was the writing of the *Ming History* by an imperially appointed commission. Every new dynasty, the Chinese believed, was under obligation to sponsor the writing of the preceding dynasty's history, and since Tang times that had been done by commissions of historians working for the central government. The Ming dynasty produced its history of the Yuan in less than two years' working time, in 1369 and 1370. A proposal to write the Ming history was presented to the

Qing court in 1645, but a formal response three years later concluded that for the time being there must be an effort to collect and organize materials. Thus the matter dragged on inconclusively until, in 1678, the Kangxi emperor announced that the court was soliciting names for membership in a commission to commence work the following year.[18] The writing of the Ming dynasty's official history would serve a number of purposes. Scholars loyal to the Ming and living as recluses would be under great pressure to come forth and help with this last service to their dynasty; that would put a large bloc of prominent holdout loyalists in the Qing government's service. Writing the history not only would promulgate an official version of events and interpretation of their meaning that the Qing could approve, and thereby undermine efforts to tell the story in a less favorable way, but would allow the emperor to patronize the work and the scholars doing it as well. Producing the official history also would formally mark the end of the Ming, signaling to all that efforts to revive or restore the former dynasty were in vain, in the view of everyone who contributed to the history's compilation.

Very few of the distinguished senior figures that the government most wanted to co-opt by this effort were willing to come forth and serve. The emperor again called on all court and local officials to nominate "scholars of broad learning and outstanding eminence" *(boxue hongru)* to sit for a special examination at the capital in 1679; it was contrived to give prestige to and accommodate the senior status of men who, it was disingenuously explained, had been unable to sit for the *jinshi* examinations at the expected times in their lives because of war and disorder. This project clearly was designed to force Ming loyalists to come to the capital. A final list was compiled of 188 men summoned for the examination. Thirty-six of them, through their strenuous efforts, were excused, although among those who went, some had to be forcibly dragged off, tied up, and put in mule carts, treated like indicted felons. There were indignant protests; tales of sardonic humor about the unwilling participants made mockery of the honor and dignity the examination was supposed to confer.[19] Of those who finally sat for it, only fifty were awarded the special degrees, forty of them from the lower Yangzi provinces of Jiangsu and Zhejiang. Assigned to literary postings at court, all concurrently served with the Ming history commission that got under way formally in 1679. The biggest fish, like Gu Yanwu and Huang Zongxi (discussed in Chapter 32), all escaped this net. Nevertheless, it was considered a breakthrough in getting a bloc of well-known and respected southern (meaning lower Yangzi region) scholars into the court, almost the first to be appointed to office since the founding of the Qing.

The official Ming history commission at first made little progress, but a curious event rescued the effort. The best-qualified historian of the Ming then alive was Wan Sitong (1638–1702), from a famed family of scholars in northern Zhejiang and a student of Huang Zongxi. He was nominated to sit for the special examination in 1679 but was among the thirty-six who successfully refused. He was, however, on friendly relations with the southern scholar Xu Yuanwen,[20] who headed the commission, a much-respected man of his own generation. Xu prevailed upon Wan Sitong to assist, not officially and not requiring that he go to the offices of the history commission, but as a private scholar living in the Xu residence in Beijing. This offer Wan could not refuse; through the next twelve years, devoting his full time assiduously to the task, he managed to review, correct, put in order, and in many cases write anew the major bloc of chapters (more than 300) subsequently incorporated into the *Ming History*.

After Wan Sitong's death in 1702, not much more was done to the manuscript; in 1723, in the first year of the Yongzheng reign, the history commission was established anew, to make minor refinements of the text and add a few missing sections. It was finally submitted to the throne in 1736, the first year of the Qianlong reign, and in 1739 was approved for publication after another critical reading led to a final round of superficial changes. The delays and reviews over a span of ninety years were caused by fears that in some obscure ways the wording might contain insults to the Manchus.

The contorted story of how the official Ming dynastic history was compiled shows how far the sensitivity to sedition affected the relations between the Qing imperial court and the Chinese elite, and through them the Chinese population at large. Xuanye, the Kangxi emperor, was a complex figure, but withal a man striving to work out rational solutions to the real problems of governing. He fully understood the significance of getting scholars from the South involved in his regime. The expression "simultaneously employing favors and threats" *(en wei bingyong),* which might be translated "concurrent enticement and intimidation," has been used to describe the manner he employed to win greater personal favor with the Chinese public while holding a tight rein. Some have called that hypocrisy—making a show of displaying his grace while at the same time reminding people that he was all-powerful and unrelenting in maintaining Manchu superiority. Some of his pronouncements have been analyzed to show, for example, that when he spoke sympathetically about those who suffered hardship and punishment, his real purpose was to remind others that they were under threat of the same. The charge of hypocrisy is thus not unfounded, but such hypocritical acts appear to be within the standard behavior of monarchs. More important, he was genuinely interested in his realm. He was eager to know it more directly, and at times rather self-effacing in maintaining what was, for an emperor, a non-pompous manner and a simple style, especially when traveling among and associating with members of Chinese society.

He began the practice of making long tours through the realm, especially six famous tours of the Yangzi South, or Jiangnan, meaning the lower Yangzi region. His declared purpose was to inspect the great waterworks controlling floods and supplying irrigation and transport between the Yellow River and the Yangzi Delta. He was deeply interested in the technology, and made a serious effort to learn about it.

On the first of those tours, in 1684, he avoided passing through Yangzhou, feeling that the smoldering resentment dating from the Qing massacre of that famous city in 1645 might still make it unsafe for him to go there. He of course could have gone safely with a great show of force, but he chose not to display that face to his subjects. On his second southern tour, in 1689, he quietly visited Yangzhou, staying at a temple in the suburbs, and after that he always included it in his itinerary. The last of the southern inspections was in 1707, when he made a special effort to enjoy performances of Chinese southern-style opera *(kun qu)*, of which he had grown inordinately fond. Other than the six extended tours of the South, he also made dozens of other tours. He visited the capitals of the provinces to the west, went to the home of Confucius in Shandong Province, ascended nearby Mount Tai to conduct sacrifices to the spirits of the sacred mountains as earlier emperors had done since the time of the First Emperor, Qin Shihuang, in the third century B.C.E., but which no Ming ruler had ever done. He was an active, inquisitive man, serious about broadening his direct experience of China, not merely seeking the luxurious indulgences afforded by such travel.

He nonetheless was forced to investigate further instances of scandal in the examinations later in his reign, and he also had to impose punishments from time to time on Chinese who, intentionally or not, offended against Manchu priorities. Keeping docile and relatively content the elite of China, from whose ranks he had to staff his government, was a task of unending complexity; eventually it wore him down. He disappoints by not always continuing to devote his undoubted intelligence and his energies to that task with his earlier rigor and relentless efficiency. It became clear by his middle years that he was susceptible to favoritism, tolerant of sycophants, and prey to laxity in domestic governing. Yet he was alert to the great issues of power and state interest, vigorous in pursuit of the wars against the western Mongols, aware that the Russian penetration of Siberia violated his northern border regions and required vigilant attention. These aspects of the Kangxi emperor's impressive—if not faultless—governing also merit attention.

III. THE MONGOLS ON THE NORTHERN BORDERS

The Manchus' rise to power in Inner Asia depended in the beginning on their ties to their Mongol neighbors in western Manchuria, and thereafter on their continuing skill in exploiting the sphere of Mongol relationships.[21] Under Hung Taiji (Qing emperor Taizong, 1626–1643), as early as the 1630s, before the fall of the Ming, when the Manchu Qing state still had its capital at Shenyang (Mukden) in Manchuria, it established an office for dealing with the Mongols which became known by the name Lifan Yuan, or "Office for Relations with (Mongol) Principalities." Later, other principalities were created on other borders, and heads of other polities, nearer or farther, were recognized as subordinate princes, so the Lifan Yuan became in essence the "foreign office" of the Qing government. This office managed relations with any territory not directly administered by the Qing government, which in any event looked upon all foreign nations as actual or potential vassal states. At this time the focus was entirely on relations with the Mongols; that focus dominated Manchu concerns for a century.[22]

Many individuals of the Manchu Aisin Gioro imperial clan and other Manchu princely families intermarried with Mongols. For example, nine of Hung Taiji's daughters married Mongol princes; Hung Taiji himself married two Mongol princesses, sisters, one of whom, the later Empress Xiaozhuang (1613–1688), was the mother of Fulin, the Shunzhi emperor. She was the beloved grandmother and trusted adviser of Xuanye, the Kangxi emperor, having reared him after his own mother's early death when he was nine.

Qing relations with the Mongols were, as we might expect, entirely different from Chinese-Mongol relations in the Ming period. The Manchus understood better the conditions of Mongol life in the steppe and the past failures of the Chinese to manage that relationship effectively. Under the Qing dynasty, the Manchus had adopted long-standing Chinese concepts of divide and rule, described in the old Chinese phrase about "using barbarians to control barbarians," or at least to defend the borders against other peoples. But the Qing dynasty also utilized the Mongols to do far more than that: while keeping them divided and under their control, they also depended on them militarily. Mongol military might was essential as the Qing dynasty was being established, and thereafter to protect their Inner Asian empire. The Qing "empire" was an extension of Chinese government beyond China's culture zone to an extent that has no precedent in Chinese history.[23]

With an exception of Tibet, which was a distinct polity *not* made administratively subordinate to the Qing, the new regions of Xinjiang, Mongolia (Inner Mongolia only, after 1949), and Manchuria are today equal in area to China Proper within the Great Wall (see Map 22 in Chapter 36). These Asian lands were added to the traditional Chinese state by the force of Manchu cavalry, with large components of Mongol cavalry and, to a lesser extent, Chinese military units supplying strategic auxiliary services as well as foot soldiers. The Mongols' participation was crucial to the success of an empire-building process in which they were at first essential allies, gradually thereafter reduced to the status of mere subjects, albeit privileged ones.

It is somewhat puzzling that the Manchus were able to impose their will on the larger and more potent Mongol nation; they did so by allowing their Mongol subordinates a high degree of autonomy in governing their own tribal affairs, sharing with them the material benefits derived from the control over China, while utilizing the inner divisions within the Mongol people to prevent their reunification under a strong national leader. Not least among the explanations, however, was that the Manchus' success in warfare bred expectations in the steppe of further successes. They had to keep expanding against all challenges to their hegemony. In that extended building process, it was the combined force of arms—Manchu, Mongol, and Chinese—under resourceful, determined Manchu leadership, that built the empire.

To accomplish the gradual absorption of the many Mongol tribes, the Manchus used political controls to keep them divided and under surveillance. Mongol tribes whose leaders surrendered voluntarily to the Manchus were given the status of border principalities *(fan wang)* and were not forced into banners. The Chahar Mongols, however, were forcibly brought under Manchu rule in the last decades of the Ming dynasty by Nurhaci and Hung Taiji; they occupied the region just outside the Great Wall and to the west of Beijing. Thereafter Manchu military and political pressure focused on the Khalkha (Qalqa) Mongols, farther north in what the Qing called Outer Mongolia, the present-day Mongolian Republic. From the 1680s onward, the Khalkhas also bore the brunt of the Western Mongols' military expansion. As the Khalkhas came under that threat of invasion and peril, the Manchus extended military protection to them, gradually turning that into full control over them.

When the Khalkha and other Mongol federations were defeated in war or forced to submit and declare allegiance to the Manchus, they were organized into banners nominally parallel to the Manchu banners, but in fact different. The Mongol banners were organized not to incorporate but to displace the original tribal authority structures, and to replace their former tribal chieftains with Qing-appointed company commanders. The intent was to eliminate the fluid steppe process of tribal buildups accompanying the rise to authority of successful war leaders. The banners imposed a static organization in place of the fluid tribal structure of command. Authority and appointment to leadership thus came to be bestowed by the Manchus.[24] By the early years of the Kangxi reign this process was completed among the Chahar tribes and other Mongols living closest to the Chinese border, and was under way among the Khalkha tribes. Although not without resistance and occasional threats of rebellion, the Manchus' tactics gradually prevailed.

The intractable Mongol problem in Qing times, from the 1670s in the Kangxi reign to the 1750s in the Qianlong reign, was that of the Western Mongols. Under the early Ming, the Oyirat Mongols (Oirat, Ölöd, Eleuth, and so on; "Oyirat" is used here as a general name for the Western Mongols) had captured the Ming emperor in 1449, but thereafter remained apart, and posed less threat to China than other Mongol tribal federations. Yet the Khoshut (Khoshote) tribal federation within the Oyirats became deeply involved in internal Tibetan affairs in the sixteenth century and thereafter, causing concern in Ming Beijing. Early in the Qing a new resurgence of Western Mongol power generated the "intractable problem," one that came from a different tribal group within the Oyirat federation. These tribal people were called the Dzungars (Sungars, Junghars, Zungars, Jüngars) after their home region, the great basin of Dzungaria that makes up the northwestern part of present-day Xinjiang. In the late seventeenth century they were led by a clan of dynamic leaders who claimed lineal descent from Esen, the Oyirat leader who captured the Ming emperor in 1449. Imposing their rule over other tribal groupings (e.g., the Khoshuts and Derbets) within the Oyirat or Western Mongol federation, they expanded to the west of the Pamir Mountains into present-day Kazakhstan, simultaneously also south of the Tian Shan Mountains into Muslim Turkic southern Xinjiang, and eastward into Khalkha Mongol territory. As sponsors and protectors of the Dalai Lamas, they also intervened in Tibetan affairs, becoming virtually the military overseers of Tibet. Their strongest leader, and the Kangxi emperor's fierce antagonist, was Galdan (1632?–1697).

Galdan claimed for himself the title of khan, or "emperor," of the Dzungar federation. His father, a powerful chieftain, had sent Galdan as a boy to Lhasa to be educated as a Yellow Sect lama. His older brother succeeded to the Dzungar chieftainship, but when that brother was killed in a family conflict, Galdan renounced his intentions to become a holy lama and, with the Dalai Lama's permission, returned to his people to avenge his brother's death and take over the chieftainship. He thus knew at firsthand both the power of the Tibetan religion and the secular and military conditions among his energized Dzungar Mongol federation. He became one of the most important Inner Asian leaders of the seventeenth century, in his impact on history ranking with the great empire builders.

The Kangxi court was well aware that a powerful Dzungar nation on the northwestern fringe of its growing Inner Asian empire could not only destabilize the Khalkha Mongols and imperil the entire northern border region but also use its influence in Tibet to project the religious authority of the Dalai Lamas; by that combination of military and religious means the Dzungars might try to exert control over all of Mongolia, where the Tibetan religion and its reincarnated leaders were venerated. That could strike at the heart of Mongol allegiance to the Qing and cause disaffection among the Mongol banner armies. The Qing government's Mongol alignment was crucial to maintaining the dynasty's military intimidation in China as well as throughout the Inner Asian components of the empire. This Dzungar challenge therefore demanded the most forceful efforts to counter it.

Beijing's northern border problems in the Kangxi reign were further complicated by the appearance on the scene of a new element in East Asian history: conflict with a European power that expanded toward China by land. Russia began to play a significant role in the history of Qing China through its penetration of Siberia, beginning in the late sixteenth century (Map 21). As that advance brought it closer to China, it ran up against the Mongols. Bilateral Qing-Mongol relations threatened to become trilateral contests, and Mongol fragmentation further complicated the scene.

Mongols occupied much of the very large zone in which the eastward push of Russian empire encountered the northern extension of Manchu empire—meaning the government of Qing China, the political instrument of Manchu power. Mongols were both drawn into the hostilities and affected by the accommodations worked out between Russia and China. Needless to say, their own interests were given scant notice by either of the imperial parties. At one point, however, when the Khalkha princes were trying to decide whether to align themselves with Russia or with the Manchus, their Living Buddha said that the Russians had no regard for Buddhism while the Qing state did, so they should throw their lot in with the Kangxi emperor's forces. That they did. Nevertheless, one can imagine that if the Ming dynasty had not fallen in 1644 or had been succeeded by another native Chinese dynasty, the various Mongol federations would have combated the Russians on their own ground, in their own way, and China might have remained a remote and not very observant neighbor to that zone of interaction. In that case, a

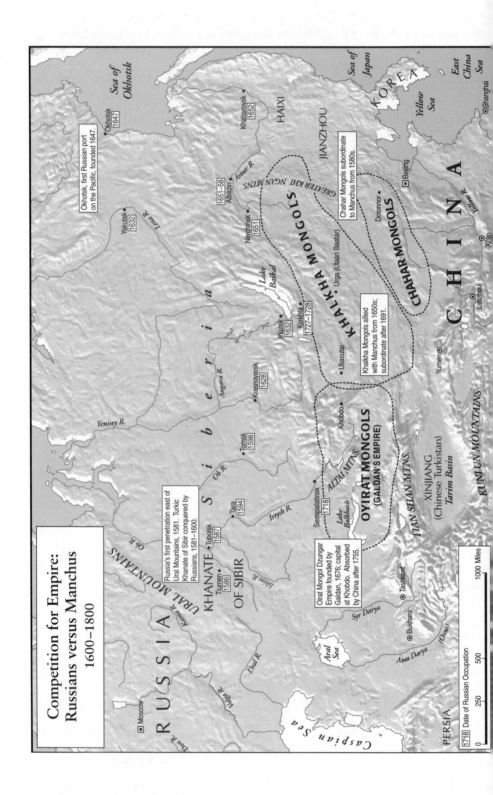

Competition for Empire: Russians versus Manchus 1600–1800

Okhotsk, first Russian port on the Pacific, founded 1647.

Russia's first penetration east of Ural Mountains, 1581. Turkic Khanate of Sibir conquered by Russians, 1581–1600.

Oirat Mongol Dzungar Empire founded by Galdan, 1676; capital at Khobdo. Absorbed by China after 1755.

Chahar Mongols subordinate to Manchus from 1580s.

Khalkha Mongols allied with Manchus from 1650s; subordinate after 1691.

Okhotsk 1647
Yakutsk 1632
Albazin 1651–58
Khabarovsk 1652
Nerchinsk 1651
Kiakhta 1727–1728
Irkutsk 1632
Krasnoyarsk 1628
Tomsk 1598
Tara 1594
Tobolsk 1587
Tyumen 1586
Semipalatinsk 1718

Moscow

RUSSIA

URAL MOUNTAINS
KHANATE OF SIBIR

S i b e r i a

Lena R.
Amur R.
GREATER KHINGAN MTS.
Lake Baikal
Angara R.
Yenisey R.
Ob R.
Irtysh R.
Ishim R.
Tobol R.
Kama R.
Ural R.
Volga R.
Don R.

KHALKHA MONGOLS
Urga (Ulaan Baatar)
Uliasutai
U?
Khobdo
ALTAI MTS.
Lake Balkhash
OYIRAT MONGOLS (GALDAN'S EMPIRE)

CHAHAR MONGOLS
Dolonnor

HAIXI
JIANZHOU

TIAN SHAN MTS.
XINJIANG (Chinese Turkistan)
Tarim Basin
KUNLUN MOUNTAINS

C H I N A
Beijing
Xi'an
Lanzhou
Yumen
Yellow R.

KOREA
Sea of Okhotsk
Sea of Japan
Yellow Sea
East China Sea
Shanghai

Tashkent
Bukhara
Syr Darya
Amu Darya (Oxus)
Aral Sea
Caspian Sea
PERSIA

1718 Date of Russian Occupation

0   250   500   1000 Miles

Sino-Russian border much closer to the Great Wall might have come into being.

What actually happened, however, is that the Mongols were caught squarely in the middle of the zone of potential Sino-Russian friction. The consequence for them has been called their "step-by-step conquest by the Manchus and the Russians."[25] The implications remain significant in the present-day history of East Asia.

Just as the pre-conquest Manchus in 1638 were establishing their Mongolian affairs office, the Lifan Yuan, the Russian government in Moscow established a "Colonial Office for Siberia" in 1637, half a century after the first Russian adventurers first began to explore the routes leading east from the Ural Mountains. Thereafter, with encouragement from the tsar's government, Russian and Cossack adventurers established forts: at Okhotsk in 1647 on the Pacific coast north of Sakhalin; at Irkutsk in 1652 on the eastern side of Lake Baikal; at Selenginsk on the Selenga River in 1666 in Buryat Mongol territory; at Nerchinsk in 1658 on the borders of Khalkha territory; and at Albazin (Albazina, Albajin) in 1658 on the western reaches of the Amur River. The Albazin outpost was almost immediately wiped out by a small Manchu force in conjunction with the local tribal (Jurchen-related) people, who were under Manchu suzerainty (they paid tribute in furs), and had appealed for aid. But Albazin was subsequently rebuilt, in the years when the Qing court was busy with the Rebellion of the Three Feudatories (1673–1681). The presence of an alien military outpost, undermining their control over tribal kin living as close as the Amur, was particularly threatening to the Manchus. The Amur, known in Chinese accounts as the Heilongjiang, or Black Dragon River, forms the northern boundary of present-day Manchuria. Lands along its course have been fiercely disputed between Russia and China from that time to the present.[26] The centuries-long struggle to define the Chinese-Russian border had begun.

At all of their many strongholds in Siberia, the Russian explorers and colonial agents coerced the local tribal peoples, Mongols and others, to pay tribute in furs and precious metals, and to supply grains and other provisions needed to sustain the population in their forts. They were highly aware of the wealth of China, and began to approach the court in Beijing, both through intermediaries and by sending official envoys. They wanted land in Siberia, but they also wanted trade with China.

The disputes that arose drew the attention of the Kangxi emperor. The entire northern defense problem rested on a number of elements: it involved the role of Tibet in Mongolia; the ambitions of Galdan and the Dzungars; the instability of Manchu control over the Khalkhas and other Mongol groups; and the Russian penetration into territories close to the Manchu homeland. Moreover, it was becoming clear that these European newcomers to the region were not going away, and that they might play a strong hand with the same local elements on which the Manchu Inner Asian empire rested. They might, for example, enter into an alliance with the Dzungars. The emperor recognized the need for decisive action.

Tibet has "long" belonged to China while disagreeing on just when that began; some indeed insist that it has "always" been part of China. A leading specialist on Qing history has written that immediately after the Manchus defeated the Dzungar chieftain Galdan in 1696, "Tibet became permanently a vassal of China." Another historian of the Qing wrote in 1935 that from the Yongzheng reign period, about 1727, "Tibet became wholly the territory of China." A work written in the 1950s for a broader audience says, "Tibet is an inseparable part of our nation's sovereign territory; from ancient times the region of Tibet has always been subject to our central governing authority."[36] The political view of this historical issue has been clearly drawn in recent times, but the historical argument turns on the peripheral issue of when the Manchus fully displaced the Western Mongols as the military guarantors of the Dalai Lamas' unquestioned civil authority.[37] No matter when that occurred, it is irrelevant to the question of Tibet's incorporation into the Chinese state: that did not happen in Qing times.

In the nineteenth century the Qing court, to head off British influence over Tibet from Britain's base in India, proclaimed that it was responsible for Tibet's foreign relations. In the mid-nineteenth century the Manchu court's two Imperial Residents (Amban) in Lhasa were ignored by the British and the heads of various Indian states as Britain succeeded in taking over management of Tibet's foreign relations. The country was opened to trade from India. That might have appeared again to orient the country away from Mongolia and China, toward India and the south, as it had been oriented a thousand years earlier, in the period of its greatest cultural development. That did not happen, although by the end of the twentieth century, with the Fourteenth Dalai Lama a refugee resident in India, Tibet had become the subject of international concern.

Closer to China, however, the northeastern Tibetan or Amdo Tibet region in the late nineteenth century was made a province, called Qinghai, and placed under direct (if administratively limited) control of officials appointed from Beijing. After 1928 the entire eastern Tibetan region was divided into the two provinces of Qinghai and Xikang. Tibet Proper, all that is labeled Tibet on modern maps, nonetheless remained autonomous. From the Revolution of 1911, the Republican government of China continued the Qing claim to be responsible for Tibet's foreign relations, to which it added the claim that Tibet is an integral part of China in terms of modern international law; it did not, however, set up any Chinese government within Tibet. That did not happen until after the Chinese army's invasion after 1949 and the flight of the Fourteenth Dalai Lama to India in 1959. Chinese control, something previously found not feasible, or perhaps traditionally not held to be highly desirable, was in the end accomplished by modern military force.[38]

To return to the empire-wide problems that faced the Kangxi emperor, the way he met the Russian challenge, absorbed the Khalkha Mongols, and destroyed Galdan to lay claim to all of Xinjiang while disallowing Mongol rivals for influence over Tibet all show him at his imperial best. True, the Qing failed to follow through on the expulsion of the Russians from the

Amur, perhaps putting too much faith in the power of the treaties to resolve that issue for all time. Eventually the Russians came back and found that the Manchus were not on guard against them; that failure, however, must be charged to the Kangxi emperor's successors. In assessing overall the complexities of the Mongol frontier, the emperor was perceptive in understanding problems and vigorous in responding. In matters of domestic governing in those same years and on to the end of his reign in 1722, he was less successful. The Kangxi reign ended in a dismaying spectacle of imperial frustration and political decline.

V. COURT FACTIONS

After the death of Nurhaci (1626), the ambitious Manchu enterprise in China was implemented under a succession of leaders: Hung Taiji (d. 1643), Dorgon (d. 1650), the Shunzhi emperor (Fulin, d. 1661), Oboi (d. 1669), Songgotu (d. 1703), and the Kangxi emperor (Xuanye, d. 1722), to name the most important among the dynasty's founding figures. One after another these men held the leadership, but they did not always share the same vision, nor did they control the same political resources. Along an uneven course to dynastic greatness, the basic weakness of Manchu imperial governing is most clearly seen in the role played by political factions. They were a disorderly element in a political system that ideally had no place for them, but in fact they became the characteristic feature of early Qing politics.

Politics in imperial China was not conducted through recognized, authorized political parties having valid status as proponents of competing political programs. Nor would emperors have wanted politics to be conducted in a way so detrimental to their solitary majesty as the font of all governing authority and wisdom.

Nevertheless, groupings of officials, imperial relatives, military leaders, and others commanding some elements of power and influence have always been present on or just under the surface of the political scene, trying to advance their special interests. In the eleventh century the great statesman Ouyang Xiu tried to defend groupings of like-minded statesmen as a good phenomenon—when, as he argued, they represented the best men banding together to promote the most worthy causes. (Did any politician ever claim to be doing otherwise?) His forceful essay "On Factions" *(Pengdang lun)* was denounced, and he was demoted for having argued the issue. In imperial times there was no acceptable basis for dignifying factions with the name "political party" and thereby making them legitimate. "Loyal opposition" was inconceivable. That would be very forcefully demonstrated again in the eighteenth century.[39] China's political development was not proceeding along that course.

The factional struggles that dominated government throughout the early Kangxi reign were essentially of two kinds. Factions of the first and most important kind represented military power groupings and were based in the banner system. Each of the eight Manchu banners controlled very large human and material resources. Leadership of the banners was undergoing that they preferred to appoint officials from the North. A basis for North-South factionalism existed.

The South meant both the geographic South, that is, all of China from the Yangzi drainage southward, and the historic South, which meant the mid- and lower Yangzi zone only, that is, Jiangnan, or "the Yangzi South"—essentially southern Jiangsu and Zhejiang. Within the larger region here called the geographic South, factions of southerners often were further divided on the basis of smaller identifications, such as provinces or dialect boundaries.[44] For example, a Jiangxi provincial faction acquired importance in mid-Ming times when that southern province produced an extraordinary number of *jinshi;* this advantage gained great influence for it both in politics and in the realm of letters. Regional or local factors such as shared dialects and parochial cultural traditions often were the unifying factors in geographic factionalism.

Hong Chengchou, the all-important turncoat official from Fujian, was one of the very few southerners in the early Qing government. The banner-based Manchu factions all had to work with Chinese officials, and they favored northerners. The relationship developed early because the northerners were on the scene when the Manchus invaded; they were useful for their knowledge of the capital region and its historic relations with Inner Asia, and they were accepted as trustworthy. The favored Chinese northerners in turn vigorously protected their dominant position and tried to prevent southerners, whose strong performance in the civil service examinations gave them a much larger number of potential appointees to high office, from gaining important posts in the central government. In this way, the long-standing North-South rivalry took on a more extreme character in early Qing than had been known during the Ming, even though some of the Ming emperors also had strongly favored men of the North.

The Kangxi emperor was astute enough to see that he could benefit by favoring southerners. He seems to have genuinely admired southern men of learning and to have enjoyed their company. He also was greatly taken by the ambience of life in the more ingratiating South, which he encountered in his tours. When he was encouraging Mingju to help him contest the factional dominance of Songgotu (who greatly favored northern Chinese officials), he took note of the fact that Mingju was well educated in Chinese, collected paintings and calligraphy, and had strong relations with a number of scholarly southerners. When the emperor established his Southern Studio (Nan shufang), it was so called because it was located in the southern part of the palace grounds, but it came to be taken as "the studio where the southerners congregated," and eventually those southerners at his court were called the "southern party" *(nandang).* That of course led to labeling the northerner Chinese officials at court the "northern party" *(beidang).*

The initial successes of the rebellion of Wu Sangui in the 1670s revealed to the Kangxi emperor that the Manchu regime was especially weak in the South. His *boxue hongru* special examination of 1679 was not a great success in capturing the most eminent of holdout scholars in the realm, but it was a success from another point of view: it brought the first large bloc of southern scholars into the Qing government, paving the way for them to encourage others to follow. They soon dominated Qing officialdom. As a factional group dependent on the emperor, they gave him an additional kind of leverage in political life. In his carefully tended policy of balancing factions and limiting the range of their influence, the emperor made strategic use of the southern party, cultivating it within the central government, and thereby enhancing his own power. The result was a period of political stability, achieved on his terms.

VI. THE SUCCESSION CRISIS

The political stability that the Kangxi emperor achieved in the decades from the end of the Rebellion of the Three Feudatories (Wu Sangui's rebellion) in 1681 until the end of the seventeenth century was gravely threatened in the first years of the eighteenth century. Again, the threat took the form of factionalism, but factionalism of a very special kind. The problem is known as the Succession Crisis. Of the emperor's thirty-five sons, twenty survived to maturity. Some were competent and ambitious, some mediocre and of little importance on the political scene. His second son, Yinreng, born to the niece of Songgotu in 1674, was declared the heir apparent when he was only two years old. He had an older brother, Prince Yinti (1672–1734), but the Manchus did not practice primogeniture, nor had they worked out a way of predetermining the succession so as to prevent crises.[45] The emperor doted on Yinreng, who was to be sure intelligent and active, handsome and talented. He was reared in an atmosphere in which he could do no wrong.

Yinreng was, however, a disturbed young man, given to fits of temper and "unspeakable" excesses of behavior. Although the Kangxi emperor continued to favor him and forgive him all his faults, the question whether he should be allowed to succeed became a political issue. His brothers came to hope that the succession would go to one of them, and politically ambitious courtiers and Manchu nobles flocked around several of them to help promote their chances of ascending the throne. Each of the factions that brought great turmoil to the Kangxi emperor's last twenty years is labeled with the name of one of the other sons.

The emperor's blind love for this second son and designated heir would not allow him to believe the stories circulating about the prince's profligacy and degenerate habits. Even so, as both emperor and father, he felt it necessary to investigate, but without revealing his need to do so. The normal instrument for gathering information was the system of memorials and reports submitted by officials at the capital or in the provinces. Incoming memorials were processed through the Office of Transmission, with copies sent to relevant agencies. Such information was immediately known throughout the entire court, and thus could not be controlled. He had another instrument for obtaining information, one that allowed incoming reports to remain secret, to be opened only by the ruler in person. This was the system of secret memorials. Only a few covertly designated high officials and imperial bond servants urban streets were supposed to hear each month: after bowing respectfully to him, their Sage Emperor, they were required to listen as elders read and explained the maxims. The emperor's text and the accompanying lectures made clear in simple language how to keep their local society pure, law-abiding, and upright, and their families free from danger.[50] As the aging ruler pondered the depth of corruption and moral decadence in his family, and among their associates throughout the elite of both Manchu and Chinese society, was he also moved to suspect that his own image—that of moral exemplar to his subjects—was received with cynicism, no less among the corrupted elite than among the people at large?

34

THE YONGZHENG EMPEROR
AS MAN AND RULER

The thirteen-year reign of Yinzhen, the Yongzheng emperor (1723–1735), was a period of central importance in the maturing of Manchu rule in China. He possessed few attractive qualities, yet he can be called the most skilled manager of the state apparatus to occupy the Qing throne. Both for his critical supervision of his government and its governors and for his institutional innovations, his brief reign was one of impressive accomplishment. The practical consequences of improved governing are evident in many aspects of Chinese life: the population resumed steady growth, and prosperity throughout society reached impressive new levels. How the achievements of his able if less than benign rule are to be assessed by other pertinent criteria is a matter that historians debate.

I. IMPERIAL STYLE, POLITICAL SUBSTANCE

It is a cliché of Qing history that the Yongzheng emperor was a man whose considerable achievements in governing are largely to be explained by defects in his character: the cold-blooded man became the exacting tyrant who made government work as never before under Manchu rule. There is some truth in that, but as always, when we know more about the man, the story becomes more interesting. Like all Ming and Qing monarchs, he is known in history by three names: his personal name was Yinzhen, his posthumous temple name was Shizong, and Yongzheng is the era name for the years 1723–1735, by which his reign is known. The thirteen-year reign of Qing Shizong marks an important turning point; the loose and still uncertain pattern of the dynasty's domestic governing under the long and praiseworthy rule of the Kangxi emperor (1661–1722) was succeeded by rigorous rule, implacably overseen by a secretive, awesome autocrat.

Corruption and inefficiency were his targets; sedition was his obsession. The tone of governing was transformed. The country's management was tightened and local governing improved. All that contributed to an undoubted growth of prosperity. The eighteenth century came to be called "sheng Qing," meaning the "flourishing" or the "splendid" phase of Qing, during which the Yongzheng emperor's son, the Qianlong emperor (r. 1736–1796), reigned in extravagant glory, thanks to the orderly administration and the treasury surpluses his father bequeathed to him. That is the essence of the cliché that dominates Chinese and other historical writings, past and recent.

This familiar summary of the Yongzheng period with its consequences for Qing dynasty grandeur is a useful starting point. But a careful look at the emperor and his reign reveals much more about imperial China in the eighteenth century, and provides a better understanding of the base from which modernizing change eventually took place. Because the Yongzheng emperor's personal qualities are looked upon as having defined the age, that is where the story must begin.

Prince Yinzhen, born in 1678, was the Kangxi emperor's fourth son. He came to the throne under the suspicion that to gain it, he had falsified his dying father's will, or worse; his clouded succession had deep repercussions within the Manchu elite and throughout government.[1] It is reported that he had been a reckless young Manchu fighter and roisterer in his twenties. By the time he came to the throne, he was forty-four years old, a mature and well-prepared prince who took his duties as ruler very seriously. There was little else that interested him. He came from a very large imperial family; many brothers and several sisters had survived to adulthood, but he probably did not really know his sisters, and his relations with his brothers were blighted by the hatreds engendered during the long years of the succession struggle. Among his relatives who survived his purges in the 1720s, he held only one of his brothers in close affection; that was his younger brother (the thirteenth) Prince Yinxiang (1686–1730), perhaps the only one whom he fully trusted and used importantly in office.[2]

It has been said that suspicion and fear were the norm in the Qing imperial clan: "The imperial household and closer relatives rarely if ever joined in informal pleasures in the palaces; the Son of Heaven maintained his august severity and the princes all bore the terrified demeanor of innocents on the way to be slaughtered. Compared with the historical record of all other dynasties, the estrangement within the imperial clan and between ruler and servitors was extreme, and constitutes another of the Qing period's special characteristics."[3] In that dismal atmosphere, Prince Yinzhen, later the Yongzheng emperor, spent his entire life. He could be close to very few people.

Even after he had arrested half a dozen of his brothers and scores of other close relatives, most of whom died under conditions of their imprisonment, Yinzhen remained uncertain about his hold on power. Whether he was afraid that secrets about the way he had seized the throne immediately upon the Kangxi emperor's death in December 1722 would be revealed, or that his imperial relatives would conspire with Manchu nobles to undermine him for other reasons, he was always alert to hints of sedition within the Manchu ruling elite, and to "rumors" spread about himself.

Fearing a return to the factional struggles in which he had come of age, in 1725 he took it upon himself to preempt all jockeying for power within the banners and the Manchu aristocracy by writing a new "Discourse on Factions," *(Pengdang lun),* using the same title Ouyang Xiu had used for his defense of factions among good servitors in Northern Song times. The Yongzheng emperor's discourse on that very sensitive issue is of course entirely different from Ouyang's earlier model; this emperor demanded that all servitors of the throne must totally accept the mind of the ruler as the sole criterion for good and evil, must follow the ruler's decisions in all matters of state, and above all must not join together to press for policies (such as supporting a claimant in a future succession) on which the ruler alone can make decisions.[4] That view of the servitor's place in the state, in its all-encompassing scope, not only denies Confucian man's moral independence but also defines a form of despotism so extreme that it could not truly be realized. Courtiers understood that the emperor's diktat was intended to bear particularly on factions among princes vying for the succession. At the same time, Yinzhen announced that his decision concerning his successor had been made, in writing, and would be kept secret until the appropriate time. No repetition of the factional infighting among imperial clan members and their adherents in the banners and throughout officialdom would be tolerated in this ruler's reign!

His "Discourse on Factions" set the tone for political behavior in the Yongzheng period. In its spirit, the emperor turned to maintaining a day-to-day surveillance of his entire governing establishment, extending from the capital throughout all the provinces. His most important tool for remaining in personal control over the vast machinery of governing was the special system of "secret" memorials, initiated by his father in the 1690s. More properly called palace memorials, to distinguish them from the far more numerous routine memorials which were sent through the Office of Transmission to the Outer Court, the palace memorials were confidential reports submitted directly to his hand by officials covertly selected by him. They contained information, and they might propose political actions.

The system of secret palace memorials, taken over from the Kangxi reign, was enlarged by the Yongzheng emperor. He expanded the list of officials who were authorized to submit them, greatly increased their flow, and used the two-way confidential communication channel they provided as his particular management tool. Having sole control over a strategic flow of sensitive information, quite apart from the much larger flow of routine reporting to the central government, he possessed the instrument needed for encouraging and intimidating his Manchu nobles and his Chinese bureaucracy. He could keep them all fearfully and hopefully responsive to his directing hand.

He wrote that during the day he played the imperial part in the unending round of governing activities, meeting his court, receiving officials, giving instructions to the ministers who headed the Outer Court. He was not particularly communicative in those face-to-face meetings. Rather, it appears that he took on an entirely different manner in the long hours each evening, sitting in his study that adjoined his bedroom deep in the inner confines of the imperial palace city, where he reviewed the day's incoming palace memorials until late into the night. He selected the most important of them, usually twenty or thirty a night, but sometimes as many as fifty or sixty.[5] He studied them carefully, checked their content against his data files and his powerful memory, and with his brush dipped in vermilion ink, he wrote on them long "rescripts," or comments expressing his judgment and initiating whatever follow-up action was called for. These incoming memorials, after the vermilion rescripts had been added in the emperor's own hand, were then dispatched confidentially back to the sender, who, after studying the emperor's words, sent them again to the palace to be preserved there, forming the reference file of palace memorials (gongzhong dang). More than 20,000 of those original documents have been preserved; through them we can study the emperor's daily reflections on the political issues of the time, and especially his manipulation of the governing personnel.[6]

The palace memorial system represented a new technique for imperial participation in governing; the secret memorials and the emperor's lengthy responses added a layer of political interaction to the regular paper flow through which governing functioned. Ordinarily, reviewing incoming memorials, proposing responses, getting the emperor's or his surrogates' acknowledgment, and sending them to the relevant ministries for action was the basic work of imperial government. It had long been a highly routinized process in which most emperors accepted the rescripts drafted for them on a separate slip of paper by their court officials and attached to the memorials before he saw them; at most the ruler might add "noted" or "approved" or "to be tabled" or whatever brief comment he chose. That work of handling the thousands of memorials received each month could mostly be done by secretaries and other aides, sometimes by eunuchs (as in some reigns of the Ming dynasty). The Kangxi emperor began the practice of using the rescripts he added to the palace memorials as his very personal, confidential communications between himself and chosen officials, yet few of his rescripts were more that ten or twenty words in length.[7] The Yongzheng emperor's rescripts often ran to several hundred or more than a thousand words. They became something quite new in the history of Chinese government.

Among the masses of original documents that were transferred from palace storage rooms to research institutes in the 1920s, the great trove of rescripted palace memorials (along with a much greater quantity of other documentation) began to be broadly studied only from the 1960s onward. It is not yet possible to assess their full importance for reconstructing the political life of the early eighteenth century. The Yongzheng emperor's vermilion rescripts, however, make it quite clear that he was acutely focused on honesty and efficiency in government operations. He scrutinized the confidential memorials sent to him for evidence of weaknesses in his appointed administrators and for signs that the structures of government were not functioning well. His confidential replies made judgments about the administrative issues but also encouraged his appointees to perform to higher standards. They show that he valued perceptive, independent-minded men who would forthrightly tell him things he might not welcome, and who would offer their own views even when they knew he might be prepared to disagree. He often rebuked his memorial writers for sycophantic excesses, for lack of clarity in their analyses, or for failure to garner all the facts. When men had gained his confidence and earned his often exaggerated praise, he would nevertheless remain alert to signs that they were growing lax, or that they might come to take advantage of their special relationship to him. Such officials might expect to receive a vermilion endorsement that deftly cut them to shreds.

Along with the overwhelming evidence that the Yongzheng emperor was in every sense a formidable executive, his vermilion rescripts also reveal that he could be humorous, sardonic, even whimsical at times. He often used vulgar colloquialisms that he must have learned from ordinary city people working in the palaces, or from soldiers in his palace guard. It also appears that occasionally he grew tired during a long night of studying memorials to frame his responses, and in his vermilion rescripts wrote mistaken characters, left sentences unfinished, said things in a quite unimperial manner. It is only in very recent years that historians have had access to those original documents, to discover in them the traces of his human fallibilities.[8]

Enigmatic evidence about his turn of mind is found in the many paintings he ordered his court artists, especially the foreign artists, to paint of him. Most important among these artists is the Italian Jesuit brother Giuseppe Castiglione (1688–1766), who entered the palace in 1715, served through the last seven years of the Kangxi reign, then through the Yongzheng reign, and for thirty more years under the Qianlong emperor.[9] Among his portraits of the Yongzheng emperor are fourteen in an album of costume portraits, action pictures depicting the ruler in various costumes and poses, many in exotic settings; a number depict the emperor in settings of Chinese folk religion and legend. There is no record of any emperor before that time having chosen to be depicted in such "curious self-fashioning" as we see in these scenes. It may simply have amused him to see his face painted onto the principal figure in each of these bizarre scenes. One can only speculate on what these remarkable pictures meant in this ruler's imagination.[10]

He was fascinated by a traditional Chinese means of reading a person's horoscope through the study of the eight characters used for recording the hour, day, month, and year of birth, and was skilled in the traditional art of analyzing them *(pi ba zi)* to reveal a man's potential. He frequently requested that information sent to him should include the "eight characters" of other military or civil officials, and then based his assessments of them and their assignments in part on that kind of information. This was not a contradiction: in this strongly rational man's mind, this too was a system of analysis. It did not appeal for divine intervention, nor did it assume supernatural forces, but analyzed what were taken to be systematic conjunctions in the cosmic process that generates human circumstances. If that was at best a pseudoscience, its thought processes nevertheless were those of calculation and reasoning.

The vermilion rescripts reveal that the Yongzheng emperor became quite fond of many of his officials, albeit at a distance; he might praise them warmly

Chinese and rescripted them in Chinese. Fully competent to function in both cultural spheres, he transcended the ethnic uneasiness of earlier Qing leaders. Putting that issue aside in itself reduced the grounds for factional involvement; by ending that diffusion of power into competing channels, he could better control the exercise of power.

With that objective in mind, he first concentrated executive power at the desk where he studied the paper flow and molded it to his uses. Only then did he transmit his executive decisions to the offices at court and throughout the country where his authority was translated into administrative action. The first step in that change was to strengthen his Inner Court cabinet. That engaged his efforts during his first three years on the throne.

The Inner Court was called that because its offices, staffed by the Grand Secretaries and their Hanlin Academy associates, were physically located within the palace precincts. The Outer Court, headed by the ministers of the Six Ministries and the two Censors-in-Chief, occupied offices outside the palace walls, and controlled a host of subsidiary offices in the capital and in provincial and local governing.[16] Strengthening the Inner Court lessened the Outer Court's prestige and reduced the scope of its initiative. The leading Inner Court officials, the Grand Secretaries, were in direct contact with the emperor on a daily basis, helped him formulate his policies, and transmitted his will to the Outer Court and all its agencies. The tension between Inner and Outer Courts was inherent in the structure of imperial governing; this emperor was not breaking new ground in striving to make it work more to his advantage, yet he brought about that change deftly and decisively. Competition for power and prestige was only one aspect of the Inner-Outer Court relationship; in this reign as always, many of the leading Inner Court figures also held concurrent, nonsubstantive posts in Outer Court ministries. Those links sustained the necessary communication and sense of shared interests among the personalities filling the leading positions in central government. Striving to make that executive agency function more efficiently, he found that there was only so much that even he could do to make the Inner Court his personal instrument.

Having rapidly gone as far as he could through strengthening his Inner Court, this emperor was determined to draw all administrative authority still more closely under his wing. In 1726 he began to focus on establishing a new, more truly "inner" Inner Court. Between that year and 1729 a new group of his highest-level assistants acquired a name, an official seal, and a new location—in a small study adjoining the emperor's apartment in the innermost sanctum of the palace. Drawing the administrative initiatives and controls entirely into his private living quarters symbolized the quality of this change.

The new agency took form as a military threat appeared, a resurgence of the Dzungar Mongols in far northwest reaches of Xinjiang. These persistent heirs of Galdan, whose defeat by the Kangxi emperor in the late 1690s did not end their threat to Xinjiang and Tibet, were again prepared to invade. Under the urgency of the planning required to counter that threat, the emperor demanded greater security of information, and speedier procedures for taking action, than the existing machinery of government allowed. He therefore organized a small group of advisers whom he called his "Junji dachen," which might be translated "High Councillors for Sensitive State Interests"; the standard translation of the new organ is "the Grand Council" (Junji chu). The first three men appointed to it included the emperor's favorite brother, Prince Yinxiang, along with Zhang Tingyu, a Chinese fluent in Manchu,[17] and another Chinese, Jiang Tingxi, a painter and poet who had served with distinction in civil administration. The latter two were southerners, and both represented the ideals of the literati. All appointees held concurrent posts such as Grand Secretary and titular heads of ministries. Their principal qualification for Grand Council seats, however, was not that they held high bureaucratic rank; it was that the ruler trusted them.

Throughout the remaining five years of the Yongzheng reign, the new Grand Council usually had only three or four appointees at a time, but it grew much larger in the succeeding reign.[18] Its working language at first appears to have been Manchu, appropriate to the security of military operations. One can surmise, however, that with or without the military emergency for which it was created, the Grand Council would have come into being. It suited the emperor's ruling style, and it quickly became the central organ of Qing administration. Its enlargement in the first years of the Qianlong reign which followed brought the Grand Council to its fullest development. The official history says of it: "From the Yongzheng and Qianlong periods onward, for 180 years the awesome imperial authority was based not in the cabinet [Neige, that is, the Inner Court] but in the Grand Council, the preeminent agency for wielding the powers of governing."[19]

Changes in the Censorate

The creation of the Grand Council was the major institutional innovation of the Yongzheng reign; beyond that the most interesting is the reorganization of the Censorate.[20] This organ traditionally had two principal functions: investigation of and surveillance over governmental operations, and remonstrance to the throne where malfunctions and abuses were noted or where policies appeared to be faulty. Officials assigned to it were relatively low in rank, and especially in Ming times were noted for their courage in speaking out against abuses of the imperial power. Its proper functioning was entirely dependent on the emperor; he could ignore it or even punish censors for meddling if he chose, though the price in "public" (meaning officialdom's) disapproval might be high. Despite that limitation it was regarded as an important agency of the administration.

The Censorate attracted much attention from the early European residents in China, from the Jesuits in late Ming and Qing times, and other Western officials and traders who began to write about China for European edification. They settled on our standard English name for it, one that does not fully convey its character. There being nothing closely similar in the West of that time, Europeans likened the Chinese institution to the office of *censor* in classical Rome. The analogy is vague at best. The Roman *censor* was a particular category of magistrate, or local official, who was responsible for registering the people (hence, the *census*), supervising their social lives and punishing their moral and political misdeeds. The Chinese "censors," in contrast, were central government officials in a cluster of parallel agencies responsible primarily to ensure that other offices of government were functioning honestly and effectively. Early European views of the Chinese Censorate tended to idealize it, seeing it as evidence that the Chinese had developed a highly rational institution for maintaining social ethics, forestalling political malpractice, and even limiting the power of the throne! Sun Yat-sen (1866–1925), called the Father of the Chinese Republic, decided to retain the Censorate (and the civil service examination system) as distinctly Chinese institutions worthy of being adapted to modern government, following the Revolution of 1911.[21]

The Chinese Censorate through later imperial times performed the tasks of investigative reporting, preparing impeachments, and offering the ruler a view of administrative issues that differed from what he might hear through the regular bureaucracy. It was not primarily for "censorship" of texts to remove offending passages, as in our present-day use of the term. Yet in the suspicious atmosphere of Qing government, censorship in that sense also was practiced by it, as well as by other agents of the throne.

Surveillance and investigation were supervisory functions important to any ruler trying to ensure that his government was effective. We might assume that the Yongzheng emperor would have extended and strengthened the censorial functions. He did the opposite. He chose to simplify and reduce the activity. He amalgamated the previously separate functions of the Censors-in-Chief and the investigative arm, the Supervising Censors who were attached to the ministries and to regional offices of government. At the same time, he reduced the remonstrance functions and lowered the status and prestige of the entire surveillance operation. He wished to relegate these venerable institutions to a kind of pro forma existence without abolishing them. In the meantime, their most sensitive functions as independent sources of information on the conduct of officials and the conditions affecting governing were superseded by his palace memorial system. That non-bureaucratized, direct, responsive means of extending his eyes and ears into all the crannies of society much better served his needs for strategic information. And its information flow did not pass through the Outer Court to be distributed to various agencies of the government, as did censors' memorials and impeachments, but remained confidential; loose information was a danger to authoritarian rulers.

To the extent that the Censorate had been able to provide genuinely independent criticism and judgment, this change weakened Chinese government, even as the emperor used his alternate instrument to strengthen his managing hand. His new Grand council had access to the secret palace memorials, and assisted him in utilizing that flow of confidential information to tighten adminstrative practices.

III. OTHER GOVERNING MEASURES

The Yongzheng emperor sought to control thought on two levels: he stressed the "guidance" that local government was to provide to the ordinary people, and he carried out various kinds of literary inquisition to intimidate the educated. On the level of the people at large, he sponsored an amplified version of his father's famous Sixteen Maxims, the so-called "Sacred Edict" that the Kangxi emperor had issued first in 1670. His "Amplified Instructions for the Sacred Edict" (1724) was a very long document, intended to be plain enough so that "ignorant rustics" could easily comprehend it.[22] Local gatherings at which it was to be read aloud and talked about were scheduled for the first and fifteenth of every month; attendance was to be compulsory, and the practice was to be continued by succeeding emperors. How soon the gatherings became irregular or ceased altogether, or attendance ceased to be enforced, following each of the successive imperial exhortations, is difficult to tell. Now and then we read that a local magistrate or other official became an enthusiastic promoter of the lectures, brought out a new illustrated edition of the text, or attracted attention by his spirited participation. Such enthusiasm was not common. If the system worked at all, it was during the short reign of the Yongzheng emperor.

Persuading the masses to be good, however, was not an entirely wasted effort; there was a widely shared ethical sense throughout all levels of society, but its existence undoubtedly had more to do with patterns of family and clan life, and of informal community leadership in relation to elite models, than it did with the government's indoctrination methods. The Yongzheng emperor surely understood that, and for this reason he was doubly concerned about thought control of the elite.

Ming loyalism within the elite was a diminishing issue, but anti-Manchu (or anti-alien) sentiment, which occasionally included Ming restorationist notions, continued to emerge in the literate sector of mid-Qing society. Several cases of suspected elite dissidence, and charges that the rulers had been defamed, were dealt with in ways designed to frighten the elite and keep them tractable. For example, poems might be discovered whose content implied criticism of the Manchu conquerors; the principals, whether the writer of the poetry, his relatives, his circle of associates, or others who contributed to the dissemination of the poetry, were beheaded, or enslaved and exiled to inhospitable border regions. All this was done to achieve the greatest publicity and most far-reaching intimidation. Or vaguely heterodox teachings might be discovered to have been used in the local schools where young men prepared for the civil service examinations; in addition to the principals' being rigorously punished, all the educated youth of the region (including the struggling poor seeking enough education to qualify for the local examinations) would be banned from the examinations for a period of time. To be cut off from the main route of advancement could bring dismay to the hearts of all. The Yongzheng administration was vigilant in tracking down (or in fabricating by exaggeration) cases of these kinds.

The most interesting thought control incident of the Yongzheng reign is that involving the doctrines of a certain Lü Liuliang (1629–1683), a man born near the end of the Ming who lived into the Kangxi reign. He was sixteen when the Manchus conquered his home region in Zhejiang, and some family members were executed at that time for supporting the Ming cause. He continued to study, and sat for the examinations under the Qing, but never successfully, so gave up and taught, then supported himself by writing and running a bookstore in Nanjing. His writings were distinctly critical of the Manchus; he specialized in studying those passages in early classical writings dealing with the non-Chinese peoples of the borders, and by his disparaging remarks about such peoples implicitly held the Manchus up to scorn. It is revealing that at that time a man of his dissident mindset could survive, even sell books and advertise his ideas, without being identified as a political agitator and punished for it. He was widely recognized as an expert on the teachings of the Song philosopher Zhu Xi, and was recommended to the court by local officials as one worthy of being invited to the special *boxue* examinations of 1679. (He refused the invitation.) This is a reminder that the atmosphere in the Kangxi reign was much more relaxed than under the Yongzheng emperor. After Lü Liuliang died, his son sat for the examinations and distinguished himself by placing second in the palace examinations for the *jinshi* in 1706; he died in 1708. The Lü family might have disappeared from history at that time but for an unexpected set of circumstances.

A generation later, a struggling scholar in Henan, Zeng Jing (1679–1736), was drawn to the writings of Lü Liuliang by his interest in the Song dynasty philosopher Zhu Xi. The anti-Manchu ideas he also found there strongly influenced his thinking. An unsuccessful candidate for the lowest-level examinations, he was forced to support himself by teaching in an elementary school. Certain staff members of the households of the Yongzheng emperor's brothers and their adherents earlier had been dismissed and sent into exile by the emperor. As they passed through the town where Zeng Jing taught in 1727 on their way to exile, he heard their lurid tales, perhaps wild fabrications, telling how the emperor had dispatched his father and stolen the throne from his brother and committed numerous other vile acts. Putting that together with the anti-Manchu content of Lü Liuliang's writings, Zeng Jing began to teach that the Manchus were an evil plague on China that must be exterminated.

A politically naive person, Zeng prepared to arouse a general revolt, although he had only a handful of followers and no organization. He dispatched his most trusted (and equally naive) follower to meet Yue Zhongqi, the governor general of Sichuan and Shaanxi Provinces. Zeng picked Yue Zhongqi as a likely co-conspirator because he guessed that Yue must be a descendant of Yue Fei, the famed patriot general of the early Southern Song dynasty, who was the outstanding symbol of military resistance to invaders, and the shining exemplar of loyalist sentiment.[23] In the letter conveyed to Governor Yue, Zeng Jing invited him to rebel with his armies and provincial resources and launch the patriotic drive to terminate the Manchu plague.

Yue Zhongqi was startled. He was one of those regional officials most trusted by the Yongzheng emperor, a writer of secret palace memorials that won the ruler's warmest responses. To gain further information and learn the identity of Zeng Jing, he first pretended to be won over by the anti-Manchu arguments. After learning what he needed to know, Yue then arrested Zeng's messenger, immediately informed the emperor in a palace memorial, and set in motion an investigation leading back to Zeng Jing in Henan. Soon Zeng Jing was under arrest with his few followers. Investigators also were sent to the site of Lü Liuliang's former home in Zhejiang to see what activities might still be based there.

The emperor was at first furious, and perhaps more than a bit unsettled by this evidence of the ease with which seditious doctrines could be nurtured and spread about in Chinese society. The worst thing was that his enemies within the imperial clan had spread rumors to undermine the legitimacy of his succession. Those were his dissenting brothers, arrested in 1725 and 1726. Their family members and household servants as well as military underlings and others of their large entourages also had been arrested, charged, and punished in varying degrees of severity. That produced thousands of unhappy people willing to express their resentment. Just at that time he was also closing elaborate traps on the two officials whose loyalty to him had been of crucial importance at the moment when his father died in 1722. One was General Nian Gengyao (arrested in 1725, died 1726), who in 1722 was in control of provincial forces in the northwest that had prevented Prince Yinti from contesting the succession. The second was his uncle Prince Lungkodo (arrested 1727, died in prison 1728), who in 1722 was commandant of the capital garrison forces. Lungkodo's support had prevented other princes and their factions from challenging the succession. The emperor had known it would be necessary to silence these two men because they knew things that could not be made public. That the exiled survivors of his purges in 1725 and 1726 should also have spread damaging reports about him, stimulating this simpleminded fool Zeng Jing to attempt rebellion, was proof that such information was circulating; it could also be used by cleverer conspirators to much more dangerous effect, he realized.

In 1729, following his arrest in Henan, Zeng Jing was brought to Beijing to be publicly tried. Some of the proceedings were conducted in the emperor's presence. The rumor-mongering princely household servants who had traveled through Henan on their way to distant exile in 1727 also were brought to the capital and made to confess that they had invented the lurid stories. The hapless Zeng Jing, declaring that he had been gravely misled, wrote a lengthy statement explaining how he had been taken in. The emperor generously granted him amnesty, saying that he could forgive a man who had defamed him, but filial duty would not permit him to forgive one who had insulted his father. Therefore the corpses of Lü Liuliang and his family were exhumed and shredded. Surviving male members of the Lü clan were severely punished; the females were sent to the imperial palaces to work as drudges.

Determined to gain as much impact as possible from the case, the emperor had a tract compiled that included essays by himself, Zeng Jing's confession, and other documents demonstrating the falseness of all the anti-Manchu stories that had surfaced during the incident. Called *Dayi juemi lu* ("A Record of Righteous Awakening from Error"), it was published in 1730, and immediately was made required reading for all persons preparing for the examinations and by officials throughout the government. Zeng Jing was sent home to serve as an honored minor official supervising public morality, and to bear witness to the magnanimity of his emperor. But the matter was not concluded. The emperor died in October 1735. His fourth son, Hongli, the Qianlong emperor, came to the throne as a mature young man of twenty-four who had his own ideas about such matters. First, he found his father's rambling account of the "truth" about imperial household affairs in the period of the succession struggle an embarrassment; it said far too much. He ordered the *Dayi juemi lu* called in and all copies destroyed, pending the preparation of a less revealing revision.[24] Then, in the name of filial piety, he declared that he too must do as his father had done: punish those who had defamed *his* father. Zeng Jing and his associate were called to the capital in 1736 and executed in the most brutal manner possible.[25] Filial piety was preserved and Qing justice was done.

The story did not end there, however. Among the people, the urge to achieve justice for the wrongly punished frequently took the form of popular legend in which wrong was righted. That kept the event alive, spreading far and wide the satisfying tale of cosmic justice, and the legend grew in detail and specificity as time passed. In the wake of these events, a stirring tale emerged in which satisfying vengeance was achieved. Lü Liuliang was said to have had a granddaughter, a remarkable young woman noted for swordsmanship taught to her by a monk who was secretly devoted to the memory of the Ming loyalist Zheng Chenggong. Her martial skills were matched only by her beauty and charm. This intrepid young woman was arrested along with female members of her family; all were sent to the palace to become household slaves; there, the tale goes, she managed to attract the emperor. His final illness and sudden death in 1735 were enough to arouse popular rumors, although there appear to be no grounds for believing that he did not die naturally. In popular belief, however, she avenged her grandfather and the Lü clan by assassinating the emperor in his bedroom; in some versions of the tale she then committed suicide, in others she fought her way out of the palace and survived.

The story is important: it cast the Manchu regime in a bad light. Many people were eager to believe that the Yongzheng emperor, and the entire conquest regime, were unworthy bearers of the Mandate, and thus might be conspired against. The eighteenth century saw the emergence of many secret societies, typically anti-Qing and loyal to the long-fallen Ming.[26] Such stories played their part in feeding the beliefs that lent coherence to clandestine groups.

IV. MILITARY CAMPAIGNS AND BORDER POLICIES

The Yongzheng emperor did not seek military expansion; he did not send, much less did he lead, armies into the field in search of dynastic and personal glory. Yet he saw the need for firm policies on the borders and was willing to commit his dynasty's resources when necessary. In these matters his brief reign was an interlude between the longer and more definitive reigns of his father and his son, yet some important steps were undertaken.

The Dzungar Wars

Relations with the Russians in Siberia were maintained by a second treaty, signed at Kiakhta in 1727 and 1728, as noted in the preceding chapter. This led to a quick growth in Sino-Russian trade, through the city of Kiakhta, on the northern boundary between what is today the Mongolian Republic (historically, Outer Mongolia) and Siberia. The treaty reduced the possibility of a Russian-Dzungar alliance against the Qing, a possibility that previously had complicated the Manchus' relations with all their Mongol subjects and partners in empire.

On the far northwestern fringe of the Qing empire, the Dzungar federation of the Western (Oyirat, Eleuth) Mongols was again active. After their great founding ruler Galdan's death in 1697, his nephew Tsewang Araptan (1643–1727) came on the scene; he gradually pulled the fragmented Dzungar state together and, leading a powerful resurgence, expanded its boundaries.[27] He invaded Tibet in 1716–17, causing great devastation and arousing the resentment of the Dalai Lama; it was the Dzungar leader's intention to supersede both rival Mongols and the Qing state in establishing his control over the Qinghai region that borders both northwest China and northeast Tibet. His planned takeover of Xining, the principal city of Qinghai, was thwarted when the Kangxi emperor in 1719 sent his fourteenth son, Prince Yinti, at the head of a large army to garrison Xining. That army was backed up by General Nian Gengyao, based in adjoining Sichuan Province. Thus all the elements were again in place for what had become the classic confrontation between northwest Mongols (whether Dzungars or Koshuts or others of the Oyirat federation) and China over dominance in Tibet.

The Yongzheng emperor inherited that tense situation when he came to the throne in 1722. Prince Yinti, his rival for the Qing throne, was recalled to Beijing and played no further part in the military action that was to ensue, but Qing armies continued to hold their ground in Xining and deny the Dzungars control over the strategic Qinghai region. Tsewang Araptan died in 1727, leaving his throne to his son Galdan Tseren (d. 1750). This able military leader became the Manchus' troublesome foe in the northwest; he had to decide how far to go in challenging the Qing state for control over Tibet. The Manchu emperor decided to preempt the Dzungar ruler; his new Grand Council was created to expedite the supervision of his Dzungar campaigns.

Neither side was able to bring off a decisive victory. In 1731 the Manchus suffered a disastrous defeat and were saved only by the intervention of a further contingent of Mongol banner forces. A truce was agreed upon in 1732 and renewed under the Qianlong emperor in 1738, after which peace reigned in Dzungaria until the 1750s. The final showdown over control in Tibet, possession of Qinghai, the Qing presence in Muslim Turkic southern Xinjiang, and Dzungaria itself was postponed until the Qianlong emperor in the 1750s launched the war that finally eliminated Dzungar power. The Yongzheng emperor's military intervention sustained the Qing claim to Xinjiang which the Kangxi emperor had for the first time attempted to add to the Qing (Manchu/Chinese) empire, but left the conclusive steps to be taken by his successor later in the eighteenth century.

The Southwest Border Region

E'ertai (1680–1745) was a Manchu official who was greatly trusted and favored by the Yongzheng emperor; he devised special policies that brought about changes in the southwest.[28] He came from a Manchu noble family distinguished for service; his father was well educated in both Manchu and Chinese and had served as head of the National Academy. E'ertai also achieved some distinction in Chinese literature early in a career in which he held mostly provincial offices. He served from 1726 to 1731 as governor, then governor general, in Guangxi and Yunnan-Guizhou provinces, becoming a specialist on the problems of governing in regions where non-Chinese native peoples constituted the majority. His reports on his administration in the southwest so impressed the Yongzheng emperor that he called him to the capital in 1732, appointed him Grand Secretary, Minister of War, and concurrently to a seat in the Grand Council. For the remainder of his career, under this emperor and the next, he was one of the most influential and most highly honored officials in the Qing government. It is his service in the southwest provinces between 1726 and 1731 that merits notice here.

Unlike the Chinese, the native peoples of the region were mostly not registered in census records nor governed under Chinese *xian* (county) administrations. The Qing government inherited the system of *tusi,* or "native chieftainships," that arose during the Yuan dynasty and had been continued and enlarged under the Ming. The tribal peoples' own hereditary chieftains were allowed to govern, were required to maintain peaceful relations among themselves and with neighboring populations of Chinese, and received official title and rank from the Ming government, which could step in at any time and remove them if necessary. It had always been assumed that the *tusi* were a temporary necessity but would in time be replaced by county governments headed by appointed Chinese civil service administrators, when their regions would be reorganized along Chinese patterns. That process was called *gaitu guiliu,* meaning "changing the *tusi* to appointed officials."

The *tusi* system represented a degree of Chinese intervention that did not benefit the native peoples, nor did it serve well the interests of the Chinese government. The native chieftains among some of the larger ethnic groups (e.g., the Yao, the Miao) were often warlike. They kept the southwest in prolonged states of disorder as they squabbled over inheritance, over control of legal and illegal trade, and over the benefits to be gained from improper collusion with Chinese officials in the region. The Manchu/Chinese government's interests, justifiable or otherwise, badly needed the strong organizing hand of a perceptive administrator. That is what E'ertai provided.

He had to conduct a number of campaigns to pacify warring tribes, but he learned to deal with their leaders directly, and to gain their compliance with his impartial if stern governing. It was his conclusion that the time was long overdue to end many of the chieftainships and impose regular Chinese local government on their regions, in which increasing numbers of Chinese were coming to live. The introduction of New World crops, especially maize (Indian corn), sweet potatoes, peanuts, and tobacco, was changing the agrarian economy. Those changes decisively favored the Chinese farmers, but in a curiously indirect way: they reduced the necessity for the native peoples to retain control of the richer valley bottoms. The New World crops made possible for the native peoples an alternate way of subsisting on poorer upland agriculture. Forced to relinquish the rice paddy lands to Chinese competitors (in a competition made unfair by government favor toward the taxpaying Chinese), they thus tended to become "hill people."

As governor and governor general in the three provinces of the southwest with the largest percentage of non-Chinese inhabitants, E'ertai imposed a stern peace, abolished half the native chieftainships, and thereby extended the Chinese pattern of taxation and governing to larger sectors in these provinces. This had the effect of extending imperial control on the soft southern borders at the same time the Manchu and Mongol armies were accomplishing much the same result in Inner Asia. E'ertai also encouraged mining, especially the mining of copper in Yunnan, and he supervised improvements in irrigation and transport systems. By establishing and supporting Confucian schools, he speeded assimilation of the border zone into Chinese cultural patterns. This was looked upon in Beijing as brilliant success, for which E'ertai was richly rewarded. It had a transforming effect on the region, although whether it brought about the betterment of the local population is debatable.

v. Population Growth and Social Conditions

The continuing story of Chinese population history through the centuries can be brought into Qing times at this point, where the Yongzheng emperor's rigorous governing is seen to have encouraged stability and growth. The final phase of this story will be discussed in the following chapter, where the Qianlong emperor's repeated efforts to achieve a more accurate counting of his subjects are discussed in relation to demographic trends.

It has been proposed in an earlier chapter that the population of Ming dynasty China was in fact considerably larger than previous estimates have shown.[29] While the figures proposed here for the end of Ming (the date 1650 is used) are no more than estimates, as are all other available figures, they are convincing enough that the previous estimates of Qing dynasty population must be adjusted accordingly. It should be kept in mind that "hard statistics" are not available until the mid-twentieth century for China's population as a whole, nor for other parts of the world before the nineteenth century. Historical demographers are becoming increasingly sophisticated in the methods by which they revise and improve their estimates, but China's population in particular demands much more of their concentrated effort. In what follows, various kinds of estimates are compared and a judgment is offered about which figures are the most apt to stand up, if only as refined estimates.[30]

To carry the discussion forward into Qing times, it is useful first to quote a summary statement found in the most influential study of Ming and Qing population: "The population of China, which was presumably in the neighborhood of 150,000,000 around 1700 or shortly after, probably increased to 275,000,000 in 1779 and 313,000,000 in 1794. If so, it had more than doubled itself within a century that offered uniquely favorable conditions for growth."[31] That set of estimates starts with a base figure of 150 million in or around 1700; although that is two and one-half times the official figures in Ming and Qing sources, it still must be considered much too low. It posits an annual growth rate as high as 0.87 percent for one fifteen-year period in the late eighteenth century, and proposes an overall annual growth rate of 0.63 for the period 1779–1850; both are considerably higher than any of the growth rates adopted here in estimating Ming population growth. Historical demographers have usually accepted a growth rate of 0.3 percent for the entire world between 1650 and 1750,[32] a rate that incidentally is in keeping with rates posited here for China.

Finally, the summary statement just quoted accepts the official Qing statistics from the end of the eighteenth century, which to be sure were more carefully produced using a new system. On that basis it states that the population "more than doubled" in the eighteenth century, and says that conditions inducing that explosive growth were "uniquely favorable."[33] Most historians agree that the censuses taken late in the eighteenth and at the beginning of the nineteenth centuries were vast improvements over those produced in the previous three centuries. For all their late improvements after 1740, however, responsible local officials still worked under conditions that induced under-reporting. The Qianlong emperor himself was well aware of that. When the startling new figures were reported to him in 1740, showing a total of 143 million (instead of the anticipated 60–70 million), he immediately pronounced them still too low and ordered annual recounts. In 1743 the reported figure grew to 160 million; he continued to be suspicious of undercounting, and continued to get rapidly increasing figures: 260 million in 1775, and 297 million near the end of his reign in 1795. The figure of 313 million for about 1800, one of the most widely quoted census figures for later Chinese history, need not be believed. It merely shows how inadequate (for counting actual population totals) the census procedures remained, after half a century during which the Qianlong emperor demanded fuller countings and implemented

new methods for reaching them. Despite those improvements, there is no reason to believe that an accurate counting was ever achieved. Underreporting
remained the basic fault; that is made clear by the comments of local officials
as well as the evaluations offered by the emperor.[34]

Nor can one accept the idea that between 1700 and 1800 China offered
"uniquely favorable conditions for growth." They appear to have been
unique only because previously accepted figures do not show another time
when growth was so rapid, but that reasoning becomes circular. From
descriptive information we have good reason to believe that growth comparable to that posited here for the eighteenth century was also probable in much
of the fifteenth and throughout the sixteenth centuries. Altogether, we have
good reason to accept a much higher starting point for Qing population
growth than the generally adopted figure of 150 million. Even if our hypothetical population total of 268 million in 1650 is high, it would seem reasonable
at the least to accept a figure somewhere between that and the so-called low
estimate's alternate figure of 231 million in 1650.[35]

The problem here, therefore, is to project figures for the first half of the
Qing period (1650 to 1800) from a base no lower than 250 million in 1650.
Descriptive information from people of the time observing conditions in various parts of the country, though scattered and fragmentary, can be used to
suggest trends and test hypotheses. How sound was the rural economy in
relation to the pressure of population on the land? What is indicated by the
growth of cities, the expansion of craft production, and the structure of marketing in domestic trade? What is reported about the recovery of devastated
areas, or about migrants fleeing depressed areas or enticed into growth areas?
Do we have micro-data for specific small samples that can corroborate or
deny the less well documented generalizations? New information along those
lines is becoming known.

There are as yet, however, no well worked-out data on which to base firm
conclusions about the Qing population overall. It is probable that the Manchu
conquest initially reduced the population totals in certain regions enough to
lower overall growth trends. For example, creation of the banner lands by
expropriation throughout Zhili, the Metropolitan Province in which Beijing
was located, probably stalled or reversed population growth there. Still more
serious devastation in Sichuan in the 1640s and 1650s, following the defeat
of the roving bandit Zhang Xianzhong, probably caused a sharp drop in the
population throughout that large and potentially rich province. The maritime
embargo and the enforced removal of coastal population in Fujian and adjoining provinces between 1660 and 1683 caused hardships on a scale that probably decreased total population there also. Those and other less severe consequences of the Manchu invasion may have kept the population from achieving
significant increase overall between 1650 and 1700; that is what most historical demographers (albeit working from lower base figures than here
employed) have always assumed to be the case.[36] It may be overly cautious
to posit virtually no net increase from 1650 to 1700, but even so, the population of China in 1700 must have been closer to 275 million than to 150

million as heretofore widely believed. If it then increased by one-third in the following century, that would have brought it to a total of 360 million by 1800; that increase implies an annual growth rate of only 0.3 percent, much lower than most demographers have calculated for the eighteenth century. Yet the slower pace of growth appears to be more reasonable than the long-held idea, cited earlier, that the population "more than doubled" between 1700 and 1794. A continuation of a modest 0.3 percent growth rate would have produced a total of 420 or 430 million by 1850. Such a conclusion loosely accords with the most widely accepted views about the population in the mid-nineteenth century,[37] just before the cataclysmic second half of the century again brought net losses, but it suggests a quite different path to that landmark point.

None of the figures used in the foregoing discussion should be looked upon as more than working hypotheses. A major implication of the proposed outline of Qing population growth is that it discredits what usually has been taken as the most significant demographic fact about Qing: the idea of a "population explosion" in the eighteenth century. That supposed phenomenon is given high explanatory value in relation to many social and political contexts. If, however, the population did *not* suddenly increase during that century, but started from a higher plateau and grew moderately, many social issues must then be otherwise explained. For example, calculations using those earlier population figures in conjunction with equally suspect official Ming and Qing figures for land in cultivation show a disastrous fall in the ratio of cultivated land to consuming population; the implicit crisis in that ratio of productive land to population must be reexamined. Related views about the "optimum population" of China, perhaps in itself a suspect notion, also must be reconsidered; calculations to determine an optimum population level for China have not given appropriate weight to the Chinese farmers' capacity for intensification of agriculture, clearly displayed in Ming and Qing times, long before new technological elements of recent times introduced further changes in agricultural and other kinds of productive activity.

With those caveats, the historian still must attempt to assess the health of Chinese society as reflected in population growth, and as sustained by social policies. The Yongzheng emperor was primarily concerned with retaining and enhancing his authority, but he did not see that as unrelated to the health of society. He tried to induce order at all levels in the society, because disorder could spawn challenges to the dynasty's continued existence, but also because a settled, prosperous, well-functioning society was more easily ruled, and provided more certain benefits to the ruling regime. In that spirit he continued his father's deep interest in water control projects to prevent flooding and ensure irrigation and water transport. He intensified corrective and preventive measures on both the Yellow River and the Grand Canal, where the major flood control operations were located. He also initiated a project, at first placed under the direction of his brother Prince Yinxiang, to improve canals and drainage projects within Zhili Province, where the Manchu banner lands were concentrated. He did not undertake ostentatious tours of inspection to observe progress in those activities, but through his network of surveillance he probably knew more about what was going on than did either his touring father or, subsequently, his parading son.

His efforts to tighten the administration not only prescribed punishment for officials guilty of malpractices but also turned his attention to the so-called bad gentry *(lie shen)*, who used their status in local society to evade taxation and abuse the common people. He may not have recognized that the "bad gentry" phenomenon itself was a by-product of diminished morale and commitment within the upper stratum in society, reflecting the cynicism induced by Qing political hypocrisy. His way of dealing with upper-class misbehavior complemented his efforts to keep the elite under intimidation; that was politically strategic to his interests because the elite not only was the source of his civil officials, but also constituted the sector with the most influence in local affairs throughout the realm. His motivation was not an urge toward petty tyranny; rather, he wished to enhance his authority over provincial and local offices of government so as to achieve disciplined and orderly governing. The exemplars of good provincial government selected by him for the greatest rewards were praised for "defending the imperial interest," not for serving the people.[38]

The Yongzheng emperor also must be given credit for eliminating some practices, long established, that were harmful to certain categories of the ordinary people—those who in one way or another were forced into legally defined debased statuses. He discovered cases where a segment of society, often centuries earlier, had been punished for supporting a rebellion and whose descendants were still confined to a degraded status, made outcasts in relation to the society about them, denied access to education and upward mobility, discriminated against under the law. Or he learned of cases where groups had been forced into hereditary servant status or given identifications that denied them ordinary subjects' rights. Where such cases came to his attention, he lifted all restrictions, allowing the affected populations to live as ordinary people in their communities. He did not take up the general category of "mean people" (*jian min,* a long-recognized category made up of prostitutes and their children, actors and stage performers, and in some times and places also butchers, barbers, and others), nor did he abolish that status with all its restrictions on freedoms, but those were in any event not strictly enforced. Total numbers of "mean people" were very small, perhaps 3 percent of the population, though the localized debased groups that he did choose to emancipate were still smaller in numbers. Their emancipation did not significantly alter Chinese social patterns, for in general the Chinese common people were not confined by such imposed inequities. Removing holdover irregularities from earlier times probably appealed to this emperor's sense of order; it also allowed him to associate his governing with altruism. It is more significant that he did not emancipate the large numbers of Chinese forced into bond tenant or bond servant status on the banner lands in North China or those reduced to slavery and exile in punishment for political resistance to Manchu rule. He introduced some minor adjustments into their situations that offered hope for future improvement, but essentially he left that problem as he found it.

VI. TAXATION AND THE YONGZHENG REFORMS

Reforms in the systems of taxation were a major focus of the emperor's attention. The Qing agrarian tax system, the principal source of revenues through most of the dynasty, followed the Ming system, but in Kangxi times reforms were begun that the Yongzheng emperor guided to completion. As in the Ming, the Qing levied taxes on agricultural landholdings, the rates of taxation varying according to the region and the productivity of the land. The basic tax rates were remarkably low, compared with tax revenues in other premodernized countries. It has been calculated that the land tax took only 5 to 6 percent of the annual harvest of the principal cereal crops, and much of that was siphoned off by regional government before it reached the central Ministry of Revenues.[39] The Qing tax system (like the Ming before it) thus left much of the surplus over subsistence in agricultural production to be consumed in the provinces, making the regions relatively strong in comparison with the center. It seems probable that a substantial amount of that surplus was taken illicitly from the producers by various other means, but because it was mostly retained in the places where it was taken, it too contributed to the local economy.

In addition to the basic tax on agricultural land, taxes also were imposed on adult males for labor services, originally (in pre-Qing times) collected in a specified number of days per year of actual physical labor. Following long-established practice, the labor service was usually commuted to payment in cash that was used to hire labor rather than force ordinary farmers themselves to perform it. These two forms of taxation—imposts on grain *(fu)* and on service *(yi)*—together provided the government's main tax revenues, and the major task of local government was to supervise and guarantee their collection.[40] The provincial governments regularly compiled books called "Complete Text of the Land *Fu* and Labor *Yi* Imposts" *(Fuyi quanshu),* which they revised for publication every few years and distributed to all offices of local government (as well as placing reference copies in the local Confucian temples where people could consult them) to regularize the work of tax collection.[41]

During the later decades of the Ming, the "Single Whip" method *(Yitiao bianfa)* of revenue reform, initiated by local officials and gradually adopted by the central government, rationalized tax collection by combining the grain tax and the service imposts and commuting a portion or all of the annual payment borne by all taxpaying households into cash. That improvement in the system was not fully carried over into the early Qing. Proposals to modify aspects of the tax system came forth regularly in the later Kangxi years, and the entire problem was then scrutinized by the Yongzheng emperor in his usual thorough manner. He concluded that a constellation of institutional weaknesses fostered corruption.

While tax rates were low, many surcharges, added at the discretion of regional officials, had become accepted practice while remaining technically illegal. There were surcharges to pay for wastage in grain transport, and surcharges to cover costs when raw silver received in tax payments was melted down and cast into bullion ingots for transport to the capital. Other surcharges were added under particular circumstances. These receipts, adding from 30 to 50 percent to the basic tax charge, made up a pool of cash that was used for public and private expenses, with much opportunity for individual administrators at all levels to profit improperly. The surcharges, however, were not entirely a matter of peculation; official salaries were so low that officials could not survive on them, and local and regional government offices had to devise ways of supplementing them and of making up deficiencies in official operating budgets. Starting with Ming times, what in earlier dynasties had been generous support of government employees turned miserly. That became a fundamental weakness in later imperial governing. Both the surcharges and regularized "gratuities" paid from lower level officials to those at the next higher level in government had become accepted ways of meeting actual needs.

Acting on a proposal from the governor of Shanxi in 1723, the emperor legalized surcharges at rates ranging from 10 to 20 percent of the tax, specified how the money was to be used, and declared that any official adding any further surcharge would be severely punished.[42] The payment of "gratuities" was correctly seen as the counterpart to the problem of surcharges. The sums involved were very large, passed upward from clerks in the counties to their magistrates, from magistrates in the counties to the prefectures, thence to the provinces, with a substantial share eventually reaching the pockets of personnel in the ministries and other agencies at the capital. Again, the emperor recognized a real need underlying this ad hoc and readily corrupted way of solving the expense funds shortage. He forbade the practice, but supplied a sum of money from the regularized surcharges with which to pay "bonuses to encourage incorruptibility" (in Chinese called *yang lian yin*); in essence they were merit increases paid to all officials, equaling as much as twenty times the official salary of a county magistrate and more for officials at higher ranks.[43]

That seems a curiously indirect way of meeting an administrative problem; in the emperor's mind it undoubtedly saved him the necessity to overturn long-established precedents, something on which he need not waste time if it could be avoided. His way of reforming the system allowed him to impose an ethical standard—the appeal to scholar-officials to be incorruptible *(lian)*, to retain their integrity—as a way to enhance the normative controls in his government. All Chinese governments, whether under native or conquest dynasties, readily perceived the economy of governing through normative means in preference to costlier coercive ones, at least in the day-to-day operations of government and society. The normative could be reinforced by coercion, usually meaning frightening examples of ruthless punishment when the occasion demanded it.

The most important reform adopted in the taxation system was to abolish the separate registers for land in cultivation and for adult males liable for labor service obligations; these were combined in one tax levied on the productivity of the land, with the labor service component now borne entirely by owners of cultivated land. This obviated the necessity to maintain the two sets of ledgers, one for landholdings *(di)* and one for adult males *(ding)*, both of which in any event bore little relation to reality. That led eventually (1772) to terminating the troublesome task of maintaining separate tax registers; to the tax on cultivated land was added a percentage for labor service. The land tax thereafter became known as the *di-ding* tax, that is, land tax combined with a labor service component. That simplification also took a tax burden off the shoulders of adult men who owned no land—mostly poor hired laborers, but also craftsmen and small merchants, even the very few rich people who were not landowners. It freed the laboring people to take up the full range of options for making their livings without being tied to a local registry of *ding* (adult males who were liable for service levies, ages fifteen to fifty-nine). The benefits of these changes were far-reaching.[44]

The Yongzheng period reforms gradually induced new procedures for reporting more precisely the amount of land in cultivation, although still without going to the expense of making actual cadastral surveys, and for registering all members of households (*hu* and *kou,* that is, households and all the individuals constituting them). The reforms eventually led to the sharply improved though still not accurate census *(hukou)* figures from the mid-Qianlong years, as discussed earlier. To summarize the consequences of the Yongzheng emperor's various administrative reforms, he made the Qing empire work at considerably higher levels of efficiency than had previously been attained. His supervision of revenue collection achieved solvency and began to accumulate operating surpluses. His understanding of corrupt practices led to their reduction, and thereby increased revenues overall. He instilled widespread fear of failure to comply with his standards, and attempted simultaneously (if not successfully) to inculcate the morale of shared purpose in complying. Those improvements appear not to have endured; both the new efficiency and the norms of incorruptibility quickly lagged after his short reign. He benefited the ordinary Chinese by making government less subject to corrupt ways of exploiting the people, and some of his reforms freed a few tiny segments of the population from inequitable limitations on their life choices. He contributed directly to the growth of the prosperity that marked the eighteenth century, with all its implications for all avenues of life.

Did he achieve the heights of authoritarian rule that are equated by some with despotism? And if so, was his despotism, his heightened autocracy by whatever criterion it can be measured, of a benevolent character? Or did it make government more oppressive than before? There is no doubt that he was a more powerful ruler than any of his Qing predecessors. His authority encountered fewer challenges, his will prevailed in more circumstances, his capacity to reward and punish was virtually unlimited. He could order any person, even his imperial relatives, arrested, exiled, or executed. Using the unchallenged power to punish and to reward, he broke the organizational bases of resistance to himself, whether those were internal to the Manchu power structure or were more broadly based in the society of his conquered subjects—Chinese, Mongol, and other. He used his power to enhance and extend his authority. That was his goal in making government work more efficiently; it was not primarily to spread the benefits of benign governing more abundantly to his subjects. When the people benefited, it was because he believed their bettered condition to be an asset to his power. He did not lack a sense of justice, and seems to have believed that the cosmic order responded to the fundamental force of justice in society, as the Chinese tradition taught, yet his concept of justice was readily adapted to the pursuit of his own governing prerogatives.

Was he an *all-powerful* ruler? Not in any practical sense of that term. When he focused on a particular political objective, he usually could more or less achieve it, but he could not limitlessly decree all manner of political objectives and realize them in practice. His officials, the agents of his governing authority, could underperform for their own reasons and could resist in countless small ways. Most pertinent to the extension of his authority through their governing acts, they could not always make their underlings, or society in general, perform to their demands, even when they wished to do so. The Yongzheng emperor became about as powerful a ruler as it was possible to become in Chinese society in premodern times, but that was not truly all-powerful. Given the keenness of his perception, he would have been the first to acknowledge that fact. He often issued commands that failed to be fully and satisfactorily observed. He had to work very hard to keep the daily governing, not to mention all the larger objectives, on a steady track. It was an exhausting occupation. None of his successors came close to meeting his level of performance.

35

SPLENDOR AND
DEGENERATION,
1736-1799

The long reign of the Qianlong emperor filled out the remaining two-thirds of the eighteenth century, from his father's death in 1735 until his own in 1799, and essentially concludes the political narrative of this volume. For the Manchu Qing imperial dynasty and for the Chinese people, this reign can be seen both as the culmination of dynastic greatness and as the forerunner of an era of deep troubles. The young and ambitious emperor had vast plans. He realized many of them, as conqueror and empire builder, aesthete and sponsor of culture, poet and artist, grand ruler over the world's largest society. Yet by the end of his reign, much of that grandeur was perceived as fraud and sham, in large part because a host of scandals revealed self-defeating elements for which he was held responsible. Yet at the same time, changing external conditions also were bearing in on China that no one of the time could have fully comprehended or prepared for. Understanding the middle century of Qing rule is an intriguing challenge to the reader of history. Here the focus is on domestic dimensions of the Qianlong reign. The new international relations are discussed in the following chapter.

I. CHANGING ASSESSMENTS

The Qianlong emperor, whose personal name was Hongli, came securely to the throne on his father's death in 1735; he was the first Qing ruler to have been formally (although secretly) designated the heir in advance of the succession, and therefore faced no competitors. He had just passed his twenty-fourth birthday when his father died on October 8, 1735; in his portrait painted the following year by Giuseppe Castiglione (along with his empress and eleven imperial consorts), he is a handsome man with an open, alert expression.[1] With great fondness he remembered his grandfather, the long-reigning Kangxi emperor, as a man of generous spirit. Toward his distant, awesome father he expressed respect, whatever his real feelings. He intended to surpass both of them to be the grandest ruler in all of Chinese history. Sixty years later he took the unusual step of formally retiring to display exceptional deference to his grandfather; he would not exceed the Kangxi reign's sixty years. But by that unusual act he only drew attention to himself as a paragon; clearly he thought of himself as having surpassed all of his forebears. Inordinately fond of self-congratulation, in 1796 this old emperor could assure himself that he had succeeded by all such measures of greatness.

The British envoys he received on his eighty-second birthday in 1793 described him as a majestic ruler who looked and moved like a man twenty years younger and seemed still in full possession of his physical and mental capacities; in their words he was truly a great monarch, "like Solomon in all his glory." George, Earl Macartney, however, who headed that first British embassy ever to be received by the Chinese court (albeit only in a tent in Inner Mongolia, and after decades of unanswered British demands for diplomatic relations), also recognized some of the Chinese empire's not-so-apparent weaknesses. In an often quoted passage he wrote in his diary:

> The empire of China is an old, crazy, first-rate Man of War, which a succession of able and vigilant officers have contrived to keep afloat for these hundred and fifty years past, and to overawe their neighbors merely by her bulk and appearance. But whenever an insufficient man happens to have the command on deck, adieu to the discipline and safety of the ship. She may, perhaps, not sink outright; she may drift sometime as a wreck, and will then be dashed to pieces on the shores; but she can never be rebuilt on the old bottom.[2]

The Qianlong emperor died in 1799, and the new century quickly brought circumstances that began to dash China to pieces on the shores of domestic and international disasters. Therein lies the dilemma that faces historians trying to assess the Qianlong reign. In the minds of progressive thinkers in the early Republican period (1911–1937), the Qianlong emperor was an embarrassment. His famous letter to King George III sent back with Macartney expressed sentiments such as: "China possesses all things"; therefore China does not need European trinkets (referring to the 600 cases of lavish gifts, including valuable scientific equipment, brought by Macartney). When you foreigners have acquired a degree of civilization sufficient to make you understand proper etiquette toward the monarch of the world, you might in that distant future then come back and take your proper place in the Chinese universe. In the meantime, take note of our generous and civil treatment of you troublesome barbarians, and go quietly.[3]

That famous reply to the king of England, for all its imperious rebuff to the ambitious and costly embassy from Great Britain in 1793, does not convey the full meaning of the event. The emperor was surely aware in some measure of its deeper significance for future Chinese-Western relations, its ritualized rebuff to Great Britain notwithstanding.[4] Yet a century or more later the letter was taken by modern-minded Chinese (and by most Westerners) as proof that at the end of the eighteenth century, when the West was firmly embarked on its course of enlightenment and modernization, the emperor of China was still ignorant, pompous, and blind to realities.[5] Historical writing of the early twentieth century focused on the decline of Chinese civilization under Qing rule, and the Qianlong emperor was taken to symbolize China's backwardness, evident in its rulers' wasteful ostentation and grandiose display, and above all in their inward-looking mentality.

Since the middle of the twentieth century, however, a marked turn toward nationalism has led Chinese historians of all political persuasions to identify with the grandeur of eighteenth-century China. The Qianlong emperor is depicted as one of the all-time great figures of history, a man whose policies were basically appropriate. He is lavishly praised for having protected and expanded the frontiers of the Qing regime's—that is, China's—Inner Asian empire. His domestic governing is seen as having encouraged the impressive economic growth of the age. Yet the same historians who praise him for those accomplishments still find him responsible for nineteenth-century China's calamitous weakness vis-à-vis the West, and for failing to stem the intensification of social problems at home. In general, however, he is at present given more sympathetic treatment than in the past.[6]

Something can be said for each of the contrasting assessments of the Qianlong emperor. He is a figure of contradictions, of sagelike demeanor combined with stubborn ignorance, apparent kindness and grace countered by cruelty and vengeance, generosity alongside avarice, occasional frankness masking the most elaborate self-serving poses. Some historians accept the sum of his positive qualities as the essential man, while others would measure him by sterner criteria.[7] Such viewpoints are far from being irrelevant, yet other questions about the man may prove more fruitful for penetrating the circumstances of his life and understanding the issues of his day.

II. HONGLI

The Manchu imperial prince who came to the throne on the Yongzheng emperor's death in the autumn of 1735 reigned until January 1796 under the era name Qianlong; upon his death in February 1799 (in the fourth year of his son's Jiaqing reign), he was given the posthumous temple name Gaozong, the "Lofty Ancestor." Before he came to the throne at age twenty-four, he had shown himself to be an intelligent and thoroughly schooled man. When he was only ten or eleven, the "Sagelike Ancestor" (Shengzu), his grandfather the Kangxi emperor, had invited him to live in the palace where they could come to know each other better. The old emperor at that time had over 100 grandchildren, most of whom he probably did not know, but his attention was drawn to this boy's alert mind and to his courage and physical skills, in the Manchu warrior mold. To be brought into the old emperor's favor in that fashion was a rare honor, granted to no more than two or three of his grandsons. Hongli, the prince, was eleven when his grandfather died at the end of that year, in December 1722.

The old emperor's last years were troubled by strife and stress, of which the young prince must have been aware. Strife and stress came much closer to his life throughout the thirteen years of his father's reign; several of his uncles, two cousins more or less his own age, even his only older brother, Prince Hongshi, fell victim to his suspicious father. In 1727, when Hongshi was twenty-four and Hongli only sixteen, Hongshi was arrested, his name was stricken from the imperial genealogy "for wanton behavior," and he soon died under the conditions of imprisonment. All the records were purged of his name; there is no way today of knowing why the father destroyed his eldest living son.[8]

The Yongzheng emperor appears, however, to have been proud of Hongli.[9] He treated this son well, while prescribing for him a rigorous course of classical studies and closely supervising his performance, which was in any case brilliant. The young Qianlong became the best trained of all the Manchu emperors in the full range of Chinese humanistic studies, including poetry, calligraphy, and painting (in all of which he displayed great enthusiasm and indifferent talent). He also fully mastered Manchu and is said to have been able to converse in Mongolian, Uighur, and Tibetan as well.

He studied in the palace under senior scholars, most of whom bore such heavy concurrent duties in government that their instruction was nominal at best, yet two or three of his less eminent teachers were fine scholars who could spend their full time guiding his learning. His father arranged that the next younger brother, Prince Hongzhou (also born in 1711, but three months younger than Hongli), and several cousins and other relatives, should study in the palace school with him. Compared with Hongli, Hongzhou was dull-witted, but the two boys became fast friends until the day Hongli ascended the throne. At that point Hongzhou and the only other surviving brother,[10] a much younger boy, were perforce estranged from him. They were mere princes; he was the emperor, who must always be addressed as another order of being. Hongzhou later became an ill-tempered profligate, the cause of much worry to his imperial brother. Of the five or six sons of imperial relatives who also studied with the two princes in the palace school, none thereafter became an important figure in government. Some were talented and congenial, yet when he became emperor, Hongli chose to exclude imperial clan members from important posts, probably in order to avoid a recurrence of the factionalism that he had witnessed in the last years of his grandfather's reign. The isolation of the emperor from family and companions was thus in part institutional, in part a matter of his own choosing.

The one person who was close in his affections was his birth mother, later elevated to the title of Empress Dowager Xiaosheng (1693–1777). It became the pattern for him to visit her every three days, attend her at a meal every five days, honor her at feasts and celebrations, give her lavish gifts, and take her along on most of his many travels. She remained physically vigorous until the end of her long life, and his devotion to her was truly extraordinary. Yet she is said to have been wholly screened from all matters of governing and was never allowed to intervene in public affairs.

Among his consorts was one with whom he formed deep attachment; she was his first empress, Xiaoxian, whom he married when he was sixteen. She died in her mid-thirties, in 1748. After that, he formed no similarly close attachment with his other consorts and palace women, although they bore him seventeen sons and ten daughters, of whom about half survived to maturity. He lived a regulated, rather disciplined life. All the historical romances to the contrary, his indulgences were poetizing, collecting art, and building gardens and palaces, not wine, women, and song.

The officially compiled collections of his own poetry run to more than 40,000 poems, all bad and many ludicrously so. No other poet in all of Chinese history produced so many poems, and we must assume that he accepted a great deal of help in churning them out, but some critics have said that their low quality is itself the best proof that they are really his. He collected art and antiquities with a passion.[11] Some praise his discernment, while others note that he accepted many forgeries as genuine works.[12] His avarice for art was notorious; art collectors feared that he would demand their best items as gifts. Some collectors hid their most prized possessions, and had clever copies made of the most noted ones in case the emperor should learn of their existence and want them. His fluid, flaccid calligraphy is very distinctive, and much of it appears to have come from his own hand, but it is not granted high ratings by expert connoisseurs. Art collectors in particular resent that he insisted in putting long colophons, that is, commemorative compositions written in his hand, on the surfaces of the finest paintings in the imperial collection. If taste and a respect for art should have prevented that, his overweening ego won out over both. Indignant critics in recent times have called his actions vandalism. Nevertheless, the imperial collections that he amassed and lovingly catalogued have never been exceeded in scope or quality.[13]

Like his grandfather, he traveled much through his realm, matching the Kangxi emperor's famous Six Tours of the South, and making well over 100 other tours. Temporary gardens and palaces were built at many places to accommodate him; roadways paved with specially fired bricks were built up many mountains and hills so that his palanquin and those of his mother, his wives, and others of his entourage could be borne to the summits. The ostentation and luxury demanded in these travels could bankrupt wealthy families designated to prepare for his visits, and impoverished the common people who lived along the route of his travels. Illustrated celebratory publications often were produced to commemorate his travels or to describe his palaces and gardens. People of the time compared the Kangxi emperor's relative restraint in such self-indulgence with the Qianlong emperor's unbridled expenditures.

He attached great importance to the Manchu virtues, and urged Manchus to learn their history and language, yet it was during the latter decades of his reign that the use of Manchu at the court and in the imperial household dwindled and nearly vanished. He was no more successful than his Jurchen forebears during the last years of the Jin dynasty in arousing a nativist revival and preserving his people's cultural distinctiveness. The Manchu elite retained their privileges and their airs, but by and large they became culturally Chinese, as did most ordinary Manchus.

He was one of the greatest builders of all Chinese imperial history. Beijing, before the great changes effected since 1950, was a city heavily marked by his hand. He restored, enlarged, and rebuilt palaces, walls, and gate towers, roadways, hydraulic works, and countless temples. He did not alter the axial layout of the imperial palace city or displace its principal buildings, but he added new structures at the sides of the Forbidden City complex, and largely redesigned the summer palaces both in the western suburbs and in Rehe, outside the Great Wall. He demanded the best-quality work using the finest materials, with no limits on expenditures, and in general his enthusiasm for those massive projects was matched by his (or others') good taste. He found the residential palaces of the Forbidden City dull, austere, and too regular in their outlines; he softened them by adding gardens, trees, water, and flowers. He built pavilions and gazebos, and designed vistas enhanced by artificial mountains and waterways. The great summer palaces in the western suburbs allowed him a still freer hand in redesigning both layouts and buildings. He even had his court Jesuit artists and engineers build there a white marble baroque palace in the European style, with belvederes on terraced slopes overlooking intricately engineered fountains, on the model of Versailles. He also ordered the governors in the provinces to restore and rebuild city walls and government office compounds and to improve roads and canals. The physical components of the Qing state, at its capitals and throughout the provinces, were greatly improved by his fever for building. Most of that was done in the first thirty years of his reign; the pace slowed thereafter but did not entirely cease.

Early in his reign, censors began submitting memorials criticizing his building projects as wasteful and burdensome. He of course could only praise their Confucian sense of frugality, but he ignored their criticisms. He wrote an essay acknowledging a degree of fault, for the sake of argument, but concluding that he had no reason to regret the fault. He also made other pronouncements defending his projects. In all such responses to criticism he turned the argument around, proudly boasting that his treasury had larger reserves in the 1780s when he wrote the essay than in the 1730s when he ascended the throne; also that he procured material by purchase on the market while paying workmen at better than standard wages. Thus, he concluded, his building projects were not a burden on the people; on the contrary, they redistributed wealth that otherwise lay unused and directly benefited the ordinary people they employed. Narrowly argued, that may in fact be true.[14] In a larger perspective, however, his lavish lifestyle encouraged waste and ostentation throughout the upper stratum of society. When heavy fiscal demands for military operations after the middle years of his reign forced the state to increase its revenues by irregular means, and when his favorites practiced corruption on an unheard-of scale, both the morale and the effectiveness of government deteriorated.

III. POLITICAL MEASURES

The Qing dynasty was ninety years old when the Qianlong emperor's reign began; its institutions, largely taken over intact from the preceding Ming dynasty, had gone through minor adjustments and worked well to meet Manchu needs and interests. Few major institutional changes were undertaken, but the supervision and management of the entire governing structure had been greatly improved during his father's reign. Dual staffing in the most important posts at the central government and in the provinces was designed to give Manchu officials superior authority over their Chinese counterparts. Confident that the system of Qing governing was solidly in place and control could be maintained, the Qianlong emperor assumed a more partisan pro-Manchu stance than had his predecessors. In high positions, Manchus possessed governing authority while their Chinese counterparts, one or more steps lower in rank, bore responsibility for carrying on the work of their offices. During the Qianlong reign, Manchu numbers in the higher offices grew as the numbers of Chinese shrank. Exceptions to this pattern became ever more rare through the years of this reign. The regime became more Manchu as the Manchus themselves became less so.

Strengthening Local Control through the Baojia System

Among the various small institutional changes, the emperor in the early 1740s expanded the role of the *baojia* system, the base-level social control mechanism through which law and order were maintained in the rural countryside.[15] The name *baojia* as a system of local security can be traced back to the reforms of Wang Anshi in the 1060s and 1070s of Northern Song times, when it was partially implemented. During the Ming dynasty it was proposed from time to time as an ideal system for extending the government's authority through sub-official structures at sub-county levels, but other than a few local experiments, no *baojia* system was ever put in place under the Ming.

As soon as the Manchu government under Prince Regent Dorgon was set up in Beijing in 1644, orders were issued to establish the *baojia* in all places. Those orders were reissued and made more specific throughout the Kangxi years; the *baojia* police system of mutual responsibility for local law and order, based in groups of ten households (called *pai*), ten of which formed a *jia,* ten *jia* (or 1,000 households) making up a *bao,* was in place when the Qianlong reign began. It was paralleled by the sub-official structure for managing tax collection, called the *lijia* system, also based on groupings of ten (the *li*) and 100 (the *jia*) households. The two were separately organized but worked side by side to carry on their specified tasks. Organizationally these extensions of local governing down to the level of direct contact with the people in the villages varied with local cultural patterns; uniformity throughout the vast expanse of China in matters so close to daily lives was not possible. Eventually the two structures merged in some places, and the distinction between the *lijia* tax collection system (sometimes called the "tithings") and the *baojia* (the mutual surveillance system) became confused, their names interchanged, and their functions sometimes fused into one system. There was of course a kind of rationality in that development. In the eighteenth century, however, the two still functioned separately, and fairly effectively.

The emperor decided in 1740 to alter the taxation system and the census on which it was based. Local officials were at this time ordered not just to register adult males on whom labor service was levied, but to combine the labor service with the land tax and to register all individuals in each household. The emperor was told by local and provincial officials that it could not be done. A strong-willed young emperor who did not like to be told something could not be done, he listened to their complaint that managing a full count of all individuals would be impossibly clumsy. After some thought (did someone propose it to him?), he proclaimed that it could indeed be easily accomplished—through the *baojia.* The head of each *pai,* the base-level unit of ten households, would assume responsibility for making a count of all individuals in each of his ten households and write their names, sex, and ages on a placard to be posted at the entrance of each house. Every year the *pai* leader could then make the rounds and record all changes. Those revised figures were to be forwarded to the head of the *jia,* thence to the head of the *bao,* and the *bao* head would report those totals to the county magistrate. That obviated the need for all the people to go to county offices to be recorded, an objection raised by some officials. It allowed for annual corrections. Above all, it showed that the emperor could outsmart his recalcitrant officials.

The new system, as we have seen, did not produce a perfect census, but it was a more reliable instrument for producing improved head counts of the Chinese population. It also extended the functions of the police system, giving the *baojia* a better surveillance mechanism. Each group of ten neighboring families was to be held mutually responsible for misdemeanors and crimes committed by all its members and for reporting the presence of strangers and all persons who committed improper deeds. It helped that their responsibilities were sharply etched on their minds by the mechanisms of the recording and registering procedures. This system suited the dynasty's local control needs, and for some decades it worked well.

Manchu-Chinese Frictions

The young Qianlong ruler in the first years of his reign was clearly conscious of the faults of his immediate predecessors. The revered Kangxi emperor had striven to incorporate the Chinese elite into his regime, but he was by nature lax and overly generous when his underlings performed poorly. The fearsome Yongzheng emperor went to the other extreme, rigorously enforcing strict standards and imposing cruel punishments. Hongli pondered those examples and, in edicts intended to guide his officials, proposed ways of reaching a golden mean. In his words, severity should be tempered by leniency, leniency kept in bounds by severity, the two applied in alternation to achieve a balance *(kuan yan xiangji).* But he noted that as soon as he spoke of leniency, his officials would draw their own conclusions and assume that he was giving them license to relax their standards. Should they do so, he warned, he would reimpose severe standards, and they would pay a heavy price for their transgressions.[16] Despite such threats, his officials did in fact judge him correctly: they concluded that he would be a compromising ruler who would not maintain strict, consistent standards throughout his government, and that prediction proved to be correct.

He was, in short, more like his relaxed grandfather than like his demanding father. He allowed his officials considerable license most of the time, especially those guilty of financial peculation and administrative underperformance. But when he scented anti-Manchu attitudes or threats to his dynasty's security, like his father he would descend in unreasoning fury to destroy sedition and make a frightening example to all. He was also sensitive to the threat of factions that might seek to misuse official authority in petty ways—to gain advancements for partisans by undermining the credibility of competitors, playing the mundane games of courtiers in all times. Unlike his father, however, when the Qianlong emperor acted against potential factionalism his concern was not about efficiency in government but about encroachments on his imperial dignity. In the last analysis, he was driven by his egoistic self-image. He was a facile man, not a truly thoughtful ruler. He no doubt perceived that the facade of awesome imperial grandeur was an indispensable political tool, and at times he used it effectively. As his long reign wore on, however, the imperial pomp came more obviously to serve his voracious need for personal gratification. He became vulnerable to self-deception and flawed judgment, in the classic mold of the very bright but fallible petty despot. His personal qualities in these ways bore directly on the life of state and society.

When he first came to the throne, he inherited two powerful ministers from his father's tightly run regime. One was the Manchu E'ertai (1680–1745), who had served for some years as governor general in the southwest before being called to Beijing in 1732 and named Grand Secretary, Minister of War, and concurrently Grand Councillor. The other was the Chinese Zhang Tingyu (1672–1755), who had been one of the three original Grand Councillors when the Council (junji chu) was created in 1729. Each had been highly trusted by the Yongzheng emperor and named to oversee the transition to the Qianlong reign. Both wielded great power in the early Qianlong years. In the normal course of governing, they could advance scores of men into important positions, who of course would remain indebted and loyal to their sponsors. The beneficiaries of their patrons' power quite understandably formed incipient factions on the basis of shared interest in continuing the patronage. That was an inevitable consequence of a ruler's trust in particular servitors. Such men could gain strong followings, while at the same time, when they lost that power, it was a signal to others that they no longer commanded the ruler's full confidence. In this instance, when the emperor transferred the two senior Grand Councillors to less consequential posts, the message was clear: there was nothing to be gained by their subordinates' continuing to identify with them. Their blocs of political followers dissolved, but among the feelings which lingered, an undercurrent of antagonism between Chinese and Manchus in officialdom took form.

The Qianlong emperor observed the underlying friction, displayed at court and throughout the government, between the Zhang Tingyu bloc (largely Chinese) and the E'ertai bloc (to which many leading Manchus adhered), and saw in it a warning: their influence in the government competed with his own. Bound by his father's injunction to honor and respect the two senior statesmen, he could not simply demolish them. He gradually distanced himself, but observed the growing ethnic tension.

That there should be such tension was curious, since both Zhang Tingyu and E'ertai were culturally dual persons, each completely in command of both languages and traditions. The Chinese Zhang had taken advantage of the opportunity to study Manchu at the Hanlin Academy after being appointed there shortly after gaining his *jinshi* degree. The Manchu E'ertai, whose father had been a director of the National Academy, had close links with the Chinese literary world and himself was a good essayist and poet in Chinese. It would be difficult to see them as symbols of antagonism between the two cultural spheres. Moreover, E'ertai's bloc of followers included some Chinese literati as well as many leading Manchu political figures. But competition between Chinese and Manchu cliques in the government was growing intense under the emperor's shifting cultural policies. He was attempting, unsuccessfully, to stem the tide of Manchu assimilation. Despite the dynasty's long adherence, at least nominally, to the oft-proclaimed policy of Manchu-Chinese equality, conditions in the Qianlong reign were not what they had been under earlier emperors. In the Kangxi reign the problem had been to get the Chinese elite to identify with the government and serve in it. Now the problem was to retain a significant role for Manchus *as* Manchus.

Manchu distinctiveness was disappearing. The emperor could not stop the deterioration of the culture, but he could attempt to compensate by giving Manchus more prestige and power in society. That led to marked increases in the dominance of Manchu officials in the highest posts, a situation that drew criticism from outspoken Chinese officials. It was noted, for example, that wise emperors of the past had always sought to unify, not to allow divisions among those who served in public life to be aroused by the ruler's partiality to one group over another. The Chinese critics also saw other kinds of faults. As tension grew, the emperor's response was to launch cultural policies intended to silence Chinese who might generate disloyalty. Enticement of the Chinese literati had been almost too successful. Although he himself provided the leading model for it, the Qianlong emperor was greatly irritated to observe that Manchus were aping the Chinese elite in their literary and artistic associations, adopting manners and forming attachments that undermined their social distinctiveness.[17] He issued bans on such behavior, but to no effect. The time had come when Chinese influence, with its threat of political disaffection, had to be curtailed by a large measure of intimidation. The scope of the ensuing cultural programs suggests that the Qianlong emperor, by the middle years of his reign, considered the continuing traces

of the project were discussed, then of course made his own decision: in March 1773 he formally launched the project, giving it the name the *Complete Library of the Four Treasuries (Siku quanshu).*[19] I have described the scope of the compilers' labors elsewhere:

> Rare books were assiduously collected. Private collectors were induced or intimidated into lending their choicest items for copying. Some new works were specially compiled. Fragments of lost ancient works were reassembled from passages quoted in later writings, in particular by drawing from the imperial library's sole, but incomplete, set of the early fifteenth-century encyclopedic compendium, the *Yongle dadian.* Salvaging those otherwise lost works from a great manuscript in danger of disappearing was one of the most stirring proposals by the scholars of the time, and one that may have moved the emperor to enlarge his still inchoate urge to achieve a grand effect. All the books collected were then assembled at the Hanlin Academy within the Palace City in Beijing, where they were collated and emended, using the resources of the various imperial libraries. Altogether 360 Hanlin scholars and other scholar-officials specially selected for this highly prestigious assignment produced new critical editings of all the works, and 3,862 expert scholar-calligraphers transcribed manuscript copies in uniform format. The project soon outgrew the facilities of the Hanlin Academy, and a special bureau was established to house and manage the work. Moreover, a large library building, called the Wenyuan Ge, was built within the palace precincts to hold the final product.[20] Thousands of works were reviewed by the scholars. One of their important assignments was to prepare critical abstracts giving information on the author, the work, and the transmission of each text. Such abstracts ultimately numbered 10,230. From among those works, 3,470 were selected to be copied completely into the *Complete Library (Siku quanshu).* The others were recorded by title only in the *General Table of Contents with Critical Abstracts,* or *Zongmu tiyao,* itself a hefty publication in 200 chapters. It became the cornerstone of Chinese scholarly bibliography.

The first manuscript copy of the *Complete Library* was presented to the throne in 1782. The 3,470 complete works in it have a combined total of 79,932 chapters, more than 360 million words, filling 36,000 large folio volumes.[21] The resulting work was far too large to be engraved on blocks and printed. Eventually seven manuscript copies were made, four to be kept at imperial palaces in and near Beijing, and three in important locations in the Yangzi South—Yangzhou, Zhenjiang, and Hangzhou—where authorized private scholars and officials were allowed access to them. During the civil turmoil of the mid-nineteenth century, most of those sets were destroyed. The emperor's premier copy survived, however, and was at last printed in 1984 in a facsimile copy made by electronically scanning the original, 200 years after it was first produced.[22]

The *Complete Library* is both praised and damned: it has preserved works that otherwise would have been lost, but those works have in many cases undergone editing that does not meet traditional Chinese scholarly criteria.[23] Editing was expertly done by competent scholars in some cases, but in many others it was done capriciously, superficially, erroneously, in irresponsible fashion: no indication is given in the copied texts that alterations and deletions have been made. Those changes range from rewording sentences to rewriting whole sections, even unmarked deletions ranging from single words to entire chapters and sections of texts. According to well-developed Chinese standards of scholarly editing, texts should have remained unaltered, with all changes set forth in notes appended to the relevant passages. That responsible way of editing would of course have been self-defeating when the purpose was to obliterate words and passages found politically offensive. Present-day scholars therefore can make use of the *Complete Library* versions of works only when no edition can be found for comparison that escaped the Qianlong emperor's tampering.

As for the claim made by the word "complete" in the work's title, that too is fraudulent. The works included are often far from "complete," and the coverage of the existing literature in eighteenth-century China also is incomplete. More works were suppressed than are included, whether one counts the 3,470 "complete" texts copied into it or the more than 7,000 preserved "by title only." One analysis places the number of destroyed works at 10,000, and still others were not in categories that fell under the purview of the compilers.[24] When a work was designated "to be destroyed," that usually included not only burning all copies of the book that could be found, but also locating the carved blocks from which the pages were printed, stored for reuse over centuries, and burning those as well.

A project that began in the spirit of serving China's literary heritage became the largest destruction ever wreaked upon that heritage. The ruler's role in fostering both aspects of it leaves him responsible for both; the negative consequences must be seen as outweighing the positive. Yet it must be granted that the destructive aspects of the project developed in a way not foreseen at the beginning. The political censorship became virulently destructive only after the project was well under way. The examination of works for inclusion in the *Complete Library* then merged with a broad literary inquisition that grew in tandem with it.

The Qianlong Reign's "Literary Inquisition"

Between 1773 and 1775 most of the books to be included in the *Complete Library* were collected and assembled in Beijing, where collating and editing continued until the first set was completed in 1782. In that work of closely examining the texts, far more examples of offensive wording, even seditious sentiment, were brought to light than had been anticipated. These were found not only in writings dating from the late Ming era of conflict between Manchus and Chinese, where they were expected, but also throughout the entire span of time covered by the assembled works, even in commentaries on the ancient classics. Especially numerous were unflattering references to the tribal peoples of the conquest dynasties, the Khitans, the Tanguts, the Jurchens, and the Mongols. They had been China's powerful enemies, and not surprisingly bore the brunt of Chinese disdain and hatred. The Qianlong emperor at first brushed those examples aside as something to be expected; he ordered that unflattering words (e.g., "malodorous savages") be replaced by harmless ones (e.g., "northern peoples"), but no more. Soon, however, he took a stronger stance; such writings, he concluded, could be used by people of his time to insinuate disdain for the Manchus. As he examined a number of such works, including some from his own time, even some written by literary-minded Manchus, he began to see ever deeper meaning, ever broader plots to defame him and the dynasty.

The emperor urged regional and local officials to make more careful searches for such writings, not with the intent to include them in the *Complete Library* but to bring them under surveillance by what was emerging as a totally distinct operation. One scholar has tabulated eighty-four major cases of censorship involving criminal indictments, from the beginning of the Qing through the Qianlong reign, of which seventy were prosecuted under the Qianlong emperor, mostly in the 1770s and 1780s. In all but five of the eighty-four cases, one or more authors' works were found to contain treasonable content; the works were ordered destroyed and the authors, their families, and associates were subjected to punishments ranging from beatings and banishment to death and enslavement.[25] The proceedings were conducted to achieve maximum effect throughout the upper stratum of society. The emperor himself produced outraged analyses of some examples, saying things such as, "What kind of debased person could have written such vile insults; were he alive today he certainly would not be allowed to live." And in many cases the long-entombed bodies of unfortunate authors were exhumed and cut to pieces, while their living descendants, and living writers who drew his wrath, were executed along with all adult males in their clans, their women made slaves.[26] The fury of his effort to cleanse the entire corpus of writings and terrorize living writers is difficult to grasp, especially when specific examples of words and phrases that infuriated him can in many cases be seen today as innocuous. If the impulse to terrify and punish was in part driven by overzealous officials trying to gain favor, or by covetous neighbors or rivals of the victims hoping to profit by destroying them, as is likely in any such fevered movement, it nonetheless could have been stopped at any time by the emperor. It never was. The issues of greatest significance to him in sustaining the literary inquisition over two decades of its most intense implementation appear to have been the following.

1. *Pro-Ming sentiment.* The Qianlong emperor was very sensitive to comparisons between the Ming and the Qing. It was important to characterize the Ming as degenerate and doomed to collapse before the Manchus invaded, to show that the Mandate had in fact been legitimately transferred to the Qing and had not been seized by force. Although he could select certain Ming personages to praise, even certain Ming emperors who merited approval or sympathy, he was suspicious of statements made by others, past or present,

that praised any facet of the Ming experience, thereby suggesting a comparison that might disparage the Qing.

2. *Ming restorationist thought.* Covert efforts to restore the Ming, or even to suggest that the time would come when the people would demand the just restoration of Ming rule, appeared to have fairly wide underground appeal, whether or not linked (as they were later, in the nineteenth century) to organized movements. Some Ming restorationist thought, truly conspiratorial, fed on repression and grew, but most of it was vague and harmless. Yet in all cases, when discovered or when merely imputed, it was brutally suppressed.

3. *Hostility to steppe peoples.* The long interaction between China and the steppe had standardized the many terms referring to "aliens," "barbarians," or "northern tribal peoples." The terms of course could be combined with unflattering adjectives that denigrated those inimical neighbors, but they were not always used with overtones of hostility; more often they were merely descriptive. There are many examples of the steppe peoples also using those standard terms, whether for themselves or to refer to other steppe peoples. At the height of the literary inquisition, 1770–1790, the emperor was ready to read hostile, seditious intent into any use of words such as *hu* or *di,* and other ethnic names for the eastern and northeastern tribal peoples. Even when the word *hu* was used in another standard sense, as a literary interrogative, he was prepared to see slyly malicious intent. He and others directed by him searched quite innocent poetry, essays, historical writings, and memorials for examples of usages deemed insulting.

4. *Salacious and licentious entertainment writings.* Disloyalty to the dynasty was seen as an issue of basic social morality; it demanded that China be cleansed and morally purified. The emperor's role was explained on analogy of rulers to fathers, of society to the family. The modern nation-state's claim on the loyalty of all its individual subjects was at that time a not yet well-defined issue. In Qing China the political crime of sedition was regarded as above all an affront to the moral social order, and to the imperial institution which capped that order; that linked sedition to all other issues of morality in society.[27] Not surprisingly, the censors of texts also recognized a connection between that moral fault and the existence of what they termed salacious fiction and drama. It may well be that the emperor was concerned about the impact of such material on his Manchu countrymen; their lives clearly had degenerated in the setting of a peaceful and prosperous China. It is also likely that publicizing the drive to eliminate sexually explicit or morally marginal materials reinforced the high moral tone claimed for the simultaneous effort to eliminate sedition. Banning licentious works began in the Kangxi reign, reversing the greater openness about sex that had developed in the late Ming. A stringent official puritanism reached its peak during the Qianlong and succeeding reigns.[28]

5. *Military writings.* A number of other possible motivations can be discerned in some cases, among which the most important may be the Qing sensitivity to the Chinese studying their own military writings. The Manchus were dependent on Chinese soldiery (also on the Mongols and other border

zone peoples) to maintain their military dominance, but restricted Chinese participation in leadership, tactical initiative, and military intelligence. The Chinese tradition in military writings, particularly strong in Ming times, was a source of concern to them; at least a dozen Ming works on military tactics and strategy were designated to be destroyed.[29]

The literary inquisition did not cease after the Qianlong reign, but its pace was greatly slowed. By the mid-nineteenth century, publication of politically offensive, previously banned late Ming works in particular was resumed with little interference.

Two further consequences of the Qianlong literary inquisition, apart from the government's destruction of books and manuscripts, can be noted. First, the entire movement's intellectual dishonesty contributed to the growing cynicism within the elite, Manchu as well as Chinese, and led to feelings of protest against hypocrisy and injustice that could transcend ethnic boundaries. Even among Chinese banner households, the specially favored Chinese who were most clearly identified with Qing dynastic interests, the widely apparent abuses of favored status produced among some of those privileged individuals a shared sense of "Chineseness" based on cultural awareness.[30] Second, especially among the sub-elite strata of society, fear led many to destroy all manner of books in their possession rather than face the uncertainties of discovery and punishment, adding further to the cultural loss. At the same time, the sense of peril may have led ordinary people to take defensive refuge for mutual protection in clandestine associations such as anti-Qing secret societies. Especially in those sub-elite settings the suppressed doctrines could gain credibility and potency that they might otherwise have lacked. Thus, from elite cynicism to popular resentment, dissident attitudes grew at all levels of society.

v. A Late Flowering of Thought and Learning

Concurrent with the Qianlong reign's drive to suppress deviant and seditious thought, a large number of Chinese thinkers were themselves in the midst of a movement that transformed Neo-Confucian "thought and learning" *(xueshu sixiang)*, as the intellectual enterprise is called. It is a paradox that an intimidating censorship was fiercely enforced through the decades when great advances in scholarship were coupled with original philosophical inquiry. Yet one must not assume that despotic regimes in premodernized societies had the means to block out all thought and expression. They could intimidate the scholarly community and deny all manner of people certain avenues of expression. They could subject individuals to the most severe punishment, especially when sedition was charged. Yet disagreement over technicalities of scholarship, even intellectual dispute over basic issues in thought, could not be wholly controlled. The philosophers found their venues for safely expressing ideas that might not in fact be harmless; historians still sought the truth in the records of human affairs even though their findings might be politically risky;[31] classical scholars might discover new meaning in ancient texts that, logically pursued, could undermine the regime's authority. All manner of such intellectual activity went on throughout the eighteenth century, much of it not formally published at the time, its full import in many cases not perceived until a century or more later. And among more ordinary people, the songs and the tales, the humor and the bitter complaint all continued to manifest the society's deep feelings, often reinforcing the feelings of the elite, with whom their lives were intertwined.

The movement that changed the character of Neo-Confucian thought and learning was above all, however, the scholars' undertaking. It was embedded in evidential research (*kaozheng xue,* sometimes translated narrowly as "philology"; also called "empirical research," "inductive method," and so on). As this trend in scholarship gained momentum, it went beyond its original concern with correcting the understanding of classical texts. It became a broad current in intellectual life, and while its proponents were mostly not philosophers, a minority were, and they included the most significant thinkers of the time. Some historians have designated their contributions to the deepening of Confucian thought the "third phase" in the development of Confucianism. According to this view, the first phase was the establishment of the Confucian school in the late preimperial centuries, when Confucius himself and later adherents such as Mencius and Xun Zi were active, in the sixth through third centuries B.C.E. The second phase witnessed the emergence of a revitalized Confucianism in late Tang and Song times, in what we in the West call Neo-Confucianism. That large undertaking reestablished the dominance of Confucian thought and values. Neo-Confucianism, however, left people the choice between the rationalist school (Lixue), defined by Song thinkers Cheng Yi and Zhu Xi (Cheng-Zhu), and that of the Lu-Wang intuitionalist (idealist) thinkers Lu Jiuyuan of Southern Song and Wang Shouren (Wang Yangming) of Ming times. The Cheng-Zhu dominant orthodoxy came to be strongly challenged by the Lu-Wang idealism in the sixteenth century, when Wang Yangming and his followers produced a many-sided intellectual and social confrontation that greatly stirred the world of thought.

At the end of Ming and into the first decades of Qing, thinkers such as Gu Yanwu and Huang Zongxi launched a critical reaction. Although they recognized that the textual foundations of all the Neo-Confucian thinkers were unsound, at that time they did not yet look beyond the boundaries of the rationalist-idealist debate; in the painful seventeenth-century transition from Ming to Qing, their immediate demands for new thinking centered on defensible principles that responded to the crises of state and society. Their methods included rigorous examination of texts in search of accurate meaning, and they reexamined history, seeking better precedents for governing. In their textual analysis they pioneered new methods in historical phonology and in philology. They were capable of being radically revisionist in many fields of scholarship and of historical understanding, but they were not engaged in redefining the bases of Neo-Confucian thought. The later full-blown movement of evidential research traced its origins to them.

Historians have come to see that during the eighteenth century, the evidential research scholars' seemingly detached and arid obsession with words—

with making critical studies of meaning and pronunciation to determine how the ancient textual sources of philosophical authority should be understood— simultaneously could engage cutting issues in philosophy as well. Striving to make the meaning of early texts more precise, the textual scholars also made the sources of authority in philosophy (and, by extension, in politics) more accessible. The motivation of the leading scholars in this effort was dual: they of course strove to perfect the ancient texts per se; and by doing that, they also sought greater clarity and certainty in the philosophical ideas that were built on those texts. The first of these two distinct impulses produced critical scholarship; the second led to new fields of philosophic thought. In the best minds of the time, the two were inseparable.

That is an important finding, because the literary inquisition often has been credited with having turned the best minds of Qing China away from socially relevant ideas into meaningless pursuits in arid scholarship. Thus, some have written, the Qing repression succeeded in turning·China's scholar-elite into drones; it wasted human abilities and detached intellectual activity from all sense of social responsibility. That is a partially true but one-sided view of the meticulous, even pedantic classical scholarship and related researches in literature and historiography. It may be more or less fair to say that routine scholarship, like much historical inquiry, even most literary expression in the Qianlong era, all display conventional-minded conformity. The atmosphere it induced can easily be parodied and satirized, as it is in the great novel *The Scholars (Rulin waishi)*, written about 1750.[32] In that mercilessly sardonic exposure of hollow moralizing and ritualized hypocrisy, the faults of "proper" society are laid bare.

For all the essential rightness of that overdrawn caricature, there are other sides to the intellectual life of mid-Qing times. The eighteenth century, and consequent endeavors continuing through the nineteenth and into the early twentieth centuries, accomplished a vast reworking of classical texts, their commentaries, and related scholarship. That spilled over into critical examination of historical writings and, further, into the editing and annotating of many other kinds of writings, especially the belles lettres of all earlier periods. Bibliography and specialized lexicography also flourished. So much of Chinese high culture's written heritage was painstakingly examined and systematically edited for publication that today one studying any phase of premodern China usually takes the corpus of Qing period scholarship as the logical starting place. While much of that outpouring appears to deserve the criticism that it was irrelevant to what we today would call the real problems of the world in which those Qing scholars lived, it is by no means unimportant. Even at its most routine, it was produced by serious scholars in full command of their heritage. It is difficult today to find their equals in that kind of competence.

Still more important, however, amidst the broad currents of Qing scholarly activity there also were, as in all ages, the rare, highly exceptional minds. Some of these were drawn or driven into paths that ran counter to the dominant trends of the age. We look to them for the critical-minded and creatively original works, whether in thought, in textual scholarship, or in artistic expression. A few important figures and works of that caliber can be mentioned here.

Evidential research *(kaozheng xue)* became so powerful a movement in intellectual life that it established the agenda for all scholarly activity. A consequence was the reordering of the debate between the Song dynasty "rationalism" of the dominant Cheng-Zhu (Lixue) tradition and the "idealism" (Xinxue) of the Song and Ming Lu-Wang tradition. As noted earlier, evidential research repudiated scholarly trends of the entire Neo-Confucian era, looking beyond the Song dynasty, farther back into antiquity to the Han dynasty for its models. Critical thinking was no longer restricted to the old arena of debate.

At the same time, a defense of the Song and post-Song orthodoxy was voiced. The more conservative scholars continued to defend the Zhu Xi mainstream in classical learning. Within that stream there were of course honest scholars and upright social leaders, but inevitably it also drew to it all the moralizing on social issues that had become central to that tradition. That tradition was coming to be seen as a stultifying substitute for critical social thought. The Qing state of course continued to patronize that conservative stance in education and in thought, with all its reliably predictable reflexes. Thus the ground was set for a new debate on philosophy's fundamental orientation.

The old debate between rationalism and idealism (Lixue versus Xinxue) that for 700 or 800 years had established the parameters of Confucian thinking, was replaced by one between traditional-minded "Song" scholars and their new opponents who formed ranks around the banner of "Han learning" (Hanxue). As the principal ground of argument was redefined using these labels, the methods employed by the Han learning (the new name that was used interchangeably with "evidential research") were traced to the great classical exegetes of Han times (206 B.C.E.–220 C.E.). Many Qing dynasty scholars were drawn to this stance, because in their minds "Han learning" stood first of all for the systematic examination of texts, and for rigorous demonstration of meaning utilizing inductive reasoning. In this new debate over principles of learned inquiry, the issues of "reason" *(li)* versus "mind" *(xin)*, both as values and as epistemological orientations in thought, were thus replaced by "Song" versus "Han." That change encouraged new emphases in the world of thought. It also may appear to have transferred attention from substance to mere matters of method.

That was not the case, however. Whether we call it evidential research or Han learning, the combative new stance engaged the essential philosophical issues in a new way. To cite a central issue of substance, Han learning came to take on overtones of anti-Buddhist awareness in the reassessment of China's long cultural history. The evidential scholars began to see something that their seventeenth-century predecessors in critical textual study had not pursued: not only were the textual foundations of Song philosophy shaky, but also *both* the Song "rationalism" and the Song-Ming "idealism," as products of the post-Buddhist era, had developed Buddhist-influenced metaphysics premised (if unknowingly) on a thought system introduced into China from India. Given those premises, Song "rationalism" was seen to be no less "idealistic" than was its idealist counterpart; its claims to be objectively "reason-based" were self-deceiving. "Han learning," therefore, starting as a methodological innovation (albeit labeled a "revival") in dealing with texts, also became an effort to recover the meaning of the classics as understood in the Han period, before the Chinese mentality was clouded by post-Han alien influence.

The critics' perceptions of Buddhist influences on Chinese culture did not, in Qing times, engender hostility toward Buddhism as a religion, the way it had in Tang and Song times, when Neo-Confucianism was taking form in an atmosphere of stark competition to survive. It did, however, lead the Han learning scholars to reject Song Confucianism's metaphysics as flawed,[33] and to correct its flaws insofar as they bore on intellectual matters. It sought to establish new philosophical ground by the time-honored means of repudiating the nearer past in favor of the greater worth of an earlier past. That stance, sometimes labeled "revolutionary archaism," is a recurrent feature of Chinese cultural history, frequently noted throughout the present work.[34]

The depth of some of the eighteenth-century critical thinkers' renewal of basic concepts has been taken to justify calling Qing Confucian philosophy the "third phase" in the history of Confucian thought's development.[35] That is an important idea, although a limited one. The third phase thinkers were few in number at the time, and their ideas did not realize their transforming potential or establish a new era in thought, as had the first two phases of Confucian thought history. They were nonetheless significant for the intrinsic originality and breadth of their new conceptions, and because they illustrated the fact that Confucianism as a thought system still possessed the vitality to engender significant new thinking. The third phase contributed more to intellectual life among a still small group of new thinkers in the twentieth-century.

In the eighteenth century, its most important original thinker was Dai Zhen (1724–1777). He was the precocious son of a poor Anhui family;[36] his father was a struggling cloth merchant who was forced to live in various places in Central and Eastern China, where he was nevertheless able to give the young Dai Zhen a sound basic education. That was aided by the early recognition of the boy's talent, something that often succeeded in interesting better-off neighbors and associates to help in the education of a poor but brilliant boy. Several learned figures were willing to give him instruction, and rich book owners gave him access to their private libraries. He was drawn especially to mathematics and to historical linguistics.

Dai Zhen eventually passed the civil service examinations at the second or *juren* level, becoming thereby eligible for lower civil service appointment, but he took the *jinshi* examinations repeatedly without ever being successful. Living in Beijing from the 1750s onward, he was accepted as an honored participant in scholarly circles. Several of his scholarly works were published, starting in the 1760s. They drew much attention among the evidential research scholars, who acknowledged him a reigning master. He also began to publish philosophical inquiries that were not greatly appreciated; the reaction of some leading Han learning experts was, "Why does so brilliant a textual-critical scholar waste his time on this sort of enterprise?" Through his connections he was appointed in 1773 to the *Four Treasuries* project (discussed in the preceding section) as an editor-compiler; he remained in that post through the remaining four and one-half years of his life. His work there was entirely devoted to one of the project's most demanding and important tasks: the recovery of otherwise lost texts from the imperial library's lone surviving copy of the *Yongle dadian,* the manuscript encyclopedia dating from the early fifteenth century. He was spared involvement in the literary inquisition that grew out of the *Four Treasuries* project; he died in 1777, about the time that the debased secondary activity of text censorship took on serious proportions.

Dai Zhen's efforts in philosophy, apart from his extensive achievements in evidential research, were directed toward achieving a more accurate and useful understanding of the natural order and of man's place in it. In his mind the natural world consisted simply of the orderly workings of an all-encompassing material reality, something readily subject to observation and study, and not requiring metaphysical explanation. He thus rejected Song Neo-Confucianism's central tenet in explaining the world, the idea of *li,* or principle. That concept is central to Zhu Xi's synthesis of Neo-Confucian philosophy; without it, the entire Neo-Confucian system of ideas lacks coherence. In Dai Zhen's mind, *li* is but a subjective concept, lacking explanatory value. He was true to Confucianism in accepting the fundamentally ethical character of mankind's place in the natural order, agreeing with Mencius in that regard. His most important philosophical work goes by the name *Mengzi ziyi shuzheng,* which may be translated "A Semantic Analysis of the Language of the Book of *Mencius.*" He also wrote three essays to which he attached great importance, called *Yuan shan* (On the Meaning of the Good), and a few other purely philosophical inquiries. No more than half a dozen persons of his time, even his admiring disciples in textual research, fully appreciated their significance.[37]

Another important thinker of the time, an acquaintance and admirer of Dai Zhen, is Zhang Xuecheng (1738–1801). He came from an impoverished official family and encountered many difficulties, but in 1778 he received the *jinshi* degree. While he had no official career, he too attracted the attention of the scholar-official elite and was patronized by some of the same eminent figures who assisted Dai Zhen. Their help enabled him to make a marginal living by teaching in academies, tutoring, and working on commissions compiling local histories. He applied the methods of evidential research to the study of history, and developed a broad theory about the nature and philosophical importance of historical study. It is for his impact on historiography that he is best known, but he also was an original thinker, and one of the few who understood the far-reaching implications of Dai Zhen's philosophic breakthrough, if not on a similar level of significance as an original thinker.[38]

Eighteenth-century intellectual life also encompassed many whose scholar-ship, if not important in philosophy per se, transformed their fields of special-ized learning. One group concentrated on the study of historical linguistics, reconstructing the pronunciation of Chinese in ancient times, analyzing the development of the writing system, delving deep into etymology and seman-tics, and clarifying the rhyme schemes and other aspects of the prosody of early poetry. Their studies, highly systematic and methodologically sound, have sometimes been seen as evidence for the "scientific method" in Qing scholarship. There also were richly productive studies of mathematics and mathematicians, of pharmacology and medicine, of astronomy, of geography and cartography, and in other areas that suggest a capacity for scientific undertakings by persons active in the traditional fields of Chinese scholarship. Modern science as such, however, had to await later developments.

As a final reflection on the mid-Qing flowering of scholarship and Confu-cian learning, one may cite another component of that milieu to explain why Dai Zhen's breakthrough in philosophical thought was not more influential, its impact confined to a small number of thinkers and not adequately appreci-ated until the early twentieth century. On the one hand, his philosophical system is subtle and difficult to grasp, and he did not live to develop its presen-tation through open discussion and debate among fellow thinkers. Yet, on the other hand, a more important reason may be that it affronted the ethical sensibilities of many by undermining the traditional ethics as taught since Song times. A vague and empty moralizing, as we have seen, was often resorted to as a substitute for critical thinking on social issues. That had become a characteristic mode of behavior; it was comfortably familiar to indi-viduals, and it was useful to the state. As we have seen in connection with the literary inquisition, ruler and government (often cynically) leaned heavily on their roles as defenders of morality to justify political policies.

Dai Zhen's standing in intellectual history has been strenuously debated from his time to the present, mostly over issues unrelated to the content of his thought, although its content was in fact what disturbed his critics. One eminent historian of Chinese philosophy noted that influential figures throughout the century and a half following Dai's death so resented his pow-erful rejection of the Cheng-Zhu orthodox position in Confucian thought that they indulged in vilification to discredit him. They charged that as an eviden-tial research scholar he had plagiarized other scholars' writings and major discoveries, claiming them as his own. This historian has demonstrated that their charges were false, often knowingly false. The writer concluded: "By stressing their private conceptions of *li* [a long line of righteous men believed] they were championing a cause of Justice [*gongli*]."[39] The "righteous men" referred to are among the most eminent historians and intellectual leaders in early twentieth-century China, men who otherwise were themselves the champions of new thought and values; all were friendly associates of the writer who made this serious charge.

From this one can grasp how difficult it is to attempt an equitable assess-ment of Dai Zhen's place in the history of thought. Because of the strongly moralistic tone of later Neo-Confucianism, one must demonstrate first that Dai—one of its most profound critics—was an ethically upright man before one can comment on his intellectual acumen and philosophical originality. It should not be necessary to prove that he did not plagiarize other men's textual scholarship before one can give his philosophical ideas serious and unbiased consideration. Yet the enduring pull (some would say "pall") of Zhu Xi's system of thought, as an embodiment of traditional values, still has not lost all of its force. In the eighteenth century, Dai could not gain a fair hearing for radically revisionist philosophical ideas. Even into the early twentieth century, moralistic considerations often stood in the way of philosophic inquiry per se.

In other fields of expression, the free spirits could go much further. The great novelists who wrote *The Scholars* and *The Dream of the Red Chamber* (*Honglou meng*, known in its best translation as *The Story of the Stone*), and other writers of fiction and poetry, could satirize the foibles of convention-ridden society and scoff at Confucian moralism gone awry more or less in safety, because they did not seem to attack the foundations of the thought system. Also, the appeal of their storytelling was so great that everyone read them. They could not be suppressed. It has been shown that *The Dream of the Red Chamber* creates an ideal imaginary world from which both the filth of corrupted elite life and the coarseness of ordinary everyday life are entirely excluded, to express the writer's rejection of Qianlong era society.[40] The faults of the real world contrast with the ideals of the imaginary one in a revealing way; in particular, the novelist (Cao Zhan, or Cao Xueqin, 1716?–1763) reveals his resentment of political corruption, rigidly conventional morality, and the Manchu elite's misuse of power, yet sets those forth as elements of a deeply moving human story, not obviously as an attack on the times. No other literary work has been so widely admired in China, so studied and commented on, so beloved by readers who have read it repeatedly throughout their lives. The repressive conditions of the Qianlong era could not prevent all such works of genius from coming into being, and in fact those conditions spurred creators and admirers alike to produce and cherish them.

VI. THE QIANLONG EMPEROR'S MILITARY CAMPAIGNS

Playing the role of the conquering hero was important to Hongli, the Qianlong emperor. He sought opportunities to send Manchu generals to the borders to put down insurgencies among non-Chinese and to maintain the awe of Manchu-Qing China on the frontiers and also among the Chinese population at home. There were, to be sure, sound military justifications for some of the border wars, but they also were part of his design to enhance Manchu prestige and improve the morale of the Manchu banner population. He did not lead armies in person, but he made a display of going to the edges of the steppe to see off departing armies and to welcome returning victors and receive the obeisances of the conquered.

In the capital he built a hall to military valor; it was a kind of military museum where portraits of victorious commanders were displayed along with

Immediately adjacent to Shigatse is the great monastery of Tashilhunpo, in the eighteenth century the seat of the Panchen Lamas. They were second to the Dalai Lamas in the hierarchy of the Gelup-ka sect of Tibetan Buddhism, and were figures of very great prestige and influence, often assuming authority after the death of a Dalai Lama and helping to determine his successor, and otherwise potentially important in secular as well as religious affairs. The remarkable incumbent in the 1760s was the Third Panchen Lama (1738–1780). He spoke Hindi, corresponded in Persian, was friendly with agents of the British East India Company in India and with Catholic missionaries in Tibet.[48] He was invited to Beijing in 1780 for the celebrations of the Qianlong emperor's seventieth (sui) birthday. There the court took special note of him, having heard about his cosmopolitan connections; they loaded him down with rich gifts and attached aides to his entourage. He would bear watching. Sadly, he contracted smallpox in China and died in Beijing at the age of forty-two.

The Nepalese rulers also were in contact with the East India Company's Governor General in Calcutta and with the Company's agents in the region.[49] When the rash rulers of Nepal decided to invade southern Tibet in 1788, they probably thought they would have British backing; the British saw Nepal as a doorway for trade into Tibet, and via Tibet on into west China, and had discussed common interests with the Gurkha leaders. Mediation by the Panchen Lamas was no longer possible following the death of the amiable Third in 1780, leaving his reincarnate successor, a young child.

The two Manchu resident agents in Lhasa (Ambans) made no attempt to defend the region against the invaders. They took the child Panchen (along with the Dalai Lama) to safety when the Nepalese troops came through and plundered the rich monastery at Shigatse on their way to attack Lhasa. The Manchu agents' only interest was to protect the two Buddhist religious leaders, not to defend the Tibetan state, nor had they military or diplomatic means to do so. As the affair was reported in urgent dispatches to Beijing, alien powers had designs on the region and on its spiritual leaders. Manchu control over Tibet and its religious influence throughout Inner Asia again appeared to be threatened, but from an entirely new quarter.

Those are the circumstances that underlay the Qianlong emperor's urgent decision to dispatch an army, made up of Manchu and Mongol forces supplemented by tribal soldiers supplied by the native chieftainships, to drive the Nepalese out of southern Tibet. Upon hearing of the first Nepalese incursions in 1788–89, the emperor commanded forces from Sichuan to proceed to Lhasa and restore order. That measure, by no means a simple logistical feat, was counted as the first of two wars with the Gurkhas. It appeared to have been successful, but the commanders lied about conditions, hoping to conceal the true state of affairs: they found that the marauding Gurkha forces had already withdrawn, and no "suppression" was accomplished. Reports continued to come to Beijing saying that the Gurkha armies had again invaded; in 1791 they returned in force. This time the emperor ordered those officers responsible for the previous effort punished, and selected more reliable military leaders to undertake a decisive operation. Fukang'an, a Manchu related to the emperor, was an able but unscrupulous military commander; he took as his second in command Hailancha, perhaps the best military tactician in the Qing armies.[50] They chose to enter Tibet from Xining (Qinghai) in the north, shortening the march but making it in the dead of winter 1791–92, crossing high mountain passes in deep snow and cold. Their entire force probably did not exceed 10,000, about 6,000 Manchus and Mongols along with units made up of Tibetan soldiers from the native chieftainships in China's northwest. They reached central Tibet in the summer of 1792 and within two or three months could report to Beijing that they had won a decisive series of encounters that pushed the warlike Gurkha armies across the crest of the Himalayas and back into the valley of Katmandu. That allowed the Qianlong emperor to produce his essay on his "ten perfections" late in 1792, although his armies fought on in Nepal into 1793, when, virtually at the gates of Katmandu, Fukang'an forced the battered Gurkha armies to accept surrender on Manchu terms. By claiming two victories over the Gurkhas, the emperor rounded out his list of ten triumphs, but in fact only the expedition under Fukang'an and Hailancha in 1791–1793 can be counted as a military victory.

Victory over the Gurkhas in 1793 did not prevent repeated Nepalese incursions thereafter; in the mid-1850s the Tibetans defeated and expelled a Gurkha invasion without informing the Manchu Amban, and negotiated a peace treaty without Beijing's knowledge. The Chinese position in Tibet under the Qianlong emperor was seen by the British as "suzerainty," like that which China claimed over many of its neighboring countries such as Korea, Vietnam, and Siam. Suzerainty implies that the Manchu-Chinese court claimed a kind of distant overlordship under which the "vassal state" retained full sovereignty. That rhetoric of empire in fact acknowledged the independence of states while claiming a nominal superiority over them. The two resident Manchu Ambans who represented the Qing emperors at the court of the Dalai Lamas in Lhasa had no role in governing the people of Tibet, nor authority to appoint or approve the Tibetan administrators; their functions, in their roles as personal representatives of the Manchu emperors, were limited to influencing the Dalai Lamas and other heads of the Tibetan Buddhist hierarchy, who had become de facto clients of the Manchu emperors. That is to say, the rulers in Beijing expected the Tibetan church to uphold policies that would not be inimical to China's interests in Inner Asia. As for the new links of Nepal with British India, the Chinese court was made aware that the British threatened their position in Tibet; they demanded that the Dalai Lamas prevent all commercial penetration by the East India Company and relations with all European powers, thereby closing Tibet to British (and later to Russian) influence. In that they succeeded for most of a century. Those were the limited goals of Qing foreign policy vis-à-vis Tibet. The Gurkha wars reveal the limits of that relationship.

the very favorable view of China in the eyes of Western observers of the time is not without substance.

That favorable view gradually changed, from mid-Qing onward, as Western interests (political, commercial, and religious) came into conflict with the Qing government (see Chapter 36). By the nineteenth century, when Westerners' frustrations in dealing with the intractable empire dimmed its aura, the general Western admiration for China began to take on a tone of contempt for its "backward institutions." Admiration for the industrious Chinese people, however, and for the refinements of China's high culture, were not diminished as contacts broadened. The point to be stressed here is that China, even under later Qing political decline, remained an impressive example of a complex society that functioned at high levels. Despite its population mass and geographic extent, its institutions continued to develop to meet the challenges of its own internal expansion and, if less impressively, to meet new challenges from abroad.

In quantitative terms, governing mid-Qing China was twice the problem that it had been in mid-Ming times, two centuries earlier. While rejecting disruptive consequences of explosive growth, one must yet be alert to qualitative adjustments in the basic activities of feeding and clothing ever larger numbers of people and maintaining peace and order among them. As a corollary to the revised view of population growth offered here, it must be noted that agricultural output kept up with that growth; the capacity of Chinese agricultural technology to innovate and to expand productivity has generally been underestimated. It is now widely accepted that population increases stimulated technological advances, especially in agriculture, in contrast with earlier views that population growth overwhelmed society, leaving no resources to devote to change and improvement. Chinese agricultural tools and implements were of high quality, ahead of those known in preindustrial Europe. Throughout the centuries of steady if moderate population growth, ingenious inventions and improvements in those kinds of applied technology continued to appear, as did techniques for enriching the soil and improving crop varieties. New World crops too were significant in this respect. To cite one example, the American sweet potato (first introduced in the 1570s) is particularly rich in nutritive value; its use spread quickly throughout China between 1700 and 1800, "accounting for half the year's food supply of the poor in Shantung [Shandong Province]," and becoming the third most important source of food in the entire country, after rice and wheat.[54] China was highly adaptive to new foods and agricultural products; its culture, although conservative in matters of social ethics and organization, was not resistant to many other kinds of change.

Accompanied by matching increases in agricultural productivity, steady population increase thus did not bring China to general destitution. Despite regional variations, narrower agricultural margins in North China, and pockets of entrenched poverty in some places, mid-Qing society remained prosperous. Secondary productive activities occupied those long periods in the agricultural year between the busier times of the spring plowing and planting and the fall harvesting. Industrial crafts and commodity production, such as processing foods for sale in local markets, supplemented farmers' incomes; "compared with medieval and early modern Europe consumer goods were plentiful, some of extremely high quality, but most designed for popular consumption."[55] Yet new lands suitable for cultivation, and surpluses of the basic foods produced on the land, were always limited. China was not poor, but it became increasingly vulnerable. It was susceptible to disaster when normal conditions were upset, whether by the acts of man or by the vagaries of nature. At the same time, its mass and social stability allowed it to absorb deep shocks without disintegrating. Through the mid- and later Qing dynasty, the interplay between factors favoring stability and the disabling effects of stress and shock was to be prolonged over a long span of time.

Local Government and Local Society

The structure of local governing during the Qing remained fundamentally unchanged from Ming. In some ways its operations became more specialized, demanding more functional differentiation among the magistrate's aides and subordinates, and for a time in the reign of the Yongzheng emperor and in the early Qianlong years, it operated more effectively than in earlier times. From the middle of the eighteenth century onward, however, performance lagged, for reasons that will be discussed. First, to review the structure of base-level administration, there were about 1,300 counties (or "districts," called *xian*), and about 200 sub-prefectures (called *zhou*); those 1,500 base-level administrative units were administered under 185 to 200 prefectures. Those numbers varied within a narrow range throughout the entire Qing period.[56] On average, thus, each prefecture contained eight sub-prefectures and counties. To simplify, whether called *zhou* or *xian*, the base-level administrations were the lowest level of formally responsible governing, normally staffed by three to eight civil service appointees. The head of each base-level administrative jurisdiction bore a title usually translated "magistrate." His staff consisted of one or more "associate magistrates" or "assistant magistrates," one or more "sub-magistrates," and further staff called by titles such as "registrar" and "director of Confucian studies," as well as locally hired sub-officials with titles such as "warden," "police captain," and the like. Each of the base-level magistrates' offices (the *yamen*) employed sub-official clerical staffs, together with more lowly aides and servants, in numbers running to the hundreds. All of that closely resembles the Ming and earlier patterns.[57]

There were many variations in kinds of prefectures, sub-prefectures, counties, and other special districts, and of their staffing, but to simplify a complex matter, it is sufficient here to think of a basic pattern of governing throughout the regions away from the capital as existing on three levels: the province *(sheng)* level, under which was the prefecture *(fu)* level, with the sub-prefectures and counties forming the base level.

One new addition complicates that simplified schema. In keeping with the Yongzheng emperor's rigorous supervision of all aspects of governing, in the

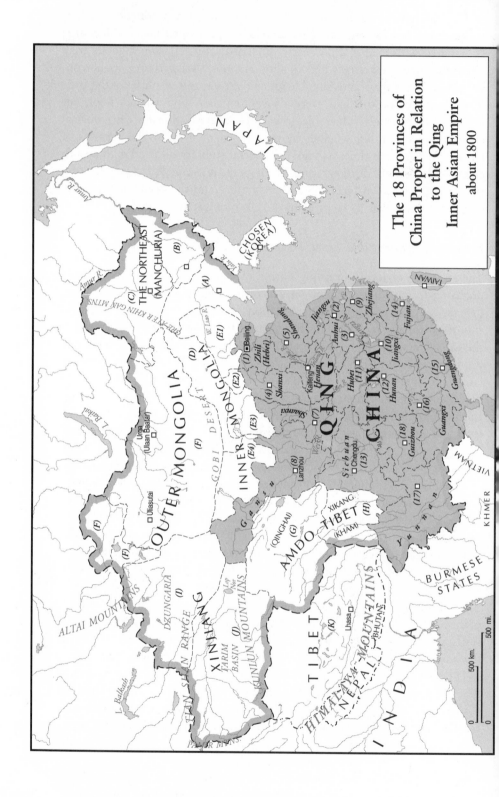

The 18 Provinces of China Proper in Relation to the Qing Inner Asian Empire about 1800

MAP 22

Inner Asian regions:

A   Shengjing (Fengtian), capital, Shenyang (Mukden); Liaoning Province after 1907.

B   Kirin (Jilin), capital Jilin, Province after 1907.

C   Heilongjiang, capital Tsitishar, Province after 1907.

D   Inner Mongolia, administratively separate from mid-18th century.

E1, E2   Portions of Inner Mongolia attached to Zhili and Shanxi Provinces 1725–1742; after 1911 made provinces of Rihe (Jehol) and Chahar.

E3, E4   Portions of Inner Mongolia made provinces of Suiyuan and Ningxia, 1911.

F   Outer Mongolia, administratively separate from mid-18th century; present-day Mongolian Republic.

G, H   Kokonor (Qinghai) and Kham regions of Amdo, Tibet, designated special military regions in early 18th century, made provinces of Qinghai and Xikang (Sikang) in 20th century, until 1950s.

I, J   Xinjiang, divided by Tianshan Mountain Range into Mongolian Dzungaria and Turkic Tarim Basin regions, both conquered and absorbed in 1750s, united to form Province of Xinjiang in 1884.

K   Tibet Proper, administratively independent of China until 1950.

mid-eighteenth century a new level of executive functions was inserted between the provinces and the prefectures. This was done by enlarging the character of what had been an investigative arm, the Circuit *(dao)*, and giving its circuit intendants enlarged staffs so that they could directly manage what were held to be particularly important strategic functions, such as irrigation, water control, and transport canal management; the salt and other production and distribution monopolies; tax grain transport; the postal relay system; customs collections; and the trade with Inner Asia in tea for horses. These crucial operations were turned over to specialists under the direct control of the provincial governors. There were in Qianlong times about ninety circuits, or on average one for two or three prefectures; they were headed by Circuit Intendants *(dao tai)* ranked 4A, higher than the highest-ranking prefects and just below the heads of provincial offices. The redefined circuits show that significant changes in the structure of governing were within the psychological and institutional means of Qing statesmen. In mid-Qing times appointment to this newly consequential office was highly desired; it incidentally offered ample opportunities to become rich by illegal and semilegal means when the general morale of government deteriorated.

The potential for corruption notwithstanding, the Qing system of regional and local governing could deliver effective governing, as it did for a short time during and following the reign of the Yongzheng emperor. The system was elastic enough for significant changes and adaptations to be made. For another example, the magistrates' staffs became more professional through the use of specialized, privately employed assistants. The old ideal of the liberally educated magistrate competent to perform all tasks and meet all circumstances, already seen to be impractical by late Ming times, was fully superseded when the Yongzheng emperor demanded higher levels of technical competence in governing. Every magistrate had to have assistants in at least two fields—specialists in law and specialists in fiscal matters. Specialists also were hired by many magistrates to draft appropriately elegant and forceful reports to their superiors, the better to maintain their reputations as men of stature. The profession of magistrates' private aides quickly developed, often employing men educated for and sometimes holding the higher civil service degrees, but who preferred lucrative and less stressful roles as advisers to those bearing direct responsibility for governing. Logically, we might expect that functions so necessary to the successful conduct of government would gradually be formalized and absorbed into the civil service in an expanded structure of local governing. That did not happen. The assistants (called *mufu* or *muyou*, "advisers" or "friends") remained privately employed, costing their employers large sums that had to come from the special supplements to official salaries regularized by the Yongzheng reforms, or putting pressure on the magistrates and prefects and higher-level administrators to find the resources in other ways. In this development we see a rational extension of professionalism in governing but a lag in institutional adaptation; that increased the pressures on administrators to raise expense funds by irregular means.

It can be argued that the rigor demanded by the Yongzheng emperor, while greatly improving performance in government, also was counterproductive and could not be long maintained. It ran counter to some features of the ruling ethos in Chinese society, where personal relations, deference patterns, and ritualized behavior all interfered with impersonal, efficient administration. In any event, the Qianlong emperor did not attempt to maintain his father's rigorous norms. He allowed a return to laxity even while making occasional displays of his commitment to upright governing. That only added to the spreading cynicism throughout the elite and in offices of government at all levels, fed by the obvious discrepancy between ideal and actual patterns. A pervading sense of falseness in the regime's stress on moral precepts, while failing to provide convincing models of virtue in high places, could not be concealed. A generalized cynicism of that kind appears to be a feature of Qing social life that has no precedent in earlier periods.

That is not to say that there were not many highly motivated, conscientious Confucian personalities striving to enter government service by the traditional route of learning and examination, in order to uphold the responsibilities of the scholar-official. Such men indeed existed, and continued to come forth to the end of the Qing dynasty. Yet the atmosphere of intellectual life, in the main, did not encourage critical thinking about real problems of society, and political thought in particular became redundant and meaningless. Few scholar-officials by mid-Qing times displayed the mentality of independent-minded thinkers. The overriding tone of Confucian scholarship and thought, while often academically brilliant, grew ever more detached from social problems. A major trend in mid- and later Qing literary expression is scorn for the incompetence of men in public life on the one hand and, on the other, satirical depictions of opportunism and corruption.

Satire of course exaggerates to make its points, but it has no point if it bears no relation to reality. Our concern, finally, must be with the issue of how the widely observed degeneration of ethics and morale in public life affected the lives of the governed. Much detail has been assembled by social historians, but their findings, often ideologically driven, often contradictory, as yet offer no clear picture of Qing society. Yet two generalizations appear to be sound. One, the society remained prosperous as population steadily grew, economic growth was supplemented by diversified forms of productivity, trade flourished, and consumption reached ever higher levels. There were regions that did not share fully in that general prosperity, and the margin in agricultural production, while not critically thin, was slender enough to subject populations to greater risk in exceptional circumstances of drought, flood, and other disasters. On the whole, however, China in 1800 probably was better fed, clothed, and housed, its people sharing in a more diversified economy, than in most other places in Asia and many in Europe. Two, the lives of ordinary people in their localities were adversely affected by the steady loss of morale in the elite sector, and therefore in the conduct of local government. The spreading cynicism allowed malpractice to replace altruistic dedication, and to be realistically if not ideally accepted as the norm. The sense of social responsibility in officialdom, and among the elite who dominated local society, became ever more a pretense, ever less a widely shared obligation. Abuses of position and power were much less apt than in earlier times to be checked by ethical concerns shared among the leading sectors of society, and ever farther beyond the supervisory arms of a corrupted central government.

This describes a general decline, but only in relative terms. It did not augur well for the future, but it did not yet represent a state of social crisis. This account of later imperial Chinese history, closing in 1799 with the death of the Qianlong emperor, leaves the reader to anticipate an uncertain next phase for the Chinese people, and inevitably to ponder the extent to which this ruler's personal leadership is a crucial explanatory factor. In 1800 the world's largest society still possessed a vital cultural tradition that gave it unity, strength, and resiliency, and kept its noblest ideals alive in the minds of most people. Although diminished, those practical aspects of traditional values were still capable of being renewed, and in some measure they were, during the nineteenth century. But the venerable civilization's late imperial governing had led it into perilous circumstances. Add to that the new threats from the outside, now meaning the maritime world dominated by the European powers, and the nineteenth century was to be one of inescapable crises and further political decline.

36

CHINA'S LEGACY IN A
CHANGING WORLD

China in 1800 was becoming embroiled in a changing world in which
the West—essentially western Europe with its North American offshoots—was coming into a dominant position. The West's industrializ-
ing nations would for the next century or two be taken as the source
of a universal civilization, contesting China's long-standing claim to be
precisely that, and testing China's ability to survive as an independent
nation with a distinctive culture. This final chapter reflects briefly on
some of the issues relevant to that contest, and to the significance of
China's historical achievement in the face of worldwide change. The
historical roots of modern China's interactions with the West, leading
up to the nineteenth century, are discussed under four topical headings,
following a brief review of earlier contacts with the world beyond China's borders. The long process of China's transforming interaction with
the West became a dominant theme in its later imperial and twentieth-
century history.

I. THE BACKGROUND OF CHINA'S
INTERNATIONAL RELATIONS

Despite geographic barriers to international contacts, China was never truly
isolated from the rest of the world. Prehistoric man roamed across Eurasia,
and the earliest humans in China, themselves having physical characteristics
of several racial types, used products brought by trade from very distant
places. Two thousand years ago contacts through Central Asia with India led
China into the Indianized sphere of international Buddhism; those contacts
were attenuated only a thousand years later, when Islamic expansion in the
twelfth century along India's northern borders broke those links, but at the
same time created new paths of interaction across Inner and Central Asia. In
the thirteenth and fourteenth centuries, as recorded in written materials from

Marco Polo and many other European and Western Asian travelers, China's awareness of other world religions—Islam, Christianity, and Judaism (among others)—grew through overland and maritime contacts. At the same time, Chinese and Arab shipping shared the seas between China, the Indian Ocean, and the Persian Gulf, encouraging exchanges of maritime technology and a range of personal and commercial contacts. Chinese exploration of the entire Pacific Basin also is at least suggested by various kinds of evidence. The exchange of products, techniques, and ideas has for millennia enriched civilization. China both gave to and took from those constant but often indirect exchanges, mostly carried out through intermediaries.

"Intermediaries" is the significant word in describing China's many kinds of long-functioning contacts with the rest of the world; few of them brought Chinese people directly into contact with their non-Chinese neighbors, still less with more remote parts of the world from which came products, ideas, and small numbers of people. Compared with the earlier civilizations in other parts of the world, China was relatively remote, insulated, self-sufficient, and self-contained. China's seafaring people were the exception, and they did not occupy a large place in the life of the nation as a whole.

In the early sixteenth century a new phase of direct European-Chinese interaction began. Portuguese empire builders first sailed to China from their newly acquired bases in India, to be followed quickly by the Spanish, who arrived via the Pacific crossing, then by the Dutch, the English, and other Europeans. Europeans came to live first at the edges, then inside China. Many of them learned the Chinese language and read its books, taught European religion as well as secular knowledge to some members of Chinese society, wrote voluminously about China to inform their fellow Europeans, even took some Chinese (mostly religious postulants) back to Europe with them. From 1517, when the first Portuguese ships reached Canton, there was steady growth in these direct contacts, up to the time when the Macartney embassy, sent by King George III of Great Britain to the Qianlong emperor, resided in Beijing from August to October 1793. Over that span of almost 300 years before 1793, China and Europe carried on a steadily growing relationship. If we call that the "first phase" of the direct contacts between China and the farther West of Europe, that phase can be said to have ended with the Macartney embassy's failure to achieve its goal of direct treaty relations with China. That failure provoked a second phase of relations in the nineteenth century, to be conducted under new modes, expressing different attitudes, a story that lies beyond the present volume.

The 300 years of that opening phase of direct European-Chinese relations, roughly 1500–1800, were divided almost evenly between the native Ming and the Manchu Qing dynasties. The new relations with Europe came to affect many aspects of Chinese life, far more than Chinese or Europeans were then aware. Today we might judge that their economic interaction was the most profound aspect of their relationship, yet at the time the least readily perceived, despite massive exchanges of New World silver for Chinese goods.

The exchanges of ideas, especially in the spheres of religion and philosophy, might appear to have had little effect, yet the subtleties of that process are difficult to judge. In other fields of knowledge, elements of Western science and technology undoubtedly had lasting and growing impact, although (as in religion and philosophy) we tend to focus on the introduction of European elements in a one-way traffic, thereby overlooking the element of interaction.

One long-range trend is particularly apparent in the relationship of China and the West over those three centuries: it is the trend away from the initial mutual respect (albeit tinged with Chinese condescension) that marked the first century or more. By the mid-eighteenth century, that trend had become one of growing European superiority, bordering on contempt for the Chinese empire. It led to the antagonism that became the dominant mood during the nineteenth century, albeit still marked at times by many Europeans' awe for the vastness and the grandeur of China. European superiority was accompanied by a related trend, one away from Europeans' search for a place *within* the Chinese political and commercial world, toward one of defying Chinese patterns and seeking to impose Western ones, by force if necessary.

Sino-Western relations in the three centuries from 1500 to 1800 can be summarized under four headings: (1) growing mutual recognition; (2) economic interactions; (3) broadened horizons of religion and philosophy, and exchanges of scientific thought and practical knowledge; and (4) a changing military and diplomatic scene. Some of those trends are more apparent at the China end of the exchange than at the other. Here the focus is on China; China's and Asia's contributions to the changing life of Europe are alluded to only occasionally in what follows.[1]

II. MUTUAL RECOGNITION

Marco Polo returned to Europe from China about 1300 to dictate his extensive description of his travels to a literate friend, creating the remarkable book that bears his name. Several other important travelers' accounts became widely known during the following decades. China and the East took on mythic proportions in the imagination of Europe, yet knowledge of the rest of Asia remained hazy. There was confusion over the ancient kingdoms Europeans called Sinim (Chinese *Qin*) and Seres (the "land of silk"), both known to the Roman Mediterranean world. Were they the same as northern and southern regions of China which Marco Polo called "Cathay" and "Manzi"? There was further confusion over the Mongol Great Khans; Marco Polo knew them as emperors of China, but he also used that title for the rulers of India. Columbus was a victim of that confusion. A century after Columbus, the Italian Jesuit missionary Matteo Ricci lived in China from 1583 until his death at Beijing in 1610. From that time onward, with the presence in China of learned Europeans who came to know the language and history, more accurate information about China was sent to Europe. For example, China and Cathay were shown to be the same; more accurate maps of China and

East Asia were drawn and published in Europe; China's geographic extent and its relation to Japan, Korea, and India were explained. From 1600 onward, the rapidly expanding body of Jesuit reporting and translating steadily raised the level of European knowledge, and Europe's image of China began to come into focus.

China's knowledge of Europe was if anything still more hazy. Arab mariners brought the word *farang* (Chinese, *falan, falanji*) into East Asian ports, where variants of this word became part of mariners' sense of the wider world. The many variants of the word all derive from the Arabic, "Farangi," for "Franks," dating from the expansion of Islam into Spain and southern France in the eighth century. Later, during the Crusades, the word was used in the Islamic world to designate all Europeans, that is, all the peoples of Christendom. Picking up this name from the seagoing Arabs who came to South China's ports as early as the eighth century, the Chinese adopted the word *farang* as a name for all things European. The word *falang* (or *folang*) continued to be used during later Ming and early Qing times as a general if vague designation for Europe and Europeans, and things brought from Europe. Under Jesuit influence it was gradually superseded in the seventeenth century by the name "Tai xi" ("Occidens extremus," or "the Far West"), for Europe and America, to differentiate the Western world from China's name for nearer Western Asia, "Xiyu," "the Western Regions."

Sixteenth-century Europe was of course no longer the Christendom known to Arabs during the Crusades. From the seventeenth century onward it slowly penetrated the Chinese consciousness that Europe had become a continent containing many independent, highly competitive kingdoms. Up-to-date knowledge was available but not widely utilized. Ricci's map of the world (1584) had circulated in printed editions since the 1590s. Missionary writings in Chinese about religion, science, and other aspects of the West had begun to appear.[2] Yet such information was seen as a trivial curiosity by most educated Chinese. Their systematic efforts to study the West as a field of knowledge that should be important to China's statesmen were not produced until the nineteenth century, two centuries after Europe had gained access to a very large quantity of good information about China.[3] Ricci himself, though a great admirer of Chinese learning, is quoted as having said, "The Chinese are so self-opinionated that they cannot be made to believe that the day will ever come when they will learn anything from foreigners which is not already set down in their own books."[4] The Europeans' efforts to make an impact on the deeply cultivated, sophisticated Chinese mentality encountered endless frustration. The sharp tool of knowledge and understanding was underused on both sides, but particularly among the Chinese who had to deal with the West in mid-Qing times. Mutual recognition had indeed grown by the time the Qianlong emperor rebuffed the Earl Macartney in 1793, yet it had not advanced enough to provide either side with sure guidance through the troubled century that followed. Nor has the barrier of mutual ignorance been adequately overcome in the present day.

III. ECONOMIC INTERACTIONS

China was an important player in the world's economy at the end of the Ming dynasty in 1644, and its importance increased during the first century and a half of the Qing. Chinese economic policy nonetheless barely recognized that fact: Chinese rulers and statesmen dealt knowingly with matters of fiscal administration without formulating anything we can properly call an economic policy. Neither in China nor in the West did there yet exist the concept of a "Chinese economy" interacting with trends in the world's economy. Chinese rulers and statesmen did not see their country as being in competition with other nations for the profits of trade or for access to resources. Protecting its ships at sea was not perceived as a matter of state concern, nor did China claim sovereignty over the far shores which its seafarers reached. Trade was conducted by traders with little official support or supervision beyond collecting modest tariffs on goods landed in Chinese ports, and those tariffs were not considered a significant item in the nation's revenues.

This is in great contrast with the role of trade as perceived by the European states, from the rise of mercantile empires in the sixteenth century on. The European states competed vigorously among themselves, fought wars and practiced piracy at sea, invested in foreign trading companies, and often claimed state's ownership (or "private" ownership licensed and protected by the state) of mines, factories, and plantations abroad. Mercantile interests led to the establishment of colonial governments across the globe. In those new imperialist forms of national development the Chinese lagged far behind, not by default but by intent. The differences were conceptual.

Imperialist expansion became a major item of Chinese state policy under the Qing after 1644, but it was focused on Inner Asia, where Manchu/Chinese administrations were imposed on newly absorbed non-Chinese regions and peoples on the nearer land frontiers. Those regions were, however, seen to be of political and military significance; they were not absorbed for economic reasons. Imperialist Chinese expansion under the Ming and Qing also turned to extending the land frontiers in the south and southwest, where, unlike the situation on the northern borders, the resident populations were close to the Chinese in their agrarian way of life; they were moreover divided into small tribal states, and were nonthreatening to Chinese national security. The motives for and the modes of expansion and absorption in the south were different from those on the "border of peril" in the north, yet many local polities on the southern frontier were made subject to Chinese political and military control, and their territories and populations eventually absorbed. Spontaneous Chinese migration was as important in that process as was state policy. The southern expansion also fits our definition of imperialism, although it was of a different character from the Manchu empire building in Inner Asia.

Overseas Chinese communities also began to develop throughout Southeast Asia from mid-Ming times, extending from the Philippines through the insular and mainland reaches of Southeast Asia all the way to Java and Sumatra, Thailand and Burma, and beyond. The creations of out-migrants from China's southeast coastal provinces, they not only were not supported by the government in Beijing, but were actually outlawed and isolated by its policies. Those communities nevertheless provided the bases for a steadily growing private commercial penetration of the region. Chinese ships and Chinese merchants, undaunted by their government's negative policies, filled the ports and garnered a large share of the profits. Yet China displayed no interest in their potential value as springboards for expansion until very recent times. Here again one can discern the contrast, frequently noted in foregoing chapters on mid-Ming and later developments: we see vigor and entrepreneurship in local society in the provinces (and out into the world beyond), strongly contrasting with the stultification of statecraft and political inertia at the center. That is especially true in matters affecting China's foreign relations. While the dynamic "rise of the West"[5] was remaking much of the world, China's government responded to the presence of the West in East Asia by clinging to the established attitudes and stable patterns of its increasingly unrealistic Sinocentric world order.

China's role in world trade grew to great size by 1700 and continued to grow thereafter. Its importance has been measured by the international flow of precious metals, especially the silver produced by Spanish colonial enterprise in the Americas starting early in the sixteenth century. Thereafter the world was suddenly flooded by great increases in the amount of silver bullion entering the world's markets, and at the same time was made subject to erratic fluctuations in those amounts.[6] Some significant indications that national economies worldwide were beginning to interact are becoming apparent to scholars analyzing the information today, but no governments, least of all China's, were able to analyze and respond to such phenomena at the time.

China produced the craft goods that the world was most eager to buy with its new excesses of silver in the sixteenth century. In addition to ordinary craft manufactures and commodities, silks and velvets, brocades and embroideries, porcelains and jade objects, intricately worked luxury goods made of lacquer and rare woods, ivory and leather, bronze and gold, along with medicines and pharmaceutical products, processed foods such as tea and ginger: these set the standard of luxury consumption throughout the world and dominated markets in Europe. Ships of the mercantile powers in Europe competed with Chinese, Japanese, Indians, and Arabs to monopolize the profitable carrying trade throughout Asia and to and from Europe. Locally made imitations of Chinese fine crafts became significant elements in Europe's diversifying economies, but the high quality of the Chinese crafts coupled with their low price made competition difficult. The Europeans brought attractive gifts of clocks, prisms and lenses, woolen textiles, and musical instruments to the Chinese court. Some of these were appreciated, but no market for them was created in Asia. The Earl Macartney's lavish gifts to the Qianlong emperor in 1793 even went so far as to include some large pieces of Wedgwood "china," that is, bone china wares made in imitation of Chinese true porcelain. Those gifts were put on display in Beijing, where they raised questions about the giver's taste, but they made no impact as art or as technology. Europe could find no export items attractive enough to the huge and rich Chinese market to reverse the one-way flow into China of the world's silver. No foreign goods attracted buyers in China's ports in significant number; only silver could be expended in exchange for the many Chinese products demanded on the world's markets. Before 1800, silver flowed in and China's products flowed out in a trade starkly unbalanced in China's favor. The Chinese government did not officially foster that situation; China succeeded grossly in the world's business without really trying. Yet the problems brought by trade would soon threaten China and all of East Asia.

Two interesting kinds of questions follow from the undeniable evidence that China was becoming a crucial player in transnational economic developments: How did the new conditions of trade affect China's domestic economy? And to what extent did economic developments in the rest of the world reverberate within China?

With regard to the first of those questions, as huge amounts of silver were absorbed into China's markets in payment for the exported products of commodity producers and craft industries, what was the impact on economic conditions in general? The incoming silver was a commodity used as money in the form of ingots (raw silver bullion). That produced a great increase in liquidity, or money in circulation, which should have driven down the value of money in relation to the goods for which it was exchanged. To state that more directly, it should have caused inflation, because much more money was available to be traded for market and export products, for labor, for land and other real property, and for the commodities such as grains and textiles on which the people's livelihood depended. Did all that silver flow directly into the market, or was much of it accumulated and held by middlemen? Did it affect the conduct of government by providing the public sector with a greater take in liquid capital than heretofore, by altering the conditions in which taxes were levied and collected, or by increasing the likelihood of bribery and corruption? Some tentative answers to questions of that kind have been proposed in foregoing chapters.

Did the inflow of money enhance the means of acquiring wealth and elite status and give persons in the elite alternate options for gaining and enjoying wealth that competed with the official career patterns? Late Ming consumption patterns were decried at the time as being of unprecedented vulgarity; but we can also see that the social vitality of the later Ming was greatly leavened by the enlargement of choices and sustained by new levels of wealth. By that measure, the spillover into Chinese society from the world's silver flow and commerce was indeed significant.

Other questions arise about the impact of trade. Its effects are most clearly seen in the coastal regions where foreign commerce was concentrated. It appears to have enlarged regional differences in economic conditions, yet some of its consequences also filtered throughout the society, changing economic processes and altering conditions on a national scale. Careful studies of the related issues confirm some of the descriptive statements made throughout foregoing chapters, but strong and convincing generalizations must be left to the specialists on later imperial China's economic history. Knowledge is more complete and analyses more convincing when one comes to the nineteenth and twentieth centuries.

The interesting hypotheses concerning the reverberations within China before 1800 from the world's economic interactions also remain tentative. It is clear that the production and export of silver from the New World was uneven throughout the centuries from 1500 to 1800; there were decades of high production alternating with periods of sharply decreased outflow. Moreover, policies adopted in the colonial states and by the major European trading nations were at times designed to control bullion flow and restrict import markets. Moreover, cycles of economic depression and prosperity affected levels of trade in Europe and with its colonies. Some economic historians have posited the thesis that there was a general economic crisis in the first half of the seventeenth century and that it had measurable impact on China, Japan, and the trading outposts of the European mercantile empires in Manila, Macao, and Batavia. If that is so, can we measure the extent to which China's economic well-being became subject to remote and (from the Chinese point of view) inexplicable factors? As these elements of an incipient worldwide economic integration began to take form, China probably was insulated from the more direct shocks by its size and its still largely autochthonous basic productive activities, yet the question remains: Could a crisis in Europe have affected China's domestic economy by causing tightened money supply, deflation, lowered incomes, scarcities, and hardships on the domestic scene?[7] Whatever economic and social historians eventually determine in detail about these questions, we must remind ourselves that China, by 1799 when the Qianlong emperor died, was becoming part of a world system that was increasingly able to affect the life of Chinese society.

IV. BROADENED HORIZONS OF RELIGION, PHILOSOPHY, AND PRACTICAL KNOWLEDGE

The "Great Tradition" of China's high culture, over a period of 2,000 years by the mid-Qing, had developed an impressive conceptual scheme to explain the origins of the cosmos and the nature of reality. This thought system's cosmogony, that is, its way of explaining the origins of the cosmos and the process by which all the discrete, differentiated elements of material existence (including humankind) were generated, had become a compelling, philosophically satisfying whole. Its basic ideas appear to date from before the beginnings of formal philosophizing in the sixth and fifth centuries B.C.E. They were never described as "revealed" from some higher authority, but were considered to be the product of human—if extraordinary—minds. At different levels of understanding, this cosmogony (or, in the larger sense of its whole conception, its "cosmology") was generally accepted as the common ground of thought. Its Confucian proponents called it Confucian (Ru) learning because its authority was founded on the set of ancient classical writings venerated by Confucian tradition, but the fundamental conceptions were not exclusively, and perhaps not originally, theirs. As we have noted in earlier chapters, this system was profoundly reconsidered, elaborated, and reconfirmed by the Neo-Confucian cosmological thinkers who dominated intellectual life in the eleventh century, in Northern Song times. They launched the new, comprehensive intellectual stance that endured into modern times as the mainstream of Chinese thought and learning. Their Neo-Confucian view of the self-contained world was that it is essentially moral and is responsive to human effort; Confucianism remained optimistic about the human condition.

That Confucian and Neo-Confucian worldview had long encountered two kinds of challenges from within. First, there were other trends within Chinese thought that rejected essential aspects of the Confucian worldview. Most important of those was Daoism, which, while agreeing with the cosmology, was less human-centered, was philosophically amoral, and was powerfully negative about the Confucian social enterprise.

In addition, as with most philosophical and religious systems, the Confucian high culture coexisted with popular beliefs and practices which mostly acknowledged the grand norms while professing and practicing what were in fact caricatures of them. Parallels in human history are many. In the histories of Christendom and of Islam, for example, it is not difficult to find saints and holy figures around whom cults developed; in the minds of the cultists, their special saints became divine agents who could be pleaded with, bribed, even threatened to make them perform magical acts that were contrary to their professed religions' higher teachings.[8] In China, too, popular thought and religious practice often led to similar distortions of philosophical ideas, turning its symbols into support for magic, alchemy, secret cult organizations, and occult doctrinal leadership, all of which were contrary to the essentially rational character of Confucian thought.

The Confucian Great Tradition was able to coexist with both those kinds of challenges. Its great figures at any time in history, not claiming to have received an inviolable revelation, were apt to regard all the differing views, even on essential matters, as mere products of human imperfection, in which they also shared. They could believe that such differences eventually would be resolved through better learning. The important point is that all such differences grew from the common ground of Chinese civilization; antidogmatic, it did not demand that everyone must hold precisely the same beliefs. Within that civilization, dissidence and divergence were readily spawned, and philosophically they could be tolerated.

In actual social life, the dissidences and divergences could take form in turbulent popular beliefs, pushing the state to the point of declaring them dangerous and seeking to suppress them. But at that level too, the little people's ignorance was accepted as explanation for their threatening behavior, and the effective remedy was seen to be moral guidance and teaching. In any event, the high philosophical concepts of the Great Tradition probably seemed far less relevant to the average Chinese (whatever his or her social status) than were the many faces of religious practice that filled daily life. How much, then, did high philosophizing matter in the ordinary life of society?

Despite frequent lack of congruence between philosophical-minded persons' conceptions and the popular mentality, something that we might expect to find in most societies, there is a special sense in which the tenets of Chinese high tradition were not unimportant to the daily life of society: the learned secular tradition generated its own continuing claims on men's minds, and those claims preempted all efforts to devise beguiling alternatives. Tradition was maintained by its affirmation in each new generation of its students, the scholar-elite in training, who were free to express their personal understanding of its texts and the accumulation of interpretive commentary embodying all the differing views ever put forth on them, but that learning process tolerated no recourse to other sources of authority on what to believe.

That traditional system of learning, by encouraging the learners to acquire their own understanding, made it difficult to launch any nonrational authority which would supersede each individual's responsibility to know and to act on one's own knowledge. Claims to possess transcendent religious authority were sure to be denied ready credence among most of the elite, who scorned them as typical of vulgarized doctrines in the popular religions. Those popular notions were, however, looked upon more with amusement than with fear or hatred.

The patronage of credulous rulers aside, rarely could religious leaders gain elite advocacy, nor could their doctrines be more than temporarily aligned with the state's ruling authority. In this way the bookish character of high tradition significantly limited the validity of popular thought (and the forms of social action springing from it), even though the learned tradition's more profound philosophical concepts may not have been widely understood within society at large. Direct challenges to Confucian dominance, from any ground within the cultural amalgam of Chinese civilization, usually were ineffectual.

What we call the Confucian high culture, however, had also long known other kinds of challenges that arose in contacts with peoples representing other civilizations. Different cosmogonic myths were found among many of the peoples living within China's border regions and in neighboring civilizations such as India. Indian Buddhism presented to the Chinese people at large an exceedingly attractive system of personal ethics and values and left an enduring mark on Chinese life. Yet by the tenth century C.E., when Chinese thinkers were prepared to reject it philosophically, much of its message had already been adapted to Chinese social patterns, and had permanently broadened intellectual horizons.

The powerful systems of Western Asian monotheisms were less adaptable than Buddhism. They presented the concept of a creator God who in a divine act created the world ex nihilo. In its Judaic, Christian, and Islamic versions, that cosmology was brought to China during the Tang dynasty (618–907 C.E.). Communities of Jews, Nestorian Christians, and Muslims were found in China at that time, and some of their learned men presented their religious ideas to Chinese audiences, orally and in written forms. Later, during the Yuan dynasty (1281–1367), representatives of medieval Roman Catholicism were sent to China as missionaries; they added a strong voice of Christian belief to the Nestorian Christianity then favored by many among the Mongol conquerors. Also during the Yuan dynasty the Islamic community grew greatly in size. Thereafter, Chinese Judaism and Christianity both waned, but Chinese Islam would gain strong followings both among the Chinese and within non-Chinese populations of border regions.

In short, competing philosophical and cosmological systems had long coexisted within China alongside the indigenous thought system, yet the imported doctrines had aroused very little interest in spheres of thought and learning. When the new era of direct European-Chinese contacts began shortly after 1500, a major focus of the European activity was to bring Christian doctrine and associated fields of Western learning directly to the attention of Chinese men of learning. That challenge to old Chinese patterns of thought was to be direct and expertly transmitted. The quality of the Jesuit mission personnel at the Chinese court throughout the seventeenth century was equal to the best that European learning had to offer at the time. Western astronomy and mathematics, as well as practical knowledge in fields such as hydraulics, cartography, and military technology, were taught with the hope of captivating the Chinese elite, thereby to bring the most sophisticated Chinese minds to the door of Christian belief. A few Chinese of mature years and great learning appear to have crossed the cosmological gulf separating China from Europe to become Christians, but these were extraordinary cases.[9] The religious message had little appeal among the elite on whom the Jesuits, by design, concentrated their efforts.

Any religion that offered dogmatic moral certitude ultimately beyond the individual's judgment was, in that respect, quite unlike anything that could be found in the accumulated wisdom of all the Confucian Sages. Religiously grounded authority continued to be looked upon with great suspicion among learned Chinese.

The new secular knowledge, in contrast, aroused a measure of genuine excitement and brought respect to the "Western literati," as the learned Jesuits were called. Those missionaries in late Ming and early Qing times therefore placed particular stress on scientific and practical knowledge; thanks to them, there soon appeared an extensive range of translations into Chinese as well as new works composed in China in the Chinese language by European scholar-missionaries working together with Chinese counterparts. Would that large undertaking in time work to the advantage of the missionaries?

In any assessment of the Jesuits' broad "effort at guided cultural change,"[10] it is important to note that scientific and practical knowledge from the West did not in itself challenge the Chinese verities. The new astronomy, for example, was not threatening to Chinese cosmological conceptions, nor did the European mathematics that so usefully supplemented Chinese mathematical thinking present clashes of values. It is ironic that the Chinese acceptance of European science was far warmer than the reception given in Rome to Galileo's new findings supporting Copernican theory; he was forced to recant and subjected to house arrest in 1633 in the attempt to discredit him.

On encountering the Christian humanism of the Jesuits, their Chinese counterparts could accept most of it as compatible with Chinese ethical thinking. On their side, the European missionaries declared that China's simpler, early (that is, pre–Neo-Confucian) teachings not only presented no bar to Christianity but in fact anticipated it. It was the Chinese family rituals that became the subject of dispute among Europeans in the different religious orders then working in China. The Jesuits maintained that elite families venerated their ancestors in ways similar to Christian practice in Europe. Franciscans and Dominicans working among lower levels of society, however, found that the same family rituals were popularly understood in different ways; they found the vulgarized versions of Chinese family religion to be idolatrous, hence incompatible with Christian doctrine. A great controversy arose among Enlightenment thinkers and their opponents in Europe over the nature of the Confucian rituals, embroiling the Catholic Church and European thinkers in serious debate.

Subsequently, the Vatican rejected the Jesuits' benign understanding of Chinese social ethics and faulted their accommodative tactics for appealing to the Chinese literati. The popes, whose authority in matters of faith and morals brooked no dissent, sent papal legates to the court of the Kangxi emperor about 1700 to forbid as "idolatrous" the Chinese family-centered rituals. The emperor, whose authority in matters of Chinese politics and culture recognized no bounds, found the pope's envoys, French clerics of highest standing, illiterate (in the relevant language) and ignorant, so sent them packing. Only then did Western learning encounter Chinese opposition at official levels. Yet even in that confrontation, the Chinese reaction against the West's dogmatic claim to superior authority in matters of learning was far less stringent than was European opposition to "heresy" among the "heathen Chinese." The Chinese at no point retaliated by trying to root out Western influences on their cultural life, and allowed the missionaries then in China to remain. These religious and philosophical disputes over Chinese civilization's very nature and meaning dominated the atmosphere of Chinese-Western relations in the eighteenth century.

The Chinese clung to their traditional modes of thought and learning throughout the centuries of purposive European missionary efforts to challenge them. China's response reveals complacency about the foreign threat more than it indicates opposition to things foreign or revulsion against foreigners. The often cited notion of a "traditional Chinese xenophobia" is groundless as a historical generalization. Moreover, when we look at China in 1800, it is difficult to find evidence showing that Europe's large and well-presented challenge to Chinese beliefs had borne significant fruit. China and the West shared much common ground in fields such as astronomy, mathematics, medicine, even ethics. And there was a pragmatic side to the Chinese mentality that facilitated the acceptance of new technology, new food products, new useful things; the widespread acceptance of these alien things raised few doubts in Chinese minds about the superiority of Chinese civilization.

Chinese cultural self-confidence was still strong in 1800. The changing circumstances of more recent times can be understood only in relation to the powerful hold that traditional Chinese ways continued to exercise on the people at large, and on their elite leaders.

V. DIPLOMATIC AND MILITARY THREATS

China in 1800 did not appear to be vulnerable to any dysfunctional consequences of the growing European presence in East Asia. While its people's knowledge about the West remained thin, China's economy absorbed the impact of what might have been destabilizing influences from foreign trade, and its sophisticated world of thought and learning was unshaken by continuing challenges from Western religion and philosophy. The same might have appeared to be true of the changing diplomatic and military scene, for on the surface the long-established patterns appeared to be unaffected. Yet the potential consequences of China's growing international involvement were in fact much more threatening.

It seems likely that even the aging Qianlong emperor, at eighty-two in 1793 when he rebuffed the Earl Macartney and rejected British efforts to engage China in new patterns of foreign relationships, was aware that this European intruder was different. This was not another sultan from the Straits of Malacca demanding the right to submit tribute so as to engage in trade. Nor were the importunate Europeans to be compared with the likes of a Galdan, self-proclaimed emperor of the Dzungar Mongols, a truly formidable opponent of the Qing empire in the seventeenth century. Those were the familiar modes of foreign problems, whether in the nuisance category or genuinely threatening to Qing interests. True, the old emperor treated the British demands as if they came from a small tribe in Inner Asia, and solved the dilemmas of protocol and ritual by acting out that pretense. He received the Macartney embassy in a grand imperial tent in Inner Mongolia, as if receiving barbarians who could not be expected to comply with the elaborate forms appropriate to the still grander court in Beijing. Yet he undoubtedly could see that Great Britain presented him with an entirely different scale of challenge. He apparently did not have the will or the intellectual energy at that late moment in his life to do more than fall back on traditional attitudes and formalities in the hope of dismissing an intractable problem. But in fact, his weak maneuvering gained very little time for his dynasty and his state; troubles would plague his son's reign (1796–1820) and would become crises soon thereafter. The Qing state's vulnerability would be made obvious both to its domestic and to its foreign enemies. Great Britain would be the leader among Western nations that sought to humble China.

During the second half of the eighteenth century, Great Britain became the world's dominant imperial power, outpacing the earlier mercantile empires of Portugal, Spain, and the Netherlands, and repeatedly defeating its strongest foe, France. In Europe, in North America, and in India, Britain decisively overcame the French and their allies, principally Spain. The Seven Years' War in Europe was settled in 1762, fully acknowledging the victory of Britain over the French. In the following year, after a succession of victories over the French in North America, the British were victorious in the French and Indian War, forcing the French to cede Canada to them. In Asia, the decisive defeat of the French by Robert Clive of the East India Company, at Plassey near Calcutta in 1757, gave the Company control over all of northeast India, where the rich states of Bengal and Bihar supported lucrative trade and also promised access to Tibet. In the 1780s and 1790s, the Company, acting for the British government, sought, though unsuccessfully, to penetrate the China market by way of Tibet.[11]

Britain's loss of the American colonies in 1781 (formally acknowledged in the peace of 1783) turned British imperial ambitions from North America to Asia, where India absorbed the bulk of attention. The privately owned East India Company underwent a transformation; it retained its monopoly on trade for another half-century, but from the 1780s onward it was transformed into a colonial government responsible to Parliament, its leaders appointed by the throne. The colonial government of India thus displaced the East India Company in the political sphere, but continued to work closely with it in economic and trade matters. The Company, for example, established its complete monopoly of all aspects of opium plantation, production, and export in 1763, and soon thereafter licensed only non-Company ships to carry opium to China. Publicly it disavowed its connections with the trade, complying superficially with the British-Indian government's policy of respecting the Chinese government's prohibition on the import of opium. In fact, the Company became the world's largest smuggler of opium, the profits from the China opium trade in particular being essential to the fiscal stability of the entire British enterprise in India. Such were the complexities of the new international relations as the European powers extended their spheres of interest to the borders of China.

In East Asia, the British and their traditional allies the Portuguese began to establish the patterns for the growing European presence at the edges of China. Britain framed the diplomatic demands intended to protect its own trade, and incidentally all the European and American trade, throughout the region. Britain brought the threat of military force onto the scene. Under British cover, all the ambitious trading interests in Europe and America were poised to intrude into the arena of Chinese tribute system relations among the Asian states. That old pattern of relations was, to be sure, already anomalous; under the intrusive new pressures it would quickly become obsolete, forcing the Chinese to meet the exigencies of living under a new international order alien to all their values and hostile to all their expectations.

None of those developments had yet broken the surface of Chinese calm when the old emperor died in 1799. That calm was deceptive. For half a century, conditions had been forming that would quickly lead into a long age of turmoil. China's cultural resiliency would be tested to the fullest measure. Its people's sense of China's place in the world would be transformed. The ancient and long-evolving civilization would absorb much of the world's culture, while finding within itself the means to become a modern nation among nations.

VI. AN OLD CIVILIZATION IN A NEW WORLD

The foregoing sections of this chapter have described the early phases in the process of China's interaction with the western European powers that had made their presence felt in East Asia beginning in the sixteenth century. These brief concluding remarks allude to the larger trends of change, and take special note of that Western presence which, as an underlying and steadily intensifying condition, was becoming a major element affecting the course of China's late imperial history.

The Western mercantile empires were invaders, pushing vigorously into East Asia following the arrival of the Portuguese in Canton in 1517 and the de facto cession of Macao to them in the 1540s. In their motives and their methods they were strikingly different from the Inner Asian invaders of earlier history; their inroads nonetheless would prove to have more profoundly transforming consequences for China, and all its Asian neighbors, than had all the past incursions of any nearer neighbors. The European impact took many forms, military, political, and cultural. Matteo Ricci, who was in China from 1583 until his death in Beijing in 1610, founded what would function as the most significant vehicle of Sino-European cultural interchange in the century or more thereafter. His company of extraordinary Jesuit intellectuals attempted nothing less than "guided cultural change," an effort that continued well into the eighteenth century. In their own minds, those and subsequent religious and educational agents of change in late imperial China also had secular goals, typically expressed in terms of enfolding East Asian civilizations into the patterns of "universal" cultural and political relations among peoples. While often meant sincerely, such statements were parochial and misleading, and with some it was a disingenuous characterization. "Universal" in such minds meant simply "European," or "Christian," or "Western," all terms we now see as having less than universal scope. At the time, those Europeans often appeared to the Chinese to be making an unwarranted challenge to Chinese definitions of "universal." In fact, the concepts of what constitute universal features of present-day civilizations continue to undergo debate and redefinition.

An interesting aspect of that pre-1800 phase of cultural guidance carried on in China by Westerners is that it closely paralleled, in underlying conception and methods, the efforts made through the ages by the Chinese to transform peoples on their borders. In the Chinese case, "universal" meant simply what today we call "Chinese," but the Chinese too used highly analogous defenses of their acculturation policies, expressed parochially, misleadingly, or disingenuously. Throughout history, the Chinese were more successful in their efforts than were those early Western missionaries; other elements favored them (for example, the Chinese and their southern neighbors were less strange to one another), and the Chinese were an overwhelming neighbor with whom it was often advantageous to achieve accord, especially for the smaller polities on China's borders. The Europeans did not acquire over-whelming advantages in their contests with the Chinese until a century or more later. Eventually the idea of Westernizing or modernizing change had acquired an appeal to a growing segment of Chinese society, apart from any elements of coercion. The eventual broad-scale acceptance of Western values in nineteenth- and twentieth-century China was less coercive than the pro-cesses of cultural change enforced upon the Vietnamese by French colonial policies, the circumstances in the Netherlands East Indies under Dutch man-agement, or Taiwan and Korea under Japanese military occupation.[12]

Chinese adaptation to the Western presence was to be a long process, one that is still under way. But by the end of the eighteenth century the character of that process was beginning to be perceived in China. Even though it was a slowly developing process, one can use the hindsight of history here in offer-ing observations on the larger patterns of cultural change during these later centuries when the Western presence constantly grew in size and significance.

For several centuries the Europeans infiltrated gradually into East Asia. Their methods would change, eventually (in the nineteenth century) to the use of military force to gain some limited objectives, such as forcing China to observe international law and diplomatic conventions, and gaining access to trade, to residence within China, and to freedom of movement for their businessmen and missionaries. Those representatives of the Western powers within China became deeply involved with Chinese society in many places and on many levels of interaction. The tides from the West were to become a tidal wave of powerful impact.

The Chinese have long used phrases such as *neiyou waihuan* (disorders within and disasters from without) to describe the way domestic weaknesses and foreign incursions could double up, each gaining strength from the dis-traction caused by the other, to bring about national calamity.[13] For more than 2,000 years, the "disasters from without" always referred to the incur-sions from across the northern land frontiers, the last major one having been the Manchu conquest in 1644. After 1800, however, "disaster from without" came to signify invasion from the maritime frontier, at first by the Western powers, then subsequently also from Japan. The identification of the source of national peril thus was transformed, to become a leading element in Chi-na's rapidly changing recent national consciousness. That, however, remained a latent problem in the late eighteenth century, and one that lies beyond the scope of this volume.

Here the focus is on the past, especially on the preeminence of the political system in that traditional civilization, on the social base as defined by its fam-ily system, and on the consequences of the open society for the way its people conducted their lives. In reflecting on the importance that the Chinese tradi-tionally assigned to governing, one must nonetheless look critically at China's political heritage: What were its strengths and weaknesses? How did China's compare with governments elsewhere in the world in the tenth century, when this history begins, and again in the eighteenth century, when it concludes? In what ways did the importance attached to governing as the high calling in human society carry over into the ways the Chinese faced their difficulties in the two centuries after 1800?

That political history reveals many things about the character of Chinese society beyond the scope of governing per se. It could not do otherwise because the Chinese imperial institution, and the succession of governments formed around it, could function only by drawing to the full on the human and cultural resources of the society it governed. This is fully evident in the period of native Chinese rule. Yet we also see, if differently, the "Chineseness of China"[14] when it was governed under the alien imperial regimes of the conquest dynasties.

Important features of Chinese society have thus been drawn into the foregoing reflections on Chinese government; governing inevitably reflected both the structure and the ruling norms of the society at large. The authority patterns in family and lineage organization were fully recognized by the state, for example, and insofar as practicable, ideal family norms were coopted by the state, as in the analogizing apparent in the formula "Good sons will be loyal servitors." That was readily extended to mean that good parents will teach their sons to be loyal servitors. Further, parents will exercise their unchallenged family authority to ensure that in their localities, the state's interests too will have moral weight, even though the tension between family and state could not be wholly resolved in the state's favor. Many ancient Confucian ethical precepts remained strong. One example is that of the good son who proudly shields his lawbreaking father from the state's punitive justice.[15] Ambiguities abounded. In imperial times the state's priorities never displaced those of family, and in fact the emperors and their policy advisers sought to gain by association with them rather than to undermine the state's principal competitor for authority over individual lives. That policy would not be radically changed until the latter half of the twentieth century.[16]

The distinctive patterns of Chinese society were well established in early imperial times. The slowly renovating changes that characterize the nine centuries with which this volume is concerned should not be taken to imply social stagnation. For one striking example of the capacity for growth, one need point only to the gradual flowering of bureaucratic society, the shift to a merit-based recruitment system, and the dominance of what has been referred to as scholar-official elite society. Those profound innovations marked a significant change from Tang and earlier times to the "new culture" of the Song period.

It has been pointed out that in traditional societies "far-reaching change in general was not expected, was not a part of the ideals of the members . . . and was in retrospect generally viewed as the result of improper functioning." That attitude is in sharp contrast with the expectations of most people in modernized societies, in which deep change "is expected, preferred, and regarded as the sign par excellence of [society's] proper functioning." That draws attention to a significant contrast between most traditional and most modernized societies. Yet there are also significant differences among traditional societies: the same author points out that China's unmatched continuity of social forms was possible because the society had "renovating structures of social change."[17] The distinctive process by which this society continuously renovated its institutions, rather than allowing them to stagnate and spawn irreconcilable conflicts, was many-sided and is difficult to describe briefly. One can observe, however, that self-renovating change was constant and gradual, not sudden and disruptive, and was always justified by reference to past models. Chinese society looked backward in order to move steadily if slowly forward, overcame institutional lag from time to time in the name of recovering antique values, obviated the need for explosive adaptations, and comfortingly convinced itself that it was virtually unchanging, while in fact it was growing with the times. Some of the best observers in the past were acutely aware of cumulative social change, and could accept it as historical reality,[18] but they were not for that reason ready to forgo the useful ideal of a golden age in the past. This presents the fascinating enigma of archaism serving the cause of renovating change; moreover, that pace of social change appeared to be sufficient to China's needs until very late in the imperial era. Eventually the attitude of complacency it fostered would be denounced by impatient modernizers and revolutionaries because it made rapid "revolutionary" change difficult to achieve. Social explosion, deferred through the centuries, would (they hoped) at last become inevitable under modern conditions.

Although we must leave China's experience in the nineteenth and twentieth centuries to be told elsewhere, it may be useful to be reminded here of some of those defining features of the old society that appear to contribute the most to our understanding of China's problems in adapting to a changing world.

Among behavior patterns common to the entire society, an outstanding source of strength to the people and to their nation was, and remains, their work ethic. Climate, topography, and the conditions of agriculture varied greatly throughout China's vast reaches, but nowhere within the country was life easy. For the vast majority, one had to work to survive, and to prosper required a combination of fortunate circumstances and the joint efforts of the entire family and clan. It was the common Chinese perception that individuals did not succeed; families with the support of their clans or lineages could. China's ordinary people were socialized to work diligently within kinship-defined groups, as well as within community contexts, to accomplish all manner of labor and productive enterprise, to be frugal and to save, and to invest their hard-earned resources for the betterment of succeeding generations. There was to be sure an expectation that the larger community of the village, the town, or the county would try to supply emergency assistance supports in times of greatest need, as in famines, floods, or epidemics. Social welfare responsibilities were recognized in government action to maintain emergency granaries and to provide disaster relief. But such philanthropic activities also were often carried out by nongovernmental agencies formed in local society to sponsor orphanages, burial associations, clinics, and free pharmacies, and to provide disaster relief.

In most situations, however, human ingenuity and human exertion were expected to ensure survival, and to make better futures possible. The earliest European observers in sixteenth- and seventeenth-century China all remarked on the industrious, cheerful, and relatively "prosperous" Chinese common people—relative, that is, to their counterparts among the common people of Europe at that time. In those same centuries and thereafter, as Chinese began to form settlements in several countries of Southeast Asia, the poor Chinese who came as laborers or petty merchants often prospered within a generation, and were looked upon with envy and even with resentment as being harder-working and more successful than the native peoples. Those overseas Chinese settlers customarily organized self-governing associations, set up schools, assumed community welfare duties, and often extended their social services to the host societies as well. They brought those social values with them and enlarged them to meet the circumstances of their new environments. Their work ethic, inculcated within the family and drawing impetus from the family-centered religion, was the outstanding feature of Chinese society in China, and was readily exported with those Chinese who settled abroad.

Because it was an open society, so was it an "achieving society," in which the rewards for achievement were open to all. The Chinese farmer who worked hard did not have to settle with the prospect of forever being at best a "rich peasant." I have argued throughout that Chinese farmers were not "peasants" in the Western historical sense that the word implies, and their achievement goals were not restricted by impenetrable class boundaries. Most families could at least imagine a long-range economic success whereby, over several generations, an able son might acquire enough education to sit for the civil service examinations, and perhaps become a member of the social elite in that way. Through practicable small steps of upward progress, ordinary people were encouraged to work for long-range goals, thus keeping meaningful the ideal of the achieving society. In the West we encounter this social phenomenon most commonly in recent centuries, in the societies of frontier regions such as North America, and subsequently in modernized societies where old social structures have been weakened. Traditional China is very unusual, probably unique, in having had two millennia of experience with an increasingly open social structure and social ethos.

Women in that traditional society, as generally true of past societies, were notably subordinate to males. Inhumane practices, especially that of foot-binding, are difficult to explain. It became common in the ninth or tenth century and persisted until early in the twentieth, and thus is a feature of Chinese society in the centuries corresponding with the time frame of this volume. We cannot satisfactorily explain why the practice came about, why it became widespread throughout society, and why it persisted for so long a time. Footbinding usually is looked upon as having degraded women, but evidence from the people who constituted that society shows that it was considered by them to bestow esteem on its victims, who were the young girls being prepared for adulthood by their mothers, aunts, and grandmothers. Its crippling impact on its victims has often been overstated: footbinding did not "immobilize" women, keeping them helpless captives of the inner quarters, as is sometimes said, but it certainly caused years of pain to the growing child, and in varying degrees it restricted some kinds of activity for the remainder of the woman's life.

What does the seemingly nonrational practice of footbinding tell us about the status of women in traditional Chinese society? The range of current interpretations is vast. Other aspects of women's lives may reveal more. It has been shown that, in the movement to strengthen family organization, women of elite statuses were made more subservient to their husbands' families in post-Song times than they had previously been. In the centuries when Neo-Confucian Lixue (the "rationalist" mainstream of Neo-Confucian thought and learning) was dominant, women tended to lose their rights to control their dowries, to own and manage property, to remarry after the loss of husband or fiancé, and to make other essential decisions concerning their own lives. Yet at the same time, exceptions to those limiting conditions are too numerous to be ignored: examples of women at all levels of society who controlled their husbands and their husbands' families through management of property, dominance of their sons, or sheer force of character displayed in other ways are standard features of entertainment literature from those same centuries. What was the social reality? The specialized (and sometimes isolating) focus on women in Chinese history is a relatively new field. It is now producing substantial scholarly descriptions and interpretations of China's social practices and personal relationships through the later imperial dynasties. We can expect it to contribute still more to important reconsiderations of social history.

Religious beliefs and practices were omnipresent in traditional Chinese society, yet, as frequently noted in the foregoing chapters, religion was "diffuse"[19] throughout society, while remaining weakly organized. None of the indigenous or long-naturalized religions had centralized institutions with governing authority over their religious professionals, much less over the practicing believers. For reasons I have noted, religions as such thus could not gain strong political influence, although individual religious leaders could find opportunities to establish personal relations with emperors or governors. The powers they gained in those situations were always briefly held and widely denounced.

While Buddhism and religious Daoism touched virtually all Chinese lives, they remained secondary to the family religion which venerated ancestors, and which validated authority relationships among all members of the family and lineage. The religious practices marking births, marriages, deaths, and burials, central to all Chinese family life, varied greatly in their forms and ritual details by region and by social status, but during the nine centuries of the later empire dealt with in this volume, great strides were made by the scholar-official elite to standardize these practices, and to strengthen family organization. In some regions of China, more in the South than in the North, family organizations became corporate property owners and could attain significant economic powers. The varieties of organized family existence are innumerable, but the core beliefs were generally adhered to.

The Chinese population was 80 or 90 percent rural through the later imperial centuries, and most of the rural population lived principally by farming. Private ownership of the land was the norm, albeit a fluid one, and one that varied from region to region. The spectrum of economic statuses among rural farming people was wide, encompassing the range from poor hired or indentured laborers to rich farmers whose lives might imitate those of prosperous businessmen (and who often had connections with business activities) or who imitated the lifestyles of the scholar gentry. The economic status of the members constituting any clan or lineage ordinarily ranged from high to low, so that some people of poor to moderate means had richer relatives, and all rich people had poorer relatives. Those in the higher economic statuses were never sure that they could retain their wealth, and those at the bottom were likely to be buffeted by changing fortunes, moving in and out of landownership within short periods of time, while aiming, of course, to become securely established landowning farmers. Many farmers owned some of their land and rented more; some who farmed their own land or worked on additional land they rented also worked as hired laborers some of the time. Many households had subsidiary occupations, such as raising silkworms or reeling and spinning silk, weaving cotton and other textiles, processing food items for the market, or producing other goods to sell. Rural social life was marked above all by fluidity and variety throughout all its economic strata.

Generalizations about the economic well-being of Chinese society are difficult to formulate. That is reason to avoid simplistic status categorizations that imply a social analysis such as the frequently encountered phrase "the Chinese peasantry," or "the Chinese gentry." Even the latter, misleading but perhaps unavoidable, must be analyzed in all its complexity to become useful. Most studies of economic life in traditional Chinese society are based on nineteenth-century or later data, and may overgeneralize about social and economic conditions from that narrow base.

To attempt, then, only the most cautious characterizations of economic conditions in traditional Chinese society, it appears justified to describe the society from mid-Ming to mid-Qing times as generally orderly and prosperous. That poses difficulties in view of the prevalent disorder evident throughout much of the succeeding nineteenth and twentieth centuries, and the dislocation and instability that accompanied widespread human suffering at that time. One must conclude that the breakdowns that soon followed the death of the Qianlong emperor in 1799 had roots in problems already present in mid-Qing society. In earlier chapters, certain of those problems have been noted: a narrowing margin in agricultural productivity caused in part by steadily increasing (but not explosive) pressure of population on the land; a growing failure of local governing induced in large part by the cynicism with which the Qing dynastic regime was viewed, and the weakening of normative influences linked to it; fundamental changes in China's relations with the outside world brought about by the Western presence in East Asia; and the challenge of foreign industrial technology, which lowered China's capacity to compete. These were potentially serious problems, yet none of them had reached crisis proportions by the end of the eighteenth century. The society, as viewed from the landmark of our Western calendar year 1800, gave reassuring evidence of being socially stable, economically productive, and culturally self-confident. Those would continue to be the essential characteristics of the old social order, even as it became ever more closely drawn into a new international setting and was forced to make painful efforts to survive. Indeed, we may conclude that its resilient social structure, its capacity for economic productivity, and its strong sense of cultural identity are what have guaranteed China's national survival into the present time.

Generalizations about the economic well-being of the ordinary Chinese people inevitably bear on the personal freedoms, the "human rights" of the Chinese. Most of the choices which people make are to be sure in some measure limited or made difficult by the lack of means to carry them out. Despite that obvious fact, it is safe to say that the ordinary Chinese of late imperial times enjoyed more personal freedom to make their basic life choices than have Chinese in very recent times. People could move about, change their livelihoods, live where their choices directed, associate with whom them wished, have children, marry, go abroad or to another province, become city dwellers if they could manage the means, and above all think as they chose, even read and write more or less as they wished.

While it belongs to another volume, the story of China's adoption of Leninist one-party rule in the 1920s, and reimposing that system with the power to implement it in the 1950s, has marked the greatest change, one brought about by culturally intrusive elements not derived from the old society but in fundamental conflict with it. From the year 1950 onward, China suffered the most profound loss of human freedoms, and little if any improvement in the economic aspects of people's lives until the last decade or two of the twentieth century. This is not understood by most residents of China today because the memory of the recent past has been obscured. It usually is not stated, and is perhaps usually not understood by non-Chinese writing about contemporary issues in Chinese life, because they often do not know Chinese history. Most of both categories of present-day experts on China—native and foreign—appear to believe that the depth of general poverty was so severe in "the old China" (before 1950) that talk of individual choices and human freedoms is rendered irrelevant. That is simply untrue. It does not match the contemporary descriptions of Ming and Qing society, nor is it supported by my own observations in the mid- and late 1940s, nor by those of many others in the nineteenth and twentieth centuries. Still less is that view in any sense true of China before 1800. China was both more generally prosperous (especially in the rural areas of most provinces) and freer than it has been since 1950.

Throughout the present volume the reader has been reminded that the high culture, as manifested especially in literature, philosophy, scholarship, and the fine arts, produced in immense quantity what many historians consider to be the true measure of Chinese civilization.

I too regard that heritage as China's timeless achievement. It provides the venues for our most rewarding encounters with China's past. It can speak directly to us today in ways that transcend the cultural differences between our modern civilization and those past millennia of China's continuous existence. One does not need to know any of the details of history to comprehend the profound identification with nature conveyed in masterworks of Chinese landscape painting, or to sense the humanism of its poetry and philosophy.

Such encounters can indeed transcend the particularities of history, yet the transcendent monuments of that high culture are nevertheless part of history. Some knowledge of the historical circumstances in which they were created can further enhance their capacity to move and instruct us. The earnest commitment of China's thinkers and scholars through the centuries, the creative force of its painters, calligraphers, and poets, the nuanced lives of its cultivated men and women—these rewarding dimensions of China's civilization are best understood in the setting of its social and political history. The present work attempts to provide a way to understand that setting.

This work, however, cannot attempt to include more than occasional references to the monuments of the high culture. The arts of China—painting, calligraphy, sculpture, ceramics, architecture, and what are sometimes called the decorative arts—can be adequately presented only in extensive historical and critical works that include a great quantity of high-quality reproductions. Literary masterworks have been extensively translated, often very well translated, as have been the crowning works of philosophy and some major works of historiography. It is not difficult to pursue one's further interests in those things through many specialized publications, apart from the narrower exploration of history that occupies this already large volume.

When we look back from the deeply transformed world of today to China before 1800, the question about that long and rich cultural history that we shall consider here is: What meaning do these aspects of the Chinese people's historical experience have for the life of China today? What part has the high cultural achievement of the past played in the transformation of a modernizing China? To be more specific than simply stating that China in 1800 remained "culturally self-confident," how was the high culture of the elite shared throughout the larger society, and how did it function in the lives of all the people?

When I commenced the serious study of China's civilization in China more than fifty years ago, my Chinese teachers and fellow students all perceived the past as alive in the culture of the present. Both the learned Chinese and the ordinary people, who lived in intimate conjunction with all the reminders of China's past life, thought of that past as continuous with the present. They were the latest—perhaps almost the last—living bearers of a tradition that resonated in their social attitudes and values, in their daily language, in the allusions by which people expressed themselves, in the images and the attitudes that were shared in all facets of their daily lives. When they wrote school examinations, they wrote in the language learned from studying the texts of Confucius and Mencius, and they had read many of the finest writings of the subsequent 2,000 years. They had read and remembered the Tang and Song poets, whose metaphors, along with images they all knew from reading the historical and romantic fiction of the Ming and Qing periods, colored their perceptions of the people and events all around them. Their newspapers were written in a style that combined past literary models with more recent forms of expression. They celebrated all the holidays of the old solar-lunar calendar, which they called the "farmer's calendar," and they followed, if often in pared-down forms, many of the ritual observances of the past. In short, tradition functioned in innumerable ways in the lives of all people at all levels of society. Their dress reinforced the traditional social patterns, and their speech retained the courtesies of deference and place. People knew who they were; their behavior, even when rebellious, reflected expected patterns. The still widely shared high culture exerted a powerful normative influence on the entire population up to the middle of the twentieth century, for it was still alive in their minds.

I am not sure to what extent that is still so today. How many Chinese still command, even indirectly (as did even the illiterate and the poorly educated of the past), enough basic knowledge to reflect the widely shared old culture in their lives, their manners, their values and attitudes? Among those educated since 1950, there is ever less evidence that it survives. The corpus of literary, historical, and artistic works from the past is of course still extant, and Chinese may again turn to it in large numbers as essential elements of their general education. But it is no longer widely internalized and shared, in differing ways, among all the educated, much less among the people at large. No longer alive in their consciousness, that immense body of cultural knowledge can no longer refine their lives. Yet, neither can we yet pronounce it dead.

Well into the twentieth century, China could and in fact did continuously experience meaningful renovation through gradual change, within the framework of the old culture. But a time came in midcentury when radical change was forcibly and destructively implemented. The nation could perhaps *not* experience profound social restructuring and rapid change without abandoning, even destroying, many aspects of the old social order and its defining cultural values. That is what has now happened.

China's history through the two centuries since 1800 can be analyzed in many ways, for different purposes, but it cannot be told apart from the story of how China's traditional social patterns and values, under the unifying and guiding influence of its high culture, responded to the changing demands and newly defined interests of the Chinese people as a whole. In the latter half of the twentieth century, that guiding influence was finally overturned and superseded, to the extent that a thoroughgoing revolutionary practice could bring that about. How far and how permanently it has succeeded is not yet clear, but that there has been a restructuring of the social base and a break with many cultural elements of the old society is not in doubt. China has been forced to experience a genuine revolution.

What this signifies for the future of the world's oldest living civilization is also not yet clear. Profound cultural change can imply both loss and gain. A new Chinese culture is rapidly taking shape. Nostalgia for the past, a feeling mostly confined to the older generations whether in China or on the outside, tends to focus on the cultural loss. China has passed through a watershed; the reality of change, and of immense cultural loss, is undeniable. Yet there also will be gains in that transformation. At the same time, one must not too hastily conclude that the losses are as complete as those who are nostalgic for some aspects of the cultural past may fear. Whatever forms and qualities may come to mark the new era of Chinese civilization's development, we can be sure that China's future cannot develop apart from its past. Nor can our observations and assessments of China's contemporary development achieve credibility without an understanding of the civilization's long history.

APPENDIX
Conversion Table
Pinyin to Wade-Giles

a–ah	chang–ch'ang	di–ti	gao–kao
ai–ai	chao–ch'ao	dian–tien	ge–ko
an–an	che–ch'e	diao–tiao	gei–kei
ang–ang	chen–ch'en	die–tieh	gen–ken
ao–ao	cheng–ch'eng	ding–ting	geng–keng
	chi–ch'ih	diu–tiu	gong–kung
ba–pa	chong–ch'ung	dong–tung	gou–kou
bai–pai	chou–ch'ou	dou–tou	gu–ku
ban–pan	chu–ch'u	du–tu	gua–kua
bang–pang	chuai–ch'uai	duan–tuan	guai–kuai
bao–pao	chuan–ch'uan	dui–tui	guan–kuan
bei–pei	chuang–ch'uang	dun–tun	guang–kuang
ben–pen	chui–ch'ui	duo–to	gui–kuei
beng–peng	chun–ch'un		gun–kun
bi–pi	chuo–ch'o	e–eh	guo–kuo
bian–pien	ci–tz'u	ei–ei	
biao–piao	cong–ts'ung	en–en	ha–ha
bie–pieh	cou–ts'ou	eng–eng	hai–hai
bin–pin	cu–ts'u	er–erh	han–han
bo–po	cuan–ts'uan		hang–hang
bu–pu	cui–ts'ui	fa–fa	hao–hao
	cun–ts'un	fan–fan	he–ho
ca–ts'a	cuo–ts'o	fang–fang	hei–hei
cai–ts'ai		fei–fei	hen–hen
can–ts'an	da–ta	feng–feng	heng–heng
cang–ts'ang	dai–tai	fo–fo	hong–hung
cao–ts'ao	dan–tan	fou–fou	hou–hou
ce–ts'e	dang–tang	fu–fu	hu–hu
cen–ts'en	dao–tao		hua–hua
ceng–ts'eng	de–teh	ga–ka	huai–huai
cha–ch'a	dei–tei	gai–kai	huan–huan
chai–ch'ai	den–tuen	gan–kan	huang–huang
chan–ch'an	deng–teng	gang–kang	hui–hui

hun–hun	lie–lieh	nu–nu	rou–jou
huo–huo	lin–lin	nü–nü	ru–ju
	ling–ling	nuan–nuan	ruan–juan
ji–chi	liu–liu	nun–nuen	rui–jui
jia–chia	long–lung	nüe–nüeh	run–jun
jian–chien	lou–lou	nuo–no	ruo–jo
jiang–chiang	lu–lu		
jiao–chiao	lü–lü	ou–ou	sa–sa
jie–chieh	luan–luan		sai–sai
jin–chin	lüe–lüeh	pa–p'a	san–san
jing–ching	lun–lun	pai–p'ai	sang–sang
jiong–chiung	luo–lo	pan–p'an	sao–sao
jiu–chiu		pang–p'ang	se–seh
ju–chü		pao–p'ao	sen–sen
juan–chüan	ma–ma	pei–p'ei	seng–seng
jue–chüeh	mai–mai	pen–p'en	sha–sha
jun–chün	man–man	peng–p'eng	shai–shai
	mang–mang	pi–p'i	shan–shan
ka–k'a	mao–mao	pian–p'ien	shang–shang
kai–k'ai	mei–mei	piao–p'iao	shao–shao
kan–k'an	men–men	pie–p'ieh	she–sheh
kang–k'ang	meng–meng	pin–p'in	shei–shei
kao–k'ao	mi–mi	ping–p'ing	shen–shen
ke–k'e	mian–mien	po–p'o	sheng–sheng
ken–k'en	miao–miao	pou–p'ou	shi–shih
keng–k'eng	mie–mieh	pu–p'u	shou–shou
kong–k'ung	min–min		shu–shu
kou–k'ou	ming–ming	qi–ch'i	shua–shua
ku–k'u	miu–miu	qia–ch'ia	shuai–shuai
kua–k'ua	mo–moh	qian–ch'ien	shuan–shuan
kuai–k'uai	mou–mou	qiang–ch'iang	shuang–shuang
kuan–k'uan	mu–mu	qiao–ch'iao	shui–shui
kuang–k'uang		qie–ch'ieh	shun–shun
kui–k'uei	na–na	qin–ch'in	shuo–shuo
kun–k'un	nai–nai	qing–ch'ing	si–ssu
kuo–k'uo	nan–nan	qiong–ch'iung	song–sung
	nang–nang	qiu–ch'iu	sou–sou
la–la	nao–nao	qu–ch'ü	su–su
lai–lai	ne–ne	quan–ch'üan	suan–suan
lan–lan	nei–nei	que–ch'üeh	sui–sui
lang–lang	nen–nen	qun–ch'ün	sun–sun
lao–lao	neng–neng		suo–so
le–le (lo)	ni–ni	ran–jan	
lei–lei	nian–nien	rang–jang	ta–t'a
leng–leng	niang–niang	rao–jao	tai–t'ai
li–li	niao–niao	re–jeh	tan–t'an
lia–lia	nie–nieh	ren–jen	tang–t'ang
lian–lien	nin–nin	reng–jeng	tao–t'ao
liang–liang	ning–ning	ri–jih	te–teh
liao–liao	niu–niu	rong–jung	teng–t'eng
	nong–nung		

ti–t'i	xi–hsi	ying–ying	zhe–che
tian–t'ien	xia–hsia	yong–yung	zhen–chen
tiao–t'iao	xian–hsien	you–yu	zheng–cheng
tie–t'ieh	xiang–hsiang	yu–yü	zhi–chih
ting–t'ing	xiao–hsiao	yuan–yuan (yüan)	zhong–chung
tong–t'ung	xie–hsieh	yue–yüeh	zhou–chou
tou–t'ou	xin–hsin	yun–yun (yün)	zhu–chu
tu–t'u	xing–hsing		zhua–chua
tuan–t'uan	xiong–hsiung	za–tsa	zhuai–chuai
tui–t'ui	xiu–hsiu	zai–tsai	zhuan–chuan
tun–t'un	xu–hsü	zan–tsan	zhuang–chuang
tuo–t'o	xuan–hsüan	zang–tsang	zhui–chui
	xue–hsüeh	zao–tsao	zhun–chun
wa–wa	xun–hsün	ze–tse	zhuo–chuo
wai–wai		zei–tsei	zi–tzu
wan–wan		zen–tsen	zong–tsung
wang–wang	ya–ya	zeng–tseng	zou–tsou
wei–wei	yan–yen	zha–cha	zu–tsu
wen–wen	yang–yang	zhai–chai	zuan–tsuan
weng–weng	yao–yao	zhan–chan	zui–tsui
wo–wo	ye–yeh	zhang–chang	zun–tsun
wu–wu	yi–i (yi)	zhao–chao	zuo–tso
	yin–yin		

NOTES

1. The Five Dynasties

1. These include Han Yu (768–824), Li Ao (d. 844), and a few like-minded contemporaries.

2. Throughout this work, "nation" is used in the traditional sense of a distinct race or people, characterized by common descent, language, or history, not in the sense of the modern nation-state. "State," by contrast, is used to refer to the polity, the political order. The boundaries of the two did not necessarily coincide.

3. Some histories list twelve states, nine of which were in Central and South China. Those are listed and discussed in Section IV of this chapter.

4. He was Xue Juzheng (912–981), whose dates show that he was born under the first of the Five Dynasties and lived through the other four, to take service under the Song founder after 960. He received his *jinshi* examination degree under the Later Tang, then held office under the remaining three of the Five Dynasties.

5. Detailed maps of all the dynasties and states can be found in Tan Qixiang's "Chinese Historical Atlas" (1991, 5:82–93), on which the maps included here are based. For a useful brief history of the period, see Tao Maobing 1985.

6. See essay by Robert Somers in CHC 3:773–787; Tao Maobing 1985, pp. 19–68.

7. See Schafer 1954b.

8. See Worthy 1983; Li Dong-hua 1993.

9. See Schafer 1954a.

10. This process is described in Ma Changshou 1962, pp. 41–68. Some traditional sources oversimplify the facts in stating that the Tang court bestowed the name "Nanzhao" and gave its ruler the title "King of Nanzhao" in 738. It was entirely independent of China throughout its history, until its collapse in the first decades of the tenth century. In 937 (some accounts say 944) it was succeeded by the independent kingdom of Dali, which survived until it was conquered by the future Khubilai Khan in 1253–54.

11. See the discussion of the Sui-Tang canal transport system in Twitchett 1970, pp. 84–96.

12. Aspects of the land and sea trade have been examined in relation to the wealthy Wu-Yue state, probably the richest of the Ten Kingdoms, in Li Donghua 1993.

13. Interstate diplomacy gave the state of Wu-Yue the opportunity to use its wealth to obtain security and political recognition; see Worthy 1983.

14. This view draws on the authoritative analysis of the period in Wang Gungwu 1963.

15. This argument draws on the analysis of David Johnson 1977. His views have been widely corroborated in more recent scholarship. The Tang elite is often described as an "aristocracy"; that is technically incorrect in that their privileged status, even though it might be perpetuated through many generations, lacked all legal foundation in the open society of Tang China. But the word "aristocratic" accurately conveys, by analogy to European feudal and post-feudal aristocracies, the tone of their lives and their social attitudes; it can be compared with the loose use of the word in describing elite strata in American society.

16. Tsien Tsuen-hsuin 1985, p. 156. Starting a decade later, another set of the Confucian classics was produced at the court of the Later Shu in Chengdu, intended by its sponsor to be sold inexpensively to poor scholars.

17. See Wang Gungwu 1962, pp. 123–145.

18. Kang-i Sun Chang 1980, pp. 63–106.

19. Among the most eminent of these painters were Dong Yuan (ca. 900–962), the monk painter Juran (fl. ca. 960–985), Gu Hongzhong (fl. 943–960), Zhou Wenju (fl. 961–975), Li Cheng (919–967), and Dong Yu (fl. 960–990), all of whom were active at the Southern Tang court at Nanjing, and many of whom later became prominent under the Song.

20. The form "Transoxania" is also used.

21. See Sinor 1990, esp. chap. 1, "Introduction: The Concept of Inner Asia" by Denis Sinor, and chap. 2, "The Geographic Setting," by Robert Taaffe; in both of those chapters, however, a larger, somewhat looser geographic definition of Inner Asia is adopted.

22. The precise figures are difficult to determine, as they vary from one reference source to another, for a variety of reasons. For example, the Republic of China regards the Republic of Mongolia (former Outer Mongolia), with its 450,000 square miles of territory, as an integral part of China; the People's Republic of China now makes no claim to that territory. Another factor is that the PRC has extended the boundaries of provinces bordering on the former boundary of Inner Mongolia northward into that region, enlarging "China Proper" at the expense of the former Inner Asian region. Officially, the area of China as reported by the government in Beijing is 3,706,564 square miles, or 9,600,000 square kilometers. By comparison, the area of the fifty United States is 3,615,123 square miles, and that of Canada is 3,851,809 square miles.

23. Today the Mongols of Inner Mongolia in China and those of the Mongolian Republic (Outer Mongolia) taken together number fewer than 5 million, of whom slightly more than half are in China.

24. See Vainshtein 1989a and Murphey 1989.

25. See Vainshtein 1989b and scholarly writings cited there. This exhibition catalog contains superb photographs of archaeological and ethnographic significance.

2. ABAOJI

1. *Liao History* 1344 (1974), p. 1. "Nine *chi*," by Tang period standards, was more than eight feet tall; we may take that as a metaphor for "very tall."

2. The term "psychic mobility" is used by Daniel Lerner (1958) to mean "the capacity for vicarious experience."

3. In the second half of the twentieth century, the Chinese government extended the

so-called Inner Mongolian Autonomous Region to the east of the Khingan Range, well into Dongbei, the "Northeast," or Manchuria.

4. Li Keyong's place in late Tang and Five Dynasties history is discussed in Chapter 1.

5. Yao Congwu 1959, pp. 193–216.

6. Wittfogel and Feng Chia-sheng 1946, pp. 428–504.

7. *Juan* 64, pp. 968–969; cited in Yang Shushen 1984, p. 291.

8. For an analysis of the nature of the Khitan scripts, see Kane 1989, chaps. 1 and 2.

9. The Khitan small script, nonetheless, was widely known among Khitans, later among Jurchens, and perhaps among other peoples as well, and its use continued through both the Liao and the Jin dynasties.

10. Li Cunxu; see Chapter 1, Section II.

11. This translation is based on the reconstruction and analysis of Yao Congwu 1959, pp. 217–247.

3. Building the Liao Empire

1. The Chinese officer was Zhao Siwen, a wounded hero of the just concluded campaign against the Bohai. See *Qidan guozhi* 1247 (1985), p. 139. Zhao's biography in *Liao History* does not include this exchange with the empress. The empress's action is well attested in *Liao History, juan* 71, p. 1200, and elsewhere.

2. See his biography in ibid., chap. 14. I follow here the dating given in Sima Guang 1084 (1956), vol. 13, *juan* 280, p. 9162.

3. The eleventh-century Chinese historian Sima Guang, noting that Wuyu's presence in Kaifeng in 947 marked his first appearance in the historical records, agrees about his ideal princely qualities, but also notes that he was "blind in one eye," a point not mentioned in Liao historical accounts. See Sima Guang 1084 (1956), vol. 13, *juan* 286, p. 9332. Sima, strongly influenced by Chinese legitimacy concepts, was pleased to see that the eldest son of Prince Bei would come to the Liao throne. The Chinese author of the *Qidan guozhi* (dating from 1247), however, reported on Shizong's (Wuyu's) character in a much less flattering manner (*juan* 4).

4. The *Qidan guozhi,* at the point cited in n. 3, tells of factional disputes and political animosities within the imperial family and among the leading members of the nobility, the army, and the tribal chieftains, making a far more complex story of the continuing resistance to Emperor Shizong than the simple summary given here indicates.

5. Unless they, writing in 1345 under the Mongol dynasty, which rejected Chinese primogeniture patterns in its imperial succession, felt it their duty to stress the rewards for behavior that adhered to Chinese norms.

6. Note that the Khitans adopted the dynastic name Liao for their imperial state only in 947, though I also refer to it by that name in the pre-947 decades of their rule.

7. See translation of these materials and accompanying analysis in Wittfogel and Feng Chia-sheng 1946, pp. 44–114 and 434–444.

8. The locations of such walls, in some cases their existence, is somewhat uncertain; see Waldron 1990, pp. 21–29.

9. See Jin Yufu 1966, pp. 22–25.

10. Waldron 1990 analyzes both the history and the myths of the Great Wall.

11. This was Li Cunxu, Emperor Zhuangzong of the Later Tang (r. 923–926). See Chapter 1, Section II.

12. For Abaoji's meeting with Yao Kun, the ambassador from the Later Tang, see Chapter 2.

13. The date of the forced cession of the Sixteen Prefectures to the Liao is given variously as 936 and 938; it may have been agreed to at the end of 936 and formalized early in 938. See Map 5.

14. This was Liu Zhiyuan; see Chapter 1, Section II.

15. Muzong had a vicious temperament and was much given to violence; coupled with his alcoholism, that rendered him an ineffectual ruler. See Herbert Franke 1992, p. 121.

16. Turn to Chapter 5 for the continuation of this story from the Song dynasty's point of view.

17. For a fuller account of the Song offensive, see Chapter 5.

18. On Song historical maps it is called Kaide; it is near Puyang in northeastern Henan on modern maps. The course of the Yellow River today flows in a channel forty or more miles to the north of its tenth-century channel.

19. The negotiations and the resulting treaty are more fully discussed from the viewpoint of Song history in Chapter 5, Section IV.

4. Liao Civilization

1. See Wittfogel and Feng Chia-sheng 1946, esp. "Social Organization, Kinship System, Customs, Traditions," pp. 191–290, from which the extracts in the text are drawn; their wording is slightly modified here. The *Liao History* 1344 (1974) was compiled by an officially sponsored commission two centuries after the fall of the dynasty, utilizing a large variety of Chinese-language sources and secondary materials. The Wittfogel-Feng volume is valuable today mostly for its extensive translations from the *Liao History*, selected and prepared by Feng Chia-sheng and others; see its "General Introduction," p. 33.

2. As noted elsewhere here, the term "barbarian" designated peoples different by cultural criteria from the Chinese; it was meant to be objectively descriptive. Although "barbarian" might convey uncomplimentary overtones, the intent in this instance is not to insult, merely to describe.

3. All of the surviving reports written by Song envoys to the Liao have been collected and translated in David C. Wright 1993.

4. Much of the foregoing draws on the analysis of Herbert Franke 1992.

5. See Wittfogel and Feng Chia-sheng 1946, "Rebellions," esp. pp. 404–407 on the Bohai and the Chinese subjects of the Liao.

6. The relevant passage in the *Liao History* 1344 (1974, *juan* 89, p. 1350), is translated in Wittfogel and Feng Chia-sheng 1946, p. 264.

7. A man marrying two or more sisters, simultaneously or in sequence.

8. Requiring or expecting widows to marry their late husband's brother.

9. See *Analects* III/5 and the discussion of racial versus cultural determinants of Chineseness in K. C. Hsiao 1982, pp. 137–141; the passage in question is discussed on p. 138.

10. See Yang Shufan 1974.

11. See the discussion of recruitment in Wittfogel and Feng Chia-sheng 1946, esp. pp. 450–463, where the use of the *yin* privilege in Chinese dynasties is compared with that under the Liao.

12. See *Liao History* 1344 (1974), *juan* 72, p. 1209.

13. Wittfogel and Feng Chia-sheng 1946, pp. 53–58 and 306.

14. Steinhardt 1994. The high achievements of Liao architecture are seen by Steinhardt as evidence of the Khitans' role in amalgamating elements from across northern Inner Asia, from Korea to the Tangut Xi Xia state, and "in moving Chinese architecture to its highest level in medieval times" (p. 25). See also her *Liao Architecture* 1997.

15. Liu Zhenhua 1973.

16. Yang 1993.

17. Feng Yongqian 1987, esp. p. 308.

18. See Mino 1973, the illustrated catalogue of the first exhibition of Liao ceramics in the United States.

19. Wittfogel and Feng Chia-sheng 1946, p. 434.

20. From *Liao History* 1344 (1974), *juan* 45, pp. 685, 686, and 688. In summary, in words quoted from Yuan Haowen, "the Northern Chancellery does not administer the people's affairs," and "the Southern Chancellery does not manage the military."

21. Lattimore 1940, chap. 8, "The 'Reservoir' and the Marginal Zone."

22. Referring to the conceptualization of Benedict 1934.

5. CREATING THE SONG DYNASTY

1. This account is based primarily on the *Old History of the Five Dynasties* 974 (1976), *juan* 112 and 120; Sima Guang 1084 (1956), vol. 13, *juan* 285 and 294; and the *New History of the Five Dynasties,* Ouyang Xiu 1053 (1974), *juan* 10–12. Otto Franke 1930–1952, vol. 4 (1948), offers a penetrating analysis of Guo Wei's rise to power (pp. 61–65), but says almost nothing about that of Zhao Kuangyin (p. 75).

2. The name was later changed to Shanyuan; it was the site of the Song-Liao treaty negotiations in 1004–1005.

3. See Chen Xuelin [Hok-lam Chan] 1993, pp. 1–57, "Da Song Guohao yu Deyun lunbian shu yi" (An analysis of the debate over the dynastic name "the Great Song" and its "accession theory"). The region of Henan called Song had been the state of Song during the preimperial Zhou dynasty (ca. 1100 into the third century B.C.E.), and was thereby identified with the pre-Zhou Shang dynasty, as well as with the ancestors of Confucius.

4. His drinking may be stressed in this account to absolve him from suspicion of having spent the night plotting, but he is known to have been a heavy drinker, not atypical of his peers.

5. This account is based on the official *Song History* 1345 (1977), *juan* 1; Bi Yuan 1796 (1957), *juan* 1; and the *Old History of the Five Dynasties* 974 (1976). The translated passages are taken from Bi Yuan's work. Modern historical scholarship mostly accepts that the usurpation was carried out with Zhao Kuangyin's full knowledge, and that his brother, Zhao Kuangyi, and Zhao Pu helped to plan it.

6. The term comes from the title of a notable book by Saeki Tomi (1967, *So no shin bunka,* "The New Culture of the Song"), which has influenced the chapters on the Song.

7. The etymology of *huangdi,* meaning something like "celestial magnificence," is not parallel to that of "emperor," from Latin *imperare,* meaning "to command," thus, "the military supreme commander." The concept of a polyethnic "imperium," or "empire," in the Western experience also is unrelated to the Chinese sense of the state as the realm of shared Chinese culture.

8. On the concept of *gengshi,* or "new beginnings," see Section III of this chapter.

9. For a brief discussion of this issue in relation to the arts, see Mote, 1976a, pp. 3–8.

10. "Chief Councillor" will be used throughout as the best functional translation of *zaixiang,* and the later (after 1172) *chengxiang* titles; these often have been translated "prime minister," "grand councillor" or "chancellor" in other writings.

11. Bi Yuan 1957, *juan* 1, p. 9. The eighteenth-century historian Bi Yuan's great compendium is closely based on a number of Song period historical works.

12. K. C. Hsiao 1979, esp. pp. 478, 495, 510, and passim.

13. I adopt here Hellmut Wilhelm's concept of military power in Chinese imperial government functioning as a "sanction of a sanction," that is, as the coercive secondary sanction of the primary normative sanction (my 1951 notes from his unpublished lectures on Chinese imperial history).

14. Bi Yuan 1795 (1957), *juan* 2, pp. 35–36.

15. Li Yu's captivity was not luxurious, and he complained bitterly about how miserable he was. His poisoning, however, was carried out in 978, under Zhao Kuangyin's less magnanimous brother and successor, Emperor Taizong.

16. His younger brother Zhao Kuangyi, observing the taboo on the use of words in the emperor's name, had changed his name to the similar-sounding Guangyi in 960, and on coming to the throne in 976 again changed it, for whatever reason, to Zhao Jiong, sometimes pronounced Gui; see Herbert Franke 1976, 3:992–995. Here I shall continue to adopt the Chinese historiographic convention of referring to emperors by their posthumous temple names: Taizu for the first Song emperor, Zhao Kuangyin; and Taizong, "Grand Ancestor," the expected temple name for a second ruler in a dynasty, for his brother.

17. See Herbert Franke 1976, biographies of "Chao Te-chao" (1:70–71) and "Chao T'ing-mei" (1:83–84), and sources cited there.

18. In the 1070s a book appeared that related a no doubt long-circulated story, according to which in 976, when Taizu lay dying, Taizong murdered him to prevent Taizu from reneging on the promise demanded by his mother in 961 (and recorded by Taizu's confidant, the high official Zhao Pu) to turn the succession first to Taizong and then to their third brother. On his deathbed Taizu is said to have asked that his own son succeed him. The story has been debated ever since, and is not widely believed by historians today, except as evidence that Taizong was made insecure by public doubts about his fitness. See Chen Xuelin 1993, pp. 13–14 and bibliography cited there. Chen (Hok-lam Chan) cites among others Sun Kekuan 1965, who explores this rumored incident in relation to Taizong's strong adherence to forms of popular religious Daoism, thereby initiating an enduring pro-Daoist stance by successive Song emperors.

19. E.g., Chen Hongjin in southern Fujian; see *Song History* 1345 (1977), chap. 483, where Chen and other such holdouts are discussed.

20. The southwest (i.e., the later provinces of Guizhou and Yunnan) would not become part of the Chinese state until Yuan and Ming times.

21. See Maps 1, 3, and 5, and discussion in Chapter 3, Section V.

22. For this event as seen from the Khitan side, see Chapter 3, Section VI.

23. The recent scholar Fu Lehuan (1913–1966) believed that Taizong was forced to flee the scene because some portion of his army actually did mutiny and would have killed him. See Fu Lehuan 1984, pp. 29–35, for this argument and other details of the battle.

24. Bi Yuan 1796 (1957), *juan* 10, pp. 244–245.

25. Emperor Gaozong, the first ruler of the Southern Song (1127–1162), having no heir, adopted two sons from different branches of Taizu's descendants. See Chapter 13, Section III, and Dynastic Succession Chart 5, "Southern Song."

26. *Song History* 1345 (1977), *juan* 5, p. 101.

27. The last sentence has been added to the passage as incompletely quoted in Rui Hezheng 1970, pp. 429–477, esp. pp. 455ff. Some but not all of Rui's views are adopted here; where his punctuation, and hence interpretation, differs, I follow *Song History* 1345 (1977), *juan* 161, p. 3768.

28. Hucker 1985, pp. 40–41.

29. It has been usual to refer to the Han, the Tang, the Song, the Ming, and the Qing as the five major dynastic periods because they lasted the longest and achieved the greatest cultural development; the Yuan is sometimes added as a sixth major dynasty because of its importance in reunifying the long-divided nation, and for its enduring domestic and international impact.

30. Also called a war party, although it was not an organized political group. Both terms will be used hereafter.

31. See Chapter 6 for a discussion of trends in early Song political and social thought.

32. See Chapter 8 on the Xi Xia state of the Tanguts.

33. This analysis draws on Chen Fangming 1977.

34. Wolfgang Franke has compared the deeds of Kou Zhun in this crisis and their consequences with the case of Yu Qian, the Minister of War who took charge at the Ming court during the crisis of Mongol invasion in 1449. See Wolfgang Franke 1989, pp. 144–151; see also Map 5.

35. These figures are drawn from Song Xi *SSJY* 1970, and are related in the following discussion to figures provided in Fang Hao 1979, pt. 2, chap. 5. Other figures cited in the text draw on Qian Mu 1947, pp. 379ff. A number of other discussions of Song state finances give similar figures; no definitive work on the subject is known to me.

36. Yang 1971, p. 45, para. 5.18.

37. The details of the protocol are discussed in Chapter 3; see also David C. Wright 1993, 1996.

6. The World of Ideas in Northern Song China

1. This interpretation of Ouyang Xiu draws on two works by James T. C. Liu, 1963 [Liu Zijian] and 1967.

2. This was Ouyang Fei. The eldest son, Ouyang Fa, who was very scholarly by nature but not interested in preparing for the examinations, received the *jinshi* degree by grace, in recognition of his father's high position. Such status by "protection" did not carry the prestige of an earned degree.

3. Some of his Song period biographies, necrologies, and epitaphs list earlier eminent forebears, but others, including the long memoir by his son Ouyang Fa, omit all of that, strongly suggesting that such links are unfounded. See Ouyang's *Collected Works*, SBCK edition, in the five appended *juan*. Ouyang's father and at least one of his father's brothers passed the *jinshi* examination in 1000, the year in which 1,548 candidates were passed, the highest number in one year in Song times. See Kracke 1953, p. 60.

4. Wang Anshi's eulogy is to be found in Ouyang's *Collected Works* in appended *juan* 1. See also James T. C. Liu 1967, p. 154.

5. James T. C. Liu 1957 provides a sound study of Fan and his reform program.

6. For the threatened Liao invasion, see Chapter 3, Section V, for the Xi Xia state's part in this event, see Chapter 8.

7. The Liao invasion and the terms of the Treaty of Shanyuan are discussed in Chapter 3, Section IV, for a discerning analysis of the crisis and the resulting treaty, see David C. Wright 1993.

8. James T. C. Liu 1957 stresses this aspect of the factional struggle. "Idealistic" here, of course, means morally idealistic; it does not refer to philosophical idealism in the technical sense.

9. The content of the Qing-li Reforms (the Minor Reform) is discussed briefly in Section V of this chapter.

10. He was slandered by reform faction enemies who charged him with having had improper sexual relations with a young women of his household; these charges did not gain credence, but added pressure for his removal from the court.

11. James T. C. Liu 1967, p. 68.

12. Dates and details in the foregoing account are in large part drawn from the 1196 biography by Hu Ke 1936. The formal biographical records typically make no mention of daughters. A tomb inscription for the Lady Xue, probably written in 1104 at the request of her son Ouyang Fei (b. 1047) by the famed literatus Su Che (1039–1112), however, states that she bore eight sons, four of whom died in infancy, and three daughters, all of whom died before reaching the age of marriage. See Su Che 1541 (1936), *juan* 25, pp. 6a–8b.

13. Zhang Jinjian 1955, chap. 3, esp. pp. 58–63 and 75–80.

14. Bol 1990, p. 151, makes the point that this caused a "shift in the identity of the national elite from those who served to those who learned." High status came, however, when those who learned were successful in attaining substantial positions in government.

15. In Song times these "debased groups" included merchants, but there are many known cases of Song merchants becoming *jinshi*; see P. T. Ho 1962, p. 42. Others disqualified were those guilty of major crimes, men shown to lack the filial virtues, former monks and Daoist priests, and so on. See *Song History* (1977), *juan* 155, p. 3605.

16. Chaffee 1985, pp. 34–35; cited and discussed in Ebrey 1988, p. 501.

17. Kracke 1953, among others, refers to these as the "departmental" examinations; see his chap. 4.

18. Ibid., pp. 62–64.

19. The system deteriorated somewhat in the latter part of the Southern Song. See Miyazaki 1976 for rich detail on the conduct of the examinations and their social impact, mostly drawn from later periods, but with some references to Song practices.

20. Kracke 1953, p. 69.

21. Ho 1962. The entire book is relevant; the statistics are summarized on pp. 111–125.

22. Hartwell 1982, pp. 405–425.

23. A perceptive and informative summary is offered in Ebrey 1988.

24. On the fictionalizing of ancestries in Northern Song times, see Johnson 1977, esp. pp. 77–78.

25. I owe this observation, made in private conversation, to Marion J. Levy, Jr. To it James Geiss added, "a situation rarely if ever encountered in their own social milieu." And to which the author added, "And the Chinese ran their world much more effectively than we can imagine our academic colleagues administering anything."

26. These and other figures here are drawn chiefly from Kracke 1953, chap. 4. The figures for civil officials of course do not include military officers, whose rapidly growing numbers remained at least half as large as those for civil officials. Qian Mu 1947, chap. 31, provides various figures and their interpretation.

27. Kracke 1953 devotes much of his emphasis to this system; see esp. chaps. 6–11.

28. The examiners were not given authority to pass all those who attained grades over a set mark; only a fixed number could pass. In the year 992, for example, 97,000 sat for an examination which only about 1,000 could expect to pass. Numbers of examinees usually were much smaller, but even when the quota for passing was as high as 10 in 100, examiners could not rigorously distinguish between those who deserved to pass and those who did not.

29. Quoted in K. C. Hsiao 1982, p. 483.

30. The term could also be translated "beneficial effectiveness," to avoid any association with the kind of calculation of profit and benefit identified as the morally good, as found in Bentham and Mill and the British Utilitarians of the eighteenth and nineteenth centuries.

31. Presented in partial translation, with analysis, in James T. C. Liu 1967, pp. 53–58 et seq.

32. James T. C. Liu 1959b offers an overview and analysis of Wang Anshi's Major Reform.

33. The *Zhouguan,* also known as the *Zhouli,* is a late Warring States period (4th–3rd century B.C.E.) work purporting to set forth the institutional structure of the ancient Zhou dynasty's government. Throughout the ages it has attracted the attention of reform-minded statesmen, because it encourages change while having the unassailable value of being ancient.

34. Wang's structural changes are referred to repeatedly throughout the *Song History,* esp. in *juan* 161–172, "Treatise of Offices and Duties" *(Zhiguan zhi),* as the "new official ordinances of the Shenzong reign." For a convenient comparison, note that Wei Wenxuan 1987, in his detailed diagrams of the structure of Song government (pp. 89–112), offers two sets of diagrams for most divisions of the government, one for "pre Yuan-feng" (1077–1085) and one for "post Yuan-feng," to show the changes resulting from Wang's reforms.

35. See K. C. Hsiao 1982, pp. 487–493.

36. The passage in the *Song History, juan* 192, pp. 4767–68, describing the establishment of the *baojia* system, is translated in K. C. Hsiao 1960, p. 27.

37. Even in the present some have continued to defame Wang Anshi. An example is the somewhat superficial if often amusing book by Lin Yutang *The Gay Genius: The Life and Times of Su Tungpo* (1947), in which Wang is depicted as an unsavory, bumbling, socially awkward, and politically misguided statesman. While the book contains many useful translations of Su Shi's writings, it seems that Lin's purpose has been to use mid–eleventh-century history to satirize mid–twentieth-century politics; as a history of Wang Anshi's career it is largely irrelevant.

38. From K. C. Hsiao 1982, pp. 492–493. Inconsistencies in Wang Anshi's policy innovations have been noted by many writers. It is possible that the two sides of Wang's political initiatives, identified here by K. C. Hsiao, can explain the incongruencies evident in his policies as analyzed by Paul J. Smith, and also the elements of statism in Wang's politics as discerned by Peter K. Bol; see their essays on Wang Anshi in Hymes and Shirokauer 1993, pp. 76–127 and 128–192, respectively. Bol's study, in particular, offers a thoughtful analysis that differs from the interpretation of Wang and his opponents as set forth here.

39. "Metaphysical" is commonly used to designate Neo-Confucianism's more abstract concerns with ontological issues; but in a strict definition it may be inaccurate, as indicated in the discussion that follows.
40. Nivison 1959, quoting de Bary 1959; Nivison's comments also have been reprinted in Liu and Golas 1969, pp. 74–78, where de Bary 1959 also is excerpted, pp. 89–93.
41. See the discussion of this in Qian Mu 1980, 3:45–52 and 82–97.
42. Translated in Wing-tsit Chan 1963a, pp. 496–500.
43. Wing-tsit Chan 1963a, p. 544. Chan's extensive and careful translations with critical commentary, pp. 460–571, partially drawn upon in the foregoing, offer a rounded introduction to Neo-Confucian philosophy, if one that is at many points debatable.
44. The importance of the *Yijing* or *Book of Changes* to the whole gamut of Song Neo-Confucian thinkers is explored in depth in Kidder Smith, Jr., et al. 1990; in that connection, note also Lynn 1997.

7. DIMENSIONS OF NORTHERN SONG LIFE

1. I should make it clear that my evaluation of Chinese philosophy here does not differ from my evaluation of all past philosophies; as a historian I am concerned with understanding their explanatory significance in history, not with any possible validity of their content per se.
2. Rudolph 1963, p. 169. Archaeology in relation to Song elite culture is discussed again in Chapter 14.
3. Since the middle of the twentieth century, changes in social values and in education have eroded the previously high level of general awareness of the traditional culture.
4. Robert P. Hymes 1986b, in his important study of "Statesmen and Gentlemen," as he calls the elite he has studied through the three centuries of the Song dynasty in a Jiangxi prefecture, carefully defines the members of that elite by seven criteria, five of which go beyond the "official elite" definition. Some of the problems involved in maintaining these criteria, and in quantifying the data that can be compiled about all the individuals in a prefecture who can be so identified so as to make generalizations and draw conclusions about the character of society, are pointed out in a thoughtful review of Hymes's book; see McDermott 1991. It is nevertheless useful to make the distinction between legal and social realities in any analysis of societies.
5. On Su Xun's thought, see K. C. Hsiao 1982, pp. 518–522; and George Hatch, "Su Hsun's Pragmatic Statecraft," in Hymes and Shirokauer 1993, pp. 59–75.
6. Qian Zhongshu 1958, p. 69.
7. Zheng Qian 1952, p. 40.
8. That this aspect of traditional Chinese civilization is difficult for present-day persons, whether Chinese or not, to comprehend has been forcefully pointed out by Elman 1995, esp. pp. 534–535.
9. For a valuable analysis of his life and thought, see Hatch 1976. Bol 1992 presents a strong interpretation of Su's mentality in his study of Northern Song literati. For a meticulous intellectual and literary biography, see Egan 1994.
10. Hatch 1976, pp. 955 and 959–961.
11. Slightly modified from the translation in Lin Yutang 1947, p. 218.

12. His letter urging that steps be taken to end infanticide is translated in Lin Yutang 1947, pp. 220–223, and is reprinted in Lin Yutang 1960, pp. 203–206.

13. Quoted in Lin Tianwei 1977, p. 157. Lin finds the failures of the examination system one of the three great sources of Northern Song weakness, the other two being the policy of diminishing the military and the impact of Lixue in diverting minds and lives away from active involvement in political and social affairs. All three points are arguable.

14. Quoted in Ebrey 1991b, p. 68; see esp. chaps. 3 and 4 on Northern Song developments in normalizing Confucian family ritual.

15. Liu Zijian 1987a, pp. 225–226.

16. This discussion draws on the specialized studies of Fang Hao, published serially in *SSYJ*, nos. 9–13 (1977–1981).

17. Kenneth K. S. Chen 1968, pp. 97–98.

18. Kenneth K. S. Chen 1964, chap. 14.

19. Bowring 1992 provides a fascinating account of the difficult last years of the Institute for Sutra Translation.

20. Kenneth K. S. Chen 1964, p. 400.

21. Sun Kekuan 1965, p. 91. Bi Yuan (1957), *juan* 37, p. 862, states that this temple complex contained 3610 *ying,* or "rooms," actually floor space, measured as the area contained within four columns.

22. The Tang imperial line claimed descent from Lao Zi, whose surname was thought to be Li, like that of the Tang imperial house. Nonetheless, Tang imperial sponsorship of Daoism, except in the reign of Emperor Xuanzong (713–755), who demoted Confucius to the status of a disciple of Lao Zi, and Wuzong (841–846), who carried out the great suppression of Buddhism in 845 in the name of Daoism, was less consistently in evidence than in Song times.

23. For a short history of Song Daoism, see Sun Kekuan 1965.

24. Ho 1967; Bielenstein 1987, using different methods, corroborates Ho on the Song, and places the Song in a continuum from 2 C.E. until 1982. For a fuller discussion see Chapter 15, Section I.

25. For an example in the northern Zhejiang region around the prefecture of Ningbo, see Shiba 1977, esp. pp. 393–396, and Map 1.

26. The best succinct account is in Rozman 1973, pp. 31–36 and 280; see also Laurence J. C. Ma 1971, which offers valuable descriptive information.

27. Laurence J. C. Ma 1971, "Appendix," pp. 165–171, lists sixty-three cities with the largest quotas for commercial taxes; see also his discussion of these data, chap. 4, esp. pp. 60–73. Figures on collection of commercial taxes cannot provide population figures as such; but they do indicate the level of commercial activity in the city or town where the tax was collected.

28. Based on Rozman 1973, esp. pp. 279–281.

29. Skinner 1977, "Introduction," esp. pp. 28–30, argues that the share of China's population that can be counted as "urban" was 10 percent or higher in Song times ("medieval times"). Perhaps this was true in some regions; the present state of knowledge does not allow us to resolve this issue.

30. Ho 1956.

31. Shiba 1975; this paraphrases his conclusions on pp. 41 and 42.

32. This is well described in Laurence J. C. Ma 1971, chap. 5; see also Kracke 1975 and Pei-yi Wu 1994.

33. Shiba 1975, pp. 44–46.

8. Origins of the Xi Xia State

1. This is the modern Chinese pronunciation of the two Chinese characters; in Tang times it probably was pronounced *tubo(t)*, suggesting the Turkic word *tubbat*, cognate with our word Tibet.

2. The word Qiang as the name of a non-Chinese people with whom the ancient Chinese interacted appears in the oracle bone inscriptions, dating to 1500 B.C.E. or earlier, and also appears in the earliest texts from Zhou times (ca. 1100–256 B.C.E.), such as the *Book of Documents (Shang Shu)*, that preserve materials which originated earlier. The Chinese census of 1982 includes a minority people called Qiang, numbering 120,768, living in what is today part of Sichuan Province, to the northwest of Chengdu. That part of Sichuan was until the 1950s part of Xikang Province, formed in the 1920s to bring the southern Amdo region under direct Chinese administration. It is assumed that these Qiang are descendants of the Tang dynasty Qiang, and perhaps also of the tribal people in that region in high antiquity who in Chinese records are called Qiang. See Ramsey 1987, pp. 273–277.

3. The subject of Tibet's historical relationship with China will be more fully discussed in Chapter 27, Section III, in my discussion of the border regions of Ming China. Whether the Qiang people of early times were genetically related to the Tibetans, by evidence of language and culture, is much disputed. For the affirmative view that has prevailed in scholarship, see Stein 1972, chaps. 1 and 2. For an incisive rejection of those linguistic and cultural relationships, see Beckwith 1987, pp. 3–10. Here my concern is with the role of the Qiang people in linking the Tanguts to Tibetan civilization, a subject not in fundamental dispute, though admittedly not fully studied.

4. Dunnell 1984.

5. Dien 1991 reviews problems of Tuoba (Xianbei) identity and the impact of that people's high culture on their Chinese and other neighbors through the middle of the first millennium C.E.

6. See the detailed "Chronology of Major Events" in Appendix III of Wu Tianchi 1980, pp. 306–337.

7. Que Haozeng 1979, pp. 263–264. Aside from paragraphs like these, Que's study is not without merit.

8. Cai Meibiao et al. 1979, pp. 143–144, 199–200, and 225–226.

9. For a discussion of these issues, see Dunnell 1994.

10. Quoted in Wu Tianchi 1980, p. 18.

11. A kingly or princely title of two Chinese syllables (e.g., Xiping) was of lower rank than one consisting of one syllable (e.g., Xia).

12. *Song History* 1345 (1977), *juan* 485, p. 13989.

13. Ibid., p. 13991.

14. Ibid., p. 13993. The significance of "over five feet" is unclear; he probably was a bit over average height.

15. Ibid.

16. Kane 1989, p. 1. Chinese, by comparison, has more than 70,000 characters, of which most are obsolete, variants, or rarely used; a knowledge of about 10,000 characters makes it possible to read scholarly writings.

17. Bai Bin 1989, p. 27.

18. The comment of Zhang Zhu (1781–1847), quoted in Shi Jinbo 1986, pp. 20–32.

19. Chinese and Japanese scholars in the 1920s and 1930s made some initial progress in deciphering Tangut, but the principal effort leading to complete success in read-

ing Tangut materials was carried out by Russian scholars in St. Petersburg (Leningrad) following World War II, using their access to extensive holdings of archaeologically recovered finds from Tangut sites in Inner Asia.

20. Bi Yuan 1795 (1957), *juan* 62, pp. 1523–24. China's ancient *Book of Documents,* Sima Guang notes, praised the great King Wen of high antiquity, saying: "The great states feared his strength; the small states cherished his virtue" (Legge, *SHOO* 1960, p. 311). That is, Xia being a small state should be induced by our sincerity to cherish us, not subjected to humiliation.

9. The "Wild Jurchens" Erupt into History

1. This site on the Sungari in modern northern Jilin (Kirin) was the regular location of the Liao rulers' spring Nabo; see Wittfogel and Feng Chia-sheng 1946, p. 132, and Chapter 4, Section V, for an explanation of Nabo, the Khitan rulers' annual cycle of encampments and tribal leadership conferences.
2. *Liao History* 1344 (1974), *juan* 27, pp. 326 and 330, n. 9.
3. On the name of the dynasty, see Hok-lam Chan 1991.
4. More cautious scholars prefer "more than 100,000" for the total strength of the Liao field army. A general mobilization could have involved the larger number of forces, but the emperor's field army would have been smaller, and the main column defeated by Aguda smaller still.
5. Herbert Franke 1970 contains translations and analyses of the texts of treaties and oath letters from 1123, 1126, and 1141.
6. This phase of Song history is told in more detail from the Song point of view in Chapter 13.
7. This Jin, here meaning an old name for the Shanxi region, is written with a character different from the word Jin meaning "gold," the name of the Jurchen dynasty. For the Liao emperor Taizong's campaign in 947, see Chapter 3, Section 5, and Map 5.
8. The Song decision to make peace in 1141 despite strong objections from a "war party" at court, backed up by military leaders in the field, had profound repercussions, and is still debated. See the discussion in Chapter 13, Section II. See also the discussion of international trade in Chapter 14 and Herbert Franke 1970 and 1983, on the treaties.
9. For these two encounters, see *Liao History* (1974), *juan* 30, pp. 355 and 349.
10. Zhenzhou, also called Kedun Cheng, is about 125 miles west of Ulaan Baatar on modern maps of Mongolia. See Map 4; also Tan Qixiang 1991, 6:6; for a map of the Western Liao, see 6:73–74. This historical atlas's maps showing Inner Asian boundaries must be used with caution, as must those in Wittfogel and Feng Chia-sheng 1946.
11. The chronology of Yelù Dashi's movements and political acts follows the critical study and summary in Yu Dajun 1987, pp. 246–249.
12. For a review of Western Liao history with translations of sources and critical analysis, see Wittfogel and Feng Chia-sheng 1946, Appendix V, pp. 619–674, where it is spelled "Qarā-Khitāy."
13. Shuihuzhuan has been variously translated as *All Men Are Brothers,* in the translation by Pearl S. Buck, and by Sidney Shapiro under the title *Outlaws of the Marsh,* as well as under the title *The Water Margins.* The famous erotic novel *Jinpingmei* also has appeared in several translations, such as that by Clement Egerton under the title *The Golden Lotus.* The translation by David T. Roy under the title *The*

Plum in the Golden Vase, of which the first volume has appeared as of this writing, undoubtedly will become the standard translation. See also Plaks 1987.

14. Kao 1962 and 1966; McKnight 1976.

15. For a good critical reconstruction of the events, along with some contentious background views, see Zhang Tianyou 1980. For a general appraisal, see Jing-shen Tao 1988, chap. 8.

16. The traditional Chinese terms *sheng* (raw) and *shu* (cooked), meaning in this context "savage" or "uncultured" in contrast to "familiar" or "assimilated," quite coincidentally suggest a correspondence with the anthropological usage of Claude Lévi-Strauss in his work *Le Cru et le cuit* (1964), translated as *The Raw and the Cooked.*

17. *Jin History* 1344 (1975), *juan* 1, pp. 2–6.

18. See note 3.

19. Quoted passages in the foregoing account are from *Jin History* 1344 (1975), *juan* 1 and 2. For contemporary Chinese descriptions of the early Jurchens, see Herbert Franke 1975.

20. This discussion, like much of this and the following chapter, is heavily indebted to the extensive researches of Mikami Tsugio 1970–1973.

21. Jurchen words are known as preserved in transcriptions using Chinese characters; they are pronounced according to the modern pronunciation of standard Chinese, which may be quite unlike their twelfth-century sound in Jurchen. The forms *minggan* and *mukun,* representing Jurchen pronunciations reconstructed on analogy to modern Manchu, a closely related language, are also encountered in some scholarly writings.

22. *Jin History* 1344 (1975), *juan* 73, p. 1684.

23. The best technical discussion of the Jurchen scripts and the present state of their study is found in Kane 1989.

24. According to Xu Mengxin (1126–1194), in his compilation *Sanchao beimeng huibian,* 1878 ed., *juan* 3, p. 11a.

10. The Jurchen State and Its Cultural Policy

1. That was the situation in the mid-twelfth century. By the early thirteenth century the Jurchens had given up half of that zone. The Liao, building their empire principally in the Inner Asian steppe, had extended their empire more than 1,500 miles to the west from their original homeland in the Khingan range in the first half-century after Abaoji. This vividly indicates a difference between Liao and Jin.

2. Total population figures for Southern Song China and Jin China in about the year 1200 are discussed in Chapter 15, Section I.

3. Note that *meng'an* and *mouke* are terms used both for the population units and for their leaders; see discussion in Chapter 9, Section V.

4. This is more or less the periodization set forth in Jing-shen Tao 1976, and reflected in several other important studies of the Jin era.

5. *Jin History* 1344 (1975), *juan* 77, pp. 1758–62; see also Chapter 9.

6. Jing-shen Tao 1976, p. 34.

7. Wakeman 1975, esp. pp. 55–65.

8. The *Jin History* 1344 (1975) provides only one comprehensive set of figures for the population of all the *meng'an* and *mouke,* under the date 1183 (*juan* 44, p. 996). Those figures show a total population of 6,158,636 persons, of whom 1,345,967 are designated as slaves. That leaves 4,812,699 Jurchens of all statuses.

Those figures cannot be accepted uncritically. It is likely that the numbers of slaves and other "attached" households and individuals are underreported, and it also seems likely that the portion of the population identified as Jurchens is over-reported, because the leaders of the *mouke* benefited from both kinds of false reporting. One must assume, therefore, that the total Jurchen population was considerably under 4 million.

9. *Qidan guozhi* 1247 (1985), *juan* 12, p. 179.
10. *Jin History* 1344 (1975), *juan* 4, p. 87.
11. This section draws on Hok-lam Chan 1982, and on Cui Wenyin 1987.
12. See, for example, Feng Menglong 1634, story 33, whose title can be translated: "Prince Hailing of Jin's Unbridled Lechery Costs Him His Life." This is often omitted from editions of Feng's story collection because it uses improper language. Other accounts dating from Song and Yuan times are still more lurid.
13. The content of Jurchen culture is discussed in relation to this phase of nativist reaction by Jin Qicong, in Tillman and West 1995, pp. 216–237.
14. *Jin History* 1344 (1975), *juan* 44, p. 993. This was Prince Zongwang, nephew of the then reigning Emperor Taizong.
15. Jing-shen Tao 1976, pp. 86 and 153, nn. 17 and 18. Chinese regarded all imperial hunting activities as destructive and wasteful.
16. Han was assassinated by Southern Song political rivals in November 1207; his embalmed head, along with that of another war party leader, was turned over to the Jurchen court in the summer of 1208. The politics of the Southern Song court in this conflict are more fully discussed in Chapter 13, Section III.
17. *Jin History* 1344 (1975), *juan* 93, p. 2067.
18. De Rachewiltz 1993; see also de Rachewiltz 1962, p. 193.
19. For more on his not very satisfying career as an adviser to the Mongol khans, see Chapter 17, Section V.
20. The views of Liu Qi (1203–1250), paraphrased from passages quoted by Tao Jinsheng 1970, esp. p. 220.
21. See Hok-lam Chan 1993d for a translation of a memoir on the last days of the Jin at Caizhou.

11. THE LATER XI XIA STATE

1. The founding of the Xi Xia state and its early history are the subject of Chapter 8; a map and the dynastic succession chart are found there. Xi Xia, meaning "Western Xia," is the Chinese name for the state, here used interchangeably with Xia.
2. Tong Guan's role in court politics at the end of Northern Song is discussed in Chapter 9, Section II.
3. *Jin History* 1344 (1975), *juan* 134, pp. 2865–66.
4. Slightly paraphrasing ibid., p. 2868.
5. Ibid., pp. 2869–70.
6. One might observe, ironically, that the "barbarian" Jin state's response was more in keeping with venerable Confucian interstate norms than was the opportunistic reply of the Song. Although that is true, it would be a mistake to accept at face value either of these essentially self-serving replies, regardless of their rhetoric. Nevertheless, both invoked the universalistic norms of ritualized ethics. On this point, see also Chapter 16, Section II.
7. See the Xi Xia succession chart in Chapter 8 for details.

8. Dunnell 1991 provides much detail on Xia-Mongol relations in the final decades of the Xi Xia.

9. Heijdra and Cao Shuwen 1992.

10. Shi Jinbo 1988, chap. 4.

11. See Wu Tianchi 1980, pp. 171–172 and 190, n. 6.

12. *Jin History* 1344 (1975), *juan* 134, p. 2877.

13. Wu Tianchi 1980, p. 18.

14. Shi Jinbo 1988 offers a book-length treatment of all aspects of Xi Xia Buddhism. I received Dunnell 1996 only after this book was undergoing editing. Subtitled *Buddhism and State Formation in Eleventh-Century Xia,* this important addition to scholarly knowledge of the Xia is cited here (instead of in Chapter 8) because its focus on Tangut Buddhism is relevant at this point.

15. The use of interlinear Tibetan script and its implications are stated most explicitly in Cai Meibiao et al. 1979, p. 222. Shi Jinbo 1988, p. 104, observes the same phenomenon but offers a more limited interpretation.

16. This point is based on private correspondence with Nancy Schatzman Steinhardt; see also her *Liao Architecture* 1997, published after this book had been submitted for publication.

17. For a scholarly catalog of Xi Xia Buddhist art in the Hermitage, St. Petersburg, see Piotrovsky 1993.

12. TRENDS OF CHANGE UNDER JIN ALIEN RULE

1. Tillman and West 1995, an important collection of studies on China under Jurchen rule, is the first book in a Western language devoted to studies of Jin intellectual and cultural history. It appeared too late to be considered when this chapter was being written, but it has been noted during final revisions, and various of its essays are cited in several chapters here. The entire volume is highly recommended.

2. I observed surprisingly similar attitudes in Nanjing immediately following the cessation of hostilities in August 1945 among the survivors of the infamous "Rape of Nanking" in the winter of 1937–38. A frequently heard response from persons whose families had suffered death and destruction, and who themselves bore physical scars, was that revenge against disarmed Japanese military personnel or against Japanese civilians who safely walked the streets where violence had occurred only seven years earlier would be unreasonable, because these individuals now on the scene were not the ones who had been involved in the earlier events. A distinctly Chinese cultural attitude appeared to prevail, much to the surprise of Western observers. The survivors still bore scars, but they had moved on with their lives.

3. This must be mentioned because after half a century of imposed strictures on what Chinese historians can write, these distortions have become thoroughly built in to the body of historical scholarship; such matters do not invalidate that entire field of scholarship, but that scholarship must be used with discernment.

4. Other, possibly useful criteria have largely been abandoned because they appear to be vague or misleading.

5. S. Robert Ramsey 1987 uses the term "dialects" to designate the seven main divisions of Chinese; see his map preceding p. 17. That format agrees with current Mainland Chinese official usage. Jerry Norman 1988, pp. 1–8, discusses the "varieties of Chinese," drawing the distinction that most linguists prefer to use to distinguish "languages" from "dialects," that is, the former mark the boundaries of

non–mutually intelligible speech, while the latter are local variants that usually do not prevent hearers from understanding. In the present work "language" and "dialect" are used in Norman's sense.

6. Some examples are given in Herbert Franke 1975.

7. Aspects of this subject are discussed in Herbert Franke 1978a.

8. The terms "political presence" and "cultural presence" are borrowed from Bol 1987a. Bol analyzes in particular the nature of Chinese learning and cultural expression in relation to the Jin dynasty's civil service examination and recruitment systems.

9. Jing-shen Tao 1976, pp. 55–65. Tao also cites the comparative figures for Northern Song compiled by Kracke 1953. Bol 1987 suggests that Tao's totals for the Jin dynasty may be too high. See also the discussion by Hoyt Cleveland Tillman in Tillman and West 1995, pp. 27–49, esp. pp. 32–35.

10. Jing-shen Tao draws a similar conclusion from his study of public schools in the Jin dynasty; see Tillman and West 1995, pp. 50–67.

11. *Jin History* 1344 (1975), *juan* 83, p. 1864; also cited in Yang Shufan 1974, esp. p. 116.

12. Jing-shen Tao 1976, pp. 59–60, citing figures from the *Jin History* 1344 (1975), *juan* 55, p. 1216.

13. *Jin History* 1344 (1975), *juan* 51, pp. 1138–39. In 1197, 925 *jinshi* degrees were awarded, but the number of candidates is not recorded. In both cases the numbers are exceptionally high because special circumstances allowed candidates to bypass the lower-level qualifying examinations. Nevertheless, these figures show that the pool of potential candidates was very large.

14. Irving Yucheng Lo 1971 offers both biographical study and translations of many of Xin Qiji's *ci* lyrics.

15. Yuan Haowen is included in the discussion of Jin dynasty poetry in Yoshikawa, Kojiro 1963, trans. Wixted 1989, chap. 2. See also Wixted 1982.

16. Bol 1987.

17. Peter Bol has focused on this aspect of Su Shi's historical importance in several of his writings; see Bol 1992 and his essay on the late Jin literary figure Zhao Bingwen (Chao Ping-wen) in Tillman and West 1995, pp. 115–144; see also Hoyt Tillman's study of Confucianism under the Jin in the same volume, esp. pp. 102–106, on Su Shi's legacy.

18. They were out of date in serious statecraft philosophy but pervasive in common beliefs. Philosophical discussions of "legitimate succession" had come to center on more meaningful issues of political uprightness and success in unifying the realm. The philosophical tenor of the original Five Agents theories advanced by Zou Yan in the third century B.C.E. had quickly degenerated thereafter, and the theories were not granted much philosophical weight, even though they remained a central element in popular magic. See Kung-chuan Hsiao 1979, pp. 61–65.

19. The "cyclical production" *(xiang sheng)* succession of the Five Agents is Wood, Fire, Earth, Metal, Water.

20. Hok-lam Chan 1984, p. 117. This work thoroughly sets forth the cultural and political elements of these late Jin period theoretical discussions on dynastic legitimacy.

21. Herbert Franke 1992; see also the discussion of Liao law in Chapter 4.

22. Idema and West 1982 well represents the new scholarship; its Introduction and chap. 1 in particular deal with the Jin antecedents of the full-blown Yuan *zaju*. Note that the drama translated in chap. 5 (pp. 205–235), "A Playboy from a

Noble House Opts for the Wrong Career," has a Jin period setting and tells of a young Jurchen nobleman's love for a Chinese actress. Idema's study of a parallel development in Jin literature, the ballad form called "all keys and modes" *(zhugongdiao)*, adds greatly to the story of popular writing under the Jin; see Idema's essay in Tillman and West 1995, pp. 238–280.

23. One of the Yuan *zaju* versions of the story is translated in Hsiung 1968.

24. Crump 1970, pp. 473–490, well describes the raucous atmosphere in which Jin period drama developed. He translates some of the Yuanben titles as follows: "Seductive Wench," "A Hick in the City," "The Horse's Ass," "A Case of the Claps," and "Two Doctors Raise Hell." See also Idema and West 1982, pp. 83–94 and passim.

25. Here I am quoting the analysis of the treaty relationships by Herbert Franke 1970.

26. The treaties with Jin followed the pattern of those between Liao and the Northern Song, discussed in Chapter 5, Section IV.

27. Kato 1953, 2:253–270.

13. THE SOUTHERN SONG AND CHINESE SURVIVAL

1. For an account of Northern Song collapse under the Jin onslaught, see Chapter 9, Section III.

2. *Song History* 1345 (1977), *juan* 24, pp. 439–440. Other accounts differ somewhat on these details.

3. This encounter occurred at Cizhou, in modern Hebei; shortly thereafter Prince Kang moved his headquarters to Xiangzhou, modern Anyang in northeast Henan. Within the next few months he continued to move, first east into Shantung, then south again into Henan.

4. This is the opinion of, among others, Zeng Qiongbi 1988, p. 244, citing the *Song History* 1345 (1977), *juan* 24.

5. The place where the Song imperial captives eventually were held as prisoners is disputed; all the possible sites are in central or northern Manchuria. Zhao Gou's mother and his principal consort were among the captives.

6. *Song History* 1345 (1977), *juan* 233, pp. 7729–37, and *juan* 246, pp. 8725–34. The first mention of the son listed thirty-first is in *juan* 22, p. 416, when he was granted his ducal title; that usually occurred within a short time after the birth of imperial sons, whose actual birthdates are seldom given. Another son, number eighteen, is mentioned as an adult in 1128, when he or an impostor was reported to have escaped from the Jurchens and made his way to Gaozong's court; see Bi Yuan 1796 (1957), *juan* 101, pp. 2668–69. If so, he must have been born no later than 1112, about five years after Zhao Gou, who was number nine in the sequence. The eldest daughter was born in 1101; other birthdates are not given. In short, the *History's* information on Song imperial children is incomplete.

7. Haeger 1975.

8. There are of course no firsthand accounts of the emperor's escape, and the numerous tellings pieced together later vary among themselves in details. The version given here, based on the critical synthesis by Bi Yuan 1796 (1957), *juan* 103, pp. 2709–20, may not be wholly accurate, but can be taken as close to the facts.

9. For a succinct account of this coup and its overthrow, see Haeger 1976.

10. *Song History* 1345 (1977), *juan* 25, p. 466.

11. Curiously, Gaozong never had another son, and appears to have had no daughters, although throughout the next forty years he had the usual complement of consorts

and palace women. Some recent historians, following court gossip of the time, have stated that he was rendered permanently impotent by the terror of his escape and feelings of personal guilt; see Deng Guangming 1945–46, p. 47, and 1983, pp. 219–221; and Wang Deyi 1978, p. 246. That suggestion appears to be borne out by the fact that in 1132, still in his mid-twenties, he adopted two very young sons from another branch of the imperial line; the elder eventually was named his heir.

12. Prince Zongbi was the founding emperor Aguda's fourth son, thus a nephew of the reigning Jin emperor.

13. For the treaty arrangements made between Jin and Southern Song in 1142, see Chapter 12. For Prince Hailing's misguided adventure in 1161, and for the Jin war against Song in 1216–1220, see Chapter 9, Section III.

14. Necessarily lying beyond direct verification, these are nevertheless the reasonable judgments of historians.

15. Quoting here James T. C. Liu 1988, his summary on the book jacket, and his book title. This is a powerfully argued study of Emperor Gaozong's reign.

16. They were the descendants of Han Qi (1008–1075), the noted conservative statesman and literatus who served prominently alongside Ouyang Xiu; see Chapter 6, Section II. Han Qi's great-grandson Han Xiaozhou (1075–1150) was the head of the family in Yue Fei's time, and according to this tradition his children were Yue Fei's companions in the Han family private school. See Deng Guangming 1945–46, p. 11; that account is considerably altered in Deng Guangming 1983.

17. This puppet state was set up with its capital at Kaifeng in 1130, and was abolished at the end of 1137. See also Chapter 9, Section III.

18. Because of these aspects of their doctrines, they have attracted the sympathies of historians in Mainland China since 1949, some of whom have gone so far as to say that Yue Fei's suppression of the movement is a "historic tragedy" and the great blemish on his otherwise noble career. See, e.g., Wang Zengyu 1983, pp. 155–174, and Yin Shixue 1988.

19. The technology of the paddle wheel ships is discussed and illustrated in Joseph Needham 1954–, vol. 4, pt. 2, pp. 418–423 and 3, p. 693; contemporary accounts of Yang Yao's and Yue Fei's battles are translated there.

20. Emperor Gaozong apparently knew as early as 1132, when he was only twenty-five, that he would not have another son of his own. By adopting a direct descendant of the Song founder, Zhao Kuangyin, instead of someone from his own branch of the imperial line (descended from Emperor Taizong, the founding emperor's younger brother), he may have calculated that he could thereby restore to the dynasty some of the luster associated with the founder.

21. Deng Guangming 1983, Appendix 1, pp. 410–413.

22. Yue Ke's "family biography" formed the basis of Yue Fei's biography in the official *Song History* (1345) and most subsequent accounts. For a critical edition of the collected works, see Wang Zengyu 1989.

23. See James T. C. Liu 1972, and Liu Zijian 1987b, pp. 185–207. Liu's studies are particularly important for critically reviewing the recent scholarship discrediting much of the myth about Yue Fei.

24. Deng Guangming 1983, p. 99.

25. From the translation in Wilhelm 1962. Since 1962 the authenticity of this famous poem, and many other elements of the Yue Fei legend, have come under serious question. See Liu Zijian [James T. C. Liu] 1987b, pp. 185–207; Rao Zongyi 1982, pp. 794–813. For more conservative (nationalistic) views, see the biographies of

Yue Fei by Deng Guangming 1983 and Wang Zengyu 1983; note, however, that these and other recent scholars do not agree on which elements of the myth are to be abandoned. Their reasoning appears to be colored by ideological commitments.

26. Wang Zengyu 1989, 2:982; cf. Liu Zijian [James T. C. Liu] 1987b, p. 206.

27. For strong statements of the counter view, see Deng Guangming 1945–46, Preface, pp. 5–8; and Zeng Qiongbi 1988.

28. Herbert Franke 1970. Also called the Treaty of Shaoxing, after the reign period during which it was concluded.

29. A Southern Song painting which may depict their arrival at Hangzhou is described in Murray 1992.

30. Herbert Franke 1970, p. 79.

31. Richard L. Davis 1986a, pp. 53–78; Davis cites Wang Deyi 1978.

32. Wang Deyi 1978 develops this point at length.

33. See Chapter 19, Section VI, for the Mongol conquest of the Southern Song in the 1270s.

34. For the Northern Song background, see Chapter 6.

35. See K. C. Hsiao 1982, pp. 541–543, on the forged Song period *Classic of Loyalty (Zhong Jing)*.

36. Concurrent trends in intellectual history are discussed in Chapter 14.

37. Cited in Lin Tianwei 1976, p. 167, n. 9.

38. He held that post somewhat unsteadily, for there was an established objection in principle to having members of the imperial clan hold executive posts of such high rank, and he was the first to break with that principle.

39. Chaffee 1992.

40. The facts, however, are not clear; the antecedents from whom he claimed descent are Han Qi and his son Han Zhongyuan, who had been Chief Councillors, the elder Han in the 1050s and 1060s and the son early in the twelfth century; a descendant of theirs, Han Xiaozhou, has been mentioned as the head of the clan, a prominent figure at court and in his home locality, where the young Yue Fei grew up.

41. For Jin cultural policy in Zhangzong's reign, see Chapter 10, Section IV.

42. Davis 1986a, pp. 89–95.

43. See Chapter 12, Section IV; and Irving Yucheng Lo 1971, pp. 51–72.

44. See Duke 1977, pp. 65–80. Lu You's seemingly contradictory support of Han Tuozhou, despite his long-standing good relations with Zhu Xi and his followers, is analyzed by Zhu Dongrun 1960, pp. 206–245. See also Chapter 15, Section VI.

45. She was also a musician, poet, calligrapher, and patron of the arts; for examples of her calligraphy and poetry, see Fong 1992, pp. 233–237.

46. See Davis 1986a, pp. 79–127, for the careers of both Shi Miyuan and the Empress Yang.

47. Han Tuozhou never officially received that title but in all respects was the equivalent of the "all-powerful Chief Councillor," and is so discussed in Chinese historical works.

48. On the earlier developments of Neo-Confucian rationalism, called Lixue, see Chapter 6, Section III. For Zhu Xi, see Chapter 14, Section III.

49. James T. C. Liu 1973.

50. *Song History* 1345 (1977), *juan* 274, pp. 13779–87.

51. See Herbert Franke 1962 and works cited there. The conventional view of Jia embedded in the *Song History* has not received much rethinking; typical is Han Rulin et al. 1986, 1:277–286.

52. *Song History* 1345 (1977), *juan* 274, p. 13786.
53. This point is developed in Herbert Franke 1962.
54. Herbert Franke 1958.
55. This point is stressed by Herbert Franke 1962, p. 231.
56. A interesting example is found in the writings of the respected modern historian Jin Yufu 1966, pp. 113–116. Jin attempts to produce a balanced judgment of Jia Sidao that is devastating to Jia's reputation, and unfairly so.
57. See James T. C. Liu 1985 and his other writings cited there for an elaboration of this point.
58. Liu Zijian 1987b, p. 80.

14. CHINESE CIVILIZATION AND THE SONG ACHIEVEMENT

1. A reference to the book by Saeki Tomi 1967; see Chapter 5, n. 6.
2. Since 1949 the loosely used scornful designation for all aspects of the traditional civilization in Mainland China has been "feudal China," a disparaging term without specific meaning apart from its ideological overtones.
3. The life of ordinary society in rural China, not susceptible to detailed description and analysis, will be touched upon in Chapter 15.
4. Needham 1954–, 1:134; see summary of Song science, 1:134–139.
5. E.g., Nathan Sivin, especially "Conclusion" and "Introduction" in Sivin 1977b; note particularly pp. xv–xxi.
6. Needham 1954–, 1:135.
7. Subrenat 1976; Sivin 1977a. Evidence for Shen's work and thought is found in his principal surviving work, his *Mengxi bitan* in 26 *juan,* written after Shen retired about 1086. *Mengxi* means "Dream Brook" (or "Dream Pool"), the name of his residence in retirement; the title means "Brush Talks from Dream Brook."
8. See their brief biographies in *Song History* 1345 (1977), *juan* 331, pp. 10651–57.
9. Needham 1969, p. 94.
10. *Song History* 1345 (1977), *juan* 351, pp. 11093–94.
11. Ibid., *juan* 444, pp. 13121–22.
12. He was Wang Gongchen (1012–1085); see ibid., *juan* 318, pp. 10359–61.
13. Hervouet 1978, pp. 199–208.
14. Rudolph 1963.
15. According to some near contemporary accounts Li was pressured by her brother into marrying in 1132 a minor official of some means, but was soon separated from him after denouncing him for embezzlement of government funds. Many scholars feel that this story has been shown to be groundless, though Julia Ching 1976a argues that it could well be true. Patricia Buckley Ebrey accepts Ching's view; see Ebrey 1993, pp. 205 and 208. The implications are discussed in Section III of this chapter, under "Zhu Xi."
16. Kai-yu Hsü 1962; Ching 1976a; Zheng Qian 1952, pp. 81–88.
17. This account is based on Davis 1986a, which provides a full history of the Shi family through Southern Song and into Yuan times, in which the story of Shi Cai is part of the opening segment. The best known of Shi Cai's eminent descendants, powerful Chief Councillor Shi Miyuan, is discussed in Chapter 13, Section III.
18. Davis 1986a, pp. 46–51.
19. Ibid., pp. 169–173.
20. The Northern Song beginnings of this process are discussed in Chapter 6.

21. This word *li*, "benefit," is different from and unrelated to the word *li* of Lixue, meaning "reason."
22. *Mencius* 7.2.14, in Legge 1960, 2:483–484, and D. C. Lau 1970, p. 196.
23. See Tillman 1982 and 1988.
24. K. C. Hsiao 1982, pp. 497–502.
25. Best analyzed by Yu Yingshi [Yü Ying-shih] 1987, esp. pp. 43–94.
26. They are two of the five masters discussed in Chapter 6, Section VI. See also Kidder Smith, Jr., 1990.
27. I refer here to the *Song Yuan Xue An*, started by Huang Zongxi in the 1680s and substantially completed under the supervision of Quan Zuwang in the 1750s.
28. Here I use wording found in Wing-tsit Chan 1967, p. xxi.
29. Siu-chi Huang 1944; Wing-tsit Chan 1963a, chap. 33.
30. The characterization of Zhu Xi's achievement as the "completion" of the Neo-Confucian development is taken from Wing-tsit Chan 1973. Elsewhere, e.g., Wing-tsit Chan 1963a, he speaks of the "Great Synthesis."
31. Quoted in Wang Zicai et al. 1838 (1962), *juan* 39, p. 6b.
32. A succinct account is found in Bi Yuan 1796 (1957), *juan* 154, pp. 4131–46. See also Chapter 13, Section III, where the affair of Han Tuozhou is discussed.
33. By which it is known in the *Song History* 1345 (1977); see *juan* 327–330.
34. See Tillman 1992 on the growth of Zhu Xi's intellectual horizons and his place in the intellectual life of his time.
35. This analysis draws on but is not confined to the conspectus offered in Wing-tsit Chan 1973.
36. Gardner 1989.
37. Extensive translations and analysis are found in Gardner 1990.
38. Translated and analyzed in Ebrey 1991a. See also Ebrey 1991b.
39. See Birge 1992, esp. chaps. 3 and 4. See also Ebrey 1993, a broad-ranging study of women and marriage in Song times.
40. Translated and analyzed by Wing-tsit Chan 1967. There has been much discussion (noted in Chapter 6, Section VI) about why Zhu Xi pointedly omitted the fifth of the great Northern Song Neo-Confucian thinkers, Shao Yong.
41. Wing-tsit Chan 1973, p. xxxix, curiously refers to Lü only as a leader of "the East Chekiang School" of thought and scholarship; for a more analytical characterization of him as a member of the utilitarian school, see K. C. Hsiao 1982, p. 493.
42. This is also apparent in his commentary on the ancient *Book of Odes (Shi)*. For an important assessment of Zhu Xi's "sense of history," see Conrad Shirokauer in Hymes and Shirokauer 1993, pp. 193–220.
43. This view draws on K. C. Hsiao 1982, pp. 539–541.
44. Here I draw on the acute analysis of Chinese history offered by Ray Huang 1988a.
45. See Fong 1992, esp. chap. 4, "Sung Imperial Art." Other chapters in this important book provide an extensive survey of Song art.
46. This point has been developed by James T. C. Liu 1985 in connection with his study of the sport of polo in Tang, Song, and later China.
47. *Song History* 1345 (1977), *juan* 461–462.
48. See Davis 1986b, pp. 63–67.
49. See Bossler 1991.
50. Anthropologists and social historians, working together, have attempted to establish a more precise English terminology than the Chinese themselves have

employed in their own language; see especially the important discussions of that problem in Ebrey and Watson 1986, Introduction and chaps. 1 and 9.

51. See Chapter 6, Section II, where Fan, an important statesman and social thinker, is discussed in conjunction with his "Minor Reforms" of the Qing-li reign period.

52. Twitchett 1959.

53. See essays by Robert P. Hymes (pp. 95–135) and Jerry Dennerline (pp. 170–209) in Buckley and Watson 1986.

54. *Song History* 1345 (1977), *juan* 460.

15. SOUTHERN SONG LIFE—A BROADER VIEW

1. The projected figures are from the United Nations Population Fund 1992.

2. Ho 1967.

3. See Maps 6 and 10 for Song (ca. 1080) and Song-Jin (ca. 1200) circuits.

4. This function was an aspect of the reorganization of the examinations and the creation of local schools in the years 1103–1120; under the Southern Song these duties fell to local magistrates.

5. Debates at court over the *baojia* system raged from the time Wang Anshi initiated it in the 1070s to the end of the Northern Song; see *Song History* 1345 (1977), *juan* 192. In Southern Song the local defense aspects of the *baojia* were supervised by the county magistrate.

6. See the discussion of the utilitarian school in Chapter 14, Section III.

7. Luo Wen 1977 is very useful for its analysis of the circuit level of administration.

8. *Song History* 1345 (1977), *juan* 167, p. 3977.

9. This figure is based on household figures for the year 1162 (Shaoxing 32) as given in *Song History* 1345 (1977), *juan* 88, p. 2173, where the figures for the "Liang Zhe" are combined; the total household figure of 2,243,000 has been multiplied by 5.5 to get the figure for individuals.

10. Ho 1967, p. 48.

11. England's population did not pass the 10 million mark until well into the nineteenth century; today England, with an area of 50,000 square miles, and Zhejiang, with about 40,000 square miles, each has roughly 50 million people.

12. See discussion of prices and money values in Hartwell 1967, pp. 136–138, n. 8.

13. Qian Mu 1947, 2:388; Fang Hao 1979, vol. 2, chap. 5. These works and other modern scholarship that could be cited give mutually conflicting figures and interpretations.

14. See Song Xi [Sung Shee] 1962, pp. 30–64 and 65–72, for an extensive discussion of commercial taxes.

15. Needham 1970, pp. 108–112. The volume in Needham 1954– devoted to mining and metallurgy had not yet appeared as of this writing.

16. Hartwell 1967. This study has been criticized for faulty interpretation of tax receipts on which its Song dynasty production figures are based, and particularly for accepting declines in those receipts as evidence of a corresponding decline in production in Southern Song and later times. Despite such criticisms and the need to modify some of its findings, it remains a landmark study of the Song economy, economic organization, and urban market development.

17. We know very little about wages in the Song: the figure of "100 cash and two and a half pints of rice" for an ordinary sailor's daily wage, given in Shiba 1970, p. 25, is one of the few recorded bits of such information.

18. See the discussion of paper currency in Lien-sheng Yang 1971, chap. 6.

19. In English, "peasant" is recorded as a term of abuse as early as the mid-sixteenth century. "Villein" or "villan," used in the sense of "villain," is attested as early as 1303, according to the *Oxford English Dictionary.*

20. Golas 1980 offers a good survey of factors in rural life.

21. This, of course, is to use "feudal" as a technical term for the political and social organization characteristic of a period in western European history, not as a catch-all name for precapitalist phases of all histories in the Marxian formula, especially as that has been vulgarized in our own day.

22. But see Pulleyblank 1958 for a well-formulated view of slavery in early China.

23. See, for one amusing example, the translation of "Country Cousin at the Theater," in Crump 1970, pp. 480–484. Names of other comedies noted there are "A Hick in the City" and "Old Granny Hayseed."

24. For Kaifeng, see Pei-yi Wu 1994 and Hartwell 1967; Hangzhou has been magnificently described in Gernet 1962, but in certain respects (e.g., chap. 2, "Society") the book is somewhat out of date. See also Ebrey 1981, pp. 100–106.

25. On theater, the entertainment quarters, and forms of pleasure-seeking, see Idema and West 1982, esp. chap. 1.

26. Compare these aspects of Song life with the discussion of the same in Ming society in Chapter 29, Section III.

27. The theme of "ideal" versus "actual" structures in the study of society is stressed in Levy 1952, pp. 123–127; and with special relevance to family structure, see Levy 1966, 2:426–430.

28. Ebrey 1995, which appeared too late to be considered here, is an important addition to our knowledge about women and marriage in Song times.

29. Birge 1992.

30. Hymes 1986a.

31. Quoting from the excellent brief biography of Lu You by D. R. Jonker, in Herbert Franke 1976, 2:691–704.

32. Watson 1973, p. 100; this is taken from the entry for the eighth lunar month, twenty-third day (October 4), 1170, in Burton Watson's partial translation of Lu You's diary of his travel to Sichuan, his *Ru Shu ji.* See also the full translation with annotation of the same work in Chang and Smythe 1981.

33. Zhu Dongrun 1960, chaps. 7 and 8, pp. 99–150, reconstructs those years and explains Lu's activities.

34. See the poems translated in Watson 1973, esp. pp. 34–35, 43–45, 48–49, 56–57; and in Michael S. Duke 1977, esp. pp. 124–131.

35. Watson 1973, p. 66.

36. Ibid., pp. 40–41.

37. Duke 1977, pp. 130 and 127.

38. Watson 1973, pp. 34, 56.

16. A MID-THIRTEENTH-CENTURY OVERVIEW

1. Rossabi 1983.

2. Cf. Chapter 1, n. 2, for the sense in which "state" and "nation" are used in the present work. To summarize, the modern "nation-state" is seen here as a conceptually new nineteenth-century development. "Nation," however, is used throughout this work in the sense of "a distinct race or people" sharing a sense of cultural identity, while "state" is taken to refer to any kind of polity, past or present. The

Chinese traditionally distinguished "dynasty" *(chao)* and "state" *(guo)*, but with other implications.

3. Fairbank 1968.

4. "Voluntary," that is, with polities that it recognized as being beyond its administrative reach; the subjection to Chinese overlordship of the smaller non-Chinese entities on its nearer borders was by no means voluntary. Much modern historical writing masks that fact by calling many of those peoples and polities "Chinese" in a newly defined sense of that word.

5. As noted previously, "barbarian" is used in the sense in which the Chinese intended it, meaning "culturally different" or simply "non-Chinese."

6. Herbert Franke 1983, p. 133; for an extended discussion, see pp. 116–148.

7. The Korean case has been analyzed by Michael C. Rogers 1983, pp. 151–172.

8. *Jin History* 1344 (1975), *juan* 60, p. 1390, and *juan* 135, p. 2885. The chronology is confused in *juan* 135, but internal evidence places this event late in 1123.

9. Ibid., *juan* 134, p. 2866.

10. Ibid., pp. 2869, 2870.

11. Mary Clabaugh Wright 1966, pp. 237–238.

12. Sinor 1990, esp. pp. 4–7.

13. The twentieth-century Chinese writer Lu Xun parodied that mind-set as "Ah-Q'ism," perhaps somewhat unfairly, in his famous parable excoriating Chinese cultural weaknesses, "The True Story of Ah-Q," *(A-Q Zheng-zhuan).*

14. See the important distinction between the rule of law and governing by laws in Kung-chuan Hsiao [K. C. Hsiao] 1979, vol. 1, esp. pp. 345–347, p. 445 n. 39, and passim.

15. See Bodde 1981, pp. 299–315, and the writings cited there.

16. Hugo Grotius, *De jure belli ac pacis,* 1625.

17. In pre-Confucian times, the *shi,* translated here as "scholars," had been a class of hereditary knights. Their transformation into a nonhereditary stratum of civil officials is one of the consequences of social changes concurrent with the life of Confucius.

18. Just as we would find it incongruous to refer to the farmers of the United States at any point in American history as "peasants," it is incongruous to apply the word, with all its weighty baggage of European postfeudal connotations, to the broad social spectrum of those who farmed the land in China.

19. Twitchett 1979, Introduction, pp. 29–31, and his earlier writings cited there.

20. This observation was made by Marion J. Levy, Jr., in personal communication.

21. Tibetan script was derived through Nagari from the Indian Brahmi script, which in turn, like Uighur, is based on Western Asian Aramaic. Both Uighur and Tibetan scripts are thus derived ultimately from Semitic writing systems, representing the other principal invention of writing in human history.

17. THE CAREER OF THE GREAT KHAN CHINGGIS

1. The name Chinggis may also be spelled Genghis, Jengiz, Ghengiz, Cingiz, Jinkiz, and so on. Most other Mongol and Inner Asian words and names are spelled in a wide variety of ways in Western-language writings. The reader of history must be prepared to make imaginative leaps in recognizing the many variant spellings.

2. *Liao History* 1343 (1974), *juan* 24, p. 289.

3. See Chapter 2, Section II, for the problems of ethnolinguistic identification of peoples.

4. For a succinct discussion of the use of "Tatar" in Russian history, see Nutsch 1984.

5. Distilled liquor made from grains, which seems to have come into human history in the twelfth century from some point of origin in Eurasia (although Joseph Needham may have evidence for it slightly earlier in China) and spread as quickly as any invention ever known, was soon to supplement the milder koumiss among the Mongols, but they did not manufacture it themselves. Their use of stills for distilling arak from koumiss apparently dates from several centuries later. See Needham 1954–, vol. 5, pt. 4, pp. 103–106 and 141–150.

6. For a view of what constitutes the state, with special consideration of nomadic societies, see Krader 1968, esp. chap. 6, "The Tatar State: Turks and Mongols." For an influential statement of the counter view, see Strayer 1970, esp. pp. 4–11.

7. For the lives of some extraordinary Mongol women, see Rossabi 1979.

8. See Cleaves 1982, Introduction.

9. Also spelled Yisugei, Yissüngge, and so on.

10. *Yuan History* 1370 (1976), *juan* 1, p. 3.

11. Ratchnevsky 1991, pp. 9–10. (This source erroneously dates the Jin emperor Xizong's accession to 1125 instead of 1135.) Ratchnevsky's source for many of the details in this period of Mongol history come from Rashid al-Din (1237–1318), Grand Vizier to the Mongol Khans who ruled in Persia, and usefully supplements the Chinese and Mongol sources, despite occasional factual errors.

12. Yuwen [Youwen] Maozhao, *Da Jin guozhi*, ca. 1160 (1986), *juan* 12.

13. That is, Hö'elun and Yesugei's second wife, mother of two younger children.

14. Paul Kahn 1984, p. 19, used here and throughout with permission granted by the poet-translator. Kahn's translation is based on Cleaves 1982. Spellings of personal names are modified to agree with the spelling of Mongolian words used throughout the present work. E.g., the name of Hö'elun is spelled Hogelun by Kahn.

15. Paul Kahn 1984, p. 40.

16. Sorghaghtani Beki, whose age is not indicated here, was to be the mother of Tolui's four sons, including the two Great Khans, Möngke and Khubilai. She became one of the most famous women in Mongol history. Tolui was ten or twelve years old at the time. See also Rossabi 1979.

17. Paul Kahn 1984, pp. 98, 99, 100.

18. Ibid., p. 118.

19. *Yuan History* 1370 (1976), *juan* 114 and 116, "Biographies of Empresses and Imperial Concubines."

20. For a brief critical review of the problems surrounding the Jasagh, see Morgan 1986, pp. 96–99, and the writings cited there.

21. On his Turkic and especially his many Uighur associates, see de Rachewiltz 1983.

18. Forging the Mongol World Empire, 1206–1260

1. Under the Qing dynasty (1644–1911), Mongolia was divided into two administrative regions, Inner Mongolia closer to China, and Outer Mongolia lying farther north. In the twentieth century Outer Mongolia became the Mongolian (People's) Republic, until the early 1990s completely under Russian domination, while Inner Mongolia has since the 1950s become the so-called Inner Mongolian Autonomous Region of the People's Republic of China, newly defined to include a portion of western Manchuria; it has a rapidly changing population in which Mongols are now only about 10 percent of the total.

2. For the organization and structure of the military forces, see Ch'i-ch'ing Hsiao 1978, esp. pp. 3–17.

3. Allsen 1987, esp. chap. 7, "Recruitment of Manpower," offers a useful succinct account of Mongol manpower recruitment and management.

4. The incident is cited in Ratchnevsky 1991, p. 126.

5. See Waley 1931 for the intriguing story of Qiu Chuji's visit to Chinggis Khan.

6. See Buell 1993b for a succinct life of Sübötei and evaluation of this campaign.

7. Zhao was the Southern Song author of an early account of the Mongols, *Mengda Beilu*, written after his diplomatic visit to the camp of Prince General Mukhali in North China in 1220; he reported on Chinggis as described to him by Mongols and others at that time.

8. Ratchnevsky 1991, p. 145; quoted with permission.

9. Ibid., p. 149.

10. Ibid., p. 151.

11. See *Yuan History* 1370 (1976), *juan* 114, p. 2870. The reference is to another chapter in the *Yuan History, juan* 106, "Table of Empresses and Imperial Concubines" *(Hou fei biao),* where forty women are named, commencing with his principal spouse and first empress, Börte; among them twenty-three are identified as "empresses" and the others as "imperial concubines." According to this account, these are only the women on whom formal, regularized status was bestowed.

12. The *Secret History,* probably composed in either 1228 or 1240, calls Chinggis "Khaghan," but that is an anachronistic interpolation. In his own lifetime he was always addressed simply as "khan," and he avoided all kinds of ostentation and formality in his personal relations with his Mongol people.

13. Henthorn 1963 offers a detailed account.

14. As for the size of the armies making up this field campaign, Han Rulin et al. 1986, 1:157, states that when the army departed in the spring of 1236 it had "about 75,000 men." Han supplies no breakdown of its components, nor does he state how many Mongol chiliarchies were included in it.

15. The Bulgars of the middle Volga, although probably an offshoot of the nation of Bulgaria lying farther west, had an independent history dating back to the fifth century C.E.; the Mongols terminated their existence as a separate national entity.

16. See de Rachewiltz 1993a.

17. For the significance of his short reign, see Allsen 1987.

18. Ibid., pp. 203–207. Once established in Persia, his forces there are calculated to have numbered 300,000, of whom half were Mongol and Turkic cavalry.

19. Although now somewhat dated, the fluent account of Hülegu's western campaign in Grousset 1970, pp. 351–391, is well worth reading.

20. Han Rulin 1986, 1:156, citing Juzjani's *Tabaqat-i nasiri,* as translated by H. G. Raverty.

21. In the mid-twentieth century small pockets of Mongol descendants of Chaghadai's horde appeared to remain in isolated regions of northern Afghanistan. See Iwamura and Schurmann 1954.

22. For a splendidly lucid account of Chaghadai and the origins of Tamerlane, see Manz 1989, esp. pp. 1–40.

19. Khubilai Khan Becomes Emperor of China

1. Doubts that Marco Polo actually visited China, or may have traveled much less within China than his account says, should have been laid to rest by the research of

Frances W. Cleaves 1976 and Yang Zhijiu 1985, pp. 89–134, other publications notwithstanding.

2. De Rachewiltz 1971.
3. See Rossabi 1988, pp. 11–14; this is the standard biography.
4. Later known as Shunde; the name on current maps is Xingtai.
5. Hok-lam Chan 1993d.
6. The three great western campaigns are discussed in Chapter 18.
7. See Jan 1993, which explains that although the Chinese official record ignores Haiyun, as have many modern historians, his place in history can be reconstructed from Buddhist materials.
8. See the biographical study by Hok-lam Chan 1993c. For a discussion of Khubilai's "Xingzhou advisers," see Sun Kekuan 1953, pp. 41–55, and 1968a, pp. 163–172.
9. See biographical studies of Yao Shu and Xu Heng by Hok-lam Chan in de Rachewiltz et al. 1993b, pp. 387–406 and 416–447.
10. This discussion draws on the analysis of Xiao Qiqing [Hsiao Ch'i-ch'ing] 1983.
11. *Yuan History* 1370 (1976), *juan* 158, p. 3713.
12. Both anecdotes are cited in Xiao Qiqing 1983, p. 291. They are taken from the Spirit Way inscription for Yao Shu; the former is also included in his *Yuan History* biography, cited in n. 11. The reference to *Mencius* is to I/I/VI, Legge 1960, p. 136.
13. See also Hok-lam Chan 1993b.
14. Rossabi 1988, pp. 34–36.
15. These events have been analyzed by Sun Kekuan 1958. Li Tan's father-in-law is an interesting example in Yuan times of the "utilitarian," or *gongli,* school of Confucian statecraft (see Chapter 14, Section III, on utilitarian statecraft in the Southern Song). That put him at odds with the more conventional-minded Confucian advisers to Khubilai, who rejoiced at Wang Wentong's fall. For a carefully balanced assessment of Wang Wentong, see Hok-lam Chan in de Rachewiltz et al. 1993b, pp. 520–538, s.v. "Wang Wen-t'ung."
16. The city and the life of its court are well described in Chen Gaohua and Shi Weimin 1988.
17. See Steinhardt 1990, esp. pp. 128–160, for analysis of city plans and maps showing the Jin dynasty Zhongdu and Yuan dynasty Shangdu and Dadu (Beijing), and other writings on Dadu by Steinhardt cited there.
18. Herbert Franke 1978a, pp. 19–20. Franke also discusses further developments, especially caesaropapist concepts from Tibetan Lamaism added to Khubilai's repertory of political ideas by his Tibetan teacher, the monk Phagspa, thus justifying the words "universal emperor and god" in the title of his study.
19. See the translation of the proclamation and discussion of its meaning in Langlois 1981a, Introduction, pp. 3–7.
20. *Song History* 1345 (1977), *juan* 45, "Annals of Lizong," 5, p. 889.
21. The accuracy of this depiction has been challenged by Herbert Franke 1962. See also Chapter 13, Section III.
22. Mote 1960.
23. The first quotation is from Gernet 1962, p. 25. The second is from the Italian Franciscan friar Oderic de Pordonone (in China 1323–1328), quoted ibid., p. 31. See also de Rachewiltz 1971, pp. 178–186.
24. Herbert Franke 1974, esp. pp. 181–184.
25. *Yuan History* 1370 (1976), *juan* 6, p. 118. Shi Shu was a nephew of Shi Tianze,

one of the "hereditary lords" discussed earlier. Shi Shu had served with Möngke in Sichuan in 1258–59.

26. See Joseph Needham 1954–, vol. 5, pt. 7 "Military Technology" (1986), pp. 174–176 and 276–284. See also Herbert Franke 1974.

27. Ch'i-ch'ing Hsiao 1993.

28. The site of this decisive engagement, then called Dingjia Islet *(zhou),* is about 100 miles southwest of modern Nanjing; it is just downriver from the modern district city of Tongling, Anhui.

29. See also the discussion of the surrounding circumstances at the Song court in Chapter 13, Section III.

30. Rossabi 1988, p. 91.

31. See the discussion of Khubilai's motives ibid., pp. 206–220.

32. Ibid., pp. 206–207; on Khubilai's relationship with Empress Chabi, see pp. 67–69.

33. Herbert Franke 1952.

34. The term "Confucian politics" to designate China-oriented policies is used by John W. Dardess 1973. Dardess supplies the authoritative account of Mongol court politics after the death of Khubilai in 1294, and in particular in the period after 1328. "Confucian" in this context does not imply a grasp of or commitment to Confucian philosophical and ethical values, or even to literacy in Chinese. It is used simply to indicate the policy of China-centered governing, in contrast to promoting the steppe interests of the Mongol people.

35. To give an emperor a posthumous title (here "Taiding") plus the designation "Di" (emperor) instead of "Zong" (ancestor) is to deny him a proper place in the dynastic succession by demoting him for some failure; in this case it is because he had participated in the murder of his cousin, the young emperor Yingzong, something sternly warned against in Chinggis Khan's code of customary law, the Jasagh. That standard, however, was not always applied, for example, in the case of Emperor Wenzong, who reigned 1329–1332.

36. One of Toghto's claims to fame is that he is named as the editor in chief of the dynastic histories of the Song, Liao, and Jin dynasties. Although he played no part in their compilation and may not have been literate enough in classical Chinese to read them, he nominally headed the commission that finally brought those long-delayed projects to completion in the early 1340s.

20. CHINA UNDER MONGOL RULE

1. As noted previously (Chapter 2, n. 2), "psychic mobility" is used here in Daniel Lerner's sense: "the capacity for vicarious experience."

2. Farquhar 1990, p. 4; this is a basic reference work for Yuan institutions.

3. See the simplified diagrams of Song and Yuan central governments in Hucker 1985, Introduction; and the more detailed ones in Wei Wenxuan 1987. The names of these political organs are translated in several ways by different writers; in general, Hucker 1985 and Farquhar 1990 are followed here for Song and Yuan governments.

4. In the Chinese civil service system, ranks inhered in the posts and not in the individual performance records of the persons who held the posts. To be rewarded for good performance, a man had to be promoted to a different post with higher rank and salary, not just moved up in grade in the same post, as in most recent and present-day civil service systems.

5. See the complete lists with descriptive notes on all the superintendencies, director-ates, and suboffices of the Six Ministries, in Farquhar 1990, pp. 175–214.

6. *Yuan History* 1370 (1976), *juan* 5, p. 89; quoted in Han Rulin et al. 1986, 1:298. See also Ch'i-ch'ing Hsiao 1978, p. 27. Elizabeth Endicott-West 1989 has reviewed the separation of civilian and military governance in detail, pp. 38–43.

7. This analysis draws on Ch'i-ch'ing Hsiao 1978, which translates chaps. 98 and 99 of the "Treatise on the Military" of the *Yuan History* 1370 (1976) and provides extensive analysis; note in particular pp. 12–32.

8. Both the title and the institution of a Buddhist "imperial preceptor" were taken over from the Xi Xia; see Dunnell 1992.

9. See Petech 1993, and Chen Qingying 1992, a well-informed if somewhat politi-cized biography of Phagspa.

10. Chen Qingying 1992, pp. 141–149.

11. His story is well told in Rossabi 1992.

12. De Rachewiltz 1971, p. 195, notes that the papal envoy John of Marignolli com-mented on discussions he had held with Jews in China in the 1340s.

13. Omitted here is the level of authority that resided in the Dao, sometimes also translated "circuit," because the Yuan dynasty Dao belonged either to the military or to the surveillance systems and did not exercise administrative responsibilities in the descending levels of local administration.

14. These figures, taken from Farquhar 1990, pp. 414–421, reflect his analysis of the government as of the year 1332, to which the geographic sections of the *Yuan History* (1370) pertain. Farquhar uses the translations "circuit" and "route" where I use "prefecture"; he uses "prefecture" where I use "sub-prefecture," and we agree on the use of "county" (or "district") for the *xian*. As elsewhere in this work, I have counted the sub-prefectures *(zhou)* together with the counties *(xian)* as forming the base level of local administration.

15. *Sheh* is more properly spelled *she;* the form *sheh* is used here both to better indicate its pronunciation and to avoid confusion with the English pronoun.

16. Khubilai's proclamation of 1270 to the *sheh* is quoted and commented on in K. C. Hsiao 1960, pp. 37–38. In many regions, local terms other than *sheh* were used for analogous groupings in rural and village society, and these were made to assume similar functions.

17. The Mongol secondary capital at Shangdu, built and maintained by Khubilai and his successors as their summer capital for escaping the heat of China Proper between May and September, was a place where Chinese court protocol also could be escaped and congenial Mongol customs could prevail. It was not, however, functionally parallel to the Khitans' Supreme Capital in Inner Asia, where primary responsibility for governing the steppe portion of the Liao empire was located.

18. *Yuan History* 1370 (1976), *juan* 17, p. 377.

19. Meng Siming [Meng Ssu-ming] 1938.

20. It has been shown, nonetheless, that a process of cultural assimilation of Mongols (mostly those of high status and resident in China) may have been incipient by the end of the Yuan dynasty; see Xiao Qiqing [Hsiao Ch'i-ch'ing] 1985.

21. Farquhar 1990 translates this as "agent."

22. This account draws on Endicott-West 1989, a book-length study of Yuan local government.

23. On Ahmad and Sangha, see Herbert Franke 1993.

24. This discussion draws on Huang Qinglian 1977.

25. The name of this sect and of others mentioned in this section cannot be adequately

translated by one simple rendering into lexical equivalents because their meanings are intentionally multilayered.

26. Sun Kekuan 1970.

27. This briefly paraphrases the translation in Waley 1931, pp. 100–101.

28. Tao-chung Yao 1986.

29. In addition to the Quanzhen sect, there were sects known as Dadao (The Great Way), Taiyi (The Supreme Oneness), and Zhenda (True and Great) in the North, as well as numerous splinterings and imitators of shorter duration and less importance.

30. For a detailed discussion of other aspects of Daoist activity in Yuan times, including the revival of the historically important Maoshan center of Daoism in Jiangsu, see Sun Kekuan 1968b.

31. See Zhaqi Siqin 1978, chaps. 13 and 14. This important work by Zhaqi (Sechen Jagchid) is devoted to the relationship of Mongolia to Tibet through history.

32. Ibid., chap. 8 and passim.

33. See, e.g., Jiang Weiqiao 1928, *juan* 3, p. 17a.

34. On the later links between Tibet and Mongolia, see Chapter 27, Sections II and III.

35. See ter Haar 1992.

36. Kenneth K. S. Chen 1964, pp. 426–433. The late Yuan popular religious uprisings are discussed in Chapter 21.

37. Collcutt 1981.

38. Ibid., esp. pp. 61–68.

39. Ping-ti Ho 1967. For a brief discussion of problems in interpreting Yuan population data, see CHC 1994, 6:618–622.

40. See Liu Zhaoyou 1978, where an appendix lists more than 200 Yuan authors published in close to 900 different old (through Ming and Qing times) extant editions in the category of "collected literary works" alone.

41. For the emergence of the "Yuan" drama known as *zaju* in Jin and Yuan times, see Chapter 12, Section IV, and further comments in this chapter.

42. Tao Zongyi ca. 1367 (1959), *juan* 10, pp. 126–127; and *juan* 18, p. 225.

43. Mote 1960.

44. Hartman 1993.

45. For those developments in Southern Song times, see Chapter 14.

46. Wing-tsit Chan 1982 discusses the extent to which Southern Song thought was known in Jin China, and the stages through which the dominance of Zhu Xi was brought about in Yuan China. More recently, Hoyt Cleveland Tillman, in Tillman and West 1995, pp. 71–114, has provided a fuller account of Jin period Confucianism, showing that it did not lack knowledge of Southern Song thought and learning, correcting the traditional view that the Southern Song Confucian Zhao Fu, taken captive and brought into North China in 1235, single-handedly brought about the revival of Confucian learning in the post-Jin North. The now superseded traditional view is reflected in Mote 1960.

47. See Hok-lam Chan 1993b.

48. Lynn, 1980. This outstanding biography of a Yuan writer includes translations of all of Guan's extant literary works, and makes a good introduction to the scholarly and literary milieu of mid-Yuan times.

49. For Liu Yin's biography, see Langlois 1993b; also Tu 1982.

50. See Chapter 14. On Wu Cheng's life and thought, see Gedalecia 1981 and 1982.

51. Hok-lam Chan 1984.

52. On Toghto's role in late Yuan government, see Dardess 1973, esp. pp. 75–94; he is briefly noted in Chapter 19, Section IX. The problems associated with the compilation of the histories are aptly reviewed in Zhou Liangxiao and Gu Juying 1993, pp. 767–772.

53. The most notable among those other works is the *Wenxian tongkao* of Ma Duanlin (1254–1323).

54. See Farquhar 1990, pp. 132–135.

55. For the emergence of Yuan drama in Jin times, see Chapter 12, Section IV. For discussions of the dramatic art in Yuan times, and translations of representative dramas, see Crump 1980 and Shih 1976, in addition to the works cited in Chapter 12.

56. The Four Masters are Huang Gongwang (1269–1354), Wu Zhen (1280–1354), Ni Zan (1301–1374), and Wang Meng (ca. 1308–1385). For the "revival and synthesis" of Yuan dynasty literati painting, see Fong 1992, pp. 431–500. For a conspectus of painting throughout the Yuan period, see Cahill 1976.

57. See Marilyn Wong Fu 1981; the reference to "revelation" is from Chu-tsing Li, quoted p. 372. Studies by Chu-tsing Li and Stephen H. West in Langlois 1981a also bear on the interaction of northern and southern influences in art and literature of this period.

58. Fong 1992, p. 440.

59. On Guan Daosheng, see Chen Baozhen 1977; this study of her life also includes examples of her painting and calligraphy.

21. FROM CHAOS TOWARD A NEW CHINESE ORDER

1. An account of this period that offers more detail is given in Mote 1988b.

2. Historians in China since 1949 have made an intense effort to study this period, which, in accordance with government objectives and political directives, has been designated a "good period" in the long history of the people's struggles. The new findings do not validate the skewed paradigm, and much contrary detail has been ignored, yet the efforts of some of the better scholars working under these conditions have added immensely to our knowledge about the age. To cite one example, Yang Ne and Chen Gaohua 1985 is a very large and systematic compilation from traditional sources published under a title meaning "Materials on Peasant Warfare in the Yuan Period." Produced by a team of good scholars starting in the 1960s, their work was finally completed and published in the 1980s. In their preface the compilers state: "Yuan period social contradictions are quite complex; the class character of some of the armed violent movements is not easily determined, so the present compilation in order to advance this study a step farther has included those. Where it has been possible to determine that particular cases represent rebellious actions undertaken by upper-stratum individuals, those have all been excluded." That comment indicates that the actions of "upper-stratum" (or "bad class background") individuals have no value for history and, it seems, no relevance for this large and complex subject. Under working conditions that demand such arbitrary judgments, the contributions of even excellent researchers are inherently flawed.

3. The reigns of the later Yuan rulers are briefly discussed in Chapter 19, Section IX. See also the Yuan Dynastic Succession Chart there.

4. See the argument for calling those objectives "Confucian policy" in Dardess 1973 and 1983, and the discussion in Chapter 19, Section IX.

5. Quoted from Yang Ne and Chen Gaohua 1985, vol. 1; see esp. pp. 192–196 for this poem and for anecdotes about the inept handling of banditry and lawlessness.

6. *Ming History* 1739 (1974), *juan* 124, p. 3717.

7. Hansen 1990, esp. chap. 6.

8. That is, as minor "deities" in a cosmos with no all-dominant major deity. Certain aspects of the Chinese cultural milieu cause many familiar Western terms to be misleading when taken as "equivalents" of Chinese terms.

9. Hansen 1990, p. 141.

10. This point has been mentioned in Chapter 19, Section II, in connection with Buddhist influences on the young Khubilai Khan. Three Teachings syncretism in Yuan thought in general is the subject of Liu Ts'un-yan and Berling 1982. The new Daoist sects are discussed in Chapter 20, Section III.

11. The doctrines and their social significance are analyzed in Hok-lam Chan 1969. An important and more recent study is ter Haar 1992.

12. "Hong jin jun," or "Red Turban army," is not a new name; for an example of its use in North China as early as 1127 at the time of the Jurchen conquest, see Bi Yuan 1796 (1957), *juan* 100, p. 2626.

13. Qiu Shushen 1977.

14. The showdown battle at Lake Boyang in 1363, and its consequences, are well analyzed in Dreyer 1982, and placed in the larger context of military history in Dreyer 1988. The story of Chen Youliang's Han Dynasty is recounted in Section III of this chapter.

15. On White Lotus and Red Turban doctrines in relation to rebellions in later Chinese history, see Hok-lam Chan 1969 and Wang Chongwu 1948a. For Han Shantong's claim to be descended from Song emperors, see Wu Han 1965, pp. 42–44, and Qian Qianyi 1626? (1982), *juan* 1. Other rumors of the time claimed that the last Yuan ruler, Emperor Shun, was a descendant of the boy emperor of the Southern Song captured at Hangzhou in 1276 and taken to the court of Khubilai Khan. See Qian Qianyi 1643 (1936), *juan* 25, p. 1.

16. *Yuan History* 1370 (1976), *juan* 98, p. 2509; this passage is translated in Ch'i-ch'ing Hsiao 1978, p. 74. The discussion draws on Hsiao's analysis, esp. pp. 27–32.

17. Dreyer 1988, p. 97; see this and Dreyer 1982 for a fuller account of the military and political history of the late Yuan.

18. John W. Dardess in DMB, pp. 724–728.

19. See, e.g., Qiu Shushen 1982, pp. 91–108. The first capital of the "restored" Song dynasty was at Bozhou in Anhui; later it was moved 120 miles southeast to Anfeng, present-day Shouchun, in Anhui; after being driven out of Kaifeng at the end of 1358, Liu Futong returned the capital to Anfeng. The chronology here follows Qian Qianyi 1626? (1982), *juan* 1.

20. The campaign's tactics and strategic implications are fully analyzed in Dreyer 1974.

21. Qian Qianyi 1626? (1982), *juan* 5; Wu Han 1965, pp. 137–138.

22. See John W. Dardess in DMB, pp. 1069–73.

23. The extracts are from pp. 1–49 of Wu Han's biography, as indicated. Parentheses are as in the original; passages in brackets contain my own interpolations. My translation omits all of the numerous footnotes in the original. Wu Han (1909–1969) was an eminent specialist in Yuan and Ming history and a principal promoter of historical study in Mainland China before his untimely death, caused by sufferings endured in prison in consequence of political factionalism. His thor-

oughly documented biography of Zhu Yuanzhang is noteworthy for its lively and engaging style, but is marred by excessive reliance on formulaic Marxian historical interpretation, mostly omitted from the excerpts translated here.

22. ZHU YUANZHANG BUILDS HIS MING DYNASTY

1. For a brief biography, see Romeyn Taylor in DMB, pp. 850–854.
2. *Ming History* 1739 (1974), *juan* 127, p. 3769.
3. Ibid., p. 3795.
4. Ibid., *juan* 136, p. 3925.
5. Guo's third son was accused of treason and executed sometime thereafter.
6. Note, e.g., Wu Han's dismissal of the idea that Zhu's religious practices reflected genuine belief; Wu Han 1965, p. 48, and elsewhere throughout this biography of Zhu.
7. Dreyer 1982, p. 12. See Dreyer 1988 for a full account of the military history of the Ming founding.
8. That aspect of political disintegration is described in Chapter 21, Section I. This period in history makes it clear that the skills were at hand to accomplish the arming of the populace and the training in military arts at levels then necessary for military success against the state's armed forces, yet many questions about this process remain unanswered.
9. Wu Han 1965 in several places (e.g., pp. 5, 54) includes Xu Da among Zhu Yuanzhang's boyhood village companions, though that is not borne out by traditional sources for Xu's life.
10. The impact of the Jinhua scholars, especially Liu Ji, on the early Ming government has been stressed by Dardess 1983, esp. pp. 121–181. His argument, while not fully followed here, merits careful consideration. See also their biographies by Hok-lam Chan and F. W. Mote in DMB, pp. 932–938 and 1225–31, respectively, and the further discussion in Section IV of this chapter.
11. Wang Chongwu 1948a, esp. pt. 2.
12. Wu Han advanced this view as early as 1940; his last statement on the subject is found in Wu Han 1965, pp. 139–147.
13. Translated from the text as quoted in Wang Chongwu 1948a, pp. 67–68.
14. Ibid.; Wang Chongwu's interpretation also is drawn upon here; see also MSL, "Taizu shilu," *juan* 26, pp. 10a–12b.
15. These ambiguities of early Ming cultural policy have been called to my attention by James Geiss in a personal communication.
16. *Mencius* 2.2.12.7; Legge 1960, 2:231.
17. Zhi Weicheng and Ren Zhiyuan 1932.
18. MSL, "Taizu shilu," *juan* 34, pp. 1aff. Most of this *juan* covers Xu Da's actions on taking the city and Taizu's responses to the news.
19. For example, the *Dictionary of Ming Biography* (1976) lists all the Ming emperors under their personal names; those are not well known to readers of historical materials, but are becoming more so as all historical writings produced in Mainland China follow that practice.
20. The anthropologists' word "patriline" is not yet found in many dictionaries, but its meaning should be obvious.
21. This discussion draws on Langlois 1988, esp. pp. 174–178, and works cited there.
22. Hucker 1961, p. 10; Wu Han 1965, p. 284.
23. The city we today call Nanjing (Nanking) was called Jiqing in 1356 when Zhu

first occupied it, but that was a recent name change, and most people (and most books) still called it Jiankang, the name it had had since the Northern Song incorporated the area in 975. Zhu Yuanzhang changed Jiqing to Yingtian in 1356; that remained its proper name throughout the Ming dynasty, although after the capital was moved to Beijing in 1420, it came to be more commonly called Nanjing, "the Southern Capital." Here it will usually be called Nanjing, its subsequent Ming and its modern name.

24. Wang Jianying 1992; Farmer 1976, esp. pp. 28–70.

25. Mote 1977a.

26. The best critical chronology of Zhu Yuanzhang's life and reign is found in Sun Zhengrong 1983.

27. Langlois 1993a analyzes the code, its revisions, and its implementation throughout the dynasty.

28. *Yi ren,* "[my] one person"; this usage echoes the ancient phrase *yu yi ren,* "my one person," used by rulers claiming omnipotence and the right to possess all within the realm. Zhu uses it here to express the limitations of the ruler's capacities.

29. This decree, found in MSL, is translated here from the critically edited Chinese text as quoted in Sun Zhengrong 1983, p. 166; Sun notes that the wording varies in the different sources preserving it.

30. For the development of the Neo-Confucian curriculum, see Chapter 14, Section III.

31. Wu Han 1948.

32. Ho 1962.

33. See F. W. Mote in DMB, p. 1575.

34. Ibid., pp. 426–433.

35. Wei Wenxuan 1987, p. 172.

36. For simplified diagrams of the Ming government and those of other dynastic periods, see Hucker 1985, Introduction; for more detailed diagrams, see Wei Wenxuan 1987.

37. See the wide-ranging general assessment of the Hongwu reign in Langlois 1988, where it is spelled "Hung-wu."

38. Wu's biography of Zhu Yuanzhang, written during World War II and with a postface dated "Qinghua University [Beijing], August 12, 1948," was published at an unnamed place (probably Shanghai) in 1949. That edition was later revised and published in a final version in 1965. In some ways the 1948 version is superior in its interpretation of the man and the period, while the 1965 version supersedes it in detail and the thoroughness of its documentation. On Wu Han, see Li Youning 1973; as of that writing, Li was still unable to know the facts surrounding Wu Han's torture and death in 1969.

39. Wu Han 1949, pp. 280–281.

40. Wu Han 1965, pp. 300–301. His earlier amateur psychiatry would seem to offer more of interest than his later doctrinaire Marxism.

41. MSL, *juan* 35, pp. 636–637; also briefly noted in Xia Xie 1873, *juan* 1, pp. 198–199.

42. *Yuan History* 1370 (1976), *juan* 43, pp. 918–919. Needham 1954–, vol. 4, pt. 2, pp. 507–508, offers a related translation from the *Yuan History* and discussion of the horological significance of the clock, but does not note this information on its ultimate fate.

43. Farquhar 1990, p. 133.

44. A third bureau, for Western astronomy, was added when the Jesuits brought European astronomy to Beijing early in the seventeenth century.
45. This is a dominant theme in Dardess 1983.
46. Langlois 1981b; Langlois acknowledges a debt to Sun Kekuan's important writings on the Jinhua school.
47. Liu Ji has been most fully studied by Hok-lam Chan, who prepared his biography in DMB 1976, pp. 932–938; see also his other writings cited there.
48. K. C. Hsiao 1982, pp. 557–563.
49. Ibid., p. 563.
50. Dardess 1983, p. 184.
51. This exchange, quoted in Gu Yingtai, *juan* 14, under the fourth year of Hongwu, is cited in Yang Yifan 1992, p. 51, which reviews (pp. 49–55) the ongoing debate between Ming Taizu and a number of his advisers on severe versus lenient laws and punishments. As quoted in Liu's biography in *Ming History* 128, p. 3781, the incident is rendered unintelligible. The emperor's letter to Liu is preserved in Liu's collected works, Liu Ji 1572, *juan* 1, p. 64; the full text of Liu's "detailed reply" does not appear to have survived.
52. This explanation, factual but no longer held to be sufficient, was set forth in Mote 1961.
53. Cited in Wu Han 1965, p. 265.

23. CIVIL WAR AND USURPATION, 1399–1402

1. F. W. Mote in DMB under the names "Ch'i T'ai," "Lien Tzu-ning" and "Fang Hsiao-ju" gives biographical accounts that bear on the special problems of the Jianwen reign.
2. Wang Chongwu 1948b.
3. Zhu Di's use of this historical analogy is discussed ibid., pp. 96–99.
4. Li Zhi 1611 (1959), *juan* 5, p. 85.
5. Daoyan later was known by the name Yao Guangxiao; see Eugen Feifel and Hok-lam Chan in DMB, pp. 1561–1565, s.v. "Yao Kuang-hsiao."
6. *Ming History* 1739 (1974), *juan* 141, pp. 4017–21.
7. The Chinese traditionally reckoned nine degrees of relationship not including that of teacher-student. Zhu Di, the Yongle emperor, in his rage against the scholar-officials who rejected him, declared that his punishment would "extend to ten degrees of relationship." That extension of guilt by association was previously unheard of, and came to symbolize utterly ruthless persecution.
8. Wang Chongwu 1948b, esp. chap. 3. See also the discussion in Hok-lam Chan 1988, pp. 182–304, esp. pp. 202–205.
9. Mote 1977b, pp. 216 and 254.
10. First promulgated in 1367, reissued in 1375, and repeatedly revised thereafter to the end of his reign. See Yang Yifan 1992.
11. The terms arose in antiquity in discussions of semi-legendary earlier rulers who passed their thrones to the most worthy, as opposed to those later heads of early dynasties who passed their thrones to their own sons. From that contrast a range of further extended meanings developed. Not even an extreme interpretation of "jia tianxia," however, implied the absence of private property, as some recent historians would have it. The term was used to criticize a ruler's excessive exploitation of his position and no more.
12. K. C. Hsiao 1982, pp. 570–571.

13. The proposed and attempted changes are discussed in Hok-lam Chan 1988, pp. 187–191. Fang's place in political thought is well analyzed in K. C. Hsiao 1982, pp. 563–575. A valuable analysis of Fang's thought in relation to the development of Ming government, presented in a focus different from that offered here, is found in Dardess 1983, esp. pp. 264–289.
14. Shang Chuan 1989, p. 15; Chao Zhongchen 1993, pp. 8–13.
15. *Ming History* 1739 (1974), *juan* 100, pp. 1505–47.
16. See Soulliere 1987 for a discussion of Empress Xu and her relationship with Empress Ma. See also Chou Tao-chi and Ray Huang in DMB, pp. 566–569.

24. THE "SECOND FOUNDING" OF THE MING DYNASTY

1. The posthumous temple name awarded him after his death in 1424 was Taizong; here, in keeping with Chinese convention, he is called Chengzu, the more elevated title awarded him in 1538.
2. On the institution and the fate of Taizu's "nobility of merit," see Romeyn Taylor 1976b.
3. Lienche Tu Fang 1966 both provides a study of the institution called Shuji shi and lists of all the persons selected.
4. Hok-lam Chan 1988, pp. 208–212.
5. The emperor favored the calligraphy of the brothers Shen Du (1357–1434) and Shen Can (1379–1453), who wrote out texts to be carved on woodblocks for printing many early Ming palace editions. See DMB, pp. 1191–92; and Mote and Chu Hung-lam 1988, pp. 121–132, which has illustrations showing examples of such editions.
6. Tsien 1985, p. 174.
7. See the discussion of "orthodoxy" and Zhu Xi's commentaries in Chapter 14, Section III.
8. There is a vast literature in many languages on Zheng He and his great voyages. See, e.g., Levathes 1994.
9. Huang Zhangjian 1961.
10. MSL, Hongwu 165, p. 2544; quoted in Huang Zhangjian 1961, p. 90. See also Hucker 1961, p. 48.
11. For the attempted usurpation in 1425, see Chapter 25, Section I. For those which occurred during the Zhengde reign, 1505–1521, see Chapter 26.
12. "Han" as an ethnic designation is used throughout this work as a synonym for "Chinese."
13. Ming China's boundaries and border zones are the subject of Chapter 27.
14. See Morris Rossabi in DMB, pp. 685–686, s.v. "Isiha."
15. Chao Zhongchen 1993, p. 283. This is typical of the way the event is interpreted in Mainland Chinese historiography.
16. Rossabi 1975, esp. pp. 28–29, stresses this point with regard to Mongolia and western Inner Asia, e.g., Hami and other polities in the Tarim Basin.
17. *Ming History* 1739 (1974), *juan* 327, pp. 8463–8569.
18. For a brief review of Oyirat (Oirat) history, see Lai Jiadu and Li Guangbi 1954, chaps. 2 and 3.
19. The basic study, with translation of an important Ming period account, is found in Wolfgang Franke 1949.
20. See Gaspardone 1976.

21. For a convenient review of this phase of Sino-Japanese relations written from the point of view of Japanese history, see Tanaka Takeo 1977, pp. 163–171.
22. See the biography of Sayid Ajall, Buell 1993a.
23. Needham 1954–, vol. 4, pt. 3, sec. 29, "Nautics," pp. 379–699, provides an extensive review of Chinese nautical technology in comparison with that in the rest of the world at that time. Significant corrections and refinements have been added by scholars writing since that was published in 1971.
24. Chang Kuei-sheng in DMB, pp. 194–200; Mote 1991.
25. In an interesting and influential argument, Needham 1970, pp. 40–70, stresses this point while exaggerating China's benign attitude.
26. I refer to the television film and the book both called *He Shang,* translated as *River Elegy,* which initiated great intellectual ferment in China in the late 1980s and early 1990s. They were written by Su Xiaokang and several associates.
27. Zhang Huiyi 1937 is the definitive monograph on the porcelain pagoda. For two paintings of it made by an English artist in 1842, see Cree 1981, pp. 107 and 118.
28. Chao Zhongchen 1993, p. 435. The divinity's name is Zhenwu dijun.
29. The palace or Forbidden City walls enclosed an area 960 meters north to south and 760 meters east to west, roughly three-fourths of a mile by three-fifths of a mile. See Steinhardt 1990, p. 172. The inner palace city at Nanjing was square and somewhat larger (roughly 1,200 meters on a side). The imperial city at Nanjing, roughly square, was similar in size to that at Beijing (2.5 kilometers, almost one mile, on a side). See Cheng Kuang-yu and Hsu Sheng-mo 1984, 2:6–7. In both Nanjing and Beijing the imperial city (enclosing the palace city) occupied only a small portion of the area within the cities' walls.
30. See Steinhardt 1990 for an illuminating discussion of the layout of successive Jin, Yuan, and Ming-Qing capitals on the site we today call Beijing.
31. For nostalgic reading about the "old Peking," see Arlington and Lewisohn 1935 (rpt. 1987); Kates 1952 (rpt. 1967); Blofeld 1961 (rpt. 1989); and Morrison 1985. The photographs in the last are particularly to be commended.

25. MING CHINA IN THE FIFTEENTH CENTURY

1. Charles O. Hucker in DMB, pp. 279–289; Hucker 1978, pp. 85, 90.
2. Wang Chongwu 1948b, pp. 135–146, analyzes Zhu Gaoxu's rebellion in comparison with Chengzu's civil war of a quarter-century earlier.
3. See biographies of the three Yangs in DMB, s.v. "Yang Jung" (by Charles O. Hucker, pp. 1519–22) and "Yang Shih-ch'i," which includes Yang P'u (by Tilemann Grimm, pp. 1535–38).
4. Cahill 1978, p. 23, calls Xuanzong "a painter of modest talent"; he discusses trends in painting at the time of the "Xuande Academy."
5. Jiao Hong 1616 (1965), *juan* 117, pp. 47a–51a. The more dramatic details of these encounters are not repeated in the official histories, yet all the historical works stress that the Grand Dowager Empress was aware of Wang Zhen's evil influence and sought to restrain him.
6. His title was "Holder of the [Imperial] Writing Brush," *bingbi taijian,* who wrote down the emperor's words, or wrote down words to be attributed to the emperor. Whether he ever became the head of the Directorate of Ceremonial is not clear. His relationship with the emperor was so close that his title was of secondary importance.

7. See the discussion of these campaigns in Jung-pang Lo 1969, esp. pp. 60–62; and Ray Huang 1976b.

8. The incident is described and analyzed in Mote 1974. The ethnic name Oyirat is also spelled Oirat, Oyirad, and, in later centuries, Eleuth, etc.

9. See the thorough monographic coverage of the events and the period in de Heer 1986. The analysis of the nature of Ming imperial rule and the dynastic institution (pp. 121–136) is particularly insightful.

10. This is a reference to Levy 1981, *Levy's Eleven Laws of the Disillusionment of the True Liberal,* in which law number four states: "Always pray that your opposition be wicked. In wickedness there is a strong strain toward rationality. Therefore there is always the possibility, in theory, of handling the wicked by outthinking them. Corollary one: Good intentions randomize behavior." Officials had no difficulty outthinking the dull-minded, willful, but not truly wicked Emperor Xianzong. When, however, their opposition was the emperor's wily, suitably wicked attendants, opponents had to be quite ingenious as well as long-suffering.

11. Cited in Bao Hongchang 1991, pp. 167–168.

12. Xia Xie 1873, *juan* 33, pp. 1258–59, discusses the alternate accounts.

13. She is known in history as Consort Ji; see *Ming History* 1739 (1974), *juan* 113, pp. 3521–23, where the complicated story of her background and the unsuccessful attempts to locate members of her family are set forth.

14. Chaoying Fang in DMB, pp. 298–304.

15. For a fuller account of the two reigns, see Mote 1988a.

16. See Yung-deh Richard Chu in DMB, pp. 651–653; also *Ming History* 1739 (1974), *juan* 304, pp. 7777–78. Note discrepancies in the information concerning his name and background, p. 7797, n. 9.

17. De Heer 1986, pp. 126–127.

18. For an important example, see Chapter 26, Section VI, on Wang Yangming.

19. *Ming History* 1739 (1974), *juan* 15, p. 196.

20. Principal items dating from the Hongwu reign are listed and analyzed in Yang Yifan 1992. A large compilation of about twenty relevant legal and statutory texts printed in 1579, called *Huang Ming Zhishu,* has been reprinted in two volumes (Tokyo, 1969) under the editorial supervision of Nagasawa Kikuya, with critical notes by Yamane Yukio. Earlier versions of the *Huang Ming Zhishu* also are cited in Chinese writings.

21. Systematized by Dong Zhongshu (179–104 B.C.E.), heaven-man correlative theories acquired a place in Confucian statecraft, although for some centuries following Dong's death they degenerated into a focus on apocryphal writings and prodigies of nature. Dong's basic idea, that there is an interaction between heaven (cosmic forces) and the ruler of men which legitimates and sustains a dynasty, retained importance in later Confucian thought. See K. C. Hsiao 1979, pp. 496–530.

22. They were Grand Secretary Peng Shi and Minister of Rites Yao Kui; for their biographies, see DMB s.v. "Yao K'uei" (by Hok-lam Chan, pp. 1557–59) and "P'eng Shih" (by Tilemann Grimm, pp. 1119–21).

23. On Liang Fang, see DMB s.v. "Liang Fang" (by Chaoying Fang, pp. 896–898).

24. *Ming History* 1739 (1974), *juan* 113, pp. 3524–25.

25. The main throne hall was constructed three times, that is, twice rebuilt after fires in Ming times; in 1562, after the second rebuilding its name was changed to Huangji Dian (Hall of the Imperial Supreme).

26. *Ming History* 1739 (1974), *juan* 72, p. 1732; cited in Wang Tianyou 1992, p. 23. The discussion that follows draws on Wang.
27. MSL, Xiaozong, *juan* 2, p. 11b, day *dingwei*.
28. Ibid., *juan* 3, pp. 6b–7a, day *dingsi*.
29. Ibid., pp. 15a and 16a.
30. See Huang Shengzhang 1982, esp. pp. 147–200.
31. *Ming History* 1739 (1974), *juan* 85 and 86, pp. 2077–2118; *juan* 83 and 84, pp. 2013–75, deal in similar fashion with the management of the Yellow River.
32. The broader subject is ably summarized in Needham 1954–, vol. 4, pt. 3, "Hydraulics," pp. 209–378, with maps, diagrams, and many excellent illustrations.
33. See the discussion and translation of relevant sections of the *Yuan History* (1370) in Schurmann 1956, pp. 108–130.
34. Fang Guozhen is discussed in Chapter 21 as one of the regional warlords, the so-called rival contenders against whom Zhu Yuanzhang fought in his rise to power.
35. Wu Jihua 1970, vol. 1, pt. 1, pp. 125–173, deals with maritime shipping in Yuan and early Ming.
36. Beiping was formally renamed Shuntian, "complying with Heaven," but commonly was called Beijing, "northern capital."
37. See Needham 1954–, vol. 4, pt. 3, p. 452, note b on tonnage; on the size of the early Ming navy in comparative context, see p. 484.
38. Wolfgang Franke in DMB, s.v. "Hsü Yu-chen," pp. 612–615; Xia Xie 1873, *juan* 27, pp. 1077–78.
39. Ray Huang in DMB, s.v. "Liu Ta-hsia," pp. 958–962.
40. Ray Huang in DMB, s.v. "P'an Chi-hsün," pp. 1107–11.
41. *Ming History* 1739 (1974), *juan* 83–86.

26. THE CHANGING WORLD OF THE SIXTEENTH CENTURY

1. This is Lynn Struve's designation of the Ming-Qing transition; see Struve 1993.
2. Peterson 1976 proposes a schematic periodization of Ming history in which he describes most of the sixteenth century as "a period of expansion and change." Plaks 1987, esp. pp. 3–52, citing Peterson 1976, offers a masterly analysis of "the age of cultural flowering" and its "burst of creativity" that commenced early in the sixteenth century.
3. For a well-analyzed factual account of the reign, see Geiss 1988a. Zhu Houzhao's biography in DMB, under "Chu Hou-chao," pp. 307–315, reflects the most critical views of Ming period historians, some of which should be modified.
4. He was Prince of Anhua, a third-generation descendant of Zhu Zhan, Prince of Qing, Ming Taizu's sixteenth son.
5. Geiss 1987 gives an account of the Leopard Quarter and the role it played in Emperor Wuzong's life and in his governing.
6. See chief Grand Secretary Yang Tinghe's long memorial sternly rebuking the emperor for his conduct and irresponsibility, citing several specific examples, in MSL, "Wuzong," *juan* 120, "first month, 1515, day *jihai*." Many such memorials were submitted; the record usually notes that they were "not responded to."
7. His formal name was Wang Shouren (1472–1529); he is discussed in Section VI of this chapter.
8. This phase of his accession is conveniently summarized in Lin Yanqing 1993, chap. 2.

9. See DMB, s.v. "Chang Fu-ching," pp. 67–70.

10. *Ming History* 1739 (1974), *juan* 196, pp. 5173–74.

11. There is little discussion of this procedure in traditional sources. See *Ta Ming huidian* (1587), ed. *Wanyou wenku* 1936, *juan* 5, p. 105, and the discussion in Lin Yanqing 1993, pp. 132–133.

12. The term *ningxing*, "scheming sycophant," is applied to them in several traditional sources; see, e.g., Fu Wei-lin ca. 1660 (1937), *juan* 155.

13. Chu Hung-lam 1994, pp. 276–277.

14. A loose translation of the phrase *zhen ji yiqie*, cited in Wang Tianyou 1991a, pp. 221–222.

15. See Chapter 22, Section III, for the radical new structure of the central administration instituted in 1380.

16. Quoted in Wang Tianyou 1991a, p. 221.

17. This interpretation draws on Chu Hung-lam 1994; for the historical setting, see Geiss 1988b, esp. pp. 443–450. See also the book-length treatment of the ritual controversy in Carney T. Fisher 1990.

18. Geiss 1988b, pp. 461–465 and 479–482.

19. See the complete listing of Ming Grand Secretaries, the senior listed first under each year, in *Ming History* 1739 (1974), *juan* 109 and 110; those for Shizong's reign in *juan* 110 are found on pp. 3351–62. For the growth of the institution called the Neige, or "cabinet," see Section I of this chapter and Chapter 25, Section II.

20. See the useful analysis in Wang Tianyou 1992, pp. 36–53.

21. He held the position until he was dismissed in 1532, then was recalled in 1534 and retired for reasons of health in 1535.

22. For a thoughtful example of the rare favorable assessment of Yan Song, see So 1976, pp. 1586–91; for condemnatory but fully argued interpretations of Yan Song, see Lin Yanqing 1993, pp. 208–235 and passim; and Zhang Xianqing's book-length treatment, 1992.

23. See Ray Huang 1981, chap. 5; Chaoying Fang, "Hai Rui," in DMB, pp. 474–479; and the works cited in both. The incident led to Wu Han's imprisonment and death in 1969 at the hands of the "Gang of Four" after having been targeted by Mao Zedong for his criticism of Mao's leadership style.

24. See the account of Wang's early years, to 1508, in Tu 1976.

25. See Wing-tsit Chan 1976 (DMB), for a succinct outline of Wang's life and thought.

26. See Julia Ching in DMB, pp. 41–42; and Tu 1976, passim. Many differences in Wang's and Zhan's philosophical orientations remained, evident in Zhan's writings from the years after Wang's death in 1529.

27. See the discussion of the Guizhou *tusi*, "native offices," in Chapter 27, Section IV.

28. Dates based on the chronological biography *(nian pu)* appended (*juan* 33–34) to his *Collected Works (Wang Wencheng Gong Quanshu)*, Ming Longqing edition, reproduced in SBCK.

29. Yü Ying-shih 1997, p. 2: "Scholars either argued with him or against him, but rarely without him. I therefore propose to call this period the age of Wang Yangming."

30. In the early Confucian school text *The Great Learning (Daxue)*, there is this sentence: "The perfection of knowledge consists in the investigation of things" [*gewu zhizhi*]." In his editing of that text, Zhu Xi focused on this sentence and added extensive commentary; see Wing-tsit Chan 1963a, pp. 86–94.

31. Zhan Juoshui was a disciple of Chen Xianzhang (1428–1500), one of whose prin-

cipal tenets was that of *zi de,* or "acquiring insight for oneself," compatible with Wang's more fully developed concepts of the self-knowing mind. See Huang P'ei and Ching 1976. Chen spent his active life mostly in distant Guangdong Province.

32. Wing-tsit Chan 1963a, p. 658; and see pp. 654–691 for translations from Wang Yangming's essential writings. See also Wing-tsit Chan 1963b for a complete translation of Wang's major works. The discussion of Wang Yangming's thought here is indebted to but does not closely follow Wing-tsit Chan's writings.

33. Wang Yangming took the term *liangzhi* from *Mencius* VII.A/XV; see Legge 1960, 2:456. It is also translated "intuitive knowledge."

34. Wing-tsit Chan 1963b, pp. xxxvi–xxxix. A useful discussion of Wang Yangming's thought is also found in Carsun Chang 1962.

35. Wing-tsit Chan 1963a, p. 687.

36. A number of Wang Yangming school followers (and other mid- and late Ming personages) appear in Pei-Yi Wu 1990, a study of autobiographical writing in China. For Wang Ji ("Wang Chi"), see pp. 216–222. Note also "Teng Huo-ch'ü (1498–1570?)" and "Hu Chih (1517–85)," pp. 116–127.

37. Quite predictably, Wang Gen's "good class background" and his concern for the poor earned him the designation of "progressive thinker" in post–1949 Mainland China; writings in that vein are numerous. The Wang Yangming school in general has not fared well there because all forms of idealist philosophy are seen as bourgeois and reactionary. But one prominent historian of thought in the PRC has proposed the starkly revisionist notion that Wang Yangming's radical idealism was in fact a breakthrough in materialist thinking (hence "good"), because the mind, in Wang's definition, was part of the physical (material) self and subject to the physical senses, and hence is well grounded in materialistic conceptions! See Li Zehou 1982, pp. 242–252.

38. Rong Zhaozu 1941, pp. 150–159.

39. Dimberg 1974.

40. K. C. Hsiao 1976 (DMB). For a guide to the vast literature on Li Zhi and an assessment of his place in Ming history, see Hok-lam Chan 1980.

41. This quotation appears in Xiao Gongquan [K. C. Hsiao] 1982, p. 603; Xiao's discussion of Wang's political thought has guided the present discussion.

42. This understanding of Wang Yangming's political and social reorientation of Neo-Confucian thought draws on Yü Ying-shih 1997.

43. A shift among scholar-officials as early as Southern Song times away from careers in central government toward pursuit of their clan interests in their home communities has been described by Robert Hymes and others. See Hymes 1986a and Hymes and Shirokauer 1993. No corresponding shift in political thought to justify the focus on elite behavior in their home communities in Song period political thought is known to me.

44. Chu Hung-lam, reviewing the history of local compacts from Song and especially in Ming times, has shown the importance of elite concern for such means of maintaining the health of local society. See Chu 1993 and his and others' relevant writings in Chinese cited there.

27. MING CHINA'S BORDERS

1. MSL, *Hongwu shilu* 68, pp. 4a–b (1277–1278). This passage is quoted in part in Wang Gungwu 1968; see esp. pp. 52–53. Wang's essay provides an excellent

introduction to Ming foreign policy. The passage is also quoted somewhat more fully (in a slightly different translation) and discussed in Rossabi 1975, p. 26.

2. Early in the fifteenth century the Mongols abandoned the oft-sacked Karakorum, their capital built in the 1230s, in favor of the newer city of Urga, 200 miles to its northeast, the principal center of Khalkha power; today Urga is called Ulaan Baatar (Ulan Bator) and is the capital of Outer Mongolia, that is, the Mongolian Republic.

3. Serruys 1972.

4. Serruys 1967, esp. pp. 19–28.

5. Oyirat is also spelled Oirat, Oyirad, Öölöd, Eleuth, and so on. Here both Oyirat and Oirat are used, in different contexts. Defined regionally and by minor dialect differences, the four tribes included the Torguts, who early in the seventeenth century emigrated to the Volga in Russia, where they became known as the Kalmuks (Kalmyks); the three other tribes were the Khoshuts, Derbets, and Khoits. By later Ming a tribe of the Oyirats had become known as the Dzungars (Zunghars), who under their leader Galdan (d. 1697) created an important state that lasted almost a century (see Chapter 33, Section III). The Western Mongols occupied the territories of the earlier Naiman, Chinggis Khan's formidable enemies at the beginning of the thirteenth century, but Naiman history from Yuan times until early Ming is difficult to reconstruct. See Farquhar 1957.

6. Ligdan Khan (1592–1634), Great Khan of the Chahar Mongols who was defeated by the Manchu leader Nurhaci, is usually declared to be the last legitimate Chinggisid khan, although others claimed that status on into Qing times. See Serruys 1958, pp. 26–28.

7. Okada Hidehiro considers Dayan Khan to be the most important figure in post-Yuan Mongol history because, among other things, he reestablished the supremacy of the Chinggisid claim to leadership over all the Mongols. Among his many writings on Ming-period Mongolia, see Okada 1966; for an assessment of his scholarship and bibliography of his writings, see *Journal of Asian and African Studies* (Tokyo), no. 45 (1993): 227–264.

8. The term "Lamaism," long in use in Western writings, has now been replaced by the more accurate "Tibetan Buddhism," or in Chinese and other Asian languages a term meaning literally "the Tibetan transmission of Buddhism." Both terms are used here to draw attention to this point. I am indebted to Elliot Sperling (personal communication) for calling my attention to this fact.

9. Stein 1972, pp. 164–189.

10. This point of interpretation is stressed in the writings of Joseph Fletcher; see esp. Fletcher 1978, pp. 356–358. On the spread of Lamaism among the Mongols in the sixteenth and seventeenth centuries, see Heissig 1980, chaps. 1, 3, and 4.

11. For an extended and insightful treatment of this subject, written from a point of view that incorporates both Mongol and Chinese historical traditions, see Jagchid and Symons 1989.

12. Henry Serruys 1955, 1957, and 1959a. Wolfgang Franke 1962 adds another dimension to the problems of Mongols living in early Ming China.

13. Despite that Chinese interest in preventing Chinese migration, the idea advanced originally by Owen Lattimore that the "great walls" throughout history were intended more to keep Chinese in than to keep the steppe invaders out does not bear up under scrutiny. See Waldron 1990, pp. 30–31 and p. 233, nn. 89 and 90, for a discussion.

14. This subject is explored in Serruys 1959b.

15. The Ming government maintained a school for oral interpreters at the Huitong Guan (Interpreters' Institute) and one for translators of written documents, the Siyi Guan (Translators' Institute), in each of which there were sections devoted to Mongolian language study. See Serruys 1967, pp. 408–442, for background information. These schools do not appear to have been utilized to raise the level of knowledge about Mongolia or other foreign lands and peoples.

16. Waldron 1990.

17. The present-day town of Jiuquan, on the rail line from Lanzhow to Urumchi (Dihua).

18. Historical maps produced in the People's Republic of China show the boundaries of Ming China extending far to the west beyond this point, to include the independent state of Hami (sometimes called Uighuristan) and all of eastern Xinjiang, because the Ming court had bestowed a military title of Garrison Commander (Wei Zhihuishi) on the rulers of Hami. That territorial fiction is one of many others in Ming historical geography that are reflected in China's historical atlases. See the discussion of Hami (Khamil) in Rossabi 1975, pp. 23–39.

19. Wu Jihua 1971, pp. 329–348, and 1970, pp. 291–308.

20. In later times called Guihua, it is present-day Huhehot, capital of the Inner Mongolian Autonomous Region. The site and the surrounding region have long been important in Inner Asian history. For Altan Khan's Great Bayising, see Serruys 1959b, esp. pp. 37–40.

21. As of this writing no archaeological investigation has reported in detail on the physical properties of the Ming Great Wall throughout its entire length.

22. Waldron 1990, p. 164. Throughout, my account greatly simplifies but follows Waldron's analysis, esp. in his chap. 9.

23. See Ray Huang 1976a. Wang's biography in *Ming History* 1739 (1974), *juan* 222, pp. 5838–43, appears to have been written by someone with a narrower outlook than Wang himself displayed. The encomium (p. 5862) probably is correct, however, in saying that Zhang Juzheng's role as senior Grand Secretary at the court was crucial to the approval of Wang's policies.

24. Serruys 1976; also Serruys 1960, and 1967, pp. 64–93.

25. For a description of the region as preserved in photographs from 1923, see Alonso 1979 (with historical text by Joseph Fletcher, pp. 21–51). In this context Fletcher refers to the Tibetans as "Bhotias."

26. On current maps Tibet is designated the Tibetan (or Xizang) Autonomous Region; the Amdo region is called Qinghai (Tsinghai, or Koko Nor, both words meaning "the Blue Lake," its principal geographic feature). The Kham region is now divided between Sichuan Province and the Tibetan Autonomous Region; from 1928 until 1955 it formed Xikang Province.

27. See Chapter 8, Section I, on the origins of the Tangut people who formed the Xi Xia dynasty in the eleventh century. The Qiang of Ming times were culturally linked to Tibet, but whether their language is genetically related to Tibetan is now a disputed question. In Ming period usage, the name Qiang is very loosely applied.

28. The fullest treatment is provided in Beckwith 1987.

29. CHC vol. 3, esp. pp. 35–36, 228–230, and passim.

30. This Mongol military action in Tibet in Yuan times appears not to be recorded in Chinese sources; see Sperling 1992, p. 742. I am grateful to Elliot Sperling for calling my attention to Petech 1990, where the incident is analyzed, pp. 29–31; also for helpful advice on Tibetan history. Saskya-pa is also spelled Sa-skya-pa, Sakyapa, and so on.

31. See Chapter 20, Section I, for a discussion of the Yuan period Bureau of Tibetan and Buddhist Affairs (Xuanzhengyuan); see also Farquhar 1990, pp. 153–157.

32. See Richardson 1976; Hok-lam Chan 1988, pp. 261–264. See also Sperling 1979; Sperling sees the invitation to the fifth Karma-pa in 1407–8 as having more complex significance. Emperor Wuzong's attempt to force Halima's successor to visit him in Beijing in 1515 was a fiasco; see Geiss 1988a, pp. 417–418.

33. Also spelled dGe-lugs-pa, Dge-lugs-pa, Geluk-pa, Gelukpa, and so on.

34. The cultural history of Tibet in these centuries is well described in Snellgrove and Richardson 1968, chaps. 4–6.

35. He was dGe-'dun-rgya-mtsho (1475–1542), counted as the second Dalai Lama. See Petech 1976, pp. 412–413. From Ming to recent times, the heads of all the great monasteries in Tibet and Mongolia were recognized as reincarnations of their founders.

36. While they are not strictly correct, these names for the monastic sects are loosely used here, reflecting their use in Western writings.

37. If the dates given here seem improbable, note that the successor to Tsong-kha-pa (1357–1419) was posthumously designated the First "Dalai Lama" (1391–1475). The Second lived 1475–1542, and the Third 1543–1588.

38. His Tibetan name is Ngag-dbang rgya-mtsho.

39. Some units of administrative geography that became the Yuan native chieftainships previously in Song times had been "sub-prefectures and counties on loose rein" *(jimi zhou xian),* a euphemism for the absence of regular Chinese administration, where native peoples maintained their own local forms of governing. In short, throughout southwest China there had long been two types of local government, one for the Chinese and one for the non-Chinese populations. It has been pointed out that the so-called "autonomous" regions and counties of the People's Republic of China after 1955, though justified in new theoretical terms, can be seen as institutional continuations of the imperial era's *tusi* system; see Wade 1994, pp. 470–472.

40. The "native peoples" are often designated "aborigines," a term that is avoided here both because it carries pejorative overtones and because we cannot say with certainty who were the "original" inhabitants of the region (although it is clear the Han Chinese were not). For some implications of "aborigine" in this connection, see Ramsey 1987, pp. 160 and 170–171.

41. The figures come from Gong Yin 1992, pp. 57–63 and passim, and omit the relatively small numbers of *tusi* that were set up in Ming times in Shaanxi Province and adjoining areas. *Tusi* in northwest China for Mongols and other steppe peoples were of significantly different character.

42. Huang Kaihua 1972, pp. 338–348.

43. For a definitive study of the southwest border regions within Ming China and beyond in Southeast Asia, see Wade 1994; pp. 127–149 are most relevant to the issue of the native offices in China. For an exhaustive listing of all native offices in Ming and Qing times and a study of the system, see Gong Yin 1992.

44. Gong Yin 1992, p. 102, n. 3; although it was held to be a requirement, that undoubtedly could not always be enforced.

45. Data in the following sections are drawn mainly from Gong Yin 1992 and Huang Kaihua 1972 under the separate sections for the Ming provinces. Information on the current status of the southwest languages and their speakers is based on Ramsey 1987, esp. chap. 11.

46. Although it would be difficult and time-consuming, it should be possible to calcu-

late the share of the area in any of the southwest provinces that was under native official administrators, and to locate all the territorially defined *tusi* on a map to show their distribution as well as their total area. To my knowledge that has never been done.

47. The use of the name "wolf soldiers" was not confined to the Zhuang of Guangxi; it was also applied to the Miao soldiers from Hunan and others.

48. The campaign is discussed in CHC 7:377–380.

49. Yi or Lolo script is discussed and illustrated in Ramsey 1987, pp. 258–261.

50. See Huang Kaihua 1972, p. 348; *Ming History* 1739 (1974), *juan* 204, pp. 8187–88; and CHC 7:381–384. In CHC, note the rare example of a Chinese official's recognition of Chinese mistreatment and a plea for more just governing over the non-Chinese minorities, esp. pp. 383–384.

51. See the carefully explained details of ethnographic and political complexity in Wade 1994, esp. chap. 4.

52. See the maps for Ming China in Tan Qixiang 1991, vol. 7, maps 40–41 (dated 1423) and 42–43 (dated 1582). On both maps the boundaries are placed a great distance west of any known Chinese populations or the jurisdictions of Chinese administrative agencies. The 1423 map puts the western boundary of Yunnan west of the Irrawaddy, virtually on the Chindwin in the north, beyond the modern city of Myitkyina, and thus includes most of upper Burma. The 1582 map still shows a western boundary formed by the Salween in the south and the Irrawaddy in the north. These western and southern boundaries as shown on both maps (and on the separate maps of Yunnan province on pp. 76–79) are at best schematic approximations that do not correspond with political events or Chinese actions. Yunnan's present-day boundaries do not extend so far in either the west or the south.

53. In Southeast Asia the new definition of international boundaries also failed to protect the many peoples of the region from the effects of placing a culturally complex region under a new nation-state of the dominant group, but that is a problem of more recent history.

54. Wade 1994, esp. pp. 468–479. The extensive appendixes to Wade's work include translations from all the MSL entries relevant to the southwest borders and the countries lying beyond, running to over 2,500 pages. That constitutes the basic Chinese documentary evidence bearing on Southeast Asia in Ming times.

55. These dates are based on the "Chronology" (Dashi nianbiao) appended to Xiang Da 1962, pp. 339–391.

56. See DMB, pp. 466–471, s.v. "Fu Yu-te."

57. The most important of these was Sayid Ajall (1211–1279), appointed in 1273 after serving for a number of years in Sichuan. His heirs continued in the hereditary position in Yunnan into the 1290s. He promoted Islam, probably already present in Yunnan, and left Muslim military households there to remain the core of the Islamic community thereafter. See Buell 1993a.

58. See the map "Ethno-Linguistic Groups of Mainland Southeast Asia" appended to Lebar et al. 1964. For a reflection of official PRC scholarship in this field, see the joint Beijing-Canberra project called *The Language Atlas of China* (Hong Kong: Longmans, 1988). The well-mapped present-day linguistic situation can be used, albeit with caution, to gain an impression of the region's language diversity in Ming times. Recent linguistic research has disputed the basic classification systems used for these languages (e.g., "Sino-Tibetan," "Austroasiatic," "Tai-Kadai"), rendering the affinities among the many languages quite uncertain.

59. Joseph Needham 1954–, vol. 5, pt. 7, pp. 306–307.

60. Ray Huang 1976b, offers a comprehensive review of the Maw Shan kings and their wars.

61. Ming Yuzhen was a Red Turban regional leader who declared himself the independent lord of Sichuan in 1360, changing his title to Emperor of Xia in 1362; after his death in 1366, his young son Ming Sheng reigned until the Ming armies captured him in 1371. Ming rule over Sichuan was quickly established thereafter. See Chapter 21, Section III.

62. The Kham region in early Republican times (the 1920s) became the province of Xikang, but in 1955 was divided between Sichuan and Tibet.

63. Yang supplied immense timbers needed for palace construction and organized a Miao labor force to transport them to the Yangzi for shipment to Beijing; he also dispensed large amounts of gold in bribes to local officials and offered indemnities for his release but never paid them.

64. See Chaoying Fang 1976b. Li was a man of undoubted integrity at a time when government was riddled by corruption, and a very effective leader of both civil and military colleagues. His career merits fuller study than it has yet received.

65. See Parsons 1976; and the account in *Ming History* 1739 (1974), *juan* 312, pp. 8039–49.

66. The study of China's maritime history has made great progress in recent decades. For one example, note the series of volumes entitled *Zhongguo haiyang fazhan shi lunwen ji* (Studies on the History of China's Maritime Development), 5 vols. to 1993, published by Sun Yat-sen Institute for Social Sciences and Philosophy, Academia Sinica, Taipei.

67. Although some of its information has been superseded, Needham 1954–, vol. 4, pt. 3, pp. 379–699 ("Nautical Technology"), still offers a useful survey and comparative information.

68. By comparison, the ships sailed by Columbus and Magellan were in the range of 250–300 tons.

69. See Ray Huang 1981, pp. 160–174, for a discussion of the coastal pirate problem and mid-Ming relations with Japan.

70. A pioneer in exploring the maritime periphery of China is John E. Wills, Jr. Of immediate relevance here is his essay on maritime China, Wills 1979.

71. For an introduction to the extensive literature on these subjects, see So Kwan-wai 1975 and Li Guangbi 1956. In DMB, see s.v. "Hu Tsung-hsien," pp. 631–638; also "Lin Feng" (Limahong), pp. 917–919.

72. Canton is located on the Pearl River, thirty-five miles from the river's mouth in the Pearl River estuary (Zhujiang kou).

73. See his brief biography in DMB, pp. 1123–25.

74. The engrossing writings of C. R. Boxer are the best possible starting point; see Boxer 1948, 1953, 1959, and 1984, among others.

28. LATE MING POLITICAL DECLINE, 1567–1627

1. The Longqing reign period began in February 1567, a few days after Muzong's enthronement, and lasted until the new year, February 1, 1573, six months after his death in July 1572.

2. For contrasting views, see Ray Huang 1988b, pp. 511–514; Lienche Tu Fang and Chaoying Fang 1976; and Wang Tianyou 1991c. Wang Tianyou offers the most favorable assessment, and adduces interesting arguments about the emperor's per-

sonal involvement in the many changes that occurred during his five-and-one-half-year reign.

3. It is almost superfluous to write at any length about the Wanli reign because it has been so effectively portrayed and analyzed in the writings of Ray Huang; see Huang 1981, 1988b, and his other writings. These have established our understanding of the period. What follows here is heavily indebted to those writings, while endeavoring to supplement them in some minor ways.

4. For a brief review of Zhang Juzheng's career, see Crawford and Goodrich 1976.

5. Quoted in and commented on in K. C. Hsiao 1982, pp. 577–578. The succinct analysis of Zhang Juzheng's political thought in this work (pp. 575–580) is very useful.

6. Virtually the only other Chinese thinker of traditional times who also was so unconventional as to praise the achievements of the First Emperor was Zhang's contemporary, the radical Neo-Confucian freethinker Li Zhi (1527–1602); see K. C. Hsiao 1976, esp. p. 811, and K. C. Hsiao [Xiao Gongquan] 1982, pp. 578–579. The latter quotes Zhang's appraisal of the First Emperor.

7. See the discussion of Qi Jiguang's relationship with Zhang Juzheng in Ray Huang 1981, pp. 176–185, where his name is spelled "Ch'i Chi-kuang."

8. On Wang Chonggu and Altan Khan, see Chapter 27, Section II.

9. For a brief account of Yang Yan's reforms, see CHC, 3:580–582.

10. On Ming fiscal history, see Ray Huang 1974a; for his summary of the Single Whip reform, see pp. 112–122. For a recent assessment of the impact of Zhang Juzheng's survey, see Heijdra 1994, esp. pp. 72–83.

11. See Tai-loi Ma 1987, an exhaustive study of private academies in Ming times.

12. The political involvement of the late Ming academies is described in Meskill 1969.

13. See Ray Huang 1988b, pp. 544–550, for an interpretation of this issue.

14. Hucker 1957.

15. Busch 1976 offers a useful assessment.

16. For the Song episode involving Ouyang Xiu, see Chapter 5, Section I.

17. Plaks 1987, esp. pp. 25, 122–131, 498.

18. "Shen" in this posthumous title means "wondrously intelligent," like a child prodigy, not "divine" in a theistic sense.

19. Tombs of some Ming princes also have been scientifically excavated and the archaeological reports published.

20. See Li and Watt 1987; this is a scholarly catalog of an exhibition devoted to the artistic life of the elite in late Ming China.

21. He was Zhang Weixian, descendant of the first Duke of Ying (guo), named to that title in 1408; see Wang Gungwu 1976. Zhang Weixian's presence had symbolic significance, but he possessed little personal importance. On the establishment of the Ming "nobility of merit," see Romeyn Taylor 1976b.

22. See Ray Huang 1976c. Zhou lived 1546–1629.

23. Recorded in MSL, "Shenzong," juan 596, pp. 13b–14a. In the translation given here some ornate phrases are paraphrased to indicate their meaning more directly. The "oral testament" (yi yu) that follows is found on pp. 14a–15a. This document is often cited as the emperor's "posthumous edict" (yi zhao); Ray Huang 1976c, p. 265, expresses the view that it probably was composed under Zhou Jiamo's influence. It appears to reflect the attitudes expressed by Shenzong at his last meetings with Zhou and the other advisers, and was not simply devised by them after his death, as in instances of several other "posthumous edicts."

24. Briefly recounted in Xia Xie 1873, *juan* 72, pp. 2820–21.

25. See Tan Qian ca. 1653 (1958), *juan* 83, pp. 5153–55, for a version of the posthumous testament and seventeenth-century comment on it.

26. See her brief biography by Chaoying Fang 1976c. Fang casts doubt on the story, alluded to here, that she later presented the new emperor with a gift of women entertainers.

27. For two of the Three Cases and a general account of the Wanli emperor's successors' reigns, see Atwell 1988, 7:590–640.

28. The other three are Wang Zhen, who controlled the government in the years 1445–1449; Wang Zhi, 1477–1481; and Liu Jin, 1506–1510, all discussed in earlier chapters.

29. See also the comments in Ray Huang 1981, esp. pp. 84–86 and passim.

29. The Lively Society of the Late Ming

1. All world population figures in history before 1800 are estimates; see discussion, diagram, and tables in Braudel 1973, pp. 6–18; and United Nations Population Fund figures as reported in the *New York Times*, May 5, 1992, p. C1. The latter figures are used here as careful recent estimates.

2. Chapter 35, Section VII, on Qing population, continues this discussion through the eighteenth century.

3. Ho 1959. The main emphasis of this important study is not on population totals per se, but on the nature of the institutional and social setting from which the Chinese census figures were produced, and on methods for using these in modern historical research. The figure of 313 million in 1794, accepted by both Ho and Bielenstein 1987, is taken from Qing dynasty official population data at a point when they became somewhat more accurate; see Ho 1959, pp. 281–282.

4. Bielenstein 1987, p. 97 and p. 287, graph 19.

5. Heijdra 1994. The study of Ming population and land-in-cultivation data forms a portion of Heijdra's work, which is a general study of base-level Ming society. It makes very thorough use of scholarship in all relevant languages and is particularly strong in its command of Japanese studies of Chinese social history. Heijdra's views on Ming population represent his own conclusions, drawing fully on Ming sources and weighing critically the pertinent modern scholarship. See esp. chap. 1, sec. 3, "Population."

6. Ibid., pp. 50–56. Heijdra's hypotheses range from high figures of .6, .5, and .4 percent annual growth for the three periods into which Ming history is arbitrarily divided for this purpose (i.e., 1400–1500, 1500–1600, and 1600–1650), to middle-range projected growth rates of .5, .4, and .3 percent, and low rates of .4, .3, and .2 percent. These three sets of growth rates are then projected from the upwardly adjusted base figure of 85 million in 1400 (i.e., the revised census of 1393). The three sets of projected growth rates produce high, medium, and low figures for 1500, 1600, and 1650. For 1650 this gives a high figure of 353 million, while the lower hypothesis (Heijdra deems it "quite implausible") gives a figure of 204 million at the end of the Ming dynasty. Here I adopt his intermediate figure.

7. Citing Ho 1959, p. 10, table 3. For annual summaries of official data that appear in MSL, see Bielenstein 1987, pp. 85–88.

8. Literally, the Ministry of Revenue was called the "ministry of households," *hubu*, because the household registers listing population figures by household and by

individual were the basic tool of fiscal management. Ray Huang 1974a, pp. 61–63, cites comments of Ming period officials ridiculing the official census data and the entire effort to compile them.

9. Heijdra 1994, pp. 72–77, credits the Zhang Juzheng survey with having accomplished more than previous scholars have usually conceded.

10. Needham 1954–, vol. 3, pp. 1–168, reviews the history of Chinese mathematics; on pp. 150–168 Needham makes interesting comparisons between mathematics in China and the West. His interpretive comments describing a general decline in Chinese scientific acumen in Ming and later times are to be used with caution, however; he misjudged that issue.

11. This point has been developed most fully by Ray Huang; see 1991, chap. 1 and passim; 1988b (for his negative assessment of Zhang Juzheng's impact on Ming government); and 1988a, chap. 20, where he briefly alludes to the point that before the twentieth century, China was "mathematically unmanageable." This concept underlies his history of worldwide capitalism in relation to China (1991), an expanded English version of which is forthcoming. As for the quality of Chinese mathematics, see Needham 1954–, vol. 3, section 19, esp. pp. 151–168, comparing mathematics in China and in the West. Needham, somewhat formulaically, denigrates the level of scientific activity in the Ming period; he sees the second great flowering of Chinese mathematics as having occurred during the Song dynasty, when "a group of truly great mathematicians, themselves either commoners or subordinate officials, broke into fields much wider than the traditional bureaucratic preoccupations [referring to the continuing preoccupation with calendrical studies and astronomy within the Chinese bureaucracy]. Intellectual curiosity could now be abundantly satisfied. But the upsurge did not last. The Confucian scholars . . . [were] . . . swept back into power in the nationalist reaction of the Ming, and mathematics was again confined to the back rooms of provincial yamens" (pp. 153–154). While this account distorts the history of intellectual life in the late imperial period, it suggests that good mathematics continued to be employed in the offices of government.

12. The true sweet potato from the Americas, *Ipomoea batatas,* is far more nutritious than the yam, *Dioscorea sativa,* native to East Asia and often confused with it. For the context in which these new foods appeared, see Mote 1977b, esp. p. 198 and passim. In this essay the author still accepted the idea of an early Qing population explosion, now considered improbable.

13. Local government in Song is discussed in Chapter 15, Sections II and III, and that of Yuan in Chapter 20, Section I. The structure of Ming central and regional governing is diagrammed in Hucker 1985, Introduction, and is shown in more detail in Wei Wenxuan 1987, pp. 159–176. For a general overview of Ming local government, see Brook 1985.

14. These are the figures given in the *Ming History* 1739 (1974), *juan* 75, pp. 1850–51. No date is given for those figures; the numbers varied somewhat at different periods of the Ming. Slightly different figures are given in the same work, *juan* 40, p. 882. Some of the differences derive from the gradual replacement of "native offices" (*tusi;* see Chapter 27, Section IV) by regularly constituted sub-prefectures and counties.

15. This somewhat simplifies the relationship, both to prefectures and to counties, of the two administrative categories (i.e., "independent" and "subordinate") of sub-prefectures, but for our purposes here the simplification is justified.

16. For a study of late Ming county magistrates' roles based on information gleaned from the genre of "magistrates' handbooks," see Nimick 1993.

17. George Jer-lang Chang 1978, p. 56. See also Andrew 1985.

18. For a pioneering study of Lü Kun (1534–1616) in this connection, see Handlin 1983; see also Chu 1993 on the "community compact" in late Ming thought.

19. *Li* literally means "hamlet" or "neighborhood."

20. The terms "administrative community" for *li* and "neighborhood" for *jia* are taken from Heijdra 1994, esp. pp. 104–150. (In some writings they are labeled the "tithings.") This discussion borrows from Heijdra's study. The Chinese use the word *lijia* to designate the system itself.

21. The issue of whether the Ming *lijia* and its Song and Yuan antecedents utilized preexisting natural villages or were artificial assemblages of households administratively imposed on the social order has long been debated; the "natural social grouping" explanation makes the stronger argument.

22. There is, however, an extensive literature on these questions, much of it produced by Japanese social historians; see Heijdra 1994, esp. chap. 2, for extensive citations and evaluations of that scholarship.

23. The government inserted a managerial level of "tax captains" *(liangzhang)*, also unpaid common people but usually from families of some affluence and standing, between the county administration and the *li* heads; they were responsible for coordinating collections and deliveries. Each oversaw a region that produced 10,000 piculs (about 30,000 bushels) of grain in the autumn grain tax levies. Tax captains did not necessarily reside within the administrative unit they served, but were from the same general locality.

24. For a thoughtful review of this historical problem in relation to recent issues in modern Chinese history, see Leys 1985, pp. 113–135.

25. The Ming household registration system also included a few household occupational categories. Other than the occupationally nonspecific *min*, the categories *jun* (military) and *jiang* (artisan) were the most important. In terms of social status, those, and a few other quite small categories of nominally hereditary occupational status, can be seen as variants of the *min* or "commoner" category; though intended to be hereditary categories, they failed to prevent ordinary people from changing their occupations.

26. An important study of life in a Ming county, describing the kinds of communities to be found there, is offered by Dardess 1996.

27. The exception today, perhaps a post-Ming development, is Sichuan Province; there the single-family, spatially isolated farm is common in some regions of this large province.

28. Naquin and Yü 1992 explore the concept and practice of religious, particularly Buddhist, pilgrimage in China.

29. Modified from the table appended to *Mathews Chinese-English Dictionary* (American ed., 1945), p. 1178.

30. On the general circumstances of traditional Chinese medicine, see Needham 1970, pp. 340–395; on public and private medicine in Ming and Qing times, see Leung 1987.

31. The largest bandit uprising of the sixteenth century, eventually a true rebellion, was of that character. Known as the "Uprising of the Liu Brothers" ("Liu the Sixth" and his brother "Liu the Seventh") in the years 1510–1512, it grew to such size that it spread throughout half a dozen provinces and required very large

government armies to suppress it. For a thorough analysis of it and of banditry in the capital region 1450–1525, see Robinson 1995.

32. See Mote 1988b, esp. pp. 384–389, for a brief account of the Jing-Xiang Rebellion and the creation of the new prefecture of Yunyang.

33. "Collective violence" is the term used to describe armed social disorder in the work of James W. Tong; see Tong 1991.

34. The event is briefly noted in MSL, *juan* 424, pp. 4a–b, under the seventh month of Jiajing, year 34; see also the brief discussion in Li Guangbi 1956, pp. 50–51, where the event is cited to demonstrate the incompetence of the Ming military forces.

35. Hsiao Kung-chuan 1979 analyzes the workings of informally institutionalized procedures of conflict resolution through compromise at the village level of society in imperial China.

36. See Lütge 1966, pp. 156 and 211, for a brief review of the legal and economic implications of the phrase "Stadtluft macht frei" in twelfth-century and later European social history.

37. Usually defined as Zhuxian zhen in Honan, Jingde zhen in Jiangxi, Foshan zhen in Guangdong, and Hankou zhen, the present-day city of Hankou, which with Hanyang and Wuchang makes up the present-day metropolitan district of Wuhan. In the more general sense of "market town," including some examples of markets (*zhen*) in towns and cities, there were hundreds of *zhen* in Ming and early Qing times. See Fan Shuzhi 1990, pp. 41–57. On Foshan, see Faure 1990; on Hankou, see Rowe 1984, esp. pp. 28–38; on Jingde zhen, see Dillon 1978 and Yuan 1978.

38. The apparent exception is the "metropolitan prefecture" at the national capitals, administered by metropolitan prefects, but they are not truly exceptions, embodying merely a variant of the usual form of county-level (or prefecture-level) administration modified to meet the special needs of the national capitals.

39. For a discussion of the special characteristics of Chinese cities, see Mote 1973 and 1977a.

40. Gallagher 1953, pp. 268–269. This is a translation of Nicholas Trigault's Latin rendering of Matteo Ricci's diaries (originally written in Italian); they are an important source of information about late Ming China. Ricci interpreted much of what he saw on analogy to Europe, as foreign observers have been doing ever since, hence his reference to the "lettered aristocracy," meaning scholar-officials of the elite.

41. Geiss 1979 offers a history of Beijing from the beginning to the end of the Ming period, with many observations on the quality of urban life.

42. These figures are based on Rozman 1973, esp. pp. 41–58 and 281–282. Rozman adopted the then-standard estimates of Ming total population. If the greatly increased estimates suggested in Section I of this chapter are accepted, the size of cities and the total urban population of China must be increased accordingly. Rozman defines seven levels of urban "central places" by size and function and analyzes their relationships comparatively for Qing China and Tokugawa Japan, but also provides historical background relevant to Ming urbanism.

43. See Chapter 26, Section VI, where Wang Yangming is discussed. It is noted there that the new Confucian thought of Wang Yangming accepted merchants into the full responsibilities and dignities due social leaders.

44. A Ming figure often cited as the best example of this new model figure and the new merchant ethos is Wang Daokun (1525–1593), who lived in the half-century

following Wang Yangming's death but was not related to him. Wang Daokun was the son of a prominent Huizhou (Anhui) merchant family, a *jinshi* of 1547, able administrator in local government, military expert in the defense of the southeast coast against the pirate raids of the 1550s, thinker, poet, playwright, and voluminous author. See Hsi 1976.

45. One twentieth-century historian of Chinese thought who has pushed this analogy to the extreme is Hou Wailu in his history (1956) of the early phase of the so-called Chinese enlightenment; enlightenment has been a common theme in intellectual history in many places and times, but to press for a specific functional counterpart in relation to the emergence of capitalism and related radical movements is to press for formulaic analogies. Hou Wailu's work is discussed, in passing, in de Bary 1975, esp. pp. 4, 33 n. 12, and 142–143; de Bary recognizes the importance of Hou's views but does not endorse them.

46. Yu Yingshi [Yü Ying-shih] 1976, p. 163. This is the pathbreaking work on this aspect of Chinese intellectual history; see in this context especially Yu's concluding remarks, pp. 161–166.

47. This was strongly argued in essentially anti-Marxist if not quite non-Marxist terms by Etienne Balazs; see Balazs 1964, pp. 34–54. Balazs believed that China was a "permanently bureaucratic society" in which the state distrusted the private sector. This has been an influential but inadequate view.

48. They call this *ziben zhuyi zhi mengya*. The concerted efforts of hundreds of scholars working under centrally directed planning over several decades produced vast amounts of scholarly documentation and interpretation. Such efforts to make hitherto underused documents available have enduring value; the interpretation, however, is largely formulaic history at its most predictable and least interesting. For a useful example of the standard cant on the subsequent failure to realize full-blown capitalism, see Fang Xing, translated by James H. Cole, 1989.

49. See the brief account in Lien-sheng Yang 1971, 7:62–70.

50. Heijdra 1994, pp. 84–102, offers a succinct review of Ming monetary history. See also William S. Atwell in CHC, vol. 8, "The Ming Dynasty, Part Two"; in the latter, pp. 376–416, Atwell places the Ming monetary system in the larger regional and world context.

51. On international silver bullion flows in relation to the Chinese economy, mid-Ming to early Qing, see the extensive writings of William S. Atwell (1982, 1988, and 1990), and his chapter "Ming China and the Emerging World Economy" in CHC, vol. 8, "The Ming Dynasty, Part Two."

52. See the very brief remarks in Atwell 1988, pp. 586–590.

53. For a careful analysis of these changes, see Heijdra 1994, chap. 4, "The Commercialization of the Countryside."

54. Heijdra 1994, p. 278; see the investigation of "the socio-economic facets of land-ownership" in this work, and its concluding discussion of "gentry" and "degree holders as a socio-economic group," pp. 329–353.

55. This discussion paraphrases Ray Huang 1988a, pp. 232–243. See also Ray Huang 1974b for a study of merchant activities as reflected in late Ming popular (and fairly "realistic") fiction; this study corroborates Huang's negative findings on the "buds of capitalism" issue.

56. For one important example, see Nelson I. Wu 1962.

57. For an analysis of one literary component of this awareness in twentieth-century China, see Chih-p'ing Chou 1988, pp. 4 and 118–122.

58. Plaks 1987.

59. A full bibliography of these large and important new fields of scholarship need not be listed here. One work on women's roles in elite society can be mentioned: Ko 1994 is of special interest in describing the broadened roles developed by cultivated women in late Ming and early Qing times. See esp. pt. 3, "Women's Culture."

60. For a penetrating analysis of the interplay between artistic and ethical concerns in early literary criticism, see Vincent Y. C. Shih 1970, Introduction. Literary thought in the Ming period has not yet been thoroughly analyzed, but see, e.g., Zhu Dongrun 1959, pp. 224–273, and Chih-p'ing Chou 1988.

61. The most famous of his plays is *Mudan ting (Peony Pavilion)*; for a translation, see Birch 1980.

62. For the four great novels, see Plaks 1987. All, including the fifth, *Honglou Meng (The Dream of the Red Chamber, The Story of the Stone)*, written in the eighteenth century, have been published in more than one English translation under the titles given in parentheses.

63. E.g., Birch 1958.

64. Plaks 1994 offers analysis and evaluation of the form along with an annotated translation of a noteworthy example.

65. Shou-chien Shih 1994; the quoted passage is found on p. 221.

66. I am indebted to Susan Cherniack (1994) for the concept of "book culture," which she uses in connection with the Song dynasty.

30. THE COURSE OF MING FAILURE

1. Ray Huang's depiction of political decline, in his *1587, A Year of No Significance* (Huang 1981), subtitled *The Ming Dynasty in Decline*, gives vivid substance to his larger argument about the reasons for Chinese failure to achieve the breakthrough transition from "traditional" to "modern" society at some point in Ming or early Qing times, in the pattern of the transition then occurring in Europe. That forceful argument is succinctly set forth in his *China: A Macro-history* (1988), and in his summary history of worldwide capitalism, *Zibenzhuyi yu nianyi shiji* (1991; English edition forthcoming). I take that argument, however important, to be irrelevant to the traditional Chinese "dynastic cycle" theory that has infiltrated the thought of many modern historians.

2. Atwell 1988, esp. pp. 595–602.

3. This is William S. Atwell's translation of the Chinese term *jingshi zhiyong*, a stance in statecraft thinking that stressed practical means of improving government and bettering the conditions of the governed. See Atwell 1975, p. 347.

4. "Orthodoxy" here designates the Cheng-Zhu mainline of Neo-Confucian Lixue dating from Song times; see Chapter 14, Section III. In Yuan and Ming times it had become the orthodox school of Neo-Confucian learning, in the limited sense of "orthodoxy" in the Chinese context, by reason of the place given its interpretations of the classics in the conduct of the civil service examinations.

5. See the discussion of "party" or "faction" *(dang)* in the eleventh century at the time of Ouyang Xiu, Chapter 6, Section V. For the Donglin party, see Chapter 28, Section II.

6. The best account of this phase of late Ming history is found in Atwell 1975. See also Chapter 29, Section IV.

7. James T. C. Liu 1959b, esp. pp. 70–79, first proposed the name "manipulative

type" to define a distinct pattern of bureaucratic behavior. His classification of traditional Chinese bureaucrats offers much insight into Chinese government. See also Liu 1959a.

8. The dismissal and execution of his leading general on the Manchurian front, Yuan Chonghuan, is discussed in Section II of this chapter.

9. Hard figures do not exist for the total number of dependents supported by the state; estimates vary widely. See the discussion of the issue in Wakeman 1985, 1:331–338. See also Ming imperial household figures (30,000 in 1549) discussed in Lienche Tu Fang 1976, p. 321.

10. The senior heirs were the eldest sons of eldest sons, hence heirs to the princely titles, in the lineages of each of Ming Taizu's twenty-six sons whose lines remained in existence.

11. See discussion and analysis of figures in Ray Huang 1974a, pp. 178–180.

12. It is not possible at this stage of historical research to produce accurate figures for these categories of persons supported by the state's revenues; the figures offered are loose conjectures meant to be usefully suggestive, and no claim is made for their accuracy. Nor, it appears, are better figures available for comparing sixteenth- and seventeenth-century China with other parts of the world in this respect. For example, Braudel 1973, pp. 681–703, offers an abundance of colorfully illustrative examples drawn from sixteenth-century Mediterranean states but little or no quantitative data. Some modern states, by comparison, support 25 percent of their population on their tax revenues.

13. See Ray Huang 1974a, chap. 8, "Concluding Observations," for a fuller discussion of several relevant aspects of the Ming at the end.

14. Ibid., p. 321.

15. These were the unsuccessful rebellions of Zhu Gaoxu, the Prince of Han, in 1426; of Zhu Zhifan, Prince of Anhua in Ningxia, in 1510; and of Zhu Chenhao, the Prince of Ning, in 1519. In his successful rebellion in 1398, Zhu Di, the later Yongle emperor, had the advantages of a base area, an army, a staff of advisers and assistants, and the opportunity to take over regional revenues. Those conditions were not allowed to exist thereafter.

16. The name had been coming into use during the twenty years before 1635; its meaning and the reasons for adopting it have never been adequately explained. The *Draft Qing History* 1927 (1977), *juan* 1, claims that the use of the name goes back to a somewhat mythical "primal ancestor" of Nurhaci's Aisin Gioro clan, apparently of post-Jin, early Yuan times in the thirteenth century, but that is not substantiated. "Manchu" and "Jurchen" are used interchangeably here in discussing the rise of the Manchus in the late Ming.

17. The Three Commanderies *(san wei)* were Doën, Taining, and Fuyu; Serruys 1967, p. 3 and passim, calls those the names of "three tribes" of Mongols given special status by the Ming. Their tribal chieftains were given princely rank and made military heads of Commanderies *(wei)*, but they remained totally autonomous and independent of China in their rule over their tribes.

18. The figure almost 400 is given in Serruys 1976, p. 161. See also the discussion in Chapter 24, Section III. Hucker 1985 translates *wei* as "guard" and its head, *zhihuishi*, as "guard commander"; the translation of the "Three (Eastern) Commanderies" is, however, standard in most of the modern scholarship on the Mongols and the Jurchens in Ming times. On that analogy, "commandery" is extended here to the *wei* offices and titles among the Jurchens, although they mostly existed only on paper.

19. Included here also is the large Jurchen population lying just north of Jianzhou in the region called Haixi, where four important Jurchen tribes, especially the Hada and the Yehe, were under special Ming protection. The Ming sought to divide the Jurchen groups to maintain influence.

20. *Draft Qing History* 1927 (1977), *juan* 1; a critical review of Nurhaci's ancestry is found in Xiao Yishan 1963, pp. 1–15. Subsequent Manchu accounts evaded the fact that Nurhaci's father and grandfather had served the Ming state to the disadvantage of other Jurchens; the incident is analyzed in Chen Jiexian 1965, pp. 55–64. Nurhaci later quite disingenuously included their deaths among his "Seven Grievances" against the Ming.

21. This brief biography and analysis draw upon Fang Chao-ying in ECCP, pp. 594–599; Roth 1979; *Draft Qing History* 1927 (1977), *juan* 1; Meng Sen 1960, pt. 2, chap. 1; and Meng Sen 1965, pp. 158–217.

22. The principal body of the Mongolian population residing in Mongolia proper at that time were the Five Khalkhas; see Farquhar 1968, p. 199, where the letter is quoted in part. Jurchen/Manchu belonged to the Tungusic branch of the Altaic languages, while Mongolian constituted a second branch, and the large group of the Turkic languages (e.g., Uighur) formed the third main division. They were "different in language," but their languages shared some characteristics and showed much lexical borrowing.

23. Serruys 1967, pp. 450–455, discusses the language question and suggests this answer.

24. The script was first devised in 1599 and improved in a modification in 1631; the two are referred to as "Old Manchu" and "New Manchu." See Li Guangtao 1962.

25. See discussion of Chinese-Mongolian relations in the sixteenth century in Chapter 27, Section II.

26. This is the *meng'an-mouke* system, described in Chapters 9 and 10.

27. Normally one adult male in three was in active military service at any time. That was a lower rate of mobilization than the Jin dynasty Jurchens had required.

28. In Chinese, the Manchus were then and still are usually called *qiren,* "people of the banners."

29. The Manchus retained their Mongol and Han Chinese banners to the end, but early in the dynasty set up a secondary army organization, the Army of the Green Standard, for the large number of Chinese soldiers who subsequently were pressed into service. The Chinese Han banners could not have accommodated such large numbers without overwhelming the Manchu and Mongol banners and diluting the elite character of all the banners.

30. Much of the foregoing is based on Meng Sen 1965, pp. 218–310; see also Roth 1979.

31. Roth 1979.

32. The Hada and Yehe tribes of the Haixi Jurchens; Nurhaci was married to a Yehe princess.

33. The Ming defeat occurred at what has come to be known as the Battle of Sa-erh-hu (Sarhu); it is analyzed in Ray Huang 1988b, pp. 577–584.

34. *Draft Qing History* 1977, *juan* 216–218, and *juan* 166, pp. 5265–68, where eight daughters are listed; *juan* 2, p. 19, gives Hung Taiji's names. Hung Taiji is also spelled Khungtaiji in some recent works.

35. Chen Jiexian 1965, pp. 137–142, shows that the name did not mean "crown prince" and proposes that it was a Manchu noble title borne by more than one of Nurhaci's sons, among others. Many other explanations have been offered; see,

e.g., Li Guangtao 1947b. Li Guangtao 1970, pp. 221–230, esp. p. 230, cites further evidence that Hung Taiji usurped the succession.

36. Other accounts say he was from Teng County in Guangxi.

37. *Ming History* 1739 (1974), *juan* 259, p. 6707.

38. The Manchus opened the bargaining by asking for 100,000 *liang* (ounces) of gold, 1 million of silver, 1 million bolts of heavy brocades, and 10 million bolts of ordinary cloth, and proposed annual payments thereafter of 10,000 *liang* of gold, 100,000 of silver, 100,000 of brocades, and 300,000 of ordinary cloth. The Jurchens' return "gifts" would be 10 pearls, 1,000 sable pelts, and 1,000 catties of ginseng. Hung Taiji indicated that some bargaining could take place to set the final amounts. These details are conveniently reported in Xiao Yishan 1963, pp. 108–116.

39. Paraphrased from *Ming History* 1739 (1974), *juan* 259, pp. 6713–14.

40. They met at a place called Shuangdao (twin islands); it lay within the precincts of present-day Dalian city.

41. Yuan's act of executing Mao was coupled with a baseless charge that he also was guilty of treason: he was said to have conspired secretly with the Manchus. The case in favor of Yuan's action has been most thoroughly argued by Li Guangtao 1948b.

42. For a moving account of a somewhat parallel case, see Ray Huang 1981, chap. 6, "Ch'i Chi-kuang, the Lonely General." Ch'i (Qi) died in 1588.

43. See Meng Sen 1965, pp. 17–27, and the succinct narrative in Wakeman 1985, pp. 126–131. Yuan's biography in *Ming History* 1739 (1974), *juan* 259 (quoted in the text) does not relegate Yuan to the category of "Treacherous Officials" as his execution for treason might suggest would be the case, but it denies him favorable evaluation (p. 6723) and includes much incorrect information that served the Manchu interest. Modern scholarship has been much more favorable. In part that is because the so-called Old Manchu Documents (Manzhou jiudang), documents written in the old form of the Manchu script that was current from its promulgation in 1599 until it was substantially revised and improved in 1631, came to light only in the early twentieth century and have been fully studied only since that time. They establish that far from being guilty of complicity with the Manchu enemy, Yuan was the victim of their false reports. The most detailed studies of the Yuan Chonghuan debacle are those by Li Guangtao: 1948a, 1948b, 1947a, and other writings. Li Guangtao's extensive and authoritative writings on the Ming-Qing transition frequently have been overlooked.

44. Heijdra 1994, table 104, pp. 57–58, and 79–80; in all of the many official data compilations and modern estimates, these percentages remain roughly the same.

45. That is, if the population of Shaanxi had been reduced by 50 percent, that would have caused no more than a 2–3 percent decrease in national total figures, and probably less, because even in so large a decline some of the population loss would have been the result of migration into neighboring provinces, hence not a net national decrease.

46. This account follows a number of traditional sources and modern authorities, some of which are cited herein. For other recent scholarship, see Parsons 1970; Wakeman 1985; Li Guangtao 1965; Fu Yiling et al. 1993, esp. pp. 433–460.

47. The name *chuang wang,* or *chuang* as an adjective, had been borne by Li Zicheng's superior; when he was killed in battle in the mid-1630s, Li took over the title. The force of the word *chuang,* "to burst through," originally merely described the person as "unstoppable," not as heroic.

48. Many traditional accounts of the roaming bandits' cruelties, vicious slaughter of people, and destruction of property are beyond belief; see, e.g., *Ming History* 1739 (1974), *juan* 309, pp. 7976–77, on Zhang Xianzhong's atrocities. In the case of Zhang Xianzhong's behavior in Sichuan in the last two and one-half years of his life, a strong case has been made that the account in the *Ming History* and others should not be believed; see Li Guangtao 1954a. Yet some measure of truth must be ascribed to other accounts of the roving bandits' cruelty, rapacity, and wanton destruction.

49. This Minister of War was Yang Sichang (1588–1641), one of the Chongzhen emperor's controversial favorites; the general who defeated Zhang Xianzhong in 1640 was the famed Zuo Liangyu, who, it was said, was unwilling to exterminate the roving bandits totally, fearing (not without reason) that once the commanders in the field were not urgently needed, the emperor would eliminate them. They resented the emperor's favorites, and the distrust between emperor and his military leaders prevented the rational implementation of policy.

50. This was again Zuo Liangyu (1598–1645), who had nearly destroyed Zhang in 1640. Zuo was an able general who had come up through the ranks and was much respected by the roaming bandits. See ECCP, pp. 761–762, s.v. "Tso Liang-yü."

51. This question has been much debated; see Des Forges 1982, 1984. One implication is that by drawing to his cause some members of the educated elite, Li Zicheng broadened and strengthened his movement. Li Yan symbolized that changing character of what had been purely a "bandit" movement. See also Li Xiaosheng 1987, who offers evidence that a man named Li Yan existed, but leaves other facts in doubt.

52. The suspiciously large figure of 1 million is given in Fu Yiling et al. 1993, p. 453, quoting the official *Ming History* 1739 (1974), *juan* 309, which claims, impossibly, "A million households within the city walls were engulfed, and those who escaped . . . were fewer than 20,000 individuals" (p. 7958). Huang Yunmei 1986, p. 2439, concludes that "households" here should be "individuals." Other traditional sources cite less specific numbers; e.g., Qian Xing (Author's Preface 1653) implies that most of the inhabitants had already starved during the long siege before the waters were released (1936a, pp. 126–127); Wen Bing (written shortly after 1644) says that the waters pouring in through the city wall's north gate "suddenly rose twenty feet, and the people who drowned, both elite and commoners, numbered several hundreds of thousands" (1946, p. 205). The destruction of the city, famed for its elegance and beauty, was virtually complete.

53. Curiously, in granting posthumous titles to his ancestors at this time, he claimed Li Jiqian (963–1004) as Taizu, that is, "Grand Progenitor," of his lineage; See *Ming History* 1739 (1974), *juan* 309, p. 7963. Li Jiqian had been given that posthumous imperial title in 1038 by his grandson Li Yuanhao, founder of the Xi Xia dynasty of the Tanguts (see Chapter 8). It is doubtful that Li Zicheng was, or thought he was, a Tangut, but he was born in the same northern Shaanxi region that was the homeland of the Xi Xia Tanguts.

54. This dating follows Fu Yiling et al. 1993, p. 459–460; it varies slightly from the chronology in Tan Qian ca. 1653 (1955), pp. 6040 et seq, but agrees with Xia Xie 1873, p. 3462, and other standard sources.

55. *Homo optator* (mankind, making choices), to devise a term for this essential human characteristic, may be as useful a key to history as the often applied parallel

terms *Homo faber* (mankind, making things), *Homo ludens* (mankind, playing), *Homo habilis* (mankind, using skills), or even *Homo sapiens.*

56. Tan Tianxing 1991, p. 336. Perhaps throwing this bone to the guardians of class warfare is merely a formulaic requirement that the reader can ignore. But, to address the issue, had the Chongzhen emperor in fact maintained "elite class interests," or any other set of interests, with clarity and consistency, his reign would have been quite different and in all probability much more successful. As Tan's account convincingly shows, this ruler's randomized petulance found its victims in the elite and official strata of society as much as among the ordinary people; all suffered the social consequences of administrative failure, while members of the elite were the usual intended victims of his vindictive and foolish acts. As for his "class prejudices," one must question whether any segment of the Chinese population, including the imperial clan, displayed actions so controlled by imputed "class interests" that they were denied a range of choices, thereby binding their behavior to consistent patterns. A wide range of individual choices by persons throughout society, but particularly in the elite (about whom we have much more knowledge), is as fully demonstrable as is subservience to any single pattern of choices.

57. One must also ask whether a Chinese emperor was a member of a social class, unless it be a class of one member. His "interests" were at most shared only by some (not all) members of his immediate family; his "family" clearly did not include the entire group of living imperial descendants. The tension between the interests of the throne and the scholar-bureaucrat elite was palpable. What then were the emperor's "class prejudices"?

58. This is Charles O. Hucker's translation of *huang guifei,* the title borne by the consort second in rank to the empress. See Hucker 1985.

59. Tan Tianxing 1991, p. 341.

60. Hung Taiji died at age fifty-one in September 1643.

61. On Hong Chengchou, see Chen-main Wang 1999; see also the section on Hong Chengchou in Struve 1993, pp. 141–155. This account has also drawn on Li Guangtao 1948c.

62. Quoted in his biography in *Ming History* 1739 (1974), *juan* 251, p. 6502.

63. Ibid., pp. 6500–6504.

64. Ming Beijing had thirteen gates on the outer perimeter and three more on the southern wall of the original city as built in the Yongle period (1402–1424); that wall was absorbed into the city when the southern extension was added in 1552, following the Mongol incursions of 1550, to enclose a previously unwalled suburb on the south. For a thorough treatment of Beijing's history in Ming times, see Geiss 1979.

65. Zhangyi Men, also called the Guang'an Men.

66. The heir and his younger brother were the sons of Empress Zhou; the third prince was the surviving son of Honored Consort Tian, who had died in 1640.

67. Many persons in the first group of such suicides are listed and their deaths briefly described in Xia Xie 1873, *juan* 90, pp. 3464–74.

31. ALIEN RULE RETURNS

1. Li's procession entered the city wall at the Desheng Gate, the western gate on the northern city wall; the procession must have traveled south along the western wall

of the Palace City to Chang'an Street, then turned east to the Chengtian Gate (its name in Qing times was changed to Tian'an Men, often translated "the Gate of Heavenly Peace") and through it into the Forbidden City via the imperial causeway and the Meridian Gate (Wumen). It was an ostentatious entrance.

2. But see note 6.

3. For a contemporary account of the perils experienced in Beijing and on the escape routes from it to the South, see Struve 1993, pp. 6–27.

4. This discussion is based on the *Draft Veritable Record (Shilu gao)* of 1644, as quoted in Li Guangtao 1954b; Li's interpretation is also drawn upon in the discussion here. On the character and compilation of the Chinese and Manchu *Veritable Records* of the Qing reigns, see Chen Jiexian 1978a.

5. This account contradicts all Qing period official and unofficial writings. It follows the study written in 1942, published as Wang Chongwu 1947. Wang Chongwu's work is followed (although not credited) and somewhat supplemented in Li Guangtao 1954b. The *Draft Qing History* of 1927 is entirely untrustworthy in all matters concerning Manchu actions in the period of the conquest, so must be used with suspicion. Other traditional sources are unexplainably confused and unreliable on the events of April through June 1644, e.g., Tan Qian ca. 1653 (1958), esp. *juan* 100–101. The *Ming-Qing shiliao*, in more than ten large collections published by CYYY starting in 1946, largely under the editorship of Li Guangtao, has been used by a few recent scholars (e.g., Struve 1984) but remains to be fully exploited. For a colorful account of Li Zicheng's capture of Beijing and a somewhat different interpretation, see Wakeman 1979, and 1985, esp. pp. 225–318.

6. Li Zicheng had several times announced that he would go through the formalities of ascending the throne, and had several times postponed his announced date for doing so.

7. Li Guangtao 1954b cites documentary evidence, p. 31; his other studies cited here supply further data.

8. Meng Sen 1965, pp. 29–43, has argued that one of those "pretenders" was actually the Chongzhen emperor's eldest son; he was arrested in or near Beijing at the end of 1645 and executed along with some who testified that he was the prince. Most historians have not accepted Meng's argument.

9. Hong has been discussed briefly; see also Chapter 30 Section IV, and Li Guangtao 1948c.

10. For the text of this document and commentary on it, see Li Guangtao 1954b, p. 44. For a different interpretation of the text and these events, see Meng Sen 1960, pp. 110–111. Meng offers a curious argument: "When a hegemon (i.e., one who rules by force) adopts benevolence and righteousness, that too can have results similar to the acts of a king (i.e., one who rules by noble principles). The essential point is that even though his intent in honoring the previous dynasty is insincere, yet if his generous concern for people's well-being causes people who have long endured grim suffering to turn to him to gain relief, then one should not deny what he has in fact accomplished" (p. 113). That appears to acknowledge Manchu hypocrisy but to discount its consequences. He goes on to say that the Manchus at first acted like fierce savages, having no conception of how to gain the empire, until Dorgon came on the scene; Meng credits this prince with having first displayed good qualities indicating a capacity to govern humanely and wisely, that is, according to Chinese ideals. He finds the conditions experienced by the people under the early Manchus not inferior to those known under the late Ming

reigns, which is perhaps true. In general, however, Meng Sen's partisan view of the Manchus as conquerors and rulers is unconvincing, and his praise of Dorgon overlooks the reasons for contemporary Manchu antipathy toward him, as well as recent historians' assessments.

11. The syllable *zu* (progenitor) in an imperial posthumous title was in Chinese usage given to a founding emperor, although in the Ming dynasty the posthumous title of the third emperor, Taizong (r. 1402–1424), was subsequently elevated to Chengzu in 1538. The Qing imperial line began with Nurhaci, who was given the posthumous temple name Taizu; then the first two emperors who ruled from the capital at Beijing were given the titles Shizu and Shengzu, thus giving the Qing dynasty three "progenitors." See the Ming and Qing succession charts in Chapter 21 and this chapter.

12. There was a rumor at the time that Fulin did not die of smallpox, but entered a monastery to live out his life as a Buddhist monk. Recent scholarship has definitively shown that to be false. Important evidence to corroborate the nature of the emperor's death has been found in the diaries of Father Johann Adam Schall von Bell, who visited him during his final illness; see Schall's modern biography, Väth 1933, which incorporates extensive extracts from Schall's diaries and personal papers. Chen Jiexian 1977, using a Chinese translation of Väth's biography, analyzes crucial points of evidence in relation to Chinese documents and concludes that Schall's diaries have high credibility.

13. See Fang Chao-ying, "Fu-lin," in ECCP, pp. 255–259, and "Yang Kuang-hsien," pp. 889–892; on Schall, see Dunne 1962, esp. pp. 324–339.

14. Those were the Embroidered Uniform Guard (Jinyi wei) and the Western and Eastern Depots (Xichang, Dongchang), which frequently during the Ming had terrorized officials and commoners alike, especially in and around the capital. The Depots were abolished, and the Guard was renamed and reconstituted to serve as no more than the ruler's formal bodyguard.

15. Struve 1988, p. 641. This (pp. 641–725) is the best brief account of the Southern Ming episode; the standard work on the subject is Struve 1984. The account that follows adopts a somewhat different narrative focus, but is indebted to Struve's work throughout.

16. The Prince of Fu's birthdate is not recorded; he appears to have been thirty-eight years old at this time. Tan Qian ca. 1653 (1958), p. 6217, gives his age as forty-one *sui* when he died "suddenly" in captivity in Beijing in the early summer (fifth month, June 13–July 12) of 1646. Xia Xie 1873, p. 3607, confirms the year and month of his death.

17. Kong Shangren's drama *The Peach Blossom Fan (Taohuashan)* depicts many historical as well as fictional characters from the world of poets and courtesans who were involved in the fall of Nanjing to the Manchu forces in 1645. For Kong Shangren (K'ung Shang-jen, 1648–1718) and the relation of his play to history, see Struve 1980 and works cited there. See also Strassberg 1983. On the special characteristics of the elite environment in late Ming times, see Kang-i Sun Chang 1991 and 1994. It has been strongly argued that the intellectual environment of the Chongzhen reign, 1627–1644, spawned an important new trend in Confucian thought that would become dominant in Qing times: see Peterson 1979; and Chapter 32, Section IV. Peterson's book also describes in great detail the milieu of elite life and its sensual distractions in the late Ming.

18. For a chronological biography, see Yang De'en (pref. date 1939).

19. The quotations are from Xia Xie 1873, p. 3494. The name of the Prince of Luh is so spelled, following Struve 1984, to distinguish him from the Prince of Lu, important in the next phase of Southern Ming history.

20. There was no shortage of commanding personalities in earlier Ming history, for example, Yu Qian in the crisis of 1449, Yang Tinghe in that of 1521–1523, and the great chief Grand Secretary Zhang Juzheng at the beginning of the Wanli reign. A crucial difference in 1645 was that the structure of central government was not in place to support a forceful leader, had there been one.

21. Li Guangtao 1948c, p. 253 and passim. For a succinct summary of Li Guangtao's views on the Ming-Qing transition, albeit without complete documentation or full argument, see Li Guangtao 1965, esp. pp. 71–126. Li's interpretive stance has not been uncritically accepted here, but his scholarship has been helpful at many points.

22. The letters are translated in part and discussed in Struve 1984, pp. 47–51, and pertinent endnotes. The originals are extensively quoted in Xia Xie 1873, pp. 3522–24 and 3542–45 and other works cited by Struve. They are intriguing documents.

23. There is a vast literature on the massacre of Yangzhou, much of it in English. See Struve 1993, pp. 28–48, for a new translation of the best-known account, and other works cited there.

24. The fall of Yangzhou to the Qing and later Qing references to it are discussed in Mote 1988a, esp. pp. 37 and 48–51.

25. The Prince of Fu died "quite unexpectedly" in captivity at Beijing early the following summer; see note 16.

26. This is briefly discussed in de Bary et al. 1960, p. 315.

27. On Jiading, see Dennerline 1981; on Jiangyin, see Wakeman 1975.

28. The Manchus' forbears, the Jurchens, in 1126 also had briefly attempted to force similar regulations on the newly conquered Chinese, but quickly abandoned the effort after seeing that it was counterproductive. The Jurchens at that point were much more confident, militarily stronger, and more resilient in adapting than were the Manchus in 1645. See Chapter 10, Section II.

29. Here the comparison with Gaozong, the first Southern Song emperor, comes to mind: he too lacked a commanding presence, but many other elements of the comparison are different. Most important perhaps is the fact that the Jurchen ancestors of the Manchus in that twelfth-century setting sought, and required, far less Chinese assistance in facing the unknowns of invading and ruling over the huge population of China's vast territorial expanses. That allowed the situation on both sides to remain simpler. See Chapter 13 for the account of Southern Song survival.

30. Also spelled Coxinga and so on; the famed Japanese dramatist Chikamatsu Monzaemon (1653–1725) is known for his puppet play *Kokusenya Kassen,* translated as "The Battles of Coxinga"; see Keene 1951.

31. On Donglin and Fu she activities in the last Ming reigns, see Chapter 30, Section I, and Atwell 1975.

32. For the most favorable assessment of Li Dingguo's loyal service, see Li Guangtao 1965, pp. 126–142. Struve 1984, chap. 5, offers a balanced view.

33. For a word portrait of Hong Chengchou, see Struve 1993, pp. 141–155. This entire volume, containing accounts of Huang Daozhou, Zheng Zhilong, and Zheng Chenggong, among others discussed here, provides valuable firsthand views of the period of Southern Ming resistance. See also Wang Chen-main 1999 for an analysis of the entire career of Hong Chengchou (Hung Ch'eng-ch'ou).

32. THE KANGXI EMPEROR

1. As noted in Part Four, "The Ming Dynasty," Ming and Qing emperors, in addition to their personal names and their posthumous temple names, also are referred to by their era or reign period names. In the case of the first Qing ruler to reign from Beijing, those three names are Fulin, Emperor Shizu, and the Shunzhi emperor; the names of his son and successor are Xuanye, Emperor Shengzu, and the Kangxi emperor. All three names of each Ming and Qing emperor appear in the present work, as they do in other historical writings.

2. His father, Fulin, was declared emperor at five and a half and assumed direct rule about the time of his thirteenth birthday; Xuanye was proclaimed emperor at age six and three-quarters years and formally assumed direct rule when he was thirteen and a half, in the summer of 1667. He was not actually free to rule directly until he brought down the regent Oboi in 1669.

3. Suspicions have been expressed about the last will and testament of his father, Emperor Shizu, suggesting that it was revised by the four regents to enhance their discretionary powers; see the discussion in Kessler 1976, pp. 20–30.

4. Compare especially the discussions of nativist reactions in Chapter 8, Sections IV and V; Chapter 10, Section IV; and passim.

5. Xuanye married the Empress Xiaocheng in 1665; she died at age twenty in 1674 giving birth to Prince Yinreng. The prince was named the heir in 1676; thereafter, and as the central figure in the succession crisis (discussed later in this chapter), he remained the heir, off and on, until he was finally deposed in 1712.

6. Kong Yude died defending his provincial capital, Guilin, which also had been one of the temporary capitals of the Southern Ming Yongli emperor, against the ex-bandit chieftain turned Ming loyalist Li Dingguo (d. 1662).

7. That family relationship did not prevent the Kangxi emperor from executing Wu Yingxiong in 1674.

8. See the discussion of Wu Sangui's actions at Shanhai Guan (the Pass at Mountains by Sea) in 1644 in Chapter 31, Section II.

9. The proclamations exchanged between Wu and the Kangxi emperor are quoted in Xiao Yishan 1963, 1:453–456.

10. Blussé 1986, esp. chaps. 5 and 6.

11. Wills 1979, p. 228. Wills offers a long-range analysis of maritime activity from late Ming to the end of the seventeenth-century in which the Zheng family and Taiwan are central elements.

12. This environment, particularly that of Nanjing, Suzhou, and the rich region of the lower Yangzi which dominated intellectual life, is described in Peterson 1979.

13. See Kang-i Sun Chang 1994, for a moving account of Wu Weiye's life and the uses to which he put his poetry. See also Xie Guozhen 1948, chap. 4 and pp. 93–94. Lo and Schultz 1986, pp. 46–54, contains a brief biography and translations of Wu Weiye's poetry; their Introduction provides a general orientation to the poetry of the Qing period.

14. Deng Zhicheng 1965.

15. For an extraordinary work of this character, see Chen Yinke 1980.

16. "Social freedoms" is of course a relative concept; many aspects of late Ming society were seen as considerably looser than previously known, but individual social freedoms even in that age might not compare favorably with those of most present-day societies.

17. Peterson 1979, pp. 9–17; the quotation is found on pp. 9–10.

18. Peterson 1968–69. Peterson quotes this evaluation of Gu Yanwu from Liang Ch'i-ch'ao 1959, as translated by Immanuel C. Y. Hsü, p. 31. Peterson's life of Gu Yanwu deals at length with the issue of Ming loyalism.

19. The obligation to refuse to serve applied most directly to those who had held office or official status under the previous dynasty, and even then individuals had to make their own ethical decisions about the matter. Gu explained his refusal to serve the Qing as a moral obligation to observe the dying command of his adoptive mother (his aunt), who had been officially honored by the Ming as a virtuous widow, and in light of that "official status" chose suicide when the Ming fell. That was considered extreme behavior. Her dying command to her stepson was only that he not serve the successor dynasty. He was and is generally looked upon as a firm Ming loyalist, and as one who served anti-Qing causes in covert ways.

20. See the discussion of Song utilitarian thought in Chapter 14, Section III. On Wang Fuzhi's philosophical stance, see McMorran 1975. Wang Fuzhi's service to the Southern Ming regimes is discussed in McMorran 1979.

21. Peterson 1979, pp. 153–154.

22. Willard J. Peterson's (1979) translation "evidential scholarship" for the Chinese term *kaoju xue* is one of several ways of rendering the Chinese term, others being "empirical research," "evidential investigation," and so on. On the history of that movement in Ming thought, tracing it back to mid-Ming times and concluding with an analysis of Fang Yizhi's thought, see Lin Qingzhang 1986.

23. See Yu Yingshi [Yü Ying-shih] 1980, esp. pp. 122–123. Yu discusses Fang Yizhi's significant contributions to the trend toward "intellectualism" (away from the overriding focus on moral philosophy that characterized Neo-Confucianism) in several of his other writings, cited in this source.

24. "Han learning" refers to the Han dynasty (206 B.C.E.–220 C.E.). Liang Qichao (Liang Ch'i-ch'ao, 1873–1929) in his influential history of Qing period thought describes the central element in the new learning as follows: "The basic method of learning was 'to get at the truth through concrete facts' and [to hold] 'no belief without evidence.' Its area of study centered in the classics and extended to include traditional linguistics, phonetics, history, astronomy and mathematics, water-works and geography, court regulations and institutions, stone and bronze inscriptions, collation of texts, assembling of lost texts, etc. Its citing of evidence and collection of materials often reached back into the two Han periods and hence it won the title of 'Han learning.'" Liang Ch'i-ch'ao 1959, as translated by Immanuel C. Y. Hsü, p. 24. Calling this movement in thought and learning "Han learning" also had the advantage of relating it to pre-Buddhist Chinese tradition, since Song and Ming Neo-Confucianism's focus on metaphysical issues was thought to reflect the unfortunate impact of Buddhism on Chinese civilization.

25. Struve 1979, p. 324.

33. THE KANGXI REIGN

1. This point has been analyzed in Wilhelm 1951.

2. Tibet is pointedly omitted from this reference to Inner Asian nations that became integral parts of the Qing Chinese empire because its status (at most a nominal dependency of the Qing at some point) was different; see the discussion of Tibet in Chapter 27, Section III, and in Section III of this chapter.

3. Silas H. L. Wu 1979, pp. 114–116.

4. The succession crisis in the late Kangxi years is the subject of Silas H. L. Wu 1979.

5. For a colorful if somewhat fanciful account of the Kangxi emperor's life, see Spence 1974. This much-admired work is presented as the emperor's "autobiography" by utilizing fragments from statements written (mostly by the emperor's court historians and drafters) in the first person.

6. On the nature of the banner system under Nurhaci, see Zhou Yuanlian 1982, esp. pp. 148–152. This article is valuable for its use of materials drawn from the "Old Manchu Documents" (Manwen laodang), but it is typical of recent historical scholarship in adhering to the crudest forms of historicism.

7. The Jurchens' "great migration" into North China in the twelfth century appears to have been a more orderly transfer of well-organized units, the *meng'an* and *mouke*, across a broader geographical expanse, with less dislocation of Chinese farming households; see Chapter 10, Section I.

8. The Mongol system is briefly discussed in Chapter 19, Section I. It existed only in a transitional period, and subsequently was looked upon by Khubilai Khan as contrary to his interest in gaining direct administrative control over the revenues from all lands populated by Chinese farmers.

9. A very extensive compilation of relevant documentary materials, *Qingdai de qidi,* 3 vols., 1989, prepared by the Center for Qing Historical Studies at Renmin Daxue, Beijing, should facilitate further studies of banner landholdings.

10. The totals on banner lands expropriated between 1644 and 1669, when it was first announced that the practice would cease, are taken from Liu Jiaju 1964, chap. 2. The total figure for the Metropolitan Province's cultivated acreage in the Ming is arrived at by adding the figures for the cultivated land in its eight prefectures as given in *Ta Ming Huidian* 1587, *juan* 17. The total figure for cultivated land given there is about 400,000 *qing* (over 6 million acres), while the total for banner lands by early Kangxi was close to 200,000 *qing.* The total area of imperial estates and lands bestowed by the Ming throne on relatives and favorites in late Ming times was much smaller. Those are said (in the *Ming History* 1739 [1974], *juan* 77, p. 1887) to have totaled 45,800 *qing,* almost entirely in the regions closest to the capital. All such figures are of questionable accuracy, but can be taken to indicate the general scope of the matter.

11. For an interesting account of this phenomenon based on case studies, see Xie Guozhen 1948.

12. Liu Jiaju 1964, esp. chap. 4. The deteriorating conditions among the conquerors described here are strikingly parallel to those reported in Jin times among the Jurchen military households in North China; see Chapter 10, Section IV, for the Jin emperor Shizong's attempts to correct similar problems.

13. Banner forces (including Mongol and Han Chinese banners) are estimated to have numbered about 200,000 male adults of military age by 1644; see Li Xinda 1982. Thereafter they increased somewhat in numbers but decreased in effectiveness. The norm of one adult male in three on active duty supplied Manchu cavalry forces of about 70,000 at any one time. Figures on Manchu military strength, secret in Qing times, have aroused much interest among recent scholars. See Chaoying Fang 1950, and Guan Donggui 1969. The *Draft Qing History* 1927 (1977), *juan* 131, p. 3891, states that the Green Standard numbered 400,000 during the early Kangxi years when it was first formally established to combat the Rebellion of the Three Feudatories. Xiao Yishan 1963, 1:572, gives a figure of almost 600,000 for 1689 and a roughly similar figure for 1764. Local militias raised the totals for armed forces somewhat higher.

14. This oversimplifies the argument in Guan Donggui 1971; see esp. his summary and conclusions, pp. 484–488.

15. See table, p. 189, and accompanying discussion in Ho 1962. Averaged figures for Northern Song, as given in Kracke 1953, pp. 58–59, are as high as 600–900 per examination; and the average for Ming (Ho 1962) is 288 per examination.

16. The work, called *Ming shi jilüe,* was based on the *Huang Ming Shigai* by Zhu Guozhen (1632). See L. C. Goodrich in ECCP, pp. 206–208, s.v. "Chuang T'ing-lung."

17. Among numerous purported examples of his essay style and his calligraphy that can be seen in libraries are the prefaces, ostensibly composed by him and in his handwriting, to the "Sacred Edict" (*Sheng yu,* 1670), to the *Peiwen yunfu* (1711), and to the *Kangxi zidian,* or "Kangxi Dictionary" (1716), and the proclamation dated 1697 about the completed version of the *Draft Ming History (Mingshi gao),* published in 1723.

18. The standard account of the compilation of the *Ming History* (1739) is found in Li Jinhua 1933.

19. See Wilhelm 1951.

20. Xu Yuanwen (1634–1691); his brother Xu Qianxue (1631–1694) also served as a director of the commission after 1682. They were nephews of Gu Yanwu and leaders of scholarly circles at the capital and in their native Jiangsu.

21. For the backgrounds of late Ming and early Qing relations with the Mongols, see Chapter 27, Sections II (Mongolia) and III (Tibet). The two problems were closely interrelated.

22. An earlier Menggu Yamen (Mongol Affairs Office) in 1638 was reorganized as the Lifan Yuan, the name commonly translated "Court [Office] of Colonial Affairs" (see, e.g., Hucker 1985). The use of "colonial" here is misleading. Mancall 1968, p. 72, proposes "Barbarian Control Office" as a more appropriate rendering, but because some of the *fan wang,* or "princes with fiefs," were Chinese, that name too seems inappropriate. The piquancy of designating the Europeans, whose affairs were shared by this office and the Ministry of Rites, as "barbarians" seems to have become a reason for so translating the name. Demands from the European powers in negotiating the treaties of 1861 and 1862 led to the establishment of the Zongli Yamen (Office in General Charge of Foreign Affairs), through which they expected to teach the Qing court about international law and how to conduct diplomacy.

23. Eventually, by the late nineteenth century, the Chinese (Qing) imperial boundaries came to be recognized in international law, imposed by the West; that gave them stability under (foreign) law at a time when otherwise they might well have disappeared, along with Qing China's fading imperial might.

24. Fletcher 1978, esp. pp. 48–54, distinguishes between the status of Mongols organized early into the Mongol banners, called Mongol bannermen, and that of the populations of Mongol federations such as Khalkha and Oyirat (Oirat) on whom Qing authority was later imposed, whom he calls "banner subjects." Meng Sen 1965 analyzes parallel control mechanisms in Manchu and Mongol banners.

25. Sebes 1977. For a lucid overview of the historical events, see also Rossabi 1975, esp. chaps. 4–6.

26. After armed conflict along the Amur in the early 1960s, both the Russians and the Chinese began producing historical justifications for territorial claims and charging each other with distortions and historical crimes. See the items cited in Sebes 1977, pp. 25–26, fn.

27. There is a large literature on the Treaty of Nerchinsk and the Sino-Russian relationship that followed, including the Treaty of Kiakhta in 1727. See Sebes 1961, Mancall 1971, and works cited in both.

28. No parallel tradition of Chinese engaging in Russian studies developed, probably because the Qing government limited the study of Russian at that time to Manchus only, among whom conditions were not conducive to such a development.

29. The importance of Manchu competition with various Mongol khans for influence in Tibet and control over the Dalai Lamas can scarcely be overstated. The leader of the Tushetu Khalkhas traveled to Tibet, acquired Tibetan Buddhist scriptures, and returned with them to convert his people; he claimed to have been awarded the title of khan by the Dalai Lama, a title that the Manchus could only recognize though they considered it their prerogative to elevate Mongol princes to that lofty title when they thought it appropriate. The account of the Kangxi emperor's involvement with the Khalkhas and the Dzungars in these years abounds with references to actions taken by Mongols competing to control the Dalai Lama, and with actions taken by Tibetan lamas (at times clearly directed by the Dalai Lama) to intervene in politics among the Mongols and in their relations with the Qing court. For citations of some of the documentary material, see Xiao Yishan 1963, 1:821–835. It is eminently clear that the Kangxi emperor and his successors considered Tibet and the Dalai Lamas the key to stability in the Mongol portions of their empire.

30. What had been "five tribes" (*aimak,* federations) of Khalkhas in late Ming times had become four in early Qing, each headed by a khan. In addition to the Tushetu khanate, whose khan controlled the principal Khalkha city of Urga, the other three were Setsen (Sechen) khanate in the east, the Sain Noyan (Sayin Noyan) khanate to the west of Tushetu (in whose territories the Qing placed their Manchu governor general, based at Uliasutai), and the Zasagtu (Jasaghtu) khanate, which bordered the Khobdo region (formerly a Khalkha khanate of Altyn), by this time the base region for Galdan's government. The map in Rosssabi 1975, p. 169, shows the disposition of Mongol federations on the eve of the Dzungars' rise.

31. Wei Yuan 1842, *juan* 3, pp. 25a–b.

32. On Phagspa, see Chapter 20, Section I. Yellow Sect hierarchs resident at the Qing court were the Lcang-skya Lamas (also spelled lCangs-skya Khutughtu; see Fletcher 1978, p. 52); I am indebted to Elliot Sperling (personal communication, February 17, 1995) for correcting my understanding of this matter.

33. The Sixth Dalai Lama, by name Tshangs-dbyangs rGya-mtsho, or Tsangyang Gyatso (1683–1706), is famous, or notorious, for his amorous life and erotic poetry of high quality; see Snellgrove and Richardson 1968, pp. 204–208. The Kangxi emperor did not object to the Sixth Dalai Lama's unconventional lifestyle (highly unusual within the sequence of spiritually dedicated Dalai Lamas though that was); he wanted him replaced because his control over Tibet's religious-political institutions was slipping. See also Fang Chao-ying in ECCP 1943–44, pp. 759–761, s.v. "Tshangs-dbyangs-rgya-mtsho."

34. This is the phrase used by Snellgrove and Richardson 1968, p. 218.

35. The chapter on Tibet's geography in the *Draft Qing History* 1927 (1977), *juan* 80, pp. 2469–82, not only does not claim Qing annexation, but also states that in 1720 the Manchu-Chinese army invading Tibet to escort the Seventh Dalai Lama to Lhasa "granted the territories of Tibet to the Dalai Lama[s]," while placing the region under the military protection of the Tibetan official Poluonai (Sonam Stöbgyal) and others. Cf. Fang Chao-ying in ECCP, p. 395. Throughout

ECCP (e.g., pp. 907–908, 935, and 395–396) Fang Chao-ying appears to accept uncritically the information offered in the *Draft Qing History* and other official Qing compilations. See also *Draft Qing History, juan* 525, on Tibet as a border principality, where the complex story of the Kangxi emperor's maneuvering in the death of the Sixth Dalai Lama and the seating of the seventh is related in obfuscating detail.

36. Almost all Chinese-language histories, whether of Nationalist, Communist, or other persuasion, agree on this issue but disagree on the date of Tibet's subjugation and cite contradictory evidence, if any. The quotations here are from Xiao Yishan 1923 (1963), 1:558; Jin Zhaofeng 1935, p. 231; and Wu Han 1964, 4:72. Xiao Yishan's discussions of Tibet in sections 113 and 114, pp. 849–855, is riddled with errors and inspires little confidence. Jin Zhaofeng, a careful but partial (pro-Manchu) historian, offers little or no support for his view. The popular work edited by Wu Han is typical of many more recent writings on the subject in that it does not attempt to offer historical evidence.

37. A better date for final Chinese displacement of their Mongol rivals for influence in (but not rule over) Tibet might be 1750; in that year the Imperial Resident (Amban) representing the Manchu court at Lhasa became firmly established there after a rebellion favorable to lingering Oyirat (Dzungar) power was put down, and shortly before the Qianlong emperor's victories that ended Dzungar power forever. Cf. Fang Chao-ying in ECCP, pp. 249–251, s.v. "Fu-ch'ing." It is nevertheless clear that no Chinese or Manchu officials ever held governing responsibilities in Tibet. The account of Tibet as a border principality in the *Draft Qing History* 1927 (1977), *juan* 525, esp. pp. 14531–39, makes that abundantly clear.

38. This is not to argue what international law should decide about the status of Tibet today; it is merely to point out that Chinese claims to possess and govern Tibet are of very recent origin and have no factual basis in longer historical perspective.

39. The persistence of this political style in China today reflects new realities, but the tendency to regard those who disagree with one's political stance as morally deficient echoes the imperial age.

40. This was Guo Xiu (1638–1715), a northerner from Shandong, who had an eminent but controversial career lasting to 1703, when he was cashiered for incompetence, with imputations of corruption.

41. Mingju, a grandson through his mother of Nurhaci, was among the early Qing Manchu nobles most friendly to Chinese culture and to southern Chinese men of letters. His eldest son, Singde (1655–1685), was the finest poet (in Chinese, especially in the *ci* genre of lyrical verse) of his time. See biographical sketch and translations by William Schultz in Lo and Schultz 1986, pp. 152–160. Singde's personal relations with many of the first southern Chinese literati to come into the government were important to the growth of the Southern Party (Nandang) at that time.

42. This argument is fully developed in Miller 1974, esp. chaps. 4 and 5.

43. One might argue that "nativist reaction" ideas were a cohering element in Oboi's factional leadership, from the later years of the Shunzhi emperor's reign until Oboi's fall in 1669. We have no evidence that such ideas were articulated as doctrine and given the character of an ideology, however.

44. To some extent that was also true in the North.

45. This Prince Yinti, the Kangxi emperor's first son, should not be confused with the fourteenth son, whose name is also spelled "Yinti" but is pronounced differently in Chinese. In fact, some dictionaries give the first son's name the reading "Yinzhi," but the pronunciation "Yinti" is widely seen in Western writings; see

Fang Chao-ying in ECCP, pp. 929–931, for brief biographies of the two princes, both under "Yin-t'i," the equivalent of "Yinti" as used in the present work. Pei Huang 1974, p. 313, n. 4, gives evidence from Manchu for pronouncing the first son's name "Yinshi." This prince was placed under permanent house arrest in 1708, and thus played no further part in the succession crisis.

46. See Silas H. L. Wu 1970, esp. chap. 5. The secret memorial system reached the height of its importance under the Yongzheng emperor, 1723–1735.

47. This scholar-official was Wang Hongxu (1645–1723) from Huating, near Shanghai. He was not a reputable scholar, but was famed for his calligraphy, and served for many years as head of the commission to compile the *Ming History*.

48. Quoted in Silas H. L. Wu 1979, p. 91. The implication of sexual perversion is strong.

49. Here I follow the conclusions reached in ibid., chap. 15. The view that Yinzhen usurped the throne by manipulating the succession immediately upon his father's death has long been a standard view; see, e.g., Fang Chao-ying in ECCP, pp. 915–920, s.v. "Yin-chen." Pei Huang 1974, esp. pp. 75–80, believes that there is "reason to doubt the legitimacy of his accession," but says that there is no way to prove the matter. Most other historians state that Yinzhen usurped the throne. As will be seen in Chapter 34, his behavior after coming to the throne strongly suggests that he did. For a critical review of scholarship on the subject, see T. S. Fisher 1978.

50. The Sacred Edict and its Sixteen Maxims are translated and discussed in K. C. Hsiao 1960, pp. 184–191.

34. The Yongzheng Emperor as Man and Ruler

1. For a critical review of scholarship bearing on Yinzhen's succession, see T. S. Fisher 1978.

2. The Yongzheng emperor (b. 1678) also maintained relatively friendly if not intimate relations with two brothers much younger than himself, Princes Yinlu (1695–1767) and Yinli (1697–1738), who apparently played no part in the succession struggles.

3. Meng Sen 1965, p. 290. The phrase "terrified demeanor" *(hu su)* is an allusion to *Mencius* I/I/vii/4, where it describes the pitiful look of a sacrificial ox on its way to be slaughtered.

4. The text is quoted and briefly discussed in Xiao Yishan 1963, 1:859–860.

5. See the emperor's statement, quoted in Silas H. L. Wu 1970, p. 71.

6. For a study of the governing system of mid-Qing China, see Bartlett 1991; on the system of palace memorials, see particularly pp. 46–64. The entire work is indispensable for its analysis of Qing imperial governing. See also Chen Jiexian 1978b, devoted to Yongzheng period issues, and which on pp. 1–24 offers illuminating examples of the ways the Yongzheng emperor's use of the palace memorial system reveals his methods and his psychological involvement.

7. This is an assumption about the length and content of the Kangxi period vermilion rescripts. The Kangxi emperor's rescripted memorials were sent back to the sender and in most cases were not to be returned to the palace for preservation; thus, most of them have not been preserved.

8. Late in his reign he announced that he would make a selection (about 7,000, approximately one-third of the total) of the palace memorials with his vermilion endorsements to be published for the edification of officialdom. He died before

the editing was completed. When the work was at last printed (in 1738, in a two-color blockprinting, preserving the black and red of the originals), his son the Qianlong emperor, was embarrassed by the intimate and imprudent tone of his father's rescripts. He ordered that even these, selected as innocuous, be "cleaned up" to present the Emperor Shizong in a more fitting manner. The extent to which those redacted versions differ from the originals was not clearly established until the 1960s. See Bartlett 1974; and Chen Jiexian 1978b, pp. 1–24.

9. For a study of Castiglione's life and work at the Qing court, see Howard Rogers 1988.

10. Wu Hung 1995, p. 31. Wu Hung offers a convincing explanation for the introduction of the genre of costume portraits or "masquerade paintings" to the Qing court by European artists, but the question of what these paintings may mean for our understanding of this emperor remains. I am grateful to Naomi N. Richard for drawing this article to my attention. See also Wu Hung 1996, chap. 4.

11. Chen Jiexian 1978b, pp. 1–24.

12. This is explored in fascinating detail ibid., pp. 25–76. See also Fang Chao-ying in ECCP, pp. 719–721, s.v. "T'ien Wen-ching."

13. Earlier chapters have described the variants on this classic problem of conquest dynasties in Liao, Jin, and Yuan times.

14. Silas H. L. Wu 1970, discussing the early Kangxi reign, translates Yizheng Wang Dachen Huiyi (more commonly, Yizheng Chu) as "the Assembly of [or Council of] Deliberative Princes and Ministers"; see pp. 10–13. Bartlett 1991, pp. 31–32, in the context of early Yongzheng times, translates the name of this conciliar organ "the Plenipotentiary Council." Its functions changed over time.

15. See Pei Huang 1974, pp. 168–184.

16. Qing sources speak of the Council of the Nine Ministers, made up of the heads of the Six Ministries, the two Censors-in-Chief, and the Director of the Office of Transmissions, which managed the paper flow in court and government.

17. A certain number of *jinshi* who placed highest in the palace examinations, as in Ming times, were designated "Hanlin Bachelors," *shuji shi,* and given preferential treatment for advancement thereafter in court and central government posts. In early Qing times, a school for Manchu language studies for which selected *jinshi* were eligible was established in the Hanlin Academy. Some of the early Qing Chinese Hanlin Bachelors who elected to take the three-year course became fluent in written and spoken Manchu.

18. See the lists of names in *Draft Qing History* 1927 (1977), *juan* 176. Manchus dominated the Grand Council, which averaged eight to twelve members after 1735.

19. Ibid., p. 6229. See Bartlett 1991, chaps. 5 and 6, for the Grand Council's further development under the Qianlong emperor.

20. In earlier times the Censorate was called *yushi tai;* that was changed in early Ming to *ducha yuan;* the name *jiancha yushi* was used in a more general sense. Ming censorial functions were significantly supplemented by the surveillance of government offices conducted by the *jishizhong,* called "supervising censors" or "supervising secretaries," attached to the Six Ministries. After the Yongzheng changes, they and the circuit censors were called *kedao;* their functions were combined and they were attached to the *ducha yuan,* the Office of the Censors-in-Chief. All of the institutionally distinct branches of investigating and supervisory activity are included in the use of "Censorate" here. The standard study of these institutions is Hucker 1966.

21. Sun Yat-sen's so-called Five Power Constitution was adopted by the Guomindang in 1923. Its Five Powers were institutionalized as the Legislative Yuan (Lifa Yuan), Executive Yuan (Xingzheng Yuan), Judicial Yuan (Sifa Yuan), representing the usual tripartite division of modern Western governments, plus the Control Yuan or Control and Impeachment Yuan (Jiancha Yuan) and the Examination Yuan (Kaoshi Yuan), the latter two being the modernized forms of the traditional Censorate and civil service examination systems.

22. K. C. Hsiao 1960, p. 185.

23. Yue Zhongqi's biography in the *Draft Qing History* 1927 (1977), *juan* 296, gives no indication that Yue Zhongqi was a descendant of Song dynasty general Yue Fei. Fang Chao-ying in ECCP, p. 957, assumes he was. It seems more likely that reports at that time saying he was, and that he planned to revolt, were intended by Yue's enemies to undermine him, and were false. When Governor Yue on one occasion learned about such rumors and reported them to the Yongzheng emperor, the emperor replied that he had already received many such reports and did not credit them.

24. A few copies have survived; one is in the Gest Oriental Research Library at Princeton University.

25. The Yongzheng literary inquisition is discussed in Pei Huang 1974, pp. 187–225, where it is more benignly interpreted than here. Huang calls the Yongzheng emperor "a benevolent despot."

26. See the discussion of secret societies in Xiao Yishan 1963, 1:896–932.

27. For Galdan and the rise of the Dzungar state, see Chapter 33 Section III. On Tsewang Araptan, see Fang Chao-ying in ECCP, pp. 757–759; and Rossabi 1975, pp. 142–147.

28. For a study of E'ertai's governing in southwest China, see Kent C. Smith 1970.

29. See Chapter 29, Section I, where the hypotheses about Ming dynasty population worked out in Heijdra 1994, chap. 1, are accepted as the most useful basis presently available for estimating Ming population.

30. For an expert review of the technical problems encountered in estimating the Qing dynasty population, see Rozman 1982, esp. pp. 1–40. Rozman's figures for total population of Qing China are, however, considerably lower than those adopted here.

31. Ho 1959, p. 270, summarizing the conclusions to his important methodological study.

32. See, e.g., *International Encyclopedia of the Social Sciences*, 12:378. The absolute figures are 545 million in 1650, increasing to 728 million in 1750, described as an overall annual growth rate of 0.3 percent. Those totals undoubtedly err by using figures for China that were at that time (1968) widely accepted, but now are considered to be much too low.

33. An estimate of 430 million for 1850, before the calamitous domestic wars and disorders of the late nineteenth century, is more or less standard in recent historical writings; a figure of 583 million was produced a century later by the first census taken under the Chinese Communist government, in 1953.

34. See the discussion in Dai Yi 1992, pp. 305–311, for comments by the emperor and others on the new population figures produced during the Qianlong reign. Despite evidence Dai Yi presents, he accepts (uncritically) the notion of explosive growth through the eighteenth century; he has not attempted to place the Qing figures in a longer-range context. That is, he accepts a starting point in the seventeenth century that is (in light of the hypotheses invoked here) much too low.

35. Heijdra 1994, pp. 50–56, summarizes his conclusions about the population of late Ming China; these are accepted in Chapter 29 as the basis for estimating Ming population and as the starting point for this discussion of Qing population 1650–1800.

36. Ho 1959, p. 266: "One cannot be certain whether by 1700 the population of China was as large as that of 1600."

37. This is not to suggest that the argument is strengthened by agreeing with "widely accepted views," which are not adopted elsewhere in these discussions of Ming and Qing population; it is merely to point out that the assumptions about eighteenth-century population tentatively adopted here are if anything too cautious.

38. The quoted words are found in Pei Huang 1974, p. 235. Huang's discussion of the Yongzheng emperor's impact on society and local governing, pp. 245–272, is pertinent here, although his assessment of the emperor's character and motivation is quite generous.

39. The estimate of 5 to 6 percent includes the "labor service tax" that, starting in 1723, came to be incorporated into the land *(di-ding)* tax. See Perkins 1969, p. 176.

40. The tax receipts commuted to the equivalent value in money, that is, silver bullion, in relation to those received in grain or other products was roughly three-fourths in silver and one-fourth in kind. For the year 1753, for example, official records give the following figures: 29,611,201 taels (silver ounces) in money and 8,406,422 *shi* of grain received in kind. The official *shi* in Qing times was the equivalent of 131.6 pounds of husked grain, and was, on average, worth one tael of silver. A critical study of those and other figures concludes that the agrarian tax produced somewhat more than that amount, when all statutory and unauthorized surcharges are figured in. For 1753 this study calculates that the total land *(di-ding)* tax revenue amounted to the value of 54 million silver taels, of which 37 million was collected in silver. See Yeh-chien Wang 1973, pp. 26–29 and table 27. In an earlier work Wang is quoted as estimating the revenues in 1753 at the equivalent of 48 million taels, with the total state revenue including the salt distribution monopoly, customs tariffs, and so on at 58 million; see Perkins 1969, p. 176. K. C. Hsiao 1960, p. 585, n. 9, quotes the official figures cited here; Hsiao offers a lucid and succinct account of Qing taxation and collection procedures, pp. 84–143.

41. A privately compiled work intended to guide county magistrates in performing their duties is the *Fuhui quanshu* (1696). It complements the official *Fuyi quanshu* in giving practical information in great detail about the administration of tax collection in the counties. See the translation, Djang Chu 1984, under the title *A Complete Book Concerning Happiness and Benevolence*. Note in particular the "Translator's Introduction," pp. 1–40.

42. Yeh-chien Wang 1973, pp. 28–29, calculates that the average figure for the newly legalized surcharge nationwide was 12 percent, and that an equal amount of unauthorized surcharge continued to be regularly collected at local levels to cover costs of the county and prefectural clerical staff salaries. He therefore adds 25 percent to the *di-ding* quotas in 1753, his representative year for the mid-Qing. See also note 35.

43. See Madeleine Zelin 1984, a book-length treatment of the Yongzheng fiscal reform. For official salaries compared with the *yanglian* bonuses, see pp. 37 and 123–124.

44. See also the discussion of the tax reforms under the Yongzheng emperor in Pei Huang 1974, pp. 245–272.

35. SPLENDOR AND DEGENERATION, 1736–1799

1. This portrait has been published in Lee et al. 1980, cat. no. 262; and (in color) in Chou and Brown 1985, cat. no. 4. On Castiglione, an Italian lay brother in the Jesuit order, well known in Chinese art history by his Chinese name Lang Shining, see Chapter 34, notes 8 and 9.
2. See the discussion in Immanuel C. Y. Hsü 1983, pp. 155–163, where this passage is quoted from J. L. Cranmer-Byng; for a scholarly editing of Macartney's diary, from which this is quoted, see J. L. Cranmer-Byng 1963.
3. The letter is translated in part in Teng and Fairbank 1954, p. 19.
4. That the Macartney embassy held deeper meaning for both the British and the Manchu/Chinese sides in the context of the times is perceptively explored in Hevia 1989.
5. The English philosopher and mathematician Bertrand Russell, who came to know China during an extended lecture tour in 1920 and 1921, felt its civilization's values included elements that the West could admire and emulate. He wrote that no one understands China until the Qianlong emperor's letter to King George III ceases to seem absurd. Yet he must have encountered many highly cultured Chinese who found it absurd, and their understanding of China was at least equal to his own. Moreover, it is quite likely that many educated Englishmen today may find Macartney's behavior in China equally absurd. Both the emperor and the ambassador are understandable, which is more to the point.
6. The dilemmas of assessing the Qianlong emperor and his reign from a nationalistic point of view are well exemplified by the internally contradictory discussion in Dai Yi 1992, esp. pp. 3–37 and passim.
7. The present writer has occasionally adopted a highly critical view of the Qianlong emperor; see Mote 1988a. In the present work, however, the emphasis is placed less on such judgments and more on factors which may help to explain his governing.
8. See the speculation on this event in Dai Yi 1992, pp. 50–51, 58–60, and other information there on the violent deaths of imperial relatives in these years who were close to Hongli.
9. In 1733, when they were twenty-two, Hongli and his brother Hongzhou were elevated to Princes of the First Rank *(qin wang);* Hongli was given the title "Prince Bao."
10. Prince Hongyan, 1733–1765.
11. For a valuable collection of essays on painting and on the state of the arts during the Qianlong reign, see the symposium edited by Chou and Brown, 2 vols., 1988, 1991.
12. For a defense of Hongli's connoisseurship, see the essay by Kohara Hironobu, ibid., 1988, pp. 56–73.
13. The best items that were in the imperial palace in Beijing after the Revolution of 1911 became the Imperial Palace Collection, now in the Palace Museum in Taipei. A large number of valuable items were in the household of the "Last Emperor" in Manchuria when the Japanese established the puppet state of Manchukuo in 1932. Some of those were plundered in 1945 at the end of the Sino-Japanese War

and entered the international art market, but many are now in museums in China. The Palace Museum in Beijing has assembled a collection since 1949 that vies with the Taipei Palace Museum collection in size and quality. Many of its works also are documented as having once belonged to the Qianlong emperor.

14. In a detailed survey of the Qianlong emperor's building projects, Dai Yi 1992 discusses the emperor's arguments answering his critics; see pp. 433–498 and esp. pp. 438–441.

15. Qing police control imposed through the *baojia* system is the subject of chap. 3 in K. C. Hsiao 1960.

16. Several of the emperor's pronouncements on this subject are quoted at length and discussed in Xiao Yishan 1963, 2:3–13.

17. Yu Yingshi [Yü Ying-shih] 1978, pp. 197–199. See also Xiao Yishan 1963, 2:21–23, where some of the relevant documents are cited.

18. *Qing Shilu*, Qianlong 31 (1766), *juan* 754, second month, day *jiachen*, as quoted in Dai Yi 1992, p. 9.

19. The story is well told, and the work soundly analyzed, in Guy 1987. Guy's study is particularly valuable for the analysis of the *Siku* catalogue, which contains useful descriptive and critical notes on all the works included in it as well as on the much larger number of those not copied into the final compilation but "preserved by title only" *(cunmu)*. Guy's study, however, offers a somewhat more benign view of the emperor's role than is presented here. On the reasons for adopting the fourfold classification system, see also Cary Y. Liu 1997.

20. The Wenyuan Ge holds an important place in architectural history; see Cary Liu 1997.

21. The quoted passage is slightly modified from Mote, 1987, p. 27; Tsien Tsuen-hsiun 1985, p. 185, gives the figures as "3511 titles [i.e., complete works] in 36,275 volumes." Compare the *Siku quanshu* with the *Yongle dadian* of the Yongle reign (1402–1424), described in Chapter 24, Section I.

22. By reducing the size, it was possible to put four of the original manuscript pages of the so-called Wenyuan Ge set on one page of the 1984 printing, which fills 1,500 large bound volumes and occupies several bays in most libraries' stacks.

23. See the discussion of these aspects of the *Siku quanshu* in Mote 1987, and the accompanying essay Chu 1987.

24. Wu Zhefu 1969, esp. pp. 98–112. In the "Index list of destroyed works" appended to this work, Wu Zhefu identifies about 3,500 of the banned writings.

25. See tabular presentation in Wu Zhefu 1969, pp. 20–26.

26. Documents relevant to a number of such cases are quoted in Xiao Yishan 1963, 2:14–33. Guy 1987 analyzes the "literary inquisition" and examines some examples, pp. 157–200.

27. Today also one may associate a political crime such as treason with moral failing, as when a citizen collaborates with an enemy state in a time of war. But that is an extreme example. The overtones of moral degeneracy with which the Chinese state could convincingly impugn any subject who dissented on any of a broad range of issues was far more generally threatening. Loyalty to dynasty was demanded in innumerable ordinary contexts of life. A standard Chinese axiom was "Show me a filial son and I will show you a loyal servitor," equating loyalty with filial responsibility, the highest moral obligation in Chinese society. By Song times, that extension of social ethics to include loyalty to ruler and dynasty became firmly established, and grew stronger under the ever more highly authoritarian later dynasties. Manchu sensitivities greatly enlarged the problem.

28. Wu Zhefu 1969, pp. 64–83; this source lists 190 works of fiction and drama known to have been censored.

29. Twelve such works are listed ibid., pp. 58–59.

30. Yu Yingshi [Yü Ying-shih] 1978, pp. 181–208.

31. Among historians whose researches were particularly risky, the most interesting is Quan Zuwang (1705–1755). See his brief biography by Fang Chao-ying in ECCP, pp. 203–205, s.v. Ch'üan Tsu-wang; and discussion in Mote 1988a, esp. pp. 47–51.

32. Written by Wu Jingzi (1701–1754), it was first published in mid-Qianlong times, after the writer's death. The excellent translation by Yang Hsien-yi and Gladys Yang (Beijing, 1957) has been republished with a critical introduction, dated 1972, by C. T. Hsia, who calls it a "comedy of manners," a "comic satire of panoramic proportions." See under Wu Ching-Tzu ca. 1750 in Bibliography.

33. More precisely, they rejected both the ontology and the epistemology of all Song-Ming Neo-Confucian thought.

34. Analogous patterns are found in the cultural histories of many times and places; see the discussion in comparative terms in Yu Yingshi [Yü Ying-shih] 1976, pp. 143–145, for some examples drawn from Western intellectual and religious history.

35. The term, and the historical interpretation, are drawn from the writings of Yu Yingshi [Yü Ying-shih], esp. 1975 and 1976. He is not, however, to be held responsible for my use of those ideas here.

36. He was from Xiuning County in Huizhou Prefecture, the region that produced many of the age's richest merchants, who also had strong ties to the elite of politics and of scholarship. The young Dai Zhen undoubtedly benefited from being of the Huizhou network in eighteenth-century society.

37. For a brief introduction and selected translations, see Wing-tsit Chan 1963a, pp. 709–722. Chan is among those who, although trying to be fair, offers an unsatisfactory understanding of Dai Zhen. For a better analysis of Dai's importance, see Yu Yingshi [Yü Ying-shih] 1976; and Yü Ying-shih 1989.

38. For a book-length study, see Nivison 1966; see also Yu Yingshi [Yü Ying-shih] 1976.

39. The original uses the spelling *kung li* for the term translated "Justice." This is from Hu Shih, "A Note on Tai Chen [Dai Zhen]," in ECCP, pp. 970–982. The "righteous men" accused of failing to employ their scholarly acumen in accepting the long-standing charges against Dai Zhen are Liang Qichao (1873–1929), one of the leaders of new thought, Meng Sen (1868–1937), one of the most important figures in the new historical study, and Wang Guowei (1877–1927), a leading expert in critical scholarship.

40. Yu Yingshi [Yü Ying-shih] 1978, esp. pp. 39–141 and 181–195. This revelatory study also shows that literal-minded historians' searches for real persons, places, and events underlying this great novel of the imagination are misplaced. That, however, is not to deny its value as a reflection of social realities in the Qianlong era.

41. The hall used for this purpose was the Ziguang Ge (erroneously translated "pavilion of purple effulgence"; "purple" should be taken as an allusion to the Pole Star, a symbol of the imperial position, as in "purple forbidden city," *zijin cheng*, a standard but equally erroneous translation of the name for the Forbidden City). The Ziguang Ge, in the Zhonghai portion of the imperial palace city, was built in the Shunzhi reign at the beginning of the Qing; it appears that the Qianlong

emperor added to it a "Hall of Military Accomplishment" (Wucheng dian), in which the military objects, portraits, and murals were displayed, and held receptions and banquets to honor victorious commanders, and to receive heads of vassal states, in the adjoining pavilion. See Arlington and Lewisohn 1987, pp. 101–102.

42. *Les conquêtes de l'Empereur de la Chine,* a set of sixteen engravings produced in large folio format by the firm of Helman in Paris between 1767 and 1774; all hundred sets were to have been sent to the emperor in Beijing, and the copper plates were to have been destroyed to prevent their unauthorized use. The Helman firm illicitly made a new set in slightly smaller format, supplemented by four new plates, which it issued for sale in 1783–1786. Rare copies of both sets are found in libraries; for example, the original set is in the Library of Congress, and a complete set of the 1783–1786 reengraving at Gest Oriental Research Library and East Asian Collections, Princeton University.

43. One of the more noteworthy Chinese uprisings was that of Wang Lun in 1774, a rebellious movement proclaiming White Lotus secret society tenets; it provides a case study of local popular discontent in mid-Qing times. See Naquin 1981.

44. See the brief accounts by Fang Chao-ying in ECCP, pp. 9–11, s.v. "Amursana," and pp. 72–75, s.v. "Chao-hui."

45. For their organization under local chieftainships, see Gong Yin 1992, pp. 256–264.

46. See the accounts, with extensive quotations from relevant documents, in Xiao Yishan 1963, 2:87–146. Xiao draws heavily on Wei Yuan 1842.

47. This king was Shah Prithvi Narayan, who came to the throne of Gurkha in 1742, completed the conquest of Nepal in 1768, and died in 1775. His successors vigorously expanded Nepal's borders and encouraged trade. The British success in their Gurkha wars of 1814–1816 stabilized Nepal's borders and determined Nepal's place among the states on the edge of British India.

48. By name Paldan Yeshe (or Lopsang Palden Yeshe), he is sometimes referred to as the Sixth Panchen Lama. His relations with the British East India Company's agents and with Catholic missionaries are described in Cammann 1951, where he is referred to as the Sixth Panchen Lama. Cammann offers colorful detail coupled with sound judgment on a complex phase of history. See also Stein 1972, pp. 88–89.

49. The Gurkha throne was at this time occupied by Prithvi Narayan's grandson, under the guidance of regents in the royal family; they were rashly aggressive and eager for the profits of trading and raiding. The Governor General of the Company in India, 1786–1793 and again 1804–1805, was Charles, Lord (later First Marquis) Cornwallis (1738–1805), who had surrendered to George Washington at Yorktown, Virginia, on October 19, 1781. The hard-pressed Company was eager to find new outlets for trade.

50. For Fukang'an, see Knight Biggerstaff in ECCP, pp. 253–255, s.v. "Fu-k'ang-an"; for Hailancha, see Fang Chao-ying in ECCP, pp. 273–274, s.v. "Hai-lan-ch'a." Hailancha rose from the ranks to become a highly regarded general; he was descended from the ruling clan of the Khitans of the Liao dynasty which ended in the early twelfth century.

51. For a somewhat exculpatory evaluation of Fukang'an, in contrast with Heshen, see Dai Yi 1992, pp. 499–511.

52. Harold L. Kahn 1985, p. 288. In addition to this essay on the taste of the age, see also Harold L. Kahn 1971 for a full biographical study of the Qianlong emperor.

53. Kang-yi Sun Chang 1992.

54. Much of this discussion draws on Bray 1984. Bray offers a convenient synthesis of information about Chinese agriculture. Her entire section called "Conclusions: Agricultural Changes and Society—Stagnation or Revolution," pp. 553–616, merits reading for stimulating insight and interpretation. Specific references here are to pp. 603 and 532; the cited passage is quoted by Bray from Ping-ti Ho, 1959.

55. Bray 1984, p. 612. Bray concludes that the economy was resilient, with potential for expansion through mid-Qing, if somewhat less so in the nineteenth century.

56. By the end of the Qing dynasty, the Eastern Three Provinces (Dong san sheng; also called just the "Northeast," Dongbei) separately established in Manchuria in 1907, and the Inner Asian province of Xinjiang (Chinese Turkestan, first established as a province in 1884) had acquired six prefectural administrative subdivisions having under them between forty and fifty sub-prefectures and counties. Those in Xinjiang mostly were created as certain native chieftainships were changed over into civil service–managed local governments on the model of China Proper.

57. The standard work on structure and functioning of Qing local government is Ch'ü T'ung-tsu 1962. Watt 1972 offers the best description and analysis of the roles of Qing period county magistrates.

36. China's Legacy in a Changing World

1. For an extensive survey of China's and Asia's impact on Europe in these centuries, see Lach 1965 and Lach and van Kley 1993.

2. One of the earliest was the work by three missionaries, Fathers L. Buglio, G. Magalhaens, and F. Verbiest, called *Xifang yaoji* (Essential Information about the West), submitted to the young Kangxi emperor in 1669. It was printed and reprinted in a number of editions, but had very little impact in clearing up misconceptions about Europe.

3. This information was both extensive and of high quality. For example, a widely used comprehensive history of China, the "Outline Condensation of the Mirror of Universal History" *(Zizhi tongjian gangmu)*, credited to Zhu Xi and followers at the end of the twelfth century, was fully translated by Joseph de Moyriac de Mailla, a French Jesuit resident in Beijing from 1703 until his death there in 1748, and published in French in thirteen volumes (Paris, 1777–1783) under the title *Histoire Générale de la Chine, ou Annales de Cet Empire . . . Ouvrage enrichi de Figures & de nouvelles Cartes Géographique de la Chine ancienne & moderne.* Still earlier is a large work by the French missionary Jean-Baptiste Du Halde, *Description Géographique, Historique, Chronologique, Politique, et Physique de l'Empire de la Chine et de la Tartarie Chinoise* (Paris, 1735), quickly reprinted in several European countries and translated into other languages. Translations of early Confucian texts reached Europe in the seventeenth century, and were widely known among the important figures in European intellectual history such as Montesquieu, Leibnitz, Quesnay, Turgot, Voltaire, and others in the late seventeenth and eighteenth centuries.

4. Gallagher 1953, p. 142. Gallagher's work is an English translation of the Latin translation (i.e., based on Ricci's Italian diaries and journals); the Latin version was first published in 1615 by Nicola Trigault, one of Ricci's missionary companions in China. The Ricci-Trigault *Journals* is a valuable and influential work, although it varies somewhat in content and tone from Ricci's Italian original. One need not doubt, however, that the sentiment expressed in the quoted sentence

could have been uttered by Ricci and many other sympathetic observers of the Chinese scene in the seventeenth and eighteenth centuries.

5. This alludes to the title of the influential historical work by W. H. McNeill 1963, *The Rise of the West: A History of the Human Community.*

6. The most important contributions to our understanding of this phenomenon have been made by William S. Atwell, and are cited along with related items in Chapter 29; see esp. Atwell 1982, 1988, and 1990.

7. On the hypotheses concerning a "seventeenth-century general crisis" and its possible impact on China, see the discussions in Atwell 1986, Wakeman 1986, and works cited in them.

8. "Magic" is used here in the functional sense of "non-material means to material ends." See discussion and definition in Levy 1952, pp. 243–244, and 1966, p. 357.

9. See the analysis of the convert's thought processes in Peterson 1988; see also the more general discussion in Peterson 1998.

10. This phrase is used in the title of the study by George L. Harris 1966 focusing on the earlier phase of this initiative as initiated by Matteo Ricci between 1583 and his death in China in 1610.

11. See the discussion of the Qianlong emperor's Gurkha wars in the early 1790s, and the effort to control Tibet as a point of access to West China, in Chapter 35, Section VI.

12. South Asia under British domination from the eighteenth century onward displays elements again different from these other examples.

13. Variously worded (e.g., *neiluan waihuo* and so on), such phrases have been used since before the imperial era began in the third century B.C.E.

14. This is the title of a volume of relevant essays; see Wang Gungwu 1991.

15. *Analects* 13.18; Legge 1895 (1960), p. 270. See discussion in K. C. Hsiao 1979, pp. 386–387 and n. 39.

16. To nullify family authority would become a principal focus of government action only in the mid-twentieth century, when Leninist, not liberal Western, goals were being pursued. Western ideals also had contributed to the weakening of family values, but at other times and in other contexts.

17. All of the quotations here are from Levy 1966, 2:488.

18. E.g., the great synthesizer of Neo-Confucian thought Zhu Xi (1130–1200).

19. The term is applied to China by C. K. Yang 1961, esp. chap. 12; it is used here with a slightly more general meaning than is implied by his contrasting of "diffused" and "institutionalized" religions.

BIBLIOGRAPHY

Note: Most works are alphabetized under surname of author. Chinese and Japanese authors' names are given surname first, not followed by a comma, for their publications in those languages; the forms used on their publications in Western languages, and some others transcribed from other scripts (i.e., Cyrillic), are adopted here for their Western-language publications. In some cases that has required the use of more than one Western-language form of a single name. Some traditional Chinese works are alphabetized under the title of the work; for example, the official dynastic histories are listed by the English translation of the title, such as *Liao History,* but the cross-reference to *Liaoshi* is also entered. Note that the dynastic histories are *not* listed under names of compilers or authors. In some cases other traditional works also are entered by title, for example, *Qidan guozhi* (1247), for which a cross-reference under the name of the author, Ye Longli, is also listed. The primary listing for the eminent work of Song historiography, the *Zizhi tongjian* (1086), however, is by the name of its principal compiler, Sima Guang, as are some other works by very well known authors; they are cross-referenced under their titles. Wade-Giles romanization equivalents of all single syllables are given in an appendix to this volume.

The following abbreviations are used:

AM   *Asia Major*

CHC   *The Cambridge History of China,* 1978–; 10 vols. to date.

CYYY   *Zhongyang yanjiu yuan* (Chung-yang Yen-chiu Yuan), [Bulletin of the Institute of History and Philology, Academia Sinica], Beijing, Nanjing, and Taipei, 1929–.

DMB   *Dictionary of Ming Biography.* Ed. L. Carrington Goodrich and Chaoying Fang. 2 vols. New York: Columbia University Press, 1976.

ECCP   *Eminent Chinese of the Ch'ing Period.* Ed. Arthur W. Hummel. 2 vols. Washington D.C.: Library of Congress, 1943, 1944.

HJAS   *Harvard Journal of Asiatic Studies*

MSL   *Ming Shilu* [The Veritable Records of the Ming Dynasty]. "Taizu Shilu." 10 vols. Taipei, 1963; other reigns, Nanjing, 1940.

SBCK   *Sibu congkan* [SPTK, *Ssu-pu ts'ung-k'an*], reduced size facsimile *(suoben),* 400 vols. Shanghai, 1936.

SSYJ   *Songshi yanjiu ji* [Collected Studies on Song History], annual volumes from 1967, Taipei.

Allsen, Thomas T. 1987. *Mongol Imperialism: The Policies of the Grand Khan Möngke in China, Russia, and the Islamic Lands, 1251–1259.* Berkeley: University of California Press.

Alonso, Mary Ellen. 1979. *China's Inner Asian Frontier: Photographs of the Wulsin Expedition to Northwest China in 1923.* Cambridge, Mass.: Peabody Museum, Harvard University.

Andrew, Anita M. 1985. "The Local Community in Early Ming Social Legislation." *Ming Studies* 20 (Spring):57–68.

Arlington, L. C., and William Lewisohn. 1987. *In Search of Old Peking* [1935]. Reprint, Oxford: Oxford University Press.

Atwell, William S. 1975. "From Education to Politics: The *Fu She.*" In de Bary 1975, pp. 333–368.

——— 1982. "International Bullion Flows and the Chinese Economy, ca. 1530–1650." *Past and Present* 95 (May):68–90.

——— 1988. "The T'ai-ch'ang, T'ien-ch'i, and Ch'ung-chen Reigns, 1620–1644." In CHC 7:585–640.

——— 1990. "A Seventeenth-Century General Crisis in China?" *Modern Asian Studies* 24, no. 4:661–682.

Bai Bin. 1989. *Dangxiang shi yanjiu.* Jilin.

Balazs, Étienne. 1964. *Chinese Civilization and Bureaucracy.* Translated by Hope M. Wright. New Haven: Yale University Press.

Bao Hongchang. 1991. "Ming Xianzong Zhu Jianshen." In *Mingchao shiliu di,* ed. Xu Daling and Wang Tianyou, pp. 159–172. Beijing.

Bartlett, Beatrice S. 1974. "The Secret Memorials of the Yung-cheng Period (1723–1735), Archival and Published Versions." *National Palace Museum Bulletin* 9, no. 4 (September–October):1–12.

——— 1991. *Monarchs and Ministers: The Grand Council in Mid-Ch'ing China, 1723–1820.* Berkeley: University of California Press.

Basilov, Vladimir N., ed. 1989. *Nomads of Eurasia.* Los Angeles and Seattle: Natural History Museum of Los Angeles County and University of Washington Press.

Beckwith, Christopher I. 1987. *The Tibetan Empire in Central Asia.* Princeton: Princeton University Press.

Benedict, Ruth. 1934. *Patterns of Culture.* Boston: Houghton Mifflin.

Bi Yuan. 1957. *Xu zizhi tongjian* [Continuation of the Comprehensive Mirror for Aid in Government, 1796, punctuated edition]. 12 vols. Beijing.

Bielenstein, Hans. 1987. "Chinese Historical Demography, A.D. 2–1982." *Museum of Far Eastern Antiquities: Bulletin* (Stockholm), no. 59:1–288.

Birch, Cyril, trans. 1958. *Stories from a Ming Collection.* New York: Grove Press.

——— trans. 1980. *The Peony Pavilion* [*Mudan Ting*] by Tang Xianzu. Bloomington: Indiana University Press.

Birge, Bettine. 1992. "Women and Property in Sung China (960–1279): Neo-Confucianism and Social Change in Chien-chou, Fukien." Ph.D. diss., Columbia University.

Blofeld, John. 1989. *City of Lingering Splendour: A Frank Account of Old Peking's Exotic Pleasures* [1961]. Reprint, Boston: Shambhala.

Blussé, Leonard. 1986. *Strange Company: Chinese Settlers, Mestizo Women, and the Dutch in VOC Batavia.* Dordrecht: Foris Publications.

Bodde, Derk. 1981. "Chinese 'Laws of Nature': A Reconsideration." In *Essays on Chinese Civilization,* pp. 299–315. Princeton: Princeton University Press.

Bol, Peter K. 1987. "Seeking Common Ground: Han Literati under Jurchen Rule." HJAS 47:461–538.

—— 1990. "The Sung Examination System and the *Shih*." AM, 3rd ser. Vol. 3, pt. 2, pp. 149–171.

—— 1992. *"This Culture of Ours": Intellectual Transitions in T'ang and Sung China*. Stanford: Stanford University Press.

Bossler, Beverly Jo. 1991. "Powerful Relations and Relations of Power: Family and Society in Song China (960–1279)." Ph.D. diss., University of California at Berkeley.

Bowring, Richard. 1992. "Buddhist Translations in the Northern Sung." AM, ser. 3, 5, no. 2:79–93.

Boxer, C. R. 1948. *Fidalgos in the Far East, 1550–1770: Fact and Fancy in the History of Macao*. The Hague: M. Nijhoff.

—— ed. 1953. *South China in the Sixteenth Century*. London: Hakluyt Society.

—— 1959. *The Great Ship from Amacon: Annals of Macao and the Old Japan Trade*. Lisbon: Centro de Estudos Historicos ultramarinos.

—— ed. and trans. 1984. *Seventeenth-Century Macao in Contemporary Documents and Illustrations*. Hong Kong: Heinemann.

Boyle, John A. 1958. *History of the World Conqueror*. Translation of 'Ata-Malik Juvaini, *Ta'rikh-i Jahan gusha*. 2 vols. Cambridge, Mass.: Harvard University Press.

—— 1971. *The Successors of Genghis Khan*. Translation of Rashid ad-Din, *Jami-at-Tawarikh*. New York: Columbia University Press.

Braudel, Fernand. 1973. *Capitalism and Material Life, 1400–1800* [1967]. Translated by Miriam Kochan. New York: Harper and Row.

Bray, Francesca. 1984. *Agriculture*. In Needham 1954–, vol. 6, pt. 2, 1984.

Buell, Paul D. 1993a. "Sayid Ajall, 1211–1279." In de Rachewiltz et al. 1993, pp. 466–479.

—— 1993b. "Sübötei Ba'atur (1176–1248)." In de Rachewiltz et al. 1993, pp. 13–26.

Busch, Heinrich. 1976. In DMB, pp. 736–744, s.v. "Ku Hsien-ch'eng."

Cahill, James. 1976. *Hills beyond a River: Chinese Painting of the Yuan Dynasty, 1279–1368*. New York: Weatherhill.

—— 1978. *Parting at the Shore: Chinese Painting of the Early and Middle Ming Dynasty, 1368–1580*. New York: Weatherhill.

Cai Meibiao et al. 1979. *Zhongguo tongshi*. Vol. 6. Beijing.

Cammann, Schuyler. 1951. *Trade through the Himalayas: The Early British Attempts to Open Tibet*. Princeton: Princeton University Press.

Chaffee, John W. 1985. *The Thorny Gates of Learning in Sung China: A Social History of the Examinations*. Cambridge: Cambridge University Press.

—— 1992. "Chao Ju-yü, Spurious Learning, and Southern Sung Political Culture." *Journal of Sung-Yuan Studies*, no. 22:23–62.

Chan, Hok-lam. 1969. "The White Lotus–Maitreya Doctrine and Popular Uprisings in Ming and Ch'ing China." *Sinologica* (Basel) 10, no. 4:211–233.

—— 1976. "Liu Chi." In DMB, pp. 932–938.

—— 1980. *Li Chih, 1527–1602, in Contemporary Chinese Historiography*. White Plains, N.Y.: M. E. Sharpe.

—— 1982. "From Dualistic Administration to Centralized Rule: Chin Governing under Emperor Wan-yen Liang (r. 1150–1161)." Unpublished paper.

——— 1984. *Legitimation in Imperial China: Discussions under the Jurchen-Chin Dynasty (1115–1234).* Seattle: University of Washington Press.

——— 1988. "The Chien-wen, Yung-lo, Hung-hsi, and Hsüan-te Reigns, 1399–1435." In CHC 7:182–304.

——— 1991. " 'Ta-chin' (Great Golden): The Origins and Changing Interpretations of the Jurchen State Name." *T'oung Pao* (Leiden) 77:4–5.

——— 1993a. *The Fall of the Jurchen Chin: Wang E's Memoir on Ts'ai-chou under the Mongol Siege (1233–1234).* Stuttgart: F. Steiner.

——— 1993b. "Hsü Heng (1209–1281)." In de Rachewiltz et al. 1993, pp. 416–447.

——— 1993c. "Liu Ping-chung (1216–1274)." In de Rachewiltz et al. 1993, pp. 245–269.

——— 1993d. "Tou Mo (1196–1280)." In de Rachewiltz et al. 1993, pp. 407–415.

Chan, Hok-lam, and Wm. Theodore de Bary, eds. 1982. *Yuan Thought: Chinese Thought and Religion under the Mongols.* New York: Columbia University Press.

Chan, Wing-tsit. 1963a. *A Source Book in Chinese Philosophy.* Princeton: Princeton University Press.

——— trans. 1963b. *Instructions for Practical Living and Other Neo-Confucian Writings* by Wang Yang-ming. New York: Columbia University Press.

——— trans. 1967. *Reflections on Things at Hand: The Neo-Confucian Anthology Compiled by Chu Hsi and Lü Tsu-ch'ien* [Zhu Xi and Lü Zuqian]. New York: Columbia University Press.

——— 1973. "Chu Hsi's Completion of Neo-Confucianism." *Études Song* (Paris), ed. Françoise Aubin. Ser. 2, no. 1, pp. 59–90.

——— 1976. In DMB, pp. 1408–16, s.v. "Wang Shou-jen."

——— 1982. "Chu Hsi and Yuan Neo-Confucianism." In *Yuan Thought,* ed. Hok-lam Chan and Wm. Theodore de Bary, pp. 197–231. New York: Columbia University Press.

Chang, Carsun. 1962. *Wang Yang-ming, the Idealist Philosopher of Sixteenth-Century China.* Jamaica, N.Y.: St. John's University Press.

Chang, Chun-shu, and Joan Smythe, trans. 1981. *South China in the Twelfth Century: A Translation of Lu Yu's Travel Diaries, July 3–December 6, 1170.* Hong Kong: Chinese University Press.

Chang, George Jer-lang. 1978. "The Village Elder System of the Early Ming Dynasty." *Ming Studies* 7 (Fall):53–72.

Chang, Kang-i Sun. 1980. *The Evolution of Chinese Tz'u Poetry: From Late T'ang to Northern Sung.* Princeton: Princeton University Press.

——— 1991. *The Late-Ming Poet Ch'en Tzu-lung: Crises of Love and Loyalism.* New Haven: Yale University Press.

——— 1992. "A Guide to Ming-Ch'ing Anthologies of Female Poetry and Their Selection Strategies." *Gest Library Journal* 5, no. 2 (Winter):119–160.

——— 1994. "The Device of the Mask in the Poetry of Wu Wei-yeh (1609–1671)." In *The Power of Culture: Studies in Chinese Cultural History,* ed. Willard J. Peterson, Andrew H. Plaks, and Ying-shih Yü, pp. 247–274. Hong Kong: Chinese University Press.

Chang, Kuei-sheng. 1976. In DMB, pp. 194–200, s.v. "Cheng Ho."

Chao Zhongchen. 1993. *Ming Chengzu zhuan.* Beijing: Renmin Daxue.

Chen Baozhen [Ch'en Pao-chen]. 1977. "Guan Daosheng he ta de zhushi tu."
Gugong jikan (National Palace Museum Quarterly, Taipei) 11, no. 4:51–84.

Chen Fangming. 1977. "Songchu mibinglun de jiantao (960–1004)." In SSYJ, no. 9:63–97.

Chen Gaohua and Shi Weimin. 1988. *Yuan Shangdu*. Jilin: Xinhua Shuju.

Chen Jiexian. 1965. *Manzhou congkao* [Studies on the early Qing dynasty]. 2nd printing. Taipei.

—— 1977. *"Tang Ruowang zhuan* zhong zhi Qingchu shiliao." In *Qingshi zabi*, 2:113–126. Taipei.

—— 1978a. "Manwen Qing shihlu yanjiu." Taipei.

—— 1978b. In *Qingshi zabi*, 3: Taipei.

Chen, Kenneth K. S. 1964. *Buddhism in China: A Historical Survey*. Princeton: Princeton University Press.

—— 1968. *Buddhism, the Light of Asia*. Woodbury, N.Y.: Barron's.

Chen Qingying. 1992. *Yuanchao dishi Basiba* [Life of the Yuan dynasty Imperial Preceptor Phagspa]. Beijing: China Tibetan Studies Publication Society.

Chen Shu, ed. 1987. *Liao Jin shi lunji*. Shanghai.

Chen Xuelin [Hok-lam Chan]. 1993. *Songshi lunji* [Excursions in Song history]. Taipei.

Chen Yinke. 1980. *Liu Rushi Biezhuan*. 3 vols. Shanghai: Guji Chubanshe.

Cheng Kuang-yu and Hsu Sheng-mo. 1984. *Historical Atlas of China* [*Zhongguo lishi ditu*]. 2 vols. Taipei: Chinese Culture University.

Cherniack, Susan. 1994. "Book Culture and Textual Transmission in Sung China." HJAS 54:5–125.

Ching, Julia. 1976a. "Li Ch'ing-chao." In Franke 1976, 2:530–539.

—— 1976b. In DMB, pp. 41–42, s.v. "Chan Jo-shui."

Chou, Chih-p'ing. 1988. *Yüan Hung-tao and the Kung-an School*. Cambridge: Cambridge University Press.

Chou, Ju-hsi, and Claudia Brown. 1985. *The Elegant Brush: Chinese Painting under the Qianlong Emperor, 1735–1795*. Phoenix: Phoenix Art Museum.

—— eds. 1988, 1991. "Chinese Painting under the Qianlong Emperor." *Phoebus* (Arizona State University) 6, nos. 1 and 2.

Chou, Tao-chi, and Ray Huang. 1976. In DMB, pp. 566–569, s.v. "Hsü, Empress."

Chu, Hung-lam. 1987. "High Ch'ing Intellectual Bias as Reflected in the Imperial Catalogue." *Gest Library Journal* 1, no. 2 (Spring):51–66.

—— 1993. "The Community Compact in Late Imperial China: Notes on Its Nature, Effectiveness, and Modern Relevance." Woodrow Wilson Center Asia Program Occasional Paper no. 52.

—— 1994. Review of *The Chosen One* by Carney T. Fisher. HJAS 54, no. 1 (June):266–277.

Ch'ü, Tung-tsu. 1962. *Local Government in China under the Ch'ing*. Stanford: Stanford University Press. Reprint, 1969.

Cleaves, Francis Woodman. 1976. "A Chinese Source Bearing on Marco Polo's Departure from China and a Persian Source on His Arrival in Persia." HJAS 36 (1976):181–203.

——, trans. and ed. 1982. *The Secret History of the Mongols, for the First Time Done into English out of the Original Tongue*. Vol. 1. Cambridge, Mass.: Harvard University Press.

Collcutt, Martin. 1981. *Five Mountains: The Rinzai Zen Monastic Institution in*

Medieval Japan. Cambridge, Mass.: Council on East Asian Studies, Harvard University.

Cranmer-Byng, J. L., ed. 1963. *An Embassy to China: Being the Journal Kept by Lord Macartney during His Embassy to the Emperor Ch'ien-lung, 1793–94.* London: Longman's.

Crawford, Robert C., and L. C. Goodrich. 1976. In DMB, pp. 53–61, s.v. "Chang Chü-cheng."

Cree, Edward. 1981. *The Cree Journals.* Edited and with an introduction by Michael Levien. Exeter, England: Webb & Bower.

Crump. J. I. 1980. *Chinese Theater in the Days of Kublai Khan.* Tucson: University of Arizona Press.

Crump, James I. 1970. "Yuan-pen, Yuan Drama's Rowdy Ancestor." *Literature East & West* 14, no. 4 (December):473–490.

Cui Wenyin. 1987. "Lüe tan Jin Hailing Wang Wanyan Liang de pingjia wenti." In Chen Shu 1987, pp. 357–370.

Dai Yi. 1992. *Qianlong di ji qi shidai.* Beijing: Zhongguo Renmin Daxue chubanshe.

Da Ming huidian [1587]. 1936. Compiled under the direction of Shen Shixing et al. *Wanyou wenku* ed. (Shanghai). 40 vols.

Dardess, John W. 1973. *Conquerors and Confucians: Aspects of Political Change in Late Yuan China.* New York: Columbia University Press.

———— 1983. *Confucianism and Autocracy: Professional Elites in the Founding of the Ming Dynasty.* Berkeley: University of California Press.

———— 1996. *A Ming Society: T'ai-ho County, Kiangsi, Fourteenth to Seventeenth Centuries.* Berkeley: University of California Press.

Davis, Richard L. 1986a. *Court and Family in Sung China, 900–1279.* Chapel Hill: Duke University Press.

———— 1986b. "Political Success and the Growth of Descent Groups: The Shih of Ming-chou during the Sung." In Ebrey and Watson 1986, pp. 62–94.

de Bary, W. T. 1959. "Some Common Tendencies in Neo-Confucianism," In Nivison and Wright 1959, pp. 25–49.

———— 1975. *The Unfolding of Neo-Confucianism.* New York: Columbia University Press.

de Bary, W. T., et al. 1960. *Sources of Chinese Tradition.* New York: Columbia University Press.

de Heer, Philip. 1986. *The Care-Taker Emperor.* Leiden: Brill.

Deng Guangming. 1945–46. *Yue Fei.* Shanghai.

———— 1983. *Yue Fei Zhuan.* Beijing.

Deng Zhicheng. 1965. *Qingshi jishi chubian.* 2 vols. Beijing: Zhonghua Shuju.

Dennerline, Jerry. 1981. *The Chia-ting Loyalists.* New Haven: Yale University Press.

de Rachewiltz, Igor. 1962. "Yeh-lü Ch'u-ts'ai (1189–1243): Buddhist Idealist and Confucian Statesman." In Wright and Twitchett 1962, pp. 189–216.

———— 1971. *Papal Envoys to the Great Khans.* Stanford: Stanford University Press.

———— 1983. "Turks in China under the Mongols." In *China among Equals,* ed. Morris Rossabi, pp. 281–310. Berkeley: University of California Press.

———— 1993a. "Yeh-lü Ch'-ts'ai (1189–1243); Yeh-lü Chu (1221–1285)." In de Rachewiltz et al. 1993, pp. 136–175.

——— et al., eds. 1993b. *In the Service of the Khan: Eminent Personalities of the Early Mongol-Yuan Period (1200–1300)*. Wiesbaden: Harrassowitz.

Des Forges, Roger. 1982. "The Story of Li Yen: Its Growth and Function from the Early Ch'ing to the Present." HJAS 42, no. 2:535–587.

——— 1984. "The Legend of Li Yen: Its Origins and Implications for the Study of the Ming-Ch'ing Transition in Seventeenth-Century China." *Journal of the American Oriental Society* 104, no. 3:411–436.

Dien, Albert. 1991. "A New Look at the Xianbei and Their Impact on Chinese Culture." In *Ancient Mortuary Traditions of China*, ed. George Kuwayama, pp. 40–59. Los Angeles: Far Eastern Art Council, Los Angeles County Museum of Art.

Dillon, Michael. 1978. "Jingdezhen as a Ming Industrial Center." *Ming Studies* 6 (Spring):37–44.

Dimberg, Ronald G. 1974. *The Sage and Society: The Life and Thought of Ho Hsin-yin*. Honolulu: University of Hawaii Press.

Djang Chu, trans. 1984. *A Complete Book Concerning Happiness and Benevolence*. Translation of Huang Liuhong, *Fuhui quanshu*, 1696. Tucson: University of Arizona Press.

Draft Qing History [1927]. 1977. [*Qing shi gao*]. Comp. Zhao Erxun et al. 48 vols. Beijing: Zhonghua.

Dreyer, Edward L. 1982. *Early Ming China: A Political History, 1355–1435*. Stanford: Stanford University Press.

——— 1988. "Military Origins of Ming China." In CHC 7:58–105.

Duke, Michael S. 1977. *Lu You*. New York: Twayne.

Dunne, George H. S.J. 1962. *Generation of Giants*. Notre Dame, Ind.: University of Notre Dame Press.

Dunnell, Ruth W. 1984. "Who Are the Tanguts?: Remarks on Tangut Ethnogenesis and the Ethnonym Tangut." *Journal of Asian History* 18, no. 1:78–89.

——— 1991. "The Fall of the Xia Empire: Sino-Tangut Relations in the Late 12th to Early 13th Centuries." In *Rulers from the Steppe: State Formation on the Eurasian Periphery*, ed. Gary Seaman and Daniel Marks, pp. 158–183. Los Angeles: Ethnographics Press.

——— 1992. "The Hsia Origins of the Yuan Institution of the Imperial Preceptor." AM, 3rd ser., 5, no. 1:85–111.

——— 1994. "Significant Peripheries: Inner Asian Perspectives on Song Studies." *Journal of Sung-Yuan Studies* 24:334–339.

——— 1996. *The Great State of White and High: Buddhism and State Formation in Eleventh-Century Xia*. Honolulu: University of Hawaii Press.

Ebrey, Patricia Buckley. 1981. *Chinese Civilization and Society: A Sourcebook*. New York: Free Press.

——— 1988. "The Dynamics of Elite Domination in Sung China." HJAS 48, no. 2 (December):493–519.

——— trans. and intro. 1991a. *Chu Hsi's Family Rituals*. Princeton: Princeton University Press.

——— 1991b. *Confucianism and Family Rituals in Imperial China: A Social History of Writing about Rites*. Princeton: Princeton University Press.

——— 1993. *The Inner Quarters: Marriage and the Lives of Chinese Women in the Sung Period*. Berkeley: University of California Press.

Ebrey, Patricia Buckley, and James L. Watson, eds. 1986. *Kinship Organization in Late Imperial China, 1000–1940*. Berkeley: University of California Press.

Egan, Ronald C. 1994. *Word, Image, and Deed in the Life of Su Shi*. Cambridge, Mass.: Harvard University Press.

Elman, Benjamin. 1995. Book review. HJAS 55, no. 2 (December):519–535.

Endicott-West, Elizabeth. 1989. *Mongolian Rule in China*. Cambridge, Mass.: Council on East Asian Studies, Harvard University.

Fairbank, John K., ed. 1968. *The Chinese World Order: Traditional China's Foreign Relations*. Cambridge, Mass.: Harvard University Press.

Fan Shuzhi. 1990. *Ming-Qing jiangnan shizhen tanwei*. Shanghai: Fudan University Press.

Fang, Chao-ying. 1950. "A Technique for Estimating the Numerical Strength of the Early Manchu Forces." HJAS 13 (1950):192–215. Reprinted in John L. Bishop, *Studies of Governmental Institutions in Chinese History*. Cambridge, Mass.: Harvard University Press, 1968, pp. 244–267.

—— 1976a. In DMB, pp. 759–761, s.v. "Tshangs-dbyangs-rgya-mtsho."

—— 1976b. In DMB, pp. 822–826, s.v. "Li Hua-lung."

—— 1976c. In DMB, pp. 208–210, s.v. "Cheng Kuei-fei."

Fang Chaoying and Albert Chan. 1976. In DMB, pp. 1538–42, s.v. "Yang Ssu-ch'ang."

Fang Hao. 1977–1981. "Songdai fojiao dui shufa zhih gongxian" etc. In SSYJ, annual nos. 9–13.

—— 1979. *Song Shi*. 2 vols. First printing of new edition *(Xin Yi Ban)*. Taipei.

Fang, Lienche Tu. 1966. *Mingchao guanxuan lu*. Ming Biographical History Project Monograph no. 1. Reprinted from *Tsing Hua Journal of Chinese Studies* 5, no. 2.

—— 1976. In DMB, pp. 315–322, s.v. "Chu Hou-ts'ung."

Fang Lienche Tu and Chaoying Fang. 1976. In DMB, pp. 365–367, s.v. "Chu Tsai-hou."

Fang Xing. 1989. "Why the Sprouts of Capitalism Were Delayed in China." Trans. James H. Cole. *Late Imperial China* 10, no. 2 (December):106–138.

Farmer, Edward L. 1976. *Early Ming Government: The Evolution of Dual Capitals*. Cambridge, Mass.: Harvard University Press.

Farquhar, David M. 1957. "Oirat-Chinese Tribute Missions, 1408–1446." In *Studia Altaica: Festschrift für Nikolaus Poppe zum 60. Geburtstag am 8. August, 1957*, pp. 60–68. Ural-altaische Bibliothek ser. no. 5, ed. Julius von Farkas and Omeljan Pritsak. Wiesbaden: O. Harrassowitz.

—— 1968. "The Origins of the Manchus' Mongolian Policy." In Fairbank 1968, pp. 198–205.

—— 1990. *The Government of China under Mongolian Rule: A Reference Guide*. Stuttgart: Steiner.

Faure, David. 1990. "What Made Foshan a Town? The Evolution of Rural-Urban Identities in Ming-Qing China." *Late Imperial China* 11, no. 2 (December): 1–31.

Feifel, Eugen, and Hok-lam Chan. 1976. In DMB, pp. 1561–65, s.v. "Yao Kuang-hsiao."

Feng Menglong. 1634. "Jin Hailing zongyu wangshen." In *Xingshi hengyan, juan* 23 (omitted from most modern editions).

Feng Yongqian. 1987. "Jianguo yilai Liaodai kaogu de zhongyao faxian." In Chen Shu 1987, pp. 295–334.

Fisher, Carney T. 1990. *The Chosen One: Succession and Adoption in the Court of Ming Shizong*. Boston: Allen and Unwin.

Fisher, T. S. 1978. "New Light on the Accession of the Yung-cheng Emperor." *Papers on Far Eastern History* 17 (March):103–136.

Fletcher, Joseph. 1978. "Ch'ing Inner Asia, c. 1800" and "The Heyday of the Ch'ing Order." In CHC 10:35–106 and 351–408.

Fong, Wen C. 1992. *Beyond Representation: Chinese Painting and Calligraphy, 8th to 14th Century.* New York: Metropolitan Museum of Art/New Haven: Yale University Press.

Franke, Herbert. 1952. "Could the Mongol Emperors Read and Write Chinese?" AM 3:28–41.

———— 1958. "Die Agrarreformen des Chia Ssu-tao: Ein Beitrag zur Wirtschaft-geschichte Chinas im 13. Jahrhundert." *Saeculum* 9:345–369.

———— 1962. "Chia Ssu-tao (1213–1275): A 'Bad Last Minister'?" In Wright and Twitchett 1962, pp. 217–234.

———— 1970. "Treaties between Sung and Chin." *Études Song in Memoriam Étienne Balazs* (Paris), ed. Françoise Aubin. Ser. 1, pp. 55–84.

———— 1974. "Siege and Defense of Towns in Medieval China." In *Chinese Ways in Warfare*, ed. Frank A. Kierman, Jr., and John K. Fairbank, pp. 151–201. Cambridge, Mass.: Harvard University Press.

———— 1975. "Chinese Texts on the Jurchen: A Translation of the Jurchen Monograph in the *San-ch'ao Pei-meng Hui-pien*." *Zentralasiatische Studien* 9:119–186.

———— ed. 1976. *Sung Biographies.* 3 vols. Wiesbaden: Steiner.

———— 1978a. *From Tribal Chieftain to Universal Emperor and God: The Legitimation of the Yuan Dynasty.* Munich: Verlag der Bayerischen Akademie der Wissenschaften.

———— 1978b. "Nordchina am Vorabend der mongolischen Eroberungen: Wirtschaft und Gesellschaft unter der Chin-dynastie (1115–1234)." Rheinisch-Westfälische Akademie der Wissenschaften (Düsseldorf), *Vorträge G 228*, pp. 7–45.

———— 1983. "Sung Embassies: Some General Observations." In Rossabi 1983, pp. 116–148.

———— 1992. "Chinese Law in a Multinational Society: The Case of the Liao (907–1125)." AM, ser. 3, vol. 5, pt. 2, 111–127.

———— 1993. "Ahmad (?–1282)" and "Sangha (?–1291)." In de Rachewiltz et al. 1993, pp. 539–583.

Franke, Otto. 1930–1952. *Geschichte des Chinesischen Reiches.* 5 vols. Berlin: Walter De Gruyter.

Franke, Wolfgang. [1945]. 1989. "Yunglo's Mongoleifeldzüge." In *Sino Malaysiana*, pp. 1–54. Singapore.

———— 1962. "Zur Frage der Mongolen in China nach dem Sturz der Yüan Dynastie." *Oriens Extremus* 9, no. 1 (February):57–68.

———— [1976]. 1989. "Historical Precedent or Accidental Repetition of Events: K'ou Chun in 1004 and Yü Ch'ien in 1449?" In *Sino-Malaysiana*, pp. 144–151. Singapore: South Seas Society.

Fu Lehuan. 1984. *Liaoshi Congkao.* Beijing.

Fu, Marilyn Wong. 1981. "The Impact of the Reunification: Northern Elements in the Life and Art of Hsien-yü Shu (1257?–1302) and Their Relation to Early Yuan Literati Culture." In Langlois 1981, pp. 371–433.

Fu Weilin [ca. 1660]. 1937. *Ming Shu.* Shanghai: Commercial Press.

Fu Yiling et al. 1993. *Mingshi xinbian.* Beijing: Renmin.

Gallagher, Louis J. 1953. *China in the Sixteenth Century: The Journals of Matthew Ricci, 1583–1610.* New York: Random House.

Gardner, Daniel K. 1989. "Chu Hsi and His Program of Learning." HJAS 49, no. 1:141–172.

——— 1990. *Learning to be a Sage: Selections from the "Conversations of Master Chu, Arranged Topically."* Berkeley: University of California Press.

Gaspardone, Emile. 1976. In DMB, pp. 793–801, s.v. "Lê Lo'i."

Gedalecia, David. 1981. "Wu Ch'eng and the Perpetuation of the Classical Heritage in the Yuan." In Langlois 1981, pp. 186–211.

——— 1982. "Wu Ch'eng's Approach to Internal Self-cultivation and External Knowledge-seeking." In Chan and de Bary 1982, pp. 279–326.

Geiss, James. 1987. "The Leopard Quarter During the Cheng-te Reign." *Ming Studies* 24 (Spring):1–38.

——— 1988a. "The Cheng-te Reign, 1506–1521." In CHC 7:403–439.

——— 1988b. "The Chia-ching Reign, 1522–1566." In CHC 7:440–510.

Geiss, James P. 1979. "Peking under the Ming (1368–1644)." Ph.D. diss., Princeton University.

Gernet, Jacques. 1962. *Daily Life in China on the Eve of the Mongol Invasion, 1250–1276.* London: Allen and Unwin. Translated by H. M. Wright from *La vie quotidienne en Chine a la veille de l'invasion mongole, 1250–1276.* Paris, 1959.

Golas, Peter J. 1980. "Rural China in the Song." HJAS 39, no. 2 (February):291–325.

Gong Yin. 1992. *Zhongguo tusi zhidu.* Kunming.

Grousset, René. 1970. *The Empire of the Steppes: A History of Central Asia* [1939; rev. ed., 1952]. Translated by Naomi Walford. New Brunswick, N.J.: Rutgers University Press.

Gu Yingtai [1658]. 1934. *Mingshi jishi benmo.* Shanghai: Commercial Press.

Guan Donggui [Kuan Tung-kuei]. 1969. "Ruguan qian Manzu bingshu yu renkou wenti de tantao." CYYY 41 (Taipei), pp. 179–194.

——— 1971. "Manzu de ruguan yu hanhua." CYYY 43, no. 3 (November): 445–488.

Guy, R. Kent. 1987. *The Emperor's Four Treasuries.* Cambridge, Mass.: Council on East Asian Studies, Harvard University.

Haeger, John Winthrop. 1975. "1126–27: Political Crisis and the Integrity of Culture." In *Crisis and Prosperity in Sung China,* ed. John Winthrop Haeger, pp. 143–162. Tucson: University of Arizona Press.

——— 1976. "Miao Fu." In Franke 1976, 2:787–790.

Han Rulin et al. 1986. *Yuan chao shi.* 2 vols. Beijing.

Handlin, Joanna F. 1983. *Action in Late Ming Thought: The Reorientation of Lü K'un and Other Scholar Officials.* Berkeley: University of California Press.

Hansen, Valery. 1990. *Changing Gods in Medieval China, 1127–1276.* Princeton: Princeton University Press.

Hartman, Charles. 1993. "Literary and Visual Interactions in Lo Chih-ch'uan's *Crows in Old Trees.*" *Metropolitan Museum Journal* 28:129–167.

Hartwell, Robert. 1967. "A Cycle of Economic Change in Imperial China: Coal and Iron in Northeast China, 750–1350." *Journal of the Economic and Social History of the Orient* 10, pt. 1:102–159.

———— 1982. "Demographic, Political, and Social Transformations of China, 750–1550." HJAS 42, no. 2 (December):365–442.

Hatch, George C. 1976. "Su Shih." In Franke 1976, 3:900–968.

Heijdra, Martin J. [Martinus]. 1994. "The Socio-economic Development of Ming Rural China (1368–1644)." Ph.D. diss., Princeton University.

Heijdra, Martin, and Cao Shuwen. 1992. "The World's Earliest Extant Book Printed from Wooden Movable Type?" *Gest Library Journal* 5, no. 1:70–89.

Heissig, Walter. 1980. *The Religions of Mongolia*. Berkeley: University of California Press.

Henthorn, W. E. 1963. *Korea: The Mongol Invasions*. Leiden: E. J. Brill.

Hervouet, Ives, ed. 1978. *A Sung Bibliography*. Hong Kong: Chinese University Press.

Hevia, James L. 1989. "A Multitude of Lords: Qing Court Ritual and the Macartney Embassy of 1793." *Late Imperial China* 10:2 (December):72–105.

Ho, P. T. 1956. "Early-ripening Rice in Chinese History." *Economic History Review* (December):200–218.

Ho, Ping-ti. 1959. *Studies on the Population of China, 1368–1953*. Cambridge, Mass.: Harvard University Press.

———— 1962. *The Ladder of Success in Imperial China: Aspects of Social Mobility, 1368–1911*. New York: Columbia University Press.

———— 1967. "An Estimate of the Total Population of Sung-Chin China." In *Études Song: In Memoriam Étienne Balazs*, ed. Françoise Aubin, "Démographie," pp. 33–53. Paris: Mouton.

Hou Wailu. 1956. *Zhongguo zaoqi qimeng sixiangshi*. Beijing.

Hsi, Angela. 1976. In DMB, pp. 1427–30, s.v. "Wang Tao-k'un."

Hsiao, Ch'i-ch'ing. 1978. *The Military Establishment of the Yuan Dynasty*. Cambridge, Mass.: Harvard University Press.

———— 1993. "Bayan (1237–1295)." In de Rachewiltz et al. 1993, pp. 584–607.

Hsiao, K. C. [Kung-chuan Hsiao]. 1960. *Rural China: Imperial Control in the Nineteenth Century*. Seattle: University of Washington Press.

———— 1976. In DMB, pp. 807–818, s.v. "Li Chih."

———— 1979. *A History of Chinese Political Thought*. Translated by F. W. Mote. Vol. 1. Princeton: Princeton University Press.

———— [Xiao Gongquan], ed. 1982. *Zhongguo zhengzhi sixiang shi* [1946]. New ed. Taipei: Lien-ching.

Hsiao, Kung-chuan [K. C. Hsiao]. 1979. "Compromise in Imperial China." *Parerga: Occasional Papers on China*. Vol. 6. Seattle: University of Washington Press.

Hsiung, Shih-i, trans. 1935. *Xi Xiang Ji* [The romance of the western chamber]. London: Methuen. Reprint, New York, 1968.

Hsü, Immanuel C. Y. 1983. *The Rise of Modern China*, 3rd ed. New York: Oxford University Press.

Hsu, Kai-yu. 1962. "The Poems of Li Ch'ing-chao (1084–1141)." *Publications of the Modern Language Association of America* 77 (December):521–528.

Hu Ke [1196]. 1936. *Luling Ouyang wenzhong gong nianpu*. [Ouyang Xiu, Collected Works, 1541 ed.]. SBCK 1:11–27.

Huang Kaihua. 1972. "Mingdai tusi zhidu sheshi yu xi'nan kaifa." In *Mingshi lunji*, pp. 221–414. Hong Kong.

Huang Pei. 1974. *Autocracy at Work: A Study of the Yung-cheng Period, 1723–1735*. Bloomington: Indiana University Press.

Huang P'ei, and Julia Ching. 1976. In DMB, pp. 153–156, s.v. "Ch'en Hsien chang."

Huang Qinglian [Huang Ch'ing-lien]. 1977. *Yuandai huji zhidu yanjiu.* Taipei: National Taiwan University.

Huang, Ray. 1974a. *Taxation and Government Finance in Sixteenth-Century Ming China.* Cambridge: Cambridge University Press.

—— [Huang Renyu]. 1974b. "Cong 'sanyan' kan wan Ming shangren" [Merchants of the late Ming as presented in the *San-yen* stories]. *Journal of the Institute of Chinese Studies* (Chinese University, Hong Kong) 7, no. 1:133–154.

—— 1976a. In DMB, pp. 1369–74, s.v. "Wang Ch'ung-ku."

—— 1976b. In DMB, pp. 1208–14, s.v. "Ssu Jen-fa."

—— 1976c. In DMB, pp. 263–265, s.v. "Chou Chia-mu."

—— 1981. *1587, A Year of No Significance: The Ming Dynasty in Decline.* New Haven: Yale University Press.

—— 1988a. *China: A Macro History.* Armonk, N.Y.: M. E. Sharpe.

—— 1988b. "The Lung-ch'ing and Wan-li Reigns." In CHC 7:511–584.

—— [Huang Renyu]. 1991. *Zibenzhuyi yu nianyi shiji* [Capitalism and the twenty-first century]. Taipei: Lien-ching.

Huang Shengzhang. 1982. *Lishi dili luncong.* Beijing: Xinhua.

Huang, Siu-chi. 1944. *Lu Hsiang-shan: A Twelfth-Century Chinese Idealist Philosopher.* New Haven: American Oriental Society.

Huang Yunmei. 1979–1986. *Mingshi Kaocheng.* 8 vols. Beijing: Zhonghua Shuju.

Huang Zhangjian. 1961. "Lun *Huangming zuxun lu* suo ji Mingchu huangguan zhidu." CYYY 32 (July):77–98.

Hucker, Charles O. 1957. "The Tung-lin Movement of the Late Ming Period." In *Chinese Thought and Institutions,* ed. John K. Fairbank, pp. 132–162. Chicago: University of Chicago Press.

—— 1961. *The Traditional Chinese State in Ming Times (1368–1644).* Tucson: University of Arizona Press.

—— 1966. *The Censorial System of Ming China.* Stanford: Stanford University Press.

—— 1978. *The Ming Dynasty: Its Origins and Evolving Institutions.* Ann Arbor: University of Michigan, Center for Chinese Studies.

—— 1985. *A Dictionary of Official Titles in Imperial China.* Stanford: Stanford University Press.

Hymes, Robert P. 1986a. "Marriage, Descent Groups, and the Localist Strategy in Sung and Yuan Fu-chou." In Ebrey and Watson 1986, pp. 95–136.

—— 1986b. *The Elite of Fu-chou, Chiang-hsi, in Northern and Southern Sung.* Cambridge: Cambridge University Press.

Hymes, Robert P., and Conrad Shirokauer. 1993. *Ordering the World: Approaches to State and Society in Sung Dynasty China.* Berkeley: University of California Press.

Idema, Wilt, and Stephen H. West. 1982. *Chinese Theater, 1100–1400: A Source Book.* Wiesbaden: Steiner.

International Encyclopedia of the Social Sciences. 1968. 17 vols. New York: Macmillan/Free Press.

Iwamura Shinobu and H. F. Schurmann. 1954. "Notes on Mongolian Groups in

Afghanistan." In *Silver Jubilee Volume of the Zinbun-Kagaku Kenkyusyo*, Kyoto University, pp. 480–515.

Jagchid, Sechin, and Van Jay Symons. 1989. *Peace, War, and Trade along the Great Wall: Nomadic-Chinese Interaction through Two Millennia.* Bloomington: Indiana University Press.

Jan, Y. H. 1993. "Hai-yün (1203–1257)." In de Rachewiltz et al. 1993, pp. 224–242.

Jiang Weiqiao. 1928. *Zhongguo fojiao shi.* In *Foxue congshu.* 3 vols. N.p.

Jiao Hong [1616]. 1965. *Guochao xianzheng lu.* 8 vols. Reprint, Taipei.

Jin History [1344]. 1975. *Jin Shi.* Edited by Tuotuo et al. Beijing.

Jin, Qicong. 1995. "Jurchen Literature under the Chin." In Tillman and West 1995, pp. 216–237.

Jin Yufu [Chin Yü-fu]. 1966. *Song, Liao, Jin shi* [1946]. Reprint, Hong Kong: Longmen Shudian.

Jin Zhaofeng. 1935. *Qingshi Dagang.* Shanghai: Kaiming Shujudian.

Jiu Wudai Shi. See *Old History of the Five Dynasties.*

Johnson, David. 1977. "The Last Days of a Great Clan: The Li Family of Chao Chün in Late T'ang and Early Sung." HJAS 37, no. 1 (June):5–102.

Kahn, Harold L. 1971. *Monarchy in the Emperor's Eyes.* Cambridge, Mass.: Harvard University Press.

——— 1985. "A Matter of Taste: The Monumental and the Exotic in the Qianlong Reign." In Chou and Brown 1985, pp. 288–302.

Kahn, Paul. 1984. *The Secret History of the Mongols: The Origin of Chinghis Khan: An Adaptation of the "Yuan Ch'ao Pi Shih," Based Primarily on the English Translation by Francis Woodman Cleaves.* San Francisco: North Point Press.

Kane, Daniel. 1989. *The Sino-Jurchen Vocabulary of the Bureau of Interpreters.* Bloomington: Indiana University, Research Institute for Inner Asian Studies.

Kao, Yu-kung. 1962. "A Study of the Fang La Rebellion." HJAS 24:17–63.

——— 1966. "Source Materials on the Fang La Rebellion." HJAS 26:211–240.

Kates, George N. 1967. *The Years That Were Fat: The Last of Old China* [1952]. Reprint, New York: Harper.

Kato Shigeshi. 1953. "Sô to Kin-koku to no bôeki ni tsuite." *Shina Keizaishi Kôshô* (Tokyo) 2:253–270.

Keene, Donald. 1951. *The Battles of Coxinga: Chikamatsu's Puppet Play, Its Background and Importance.* London: Taylor's Foreign Press.

Kessler, Lawrence D. 1976. *K'ang-hsi and the Consolidation of Ch'ing Rule, 1661–1684.* Chicago: University of Chicago Press.

Ko, Dorothy. 1994. *Teachers of the Inner Chambers: Women and Culture in Seventeenth-Century China.* Stanford: Stanford University Press.

Kracke, E. A., Jr. 1953. *Civil Service in Early Sung China, 960–1067.* Cambridge, Mass.: Harvard University Press.

——— 1975. "Sung K'ai-feng: Pragmatic Metropolis and Formalistic Capital." In *Crisis and Prosperity in Sung China,* ed. John Winthrop Haeger, pp. 49–77. Tucson: University of Arizona Press.

Krader, Lawrence. 1968. *The Formation of the State.* Englewood Cliffs, N.J.: Prentice-Hall.

Lach, Donald F. 1965; 1970. *Asia in the Making of Europe.* Vol. 1, bks. 1 and 2; vol. 2, bks. 1 and 2. Chicago: University of Chicago Press.

Lach, Donald F., with Edwin J. van Kley. 1993. Vol. 3, bks. 1–3, of *Asia in the Making of Europe*. Chicago: University of Chicago Press.

Lai Jiadu and Li Guangbi. 1954. *Mingchao dui Wala de zhanzheng*. Shanghai.

Langlois, John D., Jr., ed. 1981a. *China under Mongol Rule,* Princeton: Princeton University Press.

———— 1981b. "Political Thought in Chin-hua under Mongol Rule." In Langlois 1981a, pp. 137–185.

———— 1988. "The Hung-wu Reign, 1368–1398." In CHC 7:107–181.

———— 1993a. "The Code and *Ad Hoc* Legislation in Ming Law." *AM,* 3rd ser., 6, no. 2:85–112.

———— 1993b. "Liu Yin." In de Rachewiltz et al. 1993, pp. 448–465.

Lattimore, Owen. 1962. *Inner Asian Frontiers of China* [1940]. New York: American Geographical Society. Reprint, Boston: Beacon Press.

Lau, D. C., trans. 1970. *Mencius*. Harmondsworth: Penguin Books.

Lebar, Frank M., et al. 1964. *Ethnic Groups of Mainland Southeast Asia*. New Haven: Human Relations Area Files Press.

Lee, Sherman, et al. 1980. *Eight Dynasties of Chinese Painting*. Cleveland and Bloomington: Cleveland Art Museum/Indiana University Press.

Legge, James, trans. 1960. *The Chinese Classics* [1895]. Reprint. 5 vols. Hong Kong: Chinese University Press.

Lerner, Daniel. 1958. *The Passing of Traditional Society: Modernizing the Middle East*. Glencoe, Ill.: Free Press.

Leung, Angela Ki Che. 1987. "Organized Medicine in Ming-Ch'ing China: State and Private Medical Institutions in the Lower Yangtze Region. *Late Imperial China* 8, no. 1 (June):134–166.

Levathes, Louise. 1994. *When China Ruled the Seas: The Treasure Fleet of the Dragon Throne, 1405–33*. New York: Simon & Schuster.

Lévi-Strauss, Claude. 1964. *Le cru et le cuit*. Paris: Plon.

Levy, Marion J., Jr. 1952. *The Structure of Society*. Princeton: Princeton University Press.

———— 1966. *Modernization and the Structure of Societies*. 2 vols. Princeton: Princeton University Press.

———— 1981. *Levy's Eleven Laws of the Disillusionment of the True Liberal*. Princeton, N.J.

Leys, Simon [Pierre Ryckmans]. 1985. "Human Rights in China" [1978]. In *The Burning Forest: Essays on Chinese Culture and Politics,* pp. 113–135. New York: Holt, Rinehart, and Winston.

Li Chu-tsing and James C. Y. Watt, eds. 1987. *The Chinese Scholar's Studio: Artistic Life in the Late Ming Period*. New York and London: The Asia Society with Thames and Hudson.

Li Donghua [Li Tung-hua]. 1993. "Wudai Wu-Yue de duiwai guanxi." In *Zhongguo haiyang fazhanski lunwenji* [Essays in Chinese Maritime History], ed. Zhang Bincun [Chang Pin-tsun] and Liu Shiji [Liu Shih-chi], 5:17–59. Taipei.

Li Guangbi. 1956. *Mingdai yuwo zhanzheng*. Shanghai: Renmin Chubanshe.

Li Guangtao. 1947a. "Qingren ruguanqian qiukuan zhi shimo." CYYY 9:275–328.

———— 1947b. "Ji Qing Taizong huangtaiji sanzi chenghao zhi youlai." CYYY 12: 237–239.

———— 1948a. "Lun Chongzhen ernian 'jisi lubian.'" CYYY 18:445–484.

———— 1948b. "Mao Wenlong niangluan dongjiang benmo." CYYY 19:367–488.

———— 1948c. "Hong Chengchou bei Ming shimo." CYYY 17:227–301.

———— 1954a. "Zhang Xianzhong shishi." CYYY 25:21–30.

———— 1954b. "Duoergun ruguan shimo." CYYY 25:31–57.

———— 1962. "*Lao Manwen shiliao* xu." CYYY 34:323–332.

———— 1965. *Mingji liukou shimo*. Rev. ed., Taipei: Academia Sinica.

Li Jinhua [Li Chin Hua]. 1933. *Mingshi zuanxiu kao*. Beijing: Harvard-Yenching Institute.

Li Xiaosheng. 1987. "The Question of Li Yan as Seen from *The Genealogical Records of the Li Clan* of Qi County." Translated by Roger V. Des Forges. *Ming Studies* 24, (Fall):39–57.

Li Xinda. 1982. "Ruguan qian de baqi bingshu wenti." *Qingshi luncong* 3:155–163.

Li Youning. 1973. *Wu Han zhuan*. Hong Kong: Ming Bao.

Li Zehou. 1982. *Zhongguo gudai sixiangshi lun*. Beijing: Renmin Chubanshe.

Li Zhi [1611]. 1959. *Xu cangshu*. Edited by Li Guangshu. 2 vols. Beijing.

Liang Ch'i-ch'ao. 1959. *Intellectual Trends in the Ch'ing Period*. Translated by Immanuel C. Y. Hsü. Cambridge, Mass.: Harvard University Press.

Liao History [1344]. 1974. Beijing.

Liaoshi 1344. Tuotuo et al. See *Liao History*.

Lin Qingzhang. 1986. *Mingdai Kaojuxue yanjiu*. Rev. ed., Taipei.

Lin Tianwei. 1976. "Song dai xiangquan xingcheng zhi fenxi." SSYJ 8:141–170.

———— 1977. "Bei Song jiruo de sanzhong xin fenxi." SSYJ 9:147–198.

Lin Yanqing. 1993. *Jiajing huangdi dazhuan*. Shenyang.

Lin Yutang. 1947. *The Gay Genius: The Life and Times of Su Tungpo*. New York: J. Day Co.

———— 1960. *Translations from the Chinese [The Importance of Understanding]*. Cleveland: World Publishing Co.

Liu, Cary Y. 1997. "The Ch'ing Dynasty Wen Yüan-Ko Imperial Library: Architecture and the Ordering of Knowledge." Ph.D. diss., Princeton University.

Liu, James T. C. 1957. "An Early Sung Reformer: Fan Chung-yen." In *Chinese Thought and Institutions*, ed. John K. Fairbank, pp. 105–131. Chicago: University of Chicago Press.

———— 1959a. "Eleventh-Century Chinese Bureaucrats: Some Historical Classifications and Behavioral Types." *Administrative Science Quarterly* 4, no. 2 (September):207–226.

———— 1959b. *Reform in Sung China: Wang An-shih (1021–1086) and His New Policies*. Cambridge, Mass.: Harvard University Press.

———— 1967. *Ou-yang Hsiu: An Eleventh-Century Neo-Confucian*. Stanford: Stanford University Press.

———— 1972. "Yueh Fei (1103–41) and China's Heritage of Loyalty." JAS 31 no. 2 (February):291–297.

———— 1973. "How Did a Neo-Confucian School Become the State Orthodoxy?" *Philosophy East and West* (Honolulu), 23, 4:483–505.

———— 1985. "Polo and Cultural Change: From T'ang to Sung China." HJAS 45, no. 1 (June):203–224.

———— 1988. *China Turning Inward*. Cambridge, Mass.: Harvard University Press.

Liu, James T. C., and Peter Golas, eds. 1969. *Change in Sung China: Innovation or Renovation?* Lexington, Mass.: D. C. Heath.

Liu Ji. 1592. *Chengyi Bo wenji*. SBCK.

Liu Jiaju. 1964. *Qingchao chuqi de baqi quandi*. Taipei: Taiwan University Press.

Liu Ts'un-yan and Judith Berling. 1982. "The 'Three Teachings' in the Mongol Yuan Period." In Chan and de Bary 1982, pp. 479–512.

Liu Zhaoyou. 1978. *Siku zhulu Yuanren bieji tiyao buzheng*. Taipei: Dongwu [Tung-wu] University.

Liu Zhenhua. 1973. "Nong'an wanjin ta ji chutu wenwu." *Wen wu* 8.

Liu Zijian [James T. C. Liu]. 1963. *Ouyang xiu de zhixue yu congzheng*. Hong Kong: New Asia.

―――― 1987a. "Lüe lun Songdai Difang guanxue he sixue de xiaozhang" [1965]. In *Liang Song shi yanjiu huibian*, pp. 211–227. Taipei.

―――― 1987b. *Liang Song shi yanjiu huibian*. Taipei.

―――― 1987c. "Yue Fei" [1970, 1986]. In Liu Zijian 1987b, pp. 185–207.

Lo, Irving Yucheng. 1971. *Hsin Ch'i-chi*. New York: Twayne.

Lo, Irving Yucheng, and William Schultz, eds. 1986. *Waiting for the Unicorn: Poems and Lyrics of China's Last Dynasty, 1644–1911*. Bloomington: Indiana University Press.

Lo, Jung-pang. 1969. "Policy Formation and Decision-Making on Issues Respecting Peace and War." In *Chinese Government in Ming Times: Seven Studies*, ed. Charles O. Hucker, pp. 41–72. New York: Columbia University Press.

Luo Wen. 1977. "Songdai zhongyang dui difang shizheng zhi lu de quhua." SSYJ 9:475–483.

Lütge, Friedrich. 1966. *Deutsche Sozial-und Wirtschaftsgeschichte*. Berlin: Springer Verlag.

Lynn, Richard John. 1980. *Kuan Yun-shih [Guan Yunshi]*. Boston: Twayne.

―――― 1997. Review of *Sung Dynasty Uses of the I Ching* by Kidder Smith, Jr., et al. *Journal of Sung-Yuan Studies* 27:152–167.

Ma Changshou. 1962. *Nanzhao guonei de buzu zucheng he nudi zhidu*. Shanghai: Renmin Chubanshe.

Ma, Laurence J. C. 1971. *Commercial Development and Urban Change in Sung China (960–1279)*. Ann Arbor: University of Michigan, Department of Geography.

Ma, Tai-loi. 1987. "Private Academies in Ming China (1368–1644): Historical Development, Organization, and Social Impact." Ph.D. diss., University of Chicago.

Mancall, Mark. 1968. "The Ch'ing Tributary System: An Interpretative Essay." In Fairbank 1968, pp. 63–89.

―――― 1971. *Russia and China: Their Diplomatic Relations to 1728*. Cambridge, Mass.: Harvard University Press.

Manz, Beatrice F. 1989. *The Rise and Rule of Tamerlane*. Cambridge: Cambridge University Press.

McDermott, Joseph P. 1991. Review of Robert P. Hymes 1986b. HJAS 51, 1 (June):333–357.

McKnight, Brian E. 1976. "T'ung Kuang." In Franke 1976, 3:1090–97.

McMorran, Ian. 1975. "Wang Fu-chih and the Neo-Confucian Tradition." In de Bary 1975, pp. 413–468.

―――― 1979. "The Patriot and the Partisans: Wang Fu-chih's Involvement in the Politics of the Yung-li Court." In Spence and Wills 1979, pp. 133–166.

McNeill, W. H. 1963. *The Rise of the West: A History of the Human Community*. Chicago: University of Chicago Press.

Meng Sen. 1960. *Qingdai shi*. Taipei: Zhengzhong. (Circulated as ms., 1935–1937.)

———— 1965. *Ming-Qing shi lunzhu jikan* [1934]. Taipei: Shijie.

Meng Siming [Meng Ssu-ming]. 1938. *Yuandai Shehui jieji zhidu* [Social classes in China under the Yuan Dynasty]. Peiping: Yenching University.

Meskill, John. 1969. "Academies and Politics in the Ming Dynasty." In *Chinese Government in Ming Times: Seven Studies,* ed. Charles O. Hucker, pp. 149–174. New York: Columbia University Press.

Mikami Tsugio. 1970–1973. *Kinshi Kenkyu.* 3 vols. Tokyo.

Miller, Harold Lyman. 1974. "Factional Conflict and the Integration of Ch'ing Politics." Ph.D. diss., George Washington University.

Ming History [1739]. 1974. Edited by Zhang Tingyu et al. Beijing: Zhonghua shuju.

Mino Yutaka. 1973. *Ceramics in the Liao Dynasty.* Exhibition Catalog. New York: China Institute in America.

Miyazaki Ichisada. 1976. *China's Examination Hell: The Civil Service Examinations of Imperial China* [1963]. Translated by Conrad Shirokauer. New York: Weatherhill.

Morgan, D. O. 1986. *The Mongols.* Oxford: Blackwell.

Morrison, Hedda. 1985. *A Photographer in Old Peking.* Hong Kong: Oxford University Press.

Mote, F. W. 1960. "Confucian Eremitism in the Yuan Period." In *The Confucian Persuasion,* ed. Arthur F. Wright, pp. 202–240. Stanford: Stanford University Press.

———— 1961. "The Growth of Chinese Despotism." *Oriens Extremus* (Hamburg), 8:1–41.

———— 1973. "A Millennium of Chinese Urban History: Form, Time, and Space Concepts in Soochow." *Rice University Studies* 59, no. 4 (Fall):35–66.

———— 1974. "The T'u-mu Incident of 1449." In *Chinese Ways in Warfare,* ed. Frank A. Kierman, Jr., and John K. Fairbank. pp. 243–272. Cambridge, Mass.: Harvard University Press.

———— 1976a. "The Arts and the 'Theorizing Mode' of the Civilization." In Murck 1976, pp. 3–8.

———— 1976b. "Song Lien." In DMB, pp. 1225–31.

———— 1977a. "The Transformation of Nanking, 1350–1400." In Skinner 1977, pp. 101–154.

———— 1977b. "Yuan and Ming." In *Food in Chinese Culture,* ed. K. C. Chang, pp. 193–258. New Haven: Yale University Press.

———— 1987. "Reflections on the First Complete Printing of the *Ssu-k'u Ch'üan-shu.*" *Gest Library Journal* 1, no. 2 (Spring):26–50.

———— 1988a. "The Intellectual Climate in Eighteenth-Century China: Glimpses of Beijing, Suzhou, and Yangzhou in the Qianlong Period." *Phoebus* (Arizona State University) 6, no. 1:17–55 and 169–177.

———— 1988b. "The Rise of the Ming Dynasty, 1330–1367," and "The Ch'eng-hua and Hung-chih Reigns, 1465–1505." In CHC 7:11–5 and 343–402.

———— 1991. "China in the Age of Columbus." In *Circa 1492,* ed. Jay Levenson, pp. 337–350. Washington, D.C.: National Gallery of Art.

Mote, F. W., and Chu Hung-lam et al. 1988. *Calligraphy and the East Asian Book.* Special Catalog Issue. *Gest Library Journal* 2, no. 2 (Spring). Reprint, Boston: Shambala Press.

Murck, Christian F., ed. 1976. *Artists and Traditions: Uses of the Past in Chinese Culture.* Princeton: Princeton University Press.

Murphey, Rhoads. 1989. "An Ecological History of Central Asian Nomadism." In Seaman 1989, pp. 41–72.

Murray, Julia K. 1992. "A Southern Sung Painting Regains Its Memory: *Welcoming the Imperial Carriage (Ying-luan T'u)* and Its Colophon." *Journal of Sung Yuan Studies* 22:109–124.

Naquin, Susan. 1981. *Shantung Rebellion: The Wang Lun Uprising of 1774.* New Haven: Yale University Press.

Naquin, Susan, and Chün-fang Yü, eds. 1992. *Pilgrims and Sacred Sites in China.* Berkeley: University of California Press.

Needham, Joseph. 1954–. *Science and Civilization in China.* 15 vols. Cambridge: Cambridge University Press.

——— 1969. *Within the Four Seas: The Dialogue of East and West.* London: Allen and Unwin.

——— 1970. *Clerks and Craftsmen in China and the West.* Cambridge: Cambridge University Press.

New History of the Five Dynasties [1053]. 1974. [*Xin wudai shi* by Ouyang Xiu]. 3 vols. Beijing.

Nimick, Thomas G. 1993. "The County, the Magistrate, and the Yamen in Late Ming China." Ph.D. diss., Princeton University.

Nivison, David S. 1959. Introduction. In Nivison and Wright 1959, pp. 3–24.

——— 1966. *The Life and Thought of Chang Hsueh-ch'eng.* Stanford: Stanford University Press.

Nivison, David S., and Arthur F. Wright, eds. 1959. *Confucianism in Action.* Stanford: Stanford University Press.

Norman, Jerry. 1988. *Chinese.* Cambridge Language Surveys series. Cambridge: Cambridge University Press.

Nutsch, James G. 1984. "Tatars." In *The Modern Encyclopedia of Russian and Soviet History,* ed. Joseph L. Wieczynski, 38:184–187. Gulf Breeze, Fla.: Academic International Press.

Okada, Hidehiro. 1966. "Life of Dayan Khan." In *Acta Asiatica* 11 (September): 46–55.

Old History of the Five Dynasties [974]. 1976. [*Jiu wudai shi* by Xue Juzheng et al.]. 5 vols. Beijing.

Ouyang Xiu. 1936. *Collected Works* [*Ouyang wenzhong gong wenji*]. SBCK.

Parsons, James B. 1976. In DMB, pp. 1553–56, s.v. "Yang Ying-lung."

Parsons, James Bunyan. 1970. *Peasant Rebellions of the Late Ming Dynasty.* Tucson: University of Arizona Press.

Perkins, Dwight H. 1969. *Agricultural Development in China, 1368–1968.* Chicago: Aldine.

Petech, Luciano. 1976. In DMB, pp. 412–413, s.v. "dGe-'dun-rgya-mtsho."

——— 1990. *Central Tibet and the Mongols.* Vol. 65. Serie Orientale Roma. Rome.

——— 1993. " 'P'ags-pa (1235–1280)." In de Rachewiltz et al. 1993, pp. 646–654.

Peterson, Willard J. 1968–69. "The Life of Ku Yen-wu (1613–1682)." HJAS 28 (1968):114–156, and 29 (1969):201–247.

——— 1976. "Ming Periodization: An Immodest Proposal." *Ming Studies* 3:7–8.

——— 1979. *Bitter Gourd: Fang I-chih and the Impetus for Intellectual Change.* New Haven: Yale University Press.

——— 1988. "Why Did They Become Christians?" In *East Meets West: The Jesu-*

its in China, 1582–1773, ed. Charles E. Ronan and Bonnie B. C. Oh, pp. 129–152. Chicago: Loyola University Press.

———— 1998. "Learning from Heaven: The Introduction of Christianity and Other Western Ideas Into Late Ming China." In CHC 8:789–839.

Piotrovsky, Mikhail. 1993. *Lost Empire of the Silk Road: Buddhist Art from Khara Khoto (x–xiii Centuries)*. Exhibition Catalogue. Milan: Electa and Thyssen-Bornemisza Foundation.

Plaks, Andrew H. 1987. *The Four Masterworks of the Ming Novel*. Princeton: Princeton University Press.

———— 1994. "The Prose of Our Time." In *The Power of Culture: Studies in Chinese Cultural History*, ed. Willard J. Peterson, Andrew H. Plaks, and Ying-shih Yü, pp. 206–217. Hong Kong: Chinese University Press.

Pulleyblank, Edwin G. 1958. "The Origins and Nature of Chattel Slavery in China." *Journal of the Economic and Social History of the Orient* 1, pt. 2 (April):185–220.

Qian Mu. 1947. *Guoshi dagang* [1940]. 2nd Shanghai ed.

———— 1980. *Zhu Zi xin xuean*. 5 vols. Taipei.

Qian Qianyi [1626?]. 1982. *Guochu qunxiong shilüe*. New ed. Beijing: Zhonghua shuju.

———— [1643]. 1936. *Muzhai chuxue ji*. Facsimile reprint. Shanghai.

———— [1653]. 1936. *Jiashen chuanxin lu*. In *Zhongguo neiluan waihuo lishi congshu* 8:1–161. Shanghai.

Qian Zhongshu. 1958. *Song shi xuanzhu*. Beijing.

Qidan guozhi [1247, by Ye Longli]. 1985. Shanghai: Shanghai guji chubanshe.

Qing Shi Gao. See *Draft Qing History*.

Qiu Shushen. 1977. "Yuanmo hongjinjun lingxiu Peng Yingyu xisheng de shijian he didian wenti." *Yuanshi ji beifang minzushi yanjiu jikan*, no. 1, 25–29. Nanjing.

———— 1982. "Yuan mo hongjinjun de zhengquan jianshe." *Yuanshi luncong* 1: 91–108. Beijing: Zhonghua Shuju.

Que Haozeng. 1979. "Song-Xia guanxi zhi yanjiu." SSYJ 11:263–357.

Ramsey, S. Robert. 1987. *The Languages of China*. Princeton: Princeton University Press.

Rao Zongyi. 1982. *Xuantang jilin*. 3 vols. Taipei.

Ratchnevsky, Paul. 1991. *Genghis Khan: His Life and Legacy* [*Cinggis-Khan: Sein Leben und Wirken*]. Translated by Thomas N. Haining. Oxford: Blackwell.

Ricci, Matteo. See Gallagher 1953.

Richardson, Hugh. 1976. In DMB, pp. 481–483, s.v. "Halima."

Robinson, David M. 1995. "Banditry and Rebellion in the Capital Region during the Mid-Ming (1450–1525)." Ph.D. diss., Princeton University.

Rogers, Howard. 1988. "For Love of God: Castiglione at the Court of Qianlong." *Phoebus* (University of Arizona) 6, no. 1:141–160.

Rogers, Michael C. 1983. "National Consciousness in Medieval Korea: The Impact of Liao and Chin on Koryô." In Rossabi 1983, pp. 151–172.

Rong Zhaozu. 1941. *Mingdai sixiangshi*. Shanghai: Kaiming.

Rossabi, Morris. 1975. *China and Inner Asia: From 1368 to the Present Day*. London: Thames and Hudson.

———— 1976. In DMB, pp. 685–686, s.v. "Isiha."

———— 1979. "Khubilai Khan and the Women of His Family." In *Studia Sino-Mongolica*, ed. Wolfgang Bauer, pp. 153–180. Wiesbaden: Steiner.

—— ed. 1983. *China among Equals: The Middle Kingdom and Its Neighbors, 10th–14th Centuries.* Berkeley: University of California Press.

—— 1988. *Khubilai Khan: His Life and Times.* Berkeley: University of California Press.

—— 1992. *Voyager from Xanadu: Rabban Sauma and the First Journey from China to the West.* New York: Kodansha International.

Roth, Gertraude. 1979. "The Manchu-Chinese Relationship, 1618–1636. In Spence and Wills 1979, pp. 1–38.

Rowe, William T. 1984. *Hankow: Commerce and Society in a Chinese City, 1796–1889.* Stanford: Stanford University Press.

Roy, David T., trans. 1993. *The Plum in the Golden Vase: or, Chin P'ing Mei.* Princeton: Princeton University Press.

Rozman, Gilbert. 1973. *Urban Networks in Ch'ing China and Tokugawa Japan.* Princeton: Princeton University Press.

—— 1982. *Population and Marketing Settlements in Ch'ing China.* Cambridge: Cambridge University Press.

Rudolph, Richard C. 1963. "Preliminary Notes on Sung Archaeology." JAS 22, no. 2 (February):169–177.

Rui Hezheng. 1970. "Lun Song Taizu zhi chuangye kaiguo." SSYJ no. 5: 429–477.

Saeki Tomi. 1967. *So no shin bunka* [The New Culture of the Song]. Tokyo.

Schafer, Edward H. 1954a. *The Empire of Min.* Rutland, Vt., and Tokyo: Charles E. Tuttle Co., published for the Harvard-Yenching Institute.

—— 1954b. "The History of the Empire of Southern Han According to Chapter 65 of the *Wu-tai-shih* of Ou-yang Hsiu." In *Silver Jubilee Volume of the Zinbun-Kagaku-Kenkyusyo,* pp. 339–369. Kyoto University.

Schurmann, Herbert Franz. 1956. *Economic Structure of the Yuan Dynasty.* Cambridge, Mass.: Harvard University Press.

Seaman, Gary, ed. 1989. *Ecology and Empire: Nomads in the Cultural Evolution of the Old World.* Ethnographics no. 1. Los Angeles: University of Southern California, Center for Visual Anthropology.

Sebes, Joseph S. 1961. *The Jesuits and the Sino-Russian Treaty of Nerchinsk, 1689: The Dairy of Thomas Pereira, S.J.* Rome: Institutum Historicum.

—— 1977. "The Fragmentation of the Mongols during the Ming Dynasty and Their Step-by-Step Conquest by the Manchus and the Russians." Pt. 2. *Canada-Mongolia Review* 3, no. 1 (May):24–32.

Serruys, Henry. 1955. *The Mongols of Kansu during the Ming.* In *Mélanges chinois et bouddhique* 10:215–346. Brussels: L'Institut Belge des Hautes Études Chinoises.

—— 1957. "Remains of Mongol Customs during the Early Ming." *Monumenta Serica* 16:137–190.

—— 1958. *Genealogical Tables of the Descendants of Dayan-Qan.* The Hague: Mouton.

—— 1959a. "Chinese in Southern Mongolia during the Sixteenth Century." *Monumenta Serica* 18:1–95.

—— 1959b. *The Mongols in China during the Hung-wu Period (1368–1398).* In *Mélanges chinois et bouddhique* 11:1–328 Brussels: L'Institut Belge des Hautes Études Chinoises.

—— 1960. "Four Documents Relating to the Sino-Mongol Peace of 1570–1571." *Monumenta Serica* 19:1–66.

——— 1967. *Sino-Mongol Relations during the Ming. Pt. 2. The Tribute System and Diplomatic Missions (1400–1600).* In *Mélanges chinois et bouddhique* 14. Brussels: L'Institut Belge des Hautes Études Chinoises.

——— 1972. "A Manuscript Version of the Legend of the Mongol Ancestry of the Yung-lo Emperor." *Analecta Mongolica.* Mongolia Society Occasional Papers, no. 8, pp. 19–61. Bloomington, Ind.

——— 1976. In DMB, pp. 6–9, s.v. "Altan-qaᠠan."

Shang Chuan. 1989. *Yongle huangdi.* Beijing.

Shi Jinbo. 1986. *Xi Xia wenhua.* Changchun.

——— 1988. *Xi Xia fojiao shi lüe.* Yinchuan.

Shiba, Yoshinobu. 1970. *Commerce and Society in Sung China.* Translated by Mark Elvin. Ann Arbor: University of Michigan, Center for Chinese Studies.

——— 1975. "Urbanization and the Development of Markets in the Lower Yang-tze Valley." In *Crisis and Prosperity in Sung China,* ed. John Winthrop Haeger, pp. 13–48. Tucson: University of Arizona Press.

——— 1977. "Ningpo and Its Hinterland." In Skinner 1977, pp. 390–439.

Shih, Chung-wen. 1976. *The Golden Age of Chinese Drama: Yuan Tsa-chü.* Princeton: Princeton University Press.

Shih, Shou-ch'ien. 1994. "The Landscape Painting of Frustrated Literati: The Wen Cheng-ming Style in the Sixteenth Century." In *The Power of Culture: Studies in Chinese Cultural History,* ed. Willard J. Peterson et al., pp. 219–246. Princeton: Princeton University Press.

Sima Guang [1084]. 1956. *Zizhi tongjian* [Comprehensive mirror for aid in government, with critical notes by Hu Sanxing, 1230–1287]. 14 vols. Beijing.

Sinor, Denis, ed. 1990. *The Cambridge History of Early Inner Asia.* Cambridge: Cambridge University Press.

Sivin, Nathan. 1977a. "Shen Kua." *Sung Studies Newsletter* 13:31–56.

——— ed. 1977b. *Science and Technology in East Asia.* New York: Science History Publications.

Skinner, G. William, ed. 1977. *The City in Late Imperial China.* Stanford: Stanford University Press.

Smith, Kent C. 1970. "Ch'ing Policy and the Development of Southwest China: Aspects of Ortai's Governor-Generalship 1726–31." Ph.D. diss., Yale University.

Smith, Kidder, Jr., et al. 1990. *Sung Dynasty Uses of the I Ching.* Princeton: Princeton University Press.

Snellgrove, David, and Hugh Richardson. 1968. *A Cultural History of Tibet.* Boston: Shambala Press.

So, Kwan-wai. 1975. *Japanese Piracy in Ming China during the Sixteenth Century.* East Lansing: Michigan State University Press.

——— 1976. In DMB, pp. 1586–91, s.v. "Yen Sung."

Song History [1345]. 1977. [*Songshi,* edited by Tuotuo et al.]. Beijing.

Song Xi [Sung Shee]. 1962. *Songshi yanjiu luncong.* Taipei.

Soulliere, Ellen. 1987. "Palace Women in the Ming Dynasty." Ph.D. diss., Princeton University.

Spence, Jonathan D. 1974. *Emperor of China: Self-Portrait of K'ang-hsi.* New York: Knopf.

Spence, Jonathan D., and John E. Wills, Jr., eds. 1979. *From Ming to Ch'ing.* New Haven: Yale University Press.

Sperling, Elliot. 1979. "The Fifth Karma-pa and Some Aspects of the Relationship between Tibet and the Early Ming." In *Tibetan Studies in Honour of Hugh Richardson,* ed. Michael Aris and Aung San Suu Kyi, pp. 280–289. Warminster, England: Aris and Phillips.

——— 1988. "The Szechwan-Tibet Frontier in the Fifteenth Century." *Ming Studies* 26 (Fall):37–55.

——— 1992. "Notes on References to 'Bri-Gung-Pa—Mongol Contact in the Late Sixteenth and Early Seventeenth Centuries." *Tibetan Studies, NARITA 1989* (Japan): 741–750.

Stein, Rolf. 1972. *Tibetan Civilization.* Stanford: Stanford University Press.

Steinhardt, Nancy Shatzman. 1990. *Chinese Imperial City Planning.* Honolulu: University of Hawaii Press.

——— 1994. "Liao: An Architectural Tradition in the Making." *Artibus Asiae* 54, no. 1–2:5–39.

——— 1997. *Liao Architecture.* Honolulu: University of Hawaii Press.

Strassberg, Richard. 1983. *The World of K'ung Shang-jen.* New York: Columbia University Press.

Strayer, Joseph R. 1970. *On the Medieval Origins of the Modern State.* Princeton: Princeton University Press.

Struve, Lynn A. 1979. "Ambivalence and Action: Some Frustrated Scholars of the K'ang-hsi Period." In Spence and Wills 1979, pp. 323–365.

——— 1980. "History and *The Peach Blossom Fan.*" *Chinese Literature: Essays, Articles, Reviews* 2, no. 1 (January):55–72.

——— 1984. *The Southern Ming, 1644–1662.* New Haven: Yale University Press.

——— 1988. "The Southern Ming, 1644–1662." In CHC 7:641–725.

——— ed. and trans. 1993. *Voices from the Ming-Qing Cataclysm: China in Tiger's Jaws.* New Haven: Yale University Press.

Su Che [ed. 1541]. 1936. "Ouyang wenzhong gong furen Xue shi muzhiming." *Luancheng ji.* SBCK *juan* 25, pp. 6a–8b.

Su Xiaokang et al. 1988. *He Shang* [River elegy]. Hong Kong.

Subrenat, Jean-Jacques. 1976. "Shen Kua." In Franke 1976, 2:857–863.

Sun Kekuan [Sun K'e-K'uan]. 1953. *Yuanchu ruxue.* Taipei: Yiwen.

——— 1958. *Menggu hanjun yu hanwenhua yanjiu,* pp. 44–65. Taipei.

——— 1965. *Song-Yuan daojiao zhi fazhan.* 2 vols, Taipei.

——— 1968a. *Yuandai daojiao zhi fazhan.* Taipei.

——— 1968b. *Yuandai hanwenhua zhi huodong.* Taipei: Taiwan Zhonghua.

——— 1969. "Jin Yuan quanzhen jiao de chuqi huodong." *Jingfeng* (Hong Kong) 20.

Sun Zhengrong. 1983. *Zhu Yuanzhang xinian yaolu.* Hangzhou.

Tan Qian [ca. 1653]. 1958. *Guo Que.* Edited by Zhang Zongxiang. 6 vols., Beijing: Zhonghua.

Tan Qixiang. 1991. *Zhongguo lishi ditu ji* [Chinese historical atlas, 1975]. 8 vols. Rev. ed., Hong Kong.

Tan Tianxing. 1991. "Wangguo zhi jun chongzhen di." In Xu Daling and Wang Tianyou 1991, pp. 320–355.

Tanaka Takeo 1977. "Japan's Relations with Overseas Countries." In *Japan in the Muromachi Age,* ed. John Whitney Hall, pp. 159–181. Berkeley: University of California Press.

Tao, Jing-shen [Tao Jinsheng]. 1976. *The Jurchen in Twelfth-Century China: A Study of Sinicization.* Seattle: University of Washington Press.

———— 1988. *Two Sons of Heaven: Studies in Sung-Liao Relations.* Tucson: University of Arizona Press.

Tao Jinsheng [Tao, Jing-shen]. 1970. "Liu Qi yu *Guiqian zhi.*" SSYJ, no. 5:203–228.

Tao Mao-bing. 1985. *Wudai shi lüe.* Beijing: Xinhua Shuju.

Tao Zongyi [ca. 1367]. 1959. [*Nancun*] *Chuogeng lu.* Beijing: Zhonghua.

Taylor, Romeyn. 1976a. "Li Shan-ch'ang." In DMB, pp. 850–854.

———— 1976b. "Ming T'ai-tsu and the Nobility of Merit." *Ming Studies* 2:57–69.

Teng, Ssu-yü, and John K. Fairbank. 1954. *China's Response to the West.* Cambridge, Mass.: Harvard University Press.

ter Haar, Barend J. 1992. *The White Lotus Teachings in Chinese Religious History.* Leiden: E. J. Brill.

Tillman, Hoyt Cleveland. 1982. *Utilitarian Confucianism: Ch'en Liang's Challenge to Chu Hsi.* Cambridge, Mass.: Harvard University Press.

———— 1988. "Ch'en Liang on Statecraft: Reflections from Examination Essays Preserved in a Song Rare Book." HJAS 48, no. 2 (December):403–431.

———— 1992. *Confucian Discourse and Chu Hsi's Ascendancy.* Honolulu: University of Hawaii Press.

Tillman, Hoyt Cleveland, and Stephen H. West, eds. 1995. *China under Jurchen Rule.* Albany: State University of New York Press.

Tong, James W. 1991. *Disorder under Heaven: Collective Violence in the Ming Dynasty.* Stanford: Stanford University Press.

Tsien, Tsuen-hsuin. 1985. "Paper and Printing." In Needham 1985, 5:1.

Tu, Wei-ming. 1976. *Neo-Confucian Thought in Action: Wang Yang-ming's Youth (1472–1509).* Berkeley: University of California Press.

———— 1982. "Toward an Understanding of Liu Yin's Confucian Eremitism." In Chan and de Bary 1982, pp. 233–278.

Twitchett, Denis C. 1959. "The Fan Clan's Charitable Estate, 1050–1760." In Nivison and Wright 1959, pp. 97–133.

———— 1970. *Financial Administration under the T'ang Dynasty.* 2nd ed. Cambridge: Cambridge University Press.

———— ed. 1979. In CHC Vol. 3, *Sui and T'ang China, 589–906.*

United Nations Population Fund. 1992. Report in *New York Times,* May 5, 1992, p. C1.

Vainshtein, Sevyan I. 1989a. "One of the Origins of Nomadism." In Seaman 1989, pp. 75–80.

———— 1989b. "The Turkic Peoples, Sixth to Twelfth Centuries." In Basilov 1989, pp. 55–65.

Väth, Alfons, S.J. 1933. *Johann Adam Schall von Bell, S.J.* Cologne: J. P. Bachen.

Wade, Geoffrey Philip. 1994. "The Ming Shi-lu (Veritable Records of the Ming Dynasty) as a Source for Southeast Asian History: Fourteenth to Seventeenth Centuries." Ph.D. thesis, Hong Kong University.

Wakeman, Frederic, Jr. 1975. "Localism and Loyalism during the Ch'ing Conquest of Kiangnan: The Tragedy of Chiang-yin." In *Conflict and Control in Late Imperial China,* ed. Frederic Wakeman, Jr., and Carolyn Grant, pp. 43–85. Berkeley: University of California Press.

———— 1979. "The Shun Interregnum of 1644." In Spence and Wills 1979, pp. 39–87.

———— 1985. *The Great Enterprise: The Manchu Reconstruction of Imperial*

Order in Seventeenth-Century China. 2 vols. Berkeley: University of California Press.

———— 1986. "China and the Seventeenth-Century Crisis." *Late Imperial China* 7, no. 1 (June):1–26.

Waldron, Arthur N. 1990. *The Great Wall of China: From History to Myth*. Cambridge: Cambridge University Press.

Waley, Arthur. 1931. *The Travels of an Alchemist: The Journey of the Taoist Ch'ang-ch'un from China to the Hindukush at the Summons of Chingiz Khan*. London: G. Routledge & Sons.

Wang Chen-main. Forthcoming. *The Life and Career of Hung Ch'eng-ch'ou*.

Wang Chongwu. 1947. "Wu Sangui yu Shanhaiguan zhi zhan" [1942]. *Yanjing xuebao* 33 (December):153–162.

———— 1948a. "Lun Ming Taizu qibing ji qi zhengce zhi zhuanbian." CYYY 10: 57–71.

———— 1948b. *Ming jingnan shishi kaozheng gao*. CYYY *Zhuankan* 25.

———— 1978. *Fengtian jingnan ji zhu*. CYYY *Zhuankan* 28.

Wang Deyi [Wang Teh-yi]. 1978. "Song Xiaozong ji qi shidai." In SSYJ 10:245–302.

Wang, Gungwu. 1962. "Feng Tao: An Essay on Confucian Loyalty." In Wright and Twitchett 1962, pp. 123–145.

———— 1963. *The Structure of Power in North China during the Five Dynasties*. Kuala Lumpur: University of Malaya Press.

———— 1968. "Early Ming Relations with Southeast Asia: A Background Essay." In Fairbank 1968, pp. 34–62.

———— 1976. In DMB, pp. 64–67, s.v. "Chang Fu."

———— 1991. *The Chineseness of China: Selected Essays*. Hong Kong: Oxford University Press.

Wang Jianying. 1992. *Ming Zhongdu*. Beijing: Zhonghua Shuju.

Wang Tianyou. 1991a. "Buke yishi de Ming Shizong." in Xu Daling and Wang Tianyou 1991, pp. 214–244.

———— 1991b. "Shenzong Xian huangdi Zhu Yijun." In Xu Daling and Wang Tianyou 1991, pp. 263–293.

———— 1991c. "Shi cheng 'Lingzhu' de Ming Muzong." In Xu Daling and Wang Tianyou 1991, pp. 245–262.

———— 1992. *Mingdai guojia jigou yanjiu*. Beijing: Beijing Daxue.

Wang, Yeh-chien. 1973. *An Estimate of the Land-Tax Collection in China, 1753 and 1908*. Cambridge, Mass.: East Asian Research Center, Harvard University.

Wang Zengyu. 1983. *Yue Fei xin zhuan*. Shanghai.

———— 1989. *Eguo jintuo zuibian, xubian jiaozhu*. [Critical edition of Yue Ke, 1234]. 2 vols. Beijing.

Wang Zicai et al. 1962. *Song-Yuan xue'an buyi* [1838]. 8 vols. Reprint, Shijie shuju.

Watson, Burton, trans. 1973. *The Old Man Who Does as He Pleases*. [Translations from Lu You]. New York: Columbia University Press.

Watt, John R. 1972. *The District Magistrate in Late Imperial China*. New York: Columbia University Press.

Wei Wenxuan. 1987. *Zhongguo lidai guanzhi jianbiao*. Taiyuan: Shanxi Renmin Chuban She.

Wei Yuan. 1842 [1938?]. *Shengwu ji, juan 3, Sibu beiyao* ed., pp. 25a–b. Shanghai: Zhonghua shuju.

Wen Bing [ca. 1645]. 1946. *Liehuang xiaozhi.* In *Zhongguo neiluan waihuo lishi congshu,* 17:3–241. Shanghai.

Wilhelm, Hellmut. 1951. "The Po-hsueh Hung-ju Examination of 1679." *Journal of the American Oriental Society* 71:60–66.

—— 1960. *Gesellschaft und Staat in China: Zur Geschichte eines Weltreiches* [1944]. Reprint, Hamburg: Rowohlt.

—— 1962. "From Myth to Myth: The Case of Yueh Fei's Biography." In Wright and Twitchett 1962, pp. 146–161.

Wills, John E. 1979. "Maritime China from Wang Chih to Shih Lang: Themes in Peripheral History." In Spence and Wills 1979, pp. 201–238.

Wittfogel, Karl A., and Feng Chia-sheng. 1949. *History of Chinese Society: Liao (907–1125)* [1946]. Reprint, New York: Macmillan.

Wixted, John Timothy. 1982. *Poems on Poetry: Literary Criticism by Yuan Hao-wen (1190–1257).* Wiesbaden: Steiner.

Worthy, Edmund H., Jr. 1983. "Diplomacy for Survival: Domestic and Foreign Relations of Wu Yüeh, 907–978." In Rossabi 1983, pp. 17–44.

Wright, Arthur F., and Denis C. Twitchett, eds. 1962. *Confucian Personalities.* Stanford: Stanford University Press.

Wright, David C. 1993. "Sung-Liao Diplomatic Practices." Ph.D. diss., Princeton University.

—— 1996. "Parity, Pedigree, and Peace: Routine Sung Diplomatic Missives to the Liao." *Journal of Sung-Yuan Studies* 26:55–85.

Wu Ching-tzu [Wu Jingzi]. [ca. 1750]. 1972. *The Scholars [Rulin Waishi].* Translated by Gladys Yang and Yang Hsien-yi. Beijing: Foreign Languages Press, 1957. Republished with foreword by C. T. Hsia. New York: Grosset and Dunlap Universal Library.

Wu Han. 1948. "Mingchu de xuexiao." Reprinted in Wu Han 1956a, pp. 317–341.

—— 1949. *Zhu Yuanzhang zhuan.* Xin Zhongguo Shuju: N.p. (Shanghai?).

—— 1956a. *Dushi Zhaji.* Beijing: Sanlian.

—— 1956b. "Mingjiao yu Da Ming diguo" [1940]. Reprinted in Wu Han 1956a, pp. 235–270.

—— 1964. *Zhongguo lishi changshi.* Vols. 1–7. Reprint, Wuhan.

—— 1965. *Zhu Yuanzhang zhuan.* Rev. and suppl. ed. Beijing: San-lian.

Wu Hung. 1995. "Emperor's Masquerade—Costume Portraits of Yongzheng and Qianlong." *Orientations* 26, no. 7 (July–August):25–41.

—— 1996. *The Double Screen: Medium and Representation in Chinese Painting.* Chicago: University of Chicago Press.

Wu Jihua. 1970. *Mingdai shehui jingji shi luncong.* 2 vols. Taipei.

—— 1971. *Mingdai zhidushi luncong.* 2 vols. Taipei.

Wu, Nelson. 1962. "Tung Ch'i-ch'ang (1555–1636): Apathy in Government and Fervor in Art." In *Confucian Personalities,* ed. Arthur Wright and Denis Twitchett, pp. 260–293. Stanford: Stanford University Press.

Wu, Pei-yi. 1990. *The Confucian's Progress: Autobiographical Writings in Traditional China.* Princeton: Princeton University Press.

—— 1994. "Memories of K'ai-feng." *New Literary History* 25, no. 1 (Winter): 47–60.

Wu, Silas H. L. 1970. *Communication and Imperial Control in China: Evolution of the Palace Memorial System, 1693–1735.* Cambridge, Mass.: Harvard University Press.

——— 1979. *Passage to Power: K'ang-hsi and His Heir Apparent, 1661–1722.* Cambridge, Mass.: Harvard University Press.

Wu Tianchi. 1980. *Xi Xia Shigao.* Chengdu.

Wu Zhefu. 1969. *Qingdai jinhui shumu yanjiu.* Taipei.

Xia Xie. [1873]. 1959. *Ming Tongjian.* New ed. by Shen Zhongjiu. 4 vols. Beijing.

Xiang Da. 1962. *Man shu jiao zhu.* [Critical edition of Fan Chuo, *Man shu,* ca. 865]. Beijing.

Xiao Qiqing [Hsiao Ch'i-ch'ing]. 1983. "Hubilie 'Qiandi jiulü' kao." In *Yuandaishi xintan,* pp. 263–301. Taipei.

——— 1985. "Yuandai Mengguren de Hanxue." In *Proceedings of the International Conference on China Border Area Studies,* pp. 369–485. Taipei: Zhengzhi University.

Xiao Yishan. 1963. *Qingdai tongshi.* 5 vols. Taipei: Shangwu Yinshuguan.

Xie Guozhen. 1948. *Qingchu liuren kaifa dongbei kao.* Shanghai: Kaiming Shudian.

Xin Wudai Shi. See *New History of the Five Dynasties.*

Xu Daling and Wang Tianyou, eds. 1991. *Mingchao shiliu di.* Beijing: Xinhua.

Xu Mengxin [1126–1194, ed. 1878]. *Sanchao beimeng huibian.* Reprint, Wen-hai, Taipei, 1962.

Yang, C. K. 1961. *Religion in Chinese Society.* Berkeley: University of California Press.

Yang De'en [Pref. date 1939]. *Shi Kefa Nianpu.* N.p., n.d.

Yang, Lien-sheng. 1971. *Money and Credit in China: A Short History* [1952]. Cambridge, Mass.: Harvard University Press.

Yang Ne and Chen Gaohua. 1985. *Yuandai nongmin zhanzheng shiliao huibian.* 4 vols. Beijing: Zhonghua shuju.

Yang, Ruowei. 1993. "The Liao-Dynasty Stone Inscriptions and Their Importance to the Study of Liao History." *Gest Library Journal* 6, no. 2 (Winter):55–72.

Yang Shufan. 1974. "Liao Jin Gongju Zhidu." In SSYJ 7:115–149.

Yang Shushen. 1984. *Liaoshi jianbian.* Shenyang, Liaoning Renmin chubanshe.

Yang Yifan. 1992. *Hongwu falü dianji kaozheng.* Beijing: Xinhua.

Yang Zhijiu. 1985. *Yuan shi san lun,* pp. 89–134. Beijing: Renmin Chubanshe.

Yao Congwu [Yao Ts'ung-wu]. 1959. *Dongbeishi luncong.* 2 vols. Taipei.

Yao Tao-chung. 1986. "Ch'iu Ch'u-chi and Chinggis Khan." HJAS 46, no. 1:201–220.

Yin Shixue. 1988. "Yue Fei ping Yang Yao shi yi chang lishi beiju." In *Yue Fei Yanjiu,* pp. 278–283. Hangzhou.

Yoshikawa Kojiro. 1967. *An Introduction to Sung Poetry.* Translated by Burton Watson. New York: Columbia University Press.

——— 1989. *Five Hundred Years of Chinese Poetry, 1150–1650* [*Gen Minshi Gaisetsu,* 1963]. Translated by John Timothy Wixted. Princeton: Princeton University Press.

Yu Dajun. 1987. "Yelü Dashi chuangjian diguo guocheng ji jinian xintan." In Chen Shu 1987, pp. 234–252.

Yu Yingshi [Yü Ying-shih]. 1976. *Lun Dai Zhen yu Zhang Xuecheng.* Hong Kong: Longmen Shudian.

——— 1978. *Hongloumeng de liangge shihjie.* Taipei: Lianjing.

———— 1987. *Zhongguo jinshi zongjiao lunli yu shangren jingshen*, Taipei: Lianjing.

———— 1989. "Tai Chen's Choice between Philosophy and Philology." *AM*, 3rd ser., 2:1, pp. 79–108.

———— 1997. "Reorientation of Confucian Social Thought in the Age of Wang Yang-ming." *Third Global Future Generations Kyoto Forum: Wang Yang-ming Conference*. Published text of Keynote Speech, August 11, 1997, Kyoto.

Yü Ying-shih. 1975. "Some Preliminary Observations on the Rise of Ch'ing Confucian Intellectualism." *Tsing Hua Journal of Chinese Studies*, n.s., 11, nos. 1–2 (December):105–146.

———— 1980. "Review Article: Toward an Interpretation of the Intellectual Transition in Seventeenth-Century China." *Journal of the American Oriental Society* 100, no. 2:115–125.

Yuan History [1370]. 1976. [*Yuanshi*]. Edited by Song Lien et al. Beijing.

Yuan, Tsing. 1978. "The Porcelain Industry at Ching-te-chen, 1550–1700." *Ming Studies* 6 (Spring):45–54.

Yue Fei Yanjiuhui. 1988. *Yue Fei yanjiu*. Hangzhou.

Yuwen Maozhao [ca. 1160]. 1986. *Da Jin Guozhi*. Critical edition by Cui Wenyin. 2 vols. Beijing.

Zelin, Madeleine. 1984. *The Magistrate's Tael: Rationalizing Fiscal Reform in Eighteenth-Century China*. Berkeley: University of California Press.

Zeng Qiongbi. 1988. "Zhao Gou yu Qin Gui." In Yue Fei Yanjiuhui 1988, pp. 285–305.

Zhang Huiyi. 1937. *Jinling da baoensi ta zhi*. Shanghai.

Zhang Jinjian [Chang Chin-chien]. 1955. *Zhongguo wenguan zhidu shi*. Taipei.

Zhang Tianyu. 1980. "Song-Jin Haishang lianmeng de yanjiu." *SSYJ*, no. 12:185–245.

Zhang Xianqing. 1992. *Yan Song Zhuan*. Hefei.

Zhaqi Siqin [Sechin Jagchid]. 1978. *Menggu yu xizang lishi guanxi zhi yanjiu*. Taipei.

Zheng Qian [Cheng Ch'ien]. 1952. *Ci Xuan*. Taipei.

Zheng Suchun. 1987. *Quanzhen jiao yu damengguguo dishi*. Taipei.

Zheng Zhenduo. 1958. *"Qingming shanghe tu" de yanjiu* [n.d.]. Booklet published with reproduction of the painting under title *Qingming shanghe tu*, Beijing: Wenwu chuban she.

Zhi Weicheng and Ren Zhiyuan. 1932. *Wu Wang Zhang Shicheng zaiji*. 5 vols. Shanghai.

Zhou Liangxiao and Gu Juying. 1993. *Yuandai shi*. Shanghai: Renmin.

Zhou Yuanlian. 1982. "Guanyu baqi zhidu de jige wenti." In *Qingshi luncong*, no. 3, pp. 140–183. Beijing: Zhonghua.

Zhu Dongrun. 1959. *Zhongguo wenxue pipingshi dagang*. Hong Kong: Jianwen Shuju.

———— 1960. *Lu You Zhuan*. Shanghai: Zhonghua Shuju.

INDEX

Abaoji, 12–13, 32–48, 81, 88, 90, 380, 475, 785; death, 47–48

Academies (shuyuan), private: in late Ming, 732–733, 736–738

Acculturation (cultural adaptation), 28, 42–44, 72–75, 76–81, 203, 214–216, 229; in Jin, 265, 270–271; in re Jin nativist movement, 236–237, 240–241; in Xia, 252, 260–261; of non-Chinese in southern provinces, Ming/Qing, 705–706; of Manchus, 916–918, 921–923; China and West compared, 963–964

Achieving society, 367, 967

Adoption, 369

Agrarian reforms: of Jia Sidao, 319–320

Agriculture: in Inner Asia, 27–28, 35, 40, 90; in Song China, 165; in Xia, 257, 259–260; among Jurchens, 214, 217; factor in North-South divide, 266; commodities taxed in kind, in Song, 362; use of iron and steel implements, in Song, 363; the agricultural year (calendar), 368, 756–757; similar village agriculture in non-Chinese districts of south, 706; rehabilitation of, in early Ming, 748–749; technological development, 749–750; commercialization of, 749; New World crops, 903; growth of, in Qing, 942–943, 1055nn54,55

Aguda, 194–195, 202, 210, 214, 219–220, 224, 225, 274, 381, 382, 784, 785. See also Jurchens

"All-powerful Chief Councillors" in Southern Song, 308–320, 574

"Alliance conducted at sea," 208–210

Alphabets. See Scripts

Altai Mountains, 25, 407, 421, 422, 875

Altaic languages, 33–35, 61, 170, 211, 404, 405

Altan Khan: 689, 696, 701; achieves trade agreement with Ming, 697; granted title, 726

Ambans, Manchu agents in Tibet, 938–939

Amdo (A-mdo) region of Tibet, 169, 258, 698, 877, 878, 936–937

Amur River, 33, 211, 608, 873

Ancestor veneration, 75, 98, 158–159, 332, 368, 763–764, 859–860, 968–969

"Ancestral Injunctions" (Zu Xun, Ming), 559, 585–587, 606; "charade," 594–595, 618, 781

Ancient prose. See Gu wen

Annam, relations with early Ming, 607, 611–612, 625

Anti-Manchu sentiment, in Qing, 898–900

Anti-Mongol feeling, in Ming founding, 559–561

Antiquity. See Fugu

Appanages, in Mongol system, 446, 447, 450–451, 481, 503

Aquinas, St. Thomas, 149

Archaeology: evidence from, 84–86, 258,

Archaeology *(cont.)*
264, 513; as practiced in Song times,
151, 328–329
Architecture: Buddhist, 84–85; Daoist,
163; of Imperial Qing court, 917
Aristocracy: Europe compared with
China, 349, 554, 980n15; tribal, 397
Armed society. *See* Militarization of
society
Arts: in Five Dynasties, 21–23; in Song,
152–158, 325; in Jin, 277–278; in
Yuan, 511–513, in late Ming, 769–
770, 775
Assimilation. *See* Acculturation
Astronomy, 326, 483, 510–511; Muslim,
577–578; Western, 823, 1014n44
Audiences, at Ming court, 639–642
Authoritarianism: in Song, 100–101;
under Qing Shizong, 910–911

"Bad last minister." *See* Jia Sidao
Banchen (Panchen) Lama, 875, 938
"bandits," in Chinese usage, 300, 520–
521, 524, 525, 529, 559–560, 757–
760
Banner organization (Manchu). *See* Manchu banner system
Baojia organization: in Song, 140, 355; in
Ming, 753; in Qing, 918–919
Bagu wen. See Civil service: examination
essay, in Ming
Barbarians: defined, 28, 73, 77, 124; used
to control barbarians, 36, 124; sense
of, 266–267, 279, 385; relations
with, 376–378, 379
Bei, Prince, 46, 49–52, 64, 81
Beijing (Beiping): as Ming capital, 567,
763; rebuilt by Ming Chengzu, 617–
621; at fall of Ming, 801, 806–810,
813–815; as Qing capital, 818–819
Bi Yuan, 97
Bian, Bianliang. *See* Kaifeng
"Blue" (maritime) China, defined by maritime involvement, 616–617. *See also*
"Yellow" (land-oriented) China
Bohai: nation, 33, 34, 44, 47, 60–61,
113, 200, 202, 212–213, 240, 381,
394; Bohai figures in Jin, 225, 228,
238, 274
Borders of Ming state, 685–722; southern and northern borders compared,
706
Börte, 416–419

Bourgeoisie, in Europe, compared with
China, 764–765
Buddhism: in Liao empire, 43–44, 81–86;
in Song life, 158, 160–163; in Xia,
261–264; mental disciplines of, 338,
339; international character of, 398–
399; in Inner Asia, 408; in Yuan,
501–503; life in Buddhist temple,
late Yuan, 544–546; in Ming intellectual life, 678; deplored, by Qing
thinkers, 931–932
Buddhist scriptures (Sutras), 82, 84, 85–
86, 162–163, 262–264. *See also* Tripitaka
"Buds of Capitalism" hypotheses, 765,
768–769, 1031n48
Bureaucracy: size of, in Song, 115, 308;
in Liao state, 204, in Jin, 275–276;
characteristics of, in Song, 332; in
Yuan, 482–483, 490–491, 492–494;
size of, in Ming, 636; declining performance of, late Ming, 728–729;
"manipulative" bureaucrats, 780
Bureaucratization, contrasted with entrepreneurship: 617, 652–653; in re
maritime developments, 719–720
Burial sacrifice (human), Khitan practice,
50, 52
Burma (Ava Burma, etc.), 712–713
Buryat Mongols, in Ming and later,
689

Cai Jing, 142–143, 207–210
Calendar (Chinese), 41, 368, 510, 756–
757; use by non-Chinese states, 81,
182; calendrical studies, 578
Calligraphy, 22, 152, 155, 511–512, 625,
916
Canal systems, 17, 18, 646, 652. *See also*
Grand Canal
Cannons: true cannons first used in Chinese warfare, 712; on Portuguese
ships, 721; made in Macao arsenal,
722; cast by European missionaries
for Manchus, 937
Capitalism, components of, 765, 768–
769. *See also* "Buds of Capitalism"
hypotheses
Caravan trade: in Xia, 172, 259; with
Central Asia, 392, 429; in Ming
period, 767
Castiglione, Giuseppe (Lang Shining),
891, 912, 1051n1

Catapults, used by Yuan armies, 462–463

Cathay (Khitai), 60, 445, 951

Cavalry warfare, 36, 77, 115–116, 182, 190–214, 242, 243, 260, 410–411, 427, 435, 461, 462, 480–481, 534–535

Censorate (and surveillance): in Yuan, 478; in Ming, 605, 726; reorganized in Qing, 895–896, 1048n20

Census records. *See* Demographic methods

Central Asia: defined, 23, 24; in re Mongol empire, 428–433, 435

Central Asian (Semu) advisors in Yuan, 456, 490, 493–495

Centralization of political power: Five Dynasties, 20; in Silla and Bohai, 44; in Liao, 54–55; in Song, 102, 109–112; in Xia, 186–188; in Jin, 227, 229–236, 238–239, 271; excessive, 337, 355; under Mongols, 450–451; in Ming, 566, 573–575, 639–643; Qing, 892–894

Ceramics: in Liao, 86–87; in Yuan, 513; in Ming, 625

Chan, W. T., 148

Chan (Zen) school of Buddhism, 147, 151, 154, 162, 337, 346, 448, 483, 501, 677, 823

Chang'an (Xi'an), 17, 39, 646

Change, in Chinese society, 99–100, 126, 267–268, 323–325, 345, 376, 399, 965–966

Changes, Book of (Yijing), 146–147, 149, 338

Chen Liang, 335–336

Chen Youliang (of rebel "Han" state), 530–531, 539, 558

Cheng Yi (Cheng brothers), 147–148, 154, 338, 342

Cheng-Zhu thought, 148, 929, 931

Chief Councillors, 101, 109–110, 308. *See also* "All-powerful Chief Councillors" in Southern Song

"China among Equals," 377–378

China Proper, 25, 26, 640, 944

"China Turning Inward," in Southern Song, 298–299

Chinese cultural forms, adopted by non-Chinese, 41, 74–75, 180–182, 227, 232, 238, 251–252, 260–261, 272, 274–276, 280, 386, 439, 450, 545; imperial institution under Mongols,

458–459, 506; Qing sponsorship of, 865; policy toward, in Qianlong period, 921–922

Chinese cultural unity, sense of, 269–271

Chinese ethnic identity: under Jin rule, 268–271; in Ming founding, 560

Chinese language and script, 266–267, 268–269; "Mandarin," 620, 994n5

"Chinese World Order," 376

"Chineseness," 269–271, 928, 962–963, 965

Chinggis Khan. *See* Mongol khans

Chinggisid lineages, 442, 448, 610; opposition to Khubilai Khan, 465–466; in Ming and later times, 687, 688, 1021nn6,7

Choice, as factor in social process, 802, 970, 1036nn55,56

Christianity, 83, 261, 407, 408, 424, 440, 446, 484, 501, 618, 823, 950

Circuits: *(lu)*, in Song and Jin, 354–359; *(dao)*, in Yuan, 1008n13, 1008n14; in Qing, 946

Cities: in Inner Asia, 27, 35, 41, 696; in Central Asia, 205, 206, 429, 432; in Song China, 164–166, 324–325, 367–368, 371; in Xia, 257; in Jin, 282–283, 286; in Russia, 435–436; in Yuan, 458, in Mongol conquest of Song, 464; along Grand Canal, 652; European urbanism compared with China, 760–761, 763; functions of city walls, 762; cities slaughtered by Manchus, 833. *See also* urbanization

Civil bureaucracy, special conditions of, in Yuan, 478, 490–493

Civil service: examinations, in Liao, 79–81, in Northern Song, 125, 126–135, 141, criticism of, 156–157; in Jin, 242, 272–277; in re unsuccessful candidates, 276, 311–312, 348; in Southern Song, 332, Zhu Xi's influence on, 343; system restored under Mongols, 490–491, 508; in re military careers, 554; resumed in Ming, 572, 601; among non-Chinese in native districts, 706; examination essay *(bagu wen)*, in Ming, 774–775; in Qing, 824, 861–868; cheating scandals, in Qing, 863–864, 868

Civil vs. military power, 103–104, 114, 227–228, 254, 271, 306–307, 506, 554, 555–556

Clan. *See* Family

Class warfare (conflict) interpretations of history, 302, 518, 576, 803, 1010n2, 1020n37, 1037nn56,57

Classics Mat lectures, in Ming, 655, 780

Clerks, 127, 141, 330, 358, 360, 487–488, 494, 752–753, 864, 943

Climate history, 520

Clock, made for Yuan emperor Shun, 577–578, 1013n42

"Closed" social order, compared with China, 634

Coal, 286, 363

Coastal shipping, in Ming, 651–652, 722, 749

Collections, of art and antiquities, 328–330, 775, 916

"Commercial revolution," 391

Common people: contributions to civilization, 327–328; importance of, 334; lives of, in Song, 351–374; in Yuan, 497, 503–504; impact of Wang Yangming thought on, 680–681, 752, 753; lives of, in Ming period, 754–757; subjected to moral teachings, in Qing, 897; protected from "bad gentry," in Qing, 907; in re Qing cultural policy, 928; in Qing, 941–942; their work ethic, 966–967

Commoner status: *(min)*, 152, 365–366; *bu-yi*, 333, 348, 550; *liang min* (good people), 365–366

Community: organs of governing, in Yuan, 488–489; in re popular religions, 500–501; community self-defense, in Yuan, 521, 524; place of, in thought of Fang Xiaoru, 592–593; focus on, in Wang Yangming school, 682; functioning of, in Ming rural society, 752–754

Compromise, in solving social problems, 760

Concubinage, 76

Confucian classics: printed 21; translated, into Jurchen, 240; basis of education, 336; textual basis of Neo-Confucian authority, 341–342; with Zhu Xi's exegesis, 343; standard for civil service examinations, 343, 508; traditions of learning in, Yuan, 508–510; in re Qing thought and learning, 930

"Confucian policy" in late Yuan, 519

Confucian thinkers: spectrum of, in Southern Song, 333–340; among advisors to Ming Taizu, 557–558; in Qing, 928–935

Confucian values: in Liao, 81; in Song, 100, 135, 145, 150–151, 154, 159–161, 207; in Jin, 223, 238; in Xia, 187–190, 252, 254, 273–274, 333–334; standardized throughout society, 343–344; basis of ritualized interstate relations, 379, 382, 383; ignored under Mongols, 439; in re Khubilai Khan, 448–451, 452–454; in Yuan, 506, 508; in Ming Yuzhen's rebel Xia state, 540; of advisors to Ming Taizu, 551–552; Ming Xiaozong's devotion to, 634–635; in re Qing policy, 865; Confucian man's moral independence, 889; in re China's "Great Tradition," 957–961. *See also* Neo-Confucianism

Conquest dynasties: 8, 29–30, 32, 71, 77; compared, 190, 241, 261, 265–266, 375–376; in re Buddhism, 261–262; overall impact, 376, 377. *See also* Liao *entries;* Xi Xia state; Jin *entries;* Yuan *entries;* Qing *entries*

Consort clans, 88, 100; in Chinggisid lineages, 414–416; mid-Ming, 631

Correlative interaction. *See* Heaven-man relationship

Cosmology: Neo-Confucian, 135, 144–149, 341–342, 637–639, 956–959

Counties, and county *yamen* offices: in Song, 355, 359; in Yuan, 487–489; in Qing, 943–946

Court procedures, Ming, 639–642

Crafts, 86–87, 151–152, 257, 286, 327, 390; among Mongols, 411; in re trade, 767, 954–955

"Creative misunderstanding," 87–88

Cultural interaction: in period of conquest dynasties, 394–399; among Chinese and non-Chinese in south China, 705–706; China and the West, 956–961, 963–964

Currency: in Song, 116–117, 140; in Jin, 284; in Yuan, 495, 520; in Ming, 766–768, 807

Cyclical theory. *See* Dynastic cycle theory

Cynicism, characteristic of Qing period, 820, 886, 928, 947, 969

Dadu, 457, 464, 485, 491, 518, 533, 559, 646; falls to Ming armies, 563, 687. *See also* Beijing

Dai Zhen, 932–933, 934–935, 1053n39

Dalai Lamas, 688, 700, 701–702, 870–871, 876–878, 901, 937–939

Dali, kingdom, city, 452–454, 710–711

Dangxiang tribes, 57, 169–170, 185, 200, 258

Dao: as Confucian value (Daoxue), 338, 345, 678; term of reproach, 341; transmission of, *Dao Tong,* 342, 682

Daoism: in Liao, 81; patronized by Song rulers, 104, 114, 147, 163–164, 207; religious Daoism in society, 158, 163–164; philosophical, 163–164, 337–338, 342, 497–498; in re science, 325–326; of Qiu Chuji, 438; new sects in Yuan, 498–501, 527; Daoist-Buddhist rivalry, Yuan, 500; Wudang Mt. complex patronized by Ming Chengzu, 618; magical Daoism, of Ming Shizong, 668–669; Daoist philosophy in Ming intellectual life, 678; impact on Chinese worldview, 957

Darughachi, institution of, in Yuan, 493–494. *See also* Dual staffing

De Bary, W. T., 146

Debased occupations. *See* "Mean people"

Demographic methods, 351–353, 496, 743–747, 904–906, 919

Demography. *See* Population

Despotism: in Northern Song, 99, 112, 137; in Jin, 233, 397; sources of, in Ming, 579–581; of Ming Taizu, compared with Ming Shizong, 669; of Qing Shizong, 889, 910–911; of Qing Gaozong, 920

Diplomacy. *See* Interstate relations

Donglin "party" in late Ming, 736–738, 741, 778–780, 835, 836, 881

Drama: emergence of, in Jin, 280–283; relation to Yuan *zaju,* 282–283; in Yuan, 511–512; in late Ming, 773–774

Dual administration: of Liao empire, 31, 39–40, 42, 72–75, 88–89, 475; of Xia state, 181; Liao pattern of, in Jin, 223, 225–229, 231, 271, 273–274, 475–476; rejected by Mongols, 476–477

Dual civil service examinations: in Jin, 273; in Qing, 863

Dual culture, individuals of, 39, 42, 51, 90–91, 202–203, 206, 230–231, 232, 241, 865, 894, 921

Dual staffing: under Mongols, 489–490, 492–494; in Qing, 863, 918

Dual systems of law, 73–74, 271, 279–280

Duke of Zhou analogy, in Ming usurpation, 588–589

Dutch penetration of East Asia, 720–722, 835, 840, 848

Dynastic cycle theory, 204, 518, 776–777, 781–784, 801, 1032n1

Dynastic succession charts: Liao, 53; Northern Song, 105; Xi Xia, 184; Jin, 215; Southern Song, 309; Mongol Khans, 415; Yuan, 468; Ming, 624; Qing, 822

"Dynasty": meanings of, 564–566; dynasty as private family matter, in Ming, 586–587, 589, 590–591, 667, 734, 742, 1014n11

Dzungaria, 25, 205, 206, 407, 435; in re Galdan and Qing wars, 870–872, 874–876, 894–895, 901–902, 936

Eastern Depot, Western Depot *(Dongchang, Xichang),* in Ming. *See* Prisons

Eastern Han. *See* Northern Han state

Eastern Mongols, in Ming and later times, 688–689, 784, 785

Ecological divide: in north, not found on southern boundaries of China, 706

Economic interaction, China and the West, 950–951, 953–956

Education: policy in Song, 141, 159–160; promoted in Yuan, 508; of common people and of women, in Ming, 680–681

Elite stratum: "open," 79–80, 132–135, 157, 367; in Song society, 120–121, 126–127, 150, 151–152, 340, 988n4; elite of learning, in Jin, 272–278; in Song, 311–312; elite dominance of Song and thereafter, 311–322, 323–350; elite-commoner relations, 327–328; economic status of, 333, 341; other than scholar-officials, 346–350; definition of elite in Song, 347–349; shared lifestyle of,

Elite stratum *(cont.)*
348; elite sector of Yuan society, 504–507, 519–520; elites in re "popular" religions, 527–528, 558–559; new elite of Ming, 572; elite of merit compared with hereditary monarchy, 634–635; alternate modes of elite behavior encouraged by Wang Yangming, 683–684; intellectual vigor and moral commitment of, in late Ming, 729, 732–733, 734, 736–738, 769–775; elite lifestyles not confined to cities, 763–764; components of, at Ming fall, 825–826; corrupted elite, of Kangxi period, 885–886; thought control of, in Qing, 897; degeneration of, in mid-Qing, 947–948

Elixirs, Daoist, used by Ming Shizong, 668–669

"Eminent clans" (lineages), post-Tang, 20, 120, 127, 159

Emperorship in China, 98–101; compared with Inner Asian khanate, 100, 182–183; compared with European kings, 296; threats to rulers, Tang and Song, 313; emperors as bureaucrats, 361; emperors' family rituals, 385, 666

"Empire," concept of, 183; realized under Manchu/Qing rule, 856–857, 953–954

Empresses and dowager empressess: in Liao, 49–54, 76, 113; roles in successions and usurpations, 93–98, 104, 587, 659–660; in Xia, 188, 253; in Ming, 550, 559, 569, 596, 626–627, 660–661, 727–728, 740; in Qing, 915–916

Encyclopedic compilations: in Ming, 601–602; Qing *Complete Library of the Four Treasuries (Siku quanshu)*, 923–925, 933

England. *See* Great Britain

Epidemics, 520

Epistemology: Neo-Confucian, 338–339, 509, 676–677, 929–931; comparisons with other cultures, 339

Equality (parity), between states, 377–379, 380, 385, 386

Eremitism: in Yuan, 507; late Ming withdrawal from political careers, 770

Erotic literature, 645, 765, 927

"Escape by sea" of Southern Song Gaozong's court, 297–298

Esen, Oyirat khan, and Tumu incident, 627–628, 688

Ethnic diversity: of Inner Asia, 33–35, 406; in Liao, 59–60, 73–75; diminished under Mongols, 59–60, 405; in China's southern tier provinces, 702–717

Ethnic identity: in re social status, in Yuan, 489; in native regions of south, 705

Eunuchs, 100, 296, 662–663; in Ming, 575, 602–605, 614; palace school for, Ming, 626; "eunuch dictators" in Ming, 626–629, 632–634, 655–657, 674, 741, 776, 777–778, 792; "good eunuchs" versus "bad eunuchs," 631–634; numbers of, in Ming, 636; powers of, reduced under Emperor Shizong, 724; good eunuch Feng Bao, in Ming Wanli reign, 728, 733

European (Western) presence in China, 950–964

Evidential Learning *(kaozheng)*, movement in Qing, 854–855, 923, 929–935

Examination system. *See* Civil service

Exports: in Jin-Song period, 287; in Southern Song, 393; in late Ming, 767–768; in Qing, 954–956

Factions: in Liao, 55–57, 200–202, 204; in Song, 73, 112–115, 122, 123, 124, 136–137, 154, 207; in Xia, 186–189; in Jin, 229, 247; in early Southern Song, 293, 296, 298–299; in Mongol governing, 446, 472–473, 518–519, 536; in late Ming, 728–729, 732–733, 736–738, 778–781; at Qing court, 879–884, 920–921; Qing Shunzhi emperor's discourse on, 889

Family, 132, 311, 332, 340, 965, 966, 1056n16; family rituals, in Song, 343–344, 369, 384; corporate property (charitable estates), 349–350, 968–969; clan organization, 350; size of, 353, 368–369; in Mongol society, 411–413; Chinese family rules the norm for imperial clans, 587, 594–595; responsibilities of families and clans, in Fang Xiaoru's thought, 593; obligations of mourning, in Ming, 732, 763–764

Family armies, 302

Family-centered religion, 98, 157–158, 368, 755–756, 968–969

Fan Zhongyan, 123, 124, 136–138, 349

Fang Xiaoru, 573, 588–589, 591–594

"Farang," as general designation for Europeans, 952

Farmers, status of: 348, 365; range of economic statuses among, 366; changing relation to market, 392; life of tenant farmers, late Yuan, 541–544; military skills found among, 555; manner of life, in Ming, 749–750, 752–759; enslaved under Manchus, 859–860

Feng, Chia-sheng, 87

Festivals, cycle of, 368, 756

Feudalism in Europe, contrasted with absence of, in China, 364–365, 999n2, 1002n21

"Feudatories" (princedoms): reduced by Ming Jianwen emperor, 585–586, 588; compared with Western feudal princedoms, 586; reduced by Ming Chengzu, 606–607, 623; rebellion of, in Qing Kangxi reign, 844–848

Fiction: in late Ming, 774; in Qing 930, 935

Fictive kinship: in interstate relations, 70–71, 118, 196, 202, 251, 307, 379, 380–381, 383, 384–385

Filial piety *(xiao)*, 162, 308, 330, 508, 664; filiality versus loyalty, 665–667; in re Manchu "hair and dress regulations," 832

Fiscal administration: in Northern Song, 112, 117–118, 139, 283; in Jin, 283–284, 286; under Jia Sidao, 319–320; in Southern Song, 361; modes of, under Yuan, 494–495; Ming reforms under Zhang Juzheng, 731–732; census registers in re Ming fiscal management, 746–747, 766; in re imperial clan 781–782; improvedby Qing Yongzheng emperor, 908–911

Five Agents theory, 279, 510

Five Dynasties, 3–23, 39, 44, 62–68, 92–95, 97, 279, 505

Five Dynasties and Ten States: 11, 19, 44; names and dates, 12–16; ended, 100, 106

Floods, 650, 653

Footbinding, 78, 505, 967–968

Four Books, of Neo-Confucianism, 342, 509, 571, 634, 679

"Four-tiered ranking" (or "four social classes," *simin*) in Yuan, 390–391, 489–490, 492–493

"*Four Treasures.*" *See* Encyclopedic compilations

Fugu (returning to antiquity), 99, 146; in Zhu Xi, 345

Fu She (Restoration Society), in late Ming, 779–780, 836

Gaitu guiliu (changing native offices to civil service appointments), 705, 902

Galdan. *See* Dzungaria

Gansu Corridor, 178–179, 186, 259–260, 408; in re Mongol-Tibetan relations, 698, 702

Golden Horde, 409

gongyuan, "the common era" or C.E., 4

Government, structure of: in Northern Song, 109–112, 139–140; in re economic management, 283–284; reconstructed in Southern Song, 293; criticisms of Song government, 335–336; functions analyzed, 337, 359–360; costs of, 359–364; imperial government not omnicompetent, in Ming thought, 592–593, 634; structure and workings of, in Ming, 636–646; weaknesses in Ming bureaucracy, 728–729, 783; in Qing, 892–896

Grand Canal: in Yuan, 525, 532, 535, 557; in Ming and Qing, 621, 646–653, 867

Grand Council (Junji Chu), in Qing, 895, 896, 901, 919, 920–921, 923

Grand Secretaries: in Ming, 575, 600, 625, 641, 643, 659, 661, 667, 669, 1019n19; served under Ming Shizong, 669–672; role of Zhang Juzheng, 724–734; under Ming Sizong, 803; under Qing Shizong, 894

Gratuities paid to officials, regularized by Yongzheng reforms, 909–910

Great Britain: in re Tibet, 878, 937–939; embassy to Qianlong court, 913–914, 961; world's dominant imperial power, 961–962

Great Wall, 62–63, 693, 695, 794, 796, 858; building of, 695–696. *See also* Nine Defense Areas

Great Wall line, 62, 64, 610, 693
Greater Khingan (Da Xing'an) Moun-
    tains, 26, 32, 223, 259, 404
Gu wen (ancient prose), 121, 122, 125,
    130, 153
Gu Yanwu, 801, 852–853, 864, 929
Guo Rong (a.k.a. Chai Rong), 14, 96, 97
Guo Wei, 92–95, 97
Gurkha nation, 937–939
"Gurkhan," title, 205

Hai Jui, 671–672, 724
"Hair and dress" regulations: in Jurchen
    conquest, 228: under Manchus, 828–
    829, 832–833, 847, 1040n28
Hami, 610, 1022n18
"Han" and "non-Han": ethnic terms as
    used today, 28, 173, 176, 268,
    994n3, 1003n4; special meaning in
    Yuan, 490
Han dynasty, as model for Ming, 550,
    564, 566
"Han Learning" in early Qing. *See* Evi-
    dential Learning
Han Linerh ("Young Prince of Radi-
    ance"), 533, 537–538, 552, 558
Han Tuozhou, 312–315, 335, 341, 371
Han Yu, 121, 160
"handles of power" *(quan bing)*, 110,
    297, 397
Hangzhou, 15, 21, 22–23; as Southern
    Song capital, 295, 296–298, 460; as
    recreation site, 367; under Mongols,
    460, 461, 464–465, 502, 537
Hanlin Academy: in Ming, 599–600, 673
Head-shaving command. *See* "Hair and
    dress" regulations
Heaven-man relationship, in Chinese cos-
    mology, 580, 637–639, 1017n21
Heijdra, Martin J., on Ming population
    estimates, 745–747, 1027nn5,6
High culture: of Song, 151–157, 325–
    334; in Jin, 277–279; in Yuan, 507,
    510–511; of late Ming, 769–775; of
    Qing, 922–923, 958–959, 970–971
"High politics," in Southern Song, 307–
    322
Himalaya Mountains, 25, 937, 939
Hong Chengchou, 799, 804–805, 820,
    830, 833, 836, 838
Hongwu reign. *See* Ming dynasty emper-
    ors: Taizu
Horological science, 577–578

Horse, defined nomad mobility, 410–411
Households: ratios to individuals, 353;
    registration categories of, in Song,
    365–366, 367; household registra-
    tion system, Yuan, 495–497; house-
    hold registers in re Ming taxation,
    746–747, 748, in re family's native
    place, 764; in re Qing taxation, 910,
    918–919
Huai River, 198, 227, 286, 301, 304,
    315, 362, 504, 530, 532–533, 556,
    571, 646, 648, 649
Huang Zongxi, 801, 835–837, 852–853,
    866, 929
Huangdi, translated "emperor," 98, 182–
    183, 983n7
Human rights, in Ming China, 754
Hunting, in tribal life, 238, 241
Hydraulics: works projects, 511, 532,
    547, 646–653, 867

Ideal and actual patterns, 72, 368–369,
    376, 378, 947
Il-khanate. *See* Persia
Impeachment: improper uses of, 728–
    729, 733, 778
Imperial clan members: in Song, 348–
    349; in Ming, 565–566; size of, in
    late Ming, 781–782; in Qing, 879–
    880, 883–886, 888–889, 899, 915
    See also Ming imperial clan
Imperial institution, Chinese, 40, 54–55,
    81, 179, 232, 234, 238, 396–397,
    398, 459, 965; checks on, in Ming,
    637–639; weaknesses recognized, by
    Ming thinkers, 672; Wang Yang-
    ming's disillusionment with, 682–
    684; weaknesses of, in late Ming, 742
"Imperialism." *See* "Empire," concept of
Imports: in Jin-Song period, 287; in
    Southern Song, 393–394
Incense-burning ceremonies, 529–530,
    533, 548
Indemnified peace. *See* Treaties
Industry, in Song, 363. *See also* Iron and
    steel
Infanticide, 155
Inner Asia: defined, 23–30, 36; as dimen-
    sion of Chinese history, 5–9, 394–
    399; transformed by Mongols, 403–
    404; ethnic geography in twelfth
    century, 406–410; administrative
    modes, 519; trade routes, 610;

absorbed into Manchu/Qing empire, 857, 868–876, 914, 936, 953

Inner Court: Southern Song, 317; Ming, 625, 732; strengthened in Qing Shunzhi reign, 893–895

Inner Mongolia, 24, 25, 609, 688–689, 690, 875. *See also* Mongolia

Institutes of Zhou (Zhou Guan, Zhou Li), 139, 591, 593

"Institutional lag," 20. *See also* Renovating change

Intellectual independence of scholar-elite, 311

International law, Western, 377–378, 379–380, 384, 962; in re boundaries, 709–710, 1044n23, 1046n38

Interstate relations, 35, 61–62, 118, 183, 196, 251–252, 284–285; pre-Mongol patterns of, 377–379, 386; under Mongols, 437; under Ming, 611–617, 685–686; in Qing period, 913–914, 962. *See also* Ritualized interstate relations; Tribute system of interstate relations

Iron and steel, 41, 213, 214, 286; production levels, in Song, 363

Irrigation, in Xia state, 257

Islam, 83, 261, 408, 440, 950; conversion of Mongols, 442; contacts with Islamic lands, in Yuan, 510–511; in re Ming maritime expeditions, 614; in Ming, 698; in Yunnan, Ming/ Qing, 711

Japan, Japanese: 34, 60; Mongol invasions, 466–467; Buddhist contacts with, in Yuan, 502–503; Ashikaga shogunate, relations with Ming, 613; Japanese pirates, 671, 672, 720, 759; invasion of mainland under Hideyoshi, 735, 786; links to Koxinga, 835

Jasagh (Yasa), 423–424, 434, 439

Jesuit order in China, 722, 857, 917, 937, 951–952, 959–961, 963

Jews, 83; in Yuan China, 484–485, 501; in China generally, 950

Jia Sidao, 318–320, 461, 463

Jianzhou Jurchens (Manchus). *See* Manchu nation

Jiedushi. *See* Regional Military Governors

Jin (Gold) dynasty: rise of, 194–195; conquest of the Liao, 195–196, 199–202; conquest of the Song, 196–199, 206–210, 289–298; puppet regimes, 198, 227, 301; post-conquest political developments, 222–243, 271–277; turned away from steppe, 223, 228–229; four periods of, 225; capital moved into China, 233–235, 244; rebellions, 235–236, 237; Mongol invasions, 243–248; relations with Xia, 250–251, wealth of, 285–286; later Jurchen/Manchu "Jin" dynasty, 788–790

Jin emperors, and imperial family: Taizu (Aguda), 194–195, 219–220; Taizong (Wuqimai), 195–196, 220–221, 225–229, 290; Prince Hailing, 232–236, 274, 303, 459; Shizong, 236–241, 274, 499; Zhangzong, 241–243, 278–279, 280, 499; last rulers, 244–248

Jinhua, school of Neo-Confucian studies, 557, 579–580; critical of Yuan governing, 580; influence on Ming Taizu, 580–581, 1012n10; and Fang Xiaoru, 592

Jinshi degree, 80, 129–130, 134, 156, 273, 491, 572

Juangyuan, 129–130

Jurchen/Manchu tribes of sixteenth–seventeenth centuries. *See* Manchu *entries*

Jurchens, 35, 91; emerge into history, 211–216; "cultural style," 219–220, 222, 269–270; changing social factors, 222–225, 227–229; "Great Migration," 224–225, 229, 233, 235; ideal of landowning, 229; Chinese feelings toward, 268; impact of invasions on elite lives, 328–330. *See also* Jin (Gold) dynasty; *Meng'anmouke* organization system

Juren, examination degree, 129

Kahn, Paul (translator), xvii, 1004n14

Kaifeng (Bian), 17, 19, 21, 39, 66, 166, 649; as Jin Southern Capital, 235, 245, 248; as Song city, 367, 567; Yuan rebel base, 538; as Ming "Northern Capital," 568

Kara Khitai (Western Liao), 198, 205–206, 246, 250, 407–408, 428, 429

Karakorum, 412, 435, 447, 448, 449, 454, 456, 465; superseded by Dadu, 457–458, 466, 536; in early Ming, 610, 687

Keju. See Civil service
Khaghan (title), 38, 435
Khan (title), 37–38, 786, 789, 871
Khanate: in Liao, 54–55. *See also* Mongol khanates
Khingan mountains. *See* Greater Khingan
Khitans, 8, 31–44, 75–76, 87, 91, 405; under Jurchens, 228, 235, 237, 239–240, 244, 245; multi-tribal empire, 49–71, 404; state and culture, compared with Mongols, 412–413, 422, 426. *See also* Liao dynasty
Khubilai Khan. *See* Yuan dynasty rulers
Khuriltai, 39, 425, 455; of 1206, 425–426; of 1219, 429; of 1235, 435; of 1241, 439; of 1246, 439; of 1249, 439, 447; of 1260, 442, 455; planned for 1267, 465
Kiakhta (Kiachta), Treaties of, 874, 901
Kinship, 75, 118, 159
Kirghiz, 32, 36, 407, 408
Kökö Temür, 522–523, 535–536, 539
Korea, Koreans: 33, 34, 36, 61, 86, 537; relations with Liao, 60–62, 200; with Song and Jin, 113, 212; in ritualized interstate relations, 380, 381–382; Yi dynasty (Chôsen), relations with Ming, 612–613, 625; expedition to defend, in 1590s, 735
Koryô Kingdom. *See* Korea, Koreans
Kozlov, Colonel P. K., 263–264

Lady Wan, 630–634, 644–645
Lamaism. *See* Tibetan transmission of Buddhism
Landholding interests, 318, 319; absentee landlords, 765, 768–769
Landowning, 365; in re taxation, 746–747
Later Zhou dynasty, 13–14, 67–68, 92–98
Lattimore, Owen, 25, 90
Law: in Liao, 73–74, 279–280; in Zhu Xi's thought, 335–346; conceptions of, 379–380; compared with *li*, ritual, 379–380, 387–389; transcendant, in Western traditions, 387; China and West compared, 387–389, 637, 1003n14; customary law (Jasagh) of Mongols, 424, 569; inequities of, in Yuan, 489–490; Great Ming Code, 570, 582, 759–760; emperor sole source of, 636–637; statutory codes and regulations, 637

Legalism: as pejorative term, 140; statecraft tradition, 181, 182, 189; as favorable term, 336
Legitimacy, dynastic. *See* Mandate of Heaven
Levies: military, 255; precious metals and other commodities, 362; labor (corvée), commuted to silver in late Ming, 731, 753; system revised, in Qing, 908–910, 919
Levirate, among non-Chinese, 76, 446
Li Gang, 292–293
Li Keyong, 6, 10, 12–13, 38, 44, 63
Li Qingzhao, 328–330, 350
Li Yuanhao. *See* Yuanhao
Li Zanhua. *See* Bei, Prince
Li Zicheng, 589, 796, 798–801, 814–819, 829
Liao dynasty, 8, 29, 39; dynasty proclaimed, 65–66; rulers, 53; rebellions, 40–41, 56, 88; succession crises, 49–56; expansion into North China, 65–67; civilization, 72–91; fall of, 195–196, 199–205; highpoint of, 199–200. *See also* Khitans
Liao empire: structure, 49–71, 404; relations with Korea, 60–62; relations with Song, 68–71, 112, 115–117, 138; relations with Xia, 176–177
Liao and Jin institutions compared, 216–217
Liao (Western Liao) River, 409, 789
Liaodong, in late Ming, 789, 791–795
Lifan Yuan. *See* Mongolian Affairs Office
Lineage. *See* Family
Literacy: non-Chinese, 44, 78–79, 395–396, 407, 408, 424, 493; among Chinese, 325; among women, 328, 330, 350, 941; functions of, 395–396, 424; in re officeholders, in Yuan, 489, 493; encouraged by Wang Yangming school, 680, 681; in Qing, in re Buddhism in Mongolia, 690; demanded of native leaders in south, 705–706; increase of, in Qing, 941
Literary arts: 156, 276–277; value equal to classical studies, 278; heritage of Chinese, 396; literary output, in Yuan, 504–505; Ming Taizu suspicious of, 578–579; late Ming flowering of, 769–771, 773–774
Literary inquisition: early Ming, 579; in Qing, 865, 922, 925–928

Literary societies *(wen she)*, late Ming, 770, 778–781

Literary thought, 122–123; in Ming period, 772–774

"Little (Young) Prince of Radiance." *See* Han Linerh

Liu Bingzhong, 449, 452, 457, 458

Liu Ji, 558, 570, 580–581

"Liu Kou." See Roving Bandits of late Ming

"Living Buddhas," in Tibet and Mongolia, 690, 871, 874, 875. *See also* Dalai Lamas

Lixue (school of reason or principle), 135, 144–145, 278, 316, 333, 335, 338, 340–346, 601–602, 676–677, 737, 929, 931, 968

Local cultures, 266, 269–270

Local and regional government: in Song, 137, 139, 325, 354–359; comparisons, 359, 487, 491; structure of, in Yuan, 487–489, 518; local defense measures, in late Yuan, 524; in Ming, 639, 750–754, 796; in Qing, 918–919, 943–946. *See also* Community

Loess soils, 649

"Low culture," 281

Loyalists: Yuan, 522–524; response to Ming usurpation, 588–590; end of Ming, 835–836, 837–840; Ming loyalism in early Qing, 850–852; punishment of, 864–865; in re *Ming History,* 866; intimidation of Ming loyalists, in Qing, 897–900, 926–927

Loyalty *(zhong),* 162, 311, 512, 560; loyalty in re filiality, 665–667, 922, 1052n27

Lü Liuliang case, in Qing Shunzhi reign, 898–900

Lu Xiangshan (Lu Jiuyuan), 339–340, 676–677, 678, 929

Lu You, 315; observations of ordinary lives, 370–374

Luoyang, 17, 21, 147, 328, 367

Lyric poetry *(ci),* 21–22, 122, 153; attributed to Yue Fei, 305; of Li Qingzhao, 329–330; of Guan Yunshi, 508–509; in Yuan, 511

Macao: founded, 721–722; place in trade, 767, 963–964

Magistrates: duties defined, 355–358,

750–751, 757, 761, 943–946. *See also Yamen*

Maitreyan doctrines, 502, 528–530, 540, 548

"Major Reforms" of Wang Anshi, 126, 138–144, 326–327, 334–335, 591; opposition to, 153, 154, 207; reinstatement of, 142–143, 207; evaluation of, 143–144; discredited in Southern Song, 293; compared with Jia Sidao, 319; influence on Zhu Xi, 345

"Man (people) of the steppe" concept, 31–32, 34, 91, 170, 408, 476

Manchu banner system, 218, 689, 787–788, 824; banner lands in China, 857–862; factions based in, 879–881; bureaucratized by Yongzheng emperor, 893

Manchu nation: emerges from Jurchens, 687, 689; rise of Nurhaci, 735, 785–790; cut off from farming and other non-military pursuits, 860, 862; migration into China, 862; Manchu virtues, 916–917, 921. *See also* Qing dynasty

Manchuria (the Northeast, Dongbei), 26, 33, 44, 409, 859

Mandate of Heaven *(Tian ming),* 8–10; defined, 102; claimed by non-Chinese, 81, 182; debates over, in Jin, 278–279; claimed by Southern Song, 292; in re ritual correctness, 359; claimed by Yuan emperors, 460, 506, 519–520; in re historiography, in Yuan, 510; in Ming founding, 553, 559; in Qing, 819, 861–862, 900

Manichean religion, 35, 83, 261, 408, 501, 528–530, 533, 540, 558

Mao Zedong, 189, 672

Maps, xiii, 11, 18, 24, 58, 111, 171, 230, 294, 356, 406, 430, 486, 531, 640, 648, 694, 699, 704, 718, 872, 944

Markets, market towns: 165, 283; periodic markets, 755

Maritime trade and transport: in tenth century, 18, 392; in Yuan, 526; Zheng He's expeditions, 613–617, 652, 719; Ming China as maritime power, 717–722; European role in Ming China's maritime trade, 767–768, 950

Marriage: in Khitan society, 75–76; companionate, 328–329, 369, 513, 770; arranged, 369; elite-merchant family intermarriage, 348, 764; rituals of, 369; in re incest taboo, 369, 412, 755; among Mongols, 412

Mathematics, 147, 151, 326–327, 510–511, 746, 747, 1028n11

"Mean people" ("base people," *jianmin*), 128–129, 152, 366, 907

Medical knowledge and pharmacology, 326, 347, 510, 757

Memorials, for submission to the emperor: Ming, 642–644; secret memorials, in Qing, 883–884, 889–891

Mencius, 334, 335, 336, 342, 562, 592, 682, 922, 933

Meng'an-mouke organization system, of Jurchens, 217–219, 224, 239–241, 242, 271

Merchants: relations with elite in Song, 347, 348; place of, in society, 391; social value of, in thought of Wang Yangming, 683; in Ming society, 764–765

Meritocracy, 332, 349

Messianic doctrines. *See* Religions

Miao tribespeople, 673

Militarization of society: in fourteenth century, 521–522, 554; unarmed society of rural Ming China, 757–759

Military arts: Yue Fei's training in, 300; in founding of Ming, 554–556, studied by Wang Yangming, 674, 675

Military, component of government: in Song, 112–116, 137–138; in Xia, 181–182, in Jin, 271–272; size of, in Song, 360; in Yuan, 479–482; in Ming, reformed under Zhang Juzheng, 730–731; at end of Ming, 794, 806–807

Military classics, 554, 927

Military Governors. *See* Regional Military Governors

Military heroes in history: Guan Yu, 304; Yue Fei, 304–305

Military households: in Yuan, 481, 534; in Ming, 731

Military profession, status of: in Song, 346; in Yuan, 480–482; in China generally, 524; in Ming, 727

Military threat, from the West, 961–963, 964

Millenarian movements, 518. *See also* Religions

Mind, school of. See *Xinxue*

Mines, taxes on, in Wanli reign, 735, 739

Ming dynasty: role of military in founding, 552, 557–561; name explained, 558–559; new dynasty proclaimed, 563–564; princedoms unlike European feudalism, 565, 585, 606, 727; "Central Capital" built, 567–568; purges in early Ming, 573; civil war and usurpation, 585–586, 596–597; purges of Jianwen loyalists, 587–591, 599; "second founding," 598–599; capital moved to Beijing, 617, 618–619; tensions between throne and bureaucracy, 658, 661–662, 663–668; the Ming founder's warning against imperialist expansion, 686; non-Chinese peoples within Ming China, 686, 702–717

Ming dynasty emperors and imperial family:

Taizu (Zhu Yuanzhang, Hongwu), 530, 538; youth of, 541–548; reign of, 549–582; elite advisors, 550–552; "Ancestral Injunctions," in re imperial sons and heirs, 565–566, 585, 587, 606–607; enigma of his personality, 575–582

Empress Ma, 550, 569, 579, 594, 618

Hui-di (Zhu Yunwen, Jianwen), 584–586, 615; legends about, 589–590, 615

Chengzu (Zhu Di, Yongle), 464, 594–621, 695

Empress Xu, 595, 596

Renzong (Zhu Gaozhi, Hongxi), 622–623

Xuanzong (Zhu Zhanji, Xuande), 611, 622–626

Yingzong (Zhu Qizhen, Zhengtong/Tianshun), 611, 626–630

Jing Di (Zhu Qiyu, Jingtai), 628–629

Xianzong (Zhu Jianshen, Chenghua), 630–634

Lady Wan, 630–634

Xiaozong (Zhu Youtang, Hongzhi), 631, 634–636

Wuzong (Zhu Houzhao, Zhengde), 655–658

Shizong (Zhu Houcong, Jiajing), 658–672

Muzong (Zhu Zaihou, Longqing),
723–727
Shenzong (Zhu Yijun, Wanli), 727–740
Guangzong (Zhu Changluo, Taichang),
740–741
Xizong (Zhu Youjiao, Tianqi), 741–
742
Sizong (Zhu Youjian, Chongzhen),
777–810, 813–815
Ming government: structure, 569, 570,
572–575; found unworkable by Taizu's successors, 585; staffing, 570–
572; eunuchs, 575; reforms planned
by Fang Xiaoru, 593; functions modified by Chengzu, 599–601; early border relations, 607–608; general analysis of, 636–646; *tusi* system stressed
control, not governing, 717; reactions against governing of Emperor
Shizong, 723–726; weaknesses of system in decline, 728–729, 742; Zhang
Juzheng's administrative reforms,
730–732
Ming History, compilation of, as political
device, 865–867
Ming imperial clan, 564–566, 584, 585–
586, 587, 590, 594–595, 606–607,
618, 655, 661, 781–782; rebellions
from within, 623, 656, 657–658,
675; governing of princely establishments reformed, 726; lack of normal
family life, 727–728; numbers of,
781–782
Ming Yuzhen, 539–540, 714
"Minor Reforms" of 1040s, 123, 136–
138, 334–335
Minority peoples in Ming, 675–676; in
South China, 702–717
Mobility, social, 128–129, 131–135,
331–332, 367, 557, 572
Monasteries: in Mongol society, 690; in
re governing of Tibet, 690
Money: taxes collected in cash, in Song,
363; in Ming, 731; forms of, in
Song, 363–364; in Ming, 766–768,
806. *See also* Currency
Mongol emperors. *See* Yuan dynasty
Mongol khanates, 428, 429, 435, 440,
441, 442–443, 447, 457, 465–466,
470, 535, 609–610, 687
Mongol khans, pre-Yuan:
Chinggis Khan, 243–244, 246–248;
death of, 256, 403; life of, 414–424;

military leadership, 423, 426; governing decrees become common law
(Jasagh), 423–424, 434; his sons,
428, 432–433, 434–435, 445; place
in history, 434, 445; religious beliefs,
500
Ögödei Khan, 434–437, 447; non-Mongol advisors, 438–439
Güyük Khan, 447
Möngke Khan, 439–440, 441, 442,
446; roles assigned his brothers,
439–441, relations with Khubilai,
454–455; death, 455
Khubilai Khan, 443, 444–469
See also Yuan dynasty rulers
Mongol military, pre-Yuan and Yuan:
campaigns, 419–422; attacks on Jin,
243–248, 283, 435; on Xia, 243,
246, 254–257; consequences of conquest, compared, 246–247, 375–
376, 386, 436, 450, 476; decimal
units adopted, 420, 421, 423, 475,
787; size and organization, 426–428;
three campaigns to West, 428–433,
434–436, 439–441, 447; conquest of
Korea, 435; campaigns in China,
436–437; appanages, 446, 450–451,
481; "hereditary lords" in China,
449–450, 454, 476; equivalent to
government, 475; at end of Yuan
dynasty, 535
Mongol military forces: serving under
Ming, 586, 596, 608, 609–610, 687,
691, 784–785; serving under Qing,
860–861, 869–873
Mongol peoples: emergence of, 8, 34, 81,
140, 403–410; formation of nation,
405, 421–422; social order, 409,
410–413; compared with Khitans,
Jurchens, 412–413, 422, 426, 475–
476; founding legend, 412–413; governing emerges, 422–423, 474–475;
Mongol identity, in re Jasagh, 424,
434. *See also* Yuan dynasty
Mongol rule in China. *See* Yuan dynasty
Mongolia, 25, 29, 32, 35; nation created
by Chinggis Khan, 426, 472, 475,
609; khanate of, 444; threat to Ming
China, 606, 608, 609, 672, 685;
Ming Chengzu's campaigns against,
608–611; Xuanzong's skirmishes
against, 623; Esen's control over,
627; legends about Mongol-Ming

Mongolia *(cont.)*
history, 688; Chinese living in, 690–
691; Ming Chinese ignorance of,
692; late Ming Mongol-Jurchen relations, 785–788; Qing control over,
868–876, 1004n1
Mongolian Affairs Office (of Qing government), 873
Mongolian hearthland, 246, 435, 443,
469, 609
Mongols in Ming and Qing periods,
609–611, 687–697, 701
Monks, Buddhist: roles of, 82, 161–162,
263; Tibetan, 472, 501–502, 520,
700; Ming Taizu's life as, 545–548;
in re martial arts, 555; Daoyan, advi-
sor to Ming Chengzu, 588; on Ming
court payroll, 645; monkhood, in
Mongol society, 690
Monopolies and franchises, in Song,
362–363
Monotheism, 83
Music: in re *ci* poetry, 22; in re Jin and
Yuan drama, 281

Nabo conferences (Liao), 89
Nanjing, 14, 21, 22, 301, 329, 464; as
Ming capital, 523, 530, 550–551,
557, 566–568; planning and layout,
568; Ming secondary capital, 598–
599, 619, 657, 763, 806; falls to
Manchus, 831, 832, 1012n23
Nanzhao state, 16, 453, 979n10
Nationalism, 104, 176, 268, 278, 307,
336, 341, 914, 997n25, 1051n6
"Native peoples" (non-Han, non-Chinese)
of South China, 703–717; treatment
of, in China, compared with West,
710; in Qing, 902–903
"Nativist reactions": among Tanguts,
180–181, 183, 187–188, 189–190,
260; in Jin, 236–243, 253; in Qing
period, 842, 916–917
Nature *(Tian)*, 147–148, 160
Navies, naval warfare: Song, 233, 302,
371–372; used by Yuan, 460, 461–
462, 650–651; in late Yuan uprisings, 539; in Ming founding, 526,
556–557; Zheng He's voyages, 613–
617, 719 *See also* Shipbuilding
Navigation science, 326, 719
Needham, Joseph, 325–326

Neige (cabinet). *See* Grand Secretaries
Neo-Confucianism: in Northern Song,
144–149; of Su Shi, 155–156; provided context of political discourse,
311–312; in Southern Song, 333–
350, 337–338; pedagogical system of
(Zhu Xi), 342–343; changing impact
on women, 343–344; and "Confucianization" of society, 343; weakness
of political thought, 344, 592; statecraft of, in early Ming, 579–581,
592–593; Neo-Confucian *Lixue*, in
Ming, 601–602, 854; Neo-Confucian
fundamentalism, 635; reinterpreted
by Wang Yangming, 674–675,
676–679; flourished in mid-Qing,
928
Nepal. *See* Gurkha nation
Nerchinsk, Treaty of, 874, 875
Nestorians. *See* Christianity
"New beginnings" *(gengshi)* concept, 99,
102, 110
"New culture of Song," 98, 119, 121–
122, 132–134, 144, 311–312, 323–
324, 368
"New men." *See* mobility, social
"New Policies" *(Xin fa). See* "Major
Reforms"
"Nine Chief Ministers," 643–644
Nine Defense Areas, in Ming, 611, 693–
696
Nomadism, 76–77, 404; in re Tanguts,
259; in re Mongols, 410–413,
1004n6; in re loss of mobility,
among Mongols after sixteenth cen-
tury, 690, 787
Nomads, of Inner Asian Steppe, 27–29,
32, 36
"*Nong*." *See* Farmers, status of
Normative factors, in society, 521, 522,
525, 965, 969; impacted by popular
religions, 429; role of, in local society, 751–752, 760; encouraged by
Qing reforms, 909
North-South divide in history, 265–267,
270–271, 283, 321; in re population,
353–354; in re Yuan cultural life,
507–508, 512; in re factions at
Kangxi era court, 881–883
Northeast. *See* Manchuria
Northern/Southern Chinese characteristics, 299–300, 303, 321–322, 561,
881–882

Northern Chancellery (Liao), 39, 83, 88–89

"Northern Cultural Style," 270, 277, 881

Northern Han state, 16, 67–69, 95; extinguished, 106, 112

"Nothingness (emptiness)," Buddhist philosophical concept, 148, 342

Nuns, Buddhist, 82, 162

Nurhaci. *See* Manchu nation

Nurkal (Nu'ergan) Jurchens, in Ming, 608, 609

Oases, in Xinjiang, 26–27, 35, 408

Oaths, in interstate relations, 308, 381, 382

Occupations: basis of household registration, in Yuan, 495–497, 503. *See also* Households

Office of Transmission: in Ming, 642–646; in Qing, 883, 889

Officials: *(guan)* status, 152, 348, 358; numbers of, in Song, 360; salaries and benefits, in Song, 360–361; life of a midlevel official in Song, 372; numbers of, in Yuan, 489; "by direct appointment" *(chuanfeng)* in Ming, 645, 662

"Open society" ethos, 497, 503, 754, 967

Ordos desert, 170–171, 172, 186, 259, 695

"Organismic, self-generating cosmos," 342; compared with natural law, 388

Orthodoxy, Confucian, 159; defined in Southern Song, 314, 316–317, 1032n4; as observed, in Ming, 601–602, 682; orthodox learning in re ethical norms, 679, 779; in early Qing, 854; in re Dai Zhen's thought, 934

Outer Court: Southern Song, 317; versus Inner Court, in Ming, 590, 640–641

Outer Mongolia, 24, 25, 609, 688, 690, 875. *See also* Mongolia

Ouyang Xiu: career of, 119–126, 879, 881; as historian, 125; as thinker, 135–136

Overseas Chinese, 953–954, 967

Oyirat (Western) Mongols, 407, 610, 627, 688, 698, 870–872, 1021n5

Painting and painters, 22; "literatus" (amateur), 155; by Buddhist monks, 161; by emperors, 208, 625; Qing imperial portraits by Castiglione, 891

Pamir Mountains, 23, 25, 408, 428, 870

Panchen Lamas. *See* Banchen Lama

"Paper flow" in re political power, 642–646, 890

Parhae nation. *See* Bohai

Peace party. *See* Factions

"Peasant," term not suitable for Chinese farmers, 365, 390, 969, 1003n18

Pedagogy, system of, in Zhu Xi, 342–343

Peng Yingyu ("Monk Peng"), 530, 538, 546, 558

"People of the steppe." *See* "Man of the steppe"

Persia, 428, 429, 443, 528; Il-khanate of, 440–441, 442, 452, 463, 464, 510–511

Phagspa, 483–484, 501, 877

Pilgrimages, 368

Piracy, 526, 651–652, 719–721; pirate entrepreneurs, in late Ming, 721

Poets and poetry, 152, 277–278; "patriotic poets" in Song, 315; women, 330, 513; in Yuan, 511–513; poetry of Ming loyalists, 851–852; of Qianlong emperor, 916

Political thought: in Northern Song, 135–144; in Zhu Xi, 344; of Jinhua School, in late Yuan, 579–581; of Fang Xiaoru, 591–594; of Wang Yangming, 682–684; late Ming, 737, 779. *See also* Utilitarian political thought

Polo, Marco, 367, 444, 457, 461, 490, 762, 950, 951, 1005n1

Popular religions. *See* religions

Population: Inner Asia, 26; Song China, 164, 266; of Jurchens, 224, 228, 243; China during Song and Jin dynasties, 266, 351–354, 461; comparisons with West, 351–353, 744, 745; causes of increase-decrease, 353–354; of Mongols, 426–427, 450, 458; of Yuan period, 503–504; estimates for Ming period, 743–747; distribution of, in Ming, 747–750; growth of, in Qing, 903–906, 919; implications of Qing growth, 941–943

Porcelain Pagoda, at Nanjing, 617–618

Portuguese, 672, 720–721, 962–963; first European ambassador to China, 721

Prefectures, and counties. *See* Local and
  regional government
Primogeniture: in Chinese society, 75;
  adopted in tribal societies, 40–41,
  54, 55, 76
Principle, school of. *See* Lixue
Printing: from engraved woodblocks, 7–
  8, 21, 85–86; from movable type,
  326; in Tangut script, 256–257;
  books in print, Song, 325; in Yuan,
  511; palace editions, in Ming, 601
Prisons, at Ming capital, 605, 627, 656
"Protection." *See* Yin privilege
Provinces *(sheng)*, 355; in Yuan *(xingsheng)*, 485–486; *sheng*, in Ming,
  639, 640, 750–751; in Qing, 943–945
Psychic mobility," 32, 476, 980n2
"Public lands" *(gongtian)*, 320

Qiang peoples, 169–170, 258, 263, 698,
  990nn2,3, 1022n27
Qin: First Emperor of, 274; Qin dynasty,
  334, 337, 574
Qin Gui, 299, 303–305, 331, 340, 344, 730
Qing dynasty, 63; intervention in Tibet,
  702, 937–939; attitudes toward
  Ming dynasty, 771, 926–927; dynastic "style" established, 818, 820–
  821, 862; offensive against Southern
  Ming, 827–840; Manchu tribal interests, 843; creation of the Manchu/
  Qing empire, 856–857, 902; role of
  military, 860–861, 869, 935–936;
  governing institutions, 863, 892–897,
  918–919; reliance on Mongol military, 868–870; "high Qing" era, 940
Qing (Manchu) emperors and imperial
  family: Nurhaci, 784–790; Hung
  Taiji (Abahai), 790, 791–792, 795,
  805, 808, 815, 821; Prince-regent
  Dorgon, 808, 813, 816–823, 827–
  829, 837; Shizu (Fulin, Shunzhi),
  821–824, 837; Oboi, 842–844, 865,
  880; Shengzu (Xuanye, Kangxi), 823,
  840, 841–886; Shizu (Yinzhen, Yongzheng), 884–885, 887–911; Gaozong
  (Hongli, Qianlong), 912–948, 961,
  962; Renzong (Yongyan, Jiaqing), 940
Qiu Chuji (Changchun), 433, 437–438,
  484, 499–500

Rabban Sauma, 484
Ratchnevsky, Paul, 433

Rationalism, Neo-Confucian. See *Lixue*
"Rebel," defined in re "bandit," 758–759
Red Turbans, 523, 530–533, 537–541,
  546–548, 549–560; elite disdain for,
  552, 558; Ming Taizu's break with,
  558–559, 560
Reform movements: literary and political,
  122–123, 135–144; discredited in
  Southern Song, 293; in late Ming,
  736–738
Regencies, 626, 821, 842–843. *See also*
  Empresses and dowager empresses
Regional cultural variations, in Jin–South-
  ern Song, 266
Regional Military Commanders (*Zong-
  bing, Dusi,* etc.): as warlords, in late
  Yuan, 487, 522, 524, 533–537; in
  Ming, 611, 695, 697
Regional Military Governors (*Jiedushi*),
  19–20, 38, 63, 69, 95; in early Song,
  103, 112, 354; title granted to Tangut leaders, 171, 172; title granted to
  Jurchen leaders, 213; in Song, 290
Reign-period names, 41, 81, 182, 525,
  564, 661, 740–741
Relationship (including kinship), degrees
  of, 589
Religions: in China, 6, 98; in Khitan society, 82–83; in Song life, 145, 157–
  160; in Xia, 261–262; popular sects,
  301–302; at Yuan court, 458–459;
  under Bureau of Buddhist and
  Tibetan Affairs, in Yuan, 483–484;
  Yuan supervision of religions, 484–
  485, 497–502; popular religions in
  late Yuan, 520, 526–529, 537–541;
  in Ming village life, 755–756, 758;
  in society, generally, 958–959, 968–
  969. *See also* Buddhism; Christianity;
  Daoism; Islam
Ren (benevolence, humaneness), in Neo-
  Confucianism, 342, 673
Renovating change, 126, 130, 513, 965–
  966
"Reservoir" metaphor (Lattimore), 90,
  229, 241, 258
"Restoration Society." *See* Fu She
Revealed religions, compared with Chinese religions, 528
Ricci, Matteo, 617, 763, 823, 951, 963,
  1055n4
Rites Controversy, of Ming Jiajing reign,
  663–668

Ritual *(li)*: among Chinese, 97, 98, 160, 369, 383–384, 559; adopted by tribal societies, 41, 383; providing norms of diplomacy, 118, 251, 379, 380–381; in re Ministry of Rites, 359; ritual experts, at Yuan court, 482; "ritual purists" at Ming court, in re Rites Controversy, 663

Ritual, functions compared with law, 379, 387–388

Ritualized interstate relations, 378–383, functioning beyond China, 383, 386; Chinese *vs.* non-Chinese interests served, 384–386; compared with law, 387–389; theoretical underpinnings of, 388–389

"Rival contenders," at end of Yuan, 517, 533–541, 553

Roving Bandits of late Ming, 795–801, 813–815, 817–818, 829. *See also* Li Zicheng; Zhang Xianzhong

Rozman, Gilbert, 164–165

Rural sector, 367–368; in Ming, 750–760

Russia: in re Mongols, 429, 430, 432, 434, 435–436, 442; as challenge to Manchu empire, 871–874, 878–879

Saeki, Tomi, 368

Salary reform, for government officials, in Qing, 909–910

Salt, production and distribution: in Song, 362–363; in late Yuan, 525

Sangha, in Song, 162

Sanskrit, translation from, 162–163

Schall von Bell, Adam, S.J., 823

Scholar-general ideal, 300, 301, 305, 346

Scholar-officials: dominant during and post-Song, 311–312, 314, 320–322, 333–334; *guan* status of, 347–348; Ming Taizu's suspicions of, 578–579; relations with Jianwen emperor, 584–586, 591–594; their validation of dynasty necessary, 591; high morale of, in Ming, 592, 633; roles of, enlarged by Ming Chengzu, 599–602; involvement in Rites Controversy, 664–668

Schools: village or temple, 129, 300, 372–373, 543, 755; government, 129, 141, 159, 273, 274, 330, 331; Confucian school system of Ming, 571–572; private, 159–160, 274, 763; palace school for eunuchs, Ming,

603; for non-Chinese native peoples, 903; palace school in Qing, 915

Science and technology, 151, 325–328; Chinese and Western compared, 327; Zhu Xi's negative influence on, 345; in Yuan, 483, 510–511, 578; scientific thought from West, 854, 959–960; "scientific method" in Qing thought, 934

Scripts, alphabetic, 35, 43, 180, 395, 407, 424, 438, 446, 1003n21; Phagspa script, 483–484, 786–787

Scripts, non-alphabetic, 42–43, 78–79, 180–181, 219, 238, 256–257, 263–264, 395–396, 787

Secret History of the Mongols, 412, 413–414; quoted, 416, 418, 420–421

Secret societies, 529, 928

Sect, meanings of, 526–527

Sectarian uprisings: suppressed by Yue Fei, 301–302; of fourteenth century, 518, 522, 525, 526–533, 537–541. *See also* Red Turbans

Sedition, fear of, in Qing period, 850, 864–865, 887, 888, 920–922, 925–928

Semu, 490, 493–494, 501, 506. *See also* Central Asian advisors in Yuan

Sex: techniques, 645, 668; sexual exhaustion cause of death, 740; sexual excesses of Qing elite, 885–886; sexually explicit writings, 927

Shamanism: Khitan, 82–83; Jurchen, 212; Mongols, 419, 501, 690

Shangdu (Yuan), 444, 457, 537

Shanhai Guan, 62, 806, 815–817

Shanyuan, Treaty of, 70–71, 115–117, 123–124, 178, 199, 380, 385

Shatuo Turks, 6, 10, 36, 38–39, 63, 66, 68, 93, 106

Shen Gua, 325–328

Shi Kefa, 826–827, 831

Shi Miyuan, and Shi family, 315–316, 330–332, 999n17

Shipbuilding: by Jin and Yuan, 233; in Ming, 614–615, 652, 719, 950, 1016n23

Siberia, Colonial Office for (in Russian government), 873

Silk Roads, 6, 26, 36, 408, 528

Silla (Korea), 36, 44

Silver: in Ming and Qing China, 767–768, 954–956

"Single-career elite," 333
"Single-whip" tax reforms, late Ming, 731, 908
Sinification, 44; in Xia, 187–190, 252, 261, 263. *See also* Acculturation
Sinkiang (Chinese Turkestan). *See* Xinjiang
Six Ministries, 42
Sixteen Prefectures, 13, 41, 65, 67–69, 89, 106–108, 112, 114, 195, 196, 201, 208–209, 249, 450
Slavery: in Jurchen society, 196, 224; mistranslation of Chinese status terms, 366; among Mongols, 411, 417, 419, 422, 438, 448, 450–451; imposed on Chinese by Manchus, 787, 858–860, 926
Smallpox, 757, 823, 1039n12
Smuggling, 286–287, 362, 525, 526, 562, 962
Social disorders, in Ming rural life, 757
Social statuses, 132, 152–153, 271–274, 324, 364–366, 390–391; "four-tiered system" in Yuan, 489–491, 492–493; in re "open society," 497, 754
"Son of Heaven." *See* Emperorship in China
Song dynasty: founding of, compared with Later Zhou, 72–78; revenues of, 116–118; fall of Northern Song, 196–198, 206–210, 290–291; "alliance conducted at sea" (with Jurchens), 208–210; military resistance policy in Southern Song, 290–291; Song political style, 311–312, 315, 318–319, 321–322, 581; scope of bureaucracy enlarged, 320–322; elite characteristics and roles, 323–350
Song dynasty emperors and imperial family: *Northern Song:* Zhenzong, 114, 116; Shenzong, 126, 139, 142, 144; Huizong, 142, 196, 197, 207–208, 210, 289, 625; Hui-zong's children, 291; Qinzong, 196, 197, 198–199, 210, 289–290. *Southern Song:* Gaozong, 197, 289–298; Xiaozong, 303, 304, 308–310, 331; later emperors, 310–311, 313, 319, 320, 461; Empress Yang, 315–316; Empress Dowager Xie, 318–319, 463, 464. *See also* Zhao Guangyi (Taizong); Zhao Kuangyin (Taizu)

Song dynasty, war and peace factions, 70–71, 114–116, 136–138, 291–292, 293, 297–298, 301, 306–307, 334–335, 379
Song government: structure in early Song, 109–112; changes made in Major Reform, 138–144; criticisms of, 335–336
Song-Jin relations. *See* Song dynasty, war and peace factions
Song Lian, 558, 559, 570, 580, 591–592
Song-Liao relations, 61, 69–71, 115–117, 178
Song loyalism, in re resistance to Mongols, 461, 464–465, 532, 537, 544
Song Taizong. *See* Zhao Guangyi
Song Taizu. *See* Zhao Kuangyin
Song-Xia relations, 171–173, 177–180, 326–327
Sorghaghtani Beki, 420, 446–447
Southern border peoples, in Ming, 703–717
Southern Chancellery (Liao), 39, 43, 83, 88–89
Southern Ming resistance, 824–827, 831; Hongguang (Nanjing) phase, 824, 826–827; Longwu (Fuzhou) phase, 833–837; final phase, 837–840
Southern scholar-officials, in Kangxi reign, 865, 866, 881–882
Southern Song, compared with Northern Song, 298–299, 318, 346
"Southern Study" (Nan shufang) of the Kangxi emperor, 865, 882
Southern Tang state, 14, 22
Southward migration of Chinese, 6, 702–703
Sponsorship in officialdom, in Song, 134–135
Statecraft: thought, 337, 387, 519; political instrument, 667, 779
Stein, Sir Aurel, 263
Steppe-oriented policy, in late Yuan, 519
Steppe warfare, 29, 34; Liao, 56–59, 77, 90–91; Xia, 179, 181–182, 190, 260–261; adopted by Jurchens, 214–216; of Mongols, 410–411; compared with China, 783
Su Shi and the Su family, 153–157, 278, 512
Succession problems: in Liao, 49–56, 67, 88; in early Song reigns, 104; Jurchen pattern of, 214, 241; in Xia,

254; in re Southern Song Gaozong, 291–292, 298; in re *khuriltai*, among Mongols, 425–426, 443, 447; in Ming imperial line, 587, 659–661, 735; succession crisis in Kangxi reign, 883–886; of Yongzheng emperor, 888–889; abdication and succession rituals, 97

Sun worship, in Inner Asia, 82–83

Sun Yat-sen, 584, 896

Sungari River, 212, 213, 409

Supreme Ultimate (Taiji), 342

Surnames: in tribal societies, 37–38; function of, 75, 98, 158–159, 350, 365, 369; clan surnames from tribal names, among Mongols, 422

Taiping Rebellion, 617–618

Taiwan: in early Qing, 848–849

Taizhou school, of Wang Yangming's followers, 681

Takla Makan Desert, 25–26, 649

"Tame Jurchens." *See* Jurchens

Tamerlane, 443

Tanguts, 19, 29, 57, 113, 200, 408; ethnic identity, 168–170; early history, 170–173; post-Xia, 256–257; pastoralism compared with Khitans, 259–260. *See also* Xi Xia state

Taoism. *See* Daoism

Tarim Basin, 25, 206, 408

Tartars. *See* Tatars

Tatars, 32, 57, 409, 416, 698

Tax-collectors, 373–374

Taxation: Chinese methods, 496; in Northern Song, 116–118; in Jin, 283; reforms in Southern Song, 320; in re census, 352, 496; Song system of, 361–363; in Yuan, 496–497; tax farming, 503; in re tax base of non-Chinese regions, 705; basic reforms under Zhang Juzheng in late Ming, 731–732; *lijia* rural management in Ming, 753–754; system reformed in Qing, 908–910, 918–919

Taxes: agrarian, 40, 319, 361–362, 731–732, 908, 910; commercial, 40, 117, 164, 165–166, 286, 362–363; surcharges on, 908–909. *See also* Levies

Temüjin. *See* Chinggis Khan

"Ten Perfections," military campaigns of Qianlong emperor, 935–940

"Ten States," developments in, 21–23, 106, 355

Tenancy, agrarian, 365

Thai peoples in China, 453, 711–712

Theater. *See* Drama

Thought control, in Qing, 897

"Three Cases" at late Ming court, 740

Three Eastern Commanderies. *See* Uriyangkhad

"Three Feudatories" of Ming-Qing transition, 838–839; rebellion of, 844–848

"Three Teachings" syncretism, 448, 449, 499, 527–528

Three Yangs, serving early Ming court, 625

Tian Shan Mountains, 25, 206, 407, 870

Tian'an Men Square, in Beijing, 619

Tibet, 23; early history, 168–169, 262–263, 410, 698–700; relationship with Tanguts of Xia, 258, 262, 264; during Yuan dynasty, 483–485, 700; status of, in Ming and Qing times, 698–702, 714–715; Mongol intervention in, 701–702; in Qing period, 870–871, 876–879, 901–902, 937–939, 962, 1045nn35,36,37,38

Tibetan transmission of Buddhism, 262–263, 398–399, 472, 483–484, 501–502; as the official religion of the Mongols, 689, 690, 787, 871, 939, 1021n8

Tolui, 445; sons of (Toluids), 446, 447

Tong Guan, 208–210, 249

Trade and commerce: in Northern Song, 140, 165–166, 172, 259; during Jin, 270, 284–288, in re taxation in Song, 362; growth of, from ninth century onward, 389–390, 391; international, 392–394; functions of, 394; in re Ming-Mongol tribute relations, 692–693, 697; in re Tibet, 700; maritime, in Ming, 719–721, 767–768; ban against lifted, 726; Ming negative attitudes toward, 720–721; trade, domestic, 391–394, 726; in Europe, compared with China, 953–954

Traders, denigrated, 390

Transport: in re trade, 287; of tax grains, by canal, 650, 652–653; of tax grains, by sea, 650–651, 717–720

Transport Commissioners, in Song, 355

Treaties, 116–117; Liao-Xia treaties with Song, 118, 185, 307; Jin-Song

Treaties *(cont.)*
  treaties, 118, 196, 198, 209, 303,
    306–307, 308; impact on trade, 270,
    284–286, 308; criticism of, in Song,
    336; in re Mongols, 437; with Russia
    in Qing period, 871–874, 901; fail-
    ure of Western European powers to
    gain treaty relationship, 950. *See also*
    Shanyuan, Treaty of
Tribal societies: Khitan, 54–56, 80–81,
    87–90, 200, 204–205, 211; Tangut,
    170–171, 174, 181–182, 187–188;
    Jurchen, 201, 211–216, 275–276;
    Mongol, 404–406; absorbed into
    Mongol nation, 421–422, 424, 426;
    in re trade and commerce, 392–393;
    leadership in, 396–397; transforma-
    tion of Mongol tribal society, 480;
    conciliar spirit in, 493
Tribute system of interstate relations: in
    Song, 307, 376–377; Ming restora-
    tion of, 377, 389, 608, 616, 687,
    692–693, 720, 962
Tripitaka (Buddhist canon), 85–86, 162–
    163, 263, 398–399
Tumu incident. *See* Esen, Oyirat khan,
    and Tumu incident
Tungusic languages, 34, 61, 211, 404,
Turkic peoples, 6, 27, 29–30, 32, 34, 57,
    428; absorb Mongols outside Mongo-
    lia, 442; in Ming times, 698
Tusi, "native offices" (*tuguan, tu ren,*
    etc.): from Yuan into Ming and
    Qing, 703–717, 838; distribution of,
    in southern provinces, 707–716;
    assessment of, 716–717; in Qing,
    902–903, 1023n39
Twitchett, Denis C., 392
"Two-tax system." *See* Taxation

Uighurs: 32, 34–36, 42–43, 83, 89, 380,
    405, 408, 508; relations with Tan-
    guts, 179, 259, 261, 262; relations
    with Kara Khitai, 206; relations with
    Mongols, 406, 407, 408, 424, 449
Ulaanbaatar (Ulan Bator), 407, 412
"Unchanging China" myth, 376
Ural Mountains, 872, 873
Urban-rural integration, 166–167, 364–
    365, 367–368, 763–764
Urbanization: in Song China, 164–167,
    371; in Ming China, 761–764
Urga (Ulaanbaatar), 874–875, 876

Uriyangkhad Mongols, in Ming and later,
    689, 784–785. *See also* Eastern Mon-
    gols
Ussuri River, 211
Usurpation: of Tang dynasty, 7, 10, 12,
    17; in founding of Later Zhou and
    of Song, 92–98, 102; of Ming by
    Chengzu, 587, 622; of Qing by Shi-
    zong, 884–885, 888
Utilitarian *(gongli)* political thought, 136,
    157, 334–337, 987n30; in Zhu Xi,
    344–345; in Fang Xiaoru, 592; com-
    pared with Zhang Juzheng's political
    thought, 729; in Wang Fuzhi's
    thought, 853

Vengeance: among Mongols, 417, 433–
    434, 535; for Ming usurpation, in
    Chinese legend, 589; of Wu Sangui,
    against Manchus, 846
"Vermilion Rescripts," of the Qing Shun-
    zhi emperor, 890–892
Village life: described by Lu You, 372–
    374; in Ming Taizu's youth, 541–
    545; concern of Fang Xiaoru, 592–
    593; in Ming, generally, 751–757
Violence in society, 521, 525; at Ming
    court, 573, 581–582, 605

Wang Anshi. *See* "Major Reforms" of
    Wang Anshi
Wang Yangming (Wang Shouren), 593,
    657, 673–684; Wang school, 679–
    681, 752, 764, 773, 779, 836, 853,
    929
Wanyan, tribe, surname, 212–217, 222,
    224, 226–227, 231, 234, 237, 271
War party. *See* Factions
Warfare: popular attitudes toward, 268;
    in re utilitarian thought, 335
Warlordism, 39, 66, 115, 522–524, 553.
    See also Regional Military Governors
Western Liao. *See* Kara Khitai
White Lotus Society, 502, 529–530, 533
Widows, remarriage of, 369
"Wild" Jurchens, 60, 195, 201, 211–212
Wittfogel, Karl A., 87
Women: in Khitan society, 50, 75–76,
    87, 413; in Song society, 151, 162,
    340 343–344, 350; in re marriage, in
    Song, 370; in Buddhism, 82;
    restricted, by Zhu Xi's system, 343–
    344; in Mongol society, 413, 416–

418, 434, 1004n6; mothers in re family rules in Ming, 594; procurement for Ming palace, 625–626; palace women in Ming, 630–634, 668–669; "intellectual equals of men," 681; female leaders among southern tribal peoples, 703, 709; in Ming emperor Muzong's reign, 725; enlarged opportunities for, in late Ming, 770–771; in Qing, 941; place of women in Chinese society, 967–968, 1032n59

Writing systems. *See* Scripts *entries*

Wu Han, 561, 575–576, 672, 1011n23, 1013n38, 1019n23

Wu Sangui, 808, 815–817, 838–839; rebellion of, 844–848

Wuchang, commercial prosperity of, observed by Lu You, 371

Xanadu. *See* Shangdu

Xi Xia state (dynasty): 19, 29, 60, 409; origins of, 171–173, 177–179; tribal history, 170–171; treaties with, 118, 138; trade, 172; in recent Chinese historiography, 173–176; foreign relations, 178–179, 249–251, 255, 380, 382–383; capital of, 186; Chinese influences in, 251–252, 397; rebellions in, 252; destruction of, 254–257; bi-polar development, 397

Xia state. *See* Xi Xia state

Xian. *See* Counties

Xi'an, 17, 39, 568, 646, 795, 800. *See also* Chang'an

"*Xiangxia jen*" ("country people"), 366–367

Xiao clan (Liao consorts), 38, 42, 88, 194–195, 201, 216

Xin Qiji, 277, 315

Xinjiang (Chinese Turkestan), 23, 24, 25, 405, 428, 870, 876, 902, 936

Xinxue (school of mind), 135, 144, 337–340; "minor mode" alternative to *Lixue*, 340, 509, 676, 929, 931

Xun Zi, 339

Yalu River, 61, 381, 793

Yamen (local government): staffing, in Song, 360; in lives of villagers, 373; in Ming, 751, 752–754, 757, 761–762

Yan (present-day Beijing), 41, 448, 457–458. *See also* Beijing; Dadu

Yan, Prince of. *See* Ming dynasty emperors: Chengzu

Yang Tinghe, 658–663, 664–665, 666, 667

Yangzhou, 293, 295–296, 525; "ten days' massacre," 830–831, 867–868, 1040n23

Yangzi River, 133, 295, 296, 297–298, 301, 304, 329; Lu You's travel on, 371–372, 567; in re Grand Canal, 646, 648, 652

"Yangzi South" *(jiangnan)*, 367, 371

Yao Kun's embassy, 44–48, 63–64

Yao tribespeople, at Ming court, 631–632

Yasa. *See* Jasagh

Ye Shi, 336–337

"Yellow" (land-oriented) China, 616–617

Yellow River, 408, 532; defines "yellow" China, 616–617; in re water control, 646, 648, 649–650, 653, 867; diversion of, 653

Yelü Abaoji. *See* Abaoji

Yelü clan (Liao), 38, 42, 88, 201, 216

Yelü Chucai, 245–246, 432, 437; attempted reforms of, 438–439, 476–477, 500

Yelü Dashi, 202–206. *See also* Kara Khitai

Yin privilege ("protection"), 80–81, 128, 133, 316, 319, 332, 490–491

Yingtian. *See* Nanjing

Yu Qian, 628–629

Yuan Chonghuan, 791–795

Yuan dynasty: compared with Liao, 457; reign-titles and calendar adopted, 457–458, 533; capitals, 457–460, 491; dynasty proclaimed, 459–460; Song loyalist opposition, 465–466; in re Mongol khanates, 469; Chinese elite attitudes toward, 505–507, 519–520; political disintegration, 517–521; military strength at end, 534–535

Yuan dynasty government: established at Dadu, 457; "China-centered" ("Confucian") vs. "pro-steppe" policies, 469–473; civil governing emerges, 476–477; central government structure, 477–483, 485–487; place of military in, 479–482, 484, 493; special agencies, 482–483; regional and local, 485–489, 533; sub-official

Yuan dynasty government *(cont.)*
   levels, 488–489; staffing, 489–494;
   fiscal management, 494–495; dissolution after 1330, 518–521; legitimacy
   of accepted, by Chinese, 506, 559–
   560; lasting change in political
   modes, 581–582
Yuan dynasty rulers:
   Khubilai Khan (Yuan Shizu), 401–402,
      444–469, 653–654, 877; advisors,
      448–452, 476–477, 492, 508–510;
      Yunnan campaign, 452–454, 462;
      rebellion against, 455–456, 460–
      461, 464, 465–466; suspicious of
      Chinese, 456; campaign against
      Song, 460–465; invasions of Japan,
      466–467; invasions of Annam and
      Burma, 467; sons and heirs, 467–
      473; assessment of, 492
   Chengzong, 469
   Wuzong (Kaishan), 469–470
   Renzong, 470
   Yingzong, 470–471
   Taiding Di, 471
   Wenzong, 471–472
   Ningzong, 471–472
   Emperor Shun (Shundi), 472–473,
      518–519, 522, 563, 577
Yuan Haowen, 277–278
Yuanhao (Li Yuanhao), 172–173, 179–
   187, 259–260, 263, 1036n53
Yue Fei, 268, 299–307, 554, 898–900
Yunnan: under Mongols, 451–454, 613–
   614; place of banishment, in Ming,
   668; ethnic diversity of, 709–713;
   compared with Sichuan, 714–715;
   under Wu Sangui, 839

Zhan Ruoshui, 674, 678
Zhang Juzheng, 646, 724–734, 746
Zhang Shicheng, 525–526, 535, 539,
   561–563
Zhang Xianzhong, 796, 797–798, 829,
Zhao Guangyi (Song Taizong), 96–97;
   reign of, 105–109; military fiascos,
   106–109, 112
Zhao Kuangyin (Song Taizu): 14, 68; as
   usurper, 92–98; reign of, 104–106,
   112
Zhao Mengfu, 512–513
Zhao Mingcheng, 328–330
Zhao Pu, 96–97
Zheng Chenggong (Koxinga), 834–835,
   839–840
Zheng He, 613–617, 686; voyages com-
   pared with early European, 616
Zhenjin, Prince, 448, 467
Zhongdu. *See* Ming dynasty: "Central
   Capital" built
Zhu Di. *See* Ming dynasty emperors:
   Chengzu
Zhu Yuanzhang. *See* Ming dynasty emper-
   ors: Taizu
Zhu Xi, 146, 147, 313, 315; labeled
   "false learning," 313–314, 341, 345;
   in re "orthodoxy," 314, 316, 507–
   508; achievement of, 333–334, 340–
   346; criticisms of, 341, 345; political
   thought, 344–345; impact on ethics,
   345–346; disdained "popular" reli-
   gion, 527; his thought challenged by
   Wang Yangming, 677–679. *See also*
   Cheng-Zhu thought
Zoroastrianism, 501, 528
Zu Xun. See "Ancestral Injunctions"